CROSSWORD
SOLVER

CROSSWORD
SOLVER

Edited by
Anne Stibbs

A & C Black • London

First published 1988 by Bloomsbury Publishing Plc
Second edition published 1995
Third edition published 1997
This combined edition published 2007 by
A&C Black Publishers Ltd, 38 Soho Square, London W1D 3HB
Reprinted 2008

A CIP record for this title is available from the British Library

ISBN 978 0 7136 8320 2

This book is produced using paper that is made from wood grown in managed, sustainable
forests. It is natural, renewable and recyclable. The logging and manufacturing processes
conform to the environmental regulations of the country of origin.

Text compiled and typeset by Market House Books Ltd., Aylesbury
Printed in Spain by GraphyCems

INTRODUCTION

This book consists of a set of lists of words specifically designed to help crossword-puzzle solvers. We have included over 100,000 English words organized into words with two letters, words with three letters, four letters, etc., up to fifteen letters. Within each section, the words are arranged alphabetically.

The words chosen include proper nouns, names of people and places, as well as common two- and three-word phrases. We have also given, in many cases, plurals of nouns, comparatives and superlatives of adjectives, and inflections of verbs. In general, '—ize' ending have been used for verbs. It should be noted that '—ise' endings are also possible for these.

We hope that the book will prove useful to all who enjoy doing crossword puzzles – and, in particular, to those who enjoy completing them.

AS

A	D	HI	M	PE	U
AA	DA	H'M	MA	PH	UK
AB	DJ	HO	ME	PI	UM
AC	DO	HQ	MI	PM	UN
AD			MO	PR	UP
AG	**E**	**I**	MP	PS	US
AH	EH	ID	MR	PT	UU
AI	ER	IF	MS	PX	
AM	EU	IN	MY		**V**
AN	EX	IQ		**Q**	VC
AS		IT	**N**	QC	VD
AT	**F**		NO	QT	VJ
AW	FA	**J**			VS
	FE	JP	**O**	**R**	
B	FM		OF	RE	**W**
BE		**K**	OH		WC
BO	**G**	KC	ON	**S**	WE
BY	GI	KO	OP	SH	
	GO		OR	SO	**X**
C	GP	**L**	OW		XU
CB	GS	LA	OX	**T**	
CD		LO		TA	**Y**
CO	**H**	LP	**P**	TI	YE
CV	HA	LR	PA	TO	YO
	HE		PC	TV	

1

A	BAG	CDS	DIG	ERR	GAP
ABC	BAH	CIA	DIM	ESP	GAS
ABH	BAN	CID	DIN	ESQ	GAY
ABO	BAR	CIS	DIP	EST	GCE
ACE	BAT	CJD	DIS	ETC	GDP
ACT	BAY	CND	DIY	EVE	GEC
ADD	BBC	CNS	DJS	EWE	GEE
ADJ	BBQ	COB	DNA	EYE	GEL
ADO	BED	COD	DOC		GEM
ADS	BEE	COG	DOE	**F**	GEN
ADV	BEG	COL	DOG	FAB	GET
AFT	BEN	CON	DOH	FAD	GIG
AGE	BET	COO	DON	FAG	GIN
AGM	BIB	COP	DOR	FAN	GI'S
AGO	BID	COS	DOS	FAR	GNP
AHA	BIG	COT	DOT	FAT	GNU
AID	BIN	COW	DRY	FAX	GOA
AIL	BIO-	COX	D T'S	FAY	GOB
AIM	BIT	COY	DUB	FBI	GOD
AIR	BOA	CPA	DUD	FED	GOO
A LA	BOB	CPS	DUE	FEE	GOP
ALE	BOD	CPU	DUG	FEN	GOT
ALL	BOG	CRC	DUN	FEW	GPS
AMP	BOO	CRY	DUO	FEY	GUM
AND	BOP	CSE	DYE	FEZ	GUN
ANT	BOW	CUB		FIB	GUT
ANY	BOX	CUD	**E**	FIE	GUV
AOC	BOY	CUE	EAR	FIG	GUY
APB	BPI	CUM	EAT	FIN	GYM
APE	BPS	CUP	EBB	FIR	GYP
APP	BRA	CUR	ECG	FIT	
APT	BUB	CUT	ECT	FIX	**H**
ARB	BUD	CVS	EEC	FLU	HAD
ARC	BUG	CWM	EEK	FLY	HAE
ARK	BUM		EEL	FOB	HAG
ARM	BUN	**D**	EFF	FOE	HAH
ART	BUR	DAB	EGG	FOG	HAM
ASH	BUS	DAD	EGO	FOP	HAN
ASK	BUT	DAM	EKG	FOR	HAP
ASP	BUY	DAY	ELF	FOX	HAS
ASS	BYE	DDI	ELK	FRO	HAT
ATE		DDR	ELM	FRY	HAW
ATM	**C**	DDT	ELT	FUG	HAY
AUK	CAB	DEB	EMU	FUN	HE'D
AWE	CAD	DEF	ENC	FUR	HEH
AWL	CAM	DEM	END		HEL
AXE	CAN	DEN	EON	**G**	HEM
AYE	CAP	DEP	EPS	GAB	HEN
B	CAR	DEW	ERA	GAD	HEP
BAA	CAT	DID	ERE	GAG	HER
BAD	CAW	DIE	ERG	GAL	HE'S

HET	IRE	LED	MOW	O'ER	PLY
HEW	IRK	LEE	MPS	OFF	PMS
HEX	ISM	LEG	MRI	OFT	POD
HEY	ITS	LEI	MRS	OHM	POP
HIB	ITV	LEO	MSC	OHO	POT
HIC	IUD	LET	MUD	OIK	POW
HID	IVY	LEV	MUG	OIL	POX
HIE		LIB	MUM	OLD	PPS
HIM	**J**	LID		ONE	PRE-
HIN	JAB	LIE	**N**	OOF	PRO
HIP	JAG	LIG	NAB	OPS	PRY
HIS	JAM	LIP	NAD	OPT	PTA
HIT	JAR	LIT	NAG	ORB	PTO
HOB	JAW	LOB	NAN	ORE	PUB
HOD	JAY	LOG	NAP	OTT	PUD
HOE	JET	LOO	NAV	OUR	PUG
HOG	JEW	LOP	NAY	OUT	PUN
HOM	JIB	LOT	NCO	OVA	PUP
HOO	JIG	LOW	NEC	OWE	PUS
HOP	JIT	LOX	NEE	OWL	PUT
HOT	JOB	LPS	NEG	OWN	PVC
HOW	JOG	LSD	NET		PYX
HOY	JOT	LUG	NEW	**P**	
HQS	JOY	IUV	NFL	PAD	**Q**
HRT	JPS		NHS	PAL	QCS
HSI	JUG	**M**	NIB	PAN	QUA
HUB	JUT	MAC	NIL	PAP	
HUE		MAD	NIP	PAR	**R**
HUG	**K**	MAG	NIT	PAS	RAD
HUH	KEG	MAM	NIX	PAT	RAF
HUM	KEN	MAN	NOB	PAW	RAG
HUN	KEY	MAP	NOD	PAY	RAI
HUT	KID	MAR	NON-	PCS	RAJ
	KIN	MAS	NOR	PEA	RAM
I	KIP	MAT	NOT	PEE	RAN
ICE	KIT	MAW	NOW	PEG	RAP
ICY	KOB	MAY	NRA	PEN	RAT
IDS	KOI	MEN	NSA	PEP	RAW
IFS		MET	NSU	PER	RAY
ILK	**L**	MEW	NTH	PET	REC
ILL	LAB	MIA	NUB	PEW	RED
IMP	LAD	MID	NUN	PHD	REF
INC	LAG	MIS	NUT	PHS	REP
INF	LAN	MIX		PIE	REV
INK	LAP	MOB	**O**	PIG	REX
INN	LAW	MOD	OAF	PIN	RIA
ION	LAX	MOM	OAK	PIP	RIB
IOU	LAY	MOO	OAP	PIS	RID
IPA	LCD	MOP	OAR	PIT	RIG
IQS	LCM	MOS	ODD	PIX	RIM
IRA	LEA	MOT	ODE	PLC	RIP

RNA	SEW	SUM	TOY	VET	WOO
ROB	SEX	SUN	TRY	VEX	WOP
ROC	SHE	SUP	TSK	VGA	WOT
ROD	SHY		TUB	VGC	WOW
ROE	SIC	**T**	TUC	VHF	WPC
ROM	SIN		TUG	VIA	WRY
ROT	SIP	TAB	TUT	VIE	
ROW	SIR	TAG	TVS	VIM	**Y**
RSE	SIS	TAN	TWO	VIP	
RSI	SIT	TAP		VIZ	YAK
RUB	SIX	TAR	**U**	VLF	YAM
RUE	SKA	TAT		VOW	YAP
RUG	SKI	TAX	UFO	VTR	YAW
RUM	SKY	TEA	UGH		YEA
RUN	SLY	TEC	UHF	**W**	YEN
RUT	SOB	TEE	UMP		YES
RYE	SOD	TEN	UNI-	WAD	YET
	SOH	THE	URN	WAG	YEW
S	SOL	THY	USE	WAN	YID
SAC	SON	TIA		WAR	YIN
SAD	SOP	TIC	**V**	WAX	YOB
SAE	SOS	TIE		WAY	YOU
SAG	SOT	TIN	UTC	WEB	YTS
SAP	SOU	TIP	UTD	WED	
SAT	SOW	TIT	UVA	WEE	**Z**
SAW	SOX	TNT	UVB	WET	
SAY	SOY	TOD	UVC	WHO	ZAP
SDI	SPA	TOE	UZI	WHY	ZED
SDP	SPY	TOG	VAC	WIG	ZEN
SEA	STD	TON	VAN	WIN	ZIG
SEC	STY	TOO	VAR	WIT	ZIP
SEE	SUB	TOP	VAT	WOE	ZOO
SEM	SUE	TOR	VCR	WOG	
SET	SUG	TOT	VCS	WOK	
		TOW	VDU	WON	
			VEG		

A
ABCS
ABED
ABET
ABIA
ABLE
ABLY
ABOS
ABUT
ACCT
AC/DC
ACER
ACES
ACHE
ACID
ACME
ACNE
ACRE
ACTS
ADAM
ADEN
ADZE
AEON
AERO-
AFAR
AFRO
AGAL
AGED
AGES
AGMS
AGOG
AGRA
AGUE
AHEM
AHOY
AIDE
AIDS
AIMS
AIN'T
AINU
AIRE
AIRS
AIRY
AJAR
AKIN
ALAI
ALAR
ALAS
ALBI
ALIT
ALKY

ALLY
ALMS
ALOE
ALPS
ALSO
ALTO
ALUM
AMBO
AMEN
AMEX
AMID
AMIR
AMIS
AMOK
AMOY
AMPS
ANAL
ANEW
ANKH
ANON
ANSI
ANTE
ANTI-
ANTS
ANUS
APED
APES
APEX
APSE
AQUA
ARAB
ARAN
ARCH
ARCS
ARDS
AREA
AREG
ARIA
ARID
ARKS
ARMS
ARMY
ARSE
ARTS
ARTY
ASHY
ASIA
AS IF
ASIR
ASPS
ASTI

AT IT
ATOM
ATOP
AUBE
AUDE
AUKS
AUNT
AURA
AUTO
AVER
AVID
AVON
AVOW
AWAY
AWED
AWLS
AWOL
AWRY
AXED
AXES
AXIS
AXLE
AYAH
AYES

B
BAAS
BABE
BABU
BABY
BACH
BACK
BADE
BAEZ
BAGS
BAIL
BAIT
BAJA
BAKE
BAKU
BALD
BALE
BALI
BALK
BALL
BALM
BAND
BANE
BANG
BANK
BANS

BARB
BARD
BARE
BARI
BARK
BARN
BARS
BASE
BASH
BASK
BASS
BAST
BATH
BATS
BAUD
BAWD
BAWL
BAYS
BEAD
BEAK
BEAM
BEAN
BEAR
BEAT
BEAU
BECK
BEDS
BEEF
BEER
BEES
BEET
BELL
BELT
BEND
BENS
BENT
BERK
BERN
BEST
BETA
BETS
BEVY
BIAS
BIBS
BIDE
BIDS
BIEL
BIER
BIFF
BIFU
BIKE

BILE
BILK
BILL
BIND
BINS
BIRD
BIRL
BIRO
BITE
BITS
BLAB
BLAG
BLAH
BLED
BLEW
BLIP
BLOB
BLOC
BLOT
BLOW
BLUE
BLUR
BOAR
BOAS
BOAT
BOBS
BODE
BODS
BODY
BOER
BOGS
BOIL
BOLD
BOLE
BOLL
BOLT
BOMA
BOMB
BOND
BONE
BONN
BONY
BOOB
BOOK
BOOM
BOON
BOOR
BOOS
BOOT
BOPS
BORA

BORE
BORN
BORT
BOSH
BOSS
BOTH
BOUT
BOWL
BOWS
BOYS
BOZO
BRAE
BRAG
BRAN
BRAS
BRAT
BRAY
BREW
BRIM
BRIT
BRNO
BROW
BROZ
BUBO
BUBS
BUCK
BUDS
BUFF
BUGS
BULB
BULK
BULL
BUMF
BUMP
BUMS
BUNA
BUNG
BUNK
BUNS
BUOY
BUPA
BURB
BURK
BURN
BURP
BURR
BURS
BURY
BUSH
BUSK
BUSS

BUST	CELL	COED	CROP	DAUB	DISS
BUSY	CENT	COGS	CROW	DAWN	DIVE
BUTE	CERT	COIF	CRUS	DAYS	DMSO
BUTS	CHAD	COIL	CRUX	DAZE	DOCK
BUTT	CHAP	COIN	CSES	D-DAY	DOCS
BUYS	CHAR	COIR	CUBA	DEAD	DODO
BUZZ	CHAT	COKE	CUBE	DEAF	DOER
BYES	CHEB	COLA	CUBS	DEAL	DOES
BYOB	CHEF	COLD	CUED	DEAN	DOFF
BYRE	CHER	COLS	CUES	DEAR	DOGE
BYTE	CHEW	COLT	CUFF	DEBS	DOGS
	CHIC	COMA	CULL	DEBT	DOHA
C	CHID	COMB	CULM	DECK	DO IT
CABS	CHIN	COME	CULT	DEED	DOLE
CADS	CHIP	COMO	CUNT	DEEM	DOLL
CAEN	CHIT	CONE	CUPS	DEEP	DOLT
CAFE	CHOP	CONK	CURB	DEER	DOME
CAGE	CHOU	CONS	CURD	DEFT	DONE
CAKE	CHOW	CONY	CURE	DEFY	DONS
CALF	CHUG	COOK	CURL	DELE	DON'T
CALI	CHUM	COOL	CURS	DELL	DOOM
CALK	CHUR	COON	CURT	DEMO	DOOR
CALL	C-IN-C	COOP	CUSP	DENS	DOPE
CALM	CINE-	COOS	CUSS	DENT	DORY
CALX	CITE	COOT	CUTE	DENY	DOSE
CAME	CITY	COPE	CUTS	DERV	DOSH
CAMP	CLAD	COPS	CYAN	DESK	DOSS
CAMS	CLAM	COPY	CYME	DEWY	DOTE
CANE	CLAN	CORD	CYST	DFEE	DOTS
CANS	CLAP	CORE	CZAR	DHAK	DOUR
CANT	CLAW	CORK		DHOW	DOVE
CAPE	CLAY	CORM	**D**	DIAL	DOWN
CAPO	CLEF	CORN	DABS	DICE	DOZE
CAPS	CLEW	COSH	DADO	DICK	DOZY
CARD	CLIP	COST	DADS	DIED	DRAB
CARE	CLOD	COSY	DAFT	DIET	DRAG
CARP	CLOG	COTS	DAGO	DIGS	DRAM
CARS	CLOP	COUP	DAIS	DIKE	DRAT
CART	CLOT	COVE	DALE	DILL	DRAW
CASE	CLOY	COWL	DAME	DIME	DRAY
CASH	CLUB	COWS	DAMN	DINE	DREW
CASK	CLUE	COXA	DAMP	DINK	DRIP
CAST	CLUJ	COZY	DAMS	DINS	DROP
CATS	COAL	CRAB	DANK	DINT	DRUB
CAUL	COAT	CRAG	DARE	DIPS	DRUG
CAVE	COAX	CRAM	DARK	DIRE	DRUM
CAVY	COBS	CRAP	DARN	DIRK	DUAL
CAWS	COCK	CRED	DART	DIRT	DUCK
CEDE	CODA	CREW	DASH	DISC	DUCT
CEDI	CODE	CRIB	DATA	DISH	DUDE
CELA	CODS	CROC	DATE	DISK	DUDS

DUEL	EGER	FAFF	FIRS	FOUL	GATE
DUES	EGGS	FAGS	FISH	FOUR	GAVE
DUET	EGOS	FAIL	FIST	FOWL	GAWD
DUFF	EIRE	FAIN	FITS	FOXY	GAWK
DUGS	ELAN	FAIR	FIVE	FRAP	GAWP
DUKE	ELBA	FAKE	FIZZ	FRAU	GAYA
DULL	ELBE	FALL	FLAB	FRAY	GAYS
DULY	ELIA	FAME	FLAG	FREE	GAZA
DUMA	ELKS	FANG	FLAK	FRET	GAZE
DUMB	ELMS	FANS	FLAN	FRIT	GCES
DUMP	ELSE	FARE	FLAP	FROE	GCSE
DUNE	EMIR	FARM	FLAT	FROG	G'DAY
DUNG	EMIT	FART	FLAW	FROM	GEAR
DUNK	EMUS	FAST	FLAX	FUCK	GEEK
DUNS	ENDS	FATE	FLAY	FUEL	GELD
DUOS	ENVY	FATS	FLEA	FUJI	GELS
DUPE	EONS	FAUN	FLED	FULL	GEMS
DUSK	EPEE	FAUX	FLEE	FUME	GENE
DUST	EPIC	FAWN	FLEW	FUMY	GENK
DUTY	ERAS	FAZE	FLEX	FUND	GENT
DWEM	ERGO	FEAR	FLIP	FUNK	GENU
DYAD	ERGS	FEAT	FLIT	FURL	GERA
DYED	ERIE	FEED	FLOE	FURS	GERM
DYER	ERNE	FEEL	FLOG	FURY	GERS
DYES	ERSE	FEES	FLOP	FUSE	GHAT
DYKE	ESPY	FEET	FLOW	FUSS	GHEE
DYNE	ET AL	FELL	FLUE	FUZZ	GIBE
	ETCH	FELT	FLUX		GIFT
E	ETON	FEND	FOAL	**G**	GIFU
EACH	EURE	FENS	FOAM	GAFF	GIGS
EARL	EURO	FFRN	FOBS	GAGA	GILD
EARN	EVEN	FESS	FOCI	GAGE	GILL
EARS	EVER	FEST	FOES	GAGS	GILT
EASE	EVES	FETE	FOGS	GAIA	GIMP
EAST	EVIL	FEUD	FOGY	GAIN	GINS
EASY	EWER	FIAT	FOHN	GAIT	GIRD
EATS	EWES	FIBS	FOIL	GALA	GIRL
EBBS	EXAM	FIFE	FOLD	GALE	GIRO
ECGS	EXES	FIGS	FOLK	GALL	GIRT
ECHO	EXIT	FIJI	FOND	GALS	GISH
ECRU	EYED	FILE	FONT	GAME	GIST
EDAM	EYES	FILL	FOOD	GAMY	GIVE
EDDO	EYOT	FILM	FOOL	GANG	GIZA
EDDY	EYRE	FILO	FOOT	GAOL	GLAD
EDEN		FILS	FOPS	GAPE	GLEE
EDGE	**F**	FIND	FORA	GAPS	GLEN
EDGY	FACE	FINE	FORD	GARB	GLIB
EDIT	FACT	FINN	FORE	GARD	GLOW
EDTA	FADE	FINS	FORK	GARY	GLUE
EELS	FADO	FIRE	FORM	GASH	GLUM
EFIK	FADS	FIRM	FORT	GASP	GLUT

H 4 GNAT

GNAT	GURU	HAST	HIND	HOVE	IDOL
GNAW	GUSH	HATE	HINT	HOWE	IFFY
GNUS	GUST	HATH	HIPS	HOWF	IGBO
GOAD	GUTS	HATS	HIRE	HOWL	IKBS
GOAL	GUVS	HAUL	HISS	HOYA	IKON
GOAT	GUYS	HAVE	HIST	HUBS	ILEX
GOBI	GYBE	HAWK	HITS	HUED	ILLS
GOBO	GYMS	HAZE	HIVE	HUES	IMAM
GOBS		HAZY	HOAD	HUFF	IMAX
GODS	**H**	HEAD	HOAR	HUGE	IMPI
GOER	HAAF	HEAL	HOAX	HUGO	IMPS
GOES	HAAR	HEAP	HOBO	HUGS	INCA
GO-GO	HABU	HEAR	HOBS	HULA	INCH
GOLD	HACK	HEAT	HOCK	HULK	INDO-
GOLF	HADE	HEBE	HODS	HULL	INDY
GONE	HADJ	HECK	HOED	HUME	INFO
GONG	HAEM	HEED	HOER	HUMP	INKS
GOOD	HAFT	HEEL	HOES	HUMS	INKY
GOOF	HAGS	HEFT	HOGG	HUNG	INNS
GOON	HA-HA	HEIR	HOGS	HUNK	INTI
GOOP	HAIG	HELA	HOKE	HUNT	INTO
GORE	HAIK	HELD	HOKI	HUON	IONS
GORY	HAIL	HELL	HOLD	HURD	IOTA
GOSH	HAIR	HELM	HOLE	HURL	IOUS
GOUT	HAJJ	HELP	HOLM	HURT	IOWA
GOWN	HAKE	HEMP	HOLP	HUSH	IPOH
GRAB	HALE	HEMS	HOLS	HUSK	IRAN
GRAF	HALF	HENS	HOLT	HUSS	IRAQ
GRAM	HALL	HENT	HOLY	HUTS	IRIS
GRAN	HALM	HERA	HOMA	HUTU	IRON
GRAY	HALO	HERB	HOME	HWAN	ISLE
GRAZ	HALT	HERD	HOMO	HWYL	ISMS
GREW	HAMA	HERE	HOMS	HYDE	ITCH
GREY	HAME	HERL	HOMY	HYMN	ITEM
GRID	HAMM	HERM	HONE	HYPE	IUDS
GRIM	HAMS	HERN	HONG	HYPO	
GRIN	HAND	HERO	HONK		**J**
GRIP	HANG	HERR	HOOD	**I**	JABS
GRIT	HANK	HERS	HOOF	IAMB	JACK
GROG	HARD	HESS	HOOK	IBEX	JADE
GROW	HARE	HEST	HOOP	IBID	JAGS
GRUB	HARK	HETH	HOOT	IBIS	JAIL
GUAM	HARL	HEWN	HOPE	ICBM	JAMB
GUFF	HARM	HICK	HOPI	ICED	JAMS
GULF	HARP	HIDE	HOPS	ICES	JAPE
GULL	HART	HIED	HORA	ICON	JARS
GULP	HARZ	HI-FI	HORN	IDEA	JAWS
GUMS	HASA	HIGH	HOSE	IDEM	JAYS
GUNN	HASH	HIKE	HOST	IDES	JAZZ
GUNS	HASK	HILL	HOTS	IDLE	JEEP
GURN	HASP	HILT	HOUR	IDLY	JEER

JELL	KEYS	LAID	LEWD	LOGO	MACH
JENA	KHAN	LAIN	LIAR	LOGS	MACS
JERK	KICK	LAIR	LIAS	LOGY	MADE
JEST	KIDS	LAKE	LICE	LOIN	MAFF
JETS	KIEL	LAKH	LICK	LOLL	MAGI
JEWS	KIEV	LAMA	LIDO	LONE	MAGS
JIBE	KIKE	LAMB	LIDS	LONG	MAID
JIBS	KILL	LAME	LIED	LOOK	MAIL
JIGS	KILN	LAMP	LIEF	LOOM	MAIM
JILT	KILO	LAND	LIEN	LOON	MAIN
JINN	KILT	LANE	LIES	LOOP	MAKE
JINX	KIND	LANK	LIEU	LOOS	MALE
JIVE	KINE	LAOS	LIFE	LOOT	MALI
JOBS	KING	LAPP	LIFT	LOPE	MALL
JOCK	KINK	LAPS	LIKE	LORD	MALM
JOGS	KIPS	LARD	LILO	LORE	MALT
JOHN	KIRK	LARK	LILT	LORN	MAMA
JOIN	KISS	LASH	LILY	LOSE	MAMS
JOKE	KITE	LASS	LIMA	LOSS	MANE
JOLT	KITS	LAST	LIMB	LOST	MANX
JOSH	KIVU	LATE	LIME	LOTH	MANY
JOVE	KIWI	LATH	LIMN	LOTS	MAPS
JOWL	KNAP	LAUD	LIMP	LOUD	MARE
JOYS	KNEE	LAUE	LIMY	LOUR	MARK
JUDO	KNEW	LAVA	LINE	LOUT	MARL
JUGS	KNIT	LAWN	LING	LOVE	MARS
JUJU	KNOB	LAWS	LINK	LOWS	MARY
JULY	KNOT	LAYS	LINT	LUCK	MASH
JUMP	KNOW	LAZE	LINZ	LUDO	MASK
JUNE	KOBE	LAZY	LION	LUFF	MASS
JUNK	KOFU	LEAD	LIPS	LUGO	MAST
JURA	KOGI	LEAF	LIRA	LUGS	MATE
JURY	KOHA	LEAK	LIRE	LULL	MATS
JUST	KOHL	LEAN	LISP	LUMP	MATT
JUTE	KOOK	LEAP	LIST	LUND	MAUI
	KOTA	LEAS	LITE	LUNG	MAUL
K	KRIS	LEEK	LIVE	LUNY	MAWS
KALE	KUDU	LEER	LOAD	LURE	MAYA
KANO	KURE	LEES	LOAF	LURK	MAYS
KCAL	KURU	LEFT	LOAM	LUSH	MAZE
KEEL	KYAT	LEGS	LOAN	LUST	MAZY
KEEN		LEIS	LOBE	LUTE	MEAD
KEEP	**L**	LENA	LOBS	LUVS	MEAL
KEGS	LABS	LEND	LOCH	LVIV	MEAN
KELP	LACE	LENS	LOCI	LYNX	MEAT
KENS	LACK	LENT	LOCK	LYON	MEEK
KENT	LACY	LEOS	LOCO	LYRE	MEET
KEOS	LADE	LESS	LODE		MEGA-
KEPT	LADS	LEST	LODI	**M**	MELK
KERB	LADY	LETS	LODZ	MA'AM	MELT
KERN	LAGS	LEVY	LOFT	MACE	MEMO

MEND	MOOD	NATO	NUBS	ONYX	PALP
MENU	MOON	NAVE	NUDE	OOPS	PALS
MEOW	MOOR	NAVY	NUKE	OOZE	PANE
MERE	MOOS	NAYS	NULL	OOZY	PANG
MESH	MOOT	NAZI	NUMB	OPAL	PANS
MESS	MOPE	NCOS	NUNN	OPEC	PANT
METE	MOPS	NEAR	NUNS	OPEN	PAPA
METZ	MORE	NEAT	NUPE	OPUS	PAPS
MEWS	MORN	NECK	NURD	ORAL	PARA-
MICA	MOSS	NEED	NUTS	ORAN	PARE
MICE	MOST	NEEM	NUUK	ORBS	PARK
MICK	MOTE	NE'ER		OREL	PARS
MIDI	MOTH	NEJD	**O**	ORES	PART
MIEN	MOTS	NEON	OAFS	ORGY	PASS
MIKE	MOVE	NERD	OAHU	ORLY	PAST
MILD	MOWN	NEST	OAKS	ORNE	PATE
MILE	MOYA	NETS	OAPS	ORSK	PATH
MILK	MRIA	NETT	OARS	ORYX	PATS
MILL	MUCH	NEWS	OATH	OSLO	PAVE
MILT	MUCK	NEWT	OATS	OSUN	PAWL
MIME	MUFF	NEXT	OBAN	OUCH	PAWN
MIND	MUGS	NIBS	OBEY	OUDH	PAWS
MINE	MULE	NICE	OBOE	OULU	PAYE
MINI	MULL	NICK	ODDS	OURS	PEAK
MINK	MUMS	NIFF	ODES	OUST	PEAL
MINT	MUON	NIGH	OGLE	OUZO	PEAR
MINX	MURK	NINE	OGRE	OVAL	PEAS
MIPS	MUSE	NIPS	OGUN	OVEN	PEAT
MIRE	MUSH	NISI	OHIO	OVER	PECK
MIRY	MUSK	NITS	OHMS	OVUM	PEED
MISO	MUSS	NIUE	OH MY	OWED	PEEK
MISS	MUST	NOBS	OH NO	OWEN	PEEL
MIST	MUTE	NODE	OILS	OWLS	PEEP
MITE	MUTI	NODS	OILY	OXEN	PEER
MITT	MUTT	NOEL	OINK	OYEZ	PEGS
MOAN	MYNA	NOES	OISE		PEGU
MOAT	MYTH	NO GO	OITA	**P**	PELT
MOBS		NONE	OKAY	PACE	PENN
MOCK	**N**	NON-U	OKRA	PACK	PENS
MODE	NAFF	NOOK	OKTA	PACT	PERK
MODS	NAGS	NOON	OMAN	PACY	PERL
MOJO	NAHA	NOPE	OMEN	PADS	PERM
MOKE	NAIL	NORD	OMIT	PAGE	PERT
MOLD	NAME	NORM	OMNI-	PAID	PERU
MOLE	NANA	NOSE	OMSK	PAIL	PESO
MOLL	NAPE	NOSH	ONCE	PAIN	PEST
MOLT	NAPS	NOSY	ONDO	PAIR	PETS
MOMS	NARA	NOTE	ONES	PAKI	PEWS
MONK	NARC	NOUN	ONLY	PALE	PHEW
MONO	NARK	NOUS	ONTO	PALL	PHON
MONS	NASA	NOVA	ONUS	PALM	PHOT

PHUT	PONY	PUNK	RATE	RIPE	RULE
PICA	POOF	PUNS	RATS	RIPS	RUMP
PICK	POOH	PUNT	RAVE	RISE	RUMS
PIED	POOL	PUNY	RAYS	RISK	RUNE
PIER	POOP	PUPA	RAZE	RITE	RUNG
PIES	POOR	PUPS	READ	RIVE	RUNS
PIGS	POPE	PURE	REAL	ROAD	RUNT
PIKE	POPS	PURI	REAM	ROAM	RUSE
PILE	PORE	PURL	REAP	ROAN	RUSH
PILL	PORI	PURR	REAR	ROAR	RUSK
PIMP	PORK	PUSH	RECK	ROBE	RUST
PINE	PORN	PUSS	REDD	ROCK	RUTS
PING	PORT	PUTT	REDO	ROCS	RYES
PINK	POSE	PUTZ	REDS	RODE	
PINS	POSH	PYRE	REED	RODS	**S**
PINT	POST		REEF	ROEG	SABA
PINY	POSY	**Q**	REEK	ROES	SACK
PION	POTS	QUAD	REEL	ROLE	SACS
PIPE	POUF	QUAY	REFS	ROLL	SAFE
PIPS	POUR	QUID	REGO	ROME	SAFI
PISA	POUT	QUIN	REIN	ROMO	SAGA
PISH	POWS	QUIP	RELY	ROMP	SAGE
PISS	PRAM	QUIT	REND	ROMS	SAGO
PITH	PRAT	QUIZ	RENO	ROOD	SAGS
PITS	PRAY	QUOD	RENT	ROOF	SAID
PITY	PREP		REPO	ROOK	SAIL
PLAN	PREY	**R**	REPS	ROOM	SAKE
PLAY	PRIG	RACE	REST	ROOT	SALE
PLEA	PRIM	RACK	REUS	ROPE	SALK
PLEB	PROB	RACY	REVS	ROPY	SALT
PLED	PROD	RAFT	RHEA	RORT	SAME
PLOD	PROF	RAGA	RIAL	ROSE	SAMP
PLOP	PROG	RAGE	RIBS	ROSY	SAN'A
PLOT	PROM	RAGS	RICE	ROTA	SAND
PLOW	PROP	RAID	RICH	ROTE	SANE
PLOY	PROS	RAIL	RICK	ROTH	SANG
PLUG	PROW	RAIN	RIDE	ROTS	SANK
PLUM	PRUT	RAKE	RIFE	ROUE	SAPS
PLUS	PSST	RAMP	RIFF	ROUT	SARD
PODS	PUBS	RAMS	RIFT	ROUX	SARI
POEM	PUCE	RAND	RIGA	ROVE	SARK
POET	PUCK	RANG	RIGS	ROWS	SASH
POKE	PUDS	RANI	RILE	RUBS	SASS
POKY	PUFF	RANK	RILL	RUBY	SATE
POLE	PUGS	RANT	RIME	RUCK	SAVE
POLL	PUKE	RAPE	RIMS	RUDE	SAWN
POLO	PULA	RAPS	RIMY	RUED	SAWS
POLY	PULL	RAPT	RIND	RUFF	SAYS
POMP	PULP	RARE	RING	RUGS	SCAB
POND	PUMA	RASH	RINK	RUHR	SCAG
PONG	PUMP	RASP	RIOT	RUIN	SCAM

SCAN	SHOP	SLOB	SOUP	SUMP	TART
SCAR	SHOT	SLOE	SOUR	SUMS	TASH
SCAT	SHOW	SLOG	SOWN	SUMY	TASK
SCOT	SHUN	SLOP	SOWS	SUNG	TA-TA
SCUD	SHUT	SLOT	SPAM	SUNK	TATS
SCUM	SIAN	SLOW	SPAN	SUNS	TAUT
SEAL	SICK	SLUB	SPAR	SUPS	TAXI
SEAM	SIDE	SLUE	SPAS	SURD	TEAK
SEAR	SIFT	SLUG	SPAT	SURE	TEAL
SEAS	SIGH	SLUM	SPAY	SURF	TEAM
SEAT	SIGN	SLUR	SPEC	SUSS	TEAR
SECS	SIKH	SLUT	SPED	SUVA	TEAS
SECT	SILK	SMOG	SPEW	SWAB	TEAT
SEED	SILL	SMUG	SPIC	SWAG	TEED
SEEK	SILO	SMUT	SPIK	SWAM	TEEM
SEEM	SILT	SNAG	SPIN	SWAN	TEES
SEEN	SIND	SNAP	SPIT	SWAP	TELE-
SEEP	SINE	SNIP	SPIV	SWAT	TELL
SEER	SING	SNOB	SPOD	SWAY	TEMA
SEES	SINH	SNOG	SPOT	SWIG	TEMP
SELF	SINK	SNOT	SPRY	SWIM	TEND
SELL	SINO-	SNOW	SPUD	SWOP	TENS
SEME	SINS	SNUB	SPUN	SWOT	TENT
SEMI	SION	SNUG	SPUR	SWUM	TERM
SEND	SIPS	SOAK	STAB	SYNC	TERN
SENT	SIRE	SOAP	STAG		TEST
SERA	SIRS	SOAR	STAR	**T**	TEXT
SERE	SITE	SOBS	STAY		THAN
SERF	SIZE	SOCA	STEM	TABS	THAT
SETA	SKEW	SOCK	STEP	TACH	THAW
SETI	SKID	SODA	STET	TACK	THEE
SETS	SKIM	SODS	STEW	TACO	THEM
SEWN	SKIN	SOFA	STIR	TACT	THEN
SEXY	SKIP	SOFT	STOL	TAGS	THEO-
SFAX	SKIS	SOIL	STOP	TAIL	THEY
SGML	SKIT	SOLD	STOW	TAKE	THIN
SHAD	SKUA	SOLE	STUB	TALC	THIS
SHAG	SKYE	SOLO	STUD	TALE	THOU
SHAH	SLAB	SOMA	STUM	TALK	THRU
SHAM	SLAG	SOME	STUN	TALL	THUD
SHAT	SLAM	SONG	STYE	TAME	THUG
SHED	SLAP	SONS	SUBS	TAMP	THUN
SHEW	SLAT	SOON	SUCH	TANG	THUS
SHIM	SLAV	SOOT	SUCK	TANH	TICK
SHIN	SLAY	SOPS	SUDS	TANK	TICS
SHIP	SLED	SORE	SUED	TANS	TIDE
SHIT	SLEW	SORT	SUER	TAPE	TIDY
SHOA	SLID	SO SO	SUET	TAPS	TIED
SHOD	SLIM	SO-SO	SUEZ	TARE	TIER
SHOE	SLIP	SOTS	SUIT	TARN	TIES
SHOO	SLIT	SOUL	SULK	TARO	TIFF
				TARS	

TILE	TOWS	UH OH	VILE	WEED	WISH
TILL	TOYS	ULNA	VINE	WEEK	WISP
TILT	TRAD	UNDO	VINO	WEEP	WITH
TIME	TRAM	UNIT	VIOL	WEFT	WITS
TINE	TRAP	UNIX	VIPS	WEIR	WOAD
TING	TRAY	UNTO	VISA	WELD	WOES
TINS	TREE	UPON	VISE	WELL	WOGS
TINT	TREK	UP TO	VOID	WELS	WOKE
TINY	TRIM	UPVC	VOLE	WELT	WOKS
TIPS	TRIO	URDU	VOLT	WEND	WOLD
TIRE	TRIP	URFA	VOTE	WENT	WOLF
TIRO	TROD	URGE	VOWS	WEPT	WOMB
TITI	TROT	URIC	VTOL	WEST	WONT
TITS	TRST	URNS		WETA	WOOD
TOAD	TRUE	USED	**W**	WETS	WOOF
TO BE	TRUG	USER	WADE	WHAM	WOOL
TO DO	TSAR	USES	WADI	WHAP	WOPS
TO-DO	TUBA	UTAH	WADS	WHAT	WORD
TODS	TUBE	UVEA	WAFT	WHEN	WORE
TOED	TUBS		WAGE	WHET	WORK
TOES	TUCK	**V**	WAGS	WHEW	WORM
TOFF	TUFT		WAIF	WHEY	WORN
TOGA	TUGS	VACS	WAIL	WHIG	WOVE
TOGO	TULA	VAIN	WATT	WHIM	WPCS
TOGS	TUNA	VALE	WAKE	WHIP	WRAP
TOIL	TUNE	VAMP	WALK	WHIR	WREN
TOLD	TURD	VANE	WALL	WHIT	WRIT
TOLL	TURF	VANS	WAND	WHIZ	WROT
TOMB	TURN	VARY	WANE	WHOA	WUHU
TOME	TUSH	VASE	WANK	WHOM	WUSS
TONE	TUSK	VAST	WANT	WHOP	
TONS	TUTU	VATS	WARD	WHYS	**X**
TOOK	TVEI	VAUD	WARM	WICK	XMAS
TOOL	TVER	VDUS	WARN	WIDE	X-RAY
TOOT	TWAT	VEAL	WARP	WIFE	
TOPS	TWEE	VEEP	WARS	WIGS	**Y**
TORE	TWIG	VEER	WART	WILD	YAKS
TORN	TWIN	VEIL	WARY	WILL	YAMS
TORS	TWIT	VEIN	WASH	WILT	YANG
TORT	TWOS	VELD	WASP	WILY	YANK
TORY	TYPE	VEND	WATT	WIMP	YAPS
TOSA	TYRE	VENT	WAUL	WIND	YARD
TOSH	TYRO	VERB	WAVE	WINE	YARN
TOSS	TZAR	VERY	WAVY	WING	YAWL
TOTE		VEST	WAXY	WINK	YAWN
TOTO	**U**	VETO	WAYS	WINS	YAWS
TOTS		VETS	WEAK	WINY	YAZD
TOUL	UCAS	VIAL	WEAL	WIPE	YEAH
TOUR	UCCA	VICE	WEAN	WIRE	YEAR
TOUT	UELE	VIED	WEAR	WIRY	YEAS
TOWN	UFOS	VIES	WEBS	WISE	YELL
	UGLY	VIEW			

YELP	YOBS	YOUR	**Z**	ZEST	ZIZZ
YENS	YOGA	YOWL	ZANY	ZIBO	ZOND
YETI	YOGI	YOYO	ZEAL	ZINC	ZONE
YEWS	YOKE	YUAN	ZEBU	ZINE	ZOOM
YIDS	YOLK	YUCK	ZEDS	ZION	ZOOS
YIPS	YORE	YULE	ZEIN	ZIPS	ZOUK
YLEM	YORK		ZERO	ZITS	ZULU

A	ADIEU	AILED	ALONG	ANNEX	ARIAN
AALII	ADIOS	AIMED	ALOOF	ANNOY	ARIAS
AARAU	AD LIB	AIOLI	ALOUD	ANNUL	ARICA
ABACA	AD-LIB	AIRED	ALPHA	ANODE	ARIEL
ABACK	ADMAN	AISLE	ALTAI	ANOLE	ARIEN
ABAFT	ADMEN	AISNE	ALTAR	ANOVA	ARIES
ABASE	ADMIT	AITCH	ALTER	ANTED	ARISE
ABASH	ADMIX	AJMER	ALTOS	ANTES	ARLES
ABATE	ADOBE	AKURE	AMASS	ANTIC	ARLON
ABBEY	ADOPT	ALACK	AMAZE	ANTSY	ARMCO
ABBOT	ADORE	ALAMO	AMBER	ANVIL	ARMED
ABEAM	ADORN	ALARM	AMBIT	ANZAC	AROID
ABELE	AD REM	ALARY	AMBLE	ANZIO	AROMA
ABHOR	ADUKI	ALATE	AMBRY	AORTA	AROSE
ABIDE	ADULT	ALBEE	AMEBA	AOSTA	ARRAN
ABLED	ADUWA	ALBUM	AMEND	APACE	ARRAS
ABODE	ADZES	ALCID	AMENT	APART	ARRAY
ABOHM	AEDES	ALDAN	AMICE	APEAK	ARRIS
A-BOMB	AEGIS	ALDER	AMIDE	APERY	ARROW
ABORT	AEONS	ALDOL	AMINE	APHID	ARSES
ABOUT	AESIR	ALECK	AMINO	APHIS	ARSIS
ABOVE	AFFIX	ALERT	AMIRS	APIAN	ARSON
ABUJA	AFIRE	ALGAE	AMISS	A PIED	ARTEL
ABUSE	AFOOT	ALGAL	AMITY	APING	ARTEX
ABYSS	AFOUL	ALGID	AMMAN	APISH	ARUBA
ACCRA	AFROS	ALGIN	AMNIO	APORT	ARYAN
ACHED	AFTER	ALGOL	AMONG	APPAL	ASCII
ACHES	AGAIN	ALGOR	AMOUR	APPEL	ASCOT
ACIDS	AGAMA	ALIAS	AMPLE	APPLE	ASCUS
ACKEE	AGAPE	ALIBI	AMPLY	APPLY	ASDIC
ACORN	AGATE	ALIEN	AMUCK	APRIL	ASHEN
ACRES	AGAVE	ALIGN	AMUSE	APRON	ASHES
ACRID	AGENT	ALIKE	ANCON	APSES	ASIAN
ACTED	AGGER	A LIST	ANDES	APSIS	ASIDE
ACTIN	AGGRO	ALIVE	ANGEL	APTLY	ASKED
ACTOR	AGILE	ALKYD	ANGER	AQABA	ASKER
ACT UP	AGING	ALKYL	ANGLE	ARABS	ASKEW
ACUTE	AGISM	ALLAH	ANGLO-	ARBER	ASPEN
ADAGE	AGIST	ALLAY	ANGRY	ARBOR	ASPER
ADAMS	AGLET	ALLEN	ANGST	ARDEN	ASPIC
ADANA	AGLOW	ALLEY	ANGUS	AREAL	ASSAI
ADAPT	AGNEW	ALL IN	ANHUI	AREAS	ASSAM
ADDAX	AGONY	ALLOA	ANILE	ARECA	ASSAY
ADDED	AGORA	ALLOT	ANIMA	ARENA	ASSEN
ADDER	AGREE	ALLOW	ANION	ARETE	ASSES
ADDLE	AGUES	ALLOY	ANISE	ARGIL	ASSET
ADD-ON	AHEAD	ALLYL	ANJOU	ARGOL	ASTER
ADD UP	AHERN	ALOFT	ANKLE	ARGON	ASTIR
ADEPT	AHWAZ	ALOHA	ANNAL	ARGOS	ASTRO-
A DEUX	AIDED	ALOIN	ANNAM	ARGOT	ASWAN
AD HOC	AIDES	ALONE	ANNAN	ARGUE	AT ALL

ATHOS	BABES	BARON	BEERS	BIFID	BLINI
ATLAS	BABUL	BARRA	BEERY	BIGHT	BLINK
ATOLL	BABUS	BARRE	BEETS	BIGOT	BLIPS
ATOMS	BACCY	BARRY	BEFIT	BIG UP	BLISS
ATONE	BACKS	BARTH	BEFOG	BIHAR	B LIST
ATONY	BACON	BARYE	BEGAN	BIJOU	BLITZ
ATRIA	BADGE	BASAL	BEGAT	BIKED	BLOAT
ATRIP	BADLY	BASED	BEGET	BIKES	BLOBS
AT SEA	BAGEL	BASEL	BEGIN	BILGE	BLOCH
ATTAR	BAGGY	BASER	BEGOT	BILLS	BLOCK
ATTIC	BAHAI	BASES	BEGUM	BILLY	BLOCS
AUDIO	BAHIA	BASHO	BEGUN	BINAL	BLOIS
AUDIT	BAILS	BASIC	BEIGE	BINGE	BLOKE
AUGER	BAIRN	BASIL	BEING	BINGO	BLOND
AUGHT	BAIZE	BASIN	BEIRA	BIOME	BLOOD
AUGUR	BAKED	BASIS	BELAY	BIOTA	BLOOM
AUNTS	BAKER	BASRA	BELCH	BIPED	BLOTS
AURAL	BALAS	BASSO	BELEM	BIPOD	BLOWN
AURAS	BALDY	BASTE	BELIE	BIRCH	BLOWS
AURIC	BALED	BATCH	BELLE	BIRDS	BLOWY
AUTOS	BALER	BATED	BELLS	BIROS	BLUER
AUXIN	BALES	BATHE	BELLY	BIRTH	BLUES
AVAIL	BALKH	BATHS	BELOW	BISON	BLUFF
AVENS	BALKS	BATIK	BELTS	BITCH	BLUNT
AVERT	BALLS	BATON	BEMBA	BITES	BLURB
AVIAN	BALLY	BATTY	BENCH	BITTY	BLURT
AVOID	BALMS	BATUM	BENDS	BIYSK	BLUSH
AWAIT	BALMY	BAULK	BENIN	BIZZY	BOARD
AWAKE	BALSA	BAWDS	BENTS	BLACK	BOARS
AWARD	BALTI	BAWDY	BENUE	BLADE	BOAST
AWARE	BALTI	BAYED	BENXI	BLAIN	BOATS
AWASH	BANAL	BAYOU	BERET	BLAIR	BOBBY
AWFUL	BANDA	BEACH	BERKS	BLAME	BOCHE
AWOKE	BANDS	BEADS	BERRY	BLANC	BODED
AXIAL	BANDY	BEADY	BERTH	BLAND	BODGE
AXILE	BANES	BEAKS	BERYL	BLANK	BOERS
AXING	BANFF	BEAKY	BESET	BLARE	BOGEY
AXIOM	BANGS	BEAMS	BESOM	BLASE	BOGGY
AXLES	BANJO	BEANO	BETAS	BLAST	BOGIE
AYAHS	BANKS	BEANS	BETEL	BLAZE	BOGOR
AZIDE	BANNS	BEARD	BEVEL	BLEAK	BOGUS
AZINE	BANTU	BEARS	BEVVY	BLEAR	BOHEA
AZOIC	BARBS	BEAST	BEZEL	BLEAT	BOHOL
AZOLE	BARDS	BEATS	BHAJI	BLEED	BOILS
AZOTE	BARED	BEAUS	BHANG	BLEEP	BOISE
AZTEC	BARER	BEAUT	BIBLE	BLEND	BOLES
AZURE	BARGE	BEAUX	BICKY	BLESS	BOLLS
	BARIC	BEBOP	BIDED	BLEST	BOLTS
B	BARKS	BECKS	BIDET	BLIDA	BOLUS
BAAED	BARMY	BEECH	BIERS	BLIMP	BOMBE
BABEL	BARNS	BEEFY	BIFFS	BLIND	BOMBS

BONDI	BOZOS	BROWN	BURST	CALVE	CAWED
BONDS	BRACE	BROWS	BUSBY	CALYX	CD-ROM
BONED	BRACT	BRUIN	BUSED	CAMEL	CEARA
BONES	BRAES	BRUIT	BUSES	CAMEO	CEASE
BONGO	BRAGA	BRUME	BUSHY	CAMPO	CEDAR
BONNY	BRAGG	BRUNO	BUSTS	CAMPS	CEDED
BONUS	BRAID	BRUNT	BUSTY	CANAL	CEDER
BONZE	BRAIL	BRUSH	BUTCH	CANDY	CEIBA
BOOBS	BRAIN	BRUTE	BUTTE	CANEA	CELEB
BOOBY	BRAKE	B-SIDE	BUTTS	CANED	CELLA
BOOED	BRAND	BUBAL	BUTTY	CANER	CELLE
BOOKS	BRASH	BUCHU	BUTYL	CANES	CELLO
BOOMS	BRASS	BUCKS	BUXOM	CANNA	CELLS
BOONS	BRATS	BUDDY	BUYER	CANNY	CENSE
BOORS	BRAVE	BUDGE	BWANA	CANOE	CENTO
BOOST	BRAVO	BUFFS	BYATT	CANON	CENTS
BOOTH	BRAWL	BUGGY	BYLAW	CANTO	CERES
BOOTS	BRAWN	BUGLE	BYRES	CANTS	CERIC
BOOTY	BRAXY	BUILD	BYTES	CAPER	CERTS
BOOZE	BRAYS	BUILT	BYTOM	CAPES	CETUS
BOOZY	BRAZE	BULBS	BYWAY	CAPON	CEUTA
BORAX	BREAD	BULGE		CAPRI	CHAFE
BORED	BREAK	BULGY	**C**	CAPUA	CHAFF
BORER	BREAM	BULKS	CABAL	CAPUT	CHAIN
BORES	BREDA	BULKY	CABBY	CARAT	CHAIR
BORIC	BREED	BULLA	CABER	CARDS	CHALK
BORNE	BRENT	BULLS	CABIN	CARED	CHAMP
BORNO	BREST	BULLY	CABLE	CARES	CHANT
BORNU	BREVE	BUMPH	CACAO	CARET	CHAOS
BORON	BRIAR	BUMPS	CACHE	CARGO	CHAPS
BOSKY	BRIBE	BUMPY	CACTI	CARNE	CHARD
BOSOM	BRICK	BUNCH	CADDY	CAROB	CHARM
BOSON	BRIDE	BUNDU	CADET	CAROL	CHARS
BOSSY	BRIEF	BUNGS	CADGE	CARPS	CHART
BOSUN	BRIER	BUNKS	CADIZ	CARRY	CHARY
BOTCH	BRILL	BUNNY	CADRE	CARTS	CHASE
BOUGH	BRINE	BUOYS	CAFES	CARVE	CHASM
BOULE	BRING	BURGH	CAFOD	CASED	CHATS
BOUND	BRINK	BURIN	CAGED	CASES	CHEAP
BOURN	BRINY	BURKE	CAGES	CASKS	CHEAT
BOUSE	BRISK	BURKS	CAGEY	CASTE	CHECK
BOUTS	BRITS	BURLY	CAINE	CASTS	CHEEK
BOVID	BROAD	BURMA	CAIRN	CATCH	CHEEP
BOWED	BROIL	BURNS	CAIRO	CATER	CHEER
BOWEL	BROKE	BURNT	CAJUN	CATTY	CHEFS
BOWER	BROME	BURPS	CAKED	CAULK	CHEJU
BOWIE	BRONX	BURRO	CAKES	CAUSE	CHELA
BOWLS	BROOD	BURRS	CALIX	CAVAN	CHERT
BOXED	BROOK	BURRY	CALLA	CAVED	CHESS
BOXER	BROOM	BURSA	CALLS	CAVES	CHEST
BOXES	BROTH	BURSE	CALOR	CAVIL	CHEWS

CHEWY	CIRCA	CLOUT	COMMA	COVES	CRIES
CHIBA	CISCO	CLOVE	COMPO	COVET	CRIME
CHICK	CISSY	CLOWN	CONCH	COVEY	CRIMP
CHIDE	CITED	CLUBS	CONES	COVIN	CRISP
CHIEF	CITES	CLUCK	CONEY	COWED	CROAK
CHILD	CIVET	CLUES	CONGA	COWER	CROAT
CHILE	CIVIC	CLUMP	CONGE	COWES	CROCK
CHILL	CIVIL	CLUNG	CONGO	COWLS	CROFT
CHIME	CLACK	CLUNK	CONIC	COWRY	CRONE
CHINA	CLADE	CLUNY	CONKS	COXAL	CRONY
CHINE	CLAIM	CLWYD	CONTE	COXED	CROOK
CHING	CLAMP	CLYDE	CONWY	COXES	CROON
CHINK	CLAMS	COACH	COOED	COYLY	CROPS
CHINS	CLANG	COALS	COOKS	COYPU	CRORE
CHIOS	CLANK	COALY	COOLS	COZEN	CROSS
CHIPS	CLANS	COAST	COONS	CRABS	CROUP
CHIRM	CLAPS	COATS	COOPS	CRACK	CROWD
CHIRP	CLARE	COBIA	CO-OPT	CRAFT	CROWN
CHIRR	CLARO	COBRA	COOTS	CRAGS	CROWS
CHITA	CLARY	COCKS	COPAL	CRAKE	CROZE
CHITS	CLASH	COCKY	COPED	CRAMP	CRUDE
CHIVY	CLASP	COCOA	COPES	CRANE	CRUEL
CHOCK	CLASS	CODAS	COPRA	CRANK	CRUET
CHOIR	CLAVE	CODED	COPSE	CRAPE	CRUMB
CHOKE	CLAWS	CODER	CORAL	CRAPS	CRUMP
CHOKO	CLEAN	CODES	CORDS	CRASH	CRURA
CHOKY	CLEAR	CODEX	CORED	CRASS	CRUSE
CHOMP	CLEAT	CODON	CORER	CRATE	CRUSH
CHOPS	CLEEK	COEDS	CORES	CRAVE	CRUST
CHORD	CLEFS	COGON	CORFU	CRAWL	CRYPT
CHORE	CLEFT	COHSE	CORGI	CRAZE	CUBAN
CHOSE	CLERK	COIFS	CORKS	CRAZY	CUBEB
CHOUX	CLEWS	COIGN	CORMS	CREAK	CUBED
CHOWS	CLICK	COILS	CORNS	CREAM	CUBES
CHRON-	CLIFF	COINS	CORNU	CREDO	CUBIC
CHUBB	CLIMB	COKES	CORNY	CREED	CUBIT
CHUCK	CLIME	COLDS	CORPS	CREEK	CUDDY
CHUFA	CLINE	COLEY	CORSE	CREEL	CUFFS
CHUFF	CLING	COLIC	COSTA	CREEP	CUING
CHUMP	CLINK	COLON	COSTS	CREME	CULCH
CHUMS	CLINT	COLTS	COTTA	CREPE	CULET
CHUNK	CLIPS	COLZA	COUCH	CREPT	CULEX
CHURL	CLOAK	COMAL	COUDE	CRESS	CULLS
CHURN	CLOCK	COMAS	COUGH	CREST	CULPA
CHUTE	CLODS	COMBI	COULD	CRETE	CULTS
CHYLE	CLOGS	COMBO	COUNT	CREWE	CUMIN
CHYME	CLONE	COMBS	COUPE	CREWS	CUNTS
CIDER	CLOSE	COMER	COUPS	CRIBS	CUPEL
CIGAR	CLOTH	COMET	COURT	CRICK	CUPID
CIMEX	CLOTS	COMFY	COVEN	CRIED	CUPPA
CINCH	CLOUD	COMIC	COVER	CRIER	CURBS

CURCH	DARED	DELOS	DINKY	DOORS	DRESS
CURDY	DARER	DELTA	DIODE	DOOZY	DRIBS
CURED	DARES	DELVE	DIRER	DOPED	DRIED
CURES	DARKS	DEMOB	DIRGE	DOPES	DRIER
CURET	DARKY	DEMON	DIRKS	DOPEY	DRIFT
CURIA	DARNS	DEMOS	DIRTY	DORIC	DRILL
CURIE	DARTS	DEMUR	DISCO	DOSED	DRILY
CURIO	DATED	DENAR	DISCS	DOSER	DRINK
CURLS	DATER	DENIM	DISHY	DOSES	DRIPS
CURLY	DATES	DENSE	DISKS	DOTED	DRIVE
CURRY	DATUM	DENTS	DITCH	DOTER	DROIT
CURSE	DAUBS	DEPOT	DITTO	DOTTY	DROLL
CURVE	DAUBY	DEPTH	DITTY	DOUAI	DROME
CUSEC	DAUNT	DERBY	DITZY	DOUBS	DRONE
CUSHY	DAVIT	DERMA	DIVAN	DOUBT	DROOL
CUSPS	DAVOS	DERRY	DIVED	DOUGH	DROOP
CUTER	DAWNS	DESKS	DIVER	DOURO	DROPS
CUTIN	DAZED	DETER	DIVES	DOUSE	DROSS
CUT IN	DAZES	DETOX	DIVOT	DOVER	DROVE
CUTIS	DEALS	DEUCE	DIVVY	DOVES	DROWN
CUT UP	DEALT	DEVIL	DIXIE	DOWDY	DRUGS
CUZCO	DEANS	DEVON	DIZZY	DOWEL	DRUID
CYBER	DEARS	DEWAR	DJINN	DOWER	DRUMS
CYCAD	DEARY	DHAKA	DOBBY	DOWNS	DRUNK
CYCLE	DEATH	DHOLE	DOBRO	DOWNY	DRUPE
CYDER	DEBAR	DHOTI	DOCKS	DOWRY	DRUSE
CYMAR	DEBIT	DHOWS	DODGE	DOWSE	DRYAD
CYMRY	DEBTS	DIALS	DODGY	DOYEN	DRYER
CYNIC	DEBUG	DIANA	DODOS	DOZED	DRYLY
CYSTS	DEBUT	DIARY	DOERS	DOZEN	DUALA
CYTON	DECAF	DIAZO	DO FOR	DOZER	DUBAI
CZARS	DECAL	DICED	DOGES	D PHIL	DUCAL
CZECH	DECAY	DICER	DOGGO	DRABS	DUCAT
	DECKS	DICEY	DOGGY	DRAFF	DUCHY
D	DECOR	DICKS	DOGIE	DRAFT	DUCKS
DACCA	DECOY	DICKY	DOGMA	DRAGS	DUCKY
DADDY	DECRY	DICTA	DOILY	DRAIL	DUCTS
DAGGA	DEEDS	DIETS	DOING	DRAIN	DUDES
DAGOS	DEFER	DIGIT	DOLBY	DRAKE	DUELS
DAILY	DEGAS	DIJON	DOLCE	DRAMA	DUETS
DAIRY	DE-ICE	DIKES	DOLED	DRAMS	DUFFS
DAISY	DEIFY	DILDO	DOLLS	DRANK	DUKES
DAKAR	DEIGN	DIMER	DOLLY	DRAPE	DULIA
DALES	DEISM	DIMES	DOLTS	DRAWL	DULLY
DALLY	DEIST	DIMLY	DOMED	DRAWN	DULSE
DAMAN	DEITY	DINAR	DOMES	DRAWS	DUMMY
DAMES	DEKKO	DINED	DONEE	DRAYS	DUMPS
DANCE	DELAY	DINER	DONNA	DREAD	DUMPY
DANDY	DELFT	DINGO	DONOR	DREAM	DUNCE
DANIO	DELHI	DINGY	DOOMS	DREAR	DUNES
DARAF	DELLS	DINKA	DOONA	DREGS	DUNGY

DUNKS	EDUCE	ENDED	ETUDE	FALUN	FERNY
DUPED	EDUCT	ENDER	EVADE	FAMED	FERRY
DUPER	EEJIT	END ON	EVENS	FANCY	FESSE
DUPES	EERIE	ENDOW	EVENT	FANGO	FETAL
DUPLE	EFFED	ENDUE	EVERT	FANGS	FETCH
DURAS	EGEST	ENEMA	EVERY	FANNY	FETED
DUREX	EGGER	ENEMY	EVICT	FANON	FETES
DUROC	EGHAM	ENJOY	EVILS	FANTI	FETID
DURRA	EGRET	ENNIS	EVOKE	FARAD	FETOR
DURUM	EGYPT	ENNUI	EWERS	FARCE	FETUS
DUSKY	EIDER	ENROL	EXACT	FARCI	FEUDS
DUSTY	EIFEL	ENSUE	EXALT	FARCY	FEVER
DUTCH	EIGER	ENTER	EXAMS	FARED	FEZES
DUVET	EIGHT	ENTRY	EXCEL	FARER	FIATS
DWARF	EIKON	ENUGU	EXERT	FARES	FIBRE
DWEEB	EILAT	ENURE	EXILE	FARLE	FICHU
DWELL	EJECT	ENVOY	EXIST	FARMS	FICUS
DWELT	EKMAN	EOSIN	EXITS	FARTS	FIELD
DYERS	ELAND	EPACT	EXPEL	FASTS	FIEND
DYFED	ELATE	EPEES	EXTOL	FATAL	FIERY
DYING	ELBOW	EPICS	EXTRA	FATED	FIFER
DYKES	ELCHE	EPOCH	EXUDE	FATES	FIFES
DYLAN	ELDER	EPODE	EXULT	FATTY	FIFTH
DYULA	ELECT	EPOXY	EYING	FAUGH	FIFTY
	ELEGY	EPROM	EYOTS	FAULT	FIGHT
	ELEMI	EPSOM	EYRIE	FAUNA	FILAR
E	ELFIN	EQUAL		FAUNS	FILCH
EAGER	ELGIN	EQUIP	**F**	FAVUS	FILED
EAGLE	ELIDE	ERASE		FAWNS	FILER
EAGRE	ELINT	ERBIL	FABLE	FAXED	FILES
EARED	ELITE	ERECT	FACED	FAZED	FILET
EARLS	ELOPE	ERGOT	FACER	FEARS	FILLY
EARLY	ELUDE	ERNIE	FACES	FEAST	FILMS
EAROM	ELUTE	ERODE	FACET	FEATS	FILMY
EARTH	ELVER	EROSE	FACIA	FEAZE	FILTH
EASED	ELVES	ERRED	FACTS	FECAL	FILUM
EASEL	EMBAY	ERROR	FADDY	FECES	FINAL
EASER	EMBED	ERUCT	FADED	FECIT	FINCH
EASTS	EMBER	ERUPT	FADER	FED UP	FINDS
EATEN	EMBOW	ESHER	FAERY	FEEDS	FINED
EATER	EMCEE	ESKER	FAILS	FEIGN	FINER
EAVES	EMDEN	ESPOO	FAINT	FEINT	FINES
EBBED	EMDEN	ESSAY	FAIRS	FELLS	FINGO
E BOAT	EMEND	ESSEN	FAIRY	FELON	FINIS
EBONY	EMERY	ESSEX	FAITH	FEMUR	FINNY
ECLAT	EMIRS	ESTER	FAKED	FENCE	FIORD
EDEMA	EMMEN	ESTOP	FAKER	FENNY	FIRED
EDGED	EMMER	ETHER	FAKES	FERAL	FIRER
EDGER	EMOTE	ETHIC	FAKIR	FERIA	FIRES
EDGES	EMPTY	ETHOS	FALDO	FERMI	FIRMS
EDICT	ENACT	ETHYL	FALLS	FERNS	FIRRY
EDIFY	ENATE		FALSE		

FIRST	FLOPS	FORTE	FUCUS	GALLS	GENUS
FIRTH	FLORA	FORTH	FUDGE	GAMED	GEODE
FISHY	FLORY	FORTS	FUELS	GAMER	GEOID
FISTS	FLOSS	FORTY	FUGAL	GAMES	GERMS
FITCH	FLOUR	FORUM	FUGGY	GAMEY	GESSO
FITLY	FLOUT	FOSSA	FUGUE	GAMIC	GET IT
FIVER	FLOWN	FOSSE	FULLY	GAMIN	GET ON
FIVES	FLUED	FOULS	FUMED	GAMMA	GET TO
FIXED	FLUES	FOUND	FUMER	GAMMY	GETUP
FIXER	FLUFF	FOUNT	FUMES	GAMUT	GET UP
FIXES	FLUID	FOURS	FUNDS	GANDA	GHANA
FIZZY	FLUKE	FOVEA	FUNEN	GANGS	GHATS
FJELD	FLUKY	FOWEY	FUNGI	GANJA	GHENT
FJORD	FLUME	FOWLS	FUNKS	GANSU	GHOST
FLACK	FLUNG	FOXED	FUNKY	GAOLS	GHOUL
FLAGS	FLUNK	FOXES	FUNNY	GAPED	GHYLL
FLAIL	FLUOR	FOYER	FURAN	GAPER	GIANT
FLAIR	FLUSH	FRAIL	FURRY	GAPES	GIBER
FLAKE	FLUTE	FRAME	FURZE	GARDA	GIBES
FLAKY	FLUTY	FRANC	FURZY	GASES	GIDDY
FLAME	FLYBY	FRANK	FUSED	GASPS	GIFTS
FLAMY	FLYER	FRAUD	FUSEE	GASSY	GIGOT
FLANK	FOALS	FREAK	FUSEL	GATED	GIGUE
FLANS	FOAMY	FREED	FUSES	GATES	GIJON
FLAPS	FOCAL	FREER	FUSIL	GAUDY	GILET
FLARE	FOCUS	FREON	FUSSY	GAUGE	GILLS
FLASH	FOGEY	FRESH	FUSTY	GAUNT	GILTS
FLASK	FOGGY	FRETS	FUTON	GAUSS	GIPSY
FLATS	FOILS	FRIAR	FUZZY	GAUZE	GIRLS
FLAWS	FOISM	FRIED	FYLDE	GAUZY	GIRON
FLAWY	FOIST	FRIER		GAVEL	GIRTH
FLEAM	FOLDS	FRIES	**G**	GAVLE	GIVEN
FLEAS	FOLIC	FRILL	GABBA	GAWKY	GIVER
FLECK	FOLIO	FRISE	GABBY	GAYER	GIZMO
FLEER	FOLKS	FRISK	GABES	GAZED	GLACE
FLEET	FOLLY	FRITT	GABLE	GAZER	GLADE
FLESH	FONTS	FRIZZ	GABON	GCSES	GLAIR
FLEWS	FOODS	FROCK	GADID	GEARS	GLAND
FLICK	FOOLS	FROGS	GAFFE	GECKO	GLANS
FLIER	FOOTS	FROND	GAFFS	GEESE	GLARE
FLIES	FOOTY	FRONS	GAGED	GEEST	GLARY
FLING	FORAY	FRONT	GAGES	GELID	GLASS
FLINT	FORCE	FROST	GAILY	GEMMA	GLAZE
FLIPS	FORDS	FROTH	GAINS	GENES	GLEAM
FLIRT	FORGE	FROWN	GAITS	GENET	GLEAN
FLOAT	FORGO	FROZE	GALAH	GENIC	GLEBE
FLOCK	FOR IT	FRUIT	GALAS	GENIE	GLEES
FLOES	FORKS	FRUMP	GALEA	GENII	GLEET
FLONG	FORLI	FRYER	GALES	GENOA	GLENN
FLOOD	FORME	FRY-UP	GALLA	GENRE	GLENS
FLOOR	FORMS	FUCKS	GALLE	GENTS	GLIDE

GLINT	GORKI	GRITS	GYPSY	HANOI	HEAVY
GLITZ	GORSE	GROAN	GYRAL	HANSA	HEBEI
GLOAT	GOTHA	GROAT		HANSE	HEDGE
GLOBE	GOT UP	GROIN	**H**	HANTS	HEDGY
GLOGG	GOUDA	GROOM	HABER	HAPLY	HEELS
GLOOM	GOUGE	GROPE	HABIT	HAPPY	HEFEI
GLOOP	GOURD	GROSS	HACEK	HARAR	HEFTY
GLORY	GOUTY	GROUP	HACKS	HARDS	HEGEL
GLOSS	GOWER	GROUT	HADAL	HARDY	HEIRS
GLOVE	GOWNS	GROVE	HADES	HARED	HEIST
GLUED	GRABS	GROWL	HADJI	HAREM	HEJAZ
GLUER	GRACE	GROWN	HADN'T	HARES	HEKLA
GLUEY	GRADE	GRUBS	HADST	HARPS	HELEN
GLUME	GRAFT	GRUEL	HAFIZ	HARPY	HELIX
GLUTS	GRAIL	GRUFF	HAFTS	HARRY	HELLE
GLYPH	GRAIN	GRUNT	HAGAR	HARSH	HELLO
GNARL	GRAMA	GUACO	HAGEN	HARTS	HELLS
GNASH	GRAMS	GUANO	HAGUE	HASN'T	HELMS
GNATS	GRAND	GUARD	HA-HAS	HASPS	HELOT
GNOME	GRANS	GUAVA	HAIDA	HASTE	HELPS
GOADS	GRANT	GUESS	HAIFA	HASTY	HELVE
GOALS	GRAPE	GUEST	HAIKU	HATCH	HE-MAN
GOATS	GRAPH	GUIDE	HAILS	HATED	HE-MEN
GODLY	GRASP	GUILD	HAIN'T	HATES	HENAN
GOERS	GRASS	GUILE	HAIRS	HAUGH	HENCE
GOFER	GRATE	GUILT	HAIRY	HAULM	HENGE
GOGGA	GRAVE	GUISE	HAITI	HAULS	HENIE
GOIAS	GRAVY	GULAG	HAJJI	HAUNT	HENNA
GOING	GRAYS	GULAR	HAKEA	HAUSA	HENRY
GOLDS	GRAZE	GULCH	HAKES	HAVEN	HENZE
GOLEM	GREAT	GULES	HAKIM	HAVER	HERAT
GOLLY	GREBE	GULFS	HALAL	HAVES	HERBS
GOMEL	GRECO-	GULLS	HALER	HAVOC	HERBY
GONAD	GREED	GULLY	HALIC	HAVRE	HERDS
GONDI	GREEK	GULPS	HALID	HAWES	HERES
GONER	GREEN	GUMBO	HALLE	HAWKS	HERNE
GONGS	GREER	GUMMA	HALLO	HAWSE	HEROD
GONNA	GREET	GUMMY	HALLS	HAYDN	HERON
GOODS	GREYS	GUNGE	HALMA	HAZED	HERTZ
GOODY	GRIDS	GUPPY	HALOS	HAZEL	HESSE
GOOEY	GRIEF	GURUS	HALTS	HAZER	HET UP
GOOFS	GRIFT	GUSSY	HALVE	HAZES	HEWED
GOOFY	GRIKE	GUSTO	HAMAL	H-BOMB	HEWER
GOOLE	GRILL	GUSTS	HAMMY	HEADS	HEXAD
GOONS	GRIME	GUSTY	HAMZA	HEADY	HEXED
GOOSE	GRIMY	GUTSY	HANAU	HEALY	HEXER
GOOSY	GRIND	GUTTA	HANCE	HEAPS	HEXES
GORAL	GRINS	GUYED	HANDS	HEARD	HEXYL
GORED	GRIPE	GUYOT	HANDY	HEART	HICKS
GORES	GRIPS	GWENT	HANKS	HEATH	HIDER
GORGE	GRIST	GWERU	HANKY	HEAVE	HIDES

HI-FIS	HOLLO	HOVEL	IBIZA	INKED	JAMBS
HIGHS	HOLLY	HOVER	ICIER	INK IN	JAMES
HIGHT	HOLST	HOWDY	ICILY	INKLE	JAMMU
HIJAZ	HOMER	HOWLS	ICING	IN-LAW	JAMMY
HIKED	HOMES	HOYLE	ICONS	INLAY	JAPAN
HIKER	HOMEY	HSIAN	ICTIC	INLET	JAPER
HIKES	HONAN	HUBBY	ICTUS	INNER	JAPES
HILAR	HONDO	HUBEI	IDAHO	INPUT	JAUNT
HILLA	HONED	HUBLI	IDEAL	INSET	JAWED
HILLS	HONEY	HUFFY	IDEAS	INTER	JAZZY
HILLY	HONKS	HUFUF	IDIOM	INTRO	JEANS
HILTS	HONKY	HUGER	IDIOT	INUIT	JEEPS
HILUM	HONOR	HULKS	IDLED	INURE	JEERS
HILUS	HOOCH	HULLO	IDLER	INURN	JEHOL
HINDI	HOODS	HULLS	IDOLS	INVAR	JELLO
HINDS	HOOEY	HULME	IDYLL	IODIC	JELLY
HINDU	HOO-HA	HUMAN	IGLOO	IONIC	JEMMY
HINES	HOOKE	HUMIC	IKEJA	IOTAS	JENNY
HINGE	HOOKS	HUMID	IKONS	IRAQI	JEREZ
HINNY	HOOKY	HUMPH	ILEAC	IRATE	JERKS
HI NRG	HOOPS	HUMPS	ILEUM	IRBID	JERKY
HINTS	HOOTS	HUMPY	ILEUS	IRISH	JESTS
HIPPO	HOPED	HUMUS	ILIAC	IRKED	JESUS
HIPPY	HOPEH	HUNAN	ILIAD	IRONS	JETTY
HIRAM	HOPER	HUNCH	ILIUM	IRONY	JEWEL
HIRED	HOPES	HUNKS	IMAGE	ISERE	JEWRY
HIRER	HORAE	HUNTS	IMAGO	ISLAM	JIBED
HIRST	HORAL	HUPEH	IMAMS	ISLAY	JIBES
HITCH	HORDE	HURDS	IMBED	ISLES	JIDDA
HIT ON	HOREB	HURON	IMBUE	ISLET	JIFFY
HIVED	HORME	HURRY	IMIDE	ISSUE	JIHAD
HIVES	HORNS	HURST	IMINE	ISTLE	JILIN
HOARD	HORNY	HURTS	IMPEL	ITALO-	JIMMY
HOARY	HORSA	HUSKS	IMPLY	ITALY	JINAN
HOBBS	HORSE	HUSKY	IN ALL	ITCHY	JINGO
HOBBY	HORST	HUSSY	INANE	ITEMS	JINJA
HOBOS	HORSY	HUTCH	INAPT	IVIED	JINKS
HOCKS	HORUS	HYADS	INCUR	IVIES	JINNI
HOCUS	HOSEA	HYDRA	INCUS	IVORY	JIVED
HOFEI	HOSED	HYDRO	INDEX	IZMIR	JOCKS
HOFUF	HOSES	HYENA	INDIA	IZMIT	JOINS
HOGAN	HOSTA	HYING	INDIC		JOINT
HO-HUM	HOSTS	HYMEN	INDRE	**J**	JOIST
HOICK	HOTAN	HYMNS	INDUS	JABOT	JOKED
HOIST	HOTEL	HYPED	INEPT	JACKS	JOKER
HOKKU	HOTLY	HYPER	INERT	JADED	JOKES
HOKUM	HOUGH	HYPOS	INFER	JADES	JOLLY
HOLDS	HOUND		INFIX	JAFFA	JOLTS
HOLES	HOURI	**I**	IN FOR	JAILS	JONAH
HOLEY	HOURS	IAMBS	INGOT	JALAP	JORUM
HOLLA	HOUSE	I-BEAM	INION	JAMBI	JOULE

JOUST	KEENS	KNOWS	LAMED	LEARN	LIFER
JOVES	KEEPS	KNURL	LAMER	LEASE	LIFTS
JOWLS	KELLS	KOALA	LAMPS	LEASH	LIGER
JOYED	KELLY	KOCHI	LANAI	LEAST	LIGHT
JUDAS	KENNY	KOINE	LANCE	LEAVE	LIKED
JUDGE	KENYA	KONGO	LANDS	LECCE	LIKEN
JUGAL	KERBS	KONYA	LANES	LEDGE	LIKES
JUGUM	KERCH	KOOKS	LANKY	LEDGY	LILAC
JUICE	KERRY	KOOKY	LAOAG	LED ON	LILLE
JUICY	KETCH	KORAN	LAOIS	LEECH	LILOS
JUJUS	KEVEL	KOREA	LA PAZ	LEEDS	LILTS
JULEP	KEYED	KORMA	LAPEL	LEEKS	LIMBO
JUMBO	KHAKI	KRAAL	LAPSE	LEERS	LIMBS
JUMPS	KHANS	KRAFT	LAP UP	LEERY	LIMED
JUMPY	KHMER	KRAIT	LARCH	LEFTY	LIMEN
JUNCO	KIANG	KREMS	LARGE	LEGAL	LIMES
JUNES	KICKS	KRILL	LARGO	LEGER	LIMEY
JUNKS	KIKES	KRONA	LARKS	LEGGY	LIMIT
JUNTA	KILIM	KRONE	LARNE	LEGIT	LINED
JUNTO	KILLS	KROON	LAROS	LEMMA	LINEN
JURAL	KILNS	KUDOS	LARVA	LEMON	LINER
JURAT	KILOS	KUDZU	LASER	LEMUR	LINES
JUREL	KILTS	KUFIC	LASSO	LENDL	LINGO
JUROR	KINDS	KUKRI	LASTS	LENIS	LININ
JURUA	KINGS	KULAK	LATCH	LENTO	LINKS
	KININ	KURIL	LATER	LEPER	LINTY
K	KINKS	KURSK	LATEX	LET ON	LIONS
KABUL	KINKY	KUTCH	LATHE	LETUP	LIPID
KALAT	KIOSK	KWARA	LATHS	LET UP	LIRAS
KANDY	KIRIN	KWELA	LATIN	LEVEE	LISLE
KANGA	KIRKS	KYOTO	LAUGH	LEVEL	LISTS
KANSU	KIROV		LAVAL	LEVER	LITER
KAPOK	KITES	**L**	LAVER	LEVIS	LITHE
KAPUT	KITTY	LABEL	LAWKS	LEWES	LITRE
KARAT	KITWE	LACED	LAWNS	LEWIS	LIT UP
KAREN	KIWIS	LACER	LAWNY	LEXIS	LIVED
KARMA	KLONG	LACES	LAXLY	LEYTE	LIVEN
KAROO	KNACK	LADEN	LAY-BY	LHASA	LIVER
KARST	KNAVE	LADER	LAYER	LIANA	LIVES
KASAI	KNEAD	LADLE	LAY UP	LIARS	LIVID
KASHI	KNEED	LAGAN	LAZED	LIBEL	LLAMA
KAUAI	KNEEL	LAGER	LAZIO	LIBRA	LLANO
KAURI	KNEES	LAGOS	LEACH	LIBYA	LLOYD
KAYAK	KNELL	LAHTI	LEADS	LICIT	LOACH
KAZAN	KNELT	LAIRD	LEADY	LICKS	LOADS
KAZOO	KNIFE	LAIRS	LEAFY	LIDOS	LOAMY
KBYTE	KNOBS	LAITY	LEAKS	LIEGE	LOANS
KEBAB	KNOCK	LAKER	LEAKY	LIE IN	LOATH
KEDAH	KNOLL	LAKES	LEANT	LIE-IN	LOBAR
KEDGE	KNOTS	LAMAS	LEAPS	LIENS	LOBBY
KEELS	KNOWN	LAMBS	LEAPT	LIEUS	LOBED

LOBES	LOWER	MACRO	MARRY	MERGE	MINSK
LOCAL	LOWLY	MADAM	MARSH	MERIT	MINTS
LOCHS	LOYAL	MADLY	MASAI	MERRY	MINUS
LOCKS	LUCCA	MAFIA	MASAN	MERSE	MIRED
LOCUM	LUCID	MAGIC	MASER	MESIC	MIRES
LOCUS	LUCKY	MAGMA	MASKS	MESNE	MIRID
LODEN	LUCRE	MAGUS	MASON	MESON	MIRTH
LODES	LUFFA	MAIDS	MASSA	MESSY	MISER
LODGE	LUGER	MAINE	MASTS	METAL	MISSY
LOESS	LUMEN	MAINS	MATCH	METED	MISTS
LOFTS	LUMME	MAINZ	MATED	METER	MISTY
LOFTY	LUMPS	MAIZE	MATER	METHS	MITES
LOGIC	LUMPY	MAJOR	MATES	METOL	MITIS
LOG IN	LUNAR	MAKER	MATEY	ME-TOO	MITRE
LOG ON	LUNCH	MAKES	MATIN	METRE	MITTS
LOGOS	LUNGE	MALAR	MATSU	METRO	MIXED
LOINS	LUNGS	MALAY	MATTE	MEUSE	MIXER
LOIRE	LUPIN	MALES	MAUVE	MEWED	MIXES
LOLLY	LUPUS	MALLE	MAXIM	MEZZO	MIX-UP
LONER	LURCH	MALLS	MAYAN	MIAMI	MIZAR
LOOKS	LURED	MALMO	MAYBE	MIAOW	MOANS
LOOMS	LURER	MALTA	MAYN'T	MICKS	MOATS
LOONS	LURES	MALTY	MAYOR	MICRO	MOCHA
LOONY	LUREX	MAMAS	MAYST	MIDDY	MOCKS
LOOPS	LURGY	MAMBA	MAZES	MIDGE	MODAL
LOOPY	LURID	MAMBO	MBEKI	MID-ON	MODEL
LOOSE	LUSTS	MAMET	MEADS	MIDST	MODEM
LOPED	LUSTY	MAMEY	MEALS	MIENS	MODES
LOPER	LUTES	MAMMA	MEALY	MIFFY	MOERS
LORAN	LUTON	MAMMY	MEANS	MIGHT	MOGGY
LORDS	LUXOR	MANDE	MEANT	MIKES	MOGUL
LOREN	LUZON	MANED	MEATH	MILAN	MOIRE
LORIS	LYCEE	MANES	MEATY	MILCH	MOIST
LORRY	LYING	MANGE	MECCA	MILER	MOKES
LOSER	LYMPH	MANGO	MEDAL	MILES	MOKPO
LOSSY	LYNCH	MANGY	MEDAN	MILKY	MOLAL
LOTIC	LYRES	MANIA	MEDIA	MILLS	MOLAR
LOTTA	LYRIC	MANIC	MEDIC	MIMED	MOLDS
LOTUS	LYSIN	MANLY	MEDOC	MIMER	MOLDY
LOUGH	LYSIS	MANNA	MEETS	MIMES	MOLES
LOUPE	LYSOL	MANOR	MELEE	MIMIC	MOLLS
LOUSE	LYTIC	MANSE	MELON	MINCE	MOLLY
LOUSY	LYTTA	MANTA	MELOS	MINDS	MOLTO
LOUTH		MANUS	MEMOS	MINED	MOLTS
LOUTS	**M**	MAORI	MENAI	MINER	MOMMA
LOVAT		MAPLE	MENDS	MINES	MOMMY
LOVED	MACAO	MARAE	MENUS	MINGY	MONAD
LOVER	MACAW	MARCH	MEOWS	MINIM	MONAL
LOVES	MACES	MARES	MERCA	MINIS	MONCK
LOVEY	MACHO	MARKS	MERCY	MINNA	MONEY
LOWED	MACLE	MARNE	MERES	MINOR	MONKS
	MACON				

MONTH	MUCIN	NAILS	NEVER	NOPAL	ODIUM
MONZA	MUCKY	NAIVE	NEVIS	NO-PAR	ODOUR
MOOCH	MUCRO	NAKED	NEWEL	NORMS	OFFAL
MOODS	MUCUS	NALGO	NEWER	NORSE	OFFER
MOODY	MUDDY	NAMED	NEWLY	NORTH	OFGAS
MOOED	MUFFS	NAMES	NEWRY	NOSED	OFTEL
MOOLI	MUFTI	NAMUR	NEWSY	NOSES	OFTEN
MOONS	MUGGY	NANCY	NEWTS	NOTCH	OFWAT
MOONY	MULCH	NANNY	NEXUS	NOTED	OGIVE
MOORS	MULCT	NAPES	NICAD	NOTES	OGLED
MOOSE	MULES	NAPPA	NICAM	NOTUM	OGLER
MOPED	MULEY	NAPPE	NICER	NOUNS	OGRES
MOPER	MULGA	NAPPY	NICHE	NOVAE	OILED
MOP UP	MULLS	NARES	NICKS	NOVAS	OILER
MOP-UP	MULTI-	NARKS	NIDAL	NOVEL	OINKS
MORAL	MUMMY	NARKY	NIDUS	NO WAY	OKAPI
MORAY	MUMPS	NARVA	NIECE	NO-WIN	OKAYS
MOREL	MUMSY	NASAL	NIFFY	NOYON	OLDEN
MORES	MUNCH	NASIK	NIFTY	NUCHA	OLDER
MORNS	MUNGO	NASTY	NIGER	NUDDY	OLEUM
MORON	MURAL	NATAL	NIGHT	NUDES	OLIVE
MORPH	MUREX	NATES	NIHIL	NUDGE	OLMEC
MOSEY	MURKY	NATTY	NIKKO	NUKED	OMAGH
MOSSI	MURRE	NAURU	NIMBI	NUKUS	OMAHA
MOSSO	MUSED	NAVAL	NIMBY	NURSE	OMEGA
MOSSY	MUSER	NAVAR	NIMES	NUTTY	OMENS
MOSUL	MUSES	NAVEL	NINES	NYALA	OMUTA
MOTEL	MUSHY	NAVES	NINNY	NYLON	ON AIR
MOTES	MUSIC	NAVVY	NINON	NYMPH	ON-AIR
MOTET	MUSKY	NAXOS	NINTH		ON CUE
MOTHS	MUSTH	NAZIS	NIPPY	**O**	ONEGA
MOTHY	MUSTY	NDOLA	NISEI		ON ICE
MOTIF	MUTED	'NEATH	NISUS	OAKEN	ONION
MOTOR	MUTES	NECKS	NITRE	OAKUM	ONSET
MOTTO	MUTTS	NEEDS	NITTY	OARED	ON TAP
MOULD	MUZAK	NEEDY	NIVAL	OASES	ON TOW
MOULT	MUZZY	NEGEV	NIXED	OASIS	OOMPH
MOUND	MWERU	NEGRO	NOBLE	OATEN	OOTID
MOUNT	MYALL	NEGUS	NOBLY	OATHS	OOZED
MOURN	MYNAH	NEIGH	NODAL	OBEAH	OPALS
MOUSE	MYOMA	NELLY	NODDY	OBESE	OP ART
MOUSY	MYOPE	NEMAN	NODES	OBOES	OPERA
MOUTH	MYRRH	NEMEA	NODUS	OCCUR	OPINE
MOVED	MYTHS	NEPAL	NOHOW	OCEAN	OPIUM
MOVER		NEPER	NOISE	OCHRE	OPTED
MOVES	**N**	NERDS	NOISY	OCREA	OPTIC
MOVIE	NAAFI	NERVE	NOMAD	OCTAD	ORACH
MOWED	NABOB	NERVY	NONCE	OCTAL	ORATE
MOWER	NACRE	NESTS	NOOKS	OCTET	ORBIT
MOXIE	NADIR	NEURO-	NO ONE	ODDER	ORDER
MOYLE	NAIAD	NEUSS	NOOSE	ODDLY	ORGAN
				ODEUM	

ORIBI	PACES	PARRY	PENNY	PIMPS	PLICA
ORIEL	PACKS	PARSE	PENZA	PINCH	PLIED
ORION	PACTS	PARTS	PEONY	PINED	PLIER
ORIYA	PADDY	PARTY	PERAK	PINES	PLONK
ORLON	PADRE	PASAY	PERCH	PINEY	PLOTS
ORLOP	PADUA	PASHA	PERES	PINGO	PLOWS
ORMER	PAEAN	PASSE	PERIL	PINKO	PLOYS
ORRIS	PAEON	PASTA	PERKS	PINKS	PLUCK
ORURO	PAGAN	PASTE	PERKY	PINNA	PLUGS
OSAKA	PAGED	PASTO	PERRY	PINNY	PLUMB
OSCAR	PAGER	PASTS	PERSE	PINSK	PLUME
OSIER	PAGES	PASTY	PER SE	PINTA	PLUMP
OSMIC	PAILS	PATCH	PERTH	PINTO	PLUMS
OTAGO	PAINS	PATEN	PESKY	PINTS	PLUMY
OTHER	PAINT	PATER	PESOS	PINUP	PLUNK
OTTER	PAIRS	PATES	PESTO	PIOUS	PLUSH
OUGHT	PALEA	PATHS	PESTS	PIPAL	PLUTO
OUIJA	PALED	PATIO	PETAL	PIPED	PLZEN
OUJDA	PALER	PATNA	PETER	PIPER	POACH
OUNCE	PALES	PATSY	PETIT	PIPES	PO BOX
OUTDO	PALLS	PATTY	PETTY	PIPIT	PODGY
OUTER	PALLY	PAUSE	PEWEE	PIQUE	PODIA
OUTGO	PALMA	PAVED	PEWIT	PISTE	POEMS
OUTRE	PALMS	PAVIA	PHASE	PIICH	POESY
OUTRO	PALMY	PAWED	PHIAL	PITHY	POETS
OUZEL	PALSY	PAWKY	PHLOX	PITON	POGGE
OVALS	PANDA	PAWNS	PHONE	PITTA	POILU
OVARY	PANEL	PAYEE	PHONO	PIURA	POINT
OVATE	PANES	PEACE	PHOTO	PIVOT	POISE
OVENS	PANGS	PEACH	PHUTS	PIXEL	POKED
OVERS	PANIC	PEAKS	PHYLA	PIXIE	POKER
OVERT	PANNE	PEAKY	PHYLE	PIZZA	POKES
OVINE	PANSY	PEALS	PIANO	PLACE	POLAR
OVOID	PANTS	PEARL	PIAUI	PLAGE	POLED
OVOLO	PANTY	PEARS	PICKS	PLAID	POLES
OVULE	PAPAL	PEATS	PICKY	PLAIN	POLIO
OWING	PAPAS	PEATY	PICOT	PLAIT	POLJE
OWLET	PAPAW	PECAN	PIECE	PLANE	POLKA
OWNED	PAPER	PECKS	PIERS	PLANK	POLLS
OWNER	PAPPY	PEDAL	PIETA	PLANS	POLYP
OXBOW	PAPUA	PEEPS	PIETY	PLANT	POLYS
OXEYE	PARAS	PEERS	PIGGY	PLASH	POMMY
OXFAM	PARCH	PEEVE	PIGMY	PLASM	PONCE
OXIDE	PARED	PEKOE	PIING	PLATE	PONCY
OXIME	PARER	PELTS	PIKER	PLATY	PONDS
OXLIP	PARIS	PEMBA	PIKES	PLAYS	PONGS
OZONE	PARKA	PENAL	PILAF	PLAZA	PONGY
	PARKS	PENCE	PILED	PLEAD	POOCH
P	PARKY	PENIS	PILES	PLEAS	POOFS
PACED	PARMA	PENNA	PILLS	PLEAT	POOFY
PACER	PAROL	PENNE	PILOT	PLEBS	POOLE

Q 5 POOLS

POOLS	PRILL	PULPS	QUASH	RAGED	READY
POONA	PRIME	PULPY	QUASI-	RAGES	REALM
POOPS	PRIMO	PULSE	QUAYS	RAGGA	REAMS
POPES	PRIMP	PUMAS	QUEEN	RAIDS	REARM
POPPA	PRINK	PUMPS	QUEER	RAILS	REARS
POPPY	PRINT	PUNCH	QUELL	RAINS	REBEL
POPSY	PRION	PUNKA	QUERN	RAINY	REBUS
POP-UP	PRIOR	PUNKS	QUERY	RAISE	REBUT
PORCH	PRISE	PUNTS	QUEST	RAITA	RECAP
PORED	PRISM	PUNTY	QUEUE	RAJAH	RECON
PORES	PRIVY	PUPAE	QUICK	RAKED	RECTO
PORGY	PRIZE	PUPAL	QUIET	RAKER	RECUR
PORKY	PRO-AM	PUPAS	QUIFF	RAKES	REDAN
PORNO	PROBE	PUPIL	QUILL	RALLY	REDIA
PORTS	PRODS	PUPPY	QUILT	RAMIE	REDID
POSED	PROEM	PUREE	QUINE	RAMPS	REEDS
POSER	PROFS	PURER	QUINS	RAMUS	REEDY
POSES	PROLE	PURGE	QUINT	RANCE	REEFS
POSEY	PROMO	PURRS	QUIPS	RANCH	REEKY
POSIT	PROMS	PURSE	QUIRE	R AND B	REELS
POSSE	PRONE	PUSAN	QUIRK	R AND D	REEVE
POSTS	PRONG	PUSHY	QUIRT	RANDY	REFER
POTTO	PROOF	PUSSY	QUITE	RANEE	REFIT
POTTY	PROPS	PUT ON	QUITO	RANGE	REGAL
POUCH	PROSE	PUT-ON	QUITS	RANGY	REICH
POUFS	PROST	PUTTO	QUOIN	RANKS	REIFY
POULT	PROSY	PUTTS	QUOIT	RAPED	REIGN
POUND	PROTO-	PUTTY	QUORN	RAPES	REIKI
POUTS	PROUD	PYGMY	QUOTA	RAPHE	REIMS
POWAN	PROVE	PYLON	QUOTE	RAPID	REINS
POWER	PROWL	PYOID	QUOTH	RARER	REJIG
POWYS	PROWS	PYRAN	QUR'AN	RASHT	REKEY
POXES	PROXY	PYRES		RASPS	RELAX
PRAMS	PRUDE	PYREX	**R**	RATAL	RELAY
PRANK	PRUNE	PYXES	RABAT	RATED	RELIC
PRASE	PSALM	PYXIE	RABBI	RATEL	REMEX
PRATE	PSEUD	PYXIS	RABIC	RATES	REMIT
PRATO	PSKOV		RABID	RATIO	RENAL
PRATS	PSOAS	**Q**	RABIN	RATTY	RENEW
PRAWN	PSYCH	QATAR	RACED	RAVED	RENIN
PREEN	PUBES	QUACK	RACER	RAVEL	RENTE
PREPS	PUBIC	QUADS	RACES	RAVEN	RENTS
PRESA	PUBIS	QUAFF	RACKS	RAVER	REPAY
PRESS	PUCKS	QUAIL	RADAR	RAWER	REPEL
PRICE	PUDGY	QUAKE	RADII	RAWLY	REPLY
PRICK	PUFFS	QUAKY	RADIO	RAYON	RERAN
PRICY	PUFFY	QUALE	RADIX	RAZED	RERUN
PRIDE	PUKED	QUALM	RADOM	RAZER	RESAT
PRIED	PUKKA	QUANT	RADON	RAZOR	RESET
PRIER	PULER	QUARK	RAFTS	REACH	RESIN
PRIGS	PULLS	QUART	RAGAS	REACT	RESIT

RESTS	RIVER	ROWAN	SADLY	SAUCE	SCOUT
RETCH	RIVET	ROWDY	SAFER	SAUCY	SCOWL
RETRO	RIYAL	ROWED	SAFES	SAUNA	SCRAG
RETRO-	ROACH	ROWEL	SAGAS	SAURY	SCRAM
RETRY	ROADS	ROWER	SAGES	SAUTE	SCRAP
REUSE	ROANS	ROYAL	SAGGY	SAVED	SCREE
REVEL	ROARS	RUBLE	SAHIB	SAVER	SCREW
REVET	ROAST	RUCHE	SAIDA	SAVES	SCRIM
REVUE	ROBED	RUCKS	SAIGA	SAVIN	SCRIP
REXES	ROBES	RUDDY	SAILS	SAVOY	SCRUB
RHEAS	ROBIN	RUDER	SAINT	SAVVY	SCRUM
RHEUM	ROBLE	RUFFE	SAKAI	SAWED	SCUBA
RHINE	ROBOT	RUFFS	SAKER	SAWER	SCUFF
RHINO	ROCKS	RUGBY	SAKES	SAXON	SCULL
RHONE	ROCKY	RUING	SALAD	SAYER	SCURF
RHUMB	RODEO	RUINS	SALEM	SAY SO	SCUTE
RHYME	ROGER	RULED	SALEP	SAY-SO	SEALS
RIALS	ROGUE	RULER	SALES	SCABS	SEAMS
RICIN	ROLES	RULES	SALIC	SCADS	SEAMY
RICKS	ROLLS	RUMBA	SALLY	SCALD	SEATS
RIDER	ROMAN	RUMEN	SALOL	SCALE	SEBUM
RIDES	ROMEO	RUMMY	SALON	SCALL	SECCO
RIDGE	ROMER	RUMPS	SALOP	SCALP	SECTS
RIDGY	ROMPS	RUNES	SALPA	SCALY	SEDAN
RIFFS	RONDO	RUNGS	SALTA	SCAMP	SEDGE
RIFLE	ROODS	RUNIC	SALTS	SCAMS	SEDGY
RIFTS	ROOFS	RUN IN	SALTY	SCANS	SEDUM
RIGHT	ROOKS	RUN-IN	SALVE	SCANT	SEEDS
RIGID	ROOMS	RUNNY	SALVO	SCAPE	SEEDY
RIGOR	ROOMY	RUNTS	SAMAR	SCARE	SEERS
RILED	ROOST	RUNTY	SAMBA	SCARF	SEGNO
RILEY	ROOTS	RUN-UP	SAMEY	SCARP	SEINE
RILLS	ROPED	RUPEE	SAMOA	SCARS	SEISE
RINDS	ROPES	RURAL	SAMOS	SCART	SEISM
RINGS	ROPEY	RUSES	SANDS	SCARY	SEIZE
RINKS	ROSES	RUSHY	SANDY	SCAUP	SELBY
RINSE	ROSIN	RUSKS	SANER	SCEND	SELES
RIOJA	ROTAS	RUSSO-	SAPID	SCENE	SELVA
RIOTS	ROTOR	RUSTY	SAPPY	SCENT	SEMEN
RIPEN	ROUEN	RUTTY	SARAN	SCHWA	SEMIS
RIPER	ROUES		SARGE	SCION	SENNA
RIPON	ROUGE	**S**	SARIN	SCOFF	SENOR
RISEN	ROUGH		SARIS	SCOLD	SENSE
RISER	ROUND	SABAH	SARKY	SCONE	SENZA
RISES	ROUPY	SABER	SAROS	SCOOP	SEOUL
RISKS	ROUSE	SABIN	SASSY	SCOOT	SEPAL
RISKY	ROUST	SABLE	SATAN	SCOPE	SEPIA
RITES	ROUTE	SABOT	SATED	SCORE	SEPOY
RITZY	ROUTS	SABRA	SATEM	SCORN	SERAC
RIVAL	ROVED	SABRE	SATIN	SCOTS	SERFS
RIVEN	ROVER	SACKS	SATYR	SCOUR	SERGE

29

SERIF	SHELF	SHYER	SIXTE	SLICE	SNACK
SERIN	SHELL	SHYLY	SIXTH	SLICK	SNAFU
SEROW	SHERD	SIBIU	SIXTY	SLIDE	SNAGS
SERUM	SHEWN	SIBYL	SIZAR	SLIGO	SNAIL
SERVE	SHIAH	SICKO	SIZED	SLILY	SNAKE
SERVO	SHIED	SIDED	SIZES	SLIME	SNAKY
SETAL	SHIER	SIDES	SKATE	SLIMY	SNAPS
SET ON	SHIES	SIDLE	SKEET	SLING	SNARE
SET TO	SHIFT	SIEGE	SKEIN	SLINK	SNARL
SET-TO	SHILY	SIENA	SKELP	SLIPS	SNATH
SET UP	SHINE	SIEVE	SKEWS	SLITS	SNEAK
SET-UP	SHINS	SIGHS	SKIDS	SLOBS	SNECK
SEVEN	SHINY	SIGHT	SKIED	SLOES	SNEER
SEVER	SHIPS	SIGLA	SKIEN	SLOGS	SNICK
SEWED	SHIRE	SIGMA	SKIER	SLOOP	SNIDE
SEWER	SHIRK	SIGNS	SKIES	SLOPE	SNIFF
SEXED	SHIRR	SIKHS	SKIFF	SLOPS	SNIPE
SEXES	SHIRT	SILEX	SKILL	SLOSH	SNIPS
SHABA	SHITE	SILKS	SKIMP	SLOTH	SNOBS
SHACK	SHITS	SILKY	SKINK	SLOTS	SNOEK
SHADE	SHIVE	SILLS	SKINS	SLUED	SNOGS
SHADY	SHLUH	SILLY	SKINT	SLUGS	SNOOD
SHAFT	SHOAL	SILOS	SKIPS	SLUMP	SNOOK
SHAGS	SHOAT	SILTY	SKIRL	SLUMS	SNOOP
SHAHS	SHOCK	SIMLA	SKIRT	SLUNG	SNORE
SHAKE	SHOED	SIMON	SKITS	SLUNK	SNORT
SHAKO	SHOER	SINAI	SKIVE	SLURP	SNOUT
SHAKY	SHOES	SINCE	SKUAS	SLURS	SNOWS
SHALE	SHONA	SINES	SKULK	SLUSH	SNOWY
SHALL	SHONE	SINEW	SKULL	SLUTS	SNUBS
SHALT	SHOOK	SINGE	SKUNK	SLYER	SNUFF
SHALY	SHOOT	SINKS	SLABS	SLYPE	SNUGS
SHAME	SHOPS	SINUS	SLACK	SMACK	SOAKS
SHAMS	SHORE	SIOUX	SLAGS	SMALL	SOAPS
SHANK	SHORN	SIRED	SLAIN	SMALT	SOAPY
SHAN'T	SHORT	SIREN	SLAKE	SMARM	SOBER
SHAPE	SHOTS	SIRES	SLANG	SMART	SOCHE
SHARD	SHOTT	SISAL	SLANT	SMASH	SOCHI
SHARE	SHOUT	SISSY	SLAPS	SMEAR	SOCIO-
SHARK	SHOVE	SITAR	SLASH	SMELL	SOCKS
SHARP	SHOWN	SITED	SLATE	SMELT	SOCLE
SHAVE	SHOWS	SITES	SLATS	SMILE	SODAS
SHAWL	SHOWY	SIT-IN	SLATY	SMIRK	SOFAR
SHEAF	SHRED	SITKA	SLAVE	SMITE	SOFAS
SHEAR	SHREW	SIT ON	SLAVS	SMITH	SOFIA
SHEDS	SHRUB	SIT UP	SLEDS	SMOCK	SOFTA
SHEEN	SHRUG	SIT-UP	SLEEK	SMOKE	SOFTY
SHEEP	SHUCK	SITUS	SLEEP	SMOKY	SOGGY
SHEER	SHUNT	SIVAS	SLEET	SMOLT	SOILS
SHEET	SHUSH	SIXES	SLEPT	SMOTE	SOLAR
SHEIK	SHYED	SIXMO	SLEWS	SMUTS	SOLED

SOLES	SPEND	SPUNK	STICH	STUFF	SWASH
SOL-FA	SPENT	SPURN	STICK	STULL	SWATH
SOLID	SPERM	SPURS	STIES	STUMP	SWATS
SOLOS	SPICA	SPURT	STIFF	STUNG	SWAZI
SOLTI	SPICE	SQUAB	STILE	STUNK	SWEAR
SOLUM	SPICS	SQUAD	STILL	STUNT	SWEAT
SOLVE	SPICY	SQUAT	STILT	STUPE	SWEDE
SOMME	SPIED	SQUAW	STING	STYLE	SWEEP
SONAR	SPIEL	SQUIB	STINK	SUAVE	SWEET
SONDE	SPIES	SQUID	STINT	SUCRE	SWELL
SONGS	SPIFF	STABS	STIPE	SUDAN	SWEPT
SONIC	SPIKE	STACK	STIRK	SUDOR	SWIFT
SONNY	SPIKS	STAFF	STIRS	SUDSY	SWIGS
SOOTY	SPIKY	STAGE	STOAT	SUEDE	SWILL
SOPOR	SPILE	STAGS	STOCK	SUETY	SWIMS
SOPPY	SPILL	STAGY	STOEP	SUGAR	SWINE
SORES	SPILT	STAID	STOIC	SUING	SWING
SORGO	SPINE	STAIN	STOKE	SUINT	SWIPE
SORRY	SPINS	STAIR	STOLE	SUITE	SWIRL
SORTS	SPINY	STAKE	STOMA	SUITS	SWISH
SORUS	SPIRE	STALE	STOMP	SULKS	SWISS
SOTHO	SPIRY	STALK	STONE	SULKY	SWOON
SOUGH	SPITE	STALL	STONY	SULLY	SWOOP
SOULS	SPITS	STAMP	STOOD	SUMBA	SWOPS
SOUND	SPITZ	STAND	STOOK	SUMPS	SWORD
SOUPS	SPIVS	STANK	STOOL	SUNNI	SWORE
SOUPY	SPLAT	STANS	STOOP	SUNNY	SWORN
SOUSE	SPLAY	STARE	STOPE	SUN-UP	SWOTS
SOUTH	SPLIT	STARK	STOPS	SUPER	SWUNG
SOWED	SPOCK	STARS	STORE	SUPRA	SYLPH
SOWER	SPODE	START	STORK	SURAH	SYLVA
SOYUZ	SPOIL	STASH	STORM	SURAL	SYNOD
SPACE	SPOKE	STATE	STORY	SURAT	SYRIA
SPADE	SPOOF	STAVE	STOSS	SURDS	SYRUP
SPAIN	SPOOK	STAYS	STOUP	SURER	SYSOP
SPALL	SPOOL	STEAD	STOUR	SURFY	
SPANK	SPOON	STEAK	STOUT	SURGE	**T**
SPARE	SPOOR	STEAL	STOVE	SURLY	TABBY
SPARK	SPORE	STEAM	STRAP	SUSHI	TABES
SPARS	SPORT	STEED	STRAW	SWABS	TABLE
SPASM	SPOTS	STEEL	STRAY	SWAGE	TABOO
SPATE	SPOUT	STEEP	STREW	SWAIN	TABOR
SPATS	SPRAG	STEER	STRIA	SWALE	TACET
SPAWN	SPRAT	STEIN	STRIP	SWAMI	TACIT
SPEAK	SPRAY	STELE	STROP	SWAMP	TACKS
SPEAR	SPREE	STEMS	STRUM	SWANK	TACKY
SPECK	SPRIG	STEPS	STRUT	SWANS	TACOS
SPECS	SPRIT	STERE	STUBS	SWAPS	TAEGU
SPEED	SPRUE	STERN	STUCK	SWARD	TAFFY
SPELL	SPUDS	STEWS	STUDS	SWARF	TAFIA
SPELT	SPUME	STEYR	STUDY	SWARM	TAIGA

T 5 TAILS

TAILS	TAWNY	TEXTS	TIE-UP	TOLLS	TOYED
TAINO	TAXED	THANE	TIFFS	TOLYL	TOYER
TAINT	TAXER	THANK	TIGER	TOMBS	TRACE
TA'IZZ	TAXES	THAWS	TIGHT	TOMES	TRACK
TAJIK	TAXIS	THECA	TIGON	TOMMY	TRACT
TAKEN	TAXON	THEFT	TIGRE	TOMSK	TRADE
TAKER	TAYRA	THEGN	TIKKA	TONAL	TRAIL
TAKES	TAZZA	THEIR	TILDE	TONDO	TRAIN
TAKIN	T-BONE	THEME	TILED	TONED	TRAIT
TALCA	TEACH	THERA	TILER	TONER	TRAMP
TALES	TEAKS	THERE	TILES	TONES	TRAMS
TALKS	TEAMS	THERM	TILLS	TONGA	TRANS-
TALLY	TEARS	THESE	TILTH	TONGS	TRAPS
TALON	TEASE	THETA	TILTS	TONIC	TRASH
TALUS	TEATS	THEWS	TIMED	TONNE	TRASS
TAMED	TECHY	THICK	TIMER	TON UP	TRAVE
TAMER	TEENS	THIEF	TIMES	TON-UP	TRAWL
TAMMY	TEENY	THIGH	TIMID	TONUS	TRAYS
TAMPA	TEETH	THINE	TINEA	TOOLS	TREAD
TANGA	TELEX	THING	TINES	TOOTH	TREAT
TANGO	TELIC	THINK	TINGE	TOOTS	TREEN
TANGY	TELLY	THIOL	TINGS	TOPAZ	TREES
TANKS	TEMPI	THIRD	TINNY	TOPEE	TREKS
TANSY	TEMPO	THOLE	TINTS	TOPER	TREND
TANTA	TEMPS	THONG	TIPSY	TOPIC	TRESS
TANTO	TEMPT	THORN	TIP UP	TOPOS	TREWS
TAPAS	TENCH	THOSE	TIRED	TOP UP	TRIAD
TAPED	TENET	THREE	TIREE	TOQUE	TRIAL
TAPER	TENON	THREW	TIRES	TORAH	TRIBE
TAPES	TENOR	THROB	TIROS	TORCH	TRICE
TAPIR	TENSE	THROW	TITAN	TORIC	TRICK
TAPIS	TENTH	THRUM	TITHE	TORSK	TRIED
TARDY	TENTS	THUDS	TITLE	TORSO	TRIER
TARES	TEPAL	THUGS	TITRE	TORTS	TRIES
TARGA	TEPEE	THUJA	TITTY	TORUN	TRIKE
TARNS	TEPIC	THUMB	TIZZY	TORUS	TRILL
TAROS	TEPID	THUMP	TOADS	TOTAL	TRIMS
TAROT	TERMS	THUNK	TOADY	TOTED	TRINE
TARRY	TERNE	THYME	TOAST	TOTEM	TRIOL
TARSI	TERNI	TIARA	TODAY	TOTER	TRIOS
TARTS	TERNS	TIBET	TODDY	TOTES	TRIPE
TARTU	TERRA	TIBIA	TO-DOS	TOUCH	TRIPS
TASKS	TERRY	TICAL	TOE-IN	TOUGH	TRITE
TASTE	TERSE	TICKS	TOFFS	TOURS	TROLL
TASTY	TESLA	TIDAL	TOGAS	TOUTS	TRONA
TATAR	TESOL	TIDED	TOILE	TOWED	TRONK
TATRA	TESTA	TIDES	TOILS	TOWEL	TROOP
TATTY	TESTS	TIE-IN	TOKAY	TOWER	TROPE
TAUNT	TESTY	TIE-ON	TOKEN	TOWNS	TROTH
TAUPE	TETRA	TIERS	TOKYO	TOXIC	TROTS
TAWER	TEXAS	TIE UP	TOLAN	TOXIN	TROUT

TROVE	TUTOR	UNARY	UTTER	VERVE	VOIDS
TRUCE	TUTSI	UNBAR	U-TURN	VESTA	VOILE
TRUCK	TUTTI	UNCAP	UVEAL	VESTS	VOLAR
TRUER	TUTTY	UNCLE	UVULA	VETCH	VOLES
TRUES	TUTUS	UNCUS	UZBEK	VEXED	VOLTA
TRUGO	TWAIN	UNCUT		VEXER	VOLTS
TRUGS	TWANG	UNDER	**V**	VIALS	VOLVA
TRULY	TWATS	UNDID		VIAND	VOMER
TRUMP	TWEAK	UNDUE	VAASA	VIBES	VOMIT
TRUNK	TWEED	UNFIT	VADUZ	VICAR	VOTED
TRURO	'TWEEN	UNFIX	VAGAL	VICES	VOTER
TRUSS	TWEET	UNIAT	VAGUE	VICHY	VOTES
TRUST	TWERP	UNIFY	VAGUS	VIDAL	VOUCH
TRUTH	TWICE	UNION	VALES	VIDEO	VOWED
TRYMA	TWIGS	UNITE	VALET	VIEWS	VOWEL
TRY ON	TWILL	UNITS	VALID	VIGIA	VOWER
TRY-ON	TWINE	UNITY	VALSE	VIGIL	V-SIGN
TRYST	TWINS	UNLAY	VALUE	VILER	VULVA
TSARS	TWIRL	UNMAN	VALVE	VILLA	VYING
TUBAL	TWIRP	UNPEG	VAMPS	VIMEN	
TUBAS	TWIST	UNPIN	VANDA	VINCA	**W**
TUBBY	TWITE	UNRIG	VANES	VINES	WACKY
TUBER	TWITS	UNRIP	VAPID	VINIC	WADDY
TUBES	TWIXT	UNSAY	VARIA	VINYL	WADED
TUCKS	TYING	UNSET	VARIX	VIOLA	WADER
TUDOR	TYPED	UNSEX	VARNA	VIOLS	WADGE
TUFTS	TYPES	UNTIE	VARUS	VIPER	WADIS
TUFTY	TYRES	UNTIL	VARVE	VIRAL	WAFER
TULIP	TYROL	UNZIP	VASES	VIREO	WAGED
TULLE	TYROS	UP-BOW	VAULT	VIRGA	WAGER
TULSA	TYSON	UPEND	VAUNT	VIRGO	WAGES
TUMID	TZARS	UPOLU	V-CHIP	VIRTU	WAGON
TUMMY	TZU-PO	UPPER	VEDDA	VIRUS	WAHOO
TUNAS		UPSET	VEDIC	VISAS	WAIFS
TUNED	**U**	URALS	VEERY	VISBY	WAIST
TUNER	U-BOAT	URATE	VEGAN	VISES	WAIVE
TUNES	UDDER	URBAN	VEILS	VISEU	WAJDA
TUNIC	UDINE	UREAL	VEINS	VISIT	WAKED
TUNIS	UGRIC	UREDO	VEINY	VISOR	WAKEN
TUNNY	UHURU	URGED	VELAR	VISTA	WAKER
TUQUE	UIGUR	URGER	VELUM	VITAL	WAKES
TURDS	ULCER	URGES	VENAL	VITTA	WALES
TURFS	ULNAR	URINE	VENDA	VIVID	WALKS
TURFY	ULNAS	USAGE	VENIN	VIXEN	WALLS
TURIN	ULTRA-	USERS	VENOM	V-NECK	WALLY
TURKI	ULURU	USHER	VENTS	VOCAB	WALTZ
TURKU	UMBEL	USING	VENUE	VOCAL	WANDS
TURNS	UMBER	USUAL	VENUS	VODKA	WANED
TURPS	UMBRA	USURP	VERBS	VOGUE	WANES
TUSKS	UMIAK	USURY	VERGE	VOGUL	WANEY
TUTEE	UNAPT	UTERI	VERSO	VOICE	WANLY

X 5 WANTS

WANTS	WHACK	WILDS	WOOFS	XENON	YOKES
WARDS	WHALE	WILES	WOOZY	XERIC	YOLKS
WARES	WHAMS	WILLS	WORDS	XEROX	YOLKY
WARPS	WHANG	WILLY	WORDY	XHOSA	YONKS
WARTS	WHARF	WIMPS	WORKS	X-RAYS	YONNE
WARTY	WHEAL	WIMPY	WORLD	X-UNIT	YOUNG
WASHY	WHEAT	WINCE	WORMS	XYLAN	YOURS
WASPS	WHEEL	WINCH	WORMY	XYLEM	YOUSE
WASTE	WHELK	WINDS	WORRY	XYLOL	YOUTH
WATCH	WHELP	WINDY	WORSE	XYLYL	YOWLS
WATER	WHERE	WINED	WORST		YOYOS
WATTS	WHICH	WINES	WORTH	**Y**	YPRES
WAVED	WHIFF	WINEY	WOULD	YACHT	YUCCA
WAVER	WHIGS	WINGE	WOUND	YAHOO	YUCKY
WAVES	WHILE	WINGS	WOVEN	YAKUT	YUKON
WAXED	WHIMS	WINKS	WOWED	YALTA	YULAN
WAXEN	WHINE	WINZE	WRACK	YANAN	YUMAN
WAXER	WHINY	WIPED	WRAPS	YANKS	
WEALD	WHIPS	WIPER	WRATH	YAPOK	**Z**
WEALS	WHIRL	WIPES	WREAK	YAPPY	ZAIRE
WEARY	WHIRR	WIRED	WRECK	YARDS	ZAMIA
WEAVE	WHIRS	WIRER	WRENS	YARNS	ZANTE
WEBBY	WHISK	WIRES	WREST	YAWED	ZAPPY
WEBER	WHIST	WISER	WRIED	YAWLS	ZARGA
WEDGE	WHITE	WISPS	WRIER	YAWNS	ZARIA
WEDGY	WHITS	WISPY	WRING	Y-AXIS	ZARQA
WEEDS	WHIZZ	WITCH	WRIST	YEARN	Z-AXIS
WEEDY	WHOLE	WITHE	WRITE	YEARS	ZEBRA
WEEKS	WHOOP	WITHY	WRITS	YEAST	ZEIST
WEENY	WHORE	WITTY	WRONG	YELLS	ZENIC
WEEPY	WHORL	WIVES	WROTE	YELPS	ZEROS
WEIGH	WHOSE	WIZEN	WROTH	YEMEN	ZESTY
WEIRD	WICCA	WOKEN	WRUNG	YERBA	ZIBET
WEIRS	WICKS	WOLDS	WRYER	YETIS	ZILCH
WELCH	WIDEN	WOLOF	WRYLY	YIBIN	ZINGY
WELDS	WIDER	WOMAN	WUHAN	YIELD	ZIPPY
WELLS	WIDES	WOMBS	WURST	YIKES	ZLOTY
WELLY	WIDOW	WOMEN	WUSIH	YODEL	ZOMBA
WELSH	WIDTH	WONKY		YOGIC	ZONAL
WELTS	WIELD	WOODS	**X**	YOGIS	ZONED
WENCH	WIGAN	WOODY	X-AXIS	YOKED	ZONES
WESER	WIGHT	WOOED	XENIA	YOKEL	ZOOID
WETLY	WILCO	WOOER			

A
AACHEN
AARGAU
AARHUS
ABACUS
ABADAN
ABAKAN
ABASED
ABATED
ABATIS
ABATOR
ABBACY
ABBESS
ABBEYS
ABBOTS
ABDUCT
ABELIA
ABIDED
ABIDER
ABJECT
ABJURE
ABKHAZ
ABLAUT
ABLAZE
ABOARD
ABODES
ABORAL
ABOUND
ABRADE
ABROAD
ABRUPT
ABSEIL
ABSENT
ABSORB
ABSURD
ABULIA
ABULIC
ABUSED
ABUSER
ABUSES
ABVOLT
ABWATT
ACACIA
ACADIA
ACAJOU
ACARID
ACARUS
ACCEDE
ACCENT
ACCEPT
ACCESS

ACCORD
ACCOST
ACCRUE
ACCUSE
ACETAL
ACETIC
ACETUM
ACETYL
ACHAEA
ACHENE
ACHING
ACIDIC
ACINIC
ACINUS
ACNODE
ACORNS
ACQUIT
ACROSS
ACTING
ACTION
ACTIVE
ACTORS
ACTS UP
ACTUAL
ACUITY
ACUMEN
ADAGES
ADAGIO
ADDEND
ADDERS
ADDICT
ADDING
ADDLED
ADD-ONS
ADDUCE
ADDUCT
ADEPTS
ADHERE
ADIEUS
ADIEUX
ADJOIN
ADJURE
ADJUST
ADMIRE
ADNATE
ADNOUN
ADORED
ADRIFT
ADROIT
ADSORB
ADULTS

ADVENT
ADVERB
ADVERT
ADVICE
ADVISE
ADYGEI
ADZHAR
AECIUM
AEDILE
AEGEAN
AERATE
AERIAL
AERIFY
AEROBE
AERUGO
AETHER
AFFAIR
AFFECT
AFFINE
AFFIRM
AFFLUX
AFFORD
AFFRAY
AFGHAN
AFIELD
AFLAME
AFL-CIO
AFLOAT
AFRAID
AFRESH
AFRICA
AFTERS
AGADIR
AGAMIC
AGARIC
AGATES
AGEING
AGEISM
AGEIST
AGENCY
AGENDA
AGENTS
AGE OLD
AGHAST
AGNATE
AGOGIC
AGONIC
AGOUTI
AGREED
AIDING
AIKIDO

AILING
AIMING
AIRBED
AIRBUS
AIR-DRY
AIRGUN
AIRIER
AIRILY
AIRING
AIRMAN
AIRMEN
AIRWAY
AISLES
AKIMBO
AKMOLA
AL-ANON
ALARMS
ALASKA
ALBANY
ALBEDO
ALBEIT
ALBINO
ALBION
ALBITE
ALBUMS
ALCOVE
ALDISS
ALDOSE
ALDRIN
ALECKS
ALEGAR
ALEPPO
ALERTS
A LEVEL
ALGOID
AL HASA
ALIBIS
ALIENS
ALIGHT
ALIPED
ALKALI
ALKANE
ALKENE
ALKYNE
ALLEGE
ALLELE
ALLEYS
ALLIED
ALLIER
ALLIES
ALLIUM

ALL OUT
ALLOYS
ALLUDE
ALLURE
ALMADA
AL MARJ
ALMATY
ALMOND
ALMOST
ALMUCE
ALNICO
ALPACA
ALPHAS
ALPINE
ALSACE
ALSIKE
ALTAIC
ALTAIR
ALTARS
ALTONA
ALUDEL
ALUMNA
ALUMNI
ALVINE
ALWAYS
AMADOU
AMATOL
AMAZED
AMAZON
AMBALA
AMBARY
AMBITS
AMBLED
AMBLER
AMBUSH
AMEBAS
AMEBIC
AMENDS
AMHARA
AMIDIC
AMIDOL
AMIDST
AMIENS
AMMINE
AMNION
AMOEBA
AMORAL
AMOUNT
AMOURS
AMPERE
AMPULE

AMRITA
AMULET
AMUSED
AMYLUM
AMYTAL
ANABAS
ANADYR
ANALOG
ANCHOR
ANCONA
ANDEAN
ANDONG
ANDROS
ANEMIA
ANEMIC
ANERGY
ANGARY
ANGELS
ANGERS
ANGINA
ANGKOR
ANGLED
ANGLER
ANGLES
ANGOLA
ANGORA
ANHALT
ANHWEI
ANIMAL
ANIMUS
ANKARA
ANKING
ANKLES
ANKLET
ANLAGE
ANNABA
ANNALS
ANNEAL
ANNECY
ANNEXE
ANNUAL
ANODES
ANODIC
ANOINT
ANOMIC
ANOMIE
ANORAK
ANOXIA
ANOXIC
ANQING
ANSATE

ANSHAN	ARABIC	ARRIVE	ATHENS	AVENGE	BAKERS
ANSWER	ARABLE	ARROBA	AT HOME	AVENUE	BAKERY
ANTEED	ARAGON	ARROWS	AT-HOME	AVERSE	BAKING
ANTHEM	ARARAT	ARSINE	AT LAST	AVIARY	BALATA
ANTHER	ARBOUR	ARTERY	ATOLLS	AVIATE	BALBOA
ANTICS	ARCADE	ARTFUL	ATOMIC	AVIDIN	BALDLY
ANTLER	ARCANA	ARTIER	ATONAL	AVIDLY	BALEEN
ANTRIM	ARCANE	ARTIST	ATONED	AVOCET	BALING
ANTRUM	ARCHED	ARTOIS	ATONER	AVOWAL	BALKAN
ANTUNG	ARCHER	ARUNTA	ATONIC	AVOWED	BALKED
ANURAN	ARCHES	ASARUM	AT REST	AVOWER	BALKER
ANURIA	ARCHLY	ASCEND	ATRIUM	AWAKED	BALLAD
ANUSES	ARCTIC	ASCENT	ATTACH	AWAKEN	BALLET
ANVILS	ARDENT	ASCOTS	ATTACK	AWARDS	BALLOT
ANYANG	ARDOUR	ASHDOD	ATTAIN	AWEIGH	BALSAM
ANYHOW	ARENAS	ASHIER	ATTEND	AWHILE	BALSAS
ANYONE	AREOLA	ASHLAR	ATTEST	AWNING	BALTIC
ANYWAY	ARETES	ASHORE	ATTICA	AWOKEN	BAMAKO
AORIST	AREZZO	ASIANS	ATTICS	AXENIC	BAMBOO
AORTAS	ARGALI	ASIDES	ATTIRE	AXILLA	BANABA
AORTIC	ARGENT	ASKING	ATTORN	AXIOMS	BANANA
AOUDAD	ARGOSY	ASLANT	ATTRIT	AYE AYE	BANDED
AOUITA	ARGOTS	ASLEEP	ATTUNE	AYMARA	BANDIT
APACHE	ARGUED	ASMARA	ATWOOD	AZALEA	BANDOG
APATHY	ARGUER	ASPECT	AUBADE	AZORES	BANGED
APEMAN	ARGYLE	ASPIRE	AUBURN	AZOTIC	BANGER
APERCU	ARGYLL	ASSAIL	AUDILE		BANGLE
APEXES	ARIEGE	ASSAYS	AUDITS	**B**	BANGOR
APHIDS	ARIGHT	ASSENT	AU FAIT	BAAING	BANGUI
APHTHA	ARIOSO	ASSERT	AU FOND	BABBLE	BANISH
APIARY	ARISEN	ASSESS	AUGEND	BABIED	BANJOS
APICAL	ARISTA	ASSETS	AUGERS	BABIES	BANJUL
APICES	ARKOSE	ASSIGN	AUGITE	BABOON	BANKED
APIECE	ARMADA	ASSISI	AUGURY	BACKED	BANKER
APLITE	ARMAGH	ASSIST	AUGUST	BACKER	BANNED
APLOMB	ARMFUL	ASSIZE	AUKLET	BACK UP	BANNER
APNOEA	ARMIES	ASSORT	AU LAIT	BACKUP	BANTAM
APODAL	ARMING	ASSUME	AUMBRY	BADGER	BANTER
APOGEE	ARMLET	ASSURE	AU PAIR	BADGES	BANYAN
APOLLO	ARMOUR	ASTANA	AUREUS	BAFFLE	BAOBAB
APPEAL	ARMPIT	ASSUAN	AURORA	BAGELS	BAOTOU
APPEAR	ARMURE	ASTERN	AUROUS	BAGGED	BARBED
APPEND	ARNHEM	ASTHMA	AUSSIE	BAGUIO	BARBEL
APPLES	ARNICA	ASTRAL	AUSTIN	BAILED	BARBER
APPLET	AROMAS	ASTRAY	AUSTRO-	BAILEE	BARBET
APPOSE	AROUND	ASTUTE	AUTEUR	BAILER	BARBIE
APRILS	AROUSE	ASWARM	AUTHOR	BAILEY	BARDIC
APRONS	ARRACK	ASYLUM	AUTISM	BAILOR	BARELY
APULIA	ARRANT	ATAXIA	AUTUMN	BAIL UP	BAREST
AQUILA	ARRAYS	ATAXIC	AVATAR	BAIRNS	BARGED
ARABIA	ARREST	ATBARA	AVEIRO	BAITED	BARGEE

BARGES	BATTLE	BEHEAD	BETTED	BINGOS	BLINKS
BARING	BATTUE	BEHELD	BETTER	BINMAN	BLINTZ
BARIUM	BAUBLE	BEHEST	BEVELS	BINNED	BLITHE
BARKED	BAUCHI	BEHIND	BEVIES	BIOGAS	BLOCKS
BARKER	BAULKS	BEHOLD	BEWAIL	BIOGEN	BLOKES
BARLEY	BAWLED	BEHOVE	BEWARE	BIONIC	BLONDE
BARMAN	BAWLER	BEINGS	BEXLEY	BIOPIC	BLOODS
BARMEN	BAYEUX	BEIRUT	BEYOND	BIOPSY	BLOODY
BARNET	BAYING	BELFRY	BEZIER	BIOTIC	BLOOMS
BARNEY	BAYOUS	BELIED	BEZOAR	BIOTIN	BLOTCH
BARODA	BAZAAR	BELIEF	BHOPAL	BIPEDS	BLOTTO
BARONS	BEACON	BELIER	BHUTAN	BIRDIE	BLOUSE
BARONY	BEADED	BELIZE	BHUTTO	BIRTHS	BLOWER
BARQUE	BEADLE	BELLES	BIAFRA	BISCAY	BLOWSY
BARRED	BEAGLE	BELLOW	BIASED	BISECT	BLOW-UP
BARREL	BEAKER	BELONG	BIASES	BISHOP	BLOWZY
BARREN	BEAMED	BELSEN	BIBLES	BISKRA	BLUEST
BARROW	BEARDS	BELTED	BICEPS	BISONS	BLUFFS
BARTER	BEARER	BELTER	BICKER	BISQUE	BLUISH
BARTON	BEASTS	BELUGA	BICORN	BISSAU	BLUNGE
BARYON	BEATEN	BEMOAN	BIDDEN	BISTRE	BLURBS
BARYTE	BEATER	BEMUSE	BIDETS	BISTRO	BLURRY
BASALT	BEAUNE	BENDER	BIDING	BITCHY	B-MOVIE
BASELY	BEAUTS	BENGAL	BIFFED	BITING	BOARDS
BASEST	BEAUTY	BENGBU	BIFFIN	BITMAP	BOASTS
BASHED	BEAVER	BENIGN	BIGAMY	BITOLJ	BOATED
BASHES	BECAME	BENONI	BIG CAT	BITTEN	BOATER
BASICS	BECKET	BENUMB	BIG END	BITTER	BOATIE
BASIFY	BECKON	BENZOL	BIGGER	BLACKS	BOBBED
BASING	BECOME	BENZYL	BIGGIE	BLADES	BOBBER
BASINS	BEDAUB	BERATE	BIGHTS	BLAMED	BOBBIN
BASION	BEDBUG	BEREFT	BIGOTS	BLANCH	BOBBLE
BASKED	BEDDED	BERETS	BIG TOP	BLANKS	BOBCAT
BASKET	BEDDER	BERGEN	BIGWIG	BLARED	BOCHUM
BASQUE	BEDECK	BERING	BIHARI	BLASTS	BODEGA
BASRAH	BEDLAM	BERLEY	BIKING	BLAZED	BODICE
BASSES	BEDPAN	BERLIN	BIKINI	BLAZER	BODIES
BASSET	BEDSIT	BERTHS	BILBAO	BLAZES	BODILY
BASTED	BEEFED	BERYLS	BILGES	BLAZON	BODING
BASTIA	BEETLE	BESEEM	BILKED	BLEACH	BODKIN
BASUCO	BEFALL	BESIDE	BILKER	BLEARY	BODMIN
BATHED	BEFELL	BESOMS	BILLED	BLEATS	BOFFIN
BATHER	BEFOOL	BESTED	BILLET	BLEEPS	BOGEYS
BATHOS	BEFORE	BESTIR	BILLON	BLENCH	BOGGED
BATLEY	BEFOUL	BESTOW	BILLOW	BLENDE	BOGGLE
BATMAN	BEGGAR	BETAKE	BILLY-O	BLENDS	BOGIES
BATMEN	BEGGED	BETHEL	BINARY	BLENNY	BOGOTA
BATONS	BEGONE	BETIDE	BINATE	BLIGHT	BOILED
BATTED	BEGUMS	BETONY	BINDER	BLIMEY	BOILER
BATTEN	BEHALF	BETOOK	BINGEN	BLIMPS	BOLAND
BATTER	BEHAVE	BETRAY	BINGES	BLINDS	BOLDER

BOLDLY	BOSOMY	BRAKED	BRONZY	BUNGED	BUSSED
BOLERO	BOSSED	BRAKES	BROOCH	BUNGEE	BUSTED
BOLIDE	BOSSES	BRANCH	BROODS	BUNGLE	BUSTER
BOLSHY	BOSTON	BRANDO	BROODY	BUNION	BUSTLE
BOLSON	BOSUNS	BRANDS	BROOKS	BUNKED	BUST-UP
BOLTED	BOTANY	BRANDT	BROOMS	BUNKER	BUTANE
BOLTER	BOTCHY	BRANDY	BROWNS	BUNKUM	BUTENE
BOLTON	BOTFLY	BRASHY	BROWSE	BUNK-UP	BUTLER
BOMBAY	BOTHER	BRASOV	BRUGES	BUOYED	BUTTED
BOMBED	BOTTLE	BRASSY	BRUISE	BURBLE	BUTTER
BOMBER	BOTTOM	BRAVED	BRUMAL	BURBOT	BUTTES
BONBON	BOUAKE	BRAVER	BRUMBY	BURDEN	BUTTIE
BONDED	BOUCLE	BRAVES	BRUNCH	BUREAU	BUTTON
BONGOS	BOUGHS	BRAVOS	BRUNEI	BURGAS	BUXTON
BONIER	BOUGHT	BRAWLS	BRUTAL	BURGEE	BUYERS
BONILY	BOUGIE	BRAWNY	BRUTES	BURGER	BUYING
BONING	BOULES	BRAYED	BRUTON	BURGHS	BUYOUT
BONITO	BOULLE	BRAYER	BRYONY	BURGLE	BUZZED
BON MOT	BOUNCE	BRAZEN	BUBBLE	BURGOS	BUZZER
BONNET	BOUNCY	BRAZER	BUBBLY	BURIAL	BUZZES
BONSAI	BOUNDS	BRAZIL	BUCCAL	BURIED	BY-BLOW
BONZER	BOUNTY	BREACH	BUCKED	BURIER	BYGONE
BOOBED	BOURNS	BREAKS	BUCKET	BURLAP	BYLAWS
BOOGIE	BOURSE	BREAST	BUCKLE	BURLER	BY-LINE
BOOHOO	BOVINE	BRECON	BUDDED	BURLEY	BYPASS
BOOING	BOVVER	BREECH	BUDDHA	BURNED	BYPLAY
BOOKED	BOWELS	BREEZE	BUDDLE	BURNER	BYROAD
BOOKIE	BOWERS	BREEZY	BUDGED	BURNET	BYSSUS
BOOMED	BOWERY	BREGMA	BUDGET	BURPED	BYWAYS
BOOSTS	BOWFIN	BREMEN	BUFFED	BURPEE	BYWORD
BOOTED	BOWING	BRETON	BUFFER	BURRED	
BOOTEE	BOWLED	BREVET	BUFFET	BURROS	**C**
BOOTHS	BOWLER	BREWER	BUGGED	BURROW	CABALS
BOOTLE	BOWMAN	BRIBER	BUGGER	BURSAL	CABANA
BOOZED	BOWMEN	BRIDAL	BUGLER	BURSAR	CABBIE
BOOZER	BOWSAW	BRIDGE	BUGLES	BURSTS	CABERS
BOPPED	BOWSER	BRIDLE	BUILDS	BURTON	CABINS
BORAGE	BOW TIE	BRIERY	BUKAVU	BURYAT	CABLED
BORANE	BOWWOW	BRIGHT	BULBAR	BUSBAR	CABLES
BORATE	BOWYER	BRITON	BULBIL	BUS BOY	CABLET
BORDER	BOXCAR	BROACH	BULBUL	BUSBOY	CABMAN
BOREAL	BOXERS	BROADS	BULGED	BUSHED	CACHES
BORERS	BOXING	BROCHE	BULGES	BUSHEL	CACHET
BORIDE	BOYISH	BROGUE	BULKED	BUSHES	CACHOU
BORING	BRACED	BROKEN	BULLET	BUSIED	CACKLE
BORNEO	BRACER	BROKER	BUMBLE	BUSIER	CACTUS
BORROW	BRACES	BROLLY	BUMMED	BUSILY	CAD/CAM
BORZOI	BRAIDS	BROMAL	BUMPED	BUSING	CADDIE
BOSKET	BRAINS	BROMIC	BUMPER	BUSKED	CADDIS
BOSNIA	BRAINY	BRONCO	BUNCHY	BUSKER	CADENT
BOSOMS	BRAISE	BRONZE	BUNDLE	BUSKIN	CADETS

CADGED	CAMPER	CARESS	CATION	CEROUS	CHEESY
CADGER	CAMPOS	CARETS	CATKIN	CERUSE	CHEQUE
CADRES	CAMPUS	CARGOS	CATNAP	CERVID	CHERRY
CAECUM	CANADA	CARHOP	CATNIP	CERVIX	CHERTY
CAELUM	CANALS	CARIES	CATSUP	CETANE	CHERUB
CAEOMA	CANAPE	CARINA	CATTLE	CETNIK	CHESTS
CAESAR	CANARD	CARING	CAUCUS	CEYLON	CHESTY
CAFTAN	CANARY	CARLOW	CAUDAD	CHA CHA	CHEWED
CAGIER	CANCAN	CARMAN	CAUDAL	CHA-CHA	CHEWER
CAGILY	CANCEL	CARMEL	CAUDEX	CHACMA	CHICHI
CAGING	CANCER	CARNAL	CAUDLE	CHAETA	CHICKS
CAHIER	CANDID	CARNES	CAUGHT	CHAFED	CHICLE
CAICOS	CANDLE	CARNET	CAUSAL	CHAFER	CHICLY
CAIQUE	CANINE	CAROBS	CAUSED	CHAFFY	CHIDED
CAIRNS	CANING	CAROLS	CAUSES	CHAINS	CHIDER
CAJOLE	CANKER	CARPAL	CAVEAT	CHAIRS	CHIEFS
CAKING	CANNED	CARPED	CAVE-IN	CHAISE	CHIGOE
CALAIS	CANNEL	CARPEL	CAVERN	CHAKRA	CHILES
CALASH	CANNES	CARPET	CAVIAR	CHALET	CHILLI
CALCAR	CANNON	CARPUS	CAVING	CHALKS	CHILLS
CALCES	CANNOT	CARREL	CAVITY	CHALKY	CHILLY
CALCIC	CANOED	CARROT	CAVORT	CHAMPS	CHIMED
CALICO	CANOES	CARSON	CAWING	CHANCE	CHIMES
CALIPH	CANONS	CARTED	CAXTON	CHANCY	CHINES
CALKED	CANOPY	CARTEL	CAYMAN	CHANGE	CHINKS
CALKIN	CANTAL	CARTER	CD-ROMS	CHANIA	CHINTZ
CALLAO	CANTED	CARTON	CEASED	CHANTS	CHIPPY
CALLED	CANTER	CARVED	CEDARS	CHANTY	CHIRAC
CALLER	CANTIC	CARVER	CEDING	CHAOAN	CHIRPS
CALL-IN	CANTLE	CASABA	CELAYA	CHAPEL	CHIRPY
CALLOW	CANTON	CASEFY	CELERY	CHARDS	CHISEL
CALL-UP	CANTOR	CASEIN	CELLAR	CHARGE	CHITIN
CALLUS	CANTOS	CASERN	CELLOS	CHARMS	CHITON
CALMED	CANTUS	CASHED	CELTIC	CHARTS	CHITTY
CALMER	CANVAS	CASHEW	CEMENT	CHASED	CHIVES
CALMLY	CANYON	CASING	CENSER	CHASER	CHOCKA
CALPAC	CAPERS	CASINO	CENSOR	CHASES	CHOCKS
CALQUE	CAPIAS	CASKET	CENSUS	CHASMS	CHOICE
CALVED	CAPONS	CASLON	CENTAL	CHASSE	CHOIRS
CALVES	CAPOTE	CASQUE	CENTER	CHASTE	CHOKED
CALVIN	CAPPED	CASSIA	CENTRE	CHATTY	CHOKER
CAMASS	CAPPER	CASSIS	CENTUM	CHAT UP	CHOKES
CAMBER	CAPSID	CASTER	CERATE	CHEATS	CHOLER
CAMDEN	CAPTOR	CASTES	CERCAL	CHECKS	CHOLLA
CAMELS	CARAFE	CASTLE	CERCIS	CHECKY	CHONJU
CAMEOS	CARATS	CASTOR	CERCUS	CHEEKS	CHOOSE
CAMERA	CARBON	CASTRO	CEREAL	CHEEKY	CHOOSY
CAMION	CARBOY	CASUAL	CEREUS	CHEEPS	CHOPPY
CAMISE	CARDED	CATCHY	CERISE	CHEERS	CHORAL
CAMLET	CAREEN	CATENA	CERIUM	CHEERY	CHORDS
CAMPED	CAREER	CATGUT	CERMET	CHEESE	CHOREA

CHORES	CLAMPS	CLOTHS	COGNAC	COMPER	CORBAN
CHORIC	CLAQUE	CLOUDS	COHEIR	COMPLY	CORBEL
CHORUS	CLARET	CLOUDY	COHERE	CONCHA	CORDED
CHOSEN	CLARKE	CLOUTS	COHORT	CONCHY	CORDON
CHOUGH	CLASPS	CLOVEN	COHOSH	CONCUR	CORERS
CHRISM	CLASSY	CLOVER	COHUNE	CONDOM	CORFAM
CHRIST	CLAUSE	CLOVES	COILED	CONDOR	CORGIS
CHROMA	CLAWED	CLOWNS	COILER	CONEYS	CORING
CHROME	CLAWER	CLOYED	COINED	CONFER	CORIUM
CHUBBY	CLAYEY	CLUBBY	COINER	CONGAS	CORKED
CHUCKS	CLEATS	CLUCKS	COIN-OP	CONGER	CORKER
CHUKAR	CLEAVE	CLUCKY	COITAL	CONGES	CORMEL
CHUKKA	CLEESE	CLUMPS	COITUS	CONGOU	CORNEA
CHUMMY	CLEFTS	CLUMPY	COLDER	CONICS	CORNEL
CHUMPS	CLENCH	CLUMSY	COLDLY	CONIES	CORNER
CHUNKS	CLEOME	CLUNKY	COLEUS	CONIUM	CORNET
CHUNKY	CLERGY	CLUTCH	COLEYS	CONKED	CORONA
CHURCH	CLERIC	COALED	COLIMA	CONKER	CORPSE
CHURLS	CLERKS	COALER	COLLAR	CONMAN	CORPUS
CHURNS	CLEVER	COARSE	COLLET	CONMEN	CORRAL
CHUTES	CLEVIS	COASTS	COLLIE	CONNED	CORSES
CICADA	CLICHE	COATED	COLMAR	CONOID	CORSET
CICERO	CLICKS	COAXED	COLONS	CONSUL	CORTEX
CIDERS	CLIENT	COAXER	COLONY	CONTRA-	CORVID
CIGARS	CLIFFS	COBALT	COLOUR	CONVEX	CORYMB
CILICE	CLIMAX	COBBER	COLUGO	CONVEY	CORYZA
CILIUM	CLIMBS	COBBLE	COLUMN	CONVOY	COSECH
CINDER	CLIMES	COBNUT	COLURE	COOING	COSHED
CINEMA	CLINAL	COBRAS	COMATE	COOKED	COSHES
CINEOL	CLINCH	COBURG	COMBAT	COOKER	COSIER
CINQUE	CLINES	COBWEB	COMBED	COOKIE	COSIES
CIPHER	CLINGY	COCCID	COMBER	COOLED	COSILY
CIRCLE	CLINIC	COCCUS	COMBOS	COOLER	COSINE
CIRCUM-	CLIP-ON	COCCYX	COMEDO	COOLIE	COSMIC
CIRCUS	CLIQUE	COCHIN	COMEDY	COOLLY	COSMOS
CIRQUE	CLITIC	COCKED	COMELY	COOLTH	COSSET
CIRRUS	CLOACA	COCKLE	COME ON	COOPED	COSTAL
CISKEI	CLOAKS	COCK-UP	COME-ON	COOPER	CO-STAR
CITIES	CLOCHE	COCOON	COMERS	COPALM	COSTLY
CITIFY	CLOCKS	CODDLE	COMETS	COPIED	COTTER
CITING	CLODDY	CODGER	COMFIT	COPIER	COTTON
CITRAL	CLOGGY	CODIFY	COMICS	COPIES	COUCAL
CITRIC	CLONAL	CODING	COMING	COPING	COUGAR
CITRIN	CLONES	COELOM	COMITY	COP-OUT	COUGHS
CITRON	CLONIC	COERCE	COMMAS	COPPED	COULEE
CITRUS	CLONUS	COEVAL	COMMIS	COPPER	COULIS
CIVETS	CLOSED	COFFEE	COMMIT	COPSES	COUNTS
CIVICS	CLOSER	COFFER	COMMON	COPTIC	COUNTY
CIVIES	CLOSES	COFFIN	COMORO	COPULA	COUPES
CLAIMS	CLOSET	COGENT	COMOSE	COQUET	COUPLE
CLAMMY	CLOTHE	COGGED	COMPEL	CORALS	COUPON

COURSE	CREAKY	CROWER	CURDLE	**D**	DAPPER
COURTS	CREAMS	CROWNS	CURFEW	DABBED	DAPPLE
COUSIN	CREAMY	CRUDER	CURIAE	DABBER	DARDIC
COVENS	CREASE	CRUETS	CURING	DABBLE	DARFUR
COVERS	CREATE	CRUISE	CURIOS	DACHAU	DARING
COVERT	CRECHE	CRUMBS	CURIUM	DACITE	DARKEN
COVEYS	CREDIT	CRUMBY	CURLED	DACOIT	DARKER
COWAGE	CREDOS	CRUMMY	CURLER	DACRON	DARKLY
COWARD	CREEDS	CRUNCH	CURLEW	DACTYL	DARNED
COWBOY	CREEKS	CRURAL	CURL UP	DADOES	DARNEL
COWING	CREELS	CRUSES	CURSED	DAEMON	DARNER
COWMAN	CREEPS	CRUSTS	CURSES	DAFTER	DARTED
COWMEN	CREEPY	CRUSTY	CURSOR	DAFTLY	DARTER
COWPAT	CRENEL	CRUTCH	CURTLY	DAGGER	DARWIN
COWPEA	CREOLE	CRUXES	CURTSY	DAGOES	DASHED
COWPOX	CRESOL	CRYING	CURVED	DAHLIA	DASHER
COWRIE	CRESTS	CRYPTS	CURVES	DAINTY	DASHES
COXING	CRETAN	CUBANE	CURVET	DAISES	DATARY
COYOTE	CRETIC	CUBBED	CUSCUS	DAKOTA	DATING
COYPUS	CRETIN	CUBING	CUSPID	DALASI	DATIVE
COZIER	CREUSE	CUBISM	CUSSED	DALIAN	DATURA
COZILY	CREWED	CUBIST	CUSSES	DALLAS	DAUBED
CRABBY	CREWEL	CUBITS	CUSTOM	DALLES	DAUBER
CRACKS	CRICKS	CUBOID	CUTELY	DALTON	DAVIES
CRACOW	CRIERS	CUCKOO	CUTEST	DAMAGE	DAVITS
CRADLE	CRIKEY	CUCUTA	CUTESY	DAMARA	DAWDLE
CRAFTS	CRIMEA	CUDDLE	CUTLER	DAMASK	DAWNED
CRAFTY	CRIMES	CUDDLY	CUTLET	DAMMAR	DAYBOY
CRAGGY	CRINGE	CUDGEL	CUTOFF	DAMMED	DAYGLO
CRAMBO	CRINUM	CUESTA	CUT OFF	DAMNED	DAYTON
CRAMPS	CRIPES	CUFFED	CUTOUT	DAMPED	DAZING
CRANED	CRISES	CUIABA	CUTTER	DAMPEN	DAZZLE
CRANES	CRISIS	CULLED	CUTUPS	DAMPER	DEACON
CRANIA	CRISPS	CULLER	CYANIC	DAMPLY	DEADEN
CRANKS	CRISPY	CULLET	CYBORG	DAMSEL	DEADLY
CRANKY	CRISTA	CULLIS	CYCLED	DAMSON	DEAFEN
CRANNY	CRITIC	CULTIC	CYCLES	DA NANG	DEALER
CRAPPY	CROAKS	CUMANA	CYCLIC	DANCED	DEARER
CRASIS	CROCKS	CUMBER	CYDERS	DANCER	DEARLY
CRATED	CROCUS	CUNEAL	CYGNET	DANCES	DEARTH
CRATER	CROFTS	CUPIDS	CYGNUS	DANDER	DEATHS
CRATES	CRONES	CUPOLA	CYMBAL	DANDLE	DEBARK
CRATON	CROOKS	CUPPAS	CYMENE	DANGER	DEBASE
CRAVAT	CRORES	CUPPED	CYMOID	DANGLE	DEBATE
CRAVED	CROSSE	CUPRIC	CYMOSE	DANIEL	DEBITS
CRAVEN	CROTCH	CUP TIE	CYMRIC	DANISH	DEBRIS
CRAWLS	CROTON	CUPULE	CYNICS	DANKER	DEBTOR
CRAYON	CROUCH	CURACY	CYPHER	DANUBE	DEBUNK
CRAZED	CROUPS	CURARE	CYPRUS	DANZIG	DEBUTS
CRAZES	CROWDS	CURATE	CYSTIC	DAPHNE	DECADE
CREAKS	CROWED	CURBED		DAPPED	DECALS

DECAMP	DELPHI	DERRIS	DIDDLE	DISEUR	DOLLAR
DECANE	DELTAS	DESCRY	DIEPPE	DISHED	DOLLED
DECANT	DELUDE	DESERT	DIESEL	DISHES	DOLLOP
DECARE	DELUGE	DESIGN	DIESIS	DISMAL	DOLMAN
DECCAN	DE LUXE	DESIRE	DIETED	DISMAY	DOLMAS
DECEIT	DELVED	DESIST	DIETER	DISOWN	DOLMEN
DECENT	DELVER	DESMAN	DIFFER	DISPEL	DOLOUR
DECIDE	DEMAND	DESMID	DIGAMY	DISTAL	DOMAIN
DECILE	DEMEAN	DESORB	DIGEST	DISTIL	DOMINO
DECKED	DEMISE	DESPOT	DIGGER	DISUSE	DONATE
DECKLE	DEMIST	DESSAU	DIGITS	DITHER	DONDER
DECOCT	DEMODE	DETACH	DIGLOT	DITTOS	DONJON
DECODE	DEMONS	DETAIL	DIK-DIK	DIVANS	DONKEY
DECOKE	DEMOTE	DETAIN	DIKTAT	DIVERS	DONNED
DECORS	DEMURE	DETECT	DILATE	DIVERT	DONORS
DECOYS	DEMURS	DETENT	DILDOS	DIVEST	DOODLE
DECREE	DENARY	DETEST	DILUTE	DIVIDE	DOO-DOO
DEDUCE	DENEST	DETOUR	DIMITY	DIVINE	DOOMED
DEDUCT	DENGUE	DE TROP	DIMMED	DIVING	DOPANT
DEEMED	DENIAL	DETTOL	DIMMER	DIWALI	DOPIER
DEEPEN	DENIED	DETUNE	DIMPLE	DJAMBI	DOPING
DEEPER	DENIER	DEUCED	DIMPLY	DJINNS	DORIAN
DEEPLY	DENIMS	DEVEIN	DIM SUM	DOABLE	DORIES
DEFACE	DE NIRO	DEVICE	DIMWIT	DOBBIN	DORMER
DEFAME	DENNED	DEVILS	DINARS	DOCENT	DORMIE
DEFEAT	DENOTE	DEVISE	DINERO	DOCILE	DORSAD
DEFECT	DENSER	DEVOID	DINERS	DOCKED	DORSAL
DEFEND	DENTAL	DEVOTE	DINGHY	DOCKER	DORSET
DEFIED	DENTED	DEVOUR	DINGLE	DOCKET	DORSUM
DEFIER	DENTEX	DEVOUT	DINING	DOCTOR	DOSAGE
DEFILE	DENTIL	DEWIER	DINKUM	DODDER	DO-SI-DO
DEFINE	DENTIN	DEWILY	DINNED	DODDLE	DOSING
DEFORM	DENUDE	DEWLAP	DINNER	DODGED	DOSSAL
DEFRAY	DENVER	DEWORM	DIOXAN	DODGEM	DOSSED
DEFTLY	DEODAR	DEXTER	DIOXIN	DODGER	DOSSER
DEFUSE	DEPART	DHARUK	DIPLEX	DODGES	DOTAGE
DEGAGE	DEPEND	DHOTIS	DIPLOE	DODOES	DOTARD
DEGREE	DEPICT	DIACID	DIPODY	DODOMA	DOTING
DEHORN	DEPLOY	DIADEM	DIPOLE	DO DUTY	DOTTED
DE-ICED	DEPORT	DIALED	DIPPED	DOFFED	DOTTER
DE-ICER	DEPOSE	DIAPER	DIPPER	DOFFER	DOTTLE
DEIFIC	DEPOTS	DIAPIR	DIRECT	DOG-EAR	DOUALA
DEISTS	DEPTHS	DIARCH	DIREST	DOGGED	DOUBLE
DEIXIS	DEPUTE	DIATOM	DIRGES	DOGGER	DOUBLY
DEJA VU	DEPUTY	DIBBED	DIRHAM	DOGIES	DOUBTS
DEJECT	DERAIL	DIBBER	DIRNDL	DOGLEG	DOUCHE
DE JURE	DERIDE	DIBBLE	DISARM	DOGMAS	DOUGHY
DELAYS	DERIVE	DICIER	DISBAR	DOG TAG	DOURLY
DELETE	DERMAL	DICING	DISBUD	DOINGS	DOUSED
DELIAN	DERMIC	DICKER	DISCOS	DOLINE	DOUSER
DELICT	DERMIS	DICTUM	DISCUS	DOLING	DOVISH

DOWNED	DRONES	DUPERY	ECLAIR	ELIDED	ENLACE
DOWNER	DRONGO	DUPING	ECTYPE	ELIXIR	ENLIST
DOWSED	DROOPY	DUPLET	ECURIE	ELOPED	ENMESH
DOWSER	DROPSY	DUPLEX	ECZEMA	ELOPER	ENMITY
DOYENS	DROSSY	DURBAN	EDDIED	EL PASO	ENNAGE
DOYLEY	DROVER	DURBAR	EDDIES	ELUDED	ENNEAD
DOZENS	DROVES	DURESS	EDGIER	ELUDER	ENOSIS
DOZIER	DROWSE	DURHAM	EDGILY	ELYSEE	ENOUGH
DOZILY	DROWSY	DURIAN	EDGING	EMBALM	ENRAGE
DOZING	DRUDGE	DURING	EDIBLE	EMBANK	ENRICH
DRABLY	DRUIDS	DUSTED	EDICTS	EMBARK	ENROBE
DRACHM	DRUNKS	DUSTER	EDIRNE	EMBERS	ENROOT
DRAFFY	DRYADS	DUSTUP	EDITED	EMBLEM	ENSIGN
DRAFTS	DRYERS	DUTIES	EDITOR	EMBODY	ENSILE
DRAFTY	DRY ICE	DUVETS	EDWARD	EMBOLY	ENSOUL
DRAGEE	DRYING	DWARFS	EERILY	EMBOSS	ENSUED
DRAGGY	DRY ROT	DYABLE	EFFACE	EMBRYO	ENSURE
DRAGON	DUBBED	DYADIC	EFFECT	EMERGE	ENTAIL
DRAINS	DUBBIN	DYEING	EFFETE	EMESIS	ENTICE
DRAKES	DUBLIN	DYNAMO	EFFIGY	EMETIC	ENTIRE
DRAMAS	DUCATS	DYNAST	EFFING	EMIGRE	ENTITY
DRAPED	DUCKED	DYNODE	EFFLUX	EMOTER	ENTOMB
DRAPER	DUCKER		EFFORT	EMPALE	ENTRAP
DRAPES	DUDEEN	**E**	EFFUSE	EMPIRE	ENTREE
DRAWEE	DUDLEY	EAGLES	EFTPOS	EMPLOY	ENVIED
DRAWER	DUELED	EAGLET	EGESTA	ENABLE	ENVIER
DRAWLS	DUELLO	EALING	EGGCUP	ENAMEL	ENVIES
DRAWLY	DUENNA	EARFUL	EGGNOG	ENATIC	ENVOYS
DREADS	DUFFEL	EARING	EGOISM	EN BLOC	ENWIND
DREAMS	DUFFER	EARNED	EGOIST	ENCAGE	ENWOMB
DREAMT	DUGONG	EARNER	EGRESS	ENCAMP	ENWRAP
DREAMY	DUGOUT	EARTHS	EGRETS	ENCASE	ENZYME
DREARY	DUIKER	EARTHY	EIGHTH	ENCASH	EOCENE
DREDGE	DULCET	EARWAX	EIGHTS	ENCODE	EOGENE
DREGGY	DULLED	EARWIG	EIGHTY	ENCORE	EOLITH
DRENCH	DULLER	EASELS	EITHER	ENCYST	EONISM
DRESSY	DULUTH	EASIER	EJECTA	ENDEAR	EOZOIC
DRIERS	DUMBER	EASILY	ELANDS	ENDING	EPARCH
DRIEST	DUMBLY	EASING	ELAPID	ENDIVE	EPIRUS
DRIFTS	DUMDUM	EASTER	ELAPSE	ENDUED	EPONYM
DRIFTY	DUMPED	EATERS	ELATED	ENDURE	EPOPEE
DRILLS	DUMPER	EATING	ELATER	ENEMAS	EPPING
DRINKS	DUNBAR	EBBING	ELBOWS	ENERGY	EQUALS
DRIPPY	DUNCES	ECARTE	ELDERS	ENFACE	EQUATE
DRIVEL	DUNDEE	ECESIS	ELDEST	ENFOLD	EQUINE
DRIVEN	DUNITE	ECHARD	ELEGIT	ENGAGE	EQUITY
DRIVER	DUNKED	ECHOED	ELEVEN	ENGINE	ERASED
DRIVES	DUNKER	ECHOES	ELEVON	ENGRAM	ERASER
DROGUE	DUNLIN	ECHOEY	ELFISH	ENGULF	ERBIUM
DROLLY	DUNNED	ECHOIC	EL GIZA	ENIGMA	ERFURT
DRONED	DUNNER	ECKERT	ELICIT	ENJOIN	ERLANG

ERMINE	EVOLVE	FABLES	FARMED	FENCED	FIJIAN
ERODED	EVZONE	FABRIC	FARMER	FENCER	FILETS
EROTIC	EXAMEN	FACADE	FAR-OFF	FENCES	FILIAL
ERRAND	EXARCH	FACETS	FAR-OUT	FENDED	FILING
ERRANT	EXCEED	FACIAL	FARROW	FENDER	FILLED
ERRATA	EXCEPT	FACIES	FARTED	FENIAN	FILLER
ERRING	EXCESS	FACILE	FASCIA	FENNEC	FILLET
ERRORS	EXCISE	FACING	FASTED	FENNEL	FILL-IN
ERSATZ	EXCITE	FACTOR	FASTEN	FENTON	FILLIP
ERYNGO	EXCUSE	FACULA	FASTER	FERBAM	FILMED
ESCAPE	EXEDRA	FADE-IN	FAT CAT	FERIAL	FILMIC
ESCARP	EXEMPT	FADING	FATHER	FERMAT	FILOSE
ESCHAR	EXETER	FAECAL	FATHOM	FERRET	FILTER
ESCHEW	EXEUNT	FAECES	FATTEN	FERRIC	FILTHY
ESCORT	EXHALE	FAENZA	FATTER	FERULA	FIMBLE
ESCROW	EXHORT	FAERIE	FAUCAL	FERULE	FINALE
ESCUDO	EXHUME	FAG END	FAUCES	FERVID	FINALS
ESKIMO	EXILED	FAGGED	FAUCET	FESCUE	FINDER
ESPIAL	EXILES	FAGGOT	FAULTS	FESTAL	FINELY
ESPIED	EXILIC	FAILED	FAULTY	FESTER	FINERY
ESPIER	EXITED	FAILLE	FAUNAL	FETIAL	FINEST
ESPRIT	EXODUS	FAINTS	FAUNAS	FETING	FINGAL
ESSAYS	EXONYM	FAIRER	FAVOUR	FETISH	FINGER
ESTATE	EXOTIC	FAIRLY	FAWNED	FETTER	FINIAL
ESTEEM	EXPAND	FAITHS	FAWNER	FETTLE	FINING
ESTRAY	EXPECT	FAJITA	FAXING	FEUDAL	FINISH
ETALON	EXPEND	FAKERS	FAZING	FEUDED	FINITE
ETCHED	EXPERT	FAKING	FEALTY	FEZZAN	FINNED
ETCHER	EXPIRE	FAKIRS	FEARED	FEZZED	FINNIC
ETHANE	EXPIRY	FALCON	FEARER	FEZZES	FIORDS
ETHENE	EXPORT	FALLAL	FEASTS	FIACRE	FIORIN
ETHICS	EXPOSE	FALLEN	FECULA	FIANCE	FIPPLE
ETHNIC	EXSERT	FALLER	FECUND	FIASCO	FIRING
ETHYNE	EXTANT	FALLOW	FEDORA	FIBBED	FIRKIN
ETYMON	EXTEND	FALSER	FEEBLE	FIBBER	FIRMED
EUBOEA	EXTENT	FALTER	FEEBLY	FIBRED	FIRMER
EUCHRE	EXTERN	FAMILY	FEEDER	FIBRES	FIRMLY
EULOGY	EXTINE	FAMINE	FEELER	FIBRIL	FIRSTS
EUNUCH	EXTORT	FAMISH	FEIJOA	FIBRIN	FIRTHS
EUREKA	EXTRAS	FAMOUS	FEINTS	FIBULA	FISCAL
EURO MP	EXUDED	FANDOM	FEISTY	FICKLE	FISHED
EUROPE	EYEFUL	FANGED	FELINE	FIDDLE	FISHER
EVADED	EYEING	FANGIO	FELLED	FIDDLY	FISHES
EVADER	EYELET	FANION	FELLER	FIDGET	FISTIC
EVENLY	EYELID	FANJET	FELLOE	FIELDS	FITFUL
EVENTS	EYRIES	FANNED	FELLOW	FIENDS	FITTED
EVILER		FANNER	FELONS	FIERCE	FITTER
EVILLY	**F**	FAN-TAN	FELONY	FIESTA	FIVERS
EVINCE		FARCES	FEMALE	FIFTHS	FIXATE
EVOKED	FABIAN	FARINA	FEMORA	FIGHTS	FIXERS
EVOKER	FABLED	FARING	FEMURS	FIGURE	FIXING
	FABLER				

FIXITY FLIRTS FOLIOS FOULLY FROCKS FUNKER
FIZGIG FLITCH FOLIUM FOUL-UP FROGGY FUNNEL
FIZZED FLOATS FOLKIE FOUNTS FROLIC FUN RUN
FIZZER FLOATY FOLKSY FOURTH FRONDS FURFUR
FIZZLE FLOCKS FOLLOW FOVEAL FRONTS FURIES
FJORDS FLOCKY FOLSOM FOWLER FROSTS FURLED
FLABBY FLOODS FOMENT FOWLES FROSTY FURLER
FLACON FLOORS FONDER FOXIER FROTHS FURORE
FLAGGY FLOOZY FONDLE FOXILY FROTHY FURRED
FLAGON FLOPPY FONDLY FOXING FROWNS FURROW
FLAILS FLORAL FONDUE FOYERS FROWZY FUSAIN
FLAKED FLORET FONTAL FRACAS FROZEN FUSHUN
FLAKER FLORID FOODIE FRAMED FRUGAL FUSILE
FLAKES FLORIN FOOLED FRAMER FRUITS FUSING
FLAMBE FLOSSY FOOTER FRAMES FRUITY FUSION
FLAMED FLOURY FOOTLE FRANCE FRUMPS FUSSED
FLAMER FLOWED FOOZLE FRANCS FRUMPY FUSSER
FLAMES FLOWER FORAGE FRAPPE FRUNZE FUSSES
FLANGE FLUENT FORAYS FRATER FRYERS FUSTIC
FLANKS FLUFFY FORBAD FRAUDS FRYING FUTILE
FLARED FLUIDS FORBID FRAUEN FRY-UPS FUTONS
FLARES FLUKES FORCED FRAYED FU-CHOU FUTURE
FLASHY FLUKEY FORCER FRAZIL FUCKED FUZHOU
FLASKS FLUNKY FORCES FREAKS FUCKER FUZZED
FLATLY FLURRY FORDED FREAKY FUCK-UP
FLATUS FLUTED FOREGO FREELY FUCOID **G**
FLAUNT FLUTER FOREST FREEST FUDDLE GABBED
FLAVIN FLUTES FORFAR FREEZE FUDGED GABBER
FLAWED FLYBYS FORGED FRENCH FUELED GABBLE
FLAXEN FLYERS FORGER FRENZY FUGARD GABBRO
FLAYED FLYING FORGES FRESCO FUGATO GABION
FLAYER FLYSCH FORGET FRESNO FUGING GABLED
FLECHE FOALED FORGOT FRIARS FUGUES GABLES
FLECKS FOAMED FORKED FRIARY FUHRER GADDED
FLEDGE FOBBED FORMAL FRIDAY FUJIAN GADDER
FLEECE FO'C'SLE FORMAN FRIDGE FUKIEN GADFLY
FLEECY FODDER FORMAT FRIEND FULANI GADGET
FLEETS FOETAL FORMED FRIERS FULCRA GADOID
FLENSE FOETID FORMER FRIEZE FULFIL GAELIC
FLESHY FOETOR FORMIC FRIGHT FULLER GAFFER
FLETCH FOETUS FORMYL FRIGID FULL-ON GAFFES
FLEXED FOGBOW FORNIX FRIJOL FULMAR GAGGED
FLEXES FOGDOG FORTES FRILLS FUMBLE GAGGER
FLEXOR FOGGED FORTIS FRILLY FUMING GAGGLE
FLICKS FOGGIA FORUMS FRINGE FUNDED GAGING
FLIERS FOGIES FOSHAN FRINGY FUNDIC GAIETY
FLIGHT FOIBLE FOSSIL FRISKS FUNDUS GAIJIN
FLIMSY FOILED FOSTER FRISKY FUNGAL GAINED
FLINCH FOLDED FOUGHT FRIULI FUNGIC GAINER
FLINTS FOLDER FOULED FRIVOL FUNGUS GAINLY
FLINTY FOLIAR FOULER FRIZZY FUNKED GAITER

45

GALATA	GARRET	GENIES	GLACIS	GOBBLE	GRAECO-
GALATI	GARTER	GENIUS	GLADES	GOBIAN	GRAFTS
GALAXY	GASBAG	GENOME	GLADLY	GOBLET	GRAINS
GALENA	GASCON	GENRES	GLAIRY	GOBLIN	GRAINY
GALERE	GASHED	GENTLE	GLANCE	GODARD	GRAMME
GALIBI	GASHES	GENTLY	GLANDS	GODSON	GRANDS
GALIOT	GASIFY	GENTRY	GLARED	GODWIT	GRANGE
GALLED	GASKET	GEODIC	GLARES	GOFERS	GRANNY
GALLEY	GASKIN	GERBIL	GLARUS	GOFFER	GRANTS
GALLIC	GASMAN	GERMAN	GLASSY	GOGGLE	GRAPES
GALLON	GASMEN	GERMEN	GLAZED	GOITRE	GRAPHS
GALLOP	GASPED	GERUND	GLAZER	GO-KART	GRASSY
GALORE	GASPER	GETTER	GLAZES	GOLDEN	GRATED
GALOSH	GASSED	GETUPS	GLEAMS	GOLFER	GRATER
GALWAY	GASSER	GEYSER	GLEBES	GOLLOP	GRATES
GALYAK	GASSES	GEZIRA	GLEETY	GOMUTI	GRATIS
GAMBIA	GATEAU	GHETTO	GLIBLY	GONADS	GRAVEL
GAMBIT	GATHER	GHIBLI	GLIDED	GONDAR	GRAVEN
GAMBLE	GAUCHE	GHOSTS	GLIDER	GONERS	GRAVER
GAMBOL	GAUCHO	GHOULS	GLIDES	GONION	GRAVES
GAMELY	GAUGED	GHYLLS	GLINTS	GOODLY	GRAVID
GAMETE	GAUGER	GIANTS	GLIOMA	GOOFED	GRAYED
GAMIER	GAUGES	GIAOUR	GLITCH	GOOGLY	GRAYER
GAMINE	GAVAGE	GIBBED	GLITZY	GOOGOL	GRAZED
GAMING	GAVELS	GIBBER	GLOATS	GOOIER	GRAZER
GAMMAS	GAVIAL	GIBBET	GLOBAL	GOPHER	GRAZES
GAMMED	GAWKED	GIBBON	GLOBES	GORGED	GREASE
GAMMON	GAWKER	GIBE AT	GLOBIN	GORGER	GREASY
GANDER	GAWPED	GIBEON	GLOOMY	GORGES	GREATS
GANGED	GAYEST	GIBSON	GLORIA	GORGON	GREBES
GANGER	GAZEBO	GIDDAY	GLOSSA	GORICA	GREECE
GANGES	GAZING	GIFTED	GLOSSY	GORIER	GREEDY
GANGUE	GAZUMP	GIGGLE	GLOVED	GORILY	GREENS
GANNET	GDANSK	GIGGLY	GLOVER	GORING	GREYED
GANOID	GDYNIA	GIGOLO	GLOVES	GO-SLOW	GREYER
GANTRY	GEARED	GILDED	GLOWED	GOSPEL	GRIEVE
GAOLED	GECKOS	GILDER	GLOWER	GOSSIP	GRIFFE
GAOLER	GEDACT	GILLED	GLUING	GOTHIC	GRIGRI
GAPING	GEE-GEE	GILLIE	GLUMLY	GOUGED	GRILLE
GAPPED	GEEZER	GIMLET	GLUTEN	GOUGER	GRILLS
GARAGE	GEISHA	GIMMAL	GLYCOL	GOUGES	GRILSE
GARBED	GELADA	GINGER	GNAWED	GOURDS	GRIMLY
GARBLE	GELDED	GINKGO	GNAWER	GOVERN	GRINDS
GARCON	GELDOF	GIRDED	GNEISS	GRABEN	GRINGO
GARDEN	GELLED	GIRDER	GNOMES	GRACED	GRIPED
GARGET	GEMINI	GIRDLE	GNOMIC	GRACES	GRIPER
GARGLE	GEMMED	GIRLIE	GNOMON	GRADED	GRIPES
GARISH	GENDER	GIRTHS	GNOSIS	GRADER	GRISLY
GARLIC	GENERA	GIUSTO	GOADED	GRADES	GRISON
GARNER	GENEVA	GIVE IN	GOATEE	GRADIN	GRISTS
GARNET	GENIAL	GIVING	GOBBET	GRADUS	GRITTY

GRIVET	GUITAR	HAEMAL	HANKER	HATRED	HEBRON
GROANS	GULDEN	HAEMIC	HANKIE	HATTER	HECATE
GROATS	GULLAH	HAEMIN	HANKOW	HAULED	HECKLE
GROCER	GULLED	HAERES	HANNAH	HAULER	HECTIC
GRODNO	GULLET	HAFTER	HANSEL	HAUNCH	HECTOR
GROGGY	GULLEY	HAGBUT	HANSEN	HAUNTS	HECUBA
GROINS	GULPED	HAGGAI	HANSOM	HAVANA	HEDDLE
GROOMS	GULPER	HAGGIS	HAPPEN	HAVANT	HEDGED
GROOVE	GUMBOS	HAGGLE	HAPTEN	HAVENS	HEDGER
GROOVY	GUMMED	HAIDAN	HAPTIC	HAVEN'T	HEDGES
GROPED	GUNDOG	HAIDUK	HARALD	HAVING	HEDJAZ
GROPER	GUNG-HO	HAILED	HARARE	HAWAII	HEEDED
GROPES	GUNMAN	HAILER	HARASS	HAWHAW	HEEDER
GROTTO	GUNMEN	HAINAN	HARBIN	HAWICK	HEE-HAW
GROTTY	GUNNED	HAIRDO	HARD BY	HAWKED	HEELED
GROUCH	GUNNEL	HAIRIF	HARDEN	HAWKER	HEELER
GROUND	GUNNER	HAJJES	HARDER	HAWSER	HEENAN
GROUPS	GUNSHY	HAJJIS	HARDIE	HAYBOX	HEFTER
GROUSE	GUNTUR	HAKIMS	HARDLY	HAYMOW	HEGIRA
GROUTS	GUNYAH	HALEST	HARD-ON	HAZARD	HEIDUC
GROVEL	GURGLE	HALIDE	HARD UP	HAZELS	HEIFER
GROVES	GURJUN	HALITE	HAREEM	HAZIER	HEIGHT
GROWER	GURKHA	HALLAH	HAREMS	HAZILY	HEJIRA
GROWLS	GUSHED	HALLEL	HARING	HAZING	HEKATE
GROWTH	GUSHER	HALLEY	HARKED	H-BOMBS	HELENA
GROYNE	GUSSET	HALLOO	HARKEN	HEADED	HELIOS
GROZNY	GUSTED	HALLOS	HARLEM	HEADER	HELIUM
GRUBBY	GUTTED	HALLOW	HARLEY	HEAD-ON	HELLAS
GRUDGE	GUTTER	HALLUX	HARLOT	HEALED	HELLEN
GRUGRU	GUVNOR	HALOES	HARLOW	HEALER	HELLER
GRUMPY	GUYANA	HALOID	HARMED	HEALEY	HELLES
GRUNGE	GUYING	HALTED	HARMER	HEALTH	HELLOS
GRUNGY	GUZZLE	HALTER	HARNEY	HEANEY	HELMET
GRUNTS	GYPPED	HALTON	HAROLD	HEAPED	HELPED
GUARDS	GYPSUM	HALVAH	HARPED	HEAPER	HELPER
GUAVAS	GYRATE	HALVED	HARPER	HEARER	HELVES
GUELPH	GYROSE	HALVES	HARRAR	HEARSE	HEMMED
GUFNON		HAMATE	HARRIS	HEARST	HEMMER
GUESTS	**H**	HAMELN	HARROW	HEARTH	HEMPEN
GUFFAW		HAMITE	HARTAL	HEARTS	HENBIT
GUIANA	HAAKON	HAMLET	HARVEY	HEARTY	HENDRY
GUIDED	HABANA	HAMLYN	HASHED	HEATED	HENLEY
GUIDER	HABILE	HAMMED	HASHES	HEATER	HEPCAT
GUIDES	HABITS	HAMMER	HASLET	HEATHS	HEPTAD
GUIDON	HACKED	HAMPER	HASSAN	HEATHY	HERALD
GUILDS	HACKER	HANDED	HASSLE	HEAUME	HERBAL
GUILIN	HACKLE	HANDEL	HASTEN	HEAVED	HERDED
GUILTY	HADEAN	HANDLE	HATBOX	HEAVEN	HERDER
GUIMPE	HADITH	HANGAR	HATHOR	HEAVER	HERDIC
GUINEA	HADJES	HANGER	HATING	HEAVES	HEREAT
GUISES	HADJIS	HANG-UP	HATPIN	HEBREW	HEREBY

I 6 HEREIN

HEREIN	HINGER	HOLISM	HORSEY	HULLER	HYPHEN
HEREOF	HINGES	HOLLER	HOSIER	HULLOS	HYPING
HEREON	HINTED	HOLLOW	HOSING	HUMANE	
HERERO	HINTER	HOLMES	HOSTED	HUMANS	**I**
HERESY	HIPPED	HOLMIC	HOSTEL	HUMBER	IAMBIC
HERETO	HIPPER	HOLPEN	HOSTIE	HUMBLE	IAMBUS
HERIOT	HIPPIE	HOMAGE	HOT AIR	HUMBLY	IBADAN
HERMES	HIRING	HOMBRE	HOTBED	HUMBUG	IBAGUE
HERMIT	HISPID	HOMELY	HOT DOG	HUMISM	IBERIA
HERMON	HISSED	HOMIER	HOTELS	HUMMED	IBEXES
HERNIA	HISSER	HOMILY	HOTIEN	HUMMEL	IBIBIO
HEROES	HISSES	HOMING	HOT KEY	HUMMER	IBISES
HEROIC	HI-TECH	HOMINY	HOTPOT	HUMMUS	ICE AGE
HEROIN	HITHER	HONEST	HOT ROD	HUMOUR	ICEBOX
HERONS	HITLER	HONIED	HOTTER	HUMPED	ICE CAP
HERPES	HIT MAN	HONING	HOTTIE	HUMPTY	ICEMAN
HERREN	HIT MEN	HONKED	HOUDAN	HUNGER	ICEMEN
HERZOG	HITTER	HONKER	HOUNDS	HUNGRY	ICHANG
HESIOD	HIVING	HONOUR	HOURIS	HUNKER	I CHING
HESTIA	HOARDS	HONSHU	HOURLY	HUNTED	ICICLE
HETMAN	HOARSE	HOODED	HOUSED	HUNTER	ICIEST
HEWERS	HOAXED	HOODOO	HOUSEL	HUPPAH	ICONIC
HEWING	HOAXER	HOOFED	HOUSES	HURDLE	ID CARD
HEXANE	HOAXES	HOOKAH	HOVELS	HURLED	IDEALS
HEXING	HOBART	HOOKED	HOWARD	HURLER	IDEATE
HEXONE	HOBBES	HOOKER	HOWDAH	HURLEY	IDIOCY
HEXOSE	HOBBLE	HOOKUP	HOWE'ER	HURRAH	IDIOMS
HEYDAY	HOBNOB	HOOPED	HOWLED	HURRAY	IDIOTS
HIATAL	HOBOES	HOOPER	HOWLER	HURTER	IDLEST
HIATUS	HOCKED	HOOP-LA	HOWLET	HURTLE	IDLING
HICCUP	HOCKER	HOOPOE	HOWRAH	HUSAIN	IDYLLS
HICKEY	HOCKEY	HOORAH	HOYDEN	HUSHED	IGLOOS
HICKOK	HODDEN	HOORAY	HSIANG	HUSH-UP	IGNITE
HIDDEN	HODDIN	HOOTED	HUAMBO	HUSKER	IGNORE
HIDING	HODMAN	HOOTER	HUBBLE	HUSSAR	IGUACU
HIEING	HOEING	HOOVER	HUBBUB	HUSTLE	IGUANA
HIEMAL	HOGGED	HOOVES	HUBCAP	HUSTON	ILESHA
HIGGLE	HOGGER	HOPING	HUBRIS	HUXLEY	ILEXES
HIGHER	HOGGET	HOPPED	HUCKLE	HUZZAH	ILIGAN
HIGHLY	HOGNUT	HOPPER	HUDDLE	HYADES	ILKLEY
HIJACK	HOGTIE	HOPPLE	HUDSON	HYAENA	ILL-USE
HIKERS	HOHHOT	HOPPUS	HUELVA	HYALIN	ILOILO
HIKING	HOICKS	HORACE	HUESCA	HYBRID	ILORIN
HILARY	HOIDEN	HORARY	HUFFED	HYBRIS	IMAGES
HILLEL	HOISTS	HORDES	HUGELY	HYDRAS	IMBIBE
HILLER	HOLDEN	HORMIC	HUGEST	HYDRIA	IMBRUE
HIMEJI	HOLDER	HORMUZ	HUGGED	HYDRIC	IMBUED
HINDER	HOLDUP	HORNED	HUGGER	HYENAS	IMIDIC
HINDOO	HOLD UP	HORNET	HUGHES	HYMENS	IMMUNE
HINDUS	HOLIER	HORRID	HUGHIE	HYMNAL	IMMURE
HINGED	HOLILY	HORROR	HULLED	HYMNED	IMPACT

IMPAIR	INFUSE	INTROS	ITCHED	JETSAM	JOULES
IMPALA	INGEST	INTUIT	ITCHES	JET SET	JOUNCE
IMPALE	INGOTS	INUITS	ITHACA	JETTED	JOURNO
IMPART	INHALE	INULIN	ITSELF	JETTON	JOVIAL
IMPEDE	INHAUL	INURED		JEWELS	JOYFUL
IMPEND	INHERE	INVADE	**J**	JEWESS	JOYING
IMPHAL	INHUME	INVENT	JABBED	JEWISH	JOYOUS
IMPISH	INJECT	INVERT	JABBER	JHANSI	JUDAEA
IMPORT	INJURE	INVEST	JABIRU	JIBBED	JUDAIC
IMPOSE	INJURY	INVITE	JACANA	JIBBER	JUDDER
IMPOST	INK-CAP	INVOKE	JACKAL	JIBING	JUDGED
IMPROV	INKIER	INWARD	JACKED	JIGAWA	JUDGER
IMPUGN	INKING	IODATE	JACKET	JIGGED	JUDGES
IMPURE	INKPAD	IODIDE	JACKIE	JIGGER	JUDOGI
IMPUTE	INLAID	IODINE	JAFFNA	JIGGLE	JUDOKA
INARCH	INLAND	IODISM	JAGGED	JIGGLY	JUGATE
INBORN	IN-LAWS	IODIZE	JAGUAR	JIGSAW	JUGGED
INBRED	INLAYS	IODOUS	JAILED	JIHADS	JUGGLE
INCEPT	INLETS	IONIAN	JAILER	JILTED	JUICED
INCEST	INLIER	IONIZE	JAIPUR	JILTER	JUICES
INCHED	INMATE	IONONE	JALAPA	JINGLE	JUJUBE
INCHES	INMOST	IPECAC	JALOPY	JINGLY	JULEPS
INCHON	INNATE	IREFUL	JAMMED	JINXED	JULIES
INCISE	INNING	IRENIC	JAMMER	JINXES	JUMBLE
INCITE	INNUIT	IRIDIC	JANGLE	JITTER	JUMP AT
INCOME	INROAD	IRISES	JAPERY	JIVING	JUMPED
INCUBI	INRUSH	IRITIC	JAPURA	JOBBED	JUMPER
INCUSE	INSANE	IRITIS	JARGON	JOBBER	JUNEAU
INDEED	INSECT	IRKING	JARRAH	JOBBIE	JUNGLE
INDENE	INSERT	IRONED	JARRED	JOB LOT	JUNGLY
INDENT	INSETS	IRONER	JARROW	JOCKEY	JUNIOR
INDIAN	INSIDE	IRONIC	JASPER	JOCOSE	JUNKED
INDICT	INSIST	IRRUPT	JAUNTS	JOCUND	JUNKET
INDIGO	IN SITU	IRTYSH	JAUNTY	JOGGED	JUNKIE
INDITE	INSOLE	IRVINE	JAWARA	JOGGER	JUNTAS
INDIUM	INSTAR	ISATIN	JAWING	JOGGLE	JURIED
INDOLE	INSTEP	ISCHIA	JAZZED	JOHNNY	JURIES
INDOOR	INSTIL	ISLAND	JEERED	JOHORE	JURIST
INDORE	INSULA	ISLETS	JEERER	JOINED	JURORS
INDRIS	INSULT	ISOBAR	JEJUNE	JOINER	JUSTLY
INDUCE	INSURE	ISOGON	JELLED	JOINTS	JUTTED
INDUCT	INTACT	ISOHEL	JENNET	JOISTS	JUTTER
INDULT	INTAKE	ISOLEX	JERBOA	JOKERS	
INFAMY	INTEND	ISOMER	JERKED	JOKING	**K**
INFANT	INTENT	ISOPOD	JERKER	JOLTED	KABILA
INFECT	INTERN	ISRAEL	JERKIN	JORDAN	KABYLE
INFEST	INTIMA	ISSUED	JERSEY	JOSHED	KADUNA
INFIRM	INTINE	ISSUER	JESTED	JOSHES	KAFFIR
INFLOW	INTONE	ISSUES	JESTER	JOSTLE	KAFTAN
INFLUX	IN TOTO	ISTRIA	JESUIT	JOTTED	KAISER
INFORM	IN TRIM	ITALIC	JET LAG	JOTTER	KAIZEN

KAKAPO	KEYING	KNIVES	LACKED	LAPPER	LATVIA
KALISZ	KEYWAY	KNOCKS	LACKEY	LAPPET	LAUDED
KALMAR	KHALIF	KNOLLS	LACTAM	LAPSED	LAUDER
KALMIA	KHULNA	KNOTTY	LACTIC	LAPSER	LAUGHS
KALONG	KHYBER	KNOWER	LACUNA	LAPSES	LAUNCH
KALUGA	KIBOSH	KOALAS	LADDER	LAPSUS	LAUREL
KAMALA	KICKED	KODIAK	LADDIE	LAPTOP	LAVABO
KANARA	KICKER	KOHIMA	LA-DI-DA	LAP-TOP	LAVAGE
KANBAN	KICK IN	KOKAND	LADIES	LARDED	LAVISH
KANGAS	KIDDED	KOLYMA	LADING	LARDER	LAWFUL
KANPUR	KIDDER	KOPECK	LADINO	LARDON	LAWYER
KANSAS	KIDDIE	KOPPIE	LADLED	LAREDO	LAXITY
KAOLIN	KIDNAP	KOREAN	LADLER	LARGER	LAY-BYS
KARATE	KIDNEY	KORUNA	LADLES	LARGOS	LAYERS
KARATS	KIELCE	KOSHER	LADOGA	LARIAM	LAYING
KARIBA	KIGALI	KOSICE	LAGENA	LARIAT	LAYMAN
KARMIC	KIKUYU	KOVROV	LAGERS	LARINE	LAYMEN
KARPOV	KILLED	KOWTOW	LAGGED	LARISA	LAY-OFF
KASBAH	KILLER	KRAALS	LAGOON	LARKED	LAY OUT
KASSEL	KILTED	KRISES	LAHORE	LARKER	LAYOUT
KAUNAS	KILTER	KRONER	LAICAL	LARNAX	LAZIER
KAYAKS	KIMONO	KRONOR	LAID UP	LARVAE	LAZILY
KAZAKH	KINASE	KRUGER	LAIRDS	LARVAL	LAZING
KEBABS	KINDER	KUKRIS	LALANG	LARYNX	LEADEN
KEDIRI	KINDLE	KUMASI	LAMBDA	LASCAR	LEADER
KEEGAN	KINDLY	KUMISS	LAMBED	LASERS	LEAD-IN
KEELED	KINGLY	KUMMEL	LAMELY	LASHED	LEAGUE
KEENED	KIOSKS	KUNG FU	LAMENT	LASHER	LEAKED
KEENER	KIPPED	KUNLUN	LAMEST	LASHES	LEAKER
KEENLY	KIPPER	KUOPIO	LAMINA	LASHIO	LEANED
KEEPER	KIRKBY	KURGAN	LAMING	LASH-UP	LEANER
KEEP ON	KIRKUK	KUWAIT	LAMMAS	LASKET	LEAN TO
KELLER	KIRMAN	KWACHA	LAMPAS	LASSES	LEAN-TO
KELOID	KIRSCH	KWANZA	LANATE	LASSOS	LEAPED
KELPIE	KIRUNA	KYRGYZ	LANCED	LASTED	LEAPER
KELTIC	KISMET	KYUSHU	LANCER	LASTER	LEARNT
KELVIN	KISSED		LANCES	LASTLY	LEASED
KENDAL	KISSER	**L**	LANCET	LATEEN	LEASER
KENNED	KISSES		LANDAU	LATELY	LEASES
KENNEL	KISUMU	LAAGER	LANDED	LATENT	LEAVED
KENYAN	KIT BAG	LABELS	LANDES	LATEST	LEAVEN
KERALA	KITSCH	LABIAL	LANGER	LATHER	LEAVER
KERMAN	KITTED	LABILE	LANGUE	LATHES	LEAVES
KERMES	KITTEN	LABIUM	LANGUR	LATINA	LECHER
KERNEL	KLAXON	LABLAB	LANKER	LATINO	LECTIN
KERSEY	KNAVES	LABOUR	LANKLY	LATINS	LECTOR
KETENE	KNAWEL	LABRET	LANNER	LATISH	LEDGER
KETONE	KNELLS	LABRUM	LANUGO	LATIUM	LEDGES
KETOSE	KNIFED	LACHES	LAPDOG	LATRIA	LEERED
KETTLE	KNIFER	LACIER	LAPELS	LATTEN	LEEWAY
KEVLAR	KNIGHT	LACING	LAPPED	LATTER	LEGACY

LEGATE	LIBIDO	LINKED	LOCHIA	LOPPER	LUNGER
LEGATO	LIBRAN	LINKUP	LOCKED	LOQUAT	LUNGES
LEGEND	LIBYAN	LINNET	LOCKER	LORDED	LUNULA
LEGERS	LICHEN	LINTEL	LOCKET	LORDLY	LUPINE
LEGGED	LICKED	LINTER	LOCKUP	LORICA	LUPINS
LEGION	LICKER	LIPASE	LOCULE	LOSERS	LURING
LEGIST	LIDDED	LI PENG	LOCUMS	LOSING	LURKED
LEGUAN	LIEGES	LIPIDS	LOCUST	LOSSES	LURKER
LEGUME	LIE-INS	LIPOID	LODGED	LOTION	LUSAKA
LEIDEN	LIENAL	LIPOMA	LODGER	LOTTED	LUSHES
LEKKER	LIERNE	LIQUID	LODGES	LOUDEN	LU-SHUN
LE MANS	LIFERS	LIQUOR	LOFTED	LOUDER	LUSTED
LEMNOS	LIFFEY	LISBON	LOFTER	LOUDLY	LUSTRE
LEMONS	LIFTED	LISPED	LOGGED	LOUGHS	LUTEAL
LEMONY	LIFTER	LISPER	LOGGER	LOUISE	LUVVIE
LEMURS	LIGAND	LISSOM	LOGGIA	LOUNGE	LUXATE
LENDER	LIGATE	LISTED	LOGIER	LOURED	LUXURY
LENGTH	LIGHTS	LISTEN	LOGION	LOURIE	LYCEES
LENITY	LIGNIN	LITANY	LOGJAM	LOUSED	LYCEUM
LENSES	LIGULA	LITCHI	LOGLOG	LOUVAR	LYCHEE
LENTEN	LIGULE	LITERS	LOG OUT	LOUVRE	LYNXES
LENTIC	LIKASI	LITHER	LOIRET	LOVAGE	LYRATE
LENTIL	LIKELY	LITHIA	LOITER	LOVELY	LYRICS
LEOBEN	LIKING	LITHIC	LOLLED	LOVERS	LYRIST
LEONID	LILACS	LITMUS	LOLLER	LOVEYS	LYSINE
LEPERS	LILIES	LITRES	LOLLOP	LOVING	
LEPTON	LILLEE	LITTER	LOMBOK	LOWEST	**M**
LESBOS	LIMBER	LITTLE	LOMENT	LOWING	MACACO
LESION	LIMBIC	LIVE-IN	LONDON	LOW-KEY	MACAWS
LESSEE	LIMBOS	LIVELY	LONELY	LOYANG	MACEIO
LESSEN	LIMBUS	LIVERS	LONERS	LOZERE	MACKAY
LESSER	LIMEYS	LIVERY	LONGAN	L-PLATE	MACKLE
LESSON	LIMIER	LIVING	LONGED	LUANDA	MACRON
LESSOR	LIMING	LIZARD	LONGER	LUBBER	MACULA
LETHAL	LIMITS	LLAMAS	LOOFAH	LUBECK	MADAME
LETTER	LIMNED	LOADED	LOOKED	LUBLIN	MADAMS
LETUPS	LIMNER	LOADER	LOOKER	LUCENT	MADCAP
LEVANT	LIMPED	LOAFED	LOOK-IN	LUDLOW	MADDEN
LEVEES	LIMPER	LOAFER	LOOK UP	LUFFED	MADDER
LEVELS	LIMPET	LOANED	LOOMED	LUGANO	MADE-UP
LEVERS	LIMPID	LOANER	LOONEY	LUGGED	MADMAN
LEVIED	LIMPLY	LOATHE	LOOPED	LUGGER	MADMEN
LEVIER	LINAGE	LOAVES	LOOPER	LULLED	MADRAS
LEVIES	LINDEN	LOBATE	LOOSED	LUMBAR	MADRID
LEVITY	LINEAL	LOBBED	LOOSEN	LUMBER	MADURO
LEWDLY	LINEAR	LOBITO	LOOSER	LUMMOX	MAENAD
LIABLE	LINERS	LOBOLA	LOOSES	LUMPED	MAGGOT
LIAISE	LINEUP	LOBULE	LOOTED	LUMPEN	MAGIAN
LIBBER	LINGER	LOCALE	LOOTER	LUNACY	MAGNET
LIBELS	LINGUA	LOCALS	LOPING	LUNATE	MAGNUM
LIBERO	LINING	LOCATE	LOPPED	LUNGED	MAGPIE

MAGUEY	MANILA	MASCOT	MEDICK	MESCAL	MILKED
MAGYAR	MANISA	MASERS	MEDICO	MESHED	MILKER
MAHOUT	MANLEY	MASERU	MEDICS	MESHES	MILLED
MAIDEN	MANNED	MASHED	MEDINA	MESSED	MILLER
MAIKOP	MANNER	MASHER	MEDIUM	MESSES	MILLET
MAILED	MANORS	MASHES	MEDLAR	MESS-UP	MILORD
MAILER	MANQUE	MASHIE	MEDLEY	METAGE	MILTER
MAI MAI	MANTEL	MASJID	MEEKER	METALS	MIMICS
MAIMED	MANTIC	MASKED	MEEKLY	METEOR	MIMING
MAIMER	MANTIS	MASKER	MEERUT	METERS	MIMOSA
MAINLY	MANTLE	MASONS	MEETER	METHOD	MINCED
MAJORS	MANTUA	MASQUE	MEGARA	METHYL	MINCER
MAKALU	MANUAL	MASSED	MEGILP	METIER	MINDED
MAKE DO	MANURE	MASSES	MEGOHM	METING	MINDEL
MAKE IT	MAOISM	MASSIF	MEKNES	METOPE	MINDER
MAKERS	MAOIST	MASTER	MEKONG	METRES	MINERS
MAKE UP	MAPLES	MASTIC	MELEES	METRIC	MINGLE
MAKE-UP	MAPPED	MATADI	MELLOW	METROS	MINIFY
MAKING	MAPUTO	MATING	MELODY	METTLE	MINIMA
MALABO	MAQUIS	MATINS	MELOID	MEWING	MINIMS
MALADY	MARACA	MATRIX	MELONS	MEWLER	MINING
MALAGA	MARAUD	MATRON	MELTED	MEXICO	MINION
MALANG	MARBLE	MATTED	MELTER	MEZZOS	MINIUM
MALATE	MARBLY	MATTER	MELTON	MIAOWS	MINNOW
MALAWI	MARCHE	MATURE	MEMBER	MIASMA	MINOAN
MALAYA	MARGAY	MAULED	MEMOIR	MICKEY	MINORS
MALDON	MARGIN	MAULER	MEMORY	MICMAC	MINTED
MALEIC	MARIAN	MAUNDY	MENACE	MICRON	MINTER
MALICE	MARINA	MAUSER	MENADO	MICROS	MINUET
MALIGN	MARINE	MAXIMA	MENAGE	MIDAIR	MINUTE
MALLEE	MARKED	MAXIMS	MENDED	MIDDAY	MINXES
MALLET	MARKER	MAY BUG	MENDER	MIDDEN	MIOSIS
MALLOW	MARKET	MAY DAY	MENHIR	MIDDLE	MIOTIC
MALTED	MARKKA	MAYFLY	MENIAL	MIDGES	MIRAGE
MALTHA	MARKUP	MAYHEM	MENSES	MIDGET	MIRING
MAMBAS	MARLIN	MAYORS	MENTAL	MIDGUT	MIRROR
MAMMAL	MARMOT	MAZILY	MENTON	MID-OFF	MISCUE
MAMMON	MAROON	MAZUMA	MENTOR	MIDRIB	MISERE
MANAGE	MARQUE	MCEWAN	MEOWED	MIDSTS	MISERS
MANAMA	MARRED	MEADOW	MERANO	MIDWAY	MISERY
MANANA	MARRER	MEAGRE	MERCER	MIERES	MISFIT
MANAUS	MARRON	MEALIE	MERELY	MIFFED	MISHAP
MANCHE	MARROW	MEANER	MERGED	MIGHTY	MISHIT
MANCHU	MARSHY	MEANLY	MERGER	MIKADO	MISLAY
MANEGE	MARTEN	MEASLY	MERINO	MILADY	MISLED
MANFUL	MARTIN	MEATUS	MERITS	MILDER	MISSAL
MANGER	MARTYR	MECCAS	MERLIN	MILDEW	MISSED
MANGLE	MARVEL	MEDALS	MERLON	MILDLY	MISSES
MANGOS	MARY II	MEDDLE	MERMAN	MILERS	MISSIS
MANIAC	MASCLE	MEDIAL	MERSIN	MILIEU	MISSUS
MANIAS	MASCON	MEDIAN	MERTON	MILIUM	MISTED

MISTER	MONISM	MOTTLE	MUSCID	NAGANA	NECTAR
MISUSE	MONIST	MOTTOS	MUSCLE	NAGANO	NEEDED
MITRAL	MONKEY	MOULDS	MUSCLY	NAGGED	NEEDLE
MITRES	MONTHS	MOULDY	MUSEUM	NAGGER	NEEDN'T
MITTEN	MOOING	MOULIN	MUSHES	NAGOYA	NEGATE
MIXERS	MOONED	MOULTS	MUSING	NAGPUR	NEGROS
MIXING	MOORED	MOUNDS	MUSKET	NAIADS	NEIGHS
MIX-UPS	MOOTED	MOUNTS	MUSKIE	NAILED	NEKTON
MIZZEN	MOOTER	MOUSER	MUSLIM	NAILER	NELSON
MOANED	MOPANI	MOUSEY	MUSLIN	NAKURU	NEM CON
MOANER	MOPEDS	MOUSSE	MUSSED	NAMELY	NEPALI
MOATED	MOPING	MOUTHS	MUSSEL	NAMING	NEPHEW
MOBBED	MOPOKE	MOUTON	MUSTEE	NANTES	NEREID
MOBBER	MOPPED	MOVERS	MUSTER	NAPALM	NEREIS
MOBILE	MOPPET	MOVIES	MUSTN'T	NAPIER	NERVED
MOCKED	MORALE	MOVING	MUTANT	NAPKIN	NERVES
MOCKER	MORALS	MOWERS	MUTARE	NAPLES	NESTED
MOCK UP	MORASS	MOWING	MUTATE	NAPPED	NESTER
MOCK-UP	MORBID	MOWLAM	MUTELY	NAPPER	NESTLE
MOD CON	MOREEN	MUCKED	MUTING	NARIAL	NETHER
MODELS	MORGUE	MUCKER	MUTINY	NARKED	NETTED
MODEMS	MORION	MUCOID	MUTISM	NARROW	NETTLE
MODENA	MORLEY	MUCOUS	MUTTER	NARVIK	NETTLY
MODERN	MORMON	MUDCAT	MUTTON	NASALS	NEURAL
MODEST	MORNAY	MUDDED	MUTUAL	NASIAL	NEURON
MODIFY	MORONI	MUDDLE	MUTULE	NASION	NEUTER
MODISH	MORONS	MUD PIE	MUZZLE	NASSAU	NEVADA
MODULE	MOROSE	MUESLI	MYELIN	NATANT	NEVERS
MOGULS	MORROW	MUFFED	MYNAHS	NATION	NEW AGE
MOHAIR	MORSEL	MUFFIN	MYOPIA	NATIVE	NEWARK
MOHAWK	MORTAL	MUFFLE	MYOPIC	NATRON	NEWEST
MOHOLE	MORTAR	MUFTIS	MYOSIN	NATTER	NEWHAM
MOIETY	MORULA	MUGABE	MYRIAD	NATURE	NEWISH
MOLARS	MORYAH	MUGGED	MYRICA	NAUGHT	NEWMAN
MOLDED	MOSAIC	MUGGER	MYRTLE	NAUSEA	NEWTON
MOLDER	MOSCOW	MUKLUK	MYSELF	NAUTCH	NIAMEY
MOLEST	MOSLEM	MULISH	MYSORE	NAVAHO	NIBBLE
MOLISE	MOSQUE	MULLAH	MYSTIC	NAVELS	NIBLET
MOLOCH	MOSSIE	MULLED	MYTHOS	NAVIES	NICELY
MOLOPO	MOSTLY	MULLER	MY WORD	NAZISM	NICEST
MOLTED	MOTELS	MULLET	MYXOMA	NEARBY	NICETY
MOLTEN	MOTETS	MULTAN		NEARED	NICHES
MOMENT	MOTHER	MUMBLE	**N**	NEARER	NICKED
MOMISM	MOTIFS	MUMMER	NAAFIS	NEARLY	NICKEL
MOMMAS	MOTILE	MUNICH	NABBED	NEATEN	NICKER
MONACO	MOTION	MURALS	NABLUS	NEATER	NIDIFY
MONDAY	MOTIVE	MURCIA	NABOBS	NEATLY	NIECES
MONEYS	MOTLEY	MURDER	NACHOS	NEBULA	NIELLO
MONGER	MOTMOT	MURINE	NACRED	NECKAR	NIEVRE
MONGOL	MOTORS	MURMUR	NADIRS	NECKED	NIGGER
MONIES	MOTOWN	MUSCAT	NAEVUS	NECKER	NIGGLE

NIGHTS	NOSIER	**O**	OGDOAD	OPENER	OSHAWA
NILGAI	NOSILY		OGIVAL	OPENLY	OSIERS
NIMBLE	NOSING	OAFISH	OGLING	OPERAS	OSIJEK
NIMBLY	NOSTOC	OAKHAM	OGRESS	OPERON	OSMIUM
NIMBUS	NOTARY	OAXACA	OHMAGE	OPHITE	OSMOSE
NINETY	NOTICE	OBELUS	OIDIUM	OPIATE	OSMOUS
NINGBO	NOTIFY	OBEYED	OILCAN	OPINED	OSPREY
NINGPO	NOTING	OBEYER	OILCUP	OPIOID	OSSEIN
NINTHS	NOTION	OBJECT	OILIER	OPORTO	OSSIFY
NIOBIC	NOUGAT	OBLAST	OILILY	OPPOSE	OSTEAL
NIP OUT	NOUGHT	OBLATE	OILING	OPPUGN	OSTEND
NIPPED	NOUNAL	OBLIGE	OILMAN	OPTICS	OSTIUM
NIPPER	NOVARA	OBLONG	OILMEN	OPTING	OSTLER
NIPPLE	NOVELS	OBOIST	OILRIG	OPTION	OTHERS
NIPPON	NOVENA	O'BRIEN	OIL RIG	OPUSES	OTIOSE
NITRIC	NOVICE	OBSESS	OINKED	ORACLE	OTITIS
NITWIT	NOWISE	OBTAIN	OKAYED	ORADEA	O'TOOLE
NIXING	NOZZLE	OBTECT	OLD AGE	ORALLY	OTTAVA
NO BALL	NUANCE	OBTUSE	OLD BOY	ORANGE	OTTAWA
NO-BALL	NUBBLE	OBVERT	OLDEST	ORATOR	OTTERS
NOBBLE	NUBBLY	OCCULT	OLDHAM	ORBITS	OUNCES
NOBLER	NUBILE	OCCUPY	OLD HAT	ORCEIN	OUSTED
NOBLES	NUCHAL	OCEANS	OLDISH	ORCHID	OUSTER
NOBODY	NUCLEI	OCELOT	OLD LAG	ORCHIL	OUTAGE
NODDED	NUDGED	O'CLOCK	OLD MAN	ORCHIS	OUTBID
NODDLE	NUDGER	OCTANE	OLEATE	ORDAIN	OUTCRY
NOD OFF	NUDGES	OCTANT	O LEVEL	ORDEAL	OUTDID
NODOSE	NUDISM	OCTAVE	OLIVES	ORDERS	OUTFIT
NODULE	NUDIST	OCTAVO	OMASUM	ORDURE	OUTFOX
NOESIS	NUDITY	OCTETS	OMEGAS	OREBRO	OUTGAS
NOETIC	NUGGET	OCTOPI	ONAGER	OREGON	OUTING
NOGGIN	NUKING	OCTROI	ONCOST	ORENSE	OUTLAW
NOISES	NUMBAT	OCULAR	ON EDGE	ORGANS	OUTLAY
NOMADS	NUMBED	ODDEST	ONE-OFF	ORGASM	OUTLET
NOMISM	NUMBER	ODDITY	ONE-WAY	ORGEAT	OUTMAN
NONAGE	NUMBLY	ODD JOB	ONIONS	ORGIES	OUTPUT
NONCES	NUNCIO	ODDS ON	ONLINE	ORIENT	OUTRAN
NONEGO	NURSED	ODDS-ON	ONRUSH	ORIGAN	OUTRUN
NOODLE	NURSES	ODENSE	ONSIDE	ORIGIN	OUTSET
NOOSES	NUTANT	ODESSA	ONWARD	ORIOLE	OUTWIT
NOOTKA	NUTLET	ODIOUS	OOCYTE	ORISON	OVERDO
NORDIC	NUTMEG	ODOURS	OODLES	ORISSA	OVERLY
NORITE	NUTRIA	OEDEMA	OOGAMY	ORMOLU	OVIEDO
NORMAL	NUTTED	OEUVRE	OOLITE	ORNATE	OVISAC
NORMAN	NUTTER	OFFALY	OOLOGY	ORNERY	OVOIDS
NORTHS	NUZZLE	OFFEND	OOLONG	OROIDE	OVULAR
NORWAY	NYLONS	OFFERS	OOZIER	ORPHAN	OWELTY
NOSHED	NYMPHA	OFFICE	OOZILY	ORPINE	OWERRI
NOSH-UP	NYMPHS	OFFING	OOZING	ORRERY	OWLETS
NO SIDE		OFFSET	OPAQUE	OSCARS	OWLISH
NO-SIDE		OFSTED	OPENED	OSCINE	OWNERS

OWNING	PAMPAS	PARSEE	PEACES	PENMAN	PHASIC
OXALIS	PAMPER	PARSER	PEACHY	PENNED	PHENOL
OXCART	PANADA	PARSON	PEAHEN	PENNEY	PHENOM
OXFORD	PANAMA	PARTED	PEAKED	PENNON	PHENYL
OXIDES	PANDAS	PARTLY	PEALED	PEN PAL	PHIALS
OXTAIL	PANDER	PARTON	PEANUT	PENTAD	PHILAE
OXYGEN	PANDIT	PARURE	PEARLS	PENT UP	PHIZOG
OYSTER	PANELS	PASHTO	PEARLY	PENTYL	PHLEGM
OZALID	PANICS	PASSED	PEBBLE	PENULT	PHLOEM
	PANJIM	PASSES	PEBBLY	PENURY	PHOBIA
P	PANNED	PASSIM	PECANS	PEOPLE	PHOBIC
PACIFY	PANTED	PASTED	PECKED	PEORIA	PHOBOS
PACING	PANTRY	PASTEL	PECKER	PEPLUM	PHOEBE
PACINO	PANZER	PASTES	PECTEN	PEPPED	PHONED
PACKED	PAOTOW	PASTOR	PECTIC	PEPPER	PHONES
PACKER	PAPACY	PASTRY	PECTIN	PEPSIN	PHONEY
PACKET	PAPAIN	PATCHY	PEDALS	PEPTIC	PHONIC
PADANG	PAPAYA	PATENT	PEDANT	PERFIN	PHONON
PADAUK	PAPERS	PATERS	PEDATE	PERILS	PHOOEY
PADDED	PAPERY	PATHAN	PEDDLE	PERIOD	PHOTIC
PADDLE	PAPHOS	PATHOS	PEDLAR	PERISH	PHOTON
PADRES	PAPIST	PATINA	PEDWAY	PERKED	PHOTOS
PAEANS	PAPPUS	PATIOS	PEEING	PERLIS	PHRASE
PAELLA	PAPUAN	PAIMOS	PEEKED	PERMED	PHUKET
PAEONY	PAPULE	PATOIS	PEELED	PERMIT	PHYLUM
PAGANS	PAPYRI	PATRAS	PEELER	PERNIK	PHYSIC
PAGING	PARADE	PATROL	PEEPBO	PERNOD	PHYSIO
PAGODA	PARAMO	PATRON	PEEPED	PER PRO	PHYTON
PAHANG	PARANA	PATTED	PEEPER	PERRON	PIAFFE
PAID-UP	PARANG	PATTEN	PEEPUL	PERSIA	PIANOS
PAINED	PARAPH	PATTER	PEERED	PERSON	PIAZZA
PAINTS	PARCEL	PAUCAL	PEEVED	PERTLY	PICKED
PAIRED	PARDON	PAUNCH	PEEWIT	PERUKE	PICKER
PAJAMA	PARENT	PAUPER	PEGGED	PERUSE	PICKET
PALACE	PARGET	PAUSED	PEG LEG	PESADE	PICKLE
PALAIS	PARIAH	PAUSER	PEKING	PESARO	PICK-UP
PALATE	PARIAN	PAUSES	PELAGE	PESETA	PICNIC
PALELY	PARIES	PAVANE	PELITE	PESTER	PIDDLE
PALEST	PARING	PAVING	PELLET	PESTLE	PIDGIN
PALING	PARISH	PAWING	PELMET	PETALS	PIECED
PALISH	PARITY	PAWNED	PELOTA	PETARD	PIECER
PALLAS	PARKAS	PAWPAW	PELTED	PETERS	PIECES
PALLED	PARKED	PAXWAX	PELTER	PETITE	PIERCE
PALLET	PARKIN	PAYBED	PELTRY	PETREL	PIERRE
PALLID	PARLEY	PAYDAY	PELVES	PETROL	PIFFLE
PALLOR	PARODY	PAYEES	PELVIC	PETTED	PIGEON
PALMAR	PAROLE	PAYING	PELVIS	PETTER	PIGGED
PALMED	PARREL	PAYOFF	PENANG	PEWITS	PIGGIN
PALTER	PARROT	PAYOLA	PENCHI	PEWTER	PIGLET
PALTRY	PARSEC	PAYOUT	PENCIL	PHASED	PIGNUS
PAMIRS	PARSED	PCMCIA	PENGPU	PHASES	PIGNUT

PIGSTY	PISS-UP	PLEBBY	POLISH	PORTED	PREFAB
PILAFS	PISTIL	PLEDGE	POLITE	PORTER	PREFER
PILEUM	PISTOL	PLEIAD	POLITY	PORTLY	PREFIX
PILEUP	PISTON	PLENTY	POLKAS	POSERS	PREPAY
PILEUS	PITCHY	PLENUM	POLLAN	POSEUR	PREPPY
PILFER	PITHOS	PLEURA	POLLED	POSHER	PRESET
PILING	PITIED	PLEVEN	POLLEN	POSIES	PRESTO
PILLAR	PITIES	PLEXOR	POLLEX	POSING	PRETTY
PILLOW	PITMAN	PLEXUS	POLLUX	POSSES	PREWAR
PILOSE	PITMEN	PLIANT	POLONY	POSSET	PREYED
PILOTS	PITSAW	PLICAL	POL POT	POSSUM	PREYER
PILULE	PITTED	PLIERS	POLYPS	POSTAL	PRICED
PIMPED	PIVOTS	PLIGHT	POMACE	POSTED	PRICES
PIMPLE	PIXELS	PLINTH	POMADE	POSTER	PRICEY
PIMPLY	PIXIES	PLISSE	POMMEL	POSTIE	PRICKS
PINCER	PIZZAS	PLOUGH	POMPOM	POSTIL	PRIDED
PINEAL	PLACED	PLOVER	POMPON	POTAGE	PRIDES
PINENE	PLACER	PLOWED	PONCES	POTASH	PRIEST
PINERY	PLACES	PLUCKS	PONCEY	POTATO	PRIMAL
PINGED	PLACET	PLUCKY	PONCHO	POTBOY	PRIMED
PINIER	PLACID	PLUMED	PONDER	POTEEN	PRIMER
PINING	PLAGAL	PLUMES	PONDOK	POTENT	PRIMES
PINION	PLAGUE	PLUMMY	PONGED	POTFUL	PRIMLY
PINITE	PLAGUY	PLUNGE	PONGEE	POTHER	PRIMUS
PINKED	PLAICE	PLURAL	PONGID	POTION	PRINCE
PINKER	PLAIDS	PLUSES	PONIES	POTTED	PRINTS
PINKIE	PLAINS	PLUTON	PONTIC	POTTER	PRIORS
PINKOS	PLAINT	PLYING	PONTIL	POUCHY	PRIORY
PINNED	PLAITS	PNEUMA	POODLE	POUNCE	PRIPET
PINNER	PLANAR	POCKED	POOLED	POUNDS	PRISED
PINTAS	PLANED	POCKET	POOPED	POURED	PRISMS
PINTER	PLANER	PODDED	POOPER	POURER	PRISON
PINTLE	PLANES	PODIUM	POORER	POUTED	PRISSY
PINUPS	PLANET	PODZOL	POORLY	POUTER	PRIVET
PINXIT	PLANKS	POETIC	POOTLE	POWDER	PRIZED
PIPAGE	PLANTS	POETRY	POP ART	POWELL	PRIZES
PIPALS	PLAQUE	POGROM	POPERY	POWERS	PRO-AMS
PIPERS	PLASHY	POINTE	POPGUN	POWWOW	PROBED
PIPING	PLASMA	POINTS	POPISH	POZNAN	PROBER
PIPITS	PLATAN	POISED	POPLAR	PRAGUE	PROBES
PIPKIN	PLATED	POISON	POPLIN	PRAISE	PROFIT
PIPPED	PLATEN	POKERS	POPPAS	PRANCE	PROJET
PIPPIN	PLATER	POKIER	POPPED	PRANKS	PROLEG
PIQUED	PLATES	POKILY	POPPER	PRATED	PROLES
PIQUES	PLAUEN	POKING	POPPET	PRATER	PROLIX
PIQUET	PLAYED	POLAND	POPPLE	PRAWNS	PROLOG
PIRACY	PLAYER	POLDER	PORING	PRAXIS	PROMOS
PIRATE	PLAZAS	POLEYN	PORISM	PRAYED	PROMPT
PISCES	PLEACH	POLICE	PORKER	PRAYER	PRONGS
PISSED	PLEASE	POLICY	POROUS	PREACH	PRONTO
PISSES	PLEATS	POLING	PORTAL	PRECIS	PROOFS

PROPEL PUNDIT PUTTEE QUINSY RAGTAG RARELY
PROPER PUNIER PUTTER QUIRES RAGUSA RAREST
PROPYL PUNISH PUZZLE QUIRKS RAIDED RARING
PROSES PUNJAB PYKNIC QUIRKY RAIDER RARITY
PROTEA PUNKAH PYLONS QUIVER RAILED RASCAL
PRO TEM PUNNED PYOSIS QUOITS RAILER RASHER
PROTON PUNNET PYRENE QUORUM RAILEX RASHES
PROVED PUNTED PYRITE QUOTAS RAINED RASHLY
PROVEN PUNTER PYRONE QUOTED RAISED RASPED
PROVIE PUPATE PYROPE QUOTES RAISER RASPER
PROWLS PUPILS PYTHON QWERTY RAISES RASTER
PROZAC PUPPED PYURIA RAISIN RATBAG
PRUDES PUPPET **R** RAJAHS RATHER
PRUNED PUPPIS **Q** RABATO RAJKOT RATIFY
PRUNER PURDAH RABAUL RAJPUT RATINE
PRUNES PUREED QATARI RABBIS RAKING RATING
PRYING PUREES QINTAR RABBIT RAKISH RATION
PSALMS PURELY QUACKS RABBLE RAMBLE RATIOS
PSEUDO- PUREST QUAGGA RABIES RAMIFY RATITE
PSEUDS PURFLE QUAGGY RACEME RAMJET RATLAM
PSEUDY PURGED QUAHOG RACERS RAMMED RATOON
PSYCHE PURGER QUAILS RACHIS RAMMER RATTAN
PSYCHO- PURGES QUAINT RACIAL RAMOSE RAT-TAT
PTISAN PURIFY QUAKED RACIER RAMPUR RATTED
PTOSIS PURINE QUAKER RACILY RAMROD RATTER
PUBLIC PURISM QUAKES RACING RAMTIL RATTLE
PUCKER PURIST QUALMS RACISM RANCHI RATTLY
PUDDLE PURITY QUANGO RACIST RANCID RAVAGE
PUDDLY PURLED QUANTA RACKED RANDAN RAVENS
PUDSEY PURLER QUARKS RACKER RANDOM RAVERS
PUEBLA PURLIN QUARRY RACKET RANEES RAVE-UP
PUEBLO PURPLE QUARTO RACOON RANGED RAVINE
PUFFED PURRED QUARTS RADDLE RANGER RAVING
PUFFER PURSED QUARTZ RADIAL RANGES RAVISH
PUFFIN PURSER QUASAR RADIAN RANKED RAWEST
PUGGED PURSES QUAVER RADIOS RANKER RAZING
PUKING PURSUE QUAYLE RADISH RANKLE RAZORS
PULLED PURVEY QUEASY RADIUM RANKLY RAZZLE
PULLET PUSHED QUEBEC RADIUS RANSOM READER
PULLEY PUSHER QUEENS RADOME RANTED REALLY
PULL-IN PUSHES QUEERS RADULA RANTER REALMS
PULL-ON PUSH-UP QUEMOY RAFFIA RAPIDS REAMED
PULPED PUSSES QUENCH RAFFLE RAPIER REAMER
PULPIT PUTLOG QUESTS RAFTED RAPINE REAPED
PULSAR PUT OFF QUEUED RAFTER RAPING REAPER
PULSED PUT-OFF QUEUES RAGBAG RAPIST REARED
PULSES PUT-ONS QUICHE RAGGED RAPPED REARER
PUMICE PUT OUT QUIFFS RAGING RAPPEL REASON
PUMMEL PUTRID QUILLS RAGLAN RAPPER REBASE
PUMPED PUTSCH QUILTS RAGMAN RAPTOR REBATE
PUNCHY PUTTED QUINCE RAGOUT RAREFY REBELS
QUINOL

REBIND	REFLET	REMOTE	RESUME	RIBBED	RISKED
REBOOT	REFLEX	REMOVE	RETAIL	RIBBON	RISKER
REBORN	REFLUX	RENAME	RETAIN	RIBERA	RISQUE
REBUFF	REFORM	RENDER	RETAKE	RIBOSE	RITUAL
REBUKE	REFUEL	RENEGE	RETARD	RICHER	RIVALS
RECALL	REFUGE	RENNES	RETELL	RICHES	RIVERS
RECANT	REFUND	RENNET	RETENE	RICHLY	RIVETS
RECAPS	REFUSE	RENNIN	RETIAL	RICKED	RIYADH
RECAST	REFUTE	RENOWN	RETINA	RICTAL	RIYALS
RECEDE	REGAIN	RENTAL	RETIRE	RICTUS	ROAMED
RECENT	REGALE	RENTED	RETOLD	RIDDED	ROAMER
RECEPT	REGARD	RENTER	RETOOK	RIDDEN	ROARED
RECESS	REGENT	RENVOI	RETOOL	RIDDER	ROARER
RECIFE	REGGAE	REOPEN	RETORT	RIDDLE	ROASTS
RECIPE	REGIME	REPAID	RETUNE	RIDERS	ROBALO
RECITE	REGINA	REPAIR	RETURN	RIDGED	ROBAND
RECKED	REGION	REPAND	RETUSE	RIDGES	ROBBED
RECKON	REGLET	REPAST	REUSED	RIDING	ROBBER
RECODE	REGRET	REPEAL	REVAMP	RIFFLE	ROBBIN
RECOIL	REGULO	REPEAT	REVEAL	RIFLED	ROBING
RECORD	REHASH	REPENT	REVERE	RIFLER	ROBINS
RECOUP	REHEAR	REPINE	REVERS	RIFLES	ROBOTS
RECTAL	REHEAT	REPLAN	REVERT	RIGGED	ROBSON
RECTOR	REHOME	REPLAY	REVEST	RIGGER	ROBUST
RECTOS	REIGNS	REPONE	REVIEW	RIGHTS	ROCHET
RECTUM	REINED	REPORT	REVILE	RIGOUR	ROCKED
RECTUS	REJECT	REPOSE	REVISE	RIG-OUT	ROCKER
REDACT	REJIGS	REPUTE	REVIVE	RIJEKA	ROCKET
REDBUD	REJOIN	REREAD	REVOKE	RILEYS	ROCOCO
REDCAP	RELAID	RERUNS	REVOLT	RILING	RODENT
REDDEN	RELATE	RESALE	REVUES	RILLET	RODEOS
REDDER	RELAYS	RESCUE	REVVED	RIMINI	ROGERS
REDEEM	RELENT	RESEAT	REWARD	RIMMED	ROGUES
RED EYE	RELICS	RESEAU	REWIND	RIMOSE	ROLLED
REDFIN	RELICT	RESECT	REWIRE	RINGED	ROLLER
RED-HOT	RELIED	RESEDA	REWORD	RINGER	ROLL ON
REDONE	RELIEF	RESEED	REWORK	RING IN	ROLL-ON
REDOWA	RELINE	RESENT	RHEBOK	RINSED	ROMAIC
RED SEA	RELISH	RESHIP	RHESUS	RINSER	ROMANO
REDUCE	RELIVE	RESIDE	RHEUMY	RINSES	ROMANS
REECHO	RELOAD	RESIGN	RHEYDT	RIOTED	ROMANY
REEFED	REMADE	RESILE	RHINAL	RIOTER	ROMEOS
REEFER	REMAIN	RESINS	RHODES	RIPEST	ROMPED
REEKED	REMAKE	RESIST	RHODIC	RIP-OFF	RONDEL
REELED	REMAND	RESITS	RHOTIC	RIPPED	RONDOS
REELER	REMARK	RESIZE	RHYMED	RIPPER	ROOFED
REEVES	REMEDY	RESORB	RHYMES	RIPPLE	ROOKED
REFACE	REMIND	RESORT	RHYTHM	RIPPLY	ROOKIE
REFILL	REMISE	RESTED	RHYTON	RIPSAW	ROOMED
REFINE	REMISS	RESTER	RIALTO	RISERS	ROOMER
REFITS	REMORA	RESULT	RIBALD	RISING	ROOSTS

ROOTED	RUEFUL	SACRUM	SAMITE	SAWFLY	SCORES
ROOTER	RUFFLE	SADDEN	SAMOAN	SAWING	SCORIA
ROOTSY	RUFFLY	SADDER	SAMOSA	SAWYER	SCORNS
ROPIER	RUFOUS	SADDLE	SAMPAN	SAXONS	SCOTCH
ROPILY	RUGGED	SADHUS	SAMPLE	SAXONY	SCOTER
ROPING	RUGOSA	SADISM	SAMSUN	SAYING	SCOTIA
ROQUET	RUGOSE	SADIST	SANDAL	SCABBY	SCOUSE
ROSARY	RUINED	SAFARI	SANDED	SCALAR	SCOUTS
ROSIER	RUINER	SAFELY	SANDER	SCALDS	SCOWLS
ROSILY	RULERS	SAFEST	SANDHI	SCALED	SCRAPE
ROSINY	RULING	SAFETY	SANELY	SCALER	SCRAPS
ROSTER	RUMBAS	SAGELY	SANEST	SCALES	SCRAWL
ROSTOV	RUMBLE	SAGGAR	SANIES	SCALPS	SCREAM
ROSTRA	RUMBLY	SAGGED	SANITY	SCAMPI	SCREED
ROTARY	RUMMER	SAHARA	SANTER	SCAMPS	SCREEN
ROTATE	RUMOUR	SAHIBS	SANTOS	SCANTY	SCREWS
ROTGUT	RUMPLE	SAIGON	SAPELE	SCARAB	SCREWY
ROTORS	RUMPLY	SAILED	SAPOTA	SCARCE	SCRIBE
ROTTED	RUMPUS	SAILER	SAPPED	SCARED	SCRIMP
ROTTEN	RUNDLE	SAILOR	SAPPER	SCARER	SCRIPT
ROTTER	RUNNEL	SAINTS	SARGES	SCARES	SCROLL
ROTUND	RUNNER	SAIPAN	SARNIA	SCAREY	SCROOP
ROUBLE	RUN-OFF	SAITHE	SARNIE	SCARFS	SCROTA
ROUGED	RUN-UPS	SALAAM	SARONG	SCARPS	SCRUBS
ROUNDS	RUNWAY	SALADS	SARTHE	SCATTY	SCRUFF
ROUSED	RUPEES	SALAMI	SASEBO	SCENES	SCRUMP
ROUSER	RUPIAH	SALARY	SASHAY	SCENIC	SCRUMS
ROUTED	RUSHED	SALIFY	SASHES	SCENTS	SCUBAS
ROUTER	RUSHER	SALINE	SASSED	SCHEMA	SCUFFS
ROUTES	RUSHES	SALIVA	SASSES	SCHEME	SCULPT
ROVERS	RUSSET	SALLEE	SATEEN	SCHISM	SCUMMY
ROVING	RUSSIA	SALLOW	SATING	SCHIST	SCUNGY
ROWANS	RUSTED	SALMON	SATINY	SCHLEP	SCURFY
ROWERS	RUSTIC	SALONS	SATIRE	SCHOOL	SCURRY
ROWING	RUSTLE	SALOON	SATURN	SCHORL	SCURVY
ROYALS	RUTILE	SALOOP	SATYRS	SCHUSS	SCUTCH
ROZZER	RUTTED	SALTED	SAUCED	SCHWAS	SCUTUM
RUBATO	RWANDA	SALTER	SAUCER	SCHWYZ	SCUZZY
RUBBED	RYAZAN	SALTUS	SAUCES	SCILLA	SCYLLA
RUBBER		SALUKI	SAUGER	SCIONS	SCYTHE
RUBBLE	**S**	SALUTE	SAUNAS	SCLAFF	SEABED
RUBBLY	SABBAT	SALVED	SAVAGE	SCLERA	SEA DOG
RUBIES	SABERS	SALVER	SAVAII	SCOFFS	SEALED
RUBLES	SABLES	SALVES	SAVANT	SCOLDS	SEALER
RUBRIC	SABRAS	SALVIA	SAVERS	SCOLEX	SEAMAN
RUCKED	SABRES	SALVOR	SAVING	SCONCE	SEAMEN
RUCKUS	SACHET	SALVOS	SAVOIE	SCONES	SEAMER
RUDDER	SACKED	SALYUT	SAVONA	SCOOPS	SEANCE
RUDDLE	SACKER	SAMARA	SAVORY	SCORCH	SEARCH
RUDELY	SACRAL	SAMBAR	SAVOUR	SCORED	SEARED
RUDEST	SACRED	SAMBAS	SAVOYS	SCORER	SEASON

SEATED	SENNIT	SEXPOT	SHERRY	SHROUD	SILVAN
SEATER	SENORA	SEXTET	SHEWED	SHRUBS	SILVER
SEAWAY	SENORS	SEXTON	SHIELD	SHRUGS	SIMIAN
SECANT	SENSED	SEXUAL	SHIEST	SHRUNK	SIMILE
SECEDE	SENSES	SHABBY	SHIFTS	SHTOOK	SIMMER
SECOND	SENSOR	SHACKS	SHIFTY	SHUCKS	SIMNEL
SECRET	SENTRY	SHADED	SHIITE	SHUFTI	SIMONY
SECTOR	SEPALS	SHADES	SHINER	SHUFTY	SIMOOM
SECUND	SEPSIS	SHADOW	SHINNY	SHUNTS	SIMPER
SECURE	SEPTAL	SHAFTS	SHINTO	SHYEST	SIMPLE
SEDANS	SEPTET	SHAGGY	SHINTY	SHYING	SIMPLY
SEDATE	SEPTIC	SHAKEN	SHIRAZ	SIALIC	SINDHI
SEDILE	SEPTUM	SHAKER	SHIRES	SIBYLS	SINEWS
SEDUCE	SEQUEL	SHAKES	SHIRTS	SICILY	SINEWY
SEEDED	SEQUIN	SHALOM	SHIRTY	SICKED	SINFUL
SEEDER	SERAPH	SHAMAN	SHITTY	SICKEN	SINGED
SEEING	SERBIA	SHAMED	SHIVER	SICKER	SINGER
SEEKER	SEREIN	SHAMMY	SHOALS	SICKIE	SINGES
SEEMED	SERENE	SHANDY	SHOALY	SICKLE	SINGLE
SEEMER	SERIAL	SHANKS	SHOCKS	SICKLY	SINGLY
SEEMLY	SERIES	SHANNY	SHODDY	SIDE-ON	SINING
SEEPED	SERIFS	SHANSI	SHOGUN	SIDING	SINKER
SEESAW	SERINE	SHANTY	SHOOED	SIDLED	SINNED
SEETHE	SERMON	SHANXI	SHOO-IN	SIDLER	SINNER
SEFTON	SEROSA	SHAPED	SHOOTS	SIECLE	SINTER
SEICHE	SEROUS	SHAPES	SHORAN	SIEGEN	SIOUAN
SEINES	SERUMS	SHARDS	SHORED	SIEGES	SIPHON
SEISER	SERVAL	SHARED	SHORES	SIENNA	SIPPED
SEISIN	SERVED	SHARER	SHORTS	SIERRA	SIPPER
SEIZED	SERVER	SHARES	SHORTY	SIESTA	SIPPET
SEIZER	SERVES	SHARIA	SHOULD	SIEVED	SIRENS
SEJANT	SERVOS	SHARKS	SHOUTS	SIEVES	SIRING
SELDOM	SESAME	SHARPS	SHOVED	SIFAKA	SIRIUS
SELECT	SESTET	SHAVED	SHOVEL	SIFTED	SIRRAH
SELLER	SET-OFF	SHAVEN	SHOVER	SIFTER	SISERA
SELVES	SETOSE	SHAVER	SHOVES	SIGHED	SISKIN
SEMEME	SETTEE	SHAVES	SHOWED	SIGHER	SISTER
SEMITE	SETTER	SHAWLS	SHOWER	SIGHTS	SITARS
SEMPRE	SETTLE	SHEARS	SHOW UP	SIGNAL	SITCOM
SEMTEX	SET-UPS	SHEATH	SHRANK	SIGNED	SITING
SENARY	SEVENS	SHEAVE	SHREDS	SIGNEE	SIT-INS
SENATE	SEVERE	SHEETS	SHREWD	SIGNER	SITTER
SENDAI	SEVRES	SHEIKH	SHREWS	SIGNET	SIT-UPS
SENDER	SEWAGE	SHEILA	SHRIEK	SIGN ON	SIXTHS
SEND UP	SEWERS	SHEKEL	SHRIFT	SIGNOR	SIZING
SEND-UP	SEWING	SHELLS	SHRIKE	SIKKIM	SIZZLE
SENECA	SEXIER	SHELVE	SHRILL	SILAGE	SKATED
SENEGA	SEXILY	SHENSI	SHRIMP	SILENT	SKATER
SENILE	SEXING	SHERDS	SHRINE	SILICA	SKATES
SENIOR	SEXISM	SHERIA	SHRINK	SILKEN	SKEINS
SENNAR	SEXIST	SHERPA	SHRIVE	SILTED	SKELLY

SKETCH	SLICKS	SMITER	SNORER	SOMBRE	SPEARS
SKEWED	SLIDES	SMITHS	SNORES	SOMITE	SPECIE
SKEWER	SLIGHT	SMITHY	SNORTS	SONANT	SPECKS
SKIBOB	SLIMLY	SMOCKS	SNOTTY	SONATA	SPEECH
SKIDOO	SLINGS	SMOGGY	SNOUTS	SONNET	SPEEDS
SKIERS	SLINKY	SMOKED	SNOWED	SONORA	SPEEDY
SKIFFS	SLIP-ON	SMOKER	SNUBBY	SONTAG	SPEISS
SKIING	SLIPPY	SMOKES	SNUFFY	SOONER	SPELLS
SKIKDA	SLIP-UP	SMOOCH	SNUGLY	SOOTHE	SPERMS
SKILLS	SLIVER	SMOOTH	SOAKED	SOPPED	SPEWED
SKIMPY	SLOGAN	SMUDGE	SOAKER	SORBET	SPEWER
SKINNY	SLOOPS	SMUDGY	SOAPED	SORBIC	SPEYER
SKIRTS	SLOPED	SMUGLY	SOARED	SORDID	SPHENE
SKIVED	SLOPER	SMUTCH	SOARER	SORELY	SPHERE
SKIVER	SLOPES	SMUTTY	SOARES	SORREL	SPHINX
SKIVVY	SLOPPY	SNACKS	SOBBED	SORROW	SPICED
SKOPJE	SLOSHY	SNAFUS	SOBBER	SORTED	SPICER
SKULLS	SLOTHS	SNAGGY	SO BE IT	SORTER	SPICES
SKUNKS	SLOUCH	SNAILS	SOCAGE	SORTIE	SPIDER
SKYCAP	SLOUGH	SNAKED	SOCCER	SOTHIC	SPIELS
SKYLAB	SLOVAK	SNAKES	SOCIAL	SOUGHS	SPIGOT
SKYROS	SLOVEN	SNAPPY	SOCKED	SOUGHT	SPIKED
SLACKS	SLOWED	SNARED	SOCKET	SOUNDS	SPIKES
SLAGGY	SLOWER	SNARER	SOCMAN	SOURCE	SPILLS
SLAKED	SLOWLY	SNARES	SODDED	SOURED	SPINAL
SLAKER	SLUDGE	SNARLS	SODDEN	SOURER	SPINEL
SLALOM	SLUDGY	SNARLY	SODIUM	SOURLY	SPINES
SLANGY	SLUICE	SNATCH	SODOMY	SOUSED	SPINET
SLANTS	SLUING	SNAZZY	SOEVER	SOUSSE	SPIRAL
SLAP-UP	SLUMMY	SNEAKS	SOFFIT	SOVIET	SPIRES
SLATED	SLUMPS	SNEAKY	SOFTEN	SOWERS	SPIRIT
SLATER	SLURRY	SNEERS	SOFTER	SOWETO	SPITAL
SLATES	SLUSHY	SNEEZE	SOFTIE	SOWING	SPITED
SLAVED	SLYEST	SNEEZY	SOFTLY	SPACED	SPLAKE
SLAVER	SMACKS	SNICKS	SOIGNE	SPACER	SPLASH
SLAVES	SMALLS	SNIDER	SOILED	SPACES	SPLEEN
SLAVIC	SMALTO	SNIFFS	SOIREE	SPADER	SPLICE
SLAYER	SMARMY	SNIFFY	SOKOTO	SPADES	SPLINE
SLEAVE	SMEARS	SNIPED	SOLACE	SPADIX	SPLINT
SLEAZE	SMEARY	SNIPER	SOLDER	SPANKS	SPLITS
SLEAZY	SMEGMA	SNIPES	SOLELY	SPARED	SPLOSH
SLEDGE	SMELLS	SNIPPY	SOLEMN	SPARER	SPOILS
SLEEPY	SMELLY	SNITCH	SOLENT	SPARES	SPOILT
SLEETY	SMELTS	SNIVEL	SOLIDI	SPARID	SPOKEN
SLEEVE	SMILAX	SNOBOL	SOLIDS	SPARKS	SPOKES
SLEIGH	SMILED	SNOOPS	SOLING	SPARRY	SPONGE
SLEUTH	SMILER	SNOOPY	SO LONG	SPARSE	SPONGY
SLEWED	SMILES	SNOOTY	SOLUTE	SPASMS	SPOOFS
SLICED	SMILEY	SNOOZE	SOLVED	SPATHE	SPOOKS
SLICER	SMIRCH	SNOOZY	SOLVER	SPAVIN	SPOOKY
SLICES	SMIRKS	SNORED	SOMALI	SPAYED	SPOOLS

SPOONS	STABLE	STEEDS	STOOLS	STRUNG	SULTAN
SPOORS	STABLY	STEELS	STOP-GO	STRUTS	SULTRY
SPORES	STACKS	STEELY	STOP IN	STUBBY	SUMACH
SPORTS	STADIA	STEERS	STORAX	STUCCO	SUMMAT
SPORTY	STAFFS	STEEVE	STORED	STUDIO	SUMMED
SPOT-ON	STAGED	STEINS	STORES	STUFFY	SUMMER
SPOTTY	STAGER	STELAR	STOREY	STUMER	SUMMIT
SPOUSE	STAGES	STENCH	STORKS	STUMPS	SUMMON
SPOUTS	STAGEY	STEPPE	STORMS	STUMPY	SUNBED
SPRAIN	STAINS	STEP UP	STORMY	STUNTS	SUNBOW
SPRANG	STAIRS	STEREO	STOUPS	STUPID	SUNDAE
SPRATS	STAKED	STERIC	STOVER	STUPOR	SUNDAY
SPRAWL	STAKES	STERNA	STOVES	STURDY	SUNDER
SPRAYS	STALAG	STERNS	STOWED	STYLAR	SUNDEW
SPREAD	STALED	STEROL	STRAFE	STYLED	SUNDRY
SPREES	STALER	STEWED	STRAIN	STYLER	SUN GOD
SPRIER	STALKS	STICKS	STRAIT	STYLES	SUNKEN
SPRIGS	STALKY	STICKY	STRAKE	STYLET	SUNLIT
SPRING	STALLS	STIFFS	STRAND	STYLUS	SUNNED
SPRINT	STAMEN	STIFLE	STRAPS	STYMIE	SUNNIS
SPRITE	STAMPS	STIGMA	STRATA	STYRAX	SUNRAY
SPROUT	STANCE	STILES	STRAWS	STYRIA	SUNSET
SPRUCE	STANCH	STILLS	STRAWY	SUABLE	SUNTAN
SPRUIT	STANDS	STILLY	STRAYS	SUAKIN	SUPERB
SPRUNG	STANZA	STILTS	STREAK	SUBBED	SUPER-G
SPRYLY	STAPES	STINGS	STREAM	SUBDUE	SUPINE
SPUNKY	STAPLE	STINGY	STREEP	SUBITO	SUPPED
SPURGE	STARCH	STINKS	STREET	SUBLET	SUPPER
SPURRY	STARED	STINTS	STRESS	SUBMIT	SUPPLE
SPURTS	STARER	STIPEL	STREWN	SUBORN	SUPPLY
SPUTUM	STARES	STIPES	STRICK	SUBSET	SURELY
SPYING	STARRY	STIRPS	STRICT	SUBTLE	SUREST
SQUABS	STARTS	STIR UP	STRIDE	SUBTLY	SURETY
SQUADS	STARVE	STITCH	STRIFE	SUBURB	SURFED
SQUALL	STASIS	STOATS	STRIKE	SUBWAY	SURFER
SQUAMA	STATED	STOCKS	STRING	SUCHOU	SURFIE
SQUARE	STATER	STOCKY	STRIPE	SUCKED	SURGED
SQUASH	STATES	STODGE	STRIPS	SUCKER	SURGER
SQUATS	STATIC	STODGY	STRIPY	SUCKLE	SURGES
SQUAWK	STATOR	STOICS	STRIVE	SUDDEN	SURREY
SQUAWS	STATUE	STOKED	STROBE	SUFFER	SURTAX
SQUEAK	STATUS	STOKER	STRODE	SUFFIX	SURVEY
SQUEAL	STAVED	STOKES	STROKE	SUGARS	SUSLIK
SQUIBS	STAVES	STOLEN	STROLL	SUGARY	SUSSED
SQUIDS	STAYED	STOLES	STROMA	SUITED	SUTTEE
SQUILL	STAYER	STOLID	STRONG	SUITES	SUTTON
SQUINT	STAY IN	STOLON	STROPS	SUITOR	SUTURE
SQUIRE	STEADS	STONED	STROUD	SULCUS	SUU KYI
SQUIRM	STEADY	STONER	STROVE	SULKED	SUZHOU
SQUIRT	STEAKS	STONES	STRUCK	SULKER	SVELTE
SQUISH	STEAMY	STOOGE	STRUMA	SULLEN	SWABIA

SWAGER	SYRUPY	TAMPON	TAUTLY	TENNIS	THEISM
SWAINS	SYSTEM	TANDEM	TAUTOG	TENONS	THEIST
SWAMIS	SYZRAN	TANGLE	TAVERN	TENORS	THEMES
SWAMPS	SYZYGY	TANGLY	TAWDRY	TENPIN	THEMIS
SWAMPY	SZEGED	TANGOS	TAXEME	TENREC	THENAR
SWANKS		TANKER	TAXIED	TENSED	THENCE
SWANKY	**T**	TANNED	TAXING	TENSER	THEORY
SWARDS	TABARD	TANNER	TAXMAN	TENSES	THERMS
SWARMS	TABBED	TANNIC	TAXMEN	TENSOR	THESES
SWATCH	TABLED	TANNIN	TAYLOR	TENTER	THESIS
SWATHE	TABLES	TANNOY	T-BONES	TENTHS	THETIC
SWATHS	TABLET	TAOISM	TEABAG	TENURE	THICKO
SWATOW	TABOOS	TAOIST	TEACUP	TENUTO	THIEVE
SWAYED	TABRIZ	TAPERS	TEAMED	TEPEES	THIGHS
SWAYER	TACKED	TAPING	TEAPOT	TEPEFY	THIMBU
SWEATS	TACKER	TAPIRS	TEAPOY	TERBIC	THINGS
SWEATY	TACKLE	TAPPED	TEARER	TERCEL	THINLY
SWEDEN	TACOMA	TAPPER	TEASED	TERCET	THIRDS
SWEDES	TACTIC	TAPPET	TEASEL	TEREDO	THIRST
SWEENY	TADJIK	TARAWA	TEASER	TERESA	THIRTY
SWEEPS	TAEJON	TARBES	TEASES	TERETE	THOLOS
SWEETS	TAG END	TARGET	TECHIE	TERGAL	THONGS
SWELLS	TAGGED	TARIFF	TECHNO	TERGUM	THORAX
SWERVE	TAHITI	TARMAC	TEDDER	TERMED	THORIC
SWIFTS	TAIHOA	TAROTS	TEDIUM	TERMLY	THORNS
SWILLS	TAILED	TARPAN	TEEING	TERMOR	THORNY
SWINES	TAILOR	TARPON	TEEMED	TERRET	THORON
SWINGE	TAINAN	TARRED	TEEPEE	TERROR	THOUGH
SWINGS	TAIPAN	TARSAL	TEETER	TERUEL	THRALL
SWIPED	TAIPEI	TARSUS	TEETHE	TESTED	THRASH
SWIPES	TAIWAN	TARTAN	TEFLON	TESTER	THREAD
SWIRLS	TAKERS	TARTAR	TEGMEN	TESTES	THREAT
SWIRLY	TAKEUP	TARTLY	TEHRAN	TESTIS	THREES
SWITCH	TAKING	TASKER	TELEDU	TETCHY	THRESH
SWIVEL	TALCUM	TASMAN	TELIAL	TETHER	THRICE
SWIVET	TALENT	TASSEL	TELIUM	TETRAD	THRIFT
SWOONS	TALION	TASTED	TELLER	TETRYL	THRILL
SWOOPS	TALKED	TASTER	TELPAL	TETTER	THRIPS
SWOOSH	TALKER	TASTES	TELSON	TETUAN	THRIVE
SWORDS	TALKIE	TATAMI	TEMPED	TEUTON	THROAT
SYDNEY	TALLER	TATARY	TEMPER	THAMES	THROBS
SYLVAN	TALLOW	TATTED	TEMPLE	THANES	THROES
SYMBOL	TALMUD	TATTER	TEMPOS	THANKS	THRONE
SYNCOM	TALONS	TATTIE	TEMUCO	THATCH	THRONG
SYNDIC	TAMBOV	TATTLE	TENACE	THAWED	THROVE
SYNODS	TAMELY	TATTOO	TENANT	THAWER	THROWN
SYNTAX	TAMERS	TAUGHT	TENDED	THECAL	THROWS
SYPHER	TAMEST	TAUNTS	TENDER	THEFTS	THRUSH
SYPHON	TAMING	TAURUS	TENDON	THEGNS	THRUST
SYRIAN	TAMPED	TAUTEN	TENETS	THEINE	THUMBS
SYRINX	TAMPER	TAUTER	TENNER	THEIRS	THUMPS

THWACK	TINGLY	TOLEDO	TOUCAN	TRENDY	TROVES
THWART	TIN GOD	TOLLED	TOUCHE	TRENTO	TROWEL
THYMIC	TIN HAT	TOLUCA	TOUCHY	TREPAN	TROYES
THYMOL	TINIER	TOLUYL	TOULON	TRESSY	TRUANT
THYMUS	TINKER	TOMATO	TOUPEE	TRIADS	TRUCES
THYRSE	TINKLE	TOMBAC	TOURED	TRIAGE	TRUCKS
TIARAS	TINKLY	TOMBOY	TOURER	TRIALS	TRUDGE
TIBIAE	TINNED	TOMCAT	TOUSLE	TRIBAL	TRUEST
TIBIAS	TIN-POT	TOM-TOM	TOUTED	TRIBES	TRUISM
TICINO	TINSEL	TONGAN	TOWAGE	TRICES	TRUMAN
TICKED	TINTED	TONGUE	TOWBAR	TRICKS	TRUMPS
TICKER	TIP-OFF	TONICS	TOWELS	TRICKY	TRUNKS
TICKET	TIPPED	TONING	TOWERS	TRICOT	TRUSTS
TICKLE	TIPPER	TONKIN	TOWHEE	TRIERS	TRUSTY
TIC TAC	TIPPET	TONNES	TOWING	TRIFID	TRUTHS
TIDBIT	TIPPLE	TONSIL	TOWNEE	TRIFLE	TRYING
TIDDLY	TIPTOE	TOOLED	TOWNIE	TRIGER	TRY-OUT
TIDIER	TIP-TOP	TOOLER	TOXINS	TRIKES	TRYSTS
TIDILY	TIRADE	TOOTED	TOXOID	TRILBY	T-SHIRT
TIDING	TIRANA	TOOTER	TOYAMA	TRILLS	TSINAN
TIDYED	TIRING	TOOTHY	TOYING	TRIMER	TSONGA
TIE-DYE	TISANE	TOOTLE	TRACED	TRIMLY	TSOTSI
TIE-INS	TISSUE	TOP DOG	TRACER	TRINAL	TSWANA
TIEPIN	TITANS	TOPEES	TRACES	TRIODE	TUAREG
TIERCE	TITBIT	TOPEKA	TRACKS	TRIOSE	TUBBED
TIE-UPS	TITCHY	TOP HAT	TRACTS	TRIPLE	TUBERS
TIFFIN	TITFER	TOPHUS	TRADED	TRIPOD	TUBING
TIFLIS	TITHER	TOPICS	TRADER	TRIPOS	TUBULE
TIGERS	TITHES	TOPPED	TRADES	TRIPPY	TUCKED
TIGHTS	TITLED	TOPPER	TRAGAL	TRITON	TUCKER
TIGRIS	TITLES	TOPPLE	TRAGIC	TRIUNE	TUCK-IN
TILDES	TITTER	TORBAY	TRAGUS	TRIVET	TUCSON
TILERS	TITTLE	TORERO	TRAILS	TRIVIA	TUFFET
TILING	TITTUP	TORIES	TRAINS	TROCAR	TUFTED
TILLED	TIVOLI	TOROID	TRAITS	TROCHE	TUFTER
TILLER	TMESIS	TOROSE	TRALEE	TROGON	TUGGED
TILTED	TOASTS	TORPID	TRAMPS	TROIKA	TUGGER
TILTER	TOBAGO	TORPOR	TRANCE	TROJAN	TULIPS
TIMARU	TOBRUK	TORQUE	TRANNY	TROLLS	TUMBLE
TIMBAL	TOCSIN	TORRID	TRASHY	TROMPE	TUMEFY
TIMBER	TO DATE	TORSOS	TRAUMA	TROOPS	TUMOUR
TIMBRE	TODDLE	TOSSED	TRAVEL	TROPES	TUMULI
TIMELY	TOE CAP	TOSSER	TRAWLS	TROPHY	TUMULT
TIMERS	TOEING	TOSSES	TREADS	TROPIC	TUNDRA
TIMING	TOFFEE	TOSS UP	TREATS	TROPPO	TUNERS
TINCAL	TOGGED	TOSS-UP	TREATY	TROTHS	TUNE-UP
TINDER	TOGGLE	TOTALS	TREBLE	TROTYL	TUNGUS
TINEAL	TOILED	TOTEMS	TREBLY	TROUGH	TUNICA
TINEID	TOILER	TOTING	TREMOR	TROUPE	TUNICS
TINGED	TOILET	TOTTED	TRENCH	TROUTS	TUNING
TINGLE	TOKENS	TOTTER	TRENDS	TROVER	TUNNEL

TUPELO	TWIRLS	UNCORK	UNPLUG	UPRISE	VACUUM
TUPPED	TWIRLY	UNCURL	UNREAD	UPROAR	VADOSE
TURBAN	TWIRPS	UNDEAD	UNREAL	UPROOT	VAGARY
TURBID	TWISTS	UNDIES	UNREST	UPSETS	VAGINA
TURBIT	TWISTY	UNDOER	UNRIPE	UPSHOT	VAINER
TURBOT	TWITCH	UNDONE	UNROLL	UPSIDE	VAINLY
TUREEN	TWO-BIT	UNDULY	UNRULY	UPTAKE	VALAIS
TURFED	TWO-PLY	UNEASE	UNSAFE	UPTICK	VALETA
TURGID	TWO-WAY	UNEASY	UNSAID	UPTILT	VALETS
TURGOR	TYCOON	UNESCO	UNSEAL	UPTIME	VALGUS
TURION	TYMPAN	UNEVEN	UNSEAM	UPTOWN	VALINE
TURKEY	TYPHUS	UNFAIR	UNSEAT	UPTURN	VALISE
TURKIC	TYPIFY	UNFOLD	UNSEEN	UPWARD	VALIUM
TURNED	TYPING	UNFREE	UNSEXY	UPWIND	VALLEY
TURNER	TYPIST	UNFURL	UNSHIP	URACIL	VALOUR
TURN IN	TYRANT	UNGUAL	UNSNAP	URALIC	VALUED
TURNIP	TYRONE	UNGUIS	UNSTEP	URANIC	VALUER
TURN ON	TYUMEN	UNGULA	UNSTOP	URANUS	VALUES
TURN-ON		UNHAIR	UNSUNG	URANYL	VALVES
TURN UP	**U**	UNHAND	UNSURE	URATIC	VANDAL
TURN-UP	UBANGI	UNHOLY	UNTIDY	URBANE	VANISH
TURRET	U-BOATS	UNHOOD	UNTIED	URCHIN	VANITY
TURTLE	UDDERS	UNHOOK	UNTOLD	UREASE	VAPOUR
TURVES	UDMURT	UNICEF	UNTRUE	UREIDE	VARDAR
TUSCAN	UGANDA	UNIONS	UNTUCK	URETER	VARESE
TUSCHE	UGLIER	UNIPOD	UNUSED	URETIC	VARIED
TUSHES	UGLIFY	UNIQUE	UNVEIL	URGENT	VARLET
TUSKER	UGRIAN	UNISEX	UNWARY	URGING	VASSAL
TUSSAH	UJJAIN	UNISON	UNWELL	URINAL	VASTLY
TUSSIS	ULCERS	UNISON	UNWEPT	UROPOD	VAULTS
TUSSLE	ULLAGE	UNITED	UNWIND	URSINE	VAUNTS
TUTORS	ULSTER	UNITER	UNWISE	URTEXT	VECTOR
TUTSAN	ULTIMA	UNJUST	UNWRAP	USABLE	VEERED
TUT-TUT	UMBRAL	UNKIND	UNYOKE	USAGES	VEGANS
TUVALU	UMBRIA	UNKNIT	UPBEAT	USANCE	VEILED
TUXEDO	UMLAUT	UNLACE	UPCAST	USED TO	VEILER
TUYERE	UMPIRE	UNLAID	UPDATE	USEFUL	VEINAL
TWANGS	UMTATA	UNLASH	UPDIKE	USHERS	VEINED
TWANGY	UNABLE	UNLEAD	UPHELD	USURER	VELARS
TWEAKS	UNAWED	UNLESS	UPHILL	UTAHAN	VELATE
TWEEDS	UNBELT	UNLIKE	UPHOLD	UTERUS	VELCRO
TWEEDY	UNBEND	UNLIVE	UPHROE	UTMOST	VELETA
TWEETS	UNBENT	UNLOAD	UPKEEP	UTOPIA	VELLUM
TWELVE	UNBIND	UNLOCK	UPLAND	U-TURNS	VELOCE
TWENTY	UNBOLT	UNMADE	UPLIFT	UVULAE	VELOUR
TWERPS	UNBORN	UNMAKE	UPLINK	UVULAR	VELSEN
TWIGGY	UNCIAL	UNMASK	UPLOAD	UVULAS	VELURE
TWILIT	UNCLAD	UNMOOR	UPPERS		VELVET
TWINED	UNCLES	UNPACK	UPPISH	**V**	VENDED
TWINER	UNCLOG	UNPAID	UPPITY	VACANT	VENDEE
TWINGE	UNCOIL	UNPICK	UPREAR	VACATE	VENDOR

VENEER	VIBORG	VOICES	WAKING	WASHIN	WESKER
VENERY	VIBRIO	VOIDED	WALKED	WASTED	WESTER
VENETO	VICARS	VOIDER	WALKER	WASTER	WETHER
VENIAL	VICTIM	VOLANT	WALK-IN	WASTES	WETTED
VENICE	VICTOR	VOLLEY	WALK-ON	WATERS	WETTER
VENIRE	VICUNA	VOLUME	WALK-UP	WATERY	WHACKS
VENOSE	VIDEOS	VOLUTE	WALLAH	WATTLE	WHALER
VENOUS	VIENNA	VOLVOX	WALLED	WATUSI	WHALES
VENTED	VIENNE	VOODOO	WALLET	WAVIER	WHAMMY
VENTER	VIEWED	VORTEX	WALLOP	WAVILY	WHARFS
VENUES	VIEWER	VOSGES	WALLOW	WAVING	WHARVE
VENULE	VIGILS	VOSTOK	WALNUT	WAXIER	WHEELS
VERBAL	VIGOUR	VOTARY	WALRUS	WAXILY	WHEEZE
VERBID	VIKING	VOTERS	WALTON	WAXING	WHEEZY
VERDIN	VILELY	VOTING	WAMPUM	WAYLAY	WHELKS
VERDUN	VILEST	VOTIVE	WANDER	WAY-OUT	WHELPS
VERGED	VILIFY	VOTYAK	WANGLE	WEAKEN	WHENCE
VERGER	VILLAS	VOWELS	WANING	WEAKER	WHERRY
VERGES	VILLUS	VOWING	WANKED	WEAKLY	WHEYEY
VERIFY	VINERY	VOX POP	WANKER	WEALTH	WHIFFS
VERILY	VINOUS	VOYAGE	WANNED	WEANED	WHIFFY
VERISM	VINYLS	VOYEUR	WANNER	WEAPON	WHILED
VERIST	VIOLAS	V-SIGNS	WANT AD	WEARER	WHILST
VERITY	VIOLET	VULGAR	WANTED	WEASEL	WHIMSY
VERMIN	VIOLIN	VULVAE	WANTER	WEAVER	WHINED
VERMIS	VIPERS	VULVAL	WANTON	WEAVES	WHINER
VERNAL	VIRAGO	VULVAS	WAPITI	WEBBED	WHINES
VERONA	VIRGIN	VYBORG	WARBLE	WEDDED	WHINGE
VERSED	VIRGOS		WAR CRY	WEDELN	WHINNY
VERSES	VIRILE	**W**	WARDED	WEDGED	WHIPPY
VERSOS	VIRTUE	WADDLE	WARDEN	WEDGES	WHIRLS
VERSUS	VISAED	WADERS	WARDER	WEEDED	WHISKS
VERTEX	VISAGE	WADGES	WARIER	WEEDER	WHISKY
VERVET	VISCID	WADING	WARILY	WEEING	WHITBY
VESICA	VISION	WAFERS	WARLEY	WEEKLY	WHITEN
VESPER	VISITS	WAFFLE	WARMED	WEEPER	WHITER
VESPID	VISORS	WAFTED	WARMER	WEEVER	WHITES
VESSEL	VISTAS	WAFTER	WARMLY	WEEVIL	WHIZZY
VESTAL	VISUAL	WAGERS	WARMTH	WEE-WEE	WHOLLY
VESTED	VITALS	WAGGED	WARM-UP	WEIGHT	WHOOPS
VESTRY	VITRIC	WAGGLE	WARNED	WEIHAI	WHOOSH
VETOED	VIVACE	WAGGLY	WARNER	WEIMAR	WHORES
VETOER	VIVIFY	WAGING	WARPED	WEIRDO	WHORLS
VETOES	VIXENS	WAGONS	WARPER	WELDED	WHYDAH
VETTED	VIZIER	WAILED	WARRED	WELDER	WICKED
VEXING	V-NECKS	WAILER	WARREN	WELDON	WICKER
VIABLE	VOCABS	WAISTS	WARSAW	WELKIN	WICKET
VIABLY	VOCALS	WAITED	WARTED	WELKOM	WIDELY
VIAGRA	VOGUES	WAITER	WASHED	WELLED	WIDEST
VIANDS	VOICED	WAIVED	WASHER	WELTER	WIDGET
VIBIST	VOICER	WAIVER	WASHES	WENDED	WIDISH

WIDNES	WINKED	WOODEN	XIAMEN	YEMENI	ZEALOT
WIDOWS	WINKER	WOOERS	XMASES	YENTAI	ZEBRAS
WIDTHS	WINKLE	WOOFER	X-RAYED	YEOMAN	ZENIST
WIELDY	WINNER	WOOING	XUZHOU	YEOMEN	ZENITH
WIFELY	WINNOW	WOOLLY	XYLENE	YES-MAN	ZEPHYR
WIGEON	WINTER	WORDED	XYLOID	YES-MEN	ZEROED
WIGGED	WINTRY	WORKED	XYLOSE	YIELDS	ZEROES
WIGGLE	WIPING	WORKER	XYSTER	YIPPEE	ZESTER
WIGGLY	WIRIER	WORLDS		YODELS	ZEUGMA
WIGHTS	WIRILY	WORMED	**Y**	YOGISM	ZIGONG
WIGWAG	WIRING	WORMER	YACHTS	YOGURT	ZIGZAG
WIGWAM	WIRRAL	WORSEN	YAGARA	YOKELS	ZIMMER
WILDER	WISDOM	WORTHY	YAKKED	YOKING	ZINCIC
WILDLY	WISELY	WOUNDS	YAMMER	YONDER	ZINCKY
WILFUL	WISEST	WOWING	YANGON	YORKER	ZINNIA
WILIER	WISHED	WRAITH	YANKED	YORUBA	ZIPPED
WILLED	WISHER	WRASSE	YANKEE	YOUTHS	ZIPPER
WILLER	WISHES	WREATH	YANTAI	YOWLED	ZIRCON
WILLET	WISMAR	WRECKS	YAPPED	YOWLER	ZITHER
WILLOW	WITHAL	WRENCH	YAPPER	YTTRIA	ZODIAC
WILSON	WITHER	WRETCH	YARDIE	YTTRIC	ZOMBIE
WILTED	WITHIN	WRIEST	YARNED	YUCCAS	ZONATE
WIMBLE	WIZARD	WRIGHT	YARROW	YUNNAN	ZONING
WIMPLE	WOBBLE	WRISTS	YATTER	YUPPIE	ZONKED
WINCED	WOBBLY	WRISTY	YAUPON		ZONULE
WINCER	WOEFUL	WRITER	YAUTIA	**Z**	ZOOMED
WINCES	WOKING	WRITHE	YAWING	ZABRZE	ZOSTER
WINCEY	WOLFED	WRONGS	YAWNED	ZAFFER	ZOYSIA
WINDED	WOLVER	WRYEST	YAWNER	ZAGREB	ZURICH
WINDER	WOLVES	WRYING	YEARLY	ZAMBIA	ZWOLLE
WINDOW	WOMBAT	WYVERN	YEASTY	ZANDER	ZYDECO
WIND UP	WONDER		YELLED	ZANIER	ZYGOMA
WINGED	WONSAN	**X**	YELLER	ZANILY	ZYGOSE
WINGER	WONTED	XENIAL	YELLOW	ZAPPED	ZYGOTE
WINGES	WONTON	XEROMA	YELPED	ZAPPER	ZYMASE
WINING	WOODED	XHOSAN	YELPER	ZAREBA	ZYRIAN

A	ACADIAN	ACYCLIC	AFFAIRE	AIRPORT	ALKANET
AALBORG	ACAROID	ADAGIOS	AFFAIRS	AIR RAID	ALKMAAR
ABALONE	ACAUDAL	ADAMANT	AFFIANT	AIRSHIP	ALLAYED
ABANDON	ACAUSAL	ADAMAWA	AFFIXED	AIRSICK	ALLEGED
ABASHED	ACCEDED	ADAPTED	AFFIXES	AIRWAYS	ALLEGRO
ABASING	ACCEDER	ADAPTER	AFFLICT	AITCHES	ALLELIC
ABATING	ACCENTS	ADAPTOR	AFFRAYS	AJACCIO	ALLERGY
ABAXIAL	ACCLAIM	ADAXIAL	AFFRONT	ALABAMA	ALLHEAL
ABDOMEN	ACCORDS	ADDENDA	AFGHANS	ALAGOAS	ALLONYM
ABELARD	ACCOUNT	ADDICTS	AFRICAN	A LA	ALL OVER
ABELIAN	ACCRETE	ADDRESS	AGAINST	MODE	ALLOWAY
ABERFAN	ACCRUAL	ADDUCED	AGAMETE	ALANINE	ALLOWED
ABETTED	ACCRUED	ADENINE	AGEISTS	ALARMED	ALLOYED
ABETTOR	ACCUSED	ADENOID	AGELESS	ALASKAN	ALLSEED
ABEYANT	ACCUSER	ADENOMA	AGENDAS	ALBANIA	ALL-STAR
ABFARAD	ACERATE	ADEPTLY	AGENDUM	ALBERTA	ALL-TIME
ABHENRY	ACERBIC	ADHERED	AGGRADE	ALBINIC	ALLUDED
ABIDING	ACEROSE	ADIPOSE	AGGRESS	ALBINOS	ALLURED
ABIDJAN	ACETATE	ADIVASI	AGILELY	ALBITIC	ALLURER
ABILITY	ACETIFY	ADJOINT	AGILITY	ALBUMEN	ALLUVIA
ABIOSIS	ACETONE	ADJOURN	AGITATE	ALBUMIN	ALLYING
ABJURED	ACETOUS	ADJUDGE	AGITATO	ALCAZAR	ALMA-ATA
ABJURER	ACHAEAN	ADJUNCT	AGNOMEN	ALCHEMY	ALMANAC
ABLATOR	ACHIEVE	ADJURED	AGONIES	ALCOHOL	ALMERIA
ABLEISM	ACICULA	ADJURER	AGONIST	ALCOPOP	ALMONDS
ABOLISH	ACIDIFY	ADMIRAL	AGONIZE	ALCOVES	ALMONER
ABORTED	ACIDITY	ADMIRED	AGRAFFE	AL DENTE	ALMS MAN
ABRADED	ACNODAL	ADMIRER	AGRAPHA	ALEMBIC	ALOETIC
ABRADER	ACOLYTE	ADOPTED	AGROUND	ALERTED	ALOOFLY
ABREACT	ACONITE	ADORING	AILERON	ALERTLY	ALPACAS
ABREAST	ACOUCHI	ADORNED	AILMENT	A LEVELS	ALPHORN
ABRIDGE	ACQUIRE	ADRENAL	AIMLESS	ALFALFA	ALREADY
ABRUZZI	ACREAGE	ADULATE	AIRBASE	ALGARVE	ALRIGHT
ABSCESS	ACRILAN	ADVANCE	AIRBEDS	ALGEBRA	ALSO RAN
ABSCISE	ACROBAT	ADVENTS	AIR-COOL	ALGERIA	ALSO-RAN
ABSCOND	ACROGEN	ADVERBS	AIRCREW	ALGIERS	ALTDORF
ABSENCE	ACRONYM	ADVERSE	AIRDRIE	AL HUFUF	ALTERED
ABSINTH	ACROTER	ADVICES	AIRDROP	ALIASES	ALTHAEA
ABSOLVE	ACRYLIC	ADVISED	AIRFLOW	ALI BABA	ALTHING
ABSTAIN	ACRYLYL	ADVISER	AIRGLOW	ALIDADE	ALTHORN
ABUSING	ACTABLE	AEGISES	AIRGUNS	ALIENEE	ALUMNAE
ABUSIVE	ACTINAL	AEONIAN	AIRIEST	ALIENOR	ALUMNUS
ABUTTAL	ACTINIA	AERATED	AIRINGS	ALIFORM	ALUNDUM
ABUTTED	ACTINIC	AERATOR	AIRLANE	ALIGARH	ALUNITE
ABUTTER	ACTINON	AERIALS	AIRLESS	ALIGNED	ALYSSUM
ABYSMAL	ACTIONS	AEROBIC	AIRLIFT	ALIMENT	AMADODA
ABYSSAL	ACTRESS	AEROGEL	AIRLINE	ALIMONY	AMALGAM
ABYSSES	ACTUARY	AEROSOL	AIRLOCK	ALIQUOT	AMANITA
ACACIAS	ACTUATE	AETOLIA	AIRMAIL	ALIUNDE	AMASSED
ACADEME	ACULEUS	AFFABLE	AIRMILE	ALKALIC	AMASSER
ACADEMY	ACUTELY	AFFABLY	AIRPLAY	ALKALIS	AMATEUR

AMATORY	ANATOMY	ANNUITY	APLITIC	ARCHINE	ARTISTS
AMAZING	ANCHORS	ANNULAR	APOCARP	ARCHING	ARTLESS
AMAZONS	ANCHOVY	ANNULET	APOCOPE	ARCHIVE	ARTWORK
AMBIENT	ANCHUSA	ANNULUS	APOGAMY	ARCHWAY	ARUGULA
AMBLING	ANCIENT	ANODIZE	APOGEES	ARCUATE	ARUNDEL
AMBOYNA	ANCONAL	ANODYNE	APOLOGY	ARDECHE	ASCARID
AMENDED	ANDANTE	ANOMALY	APOLUNE	ARDENCY	ASCENTS
AMENDER	ANDIRON	ANORAKS	APOMICT	ARDUOUS	ASCETIC
AMENITY	ANDORRA	ANOSMIA	APOSTIL	AREAWAY	ASCITES
AMENTIA	ANDROID	ANOTHER	APOSTLE	ARENITE	ASCITIC
AMERICA	ANEMONE	ANSWERS	APOTHEM	AREOLAR	ASCRIBE
AMHARIC	ANERGIC	ANTACID	APPAREL	ARGOLIS	ASEPSIS
AMIABLE	ANEROID	ANTEFIX	APPEALS	ARGONNE	ASEPTIC
AMIABLY	ANEURIN	ANTEING	APPEASE	ARGOTIC	ASEXUAL
AMMETER	ANGARSK	ANTENNA	APPLAUD	ARGUING	ASHAMED
AMMONAL	ANGELIC	ANTHEMS	APPLIED	ARIDITY	ASHANTI
AMMONIA	ANGELOU	ANTHERS	APPLIER	ARIETTA	ASHDOWN
AMMONIC	ANGELUS	ANT HILL	APPOINT	ARISING	ASHFORD
AMNESIA	ANGERED	ANTHILL	APPRISE	ARIZONA	ASHIEST
AMNESTY	ANGEVIN	ANT HILL	APPROVE	ARMADAS	ASHTRAY
AMNIOTE	ANGINAL	ANTHRAX	APPULSE	ARMBAND	ASIATIC
AMOEBAE	ANGIOMA	ANTIBES	APRAXIA	ARMENIA	ASININE
AMOEBAS	ANGLIAN	ANTIGEN	APRAXIC	ARMFULS	ASKANCE
AMOEBIC	ANGLIFY	ANTIGUA	APRICOT	ARMHOLE	ASOCIAL
AMORIST	ANGLING	ANTIOCH	A PRIORI	ARMIGER	ASPECTS
AMOROSO	ANGOLAN	ANTIQUE	APROPOS	ARMLESS	ASPERSE
AMOROUS	ANGORAS	ANTLERS	APSIDAL	ARMLOCK	ASPHALT
AMOUNTS	ANGRIER	ANTLION	APTERAL	ARMOIRE	ASPIRED
AMPHORA	ANGRILY	ANTONYM	APTNESS	ARMOURY	ASPIRER
AMPLIFY	ANGUINE	ANTWERP	AQUARIA	ARMPITS	ASPIRIN
AMPOULE	ANGUISH	ANUROUS	AQUATIC	ARMREST	ASSAULT
AMPULLA	ANGULAR	ANXIETY	AQUAVIT	AROUSAL	ASSAYED
AMPUTEE	ANHINGA	ANXIOUS	AQUEOUS	AROUSED	ASSAYER
AMULETS	ANILINE	ANYBODY	AQUIFER	AROUSER	ASSEGAI
AMUSING	ANILITY	ANYMORE	ARABIAN	ARRAIGN	ASSHOLE
AMYLASE	ANIMALS	ANYWAYS	ARABIST	ARRANGE	ASSIZES
AMYLENE	ANIMATE	ANYWISE	ARACAJU	ARRAYAL	ASSUAGE
AMYLOID	ANIMATO	APAGOGE	ARAL SEA	ARRAYED	ASSUMED
AMYLOSE	ANIMISM	APATITE	ARAMAIC	ARREARS	ASSUMER
ANAEMIA	ANIMIST	APELIKE	ARANEID	ARRESTS	ASSURED
ANAEMIC	ANIONIC	APETALY	ARAPAHO	ARRIVAL	ASSURER
ANAGOGE	ANISEED	APHAGIA	ARAROBA	ARRIVED	ASSYRIA
ANAGRAM	ANISOLE	APHASIA	ARBITER	ARRIVER	ASTATIC
ANAHEIM	ANKLETS	APHESIS	ARBOURS	ARROWED	ASTOUND
ANALOGY	ANNATES	APHONIA	ARBUTUS	ARSENAL	ASTRIDE
ANALYSE	ANNATTO	APHONIC	ARCADES	ARSENIC	ASTROID
ANALYST	ANNELID	APHOTIC	ARCADIA	ART DECO	ASTYLAR
ANAMBRA	ANNEXED	APHYLLY	ARCANUM	ARTICLE	ASUNDER
ANAPEST	ANNEXES	APIEZON	ARCHAIC	ARTIEST	ASYLUMS
ANARCHY	ANNOYED	APLASIA	ARCHERS	ARTISAN	ATACTIC
ANATASE	ANNUALS	APLENTY	ARCHERY	ARTISTE	ATAVISM

ATAVIST	AUXERRE	BACKERS	BALLS-UP	BARENTS	BATTENS
ATELIER	AUXESIS	BACKING	BALMIER	BARGAIN	BATTERS
AT HEART	AVAILED	BACKLOG	BALMILY	BARGEES	BATTERY
ATHEISM	AVARICE	BACK OFF	BALNEAL	BARGING	BATTIER
ATHEIST	AVATARS	BACKSAW	BALONEY	BARILLA	BATTING
ATHLETE	AVENGED	BACKUPS	BALSAMS	BARKERS	BATTLED
ATHWART	AVENGER	BACOLOD	BALTICS	BARKING	BATTLES
ATLANTA	AVENUES	BACTRIA	BALUCHI	BARMAID	BATWING
ATLASES	AVERAGE	BACULUM	BAMBARA	BARMIER	BAUBLES
ATOMISM	AVERRED	BADAJOZ	BAMBERG	BARNAUL	BAUHAUS
ATOMIST	AVERTED	BAD DEBT	BAMBINO	BARNEYS	BAULKED
ATOMIZE	AVESTAN	BAD FORM	BAMBOOS	BARONET	BAUTZEN
ATONING	AVEYRON	BADGERS	BANANAS	BAROQUE	BAUXITE
ATROPHY	AVIATOR	BADNESS	BANBURY	BAROTSE	BAVARIA
ATTACHE	AVIDITY	BAFFLED	BANDAGE	BARQUES	BAWDIER
ATTACKS	AVIGNON	BAFFLER	BANDBOX	BARRACK	BAWDILY
ATTAINT	AVIONIC	BAFFLES	BANDEAU	BARRAGE	BAWLING
ATTEMPT	AVOCADO	BAGANDA	BANDIED	BARRELS	BAYAMON
ATTIRED	AVOIDED	BAGASSE	BANDIER	BARRIER	BAYONET
ATTRACT	AVOIDER	BAGGAGE	BANDING	BARRING	BAYONNE
ATTUNED	AVOWALS	BAGGIER	BANDITS	BARROWS	BAYWOOD
AUBERGE	AVOWING	BAGGILY	BANDUNG	BARYTES	BAZAARS
AUCTION	AWAITED	BAGGING	BANEFUL	BASCULE	BAZOOKA
AUDIBLE	AWAKING	BAGHDAD	BANGERS	BASENJI	BEACHED
AUDIBLY	AWARDED	BAG LADY	BANGING	BASHFUL	BEACHES
AUDITED	AWARDEE	BAGPIPE	BANGKOK	BASHING	BEACONS
AUDITOR	AWARDER	BAGWORM	BANGLES	BASHKIR	BEADIER
AUGITIC	AWESOME	BAHAISM	BANKERS	BASILAN	BEADILY
AUGMENT	AWFULLY	BAHAIST	BANKING	BASILAR	BEADING
AUGURAL	AWKWARD	BAHAMAS	BANKSIA	BASILIC	BEADLES
AUGURED	AWLWORT	BAHRAIN	BANNERS	BASKETS	BEAGLES
AUGUSTA	AWNINGS	BAILEYS	BANNING	BASKING	BEAKERS
AU PAIRS	AXOLOTL	BAILIFF	BANNOCK	BASOTHO	BEAMING
AURALLY	AZIMUTH	BAILING	BANQUET	BAS-RHIN	BEARDED
AUREATE	AZURITE	BAIL OUT	BANSHEE	BASSEIN	BEARERS
AUREOLE	AZYGOUS	BAILOUT	BANTAMS	BASSETS	BEAR HUG
AURICLE		BAINITE	BANTOID	BASSIST	BEARING
AURORAE	**B**	BAITING	BANYANS	BASSOON	BEARISH
AURORAL	BAALBEK	BALANCE	BAODING	BASTARD	BEASTLY
AURORAS	BABASSU	BALATON	BAPTISM	BASTING	BEATERS
AUSPICE	BABBITT	BALCONY	BAPTIST	BASTION	BEATIFY
AUSSIES	BABBLED	BALDING	BAPTIZE	BATCHES	BEATING
AUSTERE	BABBLER	BALEFUL	BARBARY	BATFISH	BEATNIK
AUSTRAL	BABOONS	BALKING	BARBATE	BATHERS	BEAVERS
AUSTRIA	BABYING	BALLADE	BARBELL	BATHING	BECAUSE
AUTARKY	BABYISH	BALLADS	BARBERS	BATH MAT	BECKETT
AUTHORS	BABY-SAT	BALLARD	BARBOUR	BATHTUB	BEDBUGS
AUTOCUE	BABY-SIT	BALLAST	BARBUDA	BATHYAL	BEDDING
AUTOMAT	BACCATE	BALLETS	BARBULE	BATISTE	BEDEVIL
AUTOPSY	BACILLI	BALLOON	BARCHAN	BATSMAN	BEDEWED
AUTUMNS	BACKBAR	BALLOTS	BAR CODE	BATSMEN	BEDFORD

BEDHEAD	BEMUSED	BETTING	BILTONG	BLADDER	BLOUSES
BEDLAMS	BENARES	BETWEEN	BIMODAL	BLAMING	BLOW-DRY
BEDOUIN	BENCHER	BETWIXT	BIMORPH	BLANDER	BLOWERS
BEDPANS	BENCHES	BEVELED	BINDERS	BLANDLY	BLOWFLY
BEDPOST	BENDIGO	BEWITCH	BINDERY	BLANKET	BLOWIER
BEDRAIL	BENDING	BEXHILL	BINDING	BLANKLY	BLOWING
BEDROCK	BENEATH	BEYOGLU	BINNING	BLARING	BLOWOUT
BEDROOM	BENEFIT	BEZIQUE	BIOCIDE	BLARNEY	BLOW OUT
BEDSIDE	BENELUX	BHANGRA	BIODATA	BLASTED	BLOW-UPS
BEDSORE	BENGALI	BIASING	BIOFUEL	BLATANT	BLUBBER
BEDTIME	BENNETT	BIASSED	BIOHERM	BLATHER	BLUE GUM
BEECHES	BENTHOS	BIAXIAL	BIOLOGY	BLAUBOK	BLUEING
BEEFIER	BENZENE	BIBCOCK	BIOMASS	BLAYDON	BLUE JAY
BEEFING	BENZINE	BIBELOT	BIONICS	BLAZERS	BLUE LAW
BEEF TEA	BENZOIC	BICYCLE	BIOPICS	BLAZING	BLUE-SKY
BEEHIVE	BENZOIN	BIDDING	BIOPTIC	BLAZONS	BLUETIT
BEELINE	BENZOYL	BIEN HOA	BIOTECH	BLEAKER	BLUFFED
BEESWAX	BEOGRAD	BIFFING	BIOTITE	BLEAKLY	BLUFFER
BEETFLY	BEQUEST	BIFILAR	BIOTOPE	BLEATED	BLUFFLY
BEETLED	BERATED	BIFOCAL	BIOTYPE	BLEATER	BLUNDER
BEETLES	BERBERA	BIG CATS	BIPLANE	BLEEDER	BLUNGER
BEGGARS	BEREAVE	BIG DEAL	BIPOLAR	BLEEPED	BLUNTED
BEGGARY	BERGAMO	BIG ENDS	BIRCHED	BLEEPER	BLUNTLY
BEGGING	BERMUDA	BIGENER	BIRCHES	BLEMISH	BLURRED
BEGONIA	BERNESE	BIGFOOT	BIRD DOG	BLENDED	BLURTED
BEGUILE	BERRIES	BIG GAME	BIRDIES	BLENDER	BLUSHED
BEHAVED	BERSEEM	BIGGEST	BIRETTA	BLESBOK	BLUSHER
BEHINDS	BERSERK	BIGGIES	BISCUIT	BLESSED	BLUSHES
BEIJING	BERTHED	BIGHEAD	BISHKEK	BLETHER	BLUSTER
BEJEWEL	BESEECH	BIGHORN	BISHOPS	BLEWITS	B-MOVIES
BELARUS	BESIDES	BIG NAME	BISMUTH	BLIGHTS	BOARDED
BELATED	BESIEGE	BIGNESS	BISTORT	BLINDED	BOARDER
BELAYED	BESMEAR	BIGOTED	BISTROS	BLINDLY	BOARISH
BELCHED	BESPEAK	BIGOTRY	BITCHED	BLINKED	BOASTED
BELCHES	BESPOKE	BIG SHOT	BITCHES	BLINKER	BOASTER
BELFAST	BESTIAL	BIG TIME	BITCHIN'	BLISTER	BOATERS
BELFORT	BESTING	BIG TOPS	BIT PART	BLITZED	BOATING
BELGAUM	BEST MAN	BIGWIGS	BITTERN	BLITZES	BOATMAN
BELGIAN	BEST-OFF	BIJAPUR	BITTERS	BLOATED	BOATMEN
BELGIUM	BESTREW	BIKANER	BITTIER	BLOATER	BOBBERY
BELIEFS	BESTRID	BIKINIS	BITUMEN	BLOCKED	BOBBIES
BELIEVE	BETAINE	BILBOES	BIVALVE	BLONDER	BOBBING
BELLBOY	BETAKEN	BILIARY	BIVOUAC	BLONDES	BOBBINS
BELLEEK	BETHANY	BILIOUS	BIZARRE	BLOODED	BOBBLES
BELLIES	BETHELS	BILKING	BIZERTE	BLOOMED	BOBSLED
BELLOWS	BETHINK	BILLETS	BLABBED	BLOOMER	BOBSTAY
BELOVED	BETIDED	BILLIES	BLABBER	BLOOPER	BOBTAIL
BELTING	BETIMES	BILLING	BLACKED	BLOSSOM	BODICES
BELT MAN	BETOKEN	BILLION	BLACKEN	BLOTCHY	BODKINS
BELTWAY	BETROTH	BILLOWS	BLACKER	BLOTTED	BOFFINS
BELYING	BETTERS	BILLOWY	BLACKLY	BLOTTER	BOGARDE

BOGGIER	BOOTLEG	BOWSHOT	BRECCIA	BROODED	BUGGERY
BOGGING	BOOZERS	BOW TIES	BREEDER	BROODER	BUGGIES
BOGGLED	BOOZE UP	BOXCARS	BRENDEL	BROOKED	BUGGING
BOHEMIA	BOOZE-UP	BOXROOM	BRENNER	BROTHEL	BUGLERS
BOHRIUM	BOOZIER	BOX SEAT	BRENTON	BROTHER	BUGLOSS
BOILERS	BOOZILY	BOXWOOD	BRESCIA	BROWNED	BUILDER
BOILING	BOOZING	BOYCOTT	BREVIER	BROWNER	BUILDUP
BOK CHOY	BOPPING	BOYHOOD	BREVITY	BROWNIE	BUILD UP
BOLDEST	BORACIC	BRABANT	BREWAGE	BROWSED	BUILT-IN
BOLEROS	BORAZON	BRABHAM	BREWERY	BROWSER	BUILT-UP
BOLETUS	BORDERS	BRACING	BREWING	BRUCINE	BUKHARA
BOLIVAR	BORDURE	BRACKEN	BRIBERY	BRUISED	BULBOUS
BOLIVIA	BOREDOM	BRACKET	BRICOLE	BRUISER	BULGIER
BOLLARD	BORNEEL	BRADAWL	BRIDGET	BRUISES	BULGING
BOLOGNA	BORNITE	BRAEMAR	BRIDOON	BRUITED	BULIMIA
BOLONEY	BOROUGH	BRAGGED	BRIGADE	BRUMOUS	BULKIER
BOLSHIE	BORSCHT	BRAGGER	BRIGAND	BRUSHED	BULKILY
BOLSTER	BORSTAL	BRAHMAN	BRIMFUL	BRUSHER	BULKING
BOLTING	BORZOIS	BRAIDED	BRIMMER	BRUSHES	BULLACE
BOLZANO	BOSCAGE	BRAIDER	BRINDLE	BRUSH-UP	BULLATE
BOMBARD	BOSNIAN	BRAILLE	BRING UP	BRUSQUE	BULLDOG
BOMBAST	BOSSIER	BRAINED	BRIOCHE	BRUTISH	BULLETS
BOMBERS	BOSSILY	BRAISED	BRISKER	BRYANSK	BULLIED
BOMBING	BOSSING	BRAKING	BRISKET	BUBBLED	BULLIES
BONAIRE	BOTCHED	BRAKPAN	BRISKLY	BUBBLER	BULLION
BONANZA	BOTCHER	BRAMBLE	BRISTLE	BUBBLES	BULLISH
BONBONS	BOTCH-UP	BRAMLEY	BRISTLY	BUBONIC	BULLOCK
BONDAGE	BOTTLED	BRANAGH	BRISTOL	BUCKETS	BULRUSH
BONDING	BOTTLES	BRANDED	BRITISH	BUCKEYE	BULWARK
BONE-DRY	BOTTOMS	BRANSON	BRITONS	BUCKING	BUMBLED
BONESET	BOTTROP	BRAN TUB	BRITPOP	BUCKLED	BUMBLER
BONFIRE	BOTULIN	BRASHER	BRITTLE	BUCKLER	BUMBOAT
BONGOES	BOUCHEE	BRASHLY	BROADEN	BUCKLES	BUMMING
BONIEST	BOUDOIR	BRASSES	BROADER	BUCKRAM	BUMPERS
BONJOUR	BOULDER	BRASSIE	BROADLY	BUCKSAW	BUMPIER
BONKERS	BOUNCED	BRAVADO	BROCADE	BUCOLIC	BUMPILY
BONNETS	BOUNCER	BRAVAIS	BROCKET	BUDDIES	BUMPING
BONNIER	BOUNCES	BRAVELY	BROGLIE	BUDDING	BUMPKIN
BONUSES	BOUNDED	BRAVERY	BROGUES	BUDGETS	BUNCHED
BOOBIES	BOUNDEN	BRAVEST	BROILED	BUDGING	BUNCHES
BOOBING	BOUNDER	BRAVING	BROILER	BUFFALO	BUNDLED
BOOKEND	BOUQUET	BRAVURA	BROKERS	BUFFERS	BUNDLER
BOOKING	BOURBON	BRAWLED	BROMATE	BUFFETS	BUNDLES
BOOKISH	BOURDON	BRAWLER	BROMIDE	BUFFING	BUNGING
BOOKLET	BOURGES	BRAYING	BROMINE	BUFFOON	BUNGLED
BOOMING	BOUYANT	BRAZIER	BROMISM	BUGABOO	BUNGLER
BOORISH	BOWHEAD	BREADTH	BROMLEY	BUGANDA	BUNGLES
BOOSTED	BOWKNOT	BREAKER	BRONCHI	BUGBANE	BUNIONS
BOOSTER	BOWLERS	BREAK-IN	BRONCOS	BUGBEAR	BUNKERS
BOOTEES	BOWLINE	BREATHE	BRONZED	BUG-EYED	BUNKING
BOOTING	BOWLING	BREATHY	BRONZES	BUGGERS	BUNK OFF

BUNK-UPS	BUSKING	CADAVER	CALOTTE	CANTERS	CAREERS
BUNNIES	BUSSING	CADDIED	CALTROP	CANTHUS	CAREFUL
BUNTING	BUS STOP	CADDIES	CALUMNY	CANTING	CARFARE
BUOYAGE	BUSTARD	CADDISH	CALVARY	CANTONS	CARGOES
BUOYANT	BUSTERS	CADELLE	CALVING	CANTORS	CARHOPS
BUOYING	BUSTIER	CADENCE	CALYCES	CANVASS	CARIBOU
BURBLED	BUSTING	CADENCY	CALYCLE	CANYONS	CARIOCA
BURBLER	BUSTLED	CADENZA	CALYPSO	CANZONA	CARIOLE
BURDENS	BUSTLER	CADGERS	CALYXES	CANZONE	CARIOUS
BURDOCK	BUSTLES	CADGING	CAMBERS	CAPABLE	CARJACK
BUREAUX	BUST-UPS	CADMIUM	CAMBIAL	CAPABLY	CARLINE
BURETTE	BUSYING	CAESIUM	CAMBIST	CAP-A-	CARLING
BURGEON	BUTANOL	CAESURA	CAMBIUM	PIE	CARMINE
BURGERS	BUTCHER	CAFTANS	CAMBRAI	CAPE COD	CARNAGE
BURGESS	BUTLERS	CAGIEST	CAMBRIC	CAPELIN	CARNIFY
BURGHAL	BUTLERY	CAGOULE	CAMELOT	CAPELLA	CAROLED
BURGHER	BUTTERY	CAHOOTS	CAMERAL	CAPERED	CAROLUS
BURGLAR	BUTTIES	CAIQUES	CAMERAS	CAPITAL	CAROTID
BURGLED	BUTTING	CAISSON	CAMP BED	CAPITOL	CAROUSE
BURIALS	BUTTOCK	CAJOLED	CAMPERS	CAPORAL	CARPALE
BURLIER	BUTTONS	CAJUPUT	CAMPHOR	CAPPING	CAR PARK
BURMESE	BUTYRIC	CALABAR	CAMPING	CAPRICE	CARPETS
BURNERS	BUTYRIN	CALAMUS	CAMPION	CAPSIZE	CARPING
BURNING	BUY INTO	CALCIFY	CAM RANH	CAPSTAN	CAR POOL
BURNISH	BUYOUTS	CALCINE	CAMWOOD	CAPSULE	CARPORT
BURNLEY	BUZZARD	CALCITE	CANAPES	CAPTAIN	CARRARA
BURNOUS	BUZZERS	CALCIUM	CANARDS	CAPTION	CARRICK
BURNOUT	BUZZING	CALCULI	CANASTA	CAPTIVE	CARRIED
BURPING	BYE-BYES	CALDERA	CANCANS	CAPTORS	CARRIER
BURRING	BYELOVO	CALDRON	CANCERS	CAPTURE	CARRIES
BURRITO	BYGONES	CALENDS	CANDELA	CARABAO	CARRION
BURROWS	BY-LINES	CALGARY	CANDIED	CARABID	CARROTS
BURSARS	BYRONIC	CALIBRE	CANDIES	CARACAL	CARROTY
BURSARY	BYWORDS	CALICHE	CANDLER	CARACAS	CARRY ON
BURSTER		CALICOS	CANDLES	CARACUL	CARRY-ON
BURTHEN	**C**	CALIPEE	CANDOUR	CARAFES	CARSICK
BURTONS		CALIPHS	CANELLA	CARAMBA	CARTAGE
BURUNDI	CABARET	CALKING	CANINES	CARAMEL	CARTELS
BURWEED	CABBAGE	CALLAIS	CANKERS	CARAVAN	CARTERS
BURYING	CABBALA	CALLANT	CANNERY	CARAVEL	CARTING
BUSBIES	CABBIES	CALL BOX	CANNIER	CARAWAY	CARTONS
BUS BOYS	CABEZON	CALLBOY	CANNILY	CARBENE	CARTOON
BUSHELS	CABIMAS	CALLERS	CANNING	CARBIDE	CARVERS
BUSHIER	CABINDA	CALLING	CANNOCK	CARBINE	CARVING
BUSHING	CABINET	CALL-INS	CANNONS	CARBONS	CASCADE
BUSHIRE	CABLING	CALLOUS	CANNULA	CARBOYS	CASCARA
BUSHMAN	CABOOSE	CALMEST	CANONRY	CARCASS	CASEASE
BUSHPIG	CAB RANK	CALMING	CANOPUS	CARDIAC	CASEATE
BUSHTIT	CACHETS	CALOMEL	CANTALA	CARDIFF	CASEOSE
BUSIEST	CACKLED	CALORIC	CANTATA	CARDING	CASEOUS
BUSKERS	CACKLES	CALORIE	CANTEEN	CARDOON	CASERTA

73

CASHEWS	CATTERY	CENTURY	CHANTED	CHECK ON	CHIMNEY
CASHIER	CATTIER	CEPHEUS	CHANTER	CHECKUP	CHINESE
CASHING	CATTILY	CERAMIC	CHANTRY	CHEDDAR	CHINKED
CASINGS	CATTISH	CERATED	CHAOTIC	CHEEKED	CHINOOK
CASINOS	CATWALK	CEREALS	CHAPATI	CHEEPED	CHINTZY
CASKETS	CAUDATE	CEREBRA	CHAPEAU	CHEEPER	CHINWAG
CASPIAN	CAULINE	CERTAIN	CHAPELS	CHEERED	CHIPPED
CASQUED	CAULKED	CERTIFY	CHAPLET	CHEERIO	CHIPPER
CASQUES	CAULKER	CERUMEN	CHAPPAL	CHEESES	CHIRPED
CASSATA	CAUSING	CERVINE	CHAPPED	CHEETAH	CHIRPER
CASSAVA	CAUSTIC	CESSION	CHAPTER	CHELATE	CHIRRUP
CASSINO	CAUTERY	CESSPIT	CHARADE	CHEMISE	CHISELS
CASSOCK	CAUTION	CESTODE	CHARGED	CHEMIST	CHIVIED
CASTERS	CAVALLA	CESTOID	CHARGER	CHENGTU	CHLORAL
CASTILE	CAVALRY	CETINJE	CHARGES	CHENNAI	CHLORIC
CASTING	CAVEATS	CETOOGY	CHARIER	CHEQUER	CHOC-ICE
CASTLED	CAVE-INS	CHABLIS	CHARILY	CHEQUES	CHOCKED
CASTLES	CAVEMAN	CHABROL	CHARIOT	CHERISH	CHOCTAW
CAST OFF	CAVEMEN	CHA-CHAS	CHARITY	CHEROOT	CHOICER
CAST-OFF	CAVERNS	CHAFFED	CHARKHA	CHERUBS	CHOICES
CASTORS	CAVES IN	CHAFFER	CHARLES	CHERVIL	CHOKERS
CASUIST	CAVETTO	CHAFING	CHARLIE	CHESTED	CHOKING
CATALAN	CAVILED	CHAGRIN	CHARMED	CHESTER	CHOLERA
CATALPA	CAYENNE	CHAINED	CHARMER	CHEVIOT	CHOLINE
CATANIA	CEASING	CHAIRED	CHARNEL	CHEVRON	CHOLULA
CATARRH	CEDILLA	CHAISES	CHARPOY	CHEWIER	CHOMPED
CATBIRD	CEILING	CHALAZA	CHARQUI	CHEWING	CHOOSER
CATBOAT	CELADON	CHALCID	CHARRED	CHIANTI	CHOPPED
CATCALL	CELEBES	CHALCIS	CHARTED	CHIAPAS	CHOPPER
CATCHER	CELESTA	CHALDEA	CHARTER	CHIASMA	CHORALE
CATCHES	CELLARS	CHALETS	CHASERS	CHIBOUK	CHORDAL
CATCH IT	CELLIST	CHALICE	CHASING	CHICAGO	CHOREAL
CATCH UP	CELLNET	CHALKED	CHASMAL	CHICANE	CHORION
CATECHU	CELLULE	CHALLAH	CHASSIS	CHICANO	CHORLEY
CATERED	CELSIUS	CHALLIS	CHASTEN	CHICKEN	CHOROID
CATERER	CEMBALO	CHALONE	CHASTER	CHICORY	CHORTLE
CATFISH	CENACLE	CHAMBER	CHATEAU	CHIDDEN	CHORZOW
CATHEAD	CENSORS	CHAMFER	CHATHAM	CHIDING	CHOWDER
CATHODE	CENSUAL	CHAMOIS	CHATTED	CHIEFLY	CHROMIC
CATKINS	CENSURE	CHAMPAC	CHATTEL	CHIFFON	CHROMYL
CATLING	CENTAUR	CHAMPED	CHATTER	CHIGGER	CHRONIC
CATMINT	CENTAVO	CHANCED	CHAYOTE	CHIGNON	CHRONON
CATNAPS	CENTERS	CHANCEL	CHEAPEN	CHILEAN	CHUCKED
CAT'S-	CENTIME	CHANCES	CHEAPER	CHILIAD	CHUCK IN
EAR	CENTIMO	CHANCRE	CHEAPIE	CHILIES	CHUCKLE
CAT'S	CENTNER	CHANGDE	CHEAPLY	CHILLED	CHUFFED
EYE	CENTRAL	CHANGED	CHEATED	CHILLUM	CHUGGED
CAT'S	CENTRED	CHANGER	CHEATER	CHILUNG	CHUKCHI
PAW	CENTRES	CHANGES	CHECHEN	CHIMERA	CHUKKER
CATSUIT	CENTRIC	CHANNEL	CHECKED	CHIMERE	CHUMMED
CATTALO	CENTRUM	CHANSON	CHECK-IN	CHIMING	CHURNED

CHUTNEY	CLAPPER	CLINKER	COAXIAL	COLDISH	COMPARE
CHUVASH	CLAQUES	CLINTON	COAXING	COLDITZ	COMPASS
CHYMOUS	CLARIFY	CLIPPED	COBBERS	COLD WAR	COMPEER
CICADAS	CLARINO	CLIPPER	COBBLED	COLICKY	COMPERE
CICHLID	CLARION	CLIPPIE	COBBLER	COLITIC	COMPETE
CILIARY	CLARITY	CLIQUES	COBWEBS	COLITIS	COMPILE
CILIATE	CLARKIA	CLIQUEY	COCAINE	COLLAGE	COMPING
CIMBRIC	CLASHED	CLOACAL	COCCOID	COLLARD	COMPLEX
CINDERS	CLASHER	CLOAKED	COCCOUS	COLLARS	COMPLIN
CINDERY	CLASHES	CLOBBER	COCHLEA	COLLATE	COMPONY
CINEMAS	CLASPED	CLOCHES	COCKADE	COLLECT	COMPORT
CINERIN	CLASPER	CLOCKED	COCKIER	COLLEEN	COMPOSE
CIPHERS	CLASSED	CLOGGED	COCKING	COLLEGE	COMPOST
CIPOLIN	CLASSES	CLONMEL	COCKLES	COLLIDE	COMPOTE
CIRCLED	CLASSIC	CLOPPED	COCKNEY	COLLIER	COMPTON
CIRCLER	CLASSIS	CLOSELY	COCKPIT	COLLIES	COMPUTE
CIRCLES	CLASTIC	CLOSEST	COCK-UPS	COLLOID	COMRADE
CIRCLET	CLATTER	CLOSETS	COCONUT	COLLUDE	CONAKRY
CIRCLIP	CLAUSAL	CLOSE-UP	COCOONS	COLOBUS	CONATUS
CIRCUIT	CLAUSES	CLOSING	COCOTTE	COLOGNE	CONCAVE
CIRQUES	CLAVATE	CLOSURE	COCOYAM	COLOMBO	CONCEAL
CIRRATE	CLAVIER	CLOTHED	CODDLED	COLONEL	CONCEDE
CIRSOID	CLAVIUS	CLOTHES	CODEINE	COLONIC	CONCEIT
CISSIES	CLAWING	CLOTTED	CODFISH	COLOSSI	CONCEPT
CISSOID	CLAYPAN	CLOTURE	CODGERS	COLOURS	CONCERN
CISTERN	CLEANED	CLOUDED	CODICES	COLTISH	CONCERT
CISTRON	CLEANER	CLOUTED	CODICIL	COLUMNS	CONCHAL
CITABLE	CLEANLY	CLOWNED	CODLING	COMBATS	CONCHES
CITADEL	CLEANSE	CLOYING	COELIAC	COMBERS	CONCISE
CITHARA	CLEANUP	CLUBBED	COEQUAL	COMBINE	CONCOCT
CITIZEN	CLEAN UP	CLUBMAN	COERCED	COMBING	CONCORD
CITRATE	CLEARED	CLUCKED	COETZEE	COMB-OUT	CONCUSS
CITRINE	CLEARER	CLUMPED	COEVALS	COMBUST	CONDEMN
CITRONS	CLEARLY	CLUNIAC	COEXIST	COMECON	CONDIGN
CIVILLY	CLEAR UP	CLUPEID	COFFERS	COMEDIC	CONDOLE
CIVVIES	CLEAVED	CLUSTER	COFFINS	COMFIER	CONDOMS
CLACKED	CLEAVER	CLUTTER	COGENCY	COMFITS	CONDONE
CLADODE	CLEMENT	CLYPEAL	COGGING	COMFORT	CONDORS
CLAIMED	CLERICS	CLYPEUS	COGNACS	COMFREY	CONDUCE
CLAIMER	CLERKED	COACHED	COGNATE	COMICAL	CONDUCT
CLAMANT	CLICHED	COACHES	COGNIZE	COMINGS	CONDUIT
CLAMBER	CLICHES	COAL GAS	COHABIT	COMMAND	CONDYLE
CLAMMED	CLICKED	COALING	COHERED	COMMEND	CONFECT
CLAMOUR	CLICKER	COAL TAR	COHORTS	COMMENT	CONFESS
CLAMPED	CLIENTS	COAMING	COILING	COMMODE	CONFIDE
CLAMPER	CLIMATE	COARSEN	COIMBRA	COMMONS	CONFINE
CLANGED	CLIMBED	COARSER	COINAGE	COMMUNE	CONFIRM
CLANGER	CLIMBER	COASTAL	COINERS	COMMUTE	CONFORM
CLANGOR	CLINGER	COASTED	COINING	COMOROS	CONFUSE
CLANKED	CLINICS	COASTER	COLBERT	COMPACT	CONFUTE
CLAPPED	CLINKED	COATING	COLDEST	COMPANY	CONGEAL

CONGEST	COOLIES	CORONER	COUNTED	CRABBED	CRESSET
CONGIUS	COOLING	CORONET	COUNTER	CRACKED	CRESTED
CONICAL	COOLISH	CORPORA	COUNTRY	CRACKER	CRETINS
CONIFER	COONTIE	CORPSES	COUPLED	CRACKLE	CREVICE
CONIINE	COOPERS	CORRADE	COUPLER	CRACK UP	CREW CUT
CONJOIN	CO-OPTED	CORRALS	COUPLES	CRACKUP	CREWING
CONJURE	COPAIBA	CORRECT	COUPLET	CRADLED	CRIBBED
CONKERS	COPEPOD	CORREZE	COUPONS	CRADLES	CRICKED
CONKING	COPIERS	CORRIDA	COURAGE	CRAFTED	CRICKET
CONNATE	COPILOT	CORRODE	COURIER	CRAIOVA	CRICOID
CONNECT	COPINGS	CORRUPT	COURSED	CRAMMED	CRIMEAN
CONNERY	COPIOUS	CORSAGE	COURSER	CRAMMER	CRIMPED
CONNING	COP-OUTS	CORSAIR	COURSES	CRAMPED	CRIMPER
CONNIVE	COPPERS	CORSETS	COURTED	CRAMPON	CRIMPLE
CONNOTE	COPPERY	CORSICA	COURTLY	CRANIAL	CRIMSON
CONQUER	COPPICE	CORTEGE	COUSINS	CRANING	CRINGED
CONSENT	COPPING	CORTONA	COUTURE	CRANIUM	CRINGLE
CONSIGN	COPULAR	CORVINE	COUVADE	CRANKED	CRINITE
CONSIST	COPYCAT	COSENZA	COVERED	CRANK UP	CRINKLE
CONSOLE	COPYING	COSHING	COVERER	CRAPPED	CRINKLY
CONSOLS	COPYIST	COSIEST	COVERTS	CRAPPIE	CRINOID
CONSORT	COQUINA	COSINES	COVER-UP	CRASHED	CRIOLLO
CONSULS	COQUITO	COSMINE	COVETED	CRASHES	CRIPPLE
CONSULT	CORACLE	COSMOID	COVETER	CRASSLY	CRISPED
CONSUME	CORBEIL	COSTARD	COWARDS	CRATERS	CRISPLY
CONTACT	CORBELS	CO-STARS	COWARDY	CRATING	CRISSAL
CONTAIN	CORDAGE	COSTATE	COWBANE	CRAVATS	CRISSUM
CONTEMN	CORDATE	COSTING	COWBELL	CRAVING	CRITICS
CONTEND	CORDIAL	COSTIVE	COWBIND	CRAWLED	CRITTER
CONTENT	CORDING	COSTNER	COWBIRD	CRAWLER	CROAKED
CONTEST	CORDITE	COSTUME	COWBOYS	CRAWLEY	CROAKER
CONTEXT	CORDOBA	COTE-	COWDREY	CRAYONS	CROATIA
CONTORT	CORDONS	D'OR	COWERED	CRAZIER	CROCEIN
CONTOUR	CORINTH	COTERIE	COWFISH	CRAZILY	CROCHET
CONTROL	CORKAGE	COTIDAL	COWGIRL	CREAKED	CROCKET
CONTUSE	CORKERS	COTINGA	COWHAND	CREAMED	CROFTER
CONVENE	CORKING	COTONOU	COWHERB	CREAMER	CRONIES
CONVENT	CORMOUS	COTTAGE	COWHERD	CREASED	CROOKED
CONVERT	CORNCOB	COTTONY	COWHIDE	CREASES	CROONED
CONVICT	CORNEAL	COUCHED	COWLICK	CREATED	CROONER
CONVOKE	CORNERS	COUCHER	COWLING	CREATOR	CROPPED
CONVOYS	CORNETS	COUCHES	COWPATS	CRECHES	CROPPER
COOKERS	CORNICE	COUGARS	COWRIES	CREDENT	CROQUET
COOKERY	CORNIER	COUGHED	COWSHED	CREDITS	CROSIER
COOKIES	CORNISH	COULDN'T	COWSLIP	CREEDAL	CROSSED
COOKING	CORNUAL	COULDST	COXCOMB	CREEPER	CROSSER
COOKOUT	CORNUTE	COULOIR	COYNESS	CREMATE	CROSSES
COOKSON	COROLLA	COULOMB	COYOTES	CREMONA	CROSSLY
COOLANT	CORONAE	COULTER	COZENED	CRENATE	CROUTON
COOLERS	CORONAL	COUNCIL	COZENER	CREOLES	CROWBAR
COOLEST	CORONAS	COUNSEL	COZIEST	CREOSOL	CROWDED

CROWING	CULPRIT	CUSPATE	DADAIST	DASHEEN	DECADAL
CROWNED	CULTISH	CUSSING	DADDIES	DASHIKI	DECADES
CROYDON	CULTISM	CUSTARD	DADROCK	DASHING	DECAGON
CROZIER	CULTIST	CUSTODY	DAEMONS	DASYURE	DECANAL
CRUCIAL	CULTURE	CUSTOMS	DAFTEST	DATABLE	DECAPOD
CRUCIFY	CULVERT	CUTAWAY	DAGGERS	DATA BUS	DECAYED
CRUDELY	CUMBRIA	CUTBACK	DAGLOCK	DATIVAL	DECEASE
CRUDEST	CUMQUAT	CUT DOWN	DAHLIAS	DATIVES	DECEIVE
CRUDITY	CUMULET	CUTICLE	DAHOMAN	DAUBERY	DECENCY
CRUELLY	CUMULUS	CUTLASS	DAHOMEY	DAUBING	DECIARE
CRUELTY	CUNEATE	CUTLERS	DAILIES	DAUNTED	DECIBEL
CRUISED	CUNNING	CUTLERY	DAIRIES	DAUNTER	DECIDED
CRUISER	CUP CAKE	CUTLETS	DAISIES	DAUPHIN	DECIDER
CRUISES	CUPOLAS	CUTOFFS	DAKOTAN	DAWDLED	DECIDUA
CRUMBLE	CUPPING	CUTOUTS	DALLIED	DAWDLER	DECIMAL
CRUMBLY	CUPRITE	CUTTACK	DAMAGED	DAWKINS	DECKING
CRUMPET	CUPROUS	CUTTERS	DAMAGER	DAWNING	DECLAIM
CRUMPLE	CUP TIES	CUTTING	DAMAGES	DAYBOOK	DECLARE
CRUMPLY	CURABLE	CUTWORK	DAMMING	DAYBOYS	DECLASS
CRUNCHY	CURABLY	CUTWORM	DAMNIFY	DAY CARE	DECLINE
CRUNODE	CURACAO	CWMBRAN	DAMNING	DAY-CARE	DECODED
CRUPPER	CURATES	CYANATE	DAMPERS	DAYLONG	DECORUM
CRUSADE	CURATOR	CYANIDE	DAMPEST	DAYROOM	DECOYED
CRUSHED	CURBING	CYANINE	DAMPING	DAYTIME	DECOYER
CRUSHES	CURCUMA	CYANITE	DAMPISH	DAZEDLY	DECREED
CRUSTAL	CURDLED	CYBALER	DAMSELS	DAZZLED	DECREER
CRUZADO	CURE-ALL	CYCLING	DAMSONS	DEACONS	DECREES
CRYBABY	CURETTE	CYCLIST	DANCERS	DEAD END	DECRIAL
CRYOGEN	CURFEWS	CYCLOID	DANCING	DEADEYE	DECRIED
CRYPTAL	CURIOSA	CYCLONE	DANDERS	DEADPAN	DECRIER
CRYPTIC	CURIOUS	CYCLOPS	DANDIER	DEAD SET	DECUPLE
CRYSTAL	CURLERS	CYGNETS	DANDIES	DEAF-AID	DEDUCED
CTENOID	CURLEWS	CYMBALS	DANDIFY	DEALATE	DEEMING
CUBBING	CURLIER	CYNICAL	DANDLED	DEALERS	DEEPEST
CUBICAL	CURLING	CYPHERS	DANDLER	DEALING	DEEP FRY
CUBICLE	CURRANT	CYPRESS	DANGERS	DEANERY	DEFACED
CUBITAL	CURRENT	CYPRIOT	DANGLED	DEAREST	DEFACER
CUCKOLD	CURRIED	CYPSELA	DANGLER	DEARIES	DE FACTO
CUCKOOS	CURRIER	CYSTINE	DANKEST	DEATHLY	DEFAMED
CUDBEAR	CURRIES	CYSTOID	DANSEUR	DEBACLE	DEFAMER
CUDDLED	CURRISH	CYTHERA	DAPHNIA	DEBASED	DEFAULT
CUDGELS	CURSING	CZARDAS	DAPPING	DEBASER	DEFEATS
CUDLIPP	CURSIVE	CZARINA	DAPPLED	DEBATED	DEFECTS
CUDWEED	CURSORS		DAPSONE	DEBATER	DEFENCE
CUE BALL	CURSORY	**D**	DARESAY	DEBATES	DEFIANT
CUFFING	CURTAIL	DABBING	DARIOLE	DEBAUCH	DEFICIT
CUIRASS	CURTAIN	DABBLED	DARKEST	DEBITED	DEFILED
CUISINE	CURTESY	DABBLER	DARKIES	DEBORAH	DEFILER
CULCHIE	CURVING	DAB HAND	DARLING	DEBOUCH	DEFILES
CULICID	CUSHIER	DACTYLS	DARNING	DEBRIEF	DEFINED
CULLING	CUSHION	DADAISM	DARTING	DEBTORS	DEFINER

DEFLATE	DENEUVE	DESIRES	DHAHRAN	DILATED	DISCORD
DEFLECT	DENIALS	DESKTOP	DIABASE	DILATOR	DISCUSS
DEFORCE	DENIERS	DESMOID	DIABOLO	DILDOES	DISDAIN
DEFRAUD	DENIZEN	DESPAIR	DIADEMS	DILEMMA	DISEASE
DEFROCK	DENMARK	DESPISE	DIAGRAM	DILUENT	DISEUSE
DEFROST	DENNING	DESPITE	DIALECT	DILUTED	DISGUST
DEFUNCT	DENOTED	DESPOIL	DIALING	DILUTEE	DISHFUL
DEFUSED	DENSELY	DESPOND	DIALLED	DILUTER	DISHIER
DEFYING	DENSEST	DESPOTS	DIALLER	DIMETER	DISHING
DEGAUSS	DENSITY	DESSERT	DIALYSE	DIMMERS	DISJECT
DEGRADE	DENTATE	DESTINE	DIAMINE	DIMMEST	DISJOIN
DEGREES	DENTINE	DESTINY	DIAMOND	DIMMING	DISLIKE
DEHISCE	DENTING	DESTOCK	DIANOIA	DIMNESS	DISMAST
DEICIDE	DENTIST	DESTROY	DIAPERS	DIMORPH	DISMISS
DE-ICING	DENTOID	DETAILS	DIARCHY	DIMPLES	DISOBEY
DEICTIC	DENTURE	DETENTE	DIARIES	DIMWITS	DISPLAY
DEIFIED	DENUDED	DETERGE	DIARIST	DINERIC	DISPORT
DEIFIER	DENUDER	DETINUE	DIASTER	DINETTE	DISPOSE
DEIFORM	DENYING	DETOURS	DIAZINE	DINGIER	DISPUTE
DEIGNED	DEONTIC	DETRACT	DIAZOLE	DINGILY	DISRATE
DEISTIC	DEPISER	DETRAIN	DIBASIC	DINGLES	DISROBE
DEITIES	DEPLETE	DETROIT	DIBBING	DINGOES	DISRUPT
DEJECTA	DEPLORE	DETRUDE	DIBBLED	DINKIER	DISSECT
DE KLERK	DEPLUME	DEUTZIA	DIBBLER	DINNERS	DISSENT
DELAINE	DEPOSAL	DEVALUE	DIBBLES	DINNING	DISTAFF
DELAYED	DEPOSED	DEVELOP	DICIEST	DIOCESE	DISTANT
DELAYER	DEPOSER	DEVIANT	DICKENS	DIOPTRE	DISTEND
DELETED	DEPOSIT	DEVIATE	DICKIER	DIORAMA	DISTICH
DELIGHT	DEPRAVE	DEVICES	DICKIES	DIORITE	DISTORT
DELIMIT	DEPRESS	DEVILED	DICLINY	DIOXIDE	DISTURB
DELIVER	DEPRIVE	DEVILRY	DICTATE	DIPHASE	DISUSED
DELOUSE	DEPSIDE	DEVIOUS	DICTION	DIPLOID	DITCHED
DELPHIC	DEPUTED	DEVISAL	DICTUMS	DIPLOMA	DITCHER
DELTAIC	DERANGE	DEVISED	DIDDLED	DIPLONT	DITCHES
DELTOID	DERBIES	DEVISEE	DIDICOY	DIPNOAN	DITTANY
DELUDED	DERIDED	DEVISER	DIEBACK	DIPOLAR	DITTIES
DELUDER	DERIDER	DEVISOR	DIE-CAST	DIPPERS	DIURNAL
DELUGED	DERIVED	DEVIZES	DIEHARD	DIPPING	DIVERGE
DELUGES	DERIVER	DEVOICE	DIESELS	DIPSHIT	DIVERSE
DELVING	DERMOID	DEVOIRS	DIETARY	DIPTYCH	DIVIDED
DEMANDS	DERRICK	DEVOLVE	DIETING	DIREFUL	DIVIDER
DEMERGE	DERVISH	DEVOTED	DIFFUSE	DIRNDLS	DIVIDES
DEMERIT	DESCALE	DEVOTEE	DIGAMMA	DIRTIED	DIVINED
DEMESNE	DESCANT	DEWATER	DIGESTS	DIRTIER	DIVINER
DEMIGOD	DESCEND	DEWCLAW	DIGGERS	DIRTILY	DIVISOR
DEMIVEG	DESCENT	DEWDROP	DIGGING	DISABLE	DIVORCE
DEMONIC	DESERTS	DEWIEST	DIGITAL	DISAVOW	DIVULGE
DEMOTED	DESERVE	DEWLAPS	DIGNIFY	DISBAND	DIZZIER
DEMOTIC	DESIGNS	DEXTRAL	DIGNITY	DISCARD	DIZZILY
DEMOUNT	DESIRED	DEXTRAN	DIGRAPH	DISCERN	DNIEPER
DEMURER	DESIRER	DEXTRIN	DIGRESS	DISCOID	D-NOTICE

DOBRUJA DOODLED DRAFTED DRONING DUELLED DYNAMIC
DOCKAGE DOODLER DRAFTEE DRONISH DUELLER DYNAMOS
DOCKERS DOODLES DRAFTER DROOLED DUENNAS DYNASTY
DOCKETS DOOMING DRAGGED DROOPED DUFFERS DYSURIA
DOCKING DO-OR- DRAGGLE DROPLET DUGOUTS DYSURIC
DOCTORS DIE DRAGNET DROP OFF DUKEDOM DZONGKA
DODDERY DOORMAN DRAGONS DROPOUT DULLARD
DODDLES DOORMAT DRAGOON DROPPED DULLEST **E**
DODGEMS DOORMEN DRAINED DROPPER DULLING EACH WAY
DODGERS DOORWAY DRAINER DROSHKY DULOSIS EAGERLY
DODGIER DOPIEST DRAPERS DROUGHT DUMBEST EAGLETS
DODGING DORMANT DRAPERY DROVERS DUMMIES EARACHE
DODOISM DORMERS DRAPING DROWNED DUMPERS EARDRUM
DOESKIN DORMICE DRASTIC DROWNER DUMPIER EARFLAP
DOFFING DORNICK DRATTED DROWSED DUMPING EARHOLE
DOGBANE DOSAGES DRAUGHT DRUBBER DUNDALK EARLDOM
DOGCART DOSSERS DRAWBAR DRUDGED DUNEDIN EARLIER
DOG DAYS DOSSIER DRAWERS DRUDGER DUNGEON EARLOBE
DOGFISH DOSSING DRAWING DRUDGES DUNKING EARMARK
DOGGERY DOTAGES DRAWLED DRUGGED DUNKIRK EARMUFF
DOGGIES DOTTIER DRAWLER DRUGGET DUNNAGE EARNERS
DOGGING DOTTING DRAWS IN DRUIDIC DUNNEST EARNEST
DOGGONE DOUBLED DRAWS UP DRUMLIN DUNNING EARNING
DOGLEGS DOUBLER DREADED DRUMMED DUNNITE EARPLUG
DOG ROSE DOUBLES DREAMED DRUMMER DUODENA EARRING
DOG TAGS DOUBLET DREAMER DRUNKEN DUOTONE EARSHOT
DOGTROT DOUBTED DREDGED DRUNKER DUPABLE EARTHED
DOGVANE DOUBTER DREDGER DRUTHER DURABLE EARTHEN
DOGWOOD DOUCHES DRENTHE DRYABLE DURABLY EARTHLY
DOILIES DOUGHTY DRESDEN DRYADIC DURANGO EARWIGS
DOLEFUL DOUGLAS DRESSED DRY DOCK DURMAST EASEFUL
DOLLARS DOURINE DRESSER DRY-EYED DUSKIER EASIEST
DOLLIES DOUSING DRESSES DRY LAND DUSTBIN EAST END
DOLLING DOWABLE DRESS UP DRYNESS DUSTERS EASTERN
DOLLISH DOWAGER DRIBBLE DRY-SALT DUSTIER EASTERS
DOLLOPS DOWDIER DRIBLET DRY-SHOD DUSTING EASTING
DOLMENS DOWDILY DRIED UP DRYWALL DUSTMAN EATABLE
DOLPHIN DOWN-BOW DRIFTED DUALISM DUSTMEN EBB TIDE
DOLTISH DOWNERS DRIFTER DUALIST DUSTPAN EBONITE
DOMAINS DOWNIER DRILLED DUALITY DUSTUPS EBONIZE
DOMICAL DOWNING DRILLER DUBBING DUTIFUL ECBOLIC
DOMINEE DOWRIES DRINKER DUBIETY DUVETYN ECCRINE
DONATED DOWSERS DRIP-DRY DUBIOUS DVANDVA ECDYSIS
DONATOR DOWSING DRIPPED DUBNIUM DWARFED ECHELON
DONBASS DOYLEYS DRIVE IN DUCHESS DWARVES ECHIDNA
DONEGAL DOZENTH DRIVE-IN DUCHIES DWELLED ECHINUS
DONETSK DOZIEST DRIVERS DUCKIES DWELLER ECHOING
DON JUAN DRABBER DRIVING DUCKING DWINDLE ECHOISM
DONKEYS DRABBLE DRIZZLE DUCTILE DYARCHY ECLAIRS
DONNING DRACHMA DRIZZLY DUDGEON DYELINE ECLIPSE
DONNISH DRACHMS DROLLER DUELING DYEWOOD ECLOGUE

ECOCIDE	ELATIVE	EMITTER	ENERGID	ENTRAIN	EQUATOR
ECOLOGY	ELBOWED	EMOTION	ENFEOFF	ENTRANT	EQUERRY
ECONOMY	ELDERLY	EMOTIVE	ENFIELD	ENTREAT	EQUINOX
ECORCHE	ELEATIC	EMPALER	ENFORCE	ENTREES	ERASERS
ECOTONE	ELECTED	EMPANEL	ENGAGED	ENTRIES	ERASING
ECOTYPE	ELECTOR	EMPATHY	ENGAGER	ENTROPY	ERASION
ECSTASY	ELEGANT	EMPEROR	EN GARDE	ENTRUST	ERASURE
ECTHYMA	ELEGIAC	EMPIRES	ENGINES	ENTWINE	ERECTED
ECTOPIA	ELEGIES	EMPIRIC	ENGLAND	E NUMBER	ERECTER
ECTOPIC	ELEGIST	EMPLACE	ENGLISH	ENVELOP	ERECTLY
ECTYPAL	ELEGIZE	EMPORIA	ENGORGE	ENVENOM	ERECTOR
ECUADOR	ELEMENT	EMPOWER	ENGRAFT	ENVIOUS	EREMITE
EDACITY	ELEUSIS	EMPRESS	ENGRAIL	ENVIRON	EREPSIN
EDAPHIC	ELEVATE	EMPTIED	ENGRAIN	ENVYING	ERISTIC
EDDYING	ELEVENS	EMPTIER	ENGRAVE	ENZYMES	ERITREA
EDGIEST	ELIDING	EMPTIES	ENGROSS	EOBIONT	ERMINES
EDGINGS	ELISION	EMPTILY	ENHANCE	EOSINIC	ERODENT
EDICTAL	ELITISM	EMPYEMA	ENIGMAS	EPARCHY	ERODING
EDIFICE	ELITIST	EMULATE	ENJOYED	EPAULET	EROSION
EDIFIED	ELIXIRS	EMULOUS	ENJOYER	EPEEIST	EROSIVE
EDIFIER	ELLIPSE	ENABLED	ENLARGE	EPEIRIC	EROTEMA
EDITING	EL MINYA	ENABLER	ENLIVEN	EPERGNE	EROTICA
EDITION	EL OBEID	ENACTED	EN MASSE	EPIBOLY	ERRANCY
EDITORS	ELOPING	ENACTOR	ENNOBLE	EPICARP	ERRANDS
EDUCATE	ELUDING	ENAMOUR	ENOUNCE	EPICENE	ERRATIC
EEL-LIKE	ELUSION	ENCASED	ENPLANE	EPICURE	ERRATUM
EELPOUT	ELUSIVE	ENCHAIN	ENQUIRE	EPIDOTE	ERRHINE
EELWORM	ELUVIAL	ENCHANT	ENQUIRY	EPIGEAL	ERUDITE
EFFACED	ELUVIUM	EN CLAIR	ENRAGED	EPIGENE	ERUPTED
EFFACER	ELYSIAN	ENCLAVE	ENROBER	EPIGONE	ERZURUM
EFFECTS	ELYSIUM	ENCLOSE	EN ROUTE	EPIGRAM	ESBJERG
EFFORTS	ELYTRON	ENCODED	ENSIGNS	EPIGYNY	ESCAPED
EGGCUPS	EMANATE	ENCODER	ENSLAVE	EPIMERE	ESCAPEE
EGGHEAD	EMBARGO	ENCOMIA	ENSNARE	EPISODE	ESCAPER
EGG ROLL	EMBASSY	ENCORES	ENSUING	EPISOME	ESCAPES
EGOISTS	EMBLEMS	ENCRUST	ENSURED	EPISTLE	ESCOLAR
EGOTISM	EMBOLIC	ENDARCH	ENSURER	EPITAPH	ESCORTS
EGOTIST	EMBOLUS	ENDEMIC	ENTASIA	EPITAXY	ESERINE
EGO TRIP	EMBRACE	END GAME	ENTASIS	EPITHET	ESKIMOS
EIDETIC	EMBROIL	ENDINGS	ENTEBBE	EPITOME	ESPARTO
EIDOLON	EMBRYOS	ENDIVES	ENTENTE	EPIZOIC	ESPOUSE
EIGHTHS	EMENDED	ENDLESS	ENTERED	EPIZOON	ESPYING
EIGHTVO	EMERALD	ENDMOST	ENTERER	EPOCHAL	ESQUIRE
EINKORN	EMERGED	ENDORSE	ENTERIC	EPOCHES	ESSAYED
EJECTED	EMERSED	ENDOWED	ENTERON	EPONYMY	ESSENCE
EJECTOR	EMETICS	ENDOWER	ENTHRAL	EPSILON	ESSONNE
ELAMITE	EMETINE	ENDUING	ENTHUSE	EQUABLE	ESTATES
ELAPSED	EMIGRES	ENDURED	ENTICED	EQUABLY	ESTHETE
ELASTIC	EMINENT	END USER	ENTICER	EQUALED	ESTONIA
ELASTIN	EMIRATE	ENDWAYS	ENTITLE	EQUALLY	ESTORIL
ELATION	EMITTED	ENEMIES	ENTOPIC	EQUATED	ESTREAT

ESTUARY	EXACTOR	EXPOSAL	FADEOUT	FARADAY	FEASTED
ETAGERE	EXALTED	EXPOSED	FAEROES	FARADIC	FEASTER
ETAMINE	EXALTER	EXPOSER	FAG ENDS	FARAWAY	FEATHER
ETCHERS	EXAMINE	EXPOSES	FAGGING	FARCEUR	FEATURE
ETCHING	EXAMPLE	EXPOUND	FAGGOTS	FAR EAST	FEBRILE
ETERNAL	EXARATE	EXPRESS	FAIENCE	FAR-GONE	FEDERAL
ETESIAN	EXCERPT	EXPUNGE	FAILING	FARMERS	FEDORAS
ETHANOL	EXCIMER	EXSCIND	FAILURE	FARMING	FEEBLER
ETHERIC	EXCISED	EXTENTS	FAINTED	FARNESS	FEEDBAG
ETHICAL	EXCITED	EXTINCT	FAINTER	FARRAGO	FEEDERS
ETHMOID	EXCITER	EXTRACT	FAINTLY	FARRIER	FEEDING
ETHYLIC	EXCITON	EXTREME	FAIREST	FARTHER	FEEDLOT
ETRURIA	EXCITOR	EXTRUDE	FAIRIES	FARTING	FEELERS
EUBOEAN	EXCLAIM	EXUDING	FAIRING	FARTLEK	FEELING
EUCAINE	EXCLAVE	EXULTED	FAIRISH	FASCIAL	FEIGNED
EUGENIC	EXCLUDE	EXURBIA	FAIR SEX	FASCIAS	FEIGNER
EUGENOL	EXCRETA	EXUVIAE	FAIRWAY	FASCINE	FEINTED
EUGLENA	EXCRETE	EXUVIAL	FAJITAS	FASCISM	FELAFEL
EULOGIA	EXCUSAL	EX-WORKS	FALAFEL	FASCIST	FELINES
EUNUCHS	EXCUSED	EYEBALL	FALANGE	FASHION	FELLERS
EUPHONY	EXCUSES	EYEBATH	FALASHA	FASTEST	FELLING
EUPHROE	EXECUTE	EYEBOLT	FALBALA	FASTING	FELLOWS
EUPLOID	EXEGETE	EYEBROW	FALCATE	FATALLY	FELONRY
EUPNOEA	EXERGUE	EYELASH	FALCONS	FATBACK	FELSITE
EURASIA	EXERTED	EYELESS	FALKIRK	FAT CATS	FELSPAR
EURATOM	EXHALED	EYELETS	FALLACY	FATEFUL	FELTING
EURIPUS	EXHAUST	EYELIDS	FALL GUY	FATHEAD	FELUCCA
EUSTASY	EXHIBIT	EYESHOT	FALLING	FATHERS	FELWORT
EVACUEE	EXHUMED	EYESORE	FALLOUT	FATHOMS	FEMALES
EVADING	EXHUMER	EYESPOT	FALSELY	FATIGUE	FEMORAL
EVANGEL	EXIGENT	EYEWASH	FALSEST	FATLING	FENCERS
EVASION	EXILING		FALSIES	FATNESS	FENCING
EVASIVE	EXISTED	**F**	FALSIFY	FATSHAN	FENDERS
EVENING	EXITING	FABIANS	FALSITY	FATTEST	FENDING
EVEREST	EXMOUTH	FABRICS	FALSTER	FATTIER	FENLAND
EVERTOR	EXODERM	FACADES	FAMILLE	FATTIES	FERGANA
EVESHAM	EXOGAMY	FACEBAR	FAMINES	FATTILY	FERMATA
EVICTED	EXOTICA	FACE-OFF	FANATIC	FATTISH	FERMENT
EVICTOR	EXPANSE	FACIALS	FAN BELT	FATTISM	FERMION
EVIDENT	EX PARTE	FACINGS	FANCIED	FATUITY	FERMIUM
EVILEST	EXPENSE	FACTFUL	FANCIER	FATUOUS	FERNERY
EVIL EYE	EXPERTS	FACTION	FANCIES	FAUCETS	FERRARA
EVILLER	EXPIATE	FACTORS	FANCILY	FAULTED	FERRATE
EVINCED	EXPIRED	FACTORY	FAN CLUB	FAUVISM	FERRETS
EVOKING	EXPIRER	FACTUAL	FANFARE	FAUVIST	FERRETY
EVOLUTE	EXPLAIN	FACULAR	FANNIES	FAUX PAS	FERRIED
EVOLVED	EXPLANT	FACULTY	FANNING	FAVOURS	FERRIES
EVOLVER	EXPLODE	FADABLE	FANTAIL	FAVRILE	FERRITE
EWE-NECK	EXPLOIT	FADDISH	FANTAST	FAWNING	FERROUS
EXACTED	EXPLORE	FADDISM	FANTASY	FEARFUL	FERRULE
EXACTLY	EXPORTS	FADDIST	FANZINE	FEARING	FERTILE

FERVENT	FILBERT	FISH-EYE	FLAWING	FLOUNCE	FOGYISH
FERVOUR	FILCHED	FISHGIG	FLAYING	FLOURED	FOIBLES
FESTIVE	FILCHER	FISHIER	FLEABAG	FLOUTED	FOILING
FESTOON	FILETED	FISHING	FLEAPIT	FLOUTER	FOISTED
FETCHED	FILIATE	FISHNET	FLECKED	FLOWAGE	FOLACIN
FETCHER	FILIBEG	FISSILE	FLEECED	FLOWERS	FOLDERS
FETLOCK	FILINGS	FISSION	FLEECES	FLOWERY	FOLDING
FETTERS	FILLETS	FISSURE	FLEEING	FLOWING	FOLDOUT
FETUSES	FILLIES	FISTULA	FLEETER	FLUENCY	FOLIAGE
FEUDING	FILLING	FITMENT	FLEMING	FLUFFED	FOLIATE
FEVERED	FILL-INS	FITNESS	FLEMISH	FLUIDAL	FOLIOSE
FEWNESS	FILLIPS	FITTERS	FLENSER	FLUIDIC	FOLKISH
FEYNESS	FILMIER	FITTEST	FLESHED	FLUMMOX	FOLLIES
FIANCES	FILMILY	FITTING	FLESHER	FLUNKED	FONDANT
FIASCOS	FILMING	FIXABLE	FLESHES	FLUNKEY	FONDEST
FIBBERS	FILMSET	FIXATED	FLESHLY	FLUORIC	FONDLED
FIBBING	FILTERS	FIXEDLY	FLEURON	FLUSHED	FONDLER
FIBROID	FIMBRIA	FIXTURE	FLEXILE	FLUSHER	FONDUES
FIBROIN	FINABLE	FIZZIER	FLEXING	FLUSHES	FOOCHOW
FIBROMA	FINAGLE	FIZZING	FLEXION	FLUSTER	FOODIES
FIBROUS	FINALES	FLACCID	FLEXURE	FLUTING	FOOLERY
FIBULAE	FINALLY	FLAG DAY	FLICKED	FLUTIST	FOOLING
FIBULAR	FINANCE	FLAGGED	FLICKER	FLUTTER	FOOLISH
FIBULAS	FINBACK	FLAGGER	FLIGHTS	FLUVIAL	FOOTAGE
FICTILE	FINCHES	FLAGMAN	FLIGHTY	FLUXION	FOOTBOY
FICTION	FINDING	FLAGONS	FLINGER	FLYABLE	FOOTING
FIDDLED	FINE ART	FLAILED	FLIPPED	FLYAWAY	FOOTMAN
FIDDLER	FINE-CUT	FLAKIER	FLIPPER	FLYBACK	FOOTMEN
FIDDLES	FINESSE	FLAKING	FLIRTED	FLYBLOW	FOOTPAD
FIDEISM	FINFOOT	FLAMING	FLIRTER	FLYBOAT	FOOTSIE
FIDEIST	FINGERS	FLANEUR	FLITTED	FLYBOOK	FOOT-TON
FIDGETS	FINICKY	FLANGER	FLITTER	FLY-FISH	FOOTWAY
FIDGETY	FININGS	FLANGES	FLIVVER	FLY HALF	FOOZLER
FIELDED	FINLAND	FLANKED	FLOATED	FLYLEAF	FOPPERY
FIELDER	FINNING	FLANKER	FLOATEL	FLYOVER	FOPPISH
FIERCER	FINNISH	FLANNEL	FLOATER	FLYPAST	FORAGED
FIERIER	FIREARM	FLAPPED	FLOCCUS	FLYTRAP	FORAGER
FIESOLE	FIREBOX	FLAPPER	FLOCKED	FOALING	FORAGES
FIESTAS	FIREBUG	FLARE-UP	FLOGGED	FOAMIER	FORAMEN
FIFTEEN	FIREDOG	FLARING	FLOGGER	FOAMING	FORAYED
FIFTIES	FIREFLY	FLASHED	FLOODED	FOBBING	FORAYER
FIGHTER	FIREMAN	FLASHER	FLOODER	FO'C'SLE	FORBADE
FIG LEAF	FIREMEN	FLASHES	FLOORED	S	FORBEAR
FIGMENT	FIREPAN	FLASKET	FLOPPED	FOCUSED	FORBORE
FIG TREE	FIRMEST	FLAT-BED	FLORIDA	FOCUSER	FORCEPS
FIGURAL	FIRMING	FLATLET	FLORINS	FOCUSES	FORCING
FIGURED	FIRSTLY	FLATTEN	FLORIST	FOGGIER	FORDING
FIGURER	FIRTREE	FLATTER	FLORUIT	FOGGILY	FOREARM
FIGURES	FISCALS	FLAUNCH	FLOSSED	FOGGING	FOREGUT
FIGWORT	FISCHER	FLAVONE	FLOTAGE	FOGHORN	FOREIGN
FILARIA	FISHERY	FLAVOUR	FLOTSAM	FOG LAMP	FORELEG

FOREMAN	FOXHOLE	FRIEDAN	FUKUOKA	FUTTOCK	GAMBLER
FOREMEN	FOXHUNT	FRIENDS	FULCRUM	FUTURES	GAMBOGE
FOREPAW	FOXIEST	FRIEZES	FULGENT	FUZZIER	GAMBOLS
FORERUN	FOXLIKE	FRIGATE	FULLEST	FUZZILY	GAMBREL
FORESAW	FOXTAIL	FRIGHTS	FULMARS	FUZZING	GAMELAN
FORESEE	FOXTROT	FRILLED	FULNESS	FYZABAD	GAMETAL
FORESTS	FRACTAL	FRINGED	FULSOME		GAMIEST
FORETOP	FRACTUS	FRINGES	FULVOUS	**G**	GANDERS
FOREVER	FRAENUM	FRISBEE	FUMARIC	GABBING	GANDZHA
FORFEIT	FRAGILE	FRISEUR	FUMBLED	GABBLED	GANGERS
FORGAVE	FRAILER	FRISIAN	FUMBLER	GABBLER	GANGING
FORGERS	FRAILTY	FRISKED	FUMBLES	GABFEST	GANGTOK
FORGERY	FRAKTUR	FRISKER	FUNCHAL	GADDING	GANGWAY
FORGING	FRAME UP	FRISKET	FUNDING	GADGETS	GANNETS
FORGIVE	FRAME-UP	FRISSON	FUNERAL	GADGETY	GANTLET
FORGOER	FRAMING	FRITTER	FUNFAIR	GADROON	GAOLERS
FORGONE	FRANCIS	FRIZZED	FUNGOID	GADWALL	GAOLING
FORKFUL	FRANKED	FRIZZER	FUNGOUS	GAFFERS	GAPPING
FORKING	FRANKER	FRIZZLE	FUNICLE	GAGAUZI	GAP YEAR
FORLORN	FRANKLY	FROEBEL	FUNKIER	GAGGING	GARAGED
FORMANT	FRANTIC	FROG-BIT	FUNKING	GAHNITE	GARAGES
FORMATE	FRAPPES	FROGMAN	FUNNELS	GAINERS	GARBAGE
FORMATS	FRAUGHT	FROGMEN	FUNNIER	GAINFUL	GARBING
FORMICA	FRAYING	FROLICS	FUNNILY	GAINING	GARBLED
FORMING	FRAZIER	FRONDED	FUN RUNS	GAINSAY	GARBLER
FORMOSA	FRAZZLE	FRONTAL	FUNSTER	GAITERS	GARCONS
FORMULA	FREAKED	FRONTED	FURBISH	GALATEA	GARDENS
FORSAKE	FRECKLE	FROSTED	FURCATE	GALEATE	GARFISH
FORSOOK	FREEBIE	FROTHED	FURCULA	GALENIC	GARGETY
FORSYTH	FREEDOM	FROWARD	FURIOSO	GALICIA	GARGLED
FORTIES	FREEING	FROWNED	FURIOUS	GALILEE	GARGLER
FORTIFY	FREEMAN	FROWNER	FURLING	GALIPOT	GARGLES
FORTUNE	FREEMEN	FROWSTY	FURLONG	GALLANT	GARLAND
FORWARD	FREESIA	FRUITED	FURNACE	GALLEON	GARMENT
FORWENT	FREEWAY	FRUITER	FURNESS	GALLERY	GARNETS
FOSSILS	FREEZER	FRUSTUM	FURNISH	GALLEYS	GARNISH
FOUETTE	FREIGHT	FUCHSIA	FURRIER	GALLFLY	GARONNE
FOULARD	FREMONT	FUCHSIN	FURRING	GALLING	GARPIKE
FOULEST	FRESCOS	FUCK ALL	FURROWS	GALLIUM	GARRETS
FOULING	FRESHEN	FUCKERS	FURROWY	GALLNUT	GARTERS
FOUL-UPS	FRESHER	FUCKING	FURTHER	GALLONS	GASBAGS
FOUNDED	FRESHET	FUCK-UPS	FURTIVE	GALLOON	GASCONY
FOUNDER	FRESHLY	FUDDLED	FUSCOUS	GALLOPS	GASEOUS
FOUNDRY	FRESNEL	FUDDLES	FUSIBLE	GALLOUS	GASHING
FOURIER	FRETFUL	FUDGING	FUSILLI	GALLOWS	GASKETS
FOURTHS	FRETSAW	FUEGIAN	FUSSIER	GALUMPH	GAS MAIN
FOUR-WAY	FRETTED	FUELING	FUSSILY	GAMBADO	GAS MASK
FOVEATE	FRIABLE	FUELLED	FUSSING	GAMBIAN	GASOHOL
FOVEOLA	FRIBBLE	FUELLER	FUSSPOT	GAMBIER	GASPING
FOWLING	FRIDAYS	FUENTES	FUSTIAN	GAMBITS	GAS PIPE
FOXFIRE	FRIDGES	FUGGIER	FUSTIER	GAMBLED	GASSIER

GASSING	GENTILE	GINSENG	GLOBOID	GODSEND	GRAINER
GASTRIC	GENUINE	GIN TRAP	GLOBOSE	GOGGLED	GRAMMAR
GASTRIN	GEODESY	GIPSIES	GLOBULE	GOGGLES	GRAMMES
GATEAUX	GEOLOGY	GIRAFFE	GLORIED	GOIANIA	GRAMPUS
GATE-LEG	GEORDIE	GIRASOL	GLORIES	GO-KARTS	GRANADA
GATEWAY	GEORGIA	GIRDERS	GLORIFY	GOLDEYE	GRANARY
GATHERS	GEORGIC	GIRDING	GLOSSAL	GOLFERS	GRANDAD
GAUCHOS	GERBILS	GIRDLED	GLOSSED	GOLFING	GRANDEE
GAUDERY	GERENUK	GIRDLER	GLOSSER	GOLIATH	GRANDER
GAUDIER	GERMANE	GIRDLES	GLOTTAL	GONADAL	GRANDLY
GAUDILY	GERMANS	GIRLISH	GLOTTIC	GONDOLA	GRANDMA
GAUGING	GERMANY	GIRONDE	GLOTTIS	GOODBYE	GRANDPA
GAUHATI	GERUNDS	GIRONNY	GLOWING	GOOD DAY	GRANGES
GAUTENG	GESTALT	GISARME	GLUCOSE	GOODIES	GRANITE
GAUZIER	GESTAPO	GITTERN	GLUE EAR	GOODISH	GRANOLA
GAVOTTE	GESTATE	GIVABLE	GLUEING	GOOFIER	GRANTED
GAWKERS	GESTURE	GIZZARD	GLUMMER	GOOFILY	GRANTEE
GAWKIER	GETABLE	GLACIAL	GLUTEAL	GOOFING	GRANTER
GAWKING	GETAWAY	GLACIER	GLUTEUS	GOOIEST	GRANTOR
GAWPING	GETTING	GLADDEN	GLUTTED	GOPHERS	GRANULE
GAYNESS	GEYSERS	GLADDER	GLUTTON	GORGING	GRAPHIC
GAZEBOS	GHASTLY	GLADDON	GLYCINE	GORGONS	GRAPNEL
GAZELLE	GHAZALI	GLAD EYE	GLYPHIC	GORIEST	GRAPPLE
GAZETTE	GHERKIN	GLAMOUR	GLYPTIC	GORILLA	GRASPED
GEARBOX	GHETTOS	GLANCED	GNARLED	GORIZIA	GRASPER
GEARING	GHILLIE	GLANCES	GNASHED	GOSHAWK	GRASSED
GECKOES	GHOSTED	GLARING	GNASHES	GOSLING	GRASSES
GEE-GEES	GHOSTLY	GLASGOW	GNATHIC	GO-SLOWS	GRASS UP
GEELONG	GIBBETS	GLASSED	GNAWING	GOSPELS	GRATERS
GEEZERS	GIBBING	GLASSES	GNOCCHI	GOSPLAN	GRATIFY
GEISHAS	GIBBONS	GLAZIER	GNOMISH	GOSPORT	GRATING
GELATIN	GIBBOUS	GLAZING	GNOSTIC	GOSSIPS	GRAUPEL
GELDING	GIBLETS	GLEAMED	GOADING	GOSSIPY	GRAVELY
GELLING	GIDDIER	GLEANED	GO-AHEAD	GOTLAND	GRAVEST
GEMMATE	GIDDILY	GLEANER	GOATEED	GOUACHE	GRAVITY
GEMMING	GIESSEN	GLEEFUL	GOATEES	GOUGING	GRAVLAX
GEMMULE	GIGGLED	GLENCOE	GOBBETS	GOULASH	GRAVURE
GEMSBOK	GIGGLER	GLENOID	GOBBLED	GOURAMI	GRAYEST
GENAPPE	GIGGLES	GLIADIN	GOBBLER	GOURMET	GRAYING
GENDERS	GIG LAMP	GLIBBER	GOBBLES	GRAB BAG	GRAZIER
GENERAL	GIGOLOS	GLIDERS	GOBELIN	GRABBED	GRAZING
GENERIC	GILBERT	GLIDING	GOBIOID	GRABBER	GREASED
GENESIS	GILDING	GLIMMER	GOBLETS	GRABBLE	GREASER
GENETIC	GILLIES	GLIMPSE	GOBLINS	GRACILE	GREATER
GENEVAN	GIMBALS	GLINTED	GODDAMN	GRACING	GREATLY
GENIPAP	GIMLETS	GLISTEN	GODDESS	GRACKLE	GREAVES
GENITAL	GIMMICK	GLITTER	GODHEAD	GRADATE	GRECIAN
GENITOR	GINGERY	GLIWICE	GODHOOD	GRADING	GREENED
GENOESE	GINGHAM	GLOATED	GODLESS	GRADUAL	GREENER
GENTEEL	GINGILI	GLOATER	GODLIER	GRAFTED	GREENIE
GENTIAN	GINGIVA	GLOBATE	GODLIKE	GRAFTER	GREETED

GREETER	GROSSES	GUISING	GYPSIES	HALIBUT	HANKIES
GREISEN	GROSSLY	GUITARS	GYRATED	HALIDOM	HANOVER
GREMIAL	GROTTOS	GUIYANG	GYRATOR	HALIFAX	HANSARD
GREMLIN	GROUCHY	GUIZHOU		HALLWAY	HANSOMS
GRENADA	GROUNDS	GUJARAT	**H**	HALOGEN	HANUMAN
GRENADE	GROUPED	GULCHES	HAARLEM	HALTERE	HANYANG
GREYEST	GROUPER	GULDENS	HABDABS	HALTERS	HA'PENNY
GREYHEN	GROUPIE	GULLETS	HABITAT	HALTING	HAPLESS
GREYING	GROUSED	GULLIES	HABITED	HALVING	HAPLITE
GREYISH	GROUSER	GULLING	HABITUE	HALYARD	HAPLOID
GREYLAG	GROUSES	GULPING	HABITUS	HAMADAN	HAP'ORTH
GRIBBLE	GROUTER	GUMBOIL	HACHURE	HAMBURG	HAPPIER
GRIDDLE	GROWERS	GUMBOOT	HACKBUT	HAMELIN	HAPPILY
GRIEVED	GROWING	GUMDROP	HACKERS	HAMHUNG	HAPTENE
GRIEVER	GROWLED	GUMMIER	HACKING	HAMITIC	HARAPPA
GRIFFIN	GROWLER	GUMMING	HACKLER	HAMLETS	HARBOUR
GRIFFON	GROWN-UP	GUMMITE	HACKLES	HAMMERS	HARDEST
GRILLED	GROWTHS	GUMSHOE	HACKNEY	HAMMING	HARDIER
GRILLER	GROYNES	GUM TREE	HACKSAW	HAMMOCK	HARDILY
GRILLES	GRUBBED	GUNBOAT	HADAWAY	HAMMOND	HARDING
GRIMACE	GRUBBER	GUNDOGS	HADDOCK	HAMPDEN	HARD NUT
GRIMIER	GRUDGED	GUNFIRE	HADRIAN	HAMPERS	HARD-ONS
GRIMMER	GRUDGER	GUNLOCK	HAEMOID	HAMPTON	HARD PAD
GRIMSBY	GRUDGES	GUNNELS	HAFNIUM	HAMSTER	HARDPAN
GRINDER	GRUFFER	GUNNERS	HAGFISH	HAMULAR	HARDTOP
GRINGOS	GRUFFLY	GUNNERY	HAGGARD	HAMULUS	HARELIP
GRINNED	GRUMBLE	GUNNING	HAGGISH	HANAPER	HARICOT
GRINNER	GRUMOUS	GUNSHOT	HAGGLED	HANCOCK	HARIJAN
GRIPERS	GRUNTED	GUNWALE	HAGGLER	HANDBAG	HARKING
GRIPING	GRUNTER	GURGLED	HAGLIKE	HANDFUL	HARLECH
GRIPPED	GRUYERE	GURNARD	HAHNIUM	HANDGUN	HARLOTS
GRIPPER	GRYPHON	GUSHERS	HAILING	HANDIER	HARMFUL
GRISTLE	G-STRING	GUSHING	HAINAUT	HANDILY	HARMING
GRISTLY	GUANACO	GUSSETS	HAIRCUT	HANDING	HARMONY
GRITTED	GUANASE	GUSTIER	HAIRDOS	HANDLED	HARNESS
GRIZZLE	GUANINE	GUSTILY	HAIRIER	HANDLER	HARPIES
GRIZZLY	GUARANI	GUSTING	HAIRNET	HANDLES	HARPING
GROANED	GUARDED	GUTLESS	HAIRPIN	HANDOUT	HARPINS
GROANER	GUARDER	GUTSIER	HAITIAN	HANDSAW	HARPIST
GROCERS	GUAYULE	GUTTATE	HAITINK	HANDSEL	HARPOON
GROCERY	GUDGEON	GUTTERS	HAKLUYT	HANDSET	HARRIED
GROGRAM	GUESSED	GUTTING	HALAKAH	HANDS-ON	HARRIER
GROLIER	GUESSER	GUVNORS	HALAKIC	HANDS UP	HARROWS
GROMMET	GUESSES	GUZZLED	HALAVAH	HANGARS	HARSHER
GROOMED	GUESTED	GUZZLER	HALBERD	HANGDOG	HARSHLY
GROOMER	GUFFAWS	GWALIOR	HALCYON	HANGERS	HARSLET
GROOVED	GUIDING	GWYNEDD	HALDANE	HANGING	HARTLEY
GROOVES	GUILDER	GWYNIAD	HALF-CUT	HANGMAN	HARVARD
GROPING	GUINEAN	GYMNAST	HALFWAY	HANGMEN	HARVEST
GROSSED	GUINEAS	GYMSLIP	HALF WIT	HANGOUT	HARWICH
GROSSER	GUIPURE	GYPPING	HALF-WIT	HANG-UPS	HARYANA

HAS BEEN	HAZIEST	HEINOUS	HERNIAS	HIPLIKE	HOGLIKE
HAS-BEEN	HAZLITT	HEIRDOM	HEROICS	HIPPEST	HOGNOSE
HASHING	HEADERS	HEIRESS	HEROINE	HIPPIES	HOGWASH
HASHISH	HEADIER	HEISTER	HEROISM	HIPSTER	HOGWEED
HASIDIC	HEADILY	HEITIKI	HERONRY	HIRABLE	HOISTED
HASIDIM	HEADING	HELICAL	HERRICK	HIRCINE	HOISTER
HASSELT	HEADMAN	HELICES	HERRING	HIRSUTE	HOKONUI
HASSIUM	HEADMEN	HELICON	HERSELF	HIRUDIN	HOKUSAI
HASSLED	HEADPIN	HELIPAD	HERTZOG	HIS NIBS	HOLDALL
HASSLES	HEADSET	HELLBOX	HESIONE	HISSING	HOLDERS
HASSOCK	HEADWAY	HELLCAT	HESSIAN	HISTOID	HOLDING
HASTATE	HEALERS	HELLENE	HESSITE	HISTONE	HOLD OUT
HASTIER	HEALING	HELLERY	HETAERA	HISTORY	HOLDUPS
HASTILY	HEALTHS	HELLION	HETAIRA	HITACHI	HOLIBUT
HATBAND	HEALTHY	HELLISH	HEXADIC	HITCHED	HOLIDAY
HATCHED	HEAPING	HELLUVA	HEXAGON	HITCHER	HOLIEST
HATCHEL	HEARING	HELMAND	HEXAPLA	HITCHES	HOLLAND
HATCHER	HEARKEN	HELMETS	HEXAPOD	HIT LIST	HOLLERS
HATCHES	HEARSAY	HELOISE	HEXOSAN	HITTING	HOLLOWS
HATCHET	HEARSES	HELOTRY	HEYDUCK	HITTITE	HOLMIUM
HATEFUL	HEARTEN	HELPFUL	HEYSHAM	HOARDED	HOLSTER
HATLESS	HEARTHS	HELPING	HEYWOOD	HOARDER	HOLY SEE
HATLIKE	HEATERS	HEMIOLA	HIALEAH	HOARIER	HOMBURG
HATPINS	HEATHEN	HEMIPOD	HIBACHI	HOARILY	HOMERIC
HATTERS	HEATHER	HEMLINE	HICCUPS	HOARSEN	HOME RUN
HAUBERK	HEATING	HEMLOCK	HICKORY	HOARSER	HOMIEST
HAUGHTY	HEAVENS	HEMMING	HIDABLE	HOATZIN	HOMINID
HAULAGE	HEAVIER	HENBANE	HIDALGO	HOAXERS	HOMOLOG
HAULIER	HEAVIES	HENCOOP	HIDEOUS	HOAXING	HOMONYM
HAULING	HEAVILY	HEN COOP	HIDINGS	HOBBEMA	HONESTY
HAUNTED	HEAVING	HENDRIX	HIELAND	HOBBIES	HONEYED
HAUNTER	HEBETIC	HENGELO	HIGHBOY	HOBBISM	HONIARA
HAURAKI	HEBRAIC	HENGIST	HIGHEST	HOBBIST	HONITON
HAUTBOY	HEBREWS	HENNERY	HIGH HAT	HOBBLED	HONKIES
HAUTEUR	HECKLED	HENPECK	HIGH TEA	HOBBLER	HONKING
HAVE-A-	HECKLER	HEPARIN	HIGHWAY	HOBLIKE	HONOURS
GO	HECTARE	HEPATIC	HIJACKS	HOBNAIL	HOODLUM
HAWKBIT	HEDGING	HEPBURN	HILBERT	HOBOISM	HOODOOS
HAWKERS	HEDONIC	HEPTANE	HILLARY	HOBOKEN	HOOGHLY
HAWKING	HEEDFUL	HEPTOSE	HILLERY	HOCKING	HOOKAHS
HAWKINS	HEEDING	HERALDS	HILLIER	HOCKNEY	HOOKERS
HAWKISH	HEELING	HERBAGE	HILLMAN	HODEIDA	HOOKIES
HAWORTH	HEELTAP	HERBALS	HILLOCK	HODGKIN	HOOKING
HAWSERS	HEERLEN	HERBERT	HIMSELF	HOEDOWN	HOOKUPS
HAYCOCK	HEFTIER	HERDING	HINDGUT	HOELIKE	HOORAYS
HAYFORK	HEFTILY	HEREDES	HINGING	HOFFMAN	HOOTERS
HAYRACK	HEGUMEN	HERETIC	HINTING	HOGARTH	HOOTING
HAYSEED	HEIFERS	HERISAU	HIONATE	HOGBACK	HOOVERS
HAYWARD	HEIFETZ	HERITOR	HIPBATH	HOGFISH	HOPEFUL
HAYWIRE	HEIGH-HO	HERMITS	HIPBONE	HOGGING	HOPHEAD
HAZARDS	HEIGHTS	HERNIAL	HIPLESS	HOGGISH	HOPKINS

HOPLITE	HOVERER	HURDLED	ICEBALL	IMPACTS	INCOMES
HOPPERS	HOWBEIT	HURDLER	ICEBERG	IMPALAS	INCROSS
HOPPING	HOWDAHS	HURDLES	ICE CAPS	IMPALED	INCUBUS
HOPPLER	HOWEVER	HURLING	ICE-COLD	IMPALER	INCURVE
HOPSACK	HOWLAND	HURRAYS	ICEFALL	IMPANEL	INDENTS
HORDEIN	HOWLERS	HURRIED	ICELAND	IMPASSE	IN DEPTH
HORDERN	HOWLING	HURTFUL	ICE PACK	IMPASTE	IN-DEPTH
HORIZON	HOYDENS	HURTING	ICE PICK	IMPASTO	INDEXED
HORMONE	HOYLAKE	HURTLED	ICE RINK	IMPEACH	INDEXER
HORNETS	HSIA-MEN	HUSBAND	ICHNITE	IMPEDED	INDEXES
HORNIER	HSINING	HUSHABY	ICICLED	IMPEDER	INDIANA
HORNILY	HSU-CHOU	HUSHING	ICICLES	IMPERIL	INDIANS
HORRIFY	HUAINAN	HUSKIER	ICINESS	IMPETUS	INDICAN
HORRORS	HUAI-NAN	HUSKIES	ICTERIC	IMPIETY	INDICIA
HORSENS	HUBBIES	HUSKILY	ICTERUS	IMPINGE	INDOORS
HORSIER	HUBCAPS	HUSSARS	ID CARDS	IMPIOUS	INDORSE
HORSILY	HUDDLED	HUSSEIN	IDEALLY	IMPLANT	INDOXYL
HOSANNA	HUDDLER	HUSSIES	IDEATUM	IMPLEAD	INDRAWN
HOSIERS	HUDDLES	HUSSISM	IDENTIC	IMPLIED	INDUCED
HOSIERY	HUFFIER	HUSSITE	IDIOTIC	IMPLODE	INDUCER
HOSPICE	HUFFILY	HUSTLED	IDOLIZE	IMPLORE	INDULGE
HOSTAGE	HUFFING	HUSTLER	IDYLLIC	IMPORTS	INEPTLY
HOSTELS	HUFFISH	HUTCHES	IGNEOUS	IMPOSED	INERTIA
HOSTESS	HUGGING	HUTCHIE	IGNITED	IMPOSER	INCRTLY
HOSTILE	HUHEHOT	HUTLIKE	IGNITER	IMPOUND	INEXACT
HOSTING	HULKING	HUTMENT	IGNOBLE	IMPRESA	INFANCY
HOSTLER	HULLING	HUYGENS	IGNOBLY	IMPRESS	INFANTA
HOTBEDS	HUMANLY	HWANG HO	IGNORED	IMPREST	INFANTE
HOT DOGS	HUMBLED	HYAENAS	IGNORER	IMPRINT	INFANTS
HOTFOOT	HUMBLER	HYAENIC	IGUANAS	IMPROVE	INFARCT
HOTHEAD	HUMBUGS	HYALINE	IKEBANA	IMPULSE	INFERNO
HOTLINE	HUMDRUM	HYALITE	ILEITIS	IMPUTED	INFIDEL
HOT LINE	HUMERAL	HYALOID	ILL-BRED	IMPUTER	INFIELD
HOT LINK	HUMERUS	HYBRIDS	ILLEGAL	INANELY	INFLAME
HOTNESS	HUMIDLY	HYDATID	ILLICIT	INANITY	INFLATE
HOTPOTS	HUMIDOR	HYDRANT	ILLNESS	INAPTLY	INFLECT
HOT RODS	HUMMING	HYDRATE	ILL WILL	IN A	INFLICT
HOT SEAT	HUMMOCK	HYDRIDE	IMAGERY	WORD	INFLOWS
HOT SPOT	HUMORAL	HYDROID	IMAGINE	INBOARD	INFRACT
HOTSPUR	HUMOURS	HYGIENE	IMAGISM	INBOUND	INFUSED
HOTTEST	HUMPING	HYMNALS	IMAGIST	INBREED	INFUSER
HOTTING	HUNCHED	HYMNING	IMAMATE	INCENSE	INGENUE
HOUDINI	HUNCHES	HYPED UP	IMBIBED	INCHING	INGESTA
HOUMOUS	HUNDRED	HYPHENS	IMBIBER	INCIPIT	INGOING
HOUNDED	HUNGARY	HYPONYM	IMBRUTE	INCISED	INGRAIN
HOUNDER	HUNGNAM		IMBUING	INCISOR	INGRATE
HOUSING	HUNKERS	**I**	IMITATE	INCITED	INGRESS
HOUSMAN	HUNLIKE	IAMBICS	IMMENSE	INCITER	IN-GROUP
HOUSTON	HUNNISH	IAPETUS	IMMERSE	INCLINE	INGROWN
HOUTING	HUNTERS	IBERIAN	IMMORAL	INCLOSE	INHABIT
HOVERED	HUNTING	ICE AGES	IMMURED	INCLUDE	INHALED

INHALER	INTERNS	ISOCHOR	JAMAICA	JIBBING	JOTTERS
INHERIT	INTIMAL	ISOGAMY	JAMES II	JIGGERS	JOTTING
INHIBIT	INTONED	ISOGENY	JAMMIER	JIGGING	JOURNAL
IN-HOUSE	INTONER	ISOHYET	JAMMING	JIGGLED	JOURNEY
INHUMAN	INTROIT	ISOLATE	JANGLED	JIGGLES	JOURNOS
INHUMER	INTRUDE	ISOLINE	JANGLER	JIGSAWS	JOUSTED
INITIAL	INTRUST	ISONOMY	JANITOR	JILTING	JOUSTER
INJURED	INURING	ISOTONE	JANUARY	JIM CROW	JOYLESS
INJURER	INUTILE	ISOTOPE	JARGONS	JIMJAMS	JOYRIDE
INKATHA	IN VACUO	ISOTOPY	JARRING	JIMMIES	JUBILEE
INKIEST	INVADED	ISOTRON	JASMINE	JINGLED	JUDAEAN
INKLING	INVADER	ISRAELI	JAUNTED	JINGLER	JUDAICA
INKPADS	INVALID	ISSUING	JAVELIN	JINGLES	JUDAISM
INKWELL	INVEIGH	ISTHMUS	JAWBONE	JINXING	JUDAIST
INLAYER	INVERSE	ISTRIAN	JAYWALK	JINZHOU	JUDAIZE
INMATES	INVITED	ITALIAN	JAZZIER	JITTERS	JUDASES
INNARDS	INVITER	ITALICS	JAZZILY	JITTERY	JUDGING
INNERVE	IN VITRO	ITCHIER	JAZZING	JOBBERS	JUDOIST
INNINGS	INVOICE	ITCHING	JEALOUS	JOBBERY	JUGGING
IN ORDER	INVOKED	ITEMIZE	JEERING	JOBBING	JUGGLED
INQUEST	INVOKER	ITERANT	JEHOVAH	JOBCLUB	JUGGLER
INQUIET	INVOLVE	ITERATE	JEJUNAL	JOBLESS	JUGULAR
INQUIRE	INWARDS	ITHACAN	JEJUNUM	JOB LOTS	JUICIER
INQUIRY	INWEAVE	IVANOVO	JELLABA	JOCKEYS	JUICILY
INROADS	IODIZER	IVORIAN	JELLIED	JOCULAR	JUICING
INSECTS	IONIZED	IVORIES	JELLIES	JODHPUR	JUJITSU
INSERTS	IONIZER	IZHEVSK	JELLIFY	JOGGING	JUJUBES
INSHORE	IPOMOEA		JELLING	JOGGLED	JUKEBOX
INSIDER	IPSWICH	**J**	JEMMIED	JOGGLER	JUMBLED
INSIDES	IQUIQUE	JABBING	JEMMIES	JOGGLES	JUMBLER
INSIGHT	IQUITOS	JACAMAR	JENNIES	JOG TROT	JUMBLES
INSIPID	IRANIAN	JACKALS	JERICHO	JOHN DOE	JUMPERS
INSOFAR	IRATELY	JACKASS	JERKIER	JOHNSON	JUMPIER
INSOLES	IRELAND	JACKDAW	JERKILY	JOINDER	JUMPILY
INSPECT	IRENICS	JACKETS	JERKING	JOINERS	JUMPING
INSPIRE	IRIDIUM	JACKING	JERKINS	JOINERY	JUMP-OFF
INSTALL	IRKSOME	JACKPOT	JERK OFF	JOINING	JUNDIAI
INSTANT	IRKUTSK	JACKSON	JERSEYS	JOINTED	JUNGIAN
INSTATE	IRON AGE	JACK TAR	JESTERS	JOINTER	JUNGLES
INSTEAD	IRONIES	JACOBIN	JESTING	JOINTLY	JUNIORS
INSTEPS	IRONING	JACONET	JESUITS	JOLLIED	JUNIPER
INSULAR	IRONIST	JACUZZI	JETFOIL	JOLLIER	JUNKETS
INSULIN	IRON ORE	JADEITE	JETPORT	JOLLIFY	JUNKIES
INSULTS	ISAGOGE	JAGGERY	JETTIES	JOLLILY	JUNKING
INSURED	ISCHIAL	JAGGING	JETTING	JOLLITY	JUPITER
INSURER	ISCHIUM	JAGUARS	JEWFISH	JOLTING	JURISTS
INSWING	ISFAHAN	JAILERS	JEW'S-	JONESES	JURY BOX
INTAKES	ISLAMIC	JAILING	EAR	JONQUIL	JURYMAN
INTEGER	ISLANDS	JAKARTA	JEZEBEL	JOSHING	JUSSIVE
INTENSE	ISOBARS	JALAPIC	JIANGSU	JOSTLED	JUSTICE
INTERIM	ISOBATH	JALISCO	JIANGXI	JOSTLER	JUSTIFY

JUTLAND	KERBING	KINGPIN	KOKANEE	LADDERS	LAPSING
JUTTING	KERNELS	KINKIER	KOKOBEH	LADDIES	LAPWING
	KERNITE	KINKILY	KOLDING	LADDISH	LARCENY
K	KESTREL	KINNOCK	KOLKHOZ	LADINGS	LARCHES
KABADDI	KESWICK	KINSHIP	KOLOMNA	LADLING	LARDERS
KAFFIRS	KETCHES	KINSMAN	KONGONI	LAGGARD	LARDING
KAFTANS	KETCHUP	KINSMEN	KOOKIER	LAGGING	LARGELY
KAIFENG	KETONIC	KIPPERS	KOONING	LAGOONS	LARGESS
KAINITE	KETOSIS	KIPPING	KOPECKS	LAICISM	LARGEST
KAISERS	KETTLES	KIRGHIZ	KOPEISK	LAICIZE	LARGISH
KALENDS	KEYED UP	KIRUNDI	KOUPREY	LALLANS	LARIATS
KALININ	KEYHOLE	KISSERS	KOWLOON	LAMAISM	LARKING
KALMUCK	KEYNOTE	KISSING	KREFELD	LAMAIST	LARWOOD
KAMPALA	KEY RING	KIT BAGS	KREMLIN	LAMBADA	LASAGNA
KANANGA	KHADDAR	KITCHEN	KRISHNA	LAMBAST	LASAGNE
KANNADA	KHAKASS	KITSCHY	KRYPTON	LAMBENT	LA SALLE
KANTIAN	KHALIFS	KITTENS	KUBELIK	LAMBERT	LA SCALA
KAOLACK	KHALKHA	KITTIES	KUBRICK	LAMBETH	LASCAUX
KAPITZA	KHAMSIN	KITTING	KUCHING	LAMBING	LASHING
KARACHI	KHANATE	KLAXONS	KUMAYRI	LAMELLA	LASH OUT
KARAKUL	KHARKOV	KLEENEX	KUMQUAT	LAMENTS	LASH-UPS
KARBALA	KHERSON	KNAPPER	KUNDERA	LAMINAR	LASSOED
KARELIA	KHINGAN	KNAVERY	KUNMING	LAMPERN	LASSOER
KAROSHI	KHOISAN	KNAVISH	KUNZITE	LAMPOON	LAST END
KARSTIC	KIANGSI	KNEADED	KURDISH	LAMPREY	LASTING
KASHGAR	KIANGSU	KNEADER	KUTAISI	LANCERS	LATAKIA
KASHMIR	KIBBUTZ	KNEECAP	KUWAITI	LANCETS	LATCHED
KASSALA	KICKING	KNEEING	KWANGJU	LANCHOW	LATCHES
KATANGA	KICKOFF	KNEELED	KWAZULU	LANCING	LATCHET
KATSINA	KICK OFF	KNEEPAD	KWEILIN	LANDAUS	LATENCY
KATYDID	KIDDERS	KNEES UP	KYANIZE	LANDING	LATERAL
KAYAKER	KIDDIES	KNIFING		LANDTAG	LATHERY
KAYSERI	KIDDING	KNIGHTS	**L**	LANGRES	LATIMER
KEATING	KIDNEYS	KNITTED	LABELED	LANGUID	LATRINE
KEELING	KIDSKIN	KNITTER	LABIALS	LANGUOR	LATTICE
KEELSON	KILDARE	KNOBBLY	LABIATE	LANIARY	LATVIAN
KEENEST	KILLERS	KNOCKED	LABOURS	LANKEST	LAUDING
KEENING	KILLICK	KNOCKER	LABROID	LANKIER	LAUGHED
KEEPERS	KILLING	KNOCK-ON	LACIEST	LANKILY	LAUGHER
KEEPING	KILLJOY	KNOCK-UP	LACKEYS	LANOLIN	LAUNDER
KEEPNET	KILOTON	KNOSSOS	LACKING	LANSING	LAUNDRY
KEITLOA	KILTERS	KNOTTED	LACONIC	LANTANA	LAURELS
KELVINS	KIMONOS	KNOTTER	LACQUER	LANTERN	LAWLESS
KENDREW	KINDEST	KNOW-ALL	LACTASE	LANYARD	LAW LORD
KENNEDY	KINDLED	KNOW-HOW	LACTATE	LAOTIAN	LAWSUIT
KENNELS	KINDLER	KNOWING	LACTEAL	LA PALMA	LAWYERS
KENNING	KINDRED	KNUCKLE	LACTONE	LAPDOGS	LAXNESS
KENOSIS	KINETIC	KNUCKLY	LACTOSE	LAPLACE	LAYERED
KENOTIC	KINFOLK	KOBARID	LACUNAE	LAPLAND	LAYETTE
KENTISH	KINGCUP	KOBLENZ	LACUNAR	LA PLATA	LAY-OFFS
KERATIN	KINGDOM	KOFTGAR	LACUNAS	LAPPING	LAYOUTS

LAZIEST	LEGIBLE	LEVERED	LIMPING	LIVENED	LOLLAND
L-DRIVER	LEGIBLY	LEVERET	LIMPKIN	LIVENER	LOLLARD
LEACHED	LEGIONS	LEVYING	LIMPOPO	LIVIDLY	LOLLIES
LEACHER	LEGLESS	LEXICAL	LIMULUS	LIVINGS	LOLLING
LEADERS	LEGNICA	LEXICON	LINABLE	LIVONIA	LOMBARD
LEADING	LEG-PULL	LIAISED	LINARES	LIVORNO	LONG AGO
LEAD-INS	LEGROOM	LIAISON	LINCOLN	LIZARDS	LONGBOW
LEAD OFF	LEG ROOM	LIANOID	LINCTUS	LOADING	LONGEST
LEAFAGE	LEG SIDE	LIASSIC	LINDANE	LOAFERS	LONGING
LEAFIER	LEGUMES	LIBBERS	LINDENS	LOAFING	LONGISH
LEAFLET	LEGUMIN	LIBELED	LINEAGE	LOANING	LONG TON
LEAGUED	LEGWORK	LIBERAL	LINEATE	LOATHED	LOOFAHS
LEAGUES	LE HAVRE	LIBEREC	LINEMAN	LOATHER	LOOKERS
LEAKAGE	LEIPZIG	LIBERIA	LINEMEN	LOATHLY	LOOKING
LEAKIER	LEISTER	LIBERTY	LINE-OUT	LOBBIED	LOOKOUT
LEAKING	LEISURE	LIBIDOS	LINEUPS	LOBBIES	LOOK OUT
LEANEST	LEITRIM	LIBRARY	LINGCOD	LOBBING	LOOMING
LEANING	LEMBERG	LIBRATE	LINGOES	LOBBYER	LOONIER
LEAN-TOS	LEMMING	LICENCE	LINGUAL	LOBELIA	LOONIES
LEAPING	LEMPIRA	LICENSE	LININGS	LOBSTER	LOOPING
LEARNED	LENDERS	LICKING	LINKAGE	LOBULAR	LOOSELY
LEARNER	LENDING	LIE-DOWN	LINKING	LOCALES	LOOSEST
LEASHES	LENGTHS	LIESTAL	LINKMAN	LOCALLY	LOOSING
LEASING	LENGTHY	LIFTING	LINKUPS	LOCARNO	LOOTERS
LEATHER	LENIENT	LIFTOFF	LINNETS	LOCATED	LOOTING
LEAVENS	LENTIGO	LIFT-OFF	LINOCUT	LOCATER	LOPPING
LEAVING	LENTILS	LIGHTED	LINSANG	LOCHIAL	LOQUATS
LEBANON	LEONINE	LIGHTEN	LINSEED	LOCKAGE	LORDING
LECHERS	LEOPARD	LIGHTER	LINTELS	LOCKERS	LORELEI
LECHERY	LEOTARD	LIGHTLY	LIONESS	LOCKETS	LORGNON
LECTERN	LEPANTO	LIGNIFY	LIONIZE	LOCKING	LORIENT
LECTION	LEPORID	LIGNITE	LIPETSK	LOCKJAW	LORRIES
LECTURE	LEPROSE	LIGROIN	LIP-READ	LOCKNUT	LOSABLE
LEDGERS	LEPROSY	LIGULAR	LIQUATE	LOCKOUT	LOSINGS
LEECHES	LEPROUS	LIGURIA	LIQUEFY	LOCKUPS	LOTIONS
LEERIER	LERWICK	LIKABLE	LIQUEUR	LOCOISM	LOTTERY
LEERING	LESBIAN	LIKENED	LIQUIDS	LOCULAR	LOTTING
LEE TIDE	LESIONS	LIKINGS	LISBURN	LOCUSTS	LOTUSES
LEEWARD	LESOTHO	LILTING	LISIEUX	LODGERS	LOUDEST
LEFTIES	LESSEES	LIMACON	LISPING	LODGING	LOUNGED
LEFTISM	LESSONS	LIMBATE	LISTING	LOFTIER	LOUNGER
LEFTIST	LESSORS	LIMBURG	LITCHIS	LOFTILY	LOUNGES
LEGALLY	LETDOWN	LIMEADE	LITERAL	LOFTING	LOURDES
LEGASPI	LETTERS	LIMIEST	LITHELY	LOGBOOK	LOURING
LEGATEE	LETTING	LIMINAL	LITHEST	LOGGERS	LOUSIER
LEGATES	LETTUCE	LIMITED	LITHIUM	LOGGIAS	LOUSILY
LEGATOR	LEUCINE	LIMITER	LITHOID	LOGGING	LOUSING
LEGENDS	LEUCITE	LIMNING	LITOTES	LOGICAL	LOUTISH
LEGGIER	LEUCOMA	LIMOGES	LITTERS	LOGIEST	LOUVAIN
LEGGING	LEVATOR	LIMPEST	LITURGY	LOGJAMS	LOUVRES
LEGHORN	LEVELED	LIMPETS	LIVABLE	LOGWOOD	LOVABLE

LOWBORN	LUPULIN	MAGHREB	MALVERN	MANXMAN	MARTYRS
LOWBROW	LURCHED	MAGICAL	MAMILLA	MAOISTS	MARTYRY
LOW BROW	LURCHER	MAGNATE	MAMMALS	MAPPING	MARVELS
LOW DOWN	LURCHES	MAGNETO	MAMMARY	MARABOU	MARXIAN
LOW-DOWN	LURGIES	MAGNETS	MAMMIES	MARACAS	MARXISM
LOWERED	LURIDLY	MAGNIFY	MAMMOTH	MARACAY	MARXIST
LOWLAND	LURKING	MAGNUMS	MANACLE	MARASCA	MASBATE
LOWLIER	LUSATIA	MAGPIES	MANAGED	MARATHA	MASCARA
LOW LIFE	LUSTFUL	MAHATMA	MANAGER	MARATHI	MASCOTS
LOWNESS	LUSTILY	MAHFOUZ	MANAGUA	MARBLED	MASHHAD
LOW-RISE	LUSTING	MAHICAN	MANAKIN	MARBLER	MASHING
LOW TIDE	LUSTRAL	MAH JONG	MANATEE	MARBLES	MASKING
LOYALLY	LUSTRES	MAH-JONG	MANDATE	MARBURG	MASONIC
LOYALTY	LUTEOUS	MAHONIA	MANDELA	MARCHED	MASONRY
LOZENGE	LUTHIER	MAHOUTS	MANDREL	MARCHER	MASQUES
L-PLATES	LYCHEES	MAIDENS	MANGERS	MARCHES	MASSAGE
LUALABA	LYCHNIS	MAILBAG	MANGIER	MAREMMA	MASSAWA
LUBBOCK	LYCOPOD	MAILBOX	MANGILY	MARGATE	MASSEUR
LUCERNE	LYDDITE	MAILING	MANGLED	MARGAUX	MASSIFS
LUCIDLY	LYING-IN	MAILMAN	MANGLER	MARGINS	MASSING
LUCIFER	LYNCEAN	MAILMEN	MANGLES	MARIBOR	MASSIVE
LUCKIER	LYNCHED	MAIMING	MANGOES	MARIMBA	MASTERS
LUCKILY	LYNCHER	MAINTOP	MANHOLE	MARINAS	MASTERY
LUCKNOW	LYRICAL	MAJESTY	MANHOOD	MARINER	MASTIFF
LUDDITE		MAJORCA	MANHOUR	MARINES	MASTOID
LUFFING	**M**	MAJORED	MANHUNT	MARITAL	MASURIA
LUGANDA	MACABRE	MAJORLY	MANIACS	MARKERS	MATADOR
LUGANSK	MACADAM	MAKASAR	MANIKIN	MARKETS	MATCHED
LUGGAGE	MACAQUE	MAKE OUT	MANIPUR	MARKHOR	MATCHES
LUGGERS	MACEDON	MAKES DO	MAN JACK	MARKING	MATHURA
LUGGING	MACHETE	MAKINGS	MANKIND	MARKUPS	MATINEE
LUGHOLE	MACHINE	MAKURDI	MANLIER	MARLINE	MATLOCK
LUGSAIL	MACLEAN	MALABAR	MANLIKE	MARLINS	MATRONS
LUGWORM	MACRAME	MALACCA	MAN-MADE	MARLITE	MATTERS
LULLABY	MACULAR	MALAISE	MANNERS	MARMITE	MATTING
LULLING	MADDEST	MALARIA	MANNING	MARMOTS	MATTINS
LUMBAGO	MADEIRA	MALATYA	MANNISH	MAROONS	MATTOCK
LUMENAL	MADE OUT	MALAYAN	MANNITE	MARQUEE	MATURED
LUMPIER	MADISON	MALEATE	MANNOSE	MARQUIS	MAUDLIN
LUMPILY	MADNESS	MALEFIC	MANRESA	MARRIED	MAULING
LUMPING	MADONNA	MALINES	MANROPE	MARRIER	MAUNDER
LUMPISH	MADRONA	MALINKE	MANSARD	MARRING	MAWKISH
LUMP SUM	MADURAI	MALLARD	MANSELL	MARROWS	MAXILLA
LUMUMBA	MADWORT	MALLETS	MANSION	MARSALA	MAXIMAL
LUNATIC	MAENADS	MALLEUS	MANTLED	MARSHAL	MAXIMIN
LUNCHED	MAESTRI	MALLOWS	MANTLES	MARSHES	MAXIMUM
LUNCHER	MAESTRO	MALMSEY	MANUALS	MARTENS	MAXIMUS
LUNCHES	MAFIOSO	MALTASE	MANUKAU	MARTIAL	MAXWELL
LUNETTE	MAGENTA	MALTESE	MANURED	MARTIAN	MAY DAYS
LUNGING	MAGGOTS	MALTING	MANURER	MARTINI	MAYENNE
LUOYANG	MAGGOTY	MALTOSE	MANX CAT	MARTINS	MAYFAIR

MAYORAL	MENACES	MICRONS	MINGIER	MISTERS	MOLLUSC
MAYOTTE	MENAGES	MIDDENS	MINGLED	MISTILY	MOLOKAI
MAYPOLE	MENDERS	MIDDLE C	MINIBAR	MISTIME	MOLTING
MAYWEED	MENDING	MIDGETS	MINIBUS	MISTING	MOMBASA
MAZURKA	MENDIPS	MIDIRON	MINICAB	MISTOOK	MOMENTA
MAZZARD	MENDOZA	MIDLAND	MINIMAL	MISTRAL	MOMENTS
MBABANE	MENFOLK	MIDMOST	MINIMAX	MISUSED	MOMMIES
MCENROE	MENIALS	MIDRIFF	MINIMUM	MISUSER	MONACAN
MEADOWS	MENTHOL	MIDTERM	MINIMUS	MISUSES	MONADIC
MEALIER	MENTION	MIDWEEK	MINIONS	MITCHUM	MONARCH
MEANDER	MENTORS	MIDWEST	MINIVER	MITHRAS	MONARDA
MEANEST	MEOWING	MIDWIFE	MINIVET	MITOSIS	MONCTON
MEANING	MERCIES	MIDYEAR	MINNOWS	MITOTIC	MONDAYS
MEASLES	MERCURY	MIGHTN'T	MINORCA	MITTENS	MONEYED
MEASURE	MERGERS	MIGRANT	MINSTER	MITZVAH	MONGOLS
MEATIER	MERGING	MIGRATE	MINTAGE	MIXABLE	MONGREL
MEATILY	MERITED	MIKADOS	MINTING	MIXED UP	MONITOR
MEDDLED	MERMAID	MILAZZO	MINUETS	MIXTURE	MONKEYS
MEDDLER	MERRIER	MILDEST	MINUSES	MIZORAM	MONKISH
MEDIACY	MERRILY	MILDEWY	MINUTED	MOANERS	MONOCLE
MEDIANS	MESARCH	MILEAGE	MINUTES	MOANING	MONOMER
MEDIANT	MESHING	MILIARY	MINXISH	MOBBING	MONSOON
MEDIATE	MESSAGE	MILIEUS	MIOCENE	MOBILES	MONSTER
MEDICAL	MESSIAH	MILIEUX	MIRACLE	MOBSTER	MONTAGE
MEDICOS	MESSIER	MILITIA	MIRADOR	MOCKERS	MONTANA
MEDIUMS	MESSILY	MILKERS	MIRAGES	MOCKERY	MONTANE
MEDLARS	MESSINA	MILKIER	MIRRORS	MOCKING	MONTHLY
MEDLEYS	MESSING	MILKILY	MISCALL	MOCK-UPS	MOOCHED
MEDULLA	MESS-UPS	MILKING	MISCAST	MODALLY	MOOCHER
MEEKEST	MESTIZA	MILKMAN	MISDEAL	MOD CONS	MOODIER
MEERKAT	MESTIZO	MILKMEN	MISDEED	MODELED	MOODILY
MEETING	METALED	MILK RUN	MISERLY	MODERAS	MOONEYE
MEGATON	METAMER	MILKSOP	MISFILE	MODERNS	MOONILY
MEIOSIS	METEORS	MILLDAM	MISFIRE	MODESTY	MOONING
MEIOTIC	METERED	MILLERS	MISFITS	MODICUM	MOONLIT
MEISSEN	METHANE	MILLINE	MISHAPS	MODISTE	MOONSET
MELANGE	METHODS	MILLING	MISHEAR	MODULAR	MOORAGE
MELANIC	METIERS	MILLION	MISKOLC	MODULES	MOORHEN
MELANIN	METONYM	MILLRUN	MISLAID	MODULUS	MOORING
MELILLA	METOPIC	MIMESIS	MISLEAD	MOFETTE	MOORISH
MELILOT	METRICS	MIMETIC	MISNAME	MOGADOR	MOOTING
MELISMA	METRIFY	MIMICRY	MISPLAY	MOGGIES	MOPPETS
MELODIC	METRIST	MINABLE	MISREAD	MOGILEV	MOPPING
MELTAGE	MEXICAN	MINARET	MISRULE	MOHICAN	MORAINE
MELTING	MIAOWED	MINCERS	MISSALS	MOIDORE	MORALLY
MEMBERS	MIASMAL	MINCING	MISSIES	MOISTEN	MORAVIA
MEMENTO	MIASMAS	MINDERS	MISSILE	MOISTLY	MORCEAU
MEMOIRS	MICELLE	MINDFUL	MISSING	MOLDIER	MORDANT
MEMPHIS	MICHAEL	MINDING	MISSION	MOLDING	MORDENT
MENACED	MICKEYS	MINDORO	MISSIVE	MOLDOVA	MORDVIN
MENACER	MICROBE	MINERAL	MISTAKE	MOLLIFY	MOREISH

MORELIA	MUCKILY	MURKIER	**N**	NEAREST	NEST EGG
MORELLO	MUCKING	MURKILY	NABBING	NEARING	NESTING
MORELOS	MUD BATH	MURMURS	NACELLE	NEATEST	NESTLED
MORGUES	MUDDIED	MURRAIN	NAEVOID	NEBULAE	NESTLER
MORMONS	MUDDIER	MUSCLED	NAGGERS	NEBULAR	NETBALL
MORNING	MUDDILY	MUSCLES	NAGGING	NEBULAS	NETSUKE
MOROCCO	MUDDING	MUSEFUL	NAHUATL	NECKING	NETTING
MORONIC	MUDDLED	MUSEUMS	NAIADES	NECKLET	NETTLED
MORROWS	MUDDLER	MUSHIER	NAILING	NECKTIE	NETTLES
MORSELS	MUDDLES	MUSHILY	NAIPAUL	NECROSE	NETWORK
MORTALS	MUDFISH	MUSICAL	NAIROBI	NECTARY	NEUROMA
MORTARS	MUDFLAP	MUSKETS	NAIVELY	NEEDFUL	NEURONE
MORTIFY	MUDFLAT	MUSKIER	NAIVETE	NEEDIER	NEUTRAL
MORTISE	MUDPACK	MUSKRAT	NAIVETY	NEEDING	NEUTRON
MORULAR	MUD PIES	MUSLIMS	NAKEDLY	NEEDLED	NEWBORN
MOSAICS	MUEZZIN	MUSSELS	NALCHIK	NEEDLES	NEW BORN
MOSELEY	MUFFING	MUSSING	NAMABLE	NEGATED	NEWBURY
MOSELLE	MUFFINS	MUSTANG	NAME DAY	NEGATOR	NEW CHUM
MOSEYED	MUFFLED	MUSTARD	NAMIBIA	NEGLECT	NEW DEAL
MOSLEMS	MUFFLER	MUSTERS	NANJING	NEGRESS	NEW MOON
MOSOTHO	MUGGERS	MUSTIER	NANKEEN	NEGRITO	NEWNESS
MOSQUES	MUGGIER	MUSTILY	NANKING	NEGROES	NEWPORT
MOSSIER	MUGGILY	MUTABLE	NANNIES	NEGROID	NEWTOWN
MOTHERS	MUGGING	MUTABLY	NANNING	NEIGHED	NEW TOWN
MOTIONS	MUGGINS	MUTAGEN	NANTONG	NEITHER	NEW WAVE
MOTIVES	MUGSHOT	MUTANTS	NANTUNG	NELLIES	NEW YEAR
MOTORED	MUGWORT	MUTTONY	NAPHTHA	NELUMBO	NEW YORK
MOTTLED	MUGWUMP	MUZZIER	NAPKINS	NEMATIC	NEXUSES
MOTTOES	MULATTO	MUZZILY	NAPPIES	NEMESES	NIAGARA
MOUFLON	MULCHED	MUZZLED	NAPPING	NEMESIS	NIBBLED
MOUILLE	MULCTED	MUZZLER	NARKIER	NEOCENE	NIBBLER
MOULDED	MULLAHS	MUZZLES	NARKING	NEOGAEA	NIBBLES
MOULDER	MULLEIN	MYALGIA	NARRATE	NEOGENE	NICKELS
MOULTED	MULLETS	MYALGIC	NARROWS	NEOLITH	NICKING
MOULTER	MULLING	MYALISM	NARTHEX	NEONATE	NICOBAR
MOUNTED	MULLION	MYANMAR	NARWHAL	NEOTENY	NICOSIA
MOUNTER	MULLITE	MYCENAE	NASALLY	NEOTYPE	NIFTIER
MOUNTIE	MUMBLED	MYCOSIS	NASCENT	NEOZOIC	NIFTILY
MOURNED	MUMBLER	MYCOTIC	NASTIER	NEPHEWS	NIGELLA
MOURNER	MUMMERS	MYELOID	NASTILY	NEPHRON	NIGERIA
MOUSERS	MUMMERY	MYELOMA	NATIONS	NEPOTIC	NIGGARD
MOUSIER	MUMMIES	MYIASIS	NATIVES	NEPTUNE	NIGGERS
MOUSING	MUMMIFY	MYKONOS	NATTIER	NEREIDS	NIGGLED
MOUSSES	MUMMING	MYNHEER	NATTILY	NERITIC	NIGGLER
MOUTHED	MUNCHED	MYOLOGY	NATURAL	NERVATE	NIGHTIE
MOUTHER	MUNCHER	MYOTOME	NATURES	NERVIER	NIGHTLY
MOVABLE	MUNDANE	MYRIADS	NAUGHTY	NERVILY	NIIGATA
MOVABLY	MUNSTER	MYRTLES	NAURUAN	NERVINE	NILOTIC
MOVIOLA	MUNTJAC	MYSTERY	NAVARRE	NERVING	NIMBLER
MUBARAK	MURDERS	MYSTICS	NAVVIES	NERVOUS	NINEPIN
MUCKIER	MURDOCH	MYSTIFY	NAYARIT	NERVURE	NINNIES

NIOBITE
NIOBIUM
NIOBOUS
NIPPERS
NIPPIER
NIPPILY
NIPPING
NIPPLES
NIRVANA
NITEROI
NITRATE
NITRIDE
NITRIFY
NITRILE
NITRITE
NITROSO
NITROUS
NITWITS
NIVEOUS
NO BALLS
NOBBLED
NOBBLER
NOBLEST
NOCTUID
NOCTULE
NOCTURN
NODDING
NODDLES
NODICAL
NO DOUBT
NODULAR
NODULES
NO ENTRY
NOGGING
NOGGINS
NOISIER
NOISILY
NOISOME
NOMADIC
NOMBRIL
NOMINAL
NOMINEE
NONAGON
NON-IRON
NONPLUS
NON-PROS
NONSTOP
NON STOP
NONSUIT
NON USER
NOODLES

NOONDAY
NO-PLACE
NORFOLK
NORMANS
NORWICH
NOSEBAG
NOSEGAY
NOSHING
NOSIEST
NOSTRIL
NOSTRUM
NOTABLE
NOTABLY
NOTCHED
NOTCHES
NOTELET
NOTEPAD
NOTHING
NOTICED
NOTICES
NOTIONS
NO TRUMP
NO-TRUMP
NOUGATS
NOUGHTS
NOURISH
NOUVEAU
NOVALIS
NOVELLA
NOVELLE
NOVELTY
NOVICES
NOVI SAD
NOWHERE
NOXIOUS
NOZZLES
NUANCES
NUCLEAR
NUCLEIN
NUCLEON
NUCLEUS
NUCLIDE
NUDGING
NUDISTS
NUGGETS
NUGGETY
NULLIFY
NULLITY
NULL SET
NUMBERS
NUMBING

NUMERAL
NUMMARY
NUNATAK
NUNAVUT
NUN BUOY
NUNCIOS
NUNNERY
NUPTIAL
NURSERY
NURSING
NURTURE
NUTCASE
NUTGALL
NUTMEGS
NUTRIAS
NUTTIER
NUTTILY
NUTTING
NUTWOOD
NUZZLED
NYMPHAL
NYMPHET
NYUNGAR

O

OAKLAND
OARFISH
OARLOCK
OARSMAN
OARSMEN
OATCAKE
OATMEAL
OBCONIC
OBELISK
OBELIZE
OBESITY
OBEYING
OBJECTS
OBLIGED
OBLIGEE
OBLIGER
OBLIGOR
OBLIQUE
OBLONGS
OBLOQUY
OBOISTS
OBOVATE
OBOVOID
OBSCENE
OBSCURE
OBSERVE

OBTRUDE
OBVERSE
OBVIATE
OBVIOUS
OCARINA
OCCIPUT
OCCLUDE
OCEANIA
OCEANIC
OCELLAR
OCELLUS
OCELOTS
OCHROID
OCREATE
OCTADIC
OCTAGON
OCTANES
OCTAVES
OCTOBER
OCTOPOD
OCTOPUS
OCTUPLE
OCULIST
ODDBALL
ODDMENT
ODDNESS
ODOROUS
ODYSSEY
OEDIPAL
OERSTED
OESTRUS
OFFBEAT
OFFENCE
OFFERED
OFFERER
OFFHAND
OFFICER
OFFICES
OFFINGS
OFF-LOAD
OFF-PEAK
OFFSIDE
OGREISH
OHM'S
LAW
OILBIRD
OILCANS
OILIEST
OILRIGS
OILSKIN
OIL WELL

OINKING
OKAYAMA
OKAYING
OKINAWA
OLD BOYS
OLD HAND
OLD LADY
OLD LAGS
OLD MAID
OLD NICK
OLDSTER
OLDTIME
OLDUVAI
OLEFINE
O LEVELS
OLIVARY
OLIVINE
OLOMOUC
OLSZTYN
OLYMPIA
OLYMPIC
OLYMPUS
OMENTUM
OMICRON
OMINOUS
OMITTED
OMITTER
OMNIBUS
ON A
WHIM
ONE EYED
ONENESS
ONE-OFFS
ONEROUS
ONESELF
ONE-STAR
ONE STEP
ONE-STEP
ONETIME
ON-GLIDE
ONGOING
ONITSHA
ON LEAVE
ONSHORE
ON SIGHT
ON STAGE
ONTARIO
ONWARDS
OOLITIC
OOPHYTE
OOSPERM

OOSPORE
OOTHECA
OOZIEST
OPACITY
OPALINE
OPEN-AIR
OPEN DAY
OPENERS
OPENING
OPERAND
OPERANT
OPERATE
OPHITIC
OPIATES
OPINING
OPINION
OPOSSUM
OPPOSED
OPPOSER
OPPRESS
OPSONIC
OPSONIN
OPTICAL
OPTIMAL
OPTIMUM
OPTIONS
OPULENT
OPUNTIA
OQUASSA
ORACLES
ORALISM
ORANGES
ORATION
ORATORS
ORATORY
ORBITAL
ORBITED
ORCHARD
ORCHIDS
ORCINOL
ORDEALS
ORDERED
ORDERER
ORDERLY
ORDINAL
ORECTIC
OREGANO
ORGANIC
ORGANON
ORGANUM
ORGANZA

ORGASMS	OUTBACK	OVATION	PACKERS	PANAMAS	PARESIS
ORIENTE	OUTCAST	OVERACT	PACKETS	PAN-ARAB	PARETIC
ORIFICE	OUTCOME	OVERAGE	PACK ICE	PANCAKE	PARFAIT
ORIGAMI	OUTCROP	OVERALL	PACKING	PANCHAX	PARIAHS
ORIGINS	OUTDATE	OVERARM	PADDIES	PANDECT	PARINGS
ORINOCO	OUTDONE	OVERAWE	PADDING	PANDITS	PARKIER
ORISONS	OUTDOOR	OVERBID	PADDLED	PANDORE	PARKING
ORIZABA	OUTFACE	OVERDID	PADDLER	PANELED	PARKWAY
ORKNEYS	OUTFALL	OVERDUE	PADDLES	PANGAEA	PARLEYS
ORLANDO	OUTFITS	OVERFLY	PADDOCK	PANICKY	PARLOUR
ORLEANS	OUTFLOW	OVERJOY	PADLOCK	PANICLE	PARLOUS
OROGENY	OUTGREW	OVERLAP	PADRONE	PANNIER	PARODIC
OROLOGY	OUTGROW	OVERLAY	PAGEANT	PANNING	PAROLED
OROTUND	OUTHAUL	OVERLIE	PAGEBOY	PANOCHA	PAROLES
ORPHANS	OUTINGS	OVERMAN	PAGINAL	PANOPLY	PARONYM
ORPHREY	OUTLAST	OVERPAY	PAGODAS	PANSIES	PAROTIC
ORTOLAN	OUTLAWS	OVERRAN	PAHSIEN	PANTHER	PAROTID
ORVIETO	OUTLAYS	OVERRUN	PAINFUL	PANTIES	PARQUET
OSCULAR	OUTLETS	OVERSAW	PAINING	PANTILE	PARRIED
OSCULUM	OUTLIER	OVERSEE	PAINTED	PANTING	PARRIES
OSHOGBO	OUTLINE	OVERSET	PAINTER	PANTOUM	PARROTS
OSMIOUS	OUTLIVE	OVERSEW	PAIRING	PANZERS	PARSEES
OSMOSIS	OUTLOOK	OVERTAX	PAIR-OAR	PAOTING	PARSERS
OSMOTIC	OUTMOST	OVERTLY	PAISLEY	PAPAYAS	PARSING
OSMUNDA	OUTPACE	OVERTOP	PAJAMAS	PAPEETE	PARSLEY
OSPREYS	OUTPLAY	OVERUSE	PALACES	PAPERED	PARSNIP
OSSEOUS	OUTPORT	OVIDUCT	PALADIN	PAPERER	PARSONS
OSSETIA	OUTPOST	OVIFORM	PALATAL	PAPILLA	PARTAKE
OSSETIC	OUTPOUR	OVULATE	PALATES	PAPISTS	PARTIAL
OSSICLE	OUTPUTS	OWN GOAL	PALAVER	PAPOOSE	PARTIED
OSSUARY	OUTRAGE	OXALATE	PALE ALE	PAPPIES	PARTIES
OSTEOID	OUTRANK	OXAZINE	PALERMO	PAPPOSE	PARTING
OSTEOMA	OUTRIDE	OXBLOOD	PALETTE	PAPRIKA	PARTITA
OSTIOLE	OUTRODE	OXCARTS	PALFREY	PAPYRUS	PARTITE
OSTLERS	OUTSELL	OXHEART	PALINGS	PARABLE	PARTNER
OSTMARK	OUTSIDE	OXIDANT	PALLETS	PARADED	PARTOOK
OSTOSIS	OUTSIZE	OXIDASE	PALLIER	PARADER	PARVENU
OSTRAVA	OUTSOLD	OXIDATE	PALLING	PARADES	PASCHAL
OSTRICH	OUTSOLE	OXIDIZE	PALLIUM	PARADOR	PASMORE
OTOCYST	OUTSTAY	OXONIAN	PALMATE	PARADOX	PASSADE
OTOLITH	OUT-TAKE	OXYACID	PALMIER	PARAGON	PASSAGE
OTOLOGY	OUTTALK	OXYSALT	PALMING	PARAIBA	PASSANT
OTRANTO	OUT-TRAY	OXYTONE	PALMIRA	PARAPET	PAS SEUL
OTTOMAN	OUTVOTE	OYSTERS	PALMIST	PARASOL	PASS FOR
OUABAIN	OUTWARD	OZONIZE	PALM OIL	PARATHA	PASSING
OUGHTN'T	OUTWASH		PALMYRA	PARBOIL	PASSION
OUR LADY	OUTWEAR	**P**	PALPATE	PARCELS	PASSIVE
OUR LORD	OUTWORK	PABULUM	PALSIED	PARCHED	PASSKEY
OURSELF	OUTWORN	PACHUCA	PAMPEAN	PARDONS	PASS OFF
OUSTERS	OVARIAN	PACIFIC	PANACEA	PAREIRA	PASS OUT
OUSTING	OVARIES	PACKAGE	PANACHE	PARENTS	PASTELS

PASTERN	PAYSLIP	PELTING	PERFUSE	PETTISH	PICKLES
PASTE UP	PEACHES	PENALLY	PERGOLA	PETUNIA	PICK-UPS
PASTE-UP	PEACOCK	PENALTY	PERHAPS	PFENNIG	PICNICS
PASTIER	PEAFOWL	PENANCE	PERIDOT	PHAETON	PICOTEE
PASTIES	PEAHENS	PENDANT	PERIGEE	PHALANX	PICRATE
PASTILY	PEAKIER	PENDENT	PERIGON	PHALLIC	PICRITE
PASTIME	PEAKING	PENDING	PERIODS	PHALLUS	PICTISH
PASTING	PEALING	PENGUIN	PERIQUE	PHANTOM	PICTURE
PASTORS	PEANUTS	PENISES	PERIWIG	PHARAOH	PIDDLED
PASTURE	PEARLER	PEN NAME	PERJURE	PHARYNX	PIDDOCK
PATCHED	PEASANT	PENNANT	PERJURY	PHASING	PIDGINS
PATCHER	PEBBLES	PENNATE	PERKIER	PHASMID	PIEBALD
PATCHES	PECCANT	PENNIES	PERKILY	PHELLEM	PIECING
PATELLA	PECCARY	PENNING	PERKING	PHILTRE	PIE-EYED
PATENCY	PECCAVI	PENNONS	PERLITE	PHIZOGS	PIERCED
PATENTS	PECKERS	PEN PALS	PERMIAN	PHLOXES	PIERCER
PATHANS	PECKING	PENRITH	PERMING	PHOBIAS	PIETIES
PATHWAY	PECKISH	PENROSE	PERMITS	PHOBICS	PIGEONS
PATIALA	PECTASE	PENSILE	PERMUTE	PHOCINE	PIGFISH
PATIENT	PECTATE	PENSION	PERPEND	PHOENIX	PIGGERY
PATRIAL	PECTIZE	PENSIVE	PERPLEX	PHONATE	PIGGIER
PATRICK	PEDALED	PENTANE	PERSEID	PHONE-IN	PIGGIES
PATRIOT	PEDANTS	PENTENE	PERSIAN	PHONEME	PIGGING
PATROLS	PEDDLED	PENTODE	PERSIST	PHONEYS	PIGGISH
PATRONS	PEDDLER	PENTOSE	PERSONA	PHONICS	PIG IRON
PATTENS	PEDICEL	PEONIES	PERSONS	PHONIER	PIG LEAD
PATTERN	PEDICLE	PEOPLED	PERSPEX	PHONING	PIGLETS
PATTERS	PEDLARS	PEOPLES	PERTAIN	PHRASAL	PIGMENT
PATTIES	PEDOCAL	PEPPERS	PERTURB	PHRASED	PIGMIES
PATTING	PEEBLES	PEPPERY	PERUGIA	PHRASES	PIGSKIN
PAUCITY	PEEKING	PEP PILL	PERUSAL	PHRATRY	PIGTAIL
PAULINE	PEELING	PEPPING	PERUSED	PHRENIC	PIGWEED
PAULIST	PEEPERS	PEP TALK	PERUSER	PHYSICS	PIKEMAN
PAUNCHY	PEEPING	PEPTIDE	PERVADE	PHYSIOS	PIKEMEN
PAUPERS	PEERAGE	PEPTIZE	PERVERT	PIANISM	PILEATE
PAUSING	PEERESS	PEPTONE	PESCARA	PIANIST	PILEOUS
PAVANES	PEERING	PERACID	PESETAS	PIANOLA	PILEUPS
PAVINGS	PEEVING	PERCALE	PESKIER	PIASTRE	PILGRIM
PAVIOUR	PEEVISH	PER CENT	PESSARY	PIAZZAS	PILLAGE
PAWKIER	PEEWITS	PERCEPT	PESTLES	PIBROCH	PILLARS
PAWKILY	PEGGING	PERCHED	PETARDS	PICADOR	PILLBOX
PAWNAGE	PEG LEGS	PERCHER	PETCOCK	PICARDY	PILLION
PAWNING	PELAGIC	PERCHES	PETIOLE	PICCOLO	PILLOCK
PAWPAWS	PELICAN	PERCOID	PET NAME	PICEOUS	PILLORY
PAYABLE	PELITIC	PERCUSS	PETRELS	PICKAXE	PILLOWS
PAYBEDS	PELLETS	PER DIEM	PETRIFY	PICKERS	PILOTED
PAY DIRT	PELMETS	PEREIRA	PETROUS	PICKETS	PILSNER
PAYLOAD	PELORIA	PERFECT	PETSAMO	PICKIER	PILULAR
PAYMENT	PELORUS	PERFIDY	PETTIER	PICKING	PIMENTO
PAYOUTS	PELOTAS	PERFORM	PETTILY	PICKLED	PIMPING
PAYROLL	PELTATE	PERFUME	PETTING	PICKLER	PIMPLED

PIMPLES	PISTOLS	PLASTID	PLUMAGE	POLYGON	PORTICO
PINBALL	PISTONS	PLATEAU	PLUMATE	POLYMER	PORTING
PINCERS	PIT A	PLATINA	PLUMBED	POLYNYA	PORTION
PINCHED	PAT	PLATING	PLUMBER	POLYPOD	PORTRAY
PINCHES	PIT-A-	PLATOON	PLUMBIC	POLYPUS	POSEURS
PINE NUT	PAT	PLATTER	PLUMING	POMMELS	POSHEST
PINETUM	PITCHED	PLAUDIT	PLUMMET	POMMIES	POSITED
PINFISH	PITCHER	PLAY-ACT	PLUMPED	POMPANO	POSITIF
PINFOLD	PITCHES	PLAYBOY	PLUMPER	POMPEII	POSSESS
PINGING	PITEOUS	PLAYERS	PLUMULE	POMPOMS	POSSETS
PINGUID	PITFALL	PLAYFUL	PLUNDER	POMPOUS	POSSUMS
PINHEAD	PITHEAD	PLAYING	PLUNGED	PONCHOS	POSTAGE
PINHOLE	PITHIER	PLAYLET	PLUNGER	PONGIER	POSTBAG
PINIEST	PITHILY	PLAY OFF	PLURALS	PONGING	POSTBOX
PINIONS	PITIFUL	PLAY-OFF	PLUSHER	PONIARD	POSTERN
PINKEST	PIT PONY	PLAYPEN	PLUVIAL	PONTIFF	POSTERS
PINKEYE	PIT PROP	PLEADED	PLYWOOD	PONTINE	POSTFIX
PINK GIN	PITTING	PLEADER	POACHED	PONTOON	POSTIES
PINKIES	PITYING	PLEASED	POACHER	POOCHES	POSTING
PINKING	PIVOTAL	PLEASER	PO BOXES	POODLES	POSTMAN
PINKISH	PIVOTED	PLEATED	POCHARD	POOFIER	POSTMEN
PINKOES	PIZZAZZ	PLEATER	POCKETS	POOH-BAH	POSTURE
PINNACE	PLACARD	PLEDGED	PODAGRA	POOLING	POSTWAR
PINNATE	PLACATE	PLEDGER	PODDING	POOPERS	POTABLE
PINNIES	PLACEBO	PLEDGES	PODESTA	POOR BOX	POTAGER
PINNING	PLACING	PLEDGET	PODGIER	POOREST	POTENCY
PINNULE	PLACKET	PLEDGOR	PODGILY	POOR LAW	POTFULS
PINTAIL	PLACOID	PLENARY	PODIUMS	POPADUM	POTHEEN
PINWORK	PLAFOND	PLEURAL	PODOLSK	POPCORN	POTHERB
PINWORM	PLAGUED	PLEURON	POETESS	POPEDOM	POTHOLE
PIONEER	PLAGUER	PLIABLE	POETICS	POP-EYED	POTHOOK
PIOUSLY	PLAGUES	PLIANCY	PO-FACED	POPGUNS	POTICHE
PIPETTE	PLAINER	PLICATE	POGONIA	POPLARS	POTIONS
PIPPING	PLAINLY	PLIGHTS	POGROMS	POPOVER	POT LUCK
PIPPINS	PLAINTS	PLINTHS	POINTED	POPPERS	POTLUCK
PIQUANT	PLAITED	PLODDED	POINTER	POPPETS	POTOMAC
PIQUING	PLANETS	PLODDER	POISING	POPPIES	POTSDAM
PIRAEUS	PLANING	PLOESTI	POISONS	POPPING	POTSHOT
PIRANHA	PLANISH	PLONKED	POKIEST	POP STAR	POTTAGE
PIRATED	PLANNED	PLOPPED	POLARIS	POPULAR	POTTERS
PIRATES	PLANNER	PLOSION	POLEAXE	PORCHES	POTTERY
PIRATIC	PLANTAR	PLOSIVE	POLECAT	PORCINE	POTTIER
PISCARY	PLANTED	PLOTTED	POLEMIC	PORIRUA	POTTIES
PISCINA	PLANTER	PLOTTER	POLICED	PORKERS	POTTING
PISCINE	PLANULA	PLOUGHS	POLITIC	PORKIER	POUCHED
PISHPEK	PLAQUES	PLOVDIV	POLLACK	PORK PIE	POUCHES
PISSING	PLASMID	PLOVERS	POLLARD	PORTAGE	POULARD
PISS-UPS	PLASMIN	PLOWING	POLLING	PORTALS	POULTRY
PISTEUR	PLASMON	PLUCKED	POLL TAX	PORTEND	POUNCED
PISTILS	PLASTER	PLUCKER	POLLUTE	PORTENT	POUNCES
PISTOIA	PLASTIC	PLUGGED	POLTAVA	PORTERS	POUNDAL

POUNDED	PRESAGE	PRIZING	PROTEGE	PUFFINS	PURSUIT
POUNDER	PRESENT	PROBANG	PROTEIN	PUGGING	PURVIEW
POURING	PRESIDE	PROBATE	PROTEST	PULLETS	PUSHERS
POUTING	PRESSED	PROBING	PROTIST	PULLEYS	PUSHIER
POVERTY	PRESSES	PROBITY	PROTIUM	PULLING	PUSHILY
POWDERS	PRESSOR	PROBLEM	PROTONS	PULL-INS	PUSHING
POWDERY	PRESS UP	PROCARP	PROTYLE	PULLMAN	PUSHKIN
POWERED	PRESS-UP	PROCEED	PROUDER	PULLOUT	PUSHROD
POWWOWS	PRESTON	PROCESS	PROUDLY	PULPIER	PUSH-UPS
PRAIRIE	PRESTOS	PROCTOR	PROVERB	PULPING	PUSSIES
PRAISED	PRESUME	PROCURE	PROVIDE	PULPITS	PUSTULE
PRAISER	PRETEEN	PRODDED	PROVING	PULSARS	PUTAMEN
PRAISES	PRETEND	PRODDER	PROVISO	PULSATE	PUT DOWN
PRALINE	PRETEST	PRODIGY	PROVOKE	PULSING	PUT-DOWN
PRANCED	PRETEXT	PRODUCE	PROVOST	PUMPING	PUT-OFFS
PRANCER	PRETZEL	PRODUCT	PROWESS	PUMPKIN	PUTREFY
PRATING	PREVAIL	PROFANE	PROWLED	PUNCHED	PUTTERS
PRATTLE	PREVENT	PROFESS	PROWLER	PUNCHER	PUTTING
PRAWNER	PREVIEW	PROFFER	PROXIES	PUNCHES	PUTTNAM
PRAYERS	PREYING	PROFILE	PROXIMA	PUNCH UP	PUT-UPON
PRAYING	PREZZIE	PROFITS	PRUDENT	PUNCH-UP	PUZZLED
PREBEND	PRICIER	PRO-FORM	PRUDERY	PUNDITS	PUZZLER
PRECAST	PRICING	PROFUSE	PRUDISH	PUNGENT	PUZZLES
PRECEDE	PRICKED	PROGENY	PRUNING	PUNIEST	PYAEMIA
PRECEPT	PRICKER	PROGRAM	PRURIGO	PUNJABI	PYAEMIC
PRECESS	PRICKET	PROJECT	PRUSSIA	PUNKAHS	PYGMIES
PRECISE	PRICKLE	PROLATE	PSALMIC	PUNNETS	PYJAMAS
PRECOOK	PRICKLY	PRO-LIFE	PSALTER	PUNNING	PYLORUS
PREDATE	PRIDING	PROLINE	PSYCHED	PUNSTER	PYNCHON
PREDICT	PRIESTS	PROLONG	PSYCHES	PUNTERS	PYRALID
PREEMPT	PRIMACY	PROMISE	PSYCHIC	PUNTING	PYRAMID
PREENED	PRIMARY	PROMMER	PSYLLID	PUPPETS	PYRETIC
PREENER	PRIMATE	PROMOTE	PTERYLA	PUPPIES	PYREXIA
PREFABS	PRIMERS	PROMPTS	PTYALIN	PUPPING	PYRITES
PREFACE	PRIMINE	PRONATE	PUBERTY	PURCELL	PYRITIC
PREFECT	PRIMING	PRONOUN	PUBLISH	PURGING	PYROGEN
PREHEAT	PRIMMER	PROOFED	PUCCOON	PURISTS	PYROSIS
PRELACY	PRIMULA	PROPANE	PUCKERS	PURITAN	PYRRHIC
PRELATE	PRINCES	PROPEND	PUCKISH	PURLIEU	PYRROLE
PRELIMS	PRINKER	PROPENE	PUDDING	PURLING	PYTHONS
PRELUDE	PRINTED	PROPHET	PUDDLED	PURLOIN	
PREMIER	PRINTER	PROPOSE	PUDDLER	PURPLES	**Q**
PREMISE	PRISING	PROPPED	PUDDLES	PURPORT	Q-FACTOR
PREMISS	PRISONS	PRO RATA	PUDENDA	PURPOSE	QINGDAO
PREMIUM	PRITHEE	PROSAIC	PUDGIER	PURPURA	QUACKED
PREPACK	PRIVACY	PROSIER	PUDGILY	PURPURE	QUADRAT
PREPAID	PRIVATE	PROSILY	PUERILE	PURRING	QUADRIC
PREPARE	PRIVIER	PROSODY	PUFFERY	PURSERS	QUAFFER
PREPONE	PRIVIES	PROSPER	PUFFIER	PURSING	QUAILED
PREPOSE	PRIVILY	PROTEAN	PUFFILY	PURSUED	QUAKERS
PREPUCE	PRIVITY	PROTECT	PUFFING	PURSUER	QUAKILY

QUAKING	QUININE	RAGBAGS	RANGING	RAVENNA	RECEDED
QUALIFY	QUINONE	RAGGING	RANGOON	RAVE-UPS	RECEIPT
QUALITY	QUINTAL	RAGOUTS	RANKERS	RAVINES	RECEIVE
QUANGOS	QUINTAN	RAGTAIL	RANKING	RAVINGS	RECIPES
QUANTAL	QUINTET	RAGTIME	RANKLED	RAVIOLI	RECITAL
QUANTIC	QUINTIC	RAGWEED	RANSACK	RAW DEAL	RECITED
QUANTUM	QUIPPED	RAG WEEK	RANSOMS	RAWHIDE	RECITER
QUARREL	QUITTED	RAGWORM	RANTERS	RAWNESS	RECKING
QUARTAN	QUITTER	RAGWORT	RANTING	RAZZLES	RECLAIM
QUARTER	QUITTOR	RAIDERS	RAPHIDE	REACHED	RECLINE
QUARTET	QUIVERS	RAIDING	RAPIDLY	REACHER	RECLUSE
QUARTIC	QUIVERY	RAILING	RAPIERS	REACHES	RECORDS
QUARTOS	QUI VIVE	RAILWAY	RAPISTS	REACTED	RECOUNT
QUASARS	QUIZZED	RAIMENT	RAPPING	REACTOR	RECOVER
QUASHED	QUIZZER	RAINBOW	RAPPORT	READERS	RECRUIT
QUASSIA	QUIZZES	RAINIER	RAPTURE	READIED	RECTIFY
QUAVERS	QUONDAM	RAINILY	RAREBIT	READIER	RECTORS
QUAVERY	QUORATE	RAINING	RASBORA	READIES	RECTORY
QUAYAGE	QUORUMS	RAINOUT	RASCALS	READILY	RECTRIX
QUECHUA	QUOTHED	RAISERS	RASHERS	READING	RECTUMS
QUEENED	QUOTING	RAISING	RASHEST	READOUT	RECURVE
QUEENLY		RAISINS	RASPING	REAGENT	RECYCLE
QUEERED	**R**	RAISINY	RATABLE	REALGAR	RED BOOK
QUEERER	RABBITS	RAKE-OFF	RATABLY	REALIGN	RED CARD
QUEERLY	RABBLER	RALEIGH	RATAFIA	REALISM	REDCOAT
QUELLED	RABBLES	RALLIED	RAT-A-	REALIST	RED DEER
QUELLER	RACCOON	RALLIER	TAT	REALITY	REDDEST
QUERIED	RACEMIC	RALLIES	RATBAGS	REALIZE	REDDISH
QUERIES	RACHIAL	RALLINE	RATCHET	REALTOR	REDFISH
QUERIST	RACIEST	RAMADAN	RATE-CAP	REAMERS	RED FLAG
QUESTED	RACISTS	RAMBLED	RATINGS	REAMING	REDFORD
QUESTER	RACKETS	RAMBLER	RATIONS	REAPERS	REDHEAD
QUETZAL	RACKETY	RAMBLES	RATLINE	REAPING	RED MEAT
QUEUING	RACKING	RAMEKIN	RATPACK	REARING	REDNECK
QUIBBLE	RACOONS	RAMMING	RAT RACE	REARMED	REDNESS
QUICHES	RACQUET	RAMMISH	RATTIER	REASONS	REDOING
QUICKEN	RADIALS	RAMPAGE	RATTILY	REBADGE	REDOUBT
QUICKER	RADIANT	RAMPANT	RATTING	REBATER	REDOUND
QUICKIE	RADIATE	RAMPART	RATTISH	REBATES	REDPOLL
QUICKLY	RADICAL	RAMPION	RATTLED	REBIRTH	REDRAFT
QUIETEN	RADICEL	RAM RAID	RATTLES	REBOUND	REDRESS
QUIETER	RADICES	RAMRODS	RAT TRAP	REBRAND	REDROOT
QUIETLY	RADICLE	RAMSONS	RAUCOUS	REBUFFS	REDSKIN
QUIETUS	RADIOED	RANCHER	RAUNCHY	REBUILD	RED SPOT
QUILMES	RADULAR	RANCHES	RAVAGED	REBUILT	RED TAPE
QUILTED	RAFFISH	RANCOUR	RAVAGER	REBUKED	REDUCED
QUILTER	RAFFLED	RANDERS	RAVAGES	REBUKER	REDUCER
QUIMPER	RAFFLER	RANDIER	RAVELED	REBUKES	REDWING
QUINARY	RAFFLES	RANDOMS	RAVELIN	REBUSES	REDWOOD
QUINATE	RAFTERS	RANGERS	RAVELLY	RECALLS	REEDIER
QUINCES	RAFTING	RANGILY	RAVENER	RECAPED	REEDING

REEFERS	REISSUE	REPASTS	RESTING	REVIVAL	RIGHTER
REEFING	REJECTS	REPEATS	RESTIVE	REVIVED	RIGHTLY
REEKING	REJOICE	REPINED	RESTOCK	REVIVER	RIGHT-ON
RE-ELECT	RELAPSE	REPLACE	RESTORE	REVOICE	RIGIDLY
REELING	RELATED	REPLAYS	RESTYLE	REVOKED	RIG-OUTS
REELMAN	RELATER	REPLETE	RESULTS	REVOKER	RIM-FIRE
RE-ENTER	RELATOR	REPLEVY	RESUMED	REVOLTS	RIMLESS
RE-ENTRY	RELATUM	REPLICA	RESUMES	REVOLVE	RIMMING
REFACED	RELAXED	REPLIED	RETABLE	REVVING	RIMROCK
REFEREE	RELAXER	REPLIER	RETAKEN	REWARDS	RINGENT
REFILLS	RELAXIN	REPLIES	RETAKER	REWIRED	RINGERS
REFINED	RELAYED	REPORTS	RETAKES	REWRITE	RINGING
REFINER	RELEASE	REPOSAL	RETCHED	REWROTE	RINGLET
REFLATE	RELIANT	REPOSED	RETHINK	REYNOSA	RINSING
REFLECT	RELIEFS	REPOSER	RETICLE	RHAETIC	RIOT ACT
REFORMS	RELIEVE	REPOSIT	RETINAE	RHATANY	RIOTERS
REFRACT	RELINED	REPRESS	RETINAL	RHENIUM	RIOTING
REFRAIN	RELIVED	REPRINT	RETINAS	RHEUMIC	RIOTOUS
REFRESH	RELYING	REPRISE	RETINOL	RHIZOID	RIPCORD
REFUGEE	REMAINS	REPROOF	RETINUE	RHIZOME	RIPENED
REFUGES	REMAKES	REPROVE	RETIRED	RHODIUM	RIPENER
REFUNDS	REMANDS	REPTANT	RETIRER	RHOMBIC	RIP-OFFS
REFUSAL	REMARKS	REPTILE	RETITLE	RHOMBUS	RIPOSTE
REFUSED	REMARRY	REPULSE	RETORTS	RHONDDA	RIPPING
REFUSER	REMATCH	REPUTED	RETOUCH	RHUBARB	RIPPLED
REFUTED	REMNANT	REQUEST	RETRACE	RHYMING	RIPPLER
REFUTER	REMODEL	REQUIEM	RETRACT	RHYTHMS	RIPPLES
REGALIA	REMORSE	REQUIRE	RETREAD	RIBBAND	RIPPLET
REGALLY	REMOTER	REQUITE	RETREAT	RIBBING	RIPSAWS
REGARDS	REMOULD	REREDOS	RETRIAL	RIBBONS	RIPTIDE
REGATTA	REMOUNT	RESCIND	RETSINA	RIB CAGE	RISIBLE
REGENCY	REMOVAL	RESCUED	RETURNS	RIBWORT	RISIBLY
REGENTS	REMOVED	RESCUER	REUNIFY	RICHARD	RISINGS
REGIMEN	REMOVER	RESCUES	REUNION	RICHEST	RISKIER
REGIMES	REMOVES	RESERVE	REUNITE	RICHLER	RISKILY
REGINAS	RENAMED	RESHAPE	REUSING	RICHTER	RISKING
REGIONS	RENDELL	RESIDED	REVALUE	RICKETS	RISOTTO
REGNANT	RENDING	RESIDER	REVELED	RICKETY	RISSOLE
REGOSOL	RENEGED	RESIDUE	REVELRY	RICKING	RITUALS
REGRATE	RENEGER	RESKILL	REVENGE	RIDDING	RIVALED
REGRESS	RENEWAL	RESNAIS	REVENUE	RIDDLED	RIVALRY
REGRETS	RENEWED	RESOLVE	REVERED	RIDDLER	RIVETED
REGROUP	RENEWER	RESORTS	REVERER	RIDDLES	RIVETER
REGULAR	RENFREW	RESOUND	REVERIE	RIDGING	RIVIERA
REGULOS	RENTALS	RESPECT	REVERSE	RIDOTTO	RIVIERE
REGULUS	RENT BOY	RESPIRE	REVIEWS	RIFFLED	RIVULET
REHOUSE	RENTERS	RESPITE	REVILED	RIFFLER	ROACHES
REIFIER	RENTIER	RESPOND	REVILER	RIFLERY	ROADBED
REIGATE	RENTING	RESTAGE	REVISAL	RIFLING	ROAD HOG
REIGNED	REORDER	RESTATE	REVISED	RIGGING	ROADMAN
REINING	REPAIRS	RESTFUL	REVISER	RIGHTED	ROAD MAP

ROADMEN	ROOMIER	ROWLOCK	RUPTURE	SALLIES	SAO LUIS
ROAD TAX	ROOMILY	ROYALLY	RUSHDIE	SALLOWS	SAPHENA
ROADWAY	ROOMING	ROYALTY	RUSHING	SALMONS	SAPIENT
ROAMERS	ROOSTED	ROZZERS	RUSSIAN	SALOONS	SAPLESS
ROAMING	ROOSTER	RUBBERS	RUSTICS	SALPINX	SAPLING
ROARING	ROOTAGE	RUBBERY	RUSTIER	SALSIFY	SAPONIN
ROASTED	ROOTING	RUBBING	RUSTILY	SALTANT	SAPPERS
ROASTER	ROOTLET	RUBBISH	RUSTING	SALTBOX	SAPPIER
ROBBERS	ROPIEST	RUBDOWN	RUSTLED	SALTERN	SAPPILY
ROBBERY	RORAIMA	RUBELLA	RUSTLER	SALTIER	SAPPING
ROBBING	RORQUAL	RUBEOLA	RUTLAND	SALTILY	SAPPORO
ROBUSTA	ROSARIO	RUBICON	RUTTILY	SALTING	SAPROBE
ROCK BUN	ROSEATE	RUBIDIC	RUTTING	SALTIRE	SAPSAGO
ROCKERS	ROSEBUD	RUBIOUS	RUTTISH	SALTPAN	SAPWOOD
ROCKERY	ROSE HIP	RUBRICS	RYBINSK	SALTPOT	SARACEN
ROCKETS	ROSELLA	RUCHING		SALUTED	SARANSK
ROCKIER	ROSEOLA	RUCKING	**S**	SALUTER	SARATOV
ROCKIES	ROSETTA	RUCTION	SABBATH	SALUTES	SARAWAK
ROCKING	ROSETTE	RUDDERS	SACATON	SALVAGE	SARCASM
ROCKOON	ROSIEST	RUDDIER	SACCATE	SALVERS	SARCOID
RODENTS	ROSINED	RUDDILY	SACCULE	SALVING	SARCOMA
RODLIKE	ROSTERS	RUDERAL	SACHETS	SALVOES	SARCOUS
ROEBUCK	ROSTOCK	RUFFIAN	SACKING	SALWEEN	SARDINE
ROE DEER	ROSTRAL	RUFFLED	SADDEST	SAMISEN	SARDIUS
ROGUERY	ROSTRUM	RUFFLER	SADDLED	SAMNIUM	SARKIER
ROGUISH	ROTATED	RUFFLES	SADDLER	SAMOSAS	SARNIES
ROISTER	ROTATOR	RUINING	SADDLES	SAMOVAR	SARONGS
ROLL BAR	ROTIFER	RUINOUS	SADIRON	SAMOYED	SARONIC
ROLLERS	ROTORUA	RULABLE	SADISTS	SAMPANS	SASSABY
ROLLICK	ROTTERS	RULINGS	SADNESS	SAMPLED	SASSARI
ROLLING	ROTTING	RUMANIA	SAFARIS	SAMPLER	SASSIER
ROLLMOP	ROTUNDA	RUMBLED	SAFFIAN	SAMPLES	SASSING
ROLL-ONS	ROUBAIX	RUMBLER	SAFFRON	SAMPRAS	SATANIC
ROLL-TOP	ROUBLES	RUMBLES	SAFROLE	SAMURAI	SATCHEL
ROLLWAY	ROUGHEN	RUMMAGE	SAGGIER	SANCTUM	SATIATE
ROMAGNA	ROUGHER	RUMMEST	SAGGING	SANCTUS	SATIETY
ROMANCE	ROUGHLY	RUMOURS	SAGUARO	SANDALS	SATINET
ROMANIA	ROUGING	RUMPLED	SAHARAN	SANDBAG	SATIRES
ROMPERS	ROULEAU	RUNAWAY	SAILING	SANDBAR	SATISFY
ROMPING	ROULERS	RUNCORN	SAILORS	SANDBOX	SATSUMA
RONDEAU	ROUNDED	RUN DOWN	SAINTED	SANDERS	SATYRIC
RONDURE	ROUNDEL	RUN-DOWN	SAINTLY	SAND FLY	SATYRID
RONTGEN	ROUNDER	RUN INTO	SALAAMS	SANDIER	SAUCERS
ROOFING	ROUNDLY	RUNNELS	SALABLE	SANDING	SAUCIER
ROOFTOP	ROUNDUP	RUNNERS	SALAMIS	SANDPIT	SAUCILY
ROOINEK	ROUND UP	RUNNIER	SALERNO	SANGRIA	SAUCING
ROOKERY	ROUSING	RUNNING	SALFORD	SANICLE	SAUNTER
ROOKIES	ROUTINE	RUN-OFFS	SALICIN	SAN JOSE	SAURIAN
ROOKING	ROUTING	RUN OVER	SALIENT	SAN JUAN	SAUSAGE
ROOMERS	ROWDIER	RUNTISH	SALLIED	SAN REMO	SAUTEED
ROOMFUL	ROWDILY	RUNWAYS	SALLIER	SANTA FE	SAVABLE

SAVAGED	SCHEMES	SCREWER	SEASIDE	SELL-OUT	SESOTHO
SAVAGES	SCHERZO	SCREW UP	SEASONS	SELTZER	SESSILE
SAVANNA	SCHISMS	SCRIBAL	SEATING	SELVAGE	SESSION
SAVANTS	SCHLUMP	SCRIBER	SEATTLE	SEMATIC	SESTINA
SAVE-ALL	SCHMUCK	SCRIBES	SEAWALL	SEMINAL	SETBACK
SAVINGS	SCHOLAR	SCRIMPY	SEAWARE	SEMINAR	SET FREE
SAVIOUR	SCHOOLS	SCRIPTS	SEAWAYS	SEMITIC	SETLINE
SAVOURY	SCIATIC	SCROLLS	SEAWEED	SENATES	SETTEES
SAWBILL	SCIENCE	SCROOGE	SECEDED	SENATOR	SETTERS
SAWDUST	SCISSOR	SCROTUM	SECEDER	SENDERS	SETTING
SAWFISH	SCOFFED	SCRUBBY	SECLUDE	SENDING	SETTLED
SAWMILL	SCOFFER	SCRUFFS	SECONDO	SEND-OFF	SETTLER
SAWN-OFF	SCOLDED	SCRUFFY	SECONDS	SEND-UPS	SETTLES
SAXHORN	SCOLDER	SCRUMPY	SECRECY	SENEGAL	SEVENTH
SAXTUBA	SCOLLOP	SCRUNCH	SECRETE	SENIORS	SEVENTY
SAYINGS	SCONCES	SCRUPLE	SECRETS	SENORAS	SEVERAL
SCABBLE	SCOOPED	SCUDDED	SECTARY	SENSATE	SEVERED
SCABIES	SCOOPER	SCUFFED	SECTILE	SENSING	SEVILLE
SCALARS	SCOOTED	SCUFFLE	SECTION	SENSORS	SEXIEST
SCALDED	SCOOTER	SCULLED	SECTORS	SENSORY	SEXISTS
SCALENE	SCOPULA	SCULLER	SECULAR	SENSUAL	SEXLESS
SCALIER	SCORERS	SCULPIN	SECURED	SEPTATE	SEXPOTS
SCALING	SCORIFY	SCUMBLE	SECURER	SEPTETS	SEXTANT
SCALLOP	SCORING	SCUMMER	SEDATED	SEPTIME	SEXTETS
SCALPED	SCORNED	SCUPPER	SEDILIA	SEQUELA	SEXTILE
SCALPEL	SCORNER	SCUTATE	SEDUCED	SEQUELS	SEXTONS
SCALPER	SCORPER	SCUTTLE	SEDUCER	SEQUENT	SFUMATO
SCAMPER	SCORPIO	SCYTHED	SEEDBED	SEQUINS	SHAANXI
SCANDAL	SCOTOMA	SCYTHES	SEED BED	SEQUOIA	SHACKED
SCANDIC	SCOURED	SEABIRD	SEEDIER	SERAPHS	SHACKLE
SCANNED	SCOURER	SEACOCK	SEEDILY	SERBIAN	SHADIER
SCANNER	SCOURGE	SEA DOGS	SEEDING	SERFDOM	SHADILY
SCAPOSE	SCOUSES	SEAFOOD	SEEKERS	SERGIPE	SHADING
SCAPULA	SCOUTED	SEAGIRT	SEEKING	SERIALS	SHADOOF
SCARABS	SCOUTER	SEA GULL	SEEMING	SERIATE	SHADOWS
SCARCER	SCOWLED	SEAGULL	SEEPAGE	SERICIN	SHADOWY
SCARIER	SCOWLER	SEA-LANE	SEEPING	SERIEMA	SHAFTED
SCARIFY	SCRAGGY	SEALANT	SEESAWS	SERINGA	SHAGGED
SCARING	SCRAPED	SEA LEGS	SEETHED	SERIOUS	SHAHDOM
SCARLET	SCRAPER	SEALERS	SEGMENT	SERMONS	SHAKERS
SCARPER	SCRAPES	SEALERY	SEGOVIA	SERPENT	SHAKE UP
SCARRED	SCRAPPY	SEALING	SEISMIC	SERPIGO	SHAKE-UP
SCARVES	SCRATCH	SEA LION	SEIZING	SERRATE	SHAKHTY
SCATTED	SCRAWLS	SEAMARK	SEIZURE	SERRIED	SHAKIER
SCATTER	SCRAWLY	SEAMIER	SEKONDI	SERUMAL	SHAKILY
SCENERY	SCRAWNY	SEA MILE	SELENIC	SERVANT	SHAKING
SCENTED	SCREAMS	SEA MIST	SELFISH	SERVERS	SHALLOP
SCEPTIC	SCREECH	SEANCES	SELLERS	SERVERY	SHALLOT
SCEPTRE	SCREEDS	SEAPORT	SELLING	SERVICE	SHALLOW
SCHEMED	SCREENS	SEARING	SELL OFF	SERVILE	SHAMANS
SCHEMER	SCREWED	SEASICK	SELL OUT	SERVING	SHAMBLE

SHAMING	SHINGLE	SHRINKS	SIGHTLY	SIPHONS	SKITTER
SHAMMED	SHINGLY	SHRIVEL	SIGMATE	SIPPING	SKITTLE
SHAMMER	SHINIER	SHRIVER	SIGMOID	SIRLOIN	SKIVERS
SHAMPOO	SHINING	SHROUDS	SIGNALS	SIROCCO	SKIVING
SHANKLY	SHINNED	SHRUBBY	SIGNETS	SIRRAHS	SKULKED
SHANNON	SHIPPED	SHUCKED	SIGNIFY	SISSIER	SKULKER
SHANTOU	SHIPPER	SHUCKER	SIGNING	SISSIES	SKY BLUE
SHAPELY	SHIPWAY	SHUDDER	SIGN OFF	SISTERS	SKY-BLUE
SHAPING	SHIRKED	SHUFFLE	SIGNORA	SITCOMS	SKYCAPS
SHARERS	SHIRKER	SHUNNED	SIGNORE	SIT-DOWN	SKYDIVE
SHARING	SHITBAG	SHUNNER	SIGNORS	SITTERS	SKY-HIGH
SHARPEN	SHITTED	SHUNTED	SILENCE	SITTING	SKYJACK
SHARPER	SHIVERS	SHUNTER	SILENTS	SITUATE	SKYLARK
SHARPLY	SHIVERY	SHUSHED	SILESIA	SIXFOLD	SKYLINE
SHATTER	SHOCKED	SHUT-EYE	SILICIC	SIX-PACK	SKYSAIL
SHAVERS	SHOCKER	SHUT-OFF	SILICLE	SIXTEEN	SKYWALK
SHAVING	SHOEING	SHUTOUT	SILICON	SIXTIES	SLACKED
SHAWNEE	SHOGUNS	SHUTTER	SILIQUA	SIZABLE	SLACKEN
SHEARED	SHOOING	SHUTTLE	SILKIER	SIZZLED	SLACKER
SHEARER	SHOOTER	SHYLOCK	SILKILY	SIZZLER	SLACKLY
SHEATHE	SHOPPED	SHYNESS	SILLIER	SKATING	SLAGGED
SHEATHS	SHOPPER	SHYSTER	SILLIES	SKATOLE	SLAKING
SHEAVES	SHORING	SIALKOT	SILTING	SKEPTIC	SLALOMS
SHEBANG	SHORTED	SIALOID	SILURID	SKETCHY	SLAMMED
SHE BEAR	SHORTEN	SIAMANG	SILVERS	SKEWERS	SLANDER
SHEBEEN	SHORTER	SIAMESE	SILVERY	SKEWING	SLANGED
SHEDDER	SHORTIE	SIBERIA	SIMIANS	SKIABLE	SLANTED
SHEERED	SHORTLY	SIBLING	SIMILAR	SKIBOBS	SLAPPED
SHEERER	SHOTGUN	SICHUAN	SIMILES	SKIDDED	SLAPPER
SHEIKHS	SHOT PUT	SICKBAY	SIMIOUS	SKIDPAN	SLASHED
SHEILAS	SHOTTEN	SICKBED	SIMPERS	SKID ROW	SLASHER
SHEKELS	SHOUTED	SICKEST	SIMPLER	SKIFFLE	SLASHES
SHELLAC	SHOUTER	SICKING	SIMPLEX	SKI JUMP	SLATING
SHELLED	SHOVELS	SICKLES	SIMULAR	SKILFUL	SLATTED
SHELTER	SHOVING	SICK PAY	SINALOA	SKI LIFT	SLAVERS
SHELVED	SHOWERS	SIDEARM	SINCERE	SKILLED	SLAVERY
SHELVER	SHOWERY	SIDECAR	SINE DIE	SKILLET	SLAVING
SHELVES	SHOWIER	SIDE CAR	SINGING	SKIMMED	SLAVISH
SHEPARD	SHOWILY	SIDINGS	SINGLED	SKIMMER	SLAYERS
SHEPPEY	SHOWING	SIDLING	SINGLES	SKIMMIA	SLAYING
SHERBET	SHOWMAN	SIEMENS	SINGLET	SKIMPED	SLEDDED
SHERIFF	SHOWMEN	SIERRAN	SINITIC	SKINFUL	SLEDDER
SHERPAS	SHOWN UP	SIERRAS	SINKERS	SKINNED	SLEDGED
SHEWING	SHOW OFF	SIESTAS	SINKING	SKINNER	SLEDGES
SHIELDS	SHOW-OFF	SIEVERT	SINLESS	SKI POLE	SLEEKED
SHIFTED	SHRIEKS	SIEVING	SINNERS	SKIPPED	SLEEKER
SHIFTER	SHRIFTS	SIFTERS	SINNING	SKIPPER	SLEEKLY
SHIITES	SHRIKES	SIFTING	SINUATE	SKIPPET	SLEEPER
SHIKOKU	SHRILLY	SIGHING	SINUIJU	SKIPTON	SLEETED
SHIMMER	SHRIMPS	SIGHTED	SINUOUS	SKIRRET	SLEEVES
SHINDIG	SHRINES	SIGHTER	SINUSES	SKIRTED	SLEIGHS

SLEIGHT	SMALL AD	SNEEZED	SOBBING	SOOTHER	SPANKED
SLENDER	SMALLER	SNEEZER	SOBERED	SOOTIER	SPANKER
SLEUTHS	SMARTED	SNEEZES	SOBERLY	SOOTILY	SPANNED
SLEWING	SMARTEN	SNICKED	SOCAGER	SOPHISM	SPANNER
SLICING	SMARTER	SNICKER	SOCIALS	SOPHIST	SPARING
SLICKED	SMARTLY	SNIDELY	SOCIETY	SOPPIER	SPARKED
SLICKER	SMASHED	SNIDEST	SOCKETS	SOPPILY	SPARKLE
SLICKLY	SMASHER	SNIFFED	SOCKEYE	SOPPING	SPARRED
SLIDING	SMASHES	SNIFFER	SOCKING	SOPRANO	SPARROW
SLIGHTS	SMASH-UP	SNIFFLE	SODDING	SORBETS	SPARSER
SLIMIER	SMATTER	SNIFTER	SOD'S	SORBOSE	SPARTAN
SLIMILY	SMEARED	SNIGGER	LAW	SORCERY	SPASTIC
SLIMMED	SMEARER	SNIGGLE	SOFA BED	SORDINO	SPATHIC
SLIMMER	SMECTIC	SNIPERS	SOFTEST	SORGHUM	SPATIAL
SLINGER	SMELLED	SNIPING	SOFTIES	SORITES	SPATTER
SLIP-ONS	SMELTED	SNIPPED	SOGGIER	SOROSIS	SPATULA
SLIPPED	SMELTER	SNIPPET	SOGGILY	SORRIER	SPAWNED
SLIPPER	SMIDGIN	SNOGGED	SOILAGE	SORRILY	SPAWNER
SLIP-UPS	SMILING	SNOOKER	SOILING	SORROWS	SPAYING
SLIPWAY	SMIRKED	SNOOPED	SOIREES	SORTIES	SPEAKER
SLITHER	SMIRKER	SNOOPER	SOJOURN	SORTING	SPEARED
SLITTED	SMITING	SNOOZED	SOLACED	SORT-OUT	SPEARER
SLITTER	SMITTEN	SNOOZER	SOLACER	SO THERE	SPECIAL
SLIVERS	SMOKERS	SNOOZES	SOLACES	SOTTISH	SPECIES
SLOBBER	SMOKIER	SNORERS	SOLANUM	SOUFFLE	SPECIFY
SLOGANS	SMOKILY	SNORING	SOLARIA	SOUGHED	SPECKLE
SLOGGED	SMOKING	SNORKEL	SOLDIER	SOUKOUS	SPECTRA
SLOGGER	SMOLDER	SNORTED	SOLICIT	SOULFUL	SPECTRE
SLOPING	SMOTHER	SNORTER	SOLIDLY	SOUNDED	SPEEDED
SLOPPED	SMUDGED	SNOWCAP	SOLIDUS	SOUNDER	SPEEDER
SLOSHED	SMUDGES	SNOWIER	SOLOIST	SOUNDLY	SPELLED
SLOTTED	SMUGGER	SNOWILY	SOLOMON	SOUPCON	SPELLER
SLOTTER	SMUGGLE	SNOWING	SOLUBLE	SOUPFIN	SPELTER
SLOUCHY	SMUTCHY	SNOWMAN	SOLVATE	SOURCES	SPENCER
SLOUGHS	SNACKED	SNOWMEN	SOLVENT	SOUREST	SPENDER
SLOUGHY	SNAFFLE	SNUBBED	SOLVERS	SOURING	SPEWING
SLOVENE	SNAGGED	SNUBBER	SOLVING	SOURSOP	SPHENIC
SLOWEST	SNAKILY	SNUFFED	SOMALIA	SOUSING	SPHERAL
SLOWING	SNAKING	SNUFFER	SOMATIC	SOUTANE	SPHERES
SLUGGED	SNAPPED	SNUFFLE	SOMEDAY	SOUTHER	SPICATE
SLUICED	SNAPPER	SNUFFLY	SOMEHOW	SOVIETS	SPICERY
SLUICES	SNARING	SNUGGLE	SOMEONE	SOVKHOZ	SPICIER
SLUMBER	SNARLED	SOAKAGE	SOMEWAY	SOWETAN	SPICILY
SLUMMED	SNARLER	SOAKING	SOMITAL	SOZZLED	SPICING
SLUMMER	SNARL UP	SO-AND-	SONANCE	SPACING	SPICULE
SLUMPED	SNARL-UP	SO	SONATAS	SPANCEL	SPIDERS
SLURPED	SNATCHY	SOAPBOX	SONDAGE	SPANDEX	SPIDERY
SLURRED	SNEAKED	SOAPIER	SONGFUL	SPANGLE	SPIELER
SLYNESS	SNEAKER	SOAPILY	SONNETS	SPANGLY	SPIGNEL
SMACKED	SNEERED	SOAPING	SOOCHOW	SPANIEL	SPIGOTS
SMACKER	SNEERER	SOARING	SOOTHED	SPANISH	SPIKIER

SPIKILY	SPORRAN	SQUELCH	STANNIC	STEERER	STIPEND
SPIKING	SPORTED	SQUIDGY	STANZAS	STELLAR	STIPPLE
SPILLED	SPORTER	SQUIFFY	STAPLED	STEMMED	STIPULE
SPILLER	SPORULE	SQUILLA	STAPLER	STEMMER	STIR-FRY
SPINACH	SPOTLIT	SQUINCH	STAPLES	STEMSON	STIRRED
SPINDLE	SPOTTED	SQUINTS	STARCHY	STENCIL	STIRRER
SPINDLY	SPOTTER	SQUINTY	STARDOM	STEN GUN	STIRRUP
SPIN-DRY	SPOUSAL	SQUIRES	STARING	STENTOR	STOCKED
SPINETS	SPOUSES	SQUIRMS	STARKER	STEPDAD	STOCKER
SPINNER	SPOUTED	SQUIRMY	STARKLY	STEPMUM	STOICAL
SPINNEY	SPOUTER	SQUIRTS	STARLET	STEPPED	STOKERS
SPIN-OFF	SPRAINS	SQUISHY	STARLIT	STEPPER	STOKING
SPINOSE	SPRAINT	STABBED	STARRED	STEPPES	STOMACH
SPINOUS	SPRAWLS	STABBER	STARTED	STEPSON	STOMPED
SPIN OUT	SPRAWLY	STABILE	STARTER	STEPS UP	STOMPER
SPINULE	SPRAYED	STABLED	STARTLE	STEREOS	STONIER
SPIRAEA	SPRAYER	STABLES	START UP	STERILE	STONILY
SPIRALS	SPREADS	STACKED	STARVED	STERLET	STONING
SPIRANT	SPRIEST	STACKER	STARVER	STERNAL	STOOD UP
SPIREME	SPRIGGY	STADDLE	STASHED	STERNER	STOOGES
SPIRITS	SPRINGE	STADIUM	STASHES	STERNLY	STOOKER
SPIROID	SPRINGS	STAFFED	STATANT	STERNUM	STOOPED
SPIRULA	SPRINGY	STAFFER	STATELY	STEROID	STOOPER
SPITING	SPRINTS	STAGGER	STATICS	STERTOR	STOPGAP
SPITTER	SPRITES	STAGILY	STATING	STETSON	STOPING
SPITTLE	SPROUTS	STAGING	STATION	STEWARD	STOPPED
SPLASHY	SPRUCED	STAIDLY	STATISM	STEWART	STOPPER
SPLAYED	SPRUCES	STAINED	STATIST	STEWING	STORAGE
SPLEENS	SPUMONE	STAINER	STATIVE	STHENIC	STOREYS
SPLENIC	SPUMOUS	STAINES	STATUED	STIBINE	STORIED
SPLICED	SPURNED	STAKING	STATUES	STICHIC	STORIES
SPLICER	SPURNER	STALEST	STATURE	STICKER	STORING
SPLICES	SPURRED	STALING	STATUTE	STICKLE	STORMED
SPLINTS	SPURTED	STALKED	STAUNCH	STICK-ON	STOUTER
SPLODGE	SPUTNIK	STALKER	STAVING	STICK UP	STOUTLY
SPLODGY	SPUTTER	STALLED	STAYERS	STICK-UP	STOWAGE
SPLURGE	SQUABBY	STAMBUL	STAYING	STIFFEN	STOWING
SPOILED	SQUACCO	STAMENS	STEALER	STIFFER	STRAFED
SPOILER	SQUALID	STAMINA	STEALTH	STIFFLY	STRAFER
SPOKANE	SQUALLS	STAMMEL	STEAMED	STIFLED	STRAINS
SPONDEE	SQUALLY	STAMMER	STEAMER	STIFLER	STRAITS
SPONGED	SQUALOR	STAMPED	STEAM UP	STIGMAS	STRANDS
SPONGER	SQUARED	STAMPER	STEARIC	STILLED	STRANGE
SPONGES	SQUARER	STANCES	STEARIN	STILLER	STRATAL
SPONGIN	SQUARES	STANDBY	STEELED	STILTED	STRATAS
SPONSON	SQUASHY	STAND BY	STEEPED	STILTON	STRATUM
SPONSOR	SQUAWKS	STANDER	STEEPEN	STIMULI	STRATUS
SPOOFER	SQUEAKS	STAND-IN	STEEPER	STINGER	STRAYED
SPOOKED	SQUEAKY	STAND UP	STEEPLE	STINKER	STRAYER
SPOONED	SQUEALS	STAND-UP	STEEPLY	STINTED	STREAKS
SPOORER	SQUEEZE	STANLEY	STEERED	STINTER	STREAKY

STREAMS	STYLIST	SUCRASE	SUNROOF	SWANSEA	SYLPHIC
STREETS	STYLIZE	SUCROSE	SUNSETS	SWAPPED	SYLPHID
STRETCH	STYLOID	SUCTION	SUNSPOT	SWAPPER	SYLVITE
STRETTA	STYLOPS	SUDANIC	SUNSTAR	SWARMED	SYMBOLS
STRETTO	STYMIED	SUDBURY	SUNTANS	SWARTHY	SYMPTOM
STREWED	STYPSIS	SUDETES	SUNTRAP	SWATHED	SYNAPSE
STREWER	STYPTIC	SUFFICE	SUNWISE	SWATTED	SYNCARP
STREWTH	STYRENE	SUFFOLK	SUPPERS	SWATTER	SYNCHRO
STRIATE	SUAVELY	SUFFUSE	SUPPING	SWAYING	SYNCOPE
STRIDES	SUAVITY	SUGARED	SUPPLER	SWEARER	SYNERGY
STRIDOR	SUBACID	SUGGEST	SUPPORT	SWEATED	SYNESIS
STRIKER	SUB-AQUA	SUICIDE	SUPPOSE	SWEATER	SYNGAMY
STRIKES	SUBARID	SUITING	SUPREME	SWEDISH	SYNODAL
STRINGS	SUBBASE	SUITORS	SUPREMO	SWEEPER	SYNODIC
STRINGY	SUBBASS	SUKHUMI	SURBASE	SWEETEN	SYNONYM
STRIPED	SUBBING	SULCATE	SURCOAT	SWEETER	SYNOVIA
STRIPER	SUBDUAL	SULKIER	SURFACE	SWEETIE	SYPHONS
STRIPES	SUBDUCT	SULKILY	SURFEIT	SWEETLY	SYRINGA
STRIPEY	SUBDUED	SULKING	SURFERS	SWELLED	SYRINGE
STRIVEN	SUBEDIT	SULLAGE	SURFING	SWELTER	SYRPHID
STRIVER	SUBERIN	SULLIED	SURGEON	SWERVED	SYSTEMS
STROBIC	SUBFUSC	SULPHUR	SURGERY	SWERVER	SYSTOLE
STROKED	SUBJECT	SULTANA	SURGING	SWERVES	SZILARD
STROKES	SUBJOIN	SULTANS	SURINAM	SWIFTER	
STROLLS	SUBLIME	SUMATRA	SURLIER	SWIFTLY	**T**
STROPHE	SUBPLOT	SUMBAWA	SURLILY	SWIGGED	
STROPPY	SUB ROSA	SUMMAND	SURMISE	SWIGGER	TABANID
STRUDEL	SUBSETS	SUMMARY	SURNAME	SWILLED	TABASCO
STUBBED	SUBSIDE	SUMMERS	SURPASS	SWILLER	TABBIES
STUBBLE	SUBSIDY	SUMMERY	SURPLUS	SWIMMER	TABBING
STUBBLY	SUBSIST	SUMMING	SURREAL	SWINDLE	TABLEAU
STUCK-UP	SUBSOIL	SUMMITS	SURREYS	SWINDON	TABLING
STUDDED	SUBSUME	SUMMONS	SURVEYS	SWINGER	TABLOID
STUDENT	SUBTEND	SUNBEAM	SURVIVE	SWINGLE	TABORET
STUDIED	SUBTEXT	SUNBEDS	SUSPECT	SWINISH	TABORIN
STUDIES	SUBTLER	SUNBELT	SUSPEND	SWIPING	TABULAR
STUDIOS	SUBTYPE	SUNBIRD	SUSSING	SWIPPLE	TACHYON
STUFFED	SUBUNIT	SUNBURN	SUSTAIN	SWIRLED	TACITLY
STUFFER	SUBURBS	SUNDAES	SUTURAL	SWISHED	TACKIER
STUMBLE	SUBVERT	SUNDAYS	SUTURED	SWISHER	TACKIES
STUMPED	SUBWAYS	SUNDIAL	SUTURES	SWISHES	TACKILY
STUMPER	SUCCEED	SUNDOWN	SWABBED	SWIVELS	TACKING
STUNNED	SUCCESS	SUNFISH	SWABBER	SWIZZLE	TACKLED
STUNNER	SUCCOUR	SUNGLOW	SWABIAN	SWOLLEN	TACKLER
STUNTED	SUCCUBI	SUN GODS	SWADDLE	SWOONED	TACKLES
STUPEFY	SUCCUMB	SUNLAMP	SWAGGER	SWOOPED	TACNODE
STUPORS	SUCCUSS	SUNLESS	SWAHILI	SWOPPED	TACTFUL
STUTTER	SUCKERS	SUNNIER	SWALLOW	SWOTTED	TACTICS
STYGIAN	SUCKING	SUNNILY	SWAMPED	SYCOSIS	TACTILE
STYLING	SUCKLED	SUNNING	SWANKED	SYENITE	TACTUAL
STYLISH	SUCKLER	SUNRISE	SWANNED	SYLLABI	TADPOLE
					TADZHIK

TAFFETA	TANGLER	TAUNTED	TELEXES	TERRORS	THIMBLE
TAFFIES	TANGLES	TAUNTER	TELFORD	TERSELY	THIN AIR
TAGGERS	TANGOED	TAUNTON	TELLERS	TERTIAL	THINNED
TAGGING	TANGRAM	TAUREAN	TELLIES	TERTIAN	THINNER
TAG LINE	TANKAGE	TAURINE	TELLING	TESSERA	THIONIC
TAGMEME	TANKARD	TAUTEST	TELPHER	TESTACY	THIONYL
TAIL END	TANKERS	TAVENER	TELSTAR	TESTATE	THIRSTS
TAILING	TANNAGE	TAVERNS	TEMPERA	TEST BAN	THIRSTY
TAILORS	TANNATE	TAXABLE	TEMPERS	TESTERS	THISTLE
TAINTED	TANNERS	TAX-FREE	TEMPEST	TESTIER	THISTLY
TAIYUAN	TANNERY	TAXICAB	TEMPING	TESTIFY	THITHER
TAKABLE	TANNING	TAXIING	TEMPLES	TESTILY	THORITE
TAKEOFF	TANTRUM	TAXIWAY	TEMPTED	TESTING	THORIUM
TAKE OFF	TAN-TUNG	TBILISI	TEMPTER	TETANIC	THOUGHT
TAKEOUT	TAOISTS	TBILIZI	TENABLE	TETANUS	THRALLS
TAKE OUT	TAPERED	TEABAGS	TENANCY	TETHERS	THREADS
TAKEUPS	TAPERER	TEACAKE	TENANTS	TETRODE	THREADY
TAKINGS	TAPETAL	TEA CAKE	TENCHES	TEXTILE	THREATS
TALCOSE	TAPETUM	TEACHER	TENDERS	TEXTUAL	THREE
TALENTS	TAPHOLE	TEACH-IN	TENDING	TEXTURE	R'S
TALIBAN	TAPIOCA	TEA COSY	TENDONS	THALLIC	THRIFTS
TALIPED	TAPPETS	TEACUPS	TENDRIL	THALLUS	THRIFTY
TALIPES	TAPPING	TEA GOWN	TENFOLD	THANKED	THRILLS
TALIPOT	TAPROOM	TEALEAF	TENNERS	THAWING	THRIVED
TALKERS	TAPROOT	TEAMING	TENONER	THE ARTS	THROATS
TALKIES	TARANTO	TEAPOTS	TENPINS	THEATRE	THROATY
TALKING	TARDIER	TEARFUL	TENSELY	THE BARD	THRONES
TALLAGE	TARDILY	TEAR GAS	TENSEST	THEISTS	THRONGS
TALLBOY	TARGETS	TEARING	TENSILE	THEOREM	THROUGH
TALLEST	TARIFFS	TEAROOM	TENSING	THERAPY	THROWER
TALLIED	TARMACS	TEASELS	TENSION	THEREAT	THROW IN
TALLIER	TARNISH	TEASERS	TENSIVE	THEREBY	THROW-IN
TALLIES	TARRASA	TEASHOP	TENTAGE	THEREIN	THRUSTS
TALLINN	TARRIED	TEASING	TENUITY	THEREOF	THRUWAY
TALLISH	TARRING	TEA TREE	TENUOUS	THEREON	THUDDED
TALLYHO	TARSIER	TECHILY	TEPIDLY	THERETO	THULIUM
TAMABLE	TARTANS	TECHNIC	TEQUILA	THERMAL	THUMBED
TAMARAU	TARTARS	TECTRIX	TERBIUM	THERMIC	THUMPED
TAMARIN	TASSELS	TEDIOUS	TERMING	THERMIT	THUMPER
TAMBOUR	TASTERS	TEEMING	TERMINI	THERMOS	THUNDER
TAMPERE	TASTIER	TEENAGE	TERMITE	THEROID	THURGAU
TAMPICO	TASTILY	TEEPEES	TERNARY	THEROUX	THWACKS
TAMPING	TASTING	TEGULAR	TERNATE	THEURGY	THYMINE
TAMPONS	TATOUAY	TEHERAN	TERPENE	THE WASH	THYROID
TANAGER	TATTERS	TEKTITE	TERRACE	THICKEN	THYRSUS
TANBARK	TATTIER	TELAMON	TERRAIN	THICKER	THYSELF
TANDEMS	TATTILY	TEL AVIV	TERRANE	THICKET	TIANJIN
TANGELO	TATTING	TELEOST	TERRENE	THICKIE	TIBETAN
TANGENT	TATTLED	TELERAN	TERRIER	THICKLY	TICKERS
TANGIER	TATTLER	TELESIS	TERRIFY	THIEVED	TICKETS
TANGLED	TATTOOS	TELEXED	TERRINE	THIEVES	TICKING

TICKLED	TIPPERS	TOLLING	TORREFY	TRADE IN	TRELLIS
TICKLER	TIPPETT	TOLUATE	TORRENT	TRADE-IN	TREMBLE
TICKLES	TIPPING	TOLUENE	TORREON	TRADERS	TREMBLY
TIDBITS	TIPPLER	TOMBOLA	TORSADE	TRADING	TREMOLO
TIDDLER	TIPPLES	TOMBOLO	TORSION	TRADUCE	TREMORS
TIDEWAY	TIPSIER	TOMBOYS	TORTOLA	TRAFFIC	TRENTON
TIDIEST	TIPSILY	TOMCATS	TORTONI	TRAGEDY	TREPANG
TIDINGS	TIPSTER	TOMFOOL	TORTUGA	TRAILED	TRESSES
TIDYING	TIPTOED	TOM-TOMS	TORTURE	TRAILER	TRESTLE
TIE-DIED	TIPTOES	TONEPAD	TORYISM	TRAINED	TREVISO
TIEPINS	TIRADES	TONETIC	TOSSING	TRAINEE	TRIABLE
TIFFANY	TIREDLY	TONGUES	TOSS-UPS	TRAINER	TRIACID
TIGHTEN	TISSUES	TONIGHT	TOTALED	TRAIPSE	TRIADIC
TIGHTER	TITANIA	TONNAGE	TOTALLY	TRAITOR	TRIADIC
TIGHTLY	TITANIC	TONNEAU	TOTE BAG	TRAJECT	TRIBADE
TIGRESS	TITBITS	TONSILS	TOTEMIC	TRAMCAR	TRIBUNE
TIJUANA	TITFERS	TONSURE	TOTTERY	TRAMMEL	TRIBUTE
TILAPIA	TITHING	TONTINE	TOTTING	TRAMPED	TRICEPS
TILBURG	TITMICE	TOOLING	TOUCANS	TRAMPER	TRICKED
TILLAGE	TITOISM	TOOTING	TOUCHED	TRAMPLE	TRICKER
TILLERS	TITOIST	TOOTLED	TOUCHER	TRAMWAY	TRICKLE
TILLING	TITRANT	TOOTLER	TOUCHES	TRANCES	TRICKLY
TILTING	TITRATE	TOOTLES	TOUGHEN	TRANCHE	TRICKSY
TIMBALE	TITTERS	TOOTSIE	TOUGHER	TRANSIT	TRICORN
TIMBERS	TITTIES	TOPARCH	TOUGHLY	TRANSOM	TRIDENT
TIMBREL	TITULAR	TOPAZES	TOUPEES	TRAPANI	TRIDUUM
TIMBRES	TIZZIES	TOPCOAT	TOURACO	TRAPEZE	TRIED ON
TIME LAG	TLEMCEN	TOP DOGS	TOURING	TRAPPED	TRIESTE
TIME-OUT	TOADIED	TOP HATS	TOURISM	TRAPPER	TRIFLED
TIMIDLY	TOADIES	TOPIARY	TOURIST	TRASHED	TRIFLER
TIMPANI	TOADLET	TOPICAL	TOURNAI	TRAUMAS	TRIFLES
TINAMOU	TOASTED	TOPKNOT	TOURNEY	TRAVAIL	TRIGGER
TINFOIL	TOASTER	TOPLESS	TOUSLED	TRAVELS	TRILLED
TINGING	TOASTIE	TOPMAST	TOUTING	TRAVOIS	TRILOGY
TINGLED	TOBACCO	TOPMOST	TOWARDS	TRAWLED	TRIMBLE
TINGLER	TOBOLSK	TOPONYM	TOWBOAT	TRAWLER	TRIMMED
TIN GODS	TOBY JUG	TOPPERS	TOWELED	TREACLE	TRIMMER
TIN HATS	TOCCATA	TOPPING	TOWERED	TREACLY	TRINARY
TINIEST	TOCSINS	TOPPLED	TOWHEAD	TREADER	TRINITY
TINKERS	TODDIES	TOPSAIL	TOWLINE	TREADLE	TRINKET
TINKLED	TODDLED	TOPSIDE	TOWPATH	TREAD ON	TRIOLET
TINKLES	TODDLER	TOPSOIL	TOWROPE	TREASON	TRIPLED
TINNIER	TOE CAPS	TOPSPIN	TOW ROPE	TREATED	TRIPLET
TINNILY	TOEHOLD	TORCHES	TRABZON	TREATER	TRIPLEX
TINNING	TOENAIL	TORFAEN	TRACERS	TREBLED	TRIPODS
TINTACK	TOFFEES	TORMENT	TRACERY	TREBLES	TRIPODY
TINTING	TOGGING	TORNADO	TRACHEA	TREFOIL	TRIPOLI
TINTYPE	TOGGLES	TORONTO	TRACING	TREHALA	TRIPPED
TINWARE	TOHEROA	TORPEDO	TRACKED	TREKKED	TRIPPER
TINWORK	TOILETS	TORQUAY	TRACKER	TREKKER	TRIPPET
TIP-OFFS	TOILING	TORQUES	TRACTOR	TREKKIE	TRIPURA
					TRIREME

TRISECT	TRUSTED	TURNERS	TWOSOME	UNCHAIN	UNPAGED
TRISMIC	TRUSTEE	TURNERY	TWO-STAR	UNCINUS	UNPOSED
TRISMUS	TRUSTER	TURNING	TWO-STEP	UNCIVIL	UNQUIET
TRISOME	TRYPSIN	TURNIPS	TWO-TIME	UNCLASP	UNQUOTE
TRISOMY	TRYPTIC	TURNKEY	TWO-TONE	UNCLEAN	UNRAVEL
TRITELY	TRYSAIL	TURN OFF	TYCHISM	UNCLEAR	UNREADY
TRITIUM	TRYSTER	TURN-OFF	TYCOONS	UNCLOAK	UNREEVE
TRITONE	TSARDOM	TURN-ONS	TYLOSIS	UNCLOSE	UNSCREW
TRIUMPH	TSARINA	TURN OUT	TYMPANA	UNCOUTH	UNSLING
TRIVETS	TSARIST	TURNOUT	TYMPANY	UNCOVER	UNSNARL
TRIVIAL	T-SHIRTS	TURNS UP	TYNWALD	UNCROSS	UNSOUND
TROCHAL	T-SQUARE	TURN-UPS	TYPEBAR	UNCTION	UNSTICK
TROCHEE	TSUNAMI	TURPETH	TYPESET	UNDERDO	UNSTRAP
TRODDEN	TUATARA	TURRETS	TYPHOID	UNDERGO	UNSTUCK
TROIKAS	TUBBIER	TURTLER	TYPHOON	UNDOING	UNSWEAR
TROJANS	TUBBING	TURTLES	TYPHOUS	UNDRESS	UNTHINK
TROLLED	TUBIFEX	TUSCANY	TYPICAL	UNDYING	UNTRIED
TROLLEY	TUBULAR	TUSKERS	TYPISTS	UNEARTH	UNTRUSS
TROLLOP	TUCKING	TUSSIVE	TYRANNY	UNEQUAL	UNTRUTH
TROMMEL	TUCUMAN	TUSSLED	TYRANTS	UNFROCK	UNTYING
TROOPED	TUESDAY	TUSSLES	TYRONIC	UNFUSSY	UNUSUAL
TROOPER	TUGGING	TUSSOCK	TZARINA	UNGODLY	UNVOICE
TROPHIC	TUITION	TUTORED		UNGUENT	UNWAGED
TROPICS	TUMBLED	TUTUILA	**U**	UNGULAR	UNWOUND
TROPISM	TUMBLER	TUTUOLA	UDAIPUR	UNHAPPY	UP-AND-UP
TROTTED	TUMBLES	TUXEDOS	UGANDAN	UNHEARD	UP
TROTTER	TUMBREL	TWADDLE	UGLIEST	UNHINGE	UPBRAID
TROUBLE	TUMMIES	TWANGED	UKRAINE	UNHORSE	UPBUILD
TROUGHS	TUMOURS	TWEAKED	UKULELE	UNICORN	UPCHUCK
TROUNCE	TUMULAR	TWEETED	ULANOVA	UNIFIED	UPDATED
TROUPER	TUMULTS	TWEETER	ULAN-UDE	UNIFIER	UPDATER
TROUPES	TUMULUS	TWELFTH	ULLAGED	UNIFORM	UPDATES
TROUSER	TUNABLE	TWELVES	ULULANT	UNITARY	UPDRAFT
TROWELS	TUNEFUL	TWIDDLE	ULULATE	UNITIES	UPENDED
TRUANCY	TUNICLE	TWIDDLY	UMBRAGE	UNITING	UPFRONT
TRUANTS	TUNISIA	TWIGGED	UMBRIAN	UNITIVE	UP FRONT
TRUCKED	TUNNELS	TWIN BED	UMBRIEL	UNKEMPT	UPGRADE
TRUCKER	TUNNIES	TWINGES	UMLAUTS	UNKNOWN	UPHEAVE
TRUCKLE	TUPPING	TWINING	UMPIRED	UNLATCH	UPLANDS
TRUDGED	TURBANS	TWINKLE	UMPIRES	UNLEARN	UPPSALA
TRUDGEN	TURBARY	TWINNED	UMPTEEN	UNLEASH	UPRAISE
TRUDGER	TURBINE	TWIN SET	UNAIDED	UNLOOSE	UPRIGHT
TRUDGES	TURBOTS	TWIRLED	UNARMED	UNLUCKY	UPRISER
TRUFFLE	TURDINE	TWIRLER	UNAWARE	UNMAKER	UPRIVER
TRUISMS	TUREENS	TWISTED	UNBONED	UNMANLY	UPSCALE
TRUMPED	TURFING	TWISTER	UNBOSOM	UNMEANT	UPSILON
TRUMPET	TURGITE	TWITTED	UNBOUND	UNMORAL	UPSKILL
TRUNDLE	TURKEYS	TWITTER	UNBOWED	UNMOVED	UPSTAGE
TRUSSED	TURKISH	TWIZZLE	UNBRACE	UNNAMED	UPSTART
TRUSSER	TURKMEN	TWOFOLD	UNCAGED	UNNERVE	UPSURGE
TRUSSES	TURMOIL	TWONESS	UNCANNY	UNOWNED	UPSWEEP

UPSWING	UTTERED	VARMINT	VERMONT	VILNIUS	VOCALLY
UPTAKES	UTTERER	VARNISH	VERNIER	VINASSE	VOCODER
UPTHROW	UTTERLY	VARSITY	VERONAL	VINEGAR	VOETSEK
UPTIGHT	UVEITIC	VARYING	VERRUCA	VINTAGE	VOICING
UP TO	UVEITIS	VASSALS	VERSACE	VINTNER	VOIDING
YOU	UVULARS	VASTITY	VERSANT	VIOLATE	VOIOTIA
UPTURNS	UXORIAL	VATICAN	VERSIFY	VIOLENT	VOLAPUK
UPWARDS		VAUDOIS	VERSION	VIOLETS	VOLCANO
URAEMIA	**V**	VAULTED	VERTIGO	VIOLINS	VOLLEYS
URAEMIC	VACANCY	VAULTER	VERVAIN	VIOLIST	VOLOGDA
URALITE	VACATED	VAUNTED	VESICAL	VIRAGOS	VOLTAGE
URANIAN	VACCINE	VAUNTER	VESICLE	VIRELAY	VOLTAIC
URANIDE	VACUITY	VECTORS	VESPERS	VIRGATE	VOLUBLE
URANITE	VACUOLE	VEDALIA	VESPINE	VIRGINS	VOLUBLY
URANIUM	VACUOUS	VEDDOID	VESSELS	VIRGOAN	VOLUMED
URANOUS	VACUUMS	VEDETTE	VESTIGE	VIRGULE	VOLUMES
URCHINS	VAGINAL	VEERING	VESTING	VIRTUAL	VOLVATE
UREDIAL	VAGINAS	VEGETAL	VESTRAL	VIRTUES	VOMITED
UREDIUM	VAGRANT	VEHICLE	VESTURE	VIRUSES	VOMITER
URETHRA	VAGUELY	VEILING	VETCHES	VISAGES	VOMITUS
URGENCY	VAINEST	VEINING	VETERAN	VISAING	VORLAGE
URIDINE	VALANCE	VEINLET	VETIVER	VIS-A-	VOTABLE
URINALS	VALENCE	VELAMEN	VETOING	VIS	VOUCHED
URINANT	VALENCY	VELIGER	VETTING	VISAYAN	VOUCHER
URINARY	VALERIC	VELLORE	VEXEDLY	VISCERA	VOX POPS
URINATE	VALIANT	VELOURS	VIADUCT	VISCOID	VOYAGED
URINOUS	VALIDLY	VELVETY	VIBRANT	VISCOSE	VOYAGER
URMSTON	VALISES	VENALLY	VIBRATE	VISCOUS	VOYAGES
URNLIKE	VALLEYS	VENATIC	VIBRATO	VISIBLE	VOYEURS
URODELE	VALONIA	VENDACE	VICENZA	VISIBLY	VULGATE
UROLITH	VALUERS	VENDING	VICEROY	VISIONS	VULPINE
UROLOGY	VALUING	VENDORS	VICINAL	VISITED	VULTURE
URUAPAN	VALVATE	VENEERS	VICIOUS	VISITOR	
URUGUAY	VALVULE	VENISON	VICOMTE	VISTAED	**W**
URUMCHI	VAMOOSE	VENTAGE	VICTIMS	VISTULA	WADABLE
USELESS	VAMPIRE	VENTING	VICTORS	VITALLY	WADDING
USHERED	VANADIC	VENTRAL	VICTORY	VITAMIN	WADDLED
USUALLY	VANDALS	VENTURE	VICTRIX	VITEBSK	WADDLER
USURERS	VANILLA	VENULAR	VICTUAL	VITIATE	WADDLES
USURPED	VANTAGE	VERANDA	VICUNAS	VITORIA	WAFFLED
USURPER	VANUATU	VERBENA	VIDEOED	VITRAIN	WAFFLES
UTENSIL	VANWARD	VERBIFY	VIDICON	VITRIFY	WAFTAGE
UTERINE	VAPIDLY	VERBOSE	VIETNAM	VITRINE	WAFTING
UTILITY	VAPOURS	VERDANT	VIEWERS	VITRIOL	WAGERED
UTILIZE	VARIANT	VERDICT	VIEWING	VITTATE	WAGERER
UT INFRA	VARIATE	VERDURE	VIKINGS	VIVIDLY	WAGGING
UTOPIAN	VARIETY	VERGERS	VILLACH	VIYELLA	WAGGISH
UTOPIAS	VARIOLA	VERGING	VILLAGE	VIZIERS	WAGGLED
UTRECHT	VARIOLE	VERGLAS	VILLAIN	V-NECKED	WAGGLES
UTRICLE	VARIOUS	VERISMO	VILLEIN	VOCABLE	WAGONER
UT SUPRA	VARLETS	VERMEIL	VILLOUS	VOCALIC	WAGTAIL

WAILFUL	WAR GAME	WAXWING	WELLING	WHIFFLE	WIGWAMS
WAILING	WARHEAD	WAXWORK	WELL-OFF	WHILING	WILDCAT
WAISTED	WARIEST	WAYBILL	WELL-SET	WHIMPER	WILD DOG
WAITERS	WARLIKE	WAYLAID	WELSHED	WHINERS	WILDEST
WAITING	WARLOCK	WAYLAIN	WELSHER	WHINGED	WILDING
WAIVERS	WARLORD	WAYSIDE	WEMBLEY	WHINING	WILIEST
WAIVING	WARMEST	WAYWARD	WENCHED	WHIPPED	WILLIES
WAKEFUL	WARMING	WEAKEST	WENCHER	WHIPPER	WILLING
WAKENED	WARM-UPS	WEALTHY	WENCHES	WHIPPET	WILLOWS
WAKENER	WARNING	WEANING	WENDING	WHIPSAW	WILLOWY
WALCOTT	WARPAGE	WEAPONS	WENDISH	WHIRLED	WILTING
WALKERS	WARPATH	WEARIED	WEST END	WHIRLER	WIMPIES
WALKIES	WARPING	WEARIER	WESTERN	WHIRRED	WIMPISH
WALKING	WARRANT	WEARILY	WESTING	WHISKED	WIMPLES
WALKMAN	WARRENS	WEARING	WET-LOOK	WHISKER	WINCHED
WALK OFF	WARRING	WEASELS	WETNESS	WHISKEY	WINCHER
WALK-ONS	WARRIOR	WEATHER	WET SUIT	WHISPER	WINCHES
WALKOUT	WARSHIP	WEAVERS	WETTEST	WHISTLE	WINCING
WALK-UPS	WARTHOG	WEAVING	WETTING	WHITEST	WINDAGE
WALLABY	WARTIME	WEBBING	WETTISH	WHITHER	WINDBAG
WALLAHS	WARWICK	WEBFOOT	WEXFORD	WHITING	WINDIER
WALLETS	WASHDAY	WEBSITE	WHACKED	WHITLOW	WINDILY
WALLEYE	WASHERS	WEB-TOED	WHACKER	WHITSUN	WINDING
WALLIES	WASHERY	WEDDING	WHALERS	WHITTLE	WINDOWS
WALLING	WASHING	WEDGING	WHALING	WHIZZED	WINDROW
WALLOON	WASHOUT	WEDLOCK	WHANGEE	WHIZZES	WINDSOR
WALLOPS	WASHTUB	WEEDIER	WHARVES	WHOEVER	WINE BAR
WALLOWS	WASPILY	WEEDILY	WHAT FOR	WHOOPED	WINGERS
WALNUTS	WASPISH	WEEDING	WHATNOT	WHOOPEE	WINGING
WALSALL	WASSAIL	WEEKDAY	WHATSIT	WHOOPER	WINGLET
WALTZED	WASTAGE	WEEKEND	WHEATEN	WHOPPED	WING NUT
WALTZER	WASTERS	WEENIER	WHEEDLE	WHOPPER	WINKERS
WALTZES	WASTING	WEEPING	WHEELED	WHORISH	WINKING
WANGLED	WASTREL	WEEVILS	WHEELER	WHORLED	WINKLED
WANGLER	WATCHED	WEEVILY	WHEELIE	WHYALLA	WINKLES
WANGLES	WATCHER	WEIGELA	WHEEZED	WICHITA	WINLESS
WANKERS	WATCHES	WEIGHED	WHEEZER	WICKETS	WINNERS
WANKING	WATERED	WEIGHER	WHEEZES	WICKING	WINNING
WANNABE	WATERER	WEIGHTS	WHEREAS	WICKLOW	WINSOME
WANNESS	WATFORD	WEIGHTY	WHEREAT	WIDE BOY	WINTERS
WANNEST	WATTAGE	WEIRDER	WHEREBY	WIDENED	WIRETAP
WANNING	WATTEAU	WEIRDIE	WHEREIN	WIDENER	WIRIEST
WANT ADS	WATTLES	WEIRDLY	WHEREOF	WIDGEON	WISBECH
WANTING	WAVELET	WEIRDOS	WHEREON	WIDOWED	WISE GUY
WAPITIS	WAVEOFF	WELCHED	WHERETO	WIDOWER	WISHFUL
WARBLED	WAVERED	WELCOME	WHERRIT	WIELDED	WISHING
WARBLER	WAVERER	WELDERS	WHETHER	WIELDER	WISPIER
WARDENS	WAVIEST	WELDING	WHETTED	WIGGING	WISPILY
WARDERS	WAXBILL	WELFARE	WHETTER	WIGGLED	WISTFUL
WARDING	WAXIEST	WELL-FED	WHICKER	WIGGLER	WITCHES
WARFARE	WAXLIKE	WELLIES	WHIFFER	WIGGLES	WITHERS

WITHOUT	WORKERS	WRESTER	XEROXES	YIELDER	ZENITHS
WITLESS	WORKING	WRESTLE	XIPHOID	YINGKOU	ZEOLITE
WITNESS	WORKMAN	WREXHAM	X-RAYING	YINGKOW	ZEPHYRS
WITTIER	WORKMEN	WRIGGLE		YODELED	ZERMATT
WITTILY	WORKOUT	WRIGGLY	**Y**	YOGHURT	ZEROING
WIZARDS	WORKSHY	WRINGER	YACHTIE	YONKERS	ZESTFUL
WIZENED	WORKSOP	WRINKLE	YAKKING	YORKIST	ZHDANOV
WOBBLED	WORKTOP	WRINKLY	YAKUTSK	YORUBAN	ZIGZAGS
WOBBLER	WORLDLY	WRITE-IN	YANGTZE	YOUNGER	ZILLION
WOBBLES	WORMIER	WRITERS	YANKEES	YOWLING	ZINCATE
WOLFING	WORMING	WRITE-UP	YANKING	YTTRIUM	ZINCITE
WOLFISH	WORN-OUT	WRITHED	YAOUNDE	YUCATAN	ZIONISM
WOLFRAM	WORRIED	WRITHER	YAPPING	YUCKIER	ZIONIST
WOMANLY	WORRIER	WRITING	YARDAGE	YUKONER	ZIP CODE
WOMBATS	WORRIES	WRITTEN	YARDARM	YULE LOG	ZIPPERS
WONDERS	WORSHIP	WROCLAW	YARD ARM	YUPPIES	ZIPPIER
WONKIER	WORSTED	WRONGED	YARNING	YUPPIFY	ZIPPING
WOODCUT	WOTCHER	WRONGER	YASHMAK		ZITHERS
WOODIER	WOULD-BE	WRONGLY	YATHRIB	**Z**	ZODIACS
WOODMAN	WOULDN'T	WROUGHT	YAWNING	ZAGAZIG	ZOISITE
WOODSIA	WOUNDED	WRYBILL	YEAR DOT	ZAIREAN	ZOMBIES
WOOFERS	WOUNDER	WRYNECK	YEARNED	ZAIRESE	ZONALLY
WOOFTER	WOUND-UP	WRYNESS	YEARNER	ZAMBEZI	ZONULAR
WOOLLEN	WRAITHS	WYCH-ELM	YELLING	ZAMBIAN	ZOOLOGY
WOOMERA	WRANGLE	WYOMING	YELLOWS	ZANIEST	ZOOMING
WOOZIER	WRAPPED	WYVERNS	YELPING	ZAPOTEC	ZOOTOMY
WOOZILY	WRAPPER		YENISEI	ZAPPIER	ZORILLA
WORDAGE	WREAKED	**X**	YEREVAN	ZAPPING	ZWICKAU
WORDIER	WREAKER	XANTHIC	YESHIVA	ZEALAND	ZYGOSIS
WORDILY	WREATHE	XANTHIN	YEW TREE	ZEALOTS	ZYGOTIC
WORDING	WREATHS	XERARCH	Y-FRONTS	ZEALOUS	ZYMOGEN
WORKBAG	WRECKED	XEROSIS	YICHANG	ZEBRINE	ZYMOSIS
WORKBOX	WRECKER	XEROTIC	YIDDISH	ZEDOARY	ZYMOTIC
WORKDAY	WRESTED	XEROXED	YIELDED	ZEELAND	ZYMURGY

A
AARDVARK
AARDWOLF
ABACUSES
ABAMPERE
ABATTOIR
ABBATIAL
ABBESSES
ABDICATE
ABDOMENS
ABDUCENT
ABDUCTED
ABELMOSK
ABEOKUTA
ABERDARE
ABERDEEN
ABERRANT
ABETTING
ABETTORS
ABEYANCE
ABHORRED
ABHORRER
ABIDANCE
ABINGDON
AB
  INITIO
ABJECTLY
ABJURING
ABKHAZIA
ABLATION
ABLATIVE
ABLUTION
ABNEGATE
ABNORMAL
ABOMASUM
ABORTING
ABORTION
ABORTIVE
ABOUNDED
ABRADANT
ABRADING
ABRASION
ABRASIVE
ABRIDGED
ABRIDGER
ABROGATE
ABRUPTLY
ABSCISSA
ABSEILED
ABSENCES
ABSENTED

ABSENTEE
ABSENTER
ABSENTLY
ABSINTHE
ABSOLUTE
ABSOLVED
ABSOLVER
ABSORBED
ABSORBER
ABSTRACT
ABSTRUSE
ABSURDLY
ABU
  DHABI
ABUNDANT
ABUTILON
ABUTMENT
ABUTTALS
ABUTTING
ACADEMIA
ACADEMIC
ACANTHUS
ACAPULCO
ACARPOUS
ACCEDING
ACCENTED
ACCENTOR
ACCEPTED
ACCEPTOR
ACCESSED
ACCESSES
ACCIDENT
ACCOLADE
ACCORDED
ACCORDER
ACCOSTED
ACCOUNTS
ACCREDIT
ACCRUING
ACCURACY
ACCURATE
ACCURSED
ACCUSERS
ACCUSING
ACCUSTOM
ACCUTRON
ACENTRIC
ACERBATE
ACERBITY
ACERVATE
ACESCENT

ACHENIAL
ACHIEVED
ACHIEVER
ACHILLES
ACHROMAT
ACHROMIC
ACICULAR
ACICULUM
ACID
  DROP
ACID-
  FAST
ACIDNESS
ACIDOSIS
ACIDOTIC
ACID
  RAIN
ACID
  TEST
ACIERATE
ACOLYTES
ACONITIC
ACOUSTIC
ACQUAINT
ACQUIRED
ACQUIRER
ACRE-
  FOOT
ACRE-
  INCH
ACRIDINE
ACRIDITY
ACRIMONY
ACROBATS
ACRODONT
ACROLEIN
ACROLITH
ACROMION
ACRONYMS
ACROSTIC
ACRYLICS
ACTINIDE
ACTINISM
ACTINIUM
ACTINOID
ACTIVATE
ACTIVELY
ACTIVISM
ACTIVIST
ACTIVITY
ACT OF
  GOD

ACTUALLY
ACTUATED
ACTUATOR
ACULEATE
ACUTANCE
ADAMS
  ALE
ADAMSITE
ADAPTERS
ADAPTING
ADAPTIVE
ADDENDUM
ADDICTED
ADDITION
ADDITIVE
ADDUCENT
ADDUCING
ADDUCTOR
ADELAIDE
ADENITIS
ADENOIDS
ADEQUACY
ADEQUATE
ADHERENT
ADHERING
ADHESION
ADHESIVE
ADJACENT
ADJOINED
ADJUDGED
ADJUNCTS
ADJURING
ADJUSTED
ADJUTANT
ADJUVANT
AD-
  LIBBED
AD-
  LIBBER
ADMIRALS
ADMIRERS
ADMIRING
ADMITTED
ADMONISH
ADOPTING
ADOPTION
ADOPTIVE
ADORABLE
ADORNING
ADRIATIC
ADROITLY

ADULARIA
ADULATOR
ADULTERY
ADUMBRAL
ADVANCED
ADVANCER
ADVANCES
ADVERTED
ADVISERS
ADVISING
ADVISORY
ADVOCAAT
ADVOCACY
ADVOCATE
ADYNAMIA
ADYNAMIC
AEGROTAT
AERATING
AERATION
AERIALLY
AEROBICS
AERODYNE
AEROFOIL
AEROGRAM
AEROLITE
AEROLOGY
AERONAUT
AEROSOLS
AEROSTAT
AESTHETE
AFEBRILE
AFFECTED
AFFERENT
AFFIANCE
AFFINITY
AFFIRMED
AFFIRMER
AFFIXING
AFFLATUS
AFFLUENT
AFFORDED
AFFOREST
AFFRONTS
AFFUSION
AFLUTTER
AFRICANS
AGARTALA
AGE
  GROUP
AGENCIES
AGENESIS

AGENETIC
AGENTIAL
AGENTIVE
AGERATUM
AGGRIEVE
AGIOTAGE
AGITATED
AGITATOR
AGITPROP
AGMINATE
AGNOSTIC
AGONIZED
AGRAPHIA
AGRARIAN
AGRESTAL
AGRIMONY
AGROLOGY
AGRONOMY
AGUEWEED
AIGRETTE
AIGUILLE
AILERONS
AILMENTS
AIRBASES
AIRBORNE
AIRBRAKE
AIRBRICK
AIRBRUSH
AIRBURST
AIRBUSES
AIRCRAFT
AIRCREWS
AIREDALE
AIRFIELD
AIRFORCE
AIR
  FORCE
AIRFRAME
AIRINESS
AIRLANES
AIRLIFTS
AIRLINER
AIRLINES
AIRLOCKS
AIR
  MILES
AIRPLANE
AIRPORTS
AIR
  RAIDS
AIRSCREW

113

AIRSHIPS	ALKALINE	ALTER	AMPUTATE	ANFINSEN	ANTIBODY
AIRSPACE	ALKALIZE	EGO	AMPUTEES	ANGELENO	ANTIDOTE
AIRSPEED	ALKALOID	ALTERING	AMRAVATI	ANGELICA	ANTIGENS
AIRSTRIP	ALLANITE	ALTHOUGH	AMRITSAR	ANGERING	ANTIHERO
AIRTIGHT	ALLAYING	ALTITUDE	AMYGDALA	ANGINOSE	ANTI
AIR-TO-	ALL	ALTRUISM	AMYGDALE	ANGLESEY	HERO
AIR	CLEAR	ALTRUIST	ANABAENA	ANGLICAN	ANTI-
AIRWAVES	ALLEGING	ALUMROOT	ANABASIS	ANGRIEST	ICER
AIRWOMAN	ALLEGORY	ALVEOLAR	ANABATIC	ANGSTROM	ANTILLES
AIRWOMEN	ALLELISM	ALVEOLUS	ANABLEPS	ANGUILLA	ANTIMERE
A LA	ALLELUIA	AMALGAMS	ANABOLIC	ANGULATE	ANTIMONY
CARTE	ALLEPPEY	AMARANTH	ANACONDA	ANHEDRAL	ANTI-
ALACRITY	ALLERGEN	AMARELLE	ANAEROBE	ANIMATED	NAZI
ALARMING	ALLERGIC	AMARILLO	ANAGLYPH	ANIMATOR	ANTINODE
ALARMISM	ALLEYWAY	AMASSING	ANAGOGIC	ANIMISTS	ANTINOMY
ALARMIST	ALLIANCE	AMATEURS	ANAGRAMS	ANISETTE	ANTIPHON
ALBACORE	ALLOCATE	AMAZONAS	ANALCITE	ANKERITE	ANTIQUES
ALBANIAN	ALLODIAL	AMBEROID	ANALECTS	ANKYLOSE	ANTI-
ALBINISM	ALLODIUM	AMBIENCE	ANALEMMA	ANNALIST	RIOT
ALCATRAZ	ALLOGAMY	AMBITION	ANALOGUE	ANN	ANTITANK
ALCHEMIC	ALLOPATH	AMBIVERT	ANALYSED	ARBOR	ANTONINE
ALCHEVSK	ALLOTTED	AMBROSIA	ANALYSER	ANNEALED	ANTONYMS
ALCIDINE	ALLOTTEE	AMBULANT	ANALYSES	ANNEALER	ANTRORSE
ALCOHOLS	ALLOWING	AMBULATE	ANALYSIS	ANNEXING	ANURESIS
ALDEHYDE	ALLOYING	AMBUSHED	ANALYSTS	ANNOTATE	ANYPLACE
ALDERMAN	ALL	AMBUSHES	ANALYTIC	ANNOUNCE	ANYTHING
ALDERMEN	RIGHT	AMENABLE	ANAPAEST	ANNOYING	ANYWHERE
ALDERNEY	ALL	AMENDING	ANAPHASE	ANNUALLY	AORISTIC
ALDOXIME	ROUND	AMERICAN	ANAPHORA	ANNULATE	APAGOGIC
ALEATORY	ALL-	AMETHYST	ANARCHIC	ANNULLED	APATETIC
ALEHOUSE	ROUND	AMICABLE	ANASARCA	ANNULOSE	APERIENT
ALERTING	ALLSPICE	AMICABLY	ANATHEMA	ANODYNES	APERITIF
ALFRESCO	ALL	AMITOSIS	ANATOLIA	ANOINTED	APERTURE
ALGERIAN	THERE	AMITOTIC	ANCESTOR	ANOINTER	APHANITE
ALGERINE	ALLUDING	AMMETERS	ANCESTRY	ANOREXIA	APHELIAN
ALGINATE	ALLURING	AMMONIAC	ANCHORED	ANSERINE	APHELION
ALGOLOGY	ALLUSION	AMMONIFY	ANCIENTS	ANSWERED	APHORISM
ALGORISM	ALLUSIVE	AMMONITE	ANDANTES	ANTABUSE	APHORIST
ALHAMBRA	ALLUVIAL	AMMONIUM	ANDERSON	ANTEATER	APHORIZE
ALICANTE	ALLUVIUM	AMNESIAC	ANDESINE	ANTECEDE	APIARIAN
ALIENAGE	ALMANACS	AMNIOTIC	ANDESITE	ANTEDATE	APIARIES
ALIENATE	ALMIGHTY	AMOEBOID	ANDIRONS	ANTELOPE	APIARIST
ALIENISM	ALMONERS	AMORETTO	ANDIZHAN	ANTENNAS	APIOLOGY
ALIENIST	ALOPECIA	AMORTIZE	ANDORRAN	ANTE-	APLASTIC
ALIGHTED	ALPHABET	AMOUNTED	ANDROGEN	POST	APOCRINE
ALIGNING	ALPHOSIS	AMPERAGE	ANDROIDS	ANTERIOR	APODOSIS
ALIQUANT	ALPINISM	AMPHIPOD	ANECDOTE	ANTEROOM	APOGAMIC
ALIZARIN	ALPINIST	AMPHORAE	ANECHOIC	ANTEVERT	APOLOGIA
ALKAHEST	ALSATIAN	AMPHORAS	ANEMONES	ANTHELIX	APOLOGUE
ALKALIES	ALSO-	AMPOULES	ANETHOLE	ANTHESIS	APOMIXIS
ALKALIFY	RANS	AMPULLAR	ANEURYSM	ANTHILLS	APOPHYGE
					APOPLEXY

APOSPORY	ARCHAEAN	ARRIVALS	ASSAYING	ATOM	AUTOGAMY
APOSTASY	ARCHAISM	ARRIVING	ASSEGAIS	BOMB	AUTOGIRO
APOSTATE	ARCHAIST	ARROGANT	ASSEMBLE	ATOMIZER	AUTOLYSE
APOSTLES	ARCHAIZE	ARROGATE	ASSEMBLY	ATONABLE	AUTOMATA
APPALLED	ARCHDUKE	ARROWING	ASSENTED	ATONALLY	AUTOMATE
APPANAGE	ARCHIVAL	ARSENALS	ASSENTOR	ATROCITY	AUTOMATS
APPARENT	ARCHIVES	ARSENATE	ASSERTED	ATROPHIC	AUTONOMY
APPEALED	ARCHNESS	ARSENIDE	ASSERTER	ATROPINE	AUTOSOME
APPEALER	ARCHWAYS	ARSENITE	ASSESSED	ATTACHED	AUTOTOMY
APPEARED	ARC	ARSONIST	ASSESSOR	ATTACHER	AUTOTYPE
APPEASED	LIGHT	ARTEFACT	ASSHOLES	ATTACHES	AUTOTYPY
APPELLEE	ARCTURUS	ARTERIAL	ASSIGNAT	ATTACKED	AUTUMNAL
APPENDED	ARDENNES	ARTERIES	ASSIGNED	ATTACKER	AUTUNITE
APPENDIX	ARDENTLY	ARTESIAN	ASSIGNEE	ATTAINED	AUVERGNE
APPESTAT	AREA	ARTFULLY	ASSIGNER	ATTEMPTS	AVADAVAT
APPETITE	CODE	ART	ASSIGNOR	ATTENDED	AVAILING
APPLAUSE	ARENITIC	HOUSE	ASSISTED	ATTENDEE	AVE
APPLE	AREQUIPA	ARTICLED	ASSISTER	ATTESTED	MARIA
PIE	ARETHUSA	ARTICLES	ASSONANT	ATTIRING	AVENGERS
APPLIQUE	ARGENTIC	ARTIFACT	ASSORTED	ATTITUDE	AVENGING
APPLYING	ARGININE	ARTIFICE	ASSORTER	ATTORNEY	AVERAGED
APPOSITE	ARGUABLE	ARTINESS	ASSUAGED	ATTUNING	AVERAGES
APPRAISE	ARGUABLY	ARTISANS	ASSUAGER	ATYPICAL	AVERMENT
APPRISED	ARGUMENT	ARTISTES	ASSUMING	AUBUSSON	AVERRING
APPROACH	ARIANISM	ARTISTIC	ASSURING	AUCKLAND	AVERSION
APPROVAL	ARILLATE	ARTISTRY	ASSYRIAN	AUCTIONS	AVERSIVE
APPROVED	ARILLODE	ARYANIZE	ASTATINE	AUDACITY	AVERTING
APRES-	ARISTATE	ASBESTOS	ASTERISK	AUDIENCE	AVIARIES
SKI	ARKANSAS	ASCENDED	ASTERISM	AUDITING	AVIATION
APRICOTS	ARMAGNAC	ASCENDER	ASTERNAL	AUDITION	AVIATORS
APTEROUS	ARMALITE	ASCETICS	ASTEROID	AUDITORS	AVIATRIX
APTITUDE	ARMAMENT	ASCIDIAN	ASTHENIA	AUDITORY	AVIDNESS
APYRETIC	ARMATURE	ASCIDIUM	ASTHENIC	AUGSBURG	AVIEMORE
AQUALUNG	ARMBANDS	ASCOCARP	ASTONISH	AUGURIES	AVIFAUNA
AQUANAUT	ARMCHAIR	ASCORBIC	ASTRAGAL	AUGURING	AVIONICS
AQUARIST	ARMENIAN	ASCRIBED	ASTURIAS	AUGUSTLY	AVOCADOS
AQUARIUM	ARMHOLES	ASHTRAYS	ASTUTELY	AUREOLES	AVOIDING
AQUARIUS	ARMIDALE	ASNIERES	ASUNCION	AU	AVOWABLE
AQUATICS	ARMORIAL	ASPERITY	ATARAXIA	REVOIR	AVULSION
AQUATINT	ARMOURED	ASPERSER	AT	AURICLES	AWAITING
AQUEDUCT	ARMOURER	ASPHODEL	BOTTOM	AURICULA	AWAKENED
AQUILINE	ARMS	ASPHYXIA	ATHEISTS	AUSPICES	AWARDING
ARACHNID	RACE	ASPIRANT	ATHENIAN	AUSTRIAN	AWEATHER
ARAPAIMA	AROMATIC	ASPIRATE	ATHEROMA	AUTACOID	AXILLARY
ARAWAKAN	AROUSING	ASPIRING	ATHLETES	AUTARCHY	AXIOLOGY
ARBITERS	ARPEGGIO	ASPIRINS	ATHLETIC	AUTARKIC	AXLETREE
ARBITRAL	ARRANGED	ASSAILED	ATLANTIC	AUTHORED	AYRSHIRE
ARBOREAL	ARRANGER	ASSAILER	ATLANTIS	AUTISTIC	AYURVEDA
ARBROATH	ARRAYING	ASSAMESE	AT	AUTOBAHN	AZIMUTHS
ARCADIAN	ARRESTED	ASSASSIN	LENGTH	AUTOCRAT	AZOTEMIA
ARCATURE	ARRESTER	ASSAULTS		AUTOCUES	AZOTEMIC

B

BABBLERS
BABBLING
BABIRUSA
BABYHOOD
BABY
　TALK
BACCARAT
BACCHIUS
BACHELOR
BACILLUS
BACKACHE
BACKBEAT
BACKBITE
BACKBONE
BACKCHAT
BACKCOMB
BACKDATE
BACK
　DOOR
BACKDROP
BACKFILL
BACKFIRE
BACKHAND
BACKINGS
BACKLASH
BACKLESS
BACKLIST
BACKLOGS
BACKPACK
BACK
　SEAT
BACKSIDE
BACKSLID
BACKSPIN
BACKSTAY
BACKSTOP
BACK
　TALK
BACKWARD
BACKWASH
BACKYARD
BACTERIA
BACTERIN
BACTRIAN
BADALONA
BAD
　BLOOD
BAD
　DEBTS
BADGERED
BADINAGE

BADLANDS
BADLY-
　OFF
BAD-
　MOUTH
BAEDEKER
BAFFLING
BAGGAGES
BAGGIEST
BAGPIPES
BAGUETTE
BAHAMIAN
BAHRAINI
BAILABLE
BAILIFFS
BAILMENT
BAILSMAN
BAKELITE
BAKERIES
BALANCED
BALANCER
BALANCES
BALDNESS
BALEARIC
BALINESE
BALLADES
BALLADRY
BALLARAT
BALLCOCK
BALL
　GAME
BALLONET
BALLOONS
BALLOTED
BALL
　PARK
BALLROOM
BALLS-
　UPS
BALLYHOO
BALMIEST
BALMORAL
BALSAMIC
BALUSTER
BANALITY
BANDAGED
BANDAGES
BANDANNA
BANDIEST
BANDITRY
BANDPASS
BANDSMAN

BANDSMEN
BANDYING
BANISHED
BANISTER
BANKABLE
BANKBOOK
BANK
　NOTE
BANK
　RATE
BANKROLL
BANKRUPT
BANNOCKS
BANQUETS
BANSHEES
BANSTEAD
BANTERED
BANTERER
BAPTISMS
BAPTISTS
BAPTIZED
BARATHEA
BARBADOS
BARBARIC
BARBECUE
BARBERRY
BARBICAN
BARBICEL
BAR
　CHART
BAR
　CODES
BAREBACK
BAREFOOT
BAREILLY
BARENESS
BARGAINS
BAR
　GRAPH
BARITONE
BARLETTA
BARMAIDS
BARMIEST
BARNACLE
BARNSLEY
BARNYARD
BAROGRAM
BARONAGE
BARONESS
BARONETS
BARONIAL
BARONIES

BAROSTAT
BAROUCHE
BARRACKS
BARRAGES
BARRATOR
BARRATRY
BARRETTE
BARRIERS
BARTERED
BARTERER
BARTIZAN
BASEBALL
BASEHEAD
BASELESS
BASELINE
BASEMENT
BASENESS
BASE
　RATE
BASICITY
BASIDIAL
BASIDIUM
BASILARY
BASILDON
BASILICA
BASILISK
BASKETRY
BASOPHIL
BASS
　CLEF
BASS
　DRUM
BASSINET
BASSISTS
BASSOONS
BASSWOOD
BASTARDS
BASTARDY
BASTILLE
BASTIONS
BASTOGNE
BATANGAS
BATHETIC
BATH
　MATS
BATHROBE
BATHROOM
BATHTUBS
BATHURST
BATSWANA
BATTENED
BATTERED

BATTERER
BATTIEST
BATTLING
BAUHINIA
BAULKING
BAVARIAN
BAWDIEST
BAYBERRY
BAYONETS
BAYREUTH
BAZOOKAS
BDELLIUM
BEACHING
BEADIEST
BEADINGS
BEAGLING
BEAM-
　ENDS
BEANPOLE
BEARABLE
BEARABLY
BEARDING
BEAR
　HUGS
BEARINGS
BEARSKIN
BEATABLE
BEATIFIC
BEATINGS
BEATNIKS
BEAT
　TIME
BEAULIEU
BEAUMONT
BEAUTIES
BEAUTIFY
BEAUVAIS
BEAVERED
BECALMED
BECHAMEL
BECKONED
BECKONER
BECOMING
BEDAUBED
BEDAZZLE
BEDECKED
BEDIMMED
BED
　LINEN
BEDOUINS
BEDPLATE
BEDPOSTS

BEDROOMS
BEDSIDES
BEDSORES
BEDSTEAD
BEDSTRAW
BEDTIMES
BEDWORTH
BEEBREAD
BEECHNUT
BEE-
　EATER
BEEFCAKE
BEEFIEST
BEEFWOOD
BEEHIVES
BEELINES
BEESWING
BEETLING
BEETROOT
BEFALLEN
BEFITTED
BEFOULER
BEFRIEND
BEGETTER
BEGGARED
BEGGARLY
BEGINING
BEGINNER
BEGOTTEN
BEGRUDGE
BEGUILED
BEGUILER
BEHAVING
BEHEADED
BEHOLDEN
BEHOLDER
BELABOUR
BELAYING
BELCHING
BELFRIES
BELGRADE
BELIEVED
BELIEVER
BELITTLE
BELLBIRD
BELLBOYS
BELLOWED
BELLOWER
BELLPULL
BELLWORT
BELLYFUL

BELMOPAN
BELONGED
BELOVEDS
BELTWAYS
BEMOANED
BENADRYL
BEN
  BELLA
BENEFICE
BENEFITS
BENFLEET
BENGHAZI
BENGUELA
BENIGNLY
BENTINCK
BENTWOOD
BENUMBED
BENZOATE
BEQUEATH
BEQUESTS
BERATING
BERCEUSE
BEREAVED
BEREZINA
BERGAMET
BERIBERI
BERKELEY
BERTHING
BERYLINE
BESANCON
BESIEGED
BESIEGER
BESMIRCH
BESOTTED
BESOUGHT
BESPOKEN
BESTIARY
BESTOWAL
BESTOWED
BESTOWER
BESTREWN
BESTRIDE
BESTRODE
BETAKING
BETATRON
BETIDING
BETRAYAL
BETRAYED
BETRAYER
BETTERED
BEVATRON

BEVELING
BEVELLED
BEVERAGE
BEVERLEY
BEWAILED
BEWAILER
BEWARING
BEWIGGED
BEWILDER
BHATPARA
BIANNUAL
BIARRITZ
BIASSING
BIATHLON
BIBLICAL
BIBULOUS
BICKERED
BICKERER
BICOLOUR
BICONVEX
BICUSPID
BICYCLED
BICYCLES
BICYCLIC
BIDDABLE
BIENNIAL
BIFACIAL
BIFIDITY
BIFOCALS
BIGAMIST
BIGAMOUS
BIGHEADS
BIG
  NAMES
BIGNONIA
BIG
  SHOTS
BIG
  STICK
BIG-
  TIMER
BIG
  WHEEL
BIJUGATE
BILABIAL
BILBERRY
BILINEAR
BILLETED
BILLFISH
BILLFOLD
BILLHOOK
BILLIARD

BILLIONS
BILLOWED
BILOBATE
BIMANOUS
BINAURAL
BINDINGS
BINDWEED
BIN-
  LINER
BINNACLE
BINOMIAL
BIOASSAY
BIO-
  ASSAY
BIOCIDAL
BIOCYCLE
BIODATAS
BIOLYSIS
BIOLYTIC
BIOMETRY
BIONOMIC
BIOPLASM
BIOPSIES
BIOSCOPE
BIOSCOPY
BIOTITIC
BIOTYPIC
BIPAROUS
BIPHENYL
BIPLANES
BIRACIAL
BIRADIAL
BIRAMOUS
BIRCHING
BIRDBATH
BIRDCAGE
BIRD
  DOGS
BIRDLIKE
BIRDLIME
BIRDSEED
BIRDS
  EYE
BIRD'S-
  EYE
BIRETTAS
BIRTHDAY
BIRTHING
BISCUITS
BISECTED
BISECTOR
BISEXUAL

BISMARCK
BISTOURY
BITCHIER
BITCHILY
BITCHING
BITINGLY
BIT
  PARTS
BITSTOCK
BITTERLY
BITTERNS
BITTIEST
BIVALENT
BIVALVES
BIVOUACS
BIWEEKLY
BIYEARLY
BLABBING
BLACK
  ART
BLACK
  BOX
BLACKCAP
BLACKEST
BLACK
  EYE
BLACKFLY
BLACK
  ICE
BLACKING
BLACKISH
BLACKLEG
BLACKOUT
BLACK
  TIE
BLACK-
  TIE
BLACKTOP
BLADDERS
BLAMABLE
BLAMEFUL
BLANCHED
BLANDEST
BLANDISH
BLANKETS
BLASTEMA
BLASTING
BLAST-
  OFF
BLASTULA
BLATANCY
BLAZONED

BLAZONRY
BLEACHED
BLEACHER
BLEAKEST
BLEARIER
BLEARILY
BLEATING
BLEEDERS
BLEEDING
BLEEPERS
BLEEPING
BLENCHED
BLENCHER
BLENDERS
BLENDING
BLENHEIM
BLESSING
BLIGHTED
BLIGHTER
BLIMPISH
BLINDAGE
BLINDERS
BLINDING
BLINKERS
BLINKING
BLISSFUL
BLISTERS
BLITHELY
BLITZING
BLIZZARD
BLOATERS
BLOCKADE
BLOCKAGE
BLOCKING
BLOKEISH
BLONDEST
BLOODFIN
BLOODILY
BLOODING
BLOOD
  RED
BLOOMERS
BLOOMERY
BLOOMING
BLOOPERS
BLOSSOMS
BLOTCHES
BLOTTERS
BLOTTING
BLOWFISH
BLOWHARD

BLOWHOLE
BLOWIEST
BLOWLAMP
BLOWOUTS
BLOWPIPE
BLOW-
  WAVE
BLOWZIER
BLOWZILY
BLUDGEON
BLUE
  BABY
BLUEBELL
BLUEBIRD
BLUE
  BOOK
BLUE
  CHIP
BLUE
  FILM
BLUEFISH
BLUE
  FLAG
BLUEGILL
BLUE
  GUMS
BLUE
  JAYS
BLUE
  LAWS
BLUE
  MOON
BLUENESS
BLUFFING
BLUNDERS
BLUNKETT
BLUNTING
BLURRING
BLURTING
BLUSHERS
BLUSHING
BLUSTERY
BOARDERS
BOARDING
BOARFISH
BOASTERS
BOASTFUL
BOASTING
BOAT
  HOOK
BOATLOAD

BOA
VISTA
BOBBINET
BOBBY
PIN
BOBOLINK
BOBRUISK
BOBTAILS
BOBWHITE
BODILESS
BODLEIAN
BODY
BLOW
BODYWORK
BOEHMITE
BOGEYMAN
BOGGIEST
BOGGLING
BOHEMIAN
BOILABLE
BOLDFACE
BOLDNESS
BOLIVIAN
BOLLARDS
BOLLOCKS
BOLLWORM
BOLSHIER
BOLSTERS
BOLTHOLE
BOLT
HOLE
BOLTONIA
BOLTROPE
BOMBARDE
BOMBSITE
BOMBYCID
BONA
FIDE
BONANZAS
BONEFISH
BONEHEAD
BONE-
IDLE
BONELESS
BONE
MEAL
BONFIRES
BONHOMIE
BONINESS
BONNIEST
BONS
MOTS

BONTEBOK
BOOHOOED
BOOKABLE
BOOKCASE
BOOK
CLUB
BOOKENDS
BOOKINGS
BOOKLETS
BOOKMARK
BOOKRACK
BOOKSHOP
BOOKWORM
BOOSTERS
BOOSTING
BOOT
CAMP
BOOTLACE
BOOTLESS
BOOZE-
UPS
BOOZIEST
BORA
BORA
BORACITE
BORDEAUX
BORDELLO
BORDERED
BORDERER
BOREHOLE
BORINGLY
BORNHOLM
BOROUGHS
BORROWED
BORROWER
BORSTALS
BOSPORUS
BOSS-
EYED
BOSSIEST
BOTANIST
BOTANIZE
BOTCHERS
BOTCHIER
BOTCHILY
BOTCHING
BOTCH-
UPS
BOTHERED
BOTRYTIS
BOTSWANA
BOTTLING

BOTTOMRY
BOTULISM
BOUDOIRS
BOUFFANT
BOUILLON
BOULDERS
BOULLION
BOULOGNE
BOUNCERS
BOUNCIER
BOUNCILY
BOUNCING
BOUNDARY
BOUNDERS
BOUNDING
BOUNTIES
BOUQUETS
BOUTIQUE
BOUZOUKI
BOW
BELLS
BOWSHOTS
BOWSPRIT
BOXBERRY
BOXBOARD
BOXROOMS
BOYCOTTS
BOYISHLY
BOY
SCOUT
BRACELET
BRACHIAL
BRACHIUM
BRACKETS
BRACKISH
BRACTEAL
BRADAWLS
BRADBURY
BRADFORD
BRAGGART
BRAGGING
BRAHMANI
BRAHMANS
BRAIDING
BRAINBOX
BRAINIER
BRAINING
BRAINPAN
BRAISING
BRAMBLES
BRANCHED

BRANCHES
BRANCHIA
BRANDIES
BRANDING
BRANDISH
BRAND-
NEW
BRASHEST
BRASILIA
BRASSARD
BRASS
HAT
BRASSICA
BRASSIER
BRASSILY
BRATTICE
BRAUNITE
BRAWLERS
BRAWLING
BRAWNIER
BRAWNILY
BRAZENED
BRAZENLY
BRAZIERS
BRAZILIN
BREACHED
BREACHES
BREAD
BIN
BREADNUT
BREADTHS
BREAKAGE
BREAKERS
BREAKING
BREAK-
INS
BREATHER
BREECHES
BREEDING
BREEZILY
BRETHREN
BREVETCY
BREVIARY
BRIBABLE
BRICKBAT
BRIDGEND
BRIDGING
BRIEFING
BRIGHTEN
BRIGHTON
BRINDISI
BRIOCHES

BRISANCE
BRISBANE
BRISKEST
BRISLING
BRISTLED
BRISTLES
BRITCHES
BRITTANY
BROACHED
BROACHER
BROADEST
BROADWAY
BROCADED
BROCCOLI
BROCHURE
BROILERS
BROILING
BROKENLY
BROLLIES
BROMIDES
BRONCHIA
BRONCHOS
BRONCHUS
BRONZING
BROOCHES
BROODERS
BROODIER
BROODILY
BROODING
BROOKING
BROOKITE
BROOKLYN
BROOKNER
BROTHELS
BROTHERS
BROUGHAM
BROUHAHA
BROWBEAT
BROWNEST
BROWNIES
BROWNING
BROWNISH
BROWSING
BRUISERS
BRUISING
BRUITING
BRUNCHES
BRUNETTE
BRUSHING
BRUSH
OFF

BRUSH-
OFF
BRUSH-
UPS
BRUSSELS
BRUTALLY
BRYOLOGY
BRYOZOAN
BUBALINE
BUBBLIER
BUBBLING
BUCHSHEE
BUCKAROO
BUCKBEAN
BUCKETED
BUCKHORN
BUCKLERS
BUCKLING
BUCKSHEE
BUCKSHOT
BUCKSKIN
BUDAPEST
BUDDHISM
BUDDHIST
BUDDLEIA
BUDGETED
BUFFALOS
BUFFERED
BUFFETED
BUFFETER
BUFFOONS
BUGABOOS
BUGBEARS
BUGGERED
BUILDERS
BUILDING
BUILDUPS
BUKOVINI
BULAWAYO
BULGARIA
BULGIEST
BULKHEAD
BULKIEST
BULL
BARS
BULLDOGS
BULLDOZE
BULLETIN
BULLFROG
BULLHEAD
BULLHORN

BULLNECK
BULLOCKS
BULLRING
BULLS
  EYE
BULL'S-
  EYE
BULLSHIT
BULLYBOY
BULLYING
BULLY-
  OFF
BULWARKS
BUMBLING
BUMPIEST
BUMPKINS
BUNCHING
BUNDLING
BUNGALOW
BUNGHOLE
BUNGLERS
BUNGLING
BUNTLINE
BUOYANCY
BURAYDAH
BURBERRY
BURBLING
BURDENED
BURGHERS
BURGLARS
BURGLARY
BURGLING
BURGUNDY
BURLIEST
BURNOOSE
BURNOUTS
BURRITOS
BURROWED
BURROWER
BURSITIS
BURSTING
BURTHENS
BUSHBABY
BUSHBUCK
BUSHIEST
BUSHVELD
BUSINESS
BUS
  STOPS
BUSTIEST
BUSTLING
BUSYBODY

BUSYNESS
BUTANONE
BUTCHERS
BUTCHERY
BUTTERED
BUTTOCKS
BUTTONED
BUTTRESS
BUTYRATE
BUZZARDS
BUZZWORD
BY-
  BIDDER
BYPASSED
BYPASSES
BYRONISM

C

CABARETS
CABBAGES
CABIN
  BOY
CABINETS
CABLE
  CAR
CABLEWAY
CABOCHON
CABOODLE
CABOOSES
CABOTAGE
CAB
  RANKS
CABRILLA
CABRIOLE
CACHALOT
CACHEPOT
CACHEXIA
CACHUCHA
CACKLERS
CACKLING
CACTUSES
CADASTER
CADAVERS
CADDYING
CADENCES
CADENZAS
CADUCEUS
CADUCITY
CADUCOUS
CAERLEON
CAESURAS

CAFFEINE
CAGELING
CAGINESS
CAGLIARI
CAGOULES
CAISSONS
CAJOLERY
CAJOLING
CAKEWALK
CALABASH
CALABRIA
CALADIUM
CALAMINE
CALAMINT
CALAMITE
CALAMITY
CALATHUS
CALCIFIC
CALCITIC
CALCULUS
CALCUTTA
CALDRONS
CALENDAR
CALENDER
CALF
  LOVE
CALFSKIN
CALIBRED
CALIBRES
CALIPASH
CALIPERS
CALISAYA
CALLABLE
CALL
  GIRL
CALLINGS
CALLIOPE
CALLIPER
CALLISTO
CALLUSES
CALMNESS
CALOR
  GAS
CALORIES
CALUTRON
CALVADOS
CALVARIA
CALYCATE
CALYCINE
CALYPSOS
CALYPTRA

CAMAGUEY
CAMBODIA
CAMBOGIA
CAMBRIAN
CAMELEER
CAMELLIA
CAMEROON
CAMISOLE
CAMOMILE
CAMPAGNA
CAMPAIGN
CAMPANIA
CAMP
  BEDS
CAMPECHE
CAMPFIRE
CAMPHENE
CAMPINAS
CAMPSITE
CAMPUSES
CAMSHAFT
CANADIAN
CANAIGRE
CANAILLE
CANALIZE
CANARIES
CANBERRA
CANCELED
CANCROID
CANDIDLY
CANFIELD
CANISTER
CANNABIC
CANNABIN
CANNABIS
CANNIBAL
CANNIEST
CANNIKIN
CANNONED
CANNONRY
CANOEING
CANOEIST
CANONESS
CANONIST
CANONIZE
CANON
  LAW
CANOODLE
CANOPIES
CANTATAS
CANTEENS

CANTERED
CANT
  HOOK
CANTICLE
CANTONAL
CANVASES
CANZONET
CAPACITY
CAPERING
CAPESKIN
CAPE
  TOWN
CAPITALS
CAPITATE
CAPONIZE
CAPRICES
CAPRIFIG
CAPRIOLE
CAPSICUM
CAPSIZED
CAPSTANS
CAPSTONE
CAPSULAR
CAPSULES
CAPTAINS
CAPTIONS
CAPTIOUS
CAPTIVES
CAPTURED
CAPTURES
CAPUCHIN
CAPYBARA
CARACARA
CARACOLE
CARAMELS
CARANGID
CARAPACE
CARAVANS
CARAWAYS
CARBINES
CARBOLIC
CARBONIC
CARBONYL
CARBURET
CARDAMOM
CARDENAL
CARDIGAN
CARDINAL
CARDIOID
CARDITIS
CAREENED

CAREERED
CAREFREE
CARELESS
CARESSED
CARESSER
CARESSES
CAREWORN
CARIBOUS
CARILLON
CARINATE
CARLISLE
CARNAUBA
CARNIVAL
CAROLINA
CAROLINE
CAROLING
CAROLLED
CAROTENE
CAROUSAL
CAROUSED
CAROUSEL
CAR
  PARKS
CARPETED
CAR
  POOLS
CARPORTS
CARRERAS
CARRIAGE
CARRIERS
CARRYALL
CARRYCOT
CARRYING
CARRY
  OFF
CARRYOUT
CARRY
  OUT
CARTOONS
CARUNCLE
CARVINGS
CARYATID
CASANOVA
CASCADED
CASCADES
CASEMATE
CASEMENT
CASEWORK
CASHABLE
CASHBACK
CASH
  BACK

CASH-
BOOK
CASH
CARD
CASH
CROP
CASH
DESK
CASH
FLOW
CASHIERS
CASHLESS
CASHMERE
CASSETTE
CASSOCKS
CASTAWAY
CASTINGS
CAST
IRON
CAST-
IRON
CASTRATE
CASTRATO
CASTRIES
CASUALLY
CASUALTY
CASUISTS
CATACOMB
CATALASE
CATALYSE
CATALYST
CATAMITE
CATAPULT
CATARACT
CATCALLS
CATCH
ALL
CATCH-
ALL
CATCHFLY
CATCHIER
CATCHILY
CATCHING
CATECHIN
CATECHOL
CATEGORY
CATENANE
CATENARY
CATENATE
CATENOID
CATERING
CATHEDRA

CATHETER
CATHEXIS
CATHODES
CATHODIC
CATHOLIC
CATIONIC
CAT'S
EYES
CAT'S-
FOOT
CAT'S
PAWS
CATSUITS
CATTIEST
CATTLEYA
CATWALKS
CAUCASIA
CAUCASUS
CAUCUSES
CAUDALLY
CAULDRON
CAULICLE
CAULKING
CAUSABLE
CAUSALLY
CAUSERIE
CAUSEWAY
CAUTIONS
CAUTIOUS
CAVALIER
CAVATINA
CAVEATOR
CAVEFISH
CAVICORN
CAVILING
CAVILLED
CAVILLER
CAVITIES
CAVORTED
CEDILLAS
CEILINGS
CELERIAC
CELERITY
CELIBACY
CELIBATE
CELLARER
CELLARET
CELLISTS
CELLULAR
CELULOID
CEMENTED

CEMENTER
CEMENTUM
CEMETERY
CENOTAPH
CENOZOIC
CENSORED
CENSURED
CENSURES
CENSUSES
CENTAURS
CENTAURY
CENTAVOS
CENTERED
CENTIARE
CENTIMES
CENTRING
CENTRIST
CENTROID
CEPHALAD
CEPHALIC
CEPHALIN
CERAMICS
CERAMIST
CERASTES
CERATOID
CERCARIA
CEREBRAL
CEREBRIC
CEREBRUM
CEREMENT
CEREMONY
CERNUOUS
CEROTYPE
CERULEAN
CERVELAT
CERVICAL
CERVICES
CERVIXES
CESAREAN
CESSIONS
CESSPITS
CESSPOOL
CETACEAN
CEVENNES
CHACONNE
CHAFFING
CHAINING
CHAINMAN
CHAIN
SAW
CHAIRING

CHAIRMAN
CHAIRMEN
CHALAZAL
CHALDRON
CHALICES
CHALKIER
CHALKING
CHAMBERS
CHAMBRAY
CHAMONIX
CHAMPING
CHAMPION
CHANCELS
CHANCERY
CHANCIER
CHANCILY
CHANCING
CHANDLER
CHANGING
CHANGSHA
CHANGTEH
CHANNELS
CHANTIES
CHANTING
CHANUKAH
CHAOCHOW
CHAPATTI
CHAPBOOK
CHAPERON
CHAPLAIN
CHAPLETS
CHAPPING
CHAPTERS
CHARACIN
CHARADES
CHARCOAL
CHARENTE
CHARGERS
CHARGING
CHARIEST
CHARIOTS
CHARISMA
CHARLADY
CHARLIES
CHARLOCK
CHARLTON
CHARMERS
CHARMING
CHARQUID
CHARRING
CHARTERS

CHARTING
CHARTISM
CHARTIST
CHARTRES
CHASSEUR
CHASTELY
CHASTEST
CHASTISE
CHASTITY
CHASUBLE
CHAT
SHOW
CHATTELS
CHATTIER
CHATTILY
CHATTING
CHAUFFER
CHEAPEST
CHEATING
CHECKERS
CHECKING
CHECK-
INS
CHECKOUT
CHECKUPS
CHEDDITE
CHEEKIER
CHEEKILY
CHEEKING
CHEEPING
CHEERFUL
CHEERIER
CHEERILY
CHEERING
CHEETAHS
CHEKIANG
CHEMICAL
CHEMISES
CHEMISTS
CHEMNITZ
CHEMURGY
CHENILLE
CHENOPOD
CHEPSTOW
CHEQUERS
CHEROKEE
CHEROOTS
CHERRIES
CHERTSEY
CHERUBIC
CHESHIRE

CHESSMAN
CHESTIER
CHESTILY
CHESTNUT
CHEVRONS
CHEWABLE
CHEWIEST
CHEYENNE
CHIASMAL
CHIASMIC
CHIASMUS
CHIASTIC
CHICANER
CHICANOS
CHICKENS
CHICKPEA
CHICLAYO
CHIGETAI
CHIGGERS
CHIGNONS
CHIGWELL
CHILDISH
CHILDREN
CHILIASM
CHILIAST
CHILLIER
CHILLIES
CHILLING
CHILL
OUT
CHILOPOD
CHIMAERA
CHIMBOTE
CHIMERAS
CHIMKENT
CHIMNEYS
CHINAMAN
CHIN-
CHOU
CHINDWIN
CHINKING
CHINLESS
CHIPMUNK
CHIPPIES
CHIPPING
CHIP
SHOP
CHIRPIER
CHIRPILY
CHIRPING
CHIRRUPY

CHISELED
CHITCHAT
CHIT
  CHAT
CHIVALRY
CHIVYING
CHLORATE
CHLORIDE
CHLORINE
CHLORITE
CHLOROUS
CHOC-
  ICES
CHOCKING
CHOICELY
CHOICEST
CHOIRBOY
CHOIRMAN
CHOISEUL
CHOLERIC
CHOMPING
CHONGJIN
CHOOSIER
CHOP
  CHOP
CHOP-
  CHOP
CHOPPERS
CHOPPIER
CHOPPILY
CHOPPING
CHOP
  SUEY
CHORALES
CHORDATE
CHORDING
CHORIAMB
CHORTLED
CHORTLES
CHORUSED
CHORUSES
CHOW-
  CHOW
CHOW
  MEIN
CHRESARD
CHRISMAL
CHRISTEN
CHROMATE
CHROMITE
CHROMIUM
CHROMOUS

CHUBBIER
CHUCKING
CHUCKLED
CHUCKLER
CHUCKLES
CHUCK
  OFF
CHUGGING
CHUKKERS
CHUMMIER
CHUMMILY
CHUMMING
CHUNKIER
CHURCHES
CHURINGA
CHURLISH
CHURNING
CHUTZPAH
CHYMOSIN
CIABATTA
CIBORIUM
CICATRIX
CICERONE
CICHLOID
CIMBRIAN
CINCHONA
CINCTURE
CINEASTE
CINERAMA
CINERARY
CINGULUM
CINNABAR
CINNAMON
CINQUAIN
CIPHERED
CIRCLETS
CIRCLING
CIRCUITS
CIRCUITY
CIRCULAR
CIRCUSES
CISLUNAR
CISTERNA
CISTERNS
CITADELS
CITATION
CITIFIED
CITIZENS
CITREOUS
CITRUSES

CITY
  HALL
CIVILIAN
CIVILITY
CIVILIZE
CIVIL
  LAW
CIVIL
  WAR
CLACKING
CLAIMANT
CLAIMING
CLAMBAKE
CLAMMIER
CLAMMILY
CLAMMING
CLAMOURS
CLAMPING
CLANGERS
CLANGING
CLANKING
CLANNISH
CLANSMAN
CLANSMEN
CLAPPERS
CLAPPING
CLAPTRAP
CLARINET
CLARIONS
CLASHING
CLASPING
CLASSICS
CLASSIER
CLASSIFY
CLASSING
CLASSISM
CLASSIST
CLATTERS
CLATTERY
CLAVICLE
CLAYLIKE
CLAYMORE
CLEAN
  CUT
CLEAN-
  CUT
CLEANERS
CLEANEST
CLEANING
CLEANSED
CLEANSER

CLEAR-
  CUT
CLEAREST
CLEARING
CLEAROUT
CLEARWAY
CLEAVAGE
CLEAVERS
CLEAVING
CLEMATIS
CLEMENCY
CLENCHED
CLENCHES
CLERICAL
CLERIHEW
CLERKDOM
CLERKING
CLEVEITE
CLEVERLY
CLICKING
CLIENTAL
CLIMATES
CLIMATIC
CLIMAXED
CLIMAXES
CLIMBERS
CLIMBING
CLINCHED
CLINCHER
CLINCHES
CLINGING
CLINICAL
CLINKERS
CLINKING
CLIPPERS
CLIPPIES
CLIPPING
CLIQUISH
CLITORAL
CLITORIS
CLOAKING
CLOCKING
CLODDISH
CLOGGING
CLOISTER
CLOPPING
CLOSE-
  SET
CLOSETED
CLOSE-
  UPS

CLOSURES
CLOTHIER
CLOTHING
CLOTTING
CLOUDIER
CLOUDILY
CLOUDING
CLOUDLET
CLOUTING
CLOWNERY
CLOWNING
CLOWNISH
CLUBBING
CLUBFEET
CLUBFOOT
CLUBHAUL
CLUCKING
CLUELESS
CLUMPING
CLUMPISH
CLUMSIER
CLUMSILY
CLUPEOID
CLUSTERS
CLUSTERY
CLUTCHED
CLUTCHES
COACHING
COACHMAN
COACHMEN
COACTION
COACTIVE
COAGULUM
COAHUILA
COALESCE
COALFACE
COALFISH
COALHOLE
COALMINE
COALPORT
COARSELY
COARSEST
COASTERS
COASTING
COATINGS
COATROOM
COAT-
  TAIL
COAUTHOR
COBALTIC
COBBLERS

COBBLING
COBWEBBY
COCA-
  COLA
COCCYGES
COCHLEAE
COCHLEAR
COCKADES
COCKATOO
COCKCROW
COCK
  CROW
COCKEREL
COCKEYED
COCKIEST
COCKNEYS
COCKPITS
COCKSPUR
COCKSURE
COCKTAIL
COCONUTS
COCOONED
CODDLING
CODICILS
CODIFIED
CODIFIER
CODOMAIN
CODPIECE
CO
  DRIVER
COENURUS
COENZYME
COEQUALS
COERCING
COERCION
COERCIVE
COEXTEND
COGENTLY
COGITATE
COGNATES
COGNOMEN
COGWHEEL
COHERENT
COHERING
COHESION
COHESIVE
COHOBATE
COIFFEUR
COIFFURE
COINAGES
COINCIDE

COINSURE COLUMNAR COMPRISE CONJURED CONVICTS CORONERS
COLANDER COLUMNED COMPUTED CONJURER CONVINCE CORONETS
COLD COMANCHE COMPUTER CONJUROR CONVOKED CORPORAL
  CUTS COMATOSE COMRADES CONNACHT CONVOKER CORRIDOR
COLD COMBATED CONATION CONNIVED CONVOYED CORRODED
  FEET COMBATER CONATIVE CONNIVER CONVULSE CORRODER
COLD COMBINED CONCEDED CONNOTED COOKABLE CORSAGES
  FISH COMBINER CONCEITS CONODONT COOKBOOK CORSAIRS
COLDNESS COMBINES CONCEIVE CONOIDAL COOKOUTS CORSELET
COLD COMEBACK CONCEPTS CONQUEST COOLABAR CORSETED
  SNAP COMEDIAN CONCERNS CONSERVE COOLANTS CORSETRY
COLD COMEDIES CONCERTO CONSIDER COOLIBAH CORTEGES
  SORE COMEDOWN CONCERTS CONSOLED COOLNESS CORTICAL
COLD- COMELIER CONCHOID CONSOLER COONSKIN CORTICES
  WELD COMFIEST CONCLAVE CONSOLES COOPTING CORTISOL
COLESLAW COMFORTS CONCLUDE CONSOMME COOPTION CORUNDUM
COLISEUM COMITIES CONCRETE CONSORTS COPILOTS CORVETTE
COLLAGEN COMMANDO CONDENSE CONSPIRE COPLANAR CORYPHEE
COLLAGES COMMANDS CONDOLED CONSTANT COPPERAS COSECANT
COLLAPSE COMMENCE CONDOLER CONSTRUE COPULATE COSINESS
COLLARED COMMENTS CONDONED CONSULAR COPYBOOK COSMETIC
COLLATED COMMERCE CONDONER CONSUMED COPYCATS COSTLIER
COLLATOR COMMODES CONDUCED CONSUMER COPY- COSTMARY
COLLECTS COMMONER CONDUCER CONTACTS   EDIT COST-
COLLEENS COMMONLY CONDUITS CONTANGO COPYHOLD   PLUS
COLLEGES COMMUNAL CONDYLAR CONTEMPT COPYISTS COSTUMES
COLLIDED COMMUNED CONFEREE CONTENTS COQUETRY COT
COLLIDER COMMUNES CONFERVA CONTESTS COQUETTE   DEATH
COLLIERS COMMUTED CONFETTI CONTEXTS COQUILLE COTENANT
COLLIERY COMMUTER CONFIDED CONTINUA CORACLES COTERIES
COLLOGUE COMPACTS CONFIDER CONTINUE CORACOID COTOPAXI
COLLOQUY COMPADRE CONFINED CONTINUO CORDIALS COTSWOLD
COLLUDED COMPARED CONFINES CONTOURS CORDLESS COTTAGER
COLOMBES COMPARER CONFLATE CONTRACT CORDONED COTTAGES
COLOMBIA COMPARES CONFLICT CONTRAIL CORDOVAN COTYLOID
COLONELS COMPEERS CONFOCAL CONTRARY CORDUROY COUCHANT
COLONIAL COMPERED CONFOUND CONTRAST CORDWOOD COUCHING
COLONIES COMPERES CONFRERE CONTRITE CORE COUGHING
COLONIST COMPETED CONFRONT CONTRIVE   TIME COULISSE
COLONIZE COMPILED CONFUSED CONTROLS CORKWOOD COUMARIC
COLOPHON COMPILER CONFUTED CONTUSED CORNCOBS COUMARIN
COLORADO COMPLAIN CONFUTER CONVENED CORNEOUS COUNCILS
COLORANT COMPLETE CONGENER CONVENER CORNERED COUNTERS
COLOSSAL COMPLIED CONGRATS CONVENTS CORNETTE COUNTESS
COLOSSUS COMPLIER CONGRESS CONVERGE CORNICES COUNTIES
COLOTOMY COMPLINE CONIDIAL CONVERSE CORNICHE COUNTING
COLOURED COMPOSED CONIDIUM CONVERTS CORNIEST COUPLETS
COLPITIS COMPOSER CONIFERS CONVEXLY CORN COUPLING
COLUBRID COMPOTES CONJOINT CONVEYED   PONE COURANTE
COLUMBIA COMPOUND CONJUGAL CONVEYER CORNWALL COURLAND
COLUMBIC COMPRESS CONJUNCT CONVEYOR CORONARY COURSING

COURTESY	CRAM-	CREEPING	CROSSBOW	CRYOTRON	CURE-
COURTIER	FULL	CREMATED	CROSSCUT	CRYSTALS	ALLS
COURTING	CRAMMERS	CREMATOR	CROSS	CUBATURE	CURITIBA
COUSCOUS	CRAMMING	CREODONT	CUT	CUBE	CURLICUE
COUSTEAU	CRAMPING	CREOSOTE	CROSSEST	ROOT	CURLIEST
COVALENT	CRAMPONS	CRESCENT	CROSS-	CUBICLES	CURRANTS
COVENANT	CRANE	CRESTING	EYE	CUBIFORM	CURRENCY
COVENTRY	FLY	CRESYLIC	CROSSING	CUBISIST	CURRENTS
COVERAGE	CRANIATE	CRETONNE	CROSSLET	CUBISTIC	CURRICLE
COVERING	CRANIUMS	CREVASSE	CROSSPLY	CUCKOLDS	CURRIERY
COVERLET	CRANKIER	CREVICES	CROSTINI	CUCUMBER	CURRYING
COVERTLY	CRANKING	CREW	CROTCHES	CUCURBIT	CURSEDLY
COVER-	CRANKPIN	CUTS	CROTCHET	CUDDLIER	CURTAINS
UPS	CRANNIED	CREW	CROUCHED	CUDDLING	CURTNESS
COVETING	CRANNIES	NECK	CROUPIER	CUDGELED	CURTSIED
COVETOUS	CRAPPIER	CRIBBAGE	CROUPOUS	CUFF	CURTSIES
COWARDLY	CRAPPING	CRIBBING	CROUTONS	LINK	CUSHIEST
COWBELLS	CRASHING	CRICKETS	CROWBARS	CUL-DE-	CUSHIONS
COWBERRY	CRASH	CRICKING	CROWBOOT	SAC	CUSHIONY
COWERING	PAD	CRIMINAL	CROWDING	CULIACAN	CUSPIDOR
COWHANDS	CRAVENLY	CRIMPING	CROWFOOT	CULINARY	CUSSEDLY
COWHERDS	CRAVINGS	CRIMSONS	CROWNING	CULOTTES	CUSTARDS
COWHIDES	CRAWFISH	CRINGING	CROZIERS	CULOUSLY	CUSTOMER
COWLICKS	CRAWLERS	CRINKLED	CRUCIATE	CULPABLE	CUSTUMAL
COWLINGS	CRAWLING	CRINKLES	CRUCIBLE	CULPABLY	CUT A
CO-	CRAYFISH	CRIPPLED	CRUCIFER	CULPRITS	DASH
WORKER	CRAYONED	CRIPPLES	CRUCIFIX	CULTIGEN	CUTAWAYS
COWSHEDS	CRAZIEST	CRISPATE	CRUDITES	CULTIVAR	CUTBACKS
COWSLIPS	CREAKIER	CRISPIER	CRUISERS	CULTRATE	CUTENESS
COXALGIA	CREAKILY	CRISPING	CRUISING	CULTURAL	CUT
COXALGIC	CREAKING	CRISTATE	CRUMBLED	CULTURED	GLASS
COXCOMBS	CREAMERS	CRITERIA	CRUMBLES	CULTURES	CUTICLES
COXSWAIN	CREAMERY	CRITICAL	CRUMHORN	CULVERIN	CUTICULA
COZENAGE	CREAMIER	CRITIQUE	CRUMMIER	CULVERTS	CUTINIZE
COZENING	CREAMING	CRITTERS	CRUMPETS	CUMBERED	CUT-
COZINESS	CREASING	CROAKILY	CRUMPLED	CUMBRIAN	PRICE
CRABBIER	CREATINE	CROAKING	CRUNCHED	CUMQUATS	CUTPURSE
CRABBING	CREATING	CROATIAN	CRUSADED	CUMULOUS	CUTTINGS
CRABWISE	CREATION	CROCKERY	CRUSADER	CUPBOARD	CUTWATER
CRACKERS	CREATIVE	CROCOITE	CRUSADES	CUP	CUXHAVEN
CRACKING	CREATORS	CROCUSES	CRUSHING	CAKES	CYANITIC
CRACKLED	CREATURE	CROFTERS	CRUSTIER	CUP	CYANOGEN
CRACKNEL	CREDENCE	CROMLECH	CRUSTILY	FINAL	CYANOSIS
CRACKPOT	CREDENZA	CRONYISM	CRUSTOSE	CUPIDITY	CYANOTIC
CRACKUPS	CREDIBLE	CROOKING	CRUTCHES	CUPREOUS	CYBERPET
CRADLING	CREDIBLY	CROONERS	CRUZEIRO	CUPULATE	CYCLADES
CRAFTIER	CREDITED	CROONING	CRY	CURARIZE	CYCLAMEN
CRAFTILY	CREDITOR	CROPPERS	HAVOC	CURASSOW	CYCLISTS
CRAFTING	CREEPERS	CROPPING	CRYOLITE	CURATIVE	CYCLONES
CRAGGIER	CREEPIER	CROSIERS	CRYONICS	CURATORS	CYCLONIC
	CREEPILY	CROSSBAR	CRYOSTAT	CURCULIO	CYCLOSIS
				CURDLING	CYLINDER

CYMATIUM
CYMOGENE
CYNICISM
CYNOSURE
CYPHERED
CYPRINID
CYRILLIC
CYSTEINE
CYSTITIS
CYTASTER
CYTIDINE
CYTOLOGY
CYTOSINE
CZARINAS

D
DABBLERS
DABBLING
DABCHICK
DAB
  HANDS
DACTYLIC
DAEMONIC
DAFFODIL
DAFTNESS
DAGESTAN
DAINTIER
DAINTIES
DAINTILY
DAIQUIRI
DAIRYMAN
DAIRYMEN
DALESMAN
DALLYING
DALMATIA
DALMATIC
DALTONIC
DAMAGING
DAMANHUR
DAMASCUS
DAMNABLE
DAMNABLY
DAMOCLES
DAMPENED
DAMPENER
DAMPNESS
DANDIEST
DANDLING
DANDRUFF
DANDYISH
DANDYISM

DANEWORT
DANGLING
DANKNESS
DANUBIAN
DARINGLY
DARK
  AGES
DARKENED
DARKENER
DARKNESS
DARKROOM
DARK
  ROOM
DARLINGS
DARTFORD
DATABASE
DATEABLE
DATELINE
DATE
  RAPE
DATOLITE
DAUGHTER
DAUNTING
DAUPHINE
DAUPHINS
DAVENTRY
DAWDLERS
DAWDLING
DAYBREAK
DAYDREAM
DAYLIGHT
DAYROOMS
DAYTIMES
DAY-TO-
  DAY
DAZZLING
DEACONRY
DEADBEAT
DEAD
  BEAT
DEAD
  DUCK
DEAD
  ENDS
DEADENED
DEADENER
DEADFALL
DEADHEAD
DEAD
  HEAT
DEADLIER
DEADLINE

DEADLOCK
DEADNESS
DEAD
  WOOD
DEAF-
  AIDS
DEAFENED
DEAF-
  MUTE
DEAFNESS
DEALFISH
DEALINGS
DEANSHIP
DEARESTS
DEARNESS
DEATHBED
DEATH
  ROW
DEBACLES
DEBARKED
DEBARRED
DEBASING
DEBATERS
DEBATING
DEBILITY
DEBITING
DEBONAIR
DEBRECEN
DEBUGGED
DEBUGGER
DEBUNKED
DEBUNKER
DEBUTANT
DECADENT
DECAMPED
DECANOIC
DECANTED
DECANTER
DECAYING
DECEASED
DECEIVED
DECEIVER
DECEMBER
DECENTLY
DECENTRE
DECIBELS
DECIDING
DECIDUAL
DECIMALS
DECIMATE
DECIPHER
DECISION

DECISIVE
DECKHAND
DECK
  HAND
DECLARED
DECLARER
DECLASSE
DECLINED
DECLINER
DECLINES
DECODING
DECOLOUR
DECORATE
DECOROUS
DECOYING
DECREASE
DECREPIT
DECRETAL
DECRYING
DECURVED
DEDICATE
DEDUCING
DEDUCTED
DEED
  POLL
DEEMSTER
DEEPENED
DEEPENER
DEEP-
  LAID
DEEPNESS
DEERSKIN
DEFACING
DEFAMING
DEFAULTS
DEFEATED
DEFEATER
DEFECATE
DEFECTED
DEFECTOR
DEFENCES
DEFENDED
DEFENDER
DEFERENT
DEFERRED
DEFERRER
DEFIANCE
DEFICITS
DEFILERS
DEFILING
DEFINING

DEFINITE
DEFLATED
DEFLATOR
DEFLEXED
DEFLOWER
DEFOREST
DEFORMED
DEFORMER
DEFRAYAL
DEFRAYED
DEFRAYER
DEFTNESS
DEFUSING
DEGASSER
DEGRADED
DEGRADER
DEICIDAL
DEIFYING
DEIGNING
DEJECTED
DELAWARE
DELAYING
DELEGACY
DELEGATE
DELETING
DELETION
DELICACY
DELICATE
DELIGHTS
DELIRIUM
DELIVERY
DELOUSED
DELPHIAN
DELUDING
DELUGING
DELUSION
DELUSIVE
DELUSORY
DEMAGOGY
DEMANDED
DEMANDER
DEMARCHE
DEMEANED
DEMENTED
DEMENTIA
DEMERARA
DEMERGER
DEMERITS
DEMERSAL
DEMESNES
DEMIGODS

DEMIJOHN
DEMILUNE
DEMISTED
DEMISTER
DEMIVOLT
DEMOBBED
DEMOCRAT
DEMOLISH
DEMONIAC
DEMONISM
DEMONIST
DEMONIZE
DEMOTING
DEMOTION
DEMOTIST
DEMPSTER
DEMURELY
DEMUREST
DEMURRAL
DEMURRED
DEMURRER
DENATURE
DENDRITE
DENDROID
DENIABLE
DENIZENS
DENOTING
DENOUNCE
DENTICLE
DENTINAL
DENTURES
DENUDATE
DENUDING
DEPARTED
DEPENDED
DEPICTED
DEPICTER
DEPILATE
DEPLETED
DEPLORED
DEPLORER
DEPLOYED
DEPONENT
DEPORTED
DEPORTEE
DEPOSING
DEPOSITS
DEPRAVED
DEPRAVER
DEPRIVED
DEPRIVER

DEPURATE	DETESTER	DIANTHUS	DIGITATE	DIRIMENT	DISPENSE
DEPUTIES	DETHRONE	DIAPASON	DIGITIZE	DIRT	DISPERSE
DEPUTING	DETONATE	DIAPAUSE	DIGITRON	BIKE	DISPIRIT
DEPUTIZE	DETRITAL	DIAPHONE	DIGRAPHS	DIRTIEST	DISPLACE
DERAILED	DETRITUS	DIAPHONY	DIHEDRAL	DIRT	DISPLAYS
DERANGED	DEUCEDLY	DIARCHIC	DIHEDRON	ROAD	DISPOSAL
DERELICT	DEUTERON	DIARISTS	DIHYBRID	DIRTYING	DISPOSED
DERIDING	DEVALUED	DIASCOPE	DILATANT	DISABLED	DISPOSER
DERISION	DEVIANCE	DIASPORA	DILATING	DISABUSE	DISPROOF
DERISIVE	DEVIANTS	DIASPORE	DILATION	DISAGREE	DISPROVE
DERISORY	DEVIATED	DIASTASE	DILATIVE	DISALLOW	DISPUTED
DERIVING	DEVIATOR	DIASTEMA	DILATORY	DISANNUL	DISPUTER
DEROGATE	DEVILING	DIASTOLE	DILEMMAS	DISARMED	DISPUTES
DERRICKS	DEVILISH	DIASTRAL	DILIGENT	DISARMER	DISQUIET
DESCALED	DEVILLED	DIASTYLE	DILUTING	DISARRAY	DISROBED
DESCANTS	DEVISING	DIATOMIC	DILUTION	DISASTER	DISROBER
DESCENTS	DEVOLVED	DIATONIC	DILUVIAL	DISBURSE	DISSEISE
DESCRIBE	DEVONIAN	DIATRIBE	DIMERISM	DISCARDS	DISSENTS
DESCRIED	DEVOTEES	DIAZEPAM	DIMERIZE	DISCIPLE	DISSEVER
DESCRIER	DEVOTING	DIBBLING	DIMEROUS	DISCLAIM	DISSOLVE
DESEEDER	DEVOTION	DICENTRA	DIMETRIC	DISCLOSE	DISSUADE
DESERTED	DEVOURED	DICHROIC	DIMINISH	DISCORDS	DISTAFFS
DESERTER	DEVOURER	DICKERED	DINGDONG	DISCOUNT	DISTANCE
DESERVED	DEVOUTER	DICKIEST	DINGHIES	DISCOVER	DISTASTE
DESERVER	DEVOUTLY	DICROTIC	DINGIEST	DISCREET	DISTINCT
DESIGNED	DEWBERRY	DICTATED	DINKIEST	DISCRETE	DISTRACT
DESIGNER	DEWDROPS	DICTATES	DINOSAUR	DISCUSES	DISTRAIN
DESINENT	DEWINESS	DICTATOR	DIOCESAN	DISEASED	DISTRAIT
DESIRING	DEWY-	DIDACTIC	DIOCESES	DISEASES	DISTRESS
DESIROUS	EYED	DIDDLING	DIOPSIDE	DISENDOW	DISTRICT
DESISTED	DEXTROSE	DIDYMIUM	DIOPTASE	DISGORGE	DISTRUST
DESKWORK	DIABASIC	DIDYMOUS	DIOPTRAL	DISGRACE	DISUNION
DESOLATE	DIABETES	DIEHARDS	DIOPTRIC	DISGUISE	DISUNITE
DESPATCH	DIABETIC	DIELDRIN	DIORAMIC	DISHEVEL	DISUNITY
DESPISED	DIABOLIC	DIERESES	DIORITIC	DISHFULS	DITCHING
DESPOTIC	DIACIDIC	DIERESIS	DIOXIDES	DISHIEST	DITHEISM
DESSERTS	DIACONAL	DIERETIC	DIPHENYL	DISINTER	DITHEIST
DESTINED	DIAGNOSE	DIES	DIPLEGIA	DISJOINT	DITHERED
DESTRUCT	DIAGONAL	IRAE	DIPLEXER	DISJUNCT	DITHERER
DETACHED	DIAGRAMS	DIESTOCK	DIPLOMAS	DISKETTE	DIURESIS
DETACHER	DIAGRAPH	DIETETIC	DIPLOMAT	DISLIKED	DIURETIC
DETAILED	DIALECTS	DIFFERED	DIPLOPIA	DISLIKES	DIVALENT
DETAINED	DIALLAGE	DIFFRACT	DIPLOPIC	DISLODGE	DIVE-
DETAINEE	DIALLING	DIFFUSED	DIPLOPOD	DISLOYAL	BOMB
DETAINER	DIALOGUE	DIFFUSER	DIPLOSIS	DISMALLY	DIVERGED
DETECTED	DIALYSER	DIGAMIST	DIPSTICK	DISMAYED	DIVERTED
DETECTER	DIALYSIS	DIGAMOUS	DIPTERAL	DISMOUNT	DIVERTER
DETECTOR	DIALYTIC	DIGESTED	DIPTERAN	DISORDER	DIVESTED
DETENTES	DIAMANTE	DIGESTER	DIRECTED	DISOWNED	DIVIDEND
DETERRED	DIAMETER	DIGESTIF	DIRECTLY	DISOWNER	DIVIDERS
DETESTED	DIAMONDS	DIGGINGS	DIRECTOR	DISPATCH	DIVIDING

DIVI-
DIVI
DIVINELY
DIVINERS
DIVINING
DIVINITY
DIVINIZE
DIVISION
DIVISIVE
DIVISORS
DIVORCED
DIVORCEE
DIVORCER
DIVORCES
DIVULGED
DIVULGER
DIZZIEST
DJAKARTA
DJIBOUTI
DNIESTER
D-
NOTICE
S
DOCILITY
DOCKETED
DOCKLAND
DOCKSIDE
DOCKYARD
DOCTORAL
DOCTORED
DOCTRINE
DOCUMENT
DOCU-
SOAP
DODDERED
DODDERER
DODGIEST
DOGBERRY
DOGCARTS
DOG-
EARED
DOGFIGHT
DOGGEDLY
DOGGEREL
DOGGONED
DOGGY
BAG
DOGHOUSE
DOGMATIC
DO-
GOODER
DOGSBODY

DOG'S-
TAIL
DOG
TIRED
DOG-
TIRED
DOGTOOTH
DOGTROTS
DOGWATCH
DOG
WATCH
DOGWOODS
DOLDRUMS
DOLERITE
DOLOMITE
DOLOROSO
DOLOROUS
DOLPHINS
DOMELIKE
DOMESTIC
DOMICILE
DOMINANT
DOMINATE
DOMINEER
DOMINICA
DOMINION
DOMINIUM
DOMINOES
DONATING
DONATION
DONATIVE
DON
JUANS
DONLEAVY
DOODLING
DOOMSDAY
DOOMSTER
DOORBELL
DOORJAMB
DOORKNOB
DOORMATS
DOORNAIL
DOORPOST
DOORSILL
DOORSTEP
DOORSTOP
DOORWAYS
DOPAMINE
DOPINESS
DORDOGNE
DORMANCY
DORMOUSE

DORTMUND
DOSSIERS
DOTATION
DOTINGLY
DOTTEREL
DOTTIEST
DOUBLETS
DOUBLE
UP
DOUBLING
DOUBLOON
DOUBLURE
DOUBTERS
DOUBTFUL
DOUBTING
DOUGHNUT
DOUNREAY
DOURNESS
DOVECOTE
DOVETAIL
DOWAGERS
DOWDIEST
DOWNBEAT
DOWNCAST
DOWNFALL
DOWNHAUL
DOWNHILL
DOWNIEST
DOWNLOAD
DOWNPIPE
DOWNPLAY
DOWNPOUR
DOWNSIZE
DOWNSIZE
DOWNTIME
DOWNTOWN
DOWNTURN
DOWNWARD
DOWNWASH
DOWNWIND
DOXASTIC
DOXOLOGY
DOZINESS
DRABBEST
DRABNESS
DRACAENA
DRACHMAE
DRACHMAS
DRACONIC
DRAFTEES
DRAFTIER

DRAFTING
DRAGGIER
DRAGGING
DRAGGLED
DRAGLINE
DRAGNETS
DRAGOMAN
DRAGONET
DRAGOONS
DRAGROPE
DRAINAGE
DRAINING
DRAMATIC
DRAPABLE
DRATTING
DRAUGHTS
DRAUGHTY
DRAWABLE
DRAWBACK
DRAWBORE
DRAWCORD
DRAWDOWN
DRAWINGS
DRAWLING
DRAWTUBE
DREADFUL
DREADING
DREAMERS
DREAMILY
DREAMING
DREARIER
DREARILY
DREDGERS
DREDGING
DRENCHED
DRENCHER
DRESSAGE
DRESSERS
DRESSIER
DRESSILY
DRESSING
DRIBBLED
DRIBBLER
DRIBBLES
DRIBLETS
DRIFTAGE
DRIFTERS
DRIFTING
DRILLING
DRINKERS
DRINKING

DRIPPING
DRIVABLE
DRIVE-
INS
DRIVELED
DRIVEWAY
DRIZZLED
DROGHEDA
DROLLERY
DROLLEST
DROOLING
DROOPILY
DROOPING
DROP-
DEAD
DROPLETS
DROPOUTS
DROPPERS
DROPPING
DROP
SHOT
DROPSIED
DROPS
OFF
DROPWORT
DROUGHTS
DROUGHTY
DROWNING
DROWSILY
DROWSING
DRUBBING
DRUDGERY
DRUDGING
DRUGGETS
DRUGGING
DRUGGIST
DRUIDISM
DRUMBEAT
DRUMFIRE
DRUMFISH
DRUMHEAD
DRUMMERS
DRUMMING
DRUNKARD
DRUNKEST
DRUPELET
DRY-
CLEAN
DRY
DOCKS
DRY
GOODS

DRY-
STONE
DUBONNET
DUCKLING
DUCKWEED
DUCTILES
DUELLING
DUELLIST
DUE
NORTH
DUE
SOUTH
DUETTIST
DUISBURG
DUKEDOMS
DULCIANA
DULCIMER
DULLARDS
DULLNESS
DUMBBELL
DUMB-
CANE
DUMB
DOWN
DUMBNESS
DUMB
SHOW
DUMFRIES
DUMMY
RUN
DUMPIEST
DUMPLING
DUNGAREE
DUNGEONS
DUNGHILL
DUODENAL
DUODENUM
DUOLOGUE
DUPLEXES
DURATION
DURATIVE
DUSHANBE
DUSKIEST
DUSTBINS
DUSTBOWL
DUSTCART
DUSTIEST
DUSTPANS
DUTCH
CAP
DUTCHMAN
DUTIABLE

DUTY-
FREE
DWARFING
DWARFISH
DWARFISM
DWELLING
DWINDLED
DYARCHIC
DYESTUFF
DYNAMICS
DYNAMISM
DYNAMIST
DYNAMITE
DYNASTIC
DYNATRON
DYSGENIC
DYSLEXIA
DYSLEXIC
DYSPNOEA
DYTISCID

E

EALING
EARDROPS
EARDRUMS
EARLDOMS
EARLIEST
EARLOBES
EARMUFFS
EARNINGS
EARPHONE
EARPIECE
EARPLUGS
EARRINGS
EARSHOTS
EARTHIER
EARTHILY
EARTHING
EARTHNUT
EASEMENT
EASINESS
EASTERLY
EAST
SIDE
EASTWARD
EASTWOOD
EASY
CARE
EASY
MARK
EBB
TIDES

EBBW
VALE
ECCLESIA
ECDYSIAL
ECDYSONE
ECHELONS
ECHINATE
ECHINOID
ECLECTIC
ECLIPSED
ECLIPSER
ECLIPSES
ECLIPSIS
ECLIPTIC
ECLOGITE
ECLOSION
ECONOMIC
ECOTONAL
ECOTYPIC
ECRASEUR
ECSTATIC
ECTODERM
ECTOMERE
ECTOSARC
ECUMENIC
EDACIOUS
EDENTATE
EDGEWAYS
EDGINESS
EDIFICES
EDIFYING
EDITIONS
EDMONTON
EDUCABLE
EDUCATED
EDUCATOR
EDUCIBLE
EDUCTION
EDUCTIVE
EELGRASS
EERINESS
EFFACING
EFFECTED
EFFECTER
EFFECTOR
EFFERENT
EFFICACY
EFFIGIAL
EFFIGIES
EFFLUENT
EFFUSION

EFFUSIVE
EGESTION
EGESTIVE
EGGHEADS
EGGPLANT
EGG
ROLLS
EGGSHELL
EGG
TIMER
EGOISTIC
EGOMANIA
EGOTISTS
EGO
TRIPS
EGYPTIAN
EIGHTEEN
EIGHTIES
EISENACH
EITHER-
OR
EJECTING
EJECTION
EJECTIVE
EKISTICS
ELAPSING
ELASTANE
ELATERID
ELATERIN
ELBOWING
EL
DORADO
ELDRITCH
ELECTING
ELECTION
ELECTIVE
ELECTORS
ELECTRET
ELECTRIC
ELECTRON
ELECTRUM
ELEGANCE
ELEMENTS
ELENCHUS
ELENCTIC
ELEPHANT
ELEVATED
ELEVATOR
ELEVENTH
EL
FAIYUM

EL
FERROL
ELF
LOCKS
ELICITED
ELICITOR
ELIDIBLE
ELIGIBLE
ELISIONS
ELITISTS
ELKHOUND
ELLIPSES
ELLIPSIS
ELONGATE
ELOQUENT
ELYTROID
EMACIATE
EMANATED
EMANATOR
EMBALMED
EMBALMER
EMBARKED
EMBATTLE
EMBEDDED
EMBEZZLE
EMBITTER
EMBLAZON
EMBODIED
EMBOLDEN
EMBOLISM
EMBOSSED
EMBOSSER
EMBRACED
EMBRACER
EMBRACES
EMBRYOID
EMENDING
EMERALDS
EMERGENT
EMERGING
EMERITUS
EMERSION
EMIGRANT
EMIGRATE
EMINENCE
EMIRATES
EMISSARY
EMISSION
EMISSIVE
EMITTING
EMOTIONS

EMPATHIC
EMPERORS
EMPHASES
EMPHASIS
EMPHATIC
EMPLOYED
EMPLOYEE
EMPLOYER
EMPORIUM
EMPTIEST
EMPTYING
EMPYEMIC
EMPYREAL
EMPYREAN
EMULATED
EMULATOR
EMULSIFY
EMULSION
EMULSIVE
EMULSOID
ENABLING
ENACTING
ENACTIVE
ENACTORY
ENAMELED
ENCAENIA
ENCAMPED
ENCASING
ENCIPHER
ENCIRCLE
ENCLAVES
ENCLITIC
ENCLOSED
ENCLOSER
ENCODING
ENCOMIUM
ENCROACH
ENCUMBER
ENCYCLIC
ENDAMAGE
ENDANGER
END-
BLOWN
ENDBRAIN
ENDEARED
ENDEMIAL
ENDEMISM
ENDERMIC
END
GAMES
ENDOCARP

ENDODERM
ENDOGAMY
ENDOGENY
ENDORSED
ENDORSEE
ENDORSER
ENDORSOR
ENDOSOME
ENDOWING
ENDPAPER
ENDPLATE
ENDURING
END
USERS
ENERGIZE
ENERVATE
ENFEEBLE
ENFILADE
ENFOLDED
ENFOLDER
ENFORCED
ENFORCER
ENGADINE
ENGAGING
ENGENDER
ENGINEER
ENGINERY
ENGRAVED
ENGRAVER
ENGULFED
ENHANCED
ENHANCER
ENIWETOK
ENJOINED
ENJOINER
ENJOYING
ENKINDLE
ENLARGED
ENLARGER
ENLISTED
ENLISTER
ENMESHED
ENNEADIC
ENNEAGON
ENNOBLED
ENNOBLER
ENORMITY
ENORMOUS
ENQUIRED
ENQUIRER
ENRAGING

ENRICHED
ENRICHER
ENROLLED
ENROLLEE
ENROLLER
ENSCHEDE
ENSCONCE
ENSEMBLE
ENSHRINE
ENSHROUD
ENSIFORM
ENSILAGE
ENSLAVED
ENSLAVER
ENSNARED
ENSNARER
ENSPHERE
ENSURING
ENSWATHE
ENTAILED
ENTAILER
ENTANGLE
ENTELLUS
ENTENDRE
ENTENTES
ENTERING
ENTHALPY
ENTHETIC
ENTHRONE
ENTHUSED
ENTICING
ENTIRELY
ENTIRETY
ENTITIES
ENTITLED
ENTODERM
ENTOMBED
ENTOZOIC
ENTOZOON
ENTR'ACT
E
ENTRAILS
ENTRANCE
ENTRANTS
ENTREATY
ENTRENCH
ENTREPOT
ENTRESOL
ENTRYISM
ENTRYWAY
ENTWINED

E
NUMBER
S
ENURESIS
ENURETIC
ENVELOPE
ENVIABLE
ENVIABLY
ENVIRONS
ENVISAGE
ENVISION
ENWREATH
ENZOOTIC
EOLITHIC
EPAULETS
EPHEMERA
EPIBLAST
EPIBOLIC
EPICALYX
EPICOTYL
EPICURES
EPICYCLE
EPIDEMIC
EPIDOTIC
EPIDURAL
EPIFOCAL
EPIGRAMS
EPIGRAPH
EPILEPSY
EPILOGUE
EPINASTY
EPIPHANY
EPIPHYTE
EPISCOPE
EPISODES
EPISODIC
EPISTLER
EPISTLES
EPISTYLE
EPITAPHS
EPITASIS
EPITHETS
EPITOMIC
EPIZOISM
EPIZOITE
EPONYMIC
EQUALING
EQUALITY
EQUALIZE
EQUALLED
EQUATING

EQUATION
EQUINITY
EQUIPAGE
EQUIPPED
EQUIPPER
EQUITANT
EQUITIES
ERADIATE
ERASABLE
ERASTIAN
ERASURES
ERECTILE
ERECTING
ERECTION
EREMITIC
ERETHISM
ERGOTISM
ERIGERON
ERITREAN
ERLANGEN
ERRANTRY
ERUMPENT
ERUPTING
ERUPTION
ERUPTIVE
ERYTHEMA
ESCALADE
ESCALATE
ESCALOPE
ESCAPADE
ESCAPEES
ESCAPING
ESCAPISM
ESCAPIST
ESCHEWAL
ESCHEWED
ESCHEWER
ESCORTED
ESCULENT
ESKIMOAN
ESKIMOID
ESOTERIC
ESPALIER
ESPECIAL
ESPOUSAL
ESPOUSED
ESPOUSER
ESPRESSO
ESSAYING
ESSAYIST
ESSENCES

ESTANCIA
ESTEEMED
ESTERASE
ESTERIFY
ESTHETES
ESTIMATE
ESTONIAN
ESTOPPEL
ESTOVERS
ESTRAGON
ESTRANGE
ESURIENT
ET
CETERA
ETCHINGS
ETERNITY
ETERNIZE
ETHEREAL
ETHERIFY
ETHERIZE
ETHERNET
ETHICIST
ETHICIZE
ETHIOPIA
ETHIOPIC
ETHNARCH
ETHOLOGY
ETHONONE
ETHOXIDE
ETHYLATE
ETHYLENE
ETIOLATE
ETIOLOGY
ETON
CROP
ETRUSCAN
EUCHARIS
EUGENICS
EULACHON
EULOGIES
EULOGIST
EULOGIZE
EUONYMUS
EUPEPSIA
EUPEPTIC
EUPHONIC
EUPHORIA
EUPHORIC
EUPHOTIC
EUPHRASY
EUPHUISM

EUPHUIST
EUPNOEIC
EURASIAN
EUROCRAT
EURONOTE
EUROPEAN
EUROPIUM
EUSTATIC
EUTECTIC
EUXENITE
EVACUANT
EVACUATE
EVACUEES
EVADABLE
EVALUATE
EVANESCE
EVANSTON
EVASIONS
EVECTION
EVENINGS
EVENNESS
EVENSONG
EVENTFUL
EVENTIDE
EVENTUAL
EVERMORE
EVERSION
EVERYDAY
EVERYMAN
EVERYONE
EVICTING
EVICTION
EVIDENCE
EVILDOER
EVILLEST
EVILNESS
EVINCING
EVINCIVE
EVOCABLE
EVOCATOR
EVOLVING
EVONYMUS
EXACTING
EXACTION
EXALTING
EXAMINED
EXAMINEE
EXAMINER
EXAMPLES
EXARCHAL
EXCAVATE

EXCEEDED
EXCEEDER
EXCELLED
EXCEPTED
EXCERPTS
EXCESSES
EXCHANGE
EXCISING
EXCISION
EXCITANT
EXCITING
EXCLUDED
EXCLUDER
EXCRETAL
EXCRETED
EXCRETER
EXCURSUS
EXCUSING
EXECRATE
EXECUTED
EXECUTER
EXECUTOR
EXEGESES
EXEGESIS
EXEGETIC
EXEMPLAR
EXEMPLUM
EXEMPTED
EXEQUIES
EXERCISE
EXERGUAL
EXERTING
EXERTION
EXERTIVE
EX
GRATIA
EXHALANT
EXHALING
EXHAUSTS
EXHIBITS
EXHORTED
EXHORTER
EXHUMING
EXIGENCY
EXIGIBLE
EXIGUITY
EXIGUOUS
EXISTENT
EXISTING
EXITANCE

EX
  LIBRIS
EXOCRINE
EXOERGIC
EXORABLE
EXORCISE
EXORCISM
EXORCIST
EXORCIZE
EXORDIAL
EXORDIUM
EXOSPORE
EXOTERIC
EXOTOXIC
EXOTOXIN
EXPANDED
EXPANDER
EXPECTED
EXPEDITE
EXPELLED
EXPELLEE
EXPELLER
EXPENDED
EXPENDER
EXPENSES
EXPERTLY
EXPIABLE
EXPIATED
EXPIATOR
EXPIRING
EXPLICIT
EXPLODED
EXPLODER
EXPLOITS
EXPLORED
EXPLORER
EXPONENT
EXPORTED
EXPORTER
EXPOSING
EXPOSURE
EXPUNGED
EXPUNGER
EXTENDED
EXTENDER
EXTENSOR
EXTERIOR
EXTERNAL
EXTOLLED
EXTOLLER
EXTORTED

EXTORTER
EXTRACTS
EXTRADOS
EXTREMES
EXTRORSE
EXTRUDED
EXULTANT
EXULTING
EXUVIATE
EYEBALLS
EYEBROWS
EYEGLASS
EYELINER
EYEPATCH
EYEPIECE
EYESHADE
EYESIGHT
EYESORES
EYESTALK
EYETEETH
EYETOOTH

F
FABULIST
FABULOUS
FACEABLE
FACE
  CARD
FACE
  DOWN
FACELESS
FACE-
  LIFT
FACE
  PACK
FACETIAE
FACIALLY
FACILELY
FACILITY
FACTIONS
FACTIOUS
FACTOTUM
FADELESS
FADEOUTS
FAEROESE
FAHLBAND
FAILINGS
FAIL-
  SAFE
FAILURES
FAINEANT
FAINTEST

FAINTING
FAINTISH
FAIR
  COPY
FAIR
  GAME
FAIRINGS
FAIRLEAD
FAIRNESS
FAIRWAYS
FAITHFUL
FAIZABAD
FALCHION
FALCONER
FALCONET
FALCONRY
FALDERAL
FALKLAND
FALL
  BACK
FALLFISH
FALL
  GUYS
FALLIBLE
FALLOUTS
FALL
  OVER
FALMOUTH
FALSETTO
FALTBOAT
FALTERED
FALTERER
FAMILIAL
FAMILIAR
FAMILIES
FAMISHED
FAMOUSLY
FANAGALO
FANATICS
FAN
  BELTS
FANCIERS
FANCIEST
FANCIFUL
FANCYING
FANCY
  MAN
FANCY
  MEN
FAN
  DANCE
FANDANGO

FANFARES
FANLIGHT
FANTASIA
FANZINES
FARADISM
FARADIZE
FARCEUSE
FARCICAL
FAREWELL
FAR-
  FLUNG
FARINOSE
FARMABLE
FARMHAND
FARMLAND
FARMYARD
FARNESOL
FAROUCHE
FARRIERS
FARRIERY
FARROWED
FARTHEST
FARTHING
FASCIATE
FASCICLE
FASCISTS
FASHIONS
FASTBACK
FASTENED
FASTENER
FAST
  FOOD
FASTNESS
FATALISM
FATALIST
FATALITY
FATHEADS
FATHERED
FATHERLY
FATHOMED
FATHOMER
FATIGUED
FATIGUES
FATTENED
FATTENER
FATTIEST
FAUBOURG
FAULTIER
FAULTILY
FAULTING
FAUSTIAN

FAUTEUIL
FAVONIAN
FAVOURED
FAVOURER
FAYALITE
FEARLESS
FEARSOME
FEASIBLE
FEASIBLY
FEASTING
FEATHERS
FEATHERY
FEATURED
FEATURES
FEBRIFIC
FEBRUARY
FECKLESS
FECULENT
FEDERATE
FEEBLEST
FEEDABLE
FEEDBACK
FEEDBAGS
FEELINGS
FEIGNING
FEINTING
FELDSPAR
FELICITY
FELINITY
FELLABLE
FELLATIO
FELONIES
FELSITIC
FEMININE
FEMINISM
FEMINIST
FEMINIZE
FENDERED
FENESTRA
FERETORY
FEROCITY
FERREOUS
FERRETED
FERRETER
FERRIAGE
FERRITIN
FERRULES
FERRYING
FERRYMAN
FERRYMEN
FERVENCY

FERVIDLY
FESTERED
FESTIVAL
FESTOONS
FETATION
FETCHING
FETIALES
FETICIDE
FETISHES
FETLOCKS
FETTERED
FETTERER
FETTLING
FEVERFEW
FEVERISH
FIASCOES
FIBRILAR
FIBROSIS
FIBROTIC
FICTIONS
FIDDLING
FIDELITY
FIDGETED
FIDUCIAL
FIELD
  DAY
FIELDERS
FIELDING
FIENDISH
FIERCELY
FIERCEST
FIERIEST
FIFTIETH
FIGHTERS
FIGHTING
FIG
  LEAFS
FIGMENTS
FIGURANT
FIGURATE
FIGURINE
FIGURING
FILAGREE
FILAMENT
FILARIAL
FILATURE
FILCHING
FILECARD
FILEFISH
FILENAME
FILETING

FILICIDE
FILIFORM
FILIGREE
FILIPINO
FILLETED
FILLINGS
FILMIEST
FILM
 STAR
FILTERED
FILTHIER
FILTHILY
FILTRATE
FIMBRIAL
FINAGLER
FINALISM
FINALIST
FINALITY
FINALIZE
FINANCED
FINANCES
FINDABLE
FINDINGS
FINEABLE
FINE
 ARTS
FINE-
 DRAW
FINE
 GAEL
FINENESS
FINESPUN
FINE
 SPUN
FINE-
 TUNE
FINGERED
FINGERER
FINIALED
FINISHED
FINISHER
FINISHES
FINITELY
FINNMARK
FINOCHIO
FIREABLE
FIREARMS
FIREBACK
FIREBALL
FIREBOAT
FIREBRAT
FIREBUGS

FIRE-
 CURE
FIREDAMP
FIREDOGS
FIRE-
 PLUG
FIRESIDE
FIRETRAP
FIREWALL
FIREWEED
FIREWOOD
FIREWORK
FIRMNESS
FIRMWARE
FIRST
 AID
FIRST-
 DAY
FIRTREES
FISCALLY
FISHABLE
FISHBOLT
FISHBOWL
FISHCAKE
FISH
 FARM
FISH-
 HOOK
FISHIEST
FISHMEAL
FISHNETS
FISHSKIN
FISHTAIL
FISHWIFE
FISSIPED
FISSURES
FISTMELE
FITFULLY
FITMENTS
FITTABLE
FITTINGS
FIVEFOLD
FIVEPINS
FIVE-
 STAR
FIXATION
FIXATIVE
FIXTURES
FIZZIEST
FLABBIER
FLABBILY

FLAG
 DAYS
FLAG
 FALL
FLAGGING
FLAGPOLE
FLAGRANT
FLAGSHIP
FLAILING
FLAKIEST
FLAMBEAU
FLAMENCO
FLAMEOUT
FLAMINGO
FLANDERS
FLANERIE
FLANKING
FLANNELS
FLAPJACK
FLAPPING
FLARE-
 UPS
FLASHERS
FLASHEST
FLASHGUN
FLASH
 GUN
FLASHIER
FLASHILY
FLASHING
FLATBOAT
FLATETTE
FLAT
 FEET
FLATFISH
FLATFOOT
FLATHEAD
FLATLETS
FLATMATE
FLATNESS
FLAT
 RACE
FLAT
 SPIN
FLATTERY
FLATTEST
FLATTING
FLATTISH
FLATWARE
FLATWAYS
FLATWORM
FLAUNTED

FLAUNTER
FLAUTIST
FLAVOURS
FLAWLESS
FLAXSEED
FLEABAGS
FLEABANE
FLEABITE
FLEA
 BITE
FLEAPITS
FLEAWORT
FLECKING
FLECTION
FLEECING
FLEETEST
FLEETING
FLESHIER
FLESHING
FLESHPOT
FLETCHER
FLEXIBLE
FLEXIBLY
FLEXUOUS
FLEXURAL
FLICKERY
FLICKING
FLIMFLAM
FLIMSIER
FLIMSILY
FLINCHED
FLINCHER
FLINGING
FLINTIER
FLIP-
 FLOP
FLIPPANT
FLIPPERS
FLIPPEST
FLIPPING
FLIP
 SIDE
FLIRTING
FLITTING
FLOATAGE
FLOATERS
FLOATING
FLOCCOSE
FLOCCULE
FLOCKING
FLOGGING

FLOODING
FLOODLIT
FLOORAGE
FLOORING
FLOOZIES
FLOPPIER
FLOPPILY
FLOPPING
FLORALLY
FLORENCE
FLORIDLY
FLORIGEN
FLORISTS
FLOSSING
FLOTILLA
FLOUNCED
FLOUNCES
FLOUNDER
FLOURING
FLOURISH
FLOUTING
FLOWERED
FLOWERER
FLUE-
 CURE
FLUENTLY
FLUFFIER
FLUFFING
FLUIDICS
FLUIDITY
FLUIDIZE
FLUMMERY
FLUNKEYS
FLUNKING
FLUORENE
FLUORIDE
FLUORINE
FLURRIED
FLURRIES
FLUSHING
FLUTISTS
FLUTTERS
FLUTTERY
FLYBLOWN
FLYOVERS
FLYPAPER
FLYPASTS
FLYSHEET
FLYSPECK
FLYWHEEL
FLYWHISK

FOAMIEST
FOAMLIKE
FOB
 WATCH
FOCALIZE
FOCUSING
FOCUSSED
FOETUSES
FOGBOUND
FOGGIEST
FOGHORNS
FOG
 LAMPS
FOGLIGHT
FOIE
 GRAS
FOILABLE
FOILSMAN
FOISTING
FOLDABLE
FOLDAWAY
FOLDBOAT
FOLIATED
FOLKLORE
FOLK-
 ROCK
FOLKTALE
FOLKWAYS
FOLLICLE
FOLLOWED
FOLLOWER
FOLLOW-
 ON
FOLLOW-
 UP
FOMENTED
FOMENTER
FONDANTS
FONDLING
FONDNESS
FOOLSCAP
FOOTBALL
FOOTFALL
FOOTGEAR
FOOTHILL
FOOTHOLD
FOOTLING
FOOTMARK
FOOTNOTE
FOOTPACE
FOOTPADS
FOOTPATH

FOOTRACE
FOOTREST
FOOTROPE
FOOTSIES
FOOTSLOG
FOOTSORE
FOOTSTEP
FOOTWALL
FOOTWEAR
FOOTWELL
FOOTWORK
FOOTWORN
FORAGING
FOR A
SONG
FORAYING
FORBEARS
FORBORNE
FORCE-
FED
FORCEFUL
FORCIBLE
FORCIBLY
FORDABLE
FOREARMS
FOREBEAR
FOREBODE
FORECAST
FOREDECK
FOREDOOM
FOREFEET
FOREFOOT
FOREGOER
FOREGONE
FOREHAND
FOREHEAD
FOREKNOW
FORELAND
FORELEGS
FORELIMB
FORELOCK
FOREMAST
FOREMOST
FORENAME
FORENOON
FORENSIC
FOREPART
FOREPEAK
FOREPLAY
FORESAIL
FORESEEN

FORESEER
FORESIDE
FORESKIN
FORESTAL
FORESTAY
FORESTED
FORESTER
FORESTRY
FORETELL
FORETIME
FORETOLD
FOREWARN
FOREWENT
FOREWIND
FOREWING
FOREWORD
FOREYARD
FORFEITS
FORGINGS
FORGIVEN
FORGIVER
FORGOING
FORJUDGE
FORK-
LIFT
FORMABLE
FORMALIN
FORMALLY
FORMERLY
FORMLESS
FORMULAE
FORMULAS
FORMWORK
FORNICAL
FORSAKEN
FORSAKER
FORSOOTH
FORSWEAR
FORSWORE
FORSWORN
FORTIETH
FORT
KNOX
FORTRESS
FORTUITY
FORTUNES
FORWARDS
FORZANDO
FOSSETTE
FOSTERED
FOSTERER

FOULNESS
FOUL
PLAY
FOUNDERS
FOUNDING
FOUNTAIN
FOUR-
BALL
FOUR-
DEAL
FOUR-
EYED
FOUREYES
FOURFOLD
FOUR-
LEAF
FOURSOME
FOUR-
STAR
FOURTEEN
FOVEOLAR
FOWLIANG
FOWL
PEST
FOXGLOVE
FOXHOLES
FOXHOUND
FOXHUNTS
FOXINESS
FOXTROTS
FRACTION
FRACTURE
FRAGMENT
FRAGRANT
FRAILEST
FRAMABLE
FRAME-
UPS
FRANCIUM
FRANKEST
FRANKING
FRANKISH
FRANKLIN
FRASCATI
FRAULEIN
FRAZZLED
FREAKING
FREAKISH
FRECKLED
FRECKLES
FREE-
BASE

FREEBIES
FREEBOOT
FREEBORN
FREEDMAN
FREE-
FALL
FREEFONE
FREEHAND
FREEHOLD
FREE
KICK
FREELOAD
FREE
PASS
FREE
PORT
FREEPOST
FREE
REIN
FREESIAS
FREE
TIME
FREETOWN
FREEWARE
FREEWAYS
FREE
WILL
FREEZERS
FREEZE
UP
FREEZE-
UP
FREEZING
FREIBURG
FREMITUS
FRENETIC
FRENULUM
FRENZIED
FREQUENT
FRESCOES
FRESHEST
FRESHMAN
FRESHMEN
FRETLESS
FRETSAWS
FRETTING
FRETWORK
FREUDIAN
FRIARIES
FRIBBLER
FRIBOURG
FRICTION

FRIENDLY
FRIESIAN
FRIGATES
FRIGGING
FRIGHTEN
FRIGIDLY
FRILLIER
FRINGING
FRIPPERY
FRISBEES
FRISETTE
FRISKIER
FRISKILY
FRISKING
FRISSONS
FRITTATA
FRITTERS
FRIULIAN
FRIZZIER
FRIZZING
FRIZZLED
FRIZZLER
FROCKING
FROGFISH
FROMENTY
FRONDEUR
FRONTAGE
FRONTIER
FRONTING
FRONTLET
FRONT
MAN
FRONT
MEN
FROSTIER
FROSTILY
FROSTING
FROTHIER
FROTHILY
FROTHING
FROUFROU
FROWNING
FROWZIER
FRUCTIFY
FRUCTOSE
FRUGALLY
FRUITAGE
FRUIT
BAT
FRUIT
FLY
FRUITFUL

FRUITIER
FRUITING
FRUITION
FRUMENTY
FRUMPIER
FRUMPISH
FRUSTULE
FUCHSIAS
FUCOIDAL
FUDDLING
FUELLING
FUGACITY
FUGGIEST
FUGITIVE
FUGLEMAN
FULCRUMS
FULLBACK
FULL
MOON
FULLNESS
FULL-
PAGE
FULL
STOP
FULL-
TIME
FULL
TOSS
FULMINIC
FUMAROLE
FUMATORY
FUMBLING
FUMELESS
FUMIGANT
FUMIGATE
FUMINGLY
FUMITORY
FUNCTION
FUNERALS
FUNERARY
FUNEREAL
FUNFAIRS
FUNGIBLE
FUNGUSES
FUNKIEST
FUNNELED
FUNNIEST
FURBELOW
FURCATED
FURFURAN
FURLABLE
FURLONGS

FURLOUGH
FURNACES
FURRIERS
FURRIERY
FURRIEST
FURROWED
FURROWER
FURTHEST
FURUNCLE
FUSELAGE
FUSIFORM
FUSILIER
FUSSIEST
FUSSPOTS
FUSTIEST
FUTILITY
FUTURISM
FUTURIST
FUTURITY
FUZZIEST

G

GABBLING
GABBROIC
GABONESE
GABORONE
GADABOUT
GADFLIES
GADGETRY
GAFFSAIL
GAINABLE
GAINSAID
GALACTIC
GALANGAL
GALAXIES
GALBANUM
GALENISM
GALENIST
GALICIAN
GALILEAN
GALLANTS
GALLEASS
GALLEONS
GALLERIA
GALLIARD
GALLIPOT
GALLOPED
GALLOPER
GALLOWAY
GALOSHES
GALVANIC

GAMBLERS
GAMBLING
GAMBOLED
GAMECOCK
GAME
  FOWL
GAMENESS
GAMESTER
GAMINESS
GAMMA
  RAY
GAMMONER
GANDHIAN
GANG-
  BANG
GANGLAND
GANGLIAL
GANGLING
GANGLION
GANGRENE
GANGSTER
GANGWAYS
GANISTER
GANTLINE
GANTRIES
GANYMEDE
GAOLBIRD
GAOXIONG
GAPEWORM
GAPINGLY
GARAGING
GARAMOND
GARBLESS
GARBLING
GARBOARD
GARDENED
GARDENER
GARDENIA
GARGANEY
GARGLING
GARGOYLE
GARISHLY
GARLANDS
GARLICKY
GARMENTS
GARNERED
GARRISON
GARROTTE
GASIFIER
GASIFORM
GASLIGHT

GAS
  MASKS
GASOLIER
GASOLINE
GASSIEST
GASTIGHT
GASTRULA
GASWORKS
GATEFOLD
GATEPOST
GATEWAYS
GATHERED
GATHERER
GAUDIEST
GAULLISM
GAULLIST
GAUNTLET
GAUZIEST
GAVOTTES
GAWKIEST
GAZELLES
GAZETTES
GAZPACHO
GAZUMPED
GAZUMPER
GELATINE
GELATION
GELDINGS
GELIDITY
GEMINATE
GEMOLOGY
GEMSTONE
GENDARME
GENDERED
GENERALS
GENERATE
GENEROUS
GENETICS
GENIALLY
GENITALS
GENITIVE
GENIUSES
GENOCIDE
GENOTYPE
GENTIANS
GENTILES
GENTRIFY
GEODESIC
GEODETIC
GEOGNOSY
GEOMANCY

GEOMETER
GEOMETRY
GEOPHAGY
GEOPHYTE
GEOPONIC
GEORDIES
GEORGIAN
GEOTAXIS
GERANIAL
GERANIOL
GERANIUM
GERMANIC
GERM
  CELL
GERMINAL
GESTALTS
GESTAPOS
GESTURAL
GESTURED
GESTURER
GESTURES
GET
  THERE
GHANAIAN
GHERKINS
GHETTOES
GHOSTING
GHOULISH
GIANTESS
GIBBERED
GIBBSITE
GIBINGLY
GIDDIEST
GIFT-
  WRAP
GIGAFLOP
GIGANTIC
GIGGLING
GILTHEAD
GILTWOOD
GIMCRACK
GIMMICKS
GIMMICKY
GINGERED
GINGERLY
GINGIVAL
GIN
  RUMMY
GINSBERG
GIN
  SLING

GIN
  TRAPS
GIRAFFES
GIRDLING
GIRLHOOD
GISBORNE
GIVEAWAY
GIZZARDS
GLABELLA
GLABROUS
GLACIATE
GLACIERS
GLADBECK
GLADDEST
GLAD
  HAND
GLADIATE
GLADIOLI
GLADNESS
GLAD
  RAGS
GLANCING
GLANDERS
GLANDULE
GLASSIER
GLASSINE
GLASSING
GLASSMAN
GLAUCOMA
GLAUCOUS
GLAZIERS
GLAZIERY
GLEAMING
GLEANING
GLENDALE
GLIBBEST
GLIBNESS
GLIMMERS
GLIMPSED
GLIMPSER
GLIMPSES
GLINTING
GLISSADE
GLITCHES
GLITTERS
GLITTERY
GLITZIER
GLOAMING
GLOATING
GLOBALLY
GLOBULAR

GLOBULES
GLOBULIN
GLOOMFUL
GLOOMIER
GLOOMILY
GLORIOUS
GLORYING
GLOSSARY
GLOSSIER
GLOSSILY
GLOSSING
GLOWERED
GLOW-
  WORM
GLOXINIA
GLUCAGON
GLUCINUM
GLUCOSIC
GLUMMEST
GLUMNESS
GLUTELIN
GLUTTING
GLUTTONS
GLUTTONY
GLYCERIC
GLYCERIN
GLYCEROL
GLYCERYL
GLYCOGEN
GLYCOLIC
GLYPTICS
GNASHERS
GNASHING
GNATHION
GNATHITE
GNAWABLE
GNEISSIC
GNOMONIC
GOAL
  LINE
GOALPOST
GOATHERD
GOATSKIN
GOAT'S-
  RUE
GOBBLING
GOBSHITE
GOD-
  AWFUL
GODCHILD
GODLIEST
GODSENDS

GODSPEED
GODTHAAB
GOETHITE
GO-
 GETTER
GOGGLING
GOIDELIC
GOINGS
 ON
GOINGS-
 ON
GOITROUS
GOLD
 COAT
GOLD
 DUST
GOLDFISH
GOLD
 LEAF
GOLDMINE
GOLD
 RUSH
GOLF
 BALL
GOLF
 CLUB
GOLIATHS
GOLLIWOG
GOLLOPER
GOMBROON
GONDOLAS
GONIDIAL
GONIDIUM
GONOCYTE
GONOPORE
GOOD
 BOOK
GOODBYES
GOODLIER
GOODNESS
GOOD
 TURN
GOODWILL
GOODWOOD
GOOD
 WORD
GOOFIEST
GOOGLIES
GO
 PLACES
GORDIMER
GORGEDLY

GORGEOUS
GORGERIN
GORILLAS
GORINESS
GORLOVKA
GORMLESS
GOSLINGS
GOSPODIN
GOSSAMER
GOSSIPED
GOSSIPER
GOSSYPOL
GOTEBORG
GO TO
 TOWN
GOUACHES
GOURMAND
GOURMETS
GOUTWEED
GOVERNED
GOVERNOR
GRAB
 BAGS
GRABBING
GRABBLER
GRACEFUL
GRACIOUS
GRADABLE
GRADIENT
GRADUATE
GRAECISM
GRAFFITI
GRAFFITO
GRAFTERS
GRAFTING
GRAINING
GRAMPIAN
GRANDADS
GRANDEES
GRANDEST
GRANDEUR
GRAND
 MAL
GRANDMAS
GRANDPAS
GRANDSON
GRANITIC
GRANNIES
GRANTHAM
GRANTING
GRANULAR

GRANULES
GRAPHEME
GRAPHICS
GRAPHITE
GRAPNELS
GRAPPLED
GRAPPLER
GRASPING
GRASSIER
GRASSING
GRATEFUL
GRATINGS
GRATUITY
GRAVAMEN
GRAVELED
GRAVELLY
GRAVITAS
GRAVITON
GRAYLING
GREASERS
GREASIER
GREASILY
GREASING
GREATEST
GREEDIER
GREEDILY
GREENERY
GREENEST
GREENFLY
GREENING
GREENISH
GREENLET
GREENOCK
GREEN
 TEA
GREETING
GREMLINS
GRENADES
GRENOBLE
GREY
 AREA
GREYBACK
GREYNESS
GRIDDLES
GRIDIRON
GRIDLOCK
GRIEVING
GRIEVOUS
GRIFFINS
GRILLAGE
GRILLING

GRIMACED
GRIMACER
GRIMACES
GRIMIEST
GRIMMEST
GRIMNESS
GRINDERS
GRINDERY
GRINDING
GRINNING
GRIPPING
GRISEOUS
GRISETTE
GRISLIER
GRITTIER
GRITTILY
GRITTING
GRIZZLED
GRIZZLER
GROANING
GROGGIER
GROGGILY
GROMWELL
GROOMING
GROOVIER
GROSBEAK
GROSCHEN
GROSSEST
GROSSING
GROTTIER
GROTTOES
GROUCHED
GROUCHES
GROUNDED
GROUPIES
GROUPING
GROUSING
GROVELED
GROWABLE
GROWLERS
GROWLING
GROWMORE
GROWN-
 UPS
GRUBBIER
GRUBBILY
GRUBBING
GRUDGING
GRUESOME
GRUFFEST
GRUFFISH

GRUMBLED
GRUMBLER
GRUMBLES
GRUMPIER
GRUMPILY
GRUNTING
GRYPHONS
G-
 STRING
 S
GUAIACOL
GUAIACUM
GUARANTY
GUARDANT
GUARDIAN
GUARDING
GUERNSEY
GUERRERO
GUESSING
GUESTING
GUFFAWED
GUIANESE
GUIDABLE
GUIDANCE
GUILDERS
GUILEFUL
GUILTIER
GUILTILY
GUJARATI
GULFWEED
GULLIBLE
GULLIBLY
GUMBOILS
GUMBOOTS
GUMBOTIL
GUMDROPS
GUMMIEST
GUMMOSIS
GUMPTION
GUMSHOES
GUM
 TREES
GUNBOATS
GUNFLINT
GUNMETAL
GUNPAPER
GUNPOINT
GUNSHOTS
GUNSMITH
GUNSTOCK
GUNWALES

GURGLING
GURKHALI
GUSTIEST
GUTSIEST
GUTTERED
GUTTURAL
GUYANESE
GUZZLERS
GUZZLING
GYMKHANA
GYMNASTS
GYMSLIPS
GYNANDRY
GYNARCHY
GYPSEOUS
GYRATING
GYRATION
GYRATORY

H
HABAKKUK
HABANERA
HABITANT
HABITATS
HABITUAL
HABITUDE
HABITUES
HABSBURG
HACIENDA
HACKETTE
HACKNEYS
HACKSAWS
HACKWORK
HADRONIC
HAEMATIC
HAEMATIN
HAEREMAI
HA-ERH-
 PIN
HAFTARAH
HAGGADAH
HAGGADIC
HAGGLING
HAILWOOD
HAIPHONG
HAIRBALL
HAIRCUTS
HAIRGRIP
HAIRIEST
HAIRLESS
HAIRLIKE

HAIRLINE	HANDBELL	HARAMBEE	HARKENER	HAVELOCK	HEADWORK
HAIRNETS	HANDBILL	HARANGUE	HARLOTRY	HAVE-	HEALABLE
HAIRPINS	HANDBOOK	HARAPPAN	HARMLESS	NOTS	HEARABLE
HAIRTAIL	HANDCART	HARASSED	HARMONIC	HAVERING	HEAR
HAIRWORM	HANDCLAP	HARASSER	HARPINGS	HAVILDAR	HEAR
HAKODATE	HANDCUFF	HARBOURS	HARPISTS	HAVOCKER	HEARINGS
HALAFIAN	HANDFAST	HARD AT	HARPOONS	HAWAIIAN	HEARTIER
HALATION	HANDFEED	IT	HARRIDAN	HAWFINCH	HEARTILY
HALBERDS	HANDFULS	HARDBACK	HARRIERS	HAWKBILL	HEATEDLY
HALCYONE	HANDGRIP	HARDBAKE	HARRIMAN	HAWK-	HEATHENS
HALENESS	HANDGUNS	HARDBALL	HARRISON	EYED	HEATHERY
HALFBACK	HANDHOLD	HARD	HARROWED	HAWKLIKE	HEATLESS
HALFBEAK	HANDICAP	CASH	HARROWER	HAWKWEED	HEAT
HALF	HANDIEST	HARD	HARRUMPH	HAWTHORN	PUMP
COCK	HANDLERS	COPY	HARRYING	HAYCOCKS	HEAT
HALF-	HANDLESS	HARDCORE	HARSHEST	HAY	RASH
LIFE	HANDLIKE	HARD	HARTFORD	FEVER	HEAT
HALF-	HANDLING	CORE	HARTNELL	HAYFORKS	WAVE
MAST	HANDLOOM	HARDCORE	HARUSPEX	HAYMAKER	HEAVENLY
HALF	HANDMADE	HARD-	HARVESTS	HAYSTACK	HEAVIEST
MOON	HANDOUTS	CORE	HAS-	HAZARDED	HEAVY-
HALF	HANDOVER	HARD	BEENS	HAZELHEN	SET
NOTE	HANDRAIL	DISK	HASIDISM	HAZELNUT	HEBDOMAD
HALF	HANDS-	HARDENED	HASSLING	HAZINESS	HEBETATE
TERM	OFF	HARDENER	HASSOCKS	HEADACHE	HEBETUDE
HALF	HANDSOME	HARDHACK	HASTEFUL	HEADACHY	HEBRAISM
TIME	HANDYMAN	HARDIEST	HASTENED	HEADBAND	HEBRAIST
HALFTONE	HANDYMEN	HARD	HASTENER	HEADFAST	HEBRAIZE
HALF-	HANGBIRD	LINE	HASTIEST	HEADGEAR	HEBRIDES
WITS	HANGCHOW	HARD	HASTINGS	HEADHUNT	HECATOMB
HALF-	HANGER-	LUCK	HATBANDS	HEADIEST	HECKLERS
YEAR	ON	HARDNESS	HATCHERY	HEADINGS	HECKLING
HALIBUTS	HANGINGS	HARD	HATCHETS	HEADLAND	HECTARES
HALLIARD	HANGNAIL	NUTS	HATCHING	HEADLESS	HECTORED
HALLMARK	HANGOUTS	HARD	HATCHWAY	HEADLIKE	HEDGEHOG
HALLOWED	HANGOVER	SELL	HATEABLE	HEADLINE	HEDGEHOP
HALLOWER	HANGZHOU	HARDSHIP	HATFIELD	HEADLOCK	HEDGEROW
HALLWAYS	HANKERED	HARD	HATHAWAY	HEADLONG	HEDONICS
HALMSTAD	HANKERER	TACK	HATHORIC	HEADMOST	HEDONISM
HALO-	HANNIBAL	HARDTOPS	HATTERAS	HEADRACE	HEDONIST
LIKE	HANNOVER	HARD	HAT	HEADRAIL	HEEDLESS
HALYARDS	HANRATTY	UPON	TRICK	HEADREST	HEELBALL
HAMARTIA	HANUKKAH	HARDWARE	HAULIERS	HEADROOM	HEELLESS
HAMILTON	HAPLITIC	HARDWOOD	HAUNCHED	HEADSAIL	HEELPOST
HAMMERED	HAPLOSIS	HAREBELL	HAUNCHES	HEADSETS	HEFTIEST
HAMMERER	HAPPENED	HARELIKE	HAUNTING	HEADSHIP	HEGELIAN
HAMMOCKS	HAPPIEST	HARFLEUR	HAUSFRAU	HEADSMAN	HEGEMONY
HAMPERED	HAPSBURG	HARGEISA	HAUTBOIS	HEADWARD	HEIGHTEN
HAMPERER	HAPTERON	HARICOTS	HAUTBOYS	HEADWAYS	HEIMDALL
HAMSTERS	HARA-	HARIKARI	HAUT-	HEADWIND	HEIRLESS
HANDBAGS	KIRI	HARINGEY	RHIN	HEADWORD	HEIRLOOM
HANDBALL		HARKENED			HEIRSHIP

HELIACAL
HELICOID
HELIPORT
HELLADIC
HELL-
  BENT
HELLCATS
HELLENES
HELLENIC
HELLFIRE
HELLHOLE
HELMETED
HELMINTH
HELMLESS
HELMSMAN
HELMSMEN
HELOTISM
HELPABLE
HELPINGS
HELPLESS
HELPMANN
HELPMATE
HELPMEET
HELSINKI
HELVETIA
HELVETIC
HELVETII
HEMIOLIC
HEMIPODE
HEMLINES
HEMLOCKS
HENBANES
HENCHMAN
HENCHMEN
HENEQUEN
HENGYANG
HENG-
  YANG
HEN
  HOUSE
HEN
  PARTY
HENRYSON
HENSLOWE
HEPATICA
HEPTAGON
HEPTARCH
HEPWORTH
HERACLEA
HERACLES
HERALDED
HERALDIC

HERALDRY
HERBLIKE
HERCULES
HERDSMAN
HERDSMEN
HERDWICK
HEREDITY
HEREFORD
HEREINTO
HERESIES
HERETICS
HEREUNTO
HEREUPON
HEREWARD
HEREWITH
HERITAGE
HERMETIC
HERMITIC
HERODIAS
HERPETIC
HERRINGS
HERSCHEL
HERTFORD
HERTZIAN
HESIODIC
HESITANT
HESITATE
HESPERIA
HESPERUS
HESSIANS
HETAERIC
HEXAGONS
HEXAGRAM
HEXANOIC
HEXAPLAR
HEXAPODY
HEZEKIAH
HIATUSES
HIAWATHA
HIBERNAL
HIBERNIA
HIBISCUS
HICCUPED
HIDDENLY
HIDEAWAY
HIDELESS
HIDROSIS
HIDROTIC
HIERARCH
HIERATIC
HIGHBALL

HIGHBORN
HIGHBOYS
HIGHBROW
HIGHER-
  UP
HIGHJACK
HIGH
  JUMP
HIGHLAND
HIGH
  LIFE
HIGH
  MASS
HIGHNESS
HIGH
  RISE
HIGH-
  RISE
HIGH
  ROAD
HIGH
  SEAS
HIGH
  SPOT
HIGHTAIL
HIGH
  TECH
HIGH
  TIDE
HIGH
  TIME
HIGHVELD
HIGHWAYS
HIJACKED
HIJACKER
HILARITY
HILLFORT
HILL
  FORT
HILLIARD
HILLIEST
HILLOCKS
HILLSIDE
HIMATION
HINAYANA
HINCKLEY
HINDERED
HINDERER
HINDMOST
HINDUISM
HIPBATHS
HIP
  FLASK

HIPPARCH
HIPSTERS
HIRAGANA
HIRELING
HIRI
  MOTU
HIROHITO
HISPANIA
HISPANIC
HISTOGEN
HISTORIC
HITCHING
HITHERTO
HIT
  LISTS
HIVELIKE
HOACTZIN
HOARDING
HOARIEST
HOARSELY
HOARSEST
HOBBLING
HOBBYIST
HOBNAILS
HOCHHUTH
HOCKTIDE
HOGMANAY
HOGSHEAD
HOISTING
HOKKAIDO
HOLDABLE
HOLDALLS
HOLD
  DEAR
HOLDFAST
HOLDINGS
HOLDOVER
HOLIDAYS
HOLINESS
HOLISTIC
HOLLANDS
HOLLERED
HOLLIDAY
HOLLOWED
HOLLOWER
HOLLOWLY
HOLOCENE
HOLOGRAM
HOLOTYPE
HOLOZOIC
HOLSTEIN

HOLSTERS
HOLYHEAD
HOLYOAKE
HOLYTIDE
HOLY
  WEEK
HOLY
  WRIT
HOMBURGS
HOMEBODY
HOMEBRED
HOME
  BREW
HOME
  HELP
HOMELAND
HOMELESS
HOMELIER
HOMELIKE
HOMEMADE
HOME
  PAGE
HOMERIAN
HOME
  RULE
HOME
  RUNS
HOMESICK
HOMESPUN
HOMETOWN
HOMEWARD
HOMEWORK
HOMICIDE
HOMILIES
HOMILIST
HOMINESS
HOMINOID
HOMODONT
HOMOGAMY
HOMOGENY
HOMOGONY
HOMOLOGY
HOMONYMS
HONDURAN
HONDURAS
HONEGGER
HONESTLY
HONEWORT
HONEYBEE
HONEYDEW
HONG
  KONG

HONIEDLY
HONOLULU
HONORARY
HONOURED
HONOURER
HOODLESS
HOODLIKE
HOODLUMS
HOODWINK
HOOFLESS
HOOFLIKE
HOOKLESS
HOOKLIKE
HOOKNOSE
HOOKWORM
HOOLIGAN
HOOPLIKE
HOOSEGOW
HOOVERED
HOPEFULS
HOPELESS
HOPLITIC
HORATIAN
HORIZONS
HORMONAL
HORMONES
HORNBEAM
HORNBILL
HORNBOOK
HORNFELS
HORNIEST
HORNLESS
HORNLIKE
HORNPIPE
HORNTAIL
HORNWORT
HOROLOGE
HOROLOGY
HOROWITZ
HORRIBLE
HORRIBLY
HORRIDLY
HORRIFIC
HORSEBOX
HORSEFLY
HORSEMAN
HORSEMEN
HORSIEST
HOSANNAS
HOSEPIPE
HOSPICES

HOSPITAL
HOSPODAR
HOSTAGES
HOSTELRY
HOSTLERS
HOTCHPOT
HOTELIER
HOT
   FLUSH
HOTHEADS
HOTHOUSE
HOT
   LINES
HOTPLATE
HOT
   SPOTS
HOT
   STUFF
HOT
   WATER
HOUNDING
HOUNSLOW
HOUSEBOY
HOUSEFLY
HOUSEFUL
HOUSEMAN
HOUSEMEN
HOUSETOP
HOUSINGS
HOVERERS
HOVERING
HOWITZER
HRVATSKA
HSINKING
HUANG
   HUA
HUCKSTER
HUDDLING
HUFFIEST
HUGENESS
HUGGABLE
HUGUENOT
HULA
   HOOP
HULL-
   LESS
HUMANELY
HUMANISM
HUMANIST
HUMANITY
HUMANIZE
HUMANOID

HUMBLEST
HUMBLING
HUMBOLDT
HUMIDIFY
HUMIDITY
HUMILITY
HUMMOCKS
HUMMOCKY
HUMORIST
HUMOROUS
HUMOURED
HUMPBACK
HUMPHREY
HUMPLIKE
HUNCHING
HUNDREDS
HUNGERED
HUNG
   JURY
HUNGRIER
HUNGRILY
HUNTEDLY
HUNTRESS
HUNTSMAN
HUNTSMEN
HURDLERS
HURDLING
HURRYING
HURTLING
HUSBANDS
HUSH-
   HUSH
HUSKIEST
HUSKLIKE
HUSTINGS
HUSTLERS
HUSTLING
HWANG
   HAI
HYACINTH
HYDER
   ALI
HYDRACID
HYDRANTH
HYDRANTS
HYDRATED
HYDRATES
HYDRATOR
HYDROGEL
HYDROGEN
HYDROMEL
HYGIENIC

HYMENEAL
HYPERNYM
HYPNOSIS
HYPNOTIC
HYSTERIA
HYSTERIC

I

IAMBUSES
ICEBERGS
ICEBLINK
ICEBOUND
ICEBOXES
ICE
   CREAM
ICE
   LOLLY
ICE
   PACKS
ICE
   PICKS
ICE
   RINKS
ICE
   SHEET
ICE
   SKATE
ICE
   WATER
ICHTHYIC
IDEALISM
IDEALIST
IDEALITY
IDEALIZE
IDEATION
IDEATIVE
IDEE
   FIXE
IDENTIFY
IDENTITY
IDEOGRAM
IDEOLOGY
IDIOCIES
IDIOLECT
IDLENESS
IDOLATER
IDOLATRY
IDOLIZED
IDOLIZER
IDYLLIST
IGNITING
IGNITION

IGNITRON
IGNOMINY
IGNORANT
IGNORING
IGUANIAN
ILKESTON
ILLATIVE
ILL-
   FATED
ILLINOIS
ILLIQUID
ILL-
   TIMED
ILL-
   TREAT
ILLUSION
ILLUSORY
ILMENITE
IMAGINAL
IMAGINED
IMAGINER
IMBECILE
IMBEDDED
IMBIBING
IMITABLE
IMITATED
IMITATOR
IMMANENT
IMMATURE
IMMERSED
IMMINENT
IMMOBILE
IMMODEST
IMMOLATE
IMMORTAL
IMMOTILE
IMMUNITY
IMMUNIZE
IMMURING
IMPACTED
IMPAIRED
IMPAIRER
IMPALING
IMPARITY
IMPARTED
IMPARTER
IMPASSES
IMPEDING
IMPELLED
IMPELLER
IMPERIAL

IMPERIUM
IMPETIGO
IMPINGED
IMPINGER
IMPISHLY
IMPLANTS
IMPLICIT
IMPLODED
IMPLORED
IMPLORER
IMPLYING
IMPOLICY
IMPOLITE
IMPORTED
IMPORTER
IMPOSING
IMPOSTOR
IMPOTENT
IMPRINTS
IMPRISON
IMPROPER
IMPROVED
IMPROVER
IMPUDENT
IMPUGNED
IMPUGNER
IMPULSES
IMPUNITY
IMPURITY
IMPUTING
INACTION
INACTIVE
INASMUCH
IN
   CAMERA
INCENSED
INCEPTOR
INCHOATE
INCIDENT
INCISING
INCISION
INCISIVE
INCISORS
INCISURE
INCITING
INCLINED
INCLINER
INCLINES
INCLOSED
INCLUDED
INCOMING

INCREASE
INCUBATE
INCUDATE
INCURRED
INDAMINE
INDEBTED
INDECENT
INDENTED
INDENTER
INDEXERS
INDEXING
INDICANT
INDICATE
INDICIAL
INDICTED
INDICTEE
INDIGENE
INDIGENT
INDIGOID
INDIRECT
INDOCILE
INDOLENT
INDOLOGY
INDORSED
INDUCING
INDUCTED
INDUCTOR
INDULGED
INDULGER
INDULINE
INDUSIAL
INDUSIUM
INDUSTRY
INEDIBLE
INEDIBLY
INEDITED
INEQUITY
INERTIAL
INESSIVE
INEXPERT
INFAMIES
INFAMOUS
INFANTAS
INFANTRY
INFECTED
INFECTOR
INFERIOR
INFERNAL
INFERNOS
INFERRED
INFERRER

INFESTED
INFESTER
INFIDELS
INFINITE
INFINITY
INFIXION
INFLAMED
INFLAMER
INFLATED
INFLATER
INFLEXED
IN
    FLIGHT
IN-
    FLIGHT
INFLUENT
INFLUXES
INFORMAL
INFORMED
INFORMER
INFRA
    DIG
INFRARED
INFRINGE
INFUSING
INFUSION
INFUSIVE
INGATHER
INGENUES
INGESTED
INGRATES
IN-
    GROUPS
INGROWTH
INGUINAL
INHALANT
INHALERS
INHALING
INHERENT
INHUMANE
INIMICAL
INIQUITY
INITIALS
INITIATE
INJECTED
INJECTOR
INJURIES
INJURING
INKBERRY
INKINESS
INKSTAND
INKWELLS

INLANDER
INNATELY
INNER
    MAN
INNOCENT
IN NO
    TIME
INNOVATE
INNUENDO
INOCULUM
INOSITOL
INPUTTED
INQUESTS
INQUIRED
INQUIRER
INSANELY
INSANITY
INSCRIBE
INSECURE
INSERTED
INSERTER
INSETTED
INSETTER
INSIDERS
INSIGHTS
INSIGNIA
INSISTED
INSISTER
INSOLATE
INSOLENT
INSOMNIA
INSOMUCH
INSPIRED
INSPIRER
INSPIRIT
INSTANCE
INSTANTS
INSTINCT
INSTRUCT
INSULANT
INSULATE
INSULTED
INSULTER
INSURERS
INSURING
INTAGLIO
INTARSIA
INTEGERS
INTEGRAL
INTENDED
INTENDER

INTENTLY
INTERACT
INTERCOM
INTEREST
INTERIMS
INTERIOR
INTERLAY
INTERMIT
INTERMIX
INTERNAL
INTERNED
INTERNEE
INTERNET
INTERNET
INTERPOL
INTERRED
INTERREX
INTERSEX
INTERVAL
INTERWAR
IN THE
    BAG
IN THE
    END
INTIMACY
INTIMATE
INTONATE
INTONING
INTRADOS
INTRANET
INTRENCH
INTREPID
INTRIGUE
INTRORSE
INTRUDED
INTRUDER
INTUBATE
INTUITED
INUNDANT
INUNDATE
INVADERS
INVADING
INVALIDS
INVASION
INVASIVE
INVEIGLE
INVENTED
INVENTOR
INVERTED
INVERTER
INVESTED

INVESTOR
INVIABLE
INVITING
INVOICED
INVOICES
INVOKING
INVOLUTE
INVOLVED
INVOLVER
INWARDLY
IODATION
IODOFORM
IODOPSIN
IONIZERS
IONIZING
IOTACISM
IRAKLION
IRISHMAN
IRISHMEN
IRONBARK
IRONCLAD
IRON-
    GREY
IRON
    HAND
IRONWARE
IRONWOOD
IRONWORK
IROQUOIS
IRRIGATE
IRRITANT
IRRITATE
ISAGOGIC
ISATINIC
ISCHEMIC
ISLAMIST
ISLANDER
ISMAILIA
ISOBARIC
ISOCHEIM
ISOCLINE
ISOCRACY
ISOGLOSS
ISOGONIC
ISOLABLE
ISOLATED
ISOLATOR
ISOLOGUE
ISOMERIC
ISOMETRY
ISOMORPH

ISOPHONE
ISOPLETH
ISOPODAN
ISOPRENE
ISOSTASY
ISOTHERE
ISOTHERM
ISOTONIC
ISOTOPES
ISOTOPIC
ISOTROPY
ISRAELIS
ISSUABLE
ISSUANCE
ISSYK-
    KUL
ISTANBUL
ISTHMIAN
ISTHMOID
ITALIANS
ITCHIEST
ITEMIZED

J
JABALPUR
JABBERED
JABBERER
JACKBOOT
JACKDAWS
JACKFISH
JACKPOTS
JACKSTAY
JACK
    TARS
JACOBEAN
JACOBIAN
JACOBITE
JACQUARD
JACUZZIS
JAGGEDLY
JAILBAIT
JAILBIRD
JALOPIES
JALOUSIE
JAMAICAN
JAMBOREE
JAMMIEST
JAMNAGAR
JANGLING
JANITORS
JAPANESE

JAPANNED
JAPINGLY
JAPONICA
JAROSITE
JASMINES
JAUNDICE
JAUNTIER
JAUNTILY
JAUNTING
JAVANESE
JAVELINS
JAWBONES
JAYAPURA
JAZZIEST
JEALOUSY
JEHOVIAN
JEMAPPES
JEMMYING
JEOPARDY
JEREMIAD
JERKIEST
JEROBOAM
JESUITIC
JET-
    BLACK
JETFOILS
JETLINER
JETTISON
JEWELLED
JEWELLER
JEW'S
    HARP
JEZEBELS
JIGGERED
JIGGLING
JINGLING
JINGOISM
JINGOIST
JINJIANG
JIPIJAPA
JIUJITSU
JOCKEYED
JOCOSELY
JOCOSITY
JODHPURI
JODHPURS
JOGGLING
JOHN
    BULL
JOHNNIES
JOINTING

JOINTURE
JOKINGLY
JOLLIEST
JOLLYING
JOSTLING
JOTTINGS
JOURNALS
JOURNEYS
JOUSTING
JOVIALLY
JOYFULLY
JOYOUSLY
JOYRIDER
JOYRIDES
JOYSTICK
JUBILANT
JUBILATE
JUBILEES
JUDAIZER
JUDDERED
JUDGMENT
JUDICIAL
JUGGLERS
JUGGLERY
JUGGLING
JUGULARS
JUICIEST
JULIENNE
JUMBLING
JUMBO
  JET
JUMPABLE
JUMPED-
  UP
JUMPIEST
JUMPSUIT
JUNAGADH
JUNCTION
JUNCTURE
JUNGFRAU
JUNIPERS
JUNKETER
JUNK
  FOOD
JUNK
  MAIL
JUNKYARD
JURASSIC
JURATORY
JURISTIC
JUSTICES
JUSTNESS

JUVENILE

K
KAI
  MOANA
KAIROUAN
KAKEMONO
KALAHARI
KAMACITE
KAMAKURA
KAMIKAZE
KANARESE
KANAZAWA
KANDAHAR
KANGAROO
KAOLIANG
KAOLINIC
KARELIAN
KASHMIRI
KATAKANA
KATMANDU
KATOWICE
KATTEGAT
KAUMATUA
KAWASAKI
KAYAKERS
KEDGEREE
KEENNESS
KEEPSAKE
KEESHOND
KEEWATIN
KEIGHLEY
KELANTAN
KELOIDAL
KEMEROVO
KENNELED
KENTUCKY
KERATOID
KERATOSE
KERCHIEF
KERKRADE
KEROSENE
KESTEVEN
KESTRELS
KETAMINE
KETOXIME
KEYBOARD
KEYHOLES
KEY
  MONEY
KEYNOTES

KEYPUNCH
KEY
  RINGS
KEYSTONE
KHARTOUM
KHMERIAN
KHOIKHOI
KHUSKHUS
KIAOCHOW
KIBOSHES
KICKABLE
KICKBACK
KICKOFFS
KICKSHAW
KID-
  GLOVE
KIDNAPED
KILKENNY
KILLDEER
KILLINGS
KILLJOYS
KILOBYTE
KILOGRAM
KILOVOLT
KILOWATT
KIMONOED
KINABALU
KINDLIER
KINDLING
KINDNESS
KINDREDS
KINETICS
KINGBIRD
KINGBOLT
KINGDOMS
KINGFISH
KINGLIER
KINGPINS
KINGSHIP
KING-
  SIZE
KINGSTON
KINGWANA
KINGWOOD
KINKAJOU
KINKIEST
KINSFOLK
KINSHASA
KIRIBATI
KIRIGAMI
KIRKLEES

KIRKWALL
KISHINEV
KISSABLE
KITCHENS
KLAIPEDA
KLANSMAN
KLONDIKE
KLYSTRON
KNAPSACK
KNAPWEED
KNEADING
KNEECAPS
KNEE
  DEEP
KNEE-
  DEEP
KNEE-
  HIGH
KNEE-
  JERK
KNEELING
KNICKERS
KNIGHTED
KNIGHTLY
KNITTERS
KNITTING
KNITWEAR
KNOCKERS
KNOCKING
KNOCKOUT
KNOCK-
  UPS
KNOTHOLE
KNOTTIER
KNOTTILY
KNOTTING
KNOTWEED
KNOWABLE
KNOW-
  ALLS
KNOWSLEY
KNUCKLED
KNUCKLES
KOHINOOR
KOHLRABI
KOLHAPUR
KOLINSKY
KOMSOMOL
KOOKIEST
KOOTENAY
KORDOFAN
KOSTROMA

KOWTOWED
KOWTOWER
KRAKATOA
KUMAMOTO
KUMQUATS
KUROSAWA
KURTOSIS
KUZNETSK
KWEICHOW
KWEIYANG
KYPHOSIS
KYPHOTIC

L
LABDANUM
LABELING
LABELLED
LABELLER
LABELLUM
LABILITY
LABOURED
LABOURER
LABRADOR
LABURNUM
LACANIAN
LACERANT
LACERATE
LACEWING
LACEWORK
LACINESS
LA
  CORUNA
LACRIMAL
LACROSSE
LACTONIC
LACUNOSE
LADDERED
LADYBIRD
LADYLIKE
LADYSHIP
LAEVULIN
LAGGARDS
LA
  GUAIRA
LAH-DI-
  DAH
LAID-
  BACK
LAMASERY
LAMBASTE
LAMBDOID

LAMBENCY
LAMBSKIN
LAME
  DUCK
LAMELLAR
LAMENESS
LAMENTED
LAMENTER
LAMINATE
LAMPOONS
LAMPPOST
LAMPREYS
LANCELET
LANDFALL
LANDFORM
LANDINGS
LANDLADY
LANDLORD
LANDMARK
LANDMASS
LANDMINE
LANDRACE
LANDSHUT
LANDSIDE
LANDSLIP
LANDWARD
LANGLAUF
LANGUAGE
LANGUISH
LANKIEST
LANKNESS
LANNERET
LANTERNS
LANYARDS
LAPBOARD
LAP-
  CHART
LAPELLED
LAPIDARY
LAPILLUS
LAPPETED
LAPSABLE
LAPWINGS
LARBOARD
LARGESSE
LARKSOME
LARKSPUR
LARRIGAN
LARRIKIN
LARYNGES
LARYNXES

LASHINGS
LA
  SPEZIA
LASSOING
LAST
  POST
LAST
  WORD
LAS
  VEGAS
LATCHING
LATCHKEY
LATENESS
LATERALS
LATERITE
LATHERED
LATINATE
LATINISM
LATINIST
LATINITY
LATINIZE
LATITUDE
LATRINES
LATTERLY
LATTICES
LAUDABLE
LAUDABLY
LAUDANUM
LAUGHING
LAUGHTER
LAUNCHED
LAUNCHER
LAUNCHES
LAUREATE
LAUSANNE
LAVATION
LAVATORY
LAVENDER
LAVISHED
LAVISHER
LAVISHLY
LAWFULLY
LAWGIVER
LAWSUITS
LAXATION
LAXATIVE
LAYABOUT
LAYERING
LAYETTES
LAYSHAFT
LAYWOMAN
LAYWOMEN

LAZINESS
LAZULITE
LAZURITE
L-
  DRIVERS
LEACHING
LEADSMAN
LEAD
  TIME
LEADWORT
LEAFIEST
LEAF-
  LARD
LEAFLETS
LEAGUING
LEAKAGES
LEAKIEST
LEANINGS
LEANNESS
LEAPFROG
LEAP
  YEAR
LEARNERS
LEARNING
LEASABLE
LEATHERY
LEAVENED
LEAVINGS
LECITHIN
LECTERNS
LECTURED
LECTURER
LECTURES
LEEBOARD
LEERIEST
LEE
  SHORE
LEE
  TIDES
LEFT-
  HAND
LEFTISTS
LEFTOVER
LEFT
  OVER
LEFTWARD
LEFT
  WING
LEGACIES
LEGAL
  AID

LEGALESE
LEGALISM
LEGALIST
LEGALITY
LEGALIZE
LEGATEES
LEGATINE
LEGATION
LEGENDRY
LEGGIEST
LEGGINGS
LEG-
  PULLS
LEG
  SIDES
LEINSTER
LEISURED
LEMMINGS
LEMONADE
LEMUROID
LENGTHEN
LENIENCY
LENINISM
LENINIST
LENITIVE
LENTICEL
LEOPARDS
LEOTARDS
LEPIDOTE
LEPORINE
LESBIANS
LES
  CAYES
LESSENED
LETDOWNS
LETHALLY
LETHARGY
LETRASET
LETTERED
LETTERER
LETTINGS
LETTUCES
LEUCITIC
LEUKEMIA
LEVANTER
LEVELING
LEVELLED
LEVELLER
LEVERAGE
LEVERETS
LEVERING

LEVIABLE
LEVIGATE
LEVITATE
LEVKOSIA
LEWDNESS
LEWISHAM
LEWISITE
LEXICONS
LIAISING
LIAISONS
LIAONING
LIAOTUNG
LIAOYANG
LIBATION
LIBECCIO
LIBELING
LIBELLED
LIBELLEE
LIBELLER
LIBERALS
LIBERATE
LIBERIAN
LIBRETTI
LIBRETTO
LICENCES
LICENSED
LICENSEE
LICENSER
LICHENIN
LICH
  GATE
LICKINGS
LICORICE
LIE-
  DOWNS
LIENTERY
LIFE
  BELT
LIFEBOAT
LIFE
  BUOY
LIFELESS
LIFELIKE
LIFELINE
LIFELONG
LIFE
  PEER
LIFE-
  SIZE
LIFESPAN
LIFETIME

LIFE
  WORK
LIFTABLE
LIFT-
  OFFS
LIGAMENT
LIGATION
LIGATIVE
LIGATURE
LIGHT
  ALE
LIGHT
  BOX
LIGHTERS
LIGHTEST
LIGHTING
LIGNEOUS
LIGNITIC
LIGULATE
LIGULOID
LIGURIAN
LIKELIER
LIKENESS
LIKENING
LIKEWISE
LILONGWE
LIMA
  BEAN
LIMACINE
LIMASSOL
LIMAVADY
LIMBLESS
LIMEKILN
LIMERICK
LIMINESS
LIMITARY
LIMITING
LIMNETIC
LIMONENE
LIMONITE
LIMOUSIN
LIMPIDLY
LIMPNESS
LINALOOL
LINCHPIN
LINDWALL
LINEAGES
LINEALLY
LINESMAN
LINESMEN
LINGERED
LINGERER

LINGERIE
LINGUINE
LINGUIST
LINIMENT
LINKABLE
LINKAGES
LINKWORK
LINOCUTS
LINOLEUM
LINOTYPE
LINSTOCK
LIONFISH
LIONIZED
LIONIZER
LIPOGRAM
LIPOIDAL
LIPSTICK
LIQUESCE
LIQUEURS
LISSOMLY
LISTABLE
LISTENED
LISTENER
LISTEN
  IN
LISTLESS
LITANIES
LITERACY
LITERALS
LITERARY
LITERATE
LITERATI
LITHARGE
LITIGANT
LITIGATE
LITTERED
LITTORAL
LIVE
  BAIT
LIVELIER
LIVELONG
LIVENING
LIVERIED
LIVERIES
LIVERISH
LIVETRAP
LIVEWARE
LIVE
  WIRE
LIVONIAN
LIXIVIUM

LLANDAFF
LLANELLI
LOADINGS
LOADSTAR
LOANABLE
LOANWORD
LOATHING
LOBBYING
LOBBYISM
LOBBYIST
LOBELINE
LOBLOLLY
LOBOTOMY
LOBSTERS
LOCALISM
LOCALIST
LOCALITY
LOCALIZE
LOCATING
LOCATION
LOCATIVE
LOCKABLE
LOCKOUTS
LOCOWEED
LOCUTION
LODESTAR
LODGINGS
LODGMENT
LODICULE
LOESSIAL
LOFTIEST
LOGBOOKS
LOG
 CABIN
LOGICIAN
LOGICISM
LOGISTIC
LOGOGRAM
LOGOTYPE
LOGOTYPY
LOITERED
LOITERER
LOLLARDY
LOLLIPOP
LOLLOPED
LOMBARDY
LONDONER
LONDRINA
LONELIER
LONESOME

LONE
 WOLF
LONGBOAT
LONGBOWS
LONGERON
LONG
 FACE
LONGFORD
LONGHAND
LONG-
 HAUL
LONGHORN
LONGINGS
LONG
 JUMP
LONG-
 LIFE
LONGSHIP
LONG
 SHOT
LONGSPUR
LONG
 SUIT
LONG-
 TERM
LONG
 TONS
LONGUEUR
LONG
 WAVE
LONGWAYS
LOOKER-
 ON
LOOKOUTS
LOONIEST
LOONY
 BIN
LOOPHOLE
LOOSEBOX
LOOSE
 END
LOOSENED
LOOSENER
LOP-
 EARED
LOP-
 SIDED
LOQUITUR
LORDLIER
LORDOSIS
LORDOTIC
LORDSHIP
LORICATE

LORIKEET
LORRAINE
LOTHARIO
LOTHIANS
LOUDNESS
LOUNGERS
LOUNGING
LOUSIEST
LOVEBIRD
LOVELESS
LOVELIER
LOVELIES
LOVELORN
LOVESICK
LOVINGLY
LOWBROWS
LOWERING
LOWLANDS
LOWLIEST
LOW-
 LYING
LOW
 TIDES
LOW
 WATER
LOYALISM
LOYALIST
LOZENGES
LUCIDITY
LUCKIEST
LUCKLESS
LUCKY
 DIP
LUDDITES
LUDHIANA
LUGHOLES
LUGSAILS
LUGWORMS
LUKEWARM
LUMBERED
LUMBERER
LUMINARY
LUMINOUS
LUMPFISH
LUMPIEST
LUMP
 SUMS
LUNATICS
LUNATION
LUNCHEON
LUNCHING
LUNEBURG

LUNGFISH
LUNGWORM
LUNGWORT
LUNULATE
LURCHING
LURINGLY
LUSATIAN
LUSCIOUS
LUSHNESS
LUSTRATE
LUSTROUS
LUTANIST
LUTENIST
LUTEOLIN
LUTETIUM
LUTHERAN
LUXATION
LUXURIES
LYALLPUR
LYCH
 GATE
LYCHGATE
LYCH
 GATE
LYINGS-
 IN
LYMPHOID
LYMPHOMA
LYNCHING
LYNCH
 LAW
LYNCHPIN
LYONNAIS
LYREBIRD
LYRICISM
LYRICIST
LYSOSOME
LYSOZYME

M

MACADMIA
MACARONI
MACAROON
MACERATE
MACHETES
MACHINED
MACHINES
MACHISMO
MACKEREL
MACRURAL
MACRURAN

MADDENED
MADHOUSE
MADONNAS
MADRIGAL
MADURESE
MAEBASHI
MAENADIC
MAESTOSO
MAESTROS
MAFIKENG
MAGAZINE
MAGELLAN
MAGHREBI
MAGIC
 EYE
MAGICIAN
MAGNATES
MAGNESIA
MAGNETIC
MAGNETON
MAGNETOS
MAGNOLIA
MAHARAJA
MAHARANI
MAHATMAS
MAHOGANY
MAIDENLY
MAIEUTIC
MAILABLE
MAILBAGS
MAILSHOT
MAINLAND
MAIN
 LINE
MAINMAST
MAINSAIL
MAINSTAY
MAINTAIN
MAJESTIC
MAJOLICA
MAJORCAN
MAJORING
MAJORITY
MAKE
 GOOD
MAKING
 DO
MALADIES
MALAGASY
MALAISES
MALARIAL
MALARKEY

MALAYSIA
MAL DE
 MER
MALDIVES
MALENESS
MALIGNED
MALIGNER
MALIGNLY
MALINGER
MALLARDS
MALPOSED
MALTREAT
MALTSTER
MALVASIA
MAMA'S
 BOY
MAMMOTHS
MANACLED
MANACLES
MANAGERS
MANAGING
MANASSAS
MANATOID
MANCIPLE
MANDALAY
MANDAMUS
MANDARIN
MANDATED
MANDATES
MANDIBLE
MANDOLIN
MANDORLA
MANDRAKE
MANDRILL
MAN-
 EATER
MANEUVER
MANFULLY
MANGABEY
MANGANIC
MANGANIN
MANGIEST
MANGLING
MANGONEL
MANGROVE
MANHOLES
MANHOURS
MANHUNTS
MANIACAL
MANICURE
MANIFEST

MANIFOLD MARINERS MATADORS MEDICALS MENSWEAR MEZEREON
MANIKINS MARIPOSA MATANZAS MEDICARE MENTALLY MEZEREUM
MANITOBA MARITIME MATCHBOX MEDICATE MENTIONS MEZIERES
MANLIEST MARJORAM MATCHING MEDICINE MEPHITIC MIAOWING
MANNERED MARKDOWN MATERIAL MEDIEVAL MEPHITIS MICELLAR
MANNERLY MARKEDLY MATERIEL MEDIOCRE MERCHANT MICHIGAN
MANNHEIM MARKETED MATERNAL MEDITATE MERCIFUL MICROBES
MANNITIC MARKETER MATINEES MEDUSOID MERCURIC MICRODOT
MANNITOL MARKINGS MATRICES MEEKNESS MERGENCE MIDBRAIN
MAN OF MARKSMAN MATRIXES MEETINGS MERIDIAN MIDDLE
  WAR MARKSMEN MATRONAL MEGALITH MERINGUE   CS
MAN-OF- MARMOSET MATRONLY MEGATONS MERISTEM MIDDLING
  WAR MAROONED MATTERED MEGAVOLT MERISTIC MIDFIELD
MANORIAL MAROQUIN MATTRESS MEGAWATT MERITING MIDLANDS
MANPOWER MARQUEES MATURATE MELAMINE MERMAIDS MIDNIGHT
MANSARDS MARQUESS MATURELY MELANGES MERRIEST MIDPOINT
MANSHOLT MARQUISE MATURING MELANISM MERRY MIDRIFFS
MANSIONS MARRIAGE MATURITY MELANIST   MEN MIDWIVES
MAN- MARRIEDS MAUBEUGE MELANITE MESCALIN MIGHTIER
  SIZED MARRYING MAVERICK MELANOID MESDAMES MIGHTILY
MANTILLA MARSHALS MAXILLAR MELANOMA MESMERIC MIGRAINE
MANTISES MARSH MAXIMIZE MELANOUS MESOCARP MIGRANTS
MANTISSA   GAS MAXIMUMS MELINITE MESODERM MIGRATED
MANTLING MARTABAN MAYORESS MELLOWED MESOGLEA MIGRATOR
MAN-TO- MARTAGON MAYPOLES MELLOWER MESOZOIC MILANESE
  MAN MARTELLO MAZATLAN MELLOWLY MESQUITE MILCH
MANUALLY MARTIANS MAZURKAS MELODEON MESSAGES   COW
MANURING MARTINET MEA MELODIES MESSENIA MILDEWED
MANX MARTINIS   CULPA MELODIST MESSIAHS MILDNESS
  CATS MARTYRED MEAGRELY MELODIZE MESSIEST MILEAGES
MANYFOLD MARVELED MEALIEST MELTABLE MESSMATE MILEPOST
MAPPABLE MARXISTS MEALWORM MELTDOWN MESSUAGE MILIARIA
MAPPINGS MARYLAND MEANINGS MEMBRANE MESTIZOS MILITANT
MAQUETTE MARZIPAN MEANNESS MEMENTOS METALING MILITARY
MARABOUS MASSACRE MEANTIME MEMORIAL METALLED MILITATE
MARANHAO MASSAGED MEASURED MEMORIES METALLIC MILITIAS
MARASMIC MASSAGER MEASURER MEMORIZE METAMALE MILKFISH
MARASMUS MASSAGES MEASURES MEMSAHIB METAMERE MILKIEST
MARATHON MASSEDLY MEATBALL MENACING METAPHOR MILKMAID
MARAUDER MASSETER MEATIEST MENARCHE METAZOAN MILK
MARBLING MASSEURS MECHANIC MENDABLE METAZOIC   RUNS
MARCHERS MASSICOT MECHELEN MENHADEN METEORIC MILKSOPS
MARCHESA MASTERED MECONIUM MENIALLY METERING MILKWEED
MARCHESE MASTERLY MEDALLIC MENINGES METHANOL MILKWORT
MARCHING MASTHEAD MEDDLERS MENISCUS METHYLAL MILKY
MARGARIC MASTIFFS MEDDLING MEN-OF- METHYLIC   WAY
MARGINAL MASTITIS MEDELLIN   WAR METONYMY MILLABLE
MARIANAO MASTODON MEDIALLY MENOLOGY METRICAL MILLIAMP
MARIGOLD MASTOIDS MEDIATED MEN'S METRITIS MILLIARD
MARIMBAS MASURIAN MEDIATOR   ROOM MEUNIERE MILLIARY
MARINADE MATABELE MEDICAID MENSURAL MEXICALI MILLIBAR
MARINATE

MILLINER	MISLAYER	MODIFIER	MONOCRAT	MORALISM	MOULDIER
MILLIONS	MISMATCH	MODIOLUS	MONOCYTE	MORALIST	MOULDING
MILLPOND	MISNOMER	MODISHLY	MONOGAMY	MORALITY	MOULMEIN
MILLRACE	MISOGAMY	MODULATE	MONOGENY	MORALIZE	MOULTING
MILTONIC	MISOGYNY	MOHAMMED	MONOGRAM	MORASSES	MOUNTAIN
MIMETITE	MISOLOGY	MOIETIES	MONOGYNY	MORATORY	MOUNTIES
MIMICKED	MISPLACE	MOISTURE	MONOHULL	MORAVIAN	MOUNTING
MIMICKER	MISPLEAD	MOLALITY	MONOLITH	MORBIDLY	MOURNERS
MINARETS	MISPRINT	MOLASSES	MONOLOGY	MORBIFIC	MOURNFUL
MINATORY	MISQUOTE	MOLDAVIA	MONOMIAL	MORBIHAN	MOURNING
MINCE	MISSHAPE	MOLDERED	MONOPOLE	MORDANCY	MOUSIEST
PIE	MISSILES	MOLDIEST	MONOPOLY	MOREOVER	MOUSSAKA
MINDANAO	MISSIONS	MOLDINGS	MONORAIL	MORESQUE	MOUTHFUL
MINDLESS	MISSIVES	MOLECULE	MONOSEMY	MORIBUND	MOUTHING
MIND'S	MISSOURI	MOLEHILL	MONOSOME	MORNINGS	MOVABLES
EYE	MISSPELL	MOLESKIN	MONOTONE	MOROCCAN	MOVEMENT
MINERALS	MISSPELT	MOLESTED	MONOTONY	MORONISM	MOVINGLY
MINGIEST	MISSPEND	MOLESTER	MONOTYPE	MOROSELY	MOZZETTA
MINGLING	MISSPENT	MOLLUSCS	MONOXIDE	MORPHEME	MUCHNESS
MINICABS	MISSTATE	MOLUCCAS	MONROVIA	MORPHEUS	MUCILAGE
MINIMIZE	MISTAKEN	MOLYBDIC	MONSIEUR	MORPHINE	MUCINOUS
MINIMUMS	MISTAKES	MOMENTUM	MONSOONS	MORPHING	MUCKHEAP
MINISTER	MISTIMED	MONACHAL	MONSTERS	MORRISON	MUCKIEST
MINISTRY	MISTREAT	MONADISM	MONTAGES	MORTALLY	MUCKRAKE
MINORCAN	MISTRESS	MONAGHAN	MONTEITH	MORTGAGE	MUCKWORM
MINORITY	MISTRIAL	MONANDRY	MONTEREY	MORTIMER	MUCOSITY
MINOTAUR	MISTRUST	MONARCHS	MONTREAL	MORTISER	MUD
MINSTERS	MISUSAGE	MONARCHY	MONTREUX	MORTISES	BATHS
MINSTREL	MISUSING	MONASTIC	MONUMENT	MORTMAIN	MUDDIEST
MINUTELY	MITCHELL	MONAURAL	MOOCHING	MORTUARY	MUDDLING
MINUTIAE	MITICIDE	MONAZITE	MOODIEST	MOSEYING	MUDDYING
MINUTING	MITIGATE	MONETARY	MOONBEAM	MOSQUITO	MUDFLATS
MIRACLES	MITTIMUS	MONETIZE	MOONCALF	MOSSIEST	MUDGUARD
MIREPOIX	MIXED	MONEYBOX	MOONFISH	MOTHBALL	MUDPACKS
MIRRORED	BAG	MONGOLIA	MOONLESS	MOTHERED	MUDSTONE
MIRTHFUL	MIXTURES	MONGOLIC	MOONRISE	MOTHERLY	MUENSTER
MISANDRY	MNEMONIC	MONGOOSE	MOONSEED	MOTILITY	MUEZZINS
MISAPPLY	MOBILITY	MONGRELS	MOON	MOTIONED	MUFFLERS
MISCARRY	MOBILIZE	MONISTIC	SHOT	MOTIONER	MUFFLING
MISCHIEF	MOBOCRAT	MONITION	MOONWORT	MOTIVATE	MUFULIRA
MISCIBLE	MOBSTERS	MONITORS	MOORCOCK	MOTIVITY	MUGGIEST
MISCOUNT	MOCCASIN	MONITORY	MOORHENS	MOT	MUGGINGS
MISDEEDS	MOCKABLE	MONKEYED	MOORINGS	JUSTE	MUG'S
MISERERE	MODALITY	MONKFISH	MOORLAND	MOTORBUS	GAME
MISERIES	MODELING	MON-	MOORWORT	MOTORCAR	MUGSHOTS
MISFIRED	MODELLED	KHMER	MOOSE	MOTORING	MUGWUMPS
MISFIRES	MODELLER	MONKHOOD	JAW	MOTORIST	MULATTOS
MISGUIDE	MODERATE	MONMOUTH	MOPINGLY	MOTORIZE	MULBERRY
MISHEARD	MODERATO	MONOACID	MOQUETTE	MOTORMAN	MULCHING
MISHMASH	MODESTLY	MONOCARP	MORAINAL	MOTORMEN	MULCTING
MISJUDGE	MODIFIED	MONOCLES	MORAINES	MOTORWAY	MULETEER

MULHOUSE
MULISHLY
MULLIONS
MULTIFID
MULTIPED
MULTIPLE
MULTIPLY
MUMBLING
MUNCHING
MUNIMENT
MUNITION
MURALIST
MURDERED
MURDERER
MURICATE
MURKIEST
MURMANSK
MURMURED
MURMURER
MURRAINS
MURRELET
MURRHINE
MUSCATEL
MUSCLING
MUSCULAR
MUSHIEST
MUSHROOM
MUSICALE
MUSICALS
MUSICIAN
MUSINGLY
MUSKETRY
MUSKIEST
MUSQUASH
MUSTACHE
MUSTANGS
MUSTELID
MUSTERED
MUSTIEST
MUTATION
MUTENESS
MUTICOUS
MUTILATE
MUTINEER
MUTINIED
MUTINIES
MUTINOUS
MUTTERED
MUTTERER
MUTUALLY
MUZOREWA

MUZZIEST
MUZZLING
MYCELIAL
MYCELIUM
MYCELOID
MYCETOMA
MYCOLOGY
MYELINIC
MYELITIS
MYLONITE
MYOGENIC
MYOGRAPH
MYOLOGIC
MYOSOTIS
MYOTONIA
MYOTONIC
MYRIAPOD
MYSTICAL
MYSTIQUE
MYTHICAL
MYTILENE

N

NABOBERY
NACELLES
NACREOUS
NAGALAND
NAGASAKI
NAIL
 FILE
NAILHEAD
NAINSOOK
NAISSANT
NAMANGAN
NAME
 DAYS
NAMEDROP
NAMELESS
NAMESAKE
NAMETAPE
NAMIBIAN
NANCHANG
NANTERRE
NAPHTHOL
NAPHTHYL
NAPIFORM
NARBONNE
NARCEINE
NARCISSI
NARCOSIS
NARCOTIC

NARKIEST
NARRATED
NARRATOR
NARROWED
NARROWLY
NASALITY
NASALIZE
NASCENCE
NASTIEST
NATATION
NATIONAL
NATIVISM
NATIVIST
NATIVITY
NATTERED
NATTIEST
NATURALS
NATURISM
NATURIST
NAUPLIUS
NAUSEATE
NAUSEOUS
NAUTICAL
NAUTILUS
NAVICERT
NAVIGATE
NAVY
 BLUE
NAZARENE
NAZARETH
NDJAMENA
NEAP
 TIDE
NEARCTIC
NEAR
 EAST
NEAR
 MISS
NEARNESS
NEARSIDE
NEATNESS
NEBRASKA
NEBULIZE
NEBULOUS
NECKBAND
NECKLACE
NECKLETS
NECKLINE
NECKTIES
NECROSIS
NECROTIC
NEEDIEST

NEEDLESS
NEEDLING
NEGATING
NEGATION
NEGATIVE
NEGLIGEE
NEGRILLO
NEGRITIC
NEGROISM
NEIGHING
NEKTONIC
NEMATODE
NEMBUTAL
NEOGAEAN
NEOMYCIN
NEONATAL
NEOPHYTE
NEOPLASM
NEOPRENE
NEOTERIC
NEPALESE
NEPENTHE
NEPHRITE
NEPOTISM
NEPOTIST
NERVIEST
NESCIENT
NEST
 EGGS
NESTLING
NETTLING
NETWORKS
NEURITIC
NEURITIS
NEURONIC
NEUROSES
NEUROSIS
NEUROTIC
NEUTERED
NEUTRALS
NEUTRINO
NEUTRONS
NEW
 BLOOD
NEW
 BROOM
NEWCOMER
NEW
 DEALS
NEW-
 FOUND
NEWHAVEN

NEW
 HAVEN
NEWLYWED
NEW
 MOONS
NEWSCAST
NEWSPEAK
NEWSREEL
NEWSROOM
NEW
 TOWNS
NEW
 WAVES
NEW
 WORLD
NEXT-
 DOOR
NHA
 TRANG
NIARCHOS
NIBBLING
NICENESS
NICETIES
NICHROME
NICKELED
NICKELIC
NICKNACK
NICKNAME
NICOTINE
NIELLIST
NIFTIEST
NIGERIAN
NIGGARDS
NIGGLERS
NIGGLING
NIGHTCAP
NIGHTJAR
NIGHT
 OWL
NIHILISM
NIHILIST
NIHILITY
NIJMEGEN
NIMBLEST
NIMBUSES
NINEFOLD
NINEPINS
NINETEEN
NINETIES
NIPPIEST
NIRVANAS
NIRVANIC

NITRATES
NITROGEN
NITROSYL
NIVATION
NOBBLING
NOBELIUM
NOBILITY
NOBLEMAN
NOBLEMEN
NOBODIES
NOCTURNE
NODALITY
NODOSITY
NO-GO
 AREA
NOISIEST
NOMADISM
NOMINATE
NOMINEES
NOMISTIC
NOMOLOGY
NONESUCH
NON-
 EVENT
NONJUROR
NON
 LICET
NONMETAL
NON
 RIGID
NONSENSE
NONSTICK
NONTOXIC
NONUNION
NONVOTER
NONWHITE
NOONTIME
NORMALLY
NORMANDY
NORSEMAN
NORSEMEN
NORTHERN
NORTHING
NOSEBAGS
NOSEBAND
NOSE
 BAND
NOSECONE
NOSEDIVE
NOSEGAYS
NOSINESS
NOSOLOGY

NOSTRILS	NURISTAN	OBVOLUTE	OILFIELD	ONCOMING	OPINICUS
NOSTRUMS	NURSLING	OCARINAS	OIL-	ONDAATJE	OPINIONS
NOTA	NURTURED	OCCASION	FIRED	ONDOGRAM	OPIUMISM
BENE	NURTURER	OCCIDENT	OILINESS	ONE-	OPOSSUMS
NOTABLES	NUTATION	OCCLUSAL	OIL	HORSE	OPPILATE
NOTARIAL	NUT-	OCCUPANT	PAINT	ONE-ON-	OPPONENT
NOTARIES	BROWN	OCCUPIED	OILSKINS	ONE	OPPOSING
NOTARIZE	NUTCASES	OCCUPIER	OIL	ONE-	OPPOSITE
NOTATION	NUTHATCH	OCCURRED	SLICK	PIECE	OPPUGNER
NOTCHING	NUTHOUSE	OCEANIAN	OILSTONE	ONE-	OPSONIZE
NOTEBOOK	NUTRIENT	OCHREOUS	OIL	SIDED	OPTATIVE
NOTECASE	NUTSHELL	OCOTILLO	WELLS	ONE-TO-	OPTICIAN
NOTELETS	NUTTIEST	OCTAGONS	OINTMENT	ONE	OPTIMISM
NOTEPADS	NUZZLING	OCTARCHY	OKAVANGO	ONE-	OPTIMIST
NOTICING	NYMPHETS	OCTOBERS	OKLAHOMA	TRACK	OPTIMIZE
NOTIFIED	NYSTATIN	OCTOROON	OLD	ONLOOKER	OPTIONAL
NOTIFIER		OCULISTS	FLAME	ONRUSHES	OPULENCE
NOTIONAL	**O**	ODDBALLS	OLD	ON-	ORACULAR
NOTOGAEA		ODDITIES	GUARD	SCREEN	ORANGERY
NOTORNIS	OAFISHLY	ODDMENTS	OLD	ONSTREAM	ORATIONS
NOVATION	OAKVILLE	ODIOUSLY	HANDS	ONTOGENY	ORATORIO
NOVELIST	OARLOCKS	ODOMETER	OLD	ONTOLOGY	ORBITING
NOVELLAS	OATCAKES	ODONTOID	MAIDS	OOGAMOUS	ORCHARDS
NOVEMBER	OBDURACY	ODYSSEYS	OLDSTERS	OOGONIAL	ORCHITIC
NOVGOROD	OBDURATE	OENOLOGY	OLD-	OOGONIUM	ORCHITIS
NOWADAYS	OBEDIENT	OESTRIOL	TIMER	OOLOGIST	ORDAINED
NUBECULA	OBEISANT	OESTRONE	OLD	OOPHYTIC	ORDAINER
NUBILITY	OBELISKS	OESTROUS	WOMAN	OOSPHERE	ORDERING
NUCELLAR	OBERLAND	OFF AND	OLD	OOSPORIC	ORDINALS
NUCELLUS	OBITUARY	ON	WOMEN	OOTHECAL	ORDINAND
NUCLEASE	OBJECTED	OFF	OLD	OOZINESS	ORDINARY
NUCLEATE	OBJECTOR	BREAK	WORLD	OPALESCE	ORDINATE
NUDENESS	OBLATION	OFFENCES	OLEANDER	OPAQUELY	ORDNANCE
NUDICAUL	OBLATORY	OFFENDED	OLEASTER	OPENCAST	ORENBURG
NUGATORY	OBLIGATE	OFFENDER	OLEFINIC	OPEN-	ORGANDIE
NUISANCE	OBLIGING	OFFERING	OLIBANUM	EYED	ORGANISM
NULL	OBLIQUES	OFF-	OLIGARCH	OPEN	ORGANIST
SETS	OBLIVION	GLIDE	OLIGURIA	FIRE	ORGANIZE
NUMBERED	OBSCURED	OFFICERS	OLIVE	OPENINGS	ORGASMIC
NUMBFISH	OBSERVED	OFFICIAL	OIL	OPENNESS	ORIENTAL
NUMBNESS	OBSERVER	OFFPRINT	OLYMPIAD	OPEN-	ORIFICES
NUMERACY	OBSESSED	OFFSHOOT	OLYMPIAN	PLAN	ORIGINAL
NUMERALS	OBSIDIAN	OFFSHORE	OMDURMAN	OPEN	ORINASAL
NUMERARY	OBSOLETE	OFFSTAGE	OMELETTE	SHOP	ORNAMENT
NUMERATE	OBSTACLE	OFF	OMISSION	OPENWORK	ORNATELY
NUMEROUS	OBSTRUCT	STAGE	OMITTING	OPERABLE	ORNITHIC
NUMINOUS	OBTAINED	OFF-	OMNIVORE	OPERABLY	OROGENIC
NUMMULAR	OBTAINER	WHITE	OMPHALOS	OPERATED	OROMETER
NUMSKULL	OBTRUDED	OFT	ON AND	OPERATIC	ORPHANED
NUNEATON	OBTRUDER	TIMES	OFF	OPERATOR	ORPIMENT
NUPTIALS	OBTUSELY	OHMMETER	ONCE-	OPERETTA	ORRERIES
	OBVIATED	OILCLOTH	OVER	OPHIDIAN	
			ONCOLOGY		

ORTHODOX	OUTLINES	OVERDREW	OVERWORK	PALENCIA	PANPIPES
ORTHOEPY	OUTLIVED	OVERFLEW	OVIDUCAL	PALENESS	PANSOPHY
OSCITANT	OUTLOOKS	OVERFLOW	OVIPOSIT	PALETTES	PANTHEON
OSCULANT	OUTLYING	OVERGROW	OVULATED	PALFREYS	PANTHERS
OSCULATE	OUTMODED	OVERHAND	OWLISHLY	PALINODE	PANTILES
OSNABURG	OUTPOINT	OVERHANG	OWN	PALISADE	PANTRIES
OSSIFIED	OUTPOSTS	OVERHAUL	GOALS	PALLADIC	PAPACIES
OSSIFIER	OUTRAGED	OVERHEAD	OXBRIDGE	PALLIATE	PAPERBOY
OSTEITIC	OUTRAGES	OVERHEAR	OXIDASIC	PALLIDLY	PAPERING
OSTEITIS	OUTREACH	OVERHEAT	OXIDIZED	PALLIEST	PAPILLON
OSTINATO	OUTRIDER	OVERHUNG	OXIDIZER	PALL	PAPISTRY
OSTIOLAR	OUTRIGHT	OVERKILL	OXPECKER	MALL	PAPOOSES
OSTRACOD	OUTRIVAL	OVERLAID	OXTONGUE	PALMETTE	PARABLES
OTIOSITY	OUTSHINE	OVERLAIN	OXYGENIC	PALMETTO	PARABOLA
OTOSCOPE	OUTSHONE	OVERLAND	OXYMORON	PALMIEST	PARADIGM
OTTOMANS	OUTSHOOT	OVERLAPS	OXYTOCIC	PALMISTS	PARADING
OUTBLUFF	OUTSIDER	OVERLAYS	OXYTOCIN	PALMITIN	PARADISE
OUTBOARD	OUTSIDES	OVERLEAF	OZONIZER	PALO	PARADROP
OUTBOUND	OUTSMART	OVERLOAD		ALTO	PARAFFIN
OUTBRAVE	OUTSTAND	OVERLONG	**P**	PALOMINO	PARAGOGE
OUTBREAK	OUTSTARE	OVERLOOK	PACIFIED	PALPABLE	PARAGONS
OUTBREED	OUTSTRIP	OVERLORD	PACIFIER	PALPABLY	PARAGUAY
OUTBURST	OUTSWING	OVERMUCH	PACIFISM	PALPATED	PARAKEET
OUTCASTE	OUT-	OVERPAID	PACIFIST	PALTERER	PARALLAX
OUTCASTS	TAKES	OVERPASS	PACKABLE	PALTRIER	PARALLEL
OUTCLASS	OUTVOTED	OVERPLAY	PACKAGED	PALTRILY	PARALYSE
OUTCOMES	OUTWARDS	OVERRATE	PACKAGER	PAMPERED	PARAMENT
OUTCRIES	OUTWEIGH	OVERRIDE	PACKAGES	PAMPERER	PARAMOUR
OUTCROPS	OUTWORKS	OVERRIPE	PADDLING	PAMPHLET	PARANOIA
OUTCROSS	OVALNESS	OVERRODE	PADDOCKS	PAMPLONA	PARANOID
OUTDATED	OVARITIS	OVERRULE	PADLOCKS	PANACEAN	PARAPETS
OUTDOING	OVATIONS	OVERSEAS	PAEONIES	PANACEAS	PARAQUAT
OUTDOORS	OVENBIRD	OVERSEEN	PAGANISM	PANATELA	PARASITE
OUTFACED	OVENWARE	OVERSEER	PAGANIST	PANCAKES	PARASOLS
OUTFALLS	OVERALLS	OVERSELL	PAGANIZE	PANCREAS	PARAVANE
OUTFIELD	OVERARCH	OVERSHOE	PAGEANTS	PANDA	PAR
OUTFIGHT	OVERAWED	OVERSHOT	PAGINATE	CAR	AVION
OUTFLANK	OVERBEAR	OVERSIDE	PAGO	PANDANUS	PARAZOAN
OUTFLOWS	OVERBIDS	OVERSIZE	PAGO	PANDEMIC	PARCELED
OUTFLUNG	OVERBOOK	OVERSOLD	PAGURIAN	PANDERED	PARCENER
OUTFOXED	OVERBORE	OVERSTAY	PAHOEHOE	PANDERER	PARCHING
OUTGOING	OVERCALL	OVERSTEP	PAINLESS	PANELING	PARDONED
OUT-	OVERCAME	OVERTAKE	PAINTERS	PANELLED	PARDONER
GROUP	OVERCAST	OVERTIME	PAINTING	PANGOLIN	PARENTAL
OUTGROWN	OVERCOAT	OVERTIRE	PAKISTAN	PANICKED	PARHELIC
OUT-	OVERCOME	OVERTONE	PALADINS	PANICLED	PARIETAL
HEROD	OVERCOOK	OVERTOOK	PALATALS	PANMIXIA	PARISHES
OUTHOUSE	OVERCROP	OVERTURE	PALATIAL	PANNIERS	PARISIAN
OUTLAWED	OVERDONE	OVERTURN	PALATINE	PANNIKIN	PARKIEST
OUTLAWRY	OVERDOSE	OVERVIEW	PALAVERS	PANOPTIC	PARKLAND
OUTLINED	OVERDRAW	OVERWIND	PALEFACE	PANORAMA	PARKWAYS

PARLANCE
PARLANDO
PARLEYED
PARLEYER
PARLOURS
PARMESAN
PARODIED
PARODIES
PARODIST
PAROLING
PAROTOID
PAROXYSM
PARROTED
PARRYING
PARSABLE
PARSIFAL
PARSNIPS
PARTAKEN
PARTAKER
PARTERRE
PARTHIAN
PARTIBLE
PARTICLE
PARTINGS
PARTISAN
PARTNERS
PART-
SONG
PART-
TIME
PART
WORK
PARTYING
PAR
VALUE
PARVENUS
PARZIVAL
PASADENA
PASSABLE
PASSABLY
PASSAGES
PASSBOOK
PASS
BOOK
PASSERBY
PASSIBLE
PASSIONS
PASSKEYS
PASSOVER
PASSPORT
PASSWORD
PASTERNS

PASTE-
UPS
PASTICHE
PASTIEST
PASTILLE
PASTIMES
PASTINGS
PASTORAL
PASTRAMI
PASTRIES
PASTURED
PASTURES
PATAGIUM
PATCHIER
PATCHILY
PATCHING
PATELLAR
PATELLAS
PATENTED
PATENTEE
PATENTLY
PATENTOR
PATERNAL
PATERSON
PATHETIC
PATHLESS
PATHOGEN
PATHWAYS
PATIENCE
PATIENTS
PATRIALS
PATRIOTS
PATRONAL
PATTERED
PATTERNS
PATULOUS
PAUNCHES
PAVEMENT
PAVILION
PAVLODAR
PAVONINE
PAWKIEST
PAWNSHOP
PAYCHECK
PAYLOADS
PAYMENTS
PAY
PHONE
PAYROLLS
PAYSLIPS
PEACEFUL

PEACOCKS
PEAFOWLS
PEA
GREEN
PEAKIEST
PEARLIER
PEARLITE
PEARMAIN
PEASANTS
PEBBLING
PECCABLE
PECCANCY
PECTORAL
PECULATE
PECULIAR
PEDAGOGY
PEDALIER
PEDALING
PEDALLED
PEDANTIC
PEDANTRY
PEDDLERS
PEDDLING
PEDERAST
PEDESTAL
PEDICURE
PEDIFORM
PEDIGREE
PEDIMENT
PEDIPALP
PEDOLOGY
PEDUNCLE
PEEKABOO
PEELINGS
PEEPHOLE
PEEPSHOW
PEERAGES
PEERLESS
PEGBOARD
PEIGNOIR
PEKINESE
PELICANS
PELLAGRA
PELLICLE
PELL-
MELL
PELLUCID
PELVISES
PEMBROKE
PEMMICAN
PENALIZE

PENANCES
PENCHANT
PENCILED
PENDANTS
PENDULUM
PENGUINS
PENITENT
PENKNIFE
PEN
NAMES
PENNANTS
PENNINES
PENN'ORT
H
PENOLOGY
PENSIONS
PENSTOCK
PENTACLE
PENTAGON
PENTOMIC
PENTOSAN
PENUMBRA
PENZANCE
PEOPLING
PEPPERED
PEP
PILLS
PEP
TALKS
PEPTIZER
PER
ANNUM
PERCEIVE
PERCHING
PERFORCE
PERFUMED
PERFUMER
PERFUMES
PERGOLAS
PERIANTH
PERIBLEM
PERICARP
PERIDERM
PERIDIUM
PERIGEAN
PERIGEES
PERIGYNY
PERILOUS
PERILUNE
PERINEUM
PERIODIC
PERIOTIC

PERISARC
PERISHED
PERISHER
PERIWIGS
PERJURED
PERJURER
PERKIEST
PERLITIC
PERMEANT
PERMEATE
PERMUTED
PERONEAL
PERORATE
PEROXIDE
PERSONAL
PERSONAS
PERSPIRE
PERSUADE
PERTNESS
PERUSALS
PERUSING
PERUVIAN
PERVADED
PERVADER
PERVERSE
PERVERTS
PERVIOUS
PESHAWAR
PESKIEST
PESTERED
PESTERER
PESTHOLE
PETALINE
PETALODY
PETALOID
PETECHIA
PETITION
PETIT
MAL
PET
NAMES
PETRARCH
PETROLIC
PETROSAL
PETTIEST
PETTIFOG
PETULANT
PETUNIAS
PETUNTSE
PEWTERER
PFENNIGS

PHAETONS
PHALANGE
PHANTASM
PHANTASY
PHANTOMS
PHARAOHS
PHARISEE
PHARMACY
PHASE-
OUT
PHEASANT
PHENETIC
PHENOLIC
PHILLIPS
PHILTRES
PHIMOSIS
PHONE
BOX
PHONE-
INS
PHONEMES
PHONEMIC
PHONETIC
PHONIEST
PHOSGENE
PHOSPHOR
PHOTOFIT
PHOTOMAP
PHOTOPIA
PHOTOPIC
PHOTOSET
PHRASING
PHRATRIC
PHREATIC
PHTHALIC
PHTHISIC
PHTHISIS
PHYLETIC
PHYLLITE
PHYLLODE
PHYLLOID
PHYLLOME
PHYSICAL
PHYSIQUE
PIACENZA
PIACULAR
PIANISTS
PIANOLAS
PIASSAVA
PIASTRES
PICADORS

PICCANIN
PICCOLOS
PICKABLE
PICKAXES
PICKEREL
PICKETED
PICKETER
PICKIEST
PICKINGS
PICKLING
PICKLOCK
PICK ME
 UP
PICK-ME-
 UP
PICOLINE
PICTURED
PICTURES
PIDDLING
PIEBALDS
PIE
 CHART
PIECRUST
PIEDMONT
PIERCING
PIFFLING
PIGGIEST
PIGMENTS
PIGSKINS
PIGSTICK
PIGSTIES
PIGSWILL
PIGTAILS
PILASTER
PILCHARD
PILEWORT
PILFERED
PILFERER
PILGRIMS
PILIFORM
PILLAGED
PILLAGER
PILLIONS
PILLOCKS
PILLOWED
PILOTAGE
PILOTING
PIMENTOS
PIMIENTO
PINAFORE
PINASTER

PINCE-
 NEZ
PINCHING
PINETREE
PINEWOOD
PING-
 PONG
PINHEADS
PINIONED
PINK
 GINS
PINKROOT
PIN
 MONEY
PINNACES
PINNACLE
PINNIPED
PINOCHLE
PINPOINT
PINPRICK
PINTABLE
PINT-
 SIZE
PINWHEEL
PIONEERS
PIPE
 BOMB
PIPECLAY
PIPEFISH
PIPELINE
PIPE
 RACK
PIPERINE
PIPETTES
PIPEWORT
PIQUANCY
PIRACIES
PIRANHAS
PIRATING
PIS
 ALLER
PISIFORM
PISOLITE
PISS-
 TAKE
PITCHERS
PITCHING
PITFALLS
PITHEADS
PITHIEST
PITIABLE
PITIABLY

PITILESS
PIT
 PROPS
PITTANCE
PIVOTING
PIXELATE
PIZZERIA
PLACABLE
PLACARDS
PLACATED
PLACEBOS
PLACE
 MAT
PLACENTA
PLACIDLY
PLAGUILY
PLAGUING
PLAINEST
PLAITING
PLANCHET
PLANFORM
PLANGENT
PLANKING
PLANKTON
PLANNERS
PLANNING
PLANOSOL
PLANTAIN
PLANTERS
PLANTING
PLANULAR
PLASTEEL
PLASTERS
PLASTICS
PLASTRAL
PLASTRON
PLATELET
PLATFORM
PLATINIC
PLATINUM
PLATONIC
PLATOONS
PLATTERS
PLATYPUS
PLAUDITS
PLAUSIVE
PLAYABLE
PLAYBACK
PLAY
 BALL
PLAYBILL

PLAYBOYS
PLAYGOER
PLAYLIST
PLAYMATE
PLAY-
 OFFS
PLAYPENS
PLAYROOM
PLAYSUIT
PLAYTIME
PLEADING
PLEASANT
PLEASING
PLEASURE
PLEATING
PLEBBIER
PLEBEIAN
PLECTRUM
PLEDGING
PLEIADES
PLEIN-
 AIR
PLEONASM
PLETHORA
PLEURISY
PLEUSTON
PLIANTLY
PLIGHTED
PLIGHTER
PLIMSOLL
PLIOCENE
PLODDERS
PLODDING
PLONKING
PLOPPING
PLOSIVES
PLOTTING
PLOUGHED
PLOUGHER
PLUCKIER
PLUCKILY
PLUCKING
PLUGGING
PLUGHOLE
PLUMBAGO
PLUMBERS
PLUMBERY
PLUMBING
PLUMBISM
PLUMBOUS
PLUMMIER

PLUMPEST
PLUMPING
PLUNGERS
PLUNGING
PLUSHEST
PLUTONIC
PLUVIOUS
PLYMOUTH
POACEOUS
POACHERS
POACHING
POCKETED
POCKMARK
PODAGRAL
PODGIEST
PODIATRY
PODZOLIC
POETICAL
POIGNANT
POINTERS
POINTING
POISONED
POISONER
POITIERS
POKEWEED
POKINESS
POLANSKI
POLARITY
POLARIZE
POLAROID
POLEAXED
POLECATS
POLEMICS
POLE
 STAR
POLICIES
POLICING
POLISHED
POLISHER
POLISHES
POLITELY
POLITICO
POLITICS
POLITIES
POLKA
 DOT
POLLARDS
POLLICAL
POLLINIC
POLLSTER
POLLUTED

POLLUTER
POLO
 NECK
POLONIUM
POLTROON
POLYGALA
POLYGAMY
POLYGENE
POLYGLOT
POLYGONS
POLYGYNY
POLYMATH
POLYMERS
POLYPARY
POLYPODY
POLYPOID
POLYPOUS
POLYSEMY
POLYURIA
POLYURIC
POLYZOAN
POLYZOIC
POMANDER
POMOLOGY
PONDERED
PONDERER
PONDWEED
PONGIEST
PONIARDS
PONTIFEX
PONTIFFS
PONTOONS
PONYTAIL
POOFIEST
POOH-
 POOH
POOLSIDE
POOR
 LAWS
POORLIER
POORNESS
POPADUMS
POPINJAY
POPOVERS
POPPADOM
POPSICLE
POPULACE
POPULATE
POPULISM
POPULIST
POPULOUS

PORKIEST
PORK
  PIES
POROSITY
PORPHYRY
PORPOISE
PORRIDGE
PORTABLE
PORTENTS
PORTHOLE
PORTICOS
PORTIERE
PORTIONS
PORTLAND
PORTLIER
PORTRAIT
PORT
 SAID
PORT
 SIDE
PORTUGAL
POSITING
POSITION
POSITIVE
POSITRON
POSOLOGY
POSSIBLE
POSSIBLY
POSTBAGS
POSTCARD
POSTCAVA
POSTCODE
POSTDATE
POST-
  FREE
POSTGRAD
POST
  HORN
POSTICHE
POSTINGS
POSTLUDE
POSTMARK
POST-
  OBIT
POSTPAID
POSTPONE
POSTURAL
POSTURED
POSTURER
POSTURES
POTASSIC
POTATION

POTATOES
POT-AU-
  FEU
POTBELLY
POTBOUND
POTENTLY
POTHOLER
POTHOLES
POTLUCKS
POT
 PLANT
POTSHERD
POTSHOTS
POTSTONE
POTTERED
POTTERER
POTTIEST
POULTICE
POUNCING
POUNDAGE
POUNDING
POWDERED
POWDERER
POWERFUL
POWERING
POZIDRIV
POZZUOLI
PRACTICE
PRACTISE
PRAEDIAL
PRAESEPE
PRAIRIES
PRAISING
PRALINES
PRANCING
PRANDIAL
PRANKISH
PRATIQUE
PRATTLED
PRATTLER
PREACHED
PREACHER
PREAMBLE
PREAXIAL
PREBENDS
PRECEDED
PRECEPTS
PRECINCT
PRECIOUS
PRECLUDE
PREDATED

PREDATOR
PREDELLA
PREENING
PREEXIST
PRE-
 EXIST
PREFACED
PREFACER
PREFACES
PREFECTS
PREFIXAL
PREFIXED
PREFIXES
PREGNANT
PREJUDGE
PRELATES
PRELATIC
PRELUDER
PRELUDES
PREMIERE
PREMIERS
PREMISES
PREMIUMS
PREMOLAR
PREMORSE
PRENATAL
PREPARED
PREPENSE
PRESAGED
PRESAGER
PRESAGES
PRESCOTT
PRESENCE
PRESENTS
PRESERVE
PRESIDED
PRESIDER
PRESIDIA
PRESIDIO
PRESS
 BOX
PRESSING
PRESSMAN
PRESSMEN
PRESS-
 UPS
PRESSURE
PRESTIGE
PRESUMED
PRESUMER
PRETENCE

PRETEXTS
PRETORIA
PRETREAT
PRETTIER
PRETTIFY
PRETTILY
PRETZELS
PREVIEWS
PREVIOUS
PREZZIES
PRIAPISM
PRICE
 TAG
PRICIEST
PRICKING
PRICKLED
PRICKLES
PRIDEFUL
PRIE-
 DIEU
PRIESTLY
PRIGGERY
PRIGGISH
PRIGGISM
PRIMATES
PRIMEVAL
PRIMMEST
PRIMNESS
PRIMROSE
PRIMULAS
PRIMUSES
PRINCELY
PRINCESS
PRINCIPE
PRINTERS
PRINTING
PRINTOUT
PRIORATE
PRIORESS
PRIORIES
PRIORITY
PRISMOID
PRISONER
PRISSIER
PRISSILY
PRISTINE
PRIVATES
PRIVIEST
PRIZE
 DAY
PROBABLE

PROBABLY
PROBATED
PROBATES
PROBLEMS
PROCAINE
PROCEEDS
PROCLAIM
PROCTORS
PROCURED
PROCURER
PRODDING
PRODIGAL
PRODROME
PRODUCED
PRODUCER
PRODUCTS
PROEMIAL
PROFANED
PROFANER
PROFILED
PROFILES
PROFITED
PROFITER
PRO
 FORMA
PROFOUND
PROGRAMS
PROGRESS
PROHIBIT
PROJECTS
PROLAPSE
PROLIFIC
PROLOGUE
PROMISED
PROMISER
PROMISES
PROMISOR
PROMOTED
PROMOTER
PROMPTED
PROMPTER
PROMPTLY
PRONATOR
PRONOUNS
PROOFING
PROPERLY
PROPERTY
PROPHAGE
PROPHASE
PROPHECY
PROPHESY

PROPHETS
PROPOLIS
PROPOSAL
PROPOSED
PROPOSER
PROPOUND
PROPPING
PROROGUE
PROSAISM
PROSIEST
PROSODIC
PROSPECT
PROSTATE
PROSTYLE
PROTASIS
PROTEGEE
PROTEGES
PROTEINS
PROTEOSE
PROTESTS
PROTOCOL
PROTOZOA
PROTRACT
PROTRUDE
PROUDEST
PROVABLE
PROVABLY
PROVENCE
PROVENLY
PROVERBS
PROVIDED
PROVIDER
PROVINCE
PROVISOS
PROVOKED
PROVOSTS
PROWL
 CAR
PROWLERS
PROWLING
PROXIMAL
PRUDENCE
PRUINOSE
PRUNABLE
PRUNELLA
PRUNELLE
PRURIENT
PRURITIC
PRURITUS
PRUSSIAN
PSALMIST

PSALMODY
PSALTERS
PSALTERY
PSEPHITE
PSORALEA
PSYCHICS
PSYCHING
PTEROPOD
PTOMAINE
PTYALISM
PUB-
  CRAWL
PUBLICAN
PUBLICLY
PUCKERED
PUDDINGS
PUDDLING
PUDENDUM
PUDGIEST
PUFFBALL
PUFFBIRD
PUFFIEST
PUGILISM
PUGILIST
PUISSANT
PULLMANS
PULLOUTS
PULLOVER
PULMONIC
PULMOTOR
PULPIEST
PULPWOOD
PULSATED
PULSATOR
PULSEJET
PULVINUS
PUMMELED
PUMPKINS
PUMP
  ROOM
PUNCHBAG
PUNCHEON
PUNCHIER
PUNCHING
PUNCH-
  UPS
PUNCTATE
PUNCTUAL
PUNCTURE
PUNGENCY
PUNINESS

PUNISHED
PUNISHER
PUNITIVE
PUNSTERS
PUPARIAL
PUPARIUM
PUPATION
PUPPETRY
PUPPY
  FAT
PUPPYISH
PURBLIND
PURCHASE
PUREBRED
PUREEING
PURENESS
PURFLING
PURIFIED
PURIFIER
PURISTIC
PURITANS
PURLIEUS
PURPLISH
PURPOSED
PURPOSES
PURPURIN
PURSLANE
PURSUANT
PURSUERS
PURSUING
PURSUITS
PURULENT
PURVEYED
PURVEYOR
PUSHBIKE
PUSHCART
PUSHIEST
PUSHOVER
PUSH-
  PULL
PUSSYCAT
PUSTULAR
PUSTULES
PUT
  ABOUT
PUTATIVE
PUT-
  DOWNS
PUTSCHES
PUTTERED
PUT TO
  SEA

PUT-UP
  JOB
PUZZLERS
PUZZLING
PYELITIC
PYELITIS
PYGIDIAL
PYGIDIUM
PYINKADO
PYODERMA
PYOGENIC
PYRAMIDS
PYRAZOLE
PYRENEAN
PYRENEES
PYRENOID
PYREXIAL
PYRIDINE
PYRIFORM
PYROSTAT
PYROXENE
PYRROLIC
PYRRUVIC
PYTHONIC
PYXIDIUM

Q

QUACKERY
QUACKING
QUAD
  BIKE
QUADRANT
QUADRATE
QUADROON
QUAGMIRE
QUAILING
QUAINTLY
QUALMISH
QUANDARY
QUANDONG
QUANTIFY
QUANTITY
QUANTIZE
QUARRELS
QUARRIED
QUARRIER
QUARRIES
QUARTERN
QUARTERS
QUARTETS
QUARTILE

QUASHING
QUATRAIN
QUAVERED
QUAVERER
QUEASIER
QUEASILY
QUECHUAN
QUEENDOM
QUEENING
QUEEREST
QUEERING
QUELLING
QUENCHED
QUENCHER
QUERCINE
QUERYING
QUESTING
QUESTION
QUIBBLED
QUIBBLER
QUIBBLES
QUIBERON
QUICKEST
QUICKIES
QUICKSET
QUIDDITY
QUIDNUNC
QUIETEST
QUIETISM
QUIETIST
QUIETUDE
QUILL
  PEN
QUILTING
QUINCUNX
QUI
  NHONG
QUINTETS
QUINTILE
QUIPPING
QUIPSTER
QUIRKIER
QUIRKILY
QUISLING
QUITTERS
QUITTING
QUIVERED
QUIVERER
QUIXOTIC
QUIZZING
QUOTABLE

QUOTHING
QUOTIENT

R

RABBITED
RABBITER
RABBITRY
RABIDITY
RACCOONS
RACEMISM
RACEMOSE
RACIALLY
RACINESS
RACK-
  RENT
RACLETTE
RACQUETS
RADIALLY
RADIANCE
RADIATED
RADIATOR
RADICALS
RADICAND
RADIOING
RADISHES
RAFFLING
RAGGEDLY
RAG
  TRADE
RAILHEAD
RAILINGS
RAILLERY
RAILROAD
RAILWAYS
RAINBAND
RAINBOWS
RAINCOAT
RAINDROP
RAINFALL
RAINIEST
RAINLESS
RAINY
  DAY
RAISABLE
RAKE-
  OFFS
RAKISHLY
RALLYING
RAMAT
  GAN
RAMBLERS
RAMBLING

RAMBUTAN
RAMEKINS
RAMENTUM
RAMIFIED
RAMOSITY
RAMPAGED
RAMPAGER
RAMPANCY
RAMPARTS
RAMSGATE
RAMULOSE
RANCAGUA
RANCHERS
RANDIEST
RANDOMLY
RANKLING
RANKNESS
RANSOMED
RANSOMER
RAPACITY
RAPESEED
RAPIDITY
RAPTNESS
RAPTURES
RARA
  AVIS
RAREFIED
RAREFIER
RARENESS
RARITIES
RASCALLY
RASHNESS
RASORIAL
RASPINGS
RAT-
  ARSED
RATCHETS
RATIFIED
RATIFIER
RATIONAL
RATIONED
RATSBANE
RATTIEST
RATTLING
RAT
  TRAPS
RAVAGING
RAVELING
RAVELLED
RAVELLER
RAVENING

R 8 RAVENOUS

RAVENOUS
RAVISHED
RAVISHER
RAW-
 BONED
RAW
 DEALS
RAWHIDES
RAZOR-
 CUT
REACHING
REACTANT
REACTING
REACTION
REACTIVE
REACTORS
READABLE
READABLY
READIEST
READINGS
READJUST
READOUTS
READYING
READY-
 MIX
REAFFIRM
REAGENTS
REALISTS
REALIZED
REALIZER
REALNESS
REAL-
 TIME
REALTORS
REAPABLE
REAPPEAR
REARMING
REARMOST
REARWARD
REASONED
REASONER
REASSURE
REAWAKEN
REBELLED
REBOUNDS
REBUFFED
REBUKING
REBUTTAL
REBUTTED
REBUTTER
RECALLED
RECANTED

RECANTER
RECAPPED
RECEDING
RECEIPTS
RECEIVED
RECEIVER
RECENTLY
RECEPTOR
RECESSED
RECESSES
RECHARGE
RECISION
RECITALS
RECITERS
RECITING
RECKLESS
RECKONED
RECKONER
RECLINED
RECLINER
RECLUSES
RECOILED
RECOILER
RECOMMIT
RECORDED
RECORDER
RECOUNTS
RECOUPED
RECOURSE
RECOVERY
RECREANT
RECREATE
RECRUITS
RECTALLY
RECURRED
RECUSANT
RECYCLED
REDACTOR
RED
 ALERT
REDBRICK
REDCOATS
RED
 CROSS
REDDENED
REDDITCH
REDEEMED
REDEEMER
REDEMAND
REDEPLOY
REDESIGN

RED
 FACED
RED-
 FACED
RED
 FLAGS
RED
 GIANT
REDGRAVE
REDHEADS
REDIRECT
RED
 LIGHT
REDNECKS
REDOLENT
REDOUBLE
REDOUBTS
REDSHANK
RED
 SHIFT
REDSKINS
REDSTART
REDUCING
REDUVIID
REDWOODS
REECHOED
REEDBUCK
REEDIEST
REEDLING
REEF
 KNOT
REELABLE
REELABLY
RE-
 EMPLOY
RE-
 EXPORT
REFACING
REFEREED
REFEREES
REFERENT
REFERRAL
REFERRED
REFERRER
REFILLED
REFINERY
REFINING
REFINISH
REFITTED
REFLATED
REFLEXES
REFOREST

REFORMED
REFORMER
REFRAINS
REFUELED
REFUGEES
REFUGIUM
REFUNDED
REFUNDER
REFUSALS
REFUSING
REFUTING
REGAINED
REGAINER
REGALITY
REGARDED
REGATTAS
REGELATE
REGENTAL
REGICIDE
REGIMENS
REGIMENT
REGIONAL
REGISTER
REGISTRY
REGRATER
REGROWTH
REGULARS
REGULATE
REGULINE
REHASHED
REHASHES
REHEARSE
REHEATER
REHOBOAM
REHOUSED
REIGNING
REIMPORT
REIMPOSE
REINDEER
REINSURE
REINVENT
REINVEST
REISSUED
REISSUER
REISSUES
REJECTED
REJECTER
REJIGGED
REJOICED
REJOICER
REJOINED

REKINDLE
RELAPSED
RELAPSER
RELAPSES
RELATING
RELATION
RELATIVE
RELAUNCH
RELAXANT
RELAXING
RELAYING
RELEASED
RELEASER
RELEASES
RELEGATE
RELENTED
RELEVANT
RELIABLE
RELIABLY
RELIANCE
RELIEVED
RELIEVER
RELIGION
RELINING
RELISHED
RELISHES
RELIVING
RELOADED
RELOCATE
REMAINED
REMAKING
REMANDED
REMARKED
REMARKER
REMARQUE
REMEDIAL
REMEDIED
REMEDIES
REMEMBER
REMIGIAL
REMINDED
REMINDER
REMITTED
REMITTER
REMNANTS
REMOTELY
REMOTEST
REMOULDS
REMOUNTS
REMOVALS
REMOVERS

REMOVING
RENAMING
RENDERED
RENDERER
RENDIBLE
RENDZINA
RENEGADE
RENEGING
RENEWALS
RENEWING
RENIFORM
RENOUNCE
RENOVATE
RENOWNED
RENTABLE
RENT
 BOYS
RENT-
 FREE
RENTIERS
RENT-
 ROLL
REOFFEND
REOPENED
REPAIRED
REPAIRER
REPARTEE
REPAYING
REPEALED
REPEALER
REPEATED
REPEATER
REPELLED
REPELLER
REPENTED
REPENTER
REPEOPLE
REPETEND
REPHRASE
REPINING
REPLACED
REPLACER
REPLAYED
REPLEVIN
REPLICAS
REPLYING
REPORTED
REPORTER
REPOSING
REPOUSSE
REPRIEVE

150

REPRINTS
REPRISAL
REPRISES
REPROACH
REPROOFS
REPROVAL
REPROVED
REPROVER
REPTILES
REPUBLIC
REPULSED
REPULSER
REPULSES
REQUESTS
REQUIEMS
REQUIRED
REQUIRER
REQUITAL
REQUITED
REQUITER
RESCRIPT
RESCUERS
RESCUING
RESEARCH
RESEMBLE
RESENTED
RESERVED
RESERVER
RESERVES
RESETTER
RESETTLE
RESIDENT
RESIDING
RESIDUAL
RESIDUES
RESIDUUM
RESIGNAL
RESIGNED
RESIGNER
RESINATE
RESINOID
RESINOUS
RESISTED
RESISTER
RESISTOR
RESOLUTE
RESOLVED
RESOLVER
RESOLVES
RESONANT
RESONATE

RESORTED
RESORTER
RESOURCE
RESPECTS
RESPIRED
RESPITES
RESPONSE
RESTATED
REST
 CURE
REST
 HOME
RESTLESS
RESTORED
RESTORER
RESTRAIN
RESTRICT
REST
 ROOM
RESUBMIT
RESULTED
RESUMING
RETAILED
RETAILER
RETAINED
RETAINER
RETAKING
RETARDED
RETARDER
RETCHING
RETICENT
RETICULE
RETINENE
RETINITE
RETINUED
RETINUES
RETIRING
RETORTED
RETORTER
RETRACED
RETREADS
RETREATS
RETRENCH
RETRIALS
RETRIEVE
RETROACT
RETROFIT
RETRORSE
RETURNED
RETURNER
REUNIONS

REUNITED
REUNITER
REUSABLE
REVALUED
REVAMPED
REVAMPER
REVEALED
REVEALER
REVEILLE
REVELING
REVELLED
REVELLER
REVENANT
REVENGED
REVENGER
REVENUED
REVEREND
REVERENT
REVERIES
REVERING
REVERSAL
REVERSED
REVERSER
REVERSES
REVERTED
REVERTER
REVIEWAL
REVIEWED
REVIEWER
REVILERS
REVILING
REVISERS
REVISING
REVISION
REVISORY
REVIVALS
REVIVIFY
REVIVING
REVOKING
REVOLTED
REVOLTER
REVOLUTE
REVOLVED
REVOLVER
REWARDED
REWARDER
REWINDER
REWIRING
REWORDED
REWORKED
REWRITES

REYNOLDS
RHAETIAN
RHAPSODY
RHEOBASE
RHEOLOGY
RHEOSTAT
RHETORIC
RH
 FACTOR
RHINITIS
RHIZOMES
RHIZOPOD
RHIZOPUS
RHODESIA
RHODINAL
RHOMBOID
RHONCHAL
RHONCHUS
RHUBARBS
RHYOLITE
RHYTHMIC
RIBALDRY
RIB
 CAGES
RIBOSOME
RICEBIRD
RICHMOND
RICHNESS
RICKRACK
RICKSHAW
RICOCHET
RIDDANCE
RIDDLING
RIDICULE
RIESLING
RIFENESS
RIFFLING
RIFFRAFF
RIFLEMAN
RIGADOON
RIGATONI
RIGHTFUL
RIGHTING
RIGHTISM
RIGHTIST
RIGHT
 OFF
RIGIDITY
RIGORISM
RIGORIST
RIGOROUS

RIJSWIJK
RIMOSITY
RINGBOLT
RINGBONE
RINGDOVE
RING-
 DYKE
RINGETTE
RINGHALS
RINGLETS
RING
 ROAD
RINGSIDE
RINGWORM
RINKHALS
RINSABLE
RIOT
 ACTS
RIPARIAN
RIPCORDS
RIPENESS
RIPENING
RIPOSTED
RIPOSTES
RIPPABLE
RIPPLING
RIPTIDES
RISKIEST
RISOTTOS
RISSOLES
RITENUTO
RITUALLY
RIVALING
RIVALLED
RIVERBED
RIVERINE
RIVETERS
RIVETING
RIVIERAS
RIVULETS
ROAD
 HOGS
ROAD
 RAGE
ROADSHOW
ROADSIDE
ROAD
 SIGN
ROADSTER
ROAD
 TEST
ROADWORK

ROASTERS
ROASTING
ROBINSON
ROBOTICS
ROBOTISM
ROBUSTLY
ROCAILLE
ROCHDALE
ROCK
 BAND
ROCK
 CAKE
ROCK
 DASH
ROCKETED
ROCKETRY
ROCKFALL
ROCKFISH
ROCKFORD
ROCKIEST
ROCKLING
ROCKROSE
ROCK
 SALT
ROCKWEED
ROEBUCKS
ROENTGEN
ROGATION
ROGATORY
ROLE
 PLAY
ROLLAWAY
ROLL
 BARS
ROLL
 CALL
ROLLMOPS
ROLL
 OVER
ROLLOVER
ROLY-
 POLY
ROMANCED
ROMANCES
ROMANIES
ROMAN
 LAW
ROMANSCH
ROMANTIC
RONDAVEL
RONDELET
RONTGENS

ROOFLESS
ROOF
  RACK
ROOFTOPS
ROOFTREE
ROOMIEST
ROOMMATE
ROOM
  MATE
ROOSTERS
ROOSTING
ROOT
  BEER
ROOT
  CROP
ROOTLESS
ROOTLIKE
ROPEWALK
ROPINESS
ROSARIAN
ROSARIES
ROSEBUSH
ROSEFISH
ROSE
  HIPS
ROSEMARY
ROSEOLAR
ROSE-
  ROOT
ROSETTES
ROSEWOOD
ROSINESS
ROSINING
ROSKILDE
ROSTRUMS
ROTARIAN
ROTATING
ROTATION
ROTATIVE
ROTATORY
ROTENONE
ROTHESAY
ROTOTILL
ROTTENLY
ROTUNDAS
ROUGHAGE
ROUGH-
  DRY
ROUGHEST
ROUGH-
  HEW
ROUGHING

ROULETTE
ROUND-
  ARM
ROUNDELS
ROUNDERS
ROUNDEST
ROUNDING
ROUNDISH
ROUNDUPS
ROUTINES
ROVE-
  OVER
ROWDIEST
ROWDYISM
ROW
  HOUSE
ROWLOCKS
ROYALISM
ROYALIST
RUBBINGS
RUBBISHY
RUBDOWNS
RUBELITE
RUBEOLAR
RUBICONS
RUBICUND
RUBIDIUM
RUBRICAL
RUCKSACK
RUCKUSES
RUDDIEST
RUDENESS
RUDIMENT
RUEFULLY
RUFFIANS
RUFFLING
RUGGEDLY
RUGOSITY
RUINABLE
RULEBOOK
RUMANIAN
RUMBLING
RUMINANT
RUMINATE
RUMMAGED
RUMMAGER
RUMMAGES
RUMOURED
RUMPLING
RUN-
  ABOUT
RUNAWAYS

RUNDOWNS
RUNNER
  UP
RUNNER-
  UP
RUNNIEST
RUPTURED
RUPTURES
RURALISM
RURALIST
RURALITY
RURALIZE
RUSH
  HOUR
RUST
  BELT
RUSTICAL
RUSTIEST
RUSTLERS
RUSTLING
RUTABAGA
RUTHENIC
RUTHLESS
RYDER
  CUP
RYE-
  BROME
RYEGRASS

S

SAARLAND
SABADELL
SABBATIC
SABOTAGE
SABOTEUR
SABULOUS
SACKLIKE
SACK
  RACE
SACREDLY
SACRISTY
SADDENED
SADDLERS
SADDLERY
SADDLING
SADISTIC
SAFENESS
SAFE
  SEAT
SAFETIES
SAGACITY
SAGGIEST

SAGITTAL
SAILABLE
SAILFISH
SAILINGS
SAILORLY
SAINFOIN
SAKHALIN
SALAAMED
SALACITY
SALARIED
SALARIES
SALEABLE
SALEABLY
SALEROOM
SALESMAN
SALESMEN
SALES
  TAX
SALIENCE
SALIENTS
SALINGER
SALINITY
SALIVARY
SALIVATE
SALLYING
SALPICON
SALTBUSH
SALTIEST
SALTILLO
SALTLICK
SALTNESS
SALTPANS
SALTWORT
SALUTARY
SALUTING
SALVABLE
SALVABLY
SALVADOR
SALVAGED
SALVAGER
SALZBURG
SAMARIUM
SAMENESS
SAMIZDAT
SAMOVARS
SAMPHIRE
SAMPLERS
SAMPLING
SAMURAIS
SANCTIFY
SANCTION

SANCTITY
SANCTUMS
SANDAKAN
SANDARAC
SANDBAGS
SANDBANK
SANDBARS
SAND-
  CAST
SAND
  DUNE
SAN
  DIEGO
SANDIEST
SANDPITS
SANDSHOE
SANDSOAP
SAND
  TRAP
SANDWELL
SANDWICH
SANDWORM
SANDWORT
SANENESS
SANGAREE
SANGUINE
SANITARY
SANITIZE
SANSKRIT
SANTA
  ANA
SANTAREM
SANTIAGO
SANTONIN
SAO
  PAULO
SAPIDITY
SAPIENCE
SAPLINGS
SAPONIFY
SAPONITE
SAPPHIRE
SAPPIEST
SAPROBIC
SAPROPEL
SARABAND
SARACENS
SARAJEVO
SARDINES
SARDINIA
SARDONIC
SARDONYX

SARGASSO
SARGODHA
SARKIEST
SARMATIA
SARRAUTE
SASHAYED
SASH
  CORD
SASSIEST
SASTRUGA
SATANISM
SATANIST
SATCHELS
SATIABLE
SATIABLY
SATIATED
SATIRIST
SATIRIZE
SATSUMAS
SATURANT
SATURATE
SATURDAY
SAUCEPAN
SAUCIEST
SAUNTERS
SAUROPOD
SAUSAGES
SAUTEING
SAVAGELY
SAVAGERY
SAVAGING
SAVANNAH
SAVANNAS
SAVIOURS
SAVORIES
SAVOROUS
SAVOURED
SAVOYARD
SAWBONES
SAWGRASS
SAWHORSE
SAWMILLS
SAWTOOTH
SCABBARD
SCABBIER
SCABBILY
SCABIOUS
SCABROUS
SCAFFOLD
SCALABLE
SCALABLY

SCALAWAG
SCALDING
SCALENUS
SCALIEST
SCALLION
SCALLOPS
SCALPELS
SCALPERS
SCALPING
SCAMMONY
SCAMPISH
SCANDALS
SCANDIUM
SCANNERS
SCANNING
SCANSION
SCANTIER
SCANTILY
SCAPULAR
SCAPULAS
SCARCELY
SCARCEST
SCARCITY
SCARGILL
SCARIEST
SCARIOUS
SCARRING
SCATHING
SCATTIER
SCATTILY
SCATTING
SCAVENGE
SCENARIO
SCENTING
SCEPTICS
SCEPTRES
SCHEDULE
SCHEMATA
SCHEMERS
SCHEMING
SCHERZOS
SCHIEDAM
SCHILLER
SCHIZOID
SCHIZONT
SCHMALTZ
SCHMUCKS
SCHNAPPS
SCHOLARS
SCHOLIUM
SCHOOLED

SCHOOLIE
SCHOONER
SCHWERIN
SCIAENID
SCIATICA
SCIENCES
SCILICET
SCIMITAR
SCINCOID
SCIRRHUS
SCISSILE
SCISSION
SCISSORS
SCIURINE
SCIUROID
SCLAFFER
SCLERITE
SCLEROID
SCLEROMA
SCLEROUS
SCOFFING
SCOLDING
SCOLLOPS
SCOOPING
SCOOTERS
SCOOTING
SCORCHED
SCORCHER
SCORCHES
SCORNFUL
SCORNING
SCORPION
SCORPIOS
SCORPIUS
SCORSESE
SCOTCHED
SCOT
 FREE
SCOT-
 FREE
SCOTLAND
SCOTOPIA
SCOTOPIC
SCOTSMAN
SCOTTISH
SCOURERS
SCOURGED
SCOURGER
SCOURGES
SCOURING
SCOUTING

SCOWLING
SCRABBLE
SCRAGGED
SCRAGGLY
SCRAMBLE
SCRAMMED
SCRANTON
SCRAPERS
SCRAPING
SCRAP
 MAN
SCRAPPED
SCRATCHY
SCRAWLED
SCRAWLER
SCREAMED
SCREAMER
SCREECHY
SCREENED
SCREENER
SCREWIER
SCREWING
SCREW
 TOP
SCRIBBLE
SCRIMPED
SCRIPTED
SCROFULA
SCROLLED
SCROOGES
SCROTUMS
SCROUNGE
SCRUBBED
SCRUBBER
SCRUMPED
SCRUNCHY
SCRUPLED
SCRUPLES
SCRUTINY
SCUDDING
SCUFFING
SCUFFLED
SCUFFLES
SCULLERS
SCULLERY
SCULLING
SCULLION
SCULPSIT
SCULPTOR
SCUPPERS
SCURRIED

SCURVILY
SCUTTLED
SCUTTLES
SCYTHING
SEABIRDS
SEABOARD
SEABORNE
SEACOAST
SEAFARER
SEAFRONT
SEAGIRTS
SEAGOING
SEA
 GREEN
SEAGULLS
SEAHORSE
SEALABLE
SEA
 LEVEL
SEA
 LIONS
SEALSKIN
SEALYHAM
SEAMIEST
SEA
 MILES
SEA
 MISTS
SEAMLESS
SEAMOUNT
SEAPLANE
SEAPORTS
SEA
 POWER
SEAQUAKE
SEARCHED
SEARCHER
SEARCHES
SEASCAPE
SEASHELL
SEASHORE
SEA
 SNAKE
SEASONAL
SEASONED
SEASONER
SEAT
 BELT
SEA
 TROUT
SEAWALLS
SEAWARDS

SECEDING
SECLUDED
SECONDED
SECONDER
SECONDLY
SECRETED
SECRETIN
SECRETLY
SECTIONS
SECTORAL
SECURELY
SECUREST
SECURING
SECURITY
SEDATELY
SEDATING
SEDATION
SEDATIVE
SEDIMENT
SEDITION
SEDUCERS
SEDUCING
SEDULITY
SEDULOUS
SEEDBEDS
SEEDCASE
SEEDCORN
SEEDIEST
SEEDLESS
SEEDLING
SEEDSMAN
SEEDSMEN
SEESAWED
SEETHING
SEGMENTS
SEIGNEUR
SEISABLE
SEISMISM
SEIZABLE
SEIZURES
SELANGOR
SELECTED
SELECTOR
SELENATE
SELENITE
SELENIUM
SELFHEAL
SELF-
 HELP
SELFHOOD
SELFLESS

SELF-
 MADE
SELF-
 PITY
SELF-
 RULE
SELFSAME
SELF-
 WILL
SELL-
 OUTS
SELVAGES
SEMANTIC
SEMARANG
SEMESTER
SEMIARID
SEMIDOME
SEMINARS
SEMINARY
SEMIOTIC
SEMITICS
SEMITIST
SEMITONE
SEMOLINA
SEMPLICE
SENATORS
SENDABLE
SEND-
 OFFS
SENILITY
SENORITA
SENSIBLE
SENSIBLY
SENSUOUS
SENTENCE
SENTIENT
SENTINEL
SENTRIES
SEPALLED
SEPALOID
SEPARATE
SEPHARDI
SEPTUPLE
SEQUENCE
SEQUINED
SEQUOIAS
SERAGLIO
SERAJEVO
SERAPHIC
SERAPHIM
SEREMBAN
SERENADE

SERENATA
SERENELY
SERENITY
SERGEANT
SERIALLY
SERIATIM
SERMONIC
SEROLOGY
SEROSITY
SEROTINE
SERPENTS
SERPULID
SERRANID
SERRATED
SERVABLE
SERVANTS
SERVICED
SERVICES
SERVINGS
SERVITOR
SERVQUAL
SESAMOID
SESSIONS
SET
  ASIDE
SETBACKS
SETIFORM
SET
  PIECE
SET
  POINT
SET
  RIGHT
SETSCREW
SETTINGS
SETTLERS
SETTLE
  UP
SETTLING
SEVENTHS
SEVERELY
SEVERING
SEVERITY
SEWERAGE
SEXINESS
SEXOLOGY
SEX
  ORGAN
SEXTANTS
SEXTUPLE
SEXUALLY
SHABBIER

SHABBILY
SHACKING
SHACKLED
SHACKLER
SHACKLES
SHADDOCK
SHADIEST
SHADINGS
SHADOWED
SHADOWER
SHAFTING
SHAGBARK
SHAGGIER
SHAGGILY
SHAGGING
SHAGREEN
SHAKABLE
SHAKEOUT
SHAKE-
  UPS
SHAKIEST
SHALLOON
SHALLOTS
SHALLOWS
SHAMABLE
SHAMBLED
SHAMBLES
SHAMEFUL
SHAMMIES
SHAMMING
SHAMPOOS
SHAMROCK
SHANDIES
SHANDONG
SHANGHAI
SHANTIES
SHANTUNG
SHAPABLE
SHARABLE
SHARE-
  OUT
SHARP
  END
SHARPEST
SHARPISH
SHARP-
  SET
SHAVABLE
SHAVINGS
SHEADING
SHEARING
SHEATHED

SHEBEENS
SHEDABLE
SHEDDING
SHEEPDIP
SHEEPDOG
SHEEPISH
SHEEREST
SHEERING
SHEETING
SHEIKDOM
SHELDUCK
SHELLING
SHELTERS
SHELVING
SHENYANG
SHEPHERD
SHERATON
SHERBETS
SHERIFFS
SHETLAND
SHIELDED
SHIELDER
SHIELING
SHIFTIER
SHIFTILY
SHIFTING
SHIFT
  KEY
SHIITAKE
SHILLING
SHILLONG
SHIMMERY
SHINBONE
SHINDIGS
SHINGLER
SHINGLES
SHINIEST
SHINNIED
SHINNING
SHIPABLE
SHIPLOAD
SHIPMATE
SHIPMENT
SHIPPERS
SHIPPING
SHIPWORM
SHIPYARD
SHIRKERS
SHIRKING
SHIRRING
SHIRTIER

SHIRTING
SHITLESS
SHITTIER
SHITTING
SHIVERED
SHIVERER
SHIZUOKA
SHOCKERS
SHOCKING
SHODDIER
SHODDILY
SHOEBILL
SHOEHORN
SHOELACE
SHOETREE
SHOLAPUR
SHOOTERS
SHOOTING
SHOOT
  OUT
SHOOT-
  OUT
SHOPGIRL
SHOPLIFT
SHOPPERS
SHOPPING
SHOPTALK
SHORTAGE
SHORT
  CUT
SHORT-
  DAY
SHORTEST
SHORTIES
SHORTING
SHOTGUNS
SHOULDER
SHOULDN'
  T
SHOUTING
SHOVELED
SHOVELER
SHOWBOAT
SHOWCASE
SHOWDOWN
SHOWERED
SHOWGIRL
SHOWIEST
SHOWINGS
SHOW-
  OFFS
SHOWROOM

SHRAPNEL
SHREDDED
SHREDDER
SHREWDER
SHREWDLY
SHREWISH
SHRIEKED
SHRIEKER
SHRIEVAL
SHRILLER
SHRIMPER
SHRINKER
SHROUDED
SHRUGGED
SHRUNKEN
SHUCKING
SHUDDERS
SHUDDERY
SHUFFLED
SHUFFLER
SHUFFLES
SHUNNING
SHUNTERS
SHUNTING
SHUSHING
SHUTDOWN
SHUTTERS
SHUTTING
SHUTTLED
SHUTTLES
SHYSTERS
SIANGTAN
SIBERIAN
SIBILANT
SIBILATE
SIBLINGS
SICILIAN
SICKBAYS
SICKBEDS
SICK
  CALL
SICKENED
SICKENER
SICKLIER
SICKNESS
SICKROOM
SIDEARMS
SIDE
  ARMS
SIDEBAND
SIDECARS

SIDE
  DISH
SIDE-
  FOOT
SIDEKICK
SIDELINE
SIDELONG
SIDEREAL
SIDERITE
SIDE
  ROAD
SIDESHOW
SIDESLIP
SIDESMAN
SIDESTEP
SIDEWALK
SIDEWALL
SIDEWAYS
SIEGBAHN
SIFTINGS
SIGHTING
SIGHTSEE
SIGNALED
SIGNALLY
SIGNINGS
SIGNORAS
SIGNPOST
SILASTIC
SILENCED
SILENCER
SILENCES
SILENTLY
SILICATE
SILICIDE
SILICIFY
SILICONE
SILKIEST
SILKWORM
SILLABUB
SILLIEST
SILOXANE
SILURIAN
SILVERED
SILVERER
SIMBIRSK
SIMMERED
SIMONIAC
SIMONIST
SIMPERED
SIMPERER
SIMPLEST

SIMPLIFY
SIMPLISM
SIMULANT
SIMULATE
SINAITIC
SINAPISM
SINCIPUT
SINECURE
SINFONIA
SINFULLY
SINGABLE
SINGEING
SINGLETS
SINGLING
SINGSONG
SINGULAR
SINISTER
SINKABLE
SINKHOLE
SINN
  FEIN
SINOLOGY
SINUSOID
SIPHONAL
SIPHONED
SIRENIAN
SIRLOINS
SIROCCOS
SISSIEST
SISSYISH
SISTERLY
SISTROID
SITARIST
SIT-
  DOWNS
SITOLOGY
SITTINGS
SITUATED
SITZMARK
SIX-
  PACKS
SIXPENCE
SIXPENNY
SIXTEENS
SIXTIETH
SIZEABLE
SIZZLERS
SIZZLING
SKELETAL
SKELETON
SKEPTICS

SKEPTISM
SKERRICK
SKETCHED
SKETCHER
SKETCHES
SKEWBACK
SKEWBALD
SKEWERED
SKIDDING
SKIDPANS
SKIJORER
SKI
  JUMPS
SKI
  LIFTS
SKILLETS
SKIMMERS
SKIMMING
SKIMPIER
SKIMPILY
SKIMPING
SKINCARE
SKIN
  DEEP
SKIN-
  DEEP
SKIN-
  DIVE
SKINHEAD
SKINLESS
SKINNIER
SKINNING
SKIPJACK
SKI
  PLANE
SKI
  POLES
SKIPPERS
SKIPPING
SKIRMISH
SKIRTING
SKITTISH
SKITTLES
SKIVVIED
SKIVVIES
SKULKING
SKULLCAP
SKYDIVER
SKYLARKS
SKYLIGHT
SKYLINES
SKYWARDS

SLACKEST
SLACKING
SLAGGING
SLAGHEAP
SLAG
  HEAP
SLAKABLE
SLAMMING
SLANDERS
SLANGILY
SLANGING
SLANTING
SLAP-
  BANG
SLAPDASH
SLAPHEAD
SLAPPING
SLASHING
SLATTERN
SLAVERED
SLAVERER
SLAVONIA
SLAVONIC
SLEAZIER
SLEAZILY
SLEDDING
SLEDGING
SLEEKEST
SLEEKING
SLEEPERS
SLEEPIER
SLEEPILY
SLEEPING
SLEETING
SLEEVING
SLEIGHER
SLICKERS
SLICKEST
SLICKING
SLIDABLE
SLIGHTED
SLIGHTER
SLIGHTLY
SLIM
  DOWN
SLIMIEST
SLIMMERS
SLIMMEST
SLIMMING
SLIMNESS
SLINGING

SLINKIER
SLINKILY
SLINKING
SLIPCASE
SLIPKNOT
SLIP
  KNOT
SLIP
  OVER
SLIPPAGE
SLIPPERS
SLIPPERY
SLIPPIER
SLIPPING
SLIP
  ROAD
SLIPSHOD
SLIPWAYS
SLITHERY
SLITTING
SLIVERER
SLOBBERY
SLOE-
  EYED
SLOGGERS
SLOGGING
SLOPPIER
SLOPPILY
SLOPPING
SLOPWORK
SLOSHING
SLOTHFUL
SLOTTING
SLOUCHED
SLOUCHER
SLOUGHED
SLOVAKIA
SLOVENIA
SLOVENLY
SLOWDOWN
SLOW
  DOWN
SLOWNESS
SLOWWORM
SLUDGIER
SLUGGARD
SLUGGING
SLUGGISH
SLUICING
SLUMMING
SLUMPING
SLURPING

SLURRING
SLUSHIER
SLUTTISH
SMACKERS
SMACKING
SMALL
  ADS
SMALLEST
SMALL
  FRY
SMALLISH
SMALLPOX
SMALTITE
SMARMIER
SMARTEST
SMARTING
SMASHERS
SMASHING
SMASH-
  UPS
SMEARING
SMELLIER
SMELLING
SMELTERY
SMELTING
SMIRCHED
SMIRCHER
SMIRKING
SMITHERY
SMITHIES
SMOCKING
SMOKABLE
SMOKIEST
SMOLENSK
SMOOCHED
SMOOTHED
SMOOTHEN
SMOOTHER
SMOOTHIE
SMOOTHLY
SMOTHERY
SMOULDER
SMUDGILY
SMUDGING
SMUGGEST
SMUGGLED
SMUGGLER
SMUGNESS
SMUTTIER
SMUTTILY
SNACK
  BAR

SNACKING
SNAFFLED
SNAFFLES
SNAGGING
SNAPBACK
SNAPPERS
SNAPPIER
SNAPPILY
SNAPPING
SNAPPISH
SNAP
  SHOT
SNAPSHOT
SNARLING
SNARL-
  UPS
SNATCHED
SNATCHER
SNATCHES
SNAZZIER
SNAZZILY
SNEAKERS
SNEAKIER
SNEAKILY
SNEAKING
SNEERING
SNEEZING
SNICKERS
SNICKING
SNIFFING
SNIFFLED
SNIFFLER
SNIFFLES
SNIFTERS
SNIGGERS
SNIGGERY
SNIGGLER
SNIPPETS
SNIPPILY
SNIPPING
SNITCHED
SNITCHES
SNIVELED
SNIVELLY
SNOBBERY
SNOBBISH
SNOGGING
SNOOPERS
SNOOPING
SNOOTIER
SNOOTILY

SNOOZING	SOFT	SONGBOOK	SOY	SPECTRAL	SPLAYING
SNORKELS	SELL	SONGSTER	SAUCE	SPECTRES	SPLENDID
SNORTERS	SOFT	SON-IN-	SPACE	SPECTRUM	SPLENIAL
SNORTING	SOAP	LAW	AGE	SPECULAR	SPLENIUS
SNOTTIER	SOFT	SONOBUOY	SPACE-	SPECULUM	SPLICERS
SNOTTILY	SPOT	SONORANT	AGE	SPEECHES	SPLICING
SNOWBALL	SOFTWARE	SONORITY	SPACE	SPEEDIER	SPLINTER
SNOWBIRD	SOFTWOOD	SONOROUS	BAR	SPEEDILY	SPLIT
SNOWDROP	SOGGIEST	SOOTHING	SPACE-	SPEEDING	END
SNOWFALL	SOISSONS	SOOTHSAY	BAR	SPEEDWAY	SPLIT
SNOWIEST	SOJOURNS	SOOTIEST	SPACEMAN	SPELAEAN	PEA
SNOWLINE	SOLACING	SOPHISMS	SPACEMEN	SPELLING	SPLITTER
SNOWSHED	SOLANDER	SOPHISTS	SPACIOUS	SPENDERS	SPLODGES
SNOWSHOE	SOLARIUM	SOPPIEST	SPANDREL	SPENDING	SPLOSHED
SNUBBING	SOLARIZE	SOPRANOS	SPANGLED	SPERMARY	SPLOSHES
SNUFFBOX	SOLATIUM	SORBITOL	SPANGLES	SPERMINE	SPLURGED
SNUFFERS	SOLDERED	SORBONNE	SPANIARD	SPERMOUS	SPLURGES
SNUFFING	SOLDERER	SORCERER	SPANIELS	SPHAGNUM	SPLUTTER
SNUFFLED	SOLDIERS	SORDIDLY	SPANKING	SPHENOID	SPOILAGE
SNUFFLER	SOLDIERY	SOREDIUM	SPANNERS	SPHERICS	SPOILERS
SNUFFLES	SOLECISM	SORENESS	SPANNING	SPHEROID	SPOILING
SNUGGERY	SOLECIST	SORICINE	SPANSPEK	SPHERULE	SPOLIATE
SNUGGLED	SOLEMNLY	SOROCABA	SPARABLE	SPHINXES	SPONDAIC
SNUGNESS	SOLENOID	SORORATE	SPAR	SPHYGMIC	SPONDEES
SO-AND-	SOLIDAGO	SORORITY	DECK	SPICCATO	SPONGERS
SOS	SOLIDARY	SORPTION	SPARERIB	SPICIEST	SPONGIER
SOAPBARK	SOLIDIFY	SORRENTO	SPARE	SPICULUM	SPONGILY
SOAPIEST	SOLIDITY	SORRIEST	RIB	SPIKELET	SPONGING
SOAPLESS	SOLIHULL	SORROWED	SPARKING	SPIKIEST	SPONSION
SOAPSUDS	SOLINGEN	SORROWER	SPARKLED	SPILLAGE	SPONSORS
SOAPWORT	SOLITARY	SORTABLE	SPARKLER	SPILLING	SPOOKIER
SOBERING	SOLITUDE	SOUCHONG	SPARKLES	SPILLWAY	SPOOKILY
SOBRIETY	SOLOISTS	SOUFFLES	SPARLING	SPINDLES	SPOOKING
SOB	SOLONETZ	SOUGHING	SPARRING	SPINIFEX	SPOOKISH
STORY	SOLSTICE	SOUL	SPARROWS	SPINNERS	SPOON-
SO-	SOLUTION	FOOD	SPARSELY	SPINNEYS	FED
CALLED	SOLVABLE	SOULLESS	SPARSEST	SPINNING	SPOONFUL
SOCIABLE	SOLVENCY	SOUNDBOX	SPASTICS	SPIN-	SPOONING
SOCIABLY	SOLVENTS	SOUNDING	SPATTERS	OFFS	SPORADIC
SOCIALLY	SOMALIAN	SOUND	SPATULAR	SPINSTER	SPORRANS
SOCIETAL	SOMBRELY	OFF	SPATULAS	SPIRACLE	SPORTFUL
SOCRATIC	SOMBRERO	SOURDINE	SPAWNING	SPIRALED	SPORTIER
SODALITE	SOMBROUS	SOURNESS	SPEAKERS	SPIRITED	SPORTILY
SODAMIDE	SOMEBODY	SOURPUSS	SPEAKING	SPITEFUL	SPORTING
SODOMITE	SOME	SOUTACHE	SPEARING	SPITFIRE	SPORTIVE
SODOMIZE	HOPE	SOUTHERN	SPECIALS	SPITTING	SPOTLAMP
SOFTBALL	SOMERSET	SOUTHING	SPECIFIC	SPITTOON	SPOTLESS
SOFT	SOMETIME	SOUTHPAW	SPECIMEN	SPLASHED	SPOTTERS
COPY	SOMEWHAT	SOUVENIR	SPECIOUS	SPLASHER	SPOTTIER
SOFTENED	SONANTAL	SOWBREAD	SPECKLED	SPLATTED	SPOTTILY
SOFTENER	SONATINA	SOYA	SPECKLES	SPLATTER	SPOTTING
SOFTNESS	SONGBIRD	BEAN	SPECTATE		

SPOT-
WELD
SPOUTERS
SPOUTING
SPRADDLE
SPRAINED
SPRAWLED
SPRAWLER
SPRAYERS
SPRAY
GUN
SPRAYING
SPREADER
SPRIGGER
SPRINGER
SPRINKLE
SPRINTED
SPRINTER
SPRITELY
SPROCKET
SPROUTED
SPRUCELY
SPRUCING
SPRYNESS
SPUNKIER
SPUNKILY
SPURIOUS
SPURNING
SPURRING
SPURTING
SPUTTERS
SPYGLASS
SQUABBLE
SQUAD
CAR
SQUADRON
SQUALENE
SQUALLED
SQUALLER
SQUAMATE
SQUAMOUS
SQUANDER
SQUARELY
SQUAREST
SQUARING
SQUARISH
SQUASHED
SQUASHER
SQUASHES
SQUATTED
SQUATTER

SQUAWKED
SQUAWKER
SQUEAKED
SQUEAKER
SQUEALED
SQUEALER
SQUEEGEE
SQUEEZED
SQUEEZER
SQUEEZES
SQUELCHY
SQUIGGLE
SQUIGGLY
SQUINTED
SQUINTER
SQUIRMED
SQUIRMER
SQUIRREL
SQUIRTED
SQUIRTER
SQUISHED
SRI
LANKA
SRINAGAR
STABBERS
STABBING
STABLING
STACCATO
STACKING
STADIUMS
STAFFING
STAFFMAN
STAFFORD
STAGGARD
STAGGERS
STAGINGS
STAGNANT
STAGNATE
STAINING
STAIRWAY
STAKE
OUT
STALKERS
STALKILY
STALKING
STALLING
STALLION
STALWART
STAMFORD
STAMINAL
STAMMERS

STAMPEDE
STAMPING
STANCHED
STANCHER
STANDARD
STANDBYS
STANDING
STAND-
INS
STANDISH
STANDOFF
STAND
OUT
STANNARY
STANNITE
STANNOUS
STANZAIC
STAPELIA
STAPLERS
STAPLING
STARCHED
STARCHER
STARCHES
STARDUST
STARFISH
STARGAZE
STARKERS
STARKEST
STARLESS
STARLETS
STARLIKE
STARLING
STARRIER
STARRILY
STARRING
STARSHIP
STAR
SIGN
STARTERS
STARTING
STARTLED
STARTLER
STARVING
STAR
WARS
STARWORT
STASHING
STATABLE
STATELET
STATICAL
STATIONS
STATUARY

STATURES
STATUSES
STATUTES
STAYSAIL
STEADIED
STEADIER
STEADILY
STEALING
STEALTHY
STEAMERS
STEAMIER
STEAMILY
STEAMING
STEAPSIN
STEARATE
STEATITE
STEELIER
STEELING
STEEPEST
STEEPING
STEEPLES
STEERAGE
STEERING
STEINBOK
STELLATE
STELLIFY
STELLITE
STEMHEAD
STEMMING
STENCHES
STENCILS
STEN
GUNS
STENOSIS
STENOTIC
STEP
DOWN
STEPPING
STEPWISE
STERIGMA
STERLING
STERNEST
STERNSON
STERNUMS
STERNWAY
STEROIDS
STETSONS
STEWARDS
STIBNITE
STICKERS
STICKFUL

STICKIER
STICKILY
STICKING
STICKLER
STICKPIN
STICK-
UPS
STIFFEST
STIFLING
STIGMATA
STILBENE
STILBITE
STILETTO
STILLEST
STILLING
STIMULUS
STINGERS
STINGIER
STINGILY
STINGING
STINGRAY
STING
RAY
STINKERS
STINKING
STINTING
STIPENDS
STIPPLED
STIPPLER
STIPULAR
STIRLING
STIRRERS
STIRRING
STIRRUPS
STITCHED
STITCHER
STITCHES
STITCH
UP
STOCKADE
STOCKCAR
STOCK
CAR
STOCKIER
STOCKILY
STOCKING
STOCKIST
STOCKMAN
STOCKMEN
STOCKOUT
STOCKPOT
STOCKTON

STODGIER
STODGILY
STOICISM
STOLIDLY
STOMACHS
STOMACHY
STOMATAL
STOMATIC
STOMPING
STONABLE
STONE
AGE
STONEFLY
STONIEST
STONKING
STOOD
OUT
STOOPING
STOPCOCK
STOPGAPS
STOPOVER
STOPPAGE
STOPPARD
STOPPERS
STOPPING
STORABLE
STOREYED
STORMIER
STORMILY
STORMING
STORMONT
STOUTEST
STOWAWAY
STRABANE
STRADDLE
STRAFING
STRAGGLE
STRAGGLY
STRAIGHT
STRAINED
STRAINER
STRAITEN
STRANDED
STRANGER
STRANGLE
STRAPPED
STRAPPER
STRATEGY
STRATIFY
STRAW
MAN

STRAW	STUDBOOK	SUBORDER	SULPHATE	SUPPLIED	SWANKILY
MEN	STUDDING	SUBORNED	SULPHIDE	SUPPLIER	SWANKING
STRAYING	STUDENTS	SUBORNER	SULPHITE	SUPPLIES	SWANNERY
STREAKED	STUD	SUBOTICA	SULPHONE	SUPPORTS	SWANNING
STREAKER	FARM	SUBOXIDE	SULTANAS	SUPPOSED	SWANSKIN
STREAMED	STUDIOUS	SUBPLOTS	SULTANIC	SUPPOSER	SWANSONG
STREAMER	STUDWORK	SUBPOENA	SULTRIER	SUPPRESS	SWAN
STRENGTH	STUDYING	SUBSERVE	SULTRILY	SUPREMOS	SONG
STRESSED	STUFFIER	SUBSHRUB	SUMATRAN	SURABAYA	SWAP
STRESSES	STUFFILY	SUBSIDED	SUMMERED	SURCOATS	MEET
STRETCHY	STUFFING	SUBSIDER	SUMMITAL	SUREFIRE	SWAPPING
STREUSEL	STULTIFY	SUBSOLAR	SUMMONED	SURE	SWARMING
STREWING	STUMBLED	SUBSONIC	SUM	FIRE	SWASTIKA
STRIATED	STUMBLER	SUBSTAGE	TOTAL	SURENESS	SWATCHES
STRICKEN	STUMBLES	SUBSUMED	SUNBAKED	SURETIES	SWATHING
STRICKLE	STUMPIER	SUBTITLE	SUNBATHE	SURFABLE	SWATTERS
STRICTER	STUMPING	SUBTLEST	SUNBEAMS	SURFACED	SWATTING
STRICTLY	STUNNERS	SUBTLETY	SUNBELTS	SURFACER	SWAYABLE
STRIDDEN	STUNNING	SUBTONIC	SUNBURNT	SURFACES	SWAY-
STRIDENT	STUNTING	SUBTOTAL	SUNBURST	SURFBIRD	BACK
STRIGOSE	STUNT	SUBTRACT	SUNDERED	SURFBOAT	SWEARING
STRIKERS	MAN	SUBULATE	SUNDIALS	SURFLIKE	SWEATBOX
STRIKING	STUNT	SUBURBAN	SUNDRIES	SURGEONS	SWEATERS
STRIMMER	MEN	SUBURBIA	SUNGLASS	SURGICAL	SWEATIER
STRINGER	STUPIDER	SUCCINCT	SUNLAMPS	SURICATE	SWEATILY
STRIPIER	STUPIDLY	SUCCINIC	SUNLIGHT	SURLIEST	SWEATING
STRIPPED	STURDIER	SUCCUBUS	SUNNIEST	SURMISED	SWEEPERS
STRIPPER	STURDILY	SUCHLIKE	SUNRISES	SURMISER	SWEEPING
STROBILA	STURGEON	SUCKLING	SUNROOFS	SURMISES	SWEETEST
STROKING	STUTTERS	SUDANESE	SUNSHADE	SURMOUNT	SWEETIES
STROLLED	STYLISTS	SUDATORY	SUNSHINE	SURNAMES	SWEET
STROLLER	STYLIZED	SUDDENLY	SUNSHINY	SURPLICE	PEA
STRONGER	STYLIZER	SUFFERED	SUNSPOTS	SURPRINT	SWEETSOP
STRONGLY	STYLUSES	SUFFERER	SUNTRAPS	SURPRISE	SWELLING
STROPHES	STYMYING	SUFFICED	SUN	SURROUND	SWERVING
STROPHIC	STYPTICS	SUFFICER	VISOR	SURVEYED	SWIFTEST
STRUDELS	SUBACUTE	SUFFIXAL	SUNWARDS	SURVEYOR	SWIGGING
STRUGGLE	SUBADULT	SUFFIXES	SUPADRIV	SURVIVAL	SWILLING
STRUMMED	SUBAGENT	SUFFRAGE	SUPERBLY	SURVIVED	SWIMMERS
STRUMMER	SUBCLASS	SUFFUSED	SUPEREGO	SURVIVOR	SWIMMING
STRUMPET	SUBDUING	SUGARING	SUPERFIX	SUSPECTS	SWIMSUIT
STRUNG-	SUBERIZE	SUICIDAL	SUPERIOR	SUSPENSE	SWINDLED
UP	SUBEROSE	SUICIDES	SUPERMAN	SUTURING	SWINDLER
STRUTTED	SUBFLOOR	SUITABLE	SUPERMEN	SUZERAIN	SWINDLES
STRUTTER	SUBGENUS	SUITABLY	SUPERNAL	SVALBARD	SWINEPOX
STUBBIER	SUBGROUP	SUITCASE	SUPERSEX	SVENGALI	SWINGBIN
STUBBILY	SUBHUMAN	SULAWESI	SUPERTAX	SWABBING	SWINGERS
STUBBING	SUBJECTS	SULKIEST	SUPINATE	SWADDLED	SWINGING
STUBBLED	SUBLEASE	SULLENER	SUPINELY	SWALLOWS	SWIRLING
STUBBORN	SUBMERGE	SULLENLY	SUPPLANT	SWAMPING	SWISHEST
STUCCOED	SUBMERSE	SULLYING	SUPPLEST	SWANKIER	SWISHING
					SWITCHED

SWITCHER
SWITCHES
SWIVELED
SWOONING
SWOOPING
SWOPPING
SWOTTING
SYBARITE
SYCAMINE
SYCAMORE
SYCONIUM
SYENITIC
SYLLABIC
SYLLABLE
SYLLABUB
SYLLABUS
SYLVATIC
SYMBIONT
SYMBOLIC
SYMMETRY
SYMPATHY
SYMPHILE
SYMPHONY
SYMPOSIA
SYMPTOMS
SYNAPSIS
SYNAPTIC
SYNARCHY
SYNCARPY
SYNCLINE
SYNCOPIC
SYNDESIS
SYNDETIC
SYNDETON
SYNDICAL
SYNDROME
SYNERGIC
SYNGAMIC
SYNONYMS
SYNONYMY
SYNOPSES
SYNOPSIS
SYNOPTIC
SYNOVIAL
SYNTONIC
SYPHILIS
SYPHONED
SYRACUSE
SYRINGED
SYRINGES
SYSTEMIC

SYSTOLIC
SYZYGIAL
SZCZECIN
SZECHWAN

T

TABLEAUS
TABLEAUX
TABLEMAT
TABLOIDS
TABULATE
TACITURN
TACKIEST
TACKLING
TACONITE
TACTICAL
TACTLESS
TADPOLES
TAFFRAIL
TAGANROG
TAGMEMIC
TAHITIAN
TAICHUNG
TAILBACK
TAILCOAT
TAIL
  ENDS
TAILGATE
TAILINGS
TAILLESS
TAILORED
TAIL
  PIPE
TAILRACE
TAILSKID
TAILSPIN
TAIL
  SPIN
TAILWIND
TAIL
  WIND
TAINTING
TAJ
  MAHAL
TAKE A
  BOW
TAKEAWAY
TAKE
  CARE
TAKEOFFS
TAKEOUTS
TAKEOVER

TAKES
  OFF
TAKORADI
TALAPOIN
TALENTED
TALESMAN
TALISMAN
TALKABLE
TALK
  SHOW
TALLBOYS
TALLNESS
TALLYING
TALLYMAN
TALMUDIC
TAMANDUA
TAMARACK
TAMARIND
TAMARISK
TAMBOURS
TAMEABLE
TAMENESS
TAMESIDE
TAMPERED
TAMPERER
TAMWORTH
TANDOORI
TANGENCY
TANGENTS
TANGIBLE
TANGIBLY
TANGIEST
TANGLING
TANGOING
TANGOIST
TANGSHAN
TANKARDS
TANKED
  UP
TANTALIC
TANTALUM
TANTALUS
TANTRUMS
TANZANIA
TAP
  DANCE
TAPE
  DECK
TAPENADE
TAPERING
TAPESTRY
TAPEWORM

TAPPABLE
TAPROOTS
TARAKIHI
TARBOOSH
TARDIEST
TARGETED
TARLATAN
TARRAGON
TARRYING
TARTARIC
TARTNESS
TARTRATE
TASHKENT
TASKWORK
TASK
  WORK
TASMANIA
TASSELED
TASSELLY
TASTABLE
TASTE
  BUD
TASTEFUL
TASTIEST
TATARIAN
TATTERED
TATTIEST
TATTLERS
TATTLING
TATTOOED
TATTOOER
TAUNTING
TAURANGA
TAUTENED
TAUTNESS
TAUTOMER
TAUTONYM
TAVERNER
TAWDRILY
TAXATION
TAX
  HAVEN
TAXINGLY
TAXI
  RANK
TAXONOMY
TAXPAYER
TEABERRY
TEA
  BREAK
TEA
  CADDY

TEACAKES
TEACHERS
TEA
  CHEST
TEACHING
TEACH-
  INS
TEA
  CLOTH
TEAHOUSE
TEA-
  MAKER
TEAM-
  MATE
TEAMSTER
TEAMWORK
TEA
  PARTY
TEARABLE
TEARAWAY
TEARDROP
TEAROOMS
TEASE
  OUT
TEASPOON
TEA
  TOWEL
TECHNICS
TECTONIC
TEDDY
  BOY
TEENAGER
TEE
  SHIRT
TEESSIDE
TEETERED
TEETHING
TEETOTAL
TEGMINAL
TELECAST
TELECOMS
TELEGONY
TELEGRAM
TELEMARK
TELEPLAY
TELETEXT
TELETYPE
TELEVISE
TELEWORK
TELEXING
TELLABLE
TELLTALE

TELLURIC
TELSONIC
TEMERITY
TEMPERED
TEMPERER
TEMPESTS
TEMPLATE
TEMPORAL
TEMPTERS
TEMPTING
TENACITY
TENANTRY
TENDENCY
TENDERED
TENDERER
TENDERLY
TENDRILS
TENEFIFE
TENEMENT
TENERIFE
TENESMIC
TENESMUS
TEN
  GURUS
TENON
  SAW
TENORIST
TENORITE
TENOTOMY
TENSED
  UP
TENSIBLE
TENSIONS
TENTACLE
TENURIAL
TEOCALLI
TEOSINTE
TEPHRITE
TEPIDITY
TERAFLOP
TERATISM
TERATOID
TERATOMA
TERAWATT
TERCEIRA
TEREBENE
TERESINA
TERMINAL
TERMINUS
TERMITES
TERMITIC

TERMLESS	THATCHER	THORACES	THWARTER	TINNITUS	TOILSOME
TERNOPOL	THATCHES	THORACIC	THYROIDS	TINPLATE	TOKENISM
TERPENIC	THEARCHY	THORAXES	THYRSOID	TINSELLY	TOLERANT
TERRACES	THEATRES	THORNIER	TIAN	TINSMITH	TOLERATE
TERRAINS	THEBAINE	THORNILY	SHAN	TINTACKS	TOLIDINE
TERRAPIN	THE	THOROUGH	TIBERIAS	TIPPABLE	TOLL
TERRAZZO	BIBLE	THOUGHTS	TICKETED	TIPPLERS	CALL
TERRIBLE	THE	THOUSAND	TICKLING	TIPSIEST	TOLL-
TERRIBLY	BLUES	THRALDOM	TICKLISH	TIPSTAFF	FREE
TERRIERS	THE	THRASHED	TICK	TIPSTERS	TOLLGATE
TERRIFIC	BRINY	THRASHER	OVER	TIRELESS	TOMAHAWK
TERTIARY	THEISTIC	THREADED	TICKTACK	TIRESIAS	TOMATOES
TERYLENE	THEMATIC	THREADER	TICKTOCK	TIRESOME	TOMBAUGH
TERZETTO	THEOCRAT	THREATEN	TIDDLERS	TITANATE	TOMBLIKE
TESSERAL	THEOLOGY	THREE-D	TIDEMARK	TITANISM	TOM
TESTABLE	THEOREMS	THREE-	TIDEWAYS	TITANITE	BROWN
TESTATOR	THEORIES	PLY	TIDINESS	TITANIUM	TOMENTUM
TEST	THEORIST	THRENODY	TIE	TITANOUS	TOMMY
BANS	THEORIZE	THRESHED	BREAK	TITCHIER	GUN
TEST	THEREMIN	THRESHER	TIE-	TITHABLE	TOMMYROT
CARD	THERMALS	THRESHES	BREAK	TITIVATE	TOMMY
TEST	THERMION	THRILLED	TIE-	TITMOUSE	ROT
CASE	THERMITE	THRILLER	DYING	TITOGRAD	TOMORROW
TEST-	THEROPOD	THRIVING	TIENTSIN	TITTERED	TONALITY
CASE	THESIGER	THROBBED	TIGHTEST	TITTERER	TONE-
TESTICLE	THESPIAN	THROMBIN	TIGHTWAD	TJIREBON	DEAF
TESTIEST	THESSALY	THROMBUS	TIGRAYAN	TLAXCALA	TONELESS
TEST	THEURGIC	THRONGED	TILEFISH	TOADFISH	TONE
TUBE	THE	THROTTLE	TILLABLE	TOADFLAX	POEM
TETANIZE	WEALD	THROWING	TILLICUM	TOADYING	TONICITY
TETCHIER	THIAMINE	THROW-	TIMBRELS	TOADYISM	TONLE
TETCHILY	THIAZINE	INS	TIMBUKTU	TO AND	SAP
TETHERED	THIAZOLE	THRUMMED	TIME	FRO	TONNAGES
TETRACID	THICKEST	THRUMMER	BOMB	TO-AND-	TONSURES
TETRAPOD	THICKETS	THRUSHES	TIMECARD	FRO	TOOTHIER
TETRARCH	THICKSET	THRUSTER	TIME	TOASTERS	TOOTHILY
TEUTONIC	THIEVERY	THRUWAYS	LAGS	TOASTING	TOOTLING
TEXTBOOK	THIEVING	THUDDING	TIMELESS	TOBACCOS	TOOTSIES
TEXTILES	THIEVISH	THUGGERY	TIMELIER	TOBOGGAN	TOPARCHY
TEXTUARY	THIMBLES	THUMBING	TIMEWORK	TOBY	TOP
TEXTURAL	THIN-	THUMBNUT	TIMEWORN	JUGS	BRASS
TEXTURES	FILM	THUMPING	TIME	TOCCATAS	TOPCOATS
THAILAND	THINKING	THUNDERS	ZONE	TOCOLOGY	TOP-
THALAMIC	THINNESS	THUNDERY	TIMIDITY	TODDLERS	DRESS
THALAMUS	THINNEST	THURIBLE	TIMORESE	TODDLING	TOP-
THALLIUM	THINNING	THURIFER	TIMOROUS	TOEHOLDS	HEAVY
THALLOID	THIONINE	THURROCK	TINCTURE	TOENAILS	TOPKNOTS
THALLOUS	THIOUREA	THURSDAY	TINGLING	TOGETHER	TOP-
THANKFUL	THIRTEEN	THWACKED	TINKERED	TOGOLESE	LEVEL
THANKING	THIRTIES	THWACKER	TINKERER	TOILETRY	TOP-
THANKYOU	THISTLES	THWARTED	TINKLING	TOILETTE	NOTCH
THATCHED	THONBURI	THWARTER	TINNIEST		TOPOLOGY

TOPONYMY
TOPOTYPE
TOPPINGS
TOPPLING
TOP-
  SHELL
TORCHERE
TORCHIER
TOREADOR
TORE
  DOWN
TOREUTIC
TORMENTS
TORNADIC
TORNADOS
TOROIDAL
TORPIDLY
TORQUATE
TORRANCE
TORRENTS
TORRIDLY
TORTELLI
TORTILLA
TORTIOUS
TORTOISE
TORTUOUS
TORTURED
TORTURER
TORTURES
TOTALING
TOTALITY
TOTALIZE
TOTALLED
TOTE
  BAGS
TOTEMISM
TOTEMIST
TOTTERED
TOTTERER
TOUCHIER
TOUCHILY
TOUCHING
TOUGHEST
TOULOUSE
TOURAINE
TOURISTS
TOURISTY
TOURNEYS
TOUSLING
TOWELING
TOWELLED

TOWERING
TOWN
  HALL
TOWNSHIP
TOWNSMAN
TOWNSMEN
TOWPATHS
TOWPLANE
TOWROPES
TOXAEMIA
TOXAEMIC
TOXICANT
TOXICITY
TRACHEAL
TRACHEAS
TRACHEID
TRACHOMA
TRACHYTE
TRACINGS
TRACKING
TRACTATE
TRACTILE
TRACTION
TRACTIVE
TRACTORS
TRADABLE
TRADE
  GAP
TRADE
  OFF
TRADE-
  OFF
TRAD
  JAZZ
TRADUCED
TRADUCER
TRAFFORD
TRAGOPAN
TRAILERS
TRAILING
TRAINEES
TRAINERS
TRAINING
TRAIN
  SET
TRAIPSED
TRAITORS
TRAMLINE
TRAMMELS
TRAMPING
TRAMPLED
TRAMPLER

TRANNIES
TRANQUIL
TRANSACT
TRANSECT
TRANSEPT
TRANSFER
TRANSFIX
TRANSITS
TRANSKEI
TRANSMIT
TRANSOMS
TRANSUDE
TRAPDOOR
TRAPEZES
TRAPEZIA
TRAPPERS
TRAPPING
TRAPPIST
TRAPUNTO
TRASHCAN
TRASHIER
TRASHILY
TRASHING
TRAVELED
TRAVERSE
TRAVESTY
TRAWLERS
TRAWLING
TREADING
TREADLER
TREADLES
TREASURE
TREASURY
TREATIES
TREATING
TREATISE
TREATIZE
TREBLING
TREE
  FERN
TREELESS
TREELINE
TREENAIL
TREFOILS
TREKKING
TREMBLED
TREMBLER
TREMBLES
TREMOLOS
TRENCHER
TRENCHES

TRENDIER
TRENDIES
TRENDIFY
TRENDILY
TREPHINE
TRESPASS
TRESSURE
TRESTLES
TRIADISM
TRIAL
  RUN
TRIANGLE
TRIARCHY
TRIASSIC
TRIAXIAL
TRIAZINE
TRIAZOLE
TRIBADIC
TRIBASIC
TRIBRACH
TRIBUNAL
TRIBUNES
TRIBUTES
TRICHINA
TRICHITE
TRICHOID
TRICHOME
TRICKERY
TRICKIER
TRICKILY
TRICKING
TRICKLED
TRICTRAC
TRICYCLE
TRIDENTS
TRIFLING
TRIFOCAL
TRIGGERS
TRIGLYPH
TRIGONAL
TRIGRAPH
TRILBIES
TRILEMMA
TRILLING
TRILLION
TRILLIUM
TRIMARAN
TRIMETER
TRIMMERS
TRIMMEST
TRIMMING

TRIMNESS
TRIMORPH
TRINIDAD
TRINKETS
TRIOXIDE
TRIPLANE
TRIPLETS
TRIPLING
TRIPLOID
TRIPODAL
TRIPOSES
TRIPPERS
TRIPPING
TRIPTANE
TRIPTYCH
TRIPWIRE
TRIREMES
TRISOMIC
TRISTICH
TRITICUM
TRIUMPHS
TRIUNITY
TROCHAIC
TROCHEES
TROCHLEA
TROCHOID
TROLLEYS
TROLLING
TROLLOPS
TROMBONE
TROOPERS
TROOPING
TROPHIES
TROPICAL
TROTLINE
TROTTERS
TROTTING
TROUBLED
TROUBLER
TROUBLES
TROUNCED
TROUPERS
TROUPIAL
TROUSERS
TRUCKERS
TRUCKING
TRUCKLED
TRUDGING
TRUE-
  BLUE
TRUEBORN

TRUE-
  LIFE
TRUELOVE
TRUE
  LOVE
TRUENESS
TRUFFLES
TRUISTIC
TRUJILLO
TRUMPERY
TRUMPETS
TRUMPING
TRUNCATE
TRUNDLED
TRUNNION
TRUSSING
TRUSTEES
TRUSTFUL
TRUSTIER
TRUSTIES
TRUSTILY
TRUSTING
TRUTHFUL
TSARINAS
TSESSEBI
TSINGHAI
TSINGTAO
T-
  SQUARE
  S
TSUSHIMA
TUBBIEST
TUBELESS
TUBERCLE
TUBEROSE
TUBEROUS
TUBIFORM
TUBULATE
TUBULOUS
TUCKERED
TUCOTUCO
TUESDAYS
TUG OF
  WAR
TUG-OF-
  WAR
TUMBLERS
TUMBLING
TUMBRELS
TUMIDITY
TUMOROUS
TUMULOSE

TUNELESS
TUNGSTEN
TUNGSTIC
TUNGUSIC
TUNICATE
TUNISIAN
TUNNELED
TUNNELER
TUPPENCE
TUPPENNY
TURBANED
TURBINES
TURBOCAR
TURBOFAN
TURBOJET
TURGIDLY
TURKOMAN
TURMERIC
TURNABLE
TURNCOAT
TURNCOCK
TURN
 DOWN
TURNINGS
TURNKEYS
TURN-
 OFFS
TURNOUTS
TURNOVER
TURNPIKE
TURNSOLE
TURRETED
TUSKLIKE
TUSSLING
TUSSOCKS
TUSSOCKY
TUTELAGE
TUTELARY
TUTORAGE
TUTORIAL
TUTORING
TV
 DINNER
TWADDLER
TWANGING
TWEAKING
TWEETERS
TWEETING
TWEEZERS
TWELFTHS
TWELVEMO

TWENTIES
TWIDDLED
TWIDDLER
TWIDDLES
TWIGGING
TWILIGHT
TWIN
 BEDS
TWINKLED
TWINKLER
TWINNING
TWIN
 SETS
TWIRLERS
TWIRLING
TWISTERS
TWISTIER
TWISTING
TWITCHED
TWITCHER
TWITCHES
TWITTERS
TWITTERY
TWITTING
TWOCCING
TWO-
 EDGED
TWOFACED
TWO
 FACED
TWOPENCE
TWO
 PENCE
TWOPENNY
TWO-
 PHASE
TWO-
 PIECE
TWO-
 SIDED
TWOSOMES
TWO-
 STEPS
TWO-
 TIMED
TWO-
 TIMER
TYMPANIC
TYMPANUM
TYNESIDE
TYPECAST

TYPE
 CAST
TYPEFACE
TYPE
 FACE
TYPE-
 HIGH
TYPHONIC
TYPHOONS
TYPIFIED
TYPIFIER
TYPOLOGY
TYRAMINE
TYROLESE
TYROSINE
TZARINAS
TZATZIKI

U

UBIQUITY
UBI
 SUPRA
UGLIFIER
UGLINESS
UIGURIAN
UKULELES
ULCERATE
ULCEROUS
ULTERIOR
ULTIMATA
ULTIMATE
ULTRAISM
ULTRAIST
UMBONATE
UMBRAGES
UMBRELLA
UMPIRING
UNABATED
UNAWARES
UNBACKED
UNBARRED
UNBEATEN
UNBELIEF
UNBIASED
UNBIDDEN
UNBODIED
UNBOLTED
UNBRIDLE
UNBROKEN
UNBUCKLE
UNBURDEN

UNBUTTON
UNCAPPED
UNCHASTE
UNCHURCH
UNCIFORM
UNCINATE
UNCLENCH
UNCLE
 SAM
UNCLE
 TOM
UNCLOTHE
UNCOINED
UNCOMMON
UNCORKED
UNCOUPLE
UNCTUOUS
UNDAMPED
UNDERACT
UNDERAGE
UNDERARM
UNDERBID
UNDERBUY
UNDERCUT
UNDERDOG
UNDERFUR
UNDERLAY
UNDERLET
UNDERLIE
UNDERLIP
UNDERPAY
UNDERPIN
UNDERSEA
UNDERSET
UNDERTOW
UNDERUSE
UNDULANT
UNDULATE
UNEARNED
UNEASIER
UNEASILY
UNENDING
UNERRING
UNEVENLY
UNFAIRER
UNFAIRLY
UNFASTEN
UNFETTER
UNFILIAL
UNFOLDED
UNFOLDER

UNFORCED
UNFORMED
UNFREEZE
UNFURLED
UNGAINLY
UNGUENTS
UNGULATE
UNHANDED
UNHEALED
UNHINGED
UNHORSED
UNIATISM
UNIAXIAL
UNICORNS
UNICYCLE
UNIFORMS
UNIFYING
UNIONISM
UNIONIST
UNIONIZE
UNIPOLAR
UNIQUELY
UNITEDLY
UNIVALVE
UNIVERSE
UNIVOCAL
UNKENNEL
UNKINDER
UNKINDLY
UNKNOWNS
UNLAWFUL
UNLIKELY
UNLIMBER
UNLISTED
UNLOADED
UNLOADER
UNLOCKED
UNLOOSED
UNLOOSEN
UNLOVELY
UNMANNED
UNMARKED
UNMASKED
UNMASKER
UNMUZZLE
UNNERVED
UNOPENED
UNPACKED
UNPACKER
UNPEOPLE
UNPICKED

UNPLACED
UNPOLLED
UNPRICED
UNPROFOR
UNPROVEN
UNREASON
UNRIDDLE
UNRIFLED
UNROLLED
UNSADDLE
UNSEATED
UNSEEDED
UNSEEING
UNSEEMLY
UNSETTLE
UNSHAPEN
UNSHAVEN
UNSOCIAL
UNSPOKEN
UNSTABLE
UNSTEADY
UNSTRING
UNSUBTLE
UNSUITED
UNSWATHE
UNTANGLE
UNTAPPED
UNTAUGHT
UNTHREAD
UNTIDILY
UNTIMELY
UNTIRING
UNTITLED
UNTOWARD
UNTRENDY
UNTRUTHS
UNUSABLE
UNVALUED
UNVEILED
UNVERSED
UNVOICED
UNWALLED
UNWASHED
UNWEIGHT
UNWIELDY
UNWINDER
UNWISHED
UNWONTED
UNWORTHY
UNZIPPED

UP- ANCHOR	UROSCOPY	VALVULAR	VENEERED	VESUVIAN	VINOSITY
UP-AND- UPS	UROSTYLE	VAMBRACE	VENEERER	VESUVIUS	VINTAGER
UPCOMING	URSULINE	VAMOOSED	VENERATE	VETERANS	VINTAGES
UPDATING	URTICATE	VAMPIRES	VENEREAL	VEXATION	VINTNERS
UPENDING	URUSHIOL	VAMPIRIC	VENETIAN	VEXILLUM	VIOLABLE
UPGRADED	USEFULLY	VANADATE	VENGEFUL	VEXINGLY	VIOLATED
UPGRADER	USHERING	VANADIUM	VENOMOUS	VIADUCTS	VIOLATOR
UPGROWTH	USUFRUCT	VANADOUS	VENOSITY	VIA MEDIA	VIOLENCE
UPHEAVAL	USURIOUS	VANGUARD	VENTOLIN	VIATICAL	VIPERINE
UPHOLDER	USURPERS	VANILLIC	VENTOUSE	VIATICUM	VIPEROUS
UPLIFTED	USURPING	VANILLIN	VENTURED	VIBRANCY	VIRAGOES
UPLIFTER	UTENSILS	VANISHED	VENTURER	VIBRATED	VIRGINAL
UP- MARKET	UTERUSES	VANISHER	VENTURES	VIBRATOR	VIRGINIA
UPPERCUT	UTILIZED	VANQUISH	VENUSIAN	VIBRATOS	VIRIDIAN
UPRAISER	UTILIZER	VAPIDITY	VERACITY	VIBRIOID	VIRIDITY
UPRISING	UTTERING	VAPORIZE	VERACRUZ	VIBRISSA	VIRILISM
UPROOTED	UVULITIS	VAPOROUS	VERANDAS	VIBRONIC	VIRILITY
UPROOTER	UXORIOUS	VAPOURER	VERBALLY	VIBURNUM	VIROLOGY
UPSETTER		VARACTOR	VERBATIM	VICARAGE	VIRTUOSI
UPSTAGED	**V**	VARANASI	VERBIAGE	VICARIAL	VIRTUOSO
UPSTAIRS	VACANTLY	VARIABLE	VERBOTEN	VICELIKE	VIRTUOUS
UPSTARTS	VACATING	VARIABLY	VERCELLI	VICENARY	VIRULENT
UPSTREAM	VACATION	VARIANCE	VERDANCY	VICEROYS	VISCACHA
UPSTROKE	VACCINAL	VARIANTS	VERDICTS	VICINITY	VISCERAL
UPSURGES	VACCINES	VARICOSE	VERIFIED	VICTORIA	VISCOUNT
UPSWINGS	VACCINIA	VARIETAL	VERIFIER	VICTUALS	VISIONAL
UPTHRUST	VACUOLAR	VARIFORM	VERISTIC	VIDEOFIT	VISITANT
UP TO DATE	VACUUMED	VARIOLAR	VERITIES	VIDEOING	VISITING
UP-TO- DATE	VADODARA	VARIORUM	VERJUICE	VIENNESE	VISITORS
UPTURNED	VAGABOND	VARISTOR	VERLIGTE	VIETCONG	VISUALLY
URALITIC	VAGARIES	VARITYPE	VERMOUTH	VIETMINH	VITALISM
URANITIC	VAGINATE	VARMINTS	VERONESE	VIEWLESS	VITALIST
URANYLIC	VAGOTOMY	VASCULAR	VERONICA	VIGILANT	VITALITY
URBANELY	VAGRANCY	VASCULUM	VERRUCAE	VIGNETTE	VITALIZE
URBANITY	VAGRANTS	VASELINE	VERRUCAS	VIGOROSO	VITAMINS
URBANIZE	VAINNESS	VASTERAS	VERSICLE	VIGOROUS	VITELLIN
URETERAL	VALANCED	VASTNESS	VERSIONS	VILENESS	VITIABLE
URETHANE	VALANCES	VAUCLUSE	VERTEBRA	VILIFIED	VITIATED
URETHRAL	VALDIVIA	VAULTERS	VERTEXES	VILIFIER	VITIATOR
URETHRAS	VAL- D'OISE	VAULTING	VERTICAL	VILLAGER	VITI LEVU
URGENTLY	VALENCIA	VAUNTING	VERTICES	VILLAGES	VITILIGO
URGINGLY	VALERIAN	VEGETATE	VERTICIL	VILLAINS	VITREOUS
URINATED	VALIANCE	VEHEMENT	VESICANT	VILLAINY	VITULINE
URNFIELD	VALIDATE	VEHICLES	VESICATE	VILLATIC	VIVACITY
UROCHORD	VALIDITY	VEILEDLY	VESICLES	VILLEINS	VIVARIUM
UROLOGIC	VALLETTA	VELARIZE	VESPERAL	VINCULUM	VIVA VOCE
UROPODAL	VALORIZE	VELOCITY	VESPIARY	VINDALOO	VIVIFIER
	VALOROUS	VENALITY	VESTIGES	VINEGARY	VIVISECT
	VALUABLE	VENATION	VESTMENT	VINEYARD	VIXENISH
	VALUATOR	VENDETTA	VESTRIES	VINNITSA	
		VENDIBLE	VESTURAL		

VLADIMIR
VOCALESE
VOCALISE
VOCALISM
VOCALIST
VOCALITY
VOCALIZE
VOCATION
VOCATIVE
VOICE
  BOX
VOICEFUL
VOIDABLE
VOIDANCE
VOLATILE
VOLCANIC
VOLCANOS
VOLITION
VOLITIVE
VOLLEYED
VOLLEYER
VOLPLANE
VOLTAGES
VOLTAISM
VOLUTION
VOLVULUS
VOMERINE
VOMITING
VOMITIVE
VOMITORY
VONNEGUT
VOORSKOT
VORACITY
VORONEZH
VORTEXES
VORTICAL
VORTICES
VOTARESS
VOTARIES
VOTARIST
VOUCHERS
VOUCHING
VOUSSOIR
VOWELIZE
VOYAGERS
VOYAGING
VULGARLY
VULTURES
VULVITIS

W
WADDLING
WAFFLING
WAGERING
WAGGLING
WAGON-
  LIT
WAGTAILS
WAINSCOT
WAITRESS
WAKASHAN
WAKAYAMA
WAKELESS
WAKENING
WALKABLE
WALKAWAY
WALKMANS
WALKOUTS
WALKOVER
WALLAROO
WALLASEY
WALLEYED
WALL-
  LIKE
WALLOPED
WALLOPER
WALLOWED
WALLOWER
WALLSEND
WALRUSES
WALTZING
WANDERED
WANDERER
WANDEROO
WANGANUI
WANGLING
WANTONLY
WARANGAL
WARBLERS
WARBLING
WAR
  CRIES
WAR
  CRIME
WAR
  DANCE
WARDENRY
WARDRESS
WARDROBE
WARDROOM
WARDSHIP

WARFARIN
WAR
  GAMES
WARHEADS
WARHORSE
WARINESS
WARLOCKS
WARLORDS
WARMNESS
WARNINGS
WAR
  PAINT
WARPATHS
WARPLANE
WARRANTS
WARRANTY
WARRIGAL
WARRIORS
WARSHIPS
WARTBURG
WARTHOGS
WASHABLE
WASHBOWL
WASHDAYS
WASHED-
  UP
WASHOUTS
WASHROOM
WASTABLE
WASTEFUL
WASTRELS
WATCHDOG
WATCHFUL
WATCHING
WATCHMAN
WATCHMEN
WATERAGE
WATER
  BAG
WATERBED
WATER
  ICE
WATERING
WATERLOO
WATERMAN
WATER
  RAT
WATER
  SKI
WATER-
  SKI
WATERWAY

WATT-
  HOUR
WAVE
  BAND
WAVEFORM
WAVELIKE
WAVERERS
WAVERING
WAVINESS
WAXBERRY
WAXINESS
WAXPLANT
WAXWORKS
WAYBILLS
WAYFARER
WAYLAYER
WEAKENED
WEAKENER
WEAKFISH
WEAKLING
WEAKNESS
WEANLING
WEAPONED
WEAPONRY
WEARABLE
WEARIEST
WEARYING
WEASELED
WEASELLY
WEDDINGS
WEDGWOOD
WEEDIEST
WEEKDAYS
WEEKENDS
WEEKLIES
WEENIEST
WEIGHING
WEIGHTED
WEIGHTER
WEIRDEST
WELCHING
WELCOMED
WELCOMER
WELCOMES
WELDABLE
WELL-
  BRED
WELL
  DONE
WELL-
  DONE
WELLHEAD

WELL
  HEAD
WELL-
  HUNG
WELL-
  KNIT
WELL-
  NIGH
WELL
  READ
WELL-
  READ
WELL-TO-
  DO
WELL-
  WORN
WELSHERS
WELSHING
WENCHING
WEREWOLF
WESLEYAN
WEST
  BANK
WESTERLY
WESTERNS
WESTWARD
WESTWOOD
WET
  DREAM
WET
  NURSE
WET
  SUITS
WETTABLE
WETTINGS
WEYMOUTH
WHACKING
WHARFAGE
WHATEVER
WHATNOTS
WHATSITS
WHEATEAR
WHEEDLED
WHEEDLER
WHEELIES
WHEELING
WHEEZILY
WHEEZING
WHENEVER
WHEREVER
WHETTING
WHEYFACE

WHICKERS
WHIFFIER
WHIGGERY
WHIGGISH
WHIMBREL
WHIMPERS
WHIMSIES
WHINCHAT
WHINGING
WHINNIED
WHINNIES
WHIPCORD
WHIP
  HAND
WHIPLASH
WHIPLIKE
WHIPPETS
WHIPPING
WHIPWORM
WHIRLING
WHIRRING
WHISKERS
WHISKERY
WHISKIES
WHISKING
WHISPERS
WHISTLED
WHISTLER
WHISTLES
WHITE
  ANT
WHITECAP
WHITE-
  EYE
WHITEFLY
WHITE-
  HOT
WHITE
  LIE
WHITENED
WHITENER
WHITEOUT
WHITE-
  TIE
WHITINGS
WHITLOWS
WHITTLED
WHITTLER
WHIZ-
  BANG
WHIZZING

WHIZZ
KID
WHODUNIT
WHOMEVER
WHOOPEES
WHOOPING
WHOOSHES
WHOPPERS
WHOPPING
WHOREDOM
WICKEDLY
WIDE
BOYS
WIDE-
EYED
WIDENESS
WIDENING
WIDE
OPEN
WIDE-
OPEN
WIDGEONS
WIDOWERS
WIELDERS
WIELDING
WIGGINGS
WIGGLING
WILD
BOAR
WILD
CARD
WILDCATS
WILD-
EYED
WILDFIRE
WILDFOWL
WILDLIFE
WILDNESS
WILD
OATS
WILD
WEST
WILFULLY
WILINESS
WILLABLE
WILLIWAW
WINCHING
WINDABLE
WINDBAGS
WINDBURN
WINDFALL
WINDGALL

WINDHOEK
WINDIEST
WINDLASS
WINDMILL
WINDPIPE
WINDSAIL
WINDSOCK
WINDWARD
WINE
BARS
WINESKIN
WINGLESS
WINGLIKE
WING
NUTS
WINGOVER
WINGSPAN
WINKLING
WINNABLE
WINNINGS
WINNIPEG
WINNOWED
WINNOWER
WINTERED
WINTERER
WINTRIER
WINTRILY
WIPED
OUT
WIREDRAW
WIRELESS
WIRETAPS
WIRE
WOOL
WIREWORK
WIREWORM
WIRE-
WOVE
WIRINESS
WISEACRE
WISE
GUYS
WISENESS
WISHBONE
WISPIEST
WISTERIA
WITCHERY
WITCHING
WITHDRAW
WITHDREW
WITHERED
WITHERER

WITHHELD
WITHHOLD
WITTIEST
WIZARDRY
WOBBLIER
WOBBLING
WOEFULLY
WOLFFISH
WOLFLIKE
WOMANISH
WOMANIST
WOMANIZE
WOMBLIKE
WONDERED
WONDERER
WONDROUS
WONKIEST
WOODBINE
WOODCHAT
WOODCOCK
WOODCUTS
WOODENLY
WOODIEST
WOODLAND
WOODLARK
WOODLICE
WOODNOTE
WOODPILE
WOOD
PULP
WOODRUFF
WOODRUSH
WOODSHED
WOODSMAN
WOODSMEN
WOODWIND
WOODWORK
WOODWORM
WOOLLENS
WOOLLIER
WOOLLIES
WOOLLILY
WOOLPACK
WOOLSACK
WOOZIEST
WORDBOOK
WORD-
DEAF
WORDIEST
WORDLESS
WORDPLAY

WORKABLE
WORKADAY
WORKBAGS
WORKBOOK
WORKDAYS
WORKED
UP
WORKINGS
WORKLOAD
WORKOUTS
WORKROOM
WORKSHOP
WORKTOPS
WORLD
CUP
WORM
CAST
WORM
GEAR
WORMHOLE
WORMIEST
WORMLIKE
WORMSEED
WORMWOOD
WORRIERS
WORRYING
WORSENED
WORSE-
OFF
WORSHIPS
WORSTING
WORST-
OFF
WORTHIER
WORTHIES
WORTHILY
WORTHING
WOUNDING
WRANGLED
WRANGLER
WRANGLES
WRAPOVER
WRAPPERS
WRAPPING
WRATHFUL
WREAKING
WREATHED
WRECKAGE
WRECKERS
WRECKING
WRENCHED
WRENCHES

WRESTING
WRESTLED
WRESTLER
WRETCHED
WRETCHES
WRIGGLED
WRIGGLER
WRIGGLES
WRINGERS
WRINGING
WRINKLED
WRINKLES
WRISTLET
WRITE-
INS
WRITE
OFF
WRITE-
OFF
WRITE-
UPS
WRITHING
WRITINGS
WRONGFUL
WRONGING
WURZBURG

X
XANTHATE
XANTHEIN
XANTHENE
XANTHINE
XANTHOMA
XANTHOUS
XENOGAMY
XENOLITH
XEROSERE
XEROXING
XIANGTAN
X-RAY
TUBE
XYLIDINE
XYLOCARP
XYLOTOMY

Y
YACHTING
YAHOOISM
YAKITORI
YAMMERED
YAMMERER
YARDARMS

YARN-
DYED
YASHMAKS
YEANLING
YEARBOOK
YEARLING
YEARLONG
YEARNING
YEASTILY
YELLOWED
YEOMANLY
YEOMANRY
YIELDING
YODELING
YODELLED
YODELLER
YOKELISH
YOKOHAMA
YOKOSUKA
YOUNGEST
YOUNGISH
YOURSELF
YOUTHFUL
YTTERBIA
YUCKIEST
YUGOSLAV
YULE
LOGS
YULETIDE
YVELINES

Z
ZAANSTAD
ZAIBATSU
ZANINESS
ZANZIBAR
ZAPPIEST
ZARAGOZA
ZARATITE
ZEALOTRY
ZECCHINO
ZENITHAL
ZEOLITIC
ZEPPELIN
ZERO
HOUR
ZHEJIANG
ZHITOMIR
ZIBELINE
ZILLIONS
ZIMBABWE

ZIONISTS	ZLATOUST	ZOOGLOEA	ZOONOSIS	ZOOTOXIC	ZYGOTENE
ZIP	ZODIACAL	ZOOLATER	ZOOPHILE	ZOOTOXIN	ZYMOLOGY
CODES	ZOMBIISM	ZOOLATRY	ZOOPHYTE	ZUCCHINI	
ZIPPIEST	ZONATION	ZOOMETRY	ZOOSPERM	ZUGZWANG	
ZIRCONIA	ZONETIME	ZOOM	ZOOSPORE	ZULULAND	
ZIRCONIC	ZOOCHORE	LENS	ZOOTOMIC	ZWIEBACK	

A	ABSTRACTS	ACIDOPHIL	ADHERENTS	ADVOCATES
AARONS ROD	ABSURDISM	ACID TESTS	ADHESIONS	AEOLIPILE
ABACTINAL	ABSURDITY	ACIDULATE	ADHESIVES	AEPYORNIS
ABANDONED	ABUNDANCE	ACIDULOUS	ADIABATIC	AEROBATIC
ABASEMENT	ABU SIMBEL	ACINIFORM	AD INTERIM	AERODROME
ABASHEDLY	ABUSIVELY	ACOUSTICS	ADIPOCERE	AEROLOGIC
ABATEMENT	ABUTMENTS	ACQUIESCE	ADJACENCY	AEROMETER
ABATTOIRS	ABYSSINIA	ACQUIRING	ADJECTIVE	AEROMETRY
ABCOULOMB	ACADEMICS	ACQUITTAL	ADJOINING	AEROPAUSE
ABDICABLE	ACANTHINE	ACQUITTED	ADJOURNED	AEROPHONE
ABDICATED	ACANTHOID	ACQUITTER	ADJUDGING	AEROPLANE
ABDICATOR	ACANTHOUS	ACROBATIC	ADJUSTING	AEROSPACE
ABDOMINAL	ACARIASIS	ACRODROME	ADJUTANCY	AESTHESIA
ABDUCTING	ACAROLOGY	ACROGENIC	ADJUTANTS	AESTHETES
ABDUCTION	ACCEDENCE	ACRONYMIC	AD-LIBBING	AESTHETIC
ABERRANCE	ACCENTING	ACROPETAL	ADMEASURE	AESTIVATE
ABHORRENT	ACCENTUAL	ACROPOLIS	ADMINICLE	AETHEREAL
ABHORRING	ACCEPTANT	ACROSPIRE	ADMIRABLE	AETIOLOGY
ABIDINGLY	ACCEPTING	ACROSTICS	ADMIRABLY	AFFECTING
ABILITIES	ACCESSING	ACTINOPOD	ADMIRALTY	AFFECTION
A BIT	ACCESSION	ACTIVATED	ADMISSION	AFFECTIVE
THICK	ACCESSORY	ACTIVATOR	ADMISSIVE	AFFIANCED
ABJECTION	ACCIDENCE	ACTIVISTS	ADMITTING	AFFIDAVIT
ABLUTIONS	ACCIDENTS	ACTRESSES	ADMIXTURE	AFFILIATE
ABNEGATOR	ACCIPITER	ACTS OF	AD NAUSEAM	AFFIRMING
ABOLISHED	ACCLAIMED	GOD	ADNOMINAL	AFFIXTURE
ABOLISHER	ACCLIVITY	ACTUALITY	ADOPTIONS	AFFLICTED
ABOLITION	ACCOLADES	ACTUALIZE	ADORATION	AFFLUENCE
ABOMINATE	ACCOMPANY	ACTUARIAL	ADORNMENT	AFFORDING
ABORIGINE	ACCORDANT	ACTUARIES	ADRENALIN	AFFRICATE
ABORTIONS	ACCORDING	ACTUATING	ADSORBATE	AFFRONTED
ABOUNDING	ACCORDION	ACTUATION	ADSORBENT	AFLATOXIN
ABOUT TURN	ACCOSTING	ACUMINATE	ADULATION	AFORESAID
ABOUT-TURN	ACCOUNTED	ACUMINOUS	ADULATORY	A FORTIORI
ABRASIONS	ACCRETION	ACUTENESS	ADULTERER	AFRIKAANS
ABRASIVES	ACCRETIVE	ACYCLOVIR	ADUMBRATE	AFRIKANER
ABRIDGING	ACCRUMENT	ADAMANTLY	AD VALOREM	AFRO-ASIAN
ABROGATED	ACCUMBENT	ADAPTABLE	ADVANCING	AFTERBODY
ABROGATOR	ACELLULAR	ADDICTION	ADVANTAGE	AFTERCARE
ABSCESSES	ACESCENCE	ADDICTIVE	ADVECTION	AFTERDAMP
ABSCONDED	ACETAMIDE	ADDITIONS	ADVENTIVE	AFTERDECK
ABSCONDER	ACETIFIER	ADDITIVES	ADVENTURE	AFTERGLOW
ABSEILING	ACETYLATE	ADDRESSED	ADVERBIAL	AFTERHEAT
ABSENTEES	ACETYLENE	ADDRESSEE	ADVERSARY	AFTERLIFE
ABSENTING	ACETYLIDE	ADDRESSER	ADVERSELY	AFTERMATH
ABSOLVING	ACHEULIAN	ADDRESSES	ADVERSITY	AFTERNOON
ABSORBENT	ACHIEVING	ADDUCTION	ADVERTING	AFTERWORD
ABSORBING	ACICULATE	ADEMPTION	ADVERTISE	AGE GROUPS
ABSTAINED	ACID HOUSE	ADENOIDAL	ADVISABLE	AGGRAVATE
ABSTAINER	ACIDIFIED	ADENOSINE	ADVISEDLY	AGGREGATE
ABSTINENT	ACIDIFIER	ADHERENCE	ADVOCATED	AGGRESSOR

AGGRIEVED
AGITATING
AGITATION
AGITATORS
AGNOLOTTI
AGNOMINAL
AGNOSTICS
AGONISTIC
AGONIZING
AGREEABLE
AGREEABLY
AGREEMENT
AGRIGENTO
AGRONOMIC
AGTERSKOT
AHMEDABAD
AILANTHUS
AIMLESSLY
AIRBRAKES
AIRFIELDS
AIRFORCES
AIR GUITAR
AIR-INTAKE
AIRLETTER
AIRLIFTED
AIRLINERS
AIRPLANES
AIRPOCKET
AIRSTREAM
AIRSTRIPS
AIRWORTHY
AITCHBONE
ALABAMIAN
ALABASTER
ALARM BELL
ALARMISTS
ALBATROSS
ALBERTITE
ALBESCENT
ALCHEMIST
ALCHEMIZE
ALCOHOLIC
ALDEBARAN
ALDEBURGH
ALDERSHOT
ALEHOUSES
ALEMANNIC
ALEPH-NULL
ALERTNESS
ALFILARIA
ALGARROBA

ALGEBRAIC
ALGECIRAS
ALGOMETER
ALGOMETRY
ALGONQUIN
ALGORITHM
ALICE BAND
ALICYCLIC
ALIENABLE
ALIENATED
ALIENATOR
ALIGHTING
ALIGNMENT
ALIPHATIC
ALKALOSIS
ALLA BREVE
ALLAHABAD
ALLANTOIC
ALLANTOID
ALLANTOIS
ALL-AROUND
ALL AT
  ONCE
ALLEGEDLY
ALLELUIAS
ALL ENDS
  UP
ALLENTOWN
ALLERGIES
ALLERGIST
ALLETHRIN
ALLEVIATE
ALLEYWAYS
ALLIANCES
ALLIGATOR
ALLOCATED
ALLOGRAFT
ALLOGRAPH
ALLOMETRY
ALLOMORPH
ALLOPATHY
ALLOPHANE
ALLOPHONE
ALLOPLASM
ALLOTMENT
ALLOTROPE
ALLOTROPY
ALLOTTING
ALLOWABLE
ALLOWABLY
ALLOWANCE

ALLOWEDLY
ALLUSIONS
ALLUVIUMS
ALMA MATER
ALMANDINE
ALMSHOUSE
ALMS-HOUSE
ALONGSIDE
ALOOFNESS
ALPENGLOW
ALPHABETS
ALSATIANS
ALTERABLE
ALTERCATE
ALTER EGOS
ALTERNATE
ALTIMETER
ALTIMETRY
ALTIPLANO
ALTISSIMO
ALTITUDES
ALTRICIAL
ALTRUISTS
ALUMINATE
ALUMINIUM
ALUMINIZE
ALUMINOUS
ALVEOLARS
ALVEOLATE
AMAGASAKI
AMARYLLIS
AMAUROSIS
AMAUROTIC
AMAZEMENT
AMAZINGLY
AMAZONIAN
AMAZONITE
AMBERGRIS
AMBERJACK
AMBIENCES
AMBIGUITY
AMBIGUOUS
AMBITIONS
AMBITIOUS
AMBLESIDE
AMBLYOPIA
AMBLYOPIC
AMBROSIAL
AMBROTYPE
AMBULANCE
AMBUSHING

AMENDABLE
AMENDMENT
AMENITIES
AMERASIAN
AMERICANA
AMERICANS
AMERICIUM
AMERINDIC
AMETHYSTS
AMETROPIA
AMIANTHUS
AMIDSHIPS
AMINO ACID
AMMOCOETE
AMMONIATE
AMMONICAL
AMMONITIC
AMNESIACS
AMNESTIES
AMOEBAEAN
AMORALITY
AMOROUSLY
AMORPHISM
AMORPHOUS
AMORTIZED
AMOUNTING
AMPERSAND
AMPHIBIAN
AMPHIBOLE
AMPHIGORY
AMPHIOXUS
AMPLIFIED
AMPLIFIER
AMPLITUDE
AMPUTATED
AMSTERDAM
AMUSEMENT
AMUSINGLY
AMYGDALIN
AMYLOPSIN
ANABANTID
ANABIOSIS
ANABOLISM
ANABOLITE
ANACLINAL
ANACLISIS
ANACLITIC
ANACONDAS
ANACRUSIS
ANAEROBIC
ANALECTIC

ANALEPTIC
ANALGESIA
ANALGESIC
ANALOGIES
ANALOGIST
ANALOGIZE
ANALOGOUS
ANALOGUES
ANALYSAND
ANALYSING
ANALYTICS
ANAMNESIS
ANANDROUS
ANANTHOUS
ANAPAESTS
ANAPESTIC
ANAPHORAL
ANAPLASIA
ANAPLASTY
ANAPTYXIS
ANARCHISM
ANARCHIST
ANARTHRIA
ANATHEMAS
ANATOLIAN
ANATOMIES
ANATOMIST
ANATOMIZE
ANCESTORS
ANCESTRAL
ANCHORAGE
ANCHORESS
ANCHORING
ANCHORITE
ANCHOVIES
ANCILLARY
ANCIPITAL
ANDALUSIA
ANDANTINO
ANDRADITE
ANDROLOGY
ANDROMEDA
ANECDOTAL
ANECDOTES
ANECDOTIC
ANEMOLOGY
ANEUPLOID
ANGEL CAKE
ANGELFISH
ANGELICAL
ANGIOGRAM

ANGIOLOGY	ANSWERING	APERITIFS	APPOINTER	ARCTOGAEA
ANGLE IRON	ANTALKALI	APERTURES	APPOINTOR	ARCTURIAN
ANGLESITE	ANTARCTIC	APETALOUS	APPORTION	ARCUATION
ANGLEWORM	ANTEATERS	APHERESIS	APPRAISAL	ARDUOUSLY
ANGLICANS	ANTECHOIR	APHIDIOUS	APPRAISED	AREA CODES
ANGLICISM	ANTEDATED	APHORISMS	APPRAISER	ARGENTINA
ANGLICIZE	ANTEFIXAL	APHYLLOUS	APPREHEND	ARGENTINE
ANGOSTURA	ANTELOPES	APICULATE	APPRESSED	ARGENTITE
ANGUISHED	ANTENATAL	APISHNESS	APPRISING	ARGENTOUS
ANHYDRIDE	ANTENNULE	APIVOROUS	APPROBATE	ARGILLITE
ANHYDRITE	ANTEROOMS	APLANATIC	APPROVING	ARGUMENTS
ANHYDROUS	ANTHELION	APOCOPATE	APPULSIVE	ARMADILLO
ANIMALISM	ANTHEMION	APOCRYPHA	APRIL FOOL	ARMAMENTS
ANIMALIST	ANTHODIUM	APODICTIC	APRIORITY	ARMATURES
ANIMALITY	ANTHOLOGY	APOENZYME	APTITUDES	ARMCHAIRS
ANIMALIZE	ANTHOTAXY	APOGAMOUS	AQUALUNGS	ARMISTICE
ANIMATEUR	ANTHOZOAN	APOLOGIAS	AQUAPLANE	ARMOURERS
ANIMATING	ANTHURIUM	APOLOGIES	AQUARELLE	ARMOURIES
ANIMATION	ANTICHLOR	APOLOGIST	AQUARIUMS	ARMS RACES
ANIMATISM	ANTICLINE	APOLOGIZE	AQUATINTS	AROMATIZE
ANIMISTIC	ANTIDOTES	APOPHASIS	AQUEDUCTS	ARPEGGIOS
ANIMOSITY	ANTIGENIC	APOPHYSIS	AQUILEGIA	ARRAIGNED
ANISOGAMY	ANTIKNOCK	APOPTOSIS	AQUITAINE	ARRAIGNER
ANKLEBONE	ANTIMERIC	APOSTATES	ARABESQUE	ARRANGING
ANKLE BONE	ANTIMONIC	APOSTOLIC	ARABINOSE	ARRESTING
ANKYLOSIS	ANTIMONYL	APPALLING	ARACHNOID	ARRIVISTE
ANNALISTS	ANTINODAL	APPALOOSA	ARAGONESE	ARROGANCE
ANNAPOLIS	ANTINOMIC	APPARATUS	ARAGONITE	ARROGATED
ANNAPURNA	ANTIPATHY	APPARITOR	ARAUCANIA	ARROGATOR
ANNEALING	ANTIPHONY	APPEALING	ARAUCARIA	ARROWHEAD
ANNELIDAN	ANTIPODAL	APPEARING	ARBITRAGE	ARROWROOT
ANNOTATED	ANTIPODES	APPEASING	ARBITRARY	ARROWWOOD
ANNOTATOR	ANTIQUARY	APPELLANT	ARBITRATE	ARROWWORM
ANNOUNCED	ANTIQUATE	APPELLATE	ARBITRESS	ARSENICAL
ANNOUNCER	ANTIQUITY	APPENDAGE	ARBOREOUS	ARSENIOUS
ANNOYANCE	ANTISERUM	APPENDANT	ARBORETUM	ARSONISTS
ANNUITANT	ANTITOXIC	APPENDING	ARBOVIRUS	ARTEFACTS
ANNUITIES	ANTITOXIN	APPENZELL	ARCHAISMS	ARTEMISIA
ANNULLING	ANTIVENIN	APPERTAIN	ARCHAIZER	ARTERIOLE
ANNULMENT	ANTIVIRAL	APPETENCE	ARCHANGEL	ARTERITIS
ANOESTRUS	ANTIWORLD	APPETITES	ARCHDUCAL	ARTHRITIC
ANOINTING	ANTONIONI	APPETIZER	ARCHDUCHY	ARTHRITIS
ANOMALIES	ANXIETIES	APPLAUDED	ARCHDUKES	ARTHROPOD
ANOMALOUS	ANXIOUSLY	APPLAUDER	ARCHENEMY	ARTICHOKE
ANONYMITY	ANY AMOUNT	APPLE CART	ARCHETYPE	ARTICLING
ANONYMOUS	APARTHEID	APPLEJACK	ARCHFIEND	ARTICULAR
ANOPHELES	APARTMENT	APPLE PIES	ARCHICARP	ARTIFACTS
ANORTHITE	APATHETIC	APPLIANCE	ARCHITECT	ARTIFICER
ANOSMATIC	APELDOORN	APPLICANT	ARCHIVIST	ARTIFICES
ANOXAEMIA	APENNINES	APPOINTED	ARCHIVOLT	ARTILLERY
ANOXAEMIC	APERIODIC	APPOINTEE	ARCOGRAPH	ARTLESSLY

ARYTENOID
ASCENDANT
ASCENDING
ASCENSION
ASCERTAIN
ASCOSPORE
ASCRIBING
ASEPALOUS
ASEXUALLY
ASHAMEDLY
ASHKENAZI
ASHKHABAD
ASININITY
ASPARAGUS
ASPERSION
ASPERSIVE
ASPHALTED
ASPHALTIC
ASPHALTUM
ASPHYXIAL
ASPIRANTS
ASPIRATED
ASPIRATES
ASPIRATOR
ASSAILANT
ASSAILING
ASSASSINS
ASSAULTED
ASSAULTER
ASSAYABLE
ASSEMBLED
ASSEMBLER
ASSENTING
ASSERTING
ASSERTION
ASSERTIVE
ASSESSING
ASSESSORS
ASSIDUITY
ASSIDUOUS
ASSIGNING
ASSISTANT
ASSISTING
ASSOCIATE
ASSONANCE
ASSORTING
ASSUAGING
ASSUASIVE
ASSUMABLE
ASSURABLE
ASSURANCE

ASSUREDLY
ASSURGENT
ASTERISKS
ASTEROIDS
ASTHMATIC
ASTOUNDED
ASTRADDLE
ASTRAKHAN
ASTROCYTE
ASTRODOME
ASTROLABE
ASTROLOGY
ASTRONAUT
ASTRONOMY
ASYLLABIC
ASYMMETRY
ASYMPTOTE
ASYNDETIC
ASYNDETON
AT A
 GLANCE
ATARACTIC
ATAVISTIC
ATHEISTIC
ATHENAEUM
ATHLETICS
ATLANTEAN
ATMOLYSIS
ATMOMETER
ATMOMETRY
ATOM BOMBS
ATOMICITY
ATOMISTIC
ATOMIZERS
ATONALISM
ATONALITY
ATONEMENT
AT ONE
 TIME
ATONICITY
AT PRESENT
ATROCIOUS
ATROPHIED
ATTACHING
ATTACKERS
ATTACKING
ATTAINDER
ATTAINING
ATTEMPTED
ATTEMPTER
ATTENDANT

ATTENDING
ATTENTION
ATTENTIVE
ATTENUANT
ATTENUATE
ATTESTANT
ATTESTING
AT THE
 TIME
ATTITUDES
ATTORNEYS
ATTRACTED
ATTRACTOR
ATTRIBUTE
ATTRITION
ATTRITIVE
AUBERGINE
AUBRIETIA
AU COURANT
AUCTIONED
AUCTORIAL
AUDACIOUS
AUDIENCES
AUDIO BOOK
AUDIOLOGY
AUDIPHONE
AUDITIONS
AUGMENTED
AUGMENTOR
AU NATUREL
AUNT SALLY
AURICULAR
AUSCHWITZ
AUSTENITE
AUSTERELY
AUSTERITY
AUSTRALIA
AUTARCHIC
AUTARKIES
AUTHENTIC
AUTHORESS
AUTHORIAL
AUTHORITY
AUTHORIZE
AUTOCLAVE
AUTOCRACY
AUTOCRATS
AUTOCROSS
AUTOECISM
AUTOFOCUS
AUTOGRAFT

AUTOGRAPH
AUTOICOUS
AUTOLYSIN
AUTOLYSIS
AUTOLYTIC
AUTOMATED
AUTOMATIC
AUTOMATON
AUTONOMIC
AUTOPHYTE
AUTOPSIES
AUTOSOMAL
AUTOTIMER
AUTOTOMIC
AUTOTOXIC
AUTOTOXIN
AUTOTYPIC
AUXILIARY
AVAILABLE
AVAILABLY
AVALANCHE
AVERAGING
AVERSIONS
AVERTIBLE
AVIFAUNAL
AVIRULENT
AVOCATION
AVOIDABLE
AVOIDANCE
AVUNCULAR
AWAKENING
AWARDABLE
AWARENESS
AWESTRUCK
AWFULNESS
AWKWARDLY
AXIOMATIC
AYAHUASCA
AYATOLLAH
AYUTTHAYA
AZEDARACH
AZEOTROPE
AZIMUTHAL

B

BAAGANDJI
BABY TEETH
BABY TOOTH
BACCHANAL
BACCIFORM
BACHELORS

BACILLARY
BACKACHES
BACKBENCH
BACKBITER
BACKBOARD
BACKBONES
BACKCLOTH
BACKCROSS
BACKDATED
BACK DOORS
BACKDROPS
BACKFIRED
BACKHANDS
BACKPACKS
BACKPEDAL
BACK PEDAL
BACK SEATS
BACK SHIFT
BACKSIDES
BACKSIGHT
BACKSLIDE
BACKSPACE
BACKSTAGE
BACKSWEPT
BACKTRACK
BACKWARDS
BACKWATER
BACKWOODS
BACKYARDS
BACTERIAL
BACTERIUM
BACTEROID
BADGERING
BADMINTON
BAGATELLE
BAGGINESS
BAG LADIES
BAHUVRIHI
BAILIWICK
BAIN-MARIE
BAKHTARAN
BALACLAVA
BALAKLAVA
BALALAIKA
BALANCING
BALCONIES
BALEFULLY
BALKANIZE
BALLASTED
BALLCOCKS
BALLERINA

BALL GAMES	BARCELONA	BATTENING	BEERSHEBA	BERYLLIUM
BALLISTIC	BAR CHARTS	BATTERIES	BEESTINGS	BESEECHED
BALLOONED	BARE BONES	BATTERING	BEETLE OFF	BESETTING
BALLOTING	BAREFACED	BATTINESS	BEETROOTS	BESIEGING
BALLOTINI	BARE FACED	BATTLEAXE	BEFALLING	BESMEARED
BALLPOINT	BARGAINED	BATTLE CRY	BEFITTING	BESPATTER
BALLROOMS	BARGAINER	BAWDINESS	BEGETTING	BESTIALLY
BALLYMENA	BARGE POLE	BAYONETED	BEGGARING	BESTIRRED
BALMINESS	BAR GRAPHS	BAY WINDOW	BEGINNERS	BESTOWING
BALTHAZAR	BARITONES	BEACH BALL	BEGINNING	BESTREWED
BALTIMORE	BAR KOCHBA	BEACHHEAD	BEGRUDGED	BETE NOIRE
BAMBOOZLE	BARNACLES	BEACHSIDE	BEGUILING	BETE-NOIRE
BANBRIDGE	BARN DANCE	BEACHWEAR	BEHAVIOUR	BETHLEHEM
BANDAGING	BARNSTORM	BEADINESS	BEHEADING	BETHOUGHT
BANDANNAS	BARNYARDS	BEAN FEAST	BEHOLDERS	BETOKENED
BANDEROLE	BAROGRAPH	BEARBERRY	BEHOLDING	BETRAYALS
BANDICOOT	BAROMETER	BEARDLESS	BELATEDLY	BETRAYERS
BANDOLEER	BARONETCY	BEARISHLY	BELEAGUER	BETRAYING
BANDOLIER	BAROSCOPE	BEARNAISE	BELEMNITE	BETROTHAL
BANDSTAND	BARRACKED	BEAR'S-	BELGRAVIA	BETROTHED
BANDWAGON	BARRACUDA	FOOT	BELIEVERS	BETTERING
BANDWIDTH	BARRETTES	BEARSKINS	BELIEVING	BETTER-OFF
BANEBERRY	BARRICADE	BEASTLIER	BELITTLED	BEVELLING
BANEFULLY	BARRISTER	BEATIFIED	BELITTLER	BEVERAGES
BANGALORE	BARROW BOY	BEATITUDE	BELLATRIX	BEWAILING
BANISHING	BARTENDER	BEAUMARIS	BELLICOSE	BEWITCHED
BANISTERS	BARTERING	BEAU MONDE	BELLOWING	BHAGALPUR
BANJA LUKA	BASEBALLS	BEAUTEOUS	BELLYACHE	BHARATIYA
BANKBOOKS	BASEBOARD	BEAUTIFUL	BELLY FLOP	BHAVNAGAR
BANK DRAFT	BASELINES	BEAUX-ARTS	BELONGING	BHUTANESE
BANK NOTES	BASEMENTS	BEAVERING	BELVEDERE	BIALYSTOK
BANKROLLS	BASE METAL	BEBEERINE	BEMOANING	BIBLIOTIC
BANKRUPTS	BASE RATES	BEBINGTON	BENCHMARK	BICIPITAL
BANNISTER	BASHFULLY	BECCAFICO	BENCH MARK	BICKERING
BANQUETED	BASICALLY	BECKONING	BENEFICES	BICONCAVE
BANQUETTE	BASIFIXED	BECQUEREL	BENEFITED	BICYCLING
BANTERING	BASILICAN	BEDAUBING	BENEVENTO	BICYCLIST
BANTUSTAN	BASILICAS	BEDECKING	BENGALESE	BIDENTATE
BAPTISMAL	BASILISKS	BEDEVILED	BENGALINE	BIELEFELD
BAPTIZING	BASIPETAL	BEDFELLOW	BENIGHTED	BIFARIOUS
BARBADIAN	BAS RELIEF	BEDRAGGLE	BENIGNANT	BIFOLIATE
BARBARIAN	BAS-RELIEF	BEDRIDDEN	BENIGNITY	BIFURCATE
BARBARISM	BASS CLEFS	BED-SITTER	BENIN CITY	BIGAMISTS
BARBARITY	BASSINETS	BEDSPREAD	BENTONITE	BIGARREAU
BARBARIZE	BASTINADO	BEDSTEADS	BENZIDINE	BIG DIPPER
BARBAROUS	BATH CHAIR	BEEFEATER	BERBERINE	BIGENERIC
BARBECUED	BATHOLITH	BEEFINESS	BEREAVING	BIG-TIMERS
BARBECUES	BATHROBES	BEEFSTEAK	BEREZNIKI	BIGUANIDE
BARBICANS	BATHROOMS	BEEKEEPER	BERIOSOVA	BIG WHEELS
BARBITONE	BATHWATER	BEELZEBUB	BERKELIUM	BIJECTION
BARCAROLE	BATTALION	BEERINESS	BERKSHIRE	BIJECTIVE

BILABIALS	BITTERNUT	BLENNIOID	BLUE BLOOD	BOMBPROOF
BILABIATE	BITTINESS	BLESSEDLY	BLUE BOOKS	BOMBSHELL
BILATERAL	BIVALENCY	BLESSINGS	BLUE CHIPS	BOMBSIGHT
BILHARZIA	BIZARRELY	BLETHERED	BLUE FILMS	BOMBSITES
BILINGUAL	BLABBERED	BLIGHTERS	BLUEGRASS	BONA FIDES
BILIRUBIN	BLACKBALL	BLIGHTING	BLUE JEANS	BONEBLACK
BILLBOARD	BLACK BELT	BLIND DATE	BLUE PETER	BONE CHINA
BILLETING	BLACKBIRD	BLINDFISH	BLUEPRINT	BONEHEADS
BILLFOLDS	BLACKBUCK	BLINDFOLD	BLUESTONE	BONINGTON
BILLHOOKS	BLACKBURN	BLINDNESS	BLUFFNESS	BON VIVANT
BILLIARDS	BLACKCOCK	BLIND SPOT	BLUNDERED	BOOBY TRAP
BILLIONTH	BLACKDAMP	BLINKERED	BLUNDERER	BOOHOOING
BILLOWING	BLACKENED	BLISTERED	BLUNTNESS	BOOKCASES
BILLY GOAT	BLACK EYES	BLIZZARDS	BLURREDLY	BOOK CLUBS
BILOCULAR	BLACKFACE	BLOCKADED	BLUSTERED	BOOKMAKER
BIMONTHLY	BLACKFISH	BLOCKADER	BLUSTERER	BOOKMARKS
BIN-LINERS	BLACKHEAD	BLOCKADES	BOARDROOM	BOOKPLATE
BINOCULAR	BLACK HOLE	BLOCKAGES	BOARDWALK	BOOKSHELF
BINOMIALS	BLACK ISLE	BLOCKHEAD	BOARHOUND	BOOKSHOPS
BINTURONG	BLACKJACK	BLOCK VOTE	BOAT HOOKS	BOOKSTALL
BINUCLEAR	BLACK LEAD	BLONDNESS	BOATHOUSE	BOOKSTAND
BIOGRAPHY	BLACKLEGS	BLOOD BANK	BOATSWAIN	BOOK TOKEN
BIOHAZARD	BLACKLIST	BLOODBATH	BOAT TRAIN	BOOKWORMS
BIOLOGIST	BLACKMAIL	BLOOD FEUD	BOBBEJAAN	BOOMERANG
BIOMETRIC	BLACK MASS	BLOOD HEAT	BOBBY PINS	BOOMSLANG
BIONOMICS	BLACKNESS	BLOODLESS	BOBSLEIGH	BOONDOCKS
BIONOMIST	BLACKOUTS	BLOOD LUST	BOBTAILED	BOORISHLY
BIOSPHERE	BLACKPOLL	BLOODROOT	BOCCACCIO	BOOTBLACK
BIOSTATIC	BLACKPOOL	BLOODSHED	BODACIOUS	BOOTHROYD
BIOSTROME	BLACK SPOT	BLOODSHOT	BODY BLOWS	BOOTLACES
BIPARTITE	BLACKTAIL	BLOOD TYPE	BODYCHECK	BOOTMAKER
BIPINNATE	BLAMELESS	BLOODWORM	BODYGUARD	BOOTSTRAP
BIRDHOUSE	BLANCHING	BLOSSOMED	BOGGINESS	BOOZINESS
BIRD HOUSE	BLANDNESS	BLOTCHIER	BOHEMIANS	BORDELLOS
BIRD'S-	BLANKETED	BLOTCHILY	BOILINGLY	BORDERING
FOOT	BLANKNESS	BLOW-DRIED	BOLDFACED	BOREHOLES
BIRTHDAYS	BLASPHEME	BLOW-DRIES	BOLECTION	BORN-AGAIN
BIRTHMARK	BLASPHEMY	BLOWFLIES	BOLEGNESE	BORROWERS
BIRTHRATE	BLASTEMIC	BLOWHARDS	BOLIVIANO	BORROWING
BIRTHROOT	BLASTULAR	BLOWHOLES	BOLLINGER	BOSSA NOVA
BIRTHWORT	BLATANTLY	BLOWLAMPS	BOLLYWOOD	BOSSINESS
BISECTING	BLATHERED	BLOWPIPES	BOLOMETER	BOTANICAL
BISECTION	BLAZONING	BLOWTORCH	BOLSHEVIK	BOTANISTS
BISECTRIX	BLEACHERS	BLOWZIEST	BOLSHIEST	BOTANIZED
BISERRATE	BLEACHING	BLUBBERED	BOLSTERED	BOTCHIEST
BISEXUALS	BLEAKNESS	BLUDGEONS	BOLSTERER	BOTHERING
BISHOPRIC	BLEARIEST	BLUEBEARD	BOLTHOLES	BOTTLE-FED
BISMUTHAL	BLEMISHED	BLUEBELLS	BOMBARDED	BOTULINUS
BISMUTHIC	BLEMISHER	BLUEBERRY	BOMBARDON	BOUILLONS
BISULCATE	BLEMISHES	BLUEBIRDS	BOMBASTIC	BOULEVARD
BITCHIEST	BLENCHING	BLUE-BLACK	BOMBAZINE	BOUNCIEST

BOUNDLESS
BOUNTEOUS
BOUNTIFUL
BOURGEOIS
BOUTIQUES
BOWERBIRD
BOW LEGGED
BOW-LEGGED
BOWSPRITS
BOWSTRING
BOW WINDOW
BOX AND
   COX
BOXING DAY
BOX NUMBER
BOX OFFICE
BOYCOTTED
BOYFRIEND
BOYLES LAW
BOYLE'S
   LAW
BOY SCOUTS
BRACELETS
BRACHIATE
BRACINGLY
BRACKETED
BRACKNELL
BRACTEATE
BRACTEOLE
BRAGGARTS
BRAINIEST
BRAINLESS
BRAINSICK
BRAINWASH
BRAINWAVE
BRAIN WAVE
BRAINWAVE
BRAKE SHOE
BRAKESMAN
BRAMBLING
BRANCHIAL
BRANCHING
BRANDLING
BRAND NAME
BRANTFORD
BRASHNESS
BRASS BAND
BRASSERIE
BRASS HATS
BRASSIERE
BRASSIEST

BRAVENESS
BRAWNIEST
BRAZENING
BRAZILEIN
BRAZILIAN
BREACHING
BREAD BINS
BREADLINE
BREADROOT
BREAKABLE
BREAKAGES
BREAKAWAY
BREAKBEAT
BREAKDOWN
BREAKEVEN
BREAKFAST
BREAKNECK
BREATHILY
BREATHING
BREECHING
BRENTWOOD
BRIARROOT
BRIC A
   BRAC
BRIC-A-
   BRAC
BRICKWORK
BRICKYARD
BRICOLAGE
BRIEFCASE
BRIGADIER
BRIGHOUSE
BRILLIANT
BRIMSTONE
BRININESS
BRIOLETTE
BRIQUETTE
BRISKNESS
BRISTLING
BRITANNIA
BRITANNIC
BRITICISM
BRITISHER
BRITTONIC
BROACHING
BROADBAND
BROAD BEAN
BROADBILL
BROADCAST
BROADENED
BROAD JUMP

BROADLEAF
BROADLOOM
BROADNESS
BROADSIDE
BROADTAIL
BROCADING
BROCHETTE
BROCHURES
BROKERAGE
BROMELIAD
BROMEOSIN
BROMINATE
BROMOFORM
BRONCHIAL
BRONZE AGE
BROODIEST
BROOKABLE
BROOKLIME
BROOKWEED
BROOMCORN
BROOMRAPE
BROSCOPIC
BROTHERLY
BROUGHAMS
BROWN RICE
BRUNETTES
BRUNSWICK
BRUSH-OFFS
BRUSHWOOD
BRUSHWORK
BRUSQUELY
BRUTALITY
BRUTALIZE
BRUTISHLY
BRYLCREEM
BRYOPHYTE
BRYTHONIC
BUBBLE GUM
BUBBLIES!
BUCCANEER
BUCHAREST
BUCKBOARD
BUCKETING
BUCKHOUND
BUCKTEETH
BUCKTHORN
BUCKTOOTH
BUCKWHEAT
BUCKYBALL
BUCKYTUBE
BUDDH GAYA

BUDDHISTS
BUDGETARY
BUDGETING
BUFFALOES
BUFFERING
BUFFETING
BUGGER ALL
BUGGERING
BUGLE CALL
BUGLEWEED
BUHRSTONE
BUILDINGS
BUJUMBURA
BULGARIAN
BULGINESS
BULGINGLY
BULKHEADS
BULKINESS
BULLDOZED
BULLDOZER
BULLETINS
BULLFIGHT
BULLFINCH
BULLFROGS
BULLHORNS
BULLISHLY
BULLRINGS
BULL'S-
   EYES
BULLY BEEF
BULLYBOYS
BULLY-OFFS
BULRUSHES
BUMBLEBEE
BUMIPUTRA
BUMPINESS
BUMPTIOUS
BUNDABERG
BUNDESRAT
BUNDESTAG
BUNGALOWS
BUNGHOLES
BUNKHOUSE
BUOYANTLY
BUPRESTID
BURDENING
BURGEONED
BURGESSES
BURLESQUE
BURLINESS
BURMA ROAD

BURNINGLY
BURNISHED
BURNISHER
BURNOUSES
BURROUGHS
BURROWING
BURSARIAL
BURSARIES
BURSIFORM
BURTHENED
BUSHELLER
BUSHINESS
BUSHWHACK
BUTADIENE
BUTCHERED
BUTENANDT
BUTESHIRE
BUTHELEZI
BUTTERBUR
BUTTERCUP
BUTTERFAT
BUTTERFLY
BUTTERINE
BUTTERING
BUTTERNUT
BUTTONING
BUXOMNESS
BUZZWORDS
BYDGOSZCZ
BYPASSING
BY-PRODUCT
BYSTANDER
BY THE
   BOOK
BYZANTINE
BYZANTIUM

C

CABALLERO
CABIN BOYS
CABINETRY
CABLE CARS
CABLEGRAM
CABLE-LAID
CABOODLES
CABRIOLET
CACHECTIC
CACODEMON
CACOETHES
CACOETHIC
CACOPHONY

173

CACUMINAL
CAECILIAN
CAESAREAN
CAFETERIA
CAIRNGORM
CAITHNESS
CALABOOSE
CALAMANCO
CALCANEAL
CALCANEUS
CALCICOLE
CALCIFIED
CALCIFUGE
CALCIMINE
CALCULATE
CALCULOUS
CALENDARS
CALENDERS
CALENDULA
CALENTURE
CALIBRATE
CALIPHATE
CALL A
  HALT
CALL BOXES
CALL GIRLS
CALLOSITY
CALLOUSLY
CALMATIVE
CALORIFIC
CALUMNIES
CALVARIES
CALVINISM
CALVINIST
CALVITIES
CAMBISTRY
CAMBRIDGE
CAMELHAIR
CAMELLIAS
CAMEMBERT
CAMERAMAN
CAMERAMEN
CAMERA SHY
CAMISOLES
CAMPAIGNS
CAMPANILE
CAMPANULA
CAMPFIRES
CAMPHORIC
CAMPSITES
CAMSHAFTS

CANAANITE
CANAL BOAT
CANALIZED
CANAVERAL
CANCELING
CANCELLED
CANCELLER
CANCEROUS
CANDIDACY
CANDIDATE
CANDLEMAS
CANDLENUT
CANDYTUFT
CANESCENT
CANICULAR
CANISTERS
CANKEROUS
CANNELURE
CANNERIES
CANNIBALS
CANNINESS
CANNONADE
CANNONING
CANNULATE
CANOEISTS
CANONICAL
CANONIZED
CANOODLED
CAN OPENER
CANTABILE
CANTALOUP
CANTERING
CANTICLES
CANTONESE
CANVASSED
CANVASSER
CANVASSES
CAPACIOUS
CAPACITOR
CAPARISON
CAPE VERDE
CAPILLARY
CAP IN
  HAND
CAPITULAR
CAPITULUM
CAPRICCIO
CAPRICORN
CAPSAICIN
CAPSICUMS
CAPSIZING

CAPSULATE
CAPTAINCY
CAPTAINED
CAPTIVATE
CAPTIVITY
CAPTURING
CARAPACES
CARBAMATE
CARBANION
CARBAZOLE
CARBINEER
CARBOLIZE
CARBONADO
CARBONATE
CARBONIZE
CARBONOUS
CARBON TAX
CARBUNCLE
CARBURIZE
CARCASSES
CARCINOMA
CARDBOARD
CARDIGANS
CARDINALS
CARD INDEX
CARDPHONE
CARD PUNCH
CARDPUNCH
CARDSHARP
CARD SHARP
CARD TABLE
CAREENING
CAREERING
CAREERISM
CAREERIST
CAREFULLY
CARESSING
CARETAKER
CARIBBEAN
CARIBBEES
CARILLONS
CARINTHIA
CARIOSITY
CARMELITE
CARNALIST
CARNALITY
CARNATION
CARNELIAN
CARNIVALS
CARNIVORE
CARNOTITE

CAROLLING
CAROTIDAL
CAROUSALS
CAROUSELS
CAROUSING
CARPACCIO
CARPENTER
CARPENTRY
CARPETBAG
CARPETING
CARPOLOGY
CARRAGEEN
CARREFOUR
CARRIAGES
CARRYALLS
CARRYCOTS
CARRY-OVER
CARTAGENA
CARTESIAN
CARTHORSE
CARTILAGE
CARTOGRAM
CARTOUCHE
CARTRIDGE
CART TRACK
CARTULARY
CARTWHEEL
CARYATIDS
CARYOPSIS
CASANOVAS
CASCADING
CASEATION
CASEBOUND
CASE STUDY
CASH CARDS
CASH CROPS
CASH DESKS
CASHIERED
CASSAREEP
CASSATION
CASSEROLE
CASSETTES
CASSIMERE
CASSINGLE
CASSOCKED
CASSOULET
CASSOWARY
CAST ABOUT
CASTANETS
CASTAWAYS
CASTIGATE

CASTILIAN
CASTOR OIL
CASTRATED
CASTRATOR
CASUARINA
CASUISTIC
CASUISTRY
CATABASIS
CATABATIC
CATABOLIC
CATACLYSM
CATACOMBS
CATALEPSY
CATALOGUE
CATALONIA
CATALYSER
CATALYSIS
CATALYSTS
CATALYTIC
CATAMARAN
CATAMENIA
CATAMOUNT
CAT-AND-
  DOG
CATAPHYLL
CATAPLASM
CATAPLEXY
CATAPULTS
CATARACTS
CATARRHAL
CATATONIA
CATATONIC
CATCALLED
CATCH CROP
CATCHIEST
CATCHMENT
CATCHWORD
CATECHISM
CATECHIST
CATECHIZE
CATERWAUL
CATHARSES
CATHARSIS
CATHARTIC
CATHEDRAL
CATHEPSIN
CATHETERS
CATHOLICS
CATOPTRIC
CATTERIES
CATTINESS

CATTLEMAN	CENTRISTS	CHAPERONS	CHEMPADUK	CHLORIDIC
CAUCASOID	CENTURIAL	CHAPLAINS	CHEMURGIC	CHLORITIC
CAUDATION	CENTURIES	CHAPLETED	CHENGCHOW	CHLOROSIS
CAUGHT OUT	CENTURION	CHARABANC	CHEONGSAM	CHLOROTIC
CAULDRONS	CERACEOUS	CHARACTER	CHEQUERED	CHOCK-FULL
CAUSALGIA	CERATODUS	CHARBROIL	CHERBOURG	CHOCOLATE
CAUSALITY	CERCARIAL	CHARCOALS	CHERISHED	CHOCOLATY
CAUSATION	CEREBROID	CHARINESS	CHERISHER	CHOIRBOYS
CAUSATIVE	CEREBRUMS	CHARITIES	CHERNOZEM	CHOKEABLE
CAUSEWAYS	CERECLOTH	CHARIVARI	CHERRY PIE	CHOLEROID
CAUTERANT	CERTAINLY	CHARLATAN	CHESTIEST	CHOMSKIAN
CAUTERIZE	CERTAINTY	CHARLOTTE	CHESTNUTS	CHONDRIFY
CAUTIONED	CERTIFIED	CHARMEUSE	CHEVALIER	CHONDRITE
CAVALCADE	CERTITUDE	CHARTABLE	CHEVRETTE	CHONDROMA
CAVALIERS	CERUSSITE	CHARTERED	CHICALOTE	CHONDRULE
CAVENDISH	CESAREANS	CHARWOMAN	CHICANERY	CHONGQING
CAVERNOUS	CESSATION	CHARWOMEN	CHICKADEE	CHOOSIEST
CAVILLERS	CETACEANS	CHASTENED	CHICKPEAS	CHOPHOUSE
CAVILLING	CHABAZITE	CHASTENER	CHICKWEED	CHOPLOGIC
CAVORTING	CHA-CHA-	CHASTISED	CHIEFTAIN	CHOPPIEST
CEASEFIRE	CHA	CHASUBLES	CHIHUAHUA	CHOPSTICK
CEASE-FIRE	CHAETOPOD	CHATELAIN	CHILBLAIN	CHORIONIC
CEASELESS	CHAFFINCH	CHATOYANT	CHILDHOOD	CHORISTER
CELANDINE	CHAGRINED	CHAT SHOWS	CHILDLESS	CHOROLOGY
CELEBRANT	CHAIN GANG	CHATTERED	CHILDLIKE	CHORTLING
CELEBRATE	CHAIN MAIL	CHATTERER	CHILIADAL	CHORUSING
CELEBRITY	CHAIN SAWS	CHATTIEST	CHILLIEST	CHOWKIDAR
CELESTIAL	CHAIRLIFT	CHAUFFEUR	CHINATOWN	CHRISTIAN
CELESTITE	CHAIR LIFT	CHEAPENED	CHINAWARE	CHRISTMAS
CELIBATES	CHALCOGEN	CHEAP-JACK	CHINKIANG	CHROMATIC
CELLARAGE	CHALKIEST	CHEAPNESS	CHINSTRAP	CHROMATID
CELLARMAN	CHALLENGE	CHECHENIA	CHINTZIER	CHROMATIN
CELLOIDIN	CHAMELEON	CHECKABLE	CHIPBOARD	CHROMOGEN
CELLULASE	CHAMFERER	CHECKERED	CHIPMUNKS	CHRONAXIE
CELLULOID	CHAMOMILE	CHECKLIST	CHIPOLATA	CHRONICLE
CELLULOSE	CHAMPAGNE	CHECKMATE	CHIPPINGS	CHRYSALID
CELTICIST	CHAMPAIGN	CHECKOUTS	CHIROPODY	CHRYSALIS
CEMENTING	CHAMPERTY	CHECKROOM	CHIROPTER	CHTHONIAN
CEMENTITE	CHAMPIONS	CHEEKBONE	CHIRPIEST	CHUBBIEST
CENOTAPHS	CHAMPLEVE	CHEEKIEST	CHIRRUPER	CHUCKLING
CENSORIAL	CHANCIEST	CHEERIEST	CHISELING	CHUMMIEST
CENSORING	CHANCROID	CHEERLESS	CHISELLED	CHUNGKING
CENSURING	CHANCROUS	CHELASHIP	CHISELLER	CHUNKIEST
CENTAURUS	CHANDELLE	CHELATION	CHISIMAIO	CHURCHMAN
CENTENARY	CHANDLERS	CHELICERA	CHITINOID	CHURRASCO
CENTERING	CHANDLERY	CHELIFORM	CHITINOUS	CICATRICE
CENTESIMO	CHANGCHOW	CHELONIAN	CHIVALRIC	CICATRIZE
CENTIGRAM	CHANGCHUN	CHEMICALS	CHLORACNE	CICERONES
CENTIPEDE	CHANNELED	CHEMISORB	CHLORDANE	CIGARETTE
CENTRALLY	CHANTEUSE	CHEMISTRY	CHLORELLA	CIGARILLO
CENTRIOLE	CHANTILLY	CHEMOSTAT	CHLORIDES	CILIATION

CILIOLATE
CIMMERIAN
CINCTURES
CINEMATIC
CINEPHILE
CINERARIA
CINEREOUS
CINGULATE
CIPHERING
CIRALPINE
CIRCADIAN
CIRCASSIA
CIRCINATE
CIRCUITAL
CIRCUITRY
CIRCULARS
CIRCULATE
CIRRHOSED
CIRRHOSIS
CIRRHOTIC
CIRRIPEDE
CITATIONS
CITIZENRY
CITY HALLS
CITY-STATE
CIVICALLY
CIVILIANS
CIVILIZED
CIVILIZER
CIVIL LIST
CIVIL WARS
CLADOGRAM
CLAIMABLE
CLAIMANTS
CLAMBAKES
CLAMBERED
CLAMMIEST
CLAMOROUS
CLAMOURED
CLAMPDOWN
CLAMP DOWN
CLAPBOARD
CLARENDON
CLARIFIED
CLARIFIER
CLARINETS
CLASSICAL
CLASSIEST
CLASSLESS
CLASSMATE
CLASSROOM

CLATHRATE
CLATTERED
CLAVICLES
CLAVICORN
CLAYMORES
CLAYSTONE
CLAYTONIA
CLEANABLE
CLEANNESS
CLEANSERS
CLEANSING
CLEARANCE
CLEAR-EYED
CLEARINGS
CLEARNESS
CLEARWAYS
CLEARWING
CLEAVAGES
CLEMENTLY
CLENCHING
CLERGYMAN
CLERGYMEN
CLERIHEWS
CLERKSHIP
CLEVELAND
CLIENTELE
CLIMACTIC
CLIMAXING
CLIMB DOWN
CLIMB-DOWN
CLINCHERS
CLINCHING
CLINGFILM
CLINGFISH
CLINICIAN
CLINOSTAT
CLINQUANT
CLINTONIA
CLIPBOARD
CLIP JOINT
CLIPPINGS
CLITELLUM
CLOAKROOM
CLOBBERED
CLOCKWISE
CLOCKWORK
CLOG DANCE
CLOISONNE
CLOISTERS
CLOISTRAL
CLONICITY

CLOSE CALL
CLOSEDOWN
CLOSE KNIT
CLOSE-KNIT
CLOSENESS
CLOSETING
CLOTHIERS
CLOUDBANK
CLOUDIEST
CLOUDLESS
CLOUD NINE
CLOYINGLY
CLUBBABLE
CLUBHOUSE
CLUMSIEST
CLUSTERED
CLUTCH BAG
CLUTCHING
CLUTTERED
CLYDEBANK
CNIDARIAN
COACHWORK
COADJUTOR
COADUNATE
COAGULANT
COAGULASE
COAGULATE
COALESCED
COALFACES
COALFIELD
COALHOLES
COALHOUSE
COALITION
COALMINES
COARCTATE
COARSENED
COASTLINE
COAT TAILS
COAXINGLY
COBALTITE
COBALTOUS
COCA-COLAS
COCAINISM
COCAINIZE
COCCOLITH
COCCYGEAL
COCHINEAL
COCHLEATE
COCK A
  HOOP

COCK-A-
  HOOP
COCKATIEL
COCKATOOS
COCKED HAT
COCKERELS
COCKFIGHT
COCKHORSE
COCKINESS
COCKLEBUR
COCKNEYFY
COCKROACH
COCKSCOMB
COCKSFOOT
COCKTAILS
COCOONING
CODIFYING
CODPIECES
COELOSTAT
COENOBITE
COENOCYTE
COENOSARC
COEQUALLY
COERCIBLE
COEVALITY
COEXISTED
COFFEE BAR
COFFEEPOT
COFFERDAM
COGITATED
COGITATOR
COGNATION
COGNITION
COGNITIVE
COGNIZANT
COGNOMENS
COGWHEELS
COHABITED
COHERENCE
COIFFEURS
COIFFURED
COIFFURES
COINCIDED
COINTREAU
COKULORIS
COLANDERS
COLCHICUM
COLCOTHAR
COLD CREAM
COLD-DRAWN
COLD FRAME

COLD FRONT
COLD SNAPS
COLD SORES
COLD STEEL
COLD SWEAT
COLECTOMY
COLERAINE
COLICROOT
COLICWEED
COLLAGIST
COLLAPSAR
COLLAPSED
COLLAPSES
COLLARING
COLLATING
COLLATION
COLLATIVE
COLLEAGUE
COLLECTED
COLLECTOR
COLLEGIAL
COLLEGIAN
COLLEGIUM
COLLIDING
COLLIGATE
COLLIMATE
COLLINEAR
COLLINSIA
COLLISION
COLLOCATE
COLLODION
COLLOIDAL
COLLOTYPE
COLLUDING
COLLUSION
COLLUSIVE
COLLUVIAL
COLLUVIUM
COLLYRIUM
COLOCYNTH
COLOMBIAN
COLONELCY
COLONIALS
COLONISTS
COLONIZED
COLONIZER
COLONNADE
COLORIFIC
COLOR LINE
COLOSTOMY
COLOSTRAL

COLOSTRUM	COMMODORE	CONCEALED	CONFLUENT	CONSONANT
COLOUR BAR	COMMONAGE	CONCEDING	CONFORMAL	CONSORTED
COLOUREDS	COMMONERS	CONCEITED	CONFORMED	CONSORTER
COLOURFUL	COMMON LAW	CONCEIVED	CONFORMER	CONSORTIA
COLOURING	COMMON-LAW	CONCENTRE	CONFRERES	CONSPIRED
COLOURIST	COMMOTION	CONCEPTUS	CONFUCIAN	CONSTABLE
COLOURWAY	COMMUNING	CONCERNED	CONFUSING	CONSTANCE
COLTISHLY	COMMUNION	CONCERTED	CONFUSION	CONSTANCY
COLTSFOOT	COMMUNISM	CONCERTOS	CONFUTING	CONSTANTA
COLUBRINE	COMMUNIST	CONCIERGE	CONGEALED	CONSTANTS
COLUMBIAN	COMMUNITY	CONCILIAR	CONGENIAL	CONSTRAIN
COLUMBINE	COMMUNIZE	CONCISELY	CONGER EEL	CONSTRICT
COLUMBITE	COMMUTATE	CONCISION	CONGERIES	CONSTRUCT
COLUMBIUM	COMMUTERS	CONCLAVES	CONGESTED	CONSTRUED
COLUMELLA	COMMUTING	CONCLUDED	CONGOLESE	CONSTRUER
COLUMNIST	COMPACTED	CONCOCTED	CONGRUENT	CONSULATE
COLWYN BAY	COMPACTER	CONCOCTER	CONGRUITY	CONSULTED
COMATULID	COMPACTLY	CONCORDAT	CONGRUOUS	CONSULTEE
COMBATANT	COMPANDER	CONCOURSE	CONHOIDAL	CONSULTER
COMBATING	COMPANIES	CONCRETED	CONICALLY	CONSUMERS
COMBATIVE	COMPANION	CONCUBINE	CONJOINED	CONSUMING
COMBATTED	COMPARING	CONCURRED	CONJOINER	CONTACTED
COMBINING	COMPASSES	CONCUSSED	CONJUGANT	CONTACTOR
COMBUSTOR	COMPELLED	CONDEMNED	CONJUGATE	CONTAGION
COME ABOUT	COMPELLER	CONDEMNER	CONJURERS	CONTAGIUM
COMEBACKS	COMPENDIA	CONDENSED	CONJURING	CONTAINED
COMEDIANS	COMPERING	CONDENSER	CONNECTED	CONTAINER
COMEDOWNS	COMPETENT	CONDIGNLY	CONNECTOR	CONTEMNER
COMELIEST	COMPETING	CONDIMENT	CONNEMARA	CONTENDED
COME OFF	COMPILERS	CONDITION	CONNIVENT	CONTENDER
IT	COMPILING	CONDOLING	CONNIVING	CONTENTED
COMFORTED	COMPLAINT	CONDONING	CONNOTING	CONTESTED
COMFORTER	COMPLETED	CONDUCING	CONNUBIAL	CONTESTER
COMICALLY	COMPLETER	CONDUCIVE	CONQUERED	CONTINENT
COMMANDED	COMPLEXES	CONDUCTED	CONQUEROR	CONTINUAL
COMMANDER	COMPLIANT	CONDUCTOR	CONQUESTS	CONTINUED
COMMANDOS	COMPLYING	CONDYLOID	CONSCIOUS	CONTINUER
COMMENCED	COMPONENT	CONDYLOMA	CONSCRIPT	CONTINUOS
COMMENDAM	COMPORTED	CONFERRED	CONSENSUS	CONTINUUM
COMMENDED	COMPOSERS	CONFERRER	CONSENTED	CONTORTED
COMMENSAL	COMPOSING	CONFERVAL	CONSENTER	CONTOURED
COMMENTED	COMPOSITE	CONFESSED	CONSERVED	CONTRACTS
COMMENTER	COMPOSTED	CONFESSOR	CONSERVER	CONTRAILS
COMMINGLE	COMPOSURE	CONFIDANT	CONSERVES	CONTRALTO
COMMINUTE	COMPOUNDS	CONFIDENT	CONSIGNED	CONTRASTS
COMMISSAR	COMPRISAL	CONFIDING	CONSIGNEE	CONTRASTY
COMMITTAL	COMPRISED	CONFINING	CONSIGNOR	CONTRIVED
COMMITTED	COMPUTERS	CONFIRMED	CONSISTED	CONTUMACY
COMMITTEE	COMPUTING	CONFITURE	CONSOCIES	CONTUMELY
COMMITTER	COMRADELY	CONFLATED	CONSOLING	CONTUSING
COMMODITY	CONCAVITY	CONFLICTS	CONSOLUTE	CONTUSION

CONTUSIVE
CONUNDRUM
CONVECTOR
CONVENERS
CONVENING
CONVERGED
CONVERSED
CONVERSER
CONVERTED
CONVERTER
CONVEXITY
CONVEYERS
CONVEYING
CONVICTED
CONVINCED
CONVINCER
CONVIVIAL
CONVOKING
CONVOLUTE
CONVOYING
CONVULSED
COOKHOUSE
COOKSTOWN
COOPERAGE
COOPERATE
COORDINAL
COPARTNER
COPESTONE
COPIOUSLY
COPOLYMER
COPROLITE
COPULATED
COPYBOOKS
COPYRIGHT
COQUETTES
CORALLINE
CORALLOID
CORALROOT
CORBICULA
COR BLIMEY
CORDIALLY
CORDIFORM
CORDONING
COREOPSIS
CORIANDER
CORKBOARD
CORKSCREW
CORMORANT
CORN BREAD
CORNBREAD
CORNCRAKE

CORNELIAN
CORNERING
CORNETIST
CORNFIELD
CORNFLOUR
CORNSTALK
COROLLARY
CORPORALE
CORPORALS
CORPORATE
CORPOREAL
CORPOSANT
CORPULENT
CORPUSCLE
CORRALLED
CORRASION
CORRASIVE
CORRECTED
CORRECTLY
CORRECTOR
CORRELATE
CORRIDORS
CORRODANT
CORRODING
CORROSION
CORROSIVE
CORRUGATE
CORRUPTED
CORRUPTER
CORRUPTLY
CORSELETS
CORTICATE
CORTISONE
CORUSCATE
CORVETTES
CORYDALIS
CORYMBOSE
COSEISMAL
COSMETICS
COSMIC RAY
COSMOGONY
COSMOLOGY
COSMONAUT
COSMOTRON
COSSETTED
COSTA RICA
CO-STARRED
COSTLIEST
COSTOTOMY
COST PRICE
COSTUMIER

COTANGENT
COT DEATHS
COTE
  D'AZUR
COTENANCY
COTILLION
COTTAGERS
COTTONADE
COTTON GIN
COTYLEDON
COUCHETTE
COUNSELED
COUNTABLE
COUNTDOWN
COUNTERED
COUNTLESS
COUNT NOUN
COUNTRIES
COUP
  D'ETAT
COUPLINGS
COURGETTE
COURT CARD
COURTELLE
COURTEOUS
COURTESAN
COURTIERS
COURTLIER
COURTROOM
COURTSHIP
COURT SHOE
COURTYARD
COUTURIER
COVALENCY
COVENANTS
COVERALLS
COVERINGS
COVERLESS
COVERLETS
COVER NOTE
COVERTURE
COWABUNGA
COWARDICE
CO-WORKERS
COXCOMBRY
COYOTILLO
CRAB APPLE
CRABBEDLY
CRABBIEST
CRABSTICK
CRACKDOWN

CRACKLING
CRACKPOTS
CRACKSMAN
CRACKSMEN
CRAFTIEST
CRAFTSMAN
CRAFTSMEN
CRAFTWORK
CRAGGIEST
CRAIGAVON
CRANBERRY
CRANKCASE
CRANKIEST
CRAPPIEST
CRAPULOUS
CRASH-DIVE
CRASH-LAND
CRASH TEAM
CRASSNESS
CRATEROUS
CRAYONING
CRAYONIST
CRAZINESS
CREAKIEST
CREAMCUPS
CREAMIEST
CREATIONS
CREATURAL
CREATURES
CREDENDUM
CREDITING
CREDITORS
CREDULITY
CREDULOUS
CREEPIEST
CREMATING
CREMATION
CREMATORY
CRENATION
CRENULATE
CREOLIZED
CREOPHAGY
CREOSOTED
CREOSOTIC
CREPITANT
CREPITATE
CRESCENDO
CRESCENTS
CRETINISM
CRETINOID
CRETINOUS

CREVASSES
CREWELIST
CREW NECKS
CRIBELLUM
CRICKETER
CRIME WAVE
CRIMINALS
CRIMPLENE
CRIMSONED
CRINKLIER
CRINKLING
CRINOLINE
CRIPPLING
CRISPIEST
CRISPNESS
CRITERION
CRITICISM
CRITICIZE
CRITIQUES
CROCHETED
CROCHETER
CROCODILE
CROISSANT
CROMLECHS
CROOKEDLY
CROP-EARED
CROQUETTE
CROSSBARS
CROSSBEAM
CROSSBILL
CROSSBOWS
CROSSBRED
CROSS-EYED
CROSSFIRE
CROSSHEAD
CROSSINGS
CROSS-LINK
CROSSNESS
CROSSOVER
CROSS TALK
CROSSTREE
CROSSWALK
CROSSWIND
CROSSWISE
CROSSWORD
CROSSWORT
CROTCHETS
CROTCHETY
CROUCHING
CROUPIERS
CROWBERRY

CROWN LAND
CROWNWORK
CROW'S
  FEET
CROW'S
  FOOT
CROW'S
  NEST
CRUCIALLY
CRUCIBLES
CRUCIFIED
CRUCIFIER
CRUCIFORM
CRUDITIES
CRUELTIES
CRUMBLIER
CRUMBLING
CRUMMIEST
CRUMPLING
CRUNCHIER
CRUNCHILY
CRUNCHING
CRUSADERS
CRUSADING
CRUSTIEST
CRYBABIES
CRYOMETER
CRYOMETRY
CRYOPHYTE
CRYOSCOPE
CRYOSCOPY
CRYPTOGAM
CTENIDIUM
CUBBYHOLE
CUBBY HOLE
CUBE ROOTS
CUBISISTS
CUB SCOUTS
CUCKOLDED
CUCULLATE
CUCUMBERS
CUDDLIEST
CUDGELING
CUDGELLED
CUDGELLER
CUFF LINKS
CUIRASSES
CUL-DE-
  SACS
CULLENDER
CULMINANT
CULMINATE

CULTIVATE
CULTURIST
CUMBERING
CUMBRANCE
CUNEIFORM
CUNNINGLY
CUPBEARER
CUPBOARDS
CUP FINALS
CUPOLATED
CURATIVES
CURDINESS
CURETTAGE
CURIOSITY
CURIOUSLY
CURLICUES
CURLINESS
CURLPAPER
CURRENTLY
CURRICULA
CURRYCOMB
CURSIVELY
CURSORIAL
CURSORILY
CURTAILED
CURTAINED
CURTILAGE
CURTSYING
CURVATURE
CUSHINESS
CUSHIONED
CUSPIDATE
CUSPIDORS
CUSTODIAL
CUSTODIAN
CUSTOMARY
CUSTOMERS
CUSTOMIZE
CUT A
  CAPER
CUT AND
  RUN
CUTANEOUS
CUTICULAR
CUTLASSES
CUTPURSES
CUTTHROAT
CUT-THROAT
CUTTINGLY
CYANAMIDE
CYANOTYPE

CYBERCAFE
CYBERNATE
CYBERPUNK
CYBERPUNT
CYCLAMATE
CYCLOIDAL
CYCLONITE
CYCLOPSES
CYCLORAMA
CYCLOTRON
CYLINDERS
CYMBALIST
CYMOGRAPH
CYMOPHANE
CYNICALLY
CYNOSURES
CYPHERING
CYPRESSES
CYPRINOID
CYRENAICA
CYSTEINIC
CYSTOCARP
CYSTOCELE
CYSTOLITH
CYSTOTOMY
CYTOLYSIN
CYTOLYSIS
CYTOPLASM
CYTOPLAST

D

DACHSHUND
DACTYLICS
DADAISTIC
DAFFODILS
DAILY HELP
DAINTIEST
DAIQUIRIS
DAIRY FARM
DAIRYMAID
DALAI LAMA
DALLIANCE
DALMATIAN
DALTONISM
DAMASCENE
DAMNATION
DAMNATORY
DAMNEDEST
DAMPENING
DAMP SQUIB
DAMSELFLY

DANDELION
DANDIFIED
DANGEROUS
DAREDEVIL
DARKENING
DARK HORSE
DARKROOMS
DARMSTADT
DARTBOARD
DARTMOUTH
DASHBOARD
DASHINGLY
DASTARDLY
DATABASES
DATA BUSES
DATEDNESS
DATELINES
DATE STAMP
DAUGHTERS
DAUNTLESS
DAVENPORT
DAYDREAMS
DAYDREAMY
DAYFLOWER
DAYLIGHTS
DAY SCHOOL
DEACONESS
DEADBEATS
DEAD DUCKS
DEADENING
DEAD HEART
DEAD HEATS
DEADLIEST
DEADLIGHT
DEADLINES
DEADLOCKS
DEADLY SIN
DEAD MARCH
DEAFBLIND
DEAFENING
DEAF-MUTES
DEALATION
DEAMINATE
DEANERIES
DEATHBEDS
DEATHBLOW
DEATH DUTY
DEATHLESS
DEATHLIKE
DEATH MASK
DEATH RATE

DEATH TOLL
DEATH TRAP
DEATH WISH
DEAUVILLE
DEBARKING
DEBARMENT
DEBARRING
DEBATABLE
DEBAUCHED
DEBAUCHEE
DEBAUCHER
DEBAUCHES
DEBENTURE
DEBOUCHED
DEBRIEFED
DEBUGGING
DEBUNKERS
DEBUNKING
DEBUTANTE
DECADENCE
DECAGONAL
DECALCIFY
DECALOGUE
DECAMPING
DECANTERS
DECANTING
DECAPODAL
DECASTYLE
DECATHLON
DECEITFUL
DECEIVERS
DECEIVING
DECEMBERS
DECENCIES
DECENNIAL
DECEPTION
DECEPTIVE
DECIDABLE
DECIDEDLY
DECIDUOUS
DECILLION
DECIMALLY
DECIMATED
DECIMATOR
DECIMETRE
DECISIONS
DECK CARGO
DECKCHAIR
DECKHANDS
DECKHOUSE
DECLAIMED

DECLAIMER	DEFENDING	DEMEANOUR	DEPORTING	DESPERATE
DECLARANT	DEFENSIVE	DEMIJOHNS	DEPOSABLE	DESPISING
DECLARING	DEFERENCE	DEMIMONDE	DEPOSITED	DESPOILED
DECLINATE	DEFERMENT	DEMISABLE	DEPOSITOR	DESPOILER
DECLINING	DEFERRING	DEMISTING	DEPRAVING	DESPOTISM
DECLIVITY	DEFIANTLY	DEMITASSE	DEPRAVITY	DESPUMATE
DECOCTION	DEFICIENT	DEMOBBING	DEPRECATE	DESTINIES
DECOLLATE	DEFINABLE	DEMOCRACY	DEPRESSED	DESTITUTE
DECOLLETE	DEFINIENS	DEMOCRATS	DEPRESSOR	DESTROYED
DECOMPOSE	DEFLATING	DEMOTIONS	DEPRIVING	DESTROYER
DECONTROL	DEFLATION	DEMULCENT	DEPURATOR	DESUETUDE
DECORATED	DEFLECTED	DEMULSIFY	DEPUTIZED	DESULTORY
DECORATOR	DEFLECTOR	DEMURRAGE	DERAILING	DETACHING
DECOUPAGE	DEFOLIANT	DEMURRING	DERELICTS	DETAILING
DECREASED	DEFOLIATE	DEMYSTIFY	DE RIGUEUR	DETAINEES
DECREASES	DEFORMING	DENDRITIC	DERISIBLE	DETAINING
DECREEING	DEFORMITY	DENIGRATE	DERIVABLE	DETECTING
DECREMENT	DEFRAUDED	DENITRATE	DERMATOID	DETECTION
DECRETIVE	DEFRAUDER	DENITRIFY	DERMATOME	DETECTIVE
DECRETORY	DEFRAYING	DENOTABLE	DEROGATED	DETECTORS
DECUMBENT	DEFROCKED	DENOUNCED	DERRING DO	DETENTION
DECURRENT	DEFROSTED	DENOUNCER	DERRING-DO	DETERGENT
DECUSSATE	DEFROSTER	DENSENESS	DERRINGER	DETERMENT
DEDICATED	DEGRADING	DENSITIES	DERVISHES	DETERMINE
DEDICATEE	DEGREE-DAY	DENTALIUM	DESCALING	DETERRENT
DEDICATOR	DEHISCENT	DENTATION	DESCANTER	DETERRING
DEDUCIBLE	DEHYDRATE	DENTIFORM	DESCENDED	DETERSIVE
DEDUCTING	DEJECTION	DENTISTRY	DESCENDER	DETESTING
DEDUCTION	DELEGABLE	DENTITION	DESCRIBED	DETHRONED
DEDUCTIVE	DELEGATED	DENTURIST	DESCRIBER	DETHRONER
DEED POLLS	DELEGATES	DEODORANT	DESCRYING	DETONATED
DEEDS POLL	DELETIONS	DEODORIZE	DESECRATE	DETONATOR
DEEPENING	DELICIOUS	DEOXIDIZE	DESERTERS	DETRACTED
DEEP FRIED	DELIGHTED	DEPARDIEU	DESERTING	DETRACTOR
DEEP SOUTH	DELIGHTER	DEPARTING	DESERTION	DETRAINED
DEERGRASS	DELIMITED	DEPARTURE	DESERVING	DETRIMENT
DEERHOUND	DELINEATE	DEPASTURE	DESICCANT	DETRITION
DEFALCATE	DELIRIANT	DEPENDANT	DESICCATE	DETRUSION
DEFAULTED	DELIRIOUS	DEPENDENT	DESIGNATE	DEUTERIDE
DEFAULTER	DELIRIUMS	DEPENDING	DESIGNERS	DEUTERIUM
DEFEATING	DELIVERED	DEPICTING	DESIGNING	DEVALUATE
DEFEATISM	DELIVERER	DEPICTION	DESINENCE	DEVALUING
DEFEATIST	DELOUSING	DEPICTIVE	DESIRABLE	DEVASTATE
DEFECATED	DELUSIONS	DEPICTURE	DESIRABLY	DEVELOPED
DEFECATOR	DEMAGOGIC	DEPILATOR	DESISTING	DEVELOPER
DEFECTING	DEMAGOGUE	DEPLETING	DESMIDIAN	DEVIATING
DEFECTION	DEMANDANT	DEPLETION	DES MOINES	DEVIATION
DEFECTIVE	DEMANDING	DEPLETIVE	DESOLATED	DEVIATORY
DEFECTORS	DEMANTOID	DEPLORING	DESOLATER	DEVILFISH
DEFENDANT	DEMARCATE	DEPLOYING	DESPAIRED	DEVILLING
DEFENDERS	DEMEANING	DEPORTEES	DESPERADO	DEVILMENT

DEVIOUSLY	DIATRIBES	DILATABLE	DISAVOWAL	DISH TOWEL
DEVISABLE	DIATROPIC	DILATANCY	DISAVOWED	DISHWATER
DEVITRIFY	DIAZONIUM	DILIGENCE	DISAVOWER	DISINFECT
DEVOLVING	DIAZOTIZE	DILUTIONS	DISBANDED	DISINFEST
DEVOTEDLY	DIBROMIDE	DIMENSION	DISBARRED	DISK DRIVE
DEVOTIONS	DICHASIAL	DIMIDIATE	DISBELIEF	DISKETTES
DEVOURING	DICHASIUM	DIMISSORY	DISBRANCH	DISLIKING
DEVOUTEST	DICHOGAMY	DIM-WITTED	DISBURDEN	DISLOCATE
DEXEDRINE	DICHOTOMY	DINGDONGS	DISBURSED	DISLODGED
DEXTERITY	DICHROISM	DINGINESS	DISBURSER	DISMANTLE
DEXTEROUS	DICHROITE	DINING CAR	DISCALCED	DISMASTED
DEXTRORSE	DICHROMIC	DINOCERAS	DISCARDED	DISMAYING
DIABETICS	DICKERING	DINOSAURS	DISCARDER	DISMEMBER
DIABLERIE	DICKYBIRD	DINOTHERE	DISCERNED	DISMISSAL
DIABOLISM	DICLINISM	DIOECIOUS	DISCERNER	DISMISSED
DIABOLIST	DICLINOUS	DIOESTRUS	DISCHARGE	DISOBEYED
DIABOLIZE	DICROTISM	DIPHTHONG	DISCIPLES	DISOBEYER
DIACONATE	DICTATING	DIPLOIDIC	DISCLIMAX	DISOBLIGE
DIACRITIC	DICTATION	DIPLOMACY	DISCLOSED	DISORDERS
DIACTINIC	DICTATORS	DIPLOMATE	DISCLOSER	DISOWNING
DIAERESES	DIDACTICS	DIPLOMATS	DISCOIDAL	DISPARAGE
DIAERESIS	DIETETICS	DIPLOTENE	DISCOLOUR	DISPARATE
DIAGNOSED	DIETICIAN	DIPSTICKS	DISCOMFIT	DISPARITY
DIAGNOSES	DIETITIAN	DIPSWITCH	DISCOMMON	DISPELLED
DIAGNOSIS	DIFFERENT	DIPTEROUS	DISCOUNTS	DISPELLER
DIAGONALS	DIFFERING	DIRECTING	DISCOURSE	DISPENSED
DIALECTAL	DIFFICULT	DIRECTION	DISCOVERT	DISPENSER
DIALECTIC	DIFFIDENT	DIRECTIVE	DISCOVERY	DISPERSAL
DIALOGISM	DIFFUSELY	DIRECTORS	DISCREDIT	DISPERSED
DIALOGIST	DIFFUSING	DIRECTORY	DISCUSSED	DISPERSER
DIALOGIZE	DIFFUSION	DIRECTRIX	DISDAINED	DISPLACED
DIALOGUER	DIFFUSIVE	DIRECT TAX	DISEMBARK	DISPLACER
DIALOGUES	DIGASTRIC	DIREFULLY	DISEMBODY	DISPLAYED
DIAMAGNET	DIGENESIS	DIRIGIBLE	DISENABLE	DISPLAYER
DIAMETERS	DIGENETIC	DIRT BIKES	DISENGAGE	DISPLEASE
DIAMETRAL	DIGESTANT	DIRT CHEAP	DISENTAIL	DISPORTED
DIAMETRIC	DIGESTING	DIRTINESS	DISESTEEM	DISPOSING
DIANDROUS	DIGESTION	DIRT ROADS	DISFAVOUR	DISPRAISE
DIANOETIC	DIGESTIVE	DIRT TRACK	DISFIGURE	DISPROVAL
DIAPHONIC	DIGITALIN	DIRTY WORK	DISFOREST	DISPROVED
DIAPHRAGM	DIGITALIS	DISABLING	DISGORGED	DISPUTANT
DIAPHYSIS	DIGITIZED	DISABLIST	DISGORGER	DISPUTING
DIARRHOEA	DIGITIZER	DISABUSAL	DISGRACED	DISREGARD
DIASTASIC	DIGITOXIN	DISABUSED	DISGRACER	DISRELISH
DIASTASIS	DIGLOTTIC	DISACCORD	DISGUISED	DISREPAIR
DIASTATIC	DIGNIFIED	DISAFFECT	DISGUISER	DISREPUTE
DIASTOLIC	DIGNITARY	DISAFFIRM	DISGUISES	DISROBING
DIATHERMY	DIGNITIES	DISAGREED	DISGUSTED	DISRUPTED
DIATHESIS	DIGRAPHIC	DISAPPEAR	DISHCLOTH	DISRUPTER
DIATHETIC	DIGRESSED	DISARMING	DISHONEST	DISSECTED
DIATOMITE	DIGRESSER	DISASTERS	DISHONOUR	DISSECTOR

DISSEISIN	DIVORCING	DONATIONS	DRAGGIEST	DRUGGISTS
DISSEISOR	DIVORCIVE	DONCASTER	DRAGHOUND	DRUGSTORE
DISSEMBLE	DIVULGING	DONNISHLY	DRAGOMANS	DRUMBEATS
DISSENTED	DIVULSION	DONORSHIP	DRAGONESS	DRUM MAJOR
DISSENTER	DIVULSIVE	DOODLEBUG	DRAGONFLY	DRUMSTICK
DISSIDENT	DIXIELAND	DOOHICKEY	DRAGONISH	DRUNKARDS
DISSIPATE	DIZZINESS	DOOJIGGER	DRAGOONED	DRUNKENLY
DISSOLUTE	DJAJAPURA	DOOMSAYER	DRAINABLE	DUALISTIC
DISSOLVED	DOBSONFLY	DOORBELLS	DRAINPIPE	DUBIOUSLY
DISSOLVER	DOCK BRIEF	DOORFRAME	DRAMAMINE	DUBITABLE
DISSONANT	DOCKETING	DOORKNOBS	DRAMATICS	DUBROVNIK
DISSUADED	DOCKYARDS	DOORNAILS	DRAMATIST	DUCHESSES
DISSUADER	DOCTORATE	DOORPLATE	DRAMATIZE	DUCKBOARD
DISTANCED	DOCTORING	DOORSTEPS	DRAPERIED	DUCKLINGS
DISTANCES	DOCTRINAL	DORDRECHT	DRAPERIES	DUCTILITY
DISTANTLY	DOCTRINES	DORMITORY	DRAUGHTER	DUDE RANCH
DISTEMPER	DOCUMENTS	DORMOBILE	DRAVIDIAN	DUELLISTS
DISTENDED	DODDERERS	DORONICUM	DRAWBACKS	DUFFEL BAG
DISTENDER	DODDERING	DORYPHORE	DRAWKNIFE	DULCIMERS
DISTICHAL	DODECAGON	DOSIMETER	DRAWPLATE	DUMBARTON
DISTILLED	DODGE CITY	DOSIMETRY	DREAMBOAT	DUMBBELLS
DISTILLER	DOG COLLAR	DOSSHOUSE	DREAMLAND	DUMBFOUND
DISTINGUE	DOG-EAT-	DOTTINESS	DREAMLESS	DUMB SHOWS
DISTORTED	DOG	DOUBLE BED	DREAMLIKE	DUMMY RUNS
DISTORTER	DOGFIGHTS	DOUBLED UP	DREAMTIME	DUMPINESS
DISTRAINT	DOGFISHES	DOUBLETON	DREARIEST	DUMPLINGS
DISTRICTS	DOGGY BAGS	DOUBLOONS	DRENCHING	DUNCES CAP
DISTURBED	DOGHOUSES	DOUBTABLE	DRESS CODE	DUNCE'S
DISTURBER	DOGLEGGED	DOUBTLESS	DRESS DOWN	CAP
DISUNITED	DOGMATICS	DOUGHNUTS	DRESSIEST	DUNE BUGGY
DITHERING	DOGMATISM	DOUGHTIER	DRESSINGS	DUNGANNON
DITHYRAMB	DOGMATIST	DOVECOTES	DRIBBLING	DUNGAREES
DITTANDER	DOGMATIZE	DOVETAILS	DRIFTWOOD	DUNGENESS
DIURETICS	DO-GOODERS	DOWDINESS	DRILLABLE	DUNKERQUE
DIURNALLY	DOG PADDLE	DOWITCHER	DRINKABLE	DUNSINANE
DIVALENCY	DOLEFULLY	DOWNCOMER	DRIP-DRIED	DUNSTABLE
DIVERGENT	DOLERITIC	DOWNFALLS	DRIPSTONE	DUODECIMO
DIVERGING	DOLGELLAU	DOWNGRADE	DRIVE HOME	DUODENARY
DIVERSELY	DOLLY BIRD	DOWNPOURS	DRIVELING	DUODENUMS
DIVERSIFY	DOLOMITES	DOWNRANGE	DRIVELLED	DUOLOGUES
DIVERSION	DOLOMITIC	DOWNRIGHT	DRIVELLER	DUPLEXITY
DIVERSITY	DOLTISHLY	DOWNSPOUT	DRIVE-TIME	DUPLICATE
DIVERTING	DOMESTICS	DOWNSTAGE	DRIVEWAYS	DUPLICITY
DIVERTIVE	DOMICILED	DOWNSWING	DRIZZLING	DURALUMIN
DIVESTING	DOMICILES	DOWNTHROW	DROLLNESS	DURICRUST
DIVIDABLE	DOMINANCE	DOWNTURNS	DROMEDARY	DUSKINESS
DIVIDENDS	DOMINATED	DOWNWARDS	DROPLIGHT	DUSTBOWLS
DIVINABLE	DOMINATOR	DRACONIAN	DROPPINGS	DUSTCARTS
DIVISIBLE	DOMINICAL	DRAFTIEST	DROPSICAL	DUSTSHEET
DIVISIONS	DOMINICAN	DRAFTSMAN	DROPSONDE	DUST STORM
DIVORCEES	DOMINIONS	DRAFTSMEN	DRUBBINGS	DUTCH BARN

DUTCH CAPS	EARTHWARD	EFFECTIVE	ELEVATION	EMBRYONIC
DUTCH OVEN	EARTHWORK	EFFECTUAL	ELEVATORS	EMENDABLE
DUTIFULLY	EARTHWORM	EFFERENCE	ELEVENSES	EMENDATOR
DUTY-FREES	EASTBOUND	EFFICIENT	ELEVENTHS	EMERGENCE
DWARF STAR	EAST ENDER	EFFLUENCE	ELICITING	EMERGENCY
DWELLINGS	EASTER EGG	EFFLUENTS	ELIMINANT	EMIGRANTS
DWINDLING	EASTERNER	EFFLUVIAL	ELIMINATE	EMIGRATED
DYER'S-	EASTLEIGH	EFFLUVIUM	ELIZABETH	EMINENCES
WEED	EASTWARDS	EFFORTFUL	ELLESMERE	EMINENTLY
DYNAMETER	EASY CHAIR	EFFULGENT	ELLIPSOID	EMISSIONS
DYNAMITED	EASYGOING	EFFUSIONS	EL MANSURA	EMMENTHAL
DYNAMITER	EASY GOING	EGG BEATER	ELOCUTION	EMOLLIENT
DYNAMITIC	EASY TERMS	EGGPLANTS	ELONGATED	EMOLUMENT
DYNAMOTOR	EAVESDROP	EGGSHELLS	ELOPEMENT	EMOTIONAL
DYNASTIES	EBULLIENT	EGG TIMERS	ELOQUENCE	EMOTIVELY
DYSENTERY	ECCENTRIC	EGLANTINE	ELSEWHERE	EMOTIVISM
DYSGENICS	ECHOLALIA	EGOMANIAC	ELUCIDATE	EMPANELED
DYSLECTIC	ECHOLALIC	EGOTISTIC	ELUSIVELY	EMPATHIZE
DYSPEPSIA	ECLAMPSIA	EGREGIOUS	ELUTRIATE	EMPENNAGE
DYSPEPTIC	ECLAMPTIC	EGYPTIANS	EMACIATED	EMPHASIZE
DYSPHAGIA	ECLIPSING	EIDERDOWN	EMANATING	EMPHYSEMA
DYSPHAGIC	ECOLOGIST	EIGHTFOLD	EMANATION	EMPIRICAL
DYSPHASIA	ECONOMICS	EIGHTIETH	EMANATIVE	EMPLOYEES
DYSPHASIC	ECONOMIES	EINDHOVEN	EMANATORY	EMPLOYERS
DYSPHONIA	ECONOMIST	EIRENICON	EMBALMERS	EMPLOYING
DYSPHONIC	ECONOMIZE	EISEGESIS	EMBALMING	EMPORIUMS
DYSPHORIA	ECOSPHERE	EJACULATE	EMBARGOED	EMPOWERED
DYSPHORIC	ECOSYSTEM	EKISTICAL	EMBARGOES	EMPRESSES
DYSPLASIA	ECSTASIES	ELABORATE	EMBARKING	EMPTIABLE
DYSPNOEAL	ECSTATICS	EL ALAMEIN	EMBARRASS	EMPTINESS
DYSTHYMIA	ECTOBLAST	ELAN VITAL	EMBASSIES	EMPYREUMA
DYSTHYMIC	ECTOMERIC	ELASTANCE	EMBATTLED	EMULATING
DYSTROPHY	ECTOMORPH	ELASTOMER	EMBAYMENT	EMULATION
DZUNGARIA	ECTOPHYTE	ELATERITE	EMBEDDING	EMULATIVE
	ECTOPLASM	ELATERIUM	EMBEDMENT	EMULSIONS
E	ECTOPROCT	ELBOWROOM	EMBELLISH	EMUNCTORY
EACH OTHER	ECUMENISM	ELBOW ROOM	EMBEZZLED	ENACTMENT
EAGERNESS	EDDYSTONE	ELDERSHIP	EMBEZZLER	ENAMELING
EAGLE-EYED	EDELWEISS	ELECTIONS	EMBODYING	ENAMELLED
EAGLEWOOD	EDEMATOUS	ELECTORAL	EMBOLISMS	ENAMELLER
EARLINESS	EDIBILITY	ELECTRESS	EMBOSOMED	ENAMOURED
EARLY BIRD	EDIFICIAL	ELECTRICS	EMBOSSING	ENCAMPING
EARMARKED	EDINBURGH	ELECTRIFY	EMBOWMENT	ENCAUSTIC
EARNESTLY	EDITORIAL	ELECTRODE	EMBRACEOR	ENCHAINED
EARPHONES	EDUCATING	ELECTRONS	EMBRACERY	ENCHANTED
EARPIECES	EDUCATION	ELECTUARY	EMBRACING	ENCHANTER
EARTHIEST	EDUCATIVE	ELEGANTLY	EMBRASURE	ENCHILADA
EARTHLIER	EDUCATORS	ELEMENTAL	EMBROCATE	ENCHORIAL
EARTHLING	EDUCATORY	ELEOPTENE	EMBROIDER	ENCIRCLED
EARTHRISE	EDWARDIAN	ELEPHANTS	EMBROILED	ENCLOSING
EARTHSTAR	EFFECTING	ELEVATING	EMBROILER	ENCLOSURE

ENCOMIAST	ENHANCING	ENTRANCES	EPISTASIS	ESCALATOR
ENCOMIUMS	ENHANCIVE	ENTRAPPED	EPISTATIC	ESCALOPES
ENCOMPASS	ENIGMATIC	ENTRAPPER	EPISTAXIS	ESCAPABLE
ENCOUNTER	ENJOINING	ENTREATED	EPISTEMIC	ESCAPADES
ENCOURAGE	ENJOYABLE	ENTRECHAT	EPITAPHIC	ESCAPISTS
ENCRINITE	ENJOYABLY	ENTRECOTE	EPITAXIAL	ESCHEWING
ENCRUSTED	ENJOYMENT	ENTREMETS	EPITHETIC	ESCORTING
ENDAMOEBA	ENKINDLER	ENTRE NOUS	EPITOMIST	ESKISEHIR
ENDEARING	ENLARGING	ENTRUSTED	EPITOMIZE	ESOPHAGUS
ENDEAVOUR	ENLIGHTEN	ENTRYWAYS	EPIZOOTIC	ESPERANTO
ENDLESSLY	ENLISTING	ENTWINING	EPONYMOUS	ESPIONAGE
ENDOBLAST	ENLIVENED	ENUCLEATE	EQUAL-AREA	ESPLANADE
ENDOCRINE	ENLIVENER	ENUMERATE	EQUALIZED	ESPOUSALS
ENDOERGIC	ENMESHING	ENUNCIATE	EQUALIZER	ESPOUSING
ENDOLYMPH	ENNOBLING	ENVELOPED	EQUALLING	ESPRESSOS
ENDOMORPH	EN PASSANT	ENVELOPES	EQUATABLE	ESSAOUIRA
ENDOPHYTE	ENQUIRIES	ENVIOUSLY	EQUATIONS	ESSAYISTS
ENDOPLASM	ENQUIRING	ENVISAGED	EQUERRIES	ESSENTIAL
ENDORSING	ENRAGEDLY	ENVYINGLY	EQUINOXES	ESSLINGEN
ENDOSCOPE	EN RAPPORT	ENZYMATIC	EQUIPMENT	ESTABLISH
ENDOSCOPY	ENRAPTURE	EPARCHIAL	EQUIPOISE	ESTAMINET
ENDOSPERM	ENRICHING	EPHEDRINE	EQUIPPING	ESTATE CAR
ENDOSPORE	ENROLLING	EPHEMERAL	EQUISETUM	ESTEEMING
ENDOSTEAL	ENROLMENT	EPHEMERID	EQUITABLE	ESTHETICS
ENDOSTEUM	ENSCONCED	EPHEMERIS	EQUITABLY	ESTIMABLE
ENDOTOXIC	ENSEMBLES	EPHEMERON	EQUIVOCAL	ESTIMATED
ENDOTOXIN	ENSHRINED	EPICENISM	EQUIVOQUE	ESTIMATES
ENDOWMENT	ENSLAVING	EPICENTRE	ERADICANT	ESTIMATOR
ENDURABLE	ENSNARING	EPICRISIS	ERADICATE	ESTOPPAGE
ENDURANCE	ENSTATITE	EPICRITIC	ERECTABLE	ESTRANGED
ENERGETIC	ENSUINGLY	EPICUREAN	ERECTIONS	ESTRANGER
ENERGIZED	ENTAILING	EPICURISM	ERECTNESS	ESTUARIAL
ENERGIZER	ENTAMOEBA	EPICYCLIC	EREMITISM	ESTUARIES
ENERGUMEN	ENTANGLED	EPIDEMICS	ERGOGRAPH	ESTUARINE
ENERVATED	ENTANGLER	EPIDERMAL	ERGOMETER	ESURIENCE
ENERVATOR	ENTELECHY	EPIDERMIS	ERGONOMIC	ETCETERAS
EN FAMILLE	ENTENDRES	EPIDURALS	ERISTICAL	ETERNALLY
ENFEEBLED	ENTERABLE	EPIGENOUS	EROGENOUS	ETHERIZER
ENFEEBLER	ENTERALLY	EPIGRAPHY	EROSIONAL	ETHICALLY
ENFILADED	ENTERITIS	EPIGYNOUS	EROTICISM	ETHIOPIAN
ENFILADES	ENTERTAIN	EPILEPTIC	EROTICIZE	ETHMOIDAL
ENFOLDING	ENTHRONED	EPILOGIST	ERRONEOUS	ETHNARCHY
ENFORCING	ENTHUSING	EPILOGUES	ERSTWHILE	ETHNOGENY
ENGINEERS	ENTHYMEME	EPIMYSIUM	ERUDITELY	ETHNOLOGY
ENGLACIAL	ENTITLING	EPINASTIC	ERUDITION	ETHOLOGIC
ENGRAMMIC	ENTOBLAST	EPIPHANIC	ERUPTIBLE	ETHYLENIC
ENGRAVERS	ENTOMBING	EPIPHRAGM	ERUPTIONS	ETIOLATED
ENGRAVING	ENTOPHYTE	EPIPHYSIS	ERYTHRISM	ETIQUETTE
ENGROSSED	ENTOURAGE	EPIPHYTIC	ERYTHRITE	ETRAMETER
ENGROSSER	ENTRAINED	EPIROGENY	ESCALADER	ETYMOLOGY
ENGULFING	ENTRANCED	EPISCOPAL	ESCALATED	EUCHARIST

EUCLIDEAN	EXCALIBUR	EXEMPLARY	EXPLAINER	EXTRAVERT
EUDEMONIA	EXCAUDATE	EXEMPLIFY	EXPLETIVE	EXTREMELY
EUDEMONIC	EXCAVATED	EXEMPTING	EXPLICATE	EXTREMISM
EUKARYOTE	EXCAVATOR	EXEMPTION	EXPLODING	EXTREMIST
EULOGISTS	EXCEEDING	EXEQUATUR	EXPLOITED	EXTREMITY
EULOGIZED	EXCELLENT	EXERCISED	EXPLOITER	EXTRICATE
EUPHEMISM	EXCELLING	EXERCISER	EXPLORERS	EXTRINSIC
EUPHEMIST	EXCELSIOR	EXERCISES	EXPLORING	EXTROVERT
EUPHEMIZE	EXCEPTING	EXERTIONS	EXPLOSION	EXTRUDING
EUPHONIUM	EXCEPTION	EXFOLIATE	EXPLOSIVE	EXTRUSION
EUPHONIZE	EXCEPTIVE	EXHALABLE	EXPONENTS	EXTRUSIVE
EUPHORBIA	EXCERPTER	EXHAUSTED	EXPONIBLE	EXUBERANT
EUPHRATES	EXCESSIVE	EXHAUSTER	EXPORTERS	EXUBERATE
EUPLASTIC	EXCHANGED	EXHIBITED	EXPORTING	EXUDATION
EURHYTHMY	EXCHANGER	EXHIBITOR	EXPOSABLE	EXUDATIVE
EUROCRATS	EXCHANGES	EXHORTING	EXPOSITOR	EYEBALLED
EUROPHILE	EXCHEQUER	EXISTENCE	EXPOSURES	EYEBRIGHT
EUROPOORT	EXCIPIENT	EXODONTIA	EXPOUNDED	EYELASHES
EUTHENICS	EXCISABLE	EXOENZYME	EXPOUNDER	EYELETEER
EUTHENIST	EXCISEMAN	EX OFFICIO	EXPRESSED	EYE OPENER
EUTHERIAN	EXCISIONS	EXOGAMOUS	EXPRESSER	EYE-OPENER
EUTROPHIC	EXCITABLE	EXOGENOUS	EXPRESSES	EYEPIECES
EVACUATED	EXCITEDLY	EXONERATE	EXPRESSLY	EYE SHADOW
EVACUATOR	EXCLAIMED	EXORCISER	EXPULSION	EYES RIGHT
EVADINGLY	EXCLAIMER	EXORCISMS	EXPULSIVE	EYESTRAIN
EVAGINATE	EXCLUDING	EXORCISTS	EXPUNGING	EYE STRAIN
EVALUATED	EXCLUSION	EXORCIZED	EXPURGATE	
EVALUATOR	EXCLUSIVE	EXOSMOSIS	EXQUISITE	**F**
EVAPORATE	EXCORIATE	EXOSMOTIC	EXSECTION	FABACEOUS
EVAPORITE	EXCREMENT	EXOSPHERE	EXSERTILE	FABIANISM
EVASIVELY	EXCRETING	EXOSTOSIS	EXSERTION	FABRICATE
EVENTUATE	EXCRETION	EXOTICISM	EXSICCATE	FABRIKOID
EVERGREEN	EXCRETIVE	EXPANDING	EXSTROPHY	FACE CARDS
EVERSIBLE	EXCRETORY	EXPANSILE	EXTEMPORE	FACECLOTH
EVERYBODY	EXCULPATE	EXPANSION	EXTENDING	FACE-LIFTS
EVICTIONS	EXCURRENT	EXPANSIVE	EXTENSION	FACE PACKS
EVIDENTLY	EXCURSION	EXPATIATE	EXTENSITY	FACEPLATE
EVILDOERS	EXCURSIVE	EXPECTANT	EXTENSIVE	FACE SAVER
EVILDOING	EXCUSABLE	EXPECTING	EXTENUATE	FACE-SAVER
EVINCIBLE	EXCUSABLY	EXPEDIENT	EXTERIORS	FACETIOUS
EVOCATION	EXECRABLE	EXPEDITED	EXTERNALS	FACE VALUE
EVOCATIVE	EXECRABLY	EXPEDITER	EXTIRPATE	FACSIMILE
EVOLUTION	EXECRATED	EXPELLANT	EXTOLLING	FACTIONAL
EVOLVABLE	EXECUTANT	EXPELLING	EXTOLMENT	FACTITIVE
EXACTABLE	EXECUTING	EXPENDING	EXTORTING	FACTORAGE
EXACTNESS	EXECUTION	EXPENSIVE	EXTORTION	FACTORIAL
EXALTEDLY	EXECUTIVE	EXPERTISE	EXTORTIVE	FACTORIES
EXAMINERS	EXECUTORS	EXPIATING	EXTRABOLD	FACTORING
EXAMINING	EXECUTORY	EXPIATION	EXTRACTED	FACTORIZE
EXANIMATE	EXECUTRIX	EXPIATORY	EXTRACTOR	FACTUALLY
EXANTHEMA	EXEGETICS	EXPLAINED	EXTRADITE	FACULTIES

FADDINESS	FARRAGOES	FERMENTER	FILMINESS	FIRST FOOT
FADDISHLY	FARROWING	FEROCIOUS	FILM SPEED	FIRSTHAND
FADEDNESS	FAR-SEEING	FERRETING	FILM STARS	FIRST LADY
FAGACEOUS	FARTHINGS	FERROCENE	FILM STOCK	FIRSTLING
FAGGOTING	FASCICLED	FERROTYPE	FILMSTRIP	FIRST NAME
FAINEANCE	FASCICULE	FERTILITY	FILOPLUME	FIRST-RATE
FAINTNESS	FASCIITIS	FERTILIZE	FILOSELLE	FISHCAKES
FAIRBANKS	FASCINATE	FERVENTLY	FILTERING	FISHERIES
FAIRYLAND	FASCISTIC	FESTERING	FILTER TIP	FISHERMAN
FAIRY-LIKE	FASHIONED	FESTIVALS	FILTHIEST	FISHERMEN
FAIRY RING	FASHIONER	FESTIVITY	FIMBRIATE	FISH FARMS
FAIRY-TALE	FASTENERS	FESTOONED	FINALISTS	FISHGUARD
FAITHFULS	FASTENING	FETICIDAL	FINALIZED	FISHINESS
FAITHLESS	FATALISTS	FETISHISM	FINANCIAL	FISH KNIFE
FALANGISM	FATEFULLY	FETISHIST	FINANCIER	FISHPLATE
FALANGIST	FATHEADED	FETISHIZE	FINANCING	FISH SLICE
FALCONERS	FATHERING	FETTERING	FINE-GRAIN	FISH STICK
FALCONINE	FATHOMING	FETTUCINE	FINE PRINT	FISSILITY
FALDSTOOL	FATIGABLE	FEUDALISM	FINE-TOOTH	FISTULOUS
FALLACIES	FATIGUING	FEUDALIST	FINE-TUNED	FIXATIONS
FALLALERY	FATTENING	FEUDALITY	FINGERING	FIXATIVES
FALL APART	FATTINESS	FEUDALIZE	FINGERTIP	FIXED-HEAD
FALLOPIAN	FATUITOUS	FEUDATORY	FINISHING	FIXED STAR
FALSEHOOD	FATUOUSLY	FEVERWORT	FINISTERE	FIZZINESS
FALSENESS	FAULTIEST	FIBONACCI	FIRE ALARM	FLABBIEST
FALSIFIED	FAULTLESS	FIBREFILL	FIREBALLS	FLABELLUM
FALSIFIER	FAVEOLATE	FIBRIFORM	FIREBOXES	FLACCIDLY
FALSITIES	FAVOURING	FIBRINOUS	FIREBRAND	FLAGELLAR
FALTERING	FAVOURITE	FICTIONAL	FIREBREAK	FLAGELLUM
FAMAGUSTA	FAWNINGLY	FIDEISTIC	FIREBRICK	FLAGEOLET
FAMILIARS	FEARFULLY	FIDGETING	FIRECREST	FLAGPOLES
FAMILY MAN	FEATHERED	FIDUCIARY	FIRE DRILL	FLAGRANCE
FAMILY MEN	FEATURING	FIELD ARMY	FIRE-EATER	FLAGRANCY
FANATICAL	FEBRICITY	FIELD DAYS	FIREFIGHT	FLAGSHIPS
FANCINESS	FEBRIFUGE	FIELDFARE	FIREFLIES	FLAGSTAFF
FANCY-FREE	FEBRILITY	FIELD GOAL	FIREGUARD	FLAGSTONE
FANCYWORK	FECULENCE	FIELDSMAN	FIRE IRONS	FLAG-WAVER
FANDANGLE	FECUNDATE	FIELDSMEN	FIRELIGHT	FLAKINESS
FANDANGOS	FECUNDITY	FIELD-TEST	FIREPLACE	FLAMELIKE
FANLIGHTS	FEDERATED	FIELD TRIP	FIRE-PLUGS	FLAMINGOS
FAN-TAILED	FEEDSTOCK	FIELDWORK	FIREPOWER	FLAMMABLE
FANTASIES	FEEDSTUFF	FIFTEENTH	FIREPROOF	FLANNELED
FANTASIZE	FEELINGLY	FIFTIETHS	FIRESIDES	FLAPJACKS
FANTASTIC	FEE-PAYING	FIG LEAVES	FIRESTONE	FLARE PATH
FARADIZER	FELICIFIC	FIGURE OUT	FIRESTORM	FLASHBACK
FARANDOLE	FELONIOUS	FIGURINES	FIRETHORN	FLASHBULB
FAREWELLS	FEMINISTS	FILAMENTS	FIRETRAPS	FLASHCUBE
FARMHANDS	FENESTRAL	FILIATION	FIREWATER	FLASHGUNS
FARMHOUSE	FENUGREEK	FILICIDAL	FIREWORKS	FLASHIEST
FARMSTEAD	FERMANAGH	FILLETING	FIRMAMENT	FLASHOVER
FARMYARDS	FERMENTED	FILLISTER	FIRSTBORN	FLATMATES

FLAT SPINS	FLOWCHART	FOOLHARDY	FORESHORE	FORWARDLY
FLATTENED	FLOWERAGE	FOOLISHLY	FORESIGHT	FOSSILIZE
FLATTENER	FLOWERBED	FOOLPROOF	FORESKINS	FOSSORIAL
FLATTERED	FLOWERING	FOOTBALLS	FORESTALL	FOSTERAGE
FLATTERER	FLOWERPOT	FOOTBOARD	FORESTERS	FOSTERING
FLATULENT	FLOWINGLY	FOOTFALLS	FORETASTE	FOUNDERED
FLAUNTING	FLOWMETER	FOOT FAULT	FORETOKEN	FOUNDLING
FLAUTISTS	FLUCTUANT	FOOTHILLS	FORETOOTH	FOUNDRIES
FLAVOROUS	FLUCTUATE	FOOTHOLDS	FOREWOMAN	FOUNTAINS
FLAVOURED	FLUFFIEST	FOOTLOOSE	FOREWOMEN	FOURSOMES
FLAVOURER	FLUIDIZER	FOOTNOTES	FOREWORDS	FOUR-WHEEL
FLEABITES	FLUKINESS	FOOTPATHS	FORFEITED	FOVEOLATE
FLEDGLING	FLUMMOXED	FOOTPLATE	FORFEITER	FOXGLOVES
FLEETNESS	FLUORESCE	FOOT-POUND	FORFICATE	FOXHOUNDS
FLEETWOOD	FLUOROSIS	FOOTPRINT	FORGATHER	FOXHUNTER
FLENSBURG	FLUORSPAR	FOOTRACES	FORGEABLE	FRACTIONS
FLESHIEST	FLURRYING	FOOTSTALK	FORGERIES	FRACTIOUS
FLESHINGS	FLUSTERED	FOOTSTALL	FORGETFUL	FRACTURAL
FLESHPOTS	FLUTTERED	FOOTSTEPS	FORGETTER	FRACTURED
FLEURETTE	FLUTTERER	FOOTSTOOL	FORGIVING	FRACTURES
FLEXIONAL	FLUXIONAL	FORAMINAL	FORGOTTEN	FRAGILITY
FLEXITIME	FLUXMETER	FORBEARER	FORLORNLY	FRAGMENTS
FLICKERED	FLY-FISHER	FORBIDDEN	FORMALISM	FRAGONARD
FLIGHTIER	FLY HALVES	FORBIDDER	FORMALIST	FRAGRANCE
FLIGHTILY	FLYING FOX	FORCEABLE	FORMALITY	FRAILTIES
FLIMSIEST	FLYLEAVES	FORCE FEED	FORMALIZE	FRAMBOISE
FLINCHING	FLYSHEETS	FORCE-FEED	FORMATION	FRAMEWORK
FLINTIEST	FLYWEIGHT	FORCEMEAT	FORMATIVE	FRANCHISE
FLINTLOCK	FLYWHEELS	FORCINGLY	FORMATTED	FRANCOLIN
FLIP-FLOPS	FLYWHISKS	FOREARMED	FORMICARY	FRANGIBLE
FLIPPANCY	FOAMINESS	FOREBEARS	FORMULAIC	FRANGLAIS
FLOATABLE	FOCUSABLE	FOREBODED	FORMULARY	FRANKABLE
FLOAT-FEED	FOCUSSING	FOREBODER	FORMULATE	FRANKFORT
FLOCCULUS	FOETATION	FOREBRAIN	FORMULISM	FRANKNESS
FLOGGINGS	FOETICIDE	FORECASTS	FORMULIST	FRATERNAL
FLOODABLE	FOGGINESS	FORECLOSE	FORNICATE	FRAUDSTER
FLOODGATE	FOLIATION	FORECOURT	FORSAKING	FREE AGENT
FLOOD TIDE	FOLIOLATE	FOREFRONT	FORSYTHIA	FREE-BASED
FLOOR SHOW	FOLK DANCE	FOREGOING	FORTALEZA	FREEBOARD
FLOPHOUSE	FOLKLORIC	FOREHANDS	FORTALICE	FREEHOLDS
FLOPPIEST	FOLK MUSIC	FOREHEADS	FORTHWITH	FREE HOUSE
FLOPTICAL	FOLKTALES	FOREIGNER	FORTIETHS	FREE KICKS
FLORIATED	FOLLICLES	FOREJUDGE	FORTIFIED	FREELANCE
FLORIDITY	FOLLOWERS	FORELOCKS	FORTIFIER	FREE-LIVER
FLORISTIC	FOLLOWING	FORENAMED	FORTITUDE	FREEMASON
FLOS FERRI	FOLLOW-UPS	FORENAMES	FORTNIGHT	FREEPHONE
FLOTATION	FOMENTING	FORENSICS	FORTUNATE	FREE PORTS
FLOTILLAS	FOOD CHAIN	FOREREACH	FORT WORTH	FREE-RANGE
FLOUNCING	FOOD STAMP	FORESHANK	FORTY-FIVE	FREESHEET
FLOUNDERS	FOODSTUFF	FORESHEET	FORWARDED	FREE STATE
FLOURMILL	FOOLERIES	FORESHOCK	FORWARDER	FREESTONE

FREESTYLE
FREE TRADE
FREE VERSE
FREEWHEEL
FREE WORLD
FREEZABLE
FREEZE-DRY
FREIGHTED
FREIGHTER
FREMANTLE
FRENCHIFY
FRENCHMAN
FRENCHMEN
FREQUENCE
FREQUENCY
FRESHENED
FRESHENER
FRESHNESS
FRETBOARD
FRETFULLY
FRETWORKS
FRIARBIRD
FRICASSEE
FRICATIVE
FRIESIANS
FRIESLAND
FRIGHTFUL
FRIGIDITY
FRILLIEST
FRISKIEST
FRITTERED
FRITTERER
FRIVOLITY
FRIVOLLER
FRIVOLOUS
FRIZZIEST
FRIZZLING
FROCK COAT
FROGMARCH
FROGMOUTH
FROGSPAWN
FROLICKED
FROLICKER
FRONTAGES
FRONTALLY
FRONT DOOR
FRONTIERS
FRONT LINE
FRONT-PAGE
FRONT ROOM
FROSTBITE

FROSTIEST
FROSTWORK
FROTHIEST
FROWSTIER
FROWZIEST
FRUCTUOUS
FRUGALITY
FRUIT BATS
FRUITCAKE
FRUITERER
FRUITIEST
FRUITLESS
FRUMPIEST
FRUSTRATE
FRYING PAN
FUGACIOUS
FUGITIVES
FUKUSHIMA
FULFILLED
FULFILLER
FULGURITE
FULGUROUS
FULLBACKS
FULL-BLOWN
FULL BOARD
FULL DRESS
FULLERENE
FULL-FACED
FULL-GROWN
FULL HOUSE
FULL MARKS
FULL MONTY
FULL MOONS
FULL-SCALE
FULL STOPS
FULMINANT
FULMINATE
FULSOMELY
FUMAROLIC
FUMIGATED
FUMIGATOR
FUNCTIONS
FUNDAMENT
FUNGICIDE
FUNGIFORM
FUNGISTAT
FUNICULAR
FUNICULUS
FUNNELING
FUNNELLED
FUNNINESS

FUNNY BONE
FUNNY FARM
FURBISHED
FURBISHER
FURCATION
FURIOUSLY
FURLOUGHS
FURNISHED
FURNISHER
FURNITURE
FURRINESS
FURROWING
FURTHERED
FURTHERER
FURTIVELY
FUSELAGES
FUSILLADE
FUSIONISM
FUSIONIST
FUSSINESS
FUSTINESS
FUTURISTS
FUZZINESS

G

GABARDINE
GABERDINE
GABIONADE
GADABOUTS
GADOLINIC
GADROONED
GAINFULLY
GAINSAYER
GALACTOSE
GALANTINE
GALAPAGOS
GALEIFORM
GALENICAL
GALINGALE
GALLANTLY
GALLANTRY
GALLERIED
GALLERIES
GALLICISM
GALLICIZE
GALLINULE
GALLIPOLI
GALLIVANT
GALLIWASP
GALLONAGE
GALLOPING

GALLSTONE
GALUMPHED
GALVANISM
GALVANIZE
GALWEGIAN
GAMBOGIAN
GAMBOLING
GAMECOCKS
GAMMADION
GAMMA RAYS
GANDHIISM
GANG-BANGS
GANGLIONS
GANGPLANK
GANGSTERS
GAOLBIRDS
GARBOLOGY
GARDENERS
GARDENIAS
GARDENING
GARGOYLED
GARGOYLES
GARIBALDI
GARLANDED
GARNERING
GARNISHED
GARNISHER
GARNISHES
GARNITURE
GARRISONS
GARROTTED
GARROTTER
GARROTTES
GARRULITY
GARRULOUS
GAS FITTER
GAS HEATER
GASHOLDER
GASLIGHTS
GAS MANTLE
GASOLINIC
GASOMETER
GASOMETRY
GASPINGLY
GASSINESS
GASTRITIC
GASTRITIS
GASTROPOD
GASTRULAR
GATECRASH
GATEHOUSE

GATEPOSTS
GATESHEAD
GATHERING
GAUCHERIE
GAUDINESS
GAUGEABLE
GAUGEABLY
GAULEITER
GAUNTLETS
GAUNTNESS
GAUZINESS
GAWKINESS
GAZA STRIP
GAZEHOUND
GAZETTEER
GAZIANTEP
GAZUMPING
GEARBOXES
GEAR LEVER
GEAR STICK
GEARWHEEL
GEHLENITE
GELIGNITE
GELLIGAER
GELSEMIUM
GEMMATION
GEMUTLICH
GENDARMES
GENEALOGY
GENE CLONE
GENERABLE
GENERALLY
GENERATED
GENERATOR
GENIALITY
GENITALIC
GENITALLY
GENITIVAL
GENITIVES
GENOCIDAL
GENOTYPIC
GENTEELLY
GENTILITY
GENTLEMAN
GENTLEMEN
GENTLE SEX
GENUFLECT
GENUINELY
GEODESIST
GEOGRAPHY
GEOLOGIST

GEOLOGIZE	GIRANDOLE	GLOWERING	GOOD TIMES	GRAPHITIC
GEOMANCER	GIRL GUIDE	GLOWINGLY	GOOD WORDS	GRAPPELLI
GEOMANTIC	GIRLISHLY	GLOW-WORMS	GOOFINESS	GRAPPLING
GEOMETRIC	GIRONDISM	GLUCOSIDE	GOOSANDER	GRASPABLE
GEOMETRID	GIRONDIST	GLUTAMINE	GOOSEFOOT	GRASSIEST
GEOPHYTIC	GIVEAWAYS	GLUTENOUS	GOOSENECK	GRASSLAND
GEOPONICS	GIVEN NAME	GLUTINOUS	GOOSESTEP	GRASSQUIT
GEORGETTE	GLABELLAR	GLYCERIDE	GOOSINESS	GRATICULE
GEOSTATIC	GLADDENED	GLYCERINE	GORAKHPUR	GRATIFIED
GEOTACTIC	GLADDENER	GLYCOSIDE	GORGEABLE	GRATIFIER
GEOTROPIC	GLADIATOR	GOAL LINES	GORGONIAN	GRATINGLY
GERANIUMS	GLADIOLUS	GOALMOUTH	GORILLIAN	GRATITUDE
GERIATRIC	GLAIREOUS	GOALPOSTS	GORILLOID	GRAVELING
GERMANDER	GLAMORGAN	GOATHERDS	GOSPELLER	GRAVELISH
GERMANISM	GLAMORIZE	GOATSKINS	GOSSIPING	GRAVELLED
GERMANITE	GLAMOROUS	GO BETWEEN	GOTHICISM	GRAVENESS
GERMANIUM	GLANDERED	GO-BETWEEN	GO THROUGH	GRAVESEND
GERMANIZE	GLANDULAR	GODESBERG	GO TO	GRAVESIDE
GERMANOUS	GLARINGLY	GODFATHER	EARTH	GRAVEYARD
GERM CELLS	GLASSIEST	GODLESSLY	GOTTINGEN	GRAVIDITY
GERMICIDE	GLASSWARE	GODLINESS	GOURMANDS	GRAVITATE
GERMINANT	GLASSWORK	GODMOTHER	GOUTINESS	GRAVY BOAT
GERMINATE	GLASSWORT	GODPARENT	GOVERNESS	GREASE GUN
GERMISTON	GLEANABLE	GO-GETTERS	GOVERNING	GREASIEST
GERUNDIAL	GLEANINGS	GOGGLE BOX	GOVERNORS	GREAT-AUNT
GERUNDIVE	GLEEFULLY	GOING-OVER	GRACELESS	GREAT BEAR
GESTATION	GLENGARRY	GOLDCREST	GRADATION	GREAT BELT
GESTATORY	GLIDINGLY	GOLDEN AGE	GRADIENTS	GREATCOAT
GESTURING	GLIMMERED	GOLDENEYE	GRADUALLY	GREAT DANE
GETTING ON	GLIMPSING ·	GOLDEN EYE	GRADUATED	GREATNESS
GEYSERITE	GLISSADER	GOLDENROD	GRADUATES	GREEDIEST
GHASTLIER	GLISSANDO	GOLDFIELD	GRADUATOR	GREENAWAY
GHETTOIZE	GLISTENED	GOLDFINCH	GRAMPUSES	GREENBACK
GHOSTLIER	GLITTERED	GOLD MEDAL	GRANARIES	GREEN BEAN
GHOST TOWN	GLITZIEST	GOLD-MINER	GRANDADDY	GREEN BELT
GIANT STAR	GLOBALISM	GOLDMINES	GRANDIOSE	GREEN EYED
GIBBERING	GLOBALIST	GOLD PLATE	GRANDIOSO	GREENGAGE
GIBBERISH	GLOBALIZE	GOLDSMITH	GRAND JURY	GREENHEAD
GIBRALTAR	GLOBE FISH	GOLF BALLS	GRANDNESS	GREENHORN
GIDDINESS	GLOBOSITY	GOLF CLUBS	GRAND PRIX	GREENLAND
GIFT HORSE	GLOMERATE	GOLF LINKS	GRAND SLAM	GREENLING
GIGAHERTZ	GLOMERULE	GOLLIWOGS	GRANDSONS	GREENNESS
GIGANTISM	GLOOMIEST	GOMPHOSIS	GRANITITE	GREENROOM
GILSONITE	GLORIFIED	GONDOLIER	GRANIVORE	GREEN ROOM
GILT-EDGED	GLORIFIER	GONIATITE	GRANOLITH	GREENSAND
GIMMICKRY	GLORY HOLE	GONOPHORE	GRANTABLE	GREENWICH
GINGER ALE	GLOSSIEST	GONORRHEA	GRANULATE	GREENWOOD
GINGERING	GLOSSITIC	GOODLIEST	GRANULITE	GREETINGS
GINGER NUT	GLOSSITIS	GOOD LOOKS	GRANULOMA	GREGARINE
GIN SLINGS	GLOTTIDES	GOODNIGHT	GRAPESHOT	GREGORIAN
GIPSYWORT	GLOTTISES	GOOD-SIZED	GRAPEVINE	GRENADIER

GRENADINE
GREY AREAS
GREYBEARD
GREYHOUND
GREY-STATE
GREYWACKE
GREY WATER
GRIDIRONS
GRIEVANCE
GRILLROOM
GRIMACING
GRIMALKIN
GRIMINESS
GRINDELIA
GRIPINGLY
GRISAILLE
GRISLIEST
GRISTLIER
GRISTMILL
GRITTIEST
GRIZZLING
GROCERIES
GROGGIEST
GRONINGEN
GROOMSMAN
GROOVIEST
GROPINGLY
GROSGRAIN
GROSSNESS
GROTESQUE
GROTTIEST
GROUCHIER
GROUCHILY
GROUCHING
GROUNDAGE
GROUNDING
GROUNDNUT
GROUNDSEL
GROUPINGS
GROUPWARE
GROVELING
GROVELLED
GROVELLER
GRUBBIEST
GRUBSTAKE
GRUELLING
GRUFFNESS
GRUMBLERS
GRUMBLING
GRUMPIEST
GUANABARA

GUANGDONG
GUANIDINE
GUANOSINE
GUARANTEE
GUARANTOR
GUARDABLE
GUARDEDLY
GUARDIANS
GUARDRAIL
GUARDROOM
GUARDSMAN
GUARDSMEN
GUARD'S
 VAN
GUATEMALA
GUAYAQUIL
GUERRILLA
GUESSABLE
GUESSWORK
GUESTROOM
GUFFAWING
GUIDELINE
GUIDEPOST
GUIDINGLY
GUILDFORD
GUILDHALL
GUILDSMAN
GUILELESS
GUILLEMOT
GUILLOCHE
GUILTIEST
GUILTLESS
GUINEA PIG
GUITARIST
GULPINGLY
GUMMATOUS
GUMMINESS
GUMSHIELD
GUN COTTON
GUNPOWDER
GUNRUNNER
GUNSMITHS
GUSHINGLY
GUSTATORY
GUSTINESS
GUTTERING
GYMKHANAS
GYMNASIUM
GYMNASTIC
GYNAECOID
GYNARCHIC

GYNOECIUM
GYNOPHORE
GYRATIONS
GYRFALCON
GYROSCOPE

H

HABERGEON
HABITABLE
HABITABLY
HABITUATE
HACIENDAS
HACKAMORE
HACKBERRY
HACKNEYED
HADROSAUR
HAECCEITY
HAEMATEIN
HAEMATITE
HAEMATOID
HAEMATOMA
HAEMOCOEL
HAEMOCYTE
HAEMOSTAT
HAGBUTEER
HAGGADIST
HAGGARDLY
HAGGISHLY
HAGIARCHY
HAGIOLOGY
HAG-RIDDEN
HAIDAR ALI
HAILSTONE
HAILSTORM
HAIRBRUSH
HAIRCLOTH
HAIRGRIPS
HAIRINESS
HAIRLINES
HAIRPIECE
HAIR SHIRT
HAIR SLIDE
HAIRSTYLE
HALEAKALA
HALESOWEN
HALFBACKS
HALF-BAKED
HALF BOARD
HALF-BREED
HALF-CASTE
HALF CROWN

HALF DOZEN
HALF-DOZEN
HALF-HITCH
HALF LIGHT
HALF-LIGHT
HALF-LIVES
HALF MOONS
HALF NOTES
HALFPENCE
HALFPENNY
HALF-PLATE
HALFTONES
HALF-TRUTH
HALITOSIS
HALLELUJA
HALLIARDS
HALL-JONES
HALLMARKS
HALLOWEEN
HALLOWE'EN
HALLOWING
HALLOWMAS
HALLSTATT
HALMAHERA
HALOBIONT
HALOPHYTE
HALOTHANE
HALTINGLY
HAMADRYAD
HAMADRYAS
HAMAMATSU
HAMBURGER
HAMERSLEY
HAM-FISTED
HAMMERING
HAMMERTOE
HAMMER TOE
HAMMURABI
HAMPERING
HAMPSHIRE
HAMPSTEAD
HAMSTRING
HAMSTRUNG
HANDBASIN
HANDBILLS
HANDBOOKS
HANDBRAKE
HANDCARTS
HANDCLAPS
HANDCLASP
HANDCRAFT

HANDCUFFS
HANDICAPS
HANDINESS
HANDIWORK
HANDLEBAR
HANDLOOMS
HANDOVERS
HANDRAILS
HANDS DOWN
HANDSHAKE
HANDSPIKE
HANDSTAND
HANGERS ON
HANGERS-ON
HANGNAILS
HANGOVERS
HANKERING
HANSEATIC
HAPHAZARD
HAPHTARAH
HAPLESSLY
HAPLOLOGY
HAPPENING
HAPPINESS
HAPPY HOUR
HARANGUED
HARANGUER
HARANGUES
HARASSING
HARBINGER
HARBOURED
HARBOURER
HARDBACKS
HARDBOARD
HARDBOUND
HARD CIDER
HARD CORES
HARD COURT
HARDCOVER
HARD DISKS
HARD DRINK
HARDENING
HARDHEADS
HARDHOUSE
HARDIHOOD
HARDINESS
HARD-LINER
HARD LINES
HARD-NOSED
HARDSHIPS
HARD TIMES

HARDWOODS	HAWTHORNE	HEATHFOWL	HEMSTITCH	HEY PRESTO
HAREBELLS	HAWTHORNS	HEATHLAND	HENDIADYS	HIBERNATE
HARKENING	HAYMAKING	HEATHLIKE	HEN HOUSES	HIBERNIAN
HARLEQUIN	HAYSTACKS	HEAT PUMPS	HENPECKED	HICCUPING
HARMATTAN	HAZARDING	HEAT WAVES	HEOMANIAC	HICKORIES
HARMFULLY	HAZARDOUS	HEAVINESS	HEPATITIS	HIDDENITE
HARMONICA	HEADACHES	HEAVISIDE	HEPTAGONS	HIDEAWAYS
HARMONICS	HEADBANDS	HEAVY-DUTY	HEPTARCHY	HIDEBOUND
HARMONIES	HEADBOARD	HEBRAIZER	HERACLEAN	HIDEOUSLY
HARMONIST	HEADDRESS	HEBRIDEAN	HERALDING	HIERARCHY
HARMONIUM	HEADFIRST	HECTOGRAM	HERALDIST	HIERODULE
HARMONIZE	HEAD FIRST	HECTORING	HERBALIST	HIEROGRAM
HARMOTOME	HEADINESS	HEDGE FUND	HERBARIAL	HIEROLOGY
HARNESSED	HEADLANDS	HEDGEHOGS	HERBARIUM	HIFALUTIN
HARNESSER	HEADLIGHT	HEDGEROWS	HERBICIDE	HIGHBALLS
HARNESSES	HEADLINED	HEDONISTS	HERBIVORE	HIGHBROWS
HARPOONED	HEADLINER	HEEDFULLY	HERCULEAN	HIGH CHAIR
HARPOONER	HEADLINES	HEELPIECE	HERCYNIAN	HIGH-CLASS
HARQUEBUS	HEADPIECE	HEFTINESS	HEREAFTER	HIGH COURT
HARRIDANS	HEADREACH	HEGEMONIC	HERETICAL	HIGHER-UPS
HARROGATE	HEADRESTS	HEGUMENOS	HEREUNDER	HIGH-FLIER
HARROVIAN	HEADSCARF	HEILBRONN	HERITABLE	HIGH-FLOWN
HARROWING	HEADSHIPS	HEIMDALLR	HERITABLY	HIGH-FLYER
HARSHNESS	HEADSTALL	HEINOUSLY	HERITRESS	HIGH-GRADE
HARTBEEST	HEADSTAND	HEIRESSES	HERMITAGE	HIGH HOPES
HARTSHORN	HEAD START	HEIRLOOMS	HERMITIAN	HIGH HORSE
HARUSPICY	HEADSTOCK	HELGOLAND	HERNIATED	HIGH JINKS
HARVESTED	HEADSTONE	HELICALLY	HERODOTUS	HIGH JUMPS
HARVESTER	HEADWARDS	HELICLINE	HESELTINE	HIGHLANDS
HASDRUBAL	HEADWINDS	HELIOSTAT	HESITANCY	HIGH-LEVEL
HASHEMITE	HEADWORDS	HELIOTYPE	HESITATED	HIGHLIGHT
HASTENING	HEALINGLY	HELIOZOAN	HESITATER	HIGH POINT
HASTINESS	HEALTHFUL	HELIPORTS	HESPERIAN	HIGH-RISES
HATCHABLE	HEALTHIER	HELLDIVER	HESSONITE	HIGH ROADS
HATCHBACK	HEALTHILY	HELLEBORE	HESYCHAST	HIGH-SPEED
HATCHLING	HEARKENED	HELLENIAN	HETAERISM	HIGH SPOTS
HATCHMENT	HEARKENER	HELLENISM	HETAERIST	HIGH TABLE
HATCHWAYS	HEARTACHE	HELLENIST	HETAIRISM	HIGH TIDES
HATEFULLY	HEARTBEAT	HELLENIZE	HETERODOX	HIGH-TONED
HAT TRICKS	HEARTBURN	HELLHOUND	HETERONYM	HIGH WATER
HAUGHTIER	HEARTENED	HELLISHLY	HETEROSIS	HIJACKERS
HAUGHTILY	HEARTFELT	HELPFULLY	HEURISTIC	HIJACKING
HAVE A	HEARTHRUG	HELPMATES	HEXACHORD	HILARIOUS
BASH	HEARTIEST	HELVELLYN	HEXAGONAL	HILLBILLY
HAVENLESS	HEARTLAND	HELVETIAN	HEXAGRAMS	HILLOCKED
HAVERSACK	HEARTLESS	HELVETIUS	HEXAMETER	HILLSIDES
HAVERSIAN	HEARTSICK	HEMIALGIA	HEXAPODIC	HILVERSUM
HAVERSINE	HEARTSOME	HEMICYCLE	HEXASTICH	HIMALAYAS
HAWKSBILL	HEARTWOOD	HEMINGWAY	HEXASTYLE	HIMYARITE
HAWSEHOLE	HEARTWORM	HEMISTICH	HEXATEUCH	HINDBRAIN
HAWSEPIPE	HEATHERED	HEMITROPE	HEYERDAHL	HINDERING

HINDOOISM
HINDRANCE
HINDSIGHT
HINDU KUSH
HINDUSTAN
HINGELESS
HINGELIKE
HIP FLASKS
HIP POCKET
HIPPOCRAS
HIPPOLYTA
HIPPOLYTE
HIRELINGS
HIROSHIGE
HIROSHIMA
HIRUNDINE
HISPIDITY
HISTAMINE
HISTIDINE
HISTOGENY
HISTOGRAM
HISTOLOGY
HISTORIAN
HISTORIES
HIT AND
  RUN
HIT-AND-
  RUN
HITCHCOCK
HITCHHIKE
HITLERISM
HIT-OR-
  MISS
HIT PARADE
HIT WICKET
HOARDINGS
HOARFROST
HOARHOUND
HOARINESS
HOATCHING
HOBBESIAN
HOBGOBLIN
HOBNAILED
HOBNOBBED
HO CHI
  MINH
HODOMETER
HODOMETRY
HODOSCOPE
HOGGISHLY
HOGSHEADS
HOHENLOHE

HOIDENISH
HOI POLLOI
HOLARCTIC
HOLDOVERS
HOLD WATER
HOLE IN
  ONE
HOLIDAYED
HOLINSHED
HOLLANDER
HOLLANDIA
HOLLERING
HOLLOWEST
HOLLOWING
HOLLYHOCK
HOLLYWOOD
HOLOCAINE
HOLOCAUST
HOLOCRINE
HOLOGRAMS
HOLOGRAPH
HOLOPHYTE
HOLOTYPIC
HOLSTEINS
HOLSTERED
HOLY GHOST
HOLY GRAIL
HOLYSTONE
HOME ALONE
HOME FRONT
HOMEGROWN
HOME GUARD
HOME HELPS
HOMELANDS
HOMELIEST
HOMEMAKER
HOME MOVIE
HOMEOPATH
HOMEOWNER
HOMESTEAD
HOMETOWNS
HOME TRUTH
HOMEWARDS
HOMEYNESS
HOMICIDAL
HOMICIDES
HOMILETIC
HOMOGRAFT
HOMOGRAPH
HOMOLYSIS
HOMOLYTIC

HOMONYMIC
HOMOPHILE
HOMOPHONE
HOMOPHONY
HOMOPHYLY
HOMOPLASY
HOMOPOLAR
HOMOSPORY
HOMOTAXIC
HOMOTAXIS
HONEYBEES
HONEYCOMB
HONEYEDLY
HONEY-LIKE
HONEYMOON
HONEYTRAP
HONKY-TONK
HONORARIA
HONORIFIC
HONOR ROLL
HONOURING
HOODOOISM
HOOFBOUND
HOOK NOSED
HOOK-NOSED
HOOKWORMS
HOOLIGANS
HOOTNANNY
HOOVERING
HOPE CHEST
HOPEFULLY
HOP GARDEN
HOPLOLOGY
HOPSCOTCH
HOREHOUND
HORNBILLS
HORNINESS
HORNPIPES
HORNSTONE
HOROLOGIC
HOROSCOPE
HOROSCOPY
HORRIFIED
HORSEBACK
HORSE FAIR
HORSEHAIR
HORSEHIDE
HORSELESS
HORSELIKE
HORSEMINT
HORSEPLAY

HORSESHIT
HORSESHOE
HORSETAIL
HORSEWEED
HORSEWHIP
HORSINESS
HORTATIVE
HORTATORY
HOSPITALS
HOSPITIUM
HOSTELLER
HOSTESSES
HOSTILELY
HOSTILITY
HOTELIERS
HOTFOOTED
HOTHEADED
HOTHOUSES
HOTPLATES
HOT POTATO
HOTTENTOT
HOT WATERS
HOURGLASS
HOUSEBOAT
HOUSEBOYS
HOUSECARL
HOUSECOAT
HOUSEHOLD
HOUSELEEK
HOUSELESS
HOUSELINE
HOUSEMAID
HOUSEROOM
HOUSETOPS
HOUSEWIFE
HOUSEWORK
HOUSTONIA
HOVERPORT
HOW ARE
  YOU
HOWITZERS
HOWLINGLY
HOWSOEVER
HOWTOWDIE
HOYDENISH
HSUAN
  T'UNG
HUBRISTIC
HUCKABACK
HUCKSTERS

HUE AND
  CRY
HUFFINESS
HUGH CAPET
HU-HO-HAO-
  T'E
HUMANISTS
HUMANIZED
HUMANIZER
HUMANKIND
HUMAN-LIKE
HUMANNESS
HUMANOIDS
HUMAN RACE
HUMBLEBEE
HUMBUGGER
HUMDINGER
HUMECTANT
HUMERUSES
HUMIDNESS
HUMILIATE
HUMONGOUS
HUMORISTS
HUMOURFUL
HUMOURING
HUMPBACKS
HUMPINESS
HUNCHBACK
HUNDREDTH
HUNGARIAN
HUNGERING
HUNGRIEST
HUNKY DORY
HUNKY-DORY
HUNNISHLY
HURRICANE
HURRIEDLY
HURTFULLY
HUSBANDED
HUSBANDER
HUSBANDRY
HUSH MONEY
HUSKINESS
HYACINTHS
HYBRIDISM
HYBRIDITY
HYBRIDIZE
HYBRISTIC
HYDANTOIN
HYDATHODE
HYDERABAD

HYDRANGEA	IDIOPATHY	IMMOLATED	IMPOTENCE	INCLUSION
HYDRASTIS	IDIOPHONE	IMMOLATOR	IMPOUNDED	INCLUSIVE
HYDRATION	IDOLATERS	IMMORALLY	IMPOUNDER	INCOGNITO
HYDRAULIC	IDOLIZING	IMMORTALS	IMPRECATE	INCOME TAX
HYDRAZINE	IGNESCENT	IMMOVABLE	IMPRECISE	INCOMMODE
HYDRAZOIC	IGNITABLE	IMMOVABLY	IMPRESSED	INCORRECT
HYDRIODIC	IGNORAMUS	IMMUNIZED	IMPRESSER	INCORRUPT
HYDROCELE	IGNORANCE	IMMUNIZER	IMPRESSES	INCREASED
HYDROFOIL	IGNORATIO	IMMUTABLE	IMPRINTED	INCREASER
HYDROLOGY	IGUANODON	IMMUTABLY	IMPRINTER	INCREASES
HYDROLYSE	ILEOSTOMY	IMPACTING	IMPROBITY	INCREMENT
HYDROLYTE	ILL AT	IMPACTION	IMPROMPTU	INCRETION
HYGIENIST	EASE	IMPAIRING	IMPROVING	INCUBATED
HYPERBOLA	ILLAWARRA	IMPARTIAL	IMPROVISE	INCUBATOR
HYPERBOLE	ILLEGALLY	IMPARTING	IMPRUDENT	INCUBUSES
HYPERCUBE	ILLEGIBLE	IMPASSION	IMPUDENCE	INCULCATE
HYPERTEXT	ILLEGIBLY	IMPASSIVE	IMPUGNING	INCULPATE
HYPHENATE	ILL GOTTEN	IMPATIENS	IMPULSION	INCUMBENT
HYPNOTISM	ILL-GOTTEN	IMPATIENT	IMPULSIVE	INCURABLE
HYPNOTIST	ILLIBERAL	IMPEACHED	IMPUTABLE	INCURABLY
HYPNOTIZE	ILLICITLY	IMPEACHER	IN A BAD	INCURIOUS
HYPOCRISY	ILLNESSES	IMPEDANCE	WAY	INCURRENT
HYPOCRITE	ILLOGICAL	IMPELLENT	INABILITY	INCURRING
HYSTERICS	ILL-OMENED	IMPELLING	INAMORATA	INCURSION
	ILLUSIONS	IMPENDING	INANIMATE	INCURSIVE
I	IMAGINARY	IMPERFECT	INANITIES	INCURVATE
IBUPROFEN	IMAGINING	IMPERILED	INANITION	INDECENCY
ICE CREAMS	IMAGISTIC	IMPERIOUS	INAPTNESS	INDECORUM
ICE HOCKEY	IMBALANCE	IMPETRATE	INAUDIBLE	INDELIBLE
ICELANDER	IMBECILES	IMPETUOUS	INAUDIBLY	INDELIBLY
ICELANDIC	IMBEDDING	IMPETUSES	INAUGURAL	INDEMNIFY
ICE SHEETS	IMBRICATE	IMPIETIES	IN BETWEEN	INDEMNITY
ICE SKATED	IMBROGLIO	IMPINGING	INCAPABLE	INDENTING
ICE-SKATED	IMIDAZOLE	IMPIOUSLY	INCAPABLY	INDENTION
ICE-SKATER	IMITATING	IMPLANTED	INCARNATE	INDENTURE
ICE SKATES	IMITATION	IMPLANTER	INCAUTION	INDEXICAL
ICHNEUMON	IMITATIVE	IMPLEADER	INCENSING	INDIAN INK
ICHNOLOGY	IMITATORS	IMPLEMENT	INCENTIVE	INDICATED
ICHTHYOID	IMMANENCE	IMPLICATE	INCEPTION	INDICATOR
ICONOLOGY	IMMANENCY	IMPLODING	INCEPTIVE	INDICTING
IDEALISTS	IMMEDIACY	IMPLORING	INCESSANT	INDIGENCE
IDEALIZED	IMMEDIATE	IMPLOSION	INCIDENCE	INDIGNANT
IDEALIZER	IMMENSELY	IMPLOSIVE	INCIDENTS	INDIGNITY
IDENTICAL	IMMENSITY	IMPOLITIC	INCIPIENT	INDIGOTIC
IDENTIKIT	IMMERSING	IMPORTANT	INCISIONS	INDISPOSE
IDEOGRAMS	IMMERSION	IMPORTERS	INCISURAL	INDOCHINA
IDEOLOGUE	IMMIGRANT	IMPORTING	INCLEMENT	INDOLENCE
IDEOMOTOR	IMMIGRATE	IMPORTUNE	INCLINING	INDONESIA
IDIOBLAST	IMMINENCE	IMPOSABLE	INCLOSING	INDORSING
IDIOLECTS	IMMINGHAM	IMPOSTORS	INCLOSURE	INDRAUGHT
IDIOMATIC	IMMODESTY	IMPOSTURE	INCLUDING	INDUCIBLE

INDUCTILE	INFUSORIA	INOTROPIC	INSWINGER	INTERVENE
INDUCTING	IN GENERAL	IN PATIENT	INTAGLIOS	INTERVIEW
INDUCTION	INGENIOUS	IN-PATIENT	INTEGRAND	INTERWOVE
INDUCTIVE	INGENUITY	INPUTTING	INTEGRANT	INTESTACY
INDULGENT	INGENUOUS	INQUILINE	INTEGRATE	INTESTATE
INDULGING	INGESTING	INQUIRIES	INTEGRITY	INTESTINE
INEBRIANT	INGESTION	INQUIRING	INTELLECT	IN THE
INEBRIATE	INGESTIVE	INQUORATE	INTENDANT	CLUB
INEBRIETY	INGLENOOK	INSCRIBED	INTENDEDS	IN THE
INEFFABLE	INGRAINED	INSCRIBER	INTENDING	DARK
INEFFABLY	INGROWING	INSECTEAN	INTENSELY	IN THE
INELASTIC	INHABITED	INSELBERG	INTENSIFY	LINE
INELEGANT	INHALANTS	INSENSATE	INTENSION	IN THE
INEPTNESS	INHALATOR	INSERTING	INTENSITY	SOUP
INERTNESS	INHAMBANE	INSERTION	INTENSIVE	IN THE
INFANTILE	INHARMONY	IN-SERVICE	INTENTION	SWIM
INFARCTED	IN HARNESS	INSETTING	INTER ALIA	INTIMATED
INFATUATE	INHERENCE	INSIDE JOB	INTERBRED	INTIMATES
INFECTING	INHERITED	INSIDE OUT	INTERCEDE	INTORSION
INFECTION	INHERITOR	INSIDIOUS	INTERCEPT	IN TRANSIT
INFECTIVE	INHIBITED	INSINCERE	INTERCITY	INTRICACY
INFERABLE	INHIBITER	INSINUATE	INTERCOMS	INTRICATE
INFERENCE	INHIBITOR	INSIPIDLY	INTERCROP	INTRIGUED
INFERIORS	INITIALED	INSISTENT	INTERDICT	INTRIGUER
INFERRING	INITIALER	INSISTING	INTERESTS	INTRIGUES
INFERTILE	INITIALLY	IN SO FAR	INTERFACE	INTRINSIC
INFESTING	INITIATED	AS	INTERFERE	INTRODUCE
INFIELDER	INITIATES	INSOLENCE	INTERFILE	INTROITAL
INFIGHTER	INITIATOR	INSOLUBLE	INTERFUSE	INTROJECT
INFIRMARY	INJECTING	INSOLVENT	INTERIORS	INTROVERT
INFIRMITY	INJECTION	INSOMNIAC	INTERJECT	INTRUDERS
INFLAMING	INJECTIVE	INSPECTED	INTERLACE	INTRUDING
INFLATING	INJURABLE	INSPECTOR	INTERLARD	INTRUSION
INFLATION	INJURIOUS	INSPIRING	INTERLEAF	INTRUSIVE
INFLECTED	INJUSTICE	INSTALLED	INTERLINE	INTRUSTED
INFLECTOR	INKSTANDS	INSTALLER	INTERLINK	INTUITING
INFLICTED	INMIGRANT	INSTANCED	INTERLOCK	INTUITION
INFLICTER	INNER CITY	INSTANCES	INTERLOPE	INTUITIVE
INFLUENCE	INNERMOST	INSTANTER	INTERLUDE	INTUMESCE
INFLUENZA	INNER TUBE	INSTANTLY	INTERMENT	INUNCTION
INFORMANT	INNERVATE	INSTIGATE	INTERNEES	INUNDATED
INFORMERS	INNKEEPER	INSTILLED	INTERNING	INUNDATOR
INFORMING	INN KEEPER	INSTILLER	INTERNIST	INUTILITY
INFRACTOR	INNOCENCE	INSTINCTS	INTERNODE	INVADABLE
INFRADIAN	INNOCUOUS	INSTITUTE	INTERPLAY	INVALIDED
INFRINGED	INNOVATED	INSULATED	INTERPOSE	INVALIDLY
INFRINGER	INNOVATOR	INSULATOR	INTERPRET	INVARIANT
INFURIATE	INNSBRUCK	INSULTING	INTERRING	INVASIONS
INFUSCATE	INNUENDOS	INSURABLE	INTERRUPT	INVECTIVE
INFUSIBLE	INOCULATE	INSURANCE	INTERSECT	INVEIGHED
INFUSIONS	INORGANIC	INSURGENT	INTERVALS	INVEIGHER
				INVEIGLED

INVEIGLER
INVENTING
INVENTION
INVENTIVE
INVENTORS
INVENTORY
INVERARAY
INVERNESS
INVERSELY
INVERSION
INVERSIVE
INVERTASE
INVERTING
INVESTING
INVIDIOUS
INVIOLACY
INVIOLATE
INVISIBLE
INVISIBLY
INVOCABLE
INVOICING
INVOLUCEL
INVOLUCRE
INVOLVING
IODOMETRY
IONOPAUSE
IPSO FACTO
IRASCIBLE
IRASCIBLY
IRIAN JAYA
IRIDOTOMY
IRISH BULL
IRISH STEW
IRONBOUND
IRON CROSS
IRON HORSE
IRONSIDES
IRONSTONE
IRONWORKS
IROQUOIAN
IRRADIANT
IRRADIATE
IRRAWADDY
IRREGULAR
IRRIGABLE
IRRIGATED
IRRIGATOR
IRRITABLE
IRRITABLY
IRRITANTS
IRRITATED

IRRITATOR
IRRUPTION
IRRUPTIVE
ISAGOGICS
ISALLOBAR
ISCHAEMIA
ISINGLASS
ISLAMABAD
ISLANDERS
ISLE OF
   MAN
ISLINGTON
ISOBARISM
ISOBATHIC
ISOCHORIC
ISOCLINAL
ISOCRATIC
ISOGAMETE
ISOGAMOUS
ISOGENOUS
ISOLATING
ISOLATION
ISOLATIVE
ISOLOGOUS
ISOMERISM
ISOMERIZE
ISOMEROUS
ISOMETRIC
ISONIAZID
ISOOCTANE
ISOPROPYL
ISOSCELES
ISOSMOTIC
ISOSTATIC
ISOSTERIC
ISOTACTIC
ISOTHERAL
ISOTHERMS
ISOTROPIC
ISRAELITE
ISTHMUSES
ITALICIZE
ITCHINESS
ITCHY FEET
ITCHY PALM
ITEMIZING
ITERATION
ITERATIVE
ITINERANT
ITINERARY
ITINERATE

ITSY BITSY
ITSY-BITSY
IVY LEAGUE

J

JABBERERS
JABBERING
JABORANDI
JACARANDA
JACKASSES
JACKBOOTS
JACK FROST
JACKFRUIT
JACK KNIFE
JACKSHAFT
JACKSMELT
JACKSNIPE
JACOBITES
JAILBIRDS
JAILBREAK
JAILHOUSE
JALANDHAR
JAMBOREES
JAM-PACKED
JANISSARY
JANSENISM
JANSENIST
JANUARIES
JAPANNING
JAPONICAS
JARGONIZE
JAUNDICED
JAUNTIEST
JAYWALKED
JAYWALKER
JEALOUSLY
JEERINGLY
JELLY BEAN
JELLYFISH
JELLY ROLL
JEREMIADS
JERKINESS
JERKINGLY
JEROBOAMS
JERUSALEM
JESTINGLY
JESUITISM
JET ENGINE
JET-SETTER
JET STREAM
JEWELFISH

JEWELLERS
JEWELLERY
JEWELLING
JEW'S
   HARPS
JIB-HEADED
JITTERBUG
JOBCENTRE
JOB CENTRE
JOBSWORTH
JOCKEYING
JOCKSTRAP
JOCULARLY
JOCUNDITY
JOE PUBLIC
JOINTRESS
JOINTWORM
JOLLINESS
JONKOPING
JORDANIAN
JOSS STICK
JOURNEYED
JOURNEYER
JOVIALITY
JOYLESSLY
JOYRIDERS
JOYRIDING
JOYSTICKS
JUBILANCE
JUDDERING
JUDGEABLE
JUDGEMENT
JUDGESHIP
JUDGINGLY
JUDGMENTS
JUDICABLE
JUDICATOR
JUDICIARY
JUDICIOUS
JUICINESS
JUKEBOXES
JULLUNDUR
JUMBO JETS
JUMPINESS
JUMP START
JUMP-START
JUMPSUITS
JUNCTIONS
JUNCTURES
JUNGLE GYM
JUNKETING

JUNOESQUE
JURIDICAL
JURY BOXES
JUSTICIAR
JUSTIFIED
JUSTIFIER
JUTLANDER
JUVENILES
JUVENILIA
JUXTAPOSE

K

KADAITCHA
KADIYEVKA
KAGOSHIMA
KAISERDOM
KALAMAZOO
KALANCHOE
KAMA SUTRA
KAMCHATKA
KAMILAROI
KAMPUCHEA
KANAMYCIN
KANGAROOS
KAOHSIUNG
KAOLINITE
KARABINER
KARAGANDA
KARAKORAM
KARAKORUM
KARLSRUHE
KARNATAKA
KARYOGAMY
KARYOSOME
KARYOTYPE
KATABATIC
KATANGESE
KATHIAWAR
KAWAGUCHI
KEEP ORDER
KEEPSAKES
KEEP STATE
KELTICISM
KELTICIST
KENNELING
KENNELLED
KENTLEDGE
KEPT WOMAN
KEPT WOMEN
KERATITIS
KERATOSIS

KERBSTONE
KERCHIEFS
KERFUFFLE
KETONURIA
KETTERING
KEYBOARDS
KEYHOLDER
KEYSTONES
KEYSTROKE
KIBBUTZES
KIBBUTZIM
KICKBACKS
KICK-START
KID GLOVES
KIDNAPING
KIDNAPPED
KIDNAPPER
KIDSTAKES
KIESERITE
KILLARNEY
KILLIFISH
KILLINGLY
KILOBYTES
KILOCYCLE
KILOGRAMS
KILOHERTZ
KILOLITRE
KILOMETRE
KILOWATTS
KIMBERLEY
KINDLIEST
KINEMATIC
KINGLIEST
KINGMAKER
KING'S
    EVIL
KINGS HEAD
KING'S
    LYNN
KINGSTOWN
KINKINESS
KINSWOMAN
KIRGHIZIA
KIRKCALDY
KIROVABAD
KISANGANI
KISSINGER
KITCHENER
KITTENISH
KITTIWAKE
KLEENEXES

KNACKERED
KNAPSACKS
KNAVERIES
KNAVISHLY
KNIFE EDGE
KNIFE-EDGE
KNIGHTING
KNIPHOFIA
KNITTABLE
KNOBBLIER
KNOCKDOWN
KNOCKOUTS
KNOTGRASS
KNOTTIEST
KNOWINGLY
KNOWLEDGE
KNOXVILLE
KNUCKLING
KONIOLOGY
KOOKINESS
KOSCIUSKO
KOTA BHARU
KOWTOWING
KOZHIKODE
KRASNODAR
KRAUTROCK
KRIVOY ROG
KRONSTADT
KUIBYSHEV
KURDISTAN
KURRAJONG
KWANGTUNG
KYMOGRAPH

L

LABELLING
LABELLOID
LABIALISM
LABIALITY
LABIALIZE
LABORIOUS
LABOUR DAY
LABOURERS
LABOURING
LABOURISM
LABOURIST
LABOURITE
LABRADORS
LABURNUMS
LABYRINTH
LACCOLITH

LACERABLE
LACERATED
LACERTIAN
LACHRYMAL
LACINIATE
LACQUERED
LACQUERER
LACTATION
LADDERING
LADIES MAN
LADIES'
    MAN
LADIES'
    MEN
LADYBIRDS
LADYSHIPS
LAEVULOSE
LAGOMORPH
LALLATION
LAMAISTIC
LAMBASTED
LAMBSKINS
LAME DUCKS
LAMENTING
LAMINABLE
LAMINARIA
LAMINATED
LAMINATES
LAMINATOR
LAMINITIS
LAMP-BLACK
LAMPOONED
LAMPOONER
LAMPPOSTS
LAMPSHADE
LANCASTER
LANCEWOOD
LANCINATE
LAND AGENT
LANDAULET
LANDFALLS
LANDLORDS
LANDMARKS
LANDMINES
LAND OF
    NOD
LANDOWNER
LAND ROVER
LANDSCAPE
LANDSLIDE
LANDSLIPS

LANDWARDS
LANGOUSTE
LANGUAGES
LANGUEDOC
LANGUIDLY
LANKINESS
LANOLATED
LANTHANUM
LAODICEAN
LAPLANDER
LARCENIES
LARCENIST
LARCENOUS
LARGENESS
LARGHETTO
LARKSPURS
LARVICIDE
LARYNGEAL
LASHINGLY
LAS PALMAS
LASSITUDE
LAST-DITCH
LASTINGLY
LAST RITES
LAST STRAW
LAST THING
LATCHKEYS
LATECOMER
LATERALLY
LATERITIC
LATHERING
LATIMERIA
LATINIZER
LATITUDES
LATTER-DAY
LAUDATION
LAUDATORY
LAUGHABLE
LAUGHABLY
LAUNCHING
LAUNCH PAD
LAUNDERED
LAUNDERER
LAUNDRESS
LAUNDRIES
LAUREATES
LAVISHING
LAWGIVING
LAWLESSLY
LAWNMOWER
LAWN PARTY

LAW SCHOOL
LAXATIVES
LAYABOUTS
LAY FIGURE
LAYPERSON
LAY READER
LAY SISTER
LAZARETTO
LAZYBONES
LEADERENE
LEAD TIMES
LEAFINESS
LEAFLETED
LEAF MOULD
LEAFSTALK
LEAKINESS
LEAP YEARS
LEARNABLE
LEARNEDLY
LEASEBACK
LEASEHOLD
LEASTWAYS
LEAVENING
LECHEROUS
LECTORATE
LECTURERS
LECTURING
LEERINGLY
LEE SHORES
LEFTOVERS
LEFTWARDS
LEGALIZED
LEGATIONS
LEGENDARY
LEGGINESS
LEGGINGED
LEGIONARY
LEGISLATE
LEG-WARMER
LEICESTER
LEISURELY
LEITMOTIF
LEITMOTIV
LEMNISCUS
LEMON CURD
LEMON SOLE
LEND-LEASE
LENGTHIER
LENGTHILY
LENIENTLY
LENINABAD

LENINAKAN	LIFE CYCLE	LIP READER	LOBECTOMY	LOOK AFTER
LENINGRAD	LIFEGUARD	LIP-READER	LOCAL CALL	LOOK-ALIKE
LENIN PEAK	LIFELINES	LIPSTICKS	LOCALIZED	LOOK ALIVE
LEPONTINE	LIFE PEERS	LIQUATION	LOCALIZER	LOOKING UP
LEPTOSOME	LIFE-SAVER	LIQUEFIED	LOCAL TIME	LOOM-STATE
LEPTOTENE	LIFESPANS	LIQUEFIER	LOCATABLE	LOONINESS
LESSENING	LIFE STORY	LIQUIDATE	LOCATIONS	LOONY BINS
LETHALITY	LIFESTYLE	LIQUIDITY	LOCKERBIE	LOOPHOLES
LETHARGIC	LIFETIMES	LIQUIDIZE	LOCKSMITH	LOOSE ENDS
LETTERBOX	LIGAMENTS	LIQUORICE	LOCOMOTOR	LOOSE-LEAF
LETTERING	LIGATURES	LISPINGLY	LOCUTIONS	LOOSENESS
LEUCOCYTE	LIGHT BULB	LISTENERS	LODESTARS	LOOSENING
LEUCOTOMY	LIGHTENED	LISTENING	LODESTONE	LOQUACITY
LEUKAEMIA	LIGHT-FAST	LISTERISM	LODGEABLE	LORDLIEST
LEVANTINE	LIGHTNESS	LIST PRICE	LOFTINESS	LORDSHIPS
LEVELLERS	LIGHTNING	LITERALLY	LOGAOEDIC	LORGNETTE
LEVELLING	LIGHT RAIL	LITERATIM	LOGARITHM	LORRY PARK
LEVIATHAN	LIGHTSHIP	LITHENESS	LOG CABINS	LOS ALAMOS
LEVIGATOR	LIGHTS OUT	LITHIASIS	LOGICALLY	LOST CAUSE
LEVITATED	LIGHTS-OUT	LITHOLOGY	LOGICIANS	LOTTERIES
LEVITATOR	LIGHT YEAR	LITHOPONE	LOGISTICS	LOUDMOUTH
LEXICALLY	LIGNIFORM	LITHOTOMY	LOGOGRIPH	LOUISBURG
LEXINGTON	LIKELIEST	LITHUANIA	LOGOMACHY	LOUISIANA
LIABILITY	LILY-WHITE	LITIGABLE	LOINCLOTH	LOUNGE BAR
LIBATIONS	LIMA BEANS	LITIGANTS	LOITERERS	LOUSEWORT
LIBELLANT	LIME GREEN	LITIGATED	LOITERING	LOUSINESS
LIBELLING	LIMELIGHT	LITIGATOR	LOLLINGLY	LOVEBIRDS
LIBELLOUS	LIMERICKS	LITIGIOUS	LOLLIPOPS	LOVECHILD
LIBERALLY	LIMESTONE	LITTERBIN	LOLLOPING	LOVE FEAST
LIBERATED	LIMEWATER	LITTERING	LOMBARDIC	LOVELIEST
LIBERATOR	LIMITABLE	LITTORALS	LONELIEST	LOVE MATCH
LIBERTIES	LIMITLESS	LITURGICS	LONE WOLFS	LOVING CUP
LIBERTINE	LIMNOLOGY	LITURGIES	LONG BEACH	LOW COMEDY
LIBIDINAL	LIMOUSINE	LITURGISM	LONGBOATS	LOWERABLE
LIBRARIAN	LIMPIDITY	LITURGIST	LONGCLOTH	LOWER CASE
LIBRARIES	LIMPINGLY	LIVELIEST	LONG EATON	LOWERMOST
LIBRATION	LINCHPINS	LIVERPOOL	LONGEVITY	LOWESTOFT
LIBRATORY	LINEAMENT	LIVERWORT	LONGEVOUS	LOWLANDER
LIBRETTOS	LINEARITY	LIVERYMAN	LONG FACES	LOWLINESS
LIBRIFORM	LINEATION	LIVERYMEN	LONGICORN	LOW-MINDED
LICENSEES	LINEOLATE	LIVESTOCK	LONGINGLY	LOW-NECKED
LICENSING	LINGERERS	LIVE WIRES	LONGITUDE	LOW SEASON
LICHENOID	LINGERING	LIVIDNESS	LONG JOHNS	LOYALISTS
LICHENOUS	LINGUISTS	LJUBLJANA	LONG-LIVED	LOYALTIES
LIDOCAINE	LINGULATE	LLANDUDNO	LONG-RANGE	LUBRICANT
LIEGE LORD	LINKOPING	LOADSTARS	LONGSHIPS	LUBRICATE
LIENTERIC	LINOLEATE	LOADSTONE	LONGSHORE	LUBRICITY
LIFE BELTS	LINOTYPER	LOAMINESS	LONG SHOTS	LUBRICOUS
LIFEBLOOD	LIONIZING	LOAN SHARK	LONG SINCE	LUCIFERIN
LIFEBOATS	LIPOLYSIS	LOANWORDS	LONGUEUIL	LUCKINESS
LIFE BUOYS	LIPOLYTIC	LOATHSOME	LONGUEURS	LUCKY DIPS

LUCRATIVE	MACHINIST	MAINMASTS	MAN-AT-ARMS	MARCASITE
LUCUBRATE	MACHMETER	MAINSAILS	MANCHURIA	MARCH HARE
LUDICROUS	MACKENZIE	MAINSHEET	MANCUNIAN	MARCH-PAST
LUFTWAFFE	MACKERELS	MAINSTAYS	MANDARINS	MARCO POLO
LULLABIES	MACROCOSM	MAJESTICS	MANDATARY	MARDI GRAS
LULLINGLY	MACROCYST	MAJESTIES	MANDATING	MARE'S NEST
LUMBERING	MACROCYTE	MAJORDOMO	MANDATORY	MARGARINE
LUMBERMAN	MACRUROID	MAJOR DOMO	MANDIBLES	MARGARITA
LUMBERMEN	MACRUROUS	MAJORETTE	MANDOLINS	MARGARITE
LUMBRICAL	MADDENING	MAJOR SUIT	MANDRAKES	MARGINATE
LUMINAIRE	MADELEINE	MAJUSCULE	MANDRILLS	MARIEHAMN
LUMINANCE	MAD HATTER	MAKE A MOVE	MAN-EATERS	MARIENBAD
LUMINESCE	MADHOUSES	MAKE MERRY	MAN-EATING	MARIGOLDS
LUMPINESS	MADREPORE	MAKE PEACE	MANEUVERS	MARIJUANA
LUNATICAL	MADRIGALS	MAKE READY	MAN FRIDAY	MARINADES
LUNISOLAR	MAELSTROM	MAKESHIFT	MANGALORE	MARINATED
LUNITIDAL	MAGAZINES	MAKEYEVKA	MANGANATE	MARITALLY
LURIDNESS	MAGDEBURG	MALACHITE	MANGANESE	MARKDOWNS
LURKINGLY	MAGICALLY	MALADROIT	MANGANITE	MARKETEER
LUSTFULLY	MAGIC EYES	MALAGUENA	MANGANOUS	MARKETERS
LUSTINESS	MAGICIANS	MALANDERS	MANGETOUT	MARKETING
LUTANISTS	MAGIC WAND	MALATHION	MANGINESS	MARK TWAIN
LUTHERISM	MAGISTERY	MALAYALAM	MANGROVES	MARMALADE
LUXEMBURG	MAGISTRAL	MALAYSIAN	MANHANDLE	MARMOREAL
LUXURIANT	MAGMATISM	MALDIVIAN	MANHATTAN	MARMOSETS
LUXURIATE	MAGNESIAN	MALFORMED	MANHUNTER	MAROONING
LUXURIOUS	MAGNESITE	MALGRE LUI	MANICURED	MARQUETRY
LYCHGATES	MAGNESIUM	MALIC ACID	MANICURES	MARQUISES
LYME REGIS	MAGNETICS	MALICIOUS	MANIFESTO	MARRAKECH
LYMINGTON	MAGNETISM	MALIGNANT	MANIFESTS	MARRIAGES
LYMPHATIC	MAGNETITE	MALIGNING	MANIFOLDS	MARROWFAT
LYONNAISE	MAGNETIZE	MALIGNITY	MANIZALES	MARSEILLE
LYOPHILIC	MAGNETRON	MALLEABLE	MANLINESS	MARSHALCY
LYOPHOBIC	MAGNIFICO	MALLEMUCK	MANNEQUIN	MARSHALED
LYREBIRDS	MAGNIFIED	MALLEOLAR	MANNERISM	MARSUPIAL
LYRICALLY	MAGNIFIER	MALLEOLUS	MANNERIST	MARSUPIUM
LYRICISMS	MAGNITUDE	MALTINESS	MANNISHLY	MARTINETS
LYRICISTS	MAGNOLIAS	MALTSTERS	MANOEUVRE	MARTINMAS
LYSIMETER	MAHAJANGA	MALVOISIE	MANOMETER	MARTYRDOM
LYSOSOMAL	MAHARAJAH	MAMA'S BOYS	MANOMETRY	MARTYRING
	MAHARAJAS	MAMILLARY	MANSFIELD	MARVELING
M	MAHARANIS	MAMILLATE	MANTILLAS	MARVELLED
MACARONIC	MAIDSTONE	MAMMALIAN	MANUBRIAL	MARZIPANS
MACAROONS	MAIDUGURI	MAMMALOGY	MANUBRIUM	MASCULINE
MACEDOINE	MAILBOXES	MAMMOGRAM	MANY-SIDED	MASOCHISM
MACEDONIA	MAILCOACH	MAMMONISM	MAPLE LEAF	MASOCHIST
MACERATED	MAIL ORDER	MAMMONIST	MARACAIBO	MASSACRED
MACERATER	MAILSHOTS	MANACLING	MARATHONS	MASSACRER
MACHINATE	MAINFRAME		MARAUDERS	MASSACRES
MACHINERY	MAINLINED		MARAUDING	MASSAGING
MACHINING	MAIN LINES			

MASSIVELY	MEATBALLS	MEMORIALS	MESOPAUSE	MICROTOME
MASS MEDIA	MEATINESS	MEMORIZED	MESOPHYLL	MICROTOMY
MASTERDOM	MECHANICS	MEMORIZER	MESOPHYTE	MICROTONE
MASTERFUL	MECHANISM	MEMSAHIBS	MESSALINE	MICROWAVE
MASTERING	MECHANIST	MENADIONE	MESSENGER	MIDDLE AGE
MASTER KEY	MECHANIZE	MENAGERIE	MESSIANIC	MIDDLEMAN
MASTHEADS	MEDALLION	MEN-AT-	MESSIEURS	MIDDLEMEN
MASTICATE	MEDALLIST	ARMS	MESSINESS	MIDDLESEX
MASTODONS	MEDIAEVAL	MENDACITY	MESTRANOL	MIDDLETON
MATAMOROS	MEDIATING	MENDELIAN	METABOLIC	MIDHEAVEN
MATCHLESS	MEDIATION	MENDELISM	METALLINE	MIDNIGHTS
MATCHMARK	MEDIATIVE	MENDICANT	METALLING	MIDPOINTS
MATCH PLAY	MEDIATIZE	MENISCOID	METALLIST	MIDSTREAM
MATCHWOOD	MEDIATORS	MENOPAUSE	METALLIZE	MIDSUMMER
MATELASSE	MEDICABLE	MEN'S	METALLOID	MID-WICKET
MATERIALS	MEDICABLY	ROOMS	METALWORK	MIDWIFERY
MATERNITY	MEDICALLY	MENSTRUAL	METAMERAL	MIDWINTER
MATEYNESS	MEDICATED	MENSTRUUM	METAMERIC	MIFFINESS
MATRIARCH	MEDICINAL	MENTAL AGE	METAPHASE	MIGHTIEST
MATRICIDE	MEDICINES	MENTALISM	METAPHORS	MIGRAINES
MATRIMONY	MEDITATED	MENTALITY	METAPLASM	MIGRATING
MATRONAGE	MEDITATOR	MENTIONED	METAXYLEM	MIGRATION
MATSUMOTO	MEDULLARY	MENTIONER	METEORITE	MIGRATORY
MATSUYAMA	MEGACYCLE	MENTORIAL	METEOROID	MILCH COWS
MATTERING	MEGADEATH	MEPACRINE	METHADONE	MILESTONE
MATUTINAL	MEGAHERTZ	MERBROMIN	METHODISM	MILITANCY
MAULSTICK	MEGALITHS	MERCAPTAN	METHODIST	MILITANTS
MAUNDERED	MEGAPHONE	MERCENARY	METHODIZE	MILITARIA
MAUNDERER	MEGASPORE	MERCERIZE	METHOXIDE	MILITATED
MAURITIAN	MEGASTORE	MERCHANTS	METHYLATE	MILK FLOAT
MAURITIUS	MEGHALAYA	MERCILESS	METHYLENE	MILKINESS
MAUSOLEAN	MELANESIA	MERCURATE	METRALGIA	MILKMAIDS
MAUSOLEUM	MELANOSIS	MERCURIAL	METRICIZE	MILK SHAKE
MAVERICKS	MELATONIN	MERCUROUS	METRIC TON	MILK TOOTH
MAWKISHLY	MELBOURNE	MERGANSER	METRIFIER	MILLBOARD
MAXILLARY	MELIORATE	MERIDIANS	METROLOGY	MILLENARY
MAXIMALLY	MELIORISM	MERINGUES	METRONOME	MILLENNIA
MAXIMIZED	MELITOPOL	MERITEDLY	MEZZANINE	MILLEPEDE
MAXIMIZER	MELLOWEST	MERITLESS	MEZZOTINT	MILLEPORE
MAYFLOWER	MELLOWING	MEROCRINE	MICACEOUS	MILLERITE
MAYORALTY	MELODIOUS	MEROZOITE	MICHOACAN	MILLIBARS
MAYORSHIP	MELODIZER	MERRIMENT	MICROBIAL	MILLIGRAM
MBUJIMAYI	MELODRAMA	MERRINESS	MICROCHIP	MILLINERS
MCCARTNEY	MELTDOWNS	MERSEBURG	MICROCOPY	MILLINERY
MEANDERED	MELTINGLY	MESCALINE	MICROCOSM	MILLIONTH
MEANDERER	MELTWATER	MESENTERY	MICROCYTE	MILLIPEDE
MEANDROUS	MELUNGEON	MESICALLY	MICRODONT	MILLIVOLT
MEANS TEST	MEMBRANES	MESMERISM	MICROFILM	MILLPONDS
MEANTIMES	MEMORABLE	MESMERIST	MICROMESH	MILLSTONE
MEANWHILE	MEMORABLY	MESMERIZE	MICROPYLE	MILLWHEEL
MEASURING	MEMORANDA	MESOMORPH	MICROSOME	MILOMETER

MILWAUKEE	MISMANAGE	MOLECULAR	MONOMETER	MORTALITY
MIMICKING	MISNOMERS	MOLECULES	MONOPHAGY	MORTAL SIN
MINARETED	MISONEISM	MOLEHILLS	MONOPHONY	MORTGAGED
MINCEMEAT	MISONEIST	MOLESKINS	MONOPLANE	MORTGAGEE
MINCE PIES	MISPLACED	MOLESTERS	MONOPSONY	MORTGAGES
MINCINGLY	MISPRINTS	MOLESTING	MONORAILS	MORTGAGOR
MINEFIELD	MISQUOTED	MOLLIFIED	MONOSOMIC	MORTICIAN
MINELAYER	MISREPORT	MOLLIFIER	MONOSTICH	MORTIFIED
MINIATURE	MISSHAPEN	MOLLUSCAN	MONOSTOME	MORTIFIER
MINIBUSES	MISSILERY	MOLYBDATE	MONOTONIC	MOSAICIST
MINIDRESS	MISSIONER	MOLYBDOUS	MONOTREME	MOSCHATEL
MINIMALLY	MISSTATED	MOMENTARY	MONOTYPER	MOSQUITOS
MINIMIZED	MISTAKING	MOMENTOUS	MONOTYPIC	MOSS-GROWN
MINIMIZER	MISTIMING	MOMENTUMS	MONOXIDES	MOSSINESS
MINISCULE	MISTINESS	MONACHISM	MONSIGNOR	MOTHBALLS
MINISKIRT	MISTLETOE	MONADNOCK	MONSTROUS	MOTH EATEN
MINISTERS	MISTRIALS	MONARCHAL	MONTAUBAN	MOTH-EATEN
MINITRACK	MITICIDAL	MONASTERY	MONT BLANC	MOTHERING
MINNESOTA	MITIGABLE	MONATOMIC	MONTERREY	MOTHPROOF
MINOR SUIT	MITIGATED	MONEYBAGS	MONTHLIES	MOTIONING
MINSTRELS	MITIGATOR	MONEYLESS	MONTICULE	MOTIVATED
MINT JULEP	MITREWORT	MONEYWORT	MONTREUIL	MOTOCROSS
MINUSCULE	MNEMONICS	MONGERING	MONUMENTS	MOTORBIKE
MINUTE GUN	MOANINGLY	MONGOLIAN	MONZONITE	MOTORBOAT
MINUTE MAN	MOBILIZED	MONGOLISM	MOODINESS	MOTORCADE
MIRRORING	MOBOCRACY	MONGOLOID	MOONBEAMS	MOTORCARS
MIRTHLESS	MOCCASINS	MONGOOSES	MOON-FACED	MOTORHOME
MISADVISE	MOCKERIES	MONITORED	MOONINESS	MOTORISTS
MISBEHAVE	MOCKINGLY	MONITRESS	MOONLIGHT	MOTORIZED
MISBELIEF	MODELLING	MONKEYING	MOONRAKER	MOTORWAYS
MISCALLED	MODERATED	MONKEY NUT	MOONSCAPE	MOULDABLE
MISCHANCE	MODERATES	MONKSHOOD	MOONSHINE	MOULDERED
MISCHIEFS	MODERATOR	MONOBASIC	MOON SHOTS	MOULDIEST
MISCOUNTS	MODERATOS	MONOCHORD	MOONSTONE	MOULDINGS
MISCREANT	MODERNISM	MONOCLINE	MOOT POINT	MOUNTABLE
MISCREATE	MODERNIST	MONOCOQUE	MORACEOUS	MOUNTAINS
MISDEALER	MODERNITY	MONOCRACY	MORADABAD	MOUSETAIL
MISDIRECT	MODERNIZE	MONOCULAR	MORALISTS	MOUSETRAP
MISERABLE	MODIFIERS	MONOCYTIC	MORALIZED	MOUSINESS
MISERABLY	MODIFYING	MONODRAMA	MORALIZER	MOUSTACHE
MISFIRING	MODILLION	MONOGENIC	MORATORIA	MOUTHFULS
MISGIVING	MODULATED	MONOGRAMS	MORBIDITY	MOUTHPART
MISGOVERN	MODULATOR	MONOGRAPH	MORDACITY	MOUTHWASH
MISGUIDED	MOGADISHU	MONOLATER	MORDANTLY	MOVEABLES
MISGUIDER	MOISTENED	MONOLATRY	MORECAMBE	MOVEMENTS
MISHANDLE	MOISTENER	MONOLAYER	MORGANITE	MOVIE STAR
MISINFORM	MOISTNESS	MONOLITHS	MORMONISM	MOVIETONE
MISJUDGED	MOLDAVIAN	MONOLOGIC	MORPHEMES	MOVING VAN
MISJUDGER	MOLDAVITE	MONOLOGUE	MORPHEMIC	MUCIC ACID
MISLAYING	MOLDERING	MONOMANIA	MORPHOSIS	MUCKHEAPS
MISLEADER	MOLDINESS	MONOMERIC	MORSE CODE	MUCKINESS

MUCKRAKER
MUCRONATE
MUDDINESS
MUDGUARDS
MUGGINESS
MUGGINSES
MULATTOES
MULETEERS
MULLINGAR
MULLIONED
MULTICIDE
MULTIFOIL
MULTIFOLD
MULTIFORM
MULTIHULL
MULTIPARA
MULTIPLES
MULTIPLET
MULTIPLEX
MULTITUDE
MUMMIFIED
MUNDANELY
MUNICIPAL
MUNIMENTS
MUNITIONS
MURDERERS
MURDERESS
MURDERING
MURDEROUS
MURKINESS
MURMURING
MUSACEOUS
MUSCADINE
MUSCARINE
MUSCATELS
MUSCLEMAN
MUSCLEMEN
MUSCOVADO
MUSCOVITE
MUSEOLOGY
MUSHINESS
MUSHROOMS
MUSICALLY
MUSIC HALL
MUSICIANS
MUSKETEER
MUSKINESS
MUSKMELON
MUSLIMISM
MUSTACHES
MUSTACHIO

MUSTELINE
MUSTERING
MUSTINESS
MUTAGENIC
MUTATIONS
MUTILATED
MUTILATOR
MUTINEERS
MUTINYING
MUTTERERS
MUTTERING
MUTUALITY
MUTUALIZE
MUZZINESS
MYCENAEAN
MYDRIASIS
MYDRIATIC
MYOGLOBIN
MYOGRAPHY
MYOLOGIST
MYROBALAN
MYSTAGOGY
MYSTERIES
MYSTICISM
MYSTIFIED
MYSTIFIER
MYSTIQUES
MYTHICIZE
MYTHOLOGY
MYXOEDEMA
MYXOVIRUS

N
NAHUATLAN
NAILBRUSH
NAIL FILES
NAIVENESS
NAIVETIES
NAKEDNESS
NAMECHECK
NAMEPLATE
NAME PLATE
NAMESAKES
NANNY GOAT
NANOMETER
NANTUCKET
NAPHTHENE
NAPPINESS
NARCISSUS
NARCOTICS
NARCOTISM

NARCOTIZE
NARRATING
NARRATION
NARRATIVE
NARRATORS
NARROWING
NASHVILLE
NASTINESS
NATIONALS
NATROLITE
NATTERING
NATTINESS
NATURALLY
NATURISTS
NAUGHTIER
NAUGHTILY
NAUSEATED
NAUTILOID
NAVICULAR
NAVIGABLE
NAVIGABLY
NAVIGATED
NAVIGATOR
NEAP TIDES
NEAR THING
NEBULIZER
NECESSARY
NECESSITY
NECKBANDS
NECKCLOTH
NECKLACES
NECKLINES
NECKPIECE
NECROLOGY
NECROTOMY
NECTARIAL
NECTARINE
NEEDFULLY
NEEDINESS
NEFARIOUS
NEGATIONS
NEGATIVED
NEGATIVES
NEGLECTED
NEGLECTER
NEGLIGEES
NEGLIGENT
NEGOTIANT
NEGOTIATE
NEGRITUDE
NEIGHBOUR

NEMERTEAN
NEODYMIUM
NEOLITHIC
NEOLOGISM
NEOLOGIST
NEOLOGIZE
NEON LIGHT
NEOPHYTES
NEOPHYTIC
NEOPLASTY
NEOTENOUS
NEPHELINE
NEPHOGRAM
NEPHOLOGY
NEPHRITIC
NEPHRITIS
NEPHROSIS
NEPHROTIC
NEPTUNIAN
NEPTUNIUM
NERVE CELL
NERVELESS
NERVINESS
NERVOUSLY
NESCIENCE
NESTLINGS
NESTORIAN
NETANYAHU
NETWORKED
NEUCHATEL
NEURALGIA
NEURALGIC
NEUROGLIA
NEUROLOGY
NEUROPATH
NEUROTICS
NEUROTOMY
NEUTERING
NEUTRALLY
NEUTRETTO
NEVER MIND
NEVERMORE
NEW BROOMS
NEWCASTLE
NEWCOMERS
NEW FOREST
NEW GUINEA
NEW JERSEY
NEWLYWEDS
NEWLY WEDS
NEWMARKET

NEW MEXICO
NEW ROMNEY
NEWSAGENT
NEWSGROUP
NEWSHOUND
NEWSINESS
NEWSPAPER
NEWSPRINT
NEWSREELS
NEWSROOMS
NEWSSHEET
NEWSSTAND
NEWTONIAN
NEW YORKER
NICARAGUA
NICCOLITE
NICHOLSON
NICKELING
NICKELLED
NICKELOUS
NICKNACKS
NICKNAMED
NICKNAMES
NICOTIANA
NICOTINIC
NICTITATE
NIFTINESS
NIGGARDLY
NIGHTCAPS
NIGHTCLUB
NIGHTFALL
NIGHTGOWN
NIGHTHAWK
NIGHTLIFE
NIGHTLONG
NIGHTMARE
NIGHT OWLS
NIGHT SOIL
NIGHTTIME
NIGHTWEAR
NIGROSINE
NIHILISTS
NIKOLAYEV
NINETEENS
NINETIETH
NIPPINESS
NIPPONESE
NISI PRIUS
NISSEN HUT
NITPICKER
NITRAMINE

NITRATION	NOTARIZED	NURSLINGS	OBSESSIVE	OFFENSIVE
NITRIDING	NOT AT	NURTURING	OBSOLESCE	OFFERINGS
NIVERNAIS	HOME	NUTHOUSES	OBSTACLES	OFFERTORY
NO ACCOUNT	NOTATIONS	NUTRIENTS	OBSTETRIC	OFFHANDED
NO-ACCOUNT	NOTEBOOKS	NUTRIMENT	OBSTINACY	OFFICE BOY
NOBILIARY	NOTEPAPER	NUTRITION	OBSTINATE	OFFICIALS
NOBLENESS	NOTHING ON	NUTRITIVE	OBSTRUENT	OFFICIANT
NOCTILUCA	NOTIFYING	NUTSHELLS	OBTAINING	OFFICIARY
NOCTURNAL	NO-TILLAGE	NUTTINESS	OBTRUDING	OFFICIATE
NOCTURNES	NOTOCHORD	NYASALAND	OBTRUSION	OFFICIOUS
NO-GO	NOTOGAEAN	NYMPHALID	OBTRUSIVE	OFF-LOADED
AREAS	NOTORIETY	NYSTAGMIC	OBVERSION	OFF-ROADER
NOISELESS	NOTORIOUS	NYSTAGMUS	OBVIATING	OFF SEASON
NOISINESS	NOT PROVEN		OBVIATION	OFFSHOOTS
NOMINALLY	NOTRE DAME	**O**	OBVIOUSLY	OFFSPRING
NOMINATED	NOURISHED	OAST HOUSE	OCCASIONS	OFF-STREET
NOMINATOR	NOURISHER	OBBLIGATO	OCCIPITAL	OFF THE
NOMOCRACY	NOVELETTE	OBCORDATE	OCCLUDENT	PEG
NOMOGRAPH	NOVELISTS	OBEDIENCE	OCCLUSION	OGBOMOSHO
NONAGONAL	NOVELTIES	OBEISANCE	OCCLUSIVE	OILFIELDS
NONEDIBLE	NOVEMBERS	OBELISCAL	OCCULTISM	OIL PAINTS
NONENTITY	NOVITIATE	OBFUSCATE	OCCULTIST	OIL SLICKS
NON-EVENTS	NOVOCAINE	OBJECTIFY	OCCUPANCY	OIL TANKER
NON-FINITE	NOXIOUSLY	OBJECTING	OCCUPANTS	OINTMENTS
NONILLION	NUCLEATOR	OBJECTION	OCCUPIERS	OKLAHOMAN
NONLINEAR	NUCLEOLAR	OBJECTIVE	OCCUPYING	OLDENBURG
NONPAREIL	NUCLEOLUS	OBJECTORS	OCCURRENT	OLD FLAMES
NONPAROUS	NUCLEONIC	OBJET	OCCURRING	OLD MASTER
NONRACIAL	NUEVO LEON	D'ART	OCELLATED	OLD SCHOOL
NONSMOKER	NUISANCES	OBJURGATE	OCHLOCRAT	OLD STAGER
NONVERBAL	NUKU'ALOFA	OBLATIONS	OCTAGONAL	OLD-TIMERS
NONWHITES	NULLIFIED	OBLIGABLE	OCTAMETER	OLEACEOUS
NORMALITY	NULLIFIER	OBLIGATED	OCTENNIAL	OLEANDERS
NORMALIZE	NULLIPARA	OBLIGATOR	OCTILLION	OLECRANAL
NORMATIVE	NULLIPORE	OBLIQUITY	OCTOPUSES	OLECRANON
NORTH DOWN	NULLITIES	OBLIVIOUS	ODALISQUE	OLEOGRAPH
NORTHEAST	NUMBERING	OBNOXIOUS	ODD JOBMAN	OLEORESIN
NORTHERLY	NUMBER ONE	OBREPTION	ODD-JOB	OLFACTION
NORTH POLE	NUMBER TEN	OBSCENELY	MAN	OLFACTORY
NORTHWARD	NUMBSKULL	OBSCENITY	ODD MAN	OLIGARCHY
NORTHWEST	NUMERABLE	OBSCURANT	OUT	OLIGOCENE
NORTHWICH	NUMERABLY	OBSCURELY	ODD MEN	OLIGOPOLY
NORWEGIAN	NUMERATOR	OBSCURING	OUT	OLIVE DRAB
NOSEBLEED	NUMERICAL	OBSCURITY	ODOMETERS	OLIVENITE
NOSECONES	NUMMULITE	OBSEQUENT	ODOURLESS	OLYMPIADS
NOSEDIVED	NUMSKULLS	OBSEQUIES	OESTROGEN	OLYMPIANS
NOSEDIVES	NUNNERIES	OBSERVANT	OFF CHANCE	OMBUDSMAN
NOSE PIECE	NUREMBERG	OBSERVERS	OFF COLOUR	OMBUDSMEN
NOSTALGIA	NURSELING	OBSERVING	OFFENBACH	OMELETTES
NOSTALGIC	NURSEMAID	OBSESSING	OFFENDERS	OMINOUSLY
NOSTOLOGY	NURSERIES	OBSESSION	OFFENDING	OMISSIBLE

OMISSIONS
OMNIBUSES
OMNIRANGE
OMOPHAGIA
OMOPHAGIC
ON ACCOUNT
ON A
  STRING
ONCE A
  WEEK
ONCE-OVERS
ONCOGENIC
ONDOGRAPH
ONDOMETER
ONEROUSLY
ONION DOME
ONIONSKIN
ONLOOKERS
ONLOOKING
ONOMASTIC
ONRUSHING
ONSLAUGHT
ON THE
  BEAM
ON THE
  MEND
ON THE
  NAIL
ON THE
  SPOT
ON THE
  TROT
ONTOGENIC
OOGENESIS
OOGENETIC
OOLOGICAL
OPEN-ENDED
OPEN-FACED
OPEN HOUSE
OPENING UP
OPEN ORDER
OPEN SHOPS
OPERATING
OPERATION
OPERATIVE
OPERATORS
OPERCULAR
OPERCULUM
OPERETTAS
OPHIOLOGY
OPPONENCY
OPPONENTS

OPPORTUNE
OPPOSABLE
OPPOSABLY
OPPOSITES
OPPRESSED
OPPRESSOR
OPTICALLY
OPTICIANS
OPTIMISTS
OPTIMIZED
OPTOMETER
OPTOMETRY
OPULENTLY
ORANGEADE
ORANGEISM
ORANGEMAN
ORANGE TIP
ORANG-UTAN
ORATORIES
ORATORIOS
ORBICULAR
ORCHESTRA
ORDAINING
ORDER ARMS
ORDERLIES
ORDINANCE
ORGANELLE
ORGANISMS
ORGANISTS
ORGANIZED
ORGANIZER
ORGANZINE
ORGIASTIC
ORIENTALS
ORIENTATE
ORIGINALS
ORIGINATE
ORNAMENTS
ORNITHINE
OROGRAPHY
OROLOGIST
ORPHANAGE
ORPHANING
ORRIS ROOT
ORTANIQUE
ORTHODOXY
ORTHOEPIC
ORTHOPTER
ORTHOPTIC
OSCILLATE
OSCITANCY

OSMOMETER
OSMOMETRY
OSNABRUCK
OSSICULAR
OSSIFRAGE
OSSIFYING
OSTENSIVE
OSTEOLOGY
OSTEOPATH
OSTEOTOME
OSTEOTOMY
OSTRACISM
OSTRACIZE
OSTRICHES
OTHERNESS
OTHERWISE
OTOCYSTIC
OTOLITHIC
OTOLOGIST
OTOSCOPIC
OUBLIETTE
OUR FATHER
OURSELVES
OUT AND
  OUT
OUT-AND-
  OUT
OUTBRAVED
OUTBREAKS
OUTBURSTS
OUTCASTES
OUTERMOST
OUTFACING
OUTFITTED
OUTFITTER
OUTFOUGHT
OUTFOXING
OUTGOINGS
OUTGROWTH
OUTHOUSES
OUTLASTED
OUTLAWING
OUTLAYING
OUTLINING
OUTLIVING
OUTNUMBER
OUT-OF-
  DATE
OUT OF
  STEP
OUTPLAYED
OUTRAGING

OUTRANKED
OUTRIDDEN
OUTRIDERS
OUTRIDING
OUTRIGGER
OUTRUNNER
OUTSIDERS
OUTSKIRTS
OUTSOURCE
OUTSPOKEN
OUTSPREAD
OUTSTARED
OUTSTAYED
OUTTALKED
OUTVOTING
OUTWARDLY
OUT WITH
  IT
OUTWITTED
OUTWORKER
OVATIONAL
OVEN-READY
OVERACTED
OVERAWING
OVERBLOWN
OVERBOARD
OVERBORNE
OVERBUILD
OVERCHECK
OVERCLOUD
OVERCOATS
OVERCROWD
OVERDOING
OVERDOSED
OVERDOSES
OVERDRAFT
OVERDRAWN
OVERDRESS
OVERDRIVE
OVERFLOWN
OVERFLOWS
OVERGLAZE
OVERGROWN
OVERHANGS
OVERHAULS
OVERHEADS
OVERHEARD
OVERISSUE
OVERJOYED
OVERLADEN
OVERLOADS

OVERLORDS
OVERLYING
OVERNIGHT
OVERPAINT
OVERPOWER
OVERPRICE
OVERPRINT
OVERPROOF
OVERRATED
OVERREACH
OVERREACT
OVERRIDER
OVERRULED
OVERSCORE
OVERSEERS
OVERSEXED
OVERSHOES
OVERSHOOT
OVERSIGHT
OVERSIZED
OVERSKIRT
OVERSLEEP
OVERSLEPT
OVERSPEND
OVERSPILL
OVERSTATE
OVERSTOCK
OVERTAKEN
OVERTAXED
OVERTHREW
OVERTHROW
OVERTONES
OVERTRADE
OVERTRICK
OVERTRUMP
OVERTURES
OVERVIEWS
OVERWEIGH
OVERWHELM
OVERWRITE
OVIFEROUS
OVIPAROUS
OVOTESTIS
OVULATING
OVULATION
OWNERSHIP
OXIDATION
OXIDATIVE
OXIDIZING
OXYGENATE
OXYGENIZE

OYSTER BED	PALTRIEST	PARALYSIS	PARTI PRIS	PATROL CAR
OZOCERITE	PAMPERING	PARALYTIC	PARTISANS	PATROLLED
	PAMPHLETS	PARAMATTA	PARTITION	PATROLLER
P	PANATELAS	PARAMEDIC	PARTITIVE	PATROLMAN
PACEMAKER	PANDA CARS	PARAMETER	PARTNERED	PATROLMEN
PACHYDERM	PANDEMICS	PARAMORPH	PARTRIDGE	PATRONAGE
PACHYTENE	PANDERING	PARAMOUNT	PART-SONGS	PATRONESS
PACIFIERS	PANDURATE	PARAMOURS	PART WORKS	PATRONIZE
PACIFISTS	PANEGYRIC	PARANOIAC	PARTY LINE	PATTERING
PACIFYING	PANELLING	PARAPLASM	PARTY WALL	PATTERNED
PACKAGERS	PANELLIST	PARASITES	PAS DE	PAULOWNIA
PACKAGING	PANHANDLE	PARASITIC	DEUX	PAUPERISM
PACKED-OUT	PANICKING	PARATAXIS	PASO DOBLE	PAUPERIZE
PACKHORSE	PANMUNJOM	PARATHION	PASSBOOKS	PAUSINGLY
PADERBORN	PANNIKINS	PARBOILED	PASSED OUT	PAVEMENTS
PADLOCKED	PANOPLIED	PARBUCKLE	PASSENGER	PAVILIONS
PAEDERAST	PANORAMAS	PARCELING	PASSERINE	PAWKINESS
PAEDOLOGY	PANORAMIC	PARCELLED	PASSERSBY	PAWNSHOPS
PAGANIZER	PANSOPHIC	PARCENARY	PASSIONAL	PAYCHECKS
PAGEANTRY	PANTHEISM	PARCHMENT	PASSIVELY	PAYMASTER
PAILLASSE	PANTHEIST	PARDONERS	PASSIVISM	PAY PACKET
PAILLETTE	PANTHEONS	PARDONING	PASSIVIST	PAY PHONES
PAINFULLY	PANTOMIME	PARDUBICE	PASSIVITY	PEACEABLE
PAINTBALL	PANTY HOSE	PAREGORIC	PASSOVERS	PEACEABLY
PAINTERLY	PAPARAZZI	PARENTAGE	PASSPORTS	PEACE PIPE
PAINTINGS	PAPARAZZO	PARENTING	PASSWORDS	PEACETIME
PAINTWORK	PAPERBACK	PARGETING	PASTICHES	PEARLIEST
PAKISTANI	PAPERBOYS	PARHELION	PASTILLES	PEARLITIC
PALANQUIN	PAPER CLIP	PARI PASSU	PASTINESS	PEARLIZED
PALATABLE	PAPER TAPE	PARISIANS	PASTORALE	PEARMAINS
PALATABLY	PAPERWORK	PARLEYING	PASTORALS	PEASANTRY
PALEFACES	PAPETERIE	PARLOR CAR	PASTORATE	PEA SOUPER
PALEMBANG	PAPILLARY	PARNASSUS	PASTURAGE	PECCARIES
PALESTINE	PAPILLOMA	PAROCHIAL	PASTURING	PECTINATE
PALISADES	PAPILLOTE	PARODISTS	PATAGONIA	PECULATED
PALLADIAN	PAPYRUSES	PARODYING	PATCHABLE	PECULATOR
PALLADIUM	PARABLAST	PAROICOUS	PATCHIEST	PECUNIARY
PALLADOUS	PARABOLAS	PAROLABLE	PATCHOULI	PEDAGOGIC
PALLIASSE	PARABOLIC	PARONYMIC	PATCHWORK	PEDAGOGUE
PALLIATED	PARACHUTE	PAROTITIS	PATELLATE	PEDALLING
PALLIATOR	PARADIGMS	PAROXYSMS	PATENTEES	PEDATIFID
PALMATION	PARADISAL	PARQUETRY	PATENTING	PEDERASTS
PALM BEACH	PARADISES	PARRICIDE	PATERNITY	PEDERASTY
PALMETTOS	PARADOXES	PARROTING	PATHOLOGY	PEDESTALS
PALMISTRY	PARAGOGIC	PARSIMONY	PATIENTLY	PEDICULAR
PALMITATE	PARAGRAPH	PARSONAGE	PATRIARCH	PEDICURES
PALOMINOS	PARAKEETS	PARTAKING	PATRICIAN	PEDIGREED
PALPATING	PARALLELS	PARTERRES	PATRICIDE	PEDIGREES
PALPATION	PARALYSED	PARTHENON	PATRIMONY	PEDIMENTS
PALPEBRAL	PARALYSER	PARTIALLY	PATRIOTIC	PEDUNCLED
PALPITATE	PARALYSES	PARTICLES	PATRISTIC	PEEPHOLES

PEERESSES	PEPTIDASE	PERMEANCE	PETTINESS	PHOSPHENE
PEEVISHLY	PEPTONIZE	PERMEATED	PETTISHLY	PHOSPHIDE
PEGGED OUT	PERBORATE	PERMEATOR	PETTY CASH	PHOSPHINE
PEGMATITE	PERCALINE	PER MENSEM	PETULANCE	PHOSPHITE
PEKINESES	PER CAPITA	PERMITTED	PFORZHEIM	PHOTOCELL
PEKINGESE	PERCEIVED	PERMITTER	PHAGOCYTE	PHOTOCOPY
PEKING MAN	PERCEIVER	PERMUTING	PHALANGER	PHOTOGRAM
PELLITORY	PERCHANCE	PERPETUAL	PHALANGES	PHOTONICS
PELMANISM	PERCHERON	PERPIGNAN	PHALANXES	PHOTOSTAT
PELTATION	PERCOLATE	PERPLEXED	PHALAROPE	PHOTOTUBE
PEMPHIGUS	PERCUSSOR	PERSECUTE	PHALLUSES	PHOTOTYPE
PENALIZED	PERDITION	PERSEVERE	PHANTASMS	PHRENITIC
PENALTIES	PEREGRINE	PERSIMMON	PHARISAIC	PHRENITIS
PENCHANTS	PERENNATE	PERSISTED	PHARISEES	PHTHALEIN
PENCILING	PERENNIAL	PERSISTER	PHARYNXES	PHYCOLOGY
PENCILLED	PERFECTED	PERSONAGE	PHASE-OUTS	PHYLLITIC
PENCILLER	PERFECTER	PERSONALS	PHEASANTS	PHYLLOMIC
PENDRAGON	PERFECTLY	PERSONATE	PHELLOGEN	PHYLOGENY
PENDULOUS	PERFIDIES	PERSONIFY	PHENACITE	PHYSICALS
PENDULUMS	PERFORATE	PERSONNEL	PHENAZINE	PHYSICIAN
PENEPLAIN	PERFORMED	PERSPIRED	PHENETOLE	PHYSICIST
PENETRANT	PERFORMER	PERSUADED	PHENOCOPY	PHYSIQUES
PENETRATE	PERFUMERY	PERSUADER	PHENOLATE	PHYTOTRON
PEN FRIEND	PERFUMING	PERTAINED	PHENOLOGY	PIANISTIC
PENINSULA	PERFUSION	PERTINENT	PHENOMENA	PICKETING
PENITENCE	PERFUSIVE	PERTURBED	PHENOTYPE	PICKINESS
PENITENTS	PERICLASE	PERTUSSIS	PHENOXIDE	PICK-ME-
PENKNIVES	PERICLINE	PERVADING	PHEROMONE	UPS
PENNILESS	PERICYCLE	PERVASIVE	PHILANDER	PICK PURSE
PENNINITE	PERILYMPH	PERVERTED	PHILATELY	PICNICKED
PENN'ORTHS	PERIMETER	PERVERTER	PHILIPPIC	PICNICKER
PENNY-WISE	PERIMETRY	PESSARIES	PHILOLOGY	PICOLINIC
PENNYWORT	PERIMORPH	PESSIMISM	PHLEBITIC	PICTORIAL
PEN PUSHER	PERINATAL	PESSIMIST	PHLEBITIS	PICTURING
PENSILITY	PERIODATE	PESTERING	PHLYCTENA	PIECE-DYED
PENSIONED	PERIPHERY	PESTICIDE	PHNOM PENH	PIECEMEAL
PENSIONER	PERISCOPE	PESTILENT	PHOENICIA	PIECEWORK
PENSIVELY	PERISHERS	PETAL-LIKE	PHOENIXES	PIE CHARTS
PENTAGONS	PERISHING	PETALODIC	PHONATION	PIECRUSTS
PENTAGRAM	PERISPERM	PETECHIAL	PHONATORY	PIERCABLE
PENTARCHY	PERISTOME	PETERSHAM	PHONE BOOK	PIERIDINE
PENTECOST	PERISTYLE	PETIOLATE	PHONEMICS	PIGGERIES
PENTHOUSE	PERITONEA	PETIOLULE	PHONETICS	PIGGISHLY
PENTOTHAL	PERITRACK	PETIT FOUR	PHONEY WAR	PIGGYBACK
PENTOXIDE	PERJURERS	PETITIONS	PHONINESS	PIGGYBANK
PENUMBRAL	PERJURIES	PETRI DISH	PHONOGRAM	PIGHEADED
PENUMBRAS	PERJURING	PETRIFIED	PHONOLITE	PIG-HEADED
PENURIOUS	PERKINESS	PETRIFIER	PHONOLOGY	PIGTAILED
PEPPERING	PERMALLOY	PETROLEUM	PHONOTYPE	PIKEPERCH
PEPPER POT	PERMANENT	PETROLOGY	PHONOTYPY	PIKESTAFF
PEPSINATE	PERMEABLE	PETTICOAT	PHOSPHATE	PILASTERS

PILCHARDS	PLACARDED	PLAYROOMS	PODGINESS	POLYBASIC
PILFERAGE	PLACATING	PLAYTHING	POETASTER	POLYCARPY
PILFERERS	PLACATION	PLEADABLE	POETESSES	POLYESTER
PILFERING	PLACATORY	PLEADINGS	POETICIZE	POLYGLOTS
PILLAGERS	PLACEBOES	PLEASABLE	POGO STICK	POLYGONAL
PILLAGING	PLACE CARD	PLEASANCE	POIGNANCY	POLYGONUM
PILLAR BOX	PLACE MATS	PLEASEDLY	POINCIANA	POLYGRAPH
PILLBOXES	PLACEMENT	PLEASURES	POINT DUTY	POLYMATHS
PILLORIED	PLACENTAE	PLEBBIEST	POINTEDLY	POLYMERIC
PILLORIES	PLACENTAL	PLEBEIANS	POINTLESS	POLYMORPH
PILLOWING	PLACENTAS	PLECTRUMS	POINTSMAN	POLYMYXIN
PIMPERNEL	PLACIDITY	PLENARILY	POISONERS	POLYNESIA
PINACEOUS	PLACODERM	PLENITUDE	POISON GAS	POLYPHASE
PINAFORES	PLAIN-LAID	PLENTEOUS	POISONING	POLYPHONE
PINCHBECK	PLAINNESS	PLENTIFUL	POISON IVY	POLYPHONY
PINCHCOCK	PLAINSMAN	PLEONASMS	POISONOUS	POLYPLOID
PINEAPPLE	PLAINSONG	PLEURITIC	POKEBERRY	POLYPTYCH
PINETREES	PLAINTIFF	PLEXIFORM	POKER FACE	POLYSOMIC
PINEWOODS	PLAINTIVE	PLICATION	POKERWORK	POLYTHENE
PINIONING	PLANARIAN	PLIGHTING	POLAR BEAR	POLYTONAL
PINNACLES	PLANATION	PLIMSOLLS	POLARIZED	POLYTYPIC
PINNATION	PLANETARY	PLOUGHBOY	POLARIZER	POLYVINYL
PINPOINTS	PLANETOID	PLOUGHING	POLAROIDS	POMACEOUS
PINPRICKS	PLANE TREE	PLOUGHMAN	POLEAXING	POMANDERS
PINSTRIPE	PLANGENCY	PLOUGHMEN	POLEMICAL	POMERANIA
PINTABLES	PLANISHER	PLUCKIEST	POLE VAULT	POMPADOUR
PINTADERA	PLANTABLE	PLUGBOARD	POLICE DOG	POMPOSITY
PINWHEELS	PLANTAINS	PLUGHOLES	POLICEMAN	POMPOUSLY
PIONEERED	PLASMAGEL	PLUMBABLE	POLICEMEN	PONDERING
PIOUSNESS	PLASMASOL	PLUMBEOUS	POLISHING	PONDEROUS
PIPE DREAM	PLASTERED	PLUMBICON	POLITBURO	PONDOLAND
PIPELINES	PLASTERER	PLUMB LINE	POLITESSE	PONTIANAK
PIPE RACKS	PLATELETS	PLUMMETED	POLITICAL	PONTYPOOL
PIPERONAL	PLATE RACK	PLUMMIEST	POLITICOS	PONYTAILS
PIPESTONE	PLATFORMS	PLUMPNESS	POLKA DOTS	POORHOUSE
PIPSQUEAK	PLATINIZE	PLUNDERED	POLLARDED	POORLIEST
PIQUANTLY	PLATINOID	PLUNDERER	POLLINATE	POORLY OFF
PIRATICAL	PLATINOUS	PLURALISM	POLLINIUM	POOR WHITE
PIROUETTE	PLATITUDE	PLURALIST	POLLSTERS	POPE'S
PISS-TAKES	PLAUSIBLE	PLURALITY	POLL TAXES	NOSE
PISTACHIO	PLAUSIBLY	PLURALIZE	POLLUCITE	POPINJAYS
PITCH-DARK	PLAY-ACTED	PLUS FOURS	POLLUTANT	POPLITEAL
PITCHFORK	PLAYBACKS	PLUSHNESS	POLLUTING	POPPYCOCK
PITEOUSLY	PLAY DOUGH	PLUTOCRAT	POLLUTION	POPPYHEAD
PITHINESS	PLAYED-OUT	PLUTONIUM	POLLYANNA	POPSICLES
PITOT TUBE	PLAYFULLY	PNEUMATIC	POLONAISE	POPULARLY
PIT PONIES	PLAYGOERS	PNEUMONIA	POLO NECKS	POPULATED
PITTANCES	PLAYGROUP	PNEUMONIC	POLO SHIRT	POPULISTS
PITUITARY	PLAYHOUSE	POCKETFUL	POLTROONS	PORBEAGLE
PITYINGLY	PLAYMAKER	POCKETING	POLYAMIDE	PORCELAIN
PIZZICATO	PLAYMATES	POCKMARKS	POLYANDRY	PORCUPINE

PORIFERAN	POT-BOILER	PRECISION	PRESCRIBE	PRIME COST
PORKINESS	POTENTATE	PRECLUDED	PRESCRIPT	PRIMENESS
POROMERIC	POTENTIAL	PRECOCIAL	PRESENCES	PRIME RATE
PORPHYRIN	POTHOLERS	PRECOCITY	PRESENTED	PRIME TIME
PORPOISES	POTHOLING	PRECONIZE	PRESENTEE	PRIMIPARA
PORRINGER	POTHUNTER	PRECOOKED	PRESENTER	PRIMITIVE
PORTACRIB	POT PLANTS	PRECURSOR	PRESENTLY	PRIMROSES
PORTADOWN	POTPOURRI	PREDATING	PRESERVED	PRINCEDOM
PORTATIVE	POT POURRI	PREDATION	PRESERVER	PRINCETON
PORT BLAIR	POTSHERDS	PREDATORS	PRESERVES	PRINCIPAL
PORTENDED	POTTERIES	PREDATORY	PRESETTER	PRINCIPLE
PORTERAGE	POTTERING	PREDICANT	PRESHRUNK	PRINTABLE
PORTFOLIO	POTTINESS	PREDICATE	PRESIDENT	PRINTINGS
PORTHOLES	POULTERER	PREDICTED	PRESIDING	PRINTOUTS
PORTICOES	POULTICES	PREDICTOR	PRESIDIUM	PRISMATIC
PORTIONED	POULTRIES	PREDIGEST	PRESSGANG	PRISONERS
PORTLIEST	POUNDINGS	PRE-EMPTED	PRESS GANG	PRISSIEST
PORT LOUIS	POURBOIRE	PRE-EMPTOR	PRESSINGS	PRITCHETT
PORTO NOVO	POUTINGLY	PREFACING	PRESSMARK	PRIVATEER
PORTRAITS	POVERTIES	PREFATORY	PRESSROOM	PRIVATELY
PORTRAYAL	POWDERING	PREFERRED	PRESS-STUD	PRIVATION
PORTRAYED	POWDER KEG	PREFIGURE	PRESSURED	PRIVATIVE
PORTRAYER	POWER BASE	PREFIXING	PRESSURES	PRIVATIZE
PORT SUDAN	POWERBOAT	PREFLIGHT	PRESSWORK	PRIVILEGE
PORTULACA	POWER DIVE	PREGNABLE	PRESTIGES	PRIZE DAYS
POSITIONS	POWERLESS	PREGNANCY	PRESTRESS	PROACTIVE
POSITIVES	PRACTICAL	PREHEATED	PRESTWICH	PROBABLES
POSITRONS	PRACTICES	PREJUDGED	PRESTWICK	PROBATING
POSSESSED	PRACTISED	PREJUDGER	PRESUMING	PROBATION
POSSESSOR	PRAESIDIA	PREJUDICE	PRETENCES	PROBATIVE
POSSIBLES	PRAGMATIC	PRELATISM	PRETENDED	PROBEABLE
POSTAXIAL	PRANKSTER	PRELATIST	PRETENDER	PROBINGLY
POSTCARDS	PRATINGLY	PRELATURE	PRETERITE	PROBOSCIS
POSTCODES	PRATTLERS	PRELUDIAL	PRETTIEST	PROCEDURE
POSTDATED	PRATTLING	PRELUSION	PREVAILED	PROCEEDED
POSTERIOR	PRAYERFUL	PRELUSIVE	PREVAILER	PROCEEDER
POSTERITY	PRAYER RUG	PREMATURE	PREVALENT	PROCESSED
POSTHASTE	PREACHERS	PREMIERED	PREVENTED	PROCESSES
POST HORNS	PREACHIFY	PREMIERES	PREVENTER	PROCESSOR
POSTICOUS	PREACHING	PREOCCUPY	PREVIEWED	PROCLITIC
POSTILION	PREAMBLES	PREORDAIN	PREVISION	PROCONSUL
POSTMARKS	PREBENDAL	PREPACKED	PRICELESS	PROCREANT
POSTNATAL	PRECANCEL	PREPARING	PRICE TAGS	PROCREATE
POSTPONED	PRECEDENT	PREPAYING	PRICINESS	PROCTORED
POSTPONER	PRECEDING	PREPOTENT	PRICKLIER	PROCURERS
POSTULANT	PRECENTOR	PREPUTIAL	PRICKLING	PROCURING
POSTULATE	PRECEPTOR	PRERECORD	PRIESTESS	PRODIGALS
POSTURING	PRECINCTS	PRESAGING	PRIMAEVAL	PRODIGIES
POTASSIUM	PRECIPICE	PRESBYTER	PRIMARIES	PRODROMAL
POTATIONS	PRECISELY	PRESCHOOL	PRIMARILY	PRODUCERS
POTBOILER	PRECISIAN	PRESCIENT	PRIMATIAL	PRODUCING

PROFANELY
PROFANING
PROFANITY
PROFESSED
PROFESSOR
PROFFERED
PROFFERER
PROFILING
PROFITEER
PROFITING
PROFLUENT
PROFUSELY
PROFUSION
PROGESTIN
PROGNOSES
PROGNOSIS
PROGRAMED
PROGRAMER
PROGRAMME
PROJECTED
PROJECTOR
PROLACTIN
PROLAMINE
PROLAPSED
PROLAPSES
PROLEPSIS
PROLEPTIC
PROLIXITY
PROLOGUES
PROLONGED
PROLONGER
PROLUSION
PROLUSORY
PROMENADE
PROMINENT
PROMISING
PROMOTERS
PROMOTING
PROMOTION
PROMOTIVE
PROMPTING
PRONATION
PRONENESS
PRONGHORN
PRONOUNCE
PROOFREAD
PROPAGATE
PROPAGULE
PRO PATRIA
PROPELLED
PROPELLER

PROPHETIC
PROPONENT
PROPOSALS
PROPOSERS
PROPOSING
PROPRIETY
PROPTOSIS
PROPYLITE
PROROGUED
PROSCRIBE
PROSECTOR
PROSECUTE
PROSELYTE
PROSIMIAN
PROSINESS
PROSODIST
PROSPECTS
PROSPERED
PROSTATES
PROSTATIC
PROSTRATE
PROTAMINE
PROTANDRY
PROTECTED
PROTECTOR
PROTESTER
PROTHESIS
PROTHETIC
PROTHORAX
PROTOCOLS
PROTOGYNY
PROTONEMA
PROTOSTAR
PROTOTYPE
PROTOXIDE
PROTOZOAN
PROTRUDED
PROUDNESS
PROUSTITE
PROVENCAL
PROVENDER
PROVIDENT
PROVIDERS
PROVIDING
PROVINCES
PROVISION
PROVISORY
PROVOKING
PROVOLONE
PROWESSES
PROWL CARS

PROXIMATE
PROXIMITY
PRUDENTLY
PRUDISHLY
PRURIENCE
PRUSSIATE
PRYTANEUM
PSALMISTS
PSALMODIC
PSEUDONYM
PSORIASIS
PSORIATIC
PSYCHICAL
PSYCHOSES
PSYCHOSIS
PSYCHOTIC
PTARMIGAN
PTERYGOID
PTOLEMAIC
PUB-CRAWLS
PUBESCENT
PUBLICANS
PUBLIC BAR
PUBLICIST
PUBLICITY
PUBLICIZE
PUBLISHED
PUBLISHER
PUCKERING
PUCKISHLY
PUDGINESS
PUERILISM
PUERILITY
PUERPERAL
PUFF ADDER
PUFFINESS
PUGILISTS
PUGNACITY
PUISSANCE
PULLOVERS
PULL ROUND
PULLULATE
PULMONARY
PULMONATE
PULPINESS
PULSATILE
PULSATING
PULSATION
PULSATIVE
PULSATORY
PULVERIZE

PULVILLUS
PULVINATE
PUMICEOUS
PUMMELING
PUMMELLED
PUMP ROOMS
PUNCHBALL
PUNCH BALL
PUNCH BOWL
PUNCHIEST
PUNCH LINE
PUNCTILIO
PUNCTUATE
PUNCTURED
PUNCTURER
PUNCTURES
PUNGENTLY
PUNISHING
PUPILLAGE
PUPILLARY
PUPPETEER
PUPPYHOOD
PUPPY LOVE
PURCHASED
PURCHASER
PURCHASES
PUREBREDS
PURGATION
PURGATIVE
PURGATORY
PURIFIERS
PURIFYING
PURLOINED
PURLOINER
PURPORTED
PURPOSELY
PURPOSING
PURPOSIVE
PURSUANCE
PURULENCE
PURVEYING
PURVEYORS
PUSHBIKES
PUSHCARTS
PUSHCHAIR
PUSH CHAIR
PUSHINESS
PUSHINGLY
PUSSYFOOT
PUSTULANT
PUSTULATE

PUTREFIED
PUTREFIER
PUTRIDITY
PUTTERING
PUTTYROOT
PUT-UP
  JOBS
PUY DE
  DOME
PYCNIDIUM
PYONGYANG
PYORRHOEA
PYRAMIDAL
PYRETHRIN
PYRETHRUM
PYRIDOXAL
PYROGENIC
PYROLITIC
PYROLYSIS
PYROMANCY
PYROMANIA
PYROMETER
PYROMETRY
PYROXENIC
PYROXYLIN

Q

QUADRANTS
QUADRATIC
QUADRIFID
QUADRILLE
QUADRUPED
QUADRUPLE
QUADRUPLY
QUAGMIRES
QUAKERISM
QUAKINESS
QUALIFIED
QUALIFIER
QUALITIES
QUARRELED
QUARRYING
QUARTERED
QUARTERLY
QUARTZITE
QUATRAINS
QUAVERING
QUEASIEST
QUEBECKER
QUEBECOIS
QUEBRACHO

QUEEN-SIZE	RADIATING	RATIONING	RECEPTIVE	REDACTION
QUEERNESS	RADIATION	RATTINESS	RECESSING	RED ALERTS
QUENCHING	RADIATIVE	RATTLEBOX	RECESSION	REDBREAST
QUERCETIN	RADIATORS	RAUCOUSLY	RECESSIVE	REDBRICKS
QUERETARO	RADICALLY	RAUNCHIER	RECHARGED	REDBRIDGE
QUERULOUS	RADIOGRAM	RAUNCHILY	RECHARGER	RED CARPET
QUESTIONS	RADIOLOGY	RAUWOLFIA	RECHAUFFE	REDDENING
QUEUE-JUMP	RADIO STAR	RAVELLING	RECHERCHE	REDEEMERS
QUIBBLERS	RAFFINOSE	RAVISHING	RECIPIENT	REDEEMING
QUIBBLING	RAFFISHLY	RAZORBACK	RECITABLE	REDELIVER
QUICKENED	RAFFLESIA	RAZORBILL	RECKONING	REDEVELOP
QUICKLIME	RAIL GAUGE	RAZOR EDGE	RECLAIMED	RED GIANTS
QUICKNESS	RAILHEADS	REACHABLE	RECLINATE	RED-HANDED
QUICKSAND	RAILROADS	REACTANCE	RECLINING	RED-HEADED
QUICKSTEP	RAIN CHECK	REACTIONS	RECLUSION	RED INDIAN
QUIESCENT	RAINCOATS	READDRESS	RECLUSIVE	RED LIGHTS
QUIETENED	RAINDROPS	READINESS	RECOGNIZE	REDOLENCE
QUIETISTS	RAINFALLS	READY-MADE	RECOILING	REDOUBLED
QUIETNESS	RAIN GAUGE	REALIGNED	RECOLLECT	REDOUNDED
QUIETUSES	RAININESS	REALISTIC	RECOMMEND	RED-PENCIL
QUILLWORT	RAINMAKER	REALITIES	RECOMPOSE	RED PEPPER
QUINIDINE	RAINPROOF	REALIZING	RECONCILE	REDRESSED
QUINOLINE	RAINSTORM	REANIMATE	RECONDITE	REDRESSER
QUINONOID	RAINWATER	REAPPOINT	RECONVERT	REDUCIBLE
QUINTUPLE	RAJASTHAN	REARGUARD	RECORDERS	REDUCTASE
QUIRKIEST	RAMIFYING	REAR LIGHT	RECORDING	REDUCTION
QUISLINGS	RAMPAGING	REARRANGE	RECOUNTAL	REDUNDANT
QUITCLAIM	RAMPANTLY	REARWARDS	RECOUNTED	RE-ECHOING
QUITTANCE	RANCIDITY	REASONING	RECOUPING	REEDINESS
QUIVERFUL	RANCOROUS	REASSURED	RE-COVERED	RE-EDUCATE
QUIVERING	RANDINESS	REASSURER	RECOVERER	REEF KNOTS
QUIXOTISM	RANDOMIZE	REBATABLE	RECREANTS	REEKINGLY
QUIZZICAL	RANGINESS	REBELLING	RECREATED	RE-ELECTED
QUODLIBET	RANSACKED	REBELLION	RE-CREATOR	RE-ENFORCE
QUOTATION	RANSACKER	REBINDING	RECREMENT	RE-ENTRANT
QUOTIDIAN	RANSOMERS	REBOUNDED	RECRUITED	RE-ENTRIES
QUOTIENTS	RANSOMING	REBOUNDER	RECRUITER	RE-EXAMINE
	RANTINGLY	REBUFFING	RECTANGLE	REFECTION
R	RAPACIOUS	REBUKABLE	RECTIFIED	REFECTORY
RABBINATE	RAPID-FIRE	REBUTTALS	RECTIFIER	REFERABLE
RABBITING	RAPIDNESS	REBUTTING	RECTITUDE	REFERENCE
RABBITTED	RAPTORIAL	RECALLING	RECTOCELE	REFERENDA
RACEHORSE	RAPTUROUS	RECANTING	RECTORATE	REFERRALS
RACETRACK	RARE EARTH	RECAPPING	RECTORIAL	REFERRING
RACIALISM	RASCALITY	RECAPTION	RECTORIES	REFILLING
RACIALIST	RASPBERRY	RECAPTURE	RECUMBENT	REFINABLE
RACKETEER	RASPINGLY	RECASTING	RECURRENT	REFINANCE
RACONTEUR	RASTERIZE	RECEIVERS	RECURRING	REFITTING
RADIAL-PLY	RATEPAYER	RECEIVING	RECUSANCY	REFLATING
RADIANCES	RATIFYING	RECENSION	RECUSANTS	REFLATION
RADIANTLY	RATIONALE	RECEPTION	RECYCLING	REFLECTED

REFLECTOR	REINSURER	REMOULDED	REPRESSOR	RESIDUARY
REFLEXIVE	REISSUING	REMOUNTED	REPRIEVED	RESIGNING
REFORMERS	REITERANT	REMOVABLE	REPRIEVER	RESILIENT
REFORMING	REITERATE	REMOVABLY	REPRIEVES	RESINATED
REFORMISM	REJECTING	REMSCHEID	REPRIMAND	RESISTANT
REFORMIST	REJECTION	RENASCENT	REPRINTED	RESISTERS
REFRACTED	REJECTIVE	RENDERING	REPRINTER	RESISTING
REFRACTOR	REJIGGING	RENDITION	REPRISALS	RESISTORS
REFRAINED	REJOICING	RENEGADES	REPROBACY	RESITTING
REFRAINER	REJOINDER	RENEWABLE	REPROBATE	RESNATRON
REFRESHED	REJOINING	RENEWEDLY	REPROCESS	RESOLUBLE
REFRESHER	REKINDLED	RENOUNCED	REPRODUCE	RESOLVENT
REFUELING	RELAPSING	RENOUNCER	REPROVING	RESOLVING
REFUELLED	RELATABLE	RENOVATED	REPTILIAN	RESONANCE
REFULGENT	RELATIONS	RENOVATOR	REPTILOID	RESONATED
REFUNDING	RELATIVES	REOPENING	REPUBLICS	RESONATOR
REFURBISH	RELAXABLE	REPAIRING	REPUBLISH	RESORBENT
REFUSABLE	RELAXEDLY	REPAIRMAN	REPUDIATE	RESORTING
REFUSE BIN	RELEASING	REPARABLE	REPUGNANT	RESOUNDED
REFUSE TIP	RELEGATED	REPARABLY	REPULSING	RESOURCES
REFUTABLE	RELENTING	REPARTEES	REPULSION	RESPECTED
REGAINING	RELEVANCE	REPAYABLE	REPULSIVE	RESPECTER
REGARDANT	RELEVANCY	REPAYMENT	REPUTABLE	RESPIRING
REGARDFUL	RELIEF MAP	REPEALING	REPUTABLY	RESPONDED
REGARDING	RELIEVING	REPEATERS	REPUTEDLY	RESPONDER
REGENCIES	RELIGIONS	REPEATING	REQUESTED	RESPONSER
REGICIDAL	RELIGIOSE	REPECHAGE	REQUESTER	RESPONSES
REGICIDES	RELIGIOUS	REPELLENT	REQUIRING	RESTATING
REGIMENTS	RELIQUARY	REPELLING	REQUISITE	REST CURES
REGISTERS	RELISHING	REPENTANT	REQUITING	RESTFULLY
REGISTRAR	RELIVABLE	REPENTING	REREDOSES	REST HOMES
REGRESSED	RELOADING	REPERTORY	RERUNNING	RESTIFORM
REGRESSOR	RELOCATED	REPHRASED	RESALABLE	RESTIVELY
REGRETFUL	RELUCTANT	REPLACING	RESCINDED	RESTOCKED
REGRETTED	REMAINDER	REPLAYING	RESCINDER	RESTORERS
REGRETTER	REMAINING	REPLEADER	RESCUABLE	RESTORING
REGROUPED	REMANDING	REPLENISH	RESECTION	RESTRAINT
REGULABLE	REMANENCE	REPLETION	RESEMBLED	REST ROOMS
REGULARLY	REMARKING	REPLETIVE	RESEMBLER	RESULTANT
REGULATED	REMARRIED	REPLICATE	RESENTFUL	RESULTING
REGULATOR	REMEDYING	REPLY-PAID	RESENTING	RESUMABLE
REHASHING	REMINDERS	REPORTAGE	RESERPINE	RESURFACE
REHEARSAL	REMINDFUL	REPORTERS	RESERVING	RESURGENT
REHEARSED	REMINDING	REPORTING	RESERVIST	RESURRECT
REHEARSER	REMINISCE	REPOSEDLY	RESERVOIR	RETAILERS
REHOUSING	REMISSION	REPOSEFUL	RESETTING	RETAILING
REIMBURSE	REMISSIVE	REPOSSESS	RESETTLED	RETAINERS
REINFORCE	REMITTING	REPREHEND	RESHUFFLE	RETAINING
REINSTALL	REMODELED	REPRESENT	RESIDENCE	RETALIATE
REINSTATE	REMONTANT	REPRESSED	RESIDENCY	RETARDANT
REINSURED	REMONTOIR	REPRESSER	RESIDENTS	RETARDATE

RETARDING
RETELLING
RETENTION
RETENTIVE
RETHOUGHT
RETICENCE
RETICULES
RETICULUM
RETINITIS
RETORSION
RETORTING
RETORTION
RETOUCHED
RETOUCHER
RETRACING
RETRACTED
RETRACTOR
RETREADED
RETREATAL
RETREATED
RETRIEVAL
RETRIEVED
RETRIEVER
RETROCEDE
RETROFIRE
RETROFLEX
RETROPACK
RETROUSSE
RETURNING
REUNITING
REUTILIZE
REVALUING
REVAMPING
REVEALING
REVELATOR
REVELLING
REVELMENT
REVELROUS
REVENGING
REVERABLE
REVERENCE
REVERENDS
REVERSALS
REVERSING
REVERSION
REVERTING
REVERTIVE
REVETMENT
REVIEWERS
REVIEWING
REVISABLE

REVISIONS
REVIVABLE
REVIVABLY
REVOCABLE
REVOCABLY
REVOKABLE
REVOKABLY
REVOLTING
REVOLVERS
REVOLVING
REVULSION
REVULSIVE
REWARDING
REWIRABLE
REWORDING
REWORKING
REWRITING
REYKJAVIK
RHAPSODIC
RHEOMETER
RHEOMETRY
RHEOSTATS
RHEOTAXIS
RHEUMATIC
RH FACTORS
RHIGOLENE
RHINELAND
RHINOLOGY
RHIZOBIUM
RHIZOIDAL
RHIZOTOMY
RHODAMINE
RHODESIAN
RHODOLITE
RHODONITE
RHODOPSIN
RHOMBOIDS
RHOMBUSES
RHOTACISM
RHOTACIST
RHYMESTER
RHYOLITIC
RHYTHMICS
RIBOSOMAL
RICE PADDY
RICE PAPER
RICKSHAWS
RICOCHETS
RIDDANCES
RIDERLESS
RIDGELING

RIDGEPOLE
RIDICULED
RIDICULER
RIFLEBIRD
RIGHTEOUS
RIGHT-HAND
RIGHTISTS
RIGHTNESS
RIGHTSIZE
RIGHTWARD
RIGHT WING
RIGMAROLE
RING A
   BELL
RING ROADS
RIO BRANCO
RIO GRANDE
RIOTOUSLY
RIPOSTING
RISE ABOVE
RISKINESS
RITUALISM
RITUALIST
RITUALIZE
RIVALLING
RIVALRIES
RIVALROUS
RIVERBEDS
RIVERBOAT
RIVERHEAD
RIVERSIDE
ROADBLOCK
ROADHOUSE
ROADSHOWS
ROADSTEAD
ROADSTERS
ROAD TAXES
ROAD TESTS
ROADWORKS
ROAD WORKS
ROAST BEEF
ROASTINGS
ROBBERIES
ROBOT-LIKE
ROCHESTER
ROCKBOUND
ROCK CAKES
ROCKERIES
ROCKETEER
ROCKETING
ROCKFALLS

ROCKINESS
ROCK 'N'
   ROLL
ROCK PLANT
ROCKSHAFT
ROENTGENS
ROGUERIES
ROGUISHLY
ROISTERER
ROLE MODEL
ROLE PLAYS
ROLL CALLS
ROLLINGLY
ROMANCING
ROMAN NOSE
ROMANTICS
ROMPINGLY
ROOF RACKS
ROOKERIES
ROOMINESS
ROOMMATES
ROOT CROPS
ROOTINESS
ROOTSTOCK
ROPE TRICK
ROQUEFORT
ROSACEOUS
ROSCOMMON
ROSEWATER
ROSINWEED
ROSTELLUM
ROTAMETER
ROTARIANS
ROTATABLE
ROTATIONS
ROTAVATOR
ROTHERHAM
ROTIFERAL
ROTOVATOR
ROTTERDAM
ROTUNDITY
ROUGHCAST
ROUGH DEAL
ROUGHENED
ROUGH-HEWN
ROUGHNECK
ROUGHNESS
ROUGHSHOD
ROUNDELAY
ROUNDHEAD
ROUNDNESS

ROUNDSMAN
ROUNDSMEN
ROUND TRIP
ROUND-TRIP
ROUNDWORM
ROUTINELY
ROUTINISM
ROUTINIST
ROVING EYE
ROWAN TREE
ROWDINESS
ROW HOUSES
ROYAL BLUE
ROYALISTS
ROYALTIES
RUBBERIZE
RUBBISHED
RUBESCENT
RUBRICATE
RUBRICIAN
RUCKSACKS
RUDACEOUS
RUDBECKIA
RUDDINESS
RUDIMENTS
RUFESCENT
RUFFIANLY
RUINATION
RUINOUSLY
RULEBOOKS
RUMBLINGS
RUMINANTS
RUMINATED
RUMINATOR
RUMMAGING
RUMP STEAK
RUN-ABOUTS
RUN ACROSS
RUN-AROUND
RUNCINATE
RUNNERS-UP
RUNNER-UPS
RUNNYMEDE
RUNTINESS
RUN TO
   SEED
RUPTURING
RUSH HOURS
RUSHINESS
RUSHINGLY
RUSHLIGHT

RUSH LIGHT
RUSSETISH
RUSTICATE
RUSTICITY
RUSTINESS
RUSTPROOF
RUTABAGAS
RUTACEOUS
RUTHENIAN
RUTHENIUM
RUTILATED
RUTTINESS
RUWENZORI

S

SABADILLA
SABOTAGED
SABOTEURS
SACCHARIN
SACCULATE
SACKCLOTH
SACK RACES
SACRAMENT
SACRARIUM
SACRED COW
SACRIFICE
SACRILEGE
SACRISTAN
SADDENING
SADDLEBAG
SADDLEBOW
SAFEGUARD
SAFE HOUSE
SAFELIGHT
SAFETY NET
SAFETY PIN
SAFFLOWER
SAFRANINE
SAGACIOUS
SAGEBRUSH
SAGE DERBY
SAGE GREEN
SAGITTATE
SAILBOARD
SAILCLOTH
SAILOR HAT
SAILPLANE
SAINTE FOY
SAINT GALL
SAINTHOOD
SAINT JOHN

SAINTLILY
SAINT-OUEN
SAINT PAUL
SAINT'S
  DAY
SALAAMING
SALACIOUS
SALAD DAYS
SALAMANCA
SALARYMAN
SALERATUS
SALEROOMS
SALESGIRL
SALESROOM
SALES SLIP
SALES TALK
SALIMETER
SALIMETRY
SALISBURY
SALIVATED
SALMONOID
SALOON BAR
SALPIFORM
SALTATION
SALTINESS
SALTLICKS
SALTPETRE
SALT SPOON
SALTWATER
SALTWORKS
SALVAGING
SALVATION
SAMARITAN
SAMARKAND
SANATORIA
SANCTIONS
SANCTUARY
SANDALLED
SANDBANKS
SANDBLAST
SAND-BLIND
SANDBOXES
SAND DUNES
SAND FLIES
SANDHURST
SANDINESS
SANDPAPER
SANDPIPER
SANDSHOES
SANDSTONE
SANDSTORM

SAND TRAPS
SANFORIZE
SANGFROID
SANITARIA
SANITIZED
SAN MARINO
SANS SERIF
SANTA CRUZ
SANTANDER
SANTONICA
SAPHENOUS
SAPIENTLY
SAPODILLA
SAPPHIRES
SAPPINESS
SAPRAEMIA
SAPRAEMIC
SAPROLITE
SAPROZOIC
SAPSUCKER
SARABANDE
SARABANDS
SARACENIC
SARCASTIC
SARCOCARP
SARDINIAN
SARGASSUM
SARTORIAL
SARTORIUS
SASHAYING
SASKATOON
SASSAFRAS
SASSENACH
SATANISTS
SATELLITE
SATIATING
SATIATION
SATINWOOD
SATIRICAL
SATIRIZED
SATIRIZER
SATISFIED
SATISFIER
SATURABLE
SATURATED
SATURATER
SATURDAYS
SATURNIAN
SATURNIID
SATURNINE
SATURNISM

SAUCEPANS
SAUCINESS
SAUNTERED
SAUNTERER
SAUTERNES
SAVOURING
SAXIFRAGE
SAXOPHONE
SCABBARDS
SCABBIEST
SCABIETIC
SCAFFOLDS
SCAGLIOLA
SCALAWAGS
SCALDFISH
SCALINESS
SCALLIONS
SCALLOPED
SCALLOPER
SCALLYWAG
SCAMPERED
SCAMPERER
SCANTIEST
SCANTLING
SCANTNESS
SCAPA FLOW
SCAPEGOAT
SCAPHOPOD
SCAPOLITE
SCARABOID
SCARECROW
SCARFSKIN
SCARIFIED
SCARIFIER
SCARINGLY
SCARPERED
SCATOLOGY
SCATTERED
SCATTERER
SCATTIEST
SCAVENGED
SCAVENGER
SCENARIOS
SCENARIST
SCENTLESS
SCEPTICAL
SCHEDULAR
SCHEDULED
SCHEDULES
SCHEELITE
SCHEMATIC

SCHILLING
SCHISTOSE
SCHIZOPOD
SCHLEPPED
SCHLIEREN
SCHLIERIC
SCHMALTZY
SCHNAUZER
SCHNITZEL
SCHNORKEL
SCHOLARLY
SCHOLIAST
SCHOOLBOY
SCHOOLING
SCHOONERS
SCIENTIAL
SCIENTISM
SCIENTIST
SCIMITARS
SCINTILLA
SCIOMANCY
SCIRRHOID
SCIRRHOUS
SCLERITIC
SCLERITIS
SCLEROSAL
SCLEROSED
SCLEROSES
SCLEROSIS
SCLEROTIC
SCOLDABLE
SCOLDINGS
SCOLECITE
SCOLIOSIS
SCOLIOTIC
SCOLLOPED
SCOMBROID
SCOPOLINE
SCOPULATE
SCORBUTIC
SCORCHERS
SCORCHING
SCORECARD
SCORIFIER
SCORPIOID
SCORPIONS
SCOTCH EGG
SCOTCHING
SCOUNDREL
SCOURGING
SCOURINGS

SCRABBLED	SCRUMPING	SECTIONAL	SENESCENT	SERRIFORM
SCRABBLER	SCRUNCHED	SECTIONED	SENESCHAL	SERRULATE
SCRAGGIER	SCRUNCHIE	SECTORIAL	SENIORITY	SERVERIES
SCRAGGILY	SCRUPLING	SECUNDINE	SENORITAS	SERVICING
SCRAGGING	SCUFFLING	SECURABLE	SENSATION	SERVIETTE
SCRAMBLED	SCULLIONS	SEDATIVES	SENSELESS	SERVILELY
SCRAMBLER	SCULPTORS	SEDENTARY	SENSILLUM	SERVILITY
SCRAMBLES	SCULPTURE	SEDIMENTS	SENSITIVE	SERVITORS
SCRAMMING	SCUPPERED	SEDITIOUS	SENSITIZE	SERVITUDE
SCRAPABLE	SCURRYING	SEDUCIBLE	SENSORIUM	SESSILITY
SCRAPBOOK	SCUTATION	SEDUCTION	SENTENCED	SESSIONAL
SCRAP HEAP	SCUTCHEON	SEDUCTIVE	SENTENCES	SETACEOUS
SCRAPINGS	SCUTELLAR	SEEDINESS	SENTIENCE	SET FIRE
SCRAP IRON	SCUTELLUM	SEEDLINGS	SENTIMENT	TO
SCRAPPIER	SCUTIFORM	SEEMINGLY	SENTINELS	SET PIECES
SCRAPPILY	SCUTTLING	SEESAWING	SENTRY BOX	SET SPEECH
SCRAPPING	SEABOARDS	SEGMENTAL	SEPARABLE	SETSQUARE
SCRATCHED	SEA BREEZE	SEGMENTED	SEPARABLY	SET SQUARE
SCRATCHER	SEA CHANGE	SEGREGATE	SEPARATED	SET THEORY
SCRATCHES	SEAFARING	SEIGNEURS	SEPARATES	SETTLED IN
SCRAWLING	SEAFRONTS	SELACHIAN	SEPARATOR	SETTLINGS
SCRAWNIER	SEAHORSES	SELECTING	SEPHARDIC	SET-TOP
SCRAWNILY	SEAL-POINT	SELECTION	SEPIOLITE	BOX
SCREAMING	SEALYHAMS	SELECTIVE	SEPTARIAN	SEVENFOLD
SCREECHED	SEAMINESS	SELECTORS	SEPTARIUM	SEVENTEEN
SCREECHER	SEAPLANES	SELENIOUS	SEPTEMBER	SEVENTIES
SCREECHES	SEA POWERS	SELF-ABUSE	SEPTENARY	SEVERABLE
SCREENING	SEARCHING	SELF-DOUBT	SEPTICITY	SEVERALLY
SCREWBALL	SEASCAPES	SELF-DRIVE	SEPTUPLET	SEVERALTY
SCREWIEST	SEA SHANTY	SELFISHLY	SEPULCHRE	SEVERANCE
SCREW TOPS	SEASHELLS	SELLOTAPE	SEPULTURE	SEX APPEAL
SCREWWORM	SEASONING	SELL SHORT	SEQUACITY	SEXENNIAL
SCRIBBLED	SEAT BELTS	SEMANTICS	SEQUENCER	SEX OBJECT
SCRIBBLER	SEA URCHIN	SEMAPHORE	SEQUENCES	SEX ORGANS
SCRIBBLES	SEAWORTHY	SEMBLANCE	SEQUESTER	SEXTUPLET
SCRIMMAGE	SEBACEOUS	SEMESTERS	SERAGLIOS	SEXUALITY
SCRIMPILY	SECATEURS	SEMESTRAL	SERENADED	SFORZANDO
SCRIMPING	SECESSION	SEMI-BANTU	SERENADER	SGRAFFITO
SCRIMSHAW	SECLUDING	SEMIBREVE	SERENADES	SHABBIEST
SCRIPTURE	SECLUSION	SEMICOLON	SERGEANCY	SHACKLING
SCROLLING	SECLUSIVE	SEMIFINAL	SERGEANTS	SHADINESS
SCROUNGED	SECONDARY	SEMIFLUID	SERIALISM	SHADOW-BOX
SCROUNGER	SECONDERS	SEMILUNAR	SERIALIZE	SHADOWIER
SCRUBBERS	SECONDING	SEMIOTICS	SERICEOUS	SHADOWING
SCRUBBIER	SECRETARY	SEMIRIGID	SERIGRAPH	SHAGGIEST
SCRUBBING	SECRETING	SEMISOLID	SERIOUSLY	SHAKE A
SCRUBLAND	SECRETION	SEMISWEET	SERMONIZE	LEG
SCRUFFIER	SECRETIVE	SEMITONES	SEROLOGIC	SHAKEDOWN
SCRUMHALF	SECRETORY	SEMITONIC	SEROTINAL	SHAKEOUTS
SCRUM HALF	SECTARIAN	SEMIVOCAL	SEROTONIN	SHAKINESS
SCRUMMAGE	SECTILITY	SEMIVOWEL	SERRATION	SHALLOWED

S 9 SHALLOWER

SHALLOWER	SHININESS	SHOWPIECE	SIDEWARDS	SINGULARS
SHALLOWLY	SHINNYING	SHOW PIECE	SIGHTABLE	SINGULTUS
SHAMANISM	SHIPBOARD	SHOWPLACE	SIGHTINGS	SINHALESE
SHAMANIST	SHIPMATES	SHOWROOMS	SIGHTLESS	SINISTRAL
SHAMATEUR	SHIPMENTS	SHOW TRIAL	SIGHT-READ	SINOLOGUE
SHAMBLING	SHIPOWNER	SHREDDERS	SIGHTSEER	SINUOSITY
SHAMBOLIC	SHIPSHAPE	SHREDDING	SIGMATION	SINUOUSLY
SHAMELESS	SHIPWRECK	SHREWDEST	SIGNAL BOX	SINUSITIS
SHAMPOOED	SHIPYARDS	SHRIEKING	SIGNALING	SIPHONAGE
SHAMPOOER	SHIRTIEST	SHRILLEST	SIGNALIZE	SIPHONING
SHANGRI-LA	SHIRTTAIL	SHRINKAGE	SIGNALLED	SISYPHEAN
SHAN STATE	SHITTIEST	SHRINKING	SIGNALLER	SIT AT
SHAPELESS	SHIVERING	SHRIVELED	SIGNALMAN	HOME
SHAPELIER	SHOCKABLE	SHROUDING	SIGNALMEN	SITATUNGA
SHARECROP	SHODDIEST	SHRUBBERY	SIGNATORY	SITUATING
SHARE SHOP	SHOEHORNS	SHRUGGING	SIGNATURE	SITUATION
SHAREWARE	SHOELACES	SHUBUNKIN	SIGNBOARD	SITZKREIG
SHARKSKIN	SHOEMAKER	SHUDDERED	SIGNIFIED	SIX-FOOTER
SHARPENED	SHOESHINE	SHUFBOARD	SIGNIFIER	SIXPENCES
SHARPENER	SHOETREES	SHUFFLERS	SIGNORINA	SIXTEENMO
SHARP-EYED	SHOOT-'EM-	SHUFFLING	SIGNPOSTS	SIXTEENTH
SHARPNESS	UP	SHUNNABLE	SIKKIMESE	SIXTH FORM
SHATTERED	SHOOTINGS	SHUTDOWNS	SILENCERS	SIXTIETHS
SHATTERER	SHOOT-OUTS	SHUTTERED	SILENCING	SIZARSHIP
SHEARLING	SHOP FLOOR	SHUTTLING	SILICATES	SKAGERRAK
SHEATFISH	SHORELESS	SIBILANCE	SILICEOUS	SKEDADDLE
SHEATHING	SHORELINE	SIBILANTS	SILICOSIS	SKELETONS
SHEEPDIPS	SHORTAGES	SIBYLLINE	SILIQUOSE	SKEPTICAL
SHEEPDOGS	SHORTCAKE	SICCATIVE	SILKALINE	SKETCHERS
SHEEPFOLD	SHORT CUTS	SICKENING	SILKINESS	SKETCHIER
SHEEPSKIN	SHORTENED	SICK LEAVE	SILKWORMS	SKETCHILY
SHEEPWALK	SHORTENER	SICKLIEST	SILLABUBS	SKETCHING
SHEERLEGS	SHORTFALL	SICKROOMS	SILLINESS	SKETCHPAD
SHEERNESS	SHORTHAND	SIC PASSIM	SILTATION	SKEWBALDS
SHEFFIELD	SHORT-HAUL	SIDEBOARD	SILVERING	SKEWERING
SHEIKHDOM	SHORTHORN	SIDEBURNS	SIMAROUBA	SKEW-WHIFF
SHELDUCKS	SHORT LIST	SIDE-DRESS	SIMILARLY	SKIASCOPE
SHELF LIFE	SHORTNESS	SIDE ISSUE	SIMMERING	SKIASCOPY
SHELLFIRE	SHORT SLIP	SIDEKICKS	SIMPATICO	SKIDPROOF
SHELLFISH	SHORT-TERM	SIDELIGHT	SIMPERING	SKIJORING
SHELTERED	SHORT TIME	SIDELINED	SIMPLETON	SKILFULLY
SHELTERER	SHORT WAVE	SIDELINES	SIMULACRA	SKIMMINGS
SHEPHERDS	SHOT TOWER	SIDE ORDER	SIMULATED	SKIMPIEST
SHERBORNE	SHOULDERS	SIDERITIC	SIMULATOR	SKIN-DIVED
SHIELDING	SHOVELING	SIDEROSIS	SINCERELY	SKIN DIVER
SHIFTIEST	SHOVELLED	SIDEROTIC	SINCERITY	SKIN FLICK
SHIFT KEYS	SHOWCASES	SIDESHOWS	SINECURES	SKINFLINT
SHIFTLESS	SHOWDOWNS	SIDESLIPS	SINGAPORE	SKIN GRAFT
SHILLINGS	SHOWERING	SIDESTEPS	SINGINGLY	SKINHEADS
SHIMMERED	SHOWGIRLS	SIDESWIPE	SINGLETON	SKINNIEST
SHINBONES	SHOWINESS	SIDETRACK	SINGSONGS	SKIN-TIGHT

SKI PLANES	SLOBBERER	SNAKESKIN	SOARINGLY	SOLSTICES
SKIPPERED	SLOPINGLY	SNAKINESS	SOBBINGLY	SOLUTIONS
SKITTERED	SLOPPIEST	SNAPPABLE	SOBERNESS	SOLUTREAN
SKIVVYING	SLOUCH HAT	SNAPPIEST	SOBRIQUET	SOLVATION
SKULLCAPS	SLOUCHILY	SNAPSHOTS	SOB SISTER	SOMBREROS
SKYDIVERS	SLOUCHING	SNARE DRUM	SOCIALISM	SOMEPLACE
SKYDIVING	SLOUGHING	SNARINGLY	SOCIALIST	SOMETHING
SKYJACKED	SLOVAKIAN	SNATCHILY	SOCIALITE	SOMETIMES
SKYJACKER	SLOVENIAN	SNATCHING	SOCIALITY	SOMEWHERE
SKYLARKED	SLOWCOACH	SNAZZIEST	SOCIALIZE	SOMMELIER
SKYLARKER	SLOWDOWNS	SNEAKIEST	SOCIETIES	SOMNOLENT
SKYLIGHTS	SLOW MATCH	SNICKERED	SOCIOLOGY	SONGBIRDS
SKYROCKET	SLOWWORMS	SNIDENESS	SOCIOPATH	SONGBOOKS
SKYWRITER	SLUDGIEST	SNIFFLERS	SODA WATER	SONG CYCLE
SLACKENED	SLUGGARDS	SNIFFLING	SODOMITES	SONGOLOLO
SLACKNESS	SLUMBERED	SNIGGERED	SOFTENING	SONGSTERS
SLAGHEAPS	SLUMBERER	SNIPEFISH	SOFT FRUIT	SONIC BOOM
SLANDERED	SLUSH FUND	SNITCHING	SOFT GOODS	SONNETEER
SLANDERER	SLUSHIEST	SNIVELING	SOFT METAL	SON-OF-A-
SLANTWISE	SMALL ARMS	SNIVELLED	SOFT-PEDAL	GUN
SLAPHAPPY	SMALL BEER	SNIVELLER	SOFT SPOTS	SONS-IN-
SLAPSTICK	SMALLNESS	SNOOKERED	SOFT TOUCH	LAW
SLATINESS	SMALL TALK	SNOOTIEST	SOFTWOODS	SOOTINESS
SLATTERNS	SMALL-TIME	SNOTTIEST	SOGGINESS	SOPHISTER
SLAUGHTER	SMARMIEST	SNOWBALLS	SOI-DISANT	SOPHISTIC
SLAVERING	SMART ALEC	SNOWBERRY	SOJOURNED	SOPHISTRY
SLAVISHLY	SMART CARD	SNOW-BLIND	SOJOURNER	SOPHOMORE
SLAVONIAN	SMARTENED	SNOWBLINK	SOLAR CELL	SOPORIFIC
SLEAZIEST	SMARTNESS	SNOWBOUND	SOLARIUMS	SOPPINESS
SLEEKNESS	SMASHABLE	SNOWDONIA	SOLAR YEAR	SOPRANINO
SLEEPIEST	SMATTERER	SNOWDRIFT	SOLDERING	SORCERERS
SLEEPLESS	SMEAR TEST	SNOWDROPS	SOLDIERED	SORCERESS
SLEEPWALK	SMELLIEST	SNOWFALLS	SOLDIERLY	SORCEROUS
SLICEABLE	SMILINGLY	SNOWFIELD	SOLDIER ON	SORE POINT
SLICKNESS	SMIRCHING	SNOWFLAKE	SOLECISMS	SORITICAL
SLIDE RULE	SMOKELESS	SNOW GOOSE	SOLEMNIFY	SORRINESS
SLIGHTEST	SMOKINESS	SNOWINESS	SOLEMNITY	SORROWFUL
SLIGHTING	SMOLDERED	SNOWSHOER	SOLEMNIZE	SORROWING
SLIMINESS	SMOOCHING	SNOWSHOES	SOLENODON	SORTILEGE
SLINGSHOT	SMOOTHEST	SNOWSTORM	SOLFATARA	SORTITION
SLINKIEST	SMOOTHIES	SNOW-WHITE	SOLFEGGIO	SOSNOWIEC
SLIPCASES	SMOOTHING	SNUB-NOSED	SOLFERINO	SOSTENUTO
SLIPKNOTS	SMOTHERED	SNUFFLING	SOLICITED	SOTTO VOCE
SLIPNOOSE	SMUGGLERS	SNUGGLING	SOLICITOR	SOUBRETTE
SLIPPAGES	SMUGGLING	SOAKINGLY	SOLIDNESS	SOULFULLY
SLIPPIEST	SMUTTIEST	SOAPBERRY	SOLILOQUY	SOUL MUSIC
SLIP ROADS	SNACK BARS	SOAPBOXES	SOLIPSISM	SOUNDABLE
SLIPSHEET	SNAFFLING	SOAPINESS	SOLIPSIST	SOUNDINGS
SLITHERED	SNAIL MAIL	SOAP OPERA	SOLITAIRE	SOUNDLESS
SLIVOVITZ	SNAKEBITE	SOAPSTONE	SOLONCHAK	SOUNDNESS
SLOBBERED	SNAKEROOT	SOAPSUDSY	SOLOTHURN	SOUNDPOST

SOUND POST	SPEARWORT	SPINNERET	SPOROZOAN	SQUEAKERS
SOUP SPOON	SPECIALLY	SPINOSITY	SPORTIEST	SQUEAKIER
SOUR CREAM	SPECIALTY	SPINSTERS	SPORTS CAR	SQUEAKING
SOUTH BEND	SPECIFICS	SPINULOSE	SPORTSMAN	SQUEALERS
SOUTHDOWN	SPECIFIED	SPIRALING	SPORTSMEN	SQUEALING
SOUTHEAST	SPECIFIER	SPIRALLED	SPORULATE	SQUEAMISH
SOUTHERLY	SPECIMENS	SPIRILLAR	SPOT CHECK	SQUEEGEES
SOUTHPAWS	SPECTACLE	SPIRILLUM	SPOTLIGHT	SQUEEZERS
SOUTH POLE	SPECTATED	SPIRITING	SPOTTABLE	SQUEEZING
SOUTHPORT	SPECTATOR	SPIRITOSO	SPOTTIEST	SQUELCHED
SOUTHWARD	SPECULATE	SPIRITOUS	SPRAINING	SQUELCHER
SOUTHWARK	SPEECH DAY	SPIRITUAL	SPRAWLING	SQUIDGIER
SOUTHWEST	SPEECHIFY	SPIROGYRA	SPRAY GUNS	SQUIFFIER
SOUVENIRS	SPEEDBOAT	SPITFIRES	SPREADING	SQUIGGLER
SOU'WESTER	SPEEDIEST	SPIT IT	SPRIGHTLY	SQUIGGLES
SOVEREIGN	SPEEDSTER	OUT	SPRINGBOK	SQUINTING
SOVIETISM	SPEED TRAP	SPITTOONS	SPRINGIER	SQUIRMING
SOVIETIST	SPEEDWAYS	SPLASHIER	SPRINGILY	SQUIRRELS
SOVIETIZE	SPEEDWELL	SPLASHILY	SPRINGING	SQUIRTERS
SOYA BEANS	SPELLABLE	SPLASHING	SPRINKLED	SQUIRTING
SPACEBAND	SPELLBIND	SPLATTING	SPRINKLER	SQUISHIER
SPACED OUT	SPELLINGS	SPLAYFOOT	SPRINKLES	SQUISHING
SPACELESS	SPELUNKER	SPLEENFUL	SPRINTERS	SQUITTERS
SPACEPORT	SPENDABLE	SPLEENISH	SPRINTING	STABILITY
SPACESHIP	SPERMATIC	SPLENDOUR	SPRITSAIL	STABILIZE
SPACESUIT	SPERMATID	SPLENETIC	SPROCKETS	STABLE BOY
SPACE-TIME	SPHAGNOUS	SPLENITIS	SPROUTING	STAGE DOOR
SPACEWALK	SPHAGNUMS	SPLINTERS	SPUNKIEST	STAGEHAND
SPADEFISH	SPHENODON	SPLINTERY	SPUTTERED	STAGE HAND
SPADEWORK	SPHERICAL	SPLIT ENDS	SPUTTERER	STAGE NAME
SPAGHETTI	SPHEROIDS	SPLIT PEAS	SQUABBLED	STAGGERED
SPANGLING	SPHERULAR	SPLIT RING	SQUABBLER	STAGGERER
SPANIARDS	SPHINCTER	SPLITTING	SQUABBLES	STAGHOUND
SPANKINGS	SPHYGMOID	SPLOSHING	SQUAD CARS	STAGINESS
SPARENESS	SPICINESS	SPLURGING	SQUADRONS	STAGNANCY
SPARE PART	SPICULATE	SPLUTTERS	SQUALIDLY	STAGNATED
SPARERIBS	SPIDERMAN	SPODUMENE	SQUALLIER	STAG PARTY
SPARE TYRE	SPIDERWEB	SPOKEN FOR	SQUALLING	STAIDNESS
SPARINGLY	SPIELBERG	SPOKESMAN	SQUAMOSAL	STAINABLE
SPARKLERS	SPIKENARD	SPONGE BAG	SQUARE LEG	STAINLESS
SPARKLING	SPIKE-RUSH	SPONGIEST	SQUARE ONE	STAIRCASE
SPARK PLUG	SPIKINESS	SPONSORED	SQUARROSE	STAIRHEAD
SPARTEINE	SPILLIKIN	SPOOKIEST	SQUASHIER	STAIRWELL
SPASMODIC	SPILLWAYS	SPOONBILL	SQUASHILY	STALEMATE
SPATIALLY	SPINDLIER	SPOON-FEED	SQUASHING	STALENESS
SPATTERED	SPIN-DRIED	SPOONFULS	SQUATNESS	STALINISM
SPATULATE	SPINDRIFT	SPOONSFUL	SQUATTERS	STALINIST
SPEAKABLE	SPIN-DRYER	SPOROCARP	SQUATTEST	STALL-FEED
SPEAKEASY	SPINELESS	SPOROCYST	SQUATTING	STALLIONS
SPEARHEAD	SPININESS	SPOROCYTE	SQUAWKERS	STALWARTS
SPEARMINT	SPINNAKER	SPOROGONY	SQUAWKING	STAMINATE

STAMINODE	STEADFAST	STILLNESS	STONEWORK	STRESSFUL
STAMINODY	STEADIEST	STILL ROOM	STONEWORT	STRESSING
STAMMERED	STEADYING	STILTEDLY	STONINESS	STRETCHED
STAMMERER	STEAMBOAT	STIMULANT	STOPCOCKS	STRETCHER
STAMPEDED	STEAMED-UP	STIMULATE	STOPLIGHT	STRETCHES
STAMPEDER	STEAMIEST	STINGIEST	STOPOVERS	STRETFORD
STAMPEDES	STEAM IRON	STINGRAYS	STOPPABLE	STRIATION
STAMP MILL	STEAMROLL	STINK-BOMB	STOPPAGES	STRICTEST
STANCHING	STEAMSHIP	STINKHORN	STOPPERED	STRICTURE
STANCHION	STEATITIC	STINKWEED	STOP PRESS	STRIDENCE
STANDARDS	STEEL BAND	STINKWOOD	STOPWATCH	STRIDENCY
STAND FIRM	STEELHEAD	STIPIFORM	STOREROOM	STRIKE PAY
STAND OVER	STEELIEST	STIPITATE	STORMIEST	STRINGENT
STANDPIPE	STEEL WOOL	STIPPLING	STORNOWAY	STRINGIER
STAPEDIAL	STEELWORK	STIPULATE	STORYBOOK	STRINGILY
STAR-APPLE	STEELYARD	STIR-FRIED	STORY LINE	STRINGING
STARBOARD	STEEPENED	STIRRABLE	STORYLINE	STRIP CLUB
STARBURST	STEEPNESS	STITCHING	STOUTNESS	STRIPIEST
STARCHIER	STEERABLE	STOCKADED	STOVEPIPE	STRIPLING
STARCHILY	STEERSMAN	STOCKADES	STOWAWAYS	STRIPPERS
STARCHING	STEERSMEN	STOCKCARS	STRADDLED	STRIPPING
STARE DOWN	STELLULAR	STOCK CUBE	STRADDLER	STROBILUS
STARGAZER	STENCILED	STOCKFISH	STRAGGLED	STROLLERS
STARKNESS	STENOTYPE	STOCKHOLM	STRAGGLER	STROLLING
STARLIGHT	STENOTYPY	STOCKIEST	STRAIGHTS	STROMATIC
STARLINGS	STEPCHILD	STOCKINET	STRAINERS	STRONGARM
STARRIEST	STERADIAN	STOCKINGS	STRAINING	STRONGBOX
STAR SIGNS	STERILANT	STOCKISTS	STRALSUND	STRONGEST
STARTLING	STERILITY	STOCKPILE	STRANGELY	STRONGYLE
STATE DUMA	STERILIZE	STOCKPORT	STRANGERS	STRONTIAN
STATEHOOD	STERNMOST	STOCKPOTS	STRANGEST	STRONTIUM
STATELESS	STERNNESS	STOCKROOM	STRANGLED	STROPPIER
STATEMENT	STERNPOST	STOCK TAKE	STRANGLER	STRUCTURE
STATEROOM	STEVEDORE	STOCKYARD	STRANGLES	STRUGGLED
STATESIDE	STEVENAGE	STODGIEST	STRANGURY	STRUGGLER
STATESMAN	STICK AT	STOICALLY	STRANRAER	STRUGGLES
STATESMEN	IT	STOKEHOLD	STRAPLESS	STRUMATIC
STATIONED	STICKIEST	STOKEHOLE	STRAPPING	STRUMMING
STATIONER	STICKLERS	STOLIDITY	STRATAGEM	STRUMPETS
STATISTIC	STICKPINS	STOMACHED	STRATEGIC	STRUNG-OUT
STATOCYST	STICKSEED	STOMACHIC	STRAW POLL	STRUTTING
STATOLITH	STICKWEED	STONECHAT	STREAKERS	STRYCHNIC
STATUETTE	STICKY BUN	STONE-COLD	STREAKIER	STUBBIEST
STATUS QUO	STICKY END	STONECROP	STREAKILY	STUDBOOKS
STATUTORY	STIFFENED	STONE-DEAD	STREAKING	STUDHORSE
STAUNCHED	STIFFENER	STONE-DEAF	STREAMERS	STUFFIEST
STAUNCHER	STIFFNESS	STONEFISH	STREAMING	STUMBLING
STAUNCHLY	STIGMATIC	STONELESS	STREETCAR	STUMPIEST
STAVANGER	STILETTOS	STONE-LILY	STREISAND	STUPEFIED
STAVROPOL	STILLBORN	STONEWALL	STRENGTHS	STUPEFIER
ST BERNARD	STILL LIFE	STONEWARE	STRENUOUS	STUPIDEST

STUPIDITY	SUBMITTER	SUFFOCATE	SUPERHEAT	SUSPECTED
STUPOROUS	SUBMUCOSA	SUFFRAGAN	SUPERHERO	SUSPECTER
STURDIEST	SUBNORMAL	SUFFRAGES	SUPERIORS	SUSPENDED
STURGEONS	SUBORNING	SUFFUSING	SUPERNOVA	SUSPENDER
STUTTERED	SUBPHYLAR	SUFFUSION	SUPERPOSE	SUSPENSOR
STUTTERER	SUBPHYLUM	SUFFUSIVE	SUPERSEDE	SUSPICION
STUTTGART	SUBPOENAS	SUGAR BEET	SUPERSTAR	SUSTAINED
STYLEBOOK	SUBREGION	SUGAR CANE	SUPERVENE	SUSTAINER
STYLELESS	SUBROGATE	SUGARCANE	SUPERVISE	SUSURRANT
STYLIFORM	SUBSCRIBE	SUGGESTED	SUPINATOR	SUSURRATE
STYLISHLY	SUBSCRIPT	SUGGESTER	SUPPERADD	SUZERAINS
STYLISTIC	SUBSIDIES	SUITCASES	SUPPLIANT	SWADDLING
STYLIZING	SUBSIDING	SULCATION	SUPPLIERS	SWAGGERED
STYLOBATE	SUBSIDIZE	SULKINESS	SUPPLYING	SWAGGERER
STYLOLITE	SUBSISTED	SULLENEST	SUPPORTED	SWAHILIAN
STYLOPIZE	SUBSISTER	SULLIABLE	SUPPORTER	SWALLOWED
STYPTICAL	SUBSOCIAL	SULPHATES	SUPPOSING	SWALLOWER
STYROFOAM	SUBSOILER	SULPHIDES	SUPPURATE	SWAMPLAND
SUABILITY	SUBSTANCE	SULPHITIC	SUPREMACY	SWANKIEST
SUAVENESS	SUBSTRATA	SULPHURET	SUPREMELY	SWANS DOWN
SUBALPINE	SUBSTRATE	SULPHURYL	SUPREMITY	SWAN'S-
SUBALTERN	SUBSUMING	SULTANATE	SURAKARTA	DOWN
SUBARCTIC	SUBSYSTEM	SULTRIEST	SURCHARGE	SWANSONGS
SUBATOMIC	SUBTENANT	SUMMARIES	SURCINGLE	SWAP MEETS
SUBCLIMAX	SUBTENDED	SUMMARILY	SURCULOSE	SWARTHIER
SUBCORTEX	SUBTILIZE	SUMMARIZE	SURE THING	SWARTHILY
SUBDEACON	SUBTITLED	SUMMATION	SURFACING	SWASTIKAS
SUBDIVIDE	SUBTITLES	SUMMERING	SURFBOARD	SWATHABLE
SUBDUABLE	SUBTOTALS	SUMMING-UP	SURFEITED	SWAYINGLY
SUBDUEDLY	SUBVERTED	SUMMONING	SURFEITER	SWAZILAND
SUBEDITED	SUBVERTER	SUMMONSED	SURFPERCH	SWEARWORD
SUBEDITOR	SUBWOOFER	SUMMONSES	SURGEONCY	SWEATBAND
SUBFAMILY	SUCCEEDED	SUMPTUARY	SURGERIES	SWEATIEST
SUBJACENT	SUCCEEDER	SUMPTUOUS	SURLINESS	SWEATSHOP
SUBJECTED	SUCCENTOR	SUNBATHED	SURMISING	SWEEPBACK
SUBJOINED	SUCCESSES	SUNBATHER	SURPASSED	SWEEPINGS
SUB JUDICE	SUCCESSOR	SUNBURNED	SURPLICES	SWEET CORN
SUBJUGATE	SUCCINATE	SUNDERING	SURPLUSES	SWEETENER
SUBLEASED	SUCCOURED	SUNDOWNER	SURPRISED	SWEETMEAT
SUBLEASES	SUCCOURER	SUNDSVALL	SURPRISER	SWEETNESS
SUBLESSEE	SUCCULENT	SUNFLOWER	SURPRISES	SWEET PEAS
SUBLESSOR	SUCCUMBED	SUN LOUNGE	SURRENDER	SWEET TALK
SUBLIMATE	SUCCUMBER	SUNNINESS	SURROGACY	SWELLFISH
SUBLIMELY	SUCKLINGS	SUNSHADES	SURROGATE	SWELLINGS
SUBLIMITY	SUCTIONAL	SUNSTROKE	SURROUNDS	SWELTERED
SUBLUNARY	SUCTORIAL	SUNTANNED	SURTITLES	SWEPT-BACK
SUBMARINE	SUDORIFIC	SUN VISORS	SURVEYING	SWEPTWING
SUBMENTAL	SUFFERERS	SUPERABLE	SURVEYORS	SWERVABLE
SUBMERGED	SUFFERING	SUPERCOOL	SURVIVALS	SWIFTNESS
SUBMITTAL	SUFFICING	SUPEREGOS	SURVIVING	SWIMMABLE
SUBMITTED	SUFFIXION	SUPERFINE	SURVIVORS	SWIMMERET

SWINDLERS	SYNCOPATE	TAILGATED	TARGETING	TEDDY BEAR
SWINDLING	SYNCRETIC	TAILGATES	TARMACKED	TEDDY BOYS
SWINEHERD	SYNCYTIUM	TAILLIGHT	TARNISHED	TEDIOUSLY
SWINGEING	SYNDACTYL	TAIL-LIGHT	TARNISHER	TEENAGERS
SWING-WING	SYNDICATE	TAILORING	TARPAULIN	TEE SHIRTS
SWINISHLY	SYNDROMES	TAILPIECE	TARRAGONA	TEETERING
SWISS ROLL	SYNDROMIC	TAIL PIPES	TARTARIZE	TELECASTS
SWITCHING	SYNECTICS	TAILPLANE	TARTAROUS	TELEGENIC
SWITCH OFF	SYNERESIS	TAILSPINS	TASIMETER	TELEGONIC
SWIVELING	SYNERGISM	TAILSTOCK	TASIMETRY	TELEGRAMS
SWIVELLED	SYNERGIST	TAILWHEEL	TASK FORCE	TELEGRAPH
SWORDBILL	SYNIZESIS	TAILWINDS	TASMANIAN	TELEMETER
SWORDFISH	SYNKARYON	TAIWANESE	TASMAN SEA	TELEMETRY
SWORDPLAY	SYNOEKETE	TAKAMATSU	TASTE BUDS	TELEOLOGY
SWORDSMAN	SYNONYMIC	TAKEAWAYS	TASTELESS	TELEPATHY
SWORDSMEN	SYNOVITIC	TAKE LEAVE	TASTINESS	TELEPHONE
SWORDTAIL	SYNOVITIS	TAKE NOTES	TATTINESS	TELEPHONY
SYBARITES	SYNTACTIC	TAKEOVERS	TATTOOING	TELESCOPE
SYBARITIC	SYNTHESES	TAKE STEPS	TATTOOIST	TELESCOPY
SYCAMORES	SYNTHESIS	TAKE STOCK	TAUTENING	TELESTICH
SYCOPHANT	SYNTHETIC	TAKING OFF	TAUTOLOGY	TELEVISED
SYKTYVKAR	SYPHERING	TALIGRADE	TAUTONYMY	TELLINGLY
SYLLABARY	SYPHILOID	TALISMANS	TAXACEOUS	TELLTALES
SYLLABIFY	SYPHILOMA	TALKATIVE	TAX HAVENS	TELLURATE
SYLLABISM	SYPHONING	TALKING-TO	TAXIDERMY	TELLURIAN
SYLLABLES	SYRINGEAL	TALK SHOWS	TAXIMETER	TELLURIDE
SYLLABUBS	SYRINGING	TALL ORDER	TAXI RANKS	TELLURION
SYLLEPSIS	SYSTALTIC	TALL STORY	TAXONOMIC	TELLURITE
SYLLEPTIC		TALMUDISM	TAXPAYERS	TELLURIUM
SYLLOGISM	**T**	TALMUDIST	TEA BREAKS	TELLURIZE
SYLLOGIZE	TABESCENT	TAMARINDS	TEACHABLE	TELLUROUS
SYLPHLIKE	TABLATURE	TAMIL NADU	TEA CHESTS	TELOPHASE
SYLVANITE	TABLELAND	TAMOXIFEN	TEA CLOTHS	TELPHERIC
SYMBIOSIS	TABLEMATS	TAMPERING	TEA COSIES	TEMAZEPAM
SYMBIOTIC	TABLEWARE	TANDOORIS	TEAGARDEN	TEMPERATE
SYMBOLISM	TABLE WINE	TANGERINE	TEAHOUSES	TEMPERING
SYMBOLIST	TABULABLE	TANNERIES	TEAKETTLE	TEMPLATES
SYMBOLIZE	TABULATED	TANTALATE	TEALEAVES	TEMPORARY
SYMBOLOGY	TABULATOR	TANTALITE	TEAMSTERS	TEMPORIZE
SYMPATHIN	TACAMAHAC	TANTALIZE	TEARAWAYS	TEMPTABLE
SYMPATRIC	TACHYLYTE	TANTALOUS	TEARDROPS	TEMPTRESS
SYMPHONIC	TACITNESS	TANZANIAN	TEARFULLY	TENACIOUS
SYMPHYSIS	TACKINESS	TAP DANCER	TEARINGLY	TENACULUM
SYMPODIAL	TACTFULLY	TAP DANCES	TEASINGLY	TENANCIES
SYMPODIUM	TACTICIAN	TAPE DECKS	TEASPOONS	TENDEREST
SYMPOSIAC	TACTILITY	TAPEWORMS	TEA TASTER	TENDERING
SYMPOSIUM	TAENIASIS	TAPHONOMY	TEA TOWELS	TENDERIZE
SYNAGOGUE	TAGMEMICS	TARANTISM	TECHINESS	TENDINOUS
SYNALEPHA	TAILBACKS	TARANTULA	TECHNICAL	TENEBRISM
SYNCHRONY	TAILBOARD	TARAXACUM	TECHNIQUE	TENEBRIST
SYNCLINAL	TAILCOATS	TARDINESS	TECTONICS	TENEBROUS

T

TENEMENTS	TETRAPODY	THIRTIETH	TIDAL WAVE	TOADSTOOL
TENNESSEE	TETRARCHY	THITHERTO	TIDEMARKS	TOAMASINA
TENOR CLEF	TETROXIDE	THONINESS	TIDEWATER	TOAST RACK
TENSENESS	TEXTBOOKS	THORNBACK	TIED HOUSE	TOBOGGANS
TENSILITY	THALASSIC	THORNBILL	TIE-DYEING	TOCANTINS
TENSIONAL	THANJAVUR	THORNIEST	TIGER LILY	TOGLIATTI
TENSORIAL	THANKLESS	THOUSANDS	TIGHTENED	TOLERABLE
TENTACLES	THANKYOUS	THRALLDOM	TIGHTENER	TOLERABLY
TENTATION	THATCHERS	THRASHING	TIGHTEN UP	TOLERANCE
TENTATIVE	THATCHING	THREADFIN	TIGHTKNIT	TOLERATED
TENUOUSLY	THEACEOUS	THREADING	TIGHTNESS	TOLERATOR
TEPHRITIC	THEARCHIC	THREEFOLD	TIGHTROPE	TOLLBOOTH
TEREBINTH	THEATRICS	THREESOME	TIGHT SPOT	TOLLGATES
TERMAGANT	THE BROADS	THREE-STAR	TIGRESSES	TOLLHOUSE
TERMINALS	THECODONT	THREONINE	TIME BOMBS	TOLL HOUSE
TERMINATE	THE CREEPS	THRESHERS	TIME LAPSE	TOMAHAWKS
TERPINEOL	THEME PARK	THRESHING	TIME-LAPSE	TOMBOYISH
TERRAFORM	THEME SONG	THRESHOLD	TIMELIEST	TOMBSTONE
TERRAPINS	THEOCRACY	THRIFTIER	TIME LIMIT	TOMMY GUNS
TERRARIUM	THEOCRASY	THRIFTILY	TIMEPIECE	TOMORROWS
TERRIFIED	THEOMANIA	THRILLERS	TIMESAVER	TONBRIDGE
TERRIFIER	THEORISTS	THRILLING	TIME SHEET	TONE POEMS
TERRITORY	THEORIZED	THROATIER	TIMETABLE	TONKA BEAN
TERRORFUL	THEORIZER	THROATILY	TIME ZONES	TONOMETER
TERRORISM	THEOSOPHY	THROBBING	TIMISOARA	TONOMETRY
TERRORIST	THERAPIES	THRONGING	TIMOCRACY	TONSILLAR
TERRORIZE	THERAPIST	THROTTLED	TIMPANIST	TONSORIAL
TERSENESS	THERAPSID	THROTTLER	TINCTURES	TOOL-MAKER
TERVALENT	THEREFORE	THROTTLES	TINDERBOX	TOOTHACHE
TESSERACT	THEREINTO	THROWAWAY	TINGALING	TOOTHCOMB
TESSITURA	THEREUPON	THROWBACK	TINKERING	TOOTHIEST
TESTAMENT	THEREWITH	THROWSTER	TINNINESS	TOOTHLESS
TESTATORS	THERMOSES	THRUMMING	TIN OPENER	TOOTHPICK
TESTATRIX	THESAURUS	THRUSTERS	TIP AND	TOOTHSOME
TEST CARDS	THESPIANS	THRUSTING	RUN	TOOTHWORT
TEST CASES	THE STATES	THUMBNAIL	TIPPERARY	TOOWOOMBA
TESTICLES	THEURGIST	THUMBTACK	TIPSINESS	TOP DOLLAR
TESTIFIED	THICKENED	THUNDERED	TIREDNESS	TOP DRAWER
TESTIFIRE	THICKENER	THUNDERER	TITCHIEST	TOP FLIGHT
TESTIMONY	THICKHEAD	THURINGIA	TIT FOR	TOP-FLIGHT
TESTINESS	THICKLEAF	THURSDAYS	TAT	TOPIARIAN
TESTINGLY	THICKNESS	THWACKING	TITILLATE	TOPIARIST
TEST MATCH	THIGHBONE	THWARTING	TITIVATED	TOPICALLY
TEST PILOT	THINKABLE	THYLACINE	TITIVATOR	TOPMINNOW
TEST TUBES	THINK TANK	THYMIDINE	TITLE DEED	TOPOLOGIC
TETCHIEST	THINNINGS	THYRATRON	TITLE PAGE	TOPONYMIC
TETE-A-	THIO-ETHER	THYRISTOR	TITLE ROLE	TOP SECRET
TETE	THIOPHENE	THYROXINE	TITRATION	TOP-SECRET
TETHERING	THIRD-RATE	TICKETING	TITTERING	TORCHWOOD
TETRAGRAM	THIRSTIER	TIC TAC	T-JUNCTION	TOREADORS
TETRALOGY	THIRSTILY	MAN	TOADSTONE	TOREUTICS

TORMENTED	TRACEABLE	TRASHIEST	TRIBUNALS	TRIUMPHAL
TORMENTIL	TRACHYTIC	TRATTORIA	TRIBUNARY	TRIUMPHED
TORMENTOR	TRACKABLE	TRAUMATIC	TRIBUNATE	TRIUMPHER
TORNADOES	TRACKLESS	TRAVAILED	TRIBUTARY	TRIVALENT
TORPEDOED	TRACKSUIT	TRAVELING	TRICEPSES	TRIVIALLY
TORPEDOES	TRACK SUIT	TRAVELLED	TRICHITIC	TRIWEEKLY
TORPIDITY	TRACTABLE	TRAVELLER	TRICHOMIC	TROCHLEAR
TORRIDITY	TRADE GAPS	TRAVERSAL	TRICHOSIS	TROMBONES
TORSIONAL	TRADEMARK	TRAVERSED	TRICHROIC	TRONDHEIM
TORTILLAS	TRADE NAME	TRAVERSER	TRICKIEST	TROOPSHIP
TORTOISES	TRADE-OFFS	TRAVERSES	TRICKLING	TROOSTITE
TORTRICID	TRADESMAN	TREACHERY	TRICKSTER	TROPISTIC
TORTURERS	TRADESMEN	TREADMILL	TRICLINIC	TROPOLOGY
TORTURING	TRADE WIND	TREASURED	TRICOLOUR	TROSSACHS
TOTALIZER	TRADITION	TREASURER	TRICOTINE	TROUBLING
TOTALLING	TRADUCERS	TREASURES	TRICROTIC	TROUBLOUS
TOTAQUINE	TRADUCING	TREATABLE	TRICUSPID	TROUNCING
TOTEM POLE	TRAFALGAR	TREATISES	TRICYCLES	TROUSSEAU
TO THE	TRAGEDIAN	TREATMENT	TRICYCLIC	TROWELLER
FORE	TRAGEDIES	TREE FERNS	TRIDACTYL	TRPORIFIC
TOTTERING	TRAINABLE	TREENWARE	TRIENNIAL	TRUCK FARM
TOTTING UP	TRAININGS	TREE SHREW	TRIENNIUM	TRUCKLING
TOUCHABLE	TRAIN SETS	TREHALOSE	TRIFOLIUM	TRUCKLOAD
TOUCHDOWN	TRAIPSING	TREILLAGE	TRIFORIAL	TRUCK STOP
TOUCH DOWN	TRAMLINES	TRELLISES	TRIFORIUM	TRUCULENT
TOUCHIEST	TRAMMELER	TREMATODE	TRIGGERED	TRUELOVES
TOUCHLINE	TRAMPLING	TREMBLING	TRIGONOUS	TRUE NORTH
TOUCHMARK	TRANSCEND	TREMOLITE	TRIHEDRAL	TRUMP CARD
TOUCH-TYPE	TRANSEPTS	TREMOROUS	TRIHEDRON	TRUMPETED
TOUCHWOOD	TRANSEUNT	TREMULANT	TRIHYDRIC	TRUMPETER
TOUGHENED	TRANSFERS	TREMULOUS	TRILINEAR	TRUNCATED
TOUGHENER	TRANSFORM	TRENCHANT	TRILLIONS	TRUNCHEON
TOUGH LUCK	TRANSFUER	TRENCHERS	TRILOBATE	TRUNDLING
TOUGHNESS	TRANSFUSE	TRENDIEST	TRILOBITE	TRUNK CALL
TOURCOING	TRANSIENT	TRENGGANU	TRILOGIES	TRUNKFISH
TOURISTIC	TRANSLATE	TREPANNED	TRIMARANS	TRUNK ROAD
TOUT A	TRANSMUTE	TREPHINED	TRIMEROUS	TRUSTABLE
FAIT	TRANSONIC	TREPHINES	TRIMESTER	TRUST FUND
TOWELLING	TRANSPIRE	TREPONEMA	TRIMETRIC	TRUSTIEST
TOWN CLERK	TRANSPORT	TRIALLIST	TRIMMINGS	TRYING OUT
TOWN CRIER	TRANSPOSE	TRIAL RUNS	TRINITIES	TRY SQUARE
TOWN HALLS	TRANSSHIP	TRIANGLES	TRINOMIAL	TSETSE FLY
TOWN HOUSE	TRANSVAAL	TRIATHLON	TRIOELEIN	TSITSIHAR
TOWNSCAPE	TRAPDOORS	TRIATOMIC	TRIPLEXES	TUBBINESS
TOWNSHIPS	TRAPEZIAL	TRIAZOLIC	TRIPTYCHS	TUBULATOR
TOXAPHENE	TRAPEZIUM	TRIBADISM	TRIPWIRES	TUCKER BAG
TOXICALLY	TRAPEZIUS	TRIBALISM	TRISECTED	TUCKER-BAG
TOXICOSIS	TRAPEZOID	TRIBALIST	TRISECTOR	TUCKERING
TOXOPHILY	TRAPPINGS	TRIBESMAN	TRISERIAL	TUG-OF-
TRABEATED	TRAPPISTS	TRIBESMEN	TRITENESS	LOVE
TRABECULA	TRASHCANS	TRIBOLOGY	TRITURATE	

TUGS-OF-
WAR
TUILERIES
TUITIONAL
TULIP TREE
TULIPWOOD
TULLAMORE
TUMBLE-DRY
TUMESCENT
TUMULUSES
TUNEFULLY
TUNGSTITE
TUNGUSIAN
TUNING PEG
TUNNELERS
TUNNELING
TUNNELLED
TUNNELLER
TUPPENCES
TURBIDITY
TURBINATE
TURBOJETS
TURBOPROP
TURBULENT
TURFINESS
TURGIDITY
TURKESTAN
TURNABOUT
TURN ABOUT
TURNCOATS
TURNCOCKS
TURNOVERS
TURNPIKES
TURNROUND
TURN ROUND
TURNSTILE
TURNSTONE
TURNTABLE
TURPITUDE
TURQUOISE
TUSCARORA
TUTIORISM
TUTIORIST
TUTORIALS
TUT-TUTTED
TV DINNERS
TWAYBLADE
TWENTIETH
TWICE-LAID
TWICE-TOLD
TWIDDLING

TWINKLING
TWISTABLE
TWISTEDLY
TWISTIEST
TWITCHING
TWITTERED
TWITTERER
TWO-BY-
FOUR
TWO-HANDED
TWOPENCES
TWO-SEATER
TWO-STROKE
TWO-TIMERS
TWO-TIMING
TYMPANIST
TYMPANUMS
TYNEMOUTH
TYNESIDER
TYPEFACES
TYPEWRITE
TYPHLITIC
TYPHLITIS
TYPHOIDAL
TYPHOIDIN
TYPICALLY
TYPIFYING
TYRANNIES
TYRANNIZE
TYRANNOUS
TZETZE FLY

U

UITLANDER
UKRAINIAN
ULAN BATOR
ULCERATED
ULMACEOUS
ULOTRICHY
ULTIMATUM
ULTRADIAN
ULTRA HIGH
ULULATION
ULYANOVSK
UMBELLATE
UMBELLULE
UMBILICAL
UMBILICUS
UMBRELLAS
UMPTEENTH
UNABASHED

UNADOPTED
UNADVISED
UNALLOYED
UNANIMITY
UNANIMOUS
UNAPTNESS
UNASHAMED
UNASSUMED
UNAUDITED
UNBALANCE
UNBARRING
UNBEKNOWN
UNBENDING
UNBINDING
UNBLESSED
UNBOSOMED
UNBOUNDED
UNBRIDLED
UNBUCKLED
UNCANNIER
UNCANNILY
UNCEASING
UNCERTAIN
UNCHARGED
UNCHARTED
UNCHECKED
UNCLIMBED
UNCONCERN
UNCORKING
UNCOUNTED
UNCOUPLED
UNCOUTHLY
UNCOVERED
UNCREATED
UNCROWDED
UNCROWNED
UNDAUNTED
UNDECAGON
UNDECEIVE
UNDECIDED
UNDERBODY
UNDERBRED
UNDERCLAY
UNDERCOAT
UNDERCOOK
UNDERDOGS
UNDERDONE
UNDERFEED
UNDERFELT
UNDERFOOT
UNDERFUND

UNDERGIRD
UNDERGOER
UNDERGONE
UNDERHAND
UNDERHUNG
UNDERLAIN
UNDERLAYS
UNDERLIER
UNDERLINE
UNDERLING
UNDERMINE
UNDERMOST
UNDERPAID
UNDERPASS
UNDERPLAY
UNDERPLOT
UNDERPROP
UNDERRATE
UNDERSEAL
UNDERSELL
UNDERSHOT
UNDERSIDE
UNDERSOIL
UNDERSOLD
UNDERTAKE
UNDERTINT
UNDERTONE
UNDERTOOK
UNDERWEAR
UNDERWENT
UNDERWING
UNDESIRED
UNDIVIDED
UNDOUBTED
UNDRESSED
UNDULANCE
UNDULATED
UNDULATOR
UNEARTHED
UNEARTHLY
UNEASIEST
UNEATABLE
UNELECTED
UNEQUALLY
UNETHICAL
UNFAILING
UNFAIREST
UNFANCIED
UNFEELING
UNFEIGNED
UNFITNESS

UNFLEDGED
UNFOLDING
UNFOUNDED
UNFROCKED
UNFURLING
UNGUARDED
UNGUINOUS
UNHANDING
UNHAPPILY
UNHARNESS
UNHEALTHY
UNHEARD OF
UNHEARD-OF
UNHINGING
UNHORSING
UNHURRIED
UNICOLOUR
UNIFIABLE
UNIFORMED
UNIFORMLY
UNIJUGATE
UNINSURED
UNION FLAG
UNIONISTS
UNIONIZED
UNION JACK
UNION SHOP
UNIPAROUS
UNIPLANAR
UNIRAMOUS
UNISEXUAL
UNISONOUS
UNITARIAN
UNIT TRUST
UNIVALENT
UNIVERSAL
UNIVERSES
UNKINDEST
UNKNOWING
UNLEARNED
UNLEASHED
UNLIMITED
UNLOADERS
UNLOADING
UNLOCKING
UNLOOSING
UNLUCKILY
UNMARRIED
UNMASKING
UNMATCHED
UNMEANING

UNMINDFUL
UNMUSICAL
UNNATURAL
UNNERVING
UNNOTICED
UNOPPOSED
UNPACKING
UNPICKING
UNPLUGGED
UNPLUMBED
UNPOLITIC
UNPOPULAR
UNPOWERED
UNRAVELED
UNREALISM
UNREALITY
UNREFINED
UNRELATED
UNRESERVE
UNRIDDLER
UNROLLING
UNROUNDED
UNRUFFLED
UNSADDLED
UNSAVOURY
UNSCATHED
UNSCREWED
UNSEATING
UNSECURED
UNSELFISH
UNSERIOUS
UNSETTLED
UNSHACKLE
UNSHEATHE
UNSIGHTED
UNSIGHTLY
UNSKILFUL
UNSKILLED
UNSPARING
UNSPOTTED
UNSPRAYED
UNSTOPPED
UNSTRIPED
UNSTUDIED
UNTANGLED
UNTENABLE
UNTENURED
UNTOUCHED
UNTREATED
UNTUTORED
UNTYPICAL

UNUSUALLY
UNVEILING
UNWATCHED
UNWEARIED
UNWEIGHED
UNWELCOME
UNWILLING
UNWINDING
UNWITTING
UNWORLDLY
UNWRITTEN
UNZIPPING
UP AND
  DOWN
UP-AND-
  DOWN
UPBRAIDED
UPBRAIDER
UPBUILDER
UP-COUNTRY
UPGRADING
UPHEAVALS
UPHOLDERS
UPHOLDING
UPHOLSTER
UPLIFTING
UPLIGHTER
UPPER CASE
UPPERCUTS
UPPER HAND
UPPERMOST
UPRIGHTLY
UPRISINGS
UPROOTING
UPSETTING
UPSTAGING
UP THE
  ANTE
UP THE
  DUFF
UP THE
  POLE
URANINITE
URBAN MYTH
URCEOLATE
URINATING
URINATION
URINATIVE
UROCHROME
UROGENOUS
UROLITHIC
UROLOGIST

UROPYGIAL
UROPYGIUM
UROSCOPIC
URSA MAJOR
URTICARIA
URUGUAYAN
USABILITY
USELESSLY
USHERETTE
USUALNESS
UTILITIES
UTILIZING
UTRICULAR
UTTERABLE
UTTERANCE
UTTERLESS
UVAROVITE
UXORICIDE

V

VACANCIES
VACATABLE
VACATIONS
VACCINATE
VACCINIAL
VACILLANT
VACILLATE
VACUOLATE
VACUOUSLY
VACUUMING
VAGABONDS
VAGINITIS
VAGOTONIA
VAGUENESS
VAINGLORY
VALENCIES
VALENTINE
VALIANTLY
VALIDATED
VALIDNESS
VALLATION
VALLECULA
VALUABLES
VALUATION
VALUELESS
VALVELESS
VAMOOSING
VAMPIRISM
VANASPATI
VANCOUVER
VANDALISM

VANDALIZE
VANGUARDS
VANISHING
VAPIDNESS
VAPORETTO
VAPORIFIC
VAPORIZED
VAPORIZER
VAPOURISH
VARANGIAN
VARIABLES
VARIANCES
VARIATION
VARICELLA
VARICOSIS
VARIEGATE
VARIETIES
VARIFOCAL
VARIOLATE
VARIOLITE
VARIOLOID
VARIOLOUS
VARIOUSLY
VARISCITE
VARITYPER
VARNISHED
VARNISHER
VARNISHES
VARSITIES
VARYINGLY
VASECTOMY
VASOMOTOR
VASSALAGE
VASSALIZE
VECTORIAL
VEERINGLY
VEGETABLE
VEGETATED
VEHEMENCE
VEHICULAR
VEINSTONE
VELODROME
VELVETEEN
VENDETTAS
VENDITION
VENEERING
VENERABLE
VENERATED
VENERATOR
VENEZUELA ·
VENGEANCE

VENIALITY
VENTILATE
VENTRICLE
VENTURERS
VENTURING
VENUSBERG
VERACIOUS
VERANDAED
VERATRINE
VERBALISM
VERBALIST
VERBALIZE
VERBASCUM
VERBOSELY
VERBOSITY
VERDIGRIS
VERDUROUS
VERIDICAL
VERIFYING
VERITABLE
VERITABLY
VERMICIDE
VERMIFORM
VERMIFUGE
VERMILION
VERMINOUS
VERMONTER
VERNALIZE
VERNATION
VERRUCOSE
VERSATILE
VERSIFIER
VERSIONAL
VERS LIBRE
VERTEBRAE
VERTEBRAL
VERY LIGHT
VESICULAR
VESTIBULE
VESTIGIAL
VESTMENTS
VESTRYMAN
VETCHLING
VEXATIONS
VEXATIOUS
VEXEDNESS
VEXILLARY
VEXILLATE
VIABILITY
VIAREGGIO
VIBRANTLY

VIBRATILE
VIBRATING
VIBRATION
VIBRATIVE
VIBRATORS
VIBRISSAL
VICARAGES
VICARIATE
VICARIOUS
VICARSHIP
VICEGERAL
VICENNIAL
VICEREGAL
VICEREINE
VICE VERSA
VICIOUSLY
VICKSBURG
VICTIMIZE
VICTORIAN
VICTORIES
VICTUALED
VIDELICET
VIDEODISC
VIDEO GAME
VIDEO TAPE
VIDEOTAPE
VIENTIANE
VIEWPOINT
VIGESIMAL
VIGILANCE
VIGILANTE
VIGNETTES
VILIFYING
VILLAGERS
VILLIFORM
VILLOSITY
VIMINEOUS
VINACEOUS
VINCENNES
VINDICATE
VINEYARDS
VIOLATING
VIOLATION
VIOLATIVE
VIOLATORS
VIOLENTLY
VIOLINIST
VIRESCENT
VIRGINALS
VIRGINIAN
VIRGINITY

VIRGULATE
VIRTUALLY
VIRTUOSIC
VIRTUOSOS
VIRULENCE
VIRULENCY
VISCIDITY
VISCOSITY
VISCOUNTS
VISIONARY
VISITABLE
VISUAL AID
VISUALIZE
VITACEOUS
VITALIZER
VITAMINIC
VITELLINE
VITIATING
VITIATION
VITRIFIED
VITRIFORM
VITRIOLIC
VIVACIOUS
VIVARIUMS
VIVA VOCES
VIVERRINE
VIVIDNESS
VOCALISTS
VOCALIZER
VOCATIONS
VOCATIVES
VOICELESS
VOICE MAIL
VOICE-OVER
VOJVODINA
VOL-AU-
    VENT
VOLCANISM
VOLCANIZE
VOLCANOES
VOLGOGRAD
VOLLEYING
VOLTE-FACE
VOLTMETER
VOLUMETER
VOLUMETRY
VOLUNTARY
VOLUNTEER
VOODOOISM
VOODOOIST
VORACIOUS

VORTICISM
VORTICIST
VOUCHSAFE
VOYEURISM
VULCANIAN
VULCANITE
VULCANIZE
VULGARIAN
VULGARISM
VULGARITY
VULGARIZE
VULNERARY
VULTURINE
VULTUROUS
VULVIFORM

W

WACKINESS
WAD MEDANI
WAFER-THIN
WAGE SLAVE
WAGGISHLY
WAGONETTE
WAGONLOAD
WAILINGLY
WAINSCOTS
WAISTBAND
WAISTCOAT
WAISTLINE
WAIT FOR
    IT
WAKEFIELD
WAKEFULLY
WAKE ROBIN
WAKE-ROBIN
WALBRZYCH
WALCHEREN
WALKABOUT
WALKAWAYS
WALK ON
    AIR
WALKOVERS
WALLABIES
WALLBOARD
WALLCHART
WALLOPING
WALLOWING
WALLPAPER
WALVIS BAY
WANDERERS
WANDERING

WAR CLOUDS
WAR CRIMES
WAR DANCES
WARDROBES
WARDROOMS
WAREHOUSE
WARHORSES
WARM FRONT
WARMONGER
WARRANTED
WARRANTEE
WARRANTER
WARRANTOR
WASHBASIN
WASHBOARD
WASHCLOTH
WASHED-OUT
WASHINESS
WASHING-UP
WASHROOMS
WASHSTAND
WASPINESS
WASPISHLY
WASSAILER
WASTELAND
WATCHDOGS
WATCHWORD
WATER BIRD
WATERBUCK
WATER BUTT
WATER-COOL
WATERFALL
WATERFORD
WATERFOWL
WATERHOLE
WATER ICES
WATER JUMP
WATERLESS
WATER LILY
WATERLINE
WATER MAIN
WATERMARK
WATERMILL
WATER PIPE
WATER POLO
WATER RATE
WATER RATS
WATERSHED
WATER-SICK
WATERSIDE
WATER VOLE

WATERWAYS
WATERWEED
WATERWORN
WATTMETER
WAVE BANDS
WAVEGUIDE
WAVELLITE
WAVEMETER
WAXWORKER
WAYFARERS
WAYFARING
WAYLAYING
WEAKENING
WEAKER SEX
WEAK-KNEED
WEAKLINGS
WEALTHIER
WEALTHILY
WEAPONEER
WEARINESS
WEARINGLY
WEARISOME
WEARPROOF
WEASELING
WEATHERED
WEATHERER
WEB-FOOTED
WEB OFFSET
WEDNESDAY
WEEDINESS
WEEKENDED
WEEKENDER
WEEKNIGHT
WEEPINESS
WEEPINGLY
WEIGHABLE
WEIGH DOWN
WEIGHTILY
WEIGHTING
WEIRDNESS
WELCOMING
WELL-ACTED
WELL-AWARE
WELLBEING
WELL-FOUND
WELL-KNOWN
WELL-LINED
WELL-MEANT
WELL OILED
WELL-OILED
WELL-TIMED

WELL-TRIED	WHITEFISH	WINDOW BOX	WOMENFOLK	WORTHIEST
WERNERITE	WHITE FLAG	WINDPIPES	WOMEN'S	WORTHLESS
WESLEYANS	WHITEHALL	WINDROWER	LIB	WOUNDABLE
WESTBOUND	WHITE HEAT	WINDSOCKS	WONDERFUL	WOUNDWORT
WESTERING	WHITE HOPE	WINDSTORM	WONDERING	WRANGLERS
WESTERNER	WHITE LEAD	WINDSWEPT	WOODBLOCK	WRANGLING
WESTMEATH	WHITE LIES	WINEGLASS	WOODBORER	WRAPPINGS
WESTWARDS	WHITE MEAT	WINEMAKER	WOODCHUCK	WREATHING
WET DREAMS	WHITENESS	WINEPRESS	WOODCOCKS	WRECKFISH
WET-NURSED	WHITENING	WINGSPANS	WOODCRAFT	WRENCHING
WET NURSES	WHITE ROSE	WINNEBAGO	WOODINESS	WRESTLERS
WHACKINGS	WHITEWALL	WINNOWING	WOODLOUSE	WRESTLING
WHALEBOAT	WHITEWASH	WINSOMELY	WOODPRINT	WRIGGLING
WHALEBONE	WHITEWOOD	WINTERING	WOODSCREW	WRINKLING
WHANGAREI	WHITTLERS	WINTRIEST	WOOD SCREW	WRISTBAND
WHEAT GERM	WHITTLING	WIRADHURI	WOODSHEDS	WRISTLETS
WHEATWORM	WHIZZ-BANG	WIRE-GAUGE	WOODSMOKE	WRISTLOCK
WHEEDLING	WHIZZ KIDS	WIREWORKS	WOODSTOCK	WRITE-OFFS
WHEELBASE	WHODUNITS	WIREWORMS	WOOLLIEST	WRONGDOER
WHEELWORK	WHODUNNIT	WISCONSIN	WOOZINESS	WRONGNESS
WHEREFORE	WHOLEFOOD	WISECRACK	WORCESTER	WROUGHT-UP
WHEREUPON	WHOLEMEAL	WISHBONES	WORDBREAK	WULFENITE
WHEREWITH	WHOLENESS	WISPINESS	WORDINESS	WUPPERTAL
WHERRYMAN	WHOLE NOTE	WISTFULLY	WORKBENCH	WYANDOTTE
WHETSTONE	WHOLESALE	WITCH-HUNT	WORKBOOKS	WYCH-HAZEL
WHICHEVER	WHOLESOME	WITCHLIKE	WORKFORCE	
WHICKERED	WHOSOEVER	WITH A	WORKHORSE	**X**
WHIFFIEST	WIDE-ANGLE	WILL	WORKHOUSE	XENOCRYST
WHIMPERED	WIDE-AWAKE	WITHDRAWN	WORKLOADS	XENOGRAFT
WHIMPERER	WIDOWHOOD	WITHERING	WORK OF	XENOPHILE
WHIMSICAL	WIDTHWISE	WITHERITE	ART	XENOPHOBE
WHININGLY	WIELDABLE	WITHSTAND	WORKPIECE	XERICALLY
WHINNYING	WIESBADEN	WITHSTOOD	WORKPLACE	XERODERMA
WHINSTONE	WIGWAGGER	WITLESSLY	WORKROOMS	XEROPHILY
WHIPPER-IN	WILD BOARS	WITNESSED	WORKSHEET	XEROPHYTE
WHIPPINGS	WILDFIRES	WITNESSER	WORKSHOPS	XYLOGRAPH
WHIP ROUND	WILLEMITE	WITNESSES	WORK-STUDY	XYLOPHONE
WHIP-ROUND	WILLINGLY	WITTICISM	WORKTABLE	
WHIPSTALL	WILLPOWER	WITTINESS	WORLD BANK	**Y**
WHIPSTOCK	WILTSHIRE	WOBBLIEST	WORLDLIER	YACHTINGS
WHIRLIGIG	WINCINGLY	WOEBEGONE	WORLDLING	YACHTSMAN
WHIRLPOOL	WINDBLOWN	WOKINGHAM	WORLDWIDE	YACHTSMEN
WHIRLWIND	WIND-BORNE	WOLFHOUND	WORM CASTS	YAMMERING
WHISKERED	WINDBOUND	WOLFSBANE	WORM-EATEN	YANKEEISM
WHISPERED	WINDBREAK	WOLFSBURG	WORM GEARS	YARDSTICK
WHISPERER	WINDBURNT	WOLVERINE	WORMHOLES	YAROSLAVL
WHISTLING	WINDFALLS	WOMANHOOD	WORRIEDLY	YAWNINGLY
WHITE ANTS	WIND GAUGE	WOMANIZED	WORRISOME	YEA AND
WHITEBAIT	WINDINESS	WOMANIZER	WORRYWART	NAY
WHITECAPS	WINDINGLY	WOMANKIND	WORSENING	YEARBOOKS
WHITEDAMP	WINDMILLS	WOMAN-LIKE	WORSHIPED	YEARLINGS

YEARNINGS	**Z**	ZEPPELINS	ZOOGLOEAL	ZUCCHINIS
YELLOWFIN	ZACATECAS	ZESTFULLY	ZOOGRAPHY	ZUGSPITZE
YELLOWING	ZAMBEZIAN	ZEUGMATIC	ZOOLOGIST	ZUIDER ZEE
YELLOWISH	ZAMBOANGA	ZHANGZHOU	ZOOMETRIC	ZYGOMATIC
YESTERDAY	ZANZIBARI	ZHENGZHOU	ZOOPHILIA	ZYGOPHYTE
YIELDABLE	ZAPOTECAN	ZIGZAGGED	ZOOPHILIC	ZYGOSPORE
YODELLING	ZEALOUSLY	ZIGZAGGER	ZOOPHOBIA	ZYMOGENIC
YOHIMBINE	ZEBRA-LIKE	ZINKENITE	ZOOPHYTIC	ZYMOLOGIC
YORKSHIRE	ZEBRAWOOD	ZIONISTIC	ZOOPLASTY	ZYMOLYSIS
YOUNGSTER	ZEEBRUGGE	ZIRCALLOY	ZOOSPORIC	ZYMOLYTIC
YTTERBITE	ZEELANDER	ZIRCONIUM	ZOOSTEROL	ZYMOMETER
YTTERBIUM	ZEITGEIST	ZITHERIST	ZOOTOMIST	

A	ABSORBANCE	ACETIC	ADEQUATELY	AERENCHYMA
ABANDONING	ABSORBEDLY	ACID	ADIRONDACK	AEROBATICS
ABBREVIATE	ABSORBENCY	ACETOMETER	ADJECTIVAL	AEROBIOSIS
ABDICATING	ABSORBENTS	ACETYLENIC	ADJECTIVES	AEROBIOTIC
ABDICATION	ABSORPTION	ACHIEVABLE	ADJOURNING	AERODROMES
ABDICATIVE	ABSORPTIVE	ACHONDRITE	ADJUDICATE	AERO-
ABERRATION	ABSTAINERS	ACHROMATIC	ADJUNCTIVE	ENGINE
ABHORRENCE	ABSTAINING	ACHROMATIN	ADJURATION	AEROGRAMME
ABIOGENIST	ABSTEMIOUS	ACIDIFYING	ADJURATORY	AEROGRAPHY
ABIRRITANT	ABSTENTION	ACIDIMETER	ADJUSTABLE	AEROLOGIST
ABIRRITATE	ABSTERGENT	ACIDOMETER	ADJUSTMENT	AEROMETRIC
ABJURATION	ABSTINENCE	ACIERATION	ADMINISTER	AERONAUTIC
ABLE-	ABSTRACTED	ACOTYLEDON	ADMIRATION	AEROPHAGIA
BODIED	ABUNDANTLY	ACQUAINTED	ADMIRINGLY	AEROPHOBIA
ABLE	ABYSSINIAN	ACQUIESCED	ADMISSIBLE	AEROPHOBIC
SEAMAN	ACCELERANT	ACQUIRABLE	ADMISSIONS	AEROPLANES
ABLE	ACCELERATE	ACQUITTALS	ADMITTANCE	AEROSPHERE
SEAMEN	ACCENTUATE	ACQUITTING	ADMITTEDLY	AEROSTATIC
ABNEGATION	ACCEPTABLE	ACROBATICS	ADMIXTURES	AEROTOWING
ABNEY	ACCEPTABLY	ACROMEGALY	ADMONISHED	AESTHETICS
LEVEL	ACCEPTANCE	ACRONYCHAL	ADMONISHER	AESTIVATOR
ABNORMALLY	ACCEPTEDLY	ACROPHOBIA	ADMONITION	AFFABILITY
ABOLISHING	ACCESSIBLE	ACROPHOBIC	ADMONITORY	AFFECTEDLY
ABOMINABLE	ACCESSIONS	ACTABILITY	ADOLESCENT	AFFECTIONS
ABOMINABLY	ACCESS	ACTINIFORM	ADORNMENTS	AFFECTLESS
ABOMINATED	ROAD	ACTINOLITE	ADRENALINE	AFFETTUOSO
ABOMINATOR	ACCESS	ACTINOMERE	ADRENERGIC	AFFIDAVITS
ABORIGINAL	TIME	ACTINOZOAN	ADROITNESS	AFFILIATED
ABORIGINES	ACCIDENTAL	ACTIONABLE	ADSORBABLE	AFFILIATES
ABORTICIDE	ACCIPITRAL	ACTIVATING	ADSORPTION	AFFINITIES
ABORTIONAL	ACCLAIMING	ACTIVATION	ADULTERANT	AFFINITIVE
ABORTIVELY	ACCOMPLICE	ACTIVENESS	ADULTERATE	AFFLICTING
ABOUT-	ACCOMPLISH	ACTIVITIES	ADULTERERS	AFFLICTION
TURNS	ACCORDABLE	ACTOMYOSIN	ADULTERESS	AFFLICTIVE
ABOVEBOARD	ACCORDANCE	ACT THE	ADULTERINE	AFFORDABLE
ABOVE	ACCORDIONS	GOAT	ADULTEROUS	AFFORESTED
BOARD	ACCOSTABLE	ADACTYLOUS	ADUMBRATED	AFFRICATES
ABRASIVELY	ACCOUNTANT	ADAMANTINE	ADVANTAGES	AFFRONTING
ABREACTION	ACCOUNTING	ADAMS	ADVENTITIA	AFICIONADO
ABRIDGABLE	ACCREDITED	APPLE	ADVENTURER	AFRIKANDER
ABRIDGMENT	ACCRESCENT	ADAM'S	ADVENTURES	AFRIKANERS
ABROGATING	ACCRETIONS	APPLE	ADVERBIALS	AFTERBIRTH
ABROGATION	ACCUMBENCY	ADAPTATION	ADVERTENCE	AFTERBRAIN
ABRUPTNESS	ACCUMULATE	ADDICTIONS	ADVERTISED	AFTERGLOWS
ABSCISSION	ACCURATELY	ADDIS	ADVERTISER	AFTERIMAGE
ABSCONDING	ACCUSATION	ABABA	ADVOCATING	AFTERLIVES
ABSOLUTELY	ACCUSATIVE	ADDITIONAL	ADVOCATION	AFTERMATHS
ABSOLUTION	ACCUSINGLY	ADDRESSEES	ADVOCATORY	AFTERNOONS
ABSOLUTISM	ACCUSTOMED	ADDRESSING	ADZUKI	AFTERPAINS
ABSOLUTORY	ACEPHALOUS	ADDUCEABLE	BEAN	AFTERPIECE
ABSOLVABLE	ACETABULUM	ADENECTOMY	AECIOSPORE	AFTERSHAFT
ABSORBABLE		ADENOVIRUS		

AFTERSHAVE
AFTERSHOCK
AFTERTASTE
AFTERWARDS
AGAMICALLY
AGAPANTHUS
AGGLUTININ
AGGRANDIZE
AGGRAVATED
AGGREGATED
AGGREGATES
AGGRESSION
AGGRESSIVE
AGGRESSORS
AGITATIONS
AGREEMENTS
AGRONOMICS
AGRONOMIST
AGRYPNOTIC
AHMEDNAGAR
AIDE-DE-
    CAMP
AIR-
    HOSTESS
AIR-
    LETTERS
AIR-
    LIFTING
AIR
    MARSHAL
AIRPOCKETS
AIR
    WAYBILL
AKTYUBINSK
ALACRITOUS
ALARM
    CLOCK
ALARMINGLY
ALBESCENCE
ALBUMENIZE
ALBUMINATE
ALBUMINOID
ALBUMINOUS
ALCHEMISTS
ALCHERINGA
ALCOHOLICS
ALCOHOLISM
ALCOHOLIZE
ALDERMANIC
ALEXANDRIA
ALGEBRAIST
ALGOLAGNIA

ALGOLAGNIC
ALGONQUIAN
ALGOPHOBIA
ALGORISMIC
ALGORITHMS
ALIENATING
ALIENATION
ALIGNMENTS
ALIMENTARY
ALKALINITY
ALKYLATION
ALLARGANDO
ALLEGATION
ALLEGIANCE
ALLEGORIES
ALLEGORIST
ALLEGORIZE
ALLEGRETTO
ALLERGENIC
ALLEVIATED
ALLEVIATOR
ALLIACEOUS
ALLIGATORS
ALLITERATE
ALLOCATING
ALLOCATION
ALLOCUTION
ALLOGAMOUS
ALLOMERISM
ALLOMEROUS
ALLOMETRIC
ALLOPATHIC
ALLOPATRIC
ALLOPHONIC
ALLOTMENTS
ALLOTROPIC
ALLOWANCES
ALL-
    PURPOSE
ALL-
    ROUNDER
ALL THE
    TIME
ALLUREMENT
ALLUSIVELY
ALMA
    MATERS
ALMIGHTIER
ALMIGHTILY
ALMS-
    HOUSES
ALONGSHORE

ALPENSTOCK
ALPESTRINE
ALTARPIECE
ALTAZIMUTH
ALTERATION
ALTERATIVE
ALTERNATED
ALTERNATOR
ALTIMETERS
ALTOGETHER
ALTRINCHAM
ALTRUISTIC
AMALGAMATE
AMANUENSES
AMANUENSIS
AMATEURISH
AMATEURISM
AMBASSADOR
AMBIVALENT
AMBOCEPTOR
AMBULACRAL
AMBULACRUM
AMBULANCES
AMBULATION
AMBULATORY
AMELIORANT
AMELIORATE
AMENDMENTS
AMERINDIAN
AMIABILITY
AMIANTHINE
AMINO
    ACIDS
AMMONIACAL
AMMUNITION
AMOEBIASIS
AMOEBOCYTE
AMORTIZING
AMPELOPSIS
AMPERE-
    HOUR
AMPERE-
    TURN
AMPERSANDS
AMPHEATRIC
AMPHIASTER
AMPHIBIANS
AMPHIBIOUS
AMPHIBOLIC
AMPHIBRACH
AMPHICTYON

AMPHIGORIC
AMPHIMACER
AMPHIMIXIS
AMPHOTERIC
AMPLIFIERS
AMPLIFYING
AMPUTATING
AMPUTATION
AMUSEMENTS
AMYGDALATE
AMYGDALINE
AMYGDALOID
AMYLACEOUS
AMYLOLYSIS
ANABOLITIC
ANACHORISM
ANACOUSTIC
ANACRUSTIC
ANADROMOUS
ANAGLYPHIC
ANALGESICS
ANALOGICAL
ANALYSABLE
ANAMNESTIC
ANAMORPHIC
ANAPAESTIC
ANAPLASTIC
ANAPTYCTIC
ANARCHISTS
ANARTHROUS
ANASARCOUS
ANASTIGMAT
ANASTOMOSE
ANATOMICAL
ANATOMISTS
ANATOMIZER
ANATROPOUS
ANCESTRESS
ANCESTRIES
ANCHORAGES
ANCHORITES
ANDALUSITE
ANDERLECHT
ANDROECIAL
ANDROECIUM
ANDROGENIC
ANECDOTAGE
ANECDOTIST
ANEMICALLY
ANEMOCHORE
ANEMOGRAPH

ANEMOMETER
ANEMOMETRY
ANEMOPHILY
ANEMOSCOPE
ANESTHESIA
ANESTHETIC
ANEURYSMAL
ANGELOLOGY
ANGIOSPERM
ANGLEPOISE
ANGLICISMS
ANGLICIZED
ANGLOPHILE
ANGLOPHOBE
ANGLOPHONE
ANGLO-
    SAXON
ANGULARITY
ANGULATION
ANGWANTIBO
ANIMADVERT
ANIMALCULE
ANIMAL
    FARM
ANIMATEDLY
ANISOTROPY
ANKYLOSAUR
ANNALISTIC
ANNEXATION
ANNIHILATE
ANNO
    DOMINI
ANNOTATING
ANNOTATION
ANNOTATIVE
ANNOUNCERS
ANNOUNCING
ANNOYANCES
ANNULATION
ANNULLABLE
ANNULMENTS
ANNUNCIATE
ANOINTMENT
ANORTHITIC
ANSWERABLE
ANSWERABLY
ANTAGONISM
ANTAGONIST
ANTAGONIZE
ANTARCTICA
ANTEBELLUM

ANTECEDENT
ANTEDATING
ANTE-
MORTEM
ANTEPENULT
ANTHOPHORE
ANTHRACENE
ANTHRACITE
ANTHRACOID
ANTHROPOID
ANTIBARYON
ANTIBIOSIS
ANTIBIOTIC
ANTIBODIES
ANTICHRIST
ANTICIPANT
ANTICIPATE
ANTICLIMAX
ANTICLINAL
ANTIDROMIC
ANTIFREEZE
ANTIFUNGAL
ANTIHEROES
ANTILEPTON
ANTILOGISM
ANTIMATTER
ANTIMERISM
ANTIMONIAL
ANTIMONOUS
ANTIPHONAL
ANTIPODEAN
ANTIPROTON
ANTIPYRINE
ANTIQUATED
ANTI-
SEMITE
ANTISEPSIS
ANTISEPTIC
ANTISOCIAL
ANTISTATIC
ANTITHESIS
ANTITRADES
ANTITRAGUS
ANXIOLYTIC
APARTMENTS
APGAR
SCORE
APHORISTIC
APHRODISIA
APICULTURE
APIOLOGIST

APLACENTAL
APOCALYPSE
APOCARPOUS
APOCHROMAT
APOCRYPHAL
APOLITICAL
APOLOGETIC
APOLOGISTS
APOLOGIZED
APOLOGIZER
APOPHTHEGM
APOPHYSATE
APOPHYSIAL
APOPLECTIC
APOSEMATIC
APOSTASIES
APOSTATIZE
APOSTOLATE
APOSTROPHE
APOTHECARY
APOTHECIAL
APOTHECIUM
APOTHEOSES
APOTHEOSIS
APOTROPAIC
APPALACHIA
APPARELLED
APPARENTLY
APPARITION
APPEALABLE
APPEARANCE
APPEASABLE
APPENDAGES
APPENDICES
APPENDICLE
APPENDIXES
APPERCEIVE
APPETIZERS
APPETIZING
APPLAUDING
APPLE
CARTS
APPLIANCES
APPLICABLE
APPLICANTS
APPLICATOR
APPOINTEES
APPOINTING
APPOSITION
APPOSITIVE
APPRAISALS

APPRAISING
APPRAISIVE
APPRECIATE
APPRENTICE
APPROACHED
APPROACHES
APPROXIMAL
APRIL
FOOLS
APTERYGIAL
AQUAMARINE
AQUAPHOBIA
AQUAPLANED
AQUAPLANES
ARABESQUES
ARACHNIDAN
ARAKAN
YOMA
ARAUCANIAN
ARBITRABLE
ARBITRATED
ARBITRATOR
ARCHAISTIC
ARCHANGELS
ARCHBISHOP
ARCHDEACON
ARCHERFISH
ARCHESPORE
ARCHETYPAL
ARCHETYPES
ARCHIMEDES
ARCHITECTS
ARCHITRAVE
ARCHIVISTS
ARCHOPLASM
ARCTOGAEAN
ARC
WELDING
ARENACEOUS
AREOGRAPHY
AREOLATION
ARGENTEUIL
ARGILLITIC
ARGUMENTUM
ARISTOCRAT
ARITHMETIC
ARMADILLOS
ARMAGEDDON
ARMIPOTENT
ARMISTICES
ARNHEM
LAND

ARRAIGNING
ARRHYTHMIA
ARROGANTLY
ARROGATING
ARROGATION
ARROGATIVE
ARROWHEADS
ARTFULNESS
ARTHRALGIA
ARTHRALGIC
ARTHRITICS
ARTHROMERE
ARTICHOKES
ARTICULATE
ARTIFICERS
ARTIFICIAL
ART
NOUVEAU
ARTY-
CRAFTY
ASAFOETIDA
ASARABACCA
ASBESTOSIS
ASCARIASIS
ASCENDANCY
ASCENDANTS
ASCETICISM
ASCOGONIUM
ASCOMYCETE
ASCRIBABLE
ASCRIPTION
ASEXUALITY
ASPARAGINE
ASPERITIES
ASPERSIONS
AS PER
USUAL
ASPHALTING
ASPHALTITE
ASPHYXIANT
ASPHYXIATE
ASPIDISTRA
ASPIRATING
ASPIRATION
ASPIRATORY
ASSAILABLE
ASSAILANTS
ASSAILMENT
ASSAULTING
ASSEMBLAGE
ASSEMBLIES

ASSEMBLING
ASSERTIBLE
ASSERTIONS
ASSESSABLE
ASSESSMENT
ASSET
VALUE
ASSEVERATE
ASSIBILATE
ASSIGNABLE
ASSIGNMENT
ASSIMILATE
ASSISTANCE
ASSISTANTS
ASSOCIABLE
ASSOCIATED
ASSOCIATES
ASSONANTAL
ASSORTMENT
ASSUMPTION
ASSUMPTIVE
ASSURANCES
ASTATICISM
ASTERIATED
ASTERISKED
ASTEROIDAL
ASTHENOPIA
ASTHENOPIC
ASTHMATICS
ASTIGMATIC
ASTOMATOUS
ASTONISHED
ASTOUNDING
ASTRAGALUS
ASTRINGENT
ASTROLOGER
ASTROMETRY
ASTRONAUTS
ASTRONOMER
ASTUTENESS
ASYMMETRIC
ASYMPTOTIC
AT ALL
TIMES
AT A
STRETCH
ATHERMANCY
ATMOSPHERE
ATOMICALLY
ATOMIC
BOMB

ATOMIC
    PILE
ATROCITIES
ATROPHYING
ATTACHABLE
ATTACHMENT
ATTAINABLE
ATTAINMENT
ATTEMPTING
ATTENDANCE
ATTENDANTS
ATTENTIONS
ATTENUATED
ATTENUATOR
ATTESTABLE
AT THE
    READY
ATTORNMENT
ATTRACTING
ATTRACTION
ATTRACTIVE
ATTRIBUTED
ATTRIBUTER
ATTRIBUTES
ATYPICALLY
AUBERGINES
AUCTIONEER
AUCTIONING
AUDIBILITY
AUDIOGENIC
AUDIOMETER
AUDIOMETRY
AUDITIONED
AUDITORIUM
AUGMENTING
AUREOMYCIN
AURICULATE
AURIFEROUS
AUSCULTATE
AUSFORMING
AUSPICIOUS
AUSTENITIC
AUSTERLITZ
AUSTRALIAN
AUSTRALOID
AUSTRALORP
AUTARCHIES
AUTECOLOGY
AUTHORIZED
AUTHORIZER
AUTHORSHIP

AUTOCHTHON
AUTOCRATIC
AUTOECIOUS
AUTOGAMOUS
AUTOGENOUS
AUTOGRAPHS
AUTOGRAPHY
AUTOMATICS
AUTOMATING
AUTOMATION
AUTOMATISM
AUTOMATIST
AUTOMATONS
AUTOMATOUS
AUTOMOBILE
AUTOMOTIVE
AUTONOMIST
AUTONOMOUS
AUTOPHYTIC
AUTOPLASTY
AUTOSTRADA
AUTOTOMIZE
AUTUMNALLY
AUXOCHROME
AVALANCHES
AVANT
    GARDE
AVANT-
    GARDE
AVARICIOUS
AVELLANEDA
AVENTURINE
AVICULTURE
AVOCATIONS
AVUNCULATE
AWAKENINGS
AXIOLOGIST
AYATOLLAHS
AZEOTROPIC
AZERBAIJAN
AZOBENZENE

B

BABY-
    MINDER
BABY
    SITTER
BABY-
    SITTER
BACCHANALS
BACITRACIN
BACKBITERS

BACKBITING
BACKCLOTHS
BACKCOMBED
BACKDATING
BACKFIRING
BACKGAMMON
BACKGROUND
BACKHANDED
BACKHANDER
BACKLASHES
BACK
    MATTER
BACK
    NUMBER
BACKPACKER
BACKSLIDER
BACKSPACES
BACKSTAIRS
BACKSTITCH
BACK
    STREET
BACKSTROKE
BACKWARDLY
BACKWATERS
BACULIFORM
BADEN-
    BADEN
BAD HAIR
    DAY
BAD-
    MOUTHED
BAFFLEMENT
BAGGAGE
    CAR
BAHAWALPUR
BAINBRIDGE
BALACLAVAS
BALALAIKAS
BALDERDASH
BALDHEADED
BALIKPAPAN
BALLASTING
BALLERINAS
BALLFLOWER
BALLISTICS
BALLOONING
BALLOONIST
BALLPOINTS
BALLYMONEY
BALNEOLOGY
BALUSTRADE
BAMBOOZLED

BAMBOOZLER
BANALITIES
BANANA
    SKIN
BANDERILLA
BANDLEADER
BANDMASTER
BANDOLEERS
BANDSTANDS
BANDWAGONS
BANFFSHIRE
BANGLADESH
BANISHMENT
BANK
    DRAFTS
BANKROLLED
BANKRUPTCY
BANKRUPTED
BANNERETTE
BANQUETING
BAPTISTERY
BARBARIANS
BARBARISMS
BARBARIZED
BARBECUING
BARBED
    WIRE
BARBELLATE
BAREHEADED
BARELEGGED
BARGAINING
BARGE
    POLES
BARIUM
    MEAL
BARLEYCORN
BARLEY
    WINE
BAR
    MITZVAH
BARN
    DANCES
BARNSTAPLE
BAROMETERS
BAROMETRIC
BARONESSES
BARONETAGE
BARRACKING
BARRACUDAS
BARRAMUNDA
BARRAMUNDI
BARRATROUS

BARRENNESS
BARRENWORT
BARRICADED
BARRICADER
BARRICADES
BARRISTERS
BARROW
    BOYS
BARTENDERS
BARYCENTRE
BARYSPHERE
BASALTWARE
BASE
    METALS
BASILICATA
BASKETBALL
BASKET-
    STAR
BASKETWORK
BAS-
    RELIEFS
BASSE-
    TERRE
BASSETERRE
BASS
    GUITAR
BASSOONIST
BASTARDIZE
BASUTOLAND
BATH
    CHAIRS
BATHOMETER
BATHOMETRY
BATHYMETRY
BATHYSCAPH
BATON
    ROUGE
BATTALIONS
BATTLEAXES
BATTLEDORE
BATTLEMENT
BATTLESHIP
BAYONETING
BAY
    WINDOWS
BEACH
    BALLS
BEACH
    BUGGY
BEACHCHAIR
BEACHFRONT
BEACHHEADS

BEANSPROUT
BEAR
  GARDEN
BEASTLIEST
BEATIFYING
BEATITUDES
BEAUJOLAIS
BEAUTICIAN
BEAUTIFIED
BEAUTY
  SPOT
BECOMINGLY
BECQUERELS
BEDCLOTHES
BEDEVILING
BEDEVILLED
BEDFELLOWS
BED OF
  NAILS
BED OF
  ROSES
BEDRAGGLED
BED-
  SITTERS
BEDSPREADS
BEEFEATERS
BEEF
  TOMATO
BEER
  GARDEN
BEFOREHAND
BEFOULMENT
BEFRIENDED
BEGGARWEED
BEGINNINGS
BEGRUDGING
BEHIND
  BARS
BEHINDHAND
BEHIND
  TIME
BELABOURED
BELIEVABLE
BELIEVABLY
BELITTLING
BELIZE
  CITY
BELLADONNA
BELLARMINE
BELLETRIST
BELLINZONA

BELL-
  RINGER
BELL THE
  CAT
BELLWETHER
BELL
  WETHER
BELLYACHED
BELLYACHES
BELLY
  DANCE
BELLY
  FLOPS
BELLY
  LAUGH
BELONGINGS
BELORUSSIA
BENCH
  MARKS
BENCH
  PRESS
BENEDICITE
BENEFACTOR
BENEFICENT
BENEFICIAL
BENEFITING
BENEVOLENT
BENIGNANCY
BENNINGTON
BENZOCAINE
BENZODRINE
BENZOFURAN
BEQUEATHED
BEQUEATHER
BERIBBONED
BERLIN
  WALL
BERTOLUCCI
BESEECHING
BESMEARING
BESMIRCHED
BESPEAKING
BESSARABIA
BESTIALITY
BESTIALIZE
BESTIARIES
BESTIRRING
BESTREWING
BESTRIDDEN
BESTRIDING
BEST-
  SELLER

BETELGEUSE
BETHINKING
BETOKENING
BETROTHALS
BETROTHING
BETTERMENT
BETWS-Y-
  COED
BEWILDERED
BEWITCHING
BIANNULATE
BIBLIOPOLE
BIBLIOTICS
BIBLIOTIST
BICHLORIDE
BICYCLISTS
BIENNIALLY
BIFURCATED
BIGAMOUSLY
BIG
  BROTHER
BIG
  DIPPERS
BIJOUTERIE
BILBERRIES
BILINGUALS
BILIVERDIN
BILL AND
  COO
BILLBOARDS
BILLET-
  DOUX
BILLIONTHS
BILL OF
  FARE
BILL OF
  SALE
BILLY
  GOATS
BIMESTRIAL
BIMETALLIC
BINOCULARS
BINUCLEATE
BIOCELLATE
BIODYNAMIC
BIOECOLOGY
BIOGENESIS
BIOGENETIC
BIOGRAPHER
BIOGRAPHIC
BIOLOGICAL
BIOLOGISTS

BIOMEDICAL
BIOPHYSICS
BIOPLASMIC
BIOPOIESIS
BIORHYTHMS
BIOSTATICS
BIPARIETAL
BIPARTISAN
BIPETALOUS
BIQUADRATE
BIRD OF
  PREY
BIRKENHEAD
BIRMINGHAM
BIRTHMARKS
BIRTHPLACE
BIRTH-
  RATES
BIRTHRIGHT
BIRTHSTONE
BIRTWISTLE
BISEXUALLY
BISHOPBIRD
BISHOPRICS
BISMUTHOUS
BISSEXTILE
BISULPHATE
BISULPHIDE
BISULPHITE
BISYMMETRY
BITARTRATE
BITCHINESS
BIT OF
  FLUFF
BITTERLING
BITTERNESS
BITTERWEED
BITTERWOOD
BITUMINIZE
BITUMINOUS
BIVALVULAR
BIVOUACKED
BLABBERING
BLACKAMOOR
BLACK
  BELTS
BLACKBERRY
BLACKBIRDS
BLACKBOARD
BLACK
  BOXES

BLACK
  DEATH
BLACKENING
BLACKGUARD
BLACKHEADS
BLACKHEART
BLACK
  HOLES
BLACKJACKS
BLACKLISTS
BLACK
  MAGIC
BLACK
  MARIA
BLACK
  POWER
BLACK
  SHEEP
BLACKSHIRT
BLACKSMITH
BLACKSNAKE
BLACK
  SPOTS
BLACKTHORN
BLACK
  WATCH
BLACK
  WIDOW
BLADDERNUT
BLANCMANGE
BLANKETING
BLANK
  VERSE
BLASPHEMED
BLASPHEMER
BLASTOCOEL
BLASTOCYST
BLASTODERM
BLASTOMERE
BLASTOPORE
BLATHERING
BLEACHABLE
BLEARINESS
BLEATINGLY
BLEMISHING
BLETHERING
BLIND
  ALLEY
BLIND
  DATES
BLIND
  DRUNK

BLINDFOLDS
BLIND
  SPOTS
BLISSFULLY
BLISTERING
BLITHENESS
BLITHERING
BLITHESOME
BLOCKADING
BLOCKHEADS
BLOCKHOUSE
BLOCK
  VOTES
BLONDENESS
BLOOD
  BANKS
BLOODBATHS
BLOOD
  COUNT
BLOOD
  DONOR
BLOOD
  FEUDS
BLOOD
  GROUP
BLOODHOUND
BLOODINESS
BLOOD
  LUSTS
BLOOD
  MONEY
BLOOD
  SPORT
BLOODSTAIN
BLOODSTOCK
BLOODSTONE
BLOOD
  TYPES
BLOODY
  MARY
BLOOMSBURY
BLOSSOMING
BLOTCHIEST
BLOW-BY-
  BLOW
BLOW-
  DRYING
BLOWZINESS
BLUBBERING
BLUDGEONED
BLUDGEONER
BLUE
  BABIES

BLUEBEARDS
BLUEBOTTLE
BLUE
  CHEESE
BLUE-
  COLLAR
BLUE
  DEVILS
BLUE
  MURDER
BLUE-
  PENCIL
BLUEPRINTS
BLUETHROAT
BLUE
  TONGUE
BLUNDERERS
BLUNDERING
BLUSHINGLY
BLUSTERERS
BLUSTERING
BOARDROOMS
BOARDWALKS
BOASTFULLY
BOASTINGLY
BOATHOUSES
BOATSWAINS
BOAT
  TRAINS
BOBBY
  SOCKS,
BOBSLEIGHS
BODY
  DOUBLE
BODYGUARDS
BODY
  SEARCH
BOILER
  SUIT
BOISTEROUS
BOLLOCKS-
  UP
BOLL
  WEEVIL
BOLOMETRIC
BOLSHEVIKS
BOLSHEVISM
BOLSTERING
BOMBARDIER
BOMBARDING
BOMBAY
  DUCK
BOMBSHELLS

BONDHOLDER
BONEHEADED
BONE
  MARROW
BONESHAKER
BONKBUSTER
BON
  VIVANTS
BOOBY
  PRIZE
BOOBY
  TRAPS
BOOKBINDER
BOOKKEEPER
BOOKMAKERS
BOOKMOBILE
BOOKPLATES
BOOKSELLER
BOOKSTALLS
BOOK
  TOKENS
BOOMERANGS
BOOTBLACKS
BOOTLEGGED
BOOTLEGGER
BOOTLOADER
BOOTSTRAPS
BORDERLAND
BORDERLINE
BORGERHOUT
BORROWINGS
BOTANIZING
BOTCHINESS
BOTHERSOME
BOTRYOIDAL
BOTTLE
  BANK
BOTTLE-
  FEED
BOTTLENECK
BOTTLE
  SHOP
BOTTOMLESS
BOTTOM
  LINE
BOTTOMMOST
BOULEVARDS
BOUNCINESS
BOUNDARIES
BOWDLERISM
BOWDLERIZE

BOW
  WINDOWS
BOX
  NUMBERS
BOX
  OFFICES
BOYCOTTING
BOYFRIENDS
BOYISHNESS
BRACHIOPOD
BRACHYLOGY
BRACHYURAN
BRACKETING
BRADYKININ
BRAGGINGLY
BRAHMANISM
BRAINCHILD
BRAIN
  DRAIN
BRAININESS
BRAINSTORM
BRAINWAVES
BRAKE
  SHOES
BRANCHIATE
BRANDISHED
BRANDISHER
BRAND
  NAMES
BRANDY
  SNAP
BRASHINESS
BRASS
  BANDS
BRASSBOUND
BRASSED
  OFF
BRASSERIES
BRASSIERES
BRASSINESS
BRASS
  TACKS
BRATISLAVA
BRAVISSIMO
BRAWNINESS
BRAZENNESS
BREADBOARD
BREADCRUMB
BREADFRUIT
BREADLINES
BREAKAWAYS
BREAKDOWNS

BREAKFASTS
BREAKFRONT
BREAKWATER
BREASTBONE
BREASTWORK
BREATHABLE
BRECCIATED
BREEZINESS
BRICKLAYER
BRIDEGROOM
BRIDESMAID
BRIDGEABLE
BRIDGEHEAD
BRIDGEPORT
BRIDGETOWN
BRIDGEWORK
BRIDGWATER
BRIGANTINE
BRIGHTENER
BRIGHTNESS
BRIGHTWORK
BRILLIANCE
BRILLIANCY
BRIQUETTES
BRITISHERS
BROAD
  BEANS
BROADCASTS
BROADCLOTH
BROADENING
BROAD
  GAUGE
BROADSHEET
BROADSIDES
BROADSWORD
BROCATELLE
BROKEN
  DOWN
BROKEN-
  DOWN
BROKENNESS
BROMSGROVE
BRONCHIOLE
BRONCHITIC
BRONCHITIS
BRONX
  CHEER
BROODINESS
BROOMSTICK
BROWBEATEN
BROWNED-
  OFF

BROWNFIELD
BROWNSTONE
BRUTALIZED
BRYOLOGIST
BRYOPHYTIC
BUBBLE
    WRAP
BUBONOCELE
BUCCANEERS
BUCCINATOR
BUCHENWALD
BUCKBOARDS
BUCKET
    SEAT
BUCKET
    SHOP
BUCKINGHAM
BUDGERIGAR
BUFFER
    ZONE
BUFFLEHEAD
BUFFOONERY
BULLDOZERS
BULLDOZING
BULLFIGHTS
BULLHEADED
BULLNECKED
BULLROARER
BULLY
    COURT
BUMBLEBEES
BUNCHINESS
BUNKHOUSES
BUNYA-
    BUNYA
BUON
    GIORNO
BURBERRIES
BURDENSOME
BUREAUCRAT
BURGENLAND
BURGEONING
BURGLARIES
BURGUNDIAN
BURLESQUED
BURLESQUER
BURLESQUES
BURLINGTON
BURNISHING
BURTHENING
BUSHBABIES
BUSHHAMMER

BUSHMASTER
BUSHRANGER
BUSINESSES
BUS
    STATION
BUSYBODIES
BUTCHERING
BUTTER
    BEAN
BUTTERCUPS
BUTTERFISH
BUTTERMILK
BUTTERWORT
BUTTON-
    DOWN
BUTTONHOLE
BUTTONHOOK
BUTTONWOOD
BUTTRESSED
BUTTRESSES
BY-
    ELECTION
BY-
    PRODUCTS
BYSTANDERS

C

CABANATUAN
CABIN
    CLASS
CACCIATORE
CACHINNATE
CACK-
    HANDED
CACOGENICS
CACOGRAPHY
CACOMISTLE
CACOPHONIC
CACTACEOUS
CADAVERINE
CADAVEROUS
CADET
    CORPS
CAERPHILLY
CAESAREANS
CAESPITOSE
CAFETERIAS
CALABASHES
CALABOOSES
CALAMANDER
CALAMITIES
CALAMITOUS

CALAMONDIN
CALAVERITE
CALCAREOUS
CALCEIFORM
CALCIFEROL
CALCIFUGAL
CALCIFYING
CALCITONIN
CALCSINTER
CALCULABLE
CALCULATED
CALCULATOR
CALCULUSES
CALDERDALE
CALEDONIAN
CALIBRATED
CALIBRATOR
CALIFORNIA
CALIPHATES
CALL
    CENTRE
CALL IT A
    DAY
CALLOWNESS
CALORICITY
CALUMNIATE
CALUMNIOUS
CALVINISTS
CALYPTRATE
CAMEMBERTS
CAMERAWORK
CAMERLENGO
CAMOUFLAGE
CAMPAIGNED
CAMPAIGNER
CAMPANILES
CAMPESTRAL
CAMPGROUND
CAMPHORATE
CAMPOBELLO
CANAL
    BOATS
CANALIZING
CANCELLATE
CANCELLING
CANDELABRA
CANDIDATES
CANDLEFISH
CANDLEPINS
CANDLEWICK
CANDLEWOOD

CANDYFLOSS
CANKERWORM
CANNABINOL
CANNELLONI
CANNONADES
CANNONBALL
CANONICATE
CANONICITY
CANONIZING
CANOODLING
CAN
    OPENERS
CANTABRIAN
CANTALOUPE
CANTALOUPS
CANTATRICE
CANTERBURY
CANTILEVER
CANTILLATE
CANTONMENT
CANVASBACK
CANVASSERS
CANVASSING
CAOUTCHOUC
CAPABILITY
CAPACITATE
CAPACITIES
CAPACITIVE
CAPACITORS
CAPARISONS
CAPE
    COLONY
CAP-
    HAITIEN
CAPITALISM
CAPITALIST
CAPITALIZE
CAPITATION
CAPITATIVE
CAPITULATE
CAPPUCCINO
CAPREOLATE
CAPRICIOUS
CAPRICORNS
CAPTAINING
CAPTIOUSLY
CAPTIVATED
CAPTIVATOR
CARAMELIZE
CARAVAGGIO
CARBOLATED

CARBONATED
CARBON
    COPY
CARBONIZED
CARBUNCLES
CARCINOGEN
CARDIALGIA
CARDIALGIC
CARDIOGRAM
CARDIOLOGY
CARD
    READER
CARDSHARPS
CAREERISTS
CARELESSLY
CARETAKERS
CARICATURE
CARJACKING
CARMARTHEN
CARNALLITE
CARNASSIAL
CARNATIONS
CARNELIANS
CARNIVORES
CAROLINIAN
CAROTENOID
CARPATHIAN
CARPELLARY
CARPELLATE
CARPENTERS
CARPOPHORE
CARPOSPORE
CARRIER
    BAG
CARRYING-
    ON
CARRY-
    OVERS
CARSON
    CITY
CARTHORSES
CARTHUSIAN
CARTILAGES
CARTOMANCY
CARTOONIST
CARTRIDGES
CART
    TRACKS
CARTWHEELS
CARUNCULAR
CARYATIDAL
CASABLANCA

CASCARILLA
CASE-
  HARDEN
CASEINOGEN
CASEWORKER
CASHIERING
CASSEROLES
CASSIOPEIA
CASTIGATED
CASTIGATOR
CASTING
  OFF
CASTRATING
CASTRATION
CASUALNESS
CASUALTIES
CASUS
  BELLI
CATABOLISM
CATABOLITE
CATACLINAL
CATACLYSMS
CATAFALQUE
CATALECTIC
CATALEPTIC
CATALOGUED
CATALOGUER
CATALOGUES
CATAMARANS
CATAMENIAL
CATAPLASIA
CATAPULTED
CATARRHINE
CATASTASIS
CAT
  BURGLAR
CATCALLING
CATCH A
  CRAB
CATCH
  CROPS
CATCHINESS
CATCHPENNY
CATCHWORDS
CATECHESIS
CATECHISMS
CATECHISTS
CATECHIZED
CATEGORIES
CATEGORIZE
CATENARIAN
CATENATION

CATENULATE
CATHEDRALS
CATHOLICON
CATOPTRICS
CAT'S
  CRADLE
CATTLE
  GRID
CAULESCENT
CAUTERIZED
CAUTIONARY
CAUTIONING
CAUTIOUSLY
CAVALCADES
CAVALRYMAN
CAVALRYMEN
CAVITATION
CAVITY
  WALL
CEASE-
  FIRES
CEILOMETER
CELEBRATED
CELEBRATOR
CELLOBIOSE
CELLOPHANE
CELLULITIS
CELLULOSIC
CEMETERIES
CENOTAPHIC
CENSORABLE
CENSORIOUS
CENSORSHIP
CENSURABLE
CENTENNIAL
CENTESIMAL
CENTIGRADE
CENTIGRAMS
CENTILITRE
CENTILLION
CENTIMETRE
CENTIPEDES
CENTIPOISE
CENTRALISM
CENTRALITY
CENTRALIZE
CENTRE-
  FIRE
CENTRE-
  FOLD
CENTRE
  HALF

CENTRE
  PASS
CENTRICITY
CENTRIFUGE
CENTROMERE
CENTROSOME
CENTURIONS
CEPHALONIA
CEPHALOPOD
CEREBELLAR
CEREBELLUM
CEREBRALLY
CEREDIGION
CEREMONIAL
CEREMONIES
CEROGRAPHY
CERTIFYING
CERTIORARI
CERUMINOUS
CERVICITIS
CESSATIONS
CESSIONARY
CETOLOGIST
CHAGRINING
CHAIN
  GANGS
CHAINPLATE
CHAIN-
  REACT
CHAIN
  SMOKE
CHAIN-
  SMOKE
CHAIN
  STORE
CHAIR
  LIFTS
CHAIRWOMAN
CHAIRWOMEN
CHALCEDONY
CHALCIDICE
CHALCOCITE
CHALKBOARD
CHALKINESS
CHALLENGED
CHALLENGER
CHALLENGES
CHALYBEATE
CHAMBER
  POT
CHAMELEONS
CHAMOMILES

CHAMPIGNON
CHAMPIONED
CHANCELLOR
CHANCERIES
CHANCINESS
CHANDELIER
CHANDIGARH
CHANGEABLE
CHANGEABLY
CHANGELESS
CHANGELING
CHANGEOVER
CHANGE
  OVER
CHANNEL-
  HOP
CHANNELLED
CHANNELLER
CHAPERONED
CHAPFALLEN
CHAPLAINCY
CHARABANCS
CHARACTERS
CHARDONNAY
CHARGEABLE
CHARGE
  CARD
CHARGE
  HAND
CHARIOTEER
CHARITABLE
CHARITABLY
CHARLADIES
CHARLATANS
CHARLESTON
CHARMINGLY
CHARTERING
CHARTREUSE
CHASTENING
CHASTISING
CHATELAINE
CHATOYANCY
CHATTERBOX
CHATTERERS
CHATTERING
CHAUDFROID
CHAUFFEURS
CHAUVINISM
CHAUVINIST
CHEAPENING
CHEAPSKATE
CHEBOKSARY

CHECKLISTS
CHECKMATED
CHECKMATES
CHECKPOINT
CHECKROOMS
CHEEKBONES
CHEEKINESS
CHEEKPIECE
CHEERFULLY
CHEERINESS
CHEESECAKE
CHEESED
  OFF
CHEESINESS
CHEKHOVIAN
CHELICERAL
CHELMSFORD
CHELTENHAM
CHEMICALLY
CHEMISETTE
CHEMOTAXIS
CHEQUEBOOK
CHEQUE
  CARD
CHERISHING
CHERNOVTSY
CHERRYWOOD
CHERUBICAL
CHESAPEAKE
CHESSBOARD
CHESTINESS
CHEVALIERS
CHEVROTAIN
CHEWING
  GUM
CHEW THE
  CUD
CHEW THE
  FAT
CHEW THE
  RAG
CHICHESTER
CHICKEN
  POX
CHIEFTAINS
CHIFFCHAFF
CHIFFONIER
CHIHUAHUAS
CHILBLAINS
CHILDBIRTH
CHILDISHLY

CHILD'S PLAY
CHILIASTIC
CHILLINESS
CHIMERICAL
CHIMNEYPOT
CHIMPANZEE
CHINABERRY
CHINATOWNS
CHINCHILLA
CHINQUAPIN
CHINSTRAPS
CHINTZIEST
CHIPOLATAS
CHIROMANCY
CHIRPINESS
CHISELLERS
CHISELLING
CHITARRONE
CHITTAGONG
CHIVALROUS
CHLAMYDATE
CHLORAMINE
CHLORINATE
CHLOROFORM
CHOANOCYTE
CHOCKSTONE
CHOCOHOLIC
CHOCOLATES
CHOICENESS
CHOKEBERRY
CHONDRITIC
CHOPHOUSES
CHOPPINESS
CHOPSTICKS
CHORIAMBIC
CHORISTERS
CHRISTENED
CHRISTENER
CHRISTIANS
CHROMATICS
CHROMATIST
CHROMOMERE
CHROMONEMA
CHROMOSOME
CHRONICITY
CHRONICLED
CHRONICLER
CHRONICLES
CHRONOGRAM
CHRONOLOGY

CHRYSOLITE
CHRYSOTILE
CHUBBINESS
CHUCKER-OUT
CHUCKWALLA
CHUKKA BOOT
CHUMMINESS
CHUNKINESS
CHURCHGOER
CHURCHYARD
CHURLISHLY
CHYLACEOUS
CICATRICES
CICATRICLE
CICATRIZER
CIGARETTES
CINCHONINE
CINCHONISM
CINCHONIZE
CINCINNATI
CINDERELLA
CINERARIUM
CINNAMONIC
CINQUEFOIL
CIRCUITOUS
CIRCULATED
CIRCULATOR
CIRCUMCISE
CIRCUMFLEX
CIRCUMFUSE
CIRCUMVENT
CISMONTANE
CISTACEOUS
CISTERCIAN
CITRIC ACID
CITRONELLA
CITRULLINE
CITY FATHER
CITY-STATES
CIVILITIES
CIVILIZING
CLACTONIAN
CLADISTICS
CLADOCERAN
CLAMBERING
CLAMMINESS
CLAMOURING

CLAMPDOWNS
CLANGOROUS
CLANNISHLY
CLANSWOMAN
CLAPPED-OUT
CLARABELLA
CLARIFYING
CLASP KNIFE
CLASSIC CAR
CLASSICISM
CLASSICIST
CLASSIFIED
CLASSIFIER
CLASSMATES
CLASSROOMS
CLATTERING
CLAVICHORD
CLAVICULAR
CLAY PIGEON
CLEANSABLE
CLEAN SHEET
CLEAN SWEEP
CLEARANCES
CLEFT STICK
CLEMENTINE
CLERESTORY
CLERICALLY
CLEVER DICK
CLEVERNESS
CLIENTELES
CLINGINESS
CLINGSTONE
CLINICALLY
CLINKSTONE
CLINOMETER
CLINOMETRY
CLIPBOARDS
CLIP JOINTS
CLOAKROOMS
CLOBBERING
CLOCKMAKER
CLOCK TOWER

CLODDISHLY
CLODHOPPER
CLOGGINESS
CLOISTERED
CLOSE CALLS
CLOSED BOOK
CLOSEDOWNS
CLOSED SHOP
CLOSE SHAVE
CLOSE THING
CLOTHBOUND
CLOTHES PEG
CLOUDBANKS
CLOUDBERRY
CLOUDBURST
CLOUDINESS
CLOVE HITCH
CLOVERLEAF
CLOWNISHLY
CLOYEDNESS
CLUBFOOTED
CLUBHOUSES
CLUMSINESS
CLUSTERING
CLUTCH BAGS
CLUTTERING
CLYDESDALE
CNIDOBLAST
COACERVATE
COACTIVITY
COADJUTANT
COADJUTORS
COAGULABLE
COAGULATED
COALBUNKER
COALESCENT
COALESCING
COALFIELDS
COALHOUSES
COALITIONS
COAPTATION
COARSENESS
COARSENING
COASTGUARD

COASTLINES
COAT HANGER
COAT OF ARMS
COCHABAMBA
COCHINEALS
COCKABULLY
COCKALORUM
COCKCHAFER
COCKED HATS
COCKFIGHTS
COCKHORSES
COCKNEYISM
COCKSCOMBS
COCONUT SHY
CODSWALLOP
COELACANTH
COENOCYTIC
COEQUALITY
COERCIVELY
COERCIVITY
COEXISTENT
COEXISTING
COFFEE BARS
COFFEEPOTS
COFFEE SHOP
COFFERDAMS
COGITATING
COGITATION
COGITATIVE
COGNIZABLE
COGNIZANCE
COHABITANT
COHABITING
COHERENTLY
COHESIVELY
COIMBATORE
COINCIDENT
COINCIDING
COLATITUDE
COLCHESTER
COLCHICINE
COLD CHISEL
COLD FISHES

COLD
  FRAMES
COLD
  FRONTS
COLDSTREAM
COLD
  TURKEY
COLEMANITE
COLEOPTILE
COLEORHIZA
COLLAGENIC
COLLAPSING
COLLARBONE
COLLAR
  STUD
COLLATERAL
COLLATIONS
COLLEAGUES
COLLECTING
COLLECTION
COLLECTIVE
COLLECTORS
COLLEGIATE
COLLIERIES
COLLIMATOR
COLLISIONS
COLLOCATED
COLLOQUIAL
COLLOQUIES
COLLOQUIUM
COLLOTYPIC
COLONIZERS
COLONIZING
COLONNADED
COLONNADES
COLORATION
COLORATURA
COLOR
  LINES
COLOSSALLY
COLOSSUSES
COLOURABLE
COLOUR
  BARS
COLOURFAST
COLOUR
  FAST
COLOURINGS
COLOURLESS
COLUMBINES
COLUMELLAR
COLUMNISTS

COMANCHEAN
COMBATABLE
COMBATANTS
COMBATTING
COMBINABLE
COMBUSTION
COMEDIENNE
COME-
  HITHER
COMELINESS
COMESTIBLE
COME TO
  HAND
COME TO
  MIND
COMFORTERS
COMFORTING
COMIC
  OPERA
COMIC
  STRIP
COMMANDANT
COMMANDEER
COMMANDERS
COMMANDING
COMMEASURE
COMMENCING
COMMENDING
COMMENTARY
COMMENTATE
COMMENTING
COMMERCIAL
COMMISSARS
COMMISSARY
COMMISSION
COMMISSURE
COMMITMENT
COMMITTALS
COMMITTEES
COMMITTING
COMMODIOUS
COMMODORES
COMMONABLE
COMMONALTY
COMMONNESS
COMMON
  NOUN
COMMON
  ROOM
COMMONWEAL
COMMOTIONS
COMMUNIONS

COMMUNIQUE
COMMUNISTS
COMMUTABLE
COMMUTATOR
COMPACTING
COMPANIONS
COMPARABLE
COMPARABLY
COMPARATOR
COMPARISON
COMPASSION
COMPATIBLE
COMPATIBLY
COMPATRIOT
COMPELLING
COMPENDIUM
COMPENSATE
COMPETENCE
COMPETENCY
COMPETITOR
COMPLACENT
COMPLAINED
COMPLAINER
COMPLAINTS
COMPLEMENT
COMPLETELY
COMPLETING
COMPLETION
COMPLETIST
COMPLETIVE
COMPLEXION
COMPLEXITY
COMPLIANCE
COMPLICATE
COMPLICITY
COMPLIMENT
COMPONENTS
COMPORTING
COMPOSITES
COMPOSITOR
COMPOSTING
COMPOUNDED
COMPOUNDER
COMPREHEND
COMPRESSED
COMPRESSES
COMPRESSOR
COMPRISING
COMPROMISE
COMPULSION
COMPULSIVE

COMPULSORY
COMPUTABLE
CONCEALING
CONCEDEDLY
CONCEIVING
CONCENTRIC
CONCEPCION
CONCEPTION
CONCEPTIVE
CONCEPTUAL
CONCERNING
CONCERTINA
CONCERTINO
CONCESSION
CONCESSIVE
CONCHIOLIN
CONCHOLOGY
CONCIERGES
CONCILIATE
CONCINNITY
CONCINNOUS
CONCLAVIST
CONCLUDING
CONCLUSION
CONCLUSIVE
CONCOCTING
CONCOCTION
CONCOCTIVE
CONCORDANT
CONCORDATS
CONCOURSES
CONCRETELY
CONCRETING
CONCRETION
CONCRETIVE
CONCRETIZE
CONCUBINES
CONCURRENT
CONCURRING
CONCUSSING
CONCUSSION
CONCUSSIVE
CONDEMNING
CONDENSATE
CONDENSERS
CONDENSING
CONDESCEND
CONDIMENTS
CONDITIONS
CONDOLENCE
CONDUCIBLE

CONDUCTING
CONDUCTION
CONDUCTIVE
CONDUCTORS
CONEFLOWER
CONFECTION
CONFERENCE
CONFERMENT
CONFERRING
CONFERVOID
CONFESSING
CONFESSION
CONFESSORS
CONFIDANTS
CONFIDENCE
CONFIRMING
CONFISCATE
CONFLATING
CONFLATION
CONFLICTED
CONFLUENCE
CONFORMERS
CONFORMING
CONFORMIST
CONFORMITY
CONFOUNDED
CONFOUNDER
CONFRONTED
CONFRONTER
CONFUSABLE
CONFUSEDLY
CONGEALING
CONGENERIC
CONGENITAL
CONGER
  EELS
CONGESTION
CONGESTIVE
CONGLOBATE
CONGREGATE
CONGRESSES
CONGRUENCE
CONIFEROUS
CONJECTURE
CONJOINING
CONJOINTLY
CONJUGABLE
CONJUGATED
CONJUGATOR
CONNECTING
CONNECTION

CONNECTIVE
CONNIVANCE
CONQUERING
CONQUERORS
CONSCIENCE
CONSCRIPTS
CONSECRATE
CONSENSUAL
CONSENTING
CONSEQUENT
CONSERVING
CONSIDERED
CONSIDERER
CONSIGNEES
CONSIGNING
CONSIGNORS
CONSISTENT
CONSISTING
CONSISTORY
CONSOCIATE
CONSOLABLE
CONSONANCE
CONSONANTS
CONSORTIAL
CONSORTING
CONSORTIUM
CONSPECTUS
CONSPIRACY
CONSPIRING
CONSTABLES
CONSTANTAN
CONSTANTIA
CONSTANTLY
CONSTIPATE
CONSTITUTE
CONSTRAINT
CONSTRUCTS
CONSTRUING
CONSUETUDE
CONSULATES
CONSULSHIP
CONSULTANT
CONSULTING
CONSUMMATE
CONTACTING
CONTACTUAL
CONTAGIONS
CONTAGIOUS
CONTAINERS
CONTAINING
CONTENDERS

CONTENDING
CONTENTING
CONTENTION
CONTESTANT
CONTESTING
CONTEXTUAL
CONTEXTURE
CONTIGUITY
CONTIGUOUS
CONTINENCE
CONTINENTS
CONTINGENT
CONTINUANT
CONTINUING
CONTINUITY
CONTINUOUS
CONTINUUMS
CONTORTING
CONTORTION
CONTOURING
CONTRABAND
CONTRABASS
CONTRACTED
CONTRACTOR
CONTRADICT
CONTRAFLOW
CONTRALTOS
CONTRARIES
CONTRARILY
CONTRASTED
CONTRAVENE
CONTRIBUTE
CONTRITELY
CONTRITION
CONTRIVING
CONTROLLED
CONTROLLER
CONTROVERT
CONTUSIONS
CONUNDRUMS
CONVALESCE
CONVECTION
CONVECTIVE
CONVECTORS
CONVENABLE
CONVENANCE
CONVENIENT
CONVENTION
CONVENTUAL
CONVERGENT
CONVERGING

CONVERSANT
CONVERSELY
CONVERSING
CONVERSION
CONVERTERS
CONVERTING
CONVEYABLE
CONVEYANCE
CONVICTING
CONVICTION
CONVICTIVE
CONVINCING
CONVOCATOR
CONVOLUTED
CONVULSING
CONVULSION
CONVULSIVE
COOCH
  BEHAR
COOKHOUSES
COOL-
  HEADED
COOPERATED
COOPERATOR
COOPTATION
COOPTATIVE
COORDINATE
COPARCENER
COPENHAGEN
COPPER
  BELT
COPPERHEAD
COPROLALIA
COPROLITIC
COPROPHAGY
COPULATING
COPULATION
COPULATIVE
COPY
  EDITOR
COPYHOLDER
COPYRIGHTS
COPYWRITER
COQUELICOT
COQUETRIES
COQUETTISH
COR
  ANGLAIS
CORDIALITY
CORDIERITE
CORDILLERA

CORDON
  BLEU
CORIACEOUS
CORINTHIAN
CORKSCREWS
CORMOPHYTE
CORMORANTS
CORNACEOUS
CORNCOCKLE
CORNCRAKES
CORNED
  BEEF
CORNELIANS
CORNFLAKES
CORNFLOWER
CORNSTARCH
CORNUCOPIA
CORNWALLIS
CORONATION
CORPORATOR
CORPOREITY
CORPULENCE
CORPUSCLES
CORRALLING
CORRECTING
CORRECTION
CORRECTIVE
CORRELATED
CORRELATES
CORRESPOND
CORRIENTES
CORRIGENDA
CORRIGIBLE
CORROBOREE
CORRODIBLE
CORRUGATED
CORRUPTING
CORRUPTION
CORRUPTIVE
CORSETIERE
CORUSCATED
COS
  LETTUCE
COSMICALLY
COSMIC
  RAYS
COSMODROME
COSMOGONAL
COSMOGONIC
COSMONAUTS
COSSETTING

COSTA
  RICAN
CO-
  STARRING
COSTLINESS
COST
  PRICES
COSTUMIERS
COTANGENTS
COTILLIONS
COTTAGE
  PIE
COTTON
  GINS
COTTONSEED
COTTONTAIL
COTTONWOOD
COTTON
  WOOL
COUCHETTES
COUCH
  GRASS
COULOMETER
COUNCILLOR
COUNCILMAN
COUNCILMEN
COUNCIL
  TAX
COUNSELLED
COUNSELLOR
COUNTDOWNS
COUNTERACT
COUNTERING
COUNTERSPY
COUNTESSES
COUNT
  NOUNS
COUNTRYMAN
COUNTRYMEN
COUNTY
  TOWN
COUPS
  D'ETAT
COURAGEOUS
COURGETTES
COURSEBOOK
COURT
  CARDS
COURTESANS
COURTESIES
COURTHOUSE
COURTLIEST

COURTSHIPS
COURTYARDS
COUTURIERS
COVARIANCE
COVENANTAL
COVENANTED
COVENANTEE
COVENANTER
COVENANTOR
COVER
  NOTES
COVER
  POINT
COVETOUSLY
COWCATCHER
CRAB
  APPLES
CRACKBRAIN
CRACKDOWNS
CRADLE
  SONG
CRAFTINESS
CRANE
  FLIES
CRANESBILL
CRANIOLOGY
CRANIOTOMY
CRANKSHAFT
CRAPULENCE
CRAQUELURE
CRASH-
  DIVED
CRASH-
  DIVES
CRAVENNESS
CRAYFISHES
CREAKINESS
CREAMERIES
CREAMINESS
CREATININE
CREATIONAL
CREATIVELY
CREATIVITY
CREDITABLE
CREDITABLY
CREDIT
  CARD
CREDIT
  NOTE
CREEPINESS
CREMATIONS
CREMATORIA

CRENELLATE
CREOSOTING
CREPE
  PAPER
CRESCENDOS
CRESCENTIC
CRETACEOUS
CREWELWORK
CRIBRIFORM
CRICKETERS
CRIMINALLY
CRIMSONING
CRINKLIEST
CRINOLINES
CRISPATION
CRISPINESS
CRISSCROSS
CRITERIONS
CRITICALLY
CRITICISMS
CRITICIZED
CRITICIZER
CROAKINESS
CROCHETING
CROCODILES
CROISSANTS
CROQUETTES
CROSSBONES
CROSSBREED
CROSSCHECK
CROSSHATCH
CROSS-
  INDEX
CROSSPATCH
CROSSPIECE
CROSS-
  REFER
CROSSROADS
CROSS-
  SLIDE
CROSSTREES
CROSSWALKS
CROSSWINDS
CROSSWORDS
CROWDED
  OUT
CROWN
  COURT
CROWN
  DERBY
CROWNPIECE

CROW'S
  NESTS
CRUCIFIXES
CRUCIFYING
CRUMBLIEST
CRUNCHIEST
CRUSTACEAN
CRUSTINESS
CRYOGENICS
CRYOPHILIC
CRYOSCOPIC
CRYPTOLOGY
CRYPTOZOIC
CRYSTAL
  SET
CTENOPHORE
CUBBYHOLES
CUCKOLDING
CUCKOOPINT
CUCKOO
  PINT
CUCULIFORM
CUDDLESOME
CUDGELLING
CUERNAVACA
CULLENDERS
CULTIVABLE
CULTIVATED
CULTIVATOR
CULTURALLY
CUMBERSOME
CUMMERBUND
CUMULATION
CUMULATIVE
CUMULIFORM
CUPBEARERS
CURABILITY
CURATE'S
  EGG
CURATORIAL
CURMUDGEON
CURRENCIES
CURRICULAR
CURRICULUM
CURTAILING
CURTAINING
CURVACEOUS
CURVATURES
CUSHIONING
CUSSEDNESS
CUSTARD
  PIE

CUSTODIANS
CUSTOMIZED
CUSTOM
  MADE
CUSTOM-
  MADE
CUTTHROATS
CUTTLEBONE
CUTTLEFISH
CUT UP
  ROUGH
CYANOGENIC
CYBERNETIC
CYBERSPACE
CYCLAMATES
CYCLICALLY
CYCLOMETER
CYCLOMETRY
CYCLORAMIC
CYCLOSTOME
CYCLOSTYLE
CYLINDROID
CYMBALISTS
CYMIFEROUS
CYSTECTOMY
CYSTOSCOPE
CYSTOSCOPY
CYTOCHROME
CYTOLOGIST

D

DACHSHUNDS
DAIL
  EIRANN
DAILY
  BREAD
DAIMYO
  BOND
DAINTINESS
DAIRY
  FARMS
DAIRYMAIDS
DAISY
  WHEEL
DALAI
  LAMAS
DALMATIANS
DAMAGEABLE
DAMP
  COURSE
DAMP
  SQUIBS

DAMSELFISH
DANDELIONS
DAPPLE-
  GREY
DAREDEVILS
DARJEELING
DARK
  HORSES
DARLINGTON
DARTBOARDS
DASHBOARDS
DAUGAVPILS
DAUGHTERLY
DAYDREAMED
DAYDREAMER
DAY-
  NEUTRAL
DAY
  NURSERY
DAY
  SCHOOLS
DAY-
  TRIPPER
DEACONSHIP
DEACTIVATE
DEAD
  CENTRE
DEAD
  LETTER
DEADLINESS
DEADLY
  SINS
DEAD-
  NETTLE
DEAD
  RINGER
DEALERSHIP
DEATHBLOWS
DEATH
  MASKS
DEATH
  RATES
DEATH'S-
  HEAD
DEATH
  SQUAD
DEATH
  TOLLS
DEATH
  TRAPS
DEATHWATCH
DEBASEMENT
DEBAUCHEES

DEBAUCHERY
DEBAUCHING
DEBENTURES
DEBILITATE
DEBOUCHING
DEBRIEFING
DEBUTANTES
DECADENTLY
DECAHEDRAL
DECAHEDRON
DECAMPMENT
DECAPITATE
DECATHLONS
DECEIVABLE
DECELERATE
DECEPTIONS
DECIMALIZE
DECIMATING
DECIMATION
DECIPHERED
DECIPHERER
DECISIONAL
DECISIVELY
DECKCHAIRS
DECLAIMING
DECLARABLE
DECLASSIFY
DECLENSION
DECLINABLE
DECOCTIONS
DECOLLATOR
DECOLONIZE
DECOLORANT
DECOLORIZE
DECOMPOSED
DECOMPOSER
DECOMPOUND
DECOMPRESS
DECORATING
DECORATION
DECORATIVE
DECORATORS
DECOROUSLY
DECOUPLING
DECREASING
DECREEABLE
DECREE
  NISI
DECRESCENT
DECUMBENCE
DEDICATING

DEDICATION
DEDICATORY
DEDUCTIBLE
DEDUCTIONS
DEEP
  FREEZE
DEEP
  FRYING
DEEP-
  ROOTED
DEEP-
  SEATED
DE-
  ESCALATE
DEFACEABLE
DEFACEMENT
DEFALCATOR
DEFAMATION
DEFAMATORY
DEFAULTERS
DEFAULTING
DEFEASANCE
DEFEASIBLE
DEFEATISTS
DEFECATING
DEFECATION
DEFECTIONS
DEFENDABLE
DEFENDANTS
DEFENSIBLE
DEFENSIBLY
DEFENSIVES
DEFERMENTS
DEFERRABLE
DEFICIENCY
DEFILEMENT
DEFINITELY
DEFINITION
DEFINITIVE
DEFINITUDE
DEFLAGRATE
DEFLECTING
DEFLECTION
DEFLECTIVE
DEFLOWERED
DEFLOWERER
DEFOLIANTS
DEFOLIATED
DEFOLIATOR
DEFORESTED
DEFORESTER
DEFORMABLE

DEFRAUDING
DEFRAYABLE
DEFROCKING
DEFROSTERS
DEFROSTING
DEFUNCTIVE
DEGENERACY
DEGENERATE
DEGRADABLE
DEGRESSION
DEHISCENCE
DEHUMANIZE
DEHUMIDIFY
DEHYDRATED
DEHYDRATOR
DEJECTEDLY
DELAMINATE
DELAWAREAN
DELECTABLE
DELECTABLY
DELEGATING
DELEGATION
DELIBERATE
DELICACIES
DELICATELY
DELIGHTFUL
DELIGHTING
DELIMITING
DELINEATED
DELINEATOR
DELINQUENT
DELIQUESCE
DELIVERIES
DELIVERING
DELOCALIZE
DELPHINIUM
DELTIOLOGY
DELUSIONAL
DELUSIVELY
DEMAGOGUES
DEMANDABLE
DEMARCATED
DEMARCATOR
DEMEANOURS
DEMENTEDLY
DEMICANTON
DEMIVIERGE
DEMOBILIZE
DEMOCRATIC
DEMODULATE
DEMOGRAPHY

DEMOISELLE
DEMOLISHED
DEMOLISHER
DEMOLITION
DEMONETIZE
DEMONIACAL
DEMONOLOGY
DEMORALIZE
DEMOTIVATE
DEMURENESS
DEMURRABLE
DENATURANT
DENDRIFORM
DENDROGRAM
DENDROLOGY
DENEGATION
DENIGRATED
DENIGRATOR
DENOMINATE
DENOTATION
DENOTATIVE
DENOTEMENT
DENOUEMENT
DENOUNCING
DENSIMETER
DENSIMETRY
DENTIFRICE
DENUDATION
DENUNCIATE
DENVER
  BOOT
DEODORANTS
DEODORIZED
DEODORIZER
DEONTOLOGY
DEOXIDIZER
DEPARTMENT
DEPARTURES
DEPENDABLE
DEPENDABLY
DEPENDANTS
DEPENDENCE
DEPENDENCY
DEPICTIONS
DEPILATION
DEPILATORY
DEPLETABLE
DEPLORABLE
DEPLORABLY
DEPLOYMENT
DEPOLARIZE

DEPOPULATE
DEPORTABLE
DEPORTMENT
DEPOSITARY
DEPOSITING
DEPOSITION
DEPOSITORS
DEPOSITORY
DEPRECATED
DEPRECATOR
DEPRECIATE
DEPRESSANT
DEPRESSING
DEPRESSION
DEPRESSIVE
DEPRIVABLE
DEPURATION
DEPURATIVE
DEPUTATION
DEPUTIZING
DERACINATE
DERAILLEUR
DERAILMENT
DERBYSHIRE
DEREGULATE
DERISIVELY
DERISORILY
DERIVATION
DERIVATIVE
DERMATITIS
DERMATOGEN
DERMATOMIC
DERMATOSIS
DEROGATING
DEROGATION
DEROGATIVE
DEROGATORY
DESALINATE
DESALINIZE
DESCENDANT
DESCENDENT
DESCENDING
DESCRIBING
DESECRATED
DESECRATOR
DESERTIONS
DESERVEDLY
DESHABILLE
DESICCANTS
DESICCATED
DESICCATOR

DESIDERATA
DESIDERATE
DESIGNABLE
DESIGNATED
DESIGNATOR
DESIGNEDLY
DESISTANCE
DESOLATELY
DESOLATING
DESOLATION
DESPAIRING
DESPATCHED
DESPATCHER
DESPATCHES
DESPERADOS
DESPICABLE
DESPICABLY
DESPOILING
DESPONDENT
DESQUAMATE
DESSIATINE
DESTROYERS
DESTROYING
DESTRUCTOR
DETACHABLE
DETACHMENT
DETAINABLE
DETAINMENT
DETECTABLE
DETECTIVES
DETERGENCY
DETERGENTS
DETERMINED
DETERMINER
DETERRENCE
DETERRENTS
DETESTABLE
DETESTABLY
DETHRONING
DETONATING
DETONATION
DETONATIVE
DETONATORS
DETOXICANT
DETOXICATE
DETRACTING
DETRACTION
DETRACTIVE
DETRACTORS
DETRAINING
DETRIMENTS

DETRUNCATE
DEUTOPLASM
DEUX-
    SEVRES
DEVASTATED
DEVASTATOR
DEVELOPERS
DEVELOPING
DEVIATIONS
DEVILISHLY
DEVITALIZE
DEVOCALIZE
DEVOLUTION
DEVOTEMENT
DEVOTIONAL
DEVOUTNESS
DEXTRALITY
DIABOLICAL
DIACAUSTIC
DIACHRONIC
DIACRITICS
DIACTINISM
DIADROMOUS
DIAGENESIS
DIAGNOSING
DIAGNOSTIC
DIAGONALLY
DIAKINESIS
DIALECTICS
DIALYSABLE
DIAPASONAL
DIAPEDESIS
DIAPEDETIC
DIAPHANOUS
DIAPHRAGMS
DIAPHYSIAL
DIARRHOEAL
DIASTALSIS
DIASTALTIC
DIATHERMIC
DIATROPISM
DIBASICITY
DICHLORIDE
DICHROMATE
DICKENSIAN
DICKEY
    BIRD
DICKYBIRDS
DICTAPHONE
DICTATIONS
DICTATRESS

DICTIONARY
DICTOGRAPH
DICYNODONT
DIDYNAMOUS
DIE-
    CASTING
DIE-
    HARDISM
DIELECTRIC
DIETICIANS
DIFFERENCE
DIFFICULTY
DIFFIDENCE
DIFFRACTED
DIFFUSIBLE
DIGESTIBLE
DIGESTIONS
DIGESTIVES
DIGITALISM
DIGITALIZE
DIGITATION
DIGITIFORM
DIGITIZERS
DIGITIZING
DIGNIFYING
DIGRESSING
DIGRESSION
DIGRESSIVE
DILAPIDATE
DILATATION
DILEMMATIC
DILETTANTE
DILETTANTI
DILIGENTLY
DILLYDALLY
DIMENSIONS
DIMINISHED
DIMINUENDO
DIMINUTION
DIMINUTIVE
DIMORPHISM
DIMORPHOUS
DINERS
    CLUB
DINING
    CARS
DINING
    ROOM
DINNER
    BELL
DIPETALOUS
DIPHOSGENE

DIPHTHERIA
DIPHTHONGS
DIPHYLETIC
DIPHYLLOUS
DIPHYODONT
DIPLODOCUS
DIPLOMATIC
DIPSOMANIA
DIRECTIONS
DIRECTIVES
DIRECTNESS
DIRECTOIRE
DIRECTRESS
DIRIGIBLES
DIRT
    FARMER
DIRT
    TRACKS
DIRTY
    TRICK
DISABILITY
DISABUSING
DISALLOWED
DISAPPOINT
DISAPPROVE
DISARRANGE
DISASTROUS
DISAVOWALS
DISAVOWING
DISBANDING
DISBARMENT
DISBARRING
DISBELIEVE
DISBENEFIT
DISBURSING
DISCARDING
DISC
    BRAKES
DISCERNING
DISCHARGED
DISCHARGER
DISCHARGES
DISC
    HARROW
DISCIPLINE
DISC
    JOCKEY
DISCLAIMED
DISCLAIMER
DISCLOSING
DISCLOSURE
DISCOMFORT

DISCOMMODE
DISCOMPOSE
DISCONCERT
DISCONNECT
DISCONTENT
DISCOPHILE
DISCORDANT
DISCOUNTED
DISCOUNTER
DISCOURAGE
DISCOURSED
DISCOURSER
DISCOURSES
DISCOVERED
DISCOVERER
DISCREETLY
DISCREPANT
DISCRETELY
DISCRETION
DISCURSIVE
DISCUSSANT
DISCUSSING
DISCUSSION
DISDAINFUL
DISDAINING
DISEMBOGUE
DISEMBOWEL
DISEMBROIL
DISEMPOWER
DISENCHANT
DISENDOWER
DISENGAGED
DISENTHRAL
DISENTITLE
DISENTWINE
DISEPALOUS
DISFEATURE
DISFIGURED
DISFIGURER
DISGORGING
DISGRACING
DISGRUNTLE
DISGUISING
DISGUSTING
DISHABILLE
DISHARMONY
DISHCLOTHS
DISHEARTEN
DISHONESTY
DISH
    TOWELS

DISHWASHER
DISINCLINE
DISINHERIT
DISJOINTED
DISK
DRIVES
DISLIKABLE
DISLOCATED
DISLODGING
DISLOYALLY
DISLOYALTY
DISMALNESS
DISMANTLED
DISMANTLER
DISMASTING
DISMISSALS
DISMISSING
DISMISSIVE
DISMOUNTED
DISOBEYING
DISOBLIGED
DISORDERED
DISORDERLY
DISOWNMENT
DISPARAGED
DISPARAGER
DISPASSION
DISPATCHED
DISPATCHES
DISPELLING
DISPENSARY
DISPENSERS
DISPENSING
DISPERMOUS
DISPERSING
DISPERSION
DISPERSIVE
DISPERSOID
DISPIRITED
DISPLACING
DISPLAYING
DISPLEASED
DISPORTING
DISPOSABLE
DISPOSSESS
DISPRAISER
DISPROVING
DISPUTABLE
DISPUTABLY
DISQUALIFY
DISQUIETED

DISRESPECT
DISRUPTING
DISRUPTION
DISRUPTIVE
DISSATISFY
DISSECTING
DISSECTION
DISSEMBLED
DISSEMBLER
DISSENSION
DISSENTERS
DISSENTING
DISSERVICE
DISSIDENCE
DISSIDENTS
DISSIMILAR
DISSIPATED
DISSIPATER
DISSOCIATE
DISSOLUBLE
DISSOLVING
DISSONANCE
DISSUADING
DISSUASION
DISSUASIVE
DISTANCING
DISTENDING
DISTENSION
DISTICHOUS
DISTILLATE
DISTILLERS
DISTILLERY
DISTILLING
DISTINCTLY
DISTORTING
DISTORTION
DISTORTIVE
DISTRACTED
DISTRACTER
DISTRAINED
DISTRAINEE
DISTRAINOR
DISTRAUGHT
DISTRESSED
DISTRIBUTE
DISTRUSTED
DISTRUSTER
DISTURBING
DISULFIRAM
DISULPHATE
DISULPHIDE

DISUNITING
DISUTILITY
DISYLLABIC
DITHEISTIC
DITHIONITE
DIVARICATE
DIVE-
BOMBED
DIVE-
BOMBER
DIVERGENCE
DIVERGENCY
DIVERSIONS
DIVERTEDLY
DIVERTIBLE
DIVESTIBLE
DIVESTMENT
DIVINATION
DIVINATORY
DIVING
BELL
DIVINITIES
DIVISIONAL
DIVISIVELY
DIVULGENCE
DIYARBAKIR
DOCENTSHIP
DOC
MARTENS
DOCTORATES
DOCTRINISM
DOCUMENTED
DODECANESE
DOG
BISCUIT
DOGCATCHER
DOG
COLLARS
DOGGEDNESS
DOGMATISTS
DOGMATIZER
DOGSBODIES
DOLCELATTE
DOLLARFISH
DOLL'S
HOUSE
DOLLY
BIRDS
DOLOROUSLY
DOMINATING
DOMINATION
DOMINATIVE

DOMINATRIX
DOMINEERED
DOMINICANS
DONER
KEBAB
DONKEYWORK
DONNYBROOK
DOORKEEPER
DOORPLATES
DORCHESTER
DORSIGRADE
DOSIMETRIC
DOSSHOUSES
DO THE
TRICK
DOTTED
LINE
DOUBLE
BASS
DOUBLE
BEDS
DOUBLE
BIND
DOUBLE
CHIN
DOUBLE
DATE
DOUBLE-
HUNG
DOUBLE-
PARK
DOUBLE-
REED
DOUBLE-
STOP
DOUBLE
TAKE
DOUBLE-
TALK
DOUBLE
TIME
DOUBLETREE
DOUBTFULLY
DOUGHTIEST
DOVETAILED
DOWN-AND-
OUT
DOWN AT
HEEL
DOWN-AT-
HEEL
DOWNGRADED
DOWNLOADED

DOWN-
MARKET
DOWNPLAYED
DOWNSIZING
DOWNSPOUTS
DOWNSTAIRS
DOWNSTREAM
DRAGONHEAD
DRAGONROOT
DRAGOONAGE
DRAGOONING
DRAINPIPES
DRAMATISTS
DRAMATIZED
DRAMATIZER
DRAMATURGE
DRAMATURGY
DRAWBRIDGE
DRAWING
PIN
DRAWSTRING
DREADFULLY
DREADLOCKS
DREAMBOATS
DREAMINESS
DREAMINGLY
DREAMLANDS
DREAM
WORLD
DREARINESS
DRESSINESS
DRESSMAKER
DRILLSTOCK
DRIP-
DRYING
DRIVELLERS
DRIVELLING
DROLLERIES
DROOPINESS
DROSOPHILA
DROSSINESS
DROWSINESS
DRUGSTORES
DRUM
MAJORS
DRUMSTICKS
DRUPACEOUS
DRY
BATTERY
DRY-
CLEANED

DRY
   CLEANER
DUBITATION
DUCKBOARDS
DUFFEL
   BAGS
DUFFEL
   COAT
DUMBSTRUCK
DUMBWAITER
DUNCE'S
   CAPS
DUNDERHEAD
DUODECIMAL
DUODENITIS
DUPABILITY
DUPLICABLE
DUPLICATED
DUPLICATES
DUPLICATOR
DURABILITY
DURATIONAL
DUSSELDORF
DUST
   JACKET
DUSTSHEETS
DUST
   STORMS
DUTCH
   BARNS
DUTCH
   OVENS
DUTCH
   TREAT
DUTCH
   UNCLE
DYNAMISTIC
DYNAMITING
DYSENTERIC
DYSPLASTIC
DYSPROSIUM
DYSTROPHIC
DZERZHINSK

E

EAGLESTONE
EARLY
   BIRDS
EARMARKING
EARTHBOUND
EARTHINESS
EARTHLIEST

EARTHLIGHT
EARTHLINGS
EARTHQUAKE
EARTHSHINE
EARTHWARDS
EARTHWORKS
EARTHWORMS
EAR
   TRUMPET
EAST
   ANGLIA
EAST
   BERLIN
EAST
   ENDERS
EASTER
   EGGS
EASTERNERS
EASTERTIDE
EAST
   GERMAN
EAST
   INDIAN
EAST
   INDIES
EASTWARDLY
EASY
   CHAIRS
EASY DOES
   IT
EASY
   STREET
EASY
   VIRTUE
EBRACTEATE
EBULLIENCE
EBULLITION
EBURNATION
ECCENTRICS
ECCHYMOSIS
ECHINODERM
ECHOPRAXIA
ECOCENTRIC
ECOLOGICAL
ECOLOGISTS
ECONOMICAL
ECONOMISTS
ECONOMIZED
ECONOMIZER
ECOSPECIES
ECOSYSTEMS
ECOTOURISM

ECTODERMAL
ECTOENZYME
ECTOGENOUS
ECTOMORPHY
ECUADORIAN
ECUMENICAL
ECZEMATOUS
EDENTULOUS
EDIFYINGLY
EDITORIALS
EDITORSHIP
EDULCORATE
EDWARDIANS
EFFACEABLE
EFFACEMENT
EFFECTIBLE
EFFECTUATE
EFFEMINACY
EFFEMINATE
EFFERVESCE
EFFETENESS
EFFICIENCY
EFFLORESCE
EFFORTLESS
EFFRONTERY
EFFULGENCE
EFFUSIVELY
EGOCENTRIC
EGYPTOLOGY
EIDERDOWNS
EIGHTEENMO
EIGHTEENTH
EIGHTH
   NOTE
EIGHTIETHS
EISENSTADT
EISTEDDFOD
EJACULATED
EJACULATOR
ELABORATED
ELABORATOR
ELAEOPTENE
ELASTICITY
ELASTICIZE
ELATEDNESS
ELDERBERRY
ELEATICISM
ELECAMPANE
ELECTIVITY
ELECTORATE
ELECTRICAL

ELECTRODES
ELECTROJET
ELECTRONIC
ELEMENTARY
ELEVATIONS
ELEVEN-
   PLUS
ELICITABLE
ELIMINABLE
ELIMINATED
ELIMINATOR
ELLIPTICAL
ELONGATING
ELONGATION
ELONGATIVE
ELOPEMENTS
ELOQUENTLY
EL
   SALVADOR
ELUCIDATED
ELUCIDATOR
ELUTRIATOR
ELUVIATION
EMACIATION
EMANATIONS
EMANCIPATE
EMARGINATE
EMASCULATE
EMBALMMENT
EMBANKMENT
EMBARGOING
EMBARKMENT
EMBEZZLERS
EMBEZZLING
EMBITTERED
EMBITTERER
EMBLAZONED
EMBLAZONRY
EMBLEMATIC
EMBLEMENTS
EMBODIMENT
EMBOLDENED
EMBOLISMIC
EMBONPOINT
EMBOSSMENT
EMBOUCHURE
EMBRASURED
EMBRASURES
EMBRECTOMY
EMBROIDERY
EMBROILING

EMBRYOGENY
EMBRYOLOGY
EMENDATION
EMENDATORY
EMETICALLY
EMIGRATING
EMIGRATION
EMIGRATIVE
EMISSARIES
EMISSIVITY
EMMENTALER
EMMETROPIA
EMMETROPIC
EMOLLIENCE
EMOLLIENTS
EMOLUMENTS
EMPALEMENT
EMPANELING
EMPANELLED
EMPHASIZED
EMPIRICISM
EMPIRICIST
EMPLOYABLE
EMPLOYMENT
EMPOWERING
EMULSIFIED
EMULSIFIER
EMULSIONED
ENACTMENTS
ENAMELLING
ENAMELLIST
ENAMELWARE
ENAMELWORK
ENCAMPMENT
ENCASEMENT
ENCASHABLE
ENCASHMENT
ENCEPHALIC
ENCEPHALON
ENCHAINING
ENCHANTERS
ENCHANTING
ENCHILADAS
ENCIPHERER
ENCIRCLING
ENCLOSABLE
ENCLOSURES
ENCODEMENT
ENCOUNTERS
ENCOURAGED
ENCOURAGER

ENCROACHED
ENCROACHER
ENCRUSTANT
ENCUMBERED
ENCYCLICAL
ENCYSTMENT
ENDANGERED
ENDEARMENT
ENDEAVOURS
ENDOCARPAL
ENDOCRINAL
ENDOCRINIC
ENDODERMAL
ENDODERMIC
ENDODERMIS
ENDODONTIA
ENDODONTIC
ENDOENZYME
ENDOGAMOUS
ENDOGENOUS
ENDOMORPHY
ENDOPHYTIC
ENDORSABLE
ENDOSCOPIC
ENDOSMOSIS
ENDOSMOTIC
ENDOSTOSIS
ENDOWMENTS
END
  PRODUCT
ENDURINGLY
ENERGETICS
ENERGIZING
ENERVATING
ENERVATION
ENERVATIVE
ENFACEMENT
ENFEEBLING
ENFILADING
ENFLEURAGE
ENFOLDMENT
ENFORCEDLY
ENGAGEMENT
ENGAGINGLY
ENGENDERED
ENGENDERER
ENGINEERED
ENGINE
  ROOM
ENGLISHMAN
ENGLISHMEN

ENGRAVINGS
ENGROSSING
ENGULFMENT
ENHARMONIC
ENJAMBMENT
ENJOINMENT
ENJOYMENTS
ENLACEMENT
ENLISTMENT
ENLIVENING
ENORMITIES
ENORMOUSLY
ENPHYTOTIC
ENRAGEMENT
ENRAPTURED
ENRICHMENT
ENROLMENTS
ENSANGUINE
ENSCONCING
ENSHRINING
ENSHROUDED
ENSIGNSHIP
ENTAILMENT
ENTANGLING
ENTEROTOMY
ENTERPRISE
ENTHRALLED
ENTHRALLER
ENTHRONING
ENTHUSIASM
ENTHUSIAST
ENTICEMENT
ENTICINGLY
ENTIRENESS
ENTODERMAL
ENTOMBMENT
ENTOMOLOGY
ENTOPHYTIC
ENTOURAGES
ENTRAINING
ENTRANCING
ENTRAPMENT
ENTRAPPING
ENTREATIES
ENTREATING
ENTRENCHED
ENTRENCHER
ENTRUSTING
ENTRY-
  LEVEL
ENUCLEATOR

ENUMERATED
ENUMERATOR
ENUNCIABLE
ENUNCIATED
ENUNCIATOR
ENVELOPING
ENVISAGING
ENZYMOLOGY
EOSINOPHIL
EPEIROGENY
EPENTHESIS
EPENTHETIC
EPEXEGESIS
EPEXEGETIC
EPIBLASTIC
EPICANTHUS
EPICARDIAC
EPICARDIUM
EPICENTRAL
EPICENTRES
EPICUREANS
EPICYCLOID
EPIDEICTIC
EPIDEMICAL
EPIDIDYMAL
EPIDIDYMIS
EPIGASTRIC
EPIGENESIS
EPIGENETIC
EPIGLOTTAL
EPIGLOTTIS
EPIGRAPHER
EPIGRAPHIC
EPILEPTICS
EPILEPTOID
EPIMORPHIC
EPINEURIAL
EPINEURIUM
EPIPHONEMA
EPIPHYSEAL
EPIROGENIC
EPISCOPACY
EPISCOPATE
EPISIOTOMY
EPISPASTIC
EPISTERNUM
EPISTOLARY
EPITAPHIST
EPITHELIAL
EPITHELIUM
EPITOMIZED

EPITOMIZER
EPOXY
  RESIN
EPSOM
  SALTS
EQUABILITY
EQUALIZERS
EQUALIZING
EQUANIMITY
EQUANIMOUS
EQUATIONAL
EQUATORIAL
EQUESTRIAN
EQUIPOTENT
EQUITATION
EQUIVALENT
EQUIVOCATE
ERADIATION
ERADICABLE
ERADICATED
ERADICATOR
ERECTILITY
ERETHISMIC
ERGONOMICS
ERGOSTEROL
ERICACEOUS
ERINACEOUS
EROGENEITY
EROTEMATIC
EROTICALLY
EROTOGENIC
EROTOMANIA
ERRATICISM
ERUBESCENT
ERUCTATION
ERUCTATIVE
ERUPTIONAL
ERUPTIVITY
ERYSIPELAS
ERYTHRITOL
ESCADRILLE
ESCALATING
ESCALATION
ESCALATORS
ESCAPEMENT
ESCAPOLOGY
ESCARPMENT
ESCHAROTIC
ESCRITOIRE
ESCUTCHEON
ESKILSTUNA

ESPADRILLE
ESPECIALLY
ESPLANADES
ESSENTIALS
ESTATE
  CARS
ESTHETICAL
ESTIMATING
ESTIMATION
ESTIMATIVE
ESTIMATORS
ESTIPULATE
ESTRANGING
ETERNALITY
ETERNALIZE
ETERNITIES
ETHANEDIOL
ETHEREALLY
ETHNICALLY
ETHNOGENIC
ETHNOLOGIC
ETHOLOGIST
ETHYLATION
ETIOLATION
EUBACTERIA
EUCALYPTOL
EUCALYPTUS
EUCHLORINE
EUDEMONICS
EUDEMONISM
EUDIOMETER
EUDIOMETRY
EUGENICIST
EUHEMERISM
EUHEMERIST
EUHEMERIZE
EULOGISTIC
EULOGIZING
EUPATORIUM
EUPHAUSIID
EUPHEMISMS
EUPHEMIZER
EUPHONIOUS
EUPHONIUMS
EUPHORIANT
EUHUISTIC
EURE-ET-
  LOIR
EURHYTHMIC
EUROCHEQUE
EUROCLYDON

EURODOLLAR
EUROMARKET
EURYPTERID
EURYTHMICS
EURYTROPIC
EUSTACHIAN
EUTHANASIA
EVACUATING
EVACUATION
EVACUATIVE
EVALUATING
EVALUATION
EVALUATIVE
EVANESCENT
EVANGELISM
EVANGELIST
EVANGELIZE
EVANSVILLE
EVAPORABLE
EVAPORATED
EVAPORATOR
EVECTIONAL
EVEN-
  HANDED
EVENING
  ALL
EVENING
  OUT
EVENTFULLY
EVENTUALLY
EVERGLADES
EVERGREENS
EVERY
  OTHER
EVERYTHING
EVERYWHERE
EVIDENTIAL
EVIL-
  MINDED
EVISCERATE
EVOCATIONS
EVOLVEMENT
EXACERBATE
EXACTINGLY
EXACTITUDE
EXAGGERATE
EXALTATION
EXAMINABLE
EXASPERATE
EX
  CATHEDRA
EXCAVATING

EXCAVATION
EXCAVATORS
EXCEEDABLE
EXCELLENCE
EXCELLENCY
EXCEPTABLE
EXCEPTIONS
EXCHANGING
EXCITATION
EXCITATIVE
EXCITEMENT
EXCITINGLY
EXCLAIMING
EXCLUDABLE
EXCLUSIVES
EXCOGITATE
EXCORIATED
EXCRESCENT
EXCRETIONS
EXCRUCIATE
EXCULPABLE
EXCULPATED
EXCURSIONS
EXCUSATORY
EXECRATING
EXECRATION
EXECRATIVE
EXECUTABLE
EXECUTANTS
EXECUTIONS
EXECUTIVES
EXEMPTIBLE
EXEMPTIONS
EXENTERATE
EXERCISING
EXHALATION
EXHAUSTING
EXHAUSTION
EXHAUSTIVE
EXHIBITING
EXHIBITION
EXHIBITIVE
EXHIBITORS
EXHIBITORY
EXHILARANT
EXHILARATE
EXHUMATION
EXIGENCIES
EXIGUOUSLY
EXISTENCES
EXOBIOLOGY

EXOCENTRIC
EXODONTIST
EXONERATED
EXONERATOR
EXORBITANT
EXORCIZING
EXOSPOROUS
EXOTHERMIC
EXOTICALLY
EXOTICNESS
EXPANDABLE
EXPANSIBLE
EXPANSIONS
EXPATIATED
EXPATIATOR
EXPATRIATE
EXPECTABLE
EXPECTANCY
EXPEDIENCE
EXPEDIENCY
EXPEDIENTS
EXPEDITING
EXPEDITION
EXPELLABLE
EXPENDABLE
EXPERIENCE
EXPERIMENT
EXPERTNESS
EXPIRATION
EXPIRATORY
EXPLAINING
EXPLETIVES
EXPLICABLE
EXPLICABLY
EXPLICATED
EXPLICATOR
EXPLICITLY
EXPLOITERS
EXPLOITING
EXPLOSIONS
EXPLOSIVES
EXPORTABLE
EXPOSITION
EXPOSITORY
EXPOUNDING
EXPRESSAGE
EXPRESSING
EXPRESSION
EXPRESSIVE
EXPRESSWAY
EXPULSIONS

EXPUNCTION
EXPURGATED
EXPURGATOR
EXSANGUINE
EXSICCATOR
EXTENDIBLE
EXTENSIBLE
EXTENSIONS
EXTENUATED
EXTENUATOR
EXTERNALLY
EXTINCTION
EXTINCTIVE
EXTINGUISH
EXTIRPATED
EXTIRPATOR
EXTORTIONS
EXTRACTING
EXTRACTION
EXTRACTIVE
EXTRACTORS
EXTRADITED
EXTRAMURAL
EXTRANEOUS
EXTRAVERTS
EXTRICABLE
EXTRICATED
EXTROVERTS
EXTRUSIONS
EXUBERANCE
EXULTANTLY
EXULTATION
EXULTINGLY
EXUVIATION
EYEBALLING
EYE-
  CATCHER
EYEDROPPER
EYEGLASSES
EYE-
  OPENERS
EYE
  SHADOWS
EYEWITNESS

F

FABRICATED
FABRICATOR
FABULOUSLY
FACECLOTHS

FACE-
  HARDEN
FACE
  POWDER
FACE-
  SAVERS
FACE-
  SAVING
FACE TO
  FACE
FACE-TO-
  FACE
FACE
  VALUES
FACILENESS
FACILITATE
FACILITIES
FACSIMILES
FACTITIOUS
FACT OF
  LIFE
FACTORABLE
FACTORIZED
FACTORSHIP
FACTUALISM
FACTUALIST
FAHRENHEIT
FAINTINGLY
FAIR
  COPIES
FAIR
  DINKUM
FAIRGROUND
FAIR-
  MINDED
FAIR-
  SPOKEN
FAIRYLANDS
FAIRY
  LIGHT
FAIRY
  TALES
FAISALABAD
FAITHFULLY
FALLACIOUS
FALLOW
  DEER
FALLOWNESS
FALSE
  ALARM
FALSEHOODS
FALSE
  SCENT

FALSE START
FALSE TEETH
FALSIFYING
FAMILIARLY
FAMILY NAME
FAMILY TREE
FAMISHMENT
FAMOUSNESS
FANATICISM
FANATICIZE
FANCIFULLY
FANCY DRESS
FANCY WOMAN
FANCY WOMEN
FANTASIZED
FANTOCCINI
FARCICALLY
FAR EASTERN
FARFETCHED
FARMHOUSES
FARMSTEADS
FARSIGHTED
FASCIATION
FASCICULAR
FASCICULUS
FASCINATED
FASHIONING
FASTENINGS
FASTIDIOUS
FASTIGIATE
FASTNESSES
FATALISTIC
FATALITIES
FATHERHOOD
FATHERLAND
FATHERLESS
FATHER-LIKE
FATHOMABLE
FATHOMETER
FATHOMLESS
FAT-SOLUBLE
FATTENABLE

FAULTINESS
FAVOURABLE
FAVOURABLY
FAVOURITES
FEARLESSLY
FEARNOUGHT
FEATHER BED
FEATHER BOA
FEATHERING
FEBRIFUGAL
FEBRUARIES
FECKLESSLY
FECUNDATOR
FEDERALISM
FEDERALIST
FEDERALIZE
FEDERATING
FEDERATION
FEDERATIVE
FEEBLENESS
FEET OF CLAY
FEIGNINGLY
FELICITATE
FELICITIES
FELICITOUS
FELIXSTOWE
FELLMONGER
FELLOWSHIP
FELT-TIP PEN
FEMALENESS
FEMININITY
FENESTELLA
FER-DE-LANCE
FERMENTING
FEROCITIES
FERRITE-ROD
FERTILIZED
FERTILIZER
FESTOONERY
FESTOONING
FETCHINGLY
FETIPAROUS
FETISHISTS
FETTUCCINE
FEUILLETON
FEVERISHLY

FFESTINIOG
FIANNA FAIL
FIBREBOARD
FIBREGLASS
FIBRINOGEN
FIBROBLAST
FIBROSITIS
FICKLENESS
FICTIONIST
FICTITIOUS
FIDDLEHEAD
FIDDLEWOOD
FIELD EVENT
FIELDMOUSE
FIELDSTONE
FIELD-TESTS
FIELD TRIPS
FIENDISHLY
FIERCENESS
FIFTEENTHS
FIFTY FIFTY
FIFTY-FIFTY
FIGURATION
FIGURATIVE
FIGUREHEAD
FILARIASIS
FILE SERVER
FILIALNESS
FILIBUSTER
FILMSETTER
FILMSTRIPS
FILTERABLE
FILTER TIPS
FILTHINESS
FILTRATION
FINALIZING
FINANCIERS
FINE-TUNING
FINGER BOWL
FINGERLING
FINGERNAIL
FINGERTIPS

FINISTERRE
FINNO-UGRIC
FIRE ALARMS
FIREBRANDS
FIREBREAKS
FIREBRICKS
FIRE DRILLS
FIRE-EATERS
FIRE-EATING
FIRE ENGINE
FIRE ESCAPE
FIREGUARDS
FIREPLACES
FIRE-RAISER
FIRESTORMS
FIRING LINE
FIRST CLASS
FIRST-CLASS
FIRST FLOOR
FIRST NAMES
FIRST NIGHT
FISH FINGER
FISH KNIVES
FISHMONGER
FISH SLICES
FISH STICKS
FISSIPEDAL
FISTICUFFS
FIT OF ANGER
FIT OF PIQUE
FIT THE BILL
FITZGERALD

FIVE-FINGER
FIXED-POINT
FIXED STARS
FLABBINESS
FLABELLATE
FLACCIDITY
FLAGELLANT
FLAGELLATE
FLAGITIOUS
FLAGRANTLY
FLAGSTAFFS
FLAGSTONES
FLAG-WAVING
FLAMBOYANT
FLAMEPROOF
FLAMINGOES
FLANNELING
FLANNELLED
FLARE PATHS
FLASHBACKS
FLASHBOARD
FLASHBULBS
FLASHCUBES
FLASHINESS
FLASHLIGHT
FLASH POINT
FLATFISHES
FLAT-FOOTED
FLAT RACING
FLATTENING
FLATTERERS
FLATTERING
FLATULENCE
FLAVESCENT
FLAVOURFUL
FLAVOURING
FLAWLESSLY
FLEA-BITTEN
FLEA MARKET
FLECTIONAL
FLEDGLINGS
FLEECINESS

FLEETINGLY
FLESHINESS
FLESH
  WOUND
FLETCHINGS
FLEUR-DE-
  LIS
FLEUR-DE-
  LYS
FLICKERING
FLICK
  KNIFE
FLIGHT
  DECK
FLIGHTIEST
FLIGHTLESS
FLIGHT
  PATH
FLIMSINESS
FLINTINESS
FLINTLOCKS
FLINTSHIRE
FLIPPANTLY
FLIRTATION
FLIRTINGLY
FLOATATION
FLOCCULANT
FLOCCULATE
FLOCCULENT
FLOODGATES
FLOODLIGHT
FLOOD
  TIDES
FLOORBOARD
FLOOR
  CLOTH
FLOOR
  SHOWS
FLOPHOUSES
FLOPPINESS
FLOPPY
  DISK
FLORENTINE
FLORIBUNDA
FLORISTICS
FLOTATIONS
FLOUNDERED
FLOURISHED
FLOURISHER
FLOURISHES
FLOURMILLS
FLOUTINGLY

FLOWCHARTS
FLOWERBEDS
FLOWER
  GIRL
FLOWERLESS
FLOWER-
  LIKE
FLOWERPOTS
FLUCTUATED
FLUFFINESS
FLUGELHORN
FLUID
  OUNCE
FLUMMOXING
FLUORIDATE
FLUORINATE
FLUSTERING
FLUTTERING
FLY-BY-
  NIGHT
FLYCATCHER
FLY-
  FISHING
FLYING
  BOAT
FLYING
  FISH
FLYSPECKED
FLYSWATTER
FLYWEIGHTS
FOAMFLOWER
FOAM
  RUBBER
FOB
  WATCHES
FOCAL
  POINT
FOCUS
  GROUP
FOLIACEOUS
FOLK
  DANCER
FOLK
  DANCES
FOLKESTONE
FOLKLORIST
FOLKSINESS
FOLLICULAR
FOLLICULIN
FOLLOWABLE
FOLLOWINGS
FONDLINGLY

FONTANELLE
FOOD
  STAMPS
FOODSTUFFS
FOOTBALLER
FOOTBRIDGE
FOOT-
  CANDLE
FOOT
  FAULTS
FOOTLIGHTS
FOOTPLATES
FOOTPRINTS
FOOTSTOOLS
FORBEARING
FORBIDDING
FORCEDNESS
FORCEFULLY
FORE AND
  AFT
FOREARMING
FOREBODING
FORECASTED
FORECASTER
FORECASTLE
FORECLOSED
FORECOURSE
FORECOURTS
FOREDOOMED
FOREFATHER
FOREFINGER
FOREGATHER
FOREGOINGS
FOREGROUND
FOREIGN
  AID
FOREIGNERS
FOREIGNISM
FOREMOTHER
FOREORDAIN
FORERUNNER
FORESEEING
FORESHADOW
FOREST-
  LIKE
FORETELLER
FOREWARNED
FOREWARNER
FORFEITERS
FORFEITING
FORFEITURE
FORGETTING

FORGIVABLE
FORGIVABLY
FORKEDNESS
FORMALISTS
FORMALIZED
FORMALIZER
FORMATIONS
FORMATTING
FORMIC
  ACID
FORMIDABLE
FORMIDABLY
FORMLESSLY
FORMULATED
FORMULATOR
FOR MY
  MONEY
FORNICATED
FORNICATOR
FORSTERITE
FORSWEARER
FORTE-
  PIANO
FORTHRIGHT
FORTIFIERS
FORTIFYING
FORTISSIMO
FORTNIGHTS
FORTRESSES
FORT
  SUMTER
FORTUITISM
FORTUITIST
FORTUITOUS
FORTY-
  NINER
FORTY
  WINKS
FORWARDING
FOSSILIZED
FOSTERLING
FOUDROYANT
FOUNDATION
FOUNDERING
FOUNDLINGS
FOURCHETTE
FOUR-
  COLOUR
FOUR-
  HANDED
FOURIERISM
FOURIERIST

FOUR-IN-
  HAND
FOUR-
  POSTER
FOURRAGERE
FOURSQUARE
FOUR-
  STROKE
FOURTEENTH
FOXHUNTERS
FOXHUNTING
FOX
  TERRIER
FRACTIONAL
FRACTURING
FRAGMENTAL
FRAGMENTED
FRAGRANCES
FRAGRANTLY
FRAMEWORKS
FRANCHISED
FRANCHISES
FRANCISCAN
FRANCONIAN
FRANGIPANI
FRATERNITY
FRATERNIZE
FRATRICIDE
FRAUDULENT
FRAUENFELD
FRAXINELLA
FRAY
  BENTOS
FREAKINESS
FREAKISHLY
FREDERICIA
FREE
  AGENTS
FREE-
  BASING
FREEBOARDS
FREEBOOTER
FREE
  CHURCH
FREEDWOMAN
FREE FOR
  ALL
FREE-FOR-
  ALL
FREE-
  HANDED
FREEHOLDER

FREE
  HOUSES
FREELANCED
FREELANCER
FREELANCES
FREE-
  LIVING
FREELOADED
FREELOADER
FREEMARTIN
FREEMASONS
FREE
  PARDON
FREE
  PASSES
FREE-
  SPOKEN
FREE-
  TRADER
FREIGHTAGE
FREIGHTERS
FREIGHTING
FRENCH
  BEAN
FRENCH
  HORN
FRENCH
  KISS
FRENCH
  LOAF
FRENZIEDLY
FREQUENTED
FREQUENTER
FREQUENTLY
FRESHENING
FRESHWATER
FRIABILITY
FRICANDEAU
FRICASSEES
FRICATIVES
FRICTIONAL
FRIENDLESS
FRIENDLIER
FRIENDLIES
FRIENDLILY
FRIENDSHIP
FRIGHTENED
FRIGHTENER
FRILLINESS
FRISKINESS
FRITILLARY
FRITTERING

FRIZZINESS
FROCK
  COATS
FROGHOPPER
FROLICKING
FROLICSOME
FRONTALITY
FRONTBENCH
FRONT
  DOORS
FRONT
  ROOMS
FRONTWARDS
FROSTBOUND
FROSTINESS
FROTHINESS
FROWNINGLY
FROWZINESS
FROZENNESS
FRUCTIFIED
FRUCTIFIER
FRUITCAKES
FRUITERERS
FRUIT
  FLIES
FRUITFULLY
FRUITINESS
FRUIT
  SALAD
FRUSTRATED
FRUSTRATER
FRUTESCENT
FRYING
  PANS
FUDDY-
  DUDDY
FULFILLING
FULFILMENT
FULIGINOUS
FULL-
  BODIED
FULL
  HOUSES
FULL-
  LENGTH
FULL-
  RIGGED
FULL-
  SAILED
FULLY-
  GROWN
FULMINATED

FULMINATOR
FUMATORIUM
FUMBLINGLY
FUMIGATING
FUMIGATION
FUNCTIONAL
FUNCTIONED
FUNDHOLDER
FUNEREALLY
FUNGICIDAL
FUNGICIDES
FUNICULARS
FUNICULATE
FUNNELLING
FUNNY
  BONES
FUNNY
  FARMS
FURBISHING
FURNISHING
FURTHERING
FURUNCULAR
FUSIBILITY
FUSILLADES
FUSTANELLA
FUTURISTIC
FUTUROLOGY
FUZZY
  LOGIC

G
GABARDINES
GADOLINITE
GADOLINIUM
GAFF-
  RIGGED
GAILLARDIA
GAINLINESS
GAINSAYING
GALASHIELS
GALLICIZER
GALLOGLASS
GALLSTONES
GALLUP
  POLL
GALUMPHING
GALVANIZED
GALVANIZER
GAMEKEEPER
GAMETOCYTE
GAME
  WARDEN

GANG-
  BANGED
GANG-
  BANGER
GANGLIONIC
GANGPLANKS
GANGRENOUS
GANGSTA
  RAP
GANTT
  CHART
GARAGE
  SALE
GARBAGE
  CAN
GARDEN
  CITY
GARGANTUAN
GARISHNESS
GARLANDING
GARNIERITE
GARNISHING
GARRISONED
GARROTTING
GAS
  FITTERS
GASHOLDERS
GASIFIABLE
GASOMETERS
GASOMETRIC
GAS
  STATION
GASTRALGIA
GASTRALGIC
GASTROLITH
GASTRONOME
GASTRONOMY
GASTROTOMY
GAS
  TURBINE
GATEHOUSES
GATEKEEPER
GATHERABLE
GATHERINGS
GAUCHENESS
GAULTHERIA
GAUSSMETER
GAZETTEERS
GEAR
  LEVERS
GELATINIZE
GELATINOID

GELATINOUS
GELDERLAND
GEMINATION
GEMMACEOUS
GEMOLOGIST
GENERALIST
GENERALITY
GENERALIZE
GENERATING
GENERATION
GENERATIVE
GENERATORS
GENERATRIX
GENEROSITY
GENEROUSLY
GENETICIST
GENICULATE
GENIUS
  LOCI
GENTLEFOLK
GENTLENESS
GENTRIFYED
GEOCENTRIC
GEOCHEMIST
GEODYNAMIC
GEOGNOSTIC
GEOGRAPHER
GEOLOGICAL
GEOLOGISTS
GEOMETRIZE
GEOMORPHIC
GEOPHAGIST
GEOPHAGOUS
GEOPHYSICS
GEORGETOWN
GEORGE
  TOWN
GEOSCIENCE
GEOSTATICS
GEOTHERMAL
GEOTROPISM
GERATOLOGY
GERIATRICS
GERMANIZER
GERMICIDAL
GERMICIDES
GERMINABLE
GERMINATED
GERMINATOR
GERUNDIVAL
GESTATIONS

GESUNDHEIT
GET
  HITCHED
GET-UP-
  AND-GO
GHASTLIEST
GHOSTLIEST
GHOST
  TOWNS
GHOSTWRITE
GIANT
  PANDA
GIARDIASIS
GIFTEDNESS
GIFT
  HORSES
GILLINGHAM
GINGER
  ALES
GINGER
  BEER
GINGER
  NUTS
GINGIVITIS
GIPPY
  TUMMY
GIRL
  FRIDAY
GIRLFRIEND
GIRL
  GUIDES
GIVEN
  NAMES
GIVE RISE
  TO
GLACIALIST
GLACIATION
GLACIOLOGY
GLADDENING
GLADIATORS
GLAGOLITIC
GLAIRINESS
GLAMORIZED
GLAMORIZER
GLANCINGLY
GLANDEROUS
GLASS
  FIBRE
GLASSHOUSE
GLASSINESS
GLASS-
  MAKER
GLASSWORKS

GLASWEGIAN
GLAUCONITE
GLAZING-
  BAR
GLEAMINGLY
GLENROTHES
GLIMMERING
GLIOMATOUS
GLISTENING
GLITTERATI
GLITTERING
GLOATINGLY
GLOBALISTS
GLOCHIDIUM
GLOMERULAR
GLOMERULUS
GLOOMINESS
GLORIFYING
GLORIOUSLY
GLORY
  HOLES
GLOSSARIAL
GLOSSARIES
GLOSSARIST
GLOSSINESS
GLOTTIDEAN
GLOUCESTER
GLUCOSIDAL
GLUMACEOUS
GLUTTINGLY
GLUTTONOUS
GLYCOGENIC
GLYCOLYSIS
GLYCOSIDIC
GLYCOSURIA
GLYCOSURIC
GNASHINGLY
GOALKEEPER
GOALMOUTHS
GOALSCORER
GOATSBEARD
GO-
  BETWEENS
GODFATHERS
GOD-
  FEARING
GODMOTHERS
GODPARENTS
GOGGLE-
  EYED
GOINGS-
  OVER

GOLD-
  BEATER
GOLD
  DIGGER
GOLDEN
  AGES
GOLDEN
  HOUR
GOLDEN
  MEAN
GOLDEN
  RULE
GOLDENSEAL
GOLDFIELDS
GOLDILOCKS
GOLD
  MEDALS
GOLD-
  MINING
GOLD-
  PLATED
GOLD
  RUSHES
GOLDSMITHS
GOLDTHREAD
GOLF
  COURSE
GONDOLIERS
GONGOOZLER
GONIOMETER
GONIOMETRY
GONOCOCCAL
GONOCOCCUS
GONOPHORIC
GONORRHOEA
GOOD
  FRIDAY
GOOD
  HUMOUR
GOODLINESS
GOOD
  LOOKER
GOOD
  NATURE
GOODS
  TRAIN
GOODY-
  GOODY
GOOGOLPLEX
GOOSEBERRY
GOOSEFLESH
GOOSESTEPS
GORGEOUSLY

GORGONZOLA
GORMANDIZE
GORMLESSLY
GORNO-
  ALTAI
GOTHICALLY
GO
  TOGETHER
GO TO
  GROUND
GO TO
  PIECES
GOVERNABLE
GOVERNANCE
GOVERNMENT
GRACEFULLY
GRACIOUSLY
GRADATIONS
GRADUALISM
GRADUALIST
GRADUATING
GRADUATION
GRAININESS
GRAMICIDIN
GRAMINEOUS
GRAMMARIAN
GRAMOPHONE
GRANADILLA
GRANDCHILD
GRAND
  OPERA
GRANDPAPPY
GRAND
  PIANO
GRAND
  SLAMS
GRANDS
  PRIX
GRANDSTAND
GRANGERISM
GRANGERIZE
GRANNY
  KNOT
GRANOPHYRE
GRANT-IN-
  AID
GRANULATED
GRANULATOR
GRANULITIC
GRAPEFRUIT
GRAPEVINES
GRAPHITIZE

GRAPHOLOGY
GRAPH
  PAPER
GRAPTOLITE
GRASSFINCH
GRASSINESS
GRASS
  ROOTS
GRASS
  WIDOW
GRATEFULLY
GRATIFYING
GRATUITIES
GRATUITOUS
GRAUBUNDEN
GRAVELLING
GRAVESTONE
GRAVETTIAN
GRAVEYARDS
GRAVIMETER
GRAVIMETRY
GRAVITATED
GRAVITATER
GRAVY
  BOATS
GRAVY
  TRAIN
GREASE
  GUNS
GREASEWOOD
GREASINESS
GREATCOATS
GREAT
  DANES
GREAT-
  NIECE
GREAT
  STOUR
GREAT-
  UNCLE
GREEDINESS
GREEDY-
  GUTS
GREEK
  CROSS
GREENBACKS
GREEN
  BEANS
GREEN
  BELTS
GREENBRIER
GREENFINCH
GREENFLIES

GREENGAGES
GREENHEART
GREENHORNS
GREENHOUSE
GREEN
  LIGHT
GREEN
  PAPER
GREEN
  POUND
GREENSBORO
GREENSHANK
GREENSTONE
GREEN
  THUMB
GREGARIOUS
GRENADIERS
GRENADINES
GRESSORIAL
GREYHOUNDS
GREY
  MARKET
GREY
  MATTER
GRIEVANCES
GRIEVINGLY
GRIEVOUSLY
GRIM
  REAPER
GRINDSTONE
GRIPPINGLY
GRISLINESS
GRISTLIEST
GRITTINESS
GROANINGLY
GROGGINESS
GROTESQUES
GROTTINESS
GROUCHIEST
GROUND
  BAIT
GROUND
  CREW
GROUNDLESS
GROUNDLING
GROUNDMASS
GROUNDNUTS
GROUND
  PLAN
GROUND
  RENT

GROUND
  RULE
GROUNDSMAN
GROUNDSMEN
GROUNDWORK
GROUPTHINK
GROVELLERS
GROVELLING
GRUBBINESS
GRUBSTAKES
GRUDGINGLY
GRUESOMELY
GRUMPINESS
GRUNTINGLY
GUADELOUPE
GUANAJUATO
GUANTANAMO
GUARANTEED
GUARANTEES
GUARANTIES
GUARANTORS
GUARDHOUSE
GUARDRAILS
GUARDROOMS
GUARD'S
  VANS
GUERRILLAS
GUESSINGLY
GUESTHOUSE
GUESTROOMS
GUIDELINES
GUILDHALLS
GUILEFULLY
GUILLEMOTS
GUILLOTINE
GUILTINESS
GUINEA
  FOWL
GUINEA
  PIGS
GUITARFISH
GUITARISTS
GUJRANWALA
GULF
  STREAM
GUNRUNNERS
GUNRUNNING
GURGLINGLY
GYMNASIAST
GYMNASIUMS
GYMNASTICS
GYMNOSPERM

GYNANDROUS
GYNOPHORIC
GYPSOPHILA
GYROSCOPES
GYROSCOPIC
GYROSTATIC

H

HABILIMENT
HABILITATE
HABITATION
HABITUALLY
HABITUATED
HACKBUTEER
HACKNEYISM
HADHRAMAUT
HAECKELIAN
HAEMAGOGUE
HAEMATINIC
HAEMATITIC
HAEMATOSIS
HAEMATURIA
HAEMATURIC
HAEMOLYMPH
HAEMOLYSIN
HAEMOLYSIS
HAEMOLYTIC
HAEMOPHILE
HAGIOCRACY
HAGIOLATER
HAGIOLATRY
HAGIOLOGIC
HAGIOSCOPE
HAILSTONES
HAILSTORMS
HAIRPIECES
HAIR
  SHIRTS
HAIR
  SLIDES
HAIRSPRING
HAIRSTREAK
HAIRSTYLES
HALBERDIER
HALF A
  CROWN
HALF-
  BOTTLE
HALF-
  BREEDS
HALF-
  CASTES

HALF
  CROWNS
HALF-
  LENGTH
HALF-
  ROTTEN
HALF-
  SISTER
HALF-
  TRUTHS
HALF
  VOLLEY
HALF-
  WITTED
HALLELUJAH
HALLMARKED
HALOGENATE
HALOGENOID
HALOGENOUS
HALOPHYTIC
HALTER-
  LIKE
HALTERNECK
HAMBURGERS
HAMMERFEST
HAMMERHEAD
HAMMERLESS
HAMMER-
  LIKE
HAMSHACKLE
HAMSTRINGS
HANDBALLER
HANDBARROW
HANDBRAKES
HANDCUFFED
HANDICRAFT
HAND IN
  HAND
HANDLEABLE
HANDLEBARS
HANDLELESS
HANDMAIDEN
HAND-ME-
  DOWN
HANDPICKED
HANDSHAKES
HANDSOMELY
HANDSPRING
HANDSTANDS
HANDSTROKE
HANKERINGS

HANKY-
  PANKY
HANOVERIAN
HAPLOLOGIC
HAPPENINGS
HAPPY
  EVENT
HAPPY
  HOURS
HARANGUING
HARASSMENT
HARBINGERS
HARBOURAGE
HARBOURING
HARD-
  BITTEN
HARD-
  BOILED
HARD
  CIDERS
HARDHEADED
HARD
  LABOUR
HARD-
  LINERS
HARD
  LIQUOR
HARD
  PALATE
HARELIPPED
HARGREAVES
HARLEQUINS
HARMLESSLY
HARMONICAS
HARMONIOUS
HARMONIUMS
HARMONIZED
HARMONIZER
HARMSWORTH
HARNESSING
HARPOONING
HARRISBURG
HARROWMENT
HARTEBEEST
HARTLEPOOL
HARUSPICAL
HARVESTERS
HARVESTING
HARVESTMAN
HASH
  BROWNS
HASTEFULLY

HATCHBACKS
HATCHELLER
HATCHERIES
HATCHET
  JOB
HATCHET
  MAN
HATCHET
  MEN
HATSHEPSUT
HATTERSLEY
HAUBERGEON
HAUGHTIEST
HAUNTINGLY
HAUSTELLUM
HAUSTORIAL
HAUSTORIUM
HAUTE-
  LOIRE
HAUTE-
  MARNE
HAVE A
  HEART
HAVE A
  POINT
HAVERSACKS
HAZARDABLE
HAZARD-
  FREE
HEADBOARDS
HEADCHEESE
HEADHUNTED
HEADHUNTER
HEADLIGHTS
HEADLINING
HEADMASTER
HEAD OF
  HAIR
HEADPHONES
HEADPIECES
HEADSPRING
HEADSQUARE
HEADSTONES
HEADSTREAM
HEADSTRONG
HEADWATERS
HEADWORKER
HEALTH
  FOOD
HEALTHIEST
HEARING
  AID

HEARKENING
HEARTBEATS
HEARTBREAK
HEARTENING
HEARTHRUGS
HEARTINESS
HEARTSEASE
HEARTTHROB
HEATEDNESS
HEATHBERRY
HEATHENDOM
HEATHENISH
HEATHENISM
HEATHENIZE
HEAT
  RASHES
HEAT
  SHIELD
HEATSTROKE
HEAT
  STROKE
HEAVEN-
  SENT
HEAVENWARD
HEAVY-
  LADEN
HEAVY
  METAL
HEAVY
  WATER
HEBDOMADAL
HEBETATION
HEBETATIVE
HEBRAISTIC
HECTICALLY
HECTOGRAPH
HEDONISTIC
HEEDLESSLY
HEIDELBERG
HEIGHTENED
HEIGHTENER
HEISENBERG
HELIANTHUS
HELICOPTER
HELIGOLAND
HELIOGRAPH
HELIOLATER
HELIOLATRY
HELIOMETER
HELIOMETRY
HELIOPOLIS
HELIOTAXIS

HELIOTROPE
HELIOTYPIC
HELLACIOUS
HELLBENDER
HELLENIZER
HELLESPONT
HELLRAISER
HELMET-
  LIKE
HELMINTHIC
HELPLESSLY
HEMELYTRAL
HEMELYTRON
HEMICYCLIC
HEMIHEDRAL
HEMIPLEGIA
HEMIPLEGIC
HEMIPTERAN
HEMIPTERON
HEMISPHERE
HEMITROPIC
HEMOGLOBIN
HEMOPHILIA
HEMORRHAGE
HEMORRHOID
HENCEFORTH
HENDECAGON
HENOTHEISM
HENOTHEIST
HEN
  PARTIES
HEPARINOID
HEPHAESTUS
HEPHAISTOS
HEPTAGONAL
HEPTAMETER
HEPTARCHIC
HEPTASTICH
HEPTATEUCH
HEPTATHLON
HERACLIDAN
HERACLITUS
HERBACEOUS
HERBALISTS
HERBICIDAL
HERBIVORES
HEREABOUTS
HEREDITARY
HEREDITIST
HERESIARCH
HERETOFORE

HERMITAGES
HERMOSILLO
HEROICALLY
HEROPHILUS
HESITANTLY
HESITATING
HESITATION
HESITATIVE
HESPERIDES
HESPERIDIN
HETERODONT
HETERODOXY
HETERODYNE
HETEROGAMY
HETEROGONY
HETEROLOGY
HETERONOMY
HETEROTOPY
HEULANDITE
HEURISTICS
HEXADECANE
HEXAEMERIC
HEXAEMERON
HEXAHEDRAL
HEXAHEDRON
HEXAMERISM
HEXAMEROUS
HEXAMETERS
HEXAMETRIC
HEXANGULAR
HEXAVALENT
HIBERNACLE
HIBERNATED
HIBERNATOR
HIBISCUSES
HIDDENNESS
HIERARCHAL
HIEROCRACY
HIERODULIC
HIEROGLYPH
HIEROLOGIC
HIERONYMIC
HIERONYMUS
HIEROPHANT
HIGHBINDER
HIGH
  CHAIRS
HIGH
  CHURCH
HIGH
  COURTS

HIGH-
  FLIERS
HIGH-
  FLYING
HIGH-
  HANDED
HIGH
  HORSES
HIGHJACKER
HIGH
  JUMPER
HIGHLANDER
HIGHLIGHTS
HIGH
  MASSES
HIGH-
  MINDED
HIGHNESSES
HIGH-
  OCTANE
HIGH
  POINTS
HIGH
  PRIEST
HIGH
  RELIEF
HIGH
  SCHOOL
HIGH
  SEASON
HIGH
  STREET
HIGH-
  STRUNG
HIGHWAYMAN
HIGHWAYMEN
HIJACKINGS
HILDEBRAND
HILDESHEIM
HILLINGDON
HIMYARITIC
HINAYANIST
HINDENBURG
HINDERMOST
HINDRANCES
HINDUSTANI
HINTERLAND
HIPHUGGERS
HIPPARCHUS
HIP
  POCKETS
HIPPOCRENE
HIPPODROME

HIPPOGRIFF
HIPPOLYTAN
HIPPOLYTUS
HIPPOMENES
HISPANIOLA
HISTAMINIC
HISTIOCYTE
HISTOGRAMS
HISTOLYSIS
HISTOLYTIC
HISTORIANS
HISTORICAL
HISTRIONIC
HIT-AND-
MISS
HITCHHIKED
HITCHHIKER
HITHERMOST
HIT
PARADES
HIT THE
SACK
HOARSENESS
HOBBYHORSE
HOBGOBLINS
HOBNOBBING
HOCHHEIMER
HOCUS-
POCUS
HODGEPODGE
HOGARTHIAN
HOITY-
TOITY
HOKEY
COKEY
HOKEY-
POKEY
HOLDERSHIP
HOLES IN
ONE
HOLIDAYING
HOLINESSES
HOLLOWNESS
HOLLYHOCKS
HOLOCAUSTS
HOLOENZYME
HOLOFERNES
HOLOGRAPHY
HOLOHEDRAL
HOLOPHYTIC
HOLUS-
BOLUS

HOLY
ISLAND
HOLY
SPIRIT
HOMEBODIES
HOME-
BREWED
HOMECOMING
HOME
GUARDS
HOMELINESS
HOMEMAKERS
HOMEMAKING
HOME
MOVIES
HOME
OFFICE
HOMEOPATHS
HOMEOPATHY
HOMEOTYPIC
HOMESTEADS
HOME
TRUTHS
HOMEWORKER
HOMILETICS
HOMOCERCAL
HOMOCYCLIC
HOMOEOPATH
HOMOEROTIC
HOMOGAMOUS
HOMOGENATE
HOMOGENIZE
HOMOGENOUS
HOMOGONOUS
HOMOGRAPHS
HOMOLOGATE
HOMOLOGIZE
HOMOLOGOUS
HOMOLOSINE
HOMONYMITY
HOMOOUSIAN
HOMOPHONES
HOMOPHONIC
HOMOPLASTY
HOMORGANIC
HOMOSEXUAL
HOMOZYGOTE
HOMOZYGOUS
HOMUNCULAR
HOMUNCULUS
HONESTNESS
HONEYBUNCH

HONEYCOMBS
HONEYDEWED
HONEY-
EATER
HONEYMOONS
HONORARIUM
HONORIFICS
HONOURABLE
HONOURABLY
HONOURLESS
HOODLUMISM
HOODWINKED
HOODWINKER
HOOKEDNESS
HOOTENANNY
HOPE
CHESTS
HOPELESSLY
HOPPING
MAD
HORIZONTAL
HORNBLENDE
HORNEDNESS
HORN-
RIMMED
HOROLOGIST
HOROLOGIUM
HOROSCOPES
HOROSCOPIC
HORRENDOUS
HORRIDNESS
HORRIFYING
HORROR
FILM
HORSEBOXES
HORSEFLESH
HORSEFLIES
HORSELAUGH
HORSELEECH
HORSE
OPERA
HORSEPOWER
HORSE
SENSE
HORSESHOES
HORSEWOMAN
HORSEWOMEN
HOSPITABLE
HOSPITABLY
HOSPITALET
HOSTELLERS
HOSTELLING

HOSTELRIES
HOT-
BLOODED
HOTCHPOTCH
HOT
DESKING
HOT
FLUSHES
HOTFOOTING
HOUSEBOATS
HOUSEBOUND
HOUSECOATS
HOUSECRAFT
HOUSEFLIES
HOUSE
GUEST
HOUSEHOLDS
HOUSEMAIDS
HOUSE OF
GOD
HOUSE
PARTY
HOUSEPLANT
HOUSE-
PROUD
HOUSE-
TRAIN
HOUSEWIVES
HOVERCRAFT
HOVERINGLY
HOVERTRAIN
HOW DO YOU
DO
HUA KUO-
FENG
HUCKLEBONE
HUDDLESTON
HUGUENOTIC
HULLABALOO
HUMANENESS
HUMANISTIC
HUMANITIES
HUMANIZING
HUMBERSIDE
HUMBLENESS
HUMBLINGLY
HUMBUGGERY
HUMDINGERS
HUMIDIFIED
HUMIDIFIER
HUMIDISTAT
HUMILIATED

HUMILIATOR
HUMORESQUE
HUMORISTIC
HUMOROUSLY
HUMOURLESS
HUMOURSOME
HUMPBACKED
HUNCHBACKS
HUNDREDTHS
HUNGRINESS
HUNTINGDON
HUNTRESSES
HUNTSVILLE
HURDY-
GURDY
HURLY-
BURLY
HURRICANES
HURRYINGLY
HUSBANDING
HUSBANDMAN
HUSBANDMEN
HYACINTHUS
HYALOPLASM
HYALURONIC
HYBRIDIZER
HYDRANGEAS
HYDRASTINE
HYDRAULICS
HYDROCORAL
HYDROFOILS
HYDROGRAPH
HYDROLOGIC
HYDROLYSER
HYDROLYSIS
HYDROLYTIC
HYDROMANCY
HYDROPONIC
HYGIENISTS
HYPERBOLAS
HYPERBOLES
HYPERBOLIC
HYPERMEDIA
HYPERSPACE
HYPHENATED
HYPNOTISTS
HYPNOTIZED
HYPOCRITES
HYPODERMIC
HYPOTENUSE
HYPOTHESES

HYPOTHESIS
HYSTERICAL

I
IAMBICALLY
IATROGENIC
ICEBREAKER
ICE
  BREAKER
ICE
  LOLLIES
ICE-
  SKATERS
ICE-
  SKATING
ICHINOMIYA
ICHTHYOSIS
ICHTHYOTIC
ICONOCLASM
ICONOCLAST
ICONOLATER
ICONOLATRY
ICONOMATIC
ICONOSCOPE
IDEALISTIC
IDEALIZING
IDEATIONAL
IDEMPOTENT
IDENTIFIED
IDENTIFIER
IDENTIKITS
IDENTITIES
IDEOGRAPHY
IDEOLOGIES
IDEOLOGIST
IDEOLOGUES
IDIOLECTAL
IDIOPATHIC
IDIOPHONIC
IDOLATRIZE
IDOLATROUS
IGNES
  FATUI
IGNOBILITY
IGNOMINIES
IJSSELMEER
ILL-
  ADVISED
ILLEGALITY
ILLEGALIZE
ILLITERACY
ILLITERATE

ILL-
  NATURED
ILLOCUTION
ILL-
  STARRED
ILL-
  TREATED
ILLUMINANT
ILLUMINATE
ILLUMINATI
ILLUMINISM
ILLUMINIST
ILLUSORILY
ILLUSTRATE
IMAGINABLE
IMBALANCES
IMBECILITY
IMBIBITION
IMBRICATED
IMBROGLIOS
IMITATIONS
IMMACULACY
IMMACULATE
IMMATERIAL
IMMATURELY
IMMATURITY
IMMEMORIAL
IMMERSIBLE
IMMIGRANTS
IMMIGRATED
IMMIGRATOR
IMMINENTLY
IMMISCIBLE
IMMOBILITY
IMMOBILIZE
IMMODERACY
IMMODERATE
IMMODESTLY
IMMOLATING
IMMOLATION
IMMORALIST
IMMORALITY
IMMORTELLE
IMMOTILITY
IMMUNIZING
IMMUNOLOGY
IMPAIRMENT
IMPALEMENT
IMPALPABLE
IMPANATION
IMPANELLED

IMPARTIBLE
IMPASSABLE
IMPATIENCE
IMPEACHING
IMPECCABLE
IMPECCABLY
IMPEDANCES
IMPEDIMENT
IMPEDINGLY
IMPENDENCE
IMPENITENT
IMPERATIVE
IMPERIALLY
IMPERILLED
IMPERSONAL
IMPERVIOUS
IMPETRATOR
IMPISHNESS
IMPLACABLE
IMPLANTING
IMPLEMENTS
IMPLICATED
IMPLICITLY
IMPLOSIONS
IMPOLITELY
IMPORTANCE
IMPORTUNED
IMPORTUNER
IMPOSINGLY
IMPOSITION
IMPOSSIBLE
IMPOSSIBLY
IMPOSTROUS
IMPOSTURES
IMPOTENTLY
IMPOUNDAGE
IMPOUNDING
IMPOVERISH
IMPREGNATE
IMPRESARIO
IMPRESSING
IMPRESSION
IMPRESSIVE
IMPRIMATUR
IMPRINTING
IMPRISONED
IMPRISONER
IMPROBABLE
IMPROBABLY
IMPROPERLY
IMPROVABLE

IMPROVISED
IMPROVISER
IMPRUDENCE
IMPUDENTLY
IMPUISSANT
IMPULSIONS
IMPUNITIES
IMPURITIES
IMPUTATION
IMPUTATIVE
IN
  ABSENTIA
INACCURACY
INACCURATE
INACTIVATE
INACTIVELY
INACTIVITY
IN
  ADDITION
INADEQUACY
INADEQUATE
INAMORATAS
IN ANY
  EVENT
INAPPOSITE
INAPTITUDE
INARTISTIC
INAUGURATE
INBREEDING
INCANDESCE
INCAPACITY
INCAPARINA
INCARNATED
INCAUTIOUS
INCENDIARY
INCENTIVES
INCEPTIONS
INCESSANCY
INCESTUOUS
INCHOATION
INCHOATIVE
INCIDENTAL
INCINERATE
INCIPIENCE
INCIPIENCY
INCISIVELY
INCITATION
INCITEMENT
INCITINGLY
INCIVILITY
INCLEMENCY

INCLINABLE
INCLOSURES
INCLUDABLE
INCLUSIONS
INCOHERENT
INCOMMODED
INCOMPLETE
INCONSTANT
INCRASSATE
INCREASING
INCREDIBLE
INCREDIBLY
INCREMENTS
INCRESCENT
INCUBATING
INCUBATION
INCUBATIVE
INCUBATORS
INCULCATED
INCULCATOR
INCULPABLE
INCULPATED
INCUMBENCY
INCUMBENTS
INCUNABULA
INCURRABLE
INCURRENCE
INCURSIONS
INDECENTLY
INDECISION
INDECISIVE
INDECOROUS
INDEFINITE
INDELICACY
INDELICATE
INDENTURED
INDENTURES
INDEXATION
INDIAN
  CORN
INDICATING
INDICATION
INDICATIVE
INDICATORS
INDICATORY
INDICTABLE
INDICTMENT
INDIGENOUS
INDIRECTLY
INDISCREET
INDISCRETE

INDISPOSED	INFINITUDE	INIQUITOUS	INSCRIBING	INSULATORS
INDISTINCT	INFLATABLE	INITIALING	INSECURELY	INSURANCES
INDIVIDUAL	INFLATEDLY	INITIALIZE	INSECURITY	INSURGENCE
INDOCILITY	INFLECTING	INITIALLED	INSEMINATE	INSURGENCY
INDOLENTLY	INFLECTION	INITIATING	INSENSIBLE	INSURGENTS
INDOLOGIST	INFLECTIVE	INITIATION	INSENSIBLY	INTANGIBLE
INDONESIAN	INFLEXIBLE	INITIATIVE	INSENTIENT	INTANGIBLY
INDOPHENOL	INFLEXIBLY	INITIATORY	INSERTABLE	INTEGRABLE
INDUCEMENT	INFLICTING	INJECTABLE	INSERTIONS	INTEGRATED
INDUCTANCE	INFLICTION	INJECTIONS	INSIDE	INTEGRATOR
INDUCTIONS	INFLICTIVE	INJUNCTION	JOBS	INTEGUMENT
INDULGENCE	INFLUENCED	INJUNCTIVE	INSIDE	INTELLECTS
INDUSTRIAL	INFLUENCER	INJURY	LANE	INTENDANCE
INDUSTRIES	INFLUENCES	TIME	INSIGHTFUL	INTENDANCY
INEBRIATED	INFLUENZAL	INJUSTICES	INSINUATED	INTENDMENT
INEBRIATES	INFORMALLY	IN	INSINUATOR	INTENTIONS
INEDUCABLE	INFORMANTS	MEMORIAM	INSIPIDITY	INTENTNESS
INEDUCABLY	INFORMEDLY	INNER	INSISTENCE	INTERACTED
INEFFICACY	INFRACLASS	CHILD	INSOBRIETY	INTER
INELEGANCE	INFRACTION	INNER	INSOLATION	ALIOS
INELIGIBLE	INFRASONIC	TUBES	INSOLENTLY	INTERBRAIN
INELOQUENT	INFREQUENT	INNKEEPERS	INSOLVABLE	INTERBREED
INEPTITUDE	INFRINGING	INNOCENTLY	INSOLVENCY	INTERCEDED
INEQUALITY	INFURIATED	INNOMINATE	INSOLVENTS	INTERCEDER
INEQUITIES	INFUSORIAL	INNOVATING	INSOMNIACS	INTERDICTS
INEVITABLE	INGESTIBLE	INNOVATION	INSOMNIOUS	INTERESTED
INEVITABLY	INGLENOOKS	INNOVATIVE	INSOUCIANT	INTERFACED
INEXISTENT	INGLORIOUS	INNOVATORS	INSPECTING	INTERFACES
INEXORABLE	INGOLSTADT	INNUENDOES	INSPECTION	INTERFERED
INEXORABLY	INGRATIATE	INNUMERACY	INSPECTIVE	INTERFERER
INEXPERTLY	INGREDIENT	INNUMERATE	INSPECTORS	INTERFERON
INEXPIABLE	INGRESSION	INOCULABLE	INSPIRABLE	INTERFLUVE
INEXPLICIT	INGRESSIVE	INOCULATED	INSPIRITER	INTERGRADE
IN	INGUSHETIA	INOCULATOR	INSTALLING	INTERGROUP
EXTREMIS	INHABITANT	IN ONE	INSTALMENT	INTERLACED
INFALLIBLE	INHABITING	PIECE	INSTANCING	INTERLAKEN
INFALLIBLY	INHALATION	IN ONES	INSTIGATED	INTERLEAVE
INFARCTION	INHARMONIC	CUPS	INSTIGATOR	INTERLINER
INFATUATED	INHERENTLY	INOPERABLE	INSTILLING	INTERLOPER
INFECTIONS	INHERITING	INORDINACY	INSTILMENT	INTERLUDES
INFECTIOUS	INHIBITING	INORDINATE	INSTITUTED	INTERLUNAR
INFELICITY	INHIBITION	INOSCULATE	INSTITUTES	INTERMARRY
INFERENCES	INHIBITIVE	IN-	INSTITUTOR	INTERMENTS
INFERNALLY	IN HOT	PATIENTS	INSTRUCTED	INTERMEZZI
INFIBULATE	WATER	INQUIETUDE	INSTRUCTOR	INTERMEZZO
INFIDELITY	INHUMANELY	INQUISITOR	INSTRUMENT	INTERMODAL
INFIELDERS	INHUMANITY	INSALIVATE	INSUFFLATE	INTERNALLY
INFIGHTING	INHUMATION	INS AND	INSULARISM	INTERNMENT
INFILTRATE	INIMITABLE	OUTS	INSULARITY	INTERNODAL
INFINITELY	INIMITABLY	INSANITARY	INSULATING	INTERNSHIP
INFINITIVE	INIQUITIES	INSATIABLE	INSULATION	INTERPHASE

INTERPHONE
INTERPLEAD
INTERPOSAL
INTERPOSED
INTERPOSER
INTERREGNA
INTERSPACE
INTERSTATE
INTERSTICE
INTERTIDAL
INTERTWINE
INTERVENED
INTERVENER
INTERVIEWS
INTERWEAVE
INTERWOVEN
INTESTINAL
INTESTINES
IN THE
   EVENT
IN THE
   MONEY
INTIMACIES
INTIMATELY
INTIMATING
INTIMATION
INTIMIDATE
INTINCTION
INTOLERANT
INTONATION
INTOXICANT
INTOXICATE
IN
   TRAINING
INTRAMURAL
INTRENCHED
INTREPIDLY
INTRIGUING
INTRODUCED
INTRODUCER
INTROSPECT
INTROVERTS
INTRUSIONS
INTRUSTING
INTUBATION
INTUITABLE
INTUITIONS
INUNDATING
INUNDATION
INUREDNESS
INVAGINATE

INVALIDATE
INVALID
   CAR
INVALIDING
INVALIDISM
INVALIDITY
INVALUABLE
INVARIABLE
INVARIABLY
INVARIANCE
INVEIGHING
INVEIGLING
INVENTIBLE
INVENTIONS
INVERACITY
INVERCLYDE
INVERSIONS
INVERTIBLE
INVESTABLE
INVESTMENT
INVETERACY
INVETERATE
INVIGILATE
INVIGORATE
INVINCIBLE
INVINCIBLY
INVIOLABLE
INVITATION
INVITATORY
INVITINGLY
INVOCATION
INVOCATORY
INVOLUCRAL
INVOLUTION
IODIZATION
IODOMETRIC
IONIZATION
IONOSPHERE
IRENICALLY
IRIDACEOUS
IRIDECTOMY
IRIDESCENT
IRISH
   STEWS
IRISHWOMAN
IRONICALLY
IRONMONGER
IRRADIANCE
IRRADIATED
IRRADIATOR
IRRATIONAL

IRREGULARS
IRRELATIVE
IRRELEVANT
IRRELIGION
IRRESOLUTE
IRREVERENT
IRRIGATING
IRRIGATION
IRRIGATIVE
IRRITATING
IRRITATION
IRRITATIVE
IRRUPTIONS
ISENTROPIC
ISKENDERUN
ISOANTIGEN
ISOCHEIMAL
ISOCHRONAL
ISOCHROOUS
ISOCYANIDE
ISODYNAMIC
ISOGAMETIC
ISOGLOSSAL
ISOGLOTTIC
ISOLEUCINE
ISOMETRICS
ISOMORPHIC
ISOPIESTIC
ISOSEISMAL
ISOTHERMAL
ISOTROPOUS
ISRAELITES
ITALIANATE
ITALICIZED
ITCHY
   PALMS
ITINERANCY
IVORY
   TOWER

J

JACKANAPES
JACKHAMMER
JACK-
   KNIFED
JACK
   KNIVES
JACKRABBIT
JACK THE
   LAD
JACOBITISM
JAGUARONDI

JAILBREAKS
JAM
   SESSION
JAMSHEDPUR
JANITORIAL
JARDINIERE
JAUNTINESS
JAWBREAKER
JAYWALKERS
JAYWALKING
JEALOUSIES
JELLY
   BEANS
JELLY
   ROLLS
JEOPARDIZE
JERRY-
   BUILD
JERRY-
   BUILT
JERSEY
   CITY
JESUITICAL
JET
   ENGINES
JET-
   SETTERS
JETTISONED
JIANG
   ZEMIN
JIGGERMAST
JINGDEZHEN
JINGOISTIC
JITTERBUGS
JOB
   CENTRES
JOBSHARING
JOCKSTRAPS
JOCULARITY
JOGJAKARTA
JOLLY
   ROGER
JOSS
   STICKS
JOURNALESE
JOURNALISM
JOURNALIST
JOURNALIZE
JOURNEYING
JOURNEYMAN
JOURNEYMEN
JOYFULNESS

JOYOUSNESS
JUBILANTLY
JUBILATION
JUDGMENTAL
JUDICATIVE
JUDICATORY
JUDICATURE
JUDICIALLY
JUGGERNAUT
JUIZ DE
   FORA
JUMBLE
   SALE
JUMBLINGLY
JUNCACEOUS
JUNCTIONAL
JUNKETINGS
JURY-
   RIGGED
JUST AS
   WELL
JUSTICIARY
JUSTIFYING
JUST IN
   CASE
JUST-IN-
   TIME
JUVENILITY
JUXTAPOSED

K

KABARAGOYA
KALGOORLIE
KANSAS
   CITY
KANTIANISM
KAPFENBERG
KARA-
   KALPAK
KARAMANLIS
KARLSKRONA
KARYOGAMIC
KARYOLYMPH
KARYOLYSIS
KARYOLYTIC
KARYOPLASM
KARYOTYPIC
KASHMIRIAN
KAZAKHSTAN
KEEP TABS
   ON
KENILWORTH

KENNELLING
KENTUCKIAN
KERATINIZE
KERATOTOMY
KERCHIEFED
KERFUFFLES
KERMANSHAH
KERSEYMERE
KETTLEDRUM
KEYBOARDED
KEYBOARDER
KEYPUNCHED
KEYPUNCHER
KEYPUNCHES
KHABAROVSK
KIDNAPPERS
KIDNAPPING
KIDNEY
BEAN
KIESELGUHR
KILMARNOCK
KILOLITRES
KILOMETRES
KILOMETRIC
KIMBERLITE
KINCARDINE
KINDLINESS
KINDNESSES
KINEMATICS
KINGFISHER
KINGLINESS
KINGMAKERS
KING-OF-
ARMS
KING'S
BENCH
KIRITIMATI
KIROVOGRAD
KISS OF
LIFE
KITAKYUSHU
KITH AND
KIN
KITTIWAKES
KLAGENFURT
KLANGFARBE
KNEECAPPED
KNEE-
LENGTH
KNICK-
KNACK

KNIFE-
EDGES
KNIGHTHEAD
KNIGHTHOOD
KNOBBLIEST
KNOBKERRIE
KNOCKABOUT
KNOCK-
KNEED
KOEKSISTER
KOMMUNARSK
KOMSOMOLSK
KOOKABURRA
KRAGUJEVAC
KRAMATORSK
KREMENCHUG
KRIEGSPIEL
KRISHNAISM
KRUGERRAND
KU KLUX
KLAN
KUOMINTANG

L
LABIONASAL
LABIOVELAR
LABORATORY
LABOR
UNION
LABOUR
CAMP
LABOUR
DAYS
LABOUREDLY
LABYRINTHS
LACERATING
LACERATION
LACERATIVE
LACHRYMOSE
LACKLUSTRE
LACQUERING
LACRIMATOR
LACTESCENT
LACTIC
ACID
LACTOGENIC
LACTOMETER
LACTOSCOPE
LACUNOSITY
LACUSTRINE
LADY-
KILLER

LADY'S-
SMOCK
LAMARCKIAN
LAMARCKISM
LAMASERIES
LAMBASTING
LAMBDACISM
LAMBREQUIN
LAMBS
TAILS
LAMELLATED
LAMENTABLE
LAMENTABLY
LAMINATING
LAMINATION
LAMPOONERY
LAMPOONING
LAMPSHADES
LANCASHIRE
LANCEOLATE
LAND
AGENTS
LAND
FORCES
LANDING
NET
LANDLADIES
LANDLOCKED
LANDLUBBER
LANDMASSES
LAND
ROVERS
LANDSCAPED
LANDSCAPES
LANDSLIDES
LANGLAUFER
LANGUISHED
LANGUISHER
LANGUOROUS
LANIFEROUS
LANTHANIDE
LAPAROTOMY
LAP
DANCING
LAPIDARIAN
LAPIDARIES
LARGE-
SCALE
LA
ROCHELLE
LARVICIDAL
LARYNGITIC

LARYNGITIS
LASCIVIOUS
LAST
MINUTE
LATECOMERS
LATENT
HEAT
LATTERMOST
LAUGHINGLY
LAUNCESTON
LAUNCH
PADS
LAUNDERING
LAUNDROMAT
LAUNDRYMAN
LAURACEOUS
LAUREATION
LAURENTIAN
LAVATIONAL
LAVATORIAL
LAVATORIES
LAVISHNESS
LAW-
ABIDING
LAW-
BREAKER
LAWFULNESS
LAWNMOWERS
LAWN
TENNIS
LAWRENCIUM
LAY
BROTHER
LAY
FIGURES
LAYPERSONS
LAY
READERS
LAY
SISTERS
LEADERSHIP
LEAF-
HOPPER
LEAFLETING
LEASEBACKS
LEAVENINGS
LEBENSRAUM
LECTIONARY
LECTORSHIP
LEEUWARDEN
LEFT-
HANDED

LEFT-
HANDER
LEFT-
WINGER
LEGAL
EAGLE
LEGALISTIC
LEGALIZING
LEGATESHIP
LEGATORIAL
LEGIBILITY
LEGISLATED
LEGISLATOR
LEGITIMACY
LEGITIMATE
LEGITIMISM
LEGITIMIST
LEGITIMIZE
LEGUMINOUS
LEG-
WARMERS
LEISHMANIA
LEITMOTIVS
LEMNISCATE
LEMON
GRASS
LEMON
SOLES
LENGTHENED
LENGTHENER
LENGTHIEST
LENGTHWAYS
LENTAMENTE
LENTICULAR
LENTISSIMO
LEOPARDESS
LEPIDOLITE
LEPRECHAUN
LEPTOSOMIC
LESBIANISM
LESSEESHIP
LETCHWORTH
LETHBRIDGE
LETS FACE
IT
LETTER
BOMB
LETTERHEAD
LEUCOCYTES
LEUCOCYTIC
LEUCODERMA
LEUCOMAINE

LEUCOPENIA
LEUCOPENIC
LEUCOPLAST
LEVERKUSEN
LEVIATHANS
LEVIGATION
LEVITATING
LEVITATION
LEXICALITY
LEXICOLOGY
LIBATIONAL
LIBERALISM
LIBERALIST
LIBERALITY
LIBERALIZE
LIBERATING
LIBERATION
LIBERATORS
LIBERTINES
LIBIDINOUS
LIBRARIANS
LIBRETTIST
LIBREVILLE
LICENSABLE
LICENTIATE
LICENTIOUS
LIE IN
  STATE
LIEUTENANT
LIFE
  CYCLES
LIFEGUARDS
LIFE
  JACKET
LIFELESSLY
LIFE-
  SAVING
LIFESTYLES
LIGHT
  BULBS
LIGHTENING
LIGHTERAGE
LIGHTHOUSE
LIGHTNINGS
LIGHTSHIPS
LIGHT
  YEARS
LIGNOCAINE
LIKELIHOOD
LIKE-
  MINDED
LIKENESSES

LILIACEOUS
LIMICOLINE
LIMICOLOUS
LIMITARIAN
LIMITATION
LIMOUSINES
LINEAMENTS
LINECASTER
LINGUIFORM
LINGUISTIC
LINLITHGOW
LINSEED
  OIL
LIPOMATOUS
LIPOPHILIC
LIP-
  READING
LIP
  SERVICE
LIQUEFYING
LIQUESCENT
LIQUIDATED
LIQUIDATOR
LIQUIDIZED
LIQUIDIZER
LIQUORICES
LISSOMNESS
LISTENABLE
LISTLESSLY
LIST
  PRICES
LITERALISM
LITERALIST
LITERARILY
LITERATELY
LITERATION
LITERATURE
LITHOGRAPH
LITHOLOGIC
LITHOMARGE
LITHOPHYTE
LITHOTOMIC
LITHOTRITY
LITHUANIAN
LITIGATING
LITIGATION
LITTERBINS
LITTERLOUT
LITTLE
  BELT
LITTLE
  ROCK

LITURGICAL
LIVABILITY
LIVELIHOOD
LIVELINESS
LIVING
  ROOM
LIVINGSTON
LIVING
  WAGE
LIVING
  WILL
LLANGOLLEN
LOADSTONES
LOBOTOMIES
LOBSTERPOT
LOBULATION
LOCAL
  DERBY
LOCALISTIC
LOCALITIES
LOCALIZING
LOCKER
  ROOM
LOCK
  KEEPER
LOCKSMITHS
LOCKSTITCH
LOCOMOTION
LOCOMOTIVE
LOCULATION
LODESTONES
LOGANBERRY
LOGARITHMS
LOGGERHEAD
LOGICALITY
LOGISTICAL
LOGOGRAPHY
LOGOPAEDIC
LOGORRHOEA
LOGROLLING
LOINCLOTHS
LOIR-ET-
  CHER
LONELINESS
LONGBENTON
LONGHAIRED
LONG-
  HEADED
LONG
  ISLAND
LONGITUDES

LONG-
  JUMPER
LONGWINDED
LOOK-
  ALIKES
LOPHOPHORE
LOQUACIOUS
LORDLINESS
LORGNETTES
LORRY
  PARKS
LOS
  ANGELES
LOSS
  LEADER
LOST
  CAUSES
LOTUS-
  EATER
LOUDHAILER
LOUDMOUTHS
LOUISVILLE
LOUNGE
  BARS
LOUNGE
  SUIT
LOVABILITY
LOVE
  AFFAIR
LOVELINESS
LOVEMAKING
LOVING
  CUPS
LOW-
  ALCOHOL
LOWBROWISM
LOWER
  CLASS
LOWER
  HOUSE
LOWERINGLY
LOWLANDERS
LOW-
  PITCHED
LOW
  PROFILE
LOW-
  TENSION
LOXODROMIC
LUBRICANTS
LUBRICATED
LUBRICATOR
LUBRICIOUS

LUBUMBASHI
LUCUBRATOR
LUGGAGE
  VAN
LUGUBRIOUS
LULUABOURG
LUMBERJACK
LUMBER-
  ROOM
LUMBERYARD
LUMBRICOID
LUMINARIES
LUMINOSITY
LUMINOUSLY
LUMISTEROL
LUNAR
  MONTH
LURCHINGLY
LUSCIOUSLY
LUSTRATION
LUSTRATIVE
LUSTREWARE
LUSTROUSLY
LUTINE
  BELL
LUXEMBOURG
LUXURIANCE
LUXURIATED
LYCOPODIUM
LYMPHOCYTE
LYOPHILIZE

M

MAASTRICHT
MAASTRICHT
MACADAMIZE
MACEBEARER
MACEDONIAN
MACERATING
MACERATION
MACERATIVE
MACHINABLE
MACHINATOR
MACHINE
  GUN
MACHINISTS
MACH
  NUMBER
MACKINTOSH
MACROCOSMS
MACROCYTIC
MACROGRAPH

MACROPHAGE
MACROSPORE
MACULATION
MADAGASCAN
MADAGASCAR
MADCHESTER
MADREPORAL
MAELSTROMS
MAGIC
  WANDS
MAGISTRACY
MAGISTRATE
MAGNA
  CARTA
MAGNETITIC
MAGNETIZED
MAGNETIZER
MAGNIFIERS
MAGNIFYING
MAGNITUDES
MAGNUM
  OPUS
MAIDENHAIR
MAIDENHEAD
MAIDENHOOD
MAIDEN
  NAME
MAIN
  CHANCE
MAIN
  CLAUSE
MAINFRAMES
MAINLINING
MAINSPRING
MAINSTREAM
MAINTAINED
MAINTAINER
MAISONETTE
MAJOR-
  DOMOS
MAJORETTES
MAJORITIES
MAJOR
  SUITS
MAJUSCULAR
MAKE A
  POINT
MAKESHIFTS
MAKEWEIGHT
MALACOLOGY
MALADDRESS
MALAPROPOS

MALCONTENT
MALEFACTOR
MALEFICENT
MALEVOLENT
MALFEASANT
MALIGNANCY
MALINGERED
MALINGERER
MALODOROUS
MALPIGHIAN
MALTED
  MILK
MALTHUSIAN
MALTREATED
MALTREATER
MALVACEOUS
MANAGEABLE
MANAGEABLY
MANAGEMENT
MANAGERESS
MANAGERIAL
MANCHESTER
MANCHINEEL
MANCHURIAN
MANCUNIANS
MANEUVERED
MAN
  FRIDAYS
MANFULNESS
MANGOSTEEN
MANHANDLED
MANIACALLY
MANICURING
MANICURIST
MANIFESTED
MANIFESTLY
MANIFESTOS
MANIFOLDER
MANIPULATE
MANNEQUINS
MANNERISMS
MANOEUVRED
MANOEUVRER
MANOEUVRES
MAN OF
  STRAW
MANOMETERS
MANOMETRIC
MANOR
  HOUSE
MANSERVANT
MANTELTREE

MANTICALLY
MANUSCRIPT
MANZANILLA
MARASCHINO
MARCESCENT
MARCH-
  PASTS
MARCONI
  RIG
MARE'S
  NESTS
MARGARITAS
MARGINALIA
MARGINALLY
MARGUERITE
MARINATING
MARINATION
MARIONETTE
MARKEDNESS
MARKETABLE
MARKETABLY
MARKETEERS
MARKET
  TOWN
MARKSWOMAN
MARLACIOUS
MARQUISATE
MARROWBONE
MARSHALING
MARSHALLED
MARSHALLER
MARSHINESS
MARSUPIALS
MARTELLATO
MARTENSITE
MARTIAL
  ART
MARTIALISM
MARTIALIST
MARTIAL
  LAW
MARTINGALE
MARTINICAN
MARTINIQUE
MARVELLING
MARVELLOUS
MARVELMENT
MARXIANISM
MASCARPONE
MASOCHISTS
MASQUERADE
MASSACRING

MASSASAUGA
MASSETERIC
MASTECTOMY
MASTER
  CARD
MASTERHOOD
MASTER
  KEYS
MASTERMIND
MASTERSHIP
MASTERWORK
MASTICABLE
MASTICATED
MASTICATOR
MASTURBATE
MATCHBOARD
MATCHBOXES
MATCHMAKER
MATCH
  POINT
MATCHSTICK
MATERIALLY
MATERNALLY
MATO
  GROSSO
MATOZINHOS
MATRIARCHS
MATRIARCHY
MATRICIDAL
MATRICIDES
MATRILOCAL
MATTERHORN
MATTRESSES
MATURATION
MATURATIVE
MAUDLINISM
MAUNDERING
MAURITANIA
MAUSOLEUMS
MAXILLIPED
MAXIMALIST
MAXIMIZING
MAXISINGLE
MAYONNAISE
MAYORESSES
MEADOWLARK
MEAGRENESS
MEANDERING
MEANINGFUL
MEANS
  TESTS
MEASLINESS

MEASURABLE
MEASURABLY
MEASUREDLY
MECHANICAL
MECHANISMS
MECHANIZED
MECHANIZER
MECONOPSIS
MEDALLIONS
MEDALLISTS
MEDDLESOME
MEDDLINGLY
MEDICAMENT
MEDICATION
MEDICATIVE
MEDIOCRITY
MEDITATING
MEDITATION
MEDITATIVE
MEDIUM
  WAVE
MEDULLATED
MEERSCHAUM
MEFLOQUINE
MEGAGAMETE
MEGALITHIC
MEGAPHONES
MEGAPHONIC
MEGASPORIC
MEITNERIUM
MELANCHOLY
MELANESIAN
MELANISTIC
MELANOCYTE
MELANOSITY
MELBURNIAN
MELIACEOUS
MELIORABLE
MELIORATOR
MELISMATIC
MELLOPHONE
MELLOWNESS
MELODRAMAS
MELTING
  POT
MEMBERSHIP
MEMBRANOUS
MEMORANDUM
MEMORIZING
MENACINGLY
MENAGERIES

MENARCHEAL
MENDACIOUS
MENDICANCY
MENDICANTS
MENINGITIC
MENINGITIS
MEN OF
 STRAW
MENOPAUSAL
MENOPAUSIC
MENSTRUATE
MENSTRUOUS
MENSURABLE
MENTAL
 AGES
MENTAL
 NOTE
MENTIONING
MERCANTILE
MERCAPTIDE
MERCIFULLY
MERIDIONAL
MERRYMAKER
MERSEY
 BEAT
MERSEYSIDE
MESENCHYME
MESENTERIC
MESENTERON
MESITYLENE
MESMERISTS
MESMERIZED
MESMERIZER
MESOCRATIC
MESODERMAL
MESOLITHIC
MESOMORPHY
MESOPHYTIC
MESOSPHERE
MESOTHORAX
MESSENGERS
METABOLISM
METABOLITE
METABOLIZE
METACARPAL
METACARPUS
METACENTRE
METAFEMALE
METAGALAXY
METALLURGY
METAMERISM
METAPHORIC

METAPHRASE
METAPHRAST
METAPHYSIC
METAPLASIA
METASTABLE
METASTASIS
METASTATIC
METATARSUS
METATHEORY
METATHESIS
METATHETIC
METATHORAX
METEORITES
METEORITIC
METHIONINE
METHODICAL
METHODISTS
METHODIZER
METHUSELAH
METHYLATOR
METHYLDOPA
METICULOUS
METOESTRUS
METRICALLY
METRICIZED
METRIC
 TONS
METRONOMES
METRONOMIC
METRONYMIC
METROPOLIS
METTLESOME
MEXICO
 CITY
MEZZANINES
MEZZOTINTS
MIAMI
 BEACH
MICHAELMAS
MICROCHIPS
MICROCLINE
MICROCOSMS
MICROCYTIC
MICROFICHE
MICROFILMS
MICROGRAPH
MICROMETER
MICROMETRY
MICRONESIA
MICROPHONE
MICROPHYTE

MICROPRINT
MICROPYLAR
MICROSCOPE
MICROSCOPY
MICROSEISM
MICROSOMAL
MICROSPORE
MICROTOMIC
MICROTONAL
MICROWAVES
MIDAS
 TOUCH
MIDDELBURG
MIDDLE-
 AGED
MIDDLE
 AGES
MIDDLEBROW
MIDDLE
 EAST
MIDDLE
 NAME
MIDDLE
 WEST
MIDLOTHIAN
MIDSECTION
MIDSHIPMAN
MIDSHIPMEN
MIDWESTERN
MIGHTINESS
MIGNONETTE
MIGRAINOID
MIGRATIONS
MILEOMETER
MILESTONES
MILITANTLY
MILITARILY
MILITARISM
MILITARIST
MILITARIZE
MILITATING
MILITATION
MILITIAMAN
MILK
 FLOATS
MILK
 SHAKES
MILK
 TOOTHS
MILLENNIAL
MILLENNIUM
MILLEPEDES

MILLESIMAL
MILLIGRAMS
MILLILITRE
MILLIMETRE
MILLIONTHS
MILLIPEDES
MILLSTONES
MILLSTREAM
MILLWHEELS
MILLWORKER
MILLWRIGHT
MILOMETERS
MIMEOGRAPH
MINATORILY
MINDLESSLY
MIND
 READER
MINEFIELDS
MINERALIZE
MINERALOGY
MINERAL
 OIL
MINESTRONE
MINIATURES
MINIMALIST
MINIMIZING
MINISTERED
MINISTRANT
MINISTRIES
MINNESOTAN
MINORITIES
MINOR
 SUITS
MINSTRELSY
MINT
 JULEPS
MINUSCULAR
MINUTE
 HAND
MINUTENESS
MIRACIDIAL
MIRACIDIUM
MIRACULOUS
MIRTHFULLY
MISAPPLIED
MISBEHAVED
MISBEHAVER
MISCALLING
MISCARRIED
MISCASTING
MISCELLANY
MISCHANCES

MISCH
 METAL
MISCONDUCT
MISCOUNTED
MISCREANTS
MISERICORD
MISFORTUNE
MISGIVINGS
MISHANDLED
MISHEARING
MISJOINDER
MISJUDGING
MISLEADING
MISMANAGED
MISMANAGER
MISMATCHED
MISMATCHES
MISOGAMIST
MISOGYNIST
MISOGYNOUS
MISOLOGIST
MISPLACING
MISPRINTED
MISPRISION
MISQUOTING
MISREADING
MISSIONARY
MISSOURIAN
MISSPELLED
MISSTATING
MISSUPPOSE
MISTAKABLE
MISTAKABLY
MISTAKENLY
MISTRESSES
MISTRUSTED
MISTRUSTER
MITIGATING
MITIGATION
MITIGATIVE
MITTERRAND
MIXABILITY
MIXED
 GRILL
MIXOLYDIAN
MIZZENMAST
MOBILE
 HOME
MOBILIZING
MOBOCRATIC
MOCK-
 HEROIC

MODERATELY
MODERATING
MODERATION
MODERATORS
MODERNISMS
MODERNISTS
MODERNIZED
MODERNIZER
MODERNNESS
MODIFIABLE
MODISHNESS
MODULATING
MODULATION
MODULATIVE
MOGADISCIO
MOHAMMEDAN
MOISTENING
MOISTURIZE
MOLLIFYING
MOLLUSCOID
MOLYBDENUM
MONADISTIC
MONADOLOGY
MONANDROUS
MONANTHOUS
MONARCHIES
MONARCHISM
MONARCHIST
MONEGASQUE
MONETARISM
MONETARIST
MONEYBOXES
MONEYMAKER
MONEY
  ORDER
MONGRELISM
MONGRELIZE
MONILIFORM
MONITORIAL
MONITORING
MONKEY
  NUTS
MONOCARPIC
MONOCHROME
MONOCLINAL
MONOCLINIC
MONOCRATIC
MONOCYCLIC
MONOCYTOID
MONOECIOUS
MONOGAMIST

MONOGAMOUS
MONOGENOUS
MONOGRAPHS
MONOGYNIST
MONOGYNOUS
MONOHYBRID
MONOLITHIC
MONOLOGIST
MONOLOGUES
MONOMANIAC
MONOMEROUS
MONOPHOBIA
MONOPHOBIC
MONOPHONIC
MONOPLANES
MONOPLEGIA
MONOPLEGIC
MONOPODIAL
MONOPODIUM
MONOPOLIES
MONOPOLISM
MONOPOLIST
MONOPOLIZE
MONOPTEROS
MONOTHEISM
MONOTHEIST
MONOTONOUS
MONOVALENT
MONSIGNORS
MONSTRANCE
MONTE
  CARLO
MONTEGO
  BAY
MONTENEGRO
MONTEVIDEO
MONTGOMERY
MONTMARTRE
MONTPELIER
MONTSERRAT
MONUMENTAL
MONZONITIC
MOONFLOWER
MOONSCAPES
MOONSTONES
MOONSTRUCK
MOOT
  POINTS
MORALISTIC
MORALITIES
MORALIZERS

MORALIZING
MORATORIUM
MORAYSHIRE
MORBIDNESS
MORDACIOUS
MORDVINIAN
MORGANATIC
MOROSENESS
MORPHEUSES
MORPHINISM
MORPHOLOGY
MORTAL
  SINS
MORTGAGEES
MORTGAGING
MORTGAGORS
MORTICIANS
MORTIFYING
MORTUARIES
MOSQUITOES
MOSTAGANEM
MOTHERHOOD
MOTHERLESS
MOTHER'S
  BOY
MOTHER'S
  DAY
MOTHER-TO-
  BE
MOTHERWELL
MOTHERWORT
MOTIONLESS
MOTIVATING
MOTIVATION
MOTIVATIVE
MOTIVELESS
MOTONEURON
MOTORBIKES
MOTORBOATS
MOTORCADES
MOTORCYCLE
MOTORIZING
MOTOR
  LODGE
MOTS
  JUSTES
MOULDBOARD
MOULDERING
MOULDINESS
MOUNTEBANK
MOURNFULLY
MOUSETRAPS

MOUSSELINE
MOUSTACHES
MOUTH
  ORGAN
MOUTHPIECE
MOVABILITY
MOVIE
  STARS
MOVING
  VANS
MOZAMBIQUE
MOZZARELLA
MPUMALANGA
MUCKRAKERS
MUCKRAKING
MUDDLINGLY
MUDSKIPPER
MUDSLINGER
MUHAMMADAN
MUJAHEDDIN
MULBERRIES
MULIEBRITY
MULISHNESS
MULTIBIRTH
MULTIMEDIA
MULTIPLANE
MULTIPLIED
MULTIPLIER
MULTISTAGE
MULTITUDES
MUMBLINGLY
MUMBO
  JUMBO
MUMMIFYING
MUNIFICENT
MURPHY'S
  LAW
MUSCOVITES
MUSCULARLY
MUSHROOMED
MUSICAL
  BOX
MUSIC
  HALLS
MUSICOLOGY
MUSKETEERS
MUSKETRIES
MUSTACHIOS
MUSTARD
  GAS
MUTABILITY
MUTATIONAL

MUTILATING
MUTILATION
MUTILATIVE
MUTINOUSLY
MUTUAL
  FUND
MYASTHENIA
MYASTHENIC
MYCETOZOAN
MYCOLOGIST
MYCOPLASMA
MYCORRHIZA
MYCOSTATIN
MYOCARDIAL
MYOCARDIUM
MYOGRAPHIC
MYOPICALLY
MYRIAPODAN
MYRTACEOUS
MYSTAGOGIC
MYSTAGOGUE
MYSTERIOUS
MYSTICALLY
MYSTIFYING
MYTHICIZER
MYTHOMANIA
MYTHOPOEIA
MYTHOPOEIC
MYXOEDEMIC
MYXOMATOUS
MYXOMYCETE

N
NAIL-
  BITING
NAIRNSHIRE
NAMBY-
  PAMBY
NAMEPLATES
NANNY
  GOATS
NANOSECOND
NAPKIN
  RING
NAPOLEONIC
NARCISSISM
NARCISSIST
NARCOLEPSY
NARRATABLE
NARRATIONS
NARRATIVES

NARROW
  BOAT
NARROWNESS
NASTURTIUM
NATATIONAL
NATIONALLY
NATIONHOOD
NATIONWIDE
NATIVISTIC
NATIVITIES
NATTERJACK
NATURAL
  GAS
NATURALISM
NATURALIST
NATURALIZE
NATUROPATH
NAUGHTIEST
NAUSEATING
NAUSEATION
NAUSEOUSLY
NAUTICALLY
NAVIGATING
NAVIGATION
NAVIGATORS
NEAPOLITAN
NEAR
  MISSES
NEAR
  THINGS
NEBULOSITY
NEBULOUSLY
NECROLATRY
NECROMANCY
NECROPHOBE
NECROPOLIS
NEEDLEFISH
NEEDLESSLY
NEEDLEWORK
NE'ER-DO-
  WELL
NEGATIVELY
NEGATIVING
NEGATIVISM
NEGATIVIST
NEGLECTFUL
NEGLECTING
NEGLIGENCE
NEGLIGIBLE
NEGLIGIBLY
NEGOTIABLE
NEGOTIATED

NEGOTIATOR
NEIGHBOURS
NEMATOCYST
NEOLOGICAL
NEOLOGISMS
NEON
  LIGHTS
NEOPLASTIC
NEPENTHEAN
NEPHOGRAPH
NEPHOSCOPE
NEPHRALGIA
NEPHRALGIC
NEPHRIDIAL
NEPHRIDIUM
NEPHROTOMY
NEPOTISTIC
NETHERMOST
NETIQUETTE
NETTLE
  RASH
NETTLESOME
NETWORKING
NEURECTOMY
NEUROBLAST
NEUROCOELE
NEUROGENIC
NEUROLEMMA
NEUROPATHY
NEUROTOXIN
NEUTRALISM
NEUTRALIST
NEUTRALITY
NEUTRALIZE
NEUTROPHIL
NEVER-
  NEVER
NEW
  BEDFORD
NEW
  BRITAIN
NEW
  ENGLAND
NEWFANGLED
NEW
  IRELAND
NEW
  ORLEANS
NEWS
  AGENCY
NEWSAGENTS
NEWSCASTER

NEWSHOUNDS
NEWSLETTER
NEWSPAPERS
NEWSREADER
NEWSSHEETS
NEWSSTANDS
NEWSVENDOR
NEWSWORTHY
NEWTON'S
  LAW
NEW
  ZEALAND
NICARAGUAN
NICKELLING
NICKNAMING
NICOTINISM
NIDICOLOUS
NIDIFUGOUS
NIGHTCLUBS
NIGHTDRESS
NIGHTLIGHT
NIGHTMARES
NIGHTSHADE
NIGHT
  SHIFT
NIGHTSHIRT
NIGHTSTICK
NIGRESCENT
NIHILISTIC
NIMBLENESS
NINCOMPOOP
NINETEENTH
NINETIETHS
NINETY-
  NINE
NINGSIA
  HUI
NIPPLEWORT
NISSEN
  HUTS
NITPICKERS
NITPICKING
NITRIC
  ACID
NITROMETER
NO-
  ACCOUNTS
NOBEL
  PRIZE
NOBILITIES
NO-MAN'S-
  LAND

NOM DE
  PLUME
NOMINALISM
NOMINALIST
NOMINATING
NOMINATION
NOMINATIVE
NOMOGRAPHY
NOMOLOGIST
NOMOTHETIC
NONALIGNED
NONCHALANT
NONDRINKER
NONESUCHES
NONETHICAL
NONFACTUAL
NONFERROUS
NONFICTION
NONJOINDER
NONMEDICAL
NO-
  NONSENSE
NONPAREILS
NONPAYMENT
NONPLUSSED
NONSMOKERS
NONSMOKING
NONSTARTER
NONSTATIVE
NON-
  STRIKER
NONTYPICAL
NONVIOLENT
NORMALIZED
NORRKOPING
NORTHBOUND
NORTHERNER
NORTH
  POLES
NORTHWARDS
NOSEBLEEDS
NOSEDIVING
NOSOGRAPHY
NOSOLOGIST
NOSTOLOGIC
NOSY
  PARKER
NOTABILITY
NOTARIZING
NOTATIONAL
NOTEWORTHY
NOTICEABLE

NOTICEABLY
NOTIFIABLE
NOTTINGHAM
NOUAKCHOTT
NOURISHING
NOVACULITE
NOVA
  SCOTIA
NOVELETTES
NOVELISTIC
NOVITIATES
NUCLEATION
NUCLEONICS
NUCLEOSIDE
NUCLEOTIDE
NUDIBRANCH
NULLIFYING
NUMBERLESS
NUMBSKULLS
NUMERATION
NUMERATIVE
NUMERATORS
NUMEROLOGY
NUMEROUSLY
NUMISMATIC
NUMMULITIC
NUNCIATURE
NURSELINGS
NURSEMAIDS
NURSERYMAN
NURSERYMEN
NURTURABLE
NUTATIONAL
NUTCRACKER
NUTRITIOUS
NYCTALOPIA
NYCTINASTY
NYMPHOLEPT

O

OAFISHNESS
OAST
  HOUSES
OBDURATELY
OBEDIENTLY
OBEISANCES
OBELISKOID
OBERHAUSEN
OBFUSCATED
OBITUARIES
OBITUARIST

OBJECTIONS
OBJECTIVES
OBJETS
 DART
OBJETS
 D'ART
OBJURGATOR
OBLIGATING
OBLIGATION
OBLIGATIVE
OBLIGATORY
OBLIGINGLY
OBLITERATE
OBSEQUIOUS
OBSERVABLE
OBSERVABLY
OBSERVANCE
OBSESSIONS
OBSESSIVES
OBSTETRICS
OBSTRUCTED
OBSTRUCTER
OBTAINABLE
OBTAINMENT
OBTUSENESS
OBVOLUTION
OBVOLUTIVE
OCCASIONAL
OCCASIONED
OCCIDENTAL
OCCUPATION
OCCURRENCE
OCEANARIUM
OCEANGOING
OCEANOLOGY
OCELLATION
OCHLOCRACY
OCTAHEDRAL
OCTAHEDRON
OCTAMEROUS
OCTANGULAR
OCTAVALENT
OCTODECIMO
OCULOMOTOR
ODALISQUES
ODD-
 PINNATE
ODIOUSNESS
ODONTALGIA
ODONTALGIC
ODONTOLOGY

OEDEMATOUS
OENOLOGIST
OESOPHAGUS
OESTRADIOL
OFFENSIVES
OFFICE
 BOYS
OFFICIALLY
OFFICIATED
OFFICIATOR
OFF-
 LICENCE
OFF-
 LOADING
OFF-
 PUTTING
OFFSETTING
OFF THE
 CUFF
OFF THE
 HOOK
OFF-THE-
 WALL
OIL-
 BEARING
OIL
 TANKERS
OLDE
 WORLDE
OLD
 MAIDISH
OLD
 MASTERS
OLD
 SCHOOLS
OLD
 SCRATCH
OLEAGINOUS
OLEOGRAPHY
OLIGARCHIC
OLIGOCLASE
OLIGOPSONY
OLIGURETIC
OLIVACEOUS
OLIVE
 GREEN
OMMATIDIAL
OMMATIDIUM
OMNIPOTENT
OMNISCIENT
OMNIVOROUS
ONCOLOGIST

ONE
 ANOTHER
ONE-MAN
 BAND
ONE-
 SIDEDLY
ONOMASTICS
ONSLAUGHTS
ON THE
 ALERT
ON THE
 CARDS
ON THE
 ROCKS
ON THE
 ROPES
ON THE
 SPREE
OOPHORITIC
OOPHORITIS
OOPS-A-
 DAISY
OPALESCENT
OPAQUENESS
OPEN-
 HANDED
OPEN
 LETTER
OPEN
 MARKET
OPEN-
 MINDED
OPEN
 SEASON
OPEN
 SECRET
OPEN
 SESAME
OPERA
 BUFFA
OPERA
 HOUSE
OPERATIONS
OPERATIVES
OPERETTIST
OPHICLEIDE
OPHTHALMIA
OPHTHALMIC
OPPILATION
OPPOSINGLY
OPPOSITION
OPPRESSING
OPPRESSION

OPPRESSIVE
OPPRESSORS
OPPROBRIUM
OPTICAL
 ART
OPTIMISTIC
OPTIMIZING
OPTIONALLY
OPTOMETRIC
ORANGEWOOD
ORANGUTANG
ORATORICAL
ORCHESTRAL
ORCHESTRAS
ORDER
 PAPER
ORDINANCES
ORDINARILY
ORDINATION
ORDONNANCE
ORDOVICIAN
ORGANICISM
ORGANICIST
ORGANISMAL
ORGANIZERS
ORGANIZING
ORGANOLOGY
ORIENTATED
ORIGINALLY
ORIGINATED
ORIGINATOR
ORIMULSION
ORNAMENTAL
ORNAMENTED
ORNATENESS
ORNITHOPOD
ORNITHOSIS
OROGRAPHER
OROGRAPHIC
OROLOGICAL
ORPHANAGES
ORTHOCLASE
ORTHOGENIC
ORTHOGONAL
OSCILLATED
OSCILLATOR
OSCULATION
OSCULATORY
OSMIRIDIUM
OSMOMETRIC
OSSIFEROUS

OSTENSIBLE
OSTENSIBLY
OSTEOBLAST
OSTEOCLAST
OSTEOPATHS
OSTEOPATHY
OSTEOPHYTE
OSTRACIZED
OSTRACIZER
OSTRACODAN
OTOLOGICAL
OUANANICHE
OUBLIETTES
OUIJA
 BOARD
OUTBALANCE
OUTBIDDING
OUTBRAVING
OUTCLASSED
OUTFIELDER
OUTFITTERS
OUTFITTING
OUTFLANKED
OUTGENERAL
OUTGROWING
OUTGROWTHS
OUT-
 HERODED
OUTLANDISH
OUTLASTING
OUT OF
 COURT
OUT OF
 DOORS
OUT OF
 ORDER
OUT OF
 PLACE
OUT OF
 SIGHT
OUTPATIENT
OUTPERFORM
OUTPLAYING
OUTPOINTED
OUTPOURING
OUTRAGEOUS
OUTRANKING
OUTRIGGERS
OUTRIVALED
OUTRUNNING
OUTSELLING
OUTSHINING

OUTSMARTED
OUTSTARING
OUTSTATION
OUTSTAYING
OUTSTRETCH
OUTSWINGER
OUTTALKING
OUTWEIGHED
OUTWITTING
OUTWORKERS
OVARIOTOMY
OVERACTING
OVERACTIVE
OVERARCHED
OVERBOOKED
OVERBURDEN
OVERCHARGE
OVERCOMING
OVERDOSAGE
OVERDOSING
OVERDRAFTS
OVEREXPOSE
OVERFLIGHT
OVERFLOWED
OVERFLYING
OVERHAULED
OVERIJSSEL
OVERLAPPED
OVERLAYING
OVERLOADED
OVERLOOKED
OVERMANNED
OVERMASTER
OVERMATTER
OVERPASSES
OVERPLAYED
OVERRATING
OVERRIDDEN
OVERRIDING
OVERRULING
OVERSEEING
OVERSHADOW
OVERSIGHTS
OVERSPILLS
OVERSPREAD
OVERSTATED
OVERSTAYED
OVERSTRUNG
OVERTAXING
OVER THE
  TOP

OVERTHROWN
OVERTHROWS
OVERTHRUST
OVERTOPPED
OVERTURNED
OVERWEIGHT
OVERWORKED
OVIPOSITOR
OVULATIONS
OXIDIMETRY
OXYCEPHALY
OXYGENATED
OXYGENIZER
OXYGEN
  MASK
OXYGEN
  TENT
OYSTER
  BEDS
OZONOLYSIS

P
PACE
  BOWLER
PACEMAKERS
PACHYDERMS
PACIFIC
  RIM
PACK
  ANIMAL
PACKSADDLE
PACKTHREAD
PADDLEFISH
PADLOCKING
PAEDERASTS
PAEDERASTY
PAEDIATRIC
PAGANISTIC
PAGINATION
PAILLASSES
PAINKILLER
PAINLESSLY
PAINTBRUSH
PAKISTANIS
PALAEOCENE
PALAEOGENE
PALAEOLITH
PALAEOZOIC
PALANQUINS
PALATALIZE
PALATIALLY
PALATINATE

PALEACEOUS
PALIMPSEST
PALINDROME
PALLBEARER
PALLIASSES
PALLIATING
PALLIATION
PALLIATIVE
PALLIDNESS
PALMACEOUS
PALMETTOES
PALM
  SUNDAY
PALPATIONS
PALPEBRATE
PALPITATED
PALSY-
  WALSY
PALTRINESS
PALYNOLOGY
PANAMA
  CITY
PANAMANIAN
PAN-
  ARABISM
PANCAKE
  DAY
PANCREASES
PANCREATIC
PANCREATIN
PANEGYRICS
PANEGYRIST
PANEGYRIZE
PANELLISTS
PANGENESIS
PANGENETIC
PANHANDLED
PANHANDLER
PANHANDLES
PANICULATE
PANJANDRUM
PANTALOONS
PANTHEISTS
PANTOGRAPH
PANTOMIMES
PANTOMIMIC
PAPANDREOU
PAPAVERINE
PAPERBACKS
PAPERBOARD
PAPER
  CHASE

PAPER
  CLIPS
PAPERINESS
PAPER
  KNIFE
PAPER
  MONEY
PAPER
  TIGER
PAPISTICAL
PARABIOSIS
PARABIOTIC
PARABOLIST
PARABOLIZE
PARABOLOID
PARACHUTED
PARACHUTES
PARADIDDLE
PARAGRAPHS
PARAGUAYAN
PARALLELED
PARALOGISM
PARALOGIST
PARALYSING
PARALYTICS
PARAMARIBO
PARAMECIUM
PARAMEDICS
PARAMETERS
PARAMETRIC
PARAMNESIA
PARANOIACS
PARANORMAL
PARAPHRASE
PARAPHYSIS
PARAPLEGIA
PARAPLEGIC
PARAPODIUM
PARAPRAXIS
PARASELENE
PARASITISM
PARASITIZE
PARASITOID
PARASTICHY
PARATACTIC
PARATROOPS
PARBOILING
PARCELLING
PARCEL
  POST
PARCHMENTS
PARDONABLE

PARDONABLY
PARENCHYMA
PARENTERAL
PARENTHOOD
PARI-
  MUTUEL
PARISH-
  PUMP
PARKING
  LOT
PARK
  KEEPER
PARLIAMENT
PARLOR
  CARS
PARONYMOUS
PAROXYSMAL
PARRICIDAL
PARRICIDES
PARROTFISH
PARSONAGES
PARTIALITY
PARTICIPLE
PARTICULAR
PARTITIONS
PARTITIVES
PARTNERING
PARTRIDGES
PARTURIENT
PARTY
  LINES
PARTY
  PIECE
PARTY
  WALLS
PARVOVIRUS
PASQUINADE
PASSAGEWAY
PASSENGERS
PASSIONATE
PASTEBOARD
PASTELLIST
PASTEURISM
PASTEURIZE
PAST
  MASTER
PASTY-
  FACED
PATCHINESS
PATCHWORKS
PATENTABLE
PATERNALLY

PATHFINDER
PATHOGENIC
PATISSERIE
PATRIARCHS
PATRIARCHY
PATRICIANS
PATRICIATE
PATRICIDAL
PATRICIDES
PATRILOCAL
PATRIOTISM
PATROL
  CARS
PATROLLING
PATRONIZED
PATRONIZER
PATRONYMIC
PATTERNING
PAWNBROKER
PAYMASTERS
PAY
  PACKETS
PAY-PER-
  VIEW
PAY
  STATION
PEACE
  CORPS
PEACEFULLY
PEACEMAKER
PEACE
  PIPES
PEACHINESS
PEACH
  MELBA
PEARL
  DIVER
PEARLINESS
PEAR-
  SHAPED
PEASHOOTER
PEA
  SHOOTER
PEA
  SOUPERS
PEBBLEDASH
PECCADILLO
PECTIZABLE
PECULATING
PECULATION
PECULIARLY
PEDAGOGISM

PEDAGOGUES
PEDANTRIES
PEDERASTIC
PEDESTRIAN
PEDIATRICS
PEDICULATE
PEDICULOUS
PEDICURIST
PEDIMENTAL
PEDOLOGIST
PEEPING
  TOM
PEGMATITIC
PEJORATION
PEJORATIVE
PELLAGROUS
PELLICULAR
PELLUCIDLY
PENALIZING
PENCILLING
PENDENTIVE
PENDERECKI
PENETRABLE
PENETRALIA
PENETRANCE
PENETRATED
PENETRATOR
PEN
  FRIENDS
PENICILLIN
PENINSULAR
PENINSULAS
PENITENTLY
PENMANSHIP
PENNINE
  WAY
PENNY
  BLACK
PENNYCRESS
PENNYROYAL
PENNYWORTH
PENOLOGIST
PEN
  PUSHERS
PENSIONARY
PENSIONERS
PENSIONING
PENTAGONAL
PENTAGRAMS
PENTAMETER
PENTAQUINE
PENTASTICH

PENTATEUCH
PENTATHLON
PENTHOUSES
PENTIMENTO
PENTSTEMON
PEPPERCORN
PEPPER
  MILL
PEPPERMINT
PEPPER
  POTS
PEPPERWORT
PEPSINOGEN
PEPTIZABLE
PEPTONIZER
PERACIDITY
PERCEIVING
PERCENTAGE
PERCENTILE
PERCEPTION
PERCEPTIVE
PERCEPTUAL
PERCIPIENT
PERCOLATED
PERCOLATOR
PERCUSSION
PERCUSSIVE
PEREMPTORY
PERENNIALS
PERFECTING
PERFECTION
PERFECTIVE
PERFIDIOUS
PERFOLIATE
PERFORABLE
PERFORATED
PERFORATOR
PERFORMERS
PERFORMING
PERICLINAL
PERICYCLIC
PERIDERMAL
PERIDOTITE
PERIGYNOUS
PERIHELION
PERILOUSLY
PERIMETERS
PERIMETRIC
PERIMYSIUM
PERIODICAL
PERIOSTEUM

PERIPETEIA
PERIPHERAL
PERIPHYTON
PERIPTERAL
PERISARCAL
PERISCOPES
PERISCOPIC
PERISHABLE
PERISTOMAL
PERISTYLAR
PERISTYLES
PERITONEAL
PERITONEUM
PERITRICHA
PERIWINKLE
PERMAFROST
PERMANENCE
PERMANENCY
PERMANENTS
PERMEATING
PERMEATION
PERMEATIVE
PERMETHRIN
PERMISSION
PERMISSIVE
PERMITTING
PERNAMBUCO
PERNICIOUS
PERNICKETY
PERORATION
PEROXIDASE
PERPETRATE
PERPETUATE
PERPETUITY
PERPLEXING
PERPLEXITY
PERQUISITE
PERSECUTED
PERSECUTOR
PERSEVERED
PERSIAN
  CAT
PERSIENNES
PERSIFLAGE
PERSIMMONS
PERSISTENT
PERSISTING
PERSONABLE
PERSONABLY
PERSONAGES
PERSONALLY

PERSONALTY
PERSONATOR
PERSPIRING
PERSUADING
PERSUASION
PERSUASIVE
PERTAINING
PERTHSHIRE
PERTINENCE
PERTURBING
PERVERSELY
PERVERSION
PERVERSITY
PERVERTING
PESCADORES
PESSIMISTS
PESTICIDAL
PESTICIDES
PESTILENCE
PETERSBURG
PETIT
  FOURS
PETITIONED
PETITIONER
PETIT
  POINT
PETITS
  POIS
PETRIFYING
PETROGLYPH
PETROLATUM
PETROPOLIS
PETTICOATS
PETULANTLY
PHAGOCYTES
PHAGOCYTIC
PHAGOMANIA
PHALANGEAL
PHALANGIST
PHALLICISM
PHALLICIST
PHANEROGAM
PHANTASIES
PHANTASMAL
PHARISAISM
PHARMACIES
PHARMACIST
PHARYNGEAL
PHELLODERM
PHENACAINE
PHENACETIN

PHENFORMIN
PHENOCRYST
PHENOMENAL
PHENOMENON
PHENOTYPIC
PHILATELIC
PHILIPPICS
PHILIPPINE
PHILISTINE
PHILOSOPHY
PHLEBOTOMY
PHLEGMATIC
PHLOGISTIC
PHLOGISTON
PHLOGOPITE
PHOCOMELIA
PHOENICIAN
PHONE
  BOOKS
PHONE
  BOXES
PHONEYNESS
PHONEY
  WARS
PHONICALLY
PHONOGRAPH
PHONOLITIC
PHONOMETER
PHONOSCOPE
PHONOTYPIC
PHOSGENITE
PHOSPHATES
PHOSPHATIC
PHOSPHORIC
PHOSPHORUS
PHOTOFLOOD
PHOTOGENIC
PHOTOGRAPH
PHOTOLYSIS
PHOTOLYTIC
PHOTOMETER
PHOTOMETRY
PHOTOMURAL
PHOTONASTY
PHOTONOVEL
PHOTOPHILY
PHOTOPHORE
PHOTOSTATS
PHOTOTAXIS
PHOTOTONIC
PHOTOTONUS

PHOTOTYPIC
PHRASEBOOK
PHRENOLOGY
PHTHISICAL
PHYLACTERY
PHYLLODIAL
PHYLLOXERA
PHYLOGENIC
PHYSIATRIC
PHYSICALLY
PHYSICIANS
PHYSICISTS
PHYSIOCRAT
PHYSIOLOGY
PHYTOGENIC
PHYTOPHAGY
PHYTOTOXIN
PIANISSIMO
PIANOFORTE
PICARESQUE
PICCADILLY
PICCALILLI
PICCANINNY
PICHICIEGO
PICKPOCKET
PICNICKERS
PICNICKING
PICRIC
  ACID
PICROTOXIC
PICROTOXIN
PICTOGRAPH
PIED-A-
  TERRE
PIERCINGLY
PIGEONHOLE
PIGEON-
  TOED
PIGGYBACKS
PIGGYBANKS
PIGMENTARY
PIGSTICKER
PIKESTAFFS
PILE
  DRIVER
PILGRIMAGE
PILIFEROUS
PILLORYING
PILLOWCASE
PILLOW
  TALK

PILOT
  LIGHT
PIMPERNELS
PIMPLINESS
PINA
  COLADA
PINCERLIKE
PINCHPENNY
PINCUSHION
PINEAPPLES
PINE
  MARTEN
PINFEATHER
PINGUIDITY
PINNATIFID
PINNATIPED
PINPOINTED
PINSTRIPED
PINSTRIPES
PIONEERING
PIPED
  MUSIC
PIPE
  DREAMS
PIPERAZINE
PIPERIDINE
PIPSISSEWA
PIPSQUEAKS
PIROUETTED
PIROUETTES
PISTACHIOS
PISTILLATE
PISTON
  RING
PITCH-
  BLACK
PITCHFORKS
PITCHINESS
PITCHSTONE
PITH
  HELMET
PITILESSLY
PITOT
  TUBES
PITTSBURGH
PITYRIASIS
PLACARDING
PLACE
  CARDS
PLACEMENTS
PLAGIARISM
PLAGIARIST

PLAGIARIZE
PLAINCHANT
PLAIN
  FLOUR
PLAINTIFFS
PLANCHETTE
PLANETARIA
PLANE
  TREES
PLANGENTLY
PLANIMETER
PLANIMETRY
PLANK-
  SHEER
PLANKTONIC
PLANOMETER
PLANOMETRY
PLANTATION
PLASMAGENE
PLASMODIUM
PLASMOLYSE
PLASMOSOME
PLASTERERS
PLASTERING
PLASTIC
  ART
PLASTICINE
PLASTICITY
PLASTICIZE
PLAT DU
  JOUR
PLATE
  GLASS
PLATELAYER
PLATE
  RACKS
PLATITUDES
PLATTELAND
PLATYPUSES
PLAY-
  ACTING
PLAYFELLOW
PLAYGROUND
PLAYGROUPS
PLAYHOUSES
PLAYSCHOOL
PLAYTHINGS
PLAYWRIGHT
PLEASANTER
PLEASANTLY
PLEASANTRY
PLEASINGLY

PLEBISCITE
PLEIOTROPY
PLEONASTIC
PLESIOSAUR
PLEURODONT
PLEUROTOMY
PLEXIGLASS
PLIABILITY
PLODDINGLY
PLOUGHBOYS
PLOUGHLAND
PLUCKINESS
PLUMB
  LINES
PLUMMETING
PLUNDERERS
PLUNDERING
PLUNDEROUS
PLUPERFECT
PLURALISTS
PLURALIZER
PLUTOCRACY
PLUTOCRATS
PNEUMATICS
POCKETABLE
POCKETBOOK
POCKETFULS
POCKMARKED
PODIATRIST
POETASTERS
POETICALLY
POGO
  STICKS
POIGNANTLY
POINSETTIA
POINT-
  BLANK
POKER-
  FACED
POLAR
  BEARS
POLARITIES
POLARIZING
POLEMICIST
POLES
  APART
POLE
  VAULTS
POLITBUROS
POLITENESS
POLITICIAN
POLITICIZE

POLLARDING
POLLINATED
POLLINATOR
POLLINOSIS
POLLUTANTS
POLONAISES
POLYANTHUS
POLYATOMIC
POLYBASITE
POLYCARPIC
POLYCHAETE
POLYCHROME
POLYCHROMY
POLYCLINIC
POLYCOTTON
POLYCYCLIC
POLYDACTYL
POLYDIPSIA
POLYDIPSIC
POLYGAMIST
POLYGAMOUS
POLYGRAPHS
POLYGYNIST
POLYGYNOUS
POLYHEDRAL
POLYHEDRON
POLYMATHIC
POLYMERASE
POLYMERISM
POLYMERIZE
POLYMEROUS
POLYNESIAN
POLYNOMIAL
POLYPHAGIA
POLYPHONIC
POLYPLOIDY
POLYPODOUS
POLYRHYTHM
POLYSEMOUS
POLYTHEISM
POLYTHEIST
POLYVALENT
POMERANIAN
POMIFEROUS
POMOLOGIST
PONDERABLE
POND-
  SKATER
PONTEFRACT
PONTEVEDRA
PONTIFICAL

PONTYPRIDD
POOH-
  POOHED
POOL
  MALEBO
POORHOUSES
POOR
  WHITES
POPE'S
  NOSES
POPISHNESS
POPULARITY
POPULARIZE
POPULATING
POPULATION
PORCUPINES
PORIFEROUS
PORK
  BARREL
PORNOCRACY
POROUSNESS
PORPHYROID
PORTAMENTO
PORTCULLIS
PORTENDING
PORTENTOUS
PORTFOLIOS
PORT-
  GENTIL
PORTIONING
PORTLAOISE
PORTLINESS
PORTOBELLO
PORT OF
  CALL
PORTRAYALS
PORTRAYING
PORTSMOUTH
PORT
  TALBOT
PORTUGUESE
POSITIONAL
POSITIONED
POSITIVELY
POSITIVISM
POSITIVIST
POSSESSING
POSSESSION
POSSESSIVE
POSSESSORS
POSSESSORY

POST-
  BELLUM
POST-
  CYCLIC
POSTDATING
POSTERIORS
POSTHUMOUS
POSTILIONS
POSTLIMINY
POSTMARKED
POSTMASTER
POSTMORTEM
POST
  OFFICE
POSTPARTUM
POSTPONING
POSTSCRIPT
POSTULANCY
POSTULANTS
POSTULATED
POSTULATES
POSTULATOR
POTABILITY
POTATO
  CHIP
POTBELLIED
POTBELLIES
POTBOILERS
POTENTATES
POTENTIATE
POTENTILLA
POTENTNESS
POTHUNTERS
POTPOURRIS
POULTERERS
POULTRYMAN
POURPARLER
POWDER
  KEGS
POWDER
  PUFF
POWDER
  ROOM
POWER
  BASES
POWERBOATS
POWER
  DIVES
POWERFULLY
POWERHOUSE
POWER
  PLANT

POWER
  POINT
POZZUOLANA
PRACTICALS
PRACTISING
PRAESIDIUM
PRAGMATICS
PRAGMATISM
PRAGMATIST
PRAIRIE
  DOG
PRANCINGLY
PRANKSTERS
PRASELENIC
PRATINCOLE
PRAYER
  RUGS
PREACHMENT
PREADAMITE
PREAMBULAR
PREARRANGE
PREBENDARY
PRECARIOUS
PRECAUTION
PRECEDENCE
PRECEDENTS
PRECENTORS
PRECEPTIVE
PRECESSION
PRECIOSITY
PRECIOUSLY
PRECIPICED
PRECIPICES
PRECIPITIN
PRECISIONS
PRECLUDING
PRECLUSION
PRECLUSIVE
PRECOCIOUS
PRECONCERT
PRECOOKING
PRECURSORS
PRECURSORY
PREDACIOUS
PREDECEASE
PREDESTINE
PREDICABLE
PREDICATED
PREDICATES
PREDICTING
PREDICTION

PREDICTIVE
PREDISPOSE
PRE-
  EMINENT
PRE-
  EMPTING
PRE-
  EMPTION
PRE-
  EMPTIVE
PRE-
  EMPTORY
PREEXISTED
PREFECTURE
PREFERABLE
PREFERABLY
PREFERENCE
PREFERMENT
PREFERRING
PREFIGURED
PREFRONTAL
PREGLACIAL
PREGNANTLY
PREHEATING
PREHENSILE
PREHENSION
PREHISTORY
PREHOMINID
PREJUDGING
PREJUDICED
PREJUDICES
PRELEXICAL
PREMARITAL
PREMAXILLA
PREMEDICAL
PRENATALLY
PRENOMINAL
PREPACKAGE
PREPACKING
PREPAREDLY
PREPAYABLE
PREPAYMENT
PREPOSSESS
PREPOTENCY
PREP
  SCHOOL
PRESAGEFUL
PRESBYOPIA
PRESBYOPIC
PRESBYTERY
PRESCHOOLS
PRESCIENCE

PRESCRIBED
PRESCRIBER
PRESCRIPTS
PRESENT
 DAY
PRESENT-
 DAY
PRESENTERS
PRESENTING
PRESERVERS
PRESERVING
PRESETTING
PRESIDENCY
PRESIDENTS
PRESIDIUMS
PRESIGNIFY
PRESS
 AGENT
PRESS
 BARON
PRESS
 BOXES
PRESSGANGS
PRESSINGLY
PRESS-
 STUDS
PRESSURING
PRESSURIZE
PRESUMABLE
PRESUMABLY
PRESUMEDLY
PRESUPPOSE
PRETENDERS
PRETENDING
PRETENSION
PRETTIFIED
PRETTINESS
PREVAILING
PREVALENCE
PREVENIENT
PREVENTING
PREVENTION
PREVENTIVE
PREVIEWING
PREVIOUSLY
PREVISIONS
PREVOCALIC
PRICKLIEST
PRIEST-
 HOLE
PRIESTHOOD
PRIESTLIER

PRIGGISHLY
PRIMA
 DONNA
PRIMA
 FACIE
PRIMAQUINE
PRIME
 MOVER
PRIME
 RATES
PRIMITIVES
PRIMORDIAL
PRIMORDIUM
PRINCEDOMS
PRINCELING
PRINCESSES
PRINCIPALS
PRINCIPIUM
PRINCIPLED
PRINCIPLES
PRINTMAKER
PRIORITIES
PRIORITIZE
PRISMATOID
PRISMOIDAL
PRISON
 CAMP
PRISON
 GATE
PRISSINESS
PRIVATEERS
PRIVATIONS
PRIVATIZED
PRIVILEGED
PRIVILEGES
PRIVY
 PURSE
PRIZEFIGHT
PROCAMBIAL
PROCAMBIUM
PROCEDURAL
PROCEDURES
PROCEEDING
PROCESSING
PROCESSION
PROCESSORS
PROCLAIMED
PROCLIVITY
PROCONSULS
PROCREATED
PROCREATOR
PROCRYPTIC

PROCTOLOGY
PROCTORIAL
PROCUMBENT
PROCURATOR
PRODIGALLY
PRODIGIOUS
PRODUCIBLE
PRODUCTION
PRODUCTIVE
PROFESSING
PROFESSION
PROFESSORS
PROFFERING
PROFICIENT
PROFITABLE
PROFITABLY
PROFITEERS
PROFITLESS
PROFLIGACY
PROFLIGATE
PROFOUNDLY
PROFUNDITY
PROGENITOR
PROGLOTTIS
PROGNOSTIC
PROGRAMERS
PROGRAMING
PROGRAMMED
PROGRAMMER
PROGRAMMES
PROGRESSED
PROGRESSES
PROHIBITED
PROHIBITER
PROJECTILE
PROJECTING
PROJECTION
PROJECTIVE
PROJECTORS
PROKARYOTE
PROLAPSING
PROLOCUTOR
PROLONGING
PROMENADED
PROMENADER
PROMENADES
PROMETHIUM
PROMINENCE
PROMISSORY
PROMONTORY
PROMOTABLE

PROMOTIONS
PROMPTBOOK
PROMPTNESS
PROMULGATE
PRONEPHRIC
PRONEPHROS
PRONOMINAL
PRONOUNCED
PRONOUNCER
PRONUCLEAR
PRONUCLEUS
PRO-
 OESTRUS
PROPAGABLE
PROPAGANDA
PROPAGATED
PROPAGATOR
PROPELLANT
PROPELLENT
PROPELLERS
PROPELLING
PROPENSITY
PROPERNESS
PROPER
 NOUN
PROPERTIED
PROPERTIES
PROPHECIES
PROPHESIER
PROPHESIED
PROPHESIES
PROPIONATE
PROPITIATE
PROPITIOUS
PROPONENTS
PROPORTION
PROPOSABLE
PROPOSITUS
PROPOUNDED
PROPOUNDER
PROPRIETOR
PROPULSION
PROPULSIVE
PROPYLAEUM
PROROGUING
PROSCENIUM
PROSCRIBED
PROSECUTED
PROSECUTOR
PROSELYTES
PROSELYTIC

PROSPECTED
PROSPECTOR
PROSPECTUS
PROSPERING
PROSPERITY
PROSPEROUS
PROSTHESIS
PROSTHETIC
PROSTITUTE
PROSTOMIUM
PROSTRATED
PROTANOPIA
PROTANOPIC
PROTECTING
PROTECTION
PROTECTIVE
PROTECTORS
PROTECTORY
PROTEINASE
PRO
 TEMPORE
PROTESTANT
PROTESTERS
PROTHALLIC
PROTHALLUS
PROTOCTIST
PROTOHUMAN
PROTONEMAL
PROTOPATHY
PROTOPLASM
PROTOPLAST
PROTOSTELE
PROTOTYPAL
PROTOTYPES
PROTOXYLEM
PROTOZOANS
PROTRACTED
PROTRACTOR
PROTRUDENT
PROTRUDING
PROTRUSILE
PROTRUSION
PROTRUSIVE
PROVENANCE
PROVENCALE
PROVERBIAL
PROVIDENCE
PROVINCIAL
PROVISIONS
PROVITAMIN
PRUDENTIAL

PRURIENTLY
PSALMODIST
PSALTERIES
PSALTERIUM
PSEPHOLOGY
PSESPHITIC
PSEUDOCARP
PSEUDONYMS
PSILOCYBIN
PSITTACINE
PSITTACISM
PSYCHIATRY
PSYCHOLOGY
PSYCHOPATH
PSYCHOTICS
PTOLEMAIST
PUB-
  CRAWLED
PUBERULENT
PUBESCENCE
PUBLIC
  BARS
PUBLICISTS
PUBLICIZED
PUBLISHERS
PUBLISHING
PUERPERIUM
PUERTO
  RICO
PUGILISTIC
PUGNACIOUS
PUISSANCES
PULLULATED
PULSATIONS
PULSIMETER
PULVERABLE
PULVERIZED
PULVERIZER
PUMMELLING
PUNCH
  BALLS
PUNCHBOARD
PUNCH
  BOWLS
PUNCH-
  DRUNK
PUNCHINESS
PUNCH
  LINES
PUNCTATION
PUNCTILIOS
PUNCTUALLY

PUNCTUATED
PUNCTUATOR
PUNCTURING
PUNISHABLE
PUNISHMENT
PUNITIVELY
PUPIPAROUS
PUPPETEERS
PURCHASERS
PURCHASING
PURGATIVES
PURITANISM
PURLOINING
PURPLENESS
PURPORTING
PURPOSEFUL
PURSUANCES
PURSUIVANT
PURVEYANCE
PUSH-
  BUTTON
PUSHCHAIRS
PUT A STOP
  TO
PUTREFYING
PUTRESCENT
PUTRESCINE
PUZZLEMENT
PUZZLINGLY
PYCNOMETER
PYOGENESIS
PYORRHOEAL
PYRACANTHA
PYRETHROID
PYRIDOXINE
PYRIMIDINE
PYROGALLIC
PYROGALLOL
PYROGRAPHY
PYROLUSITE
PYROMANCER
PYROMANIAC
PYROMANTIC
PYROMETRIC
PYROPHORIC
PYROSTATIC
PYROXENITE
PYRRHOTITE
PYTHAGORAS

Q
QARAGHANDY
QUADRANGLE
QUADRANTAL
QUADRATICS
QUADRATURE
QUADRICEPS
QUADRILLES
QUADRISECT
QUADRIVIAL
QUADRUPEDS
QUADRUPLED
QUADRUPLET
QUADRUPLEX
QUAINTNESS
QUALIFIERS
QUALIFYING
QUANDARIES
QUANTIFIED
QUANTIFIER
QUANTITIES
QUARANTINE
QUARRELING
QUARRELLED
QUARRELLER
QUARTERAGE
QUARTER
  DAY
QUARTERING
QUARTERSAW
QUATERNARY
QUATERNION
QUATREFOIL
QUEASINESS
QUEENSLAND
QUENCHABLE
QUESTINGLY
QUESTIONED
QUESTIONER
QUEZON
  CITY
QUICKENING
QUICKSANDS
QUICKSTEPS
QUID PRO
  QUO
QUIESCENCE
QUIETENING
QUINTUPLET
QUIRKINESS
QUITTANCES

QUIZMASTER
QUONSET
  HUT
QUOTATIONS

R
RABBINICAL
RABBITFISH
RABBITTING
RACECOURSE
RACEHORSES
RACETRACKS
RACHMANISM
RACIALISTS
RACKETEERS
RACK-
  RENTER
RACONTEURS
RADARSCOPE
RADIATIONS
RADICALISM
RADIO
  ALARM
RADIOGENIC
RADIOGRAMS
RADIOGRAPH
RADIOLYSIS
RADIOMETER
RADIOMETRY
RADIOPAQUE
RADIOPHONY
RADIOSCOPE
RADIOSCOPY
RADIOSONDE
RADIOTOXIC
RAFSANJANI
RAGAMUFFIN
RAGGEDNESS
RAILROADED
RAIN
  CHECKS
RAIN
  FOREST
RAIN
  GAUGES
RAINMAKING
RAINSTORMS
RAISE A
  DUST
RAJYA
  SABHA
RAKISHNESS

RAMPAGEOUS
RAMSHACKLE
RANCH
  HOUSE
RANCIDNESS
RANDOMNESS
RANSACKING
RANUNCULUS
RAPPORTEUR
RARE
  EARTHS
RAREFIABLE
RATABILITY
RAT-A-TAT-
  TAT
RATE-
  CAPPED
RATIFIABLE
RATIONALES
RATIONALLY
RAT-
  RUNNING
RATTLETRAP
RAUNCHIEST
RAVAGEMENT
RAVENOUSLY
RAVISHMENT
RAWALPINDI
RAWINSONDE
RAZZMATAZZ
REACTIONAL
REACTIVATE
REACTIVELY
REACTIVITY
READERSHIP
READJUSTED
READJUSTER
READY
  MONEY
REAFFIRMED
REAFFOREST
REAL
  ESTATE
REALIGNING
REALIZABLE
REALIZABLY
REALLOCATE
REANIMATED
REAPPEARED
REAPPRAISE
REARGUARDS
REARMAMENT

REARRANGED	RE-	REFEREEING	REGULATING	REMINISCED
REARRANGER	COVERING	REFERENCER	REGULATION	REMISSIBLE
REASONABLE	RECREATING	REFERENCES	REGULATIVE	REMISSIONS
REASONABLY	RECREATION	REFERENDUM	REGULATORS	REMISSNESS
REASSEMBLE	RECRUDESCE	REFILLABLE	REGULATORY	REMITTABLE
REASSURING	RECRUITING	REFINEMENT	REHEARSALS	REMITTANCE
REBELLIONS	RECTANGLES	REFINERIES	REHEARSING	REMITTENCE
REBELLIOUS	RECTIFIERS	REFINISHER	REIMBURSED	REMODELING
REBIRTHING	RECTIFYING	REFLECTING	REIMBURSER	REMODELLED
REBOUNDING	RECUMBENCE	REFLECTION	REINFORCED	REMODELLER
REBUILDING	RECUPERATE	REFLECTIVE	REINSTATED	REMONETIZE
REBUKINGLY	RECURRENCE	REFLECTORS	REINSTATOR	REMORSEFUL
REBUTTABLE	RED	REFLEXIVES	REINSURING	REMOTENESS
RECALLABLE	ADMIRAL	REFORESTED	REISSUABLE	REMOULDING
RECAPTURED	RED-	REFRACTING	REITERATED	REMOUNTING
RECEIVABLE	BLOODED	REFRACTION	REJECTABLE	REMOVAL
RECENTNESS	REDBREASTS	REFRACTIVE	REJECTIONS	VAN
RECEPTACLE	REDCURRANT	REFRACTORY	REJOINDERS	REMUNERATE
RECEPTIONS	REDECORATE	REFRAINING	REJUVENATE	RENDERABLE
RECESSIONS	REDEDICATE	REFRESHFUL	REKINDLING	RENDERINGS
RECHARGING	REDEEMABLE	REFRESHING	RELATIONAL	RENDEZVOUS
RECHRISTEN	REDEEMABLY	REFRINGENT	RELATIVELY	RENDITIONS
RECIDIVISM	REDELIVERY	REFUELLING	RELATIVISM	RENEWABLES
RECIDIVIST	REDEMPTION	REFUGEEISM	RELATIVIST	RENOUNCING
RECIPIENCE	REDEPLOYED	REFULGENCE	RELATIVITY	RENOVATING
RECIPIENTS	RED	REFUNDABLE	RELAXATION	RENOVATION
RECIPROCAL	HERRING	REFUTATION	RELEGATING	RENOVATIVE
RECITATION	RED	REGAINABLE	RELEGATION	RENOWNEDLY
RECITATIVE	INDIANS	REGALEMENT	RELENTLESS	RENT
RECKLESSLY	REDIRECTED	REGARDABLE	RELEVANTLY	STRIKE
RECKONINGS	REDISCOUNT	REGARDLESS	RELIEF	REORGANIZE
RECLAIMANT	REDOUBLING	REGELATION	MAPS	REPAIRABLE
RECLAIMING	REDOUNDING	REGENERACY	RELIEF	REPARATION
RECLINABLE	RED	REGENERATE	ROAD	REPARATIVE
RECOGNIZED	PEPPERS	REGENSBURG	RELIEVABLE	REPATRIATE
RECOGNIZEE	REDRESSING	REGENTSHIP	RELINQUISH	REPAYMENTS
RECOGNIZER	REDUCTIONS	REGIMENTAL	RELISHABLE	REPEALABLE
RECOGNIZOR	REDUNDANCY	REGIMENTED	RELOCATING	REPEATABLE
RECOILLESS	RE-	REGIONALLY	RELOCATION	REPEATEDLY
RECOMMENCE	EDUCATED	REGISTERED	RELUCTANCE	REPELLENCE
RECOMPENSE	RE-	REGISTERER	REMAINDERS	REPELLENTS
RECONCILED	ELECTING	REGISTRANT	REMANDMENT	REPENTANCE
RECONCILER	RE-	REGISTRARS	REMARKABLE	REPERTOIRE
RECONSIDER	ELECTION	REGISTRIES	REMARKABLY	REPETITION
RECORDABLE	RE-	REGRESSING	REMARRYING	REPETITIVE
RECORDINGS	ENFORCER	REGRESSION	REMEDIABLE	REPHRASING
RECOUNTING	RE-	REGRESSIVE	REMEDIABLY	REPLICATED
RECOUPABLE	ENTRANCE	REGRETTING	REMEDIALLY	REPORTABLE
RECOUPMENT	RE-	REGROUPING	REMEDILESS	REPORTEDLY
RECOVERIES	EXAMINER	REGULARITY	REMEMBERED	REPOSITION
	RE-	REGULARIZE	REMEMBERER	REPOSITORY
	EXPORTER			

REPRESSING
REPRESSION
REPRESSIVE
REPRIEVING
REPRIMANDS
REPRINTING
REPROACHED
REPROACHER
REPROACHES
REPROBATER
REPROBATES
REPRODUCED
REPRODUCER
REPROVABLE
REPTILIANS
REPUBLICAN
REPUDIABLE
REPUDIATED
REPUDIATOR
REPUGNANCE
REPULSIONS
REPURCHASE
REPUTATION
REQUESTING
REQUIESCAT
REQUIRABLE
REQUISITES
REQUITABLE
RESCHEDULE
RESCINDING
RESCISSION
RESCISSORY
RESEARCHED
RESEARCHER
RESEARCHES
RESEMBLANT
RESEMBLING
RESENTMENT
RESERVABLE
RESERVEDLY
RESERVISTS
RESERVOIRS
RESETTLING
RESHIPMENT
RESHUFFLED
RESHUFFLES
RESIDENCES
RESIGNEDLY
RESILEMENT
RESILIENCE
RESILIENCY

RESISTANCE
RESISTIBLY
RESISTLESS
RESOLUTELY
RESOLUTION
RESOLVABLE
RESONANCES
RESONANTLY
RESONATING
RESONATION
RESONATORS
RESORCINOL
RESORPTION
RESORPTIVE
RESOUNDING
RESPECTERS
RESPECTFUL
RESPECTING
RESPECTIVE
RESPIRABLE
RESPIRATOR
RESPONDENT
RESPONDING
RESPONSIVE
RESPONSORY
RES
    PUBLICA
RESTAURANT
RESTHARROW
RESTLESSLY
RESTOCKING
RESTORABLE
RESTRAINED
RESTRAINER
RESTRAINTS
RESTRICTED
RESUMPTION
RESUMPTIVE
RESUPINATE
RESURFACED
RESURGENCE
RETAINABLE
RETAINMENT
RETALIATED
RETALIATOR
RETHINKING
RETICENTLY
RETICULATE
RETIREMENT
RETOUCHING
RETRACTILE

RETRACTING
RETRACTION
RETRACTIVE
RETREADING
RETREATING
RETRENCHED
RETRIEVERS
RETRIEVING
RETROCHOIR
RETROGRADE
RETROGRESS
RETROSPECT
RETROVERSE
RETROVIRUS
RETURNABLE
REUNIONISM
REUNIONIST
REUNITABLE
REUTLINGEN
REVANCHISM
REVANCHIST
REVEALABLE
REVEALEDLY
REVEALMENT
REVEGETATE
REVELATION
REVENGEFUL
REVERENCED
REVERENCER
REVERENCES
REVERENTLY
REVERSIBLE
REVERTIBLE
REVETMENTS
REVIEWABLE
REVILEMENT
REVILINGLY
REVISIONAL
REVITALIZE
REVIVALISM
REVIVALIST
REVIVIFIED
REVIVINGLY
REVOCATION
REVOCATIVE
REVOKINGLY
REVOLUTION
REVOLVABLE
REVOLVABLY
REWARDABLE

REWARD
    CARD
RHAPSODIES
RHAPSODIST
RHAPSODIZE
RHEOLOGIST
RHEOMETRIC
RHEOSTATIC
RHEOTACTIC
RHEOTROPIC
RHETORICAL
RHEUMATICS
RHEUMATISM
RHEUMATOID
RHINESTONE
RHINOCEROS
RHINOSCOPY
RHIZOGENIC
RHIZOMORPH
RHIZOPODAN
RHOMBOIDAL
RHUMBATRON
RHYMESTERS
RHYTHMICAL
RIBBONFISH
RIBOFLAVIN
RICKETTSIA
RICOCHETED
RIDGEPOLES
RIDICULING
RIDICULOUS
RIEMANNIAN
RIFLE
    RANGE
RIFT
    VALLEY
RIGHTABOUT
RIGHT
    ANGLE
RIGHTFULLY
RIGHT OF
    WAY
RIGHTWARDS
RIGMAROLES
RIGORISTIC
RIGOROUSLY
RINDERPEST
RING
    BINDER
RING
    FINGER
RINGLEADER

RINGMASTER
RING-
    NECKED
RING-
    TAILED
RIPPLINGLY
RIP-
    ROARING
RISIBILITY
RISING
    DAMP
RITARDANDO
RITORNELLO
RIVER
    BASIN
ROADBLOCKS
ROADHOUSES
ROAD
    ROLLER
ROADRUNNER
ROAD-
    TESTED
ROADWORTHY
ROBUSTNESS
ROCK
    BOTTOM
ROCK
    GARDEN
ROCK
    PLANTS
ROCK
    SALMON
ROISTERERS
ROISTEROUS
ROLE
    MODELS
ROLE-
    PLAYED
ROLLED
    GOLD
ROLLICKING
ROLLING
    PIN
ROLY-
    POLIES
ROMAN
    BLIND
ROMANESQUE
ROMAN
    NOSES
ROOD
    SCREEN

ROOF
GARDEN
ROPE
LADDER
ROSANILINE
ROSEMALING
ROSE
WINDOW
ROSTELLATE
ROTARY
CLUB
ROTATIONAL
ROTISSERIE
ROTOVATORS
ROTTENNESS
ROTTWEILER
ROUGHENING
ROUGHHOUSE
ROUGH
HOUSE
ROUGHNECKS
ROUGH
PAPER
ROUGHRIDER
ROUGH
STUFF
ROUNDABOUT
ROUNDHEADS
ROUNDHOUSE
ROUND
ROBIN
ROUND-
TABLE
ROUND
TRIPS
ROUSEDNESS
ROUSSILLON
ROUSTABOUT
ROUTE
MARCH
ROWING
BOAT
ROYAL
FLUSH
ROYALISTIC
RUB' AL
KHALI
RUBBER
BAND
RUBBERNECK
RUBBER
TREE

RUBBISH
BIN
RUBBISHING
RUBBLEWORK
RUBESCENCE
RUBIACEOUS
RUBIGINOUS
RUBRICATOR
RUDDERHEAD
RUDDERLESS
RUDDERPOST
RUEFULNESS
RUFESCENCE
RUFFIANISM
RUGBY
UNION
RUGGEDIZED
RUGGEDNESS
RUMBLINGLY
RUMINATING
RUMINATION
RUMINATIVE
RUMPUS
ROOM
RUNNER
BEAN
RUN-OF-
PAPER
RUN
THROUGH
RUN-
THROUGH
RUPESTRIAN
RUPTURABLE
RURITANIAN
RUSHLIGHTS
RUSSOPHILE
RUSSOPHOBE
RUSTICATED
RUSTICATOR
RUSTLINGLY
RUTHENIOUS
RUTHERFORD
RUTHLESSLY

S
SABBATICAL
SABOTAGING
SABULOSITY
SACCHARASE
SACCHARATE
SACCHARIDE

SACCHARIFY
SACCHARINE
SACCHAROID
SACCHAROSE
SACERDOTAL
SACRAMENTO
SACRAMENTS
SACRED
COWS
SACREDNESS
SACRIFICED
SACRIFICER
SACRIFICES
SACRILEGES
SACRISTANS
SACRISTIES
SACROILIAC
SACROSANCT
SADDLEBACK
SADDLEBAGS
SADDLEBILL
SADDLERIES
SADDLE-
SORE
SADDLETREE
SAFARI
PARK
SAFEGUARDS
SAFE
HOUSES
SAFETY
BELT
SAFETY
LAMP
SAFETY
NETS
SAFETY
PINS
SAHARANPUR
SAILBOARDS
SAILOR
SUIT
SAILPLANES
SAINT-
CLOUD
SAINT
CROIX
SAINT-
DENIS
SAINT
JOHN'S
SAINT
KILDA

SAINT
KITTS
SAINT
LOUIS
SAINT-
LOUIS
SAINT
LUCIA
SAINT'S
DAYS
SALABILITY
SALAD
CREAM
SALAMANDER
SALBUTAMOL
SALESCLERK
SALESGIRLS
SALES
PITCH
SALES
SLIPS
SALES
TAXES
SALESWOMAN
SALESWOMEN
SALICORNIA
SALICYLATE
SALIFEROUS
SALIFIABLE
SALIMETRIC
SALIVATING
SALIVATION
SALLOWNESS
SALMANAZAR
SALMONELLA
SALMON
LEAP
SALOON
BARS
SALOPETTES
SALPINGIAN
SALTARELLO
SALTCELLAR
SALTIGRADE
SALT
SHAKER
SALUBRIOUS
SALUTARILY
SALUTATION
SALUTATORY
SALVERFORM
SALZGITTER

SAMARITANS
SAMARSKITE
SAMOTHRACE
SAN
ANTONIO
SANATORIUM
SANCTIFIED
SANCTIFIER
SANCTIMONY
SANCTIONED
SANCTIONER
SANCTITUDE
SANDALWOOD
SANDBAGGED
SANDBAGGER
SANDCASTLE
SAND
CASTLE
SANDERLING
SANDGROUSE
SAND
'MARTIN
SANDPIPERS
SANDSTORMS
SANDWICHED
SANDWICHES
SANFORIZED
SANFORIZED
SANGUINARY
SANGUINELY
SANITARIAN
SANITARILY
SANITARIUM
SANITATION
SANITIZING
SANSKRITIC
SANTA
CLARA
SANTA
CLAUS
SANTA
MARIA
SANTA
MARTA
SAPIENTIAL
SAPONIFIER
SAPPANWOOD
SAPPHIRINE
SAPROGENIC
SAPROLITIC
SAPROPELIC
SAPROPHYTE

SAPROTROPH
SARCOPHAGI
SARMENTOSE
SARRACENIA
SASH
 WINDOW
SATELLITES
SATINWOODS
SATIRIZING
SATISFYING
SATURATING
SATURATION
SATURNALIA
SATYRIASIS
SAUERKRAUT
SAUNTERING
SAUSAGE
 DOG
SAVAGENESS
SAVAGERIES
SAXICOLOUS
SAXOPHONES
SAXOPHONIC
SCABBINESS
SCAFFOLDER
SCALEBOARD
SCALLOPING
SCALLYWAGS
SCALOPPINE
SCALPELLIC
SCAMPERING
SCANDALIZE
SCANDALOUS
SCANSORIAL
SCANTINESS
SCAPEGOATS
SCAPEGRACE
SCARABAEID
SCARABAEUS
SCARCEMENT
SCARCENESS
SCARCITIES
SCARECROWS
SCAREDY
 CAT
SCARIFYING
SCARLATINA
SCARPERING
SCATHINGLY
SCATTER-
 GUN
SCATTERING

SCATTINESS
SCAVENGERS
SCAVENGING
SCENICALLY
SCEPTICISM
SCHAERBEEK
SCHEDULING
SCHEMATISM
SCHEMATIZE
SCHEMINGLY
SCHERZANDO
SCHIPPERKE
SCHISMATIC
SCHIZOCARP
SCHIZOGONY
SCHLEPPING
SCHNITZELS
SCHOLASTIC
SCHOOLGIRL
SCHOOLMARM
SCHOOLMATE
SCHOOLWORK
SCHUMACHER
SCIENTIFIC
SCIENTISTS
SCILLONIAN
SCIOMANCER
SCIOMANTIC
SCLEROTIUM
SCLEROTOMY
SCOFFINGLY
SCOLDINGLY
SCOLLOPING
SCOREBOARD
SCORECARDS
SCORNFULLY
SCORNINGLY
SCORPAENID
SCORPIONIC
SCOTCH
 EGGS
SCOTCH
 MIST
SCOTCH
 SNAP
SCOTCH
 TAPE
SCOTTICISM
SCOUNDRELS
SCOWLINGLY
SCRABBLING
SCRAGGIEST

SCRAMBLING
SCRAPBOOKS
SCRAP
 HEAPS
SCRAP
 METAL
SCRAP
 PAPER
SCRAPPIEST
SCRATCHIER
SCRATCHILY
SCRATCHING
SCRATCH
 PAD
SCRATCHPAD
SCRAWNIEST
SCREECHING
SCREENABLE
SCREENINGS
SCREENPLAY
SCREEN
 TEST
SCREWBALLS
SCRIBBLERS
SCRIBBLING
SCRIMMAGED
SCRIMMAGER
SCRIMMAGES
SCRIPTURAL
SCROFULOUS
SCROLLWORK
SCROUNGERS
SCROUNGING
SCRUBBIEST
SCRUFFIEST
SCRUMMAGED
SCRUMMAGER
SCRUMMAGES
SCRUNCHING
SCRUPULOUS
SCRUTINEER
SCRUTINIES
SCRUTINIZE
SCULLERIES
SCULPTRESS
SCULPTURAL
SCULPTURED
SCULPTURES
SCUNTHORPE
SCUPPERING
SCURRILITY
SCURRILOUS

SCURVINESS
SCUTELLATE
SCYPHIFORM
SCYPHOZOAN
SEA
 ANEMONE
SEABORGIUM
SEA
 BREEZES
SEA
 CAPTAIN
SEA
 CHANGES
SEALED-
 BEAM
SEALING
 WAX
SEAMANLIKE
SEAMANSHIP
SEAMSTRESS
SEARCHABLE
SEA
 SERPENT
SEASONABLE
SEASONABLY
SEASONEDLY
SEASONINGS
SEA
 URCHINS
SEBIFEROUS
SEBORRHOEA
SECOND
 BEST
SECOND-
 HAND
SECONDMENT
SECOND-
 RATE
SECOND
 WIND
SECRETAIRE
SECRETIONS
SECTIONING
SECULARISM
SECULARIST
SECULARITY
SECULARIZE
SECUNDINES
SECUREMENT
SECURENESS
SECURITIES

SEDAN
 CHAIR
SEDATENESS
SEDUCINGLY
SEDUCTRESS
SEDULOUSLY
SEEMLINESS
SEERSUCKER
SEETHINGLY
SEE-
 THROUGH
SEGMENTARY
SEGMENTING
SEGREGABLE
SEGREGATED
SEGREGATOR
SEISMICITY
SEISMOLOGY
SELECTIONS
SELECTNESS
SELENOLOGY
SELF-
 ACTING
SELF-
 ACTION
SELF-
 DENIAL
SELF-
 ESTEEM
SELF-
 FEEDER
SELFLESSLY
SELF-
 REGARD
SELF-
 SEEKER
SELF-
 STYLED
SELF-
 WILLED
SELL-BY
 DATE
SELLOTAPED
SEMAPHORES
SEMAPHORIC
SEMATOLOGY
SEMIANNUAL
SEMIBREVES
SEMICIRCLE
SEMICOLONS
SEMIFINALS
SEMINALITY

SEMINARIAL	SERMONICAL	SHEATHBILL	SHOPLIFTED	SICKLEBILL
SEMINARIAN	SERMONIZED	SHEATHINGS	SHOPLIFTER	SICKLINESS
SEMINARIES	SERMONIZER	SHEEPISHLY	SHOPSOILED	SICKNESSES
SEMIQUAVER	SEROLOGIST	SHEEP'S	SHOPWALKER	SICK
SEMIVOWELS	SERPENTINE	EYES	SHOPWORKER	PARADE
SEMIWEEKLY	SERVICEMAN	SHEEPSHANK	SHORE	SIDEBOARDS
SENATORIAL	SERVICEMEN	SHEEPSHEAD	LEAVE	SIDE
SENEGALESE	SERVIETTES	SHEEPSKINS	SHOREWARDS	DISHES
SENEGAMBIA	SERVOMOTOR	SHEET	SHORTBREAD	SIDE
SENESCENCE	SETSQUARES	MUSIC	SHORTENING	EFFECT
SENSATIONS	SETTING	SHEIKHDOMS	SHORTFALLS	SIDE
SENSE	OUT	SHELF	SHORT	ISSUES
ORGAN	SETTLEABLE	LIVES	LISTS	SIDELIGHTS
SENSIBILIA	SETTLEMENT	SHELLPROOF	SHORT-	SIDELINING
SENSITIZED	SEVASTOPOL	SHELLSHOCK	LIVED	SIDE
SENSITIZER	SEVENTIETH	SHELTERING	SHORT-	ORDERS
SENSUALISM	SEVERANCES	SHENANIGAN	RANGE	SIDEROLITE
SENSUALIST	SEVERENESS	SHEPHERDED	SHORT	SIDEROSTAT
SENSUALITY	SEVERITIES	SHERARDIZE	STORY	SIDESADDLE
SENSUOUSLY	SEXAGENARY	SHERBROOKE	SHOULDERED	SIDE
SENTENCING	SEXAGESIMA	SHIBBOLETH	SHOVELHEAD	STREET
SENTENTIAL	SEXIVALENT	SHIFTINESS	SHOVELLING	SIDESTROKE
SENTIMENTS	SEX	SHIFTINGLY	SHOVELNOSE	SIDESWIPED
SEPARATELY	OBJECTS	SHIFT	SHOW	SIDESWIPER
SEPARATING	SEXOLOGIST	STICK	JUMPER	SIDESWIPES
SEPARATION	SEXPARTITE	SHILLELAGH	SHOWPIECES	SIDETRACKS
SEPARATISM	SEXTILLION	SHIMMERING	SHOW	SIDEWINDER
SEPARATIST	SEXTUPLETS	SHIPBOARDS	TRIALS	SIGHTSEERS
SEPARATIVE	SEYCHELLES	SHIPMASTER	SHREVEPORT	SIGNALIZED
SEPARATORS	SHABBINESS	SHIP-	SHREWDNESS	SIGNALLING
SEPARATRIX	SHADOWIEST	RIGGED	SHREWISHLY	SIGNATURES
SEPTENNIAL	SHAGGED	SHIPWRECKS	SHREWSBURY	SIGNIFYING
SEPTICALLY	OUT	SHIPWRIGHT	SHRIEVALTY	SIGNORINAS
SEPTICIDAL	SHAGGINESS	SHIRE	SHRILLNESS	SIGNPOSTED
SEPTIC	SHAKEDOWNS	HORSE	SHRINKABLE	SILENTNESS
TANK	SHALLOWEST	SHIRTFRONT	SHRINK-	SILHOUETTE
SEPTILLION	SHALLOWING	SHIRTTAILS	WRAP	SILICULOSE
SEPULCHRAL	SHAMANISMS	SHISH	SHRIVELING	SILK
SEPULCHRES	SHAMANISTS	KEBAB	SHRIVELLED	SCREEN
SEQUACIOUS	SHAMATEURS	SHOALINESS	SHROPSHIRE	SILLY
SEQUENCING	SHAMEFACED	SHOCKINGLY	SHROUD-	BILLY
SEQUENTIAL	SHAMEFULLY	SHOCKPROOF	LAID	SILVERFISH
SEQUESTRAL	SHAMPOOING	SHODDINESS	SHROVETIDE	SILVERWARE
SEQUESTRUM	SHANGHAIED	SHOEMAKING	SHUDDERING	SILVERWEED
SERBO-	SHANTYTOWN	SHOESHINES	SHUNT-	SIMFEROPOL
CROAT	SHAPELIEST	SHOESTRING	WOUND	SIMILARITY
SERENADING	SHARE	SHOGUN	SHUTTERING	SIMILITUDE
SERENENESS	PRICE	BOND	SIALAGOGIC	SIMONIACAL
SERIALIZED	SHARPENERS	SHOOT A	SIALAGOGUE	SIMPLE
SERIGRAPHY	SHARPENING	LINE	SIAMESE	LIFE
SERIOCOMIC	SHATTERING	SHOPAHOLIC	CAT	SIMPLENESS
	SHEARWATER	SHOPKEEPER	SIBILATION	SIMPLETONS

SIMPLICITY
SIMPLIFIED
SIMPLIFIER
SIMPLISTIC
SIMULACRUM
SIMULATING
SIMULATION
SIMULATIVE
SIMULATORS
SINCIPITAL
SINECURISM
SINECURIST
SINE QUA
NON
SINEWINESS
SINFULNESS
SINGHALESE
SINGLE
FILE
SINGLENESS
SINGLETONS
SINGULARLY
SINHAILIEN
SINISTROUS
SINN
FEINER
SINOLOGIST
SINUSOIDAL
SISTERHOOD
SITOSTEROL
SITUATIONS
SIX-
FOOTERS
SIX-
SHOOTER
SIXTEENTHS
SIXTH
FORMS
SIXTH
SENSE
SKATEBOARD
SKEDADDLED
SKEPTICISM
SKETCHABLE
SKETCHBOOK
SKETCHIEST
SKETCHPADS
SKIMPINESS
SKIN
DIVERS
SKIN
DIVING

SKIN
FLICKS
SKINFLINTS
SKIN
GRAFTS
SKINNINESS
SKIPPERING
SKIRMISHED
SKIRMISHER
SKIRMISHES
SKITTERING
SKITTISHLY
SKYJACKERS
SKYJACKING
SKYLARKING
SKYROCKETS
SKYSCRAPER
SKYWRITING
SLACKENING
SLANDERERS
SLANDERING
SLANDEROUS
SLANGINESS
SLANTINGLY
SLASHINGLY
SLATTERNLY
SLAVE
TRADE
SLAVOPHILE
SLEAZINESS
SLEEPINESS
SLEEPYHEAD
SLEEVELESS
SLENDERIZE
SLIDE
RULES
SLIGHTNESS
SLINGSHOTS
SLINKINESS
SLINKINGLY
SLIPPINESS
SLIPPINGLY
SLIPSTREAM
SLITHERING
SLOBBERING
SLOPPINESS
SLOPWORKER
SLOTHFULLY
SLOUCH
HATS
SLOW
MOTION

SLOW-
WITTED
SLUGGISHLY
SLUICEGATE
SLUMBERERS
SLUMBERING
SLUMBEROUS
SLUSH
FUNDS
SLUSHINESS
SMALL
HOURS
SMALL
PRINT
SMALL-
SCALE
SMALL-
TIMER
SMARAGDITE
SMART
ALECK
SMARTENING
SMARTINGLY
SMATTERING
SMEARINESS
SMEAR
TESTS
SMELLINESS
SMIRKINGLY
SMOKEHOUSE
SMOKESTACK
SMOLDERING
SMOOTHABLE
SMOOTHBORE
SMOOTHNESS
SMOTHERING
SMOULDERED
SMUDGINESS
SMUTTINESS
SNAIL'S
PACE
SNAKEMOUTH
SNAPDRAGON
SNAPPINESS
SNAPPINGLY
SNAPPISHLY
SNARE
DRUMS
SNARLINGLY
SNAZZINESS
SNEAKINESS
SNEAKINGLY

SNEAK
THIEF
SNEERINGLY
SNEEZEWORT
SNICKERING
SNIFFINGLY
SNIGGERING
SNIPPINESS
SNIVELLERS
SNIVELLING
SNOBBISHLY
SNOOKERING
SNOOTINESS
SNORKELLED
SNORTINGLY
SNOTTINESS
SNOWBALLED
SNOW-
CAPPED
SNOWDRIFTS
SNOWFIELDS
SNOWFLAKES
SNOWMAKING
SNOWMOBILE
SNOWPLOUGH
SNOWSTORMS
SNUBBINGLY
SNUFFINESS
SNUFFINGLY
SOAP
BUBBLE
SOAP
OPERAS
SOBERINGLY
SOBRIQUETS
SOB
STORIES
SOCIALISTS
SOCIALITES
SOCIALIZED
SOCIALIZER
SOCIALNESS
SOCIAL
WORK
SOCIOMETRY
SOCIOPATHY
SODDENNESS
SOFT-
BOILED
SOFT-
FINNED

SOFT
FRUITS
SOFT-
HEADED
SOFT
OPTION
SOFT
PALATE
SOFT-
SOAPED
SOFT-
SPOKEN
SOJOURNERS
SOJOURNING
SOLAR
CELLS
SOLAR
PANEL
SOLAR
YEARS
SOLDERABLE
SOLDIERING
SOLECISTIC
SOLEMNIZED
SOLEMNIZER
SOLEMNNESS
SOLENOIDAL
SOLFATARIC
SOLICITING
SOLICITORS
SOLICITOUS
SOLICITUDE
SOLIDARITY
SOLIDIFIED
SOLIDIFIER
SOLID-
STATE
SOLITAIRES
SOLITARIES
SOLITARILY
SOLSTITIAL
SOLUBILITY
SOLUBILIZE
SOLVOLYSIS
SOMALILAND
SOMATOLOGY
SOMATOTYPE
SOMBRENESS
SOMERSAULT
SOMNOLENCE
SONGSTRESS
SONGWRITER

SONIC
BOOMS
SONIFEROUS
SONOROUSLY
SONS-OF-
GUNS
SOOTHINGLY
SOOTHSAYER
SOPHOMORES
SORDIDNESS
SORORICIDE
SORORITIES
SOUBRIQUET
SOULLESSLY
SOUNDPROOF
SOUNDTRACK
SOUP
SPOONS
SOUR
GRAPES
SOURPUSSES
SOUSAPHONE
SOUTHBOUND
SOUTH
DOWNS
SOUTHERNER
SOUTH
KOREA
SOUTHWARDS
SOU'WESTER
S
SOVEREIGNS
SPACECRAFT
SPACE
PROBE
SPACESHIPS
SPACESUITS
SPACEWOMAN
SPACIOUSLY
SPADICEOUS
SPALLATION
SPARE
PARTS
SPARE
TYRES
SPARK
PLUGS
SPARSENESS
SPARTANISM
SPATCHCOCK
SPATIALITY
SPATTERING

SPEARHEADS
SPECIALISM
SPECIALIST
SPECIALITY
SPECIALIZE
SPECIATION
SPECIESISM
SPECIFYING
SPECIOSITY
SPECIOUSLY
SPECTACLES
SPECTATING
SPECTATORS
SPECULATED
SPECULATOR
SPEECH
DAYS
SPEECHLESS
SPEEDBOATS
SPEEDINESS
SPEED
LIMIT
SPEED
TRAPS
SPELEOLOGY
SPELLBOUND
SPELUNKING
SPEND
LIMIT
SPERMACETI
SPERMATIUM
SPERMICIDE
SPERM
WHALE
SPERRYLITE
SPHALERITE
SPHENOIDAL
SPHERICITY
SPHEROIDAL
SPHERULITE
SPHINCTERS
SPICEBERRY
SPIDERWEBS
SPIDERWORT
SPINAL
CORD
SPINDLIEST
SPIN-
DRYING
SPINESCENT
SPINNAKERS
SPIRACULAR

SPIRALLING
SPIRITEDLY
SPIRITLESS
SPIRITUALS
SPIRITUOUS
SPIROGRAPH
SPIROMETER
SPIROMETRY
SPITEFULLY
SPLANCHNIC
SPLASHBACK
SPLASH
BACK
SPLASHDOWN
SPLASHIEST
SPLATTERED
SPLEENWORT
SPLENDIDLY
SPLINTERED
SPLIT
HAIRS
SPLIT
LEVEL
SPLIT-
LEVEL
SPLIT
RINGS
SPLUTTERED
SPLUTTERER
SPOILSPORT
SPOKESHAVE
SPOLIATION
SPONGE
BAGS
SPONGE
CAKE
SPONGINESS
SPONSORIAL
SPONSORING
SPOOKINESS
SPOONERISM
SPORANGIAL
SPORANGIUM
SPOROPHORE
SPOROPHYLL
SPOROPHYTE
SPOROZOITE
SPORTINESS
SPORTINGLY
SPORTIVELY
SPORTS
CARS

SPORTSWEAR
SPOT
CHECKS
SPOTLESSLY
SPOTLIGHTS
SPOTTINESS
SPREADABLE
SPRINGBOKS
SPRINGHAAS
SPRINGHEAD
SPRINGIEST
SPRING
ROLL
SPRINGTAIL
SPRING
TIDE
SPRINGTIME
SPRINGWOOD
SPRINKLERS
SPRINKLING
SPRUCENESS
SPUMESCENT
SPUNKINESS
SPURIOUSLY
SPUTTERING
SPYGLASSES
SQUABBLING
SQUALIDITY
SQUALLIEST
SQUAMATION
SQUAMULOSE
SQUANDERED
SQUANDERER
SQUARE
DEAL
SQUARE
KNOT
SQUARE
MEAL
SQUARENESS
SQUARE
ROOT
SQUASHIEST
SQUEAKIEST
SQUEEZABLE
SQUEEZEBOX
SQUELCHIER
SQUELCHING
SQUETEAGUE
SQUIDGIEST
SQUIFFIEST
SQUISHIEST

STABILATOR
STABILIZED
STABILIZER
STABLE
BOYS
STABLEFORD
STABLENESS
STAFF
NURSE
STAG
BEETLE
STAGECOACH
STAGECRAFT
STAGE
DOORS
STAGEHANDS
STAGE
NAMES
STAGGERING
STAGNANTLY
STAGNATING
STAGNATION
STAIRCASES
STAIRWELLS
STALACTITE
STALAGMITE
STALEMATED
STALEMATES
STALKINESS
STALWARTLY
STAMMERERS
STAMMERING
STAMPEDING
STANCHABLE
STANCHIONS
STANDPIPES
STANDPOINT
STANDSTILL
STARCHIEST
STARFISHES
STARFLOWER
STARGAZERS
STARGAZING
STARRINESS
STARRY-
EYED
STARVATION
STARVELING
STATECRAFT
STATEMENTS
STATEROOMS
STATIONARY

STATIONERS
STATIONERY
STATIONING
STATISTICS
STATOBLAST
STATOSCOPE
STATUESQUE
STATUETTES
STATUS
  ZERO
STATUTABLE
STATUTE
  LAW
STAUNCHEST
STAUNCHING
STAUROLITE
STAVESACRE
STAY-AT-
  HOME
ST
  BERNARDS
STEADINESS
STEAKHOUSE
STEALTHIER
STEALTHILY
STEAMBOATS
STEAM-
  CHEST
STEAMINESS
STEAM
  IRONS
STEAMSHIPS
STEAMTIGHT
STEEL
  BANDS
STEELINESS
STEELWORKS
STEEPENING
STELLIFORM
STEM-
  WINDER
STENCILING
STENCILLED
STENCILLER
STENOGRAPH
STENOTYPIC
STENTORIAN
STEPFAMILY
STEPFATHER
STEPLADDER
STEPMOTHER
STEPPARENT

STEPSISTER
STEREOBATE
STEREOGRAM
STEREOPSIS
STEREOTOMY
STEREOTYPE
STEREOTYPY
STERICALLY
STERILIZED
STERILIZER
STERNWARDS
STERTOROUS
STEVEDORES
STEWARDESS
STICKINESS
STICK
  SHIFT
STICKTIGHT
STICKY
  ENDS
STIFFENERS
STIFFENING
STIFLINGLY
STIGMATISM
STIGMATIST
STIGMATIZE
STILLBIRTH
STILL
  LIFES
STIMULABLE
STIMULANTS
STIMULATED
STIMULATOR
STINGINESS
STINGINGLY
STINK-
  BOMBS
STINKINGLY
STINKSTONE
STIPELLATE
STIPULABLE
STIPULATED
STIPULATOR
STIR-
  FRYING
STIRRINGLY
STIRRUP
  CUP
STITCHWORT
STOCHASTIC
STOCKADING

STOCK
  CUBES
STOCKINESS
STOCKPILED
STOCKPILER
STOCKPILES
STOCKROOMS
STOCK-
  STILL
STOCKYARDS
STODGINESS
STOKEHOLDS
STOMACHING
STOMATITIC
STOMATITIS
STOMATOPOD
STOMODAEAL
STOMODAEUM
STONE-
  BLIND
STONE
  FRUIT
STONEHENGE
STONEMASON
STONY
  BROKE
STOOPINGLY
STOPPERING
STOREHOUSE
STOREROOMS
STORKSBILL
STORMBOUND
STORM
  CLOUD
STORMINESS
STORMPROOF
STORY
  LINES
STRABISMAL
STRABISMUS
STRADDLING
STRAGGLERS
STRAGGLIER
STRAGGLING
STRAIGHTEN
STRAIGHTER
STRAITENED
STRAITNESS
STRAMONIUM
STRANGLERS
STRANGLING
STRASBOURG

STRATAGEMS
STRATEGICS
STRATEGIES
STRATEGIST
STRATIFIED
STRATIFORM
STRATOCRAT
STRAWBERRY
STRAWBOARD
STRAW
  POLLS
STREAKIEST
STREAMLINE
STREET
  ARAB
STREETCARS
STREETWISE
STRELITZIA
STRENGTHEN
STRESS
  MARK
STRETCHERS
STRETCHIER
STRETCHING
STRIATIONS
STRICTNESS
STRICTURES
STRIDENTLY
STRIDULATE
STRIDULOUS
STRIGIFORM
STRIKINGLY
STRING
  BEAN
STRINGENCY
STRINGENDO
STRINGHALT
STRINGIEST
STRIPAGRAM
STRIP
  CLUBS
STRIPLINGS
STRIPTEASE
STROKE
  PLAY
STRONGHOLD
STRONGNESS
STRONG
  ROOM
STROPPIEST
STRUCTURAL
STRUCTURED

STRUCTURES
STRUGGLING
STRUTHIOUS
STRYCHNINE
STUBBINESS
STUBBORNER
STUBBORNLY
STUDIOUSLY
STUFFINESS
STULTIFIED
STULTIFIER
STUMPINESS
STUNNINGLY
STUPEFYING
STUPENDOUS
STUPIDNESS
STURDINESS
STUTTERERS
STUTTERING
STYLISTICS
STYLOGRAPH
STYLOLITIC
STYPTICITY
SUBACETATE
SUBACIDITY
SUBALTERNS
SUBAQUATIC
SUBAQUEOUS
SUBCALIBRE
SUBCLAVIAN
SUBCOMPACT
SUBCULTURE
SUBDIVIDED
SUBDIVIDER
SUBDUCTION
SUBEDITING
SUBEDITORS
SUBGENERIC
SUBGLACIAL
SUBHEADING
SUBJACENCY
SUBJECTIFY
SUBJECTING
SUBJECTION
SUBJECTIVE
SUBJOINING
SUBJUGABLE
SUBJUGATED
SUBJUGATOR
SUBKINGDOM
SUBLEASING

SUBLETTING
SUBLIMABLE
SUBLIMATED
SUBLIMATES
SUBLIMINAL
SUBLINGUAL
SUBMARINER
SUBMARINES
SUBMEDIANT
SUBMERGING
SUBMERSION
SUBMISSION
SUBMISSIVE
SUBMITTING
SUBMONTANE
SUBOCEANIC
SUBOPTIMAL
SUBORBITAL
SUBORDINAL
SUBPOENAED
SUBPROGRAM
SUBREPTION
SUBROUTINE
SUB-
  SAHARAN
SUBSCRIBED
SUBSCRIBER
SUBSECTION
SUBSEQUENT
SUBSIDENCE
SUBSIDIARY
SUBSIDIZED
SUBSIDIZER
SUBSISTENT
SUBSISTING
SUBSPECIES
SUBSTANCES
SUBSTATION
SUBSTITUTE
SUBSTRATUM
SUBSUMABLE
SUBTANGENT
SUBTENANCY
SUBTENANTS
SUBTENDING
SUBTERFUGE
SUBTILIZER
SUBTITULAR
SUBTLENESS
SUBTLETIES
SUBTRACTED

SUBTRACTER
SUBTRAHEND
SUBTROPICS
SUBTYPICAL
SUBVENTION
SUBVERSION
SUBVERSIVE
SUBVERTING
SUCCEEDING
SUCCESSFUL
SUCCESSION
SUCCESSIVE
SUCCESSORS
SUCCINCTLY
SUCCOURING
SUCCULENCE
SUCCULENTS
SUCCUMBING
SUCCUSSION
SUCCUSSIVE
SUCKERFISH
SUCKING
  PIG
SUDDENNESS
SUFFERABLE
SUFFERANCE
SUFFERINGS
SUFFICIENT
SUFFOCATED
SUFFRAGISM
SUFFRAGIST
SUGAR
  DADDY
SUGARINESS
SUGGESTING
SUGGESTION
SUGGESTIVE
SUICIDALLY
SULLENNESS
SULPHA
  DRUG
SULPHATION
SULPHONATE
SULPHURATE
SULPHURIZE
SULPHUROUS
SULTANATES
SULTRINESS
SUMMARIZED
SUMMARIZER
SUMMATIONS

SUMMERTIME
SUMMERWOOD
SUMMINGS-
  UP
SUMMONABLE
SUMMONSING
SUNBATHERS
SUNBATHING
SUNDAY
  BEST
SUNDERLAND
SUNDOWNERS
SUNFLOWERS
SUNGLASSES
SUNLOUNGER
SUN
  LOUNGES
SUPERBNESS
SUPERCARGO
SUPERCLASS
SUPERDUPER
SUPER
  DUPER
SUPERFLUID
SUPERGIANT
SUPERGRASS
SUPERHUMAN
SUPERLUNAR
SUPERMODEL
SUPERNOVAS
SUPERORDER
SUPEROXIDE
SUPERPOWER
SUPERSEDED
SUPERSEDER
SUPERSONIC
SUPERSTARS
SUPERTONIC
SUPERVENED
SUPERVISED
SUPERVISOR
SUPINENESS
SUPPLANTED
SUPPLANTER
SUPPLEJACK
SUPPLEMENT
SUPPLENESS
SUPPLETION
SUPPLETIVE
SUPPLETORY
SUPPLIABLE
SUPPLIANCE

SUPPLIANTS
SUPPLICANT
SUPPLICATE
SUPPORTERS
SUPPORTING
SUPPORTIVE
SUPPOSABLE
SUPPOSEDLY
SUPPRESSED
SUPPRESSOR
SUPPURATED
SUPRARENAL
SURCHARGED
SURCHARGER
SURCHARGES
SUREFOOTED
SURFACTANT
SURFBOARDS
SURFCASTER
SURFEITING
SURGICALLY
SURINAMESE
SURJECTION
SURJECTIVE
SURMISABLE
SURMISEDLY
SURMOUNTED
SURMOUNTER
SURPASSING
SURPLUSAGE
SURPRISING
SURREALISM
SURREALIST
SURRENDERS
SURROGATES
SURROUNDED
SURVEYABLE
SURVIVABLE
SUSCEPTIVE
SUSPECTING
SUSPENDERS
SUSPENDING
SUSPENSION
SUSPENSIVE
SUSPENSOID
SUSPENSORY
SUSPICIONS
SUSPICIOUS
SUSTAINING
SUSTENANCE
SUSTENTION

SUTHERLAND
SUZERAINTY
SVERDLOVSK
SWAGGERERS
SWAGGERING
SWALLOWING
SWANKINESS
SWAN-
  UPPING
SWARTHIEST
SWASHINGLY
SWEARINGLY
SWEARWORDS
SWEATBANDS
SWEAT
  GLAND
SWEATINESS
SWEATSHIRT
SWEATSHOPS
SWEEPINGLY
SWEEPSTAKE
SWEETBREAD
SWEETBRIER
SWEETENERS
SWEETENING
SWEETHEART
SWEETMEATS
SWEET
  TOOTH
SWELTERING
SWERVINGLY
SWIMMINGLY
SWINEHERDS
SWINGINGLY
SWING
  SHIFT
SWIRLINGLY
SWISHINGLY
SWISS
  CHARD
SWITCHABLE
SWITCHBACK
SWITCH
  CARD
SWITCHED-
  ON
SWITCHGEAR
SWIVELLING
SWOONINGLY
SWORDCRAFT
SWORD
  DANCE

SWORDSTICK
SYCOPHANTS
SYLLABUSES
SYLLOGISMS
SYLLOGIZER
SYLPHIDINE
SYLVESTRAL
SYMBIONTIC
SYMBOLIZED
SYMMETRIZE
SYMPATHIES
SYMPATHIZE
SYMPHONIES
SYMPHONIST
SYMPHYSIAL
SYMPHYSTIC
SYMPOSIUMS
SYNAGOGUES
SYNCARPOUS
SYNCHRONIC
SYNCLASTIC
SYNCOPATED
SYNCOPATOR
SYNCRETISM
SYNCRETIST
SYNCRETIZE
SYNDICATED
SYNDICATES
SYNDICSHIP
SYNECDOCHE
SYNECOLOGY
SYNERGETIC
SYNOECIOUS
SYNONYMITY
SYNONYMIZE
SYNONYMOUS
SYNTACTICS
SYNTHESIST
SYNTHESIZE
SYNTHETISM
SYNTHETIST
SYPHILITIC
SYSTEMATIC
SYSTEMIZER

T
TABERNACLE
TABESCENCE
TABLECLOTH
TABLE
  D'HOTE

TABLELANDS
TABLE
  LINEN
TABLESPOON
TABULARIZE
TABULATING
TABULATION
TACHOGRAPH
TACHOMETER
TACHOMETRY
TACHYLYTIC
TACHYMETER
TACHYMETRY
TACITURNLY
TACTICALLY
TACTICIANS
TACTLESSLY
TAENIACIDE
TAENIAFUGE
TAGLIATELE
TAILBOARDS
TAILGATING
TAILLIGHTS
TAILORBIRD
TAILOR-
  MADE
TAILPIECES
TAJIKISTAN
TAKE IN
  HAND
TAKINGNESS
TALCAHUANO
TALEBEARER
TALISMANIC
TALKING-
  TOS
TAMABILITY
TAMAULIPAS
TAMBOURINE
TANANARIVE
TANGANYIKA
TANGENTIAL
TANGERINES
TANGLEMENT
TANTALIZED
TANTALIZER
TANTALUSES
TANTAMOUNT
TAP
  DANCERS
TAP
  DANCING

TAPERINGLY
TAPESTRIED
TAPESTRIES
TARANTELLA
TARANTULAS
TARDIGRADE
TARMACKING
TARNISHING
TARPAULINS
TASIMETRIC
TASK
  FORCES
TASKMASTER
TASTEFULLY
TATTERSALL
TATTLETALE
TATTLINGLY
TATTOOISTS
TAUNTINGLY
TAUROMACHY
TAUTOMERIC
TAUTONYMIC
TAWDRINESS
TAXABILITY
TAXATIONAL
TAXIDERMAL
TAXIMETERS
TAXONOMIST
TAX
  SHELTER
TEA
  CADDIES
TEAGARDENS
TEAM
  SPIRIT
TEA
  PARTIES
TEARJERKER
TEA
  SERVICE
TEA
  TROLLEY
TECHNETIUM
TECHNICIAN
TECHNIQUES
TECHNOCRAT
TECHNOLOGY
TECTRICIAL
TEDDY
  BEARS
TEENY
  WEENY

TELECASTER
TELEGNOSIS
TELEGRAPHS
TELEGRAPHY
TELEMETRIC
TELEPATHIC
TELEPHONED
TELEPHONER
TELEPHONES
TELESCOPED
TELESCOPES
TELESCOPIC
TELESCRIPT
TELEVISING
TELEVISION
TELEVISUAL
TELEWRITER
TELIOSPORE
TELLING-
  OFF
TELOPHASIC
TELPHERAGE
TEMPERABLE
TEMPERANCE
TEMPORIZED
TEMPORIZER
TEMPTATION
TEMPTINGLY
TENABILITY
TENDENCIES
TENDERABLE
TENDERFEET
TENDERFOOT
TENDERIZED
TENDERIZER
TENDERLOIN
TENDERNESS
TENDRILLAR
TENEMENTAL
TENGRI
  KHAN
TENNESSEAN
TENOTOMIST
TENSIMETER
TENTACULAR
TENTERHOOK
TERATOLOGY
TERENGGANU
TERMAGANCY
TERMAGANTS
TERMINABLE

TERMINALLY
TERMINATED
TERMINATOR
TERMINUSES
TERRACOTTA
TERRA
  FIRMA
TERRAMYCIN
TERREPLEIN
TERRE-
  VERTE
TERRIFYING
TERRORISTS
TERRORIZED
TERRORIZER
TERRYCLOTH
TESSELLATE
TESTACEOUS
TESTAMENTS
TESTICULAR
TESTIFYING
TEST
  PILOTS
TESTUDINAL
TETCHINESS
TETE-A-
  TETES
TETRABASIC
TETRABRACH
TETRACHORD
TETRAGONAL
TETRAPLOID
TETRAPODIC
TETRARCHIC
TETRASPORE
TETRASTICH
TETRATOMIC
TEWKESBURY
TEXTUALISM
TEXTUALIST
TEXTURALLY
THANKFULLY
THEATRICAL
THEME
  PARKS
THEME
  SONGS
THEMSELVES
THENARDITE
THEOCRATIC
THEODOLITE
THEOLOGIAN

THEOLOGIES
THEOLOGIZE
THEOPHOBIA
THEORETICS
THEORIZING
THEOSOPHIC
THERAPISTS
THEREAFTER
THEREUNDER
THERMALIZE
THERMIONIC
THERMISTOR
THERMOGRAM
THERMOPILE
THERMOSTAT
THEROPODAN
THESSALIAN
THETICALLY
THICKENERS
THICKENING
THIEVINGLY
THIEVISHLY
THIMBLEFUL
THIMEROSAL
THINK
    TANKS
THIOURACIL
THIRD
    PARTY
THIRD
    WORLD
THIRSTIEST
THIRTEENTH
THIRTIETHS
THIXOTROPY
THORIANITE
THORNINESS
THOROUGHLY
THOUGHTFUL
THOUGHT-
    OUT
THOUSANDTH
THRASH
    PUNK
THREADBARE
THREADWORM
THREATENED
THREATENER
THREEPENCE
THREE-
    PHASE

THREE-
    PIECE
THREESOMES
THRENODIES
THRESHOLDS
THRIFTIEST
THRIFTLESS
THROATIEST
THROATLASH
THROMBOGEN
THROMBOSES
THROMBOSIS
THROMBOTIC
THROTTLING
THROUGHOUT
THROUGHPUT
THROUGHWAY
THROWBACKS
THUMBNAILS
THUMBSCREW
THUMBSTALL
THUMBTACKS
THUMPINGLY
THUNDER
    BAY
THUNDERERS
THUNDERFLY
THUNDERING
THUNDEROUS
THURINGIAN
THWARTEDLY
TICKERTAPE
TICKING
    OFF
TICKLISHLY
TIDAL
    WAVES
TIEBREAKER
TIED
    HOUSES
TIEMANNITE
TIGHTENING
TIGHTROPES
TIGLIC
    ACID
TILIACEOUS
TILLANDSIA
TIMBERHEAD
TIMBERLINE
TIMBERWORK
TIMBERYARD
TIMEKEEPER

TIMELESSLY
TIME
    LIMITS
TIMELINESS
TIMEPIECES
TIMESAVING
TIME-
    SAVING
TIMESERVER
TIME
    SHEETS
TIME
    SIGNAL
TIME
    SWITCH
TIMETABLED
TIMETABLES
TIMEWORKER
TIMOROUSLY
TIMPANISTS
TINCTORIAL
TINGALINGS
TINGLINGLY
TIN
    OPENERS
TIRELESSLY
TIRESOMELY
TITANESQUE
TITILLATED
TITIVATING
TITIVATION
TITLE
    DEEDS
TITLE
    PAGES
TITLE
    ROLES
TITRATABLE
TITUBATION
T-
    JUNCTION
    S
TOADSTOOLS
TOBOGGANED
TOBOGGANER
TOCOPHEROL
TOILETRIES
TOILET
    ROLL
TOLERANTLY
TOLERATING
TOLERATION

TOLERATIVE
TOLLBOOTHS
TOLLUIDINE
TOLUIC
    ACID
TOMBSTONES
TOMFOOLERY
TOMOGRAPHY
TONALITIES
TONELESSLY
TONGUE-
    TIED
TONIC SOL-
    FA
TONIC
    WATER
TONOMETRIC
TOOL-
    MAKING
TOOTHACHES
TOOTHBRUSH
TOOTHCOMBS
TOOTHINESS
TOOTHPASTE
TOOTHPICKS
TOPAZOLITE
TOPGALLANT
TOP-
    HEAVILY
TOPICALITY
TOPOGRAPHY
TOPOLOGIST
TOPPING
    OUT
TOPSY-
    TURVY
TORBERNITE
TORCHLIGHT
TORMENTING
TORMENTORS
TORPEDOING
TORRENTIAL
TORTELLINI
TORT-
    FEASOR
TORTUOSITY
TORTUOUSLY
TORTUREDLY
TOTEMISTIC
TOTEM
    POLES
TOTIPOTENT

TOUCH-AND-
    GO
TOUCHDOWNS
TOUCHINESS
TOUCHINGLY
TOUCHLINES
TOUCHPAPER
TOUCHSTONE
TOUCH-
    TYPED
TOUGHENING
TOURMALINE
TOURNAMENT
TOURNIQUET
TOWER
    BLOCK
TOWN
    CLERKS
TOWN
    CRIERS
TOWN
    HOUSES
TOWNSCAPES
TOWNSVILLE
TOWNSWOMAN
TOXALBUMIN
TOXICOLOGY
TRABEATION
TRABECULAR
TRACHEIDAL
TRACHEITIS
TRACHYTOID
TRACK
    EVENT
TRACKLAYER
TRACKSUITS
TRACTILITY
TRACTIONAL
TRADEMARKS
TRADE
    NAMES
TRADE
    PRICE
TRADE
    ROUTE
TRADE
    UNION
TRADE
    WINDS
TRADITIONS
TRADUCIBLE

TRAFFIC
JAM
TRAFFICKED
TRAFFICKER
TRAGACANTH
TRAGEDIANS
TRAGICALLY
TRAGICOMIC
TRAILINGLY
TRAITOROUS
TRAJECTILE
TRAJECTION
TRAJECTORY
TRAMONTANE
TRAMPOLINE
TRANCELIKE
TRANQUILLY
TRANSACTED
TRANSACTOR
TRANSDUCER
TRANSEPTAL
TRANSFEREE
TRANSFEROR
TRANSFIXED
TRANSGRESS
TRANSIENCE
TRANSIENCY
TRANSISTOR
TRANSITION
TRANSITIVE
TRANSITORY
TRANSKEIAN
TRANSLATED
TRANSLATOR
TRANSLUNAR
TRANSMUTED
TRANSMUTER
TRANSPIRED
TRANSPLANT
TRANSPOLAR
TRANSPORTS
TRANSPOSED
TRANSPOSER
TRANSPUTER
TRANSUDATE
TRANSVALUE
TRANSVERSE
TRAPEZIUMS
TRAPEZOIDS

TRASHINESS
TRAUMATISM
TRAUMATIZE
TRAVAILING
TRAVELLERS
TRAVELLING
TRAVELOGUE
TRAVELSICK
TRAVERSING
TRAVERTINE
TRAVESTIES
TREADMILLS
TREAD
WATER
TREASURERS
TREASURIES
TREASURING
TREATMENTS
TREBLE
CLEF
TREEHOPPER
TREMENDOUS
TRENCHANCY
TRENCH
COAT
TRENDINESS
TREPANNING
TREPHINING
TREPPANNER
TRESPASSED
TRESPASSER
TRESPASSES
TRIANGULAR
TRIBRACHIC
TRICHIASIS
TRICHINIZE
TRICHINOUS
TRICHOCYST
TRICHOGYNE
TRICHOLOGY
TRICHOTOMY
TRICHROISM
TRICHROMAT
TRICKINESS
TRICKINGLY
TRICKSTERS
TRICOLOURS
TRICOSTATE
TRICROTISM
TRIDENTATE
TRIDENTINE

TRIFLINGLY
TRIFOLIATE
TRIFURCATE
TRIGEMINAL
TRIGGERING
TRIGLYPHIC
TRIGRAPHIC
TRIHYDRATE
TRILATERAL
TRILINGUAL
TRILITERAL
TRILLIONTH
TRILOBITES
TRILOCULAR
TRIMESTERS
TRIMESTRAL
TRIMONTHLY
TRIMORPHIC
TRINOCULAR
TRIOECIOUS
TRIPARTITE
TRIPHAMMER
TRIPHTHONG
TRIPHYLITE
TRIPINNATE
TRIPLE
JUMP
TRIPLETAIL
TRIPLICATE
TRIPLICITY
TRIPPINGLY
TRIPTEROUS
TRIRADIATE
TRISECTING
TRISKELION
TRISTICHIC
TRITANOPIA
TRITANOPIC
TRITURABLE
TRITURATOR
TRIUMPHANT
TRIUMPHING
TRIVALENCY
TRIVANDRUM
TRIVIALITY
TRIVIALIZE
TROCHANTER
TROGLODYTE
TROLLEYBUS
TROLLEY
BUS

TROMBONIST
TROOPSHIPS
TROPAEOLIN
TROPAEOLUM
TROPICALLY
TROPICBIRD
TROPOLOGIC
TROPOPAUSE
TROPOPHYTE
TROTSKYISM
TROTSKYIST
TROTSKYITE
TROUBADOUR
TROUBLEDLY
TROUSSEAUS
TROUSSEAUX
TROWBRIDGE
TROY
WEIGHT
TRUCK
FARMS
TRUCKLOADS
TRUCK
STOPS
TRUCULENCE
TRUMP
CARDS
TRUMPETERS
TRUMPETING
TRUNCATING
TRUNCATION
TRUNCHEONS
TRUNK
CALLS
TRUNK
ROADS
TRUNK
ROUTE
TRUSTFULLY
TRUST
FUNDS
TRUSTINESS
TRUTHFULLY
TRUTH-
VALUE
TRYINGNESS
TRYPTOPHAN
TUBERCULAR
TUBERCULIN
TUBEROSITY
TUB-
THUMPER

TUBULARITY
TUBULATION
TUFFACEOUS
TUGS-OF-
LOVE
TULARAEMIA
TULARAEMIC
TUMBLEDOWN
TUMBLEWEED
TUMESCENCE
TUMULOSITY
TUMULTUOUS
TUNELESSLY
TUNING
FORK
TUNING
PEGS
TUNNELLING
TUPPERWARE
TURBOPROPS
TURBULENCE
TURGESCENT
TURNABOUTS
TURNAROUND
TURNBUCKLE
TURNROUNDS
TURNSTILES
TURNTABLES
TURPENTINE
TURQUOISES
TURTLEBACK
TURTLEDOVE
TURTLENECK
TUT-
TUTTING
TWELVE-
TONE
TWENTIETHS
TWIN-
BEDDED
TWINFLOWER
TWINKLINGS
TWISTINGLY
TWITTERING
TYMPANITES
TYMPANITIC
TYMPANITIS
TYPECASTER
TYPESCRIPT
TYPESETTER
TYPE
SETTER

TYPEWRITER
TYPHLOLOGY
TYPHOGENIC
TYPING
    POOL
TYPOGRAPHY
TYPOLOGIST
TYRANNICAL
TYRANNIZED
TYRANNIZER
TYROCIDINE
TYROSINASE

U

UBIQUITOUS
ULCERATING
ULCERATION
ULCERATIVE
ULTIMATELY
ULTIMATUMS
ULTRAFICHE
ULTRAISTIC
ULTRASHORT
ULTRASONIC
ULTRASOUND
ULTRAVIRUS
UMBILICATE
UMBILIFORM
UMBRAGEOUS
UMPIRESHIP
UMPTEENTHS
UNABRIDGED
UNACCENTED
UNADJUSTED
UNAFFECTED
UN-
    AMERICAN
UNASSISTED
UNASSUMING
UNATTACHED
UNATTENDED
UNAVAILING
UNBALANCED
UNBEARABLE
UNBEARABLY
UNBEATABLE
UNBECOMING
UNBELIEVER
UNBENDABLE
UNBLINKING
UNBLUSHING

UNBOSOMING
UNBUCKLING
UNBUNDLING
UNBURDENED
UNCANNIEST
UNCARED-
    FOR
UNCARPETED
UNCIVILITY
UNCOMMONLY
UNCONFINED
UNCOUPLING
UNCOVERING
UNCREDITED
UNCRITICAL
UNCTUOSITY
UNCTUOUSLY
UNDECEIVED
UNDECEIVER
UNDEFEATED
UNDEFENDED
UNDENIABLE
UNDENIABLY
UNDERACTED
UNDERBELLY
UNDERBRUSH
UNDERCOATS
UNDERCOVER
UNDERCROFT
UNDERDRAIN
UNDERFLOOR
UNDERGLAZE
UNDERGOING
UNDERGROWN
UNDERLINED
UNDERLINGS
UNDERLYING
UNDERMINED
UNDERMINER
UNDERNAMED
UNDERNEATH
UNDERPANTS
UNDERPRICE
UNDERPROOF
UNDERQUOTE
UNDERRATED
UNDERSCORE
UNDERSEXED
UNDERSHIRT
UNDERSHOOT
UNDERSIZED

UNDERSKIRT
UNDERSLUNG
UNDERSPEND
UNDERSTAND
UNDERSTATE
UNDERSTOCK
UNDERSTOOD
UNDERSTUDY
UNDERTAKEN
UNDERTAKER
UNDERTONES
UNDERTRICK
UNDERTRUMP
UNDERVALUE
UNDERWATER
UNDERWIRED
UNDERWORLD
UNDERWRITE
UNDERWROTE
UNDETERRED
UNDIRECTED
UNDISPUTED
UNDRESSING
UNDULATING
UNDULATION
UNDULATORY
UNEARTHING
UNEASINESS
UNECONOMIC
UNEDIFYING
UNEDUCATED
UNEMPLOYED
UNENVIABLE
UNEQUALLED
UNERRINGLY
UNEVENNESS
UNEVENTFUL
UNEXAMPLED
UNEXPECTED
UNEXPLODED
UNFAIRNESS
UNFAITHFUL
UNFAMILIAR
UNFATHERED
UNFEMININE
UNFETTERED
UNFINISHED
UNFLAGGING
UNFORESEEN
UNFORGIVEN
UNFRIENDLY

UNFROCKING
UNFRUITFUL
UNGENEROUS
UNGRATEFUL
UNGRUDGING
UNGUENTARY
UNHALLOWED
UNHAMPERED
UNHANDSOME
UNHERALDED
UNHOLINESS
UNHOPED-
    FOR
UNHYGIENIC
UNICAMERAL
UNICOSTATE
UNICYCLIST
UNIFOLIATE
UNIFORMITY
UNILATERAL
UNILOCULAR
UNIMPOSING
UNIMPROVED
UNINFORMED
UNINSPIRED
UNINTENDED
UNIONISTIC
UNIONIZING
UNIQUENESS
UNISEPTATE
UNITARIANS
UNITEDNESS
UNIT
    TRUSTS
UNIVALENCY
UNIVERSITY
UNJUSTNESS
UNKINDNESS
UNKNOWABLE
UNLAWFULLY
UNLEARNING
UNLEASHING
UNLEAVENED
UNLETTERED
UNLICENSED
UNLOCKABLE
UNLOOSENED
UNMANNERED
UNMANNERLY
UNMEASURED
UNMEDIATED

UNMERCIFUL
UNMORALITY
UNNUMBERED
UNOCCUPIED
UNOFFICIAL
UNORIGINAL
UNORTHODOX
UNPATENTED
UNPLAYABLE
UNPLEASANT
UNPREPARED
UNPROMPTED
UNPROVIDED
UNPROVOKED
UNPUNCTUAL
UNPUNISHED
UNRAVELING
UNRAVELLED
UNRAVELLER
UNREACTIVE
UNREADABLE
UNREADABLY
UNRELIABLE
UNRELIEVED
UNREQUITED
UNRESERVED
UNRESOLVED
UNRIVALLED
UNRULINESS
UNSADDLING
UNSANITARY
UNSCHOOLED
UNSCRAMBLE
UNSCREENED
UNSCREWING
UNSCRIPTED
UNSEALABLE
UNSEASONED
UNSEEINGLY
UNSETTLING
UNSHAKABLE
UNSOCIABLE
UNSPEAKING
UNSPECIFIC
UNSTEADILY
UNSTINTING
UNSTOPPING
UNSTRAINED
UNSTRESSED
UNSTRIATED
UNSUITABLE

UNSURFACED
UNSWERVING
UNTANGLING
UNTHANKFUL
UNTHINKING
UNTIDINESS
UNTIRINGLY
UNTOWARDLY
UNTRUSTING
UNTRUTHFUL
UNWIELDILY
UNWINDABLE
UNWORKABLE
UNWORTHILY
UNYIELDING
UP-AND-
    UNDER
UPBRAIDING
UPBRINGING
UPHOLSTERY
UP IN THE
    AIR
UPLIFTMENT
UPON MY
    WORD
UPPER
    CLASS
UPPER
    CRUST
UPPER
    EGYPT
UPPER
    HOUSE
UPPER
    VOLTA
UPPISHNESS
UPROARIOUS
UPSETTABLE
UPSIDE
    DOWN
UPSTANDING
UP THE
    SPOUT
UP THE
    STAKE
UP THE
    STICK
UPWARDNESS
URAL-
    ALTAIC
URBANENESS
UREDOSORUS

UREDOSPORE
URETHRITIC
URETHRITIS
URINALYSIS
UROCHORDAL
UROGENITAL
UROSCOPIST
URTICARIAL
URTICATION
USEFULNESS
USHERETTES
USQUEBAUGH
USTULATION
USURPATION
USURPATIVE
USURPINGLY
UTILIZABLE
UTO-
    AZTECAN
UTOPIANISM
UTTERANCES
UXORICIDAL
UZBEKISTAN

V

VACANTNESS
VACATIONED
VACATIONER
VACCINATED
VACILLATED
VACILLATOR
VACUUM
    PUMP
VAGINISMUS
VAGOTROPIC
VAL-DE-
    MARNE
VALENTINES
VALIDATING
VALIDATION
VALIDATORY
VALLADOLID
VALLECULAR
VALPARAISO
VALUATIONS
VALVULITIS
VAMPIRE
    BAT
VANADINITE
VANDALIZED
VAN DER
    POST

VANISHMENT
VANQUISHED
VANQUISHER
VAPORIZING
VAPOURABLE
VARIATIONS
VARICELLAR
VARICOCELE
VARICOSITY
VARICOTOMY
VARIEDNESS
VARIEGATED
VARIFOCALS
ANGLO-
    SAXON
VARIOLITIC
VARIOMETER
VARITYPIST
VARNISHING
VASTNESSES
VAUDEVILLE
VAUNTINGLY
VEGETABLES
VEGETARIAN
VEGETATING
VEGETATION
VEGETATIVE
VEHEMENTLY
VELOCIPEDE
VELOCITIES
VELUTINOUS
VENATIONAL
VENDETTIST
VENERATING
VENERATION
VENEZUELAN
VENGEANCES
VENGEFULLY
VENOMOUSLY
VENOUSNESS
VENTILABLE
VENTILATED
VENTILATOR
VENTRICLES
VENTRICOSE
VERBALIZED
VERBALIZER
VERBAL
    NOUN
VERIFIABLE
VERKRAMPTE

VERMICELLI
VERMICIDAL
VERMICULAR
VERNACULAR
VERNISSAGE
VERSAILLES
VERTEBRATE
VERTICALLY
VERY
    LIGHTS
VESICATION
VESICULATE
VESPERTINE
VESTIBULAR
VESTIBULES
VESTMENTAL
VESTMENTED
VETERINARY
VIBRACULAR
VIBRACULUM
VIBRAPHONE
VIBRATIONS
VICEGERENT
VICEREINES
VICINITIES
VICOMTESSE
VICTIMIZED
VICTIMIZER
VICTIMLESS
VICTORIANA
VICTORIANS
VICTORIOUS
VICTUALING
VICTUALLED
VICTUALLER
VIDEODISCS
VIDEO
    NASTY
VIDEOPHILE
VIDEOPHONE
VIDEOTAPED
VIETNAMESE
VIEWFINDER
VIEWPOINTS
VIGILANTES
VIGILANTLY
VIGNETTING
VIGNETTIST
VIGOROUSLY
VIJAYAWADA
VILLAINOUS

VILLANELLA
VILLANELLE
VILLANOVAN
VINA DEL
    MAR
VINDICABLE
VINDICATED
VINDICATOR
VINDICTIVE
VINIFEROUS
VINYLIDENE
VIOLACEOUS
VIOLATIONS
VIOLINISTS
VIRAGINOUS
VIRESCENCE
VIROLOGIST
VIRTUALITY
VIRTUOSITY
VIRTUOUSLY
VIRULENTLY
VISCOMETER
VISCOMETRY
VISCOUNTCY
VISIBILITY
VISITATION
VISITORIAL
VISUAL
    AIDS
VISUALIZED
VISUALIZER
VITALISTIC
VITAL
    SIGNS
VITRESCENT
VITRIFYING
VITRIOLIZE
VITUPERATE
VIVIPARITY
VIVIPAROUS
VIVISECTOR
VOCABULARY
VOCAL
    CORDS
VOCATIONAL
VOCIFERANT
VOCIFERATE
VOCIFEROUS
VOETSTOETS
VOICE
    BOXES

VOICE-
  OVERS
VOICEPRINT
VOLAPUKIST
VOLATILITY
VOLATILIZE
VOL-AU-
  VENTS
VOLITIONAL
VOLLEYBALL
VOLT-
  AMPERE
VOLTE-
  FACES
VOLUBILITY
VOLUMETRIC
VOLUMINOUS
VOLUNTEERS
VOLUPTUARY
VOLUPTUOUS
VORARLBERG
VORTICELLA
VOTIVENESS
VOUCHSAFED
VULCANIZED
VULCANIZER
VULGARIZED
VULGARIZER
VULGARNESS
VULNERABLE
VULNERABLY
VULPECULAR

W

WADDLINGLY
WADING
  POOL
WAGE
  SLAVES
WAGGA
  WAGGA
WAGGLINGLY
WAGONS-
  LITS
WAINWRIGHT
WAISTBANDS
WAISTCOATS
WAISTLINES
WAITPERSON
WAKEY
  WAKEY
WALKABOUTS

WALK OF
  LIFE
WALLCHARTS
WALLFLOWER
WALLPAPERS
WALL
  STREET
WALL-TO-
  WALL
WANDERINGS
WANDERLUST
WANDSWORTH
WANTONNESS
WAREHOUSES
WARMING
  PAN
WARMONGERS
WARRANTIES
WARRANTING
WARRINGTON
WASHBASINS
WASHCLOTHS
WASHING
  DAY
WASHINGTON
WASHSTANDS
WASTEFULLY
WASTELANDS
WASTE
  PAPER
WATCHFULLY
WATCHMAKER
WATCH
  NIGHT
WATCHSTRAP
WATCHTOWER
WATCHWORDS
WATER
  BIRDS
WATERBORNE
WATER
  BUTTS
WATERCRAFT
WATERCRESS
WATERFALLS
WATERFOWLS
WATERFRONT
WATERHOLES
WATERINESS
WATER
  JUMPS

WATER
  LEVEL
WATER
  MAINS
WATERMARKS
WATERMELON
WATER
  METER
WATERMILLS
WATER
  PIPES
WATERPOWER
WATERPROOF
WATER
  RATES
WATERSCAPE
WATERSHEDS
WATER
  SKIER
WATERSPOUT
WATER
  TABLE
WATERTIGHT
WATER
  VOLES
WATERWHEEL
WATERWINGS
WATERWORKS
WATTLEBIRD
WAVELENGTH
WAVERINGLY
WAXED
  PAPER
WEAKLINESS
WEAK-
  MINDED
WEAKNESSES
WEAK-
  WILLED
WEALTHIEST
WEARYINGLY
WEATHERING
WEATHERMAN
WEATHERMEN
WEAVERBIRD
WEDNESDAYS
WEEDKILLER
WEEKENDERS
WEEKENDING
WEEKNIGHTS
WEIGHTLESS

WELL-
  ARGUED
WELL-
  CHOSEN
WELL-
  EARNED
WELL-
  HEELED
WELL I
  NEVER
WELLINGTON
WELL-
  JUDGED
WELL-
  SPOKEN
WELLSPRING
WELL-
  TURNED
WELL-
  WISHER
WELL-
  WORDED
WENTLETRAP
WEREWOLVES
WEST
  BENGAL
WESTERLIES
WESTERNERS
WESTERNISM
WESTERNIZE
WEST
  INDIAN
WEST
  INDIES
WESTPHALIA
WEST
  RIDING
WET
  BLANKET
WET-
  NURSING
WHARFINGER
WHATSOEVER
WHEELBASES
WHEELCHAIR
WHEELHOUSE
WHEELIE
  BIN
WHEEZINESS
WHEEZINGLY
WHENSOEVER
WHEREFORES
WHETSTONES

WHICKERING
WHIMPERING
WHIPLASHES
WHIP-
  ROUNDS
WHIPSTITCH
WHIRLABOUT
WHIRLIGIGS
WHIRLINGLY
WHIRLPOOLS
WHIRLWINDS
WHIRLYBIRD
WHISPERERS
WHISPERING
WHIST
  DRIVE
WHITEBOARD
WHITE
  DWARF
WHITE
  FLAGS
WHITE
  HOPES
WHITEHORSE
WHITE
  HORSE
WHITE
  HOUSE
WHITE
  MAGIC
WHITE
  METAL
WHITE
  PAPER
WHITE
  SAUCE
WHITESMITH
WHITE
  TRASH
WHITEWATER
WHITLEY
  BAY
WHITTLINGS
WHOLEFOODS
WHOLE
  NOTES
WHOLESALER
WHOREHOUSE
WICKEDNESS
WICKERWORK
WICKET
  GATE

WIDE-
SCREEN
WIDESPREAD
WIDOWS
MITE
WIFELINESS
WILDCATTED
WILDEBEEST
WILDERNESS
WILDFOWLER
WILFULNESS
WILLEMSTAD
WILLOWHERB
WILLY-
NILLY
WILMINGTON
WINCEYETTE
WINCHESTER
WINDBREAKS
WIND-
BROKEN
WINDEDNESS
WINDFLOWER
WINDGALLED
WIND
GAUGES
WINDJAMMER
WINDLASSES
WINDOWPANE
WINDOW-
SHOP
WINDOWSILL
WINDSCREEN
WINDSHIELD
WIND
SLEEVE
WINDSTORMS
WINDSUCKER
WIND-
SURFER

WIND
TUNNEL
WINEBIBBER
WINE
COOLER
WINEMAKING
WINTERFEED
WINTERTHUR
WINTERTIME
WINTRINESS
WIRE-
HAIRED
WIRELESSES
WIREWORKER
WISECRACKS
WISHY-
WASHY
WITCHCRAFT
WITCH-
HAZEL
WITCH-
HUNTS
WITHDRAWAL
WITHDRAWER
WITHHOLDER
WITNESS
BOX
WITNESSING
WITTENBERG
WITTICISMS
WOBBLINESS
WOEFULNESS
WOLFHOUNDS
WOLFRAMITE
WOLLONGONG
WOMANIZERS
WOMANIZING
WOMENSWEAR
WONDERLAND
WONDERMENT
WONDERWORK

WOODBLOCKS
WOODCARVER
WOODCUTTER
WOODENNESS
WOODLANDER
WOODPECKER
WOODWORKER
WOOKEY
HOLE
WOOLGROWER
WOOLLINESS
WORDLESSLY
WORKAHOLIC
WORKBASKET
WORK-
HARDEN
WORKHORSES
WORKING
DAY
WORKINGMAN
WORKPEOPLE
WORKPLACES
WORK-TO-
RULE
WORLD-
CLASS
WORLDLIEST
WORLD
POWER
WORLD-
WEARY
WORRYINGLY
WORRYWARTS
WORSHIPFUL
WORSHIPING
WORSHIPPED
WORSHIPPER
WORTHINESS
WORTHWHILE
WOUNDINGLY
WRAITHLIKE

WRATHFULLY
WRETCHEDLY
WRISTBANDS
WRISTWATCH
WRITHINGLY
WRONGDOERS
WRONGDOING
WRONGFULLY
WUNDERKIND

X

XANTHATION
XENOGAMOUS
XENOLITHIC
XENOPHOBIA
XENOPHOBIC
XEROGRAPHY
XEROPHYTIC
XIPHOSURAN
XOCHIMILCO
X-
RADIATIO
N
X-RAY
BINARY
XYLOGRAPHY
XYLOPHONES
XYLOPHONIC
XYLOTOMIST
XYLOTOMOUS

Y

YARBOROUGH
YARDSTICKS
YEASTINESS
YELLOWBARK
YELLOWBIRD
YELLOWCAKE
YELLOWLEGS
YELLOWTAIL
YELLOWWEED

YELLOWWOOD
YESTERDAYS
YESTERYEAR
YIELDINGLY
YLANG-
YLANG
YOGYAKARTA
YOSHKAR-
OLA
YOUNGBERRY
YOUNGSTERS
YOUNGSTOWN
YOURSELVES
YOUTHFULLY
YUGOSLAVIA

Z

ZAPOROZHYE
ZENER
DIODE
ZIGZAGGING
ZINCOGRAPH
ZOOGRAPHER
ZOOGRAPHIC
ZOOLATROUS
ZOOLOGICAL
ZOOLOGISTS
ZOOM
LENSES
ZOOMORPHIC
ZOOPHAGOUS
ZOOPHILISM
ZOOPHILOUS
ZOOPHOBOUS
ZOOPLASTIC
ZWITTERION
ZYGODACTYL
ZYGOMYCETE
ZYGOSPORIC
ZYMOLOGIST

A
ABANDONEDLY
ABANDONMENT
ABBEVILLIAN
ABBREVIATED
ABBREVIATOR
ABDICATIONS
ABERRATIONS
ABERYSTWYTH
ABIETIC ACID
ABIOGENESIS
ABIOGENETIC
ABLUTIONARY
ABNORMALITY
ABOLISHMENT
ABOMINATING
ABOMINATION
ABORIGINALS
ABORTIONIST
ABRACADABRA
ABRANCHIATE
ABRIDGMENTS
ABROGATIONS
ABSENTEEISM
ABSORBINGLY
ABSORPTANCE
ABSTENTIONS
ABSTENTIOUS
ABSTRACTING
ABSTRACTION
ABSTRACTIVE
ABSTRICTION
ABSURDITIES
ABUSIVENESS
ACADEMICALS
ACADEMICIAN
ACADEMICISM
ACARPELLOUS
ACATALECTIC
ACAULESCENT
ACCELERANDO
ACCELERATED
ACCELERATOR
ACCENTUATED
ACCEPTANCES
ACCEPTATION
ACCESSIONAL
ACCESSORIAL
ACCESSORIES
ACCESSORILY
ACCIPITRINE

ACCLAMATION
ACCLAMATORY
ACCLIMATIZE
ACCLIVITIES
ACCLIVITOUS
ACCOMMODATE
ACCOMPANIED
ACCOMPANIER
ACCOMPANIST
ACCOMPLICES
ACCORDANCES
ACCORDINGLY
ACCOUNTABLE
ACCOUNTANCY
ACCOUNTANTS
ACCULTURATE
ACCUMULABLE
ACCUMULATED
ACCUMULATOR
ACCUSATIONS
ACCUSATIVAL
ACCUSATIVES
ACCUSTOMING
ACETANILIDE
ACETYLATION
ACHIEVEMENT
ACHONDRITIC
ACHROMATISM
ACHROMATIZE
ACHROMATOUS
ACID-FORMING
ACIDIFIABLE
ACIDIMETRIC
ACIDOPHILIC
ACIDOPHILUS
ACIDULATION
ACINACIFORM
ACKNOWLEDGE
ACLINIC LINE
ACOUSTICIAN
ACQUAINTING
ACQUIESCENT
ACQUIESCING
ACQUIREMENT
ACQUISITION
ACQUISITIVE
ACQUITTANCE
ACRIFLAVINE
ACRIMONIOUS
ACROCARPOUS
ACROMEGALIC

ACTINICALLY
ACTINOMETER
ACTINOMETRY
ACTINOMYCIN
ACTUALITIES
ACUMINATION
ACUPRESSURE
ACUPUNCTURE
ADAM'S APPLES
ADAPTATIONS
ADIAPHORISM
ADIAPHORIST
ADIAPHOROUS
AD INFINITUM
ADIPOCEROUS
ADJOURNMENT
ADJUDICATED
ADJUDICATOR
ADJUSTMENTS
ADMIRATIONS
ADMONISHING
ADMONITIONS
ADOLESCENCE
ADOLESCENTS
ADOPTIONISM
ADOPTIONIST
ADULTERATED
ADULTERATOR
ADUMBRATING
ADUMBRATION
ADUMBRATIVE
ADVANCEMENT
ADVANCINGLY
ADVENTURERS
ADVENTURESS
ADVENTURISM
ADVENTURIST
ADVENTUROUS
ADVERBIALLY
ADVERSARIAL
ADVERSARIES
ADVERSATIVE
ADVERSITIES
ADVERTENTLY
ADVERTISERS
ADVERTISING
ADVERTORIAL
AEOLIAN HARP
AERODYNAMIC
AEROGRAMMES
AERONAUTICS

AEROSTATICS
AEROSTATION
AESTIVATION
AETIOLOGIST
AFFECTATION
AFFECTINGLY
AFFECTIONAL
AFFECTIVITY
AFFILIATING
AFFILIATION
AFFIRMATION
AFFIRMATIVE
AFFLICTIONS
AFFORESTING
AFFRANCHISE
AFFRICATIVE
AFGHANISTAN
AFICIONADOS
AFRO-ASIATIC
AFTERBIRTHS
AFTERBURNER
AFTEREFFECT
AFTERSHAVES
AFTERTASTES
AGAMOSPERMY
AGELESSNESS
AGGLOMERATE
AGGLUTINANT
AGGLUTINATE
AGGRADATION
AGGRANDIZER
AGGRAVATING
AGGRAVATION
AGGREGATING
AGGREGATION
AGGRIEVEDLY
AGNOSTICISM
AGONIZINGLY
AGONY COLUMN
AGORAPHOBIA
AGORAPHOBIC
AGRARIANISM
AGRICULTURE
AGROBIOLOGY
AGROLOGICAL
AGROSTOLOGY
AIDE-MEMOIRE
AIDES-DE-CAMP
AILUROPHILE
AILUROPHOBE
AIMLESSNESS

AIRCRAFTMAN
AIRCRAFTMEN
AIRLESSNESS
AIRSICKNESS
AIR TERMINAL
AIX-LES-BAINS
ALARM CLOCKS
ALBATROSSES
ALBUMINURIA
ALBUQUERQUE
ALCOHOL-FREE
ALDERMASTON
ALDERPERSON
ALDOSTERONE
ALESSANDRIA
ALGEBRAICAL
ALGINIC ACID
ALGOLAGNIST
ALGORITHMIC
ALKALIMETER
ALKALIMETRY
ALKALIZABLE
ALL-AMERICAN
ALLANTOIDAL
ALLEGATIONS
ALLEGIANCES
ALLEGORICAL
ALLEVIATING
ALLEVIATION
ALLEVIATIVE
ALLOCATIONS
ALLOGRAPHIC
ALLOMORPHIC
ALLOPLASMIC
ALLOPURINOL
ALL-POWERFUL
ALL-ROUNDERS
ALLUREMENTS
ALMIGHTIEST
ALPHABETIZE
ALTARPIECES
ALTERATIONS
ALTERCATION
ALTERNATELY
ALTERNATING
ALTERNATION
ALTERNATIVE
ALTERNATORS
ALTITUDINAL
ALTOCUMULUS
ALTOGETHERS

ALTOSTRATUS
ALUMINOSITY
ALVEOLATION
AMABOKOBOKO
AMALGAMATED
AMARANTHINE
AMBASSADORS
AMBIGUGUITY
AMBIGUOUSLY
AMBITIOUSLY
AMBIVALENCE
AMBLYGONITE
AMELIORATED
AMELIORATOR
AMENABILITY
AMENORRHOEA
AMERICANISM
AMERICANIZE
AMETHYSTINE
AMICABILITY
AMINOPHENOL
AMINOPYRINE
AMMONIATION
AMONTILLADO
AMOROUSNESS
AMOR PATRIAE
AMORPHOUSLY
AMORTIZABLE
AMOUR-PROPRE
AMPHETAMINE
AMPHIBIOTIC
AMPHIBOLITE
AMPHIBOLOGY
AMPHICHROIC
AMPHICTYONY
AMPHISBAENA
AMPHISTYLAR
AMPHITRICHA
AMPLEXICAUL
AMPLIFIABLE
AMPUTATIONS
AMYL NITRITE
AMYLOPECTIN
ANACHRONISM
ANACOLUTHIA
ANACOLUTHIC
ANACOLUTHON
ANADIPLOSIS
ANAEMICALLY
ANAESTHESIA
ANAESTHETIC

ANALEMMATIC
ANALYSATION
ANAMORPHISM
ANAPHYLAXIS
ANARCHISTIC
ANASTOMOSIS
ANASTOMOTIC
ANCIENTNESS
ANCILLARIES
ANDROGENOUS
ANDROGYNOUS
ANDROSPHINX
ANEMOGRAPHY
ANEMOMETERS
ANEMOMETRIC
ANESTHETICS
ANESTHETIST
ANESTHETIZE
ANFRACTUOUS
ANGELICALLY
ANGIOMATOUS
ANGIOPLASTY
ANGLICANISM
ANGLICIZING
ANGLO-INDIAN
ANGLOPHILES
ANGLOPHILIA
ANGLOPHOBES
ANGLOPHOBIA
ANGLO-SAXONS
ANIMALCULAR
ANIMOSITIES
ANISEIKONIA
ANISEIKONIC
ANISODACTYL
ANISOGAMOUS
ANISOMEROUS
ANISOMETRIC
ANISOTROPIC
ANNABERGITE
ANNEXATIONS
ANNIHILABLE
ANNIHILATED
ANNIHILATOR
ANNIVERSARY
ANNOTATIONS
ANNUNCIATOR
ANOINTMENTS
ANOMALISTIC
ANOMALOUSLY
ANONYMOUSLY

ANORTHOSITE
ANTAGONISMS
ANTAGONISTS
ANTAGONIZED
ANTALKALINE
ANTECEDENCE
ANTECEDENTS
ANTECHAMBER
ANTEPENDIUM
ANTEVERSION
ANTHERIDIAL
ANTHERIDIUM
ANTHEROZOID
ANTHOCYANIN
ANTHOLOGIES
ANTHOLOGIST
ANTHOLOGIZE
ANTHRACITIC
ANTHRACNOSE
ANTIBIOTICS
ANTICATHODE
ANTICIPATED
ANTICIPATOR
ANTICLASTIC
ANTICYCLONE
ANTIFEBRILE
ANTIFOULING
ANTIMISSILE
ANTIMYCOTIC
ANTINEUTRON
ANTINUCLEAR
ANTINUCLEON
ANTIOXIDANT
ANTIPATHIES
ANTIPHONARY
ANTIPHRASIS
ANTIPYRESIS
ANTIPYRETIC
ANTIQUARIAN
ANTIQUITIES
ANTIRRHINUM
ANTI-SEMITES
ANTI-SEMITIC
ANTISEPTICS
ANTITUSSIVE
ANTOFAGASTA
ANTONOMASIA
ANXIOUSNESS
APATOSAURUS
APHETICALLY
APHRODISIAC

APICULTURAL	AQUATICALLY	ASCETICALLY	ATOMIC PILES
APOCALYPSES	AQUICULTURE	ASKING PRICE	ATOMIZATION
APOCALYPTIC	ARABICA BEAN	ASPERGILLUS	ATRABILIOUS
APOCOPATION	ARALIACEOUS	ASPHYXIATED	ATROCIOUSLY
APOCYNTHION	ARAN ISLANDS	ASPHYXIATOR	ATTACHE CASE
APOLOGETICS	ARBITRAGEUR	ASPIDISTRAS	ATTACHMENTS
APOLOGIZING	ARBITRAMENT	ASPIRATIONS	ATTAINMENTS
APOMORPHINE	ARBITRARILY	ASSASSINATE	ATTEMPTABLE
APONEUROSIS	ARBITRATING	ASSEMBLAGES	ATTENDANCES
APONEUROTIC	ARBITRATION	ASSEMBLYMAN	ATTENTIVELY
APOPHYLLITE	ARBITRATORS	ASSEMBLYMEN	ATTENUATING
APOSIOPESIS	ARBORESCENT	ASSENTATION	ATTENUATION
APOSIOPETIC	ARCHAEOLOGY	ASSERTIVELY	ATTESTATION
A POSTERIORI	ARCHAEOZOIC	ASSESSMENTS	ATTITUDINAL
APOSTROPHES	ARCHAICALLY	ASSESSORIAL	ATTRACTABLE
APOTHEOSIZE	ARCHANGELIC	ASSEVERATED	ATTRACTIONS
APPALLINGLY	ARCHBISHOPS	ASSIDUOUSLY	ATTRIBUTING
APPARATCHIK	ARCHDEACONS	ASSIGNATION	ATTRIBUTION
APPARATUSES	ARCHDIOCESE	ASSIGNMENTS	ATTRIBUTIVE
APPARELLING	ARCHDUCHESS	ASSIMILABLE	ATTRITIONAL
APPARITIONS	ARCHEGONIUM	ASSIMILATED	AUCTIONEERS
APPEALINGLY	ARCHENEMIES	ASSOCIATING	AUDACIOUSLY
APPEARANCES	ARCHENTERIC	ASSOCIATION	AUDIOLOGIST
APPEASEMENT	ARCHENTERON	ASSOCIATIVE	AUDIOMETRIC
APPELLATION	ARCHIPELAGO	ASSORTATIVE	AUDIOTYPING
APPELLATIVE	ARDUOUSNESS	ASSORTMENTS	AUDIOTYPIST
APPERTAINED	ARENICOLOUS	ASSUAGEMENT	AUDIO-VISUAL
APPLICATION	ARGENTINEAN	ASSUMPTIONS	AUDITIONING
APPLICATIVE	ARGYLLSHIRE	ASSUREDNESS	AUDITORIUMS
APPLICATORY	ARISTOCRACY	ASSYRIOLOGY	AUGMENTABLE
APPOINTMENT	ARISTOCRATS	ASTATICALLY	AURIGNACIAN
APPORTIONED	ARMED FORCES	ASTERISKING	AUSCULTATOR
APPORTIONER	ARMIPOTENCE	ASTIGMATISM	AUSTERENESS
APPRECIABLE	ARMOURED CAR	ASTONISHING	AUSTERITIES
APPRECIABLY	ARMOUR PLATE	ASTRAPHOBIA	AUSTRALASIA
APPRECIATED	AROMATICITY	ASTRAPHOBIC	AUSTRALIANA
APPREHENDED	ARONOMASTIC	ASTRINGENCY	AUSTRALIANS
APPRENTICED	ARRAIGNMENT	ASTRINGENTS	AUSTRONESIA
APPRENTICES	ARRANGEMENT	ASTROBOTANY	AUTHORITIES
APPROACHING	ARRESTINGLY	ASTROLOGERS	AUTHORIZING
APPROBATION	ARTERIALIZE	ASTROMETRIC	AUTOCHANGER
APPROBATIVE	ARTHROMERIC	ASTRONAUTIC	AUTOCRACIES
APPROPRIATE	ARTHROSPORE	ASTRONOMERS	AUTOGENESIS
APPROVINGLY	ARTICULATED	ASTROSPHERE	AUTOGENETIC
APPROXIMATE	ARTICULATOR	ATELECTASIS	AUTOGRAPHED
APPURTENANT	ARTILLERIES	ATHEISTICAL	AUTOGRAPHIC
AQUACULTURE	ARTIODACTYL	ATHERMANOUS	AUTOKINETIC
AQUAEROBICS	ARTLESSNESS	ATHLETICISM	AUTOMOBILES
AQUAMARINES	ARYTENOIDAL	ATLANTICISM	AUTOPLASTIC
AQUAPLANING	ASCENSIONAL	ATMOSPHERES	AUTOTROPHIC
AQUARELLIST	ASCERTAINED	ATMOSPHERIC	AUXANOMETER

AUXILIARIES	BALLBREAKER	BATTLE CRIES	BENEVOLENCE
AVOIRDUPOIS	BALLETOMANE	BATTLEFIELD	BENIGHTEDLY
AVUNCULARLY	BALLOONISTS	BATTLEMENTS	BEQUEATHING
AWESOMENESS	BALLOT PAPER	BATTLE ROYAL	BEREAVEMENT
AWKWARDNESS	BALUCHISTAN	BATTLESHIPS	BERGSCHRUND
AXIOLOGICAL	BALUSTRADES	BATTY RIDERS	BESMIRCHING
AXONOMETRIC	BAMBOOZLING	BEACHCHAIRS	BESPATTERED
AZERBAIJANI	BANANA SKINS	BEACHCOMBER	BEST-SELLERS
AZOTOBACTER	BANDMASTERS	BEAN COUNTER	BEST-SELLING
	BANGLADESHI	BEANSPROUTS	BETA-BLOCKER
B	BANK ACCOUNT	BEARISHNESS	BETES-NOIRES
BABY-MINDERS	BANKER'S CARD	BEAR'S-BREECH	BETULACEOUS
BABY ON BOARD	BANK HOLIDAY	BEASTLINESS	BEWILDERING
BABY'S-BREATH	BANKROLLING	BEAUHARNAIS	BHUBANESWAR
BABY-SITTERS	BANKRUPTING	BEAUTEOUSLY	BIAS BINDING
BABY-SITTING	BANNOCKBURN	BEAUTICIANS	BIBLIOLATRY
BACCHANALIA	BANTERINGLY	BEAUTIFULLY	BIBLIOMANCY
BACCIFEROUS	BARBARITIES	BEAUTIFYING	BIBLIOMANIA
BACCIVOROUS	BARBARIZING	BEAUTY QUEEN	BIBLIOPHILE
BACILLIFORM	BARBAROUSLY	BEAUTY SLEEP	BIBLIOPHISM
BACKBENCHER	BARBASTELLE	BEAUTY SPOTS	BIBLIOTHECA
BACKBENCHES	BARBITURATE	BEAVERBOARD	BICARBONATE
BACKCOMBING	BARCOO RIVER	BECKENBAUER	BICENTENARY
BACK COUNTRY	BAREFACEDLY	BED AND BOARD	BICEPHALOUS
BACKGROUNDS	BARIUM MEALS	BEDEVILLING	BICONCAVITY
BACKHANDERS	BARLEY SUGAR	BEDEVILMENT	BIEDERMEIER
BACK NUMBERS	BARLEY WATER	BEFITTINGLY	BIFOLIOLATE
BACKPACKERS	BAR MITZVAHS	BEFRIENDING	BIFURCATING
BACKPACKING	BARNSTORMED	BEGUILEMENT	BIFURCATION
BACK PASSAGE	BARNSTORMER	BEGUILINGLY	BIG BUSINESS
BACKPEDALED	BAROGRAPHIC	BEHAVIOURAL	BIKER JACKET
BACKROOM BOY	BARONETCIES	BELABOURING	BILATERALLY
BACKSLAPPER	BAROTSELAND	BELARUSSIAN	BILIOUSNESS
BACKSLIDERS	BARQUENTINE	BELATEDNESS	BILLETS-DOUX
BACKSLIDING	BARREL ORGAN	BELEAGUERED	BILLIONAIRE
BACK STREETS	BARRICADING	BELL-BOTTOMS	BILLOWINESS
BACKSTROKES	BASHFULNESS	BELLICOSITY	BILLS OF FARE
BACK TO FRONT	BASINGSTOKE	BELLIGERENT	BILLS OF SALE
BACKTRACKED	BASKERVILLE	BELL-RINGING	BIMETALLISM
BACTERAEMIA	BASS GUITARS	BELLYACHING	BIMOLECULAR
BACTERICIDE	BASSOONISTS	BELLY BUTTON	BIOCATALYST
BADDERLOCKS	BASTARDIZED	BELLY DANCER	BIOCENOLOGY
BAD-MOUTHING	BASTINADOED	BELLY DANCES	BIODYNAMICS
BAGGAGE CARS	BASTINADOES	BELLY LAUGHS	BIOENGINEER
BAGGAGE ROOM	BASTNAESITE	BENEDICTINE	BIOFEEDBACK
BAHIA BLANCA	BATHING SUIT	BENEDICTION	BIOGRAPHERS
BAKERS DOZEN	BATHOLITHIC	BENEDICTORY	BIOGRAPHIES
BAKER'S DOZEN	BATHOMETRIC	BENEFACTION	BIOPHYSICAL
BALANCEABLE	BATHYMETRIC	BENEFACTORS	BIPARTITION
BALEFULNESS	BATHYSPHERE	BENEFICENCE	BIQUADRATIC
BALL BEARING	BATSMANSHIP	BENEFICIARY	BIQUARTERLY

BIRD-BRAINED
BIRDS OF PREY
BIRD-WATCHER
BIROBIDZHAN
BIRTHPLACES
BIRTHRIGHTS
BIRTHWEIGHT
BISEXUALISM
BISEXUALITY
BISYMMETRIC
BIT OF FLUFFS
BITTERSWEET
BITTER SWEET
BIVOUACKING
BLACKAMOORS
BLACKBALLED
BLACKBOARDS
BLACK COMEDY
BLACK FOREST
BLACKGUARDS
BLACK HUMOUR
BLACKLEGGED
BLACKLISTED
BLACKMAILED
BLACKMAILER
BLACK MARIAS
BLACK MARKET
BLACK MASSES
BLACK MUSLIM
BLACK PEPPER
BLACKSHIRTS
BLACKSMITHS
BLACK WIDOWS
BLADDERWORT
BLAMELESSLY
BLAMEWORTHY
BLANCMANGES
BLANK CHEQUE
BLASPHEMERS
BLASPHEMIES
BLASPHEMING
BLASPHEMOUS
BLASTOGENIC
BLASTOMERIC
BLASTOPORIC
BLENCHINGLY
BLEPHARITIC
BLEPHATITIS
BLESSEDNESS
BLIND ALLEYS
BLINDFOLDED

BLINDSTOREY
BLOCKBUSTER
BLOCKHOUSES
BLOOD COUNTS
BLOOD GROUPS
BLOODHOUNDS
BLOODLESSLY
BLOOD PLASMA
BLOOD SPORTS
BLOODSTAINS
BLOODSTREAM
BLOODSUCKER
BLOOD VESSEL
BLOOMINGTON
BLOTCHINESS
BLUDGEONING
BLUEBERRIES
BLUE-BLOODED
BLUEBOTTLES
BLUE CHEESES
BLUE-EYED BOY
BLUE MURDERS
BLUNDERBUSS
BLURREDNESS
BOBSLEIGHED
BODHISATTVA
BODY-CENTRED
BODY POLITIC
BOGNOR REGIS
BOILERMAKER
BOILERPLATE
BOILER SUITS
BOLLOCKS-UPS
BOLL WEEVILS
BOMBARDIERS
BOMBARDMENT
BONDHOLDERS
BONE MARROWS
BONESHAKERS
BOOBY PRIZES
BOOKBINDERS
BOOKBINDERY
BOOKBINDING
BOOKISHNESS
BOOKKEEPERS
BOOKKEEPING
BOOKMOBILES
BOOKSELLERS
BOOMERANGED
BOORISHNESS
BOOTLEGGERS

BOOTLEGGING
BORDERLANDS
BORDERLINES
BOTANICALLY
BOTHERATION
BOTTLE BANKS
BOTTLEBRUSH
BOTTLE GREEN
BOTTLENECKS
BOUNDLESSLY
BOUNTEOUSLY
BOURGEOISIE
BOURNEMOUTH
BOWDLERIZED
BOYOMA FALLS
BOYSENBERRY
BRACE AND BIT
BRACHIATION
BRACTEOLATE
BRADYCARDIA
BRADYCARDIC
BRAGGADOCIO
BRAHMAPUTRA
BRAIN DRAINS
BRAINLESSLY
BRAINSTORMS
BRAINS TRUST
BRAINTEASER
BRAINWASHED
BRAINWASHER
BRANCHIOPOD
BRANDENBURG
BRANDISHING
BRATTISHING
BRAZZAVILLE
BREADBASKET
BREADBOARDS
BREADCRUMBS
BREADFRUITS
BREADTHWAYS
BREADWINNER
BREAKFASTED
BREAK THE ICE
BREASTPLATE
BREATHALYSE
BREATHINESS
BRECONSHIRE
BREECHBLOCK
BREMERHAVEN
BRIDGEBOARD
BRISTLETAIL

BRITTLENESS
BRITTLE-STAR
BROADCASTER
BROAD CHURCH
BROAD GAUGES
BROADMINDED
BROADSHEETS
BROADSWORDS
BROMINATION
BRONCHIOLAR
BRONTOSAURI
BRONX CHEERS
BRONZE MEDAL
BROOMSTICKS
BROTHERHOOD
BROWBEATING
BROWNSTONES
BRUCELLOSIS
BRUSQUENESS
BRUTALITIES
BRUTALIZING
BRUTISHNESS
BRYOLOGICAL
BUCARAMANGA
BUCKET SEATS
BUCKET SHOPS
BUCKLER-FERN
BUCOLICALLY
BUDGERIGARS
BUENOS AIRES
BUFFER STATE
BUFFER STOCK
BUFFER ZONES
BULBIFEROUS
BULLDOG CLIP
BULLETPROOF
BULLFIGHTER
BULLFINCHES
BULLISHNESS
BULLSHITTED
BULL TERRIER
BUMPTIOUSLY
BUNDELKHAND
BUPIVACAINE
BUREAUCRACY
BUREAUCRATS
BURGOMASTER
BURKINA-FASO
BURLESQUING
BURNISHABLE
BUSHWHACKER

BUSINESS END
BUSINESSMAN
BUSINESSMEN
BUS STATIONS
BUTCHERBIRD
BUTTER BEANS
BUTTERFLIES
BUTTONHOLED
BUTTONHOLES
BUTTONMOULD
BUTTRESSING
BUTYRACEOUS
BY-ELECTIONS
BYELORUSSIA

C

CABINETWORK
CABORA BASSA
CACHE MEMORY
CACOGRAPHIC
CACOPHONOUS
CALCEOLARIA
CALCICOLOUS
CALCIFEROUS
CALCIFUGOUS
CALCINATION
CALCULATING
CALCULATION
CALCULATORS
CALEFACIENT
CALEFACTION
CALEFACTORY
CALIBRATING
CALIBRATION
CALIFORNIAN
CALIFORNIUM
CALLIGRAPHY
CALLIPYGIAN
CALLOUSNESS
CALORIMETER
CALORIMETRY
CALUMNIATED
CALVINISTIC
CALYPTROGEN
CAMARADERIE
CAMERA-READY
CAMOUFLAGED
CAMOUFLAGES
CAMPAIGNERS
CAMPAIGNING
CAMPANOLOGY

CAMPANULATE
CAMPGROUNDS
CAMPO GRANDE
CANALICULAR
CANALICULUS
CANDELABRUM
CANDIDACIES
CANDLEBERRY
CANDLELIGHT
CANDLEPOWER
CANDLESTICK
CANDLEWICKS
CANINE TEETH
CANINE TOOTH
CANNIBALISM
CANNIBALIZE
CANNONBALLS
CANTHARIDES
CANTILEVERS
CAPACIOUSLY
CAPACITANCE
CAPILLARIES
CAPILLARITY
CAPITALISTS
CAPITALIZED
CAPITAL LEVY
CAPITATIONS
CAPITULATED
CAPITULATOR
CAPRICCIOSO
CAPRICORNUS
CAPSULATION
CAPTIVATING
CAPTIVATION
CARABINIERE
CARAVANNING
CARBAMIDINE
CARBONATION
CARBONIZING
CARBON PAPER
CAR-BOOT SALE
CARBORUNDUM
CARBOXYLASE
CARBOXYLATE
CARBUNCULAR
CARBURETTOR
CARBYLAMINE
CARCASSONNE
CARCINOGENS
CARDINALATE
CARD INDEXES

CARDIOGRAPH
CARDPUNCHES
CARDUACEOUS
CAREFULNESS
CARESSINGLY
CARICATURED
CARICATURES
CARMINATIVE
CARNIVOROUS
CAROLINGIAN
CARPOGONIAL
CARPOGONIUM
CARPOLOGIST
CARRAGEENAN
CARRIAGEWAY
CARRIER BAGS
CARSICKNESS
CARTOGRAPHY
CARTOONISTS
CARTWHEELED
CARUNCULATE
CARVEL-BUILT
CARVING FORK
CASE HISTORY
CASE STUDIES
CASEWORKERS
CASSITERITE
CASTELLATED
CASTER SUGAR
CASTIGATING
CASTIGATION
CASTING VOTE
CASTLEREAGH
CASTOR SUGAR
CATACAUSTIC
CATACHRESIS
CATACLASTIC
CATACLYSMIC
CATADROMOUS
CATAFALQUES
CATALOGUING
CATAPLASTIC
CATAPULTING
CATASTROPHE
CAT BURGLARS
CATCHPHRASE
CATCHWEIGHT
CATECHISMAL
CATECHISTIC
CATECHIZING
CATEGORICAL

CATEGORIZED
CATERPILLAR
CATERWAULED
CATHETERIZE
CATHOLICISM
CATHOLICITY
CATHOLICIZE
CATTLE GRIDS
CAULIFLOWER
CAUSABILITY
CAUSATIVELY
CAUSTICALLY
CAUSTICNESS
CAUTERIZING
CAVACO SILVA
CAVALIERISM
CAVERNOUSLY
CAVITY WALLS
CAVO-RELIEVO
CEASELESSLY
CELEBRATING
CELEBRATION
CELEBRATIVE
CELEBRITIES
CEMENTATION
CEMENT MIXER
CENOSPECIES
CENTENARIAN
CENTENARIES
CENTENNIALS
CENTIMETRES
CENTRALIZED
CENTREBOARD
CENTRE-FOLDS
CENTREPIECE
CENTRIFUGAL
CENTRIFUGES
CENTRIPETAL
CENTROBARIC
CENTROMERIC
CENTROSOMIC
CEPHALALGIA
CERARGYRITE
CEREBRATION
CEREBROSIDE
CEREMONIALS
CEREMONIOUS
CEROGRAPHIC
CEROPLASTIC
CERTAINTIES
CERTIFIABLE

CERTIFICATE
CETOLOGICAL
CHAETOGNATH
CHAFFINCHES
CHAFING DISH
CHAIN LETTER
CHAIN-SMOKED
CHAIN-SMOKER
CHAIN STITCH
CHAIN STORES
CHAIRPERSON
CHALCANLITE
CHALCEDONIC
CHALKBOARDS
CHALLENGERS
CHALLENGING
CHAMBERLAIN
CHAMBERMAID
CHAMBER POTS
CHAMELEONIC
CHAMPERTOUS
CHAMPIONING
CHANCELLERY
CHANCELLORS
CHANCROIDAL
CHANDELIERS
CHANGELINGS
CHANGEOVERS
CHANNELLING
CHANTERELLE
CHANTICLEER
CHAOTICALLY
CHAPERONAGE
CHAPERONING
CHARCUTERIE
CHARGE CARDS
CHARGE HANDS
CHARGE NURSE
CHARGE SHEET
CHAR-GRILLED
CHARIOTEERS
CHARISMATIC
CHASTISABLE
CHATELAINES
CHATTANOOGA
CHAUFFEURED
CHAULMOOGRA
CHAUVINISTS
CHEAPSKATES
CHECKMATING
CHECKPOINTS

CHEERLEADER
CHEERLESSLY
CHEESECAKES
CHEESECLOTH
CHEF D'OEUVRE
CHELICERATE
CHELIFEROUS
CHELYABINSK
CHEMOSMOSIS
CHEMOSMOTIC
CHEMOSPHERE
CHEMOTACTIC
CHEMOTROPIC
CHEQUE CARDS
CHEREMKHOVO
CHERISHABLE
CHESHIRE CAT
CHESSBOARDS
CHEVAL GLASS
CHIAROSCURO
CHIASTOLITE
CHICANERIES
CHICHIHAERH
CHICKENFEED
CHICKEN FEED
CHIFFONIERS
CHILDMINDER
CHIMNEYPOTS
CHIMPANZEES
CHINCHILLAS
CHINESE LEAF
CHINOISERIE
CHIPPENDALE
CHIROGRAPHY
CHIROPODIST
CHIROPTERAN
CHITCHATTED
CHLAMYDEOUS
CHLORINATED
CHLORINATOR
CHLOROPHYLL
CHLOROPLAST
CHLOROPRENE
CHLOROQUINE
CHOANOCYTAL
CHOCK-A-BLOCK
CHOIRMASTER
CHOIR SCHOOL
CHOKECHERRY
CHOLESTEROL
CHOLINERGIC

CHORDOPHONE
CHOREODRAMA
CHOREOGRAPH
CHOROGRAPHY
CHRISMATORY
CHRISTENDOM
CHRISTENING
CHRISTINGLE
CHRISTMASES
CHRISTOLOGY
CHROMATINIC
CHROMINANCE
CHROMOGENIC
CHROMONEMAL
CHROMOPHORE
CHROMOPLASM
CHROMOPLAST
CHROMOSOMAL
CHROMOSOMES
CHRONICALLY
CHRONICLERS
CHRONICLING
CHRONOGRAPH
CHRONOMETER
CHRONOMETRY
CHRONOSCOPE
CHRYSALISES
CHRYSAROBIN
CHRYSOBERYL
CHRYSOLITIC
CHRYSOPRASE
CHURCHGOERS
CHURCHGOING
CHURCHWOMAN
CHURCHYARDS
CICATRICIAL
CICATRIZANT
CINDERELLAS
CINEMASCOPE
CIRCULARITY
CIRCULARIZE
CIRCULAR SAW
CIRCULATING
CIRCULATION
CIRCULATIVE
CIRCULATORY
CIRCUMCISED
CIRCUMLUNAR
CIRCUMPOLAR
CIRCUMSPECT
CIRENCESTER

CITIZENSHIP
CITRONELLAL
CITY FATHERS
CIVIL RIGHTS
CIVVY STREET
CLAIRVOYANT
CLAMATORIAL
CLANDESTINE
CLARINETIST
CLASP KNIVES
CLASS ACTION
CLASSICISTS
CLASSIFYING
CLAVICHORDS
CLAY PIGEONS
CLEAN-LIMBED
CLEANLINESS
CLEAN-SHAVEN
CLEAN SWEEPS
CLEAR-HEADED
CLEAR THE AIR
CLEETHORPES
CLEFT PALATE
CLEFT STICKS
CLEISTOGAMY
CLERGYWOMAN
CLEVER DICKS
CLIENT STATE
CLIFFHANGER
CLIMACTERIC
CLIMATOLOGY
CLINANDRIUM
CLINOMETRIC
CLOCK TOWERS
CLODHOPPERS
CLOISTERING
CLOSED SHOPS
CLOSEFISTED
CLOSE-HAULED
CLOSE SEASON
CLOSE SHAVES
CLOSING TIME
CLOSTRIDIAL
CLOSTRIDIUM
CLOTHESLINE
CLOTHES PEGS
CLOUDBURSTS
CLOUD-CAPPED
CLOYINGNESS
CLUSTER BOMB
COADUNATION

COADUNATIVE
COAGULATING
COAGULATION
COAGULATIVE
COALBUNKERS
COALESCENCE
COALITIONAL
COALSCUTTLE
COARCTATION
COASTGUARDS
COAT HANGERS
COATS OF ARMS
COBBLESTONE
COCCIDIOSIS
COCCIFEROUS
COCK-A-LEEKIE
COCKCHAFERS
COCKLESHELL
COCKLE SHELL
COCKROACHES
CODICILLARY
COD-LIVER OIL
COEDUCATION
COEFFICIENT
COELENTERIC
COELENTERON
COERCIONARY
COERCIONIST
COESSENTIAL
COEXISTENCE
COEXTENSION
COEXTENSIVE
COFFEE BREAK
COFFEE HOUSE
COFFEE SHOPS
COFFEE TABLE
COGITATIONS
COGNITIVELY
COGNITIVIST
COGNIZANCES
COGNOSCENTI
COINCIDENCE
COINSURANCE
COLD-BLOODED
COLD CHISELS
COLD COMFORT
COLD-HEARTED
COLD STORAGE
COLEOPTERAN
COLLABORATE
COLLAPSIBLE

COLLARBONES
COLLAR STUDS
COLLECTABLE
COLLECTANEA
COLLECTEDLY
COLLECTIONS
COLLECTIVES
COLLEMBOLAN
COLLENCHYMA
COLLIGATION
COLLIGATIVE
COLLIMATION
COLLOCATING
COLLOCATION
COLOGARITHM
COLONIALISM
COLONIALIST
COLONIZABLE
COLONOSCOPY
COLORATURAS
COLORIMETER
COLOUR-BLIND
COLOURISTIC
COLTISHNESS
COLUMBARIUM
COMBATIVELY
COMBINATION
COMBINATIVE
COMBUSTIBLE
COMESTIBLES
COME-UPPANCE
COMFORTABLE
COMFORTABLY
COMFORTLESS
COMIC OPERAS
COMIC STRIPS
COMMANDANTS
COMMANDMENT
COMME IL FAUT
COMMEMORATE
COMMENDABLE
COMMENDABLY
COMMENTATED
COMMENTATOR
COMMERCIALS
COMMINATION
COMMINATORY
COMMINUTION
COMMISERATE
COMMISSIONS
COMMISSURAL

COMMITMENTS
COMMODITIES
COMMON NOUNS
COMMONPLACE
COMMON ROOMS
COMMON SENSE
COMMOTIONAL
COMMUNALISM
COMMUNALIST
COMMUNALITY
COMMUNALIZE
COMMUNICANT
COMMUNICATE
COMMUNIONAL
COMMUNIQUES
COMMUNISTIC
COMMUNITIES
COMMUTATION
COMMUTATIVE
COMMUTATORS
COMPACT DISC
COMPACTEDLY
COMPACTNESS
COMPANY TOWN
COMPARATIVE
COMPARISONS
COMPARTMENT
COMPASSABLE
COMPATRIOTS
COMPELLABLE
COMPENDIOUS
COMPENDIUMS
COMPENSATED
COMPENSATOR
COMPETENTLY
COMPETITION
COMPETITIVE
COMPETITORS
COMPILATION
COMPLACENCE
COMPLACENCY
COMPLAINANT
COMPLAINERS
COMPLAINING
COMPLAISANT
COMPLEMENTS
COMPLEXIONS
COMPLIANTLY
COMPLICATED
COMPLIMENTS
COMPORTMENT

COMPOSITION
COMPOSITORS
COMPOUNDING
COMPRESSING
COMPRESSION
COMPRESSIVE
COMPRESSORS
COMPRISABLE
COMPROMISED
COMPROMISER
COMPROMISES
COMPTOMETER
COMPTROLLER
COMPULSIONS
COMPUNCTION
COMPUTATION
COMPUTERATE
COMPUTERIZE
COMRADESHIP
CONCATENATE
CONCAVITIES
CONCEALMENT
CONCEITEDLY
CONCEIVABLE
CONCEIVABLY
CONCENTRATE
CONCEPTACLE
CONCEPTIONS
CONCERNEDLY
CONCERTANTE
CONCERTEDLY
CONCERTGOER
CONCERTINAS
CONCESSIBLE
CONCESSIONS
CONCILIATED
CONCILIATOR
CONCLUSIONS
CONCOCTIONS
CONCOMITANT
CONCORDANCE
CONCUBINAGE
CONCURRENCE
CONDEMNABLE
CONDENSABLE
CONDITIONAL
CONDITIONED
CONDITIONER
CONDOLATORY
CONDOLENCES
CONDOMINIUM

CONDONATION CONJUGATIVE CONSTRUCTED CONTROVERSY
CONDUCTANCE CONJUNCTION CONSTRUCTOR CONTUMELIES
CONDUCTIBLE CONJUNCTIVA CONSULSHIPS CONTUSIONED
CONDUCTRESS CONJUNCTIVE CONSULTANCY CONURBATION
CONFABULATE CONJUNCTURE CONSULTANTS CONVALESCED
CONFECTIONS CONJURATION CONSUMERISM CONVENIENCE
CONFEDERACY CONNECTIBLE CONSUMMATED CONVENTICLE
CONFEDERATE CONNECTICUT CONSUMMATOR CONVENTIONS
CONFERENCES CONNECTIONS CONSUMPTION CONVERGENCE
CONFERMENTS CONNOISSEUR CONSUMPTIVE CONVERGENCY
CONFESSEDLY CONNOTATION CONTACT LENS CONVERSABLE
CONFESSIONS CONNOTATIVE CONTAINMENT CONVERSANCE
CONFIDENCES CONSCIENCES CONTAMINANT CONVERSIONS
CONFIDENTLY CONSCIOUSLY CONTAMINATE CONVERTIBLE
CONFIDINGLY CONSCRIPTED CONTEMNIBLE CONVEXITIES
CONFINEMENT CONSECRATED CONTEMPLATE CONVEYANCER
CONFISCABLE CONSECRATOR CONTENTEDLY CONVEYANCES
CONFISCATED CONSECUTION CONTENTIONS CONVICTABLE
CONFISCATOR CONSECUTIVE CONTENTIOUS CONVICTIONS
CONFLATIONS CONSENSUSES CONTENTMENT CONVINCIBLE
CONFLICTING CONSENTIENT CONTESTANTS CONVIVIALLY
CONFLICTION CONSEQUENCE CONTEXTURAL CONVOCATION
CONFLICTIVE CONSERVABLE CONTINENTAL CONVOCATIVE
CONFLUENCES CONSERVANCY CONTINGENCE CONVOLUTION
CONFORMABLE CONSERVATOR CONTINGENCY CONVOLVULUS
CONFORMABLY CONSIDERATE CONTINGENTS CONVULSIONS
CONFORMANCE CONSIDERING CONTINUALLY COOKERY BOOK
CONFORMISTS CONSIGNABLE CONTINUANCE COOK ISLANDS
CONFOUNDING CONSIGNMENT CONTINUATOR COOPERATING
CONFRONTING CONSISTENCY CONTORTIONS COOPERATION
CONFUSINGLY CONSOLATION CONTRACTILE COOPERATIVE
CONFUTATION CONSOLATORY CONTRACTING COOPERATORS
CONFUTATIVE CONSOLIDATE CONTRACTION COOPER CREEK
CONGEALMENT CONSONANCES CONTRACTIVE COORDINATED
CONGELATION CONSONANTAL CONTRACTORS COORDINATES
CONGENIALLY CONSORTIUMS CONTRACTUAL COORDINATOR
CONGESTIBLE CONSPECIFIC CONTRACTURE COPARCENARY
CONGREGATED CONSPICUOUS CONTRAFLOWS COPING STONE
CONGREGATOR CONSPIRATOR CONTRAPTION COPLANARITY
CONGRESSMAN CONSTANTINE CONTRARIETY COPPERPLATE
CONGRESSMEN CONSTELLATE CONTRASTING COPPERSMITH
CONGRUENTLY CONSTERNATE CONTRASTIVE COPROCESSOR
CONGRUITIES CONSTIPATED CONTRAVENED COPROPHILIA
CONJECTURAL CONSTITUENT CONTRAVENER COPYWRITERS
CONJECTURED CONSTITUTED CONTRAYERVA CORACIIFORM
CONJECTURER CONSTITUTER CONTRETEMPS CORDILLERAS
CONJECTURES CONSTRAINED CONTRIBUTED CORMOPHYTIC
CONJOINEDLY CONSTRAINER CONTRIBUTOR CORNERSTONE
CONJUGALITY CONSTRAINTS CONTRIVANCE CORNFLOWERS
CONJUGATING CONSTRICTED CONTROLLERS CORNICULATE
CONJUGATION CONSTRICTOR CONTROLLING CORNUCOPIAS

COROLLARIES
CORONAGRAPH
CORONATIONS
CORONERSHIP
CORPORALITY
CORPORATELY
CORPORATION
CORPORATIVE
CORPOREALLY
CORPUSCULAR
CORRECTABLE
CORRECTIONS
CORRECTIVES
CORRECTNESS
CORRELATING
CORRELATION
CORRELATIVE
CORRIGENDUM
CORROBORATE
CORROSIVELY
CORRUGATION
CORRUPTIBLE
CORRUPTIONS
CORRUPTNESS
CORS ANGLAIS
CORTICATION
CORUSCATING
CORUSCATION
COSIGNATORY
COS LETTUCES
COSMETICIAN
COSMOGONIES
COSMOGONIST
COSMOLOGIST
COSMOPOLITE
COTERMINOUS
COTES-DU-NORD
COTONEASTER
COTTAGE LOAF
COTTON CANDY
COTTONTAILS
COTYLEDONAL
COUNCIL AREA
COUNCILLORS
COUNSELLING
COUNSELLORS
COUNTENANCE
COUNTERFEIT
COUNTERFOIL
COUNTERMAND
COUNTERMINE

COUNTERMOVE
COUNTERPANE
COUNTERPART
COUNTERPLOT
COUNTERSANK
COUNTERSIGN
COUNTERSINK
COUNTERSUNK
COUNTERTYPE
COUNTERVAIL
COUNTERWORD
COUNTERWORK
COUNTRIFIED
COUNTRY CLUB
COUNTRY SEAT
COUNTRYSIDE
COUNTY COURT
COUNTY TOWNS
COUP DE GRACE
COURTEOUSLY
COURTHOUSES
COURTLINESS
COVENANTING
COVER CHARGE
COWCATCHERS
CRABBEDNESS
CRACKERJACK
CRANBERRIES
CRANIOMETER
CRANIOMETRY
CRANKSHAFTS
CRASH COURSE
CRASH-DIVING
CRASH HELMET
CRASH-LANDED
CRAZY PAVING
CREAM CHEESE
CREDENTIALS
CREDIBILITY
CREDIT CARDS
CREDIT NOTES
CREDULOUSLY
CREMATORIUM
CRENELLATED
CRENULATION
CREOPHAGOUS
CREPITATION
CREPUSCULAR
CRESTFALLEN
CRIMINALITY
CRIMINOLOGY

CRINKLEROOT
CRINKLINESS
CRITICIZING
CROCIDOLITE
CROCODILIAN
CROOKEDNESS
CROP-DUSTING
CROSSBREEDS
CROSS-GARNET
CROSS-LEGGED
CROSSPIECES
CROSS-STITCH
CROWDEDNESS
CROWN COLONY
CROWN COURTS
CROWNED HEAD
CROWN JEWELS
CROWN PRINCE
CRUCIFEROUS
CRUCIFIXION
CRUNCHINESS
CRUSTACEANS
CRUSTACEOUS
CRYOBIOLOGY
CRYOHYDRATE
CRYOSURGERY
CRYOTHERAPY
CRYPTICALLY
CRYPTOGAMIC
CRYPTOGENIC
CRYPTOGRAPH
CRYPTOZOITE
CRYSTAL BALL
CRYSTALLINE
CRYSTALLITE
CRYSTALLIZE
CRYSTALLOID
CRYSTAL SETS
CTENOPHORAN
CUCKOO CLOCK
CULMIFEROUS
CULMINATION
CULPABILITY
CULTIVATING
CULTIVATION
CULTIVATORS
CUMMERBUNDS
CUNNILINGUS
CUPELLATION
CUPRIFEROUS
CUPRONICKEL

CURATORSHIP
CURIOSITIES
CURIOUSNESS
CURMUDGEONS
CURRICULUMS
CURRY POWDER
CURTAILMENT
CURTAIN CALL
CURVILINEAR
CUSPIDATION
CUSTARD PIES
CUSTOMARILY
CUSTOM-BUILT
CUSTOMIZING
CUT-AND-DRIED
CUTTING EDGE
CYANIDATION
CYANOHYDRIN
CYBERNATION
CYBERNETICS
CYBERPHOBIA
CYCADACEOUS
CYCLOALKANE
CYCLOHEXANE
CYCLOPLEGIA
CYCLOSPORIN
CYCLOSTYLED
CYCLOTHYMIA
CYCLOTHYMIC
CYLINDRICAL
CYPERACEOUS
CYPRINODONT
CYPRIPEDIUM
CYSTICERCUS
CYSTOCARPIC
CYSTOSCOPIC
CYTOGENESIS
CYTOKINESIS
CYTOLOGICAL
CYTOLOGISTS
CYTOPLASMIC
CZESTOCHOWA

D

DACTYLOLOGY
DAGGERBOARD
DAIL EIREANN
DAIRY CATTLE
DAIRY FARMER
DAISY WHEELS
DAMAN AND DIU

DAMNABILITY	DECLAMATORY	DEHYDRATION	DENSIMETRIC
DAMP COURSES	DECLARATION	DEICTICALLY	DENTAL FLOSS
DANGER MONEY	DECLARATIVE	DEIFICATION	DENTAL PLATE
DANGEROUSLY	DECLARATORY	DELECTATION	DENTICULATE
DAPPLE-GREYS	DECLENSIONS	DELEGATIONS	DENTILABIAL
DARDANELLES	DECLINATION	DELETERIOUS	DENUMERABLE
DAREDEVILRY	DECLINATORY	DELIBERATED	DENUNCIATOR
DAR ES SALAAM	DECLIVITIES	DELIBERATOR	DEODORIZING
DATABLENESS	DECLIVITOUS	DELICIOUSLY	DEOXYGENATE
DAUNTLESSLY	DECOLLATION	DELINEATING	DEOXYRIBOSE
DAWSON CREEK	DECOLLETAGE	DELINEATION	DEPARTMENTS
DAYDREAMERS	DECOLONIZED	DELINEATIVE	DEPLORINGLY
DAYDREAMING	DECOMPOSING	DELINQUENCY	DEPLUMATION
DEACCESSION	DECORATIONS	DELINQUENTS	DEPOLARIZER
DEACTIVATOR	DECORTICATE	DELIRIOUSLY	DEPOPULATED
DEAD LETTERS	DECREPITATE	DELITESCENT	DEPORTATION
DEAD MARCHES	DECREPITUDE	DELIVERABLE	DEPOSITIONS
DEAD RINGERS	DECRESCENCE	DELIVERANCE	DEPRAVATION
DEAD SOLDIER	DECRETALIST	DELIVERYMAN	DEPRAVITIES
DEAF-AND-DUMB	DECUSSATION	DELIVERYMEN	DEPRECATING
DEALERSHIPS	DEDICATEDLY	DELPHINIUMS	DEPRECATION
DEAMINATION	DEDICATIONS	DEMAGNETIZE	DEPRECATIVE
DEATH DUTIES	DEDUCTIVELY	DEMAGOGUERY	DEPRECATORY
DEATHLESSLY	DEEP FREEZES	DEMARCATING	DEPRECIABLE
DEATHLINESS	DEERSTALKER	DEMARCATION	DEPRECIATED
DEATH RATTLE	DE-ESCALATED	DEMOCRACIES	DEPRECIATOR
DEATH'S-HEADS	DEFALCATION	DEMOCRATIZE	DEPREDATION
DEATH SQUADS	DEFECTIVELY	DEMODULATOR	DEPRESSIBLE
DEATTRIBUTE	DEFENCELESS	DEMOGRAPHER	DEPRESSIONS
DEBARKATION	DEFENSIVELY	DEMOGRAPHIC	DEPRIVATION
DEBASEDNESS	DEFERENTIAL	DEMOLISHING	DEPUTATIONS
DEBASEMENTS	DEFICIENTLY	DEMOLITIONS	DERAILMENTS
DEBILITATED	DEFINIENDUM	DEMONETIZED	DERANGEMENT
DEBOUCHMENT	DEFINITIONS	DEMONICALLY	DERECOGNIZE
DEBRIDEMENT	DEFLECTIONS	DEMONOLATER	DEREGULATED
DECALCIFIER	DEFLORATION	DEMONOLATRY	DERELICTION
DECALESCENT	DEFLOWERING	DEMONSTRATE	DERIVATIONS
DECANEDIOIC	DEFOLIATING	DEMORALIZER	DERIVATIVES
DECAPITATED	DEFOLIATION	DEMOTIVATED	DERMATOLOGY
DECAPITATOR	DEFORCEMENT	DEMOUNTABLE	DESALINATED
DECARBONIZE	DEFORESTING	DEMULSIFIER	DESCENDABLE
DECEITFULLY	DEFORMATION	DEMUTUALIZE	DESCENDANTS
DECELERATED	DEFORMITIES	DEMYSTIFIED	DESCENDIBLE
DECELERATOR	DEFRAUDMENT	DENIGRATING	DESCRIBABLE
DECEPTIVELY	DEGENERATED	DENIGRATION	DESCRIPTION
DECEREBRATE	DEGENERATES	DENITRATION	DESCRIPTIVE
DECILLIONTH	DEGLUTINATE	DENOMINABLE	DESECRATING
DECIMALIZED	DEGLUTITION	DENOMINATED	DESECRATION
DECIPHERING	DEGRADATION	DENOMINATOR	DESEGREGATE
DECKLE-EDGED	DEHUMANIZED	DENOTATIONS	DESENSITIZE
DECLAMATION	DEHYDRATING	DENOUEMENTS	DESERVINGLY

DESEXUALIZE	DIACRITICAL	DIMENSIONAL	DISBELIEVED
DESICCATING	DIADELPHOUS	DIMERCAPROL	DISBELIEVER
DESICCATION	DIAGNOSABLE	DIMIDIATION	DISBURSABLE
DESICCATIVE	DIAGNOSTICS	DIMINISHING	DISCERNIBLE
DESIDERATUM	DIALECTICAL	DIMINUENDOS	DISCERNIBLY
DESIGNATING	DIALOGISTIC	DIMINUTIONS	DISCERNMENT
DESIGNATION	DIALYSATION	DIMINUTIVES	DISCHARGING
DESIGNATIVE	DIAMAGNETIC	DINING ROOMS	DISC HARROWS
DESPATCHING	DIAMONDBACK	DINING TABLE	DISCIPLINAL
DESPERADOES	DIAPHORESIS	DINNER BELLS	DISCIPLINED
DESPERATELY	DIAPHORETIC	DINNER TABLE	DISCIPLINER
DESPERATION	DIAPOPHYSIS	DINOSAURIAN	DISCIPLINES
DESPOILMENT	DIARTHROSIS	DIOPTOMETER	DISC JOCKEYS
DESPONDENCY	DIASTROPHIC	DIOPTOMETRY	DISCLAIMERS
DESPUMATION	DIATESSARON	DIPHOSPHATE	DISCLAIMING
DESSERT WINE	DIATOMICITY	DIPHTHEROID	DISCLOSURES
DESTABILIZE	DIATONICISM	DIPHTHONGAL	DISCOGRAPHY
DESTINATION	DICEPHALISM	DIPHYCERCAL	DISCOLOURED
DESTITUTION	DICEPHALOUS	DIPLOCOCCAL	DISCOMFITED
DESTROYABLE	DICHOGAMOUS	DIPLOCOCCUS	DISCOMFITER
DESTRUCTION	DICHOTOMIES	DIPLOMATIST	DISCOMFORTS
DESTRUCTIVE	DICHOTOMIST	DIPROTODONT	DISCOMMODED
DESULTORILY	DICHOTOMIZE	DIPSOMANIAC	DISCOMPOSED
DETACHMENTS	DICHOTOMOUS	DIPSWITCHES	DISCONTINUE
DETERIORATE	DICHROMATIC	DIRECT DEBIT	DISCORDANCE
DETERMINANT	DICHROSCOPE	DIRECTIONAL	DISCOTHEQUE
DETERMINATE	DICOTYLEDON	DIRECTORATE	DISCOUNTING
DETERMINERS	DICTAPHONES	DIRECTORIAL	DISCOURAGED
DETERMINING	DICTATIONAL	DIRECTORIES	DISCOURAGER
DETERMINISM	DICTATORIAL	DIRECT TAXES	DISCOURSING
DETERMINIST	DIDACTICISM	DIRT FARMERS	DISCOURTESY
DETESTATION	DIE-CASTINGS	DIRTY OLD MAN	DISCOVERERS
DETONATIONS	DIFFERENCES	DIRTY OLD MEN	DISCOVERIES
DETRAINMENT	DIFFERENTIA	DIRTY TRICKS	DISCOVERING
DETRIBALIZE	DIFFERENTLY	DISABLEMENT	DISCREDITED
DETRIMENTAL	DIFFIDENTLY	DISACCREDIT	DISCREPANCY
DEUTERANOPE	DIFFRACTING	DISACCUSTOM	DISCUSSIBLE
DEUTEROGAMY	DIFFRACTION	DISAFFECTED	DISCUSSIONS
DEUTSCHMARK	DIFFRACTIVE	DISAFFOREST	DISEMBARKED
DEVALUATION	DIFFUSENESS	DISAGREEING	DISEMBODIED
DEVASTATING	DIFFUSIVITY	DISALLOWING	DISENCUMBER
DEVASTATION	DIGESTIONAL	DISAPPEARED	DISENGAGING
DEVASTATIVE	DIGITIGRADE	DISAPPROVAL	DISENTANGLE
DEVELOPABLE	DIGNITARIES	DISAPPROVED	DISENTHRALL
DEVELOPMENT	DIGRESSIONS	DISAPPROVER	DISFIGURING
DEVIOUSNESS	DIHYBRIDISM	DISARMAMENT	DISFORESTED
DEVITALIZED	DILAPIDATED	DISARRANGED	DISGRACEFUL
DEVOLVEMENT	DILAPIDATOR	DISASSEMBLE	DISGRUNTLED
DEVOTEDNESS	DILATOMETER	DISASSEMBLY	DISGUISABLE
DEVOURINGLY	DILATOMETRY	DISAVOWEDLY	DISGUSTEDLY
DEXTEROUSLY	DILETTANTES	DISBANDMENT	DISHEVELLED

DISHONESTLY
DISHONOURED
DISHONOURER
DISHWASHERS
DISILLUSION
DISILLUSIVE
DISINCLINED
DISINFECTED
DISINFECTOR
DISINTEREST
DISINTERRED
DISJOINABLE
DISJUNCTION
DISJUNCTIVE
DISJUNCTURE
DISLOCATING
DISLOCATION
DISLODGMENT
DISMANTLING
DISMASTMENT
DISMEMBERED
DISMEMBERER
DISMISSIBLE
DISMOUNTING
DISOBEDIENT
DISOBLIGING
DISORDERING
DISORGANIZE
DISPARAGING
DISPARATELY
DISPARITIES
DISPATCH BOX
DISPATCHING
DISPENSABLE
DISPIRITING
DISPLEASING
DISPLEASURE
DISPOSITION
DISPROVABLE
DISPUTATION
DISQUIETING
DISQUIETUDE
DISREGARDED
DISREGARDER
DISRELISHED
DISROBEMENT
DISRUPTIONS
DISSECTIBLE
DISSECTIONS
DISSEMBLERS
DISSEMBLING

DISSEMINATE
DISSEMINULE
DISSENSIONS
DISSENTIENT
DISSENTIOUS
DISSEPIMENT
DISSIMILATE
DISSIMULATE
DISSIPATING
DISSIPATION
DISSIPATIVE
DISSOCIABLE
DISSOCIATED
DISSOLUTELY
DISSOLUTION
DISSOLUTIVE
DISSOLVABLE
DISSONANCES
DISSUADABLE
DISSYLLABIC
DISSYLLABLE
DISSYMMETRY
DISTASTEFUL
DISTEMPERED
DISTENSIBLE
DISTILLABLE
DISTINCTION
DISTINCTIVE
DISTINGUISH
DISTORTIONS
DISTRACTING
DISTRACTION
DISTRACTIVE
DISTRAINING
DISTRESSFUL
DISTRESSING
DISTRIBUTED
DISTRIBUTOR
DISTRUSTFUL
DISTRUSTING
DISTURBANCE
DISULPHURIC
DITHYRAMBIC
DITTOGRAPHY
DIVARICATOR
DIVE-BOMBERS
DIVE-BOMBING
DIVERGENCES
DIVERGENTLY
DIVERSIFIED
DIVERSIFIER

DIVERSIFORM
DIVERSIONAL
DIVERTINGLY
DIVESTITURE
DIVINATIONS
DIVINE RIGHT
DIVING BELLS
DIVINGBOARD
DIVISIONISM
DIVISIONIST
DIVORCEABLE
DIVORCEMENT
DOCTRINAIRE
DOCUMENTARY
DOCUMENTING
DODDERINGLY
DODECAGONAL
DODECAPHONY
DOGBERRYISM
DOG BISCUITS
DOGCATCHERS
DOLABRIFORM
DOLEFULNESS
DOLL'S HOUSES
DOLORIMETRY
DOMESTICATE
DOMESTICITY
DOMICILIARY
DOMICILIATE
DOMINEERING
DOORKEEPERS
DOORKNOCKER
DOORSTOPPER
DORMITORIES
DOTTED LINES
DOUBLE AGENT
DOUBLE BINDS
DOUBLE-BLIND
DOUBLE BLUFF
DOUBLE-CHECK
DOUBLE CHINS
DOUBLE CREAM
DOUBLE-CROSS
DOUBLE DATED
DOUBLE DATES
DOUBLE-DUTCH
DOUBLE-EDGED
DOUBLE-FACED
DOUBLE FAULT
DOUBLE-GLAZE
DOUBLE-QUICK

DOUBLE-SPACE
DOUBLESPEAK
DOUBLE TAKES
DOUBLETHINK
DOUROUCOULI
DOVETAILING
DOWN-AND-OUTS
DOWNGRADING
DOWNHEARTED
DOWNLOADING
DOWNPATRICK
DOWN PAYMENT
DOWNPLAYING
DOWN-TO-EARTH
DOWNTRODDEN
DOXOLOGICAL
DRAGONFLIES
DRAMATIZING
DRAMATURGIC
DRASTICALLY
DRAUGHTSMAN
DRAUGHTSMEN
DRAWBRIDGES
DRAWING PINS
DRAWING ROOM
DRAWSTRINGS
DREADNOUGHT
DREAMLESSLY
DREAM TICKET
DREAM WORLDS
DRESS CIRCLE
DRESSMAKERS
DRESSMAKING
DRILLMASTER
DROMEDARIES
DRUNKENNESS
DRY CLEANERS
DRY-CLEANING
DSCONTINUER
DUAL-PURPOSE
DUBIOUSNESS
DUDE RANCHES
DUFFEL COATS
DUMBFOUNDED
DUMBFOUNDER
DUMBWAITERS
DUNDERHEADS
DUNE BUGGIES
DUNFERMLINE
DUPLEX HOUSE
DUPLICATING

DUPLICATION
DUPLICATIVE
DUPLICATORS
DUST JACKETS
DUTCH TREATS
DUTCH UNCLES
DUTIABILITY
DUTIFULNESS
DYNAMICALLY
DYNAMOMETER
DYNAMOMETRY
DYSFUNCTION
DYSFUNCTION

E
EAGER BEAVER
EARNESTNESS
EARTHENWARE
EARTH-GRAZER
EARTHLINESS
EARTHQUAKES
EAR TRUMPETS
EASEFULNESS
EAST ANGLIAN
EASTERN CAPE
EASTERNMOST
EAST GERMANY
EAST LOTHIAN
EATING APPLE
EBULLIENTLY
ECCLESIARCH
ECCRINOLOGY
ECHCHYMOSED
ECHOPRACTIC
ECLECTICISM
ECOFRIENDLY
ECONOMETRIC
ECONOMIZING
ECOSPECIFIC
ECTOBLASTIC
ECTOGENESIS
ECTOMORPHIC
ECTOPLASMIC
ECTOSARCOUS
EDAPHICALLY
EDIFICATION
EDIFICATORY
EDITORIALLY
EDUCABILITY
EDUCATIONAL
EFFECTIVELY

EFFECTUALLY
EFFECTUATED
EFFERVESCED
EFFICACIOUS
EFFICIENTLY
EGALITARIAN
EGOCENTRISM
EGOMANIACAL
EGOTISTICAL
EGREGIOUSLY
EIDETICALLY
EIFFEL TOWER
EIGHTEENTHS
EINSTEINIAN
EINSTEINIUM
EISTEDDFODS
EJACULATING
EJACULATION
EJACULATIVE
EJACULATORY
EJECTOR SEAT
ELABORATELY
ELABORATING
ELABORATION
ELABORATIVE
ELASTICALLY
ELASTIC BAND
ELASTOMERIC
ELASTOPLAST
ELBOW GREASE
ELDERFLOWER
ELECTIONEER
ELECTORATES
ELECTORSHIP
ELECTRIC EYE
ELECTRICIAN
ELECTRICITY
ELECTRIFIED
ELECTRIFIER
ELECTROCUTE
ELECTROFORM
ELECTROLYSE
ELECTROLYTE
ELECTRONICS
ELECTROTYPE
ELEGIACALLY
ELEPHANTINE
ELEPHANTOID
ELICITATION
ELIGIBILITY
ELIMINATING

ELIMINATION
ELIMINATIVE
ELIZABETHAN
ELLIPSOIDAL
ELLIPTICITY
ELONGATIONS
ELUCIDATING
ELUCIDATION
ELUCIDATIVE
ELUCIDATORY
ELUSIVENESS
ELUTRIATION
EMANATIONAL
EMANCIPATED
EMANCIPATOR
EMASCULATED
EMASCULATOR
EMBANKMENTS
EMBARKATION
EMBARRASSED
EMBELLISHED
EMBELLISHER
EMBITTERING
EMBLAZONING
EMBLEMATIZE
EMBOLDENING
EMBOLECTOMY
EMBRACEABLE
EMBRACEMENT
EMBROCATION
EMBROIDERED
EMBROIDERER
EMBROILMENT
EMBRYECTOMY
EMBRYOGENIC
EMENDATIONS
EMERGENCIES
EMIGRATIONS
EMMENAGOGIC
EMMENAGOGUE
EMOTIONALLY
EMOTIONLESS
EMOTIVENESS
EMPANELLING
EMPANELMENT
EMPERORSHIP
EMPHASIZING
EMPIRICALLY
EMPLACEMENT
EMPLOYMENTS
EMPOWERMENT

EMPTY-HANDED
EMPTY-HEADED
EMULOUSNESS
EMULSIFYING
EMULSIONING
ENARTHROSIS
ENCAMPMENTS
ENCAPSULATE
ENCEPHALOMA
ENCEPHALOUS
ENCHAINMENT
ENCHANTMENT
ENCHANTRESS
ENCHONDROMA
ENCOMIASTIC
ENCOMPASSED
ENCOUNTERED
ENCOUNTERER
ENCOURAGING
ENCROACHING
ENCUMBERING
ENCUMBRANCE
ENCYCLICALS
ENDANGERING
ENDEARINGLY
ENDEARMENTS
ENDEAVOURED
ENDEAVOURER
ENDEMICALLY
ENDLESSNESS
ENDOBLASTIC
ENDOCARDIAL
ENDOCARDIUM
ENDOCENTRIC
ENDOCRANIUM
ENDOCRINOUS
ENDODONTICS
ENDODONTIST
ENDOMETRIAL
ENDOMETRIUM
ENDOMORPHIC
ENDONEURIUM
ENDOPLASMIC
ENDORSEMENT
ENDOSCOPIST
ENDOSPERMIC
ENDOSPOROUS
ENDOTHECIAL
ENDOTHECIUM
ENDOTHELIAL
ENDOTHELIUM

ENDOTHERMIC	ENTRUSTMENT	ERYSIPELOID	EVAPORATION
END PRODUCTS	ENTWINEMENT	ERYTHEMATIC	EVAPORATIVE
ENFORCEABLE	ENUCLEATION	ERYTHRISMAL	EVASIVENESS
ENFORCEMENT	ENUMERATING	ERYTHROCYTE	EVENING STAR
ENFRANCHISE	ENUMERATION	ESCAPEMENTS	EVENTUALITY
ENGAGEMENTS	ENUMERATIVE	ESCAPE WHEEL	EVENTUATION
ENGENDERING	ENUNCIATING	ESCARPMENTS	EVERLASTING
ENGINEERING	ENUNCIATION	ESCHATOLOGY	EVISCERATED
ENGLISH HORN	ENUNCIATIVE	ESCUTCHEONS	EVISCERATOR
ENGORGEMENT	ENVELOPMENT	ESEMPLASTIC	EXACERBATED
ENGRAILMENT	ENVIOUSNESS	ESOPHAGUSES	EXAGGERATED
ENGROSSEDLY	ENVIRONMENT	ESOTERICISM	EXAGGERATOR
ENGROSSMENT	ENZYMOLYSIS	ESSENTIALLY	EXALTEDNESS
ENHANCEMENT	ENZYMOLYTIC	ESTABLISHED	EXAMINATION
ENLARGEABLE	EPHEMERALLY	ESTABLISHER	EXANIMATION
ENLARGEMENT	EPIDERMISES	ESTATE AGENT	EXASPERATED
ENLIGHTENED	EPIDIASCOPE	ESTREMADURA	EXASPERATER
ENLIGHTENER	EPIGASTRIUM	ETHANEDIOIC	EXCAVATIONS
ENLISTED MAN	EPIGENESIST	ETHEREALITY	EXCEEDINGLY
ENLISTED MEN	EPIGRAPHIST	ETHEREALIZE	EXCELLENTLY
ENLISTMENTS	EPIPHYTOTIC	ETHICALNESS	EXCEPTIONAL
ENLIVENMENT	EPITHALAMIC	ETHNOBOTANY	EXCERPTIBLE
ENNEAHEDRAL	EPITHELIOMA	ETHNOGENIST	EXCERPTTION
ENNEAHEDRON	EPITOMIZING	ETHNOGRAPHY	EXCESSIVELY
ENNISKILLEN	EPOCH-MAKING	ETHNOLOGIST	EXCITEDNESS
ENNOBLEMENT	EQUIANGULAR	ETIOLOGICAL	EXCITEMENTS
ENNOBLINGLY	EQUIDISTANT	ETYMOLOGIES	EXCLAMATION
ENRAPTURING	EQUILATERAL	ETYMOLOGIST	EXCLAMATORY
ENSHROUDING	EQUILIBRANT	EUCHARISTIC	EXCLUSIVELY
ENSLAVEMENT	EQUILIBRATE	EUCHROMATIC	EXCOGITATOR
ENSNAREMENT	EQUILIBRIST	EUCHROMATIN	EXCORIATING
ENTABLATURE	EQUILIBRIUM	EUDIOMETRIC	EXCORIATION
ENTABLEMENT	EQUINOCTIAL	EUGENICALLY	EXCREMENTAL
ENTEROSTOMY	EQUIPOLLENT	EUPHEMISTIC	EXCRESCENCE
ENTEROVIRUS	EQUIVALENCE	EURHYTHMICS	EXCRESCENCY
ENTERPRISER	EQUIVALENCY	EUROCENTRIC	EXCULPATING
ENTERPRISES	EQUIVALENTS	EUROCHEQUES	EXCULPATION
ENTERTAINED	EQUIVOCALLY	EURODOLLARS	EXCULPATORY
ENTERTAINER	EQUIVOCATED	EUROPEANISM	EX-DIRECTORY
ENTHRALLING	ERADICATING	EUROPEANIZE	EXECRATIONS
ENTHRALMENT	ERADICATION	EURO-SCEPTIC	EXECUTIONER
ENTHUSIASMS	ERADICATIVE	EURYTHERMAL	EXECUTORIAL
ENTHUSIASTS	ERADICATORS	EVACUATIONS	EXEMPLARILY
ENTICEMENTS	ERASTIANISM	EVAGINATION	EXEMPLIFIED
ENTITLEMENT	ERGATOCRACY	EVALUATIONS	EXEMPLIFIER
ENTOBLASTIC	EROSIVENESS	EVANESCENCE	EXERCISABLE
ENTOMBMENTS	EROTOMANIAC	EVANGELICAL	EXFOLIATION
ENTOMOPHILY	ERRATICALLY	EVANGELISTS	EXFOLIATIVE
ENTRAINMENT	ERRONEOUSLY	EVANGELIZED	EXHAUSTIBLE
ENTREATMENT	ERUBESCENCE	EVANGELIZER	EXHIBITIONS
ENTRENCHING	ERUCTATIONS	EVAPORATING	EXHILARATED

EXHILARATOR
EXHORTATION
EXHORTATIVE
EXHUMATIONS
EXISTENTIAL
EXONERATING
EXONERATION
EXONERATIVE
EXORABILITY
EXORBITANCE
EXOSKELETAL
EXOSKELETON
EXOTERICISM
EXPANSIVELY
EXPATIATING
EXPATIATION
EXPATRIATED
EXPATRIATES
EXPECTANTLY
EXPECTATION
EXPECTATIVE
EXPECTORANT
EXPECTORATE
EXPEDIENTLY
EXPEDITIONS
EXPEDITIOUS
EXPENDITURE
EXPENSIVELY
EXPERIENCED
EXPERIENCES
EXPERIMENTS
EXPLAINABLE
EXPLANATION
EXPLANATORY
EXPLICATING
EXPLICATION
EXPLICATIVE
EXPLOITABLE
EXPLORATION
EXPLORATORY
EXPLOSIVELY
EXPONENTIAL
EXPORTATION
EXPOSEDNESS
EXPOSITIONS
EX POST FACTO
EXPOSTULATE
EXPRESSIBLE
EXPRESSIONS
EXPRESSWAYS
EXPROPRIATE

EXPURGATING
EXPURGATION
EXPURGATORY
EXQUISITELY
EXSICCATION
EXSICCATIVE
EXSTIPULATE
EXTEMPORIZE
EXTENSIONAL
EXTENSIVELY
EXTENUATING
EXTENUATION
EXTENUATORY
EXTERIORIZE
EXTERMINATE
EXTERNALISM
EXTERNALIST
EXTERNALITY
EXTERNALIZE
EXTIRPATING
EXTIRPATION
EXTIRPATIVE
EXTOLLINGLY
EXTRACTABLE
EXTRACTIONS
EXTRADITING
EXTRADITION
EXTRAPOLATE
EXTRAVAGANT
EXTRAVAGATE
EXTRAVASATE
EXTREMENESS
EXTREMITIES
EXTRICATING
EXTRICATION
EXTROVERTED
EXUBERANTLY
EYE-CATCHING

F

FABRICATING
FABRICATION
FABRICATIVE
FACE-CENTRED
FACETIOUSLY
FACILITATED
FACILITATOR
FACT-FINDING
FACTORIZING
FACTORY FARM
FACTS OF LIFE

FACTUALNESS
FACULTATIVE
FAIRGROUNDS
FAIR-WEATHER
FAIRY LIGHTS
FAITH HEALER
FAITHLESSLY
FALCONIFORM
FALLIBILITY
FALLING STAR
FALSE ALARMS
FALSE BOTTOM
FALSE STARTS
FALSIFIABLE
FALSTAFFIAN
FALTERINGLY
FAMILIARITY
FAMILIARIZE
FAMILY NAMES
FAMILY TREES
FANATICALLY
FANTASIZING
FARCICALITY
FARINACEOUS
FARNBOROUGH
FARRAGINOUS
FAR-REACHING
FARTHERMOST
FARTHINGALE
FASCINATING
FASCINATION
FASCINATIVE
FASHIONABLE
FAST-BREEDER
FAST-FORWARD
FATEFULNESS
FATHER-IN-LAW
FATHERLANDS
FATUOUSNESS
FAULT-FINDER
FAULTLESSLY
FAVOURINGLY
FAVOURITISM
FAWNINGNESS
FEARFULNESS
FEASIBILITY
FEATHER BEDS
FEATHER BOAS
FEATHEREDGE
FEATURE FILM
FEATURELESS

FECUNDATION
FECUNDATORY
FEDERALISTS
FEDERATIONS
FELDSPATHIC
FELICITATED
FELICITATOR
FELLOWSHIPS
FELT-TIP PENS
FEMME FATALE
FENESTRATED
FERMENTABLE
FEROCIOUSLY
FERRICYANIC
FERRIFEROUS
FERRIS WHEEL
FERROCYANIC
FERRUGINOUS
FERTILIZERS
FERTILIZING
FERULACEOUS
FERVENTNESS
FESTINATION
FESTSCHRIFT
FETISHISTIC
FEUDALISTIC
FIBRE OPTICS
FIBROMATOUS
FIBROUSNESS
FICTIONALLY
FIDGETINGLY
FIELD-EFFECT
FIELD EVENTS
FIELD HOCKEY
FIELD-HOLLER
FIELD-TESTED
FIELDWORKER
FIFTH COLUMN
FIFTH-DEGREE
FIGURED BASS
FIGUREHEADS
FILAMENTARY
FILIBUSTERS
FILL THE BILL
FILMOGRAPHY
FILMSETTING
FILTHY LUCRE
FILTRATABLE
FIMBRIATION
FINANCIALLY
FIN DE SIECLE

FINE-GRAINED	FLEET STREET	FOOT FAULTED	FORMULATION
FINES HERBES	FLESHLINESS	FOOT-LAMBERT	FORMULISTIC
FINGERBOARD	FLESH WOUNDS	FOOT-POUNDAL	FORNICATING
FINGER BOWLS	FLETCHERISM	FOOTSLOGGED	FORNICATION
FINGERNAILS	FLEURS-DE-LIS	FOPPISHNESS	FORSWEARING
FINGERPLATE	FLEXIBILITY	FORAMINIFER	FORTHCOMING
FINGERPRINT	FLICK KNIVES	FORASMUCH AS	FORTIFIABLE
FINGERSTALL	FLIGHT DECKS	FORBEARANCE	FORTNIGHTLY
FIRE BRIGADE	FLIGHTINESS	FORBIDDANCE	FORTUNATELY
FIRECRACKER	FLIGHT PATHS	FOREBODINGS	FORT WILLIAM
FIRE ENGINES	FLINCHINGLY	FORECASTERS	FORWARDNESS
FIRE ESCAPES	FLIRTATIONS	FORECASTING	FOSSILIZING
FIRE FIGHTER	FLIRTATIOUS	FORECLOSING	FOSTERINGLY
FIRE HYDRANT	FLOATATIONS	FORECLOSURE	FOUL-MOUTHED
FIRELIGHTER	FLOCCULENCE	FOREFATHERS	FOUNDATIONS
FIREPROOFED	FLOODLIGHTS	FOREFINGERS	FOUNTAIN PEN
FIRE-RAISERS	FLOORBOARDS	FOREGROUNDS	FOURDRINIER
FIRE-RAISING	FLOOR CLOTHS	FOREMANSHIP	FOUR-POSTERS
FIRE STATION	FLOORWALKER	FOREQUARTER	FOURTEENTHS
FIRING SQUAD	FLOPPY DISKS	FORERUNNERS	FOX TERRIERS
FIRMAMENTAL	FLORESCENCE	FORESEEABLE	FRACTIONARY
FIRST COUSIN	FLORILEGIUM	FORESHORTEN	FRACTIONATE
FIRST-DEGREE	FLOUNDERING	FORESIGHTED	FRACTIONIZE
FIRST-FOOTER	FLOURISHING	FORESTALLED	FRACTIOUSLY
FIRST NATION	FLOWCHARTED	FORESTALLER	FRACTURABLE
FIRST NIGHTS	FLOWER GIRLS	FORESTATION	FRAGMENTARY
FIRST PERSON	FLOWERINESS	FORETELLING	FRAGMENTING
FIRST STRIKE	FLUCTUATING	FORETHOUGHT	FRAME OF MIND
FIRST-STRING	FLUCTUATION	FORE-TOPMAST	FRANCHISING
FISHEYE LENS	FLUID OUNCES	FORE-TOPSAIL	FRANCISCANS
FISH-EYE LENS	FLUORESCEIN	FOR EVERMORE	FRANCOPHILE
FISH FARMING	FLUORESCENT	FOREWARNING	FRANCOPHOBE
FISH FINGERS	FLUORIDATED	FORFEITABLE	FRANCOPHONE
FISHMONGERS	FLUOROMETER	FORGATHERED	FRANKFURTER
FISSIONABLE	FLUOROMETRY	FORGETFULLY	FRANKLINITE
FISSIPAROUS	FLUOROSCOPE	FORGET-ME-NOT	FRANTICALLY
FLABBERGAST	FLUOROSCOPY	FORGETTABLE	FRATERNALLY
FLAGELLANTS	FLYCATCHERS	FORGIVENESS	FRATERNIZED
FLAGELLATED	FLYING BOATS	FORGIVINGLY	FRATERNIZER
FLAMBOYANCE	FLYING FOXES	FORJUDGMENT	FRATRICIDAL
FLANNELETTE	FLYING SQUAD	FORLORN HOPE	FRATRICIDES
FLANNELLING	FLYING START	FORLORNNESS	FRAUDULENCE
FLASHLIGHTS	FLYSWATTERS	FORMALISTIC	FREDERICTON
FLASH POINTS	FOCAL LENGTH	FORMALITIES	FREDRIKSTAD
FLAT-CHESTED	FOLK DANCERS	FORMALIZING	FREEBOOTERS
FLATTERABLE	FOLLICULATE	FORMATIONAL	FREE-FLOATER
FLAUNTINGLY	FOMENTATION	FORMATIVELY	FREE-FOR-ALLS
FLAVOURINGS	FOOLISHNESS	FORMICATION	FREE-HEARTED
FLAVOURLESS	FOOL'S ERRAND	FORMULAICLY	FREEHOLDERS
FLAVOURSOME	FOOTBALLERS	FORMULARIZE	FREELANCING
FLEA MARKETS	FOOTBRIDGES	FORMULATING	FREELOADERS

FREELOADING
FREEMASONIC
FREEMASONRY
FREE PARDONS
FREE-SWIMMER
FREETHINKER
FREEWHEELED
FREEZE-DRIED
FRENCH BEANS
FRENCH BREAD
FRENCH DOORS
FRENCH FRIES
FRENCH HORNS
FRENCH LEAVE
FRENCH TOAST
FRENCHWOMAN
FREQUENCIES
FREQUENTING
FRETFULNESS
FREUDIANISM
FRIENDLIEST
FRIENDSHIPS
FRIGHTENING
FRIGHTFULLY
FRINGILLINE
FRIVOLITIES
FRIVOLOUSLY
FROGMARCHED
FRONDESCENT
FRONTOLYSIS
FRONT-RUNNER
FROSTBITTEN
FRUCTIFYING
FRUGIVOROUS
FRUITLESSLY
FRUIT SALADS
FRUSTRATING
FRUSTRATION
FRUTESCENCE
FULGURATING
FULGURATION
FULL-BLOODED
FULL-FLEDGED
FULL-MOUTHED
FULMINATING
FULMINATION
FULMINATORY
FULSOMENESS
FUNAMBULIST
FUN AND GAMES
FUNCTIONARY

FUNCTIONING
FUNDAMENTAL
FUNDHOLDING
FUNGIBILITY
FUNGISTATIC
FURALDEHYDE
FURIOUSNESS
FURNISHINGS
FURTHERANCE
FURTHERMORE
FURTHERMOST
FURTIVENESS

G
GAFF-TOPSAIL
GAINFULNESS
GALLANTNESS
GALLANTRIES
GALL BLADDER
GALLINACEAN
GALLIVANTED
GALLUP POLLS
GALVANIZING
GAMEKEEPERS
GAMEKEEPING
GAMETANGIAL
GAMETANGIUM
GAMETOGENIC
GAMETOPHORE
GAMETOPHYTE
GAMOGENESIS
GAMOGENETIC
GANG-BANGING
GARAGE SALES
GARBAGE CANS
GARDEN PARTY
GARNISHMENT
GARRISONING
GARRULOUSLY
GASEOUSNESS
GAS STATIONS
GASTRECTOMY
GASTRONOMES
GASTRONOMIC
GASTROPODAN
GASTROSCOPE
GASTROSCOPY
GASTROSTOMY
GASTROTRICH
GAS TURBINES
GATECRASHED

GATECRASHER
GATEKEEPERS
GEANTICLINE
GEGENSCHEIN
GELATINIZER
GEMMIPAROUS
GEMMULATION
GEMOLOGICAL
GENDARMERIE
GENEALOGIES
GENEALOGIST
GENE LIBRARY
GENERALIZED
GENERALIZER
GENERALNESS
GENERALSHIP
GENERATIONS
GENERATION X
GENERICALLY
GENETICALLY
GENETIC CODE
GENETICISTS
GENTEELNESS
GENTIANELLA
GENTLEMANLY
GENTLEWOMAN
GENTLEWOMEN
GENTRIFYING
GENUFLECTED
GENUFLECTOR
GENUINENESS
GEOCHEMICAL
GEODYNAMICS
GEOGRAPHERS
GEOGRAPHIES
GEOMAGNETIC
GEOPHYSICAL
GEOPOLITICS
GEOSTRATEGY
GEOSTROPHIC
GEOSYNCLINE
GEOTECTONIC
GERATOLOGIC
GERMANENESS
GERMINATING
GERMINATION
GERM WARFARE
GERONTOLOGY
GERRYMANDER
GESTATIONAL
GESTICULATE

GET CRACKING
GET-TOGETHER
GHASTLINESS
GHOSTBUSTER
GHOSTLINESS
GHOSTWRITER
GIANT KILLER
GIANT PANDAS
GIBBERELLIN
GIBBOUSNESS
GIFT-WRAPPED
GIGANTESQUE
GILA MONSTER
GILLYFLOWER
GINGER BEERS
GINGERBREAD
GINGER GROUP
GIRL FRIDAYS
GIRLFRIENDS
GIRLISHNESS
GIVE-AND-TAKE
GLADIOLUSES
GLAMORIZING
GLAMOROUSLY
GLARINGNESS
GLASSBLOWER
GLASSCUTTER
GLASSHOUSES
GLASS-MAKING
GLASS-WORKER
GLASTONBURY
GLAUCONITIC
GLEEFULNESS
GLOBEFLOWER
GLOBIGERINA
GLOCHIDIATE
GLOMERATION
GLOMERULATE
GLORIFIABLE
GLOSSECTOMY
GLOSSOLALIA
GLOTTAL STOP
GLOVE PUPPET
GLOWERINGLY
GLUE-SNIFFER
GLUTATHIONE
GLYPHOGRAPH
GNATCATCHER
GOALKEEPERS
GOALKEEPING
GO BALLISTIC

GODCHILDREN
GODDAUGHTER
GODFORSAKEN
GODLESSNESS
GOLD-BEATING
GOLD DIGGERS
GOLD-DIGGING
GOLDEN EAGLE
GOLDEN SYRUP
GOLDFINCHES
GOLF COURSES
GONIOMETRIC
GONOCOCCOID
GONORRHOEAL
GOOD EVENING
GOOD LOOKERS
GOOD-LOOKING
GOOD MORNING
GOOD-NATURED
GOOD OFFICES
GORDIAN KNOT
GORMANDIZED
GORMANDIZER
GOSSIPINGLY
GO TO THE DOGS
GOURMANDISE
GOURMANDISM
GOVERNESSES
GOVERNMENTS
GRACELESSLY
GRADABILITY
GRADATIONAL
GRADE SCHOOL
GRADUALNESS
GRADUATIONS
GRAECO-ROMAN
GRAMMARIANS
GRAMMATICAL
GRAMOPHONES
GRANDADDIES
GRAND BAHAMA
GRAND CANARY
GRANDE-TERRE
GRANDFATHER
GRANDIOSITY
GRAND JURIES
GRAND MASTER
GRANDMOTHER
GRAND OPERAS
GRANDPARENT
GRAND PIANOS

GRAND RAPIDS
GRANDSTANDS
GRANGEMOUTH
GRANGERIZER
GRANITEWARE
GRANIVOROUS
GRANNY KNOTS
GRANOLITHIC
GRANOPHYRIC
GRANULARITY
GRANULATION
GRANULATIVE
GRANULOCYTE
GRAPEFRUITS
GRAPHICALLY
GRAPHOLOGIC
GRAPHOMOTOR
GRASSHOPPER
GRASS WIDOWS
GRAVESTONES
GRAVIMETRIC
GRAVITATING
GRAVITATION
GRAVITATIVE
GREASEPAINT
GREASY SPOON
GREAT CIRCLE
GREAT-NEPHEW
GREENBOTTLE
GREENGROCER
GREENHOUSES
GREENLANDER
GREENOCKITE
GREEN PAPERS
GREEN PEPPER
GRETNA GREEN
GRIDDLECAKE
GRIMACINGLY
GRINDELWALD
GRINDSTONES
GRISTLINESS
GRIZZLY BEAR
GROTESQUELY
GROTESQUERY
GROUCHINESS
GROUND CREWS
GROUND FLOOR
GROUND GLASS
GROUNDLINGS
GROUND PLANS
GROUND RENTS

GROUND RULES
GROUNDSHEET
GROUNDSPEED
GROUND STAFF
GROUNDSWELL
GROUPUSCULE
GRUELLINGLY
GRUMBLINGLY
GUADALAJARA
GUADALCANAL
GUARDEDNESS
GUARDHOUSES
GUELDER-ROSE
GUESSTIMATE
GUESTHOUSES
GUEST WORKER
GUILELESSLY
GUILLOTINED
GUILLOTINER
GUILLOTINES
GUILTLESSLY
GULLIBILITY
GUN CARRIAGE
GUNSMITHING
GURGITATION
GUTLESSNESS
GUTTA-PERCHA
GUTTER PRESS
GUTTERSNIPE
GUTTURALIZE
GYNAECOLOGY
GYPSIFEROUS
GYROCOMPASS
GYROSCOPICS
GYROSTATICS

H

HABERDASHER
HABILITATOR
HABITATIONS
HABITUATING
HABITUATION
HABITUDINAL
HADROSAURUS
HAEMACHROME
HAEMATOCELE
HAEMATOCRIT
HAEMATOLOGY
HAEMATOZOON
HAEMOCHROME
HAEMOCYANIN

HAEMOGLOBIN
HAEMOPHILIA
HAEMOPHILIC
HAEMOPTYSIS
HAEMORRHAGE
HAEMOSTASIA
HAEMOSTASIS
HAEMOSTATIC
HAGGADISTIC
HAGGARDNESS
HAGGISHNESS
HAGIOGRAPHA
HAGIOGRAPHY
HAGIOLOGIST
HAGIOSCOPIC
HAIRBREADTH
HAIRBRUSHES
HAIRDRESSER
HAIRPIN BEND
HAIR-RAISING
HAIRSPRINGS
HAIRSTYLIST
HAIR TRIGGER
HAIRWEAVING
HALBERSTADT
HALCYON DAYS
HALF-BROTHER
HALF-CENTURY
HALF-HEARTED
HALF-HOLIDAY
HALFPENNIES
HALF-SISTERS
HALF VOLLEYS
HALLMARKING
HALLUCINATE
HALOPHYTISM
HALTEMPRICE
HALTERNECKS
HALTINGNESS
HAMILTONIAN
HAMMERSMITH
HAMMERSTEIN
HAMMOCK-LIKE
HANDBREADTH
HANDCUFFING
HANDFASTING
HANDICAPPED
HANDICAPPER
HANDICRAFTS
HAND IN GLOVE
HAND LUGGAGE

HANDMAIDENS	HEALTH FOODS	HEMIHYDRATE	HEXAGONALLY
HAND-ME-DOWNS	HEALTHFULLY	HEMIMORPHIC	HEXAHYDRATE
HANDWRITING	HEALTHINESS	HEMIPTEROUS	HEXASTICHIC
HANDWRITTEN	HEARING AIDS	HEMISPHERES	HEXASTICHON
HANG GLIDING	HEART ATTACK	HEMISPHERIC	HEXATEUCHAL
HAPHAZARDLY	HEARTBROKEN	HEMITERPENE	HIBERNATING
HAPLESSNESS	HEARTHSTONE	HEMITROPISM	HIBERNATION
HAPLOGRAPHY	HEARTLESSLY	HEMOPHILIAC	HIBERNICISM
HAPPY EVENTS	HEARTSOMELY	HEMORRHAGES	HIDE-AND-SEEK
HAPPY MEDIUM	HEARTTHROBS	HEMORRHOIDS	HIDEOUSNESS
HARASSINGLY	HEATHENNESS	HEMSTITCHER	HIERARCHIES
HARBOURLESS	HEAT SHIELDS	HEPPLEWHITE	HIERARCHISM
HARD-AND-FAST	HEAVENWARDS	HEPTAHEDRAL	HIEROCRATIC
HARDECANUTE	HEAVY-HANDED	HEPTAHEDRON	HIEROGLYPHS
HARD-HEARTED	HEAVYWEIGHT	HEPTAMEROUS	HIEROLOGIST
HARD-HITTING	HEBDOMADARY	HEPTANGULAR	HIGH COMMAND
HARDICANUTE	HEBEPHRENIA	HEPTAVALENT	HIGHFALUTIN
HARD PALATES	HEBEPHRENIC	HERBIVOROUS	HIGH JUMPERS
HARD-PRESSED	HEBRAICALLY	HERCEGOVINA	HIGHLANDERS
HARDWEARING	HECKELPHONE	HERCULANEUM	HIGHLIGHTED
HARDY ANNUAL	HECTOGRAPHY	HEREDITABLE	HIGHLIGHTER
HAREBRAINED	HEDGEHOPPER	HEREDITABLY	HIGH-PITCHED
HARMFULNESS	HEEDFULNESS	HEREINAFTER	HIGH-POWERED
HARMONISTIC	HEGELIANISM	HERETICALLY	HIGH PRIESTS
HARMONIZING	HEIGHTENING	HERMENEUTIC	HIGH PROFILE
HARNESSLESS	HEINOUSNESS	HERMOUPOLIS	HIGH-RANKING
HARNESS-LIKE	HELICHRYSUM	HERO WORSHIP	HIGH SCHOOLS
HARPOON-LIKE	HELICOGRAPH	HERPESVIRUS	HIGH SHERIFF
HARPSICHORD	HELICOPTERS	HERPETOLOGY	HIGH-TENSION
HARRIS TWEED	HELIOCHROME	HERRINGBONE	HIGH TREASON
HARROWINGLY	HELIOGRAPHS	HERZEGOVINA	HIGHWAY CODE
HARTEBEESTS	HELIOGRAPHY	HESITATIONS	HIGH WYCOMBE
HARUM SCARUM	HELIOLITHIC	HESPERIDIAN	HILARIOUSLY
HARUM-SCARUM	HELIOMETRIC	HESPERIDIUM	HILLBILLIES
HARVEST HOME	HELIOSTATIC	HESYCHASTIC	HINDERINGLY
HARVESTLESS	HELIOTACTIC	HETAERISTIC	HINDQUARTER
HARVEST MOON	HELIOTROPES	HETEROCLITE	HINSHELWOOD
HATCHET JOBS	HELIOTROPIC	HETEROECISM	HIPPEASTRUM
HATCHET-LIKE	HELIOTROPIN	HETEROGRAFT	HIPPOCAMPAL
HATEFULNESS	HELLEBORINE	HETEROLYSIS	HIPPOCAMPUS
HAUGHTINESS	HELLENISTIC	HETEROLYTIC	HIPPOCRATES
HAUSTELLATE	HELLISHNESS	HETEROPHONY	HIPPOCRATIC
HAUTES-ALPES	HELMINTHOID	HETEROPHYTE	HIPPOPOTAMI
HAUTE-SAVOIE	HELPFULNESS	HETEROPOLAR	HIPPO REGIUS
HAUTE-VIENNE	HELPING HAND	HETEROSPORY	HIRSUTENESS
HAWKISHNESS	HELSINGBORG	HETEROSTYLY	HISPANICISM
HAZARDOUSLY	HEMERALOPIA	HETEROTAXIS	HISPANICIST
HEADDRESSES	HEMERALOPIC	HETEROTOPIA	HISPANICIZE
HEADHUNTERS	HEMIANOPSIA	HETEROTOPIC	HISTAMINASE
HEADHUNTING	HEMIELYTRAL	HETEROTYPIC	HISTIOCYTIC
HEADMASTERS	HEMIELYTRON	HEXADECIMAL	HISTOLOGIST

HISTORIATED
HISTORICISM
HISTORICIST
HISTORICITY
HISTRIONICS
HITCHHIKERS
HITCHHIKING
HOBBLEDEHOY
HOBBYHORSES
HOGGISHNESS
HOLKAR STATE
HOLLANDAISE
HOLOBLASTIC
HOLOCAUSTAL
HOLOGRAPHIC
HOLOHEDRISM
HOLOMORPHIC
HOLOTHURIAN
HOMECOMINGS
HOMEOPATHIC
HOMEOSTASIS
HOMEOSTATIC
HOMERICALLY
HOMESTEADER
HOME STRETCH
HOMICIDALLY
HOMOCENTRIC
HOMOEOPATHS
HOMOEOPATHY
HOMOEROTISM
HOMOGENEITY
HOMOGENEOUS
HOMOGENIZED
HOMOGENIZER
HOMOGRAPHIC
HOMOIOUSIAN
HOMOLOGICAL
HOMOLOGIZER
HOMOMORPHIC
HOMOPHONOUS
HOMOPHYLLIC
HOMOPLASTIC
HOMOPTEROUS
HOMO SAPIENS
HOMOSEXUALS
HOMOSPOROUS
HOMOTHALLIC
HOMOTHERMAL
HOMOZYGOSIS
HOMOZYGOTIC
HONEYCOMBED

HONEYMOONED
HONEYMOONER
HONEYSUCKER
HONEYSUCKLE
HONORARIUMS
HONOURS LIST
HOODWINKING
HOOLIGANISM
HOPEFULNESS
HOPLOLOGIST
HORIZONLESS
HORIZONTALS
HORNBLENDIC
HORNET'S NEST
HORNSWOGGLE
HORROR FILMS
HORS D'OEUVRE
HORSE DOCTOR
HORSELAUGHS
HORSE OPERAS
HORSERADISH
HORTATORILY
HOSPITALITY
HOSPITALIZE
HOSPITALLER
HOSTILITIES
HOT-CROSS BUN
HOTHEADEDLY
HOT POTATOES
HOT-TEMPERED
HOURGLASSES
HOUSE ARREST
HOUSEBROKEN
HOUSEFATHER
HOUSEHOLDER
HOUSEKEEPER
HOUSE LIGHTS
HOUSEMASTER
HOUSEMOTHER
HOUSEPARENT
HOUSEPLANTS
HOUSEWIFELY
HOUSEWIFERY
HOUSEWORKER
HOVERCRAFTS
HOW DO YOU DOS
HSIN-HAI-LIEN
HUCKLEBERRY
HUCKSTERISM
HUDIBRASTIC
HUGUENOTISM

HULLABALOOS
HUMAN RIGHTS
HUMDRUMNESS
HUMIDIFIERS
HUMIDIFYING
HUMILIATING
HUMILIATION
HUMILIATIVE
HUMILIATORY
HUMMINGBIRD
HUNCHBACKED
HUNGER MARCH
HUNNISHNESS
HURRIEDNESS
HURTFULNESS
HUSBANDLESS
HYACINTHINE
HYDNOCARPIC
HYDRARGYRIC
HYDRARGYRUM
HYDROCARBON
HYDROCYANIC
HYDROGENATE
HYDROGENIZE
HYDROGENOUS
HYDROGRAPHY
HYDROLOGIST
HYDROLYSATE
HYDROMANCER
HYDROMANTIC
HYDROMEDUSA
HYDROMETEOR
HYDROPHOBIA
HYDROPONICS
HYPERACTIVE
HYPERMARKET
HYPHENATING
HYPHENATION
HYPNOTIZING
HYPODERMICS
HYPOSTATIZE
HYPOTHERMIA

I

ICEBREAKERS
ICHNOGRAPHY
ICHTHYOLOGY
ICONOCLASTS
ICONOGRAPHY
ICONOLOGIST
ICOSAHEDRAL

ICOSAHEDRON
IDENTICALLY
IDENTIFYING
IDEOLOGICAL
IDIOBLASTIC
IDIOGRAPHIC
IDIOMORPHIC
IDIOTICALLY
IDOLATRIZER
IDOLIZATION
IDYLLICALLY
IGNIS FATUUS
IGNOMINIOUS
IGNORAMUSES
ILE-DE-FRANCE
ILL-ASSORTED
ILL-FAVOURED
ILLIBERALLY
ILLIMITABLE
ILL-MANNERED
ILLOGICALLY
ILL-TEMPERED
ILL-TREATING
ILLUMINANCE
ILLUMINATED
ILLUMINATOR
ILLUSIONARY
ILLUSIONISM
ILLUSIONIST
ILLUSTRATED
ILLUSTRATOR
ILLUSTRIOUS
ILLUVIATION
I'M A DUTCHMAN
IMAGINARILY
IMAGINATION
IMAGINATIVE
IMBRICATION
IMITABILITY
IMITATIONAL
IMITATIVELY
IMMEDIATELY
IMMEDICABLE
IMMIGRATING
IMMIGRATION
IMMOBILIZED
IMMOBILIZER
IMMORTALITY
IMMORTALIZE
IMMUNOASSAY
IMMUNOGENIC

IMMUNOLOGIC	IMPRECATION	INCOME TAXES	INDIVIDUATE
IMPANELLING	IMPRECATORY	INCOMMODING	INDIVISIBLE
IMPARTATION	IMPRECISION	INCOMPETENT	INDIVISIBLY
IMPARTIALLY	IMPREGNABLE	INCOMPLIANT	INDOCHINESE
IMPASSIONED	IMPREGNABLY	IN CONDITION	INDO-HITTITE
IMPASSIVELY	IMPREGNATED	INCONGRUITY	INDO-IRANIAN
IMPASSIVITY	IMPREGNATOR	INCONGRUOUS	INDOMITABLE
IMPASTATION	IMPRESARIOS	INCONSONANT	INDOMITABLY
IMPATIENTLY	IMPRESSIBLE	INCONSTANCY	INDO-PACIFIC
IMPEACHABLE	IMPRESSIONS	INCONTINENT	INDORSEMENT
IMPEACHMENT	IMPRESSMENT	INCORPORATE	INDUBITABLE
IMPECUNIOUS	IMPRIMATURS	INCORPOREAL	INDUBITABLY
IMPEDIMENTA	IMPRISONING	INCORRECTLY	INDUCEMENTS
IMPEDIMENTS	IMPROPRIATE	INCREASABLE	INDUCTILITY
IMPENITENCE	IMPROPRIETY	INCREASEDLY	INDUCTIONAL
IMPERATIVES	IMPROVEMENT	INCREDULITY	INDUCTIVELY
IMPERFECTLY	IMPROVIDENT	INCREDULOUS	INDULGENCES
IMPERFORATE	IMPROVINGLY	INCREMENTAL	INDULGENTLY
IMPERIALISM	IMPROVISING	INCRIMINATE	INDULGINGLY
IMPERIALIST	IMPRUDENTLY	INCULCATING	INDUPLICATE
IMPERILLING	IMPUGNATION	INCULCATION	INDUSTRIOUS
IMPERIOUSLY	IMPUISSANCE	INCULPATING	INEBRIATING
IMPERMANENT	IMPULSIVELY	INCULPATION	INEBRIATION
IMPERMEABLE	IMPUTATIONS	INCUNABULAR	INEDIBILITY
IMPERSONATE	INADVERTENT	INCURIOSITY	INEFFECTIVE
IMPERTINENT	INADVISABLE	INCURVATION	INEFFECTUAL
IMPETRATION	INALIENABLE	INCURVATURE	INEFFICIENT
IMPETRATIVE	INALTERABLE	INDECIDUOUS	INELEGANTLY
IMPETUOSITY	INATTENTION	INDEFINABLE	INELOQUENCE
IMPETUOUSLY	INATTENTIVE	INDEFINABLY	INELUCTABLE
IMPINGEMENT	INAUGURATED	INDEHISCENT	INELUCTABLY
IMPIOUSNESS	INAUGURATOR	INDEMNIFIED	INEQUITABLE
IMPLAUSIBLE	INAUTHENTIC	INDEMNIFIER	INEQUITABLY
IMPLAUSIBLY	INCALESCENT	INDEMNITIES	INERTIA REEL
IMPLEADABLE	INCANTATION	INDENTATION	INESCAPABLE
IMPLEMENTAL	INCAPSULATE	INDENTURING	INESCAPABLY
IMPLEMENTED	INCARCERATE	INDEPENDENT	INESSENTIAL
IMPLEMENTER	INCARDINATE	INDEX FINGER	INESTIMABLE
IMPLICATING	INCARNATING	INDIA RUBBER	INESTIMABLY
IMPLICATION	INCARNATION	INDICATABLE	INEXACTNESS
IMPLICATIVE	INCERTITUDE	INDICATIONS	INEXCUSABLE
IMPLORATION	INCESSANTLY	INDICATIVES	INEXCUSABLY
IMPLORATORY	INCIDENTALS	INDICTMENTS	INEXISTENCE
IMPLORINGLY	INCINERATED	INDIFFERENT	INEXPEDIENT
IMPORTANTLY	INCINERATOR	INDIGESTION	INEXPENSIVE
IMPORTATION	INCIPIENTLY	INDIGESTIVE	INFANTICIDE
IMPORTUNATE	INCLINATION	INDIGNANTLY	INFANTILISM
IMPORTUNING	INCLUSIVELY	INDIGNATION	INFANTILITY
IMPORTUNITY	INCOERCIBLE	INDIGNITIES	INFANTRYMAN
IMPOSITIONS	INCOGNIZANT	INDIRECTION	INFANTRYMEN
IMPRACTICAL	INCOHERENCE	INDIVIDUALS	INFATUATION

INFERENTIAL
INFERIORITY
INFERNALITY
INFERTILITY
INFESTATION
INFILTRATED
INFILTRATOR
INFINITIVAL
INFINITIVES
INFIRMARIES
INFIRMITIES
INFLAMINGLY
INFLAMMABLE
INFLECTIONS
INFLICTIONS
INFLUENCING
INFLUENTIAL
INFOMERCIAL
INFORMALITY
INFORMATION
INFORMATIVE
INFORMINGLY
INFRACOSTAL
INFRACTIONS
INFRANGIBLE
INFREQUENCY
INFURIATING
INFURIATION
INFUSIONISM
INFUSIONIST
INGENIOUSLY
INGENUOUSLY
INGRAINEDLY
INGRATIATED
INGRATITUDE
INGREDIENTS
INGURGITATE
INHABITABLE
INHABITANCY
INHABITANTS
INHALATIONS
INHERITABLE
INHERITANCE
INHIBITABLE
INHIBITEDLY
INHIBITIONS
INITIALLING
INITIATIONS
INITIATIVES
INITIATRESS
INJUDICIOUS

INJUNCTIONS
INJURIOUSLY
IN-LINE SKATE
INNER CITIES
INNERVATION
INNOCUOUSLY
INNOVATIONS
INNS OF COURT
INNUMERABLE
INNUTRITION
INOBSERVANT
INOCULATING
INOCULATION
INOCULATIVE
INOFFENSIVE
INOFFICIOUS
INOPERATIVE
INOPPORTUNE
IN PERPETUUM
INQUILINISM
INQUILINOUS
INQUIRINGLY
INQUISITION
INQUISITIVE
INQUISITORS
IN-RESIDENCE
INSALUBRITY
INSCRIBABLE
INSCRIPTION
INSCRIPTIVE
INSCRUTABLE
INSCRUTABLY
INSECTARIUM
INSECTICIDE
INSECTIVORE
INSEMINATED
INSEMINATOR
INSENSITIVE
INSENTIENCE
INSEPARABLE
INSEPARABLY
INSERTIONAL
INSESSORIAL
INSIDE TRACK
INSIDIOUSLY
INSINCERELY
INSINCERITY
INSINUATING
INSINUATION
INSINUATIVE
INSISTENTLY

INSOUCIANCE
INSPECTABLE
INSPECTIONS
INSPECTORAL
INSPIRATION
INSPIRATIVE
INSPIRATORY
INSPIRINGLY
INSTABILITY
INSTALMENTS
INSTATEMENT
INSTIGATING
INSTIGATION
INSTIGATIVE
INSTIGATORS
INSTINCTIVE
INSTITUTING
INSTITUTION
INSTITUTIVE
INSTRUCTING
INSTRUCTION
INSTRUCTIVE
INSTRUCTORS
INSTRUMENTS
INSUFFLATOR
INSUPERABLE
INSUPERABLY
INTAGLIATED
INTEGRATING
INTEGRATION
INTEGRATIVE
INTEGUMENTS
INTELLIGENT
INTEMPERATE
INTENSIFIED
INTENSIFIER
INTENSIONAL
INTENSIVELY
INTENTIONAL
INTERACTING
INTERACTION
INTERACTIVE
INTERATOMIC
INTERBEDDED
INTERCALARY
INTERCALATE
INTERCEDING
INTERCEPTED
INTERCEPTOR
INTERCESSOR
INTERCHANGE

INTERCOSTAL
INTERCOURSE
INTERDENTAL
INTERDICTOR
INTERESTING
INTERFACING
INTERFERING
INTERFUSION
INTERJECTED
INTERJECTOR
INTERLACING
INTERLARDED
INTERLINEAR
INTERLINGUA
INTERLINING
INTERLINKED
INTERLOCKED
INTERLOCKER
INTERLOPERS
INTERMEZZOS
INTERMINGLE
INTERMITTOR
INTERNALITY
INTERNALIZE
INTERNECINE
INTERNEURON
INTERNMENTS
INTERNSHIPS
INTERNUNCIO
INTERPOLATE
INTERPOSING
INTERPRETED
INTERPRETER
INTERRACIAL
INTERRADIAL
INTERREGNAL
INTERREGNUM
INTERRELATE
INTERROBANG
INTERROGATE
INTERRUPTED
INTERRUPTER
INTERSECTED
INTERSEXUAL
INTERSPERSE
INTERSTICES
INTERTRIBAL
INTERTWINED
INTERVENING
INTERVIEWED
INTERVIEWEE

INTERVIEWER
INTERWEAVER
INTIMATIONS
INTIMIDATED
INTIMIDATOR
INTOLERABLE
INTOLERABLY
INTOLERANCE
INTONATIONS
INTOXICABLE
INTOXICANTS
INTOXICATED
INTOXICATOR
INTRA-ATOMIC
INTRACOSTAL
INTRACTABLE
INTRACTABLY
INTRADERMAL
INTRAVENOUS
INTRENCHING
INTREPIDITY
INTRICACIES
INTRICATELY
INTRODUCING
INTROVERTED
INTRUDINGLY
INTRUSIONAL
INTUITIONAL
INTUITIVELY
INTUITIVISM
INTUITIVIST
INTUMESCENT
INUNDATIONS
INVAGINABLE
INVALIDATED
INVALIDATOR
INVENTIONAL
INVENTIVELY
INVENTORIAL
INVENTORIES
INVERTEBRAL
INVESTIGATE
INVESTITIVE
INVESTITURE
INVESTMENTS
INVIABILITY
INVIDIOUSLY
INVIGILATED
INVIGILATOR
INVIGORATED
INVIGORATOR

INVITATIONS
INVOCATIONS
INVOLUCRATE
INVOLUNTARY
INVOLVEMENT
IONOSPHERIC
IPECACUANHA
IRIDESCENCE
IRISH COFFEE
IRON CURTAIN
IRONMONGERS
IRONMONGERY
IRON RATIONS
IRRADIATING
IRRADIATION
IRRADIATIVE
IRRECUSABLE
IRREDENTISM
IRREDENTIST
IRREDUCIBLE
IRREDUCIBLY
IRREFUTABLE
IRREFUTABLY
IRREGULARLY
IRRELEVANCE
IRRELIGIOUS
IRREMOVABLE
IRREPARABLE
IRREPARABLY
IRRESOLUBLE
IRRETENTIVE
IRREVERENCE
IRREVOCABLE
IRREVOCABLY
IRRITATIONS
ISAAC NEWTON
ISOCHRONIZE
ISODIAPHERE
ISOELECTRIC
ISOGEOTHERM
ISOLABILITY
ISOLECITHAL
ISOMAGNETIC
ISOMETRICAL
ISOMETROPIA
ISOMORPHISM
ISORHYTHMIC
ISOTONICITY
ITACOLUMITE
ITALICIZING
ITEMIZATION

ITHYPHALLIC
ITINERARIES
ITINERATION
IVORY TOWERS

J

JACKHAMMERS
JACK-KNIFING
JACKRABBITS
JACTITATION
JAM SESSIONS
JANISSARIES
JAWBREAKERS
JAYAWARDENE
JEHOSHAPHAT
JELLYFISHES
JEOPARDIZED
JETTISONING
JOHORE BAHRU
JOIE DE VIVRE
JOURNALISTS
JOURNALIZER
JOYLESSNESS
JUDAIZATION
JUDGMENT DAY
JUDICATURES
JUDICIOUSLY
JUGGERNAUTS
JUGULAR VEIN
JUMBLE SALES
JUSTICESHIP
JUSTICIABLE
JUSTIFIABLE
JUSTIFIABLY
JUVENESCENT
JUXTAPOSING

K

KALASHNIKOV
KALININGRAD
KANCHIPURAM
KARLOVY VARY
KERB CRAWLER
KETTLEDRUMS
KEYBOARDERS
KEYBOARDING
KEYPUNCHERS
KIDNEY BEANS
KILIMANJARO
KILLER WHALE
KIND-HEARTED

KINDREDNESS
KINETICALLY
KINETOPLAST
KINGFISHERS
KISS OF DEATH
KITCHENETTE
KITCHENWARE
KITTENISHLY
KLEPTOMANIA
KNEECAPPING
KNICK-KNACKS
KNIGHTHOODS
KNUCKLEBONE
KOOKABURRAS
KRASNOYARSK
KRISTIANSEN
KRUGERRANDS
KRUGERSDORP
KUALA LUMPUR
KUMARATUNGE
KWANGCHOWAN
KWASHIORKOR
KYANIZATION
KYMOGRAPHIC

L

LABIODENTAL
LABORIOUSLY
LABOR UNIONS
LABOURINGLY
LABOUR PARTY
LABRADORITE
LACCOLITHIC
LACERATIONS
LACERTILIAN
LACINIATION
LACONICALLY
LACQUERWARE
LACRIMATION
LACRIMATORY
LACTALBUMIN
LACTATIONAL
LACTESCENCE
LACTIFEROUS
LADY-KILLERS
LAEVOGYRATE
LAGOMORPHIC
LAICIZATION
LAKE DWELLER
LAKE SUCCESS
LAMELLATION

LAMELLICORN	LEGATIONARY	LIGHT-FOOTED	LO AND BEHOLD
LAMELLIFORM	LEGERDEMAIN	LIGHT-HEADED	LOATHSOMELY
LAMELLOSITY	LEGIONARIES	LIGHTHOUSES	LOBSTERPOTS
LAMENTATION	LEGIONNAIRE	LIGHTWEIGHT	LOCAL COLOUR
LAMENTINGLY	LEGISLATING	LIKABLENESS	LOCALIZABLE
LAMINAR FLOW	LEGISLATION	LILLIPUTIAN	LOCAL OPTION
LAMMERGEIER	LEGISLATIVE	LILY-LIVERED	LOCKER ROOMS
LAMPROPHYRE	LEGISLATORS	LIMITATIONS	LOCK KEEPERS
LANARKSHIRE	LEGISLATURE	LIMITLESSLY	LOCOMOTIVES
LANCASTRIAN	LEGITIMIZED	LIMNOLOGIST	LOCUM TENENS
LANCINATION	LEMON SQUASH	LIMP-WRISTED	LOGARITHMIC
LANDHOLDING	LENGTHENING	LINDISFARNE	LOGGERHEADS
LANDING GEAR	LENGTHINESS	LINEAMENTAL	LOGISTICIAN
LANDING NETS	LENTIGINOUS	LINE DANCING	LOGOGRAPHER
LANDLUBBERS	LEPIDOSIREN	LINE DRAWING	LOGOGRIPHIC
LANDSCAPING	LEPRECHAUNS	LINEN BASKET	LOGOMACHIST
LANDSCAPIST	LEPROSARIUM	LINE OF SIGHT	LOGOPAEDICS
LANGUISHING	LEPTORRHINE	LINE PRINTER	LOITERINGLY
LAPAROSCOPY	LESE-MAJESTY	LINERTRAINS	LOLLIPOP MAN
LAPIS LAZULI	LET OFF STEAM	LINGERINGLY	LOLLIPOP MEN
LARGE-MINDED	LETTER BOMBS	LINGUISTICS	LONDONDERRY
LARKISHNESS	LETTERBOXES	LION-HEARTED	LONG JUMPERS
LARYNGOLOGY	LETTERHEADS	LIONIZATION	LONGSIGHTED
LARYNGOTOMY	LETTERPRESS	LIPOPROTEIN	LONGWEARING
LATITUDINAL	LEUCOCRATIC	LIPOSUCTION	LOOSE CANNON
LAUDABILITY	LEUCODERMAL	LIQUEFIABLE	LOOSE CHANGE
LAUGHING GAS	LEUCORRHOEA	LIQUESCENCE	LOOSESTRIFE
LAUNDERETTE	LEUCOTOMIES	LIQUIDAMBAR	LOPHOBRANCH
LAURUSTINUS	LEVEL-HEADED	LIQUIDATING	LORD PROVOST
LAW-BREAKERS	LIABILITIES	LIQUIDATION	LORD'S PRAYER
LAWBREAKING	LIANYUNGANG	LIQUIDATORS	LOSS LEADERS
LAWLESSNESS	LIBELLOUSLY	LIQUIDIZERS	LOTUS-EATERS
LAWN PARTIES	LIBERAL ARTS	LIQUIDIZING	LOUDHAILERS
LAY BROTHERS	LIBERALIZED	LISTERIOSIS	LOUDMOUTHED
LEADING LADY	LIBERALIZER	LITERALNESS	LOUDSPEAKER
LEAF-CLIMBER	LIBERALNESS	LITERATURES	LOUNGE SUITS
LEAPFROGGED	LIBERATRESS	LITHOGRAPHS	LOUTISHNESS
LEARNEDNESS	LIBERTARIAN	LITHOGRAPHY	LOVE AFFAIRS
LEASEHOLDER	LIBERTICIDE	LITHOLOGIST	LOW COMEDIES
LEATHERBACK	LIBERTINISM	LITHOMETEOR	LOWER SAXONY
LEATHERETTE	LIBRATIONAL	LITHOPHYTIC	LOW-PRESSURE
LEATHERHEAD	LIBRETTISTS	LITHOSPHERE	LOW PROFILES
LEATHERWOOD	LICENTIATES	LITHOTOMIST	LOW-SPIRITED
LEAVENWORTH	LICKSPITTLE	LITTERATEUR	LOXODROMICS
LEAVE TAKING	LIE DETECTOR	LITTERLOUTS	LOYALTY CARD
LECHEROUSLY	LIEUTENANCY	LITTLE WOMAN	LUBRICATING
LECITHINASE	LIEUTENANTS	LITURGISTIC	LUBRICATION
LECTURESHIP	LIFE JACKETS	LIVABLENESS	LUBRICATIVE
LEFT-HANDERS	LIFE OF RILEY	LIVELIHOODS	LUBRICATORS
LEFT-WINGERS	LIFE STORIES	LIVING ROOMS	LUCRATIVELY
LEGAL TENDER	LIGAMENTOUS	LLOYD WEBBER	LUCUBRATION

LUDICROUSLY	MAGNIFICENT	MANIFESTOES	MASS-PRODUCE
LUDWIGSBURG	MAHARASHTRA	MANIPULATED	MASTER CARDS
LUGGAGE RACK	MAIDENHEADS	MANIPULATOR	MASTERCLASS
LUGGAGE VANS	MAIDEN NAMES	MANNERISTIC	MASTERFULLY
LUMBERINGLY	MAIDSERVANT	MANNISHNESS	MASTERMINDS
LUMBERJACKS	MAILING LIST	MANOEUVRING	MASTERPIECE
LUMBER-ROOMS	MAIN CLAUSES	MANOR HOUSES	MASTERWORKS
LUMBERYARDS	MAINSPRINGS	MANSERVANTS	MASTICATING
LUMBRICALIS	MAINTAINING	MANTELPIECE	MASTICATION
LUMINESCENT	MAINTENANCE	MANTELSHELF	MASTICATORY
LUNAR MONTHS	MAIN-TOPMAST	MANTOUX TEST	MASTOIDITIS
LUSTFULNESS	MAINTOPSAIL	MANUFACTORY	MASTROIANNI
LUTHERANISM	MAISONETTES	MANUFACTURE	MASTURBATED
LUXULIANITE	MAKE-BELIEVE	MANUSCRIPTS	MATCHLESSLY
LUXURIANTLY	MAKES A POINT	MARASCHINOS	MATCHMAKERS
LUXURIATING	MAKHACHKALA	MARCESCENCE	MATCHMAKING
LUXURIATION	MALADJUSTED	MARCHIONESS	MATCH POINTS
LUXURIOUSLY	MALADROITLY	MAR DEL PLATA	MATCHSTICKS
LYMPHANGIAL	MALAPROPIAN	MARE CLAUSUM	MATERIALISM
LYMPHOBLAST	MALAPROPISM	MARE LIBERUM	MATERIALIST
LYMPHOCYTIC	MALCONTENTS	MARGINALITY	MATERIALITY
LYTHRACEOUS	MALEDICTION	MARGINATION	MATERIALIZE
	MALEDICTIVE	MARICULTURE	MATERNALISM
M	MALEFACTION	MARINE CORPS	MATHEMATICS
MACADAMIZER	MALEFACTORS	MARIONETTES	MATINEE IDOL
MACHICOLATE	MALEFICENCE	MARKETPLACE	MATRIARCHAL
MACHINATION	MALEVOLENCE	MARKET PRICE	MATRICULANT
MACHINE CODE	MALFEASANCE	MARKET TOWNS	MATRICULATE
MACHINEGUNS	MALFUNCTION	MARKOV CHAIN	MATRILINEAL
MACHINE TOOL	MALICIOUSLY	MARLBOROUGH	MATRIMONIAL
MACROBIOTIC	MALIGNANTLY	MARQUESSATE	MAUDLINNESS
MACROCOSMIC	MALINGERERS	MARQUISETTE	MAUNDY MONEY
MACROGAMETE	MALINGERING	MARRAM GRASS	MAURITANIAN
MACROPHAGIC	MALOCCLUDED	MARROWBONES	MAWKISHNESS
MACROSCOPIC	MALONIC ACID	MARSHALLING	MAYONNAISES
MADDENINGLY	MALPOSITION	MARSHMALLOW	MEADOWSWEET
MADEIRA CAKE	MALPRACTICE	MARTENSITIC	MEANDERINGS
MADRIGALIAN	MALTED MILKS	MARTIAL ARTS	MEANINGLESS
MADRIGALIST	MALTREATING	MARTINETISH	MEASURELESS
MAGDALENIAN	MAMMALOGIST	MARTINETISM	MEASUREMENT
MAGGOTINESS	MAMMIFEROUS	MARTYROLOGY	MECHANICIAN
MAGHERAFELT	MAMMOGRAPHY	MASCULINIST	MECHANISTIC
MAGIC BULLET	MAMMONISTIC	MASCULINITY	MECHANIZING
MAGISTERIAL	MANAGEMENTS	MASKING TAPE	MECKLENBURG
MAGISTRALLY	MANDATORILY	MASOCHISTIC	MEDIASTINAL
MAGISTRATES	MANDOLINIST	MASONICALLY	MEDIASTINUM
MAGLEMOSIAN	MANEUVERING	MASQUERADED	MEDICAMENTS
MAGNANIMITY	MANHANDLING	MASQUERADER	MEDICATIONS
MAGNANIMOUS	MANICHAEISM	MASQUERADES	MEDICINALLY
MAGNETIZING	MANICURISTS	MASSACHUSET	MEDICINE MAN
MAGNIFIABLE	MANIFESTING	MASSIVENESS	MEDICINE MEN

MEDIEVALISM	MERRYMAKERS	MICROMETERS	MISALLIANCE
MEDIEVALIST	MERRYMAKING	MICROMETRIC	MISANTHROPE
MEDITATIONS	MESALLIANCE	MICROPHONES	MISANTHROPY
MEERSCHAUMS	MESENCHYMAL	MICROPHONIC	MISAPPLYING
MEGACEPHALY	MESMERIZING	MICROPHYTIC	MISBEGOTTEN
MEGALOBLAST	MESOBENTHOS	MICROREADER	MISBEHAVING
MEGALOMANIA	MESOCEPHALY	MICROSCOPES	MISCARRIAGE
MEGALOPOLIS	MESOGASTRIC	MICROSCOPIC	MISCARRYING
MEIOTICALLY	MESOMORPHIC	MICROSECOND	MISCELLANEA
MELANCHOLIA	MESONEPHRIC	MICROSPORIC	MISCHIEVOUS
MELANCHOLIC	MESONEPHROS	MICROTOMIST	MISCIBILITY
MELIORATION	MESOPHYLLIC	MIDDLEBROWS	MISCONCEIVE
MELIORATIVE	MESOPOTAMIA	MIDDLE CLASS	MISCONSTRUE
MELLIFEROUS	MESOSPHERIC	MIDDLE NAMES	MISCOUNTING
MELLIFLUOUS	MESOTHELIAL	MIDDLE-SIZED	MISCREATION
MELODICALLY	MESOTHELIUM	MIDNIGHT SUN	MISDESCRIBE
MELODIOUSLY	MESOTHORIUM	MIGRATIONAL	MISDIRECTED
MELTABILITY	METABOLISMS	MILITARISTS	MISE-EN-SCENE
MELTING POTS	METACENTRIC	MILITARIZED	MISERLINESS
MEMBERSHIPS	METAGENESIS	MILLEFLEURS	MISFEASANCE
MEMORABILIA	METAGENETIC	MILLENARIAN	MISFORTUNES
MEMORANDUMS	METALLOCENE	MILLILITRES	MISGOVERNOR
MEMORIALIST	METALLOIDAL	MILLIMETRES	MISGUIDANCE
MEMORIALIZE	METALLURGIC	MILLIMICRON	MISGUIDEDLY
MEMORIZABLE	METALWORKER	MILLIONAIRE	MISHANDLING
MENAQUINONE	METAMORPHIC	MILLISECOND	MISINFORMED
MENDELEVIUM	METANEPHROS	MIMEOGRAPHS	MISJUDGMENT
MENDEL'S LAWS	METAPHYSICS	MIMETICALLY	MISMANAGING
MENORRHAGIA	METAPLASMIC	MIMOSACEOUS	MISMATCHING
MENORRHAGIC	METASTASIZE	MINAS GERAIS	MISOGYNISTS
MENSTRUATED	METATHERIAN	MIND-BENDING	MISONEISTIC
MENSURATION	METATHESIZE	MIND-BLOWING	MISPRINTING
MENSURATIVE	METEMPIRICS	MINDFULNESS	MISREMEMBER
MENTALISTIC	METEOROLOGY	MIND READERS	MISREPORTED
MENTALITIES	METHODOLOGY	MIND READING	MISSING LINK
MENTAL NOTES	METHYLAMINE	MINERALIZER	MISSISSAUGA
MENTHACEOUS	METHYLATION	MINERAL OILS	MISSISSIPPI
MENTHOLATED	METONYMICAL	MINESWEEPER	MISSPELLING
MENTIONABLE	METRICATION	MINIATURIST	MISSPENDING
MEPROBAMATE	METRICIZING	MINIATURIZE	MISTRUSTFUL
MERCENARIES	METROLOGIST	MINIMUM WAGE	MISTRUSTING
MERCENARILY	MICHIGANDER	MINISTERIAL	MITHRIDATIC
MERCHANDISE	MICHIGANITE	MINISTERING	MITOTICALLY
MERCHANTMAN	MICKEY MOUSE	MINISTERIUM	MIXED GRILLS
MERCHANTMEN	MICROCOCCUS	MINISTRANTS	MOBILE HOMES
MERCILESSLY	MICROCOSMIC	MINNEAPOLIS	MOBILE PHONE
MERCURATION	MICROFICHES	MINOR PLANET	MOBILIZABLE
MERCURIALLY	MICROFILMED	MINUTE STEAK	MOCKINGBIRD
MERITOCRACY	MICROGAMETE	MIRACLE PLAY	MODERNISTIC
MERITORIOUS	MICROGRAPHY	MIRROR IMAGE	MODERNIZING
MEROBLASTIC	MICROGROOVE	MIRTHLESSLY	MODULATIONS

MOHAMMEDANS
MOISTURIZED
MOISTURIZER
MOLESTATION
MOLLIFIABLE
MOLLYCODDLE
MOLYBDENITE
MOLYBDENOUS
MOMENTARILY
MONARCHICAL
MONARCHISTS
MONASTERIAL
MONASTERIES
MONASTICISM
MONETARISTS
MONEYLENDER
MONEYMAKERS
MONEYMAKING
MONEY ORDERS
MONEY SUPPLY
MONITORSHIP
MONOCHASIAL
MONOCHASIUM
MONOCHROMAT
MONOCHROMIC
MONOCLINISM
MONOCLINOUS
MONOCULTURE
MONOGENESIS
MONOGENETIC
MONOGRAMMED
MONOGRAPHER
MONOGRAPHIC
MONOHYDRATE
MONOHYDROXY
MONOLATROUS
MONOLINGUAL
MONOMANIACS
MONOMORPHIC
MONONUCLEAR
MONOPHAGOUS
MONOPHTHONG
MONOPOLISTS
MONOPOLIZED
MONOPOLIZER
MONOSTICHIC
MONOSTROPHE
MONOSTYLOUS
MONOTERPENE
MONOTHEISTS
MONOVALENCE

MONSEIGNEUR
MONSTRANCES
MONSTROSITY
MONSTROUSLY
MONS VENERIS
MONTENEGRAN
MONTPELLIER
MOONLIGHTER
MORAVIANISM
MORIBUNDITY
MORNING COAT
MORNING STAR
MORONICALLY
MORPHOLOGIC
MORRIS DANCE
MORTALITIES
MORTARBOARD
MORTISE LOCK
MOSQUITO NET
MOTHERBOARD
MOTHER-IN-LAW
MOTHER'S BOYS
MOTHER'S RUIN
MOTHERS-TO-BE
MOTHPROOFED
MOTORCYCLES
MOTOR LODGES
MOUNTAINEER
MOUNTAINOUS
MOUNTAINTOP
MOUNTBATTEN
MOUNTEBANKS
MOUTHORGANS
MOUTHPIECES
MOUTHWASHES
MOXIBUSTION
MUCOPROTEIN
MUCRONATION
MUDDLEDNESS
MUDSLINGING
MUHAMMADANS
MULTANGULAR
MULTINOMIAL
MULTIPARITY
MULTIPAROUS
MULTIPLEXER
MULTIPLYING
MULTIRACIAL
MULTISCREEN
MULTISTOREY
MULTIVALENT

MUMS THE WORD
MUNDANENESS
MUNICIPALLY
MUNIFICENCE
MURDERESSES
MURDEROUSLY
MURMURINGLY
MUSCLE-BOUND
MUSCOVY DUCK
MUSCULARITY
MUSCULATURE
MUSEUM PIECE
MUSHROOMING
MUSICALNESS
MUSIC CENTRE
MUSKELLUNGE
MUSTACHIOED
MUTAGENESIS
MUTILATIONS
MUTTERINGLY
MUTTONCHOPS
MUTUAL FUNDS
MYCOLOGICAL
MYCOPROTEIN
MYCORRHIZAL
MYELOMATOID
MYOCARDITIS
MYRIAPODOUS
MYRMECOLOGY
MYSTERY PLAY
MYSTERY TOUR
MYSTIFIEDLY
MYTHOLOGIES
MYTHOLOGIST
MYTHOLOGIZE
MYTHOMANIAC
MYTHOPOEISM
MYTHOPOEIST
MYXOMATOSIS

N

NAILBRUSHES
NAIL VARNISH
NAKHICHEVAN
NAMEDROPPED
NAMEDROPPER
NAPHTHALENE
NAPKIN RINGS
NARAYANGANJ
NARCISSISTS
NARCISSUSES

NARCOLEPTIC
NARRATOLOGY
NARROW BOATS
NARROW GAUGE
NASOFRONTAL
NASOGASTRIC
NASOPHARYNX
NASTURTIUMS
NATIONALISM
NATIONALIST
NATIONALITY
NATIONALIZE
NATION STATE
NATURALISTS
NATURALIZED
NATURALNESS
NATUROPATHS
NATUROPATHY
NAUGHTINESS
NEANDERTHAL
NEAR EASTERN
NEARSIGHTED
NECESSARIES
NECESSARILY
NECESSITATE
NECESSITIES
NECESSITOUS
NECKERCHIEF
NECROBIOSIS
NECROBIOTIC
NECROLOGIST
NECROMANCER
NECROMANTIC
NECROPHILIA
NECROPHILIC
NECROPHOBIA
NECROPHOBIC
NEEDFULNESS
NEEDLEPOINT
NEEDLEWOMAN
NEEDLEWOMEN
NE'ER-DO-WELLS
NEFARIOUSLY
NEGLIGENTLY
NEGOTIATING
NEGOTIATION
NEGOTIATORS
NEIGHBOURLY
NEOCOLONIAL
NEOLOGISTIC
NEPHELINITE

NEPHOLOGIST
NEPHRECTOMY
NE PLUS ULTRA
NERVE CENTRE
NERVELESSLY
NERVOUSNESS
NETHERLANDS
NEUROFIBRIL
NEUROLOGIST
NEUROMATOUS
NEUROPATHIC
NEUROPTERAN
NEUROTICISM
NEUROTOMIST
NEUTRALIZED
NEUTRALIZER
NEUTRON BOMB
NEVER-NEVERS
NEVER SAY DIE
NEW PLYMOUTH
NEWPORT NEWS
NEW POTATOES
NEWSCASTERS
NEWSLETTERS
NEWSREADERS
NEWSVENDORS
NEW YEAR'S DAY
NEW YEAR'S EVE
NICENE CREED
NICKELODEON
NICTITATION
NIETZSCHEAN
NIGHTINGALE
NIGHTLIGHTS
NIGHTMARISH
NIGHT-PORTER
NIGHT SCHOOL
NIGHTSHADES
NIGHT SHIFTS
NIGHTSHIRTS
NIGHTSTICKS
NIGRESCENCE
NINCOMPOOPS
NINETEENTHS
NINETY-NINES
NISHINOMIYA
NITRIFIABLE
NITROGENIZE
NITROGENOUS
NITROMETRIC
NITROSAMINE

NITTY-GRITTY
NIZHNI TAGIL
NOBEL PRIZES
NOCICEPTIVE
NOCTILUCENT
NOCTURNALLY
NOISELESSLY
NOISOMENESS
NOMADICALLY
NO-MAN'S-LANDS
NOMENCLATOR
NOMINATIONS
NOMINATIVES
NOMOGRAPHER
NOMOGRAPHIC
NOMOLOGICAL
NOMS DE PLUME
NONCHALANCE
NONCREATIVE
NONDESCRIPT
NONENTITIES
NONETHELESS
NONEXISTENT
NONFEASANCE
NONHARMONIC
NONILLIONTH
NONINVASIVE
NONIRRITANT
NONMETALLIC
NONOPERABLE
NONPARTISAN
NONPLUSSING
NONRESIDENT
NONSENSICAL
NON SEQUITUR
NONSTANDARD
NONSTARTERS
NONVERBALLY
NONVIOLENCE
NORMALIZING
NORTHAMPTON
NORTH DAKOTA
NORTHEASTER
NORTHERNERS
NORTH ISLAND
NORTHUMBRIA
NORTHWESTER
NOSOGRAPHER
NOSOGRAPHIC
NOSOLOGICAL
NOSY PARKERS

NOTABLENESS
NOTHINGNESS
NOTHING TO IT
NOTICE BOARD
NOTOCHORDAL
NOTORIOUSLY
NOTOTHERIUM
NOURISHMENT
NOVOSIBIRSK
NOXIOUSNESS
NUCLEAR-FREE
NUCLEIC ACID
NUCLEOPLASM
NUEVO LAREDO
NULL AND VOID
NULLIFIDIAN
NULLIPAROUS
NUMBERPLATE
NUMERATIONS
NUMERICALLY
NUMISMATICS
NUMISMATIST
NUNCUPATIVE
NURSING HOME
NUTCRACKERS
NUTRITIONAL
NYCTINASTIC
NYCTITROPIC
NYCTOPHOBIA
NYCTOPHOBIC
NYMPHOLEPSY
NYMPHOMANIA

O

OARSMANSHIP
OBFUSCATING
OBFUSCATION
OBITER DICTA
OBJECTIVELY
OBJECTIVISM
OBJECTIVIST
OBJECTIVITY
OBJET TROUVE
OBJURGATION
OBJURGATORY
OBLIGATIONS
OBLIQUITOUS
OBLITERATED
OBLITERATOR
OBLIVIOUSLY
OBNOXIOUSLY

OBSCENITIES
OBSCURATION
OBSCURITIES
OBSERVANCES
OBSERVATION
OBSERVATORY
OBSESSIONAL
OBSOLESCENT
OBSTINATELY
OBSTIPATION
OBSTRUCTING
OBSTRUCTION
OBSTRUCTIVE
OBTRUSIVELY
OBVIOUSNESS
OCCASIONING
OCCIDENTALS
OCCULTATION
OCCUPATIONS
OCCURRENCES
OCHLOCRATIC
OCHLOPHOBIA
OCTAHEDRITE
OCTILLIONTH
ODDS AND ENDS
ODONTOBLAST
ODONTOGRAPH
ODONTOPHORE
ODORIFEROUS
ODOROUSNESS
OENOLOGICAL
OESOPHAGEAL
OESTROGENIC
OFFENSIVELY
OFFERTORIES
OFFHANDEDLY
OFFICE BLOCK
OFFICIALDOM
OFFICIALESE
OFFICIATING
OFFICIATION
OFFICIOUSLY
OFF-LICENCES
OIL PAINTING
OIL-SEED RAPE
OLD-WOMANISH
OLEOGRAPHIC
OLIGARCHIES
OLIGOCHAETE
OLIGOTROPHY
OLIVE BRANCH

OMINOUSNESS
OMMATOPHORE
OMNIFARIOUS
OMNIPOTENCE
OMNIPRESENT
OMNISCIENCE
ONAGRACEOUS
ONCOLOGICAL
ONE-MAN BANDS
ONEROUSNESS
ONTOLOGICAL
OPALESCENCE
OPEN-AND-SHUT
OPENHEARTED
OPENING TIME
OPEN LETTERS
OPEN-MOUTHED
OPEN SEASONS
OPEN SECRETS
OPEN SESAMES
OPEN VERDICT
OPERABILITY
OPERATIONAL
OPHIOLOGIST
OPHTHALMIAC
OPINIONATED
OPINION POLL
OPPORTUNELY
OPPORTUNISM
OPPORTUNIST
OPPORTUNITY
OPPOSITIONS
OPPROBRIOUS
OPTICAL DISC
OPTOMETRIST
ORANGUTANGS
ORCHESTRATE
ORDER-DRIVEN
ORDERLINESS
ORDER PAPERS
ORDINATIONS
ORGANICALLY
ORIEL WINDOW
ORIENTALISM
ORIENTALIST
ORIENTALIZE
ORIENTATING
ORIENTATION
ORIGINALITY
ORIGINAL SIN
ORIGINATING

ORIGINATION
ORIGINATORS
ORNAMENTING
ORNITHOLOGY
ORNITHOPTER
ORTHOCENTRE
ORTHODONTIC
ORTHOGRAPHY
ORTHOPAEDIC
ORTHOPTERAN
ORTHOSCOPIC
ORTHOSTICHY
ORTHOTROPIC
OSCILLATING
OSCILLATION
OSCILLATORS
OSCILLATORY
OSCILLOGRAM
OSMOTICALLY
OSTENTATION
OSTEOCLASIS
OSTEOLOGIST
OSTEOPATHIC
OSTEOPHYTIC
OSTEOPLASTY
OSTRACIZING
OSTRACODERM
OSTRACODOUS
OUAGADOUGOU
OUIJA BOARDS
OUTBALANCED
OUTBUILDING
OUTCLASSING
OUTDISTANCE
OUTERCOURSE
OUTFIELDERS
OUTFIGHTING
OUTFLANKING
OUT-HERODING
OUTNUMBERED
OUT OF BOUNDS
OUT OF POCKET
OUT-OF-THE-WAY
OUTPATIENTS
OUTPOINTING
OUTPOURINGS
OUTRIVALING
OUTRIVALLED
OUTSMARTING
OUT SOURCING
OUTSPOKENLY

OUTSTANDING
OUTSTRIPPED
OUTWEIGHING
OVERACHIEVE
OVERANXIOUS
OVERARCHING
OVERBALANCE
OVERBEARING
OVERBIDDING
OVERBOOKING
OVERCHARGED
OVERCHARGES
OVERCLOUDED
OVERCROPPED
OVERCROWDED
OVERDEVELOP
OVERDRAUGHT
OVERDRAWING
OVERDRESSED
OVEREXPOSED
OVERFLOWING
OVERGARMENT
OVERHAULING
OVERHEARING
OVERINDULGE
OVERLAPPING
OVERLOADING
OVERLOOKING
OVERMANNING
OVERPLAYING
OVERPOWERED
OVERPRODUCE
OVERPROTECT
OVERREACHED
OVERREACTED
OVERRUNNING
OVERSELLING
OVERSTAFFED
OVERSTATING
OVERSTAYING
OVERSTEPPED
OVERSTOCKED
OVERSTUFFED
OVERTOPPING
OVERTURNING
OVERWEENING
OVERWHELMED
OVERWORKING
OVERWROUGHT
OVIPOSITION
OWNER-DRIVER

OXFORDSHIRE
OXIDATIONAL
OXIDIMETRIC
OXIDIZATION
OXYCEPHALIC
OXYGENATING
OXYGENATION
OXYGEN MASKS
OXYGEN TENTS
OXYHYDROGEN
OXYSULPHIDE
OZONIFEROUS
OZONIZATION
OZONOSPHERE

P

PACE BOWLERS
PACIFICALLY
PACKAGE DEAL
PACKAGE TOUR
PACK ANIMALS
PACKING CASE
PAEDIATRICS
PAEDOLOGIST
PAINFULNESS
PAINKILLERS
PAINSTAKING
PALAEARCTIC
PALATINATES
PALEOGRAPHY
PALEOLITHIC
PALESTINIAN
PALIMPSESTS
PALINDROMES
PALINDROMIC
PALLBEARERS
PALLIATIVES
PALM SPRINGS
PALPABILITY
PALPITATING
PALPITATION
PAMPAS GRASS
PAMPHLETEER
PAN-AMERICAN
PANCAKE ROLL
PANCHEN LAMA
PANDEMONIAC
PANDEMONIUM
PANDORA'S BOX
PANEGYRICAL
PANHANDLERS

PANHANDLING	PARI-MUTUELS	PATRILINEAL	PENTAMETERS
PANHELLENIC	PARIPINNATE	PATRIMONIAL	PENTANGULAR
PANIC ATTACK	PARISH CLERK	PATROL WAGON	PENTATHLONS
PANJANDRUMS	PARISHIONER	PATRONIZING	PENTAVALENT
PANTELLERIA	PARKING LOTS	PATRON SAINT	PENTECOSTAL
PANTHEISTIC	PARK KEEPERS	PATRONYMICS	PENTLANDITE
PANTOGRAPHS	PARLIAMENTS	PAUNCHINESS	PENULTIMATE
PANTOGRAPHY	PARLOUR GAME	PAVING STONE	PENURIOUSLY
PANTOMIMIST	PAROCHIALLY	PAWNBROKERS	PEOPLE MOVER
PAPER CHASES	PARONOMASIA	PAWNBROKING	PEPPERCORNS
PAPER-CUTTER	PARSON'S NOSE	PAY ENVELOPE	PEPPER MILLS
PAPERHANGER	PART COMPANY	PAY STATIONS	PEPPERMINTS
PAPER KNIVES	PARTIALNESS	PEACH MELBAS	PEPTIC ULCER
PAPER TIGERS	PARTICIPANT	PEACOCK BLUE	PEPTIZATION
PAPERWEIGHT	PARTICIPATE	PEARL DIVERS	PERAMBULATE
PAPIER-MACHE	PARTICIPIAL	PEARLY GATES	PERCEIVABLE
PAPYRACEOUS	PARTICIPLES	PEASHOOTERS	PERCENTAGES
PARABLASTIC	PARTICULARS	PECCABILITY	PERCEPTIBLE
PARACETAMOL	PARTICULATE	PECCADILLOS	PERCEPTIBLY
PARACHUTING	PARTING SHOT	PECTINATION	PERCHLORATE
PARACHUTIST	PARTITIONED	PECTIZATION	PERCHLORIDE
PARADOXICAL	PARTITIONER	PECULATIONS	PERCIPIENCE
PARAGENESIS	PARTITIVELY	PECULIARITY	PERCOLATING
PARAGENETIC	PARTNERSHIP	PECUNIARILY	PERCOLATION
PARAGLIDING	PARTURIENCY	PEDESTRIANS	PERCOLATIVE
PARAGRAPHIA	PARTURITION	PEDICULOSIS	PERCOLATORS
PARAGRAPHIC	PARTY PIECES	PEDICURISTS	PEREGRINATE
PARALDEHYDE	PARTY POOPER	PEDOLOGICAL	PERENNIALLY
PARALEIPSIS	PAS-DE-CALAIS	PEDUNCULATE	PERFECTIBLE
PARALLACTIC	PASQUINADER	PEEPING TOMS	PERFORATING
PARALLELING	PASSIBILITY	PEEVISHNESS	PERFORATION
PARALLELISM	PASSIONLESS	PELARGONIUM	PERFORATIVE
PARALLELIST	PASSION PLAY	PELLUCIDITY	PERFORMABLE
PARALLELLED	PASSIONTIDE	PELOPONNESE	PERFORMANCE
PARALYMPICS	PASSIVENESS	PENALTY AREA	PERFUNCTORY
PARAMEDICAL	PASTEBOARDS	PENDULOUSLY	PERICARDIUM
PARAMORPHIC	PASTEURIZED	PENETRALIAN	PERICARPIAL
PARAMOUNTCY	PASTEURIZER	PENETRATING	PERICLASTIC
PARAPHRASED	PAST MASTERS	PENETRATION	PERICRANIAL
PARAPHRASES	PAST PERFECT	PENETRATIVE	PERICRANIUM
PARAPLASTIC	PASTURELAND	PENICILLATE	PERIDOTITIC
PARAPLEGICS	PATCH POCKET	PENICILLIUM	PERIGORDIAN
PARASAILING	PATELLIFORM	PENITENTIAL	PERIHELIONS
PARATHYROID	PATERNALISM	PENNYWEIGHT	PERIMORPHIC
PARATROOPER	PATERNALIST	PENNYWORTHS	PERINEURIUM
PARATYPHOID	PATERNOSTER	PENOLOGICAL	PERIODICALS
PARENTHESES	PATHFINDERS	PENSIONABLE	PERIODICITY
PARENTHESIS	PATHFINDING	PENSIVENESS	PERIODONTAL
PARENTHETIC	PATHOLOGIST	PENTADACTYL	PERIODONTIC
PARESTHESIA	PATISSERIES	PENTAHEDRON	PERIOD PIECE
PARESTHETIC	PATRIARCHAL	PENTAMEROUS	PERIOSTITIC

PERIOSTITIS	PERTINENTLY	PHOTOCOPIED	PILLOWCASES
PERIPATETIC	PERTURBABLE	PHOTOCOPIER	PILLOW FIGHT
PERIPETEIAN	PERTURBABLY	PHOTOCOPIES	PILOCARPINE
PERIPHERALS	PERVASIVELY	PHOTO FINISH	PILOT LIGHTS
PERIPHERIES	PERVERSIONS	PHOTOGRAPHS	PINA COLADAS
PERIPHRASES	PERVERTEDLY	PHOTOGRAPHY	PINCUSHIONS
PERIPHRASIS	PERVERTIBLE	PHOTOMETRIC	PINEAL GLAND
PERISHABLES	PESSIMISTIC	PHOTONASTIC	PINE MARTENS
PERISHINGLY	PESTERINGLY	PHOTO-OFFSET	PINNATISECT
PERISPERMAL	PESTIFEROUS	PHOTOPERIOD	PINOCYTOSIS
PERISTALSIS	PESTILENCES	PHOTOPHOBIA	PINPOINTING
PERISTALTIC	PETITIONARY	PHOTOPHOBIC	PIPE CLEANER
PERITHECIUM	PETITIONERS	PHOTOSETTER	PIPE OF PEACE
PERITONEUMS	PETITIONING	PHOTOSPHERE	PIPERACEOUS
PERITONITIC	PETRODOLLAR	PHOTOSTATIC	PIPISTRELLE
PERITONITIS	PETROGRAPHY	PHOTOTACTIC	PIRATICALLY
PERIWINKLES	PETROLOGIST	PHOTOTROPIC	PIROUETTING
PERLOCUTION	PETTIFOGGER	PHRASAL VERB	PISCATORIAL
PERMANENTLY	PETTISHNESS	PHRASEBOOKS	PISCIVOROUS
PERMISSIBLE	PHAGOMANIAC	PHRASEOGRAM	PISTON RINGS
PERMISSIBLY	PHAGOPHOBIA	PHRASEOLOGY	PITCHBLENDE
PERMUTATION	PHAGOPHOBIC	PHTHIRIASIS	PITCHFORKED
PERORATIONS	PHALANSTERY	PHYCOLOGIST	PITCHOMETER
PERPETRATED	PHANEROZOIC	PHYCOMYCETE	PITEOUSNESS
PERPETRATOR	PHARMACISTS	PHYLLOCLADE	PITH HELMETS
PERPETUALLY	PHARYNGITIS	PHYLLOTAXIS	PITIFULNESS
PERPETUATED	PHELLOGENIC	PHYLOTACTIC	PITUITARIES
PERPLEXEDLY	PHENETIDINE	PHYSIATRICS	PLACABILITY
PERQUISITES	PHENOLOGIST	PHYSICALISM	PLAGIARISMS
PERSECUTING	PHILANDERER	PHYSICALIST	PLAGIARISTS
PERSECUTION	PHILATELIST	PHYSIOGNOMY	PLAGIARIZED
PERSECUTIVE	PHILHELLENE	PHYTOGRAPHY	PLAGIARIZER
PERSECUTORS	PHILIPPINES	PICKPOCKETS	PLAGIOCLASE
PERSEVERANT	PHILISTINES	PICKWICKIAN	PLAINSPOKEN
PERSEVERING	PHILOLOGIST	PICTORIALLY	PLAINTIVELY
PERSIAN CATS	PHILOSOPHER	PICTURE BOOK	PLANETARIUM
PERSISTENCE	PHLEBOTOMIC	PICTURE CARD	PLANETOIDAL
PERSNICKETY	PHONETICIAN	PICTURESQUE	PLANIMETRIC
PERSONALISM	PHONOGRAMIC	PIECE OF CAKE	PLANISPHERE
PERSONALIST	PHONOGRAPHS	PIECE OF WORK	PLANO-CONVEX
PERSONALITY	PHONOGRAPHY	PIEDMONTITE	PLANOGAMETE
PERSONALIZE	PHONOLOGIST	PIEDS-A-TERRE	PLANOGRAPHY
PERSONATION	PHONOMETRIC	PIEZOMETRIC	PLANOMETRIC
PERSONATIVE	PHONOTYPIST	PIGEONHOLED	PLANTAGENET
PERSONIFIED	PHOSPHATASE	PIGEONHOLES	PLANTATIONS
PERSPECTIVE	PHOSPHATIZE	PIGGISHNESS	PLANTIGRADE
PERSPICUITY	PHOSPHORATE	PIGHEADEDLY	PLASMAGENIC
PERSPICUOUS	PHOSPHORISM	PIGSTICKING	PLASMODESMA
PERSUADABLE	PHOSPHORITE	PILE DRIVERS	PLASMOLYSIS
PERSUASIONS	PHOSPHOROUS	PILGRIMAGES	PLASMOLYTIC
PERTINACITY	PHOTOACTIVE	PILLAR BOXES	PLASTER CAST

PLASTICALLY	POINSETTIAS	PONTIFICATE	PRACTICABLY
PLASTIC ARTS	POINTEDNESS	POOH-POOHING	PRACTICALLY
PLASTICIZER	POINTE-NOIRE	POPULARIZED	PRAEDIALITY
PLASTOMETER	POINTILLISM	POPULARIZER	PRAESIDIUMS
PLASTOMETRY	POINTILLIST	POPULATIONS	PRAGMATISTS
PLATELAYERS	POINTLESSLY	PORK BARRELS	PRAIRIE DOGS
PLATINOTYPE	POINT OF VIEW	PORNOGRAPHY	PRATTLINGLY
PLATS DU JOUR	POISONOUSLY	PORPHYRITIC	PRAYER WHEEL
PLATYRRHINE	POLARIMETER	PORTABILITY	PREARRANGED
PLAYER PIANO	POLARIMETRY	PORTERHOUSE	PREARRANGER
PLAYFELLOWS	POLARISCOPE	PORTMANTEAU	PRECAMBRIAN
PLAYFULNESS	POLARIZABLE	PORT MORESBY	PRECAUTIONS
PLAYGROUNDS	POLEMICALLY	PORTO ALEGRE	PRECAUTIOUS
PLAYING CARD	POLE VAULTED	PORT OF CALLS	PRECESSIONS
PLAY ON WORDS	POLE VAULTER	PORT OF ENTRY	PRECIPITANT
PLAYSCHOOLS	POLICE STATE	PORT OF SPAIN	PRECIPITATE
PLAYWRIGHTS	POLICEWOMAN	PORTRAITIST	PRECIPITOUS
PLAYWRITING	POLICEWOMEN	PORTRAITURE	PRECISENESS
PLEASANTEST	POLITICALLY	PORTRAYABLE	PRECLINICAL
PLEASURABLE	POLITICIANS	POSITIONING	PRECLUDABLE
PLEASURABLY	POLITICIZED	POSITIVISTS	PRECONCEIVE
PLEASUREFUL	POLITICKING	POSITRONIUM	PRECONTRACT
PLEBEIANISM	POLLEN COUNT	POSSESSIONS	PRECRITICAL
PLEBISCITES	POLLINATING	POSSESSIVES	PREDATORILY
PLECTOGNATH	POLLINATION	POSSIBILITY	PREDECEASED
PLEISTOCENE	POLTERGEIST	POSTAL ORDER	PREDECESSOR
PLENTEOUSLY	POLYANDROUS	POSTERITIES	PREDESTINED
PLENTIFULLY	POLYCHASIUM	POSTER PAINT	PREDICAMENT
PLEOCHROISM	POLYGAMISTS	POSTGLACIAL	PREDICATING
PLEOMORPHIC	POLYGENESIS	POSTMARKING	PREDICATION
PLICATENESS	POLYGENETIC	POSTMASTERS	PREDICATIVE
PLOUGHSHARE	POLYGLOTISM	POSTMORTEMS	PREDICATORY
PLOUGHSTAFF	POLYGRAPHIC	POSTNUPTIAL	PREDICTABLE
PLUG-AND-PLAY	POLYHYDROXY	POST OFFICES	PREDICTABLY
PLUM PUDDING	POLYNUCLEAR	POSTPONABLE	PREDICTIONS
PLUNDERABLE	POLYPEPTIDE	POSTSCRIPTS	PREDIGESTED
PLURALISTIC	POLYPHONOUS	POSTULATING	PREDISPOSAL
PLURALITIES	POLYPLOIDAL	POSTULATION	PREDISPOSED
PLUTOCRATIC	POLYSTYRENE	POTATO CHIPS	PREDOMINANT
PLUVIOMETER	POLYTECHNIC	POTATO CRISP	PREDOMINATE
PLUVIOMETRY	POLYTHEISTS	POTENTIALLY	PRE-EMINENCE
PNEUMECTOMY	POLYTROPHIC	POTTING SHED	PRE-EXISTENT
PNEUMOGRAPH	POLYVALENCY	POVERTY TRAP	PRE-EXISTING
POCKETBOOKS	POLYZOARIUM	POWDER PUFFS	PREFATORILY
POCKETKNIFE	POMEGRANATE	POWDER ROOMS	PREFECTURAL
POCKET KNIFE	POMICULTURE	POWER BROKER	PREFECTURES
POCKET MONEY	POMOLOGICAL	POWERHOUSES	PREFERENCES
POCOCURANTE	POMPOUSNESS	POWERLESSLY	PREFIGURING
POCTOSCOPIC	PONDEROUSLY	POWER PLANTS	PREGNANCIES
PODIATRISTS	PONDICHERRY	POWER POINTS	PREHISTORIC
PODOPHYLLIN	PONTIFICALS	PRACTICABLE	PRE-IGNITION

PREJUDGMENT	PRETTY PENNY	PROFANENESS	PROPER NOUNS
PREJUDICIAL	PREVALENTLY	PROFANITIES	PROPHESYING
PREJUDICING	PREVARICATE	PROFESSEDLY	PROPHYLAXES
PRELIMINARY	PREVENTABLE	PROFESSIONS	PROPHYLAXIS
PRELITERACY	PREVENTABLY	PROFICIENCY	PROPINQUITY
PRELITERATE	PREVENTIVES	PROFITEERED	PROPITIABLE
PREMATURELY	PRICKLINESS	PROFITEROLE	PROPITIATED
PREMEDITATE	PRICKLY HEAT	PROFLIGATES	PROPITIATOR
PREMIERSHIP	PRICKLY PEAR	PROFUSENESS	PROPORTIONS
PREMIUM BOND	PRIESTCRAFT	PROGENITIVE	PROPOSITION
PREMONITION	PRIESTLIEST	PROGENITORS	PROPOUNDING
PREMONITORY	PRIMA DONNAS	PROGNATHISM	PROPRANOLOL
PREMUNITION	PRIMATOLOGY	PROGNATHOUS	PROPRIETARY
PREOCCUPIED	PRIME MOVERS	PROGRAMMERS	PROPRIETIES
PREORDAINED	PRIME NUMBER	PROGRAMMING	PROPRIETORS
PREPARATION	PRIMIPARITY	PROGRESSING	PROROGATION
PREPARATIVE	PRIMIPAROUS	PROGRESSION	PROSAICALLY
PREPARATORY	PRIMITIVELY	PROGRESSIVE	PROSAICNESS
PREPOSITION	PRIMITIVISM	PROHIBITING	PROS AND CONS
PREPOSITIVE	PRIMITIVIST	PROHIBITION	PROSCENIUMS
PREP SCHOOLS	PRINCIPALLY	PROHIBITIVE	PROSCRIBING
PRERECORDED	PRINTING INK	PROHIBITORY	PROSECUTING
PREROGATIVE	PRIORITIZED	PROJECTILES	PROSECUTION
PRESBYTERAL	PRISON CAMPS	PROJECTIONS	PROSECUTORS
PRESCRIBING	PRIVATIZING	PROKOPYEVSK	PROSELYTISM
PRESENTABLE	PRIZEFIGHTS	PROLATENESS	PROSELYTIZE
PRESENTABLY	PROBABILISM	PROLEGOMENA	PROSENCHYMA
PRESENT ARMS	PROBABILIST	PROLETARIAN	PROSPECTING
PRESENTIENT	PROBABILITY	PROLETARIAT	PROSPECTIVE
PRESENTMENT	PROBATIONAL	PROLIFERATE	PROSPECTORS
PRESERVABLE	PROBATIONER	PROLIFEROUS	PROSTATITIS
PRESS AGENCY	PROBLEMATIC	PROLONGMENT	PROSTHETICS
PRESS AGENTS	PROBOSCIDES	PROMENADING	PROSTITUTED
PRESS BARONS	PROBOSCISES	PROMINENCES	PROSTITUTES
PRESSGANGED	PROCEEDINGS	PROMINENTLY	PROSTITUTOR
PRESSURIZED	PROCEPHALIC	PROMISCUITY	PROSTRATING
PRESSURIZER	PROCESSIONS	PROMISCUOUS	PROSTRATION
PRESTIGIOUS	PROCHRONISM	PROMISINGLY	PROTAGONISM
PRESTISSIMO	PROCLAIMING	PROMOTIONAL	PROTAGONIST
PRESTONPANS	PROCONSULAR	PROMPTITUDE	PROTANDROUS
PRESTRESSED	PROCREATING	PROMULGATED	PROTECTIONS
PRESUMINGLY	PROCREATION	PROMULGATOR	PROTECTORAL
PRESUMPTION	PROCRUSTEAN	PROMYCELIUM	PROTECTRESS
PRESUMPTIVE	PROCTOSCOPE	PRONOUNCING	PROTEOLYSIS
PRESUPPOSED	PROCTOSCOPY	PROOFREADER	PROTEOLYTIC
PRETENDEDLY	PROCURATION	PROOF SPIRIT	PROTEROZOIC
PRETENSIONS	PROCUREMENT	PROPAGATING	PROTESTANTS
PRETENTIOUS	PRODIGALITY	PROPAGATION	PROTHROMBIN
PRETERITION	PRODUCTIONS	PROPAGATIVE	PROTOGYNOUS
PRETERITIVE	PROFANATION	PROPAGATORS	PROTOLITHIC
PRETTIFYING	PROFANATORY	PROPELLANTS	PROTOPATHIC

PROTOSTELIC	PULAU PINANG	QUADRENNIUM	RABBIT PUNCH
PROTRACTILE	PULCHRITUDE	QUADRILLION	RABELAISIAN
PROTRACTING	PULL STRINGS	QUADRUPEDAL	RACECOURSES
PROTRACTION	PULLULATING	QUADRUPLETS	RACE MEETING
PROTRACTIVE	PULLULATION	QUADRUPLING	RACQUETBALL
PROTRACTORS	PULSATILITY	QUALIFIABLE	RADIATIONAL
PROTRUDABLE	PULVERIZING	QUALITATIVE	RADICALNESS
PROTRUSIONS	PULVERULENT	QUANGOCRACY	RADIOACTIVE
PROTUBERANT	PUMPKINSEED	QUANTIFIERS	RADIO ALARMS
PROVABILITY	PUNCHED CARD	QUANTIFYING	RADIO BEACON
PROVIDENCES	PUNCTILIOUS	QUANTUM LEAP	RADIOCARBON
PROVIDENTLY	PUNCTUALITY	QUARANTINED	RADIOGRAPHY
PROVINCIALS	PUNCTUATING	QUARRELLING	RADIOLARIAN
PROVISIONAL	PUNCTUATION	QUARRELSOME	RADIOLOGIST
PROVISIONED	PUNCTURABLE	QUARTER DAYS	RADIOLUCENT
PROVISIONER	PUNISHINGLY	QUARTERDECK	RADIOMETRIC
PROVISORILY	PUNISHMENTS	QUARTER-HOUR	RADIOPACITY
PROVOCATION	PUNTA ARENAS	QUARTERLIES	RADIOPHONIC
PROVOCATIVE	PURCHASABLE	QUARTER NOTE	RADIOSCOPIC
PROVOKINGLY	PURCHASE TAX	QUAVERINGLY	RADIOTHERMY
PROXIMATELY	PUREBLOODED	QUEENLINESS	RAFFISHNESS
PROXIMATION	PURGATORIAL	QUEEN MOTHER	RAGAMUFFINS
PRUDENTNESS	PURIFICATOR	QUEEN'S BENCH	RAILROADING
PRUDISHNESS	PURITANICAL	QUERULOUSLY	RAIN FORESTS
PRUSSIC ACID	PURPLE HEART	QUESTIONARY	RAISON D'ETRE
PSEUDOMORPH	PURPOSELESS	QUESTIONERS	RALLENTANDO
PSILOMELANE	PUSHINGNESS	QUESTIONING	RAMAN EFFECT
PSITTACOSIS	PUSSYFOOTED	QUESTION TAG	RAMBOUILLET
PSYCHEDELIA	PUSSY WILLOW	QUEUE-JUMPED	RANCH HOUSES
PSYCHEDELIC	PUSTULATION	QUEUE-JUMPER	RANCOROUSLY
PSYCHIATRIC	PUTREFIABLE	QUIBBLINGLY	RANGE FINDER
PSYCHICALLY	PUTRESCENCE	QUICK-CHANGE	RANK AND FILE
PSYCHOBILLY	PYCNOMETRIC	QUICK-FREEZE	RAPACIOUSLY
PSYCHODRAMA	PYELOGRAPHY	QUICKSILVER	RAPSCALLION
PSYCHOGENIC	PYLORECTOMY	QUICK-WITTED	RAPTUROUSLY
PSYCHOGRAPH	PYRANOMETER	QUID PRO QUOS	RAREFACTION
PSYCHOMETRY	PYRARGYRITE	QUIESCENTLY	RASPBERRIES
PSYCHOMOTOR	PYROCLASTIC	QUINCUNCIAL	RASTAFARIAN
PSYCHOPATHS	PYROGALLATE	QUINDECAGON	RATE-CAPPING
PSYCHOPATHY	PYROGRAPHER	QUINTANA ROO	RATIOCINATE
PTERIDOLOGY	PYROGRAPHIC	QUINTILLION	RATIONALISM
PTERODACTYL	PYROMANIACS	QUINTUPLETS	RATIONALIST
PTOCHOCRACY	PYROTECHNIC	QUIVERINGLY	RATIONALITY
PUB-CRAWLING	PYRRHULOXIA	QUIZMASTERS	RATIONALIZE
PUBLICATION	PYRROLIDINE	QUIZZICALLY	RATTLESNAKE
PUBLIC HOUSE	PYTHAGOREAN	QUONSET HUTS	RATTLETRAPS
PUBLICIZING	PYTHONESQUE	QUOTABILITY	RAUCOUSNESS
PUBLIC WORKS		QUOTE-DRIVEN	RAUNCHINESS
PUBLISHABLE	**Q**		RAVEN-HAIRED
PUCKISHNESS	QUADRANGLES	**R**	RAVISHINGLY
PUERTO RICAN	QUADRENNIAL	RABBIT HUTCH	REACH-ME-DOWN

REACTIONARY	RECONDITION	REFRESHMENT	REMONSTRANT
REACTIONISM	RECONNOITRE	REFRIGERANT	REMONSTRATE
REACTIVATED	RECONSTRUCT	REFRIGERATE	REMORSELESS
READABILITY	RECOVERABLE	REFRINGENCY	REMOVAL VANS
READDRESSED	RECREATIONS	REFURBISHED	REMUNERABLE
READERSHIPS	RECREMENTAL	REFUTATIONS	REMUNERATED
READJUSTING	RECRIMINATE	REGENERABLE	REMUNERATOR
READ-THROUGH	RECRUITABLE	REGENERATED	RENAISSANCE
READY-TO-WEAR	RECRUITMENT	REGIMENTALS	RENEGOTIATE
READY-WITTED	RECTANGULAR	REGIMENTING	RENOVATIONS
REAFFIRMING	RECTIFIABLE	REGIONALISM	RENTABILITY
REALIGNMENT	RECTILINEAR	REGIONALIST	RENT STRIKES
REALIZATION	RECUPERATED	REGISTERING	REORGANIZED
REALPOLITIK	RECUPERATOR	REGISTRABLE	REORGANIZER
REANIMATING	RECURRENCES	REGRETFULLY	REPARATIONS
REANIMATION	RECURRENTLY	REGRETTABLE	REPARTITION
REAPPEARING	RECURRINGLY	REGRETTABLY	REPATRIATED
REAPPORTION	REDACTIONAL	REGULARIZED	REPELLINGLY
REAPPRAISAL	RED ADMIRALS	REGULATIONS	REPENTANTLY
REAPPRAISED	RED CRESCENT	REGURGITANT	REPERTOIRES
REAR ADMIRAL	REDCURRANTS	REGURGITATE	REPERTORIAL
REARRANGING	REDECORATED	REIFICATION	REPERTORIES
REASSURANCE	REDEPLOYING	REIMBURSING	REPETITIONS
REASSUREDLY	REDEVELOPED	REINCARNATE	REPETITIOUS
REBARBATIVE	REDEVELOPER	REINFORCING	REPLACEABLE
RECALESCENT	RED HERRINGS	REINSTATING	REPLACEMENT
RECANTATION	REDIFFUSION	REINSURANCE	REPLENISHED
RECAPTURING	REDIRECTING	REINTRODUCE	REPLENISHER
RECEIVABLES	REDIRECTION	REITERATING	REPLETENESS
RECEPTACLES	REDOUBTABLE	REITERATION	REPLEVIABLE
RECEPTIVELY	REDOUBTABLY	REITERATIVE	REPLICATING
RECEPTIVITY	REDRESSABLE	REJUVENATED	REPLICATION
RECESSIONAL	REDUCTIONAL	REJUVENATOR	REPLICATIVE
RECIDIVISTS	REDUNDANTLY	RELATEDNESS	REPOSSESSED
RECIPROCATE	REDUPLICATE	RELAXATIONS	REPOSSESSOR
RECIPROCITY	RE-EDUCATING	RELIABILITY	REPREHENDED
RECITATIONS	RE-EDUCATION	RELIEF ROADS	REPREHENDER
RECITATIVES	RE-ELECTIONS	RELIGIONISM	REPRESENTED
RECLAIMABLE	REFECTORIES	RELIGIOSITY	REPRESSIBLE
RECLAMATION	REFERENDUMS	RELIGIOUSLY	REPRESSIONS
RECLINATION	REFERENTIAL	RELIQUARIES	REPRIEVABLE
RECOGNITION	REFINEMENTS	RELISHINGLY	REPRIMANDED
RECOGNIZING	REFLECTANCE	RELUCTANTLY	REPRIMANDER
RECOILINGLY	REFLECTIONS	RELUCTIVITY	REPROACHFUL
RECOLLECTED	REFORESTING	REMAINDERED	REPROACHING
RECOMBINANT	REFORMATION	REMEMBERING	REPROBATION
RECOMMENDED	REFORMATIVE	REMEMBRANCE	REPROBATIVE
RECOMMENDER	REFORMATORY	REMINISCENT	REPROCESSED
RECOMPENSED	REFRACTABLE	REMINISCING	REPRODUCERS
RECOMPENSER	REFRAINMENT	REMITTANCES	REPRODUCING
RECONCILING	REFRANGIBLE	REMODELLING	REPROGRAPHY

REPROVINGLY
REPUBLICANS
REPUBLISHER
REPUDIATING
REPUDIATION
REPUDIATIVE
REPUDIATORY
REPULSIVELY
REPUTATIONS
REQUEST STOP
REQUIREMENT
REQUISITION
REQUITEMENT
RERADIATION
RESCHEDULED
RESCINDABLE
RESCINDMENT
RESCISSIBLE
RESEARCHERS
RESEARCHING
RESECTIONAL
RESEMBLANCE
RESENTFULLY
RESERVATION
RESHUFFLING
RESIDENTIAL
RESIGNATION
RESILIENTLY
RESISTANCES
RESISTENCIA
RESISTINGLY
RESISTIVITY
RESOLUTIONS
RESOURCEFUL
RESPECTABLE
RESPECTABLY
RESPIRATION
RESPIRATORS
RESPIRATORY
RESPLENDENT
RESPONDENCE
RESPONDENTS
RESPONSIBLE
RESPONSIBLY
RESPONSIONS
RESTATEMENT
RESTAURANTS
RESTFULNESS
RESTITUTION
RESTITUTIVE
RESTIVENESS

RESTORATION
RESTORATIVE
RESTRAINING
RESTRICTING
RESTRICTION
RESTRICTIVE
RESTRUCTURE
RESURFACING
RESURRECTED
RESUSCITATE
RETALIATING
RETALIATION
RETALIATIVE
RETALIATORY
RETARDATION
RETARDATIVE
RETARDINGLY
RETENTIVELY
RETENTIVITY
RETICULATED
RETINACULAR
RETINACULUM
RETINOSCOPY
RETIREMENTS
RETOUCHABLE
RETRACEABLE
RETRACEMENT
RETRACTABLE
RETRACTIONS
RETRENCHING
RETRIBUTION
RETRIBUTIVE
RETRIEVABLE
RETRIEVABLY
RETROACTION
RETROACTIVE
RETROLENTAL
RETRO-ROCKET
RETROVERTED
REUPHOLSTER
REUSABILITY
REVALUATION
REVEALINGLY
REVELATIONS
REVENGINGLY
REVERBERANT
REVERBERATE
REVERENCING
REVERENTIAL
REVERSIONER
REVISIONISM

REVISIONIST
REVITALIZED
REVIVALISTS
REVIVIFYING
REVOCATIONS
REVOLTINGLY
REVOLUTIONS
REVOLVINGLY
RHABDOMANCY
RHABDOMYOMA
RHAMNACEOUS
RHAPSODIZED
RHEOLOGICAL
RHEOTROPISM
RHETORICIAN
RHEUMATICKY
RHINESTONES
RHINOLOGIST
RHINOPLASTY
RHINOSCOPIC
RHIZOMATOUS
RHIZOPODOUS
RHIZOSPHERE
RHODE ISLAND
RHOTACISTIC
RHYTHMICITY
RICE PADDIES
RICKETINESS
RICKETTSIAL
RICOCHETING
RICOCHETTED
RIFLE RANGES
RIFT VALLEYS
RIGHT-ANGLED
RIGHT ANGLES
RIGHTEOUSLY
RIGHT-HANDED
RIGHT-HANDER
RIGHT-MINDED
RIGHTS ISSUE
RIGHTS OF WAY
RIGHT-WINGER
RIGOR MORTIS
RING BINDERS
RING FINGERS
RINGLEADERS
RINGMASTERS
RINSABILITY
RIOTOUSNESS
RITUALISTIC
RIVER BASINS

ROADHOLDING
ROAD MANAGER
ROAD PRICING
ROAD ROLLERS
ROAD TESTING
ROCK-AND-ROLL
ROCK GARDENS
ROCKHAMPTON
RODENTICIDE
RODOMONTADE
ROENTGEN RAY
ROGUISHNESS
ROLE PLAYING
ROLLERBLADE
ROLLERBLADE
ROLLER BLIND
ROLLER SKATE
ROLLER TOWEL
ROLLICKINGS
ROLLICKSOME
ROLLING MILL
ROLLING PINS
ROLLTOP DESK
ROMAN CANDLE
ROMANTICISM
ROMANTICIST
ROMANTICIZE
ROOD SCREENS
ROOF GARDENS
ROOM SERVICE
ROPE LADDERS
ROSE WINDOWS
ROTARIANISM
ROTISSERIES
ROTOGRAVURE
ROTTENSTONE
ROTUNDITIES
ROUGHCASTER
ROUGH-SPOKEN
ROUNDABOUTS
ROUNDEDNESS
ROUND ROBINS
ROUSTABOUTS
ROWING BOATS
ROYAL TENNIS
RUBBER BANDS
RUBBER PLANT
RUBBER STAMP
RUBBER TREES
RUBBISH BINS
RUBEFACIENT

RUBEFACTION	SAGITTARIUS	SANGUINEOUS	SCHIZOPHYTE
RUBICUNDITY	SAILING BOAT	SANITARIUMS	SCHLESINGER
RUBRICATION	SAILOR SUITS	SAN MARINESE	SCHOLARSHIP
RUDESHEIMER	SAINT ALBANS	SAN SALVADOR	SCHOLIASTIC
RUDIMENTARY	SAINT-BRIEUC	SANSEVIERIA	SCHOOLCHILD
RUGBY LEAGUE	SAINT GALLEN	SANSKRITIST	SCHOOLHOUSE
RULE OF THUMB	SAINT HELENA	SAPONACEOUS	SCHOOLMARMS
RUMBUSTIOUS	SAINT HELENS	SAPOTACEOUS	SCHOOLMATES
RUMINATIONS	SAINT HELIER	SAPROPHYTIC	SCHWEINFURT
RUMMAGE SALE	SAINTLINESS	SARCOMATOID	SCIENCE PARK
RUMPUS ROOMS	SAINT MARTIN	SARCOPHAGUS	SCIENTISTIC
RUNNER BEANS	SAINT MORITZ	SARDONICISM	SCIENTOLOGY
RUNNING JUMP	SAINT THOMAS	SARGASSO SEA	SCINTILLATE
RUNNING MATE	SALACIOUSLY	SARTORIALLY	SCIRRHOSITY
RUN-THROUGHS	SALAMANDERS	SASH WINDOWS	SCLERODERMA
RUNTISHNESS	SALEABILITY	SATANICALLY	SCLEROMETER
RUSSOPHOBIA	SALESCLERKS	SATELLITIUM	SCLEROTIOID
RUSSOPHOBIC	SALESPEOPLE	SATIABILITY	SCOPOLAMINE
RUSTICATING	SALESPERSON	SATIRICALLY	SCOREBOARDS
RUSTICATION	SALICACEOUS	SATISFIABLE	SCORIACEOUS
RUSTPROOFED	SALIENTNESS	SATURNALIAS	SCORPAENOID
RUTTISHNESS	SALINOMETER	SAUDI ARABIA	SCOTCH BROTH
	SALINOMETRY	SAURISCHIAN	SCOTCH MISTS
S	SALMONBERRY	SAUROPODOUS	SCOTCH TAPED
SAARBRUCKEN	SALMON TROUT	SAUSAGE DOGS	SCOTOMATOUS
SABBATARIAN	SALPINGITIC	SAUSAGE ROLL	SCOURGINGLY
SABBATICALS	SALPINGITIS	SAVABLENESS	SCOUTMASTER
SACCULATION	SALTATORIAL	SAVING GRACE	SCRAGGINESS
SACRAMENTAL	SALTCELLARS	SAVINGS BANK	SCRAPPINESS
SACRIFICIAL	SALT SHAKERS	SAVOIR-FAIRE	SCRATCHCARD
SACRIFICING	SALUTATIONS	SAVOURINGLY	SCRATCHIEST
SACRILEGIST	SALVABILITY	SAXOPHONIST	SCRATCHINGS
SACROILIACS	SALVADORIAN	SCAFFOLDING	SCRATCHPADS
SADDENINGLY	SALVAGEABLE	SCALARIFORM	SCRAWNINESS
SADDLECLOTH	SALVATIONAL	SCAMMONIATE	SCREAMINGLY
SAFARI PARKS	SAL VOLATILE	SCANDALIZED	SCREENPLAYS
SAFEBREAKER	SAMURAI BOND	SCANDALIZER	SCREENSAVER
SAFE-CONDUCT	SAN ANTONIAN	SCANDINAVIA	SCREEN TESTS
SAFE-DEPOSIT	SANATORIUMS	SCARABAEOID	SCREWDRIVER
SAFEGUARDED	SANCTIFYING	SCARBOROUGH	SCRIMMAGING
SAFEKEEPING	SANCTIONING	SCAREDY CATS	SCRIMPINESS
SAFETY BELTS	SANCTUARIES	SCAREMONGER	SCRIPTORIUM
SAFETY CATCH	SANDBAGGING	SCARLATINAL	SCRUBBINESS
SAFETY-FIRST	SANDBLASTED	SCATOLOGIST	SCRUMHALVES
SAFETY GLASS	SANDBLASTER	SCATTERABLE	SCRUMMAGING
SAFETY LAMPS	SAND-CASTING	SCENOGRAPHY	SCRUMPTIOUS
SAFETY MATCH	SANDCASTLES	SCEPTICALLY	SCRUTINEERS
SAFETY RAZOR	SANDPAPERED	SCHEMATIZED	SCRUTINIZED
SAFETY VALVE	SANDWICHING	SCHISMATICS	SCRUTINIZER
SAGACIOUSLY	SAN FERNANDO	SCHISTOSITY	SCUBA DIVING
SAGITTARIAN	SANGUINARIA	SCHISTOSOME	SCULPTURING

SCYPHISTOMA	SELF-IMPOSED	SEPTICAEMIC	SHIFTLESSLY
SEA ANEMONES	SELF-INDUCED	SEPTIC TANKS	SHIFT STICKS
SEA CAPTAINS	SELFISHNESS	SEPTIFRAGAL	SHIMONOSEKI
SEARCHINGLY	SELF-LOADING	SEPTIVALENT	SHIP BISCUIT
SEARCHLIGHT	SELF-LOCKING	SEQUESTERED	SHIPBUILDER
SEARCH PARTY	SELF-PITYING	SEQUESTRANT	SHIPWRECKED
SEASICKNESS	SELF-RELIANT	SEQUESTRATE	SHIPWRIGHTS
SEBORRHOEAL	SELF-RESPECT	SERENDIPITY	SHIRE HORSES
SECESSIONAL	SELF-SEALING	SERIALIZING	SHIRTFRONTS
SECONDARILY	SELF-SEEKERS	SERICULTURE	SHIRTSLEEVE
SECOND CLASS	SELF-SEEKING	SERIES-WOUND	SHISH KEBABS
SECOND-CLASS	SELF-SERVICE	SERIOUSNESS	SHIVERINGLY
SECOND-GUESS	SELF-STARTER	SERMONIZING	SHOCKHEADED
SECOND HANDS	SELF-WINDING	SERPIGINOUS	SHOCK TROOPS
SECONDMENTS	SELL-BY DATES	SERRULATION	SHOESTRINGS
SECOND-RATER	SELLOTAPING	SERTULARIAN	SHOPKEEPERS
SECOND SIGHT	SELL-THROUGH	SERVICEABLE	SHOPLIFTERS
SECRET AGENT	SEMANTICIST	SERVICEABLY	SHOPLIFTING
SECRETARIAL	SEMASIOLOGY	SERVICE FLAT	SHOP STEWARD
SECRETARIAT	SEMIAQUATIC	SERVICE ROAD	SHOPWALKERS
SECRETARIES	SEMIARIDITY	SERVOMOTORS	SHORT CHANGE
SECRETIVELY	SEMICIRCLES	SESQUIOXIDE	SHORT-CHANGE
SECULARIZED	SEMIDIURNAL	SETTLEMENTS	SHORTCOMING
SECULARIZER	SEMIFLUIDIC	SEVENTEENTH	SHORT CORNER
SEDAN CHAIRS	SEMIMONTHLY	SEVENTIETHS	SHORTHANDED
SEDENTARILY	SEMIOTICIAN	SEXAGESIMAL	SHORT-HANDED
SEDIMENTARY	SEMIPALMATE	SEXLESSNESS	SHORT-LISTED
SEDIMENTOUS	SEMIQUAVERS	SEXOLOGISTS	SHORT SHRIFT
SEDITIONARY	SEMISKILLED	SEXTODECIMO	SHORT-SPOKEN
SEDITIOUSLY	SEMITONALLY	SHADOW-BOXED	SHORT-WINDED
SEDUCTIVELY	SEMITRAILER	SHADOWGRAPH	SHOULDERING
SEGREGATING	SEMITROPICS	SHADOWINESS	SHOWERPROOF
SEGREGATION	SEMIVOCALIC	SHALLOWNESS	SHOW JUMPERS
SEGREGATIVE	SEMPERVIVUM	SHAMANISTIC	SHOW JUMPING
SEIGNIORAGE	SEMPITERNAL	SHAMELESSLY	SHOWMANSHIP
SEISMICALLY	SENSATIONAL	SHANGHAIING	SHOW OF HANDS
SEISMOGRAPH	SENSELESSLY	SHANKS'S PONY	SHOWSTOPPER
SEISMOLOGIC	SENSE ORGANS	SHANTYTOWNS	SHRINKINGLY
SEISMOSCOPE	SENSIBILITY	SHAPELESSLY	SHRIVELLING
SELAGINELLA	SENSITIVELY	SHAPELINESS	SHRUBBERIES
SELECTIVELY	SENSITIVITY	SHAREHOLDER	SHRUBBINESS
SELECTIVITY	SENSITIZING	SHARPBENDER	SHUFFLE PLAY
SELENOGRAPH	SENSUALISTS	SHARP-WITTED	SHUTTLECOCK
SELF-ASSURED	SENSUALNESS	SHAVING FOAM	SIAMESE CATS
SELF-CENTRED	SENTENTIOUS	SHEATH KNIFE	SIAMESE TWIN
SELF-COMMAND	SENTIMENTAL	SHEET ANCHOR	SICKENINGLY
SELF-CONCEPT	SENTRY BOXES	SHELLACKING	SIDE EFFECTS
SELF-CONTROL	SEPARATIONS	SHENANIGANS	SIDESADDLES
SELF-DEFENCE	SEPARATISTS	SHEPHERDESS	SIDESLIPPED
SELF-DENYING	SEPTAVALENT	SHEPHERDING	SIDESTEPPED
SELF-EVIDENT	SEPTICAEMIA	SHIBBOLETHS	SIDESTEPPER

SIDE STREETS	SINO-TIBETAN	SLOUCHINESS	SOLILOQUIZE
SIDESWIPING	SINUOSITIES	SLOUCHINGLY	SOLIPSISTIC
SIDETRACKED	SINUOUSNESS	SLOWCOACHES	SOLMIZATION
SIDE-WHEELER	SISTERHOODS	SLUMGULLION	SOLUBLENESS
SIENKIEWICZ	SISTER-IN-LAW	SMALL CHANGE	SOLVABILITY
SIERRA LEONE	SITTING BULL	SMALLHOLDER	SOMATICALLY
SIERRA MADRE	SITTING DUCK	SMALL-MINDED	SOMATOLOGIC
SIGHTLINESS	SITTING ROOM	SMALL SCREEN	SOMATOPLASM
SIGHT-READER	SITUATIONAL	SMALL-TIMERS	SOMERSAULTS
SIGHTSCREEN	SIX-SHOOTERS	SMART ALECKS	SOMNOLENTLY
SIGHTSEEING	SIXTH-FORMER	SMART ALECKY	SONGFULNESS
SIGNAL BOXES	SIZABLENESS	SMARTY-PANTS	SON-OF-A-BITCH
SIGNALIZING	SKATEBOARDS	SMATTERINGS	SOOTHSAYERS
SIGNATORIES	SKEDADDLING	SMILINGNESS	SOPHISTRIES
SIGNIFIABLE	SKELETONIZE	SMITHEREENS	SORORICIDAL
SIGNIFICANT	SKELETON KEY	SMITHSONITE	SORROWFULLY
SIGNPOSTING	SKEPTICALLY	SMOKESCREEN	SOTTISHNESS
SILHOUETTED	SKETCHINESS	SMOKESTACKS	SOUBRIQUETS
SILHOUETTES	SKILFULNESS	SMOOTH-FACED	SOUGHT-AFTER
SILICON CHIP	SKIMMED MILK	SMORGASBORD	SOUL BROTHER
SILLIMANITE	SKIRMISHERS	SMOULDERING	SOULFULNESS
SILLY SEASON	SKIRMISHING	SNAPDRAGONS	SOUNDLESSLY
SILVER BIRCH	SKULDUGGERY	SNIPERSCOPE	SOUNDTRACKS
SILVERINESS	SKYJACKINGS	SNORKELLING	SOUP KITCHEN
SILVER MEDAL	SKYROCKETED	SNOWBALLING	SOUSAPHONES
SILVER PAPER	SKYSCRAPERS	SNOWMOBILES	SOUTH AFRICA
SILVER PLATE	SLAUGHTERED	SNOWPLOUGHS	SOUTHAMPTON
SILVERPOINT	SLAUGHTERER	SOAP BUBBLES	SOUTH DAKOTA
SILVERSMITH	SLAVE DRIVER	SOCIABILITY	SOUTHEASTER
SIMMERINGLY	SLAVE LABOUR	SOCIALISTIC	SOUTHERNERS
SIMPERINGLY	SLAVISHNESS	SOCIALIZING	SOUTH ISLAND
SIMPLIFYING	SLEEPING BAG	SOCIOLOGIST	SOUTHWESTER
SIMPLON PASS	SLEEPING CAR	SOCIOMETRIC	SOVEREIGNTY
SIMULACRUMS	SLEEPLESSLY	SOCIOPATHIC	SOVIETISTIC
SIMULATIONS	SLEEPWALKED	SOFTHEARTED	SPACE HEATER
SINE QUA NONS	SLEEPWALKER	SOFT LANDING	SPACE PROBES
SINFONIETTA	SLEEPYHEADS	SOFT OPTIONS	SPARINGNESS
SINGAPOREAN	SLENDERIZED	SOFT PALATES	SPARROWHAWK
SINGLE-BLIND	SLENDERNESS	SOFT-PEDALED	SPASTICALLY
SINGLE-CROSS	SLEUTHHOUND	SOFT-SOAPING	SPATHACEOUS
SINGLE-PHASE	SLICED BREAD	SOFT TOUCHES	SPEAKEASIES
SINGLE-SPACE	SLICE OF LIFE	SOLANACEOUS	SPEAKERSHIP
SINGLE-TRACK	SLICKENSIDE	SOLARIMETER	SPEARHEADED
SINGULARITY	SLIDE-ACTION	SOLAR PANELS	SPECIALISMS
SINGULARIZE	SLIDING DOOR	SOLAR PLEXUS	SPECIALISTS
SINISTRORSE	SLIGHTINGLY	SOLAR SYSTEM	SPECIALIZED
SINKING FUND	SLIPPED DISC	SOLEMNITIES	SPECIALNESS
SINLESSNESS	SLIPSTREAMS	SOLEMNIZING	SPECIFIABLE
SINN FEINISM	SLOOP-RIGGED	SOLIDIFYING	SPECIFICITY
SINOLOGICAL	SLOPINGNESS	SOLILOQUIES	SPECTACULAR
SINOLOGISTS	SLOT MACHINE	SOLILOQUIST	SPECTRALITY

SPECULATING	SPONGE CAKES	STALEMATING	STEREOGRAPH
SPECULATION	SPONSORSHIP	STALLHOLDER	STEREOMETRY
SPECULATIVE	SPONTANEITY	STANDARDIZE	STEREOSCOPE
SPECULATORS	SPONTANEOUS	STANDOFFISH	STEREOSCOPY
SPEECHIFIED	SPOONERISMS	STANDPOINTS	STEREOTAXIS
SPEECHIFIER	SPOROGENOUS	STANLEY POOL	STEREOTYPED
SPEED LIMITS	SPOROGONIAL	STARA ZAGORA	STEREOTYPER
SPEEDOMETER	SPOROGONIUM	STAR CHAMBER	STEREOTYPES
SPELLBINDER	SPOROPHYTIC	STARCHINESS	STEREOTYPIC
SPENDTHRIFT	SPORTSWOMAN	STAR-CROSSED	STERILIZERS
SPERMATHECA	SPORULATION	STAR-STUDDED	STERILIZING
SPERMATOZOA	SPOT CHECKED	STARTER HOME	STERLITAMAK
SPERMICIDES	SPOTTED DICK	STARTLINGLY	STERNUTATOR
SPERMOPHILE	SPREAD-EAGLE	STARVELINGS	STETHOSCOPE
SPERM WHALES	SPREADSHEET	STATELINESS	STETHOSCOPY
SPESSARTITE	SPRINGBOARD	STATELY HOME	STEWARDSHIP
SPHEROMETER	SPRING-CLEAN	STATESWOMAN	STICHICALLY
SPHERULITIC	SPRINGFIELD	STATISTICAL	STICHOMETRY
SPHINCTERAL	SPRINGINESS	STATOLITHIC	STICKHANDLE
SPHINGOSINE	SPRING ONION	STATUTE BOOK	STICK INSECT
SPHRAGISTIC	SPRING ROLLS	STATUTORILY	STICKLEBACK
SPINA BIFIDA	SPRING TIDES	STAUNCHABLE	STICK SHIFTS
SPINAL CORDS	SPRINKLINGS	STAUNCHNESS	STIFF-NECKED
SPINELESSLY	SPUMESCENCE	STAUROLITIC	STIGMATICAL
SPINESCENCE	SQUANDERERS	STAUROSCOPE	STIGMATIZED
SPINIFEROUS	SQUANDERING	STAY-AT-HOMES	STIGMATIZER
SPINSTERISH	SQUARE DANCE	STEADFASTLY	STILLBIRTHS
SPINY-FINNED	SQUARE KNOTS	STEALTHIEST	STILTEDNESS
SPIRACULATE	SQUARE MEALS	STEAM-BOILER	STIMULATING
SPIRIFEROUS	SQUARE ROOTS	STEAM-ENGINE	STIMULATION
SPIRIT LEVEL	SQUASHINESS	STEAMROLLER	STIMULATIVE
SPIRITUALLY	SQUEAMISHLY	STEAM SHOVEL	STIPENDIARY
SPIRKETTING	SQUELCHIEST	STEAROPTENE	STIPULATING
SPIROCHAETE	SQUIGGLIEST	STEATOLYSIS	STIPULATION
SPIROMETRIC	SQUIREARCHY	STEATOPYGIA	STIPULATORY
SPITSTICKER	SQUIRMINGLY	STEATOPYGIC	STIRRUP CUPS
SPLASHBOARD	STABILIZERS	STEELWORKER	STIRRUP PUMP
SPLASHDOWNS	STABILIZING	STEEPLEJACK	STOCKBROKER
SPLASH GUARD	STADIOMETER	STEERAGEWAY	STOCKHOLDER
SPLASHINESS	STAFF NURSES	STELLARATOR	STOCKJOBBER
SPLATTERING	STAGE FRIGHT	STENCILLING	STOCK MARKET
SPLAYFOOTED	STAGE-MANAGE	STENOGRAPHY	STOCKPILING
SPLENDOROUS	STAGESTRUCK	STENOHALINE	STOCKTAKING
SPLENECTOMY	STAGGERBUSH	STENOPHAGUS	STOICALNESS
SPLENETICAL	STAGING POST	STENOTROPIC	STOMACHACHE
SPLINTERING	STAG PARTIES	STENOTYPIST	STOMACHICAL
SPLIT SECOND	STAKEHOLDER	STEPBROTHER	STOMACH PUMP
SPLUTTERING	STALACTITES	STEPHANOTIS	STOMATOLOGY
SPOILSPORTS	STALACTITIC	STEPLADDERS	STONECUTTER
SPOKESWOMAN	STALAGMITES	STEPPARENTS	STONE FRUITS
SPONDYLITIS	STALAGMITIC	STEPSISTERS	STONE-GROUND

STONEMASONS	STROBOSCOPE	SUBMERSIBLE	SUFFICIENCY
STONE'S THROW	STRONGBOXES	SUBMISSIONS	SUFFOCATING
STONEWALLED	STRONGHOLDS	SUBMITTABLE	SUFFOCATION
STONEWALLER	STRONG POINT	SUBMULTIPLE	SUFFOCATIVE
STONEWORKER	STRONG ROOMS	SUBORDINARY	SUFFRAGETTE
STOOLPIGEON	STRUCTURING	SUBORDINATE	SUFFUMIGATE
STOPWATCHES	STRUCTURIST	SUBORNATION	SUGGESTIBLE
STOREHOUSES	STRUTTINGLY	SUBORNATIVE	SUGGESTIONS
STOREKEEPER	STUBBORNEST	SUBPOENAING	SUITABILITY
STORE KEEPER	STUDENTSHIP	SUBREGIONAL	SULPHA DRUGS
STORM CLOUDS	STUDIEDNESS	SUBROGATION	SULPHUREOUS
STORYTELLER	STUDIO COUCH	SUBROUTINES	SUMMARINESS
STOURBRIDGE	STULTIFYING	SUBSCAPULAR	SUMMARIZING
STRAGGLIEST	STUMBLINGLY	SUBSCRIBERS	SUMMATIONAL
STRAIGHTEST	STUNTEDNESS	SUBSCRIBING	SUMMERHOUSE
STRAIGHT-OUT	STUPIDITIES	SUBSECTIONS	SUMMERINESS
STRAIGHTWAY	STYLISHNESS	SUBSEQUENCE	SUMPTUOUSLY
STRAININGLY	STYLIZATION	SUBSERVIENT	SUNDRENCHED
STRAITLACED	STYLOGRAPHY	SUBSIDENCES	SUNLESSNESS
STRANGENESS	STYLOPODIUM	SUBSIDIZERS	SUNNY-SIDE UP
STRANGULATE	STYLOSTIXIS	SUBSIDIZING	SUPERABOUND
STRAPHANGER	SUBASSEMBLY	SUBSISTENCE	SUPERCHARGE
STRATEGISTS	SUBAUDITION	SUBSPECIFIC	SUPERFAMILY
STRATHCLYDE	SUBAXILLARY	SUBSTANDARD	SUPERFETATE
STRATIFYING	SUBBASEMENT	SUBSTANTIAL	SUPERFICIAL
STRATOCRACY	SUBCHLORIDE	SUBSTANTIVE	SUPERFLUITY
STRATOPAUSE	SUBCOMPACTS	SUBSTATIONS	SUPERFLUOUS
STRAWFLOWER	SUBCONTRACT	SUBSTITUENT	SUPERIMPOSE
STRAWWEIGHT	SUBCONTRARY	SUBSTITUTED	SUPERINDUCE
STREAKINESS	SUBCORTICAL	SUBSTITUTES	SUPERINTEND
STREAMLINED	SUBCULTURAL	SUBSTRATIVE	SUPERIORITY
STREETLIGHT	SUBCULTURES	SUBSUMPTION	SUPERJACENT
STREET VALUE	SUBDELIRIUM	SUBSUMPTIVE	SUPERLATIVE
STRENUOSITY	SUBDIACONAL	SUBTERFUGES	SUPERLUNARY
STRENUOUSLY	SUBDIVIDING	SUBTRACTING	SUPERMARKET
STRESS MARKS	SUBDIVISION	SUBTRACTION	SUPERNATANT
STRETCHABLE	SUBDOMINANT	SUBTRACTIVE	SUPERNORMAL
STRETCHIEST	SUBDUEDNESS	SUBTROPICAL	SUPERSCRIBE
STRETCHMARK	SUBHEADINGS	SUBURBANITE	SUPERSCRIPT
STRIDULATED	SUBIRRIGATE	SUBVENTIONS	SUPERSEDEAS
STRIDULATOR	SUBJECTABLE	SUBVERSIVES	SUPERSEDING
STRIKEBOUND	SUBJUGATING	SUCCEDANEUM	SUPERSEDURE
STRING BEANS	SUBJUGATION	SUCCEEDABLE	SUPERSONICS
STRINGBOARD	SUBJUNCTION	SUCCESSIONS	SUPERSTRUCT
STRINGENTLY	SUBJUNCTIVE	SUCCESSORAL	SUPERTANKER
STRINGINESS	SUBLIMATING	SUCCOURABLE	SUPERVENING
STRINGPIECE	SUBLIMATION	SUCH AND SUCH	SUPERVISING
STRIP MINING	SUBLITTORAL	SUCKING PIGS	SUPERVISION
STRIP-SEARCH	SUBLUXATION	SUCTION PUMP	SUPERVISORS
STRIPTEASES	SUBMARGINAL	SUDETENLAND	SUPERVISORY
STROBE LIGHT	SUBMARINERS	SUFFERINGLY	SUPPLANTING

SUPPLEMENTS
SUPPLICANTS
SUPPLICATED
SUPPORTABLE
SUPPOSITION
SUPPOSITIVE
SUPPOSITORY
SUPPRESSANT
SUPPRESSING
SUPPRESSION
SUPPRESSIVE
SUPPRESSORS
SUPPURATING
SUPPURATION
SUPPURATIVE
SUPREMACIST
SUPREMATISM
SUPREMATIST
SUPREMENESS
SURBASEMENT
SURCHARGING
SURFCASTING
SURGEONFISH
SURMOUNTING
SURPASSABLE
SURPRISEDLY
SURREALISTS
SURREBUTTAL
SURREBUTTER
SURRENDERED
SURRENDERER
SURROGATION
SURROUNDING
SURVEILLANT
SURVIVAL KIT
SUSCEPTANCE
SUSCEPTIBLE
SUSPENDIBLE
SUSPENSEFUL
SUSPENSIONS
SUSPICIONAL
SUSTAINABLE
SUSTAINEDLY
SUSTAINMENT
SUSURRATION
SWALLOWABLE
SWALLOW DIVE
SWALLOWTAIL
SWALLOWWORT
SWARTHINESS
SWEAT GLANDS

SWEATSHIRTS
SWEEPSTAKES
SWEETBREADS
SWEETHEARTS
SWEET PEPPER
SWEET POTATO
SWEET-TALKED
SWINDLINGLY
SWINISHNESS
SWISS CHARDS
SWISS CHEESE
SWITCHBACKS
SWITCHBLADE
SWITCHBOARD
SWITZERLAND
SWOLLEN HEAD
SWOLLENNESS
SWORD DANCER
SWORD DANCES
SWORDFISHES
SYCOPHANTIC
SYLLABOGRAM
SYLLOGISTIC
SYMBOLISTIC
SYMBOLIZING
SYMBOLOGIST
SYMMETRICAL
SYMPATHETIC
SYMPATHIZED
SYMPATHIZER
SYMPETALOUS
SYMPHONIOUS
SYMPTOMATIC
SYNAGOGICAL
SYNCHROMESH
SYNCHRONISM
SYNCHRONIZE
SYNCHRONOUS
SYNCHROTRON
SYNCOPATING
SYNCOPATION
SYNDESMOSIS
SYNDESMOTIC
SYNDICALISM
SYNDICALIST
SYNDICATING
SYNDICATION
SYNECDOCHIC
SYNECOLOGIC
SYNKARYONIC
SYNTHESIZED

SYNTHESIZER
SYNTHETICAL
SYPHILITICS
SYPHILOLOGY
SYSSARCOSIS
SYSSARCOTIC
SYSTEMATICS
SYSTEMATISM
SYSTEMATIST
SYSTEMATIZE
SZOMBATHELY

T

TABERNACLES
TABLECLOTHS
TABLESPOONS
TABLE TENNIS
TABULATIONS
TACHEOMETER
TACHOGRAPHS
TACHOMETERS
TACHOMETRIC
TACHYCARDIA
TACHYMETRIC
TACITURNITY
TACTFULNESS
TAGLIATELLE
TAKE AGAINST
TAKE-HOME PAY
TALEBEARERS
TALENT SCOUT
TALKABILITY
TALKING BOOK
TALLAHASSEE
TALL STORIES
TAMABLENESS
TAMBOURINES
TANGIBILITY
TANTALIZING
TAPE MACHINE
TAPE MEASURE
TARANTELLAS
TARNISHABLE
TARRADIDDLE
TARTAR SAUCE
TASKMASTERS
TASTELESSLY
TAUTOLOGIES
TAUTOLOGIZE
TAUTOMERISM
TAXIDERMIST

TAX SHELTERS
TEARFULNESS
TEARJERKERS
TEA SERVICES
TEA TROLLEYS
TECHNICALLY
TECHNICIANS
TECHNICOLOR
TECHNOCRACY
TECHNOCRATS
TECHNOPHILE
TECHNOPHOBE
TEDIOUSNESS
TEENYBOPPER
TEETOTALISM
TEETOTALLER
TEGUCIGALPA
TELEBANKING
TELECOMMUTE
TELECOTTAGE
TELEGNOSTIC
TELEGRAPHED
TELEGRAPHER
TELEGRAPHIC
TELEKINESIS
TELEKINETIC
TELEOLOGISM
TELEOLOGIST
TELEPATHIST
TELEPHONING
TELEPHONIST
TELEPRINTER
TELESCOPING
TELESELLING
TELEVISIONS
TELEWORKING
TELLING-OFFS
TELUKBETUNG
TEMERARIOUS
TEMPERAMENT
TEMPERATURE
TEMPESTUOUS
TEMPORALITY
TEMPORARILY
TEMPORIZING
TEMPTATIONS
TEMPTRESSES
TENACIOUSLY
TENDENTIOUS
TENDERFOOTS
TENDERIZING

TENEBROSITY	THEOCENTRIC	THREADINESS	TOMBOYISHLY
TENNIS ELBOW	THEODOLITES	THREATENING	TONSILLITIS
TENORRHAPHY	THEODOLITIC	THREEPENCES	TOOTH POWDER
TENSIBILITY	THEODORAKIS	THRIFTINESS	TOPDRESSING
TENSIOMETER	THEOLOGIANS	THRILLINGLY	TOPOGRAPHER
TENTATIVELY	THEOLOGICAL	THROATINESS	TOPOGRAPHIC
TENTERHOOKS	THEOLOGIZER	THROBBINGLY	TORCHBEARER
TENUOUSNESS	THEOPHOBIAC	THROMBOCYTE	TORMENTEDLY
TEPEFACTION	THEOREMATIC	THROUGHPUTS	TORONTONIAN
TERATOGENIC	THEORETICAL	THROUGHWAYS	TORSIBILITY
TERATOLOGIC	THEOSOPHISM	THUMBSCREWS	TORTICOLLAR
TEREBIC ACID	THEOSOPHIST	THUNDERBIRD	TORTICOLLIS
TERMINATING	THERAPEUTIC	THUNDERBOLT	TORTURESOME
TERMINATION	THEREABOUTS	THUNDERCLAP	TORTURINGLY
TERMINATIVE	THEREMINIST	THYROIDITIS	TORTUROUSLY
TERMINATORY	THERETOFORE	THYROTROPIN	TOTALIZATOR
TERMINOLOGY	THERIOMORPH	THYRSANURAN	TOTEMICALLY
TERRESTRIAL	THERMIONICS	TICKINGS OFF	TOTIPALMATE
TERRICOLOUS	THERMOCLINE	TICK-TACK-TOE	TOTIPOTENCY
TERRIGENOUS	THERMOGRAPH	TIDDLYWINKS	TOUCHPAPERS
TERRITORIAL	THERMOLYSIS	TIEBREAKERS	TOUCHSTONES
TERRITORIES	THERMOLYTIC	TIED COTTAGE	TOUCH-TYPING
TERRORISTIC	THERMOMETER	TIGHTFISTED	TOUCH-TYPIST
TERRORIZING	THERMOMETRY	TIGHT-LIPPED	TOUCHY-FEELY
TERTIUM QUID	THERMOSCOPE	TIME CAPSULE	TOUR DE FORCE
TESSELLATED	THERMOSTATS	TIMEKEEPERS	TOURMALINIC
TESTABILITY	THERMOTAXIC	TIMESERVERS	TOURNAMENTS
TESTAMENTAL	THERMOTAXIS	TIMESERVING	TOURNIQUETS
TESTICULATE	THESAURUSES	TIME-SHARING	TOUT LE MONDE
TESTIMONIAL	THICKHEADED	TIME SIGNALS	TOWER BLOCKS
TESTIMONIES	THICKNESSES	TIMETABLING	TOWN PLANNER
TEST MATCHES	THICK-WITTED	TINDERBOXES	TOWNSPEOPLE
TETANICALLY	THIGMOTAXIS	TIN PAN ALLEY	TOXICOGENIC
TETRADYMITE	THIMBLEFULS	TIN-PAN ALLEY	TOXOPHILITE
TETRAHEDRAL	THIMBLEWEED	TIRUNELVELI	TOXOPLASMIC
TETRAHEDRON	THINGAMAJIG	TITANICALLY	TRACHEOTOMY
TETRAMERISM	THIN-SKINNED	TITILLATING	TRACK EVENTS
TETRAMEROUS	THIOCYANATE	TITILLATION	TRACKLAYERS
TETRAPLEGIA	THIOPENTONE	TITILLATIVE	TRACK RECORD
TETRARCHATE	THIRD DEGREE	TITLEHOLDER	TRACKSUITED
TETRASPORIC	THIRD-DEGREE	TITTERINGLY	TRADE PRICES
TETRAVALENT	THIRD PERSON	TOASTMASTER	TRADE ROUTES
THALIDOMIDE	THIRSTINESS	TOAST MASTER	TRADES UNION
THALLOPHYTE	THIRTEENTHS	TOBACCONIST	TRADESWOMAN
THANKLESSLY	THISTLEDOWN	TOBOGGANING	TRADE UNIONS
THAUMATROPE	THIXOTROPIC	TOFFEE APPLE	TRADING POST
THEATREGOER	THORACOTOMY	TOFFEE-NOSED	TRADITIONAL
THEATRICALS	THOROUGHPIN	TOILET PAPER	TRADUCEMENT
THEIRSELVES	THOUGHTLESS	TOILET ROLLS	TRADUCINGLY
THENCEFORTH	THOUSANDTHS	TOILET WATER	TRAFFICATOR
THEOBROMINE	THRASH METAL	TOLBUTAMIDE	TRAFFIC JAMS

TRAFFICKERS	TRANSPORTER	TRINIDADIAN	TUNEFULNESS
TRAFFICKING	TRANSPOSING	TRIPALMITIN	TUNING FORKS
TRAGEDIENNE	TRANSPUTERS	TRIPLICATES	TURBINATION
TRAGICOMEDY	TRANSSEXUAL	TRIQUETROUS	TURBOCHARGE
TRAILBLAZER	TRANSURANIC	TRISTICHOUS	TURBULENTLY
TRAINBEARER	TRANSVAALER	TRISULPHIDE	TURGESCENCE
TRAMPOLINER	TRANSVALUER	TRITURATION	TURKISH BATH
TRAMPOLINES	TRANSVERSAL	TRIUMVIRATE	TURNAROUNDS
TRANQUILITY	TRAPSHOOTER	TRIVIALIZED	TURRICULATE
TRANSACTING	TRAUMATIZED	TROCHOPHORE	TURTLEDOVES
TRANSACTION	TRAVEL AGENT	TROCORNERED	TURTLENECKS
TRANSALPINE	TRAVELOGUES	TROGLODYTES	TUTTI FRUTTI
TRANSCEIVER	TRAVERSABLE	TROGLODYTIC	TWELVEMONTH
TRANSCENDED	TREACHERIES	TROJAN HORSE	TWITCHINGLY
TRANSCRIBED	TREACHEROUS	TROMBONISTS	TYNE AND WEAR
TRANSCRIBER	TREACLINESS	TROMPE L'OEIL	TYPECASTING
TRANSCRIPTS	TREASONABLE	TROPHICALLY	TYPESCRIPTS
TRANSECTION	TREASONABLY	TROPHOBLAST	TYPESETTERS
TRANSFERASE	TREASURABLE	TROPHOZOITE	TYPE SETTING
TRANSFERRED	TREBLE CLEFS	TROPICALITY	TYPEWRITERS
TRANSFERRIN	TRELLISWORK	TROPICALIZE	TYPEWRITING
TRANSFIGURE	TREMBLINGLY	TROPISMATIC	TYPEWRITTEN
TRANSFINITE	TREMULOUSLY	TROPOPHYTIC	TYPICALNESS
TRANSFIXING	TRENCHANTLY	TROPOSPHERE	TYPING POOLS
TRANSFIXION	TRENCH COATS	TROTSKYISTS	TYPOGRAPHER
TRANSFORMED	TRENCHERMAN	TROUBADOURS	TYPOGRAPHIC
TRANSFORMER	TRENCHERMEN	TROUBLESOME	TYPOLOGICAL
TRANSFUSION	TRENDSETTER	TROUBLE SPOT	TYRANNICIDE
TRANSFUSIVE	TREPIDATION	TROUBLINGLY	TYRANNIZING
TRANSHUMANT	TRESPASSING	TRUCULENTLY	TYROTHRICIN
TRANSISTORS	TRESTLETREE	TRUEHEARTED	TZETZE FLIES
TRANSITABLE	TRESTLEWORK	TRUK ISLANDS	
TRANSITIONS	TRIABLENESS	TRUMPETWEED	**U**
TRANSITIVES	TRIANGULATE	TRUNK ROUTES	ULOTRICHOUS
TRANS-JORDAN	TRIBULATION	TRUSTEESHIP	ULTRAFILTER
TRANSLATING	TRIBUTARIES	TRUSTWORTHY	ULTRAMARINE
TRANSLATION	TRIBUTARILY	TRYPANOSOME	ULTRAMODERN
TRANSLATORS	TRICERATOPS	TRYPSINOGEN	ULTRASONICS
TRANSLOCATE	TRICHINOSIS	TSELINOGRAD	ULTRAVIOLET
TRANSLUCENT	TRICHLORIDE	TSETSE FLIES	ULVERIZABLE
TRANSMITTAL	TRICHOMONAD	TUBERCULATE	UMBELLULATE
TRANSMITTED	TRICHOTOMIC	TUBERCULOUS	UNACCOUNTED
TRANSMITTER	TRICKLE-DOWN	TUB-THUMPERS	UNADVISEDLY
TRANSMUTING	TRICKLINGLY	TUB-THUMPING	UNALTERABLE
TRANSPADANE	TRICKSINESS	TUDORBETHAN	UNAMBIGUOUS
TRANSPARENT	TRICUSPIDAL	TUMBLE-DRIED	UNAMBITIOUS
TRANSPIERCE	TRIGGERFISH	TUMBLE DRIER	UNANIMOUSLY
TRANSPIRING	TRILLIONTHS	TUMBLE DRYER	UNANNOUNCED
TRANSPLANTS	TRIMETROGON	TUMBLE-DRYER	UNAVAILABLE
TRANSPONDER	TRIMORPHISM	TUMEFACIENT	UNAVOIDABLE
TRANSPORTED	TRINCOMALEE	TUMEFACTION	UNAWARENESS

UNBALANCING	UNDERSHIRTS	UNKEMPTNESS	UNTERWALDEN
UNBALLASTED	UNDERSIGNED	UNKNOWINGLY	UNTHEORIZED
UNBELIEVERS	UNDERSTAIRS	UNKNOWNNESS	UNTHINKABLE
UNBLEMISHED	UNDERSTATED	UNLOOKED-FOR	UNTOUCHABLE
UNBREAKABLE	UNDERTAKERS	UNLOOSENING	UNTRAVELLED
UNBURDENING	UNDERTAKING	UNLUCKINESS	UNUTTERABLE
UNCALLED-FOR	UNDERTHRUST	UNMANLINESS	UNUTTERABLY
UNCATCHABLE	UNDERVALUED	UNMITIGATED	UNVARNISHED
UNCERTAINLY	UNDERVALUER	UNNATURALLY	UNWARRANTED
UNCERTAINTY	UNDERWEIGHT	UNNECESSARY	UNWATCHABLE
UNCHARTERED	UNDERWRITER	UNOBTRUSIVE	UNWHOLESOME
UNCHASTENED	UNDESIGNING	UNORGANIZED	UNWILLINGLY
UNCHRISTIAN	UNDESIRABLE	UNPALATABLE	UNWITNESSED
UNCIVILIZED	UNDESIRABLY	UNPATRIOTIC	UNWITTINGLY
UNCLEANNESS	UNDEVELOPED	UNPERTURBED	UP-AND-COMING
UNCOMMITTED	UNDISCLOSED	UNPOLITICAL	UPHOLSTERED
UNCONCERNED	UNDISCUSSED	UNPRACTICAL	UPHOLSTERER
UNCONCLUDED	UNDISTORTED	UNPRACTISED	UPRIGHTNESS
UNCONFIDENT	UNDOUBTEDLY	UNPRINTABLE	UPS AND DOWNS
UNCONNECTED	UNDREAMED-OF	UNPROCESSED	UPSTRETCHED
UNCONSCIOUS	UNDRINKABLE	UNPROFESSED	URANOGRAPHY
UNCONSULTED	UNDULATIONS	UNPROMISING	URINIFEROUS
UNCONTESTED	UNEQUALNESS	UNPUBLISHED	UROCHORDATE
UNCONTRIVED	UNEQUIVOCAL	UNQUALIFIED	URTICACEOUS
UNCONVERTED	UNESSENTIAL	UNRAVELLING	USELESSNESS
UNCONVINCED	UNEXPLAINED	UNRAVELMENT	UTILITARIAN
UNCORRECTED	UNEXPRESSED	UNREALISTIC	UTILITY ROOM
UNCOUNTABLE	UNFAILINGLY	UNREASONING	UTILIZATION
UNCOUTHNESS	UNFALTERING	UNREFLECTED	UTRICULITIS
UNCRUSHABLE	UNFLAPPABLE	UNREHEARSED	
UNDECEIVING	UNFLAPPABLY	UNRELENTING	**V**
UNDECIDABLE	UNFLINCHING	UNREMITTING	VACATIONERS
UNDECIDEDLY	UNFORTUNATE	UNRIGHTEOUS	VACATIONING
UNDEMANDING	UNFULFILLED	UNSATISFIED	VACCINATING
UNDERACTING	UNGODLINESS	UNSATURATED	VACCINATION
UNDERBIDDER	UNGUICULATE	UNSAVOURILY	VACILLATING
UNDERCHARGE	UNGULIGRADE	UNSCHEDULED	VACILLATION
UNDEREXPOSE	UNHAPPINESS	UNSCRAMBLED	VACUOLATION
UNDERGROUND	UNHEALTHILY	UNSCRAMBLER	VACUOUSNESS
UNDERGROWTH	UNICELLULAR	UNSCRATCHED	VACUUM FLASK
UNDERLETTER	UNIFICATION	UNSHAKEABLE	VACUUM PUMPS
UNDERLINING	UNIFORMNESS	UNSOCIALIST	VAGABONDAGE
UNDERMANNED	UNINHABITED	UNSPARINGLY	VAGABONDISM
UNDERMINING	UNINHIBITED	UNSPEAKABLE	VAGINECTOMY
UNDERPASSES	UNINITIATED	UNSPEAKABLY	VAGRANTNESS
UNDERPAYING	UNINSPIRING	UNSPECIFIED	VALEDICTION
UNDERPINNED	UNINSULATED	UNSPONSORED	VALEDICTORY
UNDERPLAYED	UNIPERSONAL	UNSTOPPABLE	VALIDATIONS
UNDERRATING	UNIPOLARITY	UNSURPASSED	VALLE D'AOSTA
UNDERSCORED	UNIVERSALLY	UNSURPRISED	VALUATIONAL
UNDERSELLER	UNJUSTIFIED	UNSUSPECTED	VAMPIRE BATS

VANDALISTIC
VANDALIZING
VANISHINGLY
VANQUISHING
VAPORESCENT
VAPORIMETER
VAPORIZABLE
VAPOUR TRAIL
VARGAS LLOSA
VARIABILITY
VARIATIONAL
VARICELLATE
VARICELLOID
VARIEGATION
VARIOLATION
VARIOUSNESS
VASCULARITY
VASCULARIZE
VASECTOMIES
VASODILATOR
VASOPRESSIN
VATICAN CITY
VEGETARIANS
VELOCIPEDES
VENDIBILITY
VENEREOLOGY
VENESECTION
VENTILATING
VENTILATION
VENTILATIVE
VENTILATORS
VENTILATORY
VENTRICULAR
VENTRICULUS
VENTURESOME
VERACIOUSLY
VERATRIDINE
VERBALIZING
VERBAL NOUNS
VEREENIGING
VERISIMILAR
VERMICULATE
VERMICULITE
VERMINATION
VERMIVOROUS
VERNACULARS
VERRUCOSITY
VERSATILITY
VERSICOLOUR
VERTEBRATES
VERTICALITY

VERTIGINOUS
VESTIGIALLY
VETERANS DAY
VEXATIOUSLY
VEXILLOLOGY
VIBRACULOID
VIBRAPHONES
VIBRATILITY
VIBRATINGLY
VIBRATIONAL
VICARIOUSLY
VICEGERENCY
VICEROYALTY
VICEROYSHIP
VICHYSSOISE
VICIOUSNESS
VICISSITUDE
VICTIMIZING
VICTUALLING
VIDEOPHONIC
VIDEOTAPING
VIEWFINDERS
VINAIGRETTE
VINDICATING
VINDICATION
VINDICATORY
VINEDRESSER
VINEGARROON
VINEYARDIST
VINICULTURE
VINIFICATOR
VIOLABILITY
VIOLONCELLO
VIRGIN BIRTH
VIRIDESCENT
VIROLOGICAL
VISCOMETRIC
VISCOUNTESS
VISCOUSNESS
VISIBLENESS
VISIONARIES
VISITATIONS
VISUALIZING
VITICULTURE
VITRESCENCE
VITRIFIABLE
VITUPERATOR
VIVACIOUSLY
VIVISECTION
VLAARDINGEN
VLADIKAVKAZ

VLADIVOSTOK
VOCIFERANCE
VOCIFERATED
VOCIFERATOR
VOLCANICITY
VOLCANOLOGY
VOLTAMMETER
VOLUNTARIES
VOLUNTARILY
VOLUNTARISM
VOLUNTARIST
VOLUNTEERED
VOODOOISTIC
VOORTREKKER
VORACIOUSLY
VORTIGINOUS
VOUCHSAFING
VOYEURISTIC
VULCANIZING
VULGARITIES
VULGARIZING
VULGAR LATIN

WADING POOLS
WAGGISHNESS
WAINSCOTING
WAINSCOTTED
WAITING GAME
WAITING LIST
WAITING ROOM
WAITRESSING
WAKEFULNESS
WALKS OF LIFE
WALLFLOWERS
WALLPAPERED
WANDERINGLY
WANNE-EICKEL
WARM-BLOODED
WARM-HEARTED
WARMING PANS
WAR OF NERVES
WARRANTABLE
WASHABILITY
WASH DRAWING
WASHERWOMAN
WASHERWOMEN
WASHING DAYS
WASPISHNESS
WATCHKEEPER
WATCHMAKERS

WATCHMAKING
WATCHSTRAPS
WATCHTOWERS
WATER CANNON
WATER CLOSET
WATERCOLOUR
WATERCOURSE
WATERED-DOWN
WATERFRONTS
WATERING CAN
WATER LEVELS
WATER LILIES
WATERLOGGED
WATER MEADOW
WATERMELONS
WATERPROOFS
WATER SKIERS
WATER SKIING
WATERSPOUTS
WATER SUPPLY
WATER TABLES
WATER VAPOUR
WATERWHEELS
WATHAWURUNG
WAVELENGTHS
WAYWARDNESS
WEALTHINESS
WEARABILITY
WEAR AND TEAR
WEATHERCOCK
WEATHER SHIP
WEATHER VANE
WEATHER-WISE
WEDDING RING
WEIGHBRIDGE
WEIGHTINESS
WELCOMENESS
WELDABILITY
WELL-ADAPTED
WELL-ADVISED
WELL AND GOOD
WELLBEHAVED
WELL-DEFINED
WELL-ENDOWED
WELL-FOUNDED
WELL-GROOMED
WELLINGTONS
WELL-MEANING
WELL-ROUNDED
WELLSPRINGS
WELL-WISHERS

WELL-WISHING
WELWITSCHIA
WENSLEYDALE
WESLEYANISM
WEST COUNTRY
WESTERNIZED
WESTERNMOST
WEST GERMANY
WEST LOTHIAN
WESTMINSTER
WESTPHALIAN
WET BLANKETS
WETTABILITY
WHEEDLINGLY
WHEELBARROW
WHEELCHAIRS
WHEELHOUSES
WHEELWRIGHT
WHEREABOUTS
WHERESOEVER
WHEREWITHAL
WHIFFLETREE
WHIMSICALLY
WHIPPING BOY
WHIRLYBIRDS
WHIST DRIVES
WHITEBOARDS
WHITE-COLLAR
WHITE DWARFS
WHITE HORSES
WHITE KNIGHT
WHITE METALS
WHITE PAPERS
WHITE PEPPER
WHITE RUSSIA
WHITE-SLAVER
WHITE SPIRIT
WHITETHROAT
WHITEWASHED
WHITEWASHER
WHITEWASHES
WHITSUNTIDE
WHOLE NUMBER
WHOLESALERS

WHOREHOUSES
WICKET GATES
WILDEBEESTS
WILDFOWLING
WILLINGNESS
WINDCHEATER
WINDFALL TAX
WINDJAMMERS
WINDOW BOXES
WINDOWPANES
WINDOW SHADE
WINDOWSILLS
WINDSCREENS
WINDSHIELDS
WIND-SUCKING
WIND-SURFERS
WIND-SURFING
WIND TUNNELS
WIND TURBINE
WINEBIBBING
WINNINGNESS
WINNING POST
WINNIPEGGER
WINSOMENESS
WINTERGREEN
WIRE NETTING
WIRE-TAPPING
WISDOM TEETH
WISDOM TOOTH
WISECRACKED
WISECRACKER
WISHFULNESS
WISTFULNESS
WITCHDOCTOR
WITCH-HUNTER
WITHDRAWALS
WITHDRAWING
WITHHOLDING
WITHOUT FAIL
WITHSTANDER
WITLESSNESS
WITNESSABLE
WIZARD PRANG
WOBBLE BOARD

WOLFISHNESS
WOLF WHISTLE
WOMANLINESS
WONDERFULLY
WONDERINGLY
WONDERLANDS
WOOD ALCOHOL
WOODCARVING
WOODCUTTERS
WOODCUTTING
WOODEN SPOON
WOODPECKERS
WOODTURNING
WOODWORKING
WOOLGROWING
WORD-PERFECT
WORKABILITY
WORKAHOLICS
WORKAHOLISM
WORKBASKETS
WORKBENCHES
WORKING DAYS
WORKING WEEK
WORKMANLIKE
WORKMANSHIP
WORKSTATION
WORLD-BEATER
WORLDLINESS
WORLDLY-WISE
WORLD POWERS
WORLD SERIES
WORSHIPABLE
WORSHIPPERS
WORSHIPPING
WORTHLESSLY
WRIGGLINGLY
WRITING DESK
WRONGDOINGS
WRONGHEADED
WROUGHT IRON

X

XANTHOPHYLL
X CHROMOSOME

XENOGENESIS
XENOGENETIC
XENOGLOSSIA
XENOMORPHIC
XEROGRAPHER
XEROGRAPHIC
XEROMORPHIC
XEROPHILOUS
XEROPHYTISM
XYLOCARPOUS
XYLOGRAPHER
XYLOGRAPHIC
XYLOPHAGOUS
XYLOPHONIST

Y

YACHTSWOMAN
Y CHROMOSOME
YELLOW FEVER
YELLOWKNIFE
YELLOW PAGES
YELLOWSTONE
YEVTUSHENKO
YOUTH HOSTEL
YTTRIFEROUS
YUGOSLAVIAN
YUWAALARAAY

Z

ZANTHOXYLUM
ZEALOUSNESS
ZESTFULNESS
ZHANGJIAKOU
ZINCIFEROUS
ZINCOGRAPHY
ZOOCHEMICAL
ZOOMORPHISM
ZOOPLANKTON
ZOOTECHNICS
ZYGOMORPHIC
ZYGOTICALLY
ZYMOGENESIS
ZYMOTICALLY

A
ABBREVIATING
ABBREVIATION
ABELIAN GROUP
ABOLITIONARY
ABOLITIONISM
ABOLITIONIST
ABOMINATIONS
ABORTIONISTS
ABORTION PILL
ABRACADABRAS
ABSENT MINDED
ABSENT-MINDED
ABSOLUTENESS
ABSOLUTE ZERO
ABSORPTIVITY
ABSTEMIOUSLY
ABSTRACTEDLY
ABSTRACTIONS
ABSTRACT NOUN
ABSTRUSENESS
ACADEMICALLY
ACADEMICIANS
ACANTHACEOUS
ACCELERATING
ACCELERATION
ACCELERATIVE
ACCELERATORS
ACCENTUATING
ACCENTUATION
ACCESS COURSE
ACCIACCATURA
ACCIDENTALLY
ACCLAMATIONS
ACCLIMATIZED
ACCLIMATIZER
ACCOMMODATED
ACCOMPANISTS
ACCOMPANYING
ACCOMPLISHED
ACCOMPLISHER
ACCORDIONIST
ACCOUPLEMENT
ACCOUTREMENT
ACCUMULATING
ACCUMULATION
ACCUMULATIVE
ACCUMULATORS
ACCUSATORIAL
ACETALDEHYDE
ACHIEVEMENTS

ACHILLES' HEEL
ACHILL ISLAND
ACHLAMYDEOUS
ACHLORHYDRIA
ACKNOWLEDGED
ACKNOWLEDGER
ACOUSTICALLY
ACQUAINTANCE
ACQUIESCENCE
ACQUISITIONS
ACROSTICALLY
ACTINOMETRIC
ACTINOMYCETE
ADAPTABILITY
ADDERS TONGUE
ADDITIONALLY
ADHESIVENESS
ADJECTIVALLY
ADJOURNMENTS
ADJUDICATING
ADJUDICATION
ADJUDICATORS
ADMINISTERED
ADMINISTRATE
ADSCITITIOUS
ADULTERATING
ADULTERATION
ADUMBRATIONS
ADVANTAGEOUS
ADVENTITIOUS
ADVISABILITY
AERIFICATION
AERODONETICS
AERODYNAMICS
AEROEMBOLISM
AEROMECHANIC
AERONAUTICAL
AERONEUROSIS
AESTHETICIAN
AESTHETICISM
AETHEREALITY
AETIOLOGICAL
AFFECTATIONS
AFFECTEDNESS
AFFECTIONATE
AFFILIATIONS
AFFINITY CARD
AFFIRMATIONS
AFFIRMATIVES
AFORETHOUGHT
AFRIKANERDOM

AFRO-AMERICAN
AFTERBURNING
AFTEREFFECTS
AFTER THE FACT
AFTERTHOUGHT
AGAMOGENESIS
AGAMOGENETIC
AGARICACEOUS
AGE OF CONSENT
AGGLOMERATED
AGGLUTINABLE
AGGLUTINOGEN
AGGRAVATIONS
AGGREGATIONS
AGGRESSIVELY
AGONY COLUMNS
AGORAPHOBICS
AGRICULTURAL
AGROFORESTRY
AILUROPHILIA
AILUROPHOBIA
AIR COMMODORE
AIR-CONDITION
AIRHOSTESSES
AIR TERMINALS
ALCOHOLICITY
ALHAMBRESQUE
ALICE SPRINGS
ALIENABILITY
ALIMENTATION
ALIMENTATIVE
ALKALIMETRIC
ALL-IMPORTANT
ALL-INCLUSIVE
ALLITERATION
ALLITERATIVE
ALLOMORPHISM
ALLUSIVENESS
ALMIGHTINESS
ALPHABETICAL
ALPHABETIZER
ALPHA-BLOCKER
ALPHANUMERIC
ALSTROEMERIA
ALTERABILITY
ALTERCATIONS
ALTERNATIONS
ALTERNATIVES
ALTHORP HOUSE
ALTIMETRICAL
AMALGAMATING

AMALGAMATION
AMATEURISHLY
AMBASSADRESS
AMBIDEXTROUS
AMBITENDENCY
AMBIVALENTLY
AMELIORATING
AMELIORATION
AMELIORATIVE
AMERICANISMS
AMERICANIZED
AMERICANIZER
AMITOTICALLY
AMORTIZATION
AMORTIZEMENT
AMPHETAMINES
AMPHIBRACHIC
AMPHICOELOUS
AMPHICTYONIC
AMPHIDIPLOID
AMPHISBAENIC
AMPHITHEATRE
AMPHITHECIUM
AMPHITROPOUS
AMPULLACEOUS
AMYGDALOIDAL
ANACHRONISMS
ANAESTHETICS
ANAESTHETIST
ANAESTHETIZE
ANAGOGICALLY
ANAGRAMMATIC
ANALPHABETIC
ANALYTICALLY
ANAMORPHOSIS
ANAPHRODISIA
ANAPHYLACTIC
ANARCHICALLY
ANASTIGMATIC
ANATHEMATIZE
ANATOMICALLY
ANCHORPERSON
ANCIEN REGIME
ANDROSTERONE
ANEMOGRAPHIC
ANEMOPHILOUS
ANESTHETISTS
ANESTHETIZED
ANGLO-INDIANS
ANGLOPHILIAC
ANGUILLIFORM

ANGULARITIES
ANIMADVERTED
ANIMAL RIGHTS
ANIMATRONICS
ANNEXATIONAL
ANNIHILATING
ANNIHILATION
ANNIHILATIVE
ANNOUNCEMENT
ANNUNCIATION
ANNUNCIATIVE
ANTAGONISTIC
ANTAGONIZING
ANTANANARIVO
ANTECHAMBERS
ANTEDILUVIAN
ANTEMERIDIAN
ANTE MERIDIEM
ANTHOLOGICAL
ANTHOLOGISTS
ANTHROPOIDAL
ANTHROPOLOGY
ANTI-AIR-CRAFT
ANTICATALYST
ANTICIPATING
ANTICIPATION
ANTICIPATIVE
ANTICIPATORY
ANTICLERICAL
ANTICLIMAXES
ANTICYCLONES
ANTICYCLONIC
ANTIHALATION
ANTIMACASSAR
ANTIMAGNETIC
ANTINEUTRINO
ANTIPARALLEL
ANTIPARTICLE
ANTIPATHETIC
ANTIPERIODIC
ANTIQUARIANS
ANTIRACHITIC
ANTI-SEMITISM
ANTITHETICAL
ANTONOMASTIC
ANURADHAPURA
AORISTICALLY
APAGOGICALLY
APERIODICITY
APHRODISIACS
APICULTURIST

APLANOSPHERE
APOCHROMATIC
APOCYNACEOUS
APOGEOTROPIC
APOSTROPHIZE
APOTHECARIES
APPALACHIANS
APPARATCHIKS
APPARENTNESS
APPASSIONATO
APPEASEMENTS
APPELLATIONS
APPENDECTOMY
APPENDICITIS
APPENDICULAR
APPERCEPTION
APPERCEPTIVE
APPERTAINING
APPETIZINGLY
APPLAUDINGLY
APPLICATIONS
APPOGGIATURA
APPOINTMENTS
APPORTIONING
APPRAISINGLY
APPRECIATING
APPRECIATION
APPRECIATIVE
APPREHENDING
APPREHENSION
APPREHENSIVE
APPRENTICING
APPROACHABLE
APPROPRIABLE
APPROPRIATED
APPROXIMATED
APPURTENANCE
A PRETTY PENNY
APRON STRINGS
AQUICULTURAL
ARBITRAGEURS
ARBORESCENCE
ARBORIZATION
ARCHDEACONRY
ARCHDIOCESAN
ARCHDIOCESES
ARCHEOLOGIES
ARCHESPORIAL
ARCHETYPICAL
ARCHIPELAGIC
ARCHIPELAGOS

ARCHITECTURE
ARCHOPLASMIC
ARCTIC CIRCLE
ARGILLACEOUS
ARISTOCRATIC
ARMOURED CARS
ARMOUR-PLATED
AROMATHERAPY
AROMATICALLY
ARRAIGNMENTS
ARRANGEMENTS
ARSENOPYRITE
ARTESIAN WELL
ARTHROPODOUS
ARTHROSPORIC
ARTICULATELY
ARTICULATING
ARTICULATION
ARTICULATORY
ARTIFICIALLY
ARTILLERYMAN
ARTISTICALLY
ASCENSION DAY
ASCERTAINING
ASCOMYCETOUS
ASH WEDNESDAY
ASKING PRICES
ASPHYXIATING
ASPHYXIATION
ASSASSINATED
ASSEMBLY LINE
ASSEVERATING
ASSEVERATION
ASSIBILATION
ASSIGNATIONS
ASSIMILATING
ASSIMILATION
ASSIMILATIVE
ASSOCIATIONS
ASTONISHMENT
ASTOUNDINGLY
ASTRINGENTLY
ASTROBIOLOGY
ASTROCOMPASS
ASTROGEOLOGY
ASTROLOGICAL
ASTRONAUTICS
ASTRONOMICAL
ASTROPHYSICS
ASYMPTOMATIC
ASYNCHRONISM

ASYNCHRONOUS
ATHEROMATOUS
ATHLETE'S FOOT
ATHLETICALLY
ATHWARTSHIPS
ATLANTIC CITY
ATMOSPHERICS
ATOMIC ENERGY
ATTACHE CASES
ATTENBOROUGH
ATTESTATIONS
ATTESTED MILK
ATTITUDINIZE
ATTRACTIVELY
ATTRIBUTABLE
AUDIOLOGICAL
AUDIOMETRIST
AUGMENTATION
AUGMENTATIVE
AULD LANG SYNE
AUSCULTATION
AUSPICIOUSLY
AUSTRALASIAN
AUSTRONESIAN
AUTHENTICATE
AUTHENTICITY
AUTISTICALLY
AUTOANTIBODY
AUTOEXPOSURE
AUTOGRAPHING
AUTOHYPNOSIS
AUTOHYPNOTIC
AUTOMOBILIST
AUTONOMOUSLY
AUTOROTATION
AUTOXIDATION
AVAILABILITY
AVANT GARDISM
AVARICIOUSLY
AVICULTURIST
AVITAMINOSIS
AVOGADRO'S LAW
AWE-INSPIRING
AZATHIOPRINE

B

BABY CARRIAGE
BACCHANALIAN
BACKBENCHERS
BACKBREAKING
BACKHANDEDLY

BACK OF BEYOND
BACK PASSAGES
BACKPEDALING
BACKPEDALLED
BACKROOM BOYS
BACKSLAPPERS
BACKSLAPPING
BACKTRACKING
BACKWARDNESS
BACKWOODSMAN
BACKWOODSMEN
BACTERICIDAL
BACTERIOLOGY
BAGGAGE ROOMS
BAKING POWDER
BALANCED DIET
BALANCE SHEET
BALCONY SCENE
BALL BEARINGS
BALLOTTEMENT
BALNEOLOGIST
BALTIC STATES
BANDARANAIKE
BANDERILLERO
BANDJARMASIN
BANK ACCOUNTS
BANKER'S CARDS
BANKER'S ORDER
BANK HOLIDAYS
BANKRUPTCIES
BANTAMWEIGHT
BARBARIANISM
BARBARICALLY
BARBITURATES
BARLEY SUGARS
BARNSTORMERS
BARNSTORMING
BARORECEPTOR
BARQUISIMETO
BARRANQUILLA
BARREL ORGANS
BASIDIOSPORE
BASTARDIZING
BASTINADOING
BATAN ISLANDS
BATCH PROCESS
BATHING SUITS
BATHYSPHERES
BATTERING RAM
BATTLEFIELDS
BATTLE ROYALS

BEACH BUGGIES
BEACHCOMBERS
BEACONSFIELD
BEAT A RETREAT
BEATIFICALLY
BEAUTY QUEENS
BECHUANALAND
BEDAZZLEMENT
BEDFORDSHIRE
BEGGARLINESS
BEGRUDGINGLY
BEHAVIOURISM
BEHAVIOURIST
BELEAGUERING
BELGIAN CONGO
BELITTLEMENT
BELITTLINGLY
BELLETRISTIC
BELLIGERENCE
BELLIGERENCY
BELLIGERENTS
BELLY BUTTONS
BELLY DANCERS
BELLY-LANDING
BELOW THE BELT
BENEDICTINES
BENEDICTIONS
BENEFACTIONS
BENEFACTRESS
BENEFICENTLY
BENEFICIALLY
BENEVOLENTLY
BENZALDEHYDE
BENZOPHENONE
BENZOQUINONE
BEREAVEMENTS
BERWICKSHIRE
BESPECTACLED
BEVERLY HILLS
BEWILDERMENT
BEWITCHINGLY
BIAURICULATE
BIBLIOGRAPHY
BIBLIOMANIAC
BIBLIOPHILES
BICOLLATERAL
BIELSKO-BIALA
BIFLAGELLATE
BIFURCATIONS
BILHARZIASIS
BILINGUALISM

BILL OF HEALTH
BILL OF LADING
BILL OF RIGHTS
BIOCATALYTIC
BIOCHEMISTRY
BIODIVERSITY
BIOECOLOGIST
BIOFLAVONOID
BIOGEOGRAPHY
BIOGRAPHICAL
BIOLOGICALLY
BIOMECHANICS
BIONOMICALLY
BIOPHYSICIST
BIOSYNTHESIS
BIOSYNTHETIC
BIPROPELLANT
BIRDS-EYE VIEW
BIRD'S-EYE
 VIEW
BIRD-WATCHERS
BIREFRINGENT
BIRTH CONTROL
BISMUTHINITE
BLABBERMOUTH
BLACK AND BLUE
BLACKBALLING
BLACKBERRIES
BLACK COUNTRY
BLACKCURRANT
BLACK ECONOMY
BLACK ENGLISH
BLACKGUARDLY
BLACK-HEARTED
BLACKLEGGING
BLACKLISTING
BLACKMAILERS
BLACKMAILING
BLACK MUSLIMS
BLACK PUDDING
BLADDERWRACK
BLAENAU GWENT
BLAMEFULNESS
BLANK CHEQUES
BLARNEY STONE
BLAST FURNACE
BLASTODERMIC
BLASTOSPHERE
BLINDFOLDING
BLISSFULNESS
BLISTERINGLY

BLOCKBUSTERS
BLOCK LETTERS
BLOEMFONTEIN
BLOOD BROTHER
BLOODLETTING
BLOODSTAINED
BLOODSTREAMS
BLOODSUCKERS
BLOODTHIRSTY
BLOOD VESSELS
BLOODY-MINDED
BLUE-EYED BOYS
BLUESTOCKING
BLUNDERINGLY
BLUSTERINGLY
BOARDING CARD
BOASTFULNESS
BOBSLEIGHING
BODY LANGUAGE
BODY SNATCHER
BODY STOCKING
BOILING POINT
BOISTEROUSLY
BOLSTERINGLY
BOMBACACEOUS
BOMBARDMENTS
BOOBY-TRAPPED
BOOK-LEARNING
BOOMERANGING
BOROSILICATE
BOTTOM DRAWER
BOUGAINVILLE
BOUNCY CASTLE
BOWDLERIZING
BOWLING ALLEY
BOWLING GREEN
BRACHYLOGOUS
BRACKISHNESS
BRAINS TRUSTS
BRAIN SURGEON
BRAINTEASERS
BRAINWASHING
BREADWINNERS
BREAKFASTING
BREASTSTROKE
BREATHALYSER
BREATHALYZER
BREATHTAKING
BREECHLOADER
BREWERS YEAST
BRILLIANTINE

BRINKMANSHIP
BRISTLE-GRASS
BROADCASTERS
BROADCASTING
BRONCHOSCOPE
BRONCHOSCOPY
BRONCOBUSTER
BRONTOSAURUS
BRONZE MEDALS
BROTHERHOODS
BROTHER-IN-LAW
BROWNIE POINT
BUENAVENTURA
BUFFER STATES
BUFFER STOCKS
BULLDOG CLIPS
BULLET-HEADED
BULLFIGHTERS
BULLFIGHTING
BULLHEADEDLY
BULLSHITTING
BULL TERRIERS
BUNSEN BURNER
BUREAUCRATIC
BURGLAR ALARM
BURSERACEOUS
BUSINESSLIKE
BUSINESS SUIT
BUTTERSCOTCH
BUTTONHOLING
BUYER'S MARKET
BYELORUSSIAN

C

CABBAGE WHITE
CABIN CRUISER
CABINET-MAKER
CABLE RAILWAY
CACHINNATION
CAENOGENESIS
CAENOGENETIC
CALAMITOUSLY
CALCULATIONS
CALENDAR YEAR
CALIBRATIONS
CALISTHENICS
CALLIGRAPHER
CALLIGRAPHIC
CALLISTHENIC
CALL OF NATURE
CALORIMETRIC

CALUMNIATING
CALUMNIATION
CAMELOPARDUS
CAMI-KNICKERS
CAMOUFLAGING
CAMP FOLLOWER
CANALIZATION
CANCELLATION
CANDELABRUMS
CANDLESTICKS
CANDY-STRIPED
CANNIBALIZED
CANNON FODDER
CANONIZATION
CANTABRIGIAN
CANTANKEROUS
CAPABILITIES
CAPACITATION
CAPARISONNED
CAPE COLOURED
CAPE PROVINCE
CAPERCAILLIE
CAPILLACEOUS
CAPITAL GAINS
CAPITALIZING
CAPITULATING
CAPITULATION
CAPRICIOUSLY
CAPTIOUSNESS
CARAVANSERAI
CARBOHYDRATE
CARBONACEOUS
CARBON COPIES
CARBON DATING
CARBON PAPERS
CARBURETTORS
CARCINOGENIC
CARD-CARRYING
CARDIOGRAPHY
CARDIOLOGIST
CARDIOMEGALY
CARELESSNESS
CARIBBEAN SEA
CARICATURING
CARICATURIST
CARILLONNEUR
CARPETBAGGER
CARPET KNIGHT
CARPOLOGICAL
CARPOPHAGOUS
CARRIAGEWAYS

CARTE BLANCHE
CARTOGRAPHER
CARTOGRAPHIC
CARTWHEELING
CARVING FORKS
CARVING KNIFE
CASH AND CARRY
CASH REGISTER
CASTELLATION
CASTING VOTES
CATACHRESTIC
CATADIOPTRIC
CATASTROPHES
CATASTROPHIC
CATCHPHRASES
CATECHETICAL
CATEGORIZING
CATERPILLARS
CATERWAULING
CATS WHISKERS
CAULIFLOWERS
CAUSE CELEBRE
CAUTIOUSNESS
CAVEAT EMPTOR
CELEBRATIONS
CEMENT MIXERS
CENSORIOUSLY
CENTENARIANS
CENTRALIZING
CENTRAL KAROO
CENTREPIECES
CENTROCLINAL
CENTROSPHERE
CENTUPLICATE
CEPHALOMETER
CEPHALOMETRY
CEPHALOPODAN
CEPHALOPODIC
CEREMONIALLY
CEROGRAPHIST
CERRO DE PASCO
CERTIFICATED
CERTIFICATES
CHAIN LETTERS
CHAIN-SMOKERS
CHAIN-SMOKING
CHAIRMANSHIP
CHAIRPERSONS
CHAISE LONGUE
CHALCOGRAPHY
CHALCOPYRITE

CHAMBERLAINS
CHAMBERMAIDS
CHAMBER MUSIC
CHAMPIONSHIP
CHANGCHIAKOW
CHANGELESSLY
CHANGE OF LIFE
CHANGING ROOM
CHAPLAINCIES
CHAPTERHOUSE
CHARACTERFUL
CHARACTERIZE
CHARGE NURSES
CHARGE SHEETS
CHARLATANISM
CHARNEL HOUSE
CHASTISEMENT
CHASTITY BELT
CHATTERBOXES
CHAUFFEURING
CHAUVINISTIC
CHECKERBERRY
CHECKERBLOOM
CHEERFULNESS
CHEERLEADERS
CHEESEBURGER
CHEESEPARING
CHEESE-PARING
CHEFS D'OEUVRE
CHEMOSPHERIC
CHEMOTHERAPY
CHEMOTROPISM
.CHEQUERBOARD
CHERUBICALLY
CHESHIRE CATS
CHESTERFIELD
CHIAROSCUROS
CHIEF JUSTICE
CHIEF OF STAFF
CHILDBEARING
CHILD BENEFIT
CHILDISHNESS
CHILDMINDERS
CHILDMINDING
CHILD PRODIGY
CHILPANCINGO
CHIMNEYPIECE
CHIMNEYSTACK
CHIMNEYSWEEP
CHIROGRAPHER
CHIROGRAPHIC

CHIROPODISTS   CIRCULAR SAWS   CLOSING TIMES   COLONIZATION
CHIROPRACTIC   CIRCUMCISING   CLOTHESHORSE   COLORIMETRIC
CHIROPRACTOR   CIRCUMCISION   CLOTHESLINES   COLOURLESSLY
CHITCHATTING   CIRCUMFLUOUS   CLOTHES-PRESS   COLOUR SCHEME
CHITTERLINGS   CIRCUMFUSION   CLOTTED CREAM   COLUMNIATION
CHIVALROUSLY   CIRCUMNUTATE   CLOVE HITCHES   COMBINATIONS
CHLORAMBUCIL   CIRCUMSCRIBE   CLOVERLEAVES   COMBUSTIBLES
CHLORENCHYMA   CIRCUMSTANCE   CLOWNISHNESS   COME A CROPPER
CHLORINATING   CIRCUMVENTED   CLUB SANDWICH   COME-UPPANCES
CHLORINATION   CIRCUMVENTER   CLUSTER BOMBS   COMFORTINGLY
CHLOROFORMED   CIRROCUMULUS   COACERVATION   COMMANDEERED
CHLOROHYDRIN   CIRROSTRATUS   COACHBUILDER   COMMANDMENTS
CHLOROPICRIN   CITIZENS' BAND   COACH STATION   COMMEMORATED
CHOCOLATE BOX   CITRICULTURE   COALITIONIST   COMMEMORATOR
CHOIRMASTERS   CIVIL DEFENCE   COALSCUTTLES   COMMENCEMENT
CHOIR SCHOOLS   CIVILIZATION   COBBLESTONES   COMMENDATION
CHOLERICALLY   CIVIL LIBERTY   COCKFIGHTING   COMMENDATORY
CHONDRIOSOME   CIVIL SERVANT   COCKLESHELLS   COMMENSALISM
CHOREOGRAPHS   CIVIL SERVICE   COCONUT SHIES   COMMENSURATE
CHOREOGRAPHY   CLAIRVOYANCE   COCOS ISLANDS   COMMENTARIAL
CHOROGRAPHER   CLAIRVOYANTS   CODEPENDENCY   COMMENTARIES
CHOROGRAPHIC   CLANGOROUSLY   CODIFICATION   COMMENTATING
CHRISTCHURCH   CLANNISHNESS   COEFFICIENTS   COMMENTATORS
CHRISTENINGS   CLAPPERBOARD   COELENTERATE   COMMERCIALLY
CHRISTIAN ERA   CLARINETTIST   COENESTHESIA   COMMISERATED
CHRISTIANITY   CLASS ACTIONS   COENESTHESIS   COMMISERATOR
CHRISTIANIZE   CLASSICALITY   COENESTHETIC   COMMISSARIAL
CHRISTMAS BOX   CLASSICISTIC   COERCIVENESS   COMMISSARIAT
CHRISTMAS EVE   CLASSIFIABLE   COFFEE BREAKS   COMMISSARIES
CHRIST'S-THORN   CLASSIFIED AD   COFFEE HOUSES   COMMISSIONAL
CHROMATICISM   CLAUDICATION   COFFEE KLATCH   COMMISSIONED
CHROMATICITY   CLEAR-SIGHTED   COFFEE TABLES   COMMISSIONER
CHROMATOGRAM   CLEFT PALATES   COHABITATION   COMMITTEEMAN
CHROME YELLOW   CLERESTORIED   COHESIVENESS   COMMITTEEMEN
CHROMOPHORIC   CLERESTORIES   COINCIDENCES   COMMODIOUSLY
CHROMOSPHERE   CLERK OF WORKS   COINCIDENTAL   COMMON MARKET
CHRONOGRAPHS   CLIENT STATES   COLD SHOULDER   COMMONPLACES
CHRONOLOGIES   CLIFFHANGERS   COLEOPTEROUS   COMMONWEALTH
CHRONOLOGIST   CLIFFHANGING   COLLABORATED   COMMUNICABLE
CHRONOMETERS   CLIMACTERICS   COLLABORATOR   COMMUNICABLY
CHRONOMETRIC   CLIMATICALLY   COLLECTIVELY   COMMUNICANTS
CHRONOSCOPIC   CLIMATOLOGIC   COLLECTIVISM   COMMUNICATED
CHURCHWARDEN   CLIMBING IRON   COLLECTIVIST   COMMUNICATOR
CHURLISHNESS   CLINKER-BUILT   COLLECTIVITY   COMMUNIONIST
CHURRASCARIA   CLIQUISHNESS   COLLECTIVIZE   COMMUTATIONS
CHYMOTRYPSIN   CLODDISHNESS   COLLECTORATE   COMPACT DISCS
CINCHONIDINE   CLOSE-CROPPED   COLLOCATIONS   COMPANIONATE
CINEMATHEQUE   CLOSED SEASON   COLLOIDALITY   COMPANIONWAY
CIRCUITOUSLY   CLOSE-GRAINED   COLLOQUIALLY   COMPARTMENTS
CIRCULARIZED   CLOSE SEASONS   COLLYWOBBLES   COMPASS POINT
CIRCULARIZER   CLOSING PRICE   COLONIALISTS   COMPATRIOTIC

COMPELLINGLY
COMPENSATING
COMPENSATION
COMPENSATIVE
COMPENSATORY
COMPETITIONS
COMPILATIONS
COMPLACENTLY
COMPLAINANTS
COMPLAISANCE
COMPLEMENTED
COMPLETENESS
COMPLEXITIES
COMPLICATING
COMPLICATION
COMPLIMENTED
COMPONENTIAL
COMPOSITIONS
COMPOS MENTIS
COMPREHENDED
COMPRESSIBLE
COMPROMISING
COMPTROLLERS
COMPULSIVELY
COMPULSORILY
COMPUNCTIOUS
COMPUTATIONS
COMPUTERIZED
CONCATENATED
CONCELEBRATE
CONCENTRATED
CONCENTRATES
CONCENTRATOR
CONCEPTIONAL
CONCEPTUALLY
CONCERTGOERS
CONCERT GRAND
CONCERTINAED
CONCERT PITCH
CONCHIFEROUS
CONCHOLOGIST
CONCILIATING
CONCILIATION
CONCILIATORS
CONCILIATORY
CONCLUSIVELY
CONCOMITANCE
CONCOMITANTS
CONCORDANCES
CONCRESCENCE
CONCUPISCENT

CONCURRENCES
CONCURRENTLY
CONDEMNATION
CONDEMNATORY
CONDENSATION
CONDESCENDED
CONDITIONERS
CONDITIONING
CONDOMINIUMS
CONDUCTIVITY
CONDUPLICATE
CONFABULATED
CONFABULATOR
CONFECTIONER
CONFEDERATED
CONFEDERATES
CONFERENTIAL
CONFESSIONAL
CONFIDENTIAL
CONFINEMENTS
CONFIRMATION
CONFIRMATORY
CONFISCATING
CONFISCATION
CONFISCATORY
CONFORMATION
CONFOUNDEDLY
CONFRATERNAL
CONFUCIANISM
CONFUCIANIST
CONFUTATIONS
CONGENIALITY
CONGENITALLY
CONGLOBATION
CONGLOMERATE
CONGLUTINANT
CONGLUTINATE
CONGRATULATE
CONGREGATING
CONGREGATION
CONGREGATIVE
CONIDIOPHORE
CONJECTURING
CONJUGATIONS
CONJUNCTIONS
CONJUNCTIVAL
CONJUNCTIVES
CONJUNCTURAL
CONJUNCTURES
CONNECTIONAL
CONNING TOWER

CONNOISSEURS
CONNOTATIONS
CONNUBIALITY
CONQUISTADOR
CONSCIONABLE
CONSCRIPTING
CONSCRIPTION
CONSECRATING
CONSECRATION
CONSECRATORY
CONSENTIENCE
CONSEQUENCES
CONSEQUENTLY
CONSERVATION
CONSERVATISM
CONSERVATIVE
CONSERVATORY
CONSIDERABLE
CONSIDERABLY
CONSIGNATION
CONSIGNMENTS
CONSISTENTLY
CONSISTORIAL
CONSOCIATION
CONSOLATIONS
CONSOLIDATED
CONSOLIDATOR
CONSPECTUSES
CONSPIRACIES
CONSPIRATORS
CONSTABULARY
CONSTIPATION
CONSTITUENCY
CONSTITUENTS
CONSTITUTING
CONSTITUTION
CONSTITUTIVE
CONSTRAINING
CONSTRICTING
CONSTRICTION
CONSTRICTIVE
CONSTRICTORS
CONSTRUCTING
CONSTRUCTION
CONSTRUCTIVE
CONSTRUCTORS
CONSULTATION
CONSULTATIVE
CONSUMMATELY
CONSUMMATING
CONSUMMATION

CONSUMMATIVE
CONSUMPTIONS
CONSUMPTIVES
CONTAGIOUSLY
CONTAINERIZE
CONTAMINANTS
CONTAMINATED
CONTAMINATOR
CONTEMPLATED
CONTEMPLATOR
CONTEMPORARY
CONTEMPORIZE
CONTEMPTIBLE
CONTEMPTIBLY
CONTEMPTUOUS
CONTENTIONAL
CONTERMINOUS
CONTESTATION
CONTEXTUALLY
CONTIGUOUSLY
CONTINENTALS
CONTINGENTLY
CONTINUALITY
CONTINUATION
CONTINUATIVE
CONTINUINGLY
CONTINUOUSLY
CONTORTIONAL
CONTRABASSES
CONTRACTIBLE
CONTRACTIONS
CONTRADICTED
CONTRADICTER
CONTRAPTIONS
CONTRAPUNTAL
CONTRARINESS
CONTRARIWISE
CONTRAVENING
CONTRIBUTING
CONTRIBUTION
CONTRIBUTIVE
CONTRIBUTORS
CONTRIBUTORY
CONTRIVANCES
CONTROLLABLE
CONTROVERTER
CONTUMACIOUS
CONTUMELIOUS
CONURBATIONS
CONVALESCENT
CONVALESCING

CONVECTIONAL
CONVENIENCES
CONVENIENTLY
CONVENTICLES
CONVENTIONAL
CONVERGENCES
CONVERSATION
CONVERSIONAL
CONVERTIBLES
CONVEYANCING
CONVEYER BELT
CONVINCINGLY
CONVIVIALITY
CONVOCATIONS
CONVOLUTEDLY
CONVOLUTIONS
CONVULSIVELY
COOKERY BOOKS
COOKING APPLE
COOPERATIVES
COORDINATELY
COORDINATING
COORDINATION
COPOLYMERIZE
COPROPHAGOUS
COPROPHILOUS
COPTIC CHURCH
COQUETTISHLY
CORDUROY ROAD
CORESPONDENT
CORNERSTONES
CORN EXCHANGE
CORNISH PASTY
COROLLACEOUS
CORPORALSHIP
CORPORATIONS
CORPOREALITY
CORRECTITUDE
CORRECTIVELY
CORRELATIONS
CORRELATIVES
CORRESPONDED
CORROBORATED
CORROBORATOR
CORRUGATIONS
COSMETICALLY
COSMETICIANS
COSMOLOGICAL
COSMOPOLITAN
COSTERMONGER
COST OF LIVING

COST THE EARTH
COTYLEDONARY
COTYLEDONOUS
COUNTENANCED
COUNTENANCES
COUNTERACTED
COUNTERBLAST
COUNTERCHECK
COUNTERCLAIM
COUNTERFOILS
COUNTERPANES
COUNTERPARTS
COUNTERPARTY
COUNTERPOINT
COUNTERPOISE
COUNTERPROOF
COUNTERPUNCH
COUNTERSHAFT
COUNTERSIGNS
COUNTERTENOR
COUNTRY CLUBS
COUNTRY DANCE
COUNTRY SEATS
COUNTY COURTS
COUPS DE GRACE
COURAGEOUSLY
COURT MARTIAL
COURT-MARTIAL
COVENT GARDEN
COVER CHARGES
COVERED WAGON
COVETOUSNESS
COWARDLINESS
CRACKBRAINED
CRANIOLOGIST
CRANIOMETRIC
CRASH BARRIER
CRASH HELMETS
CRASH LANDING
CREEPY-CRAWLY
CREMATIONISM
CREMATIONIST
CREMATORIUMS
CRENELLATION
CRISSCROSSED
CRISSCROSSES
CROP-SPRAYING
CROSSBENCHER
CROSS BENCHER
CROSSBENCHES
CROSSCHECKED

CROSS-COUNTRY
CROSSCURRENT
CROSS-DRESSER
CROSS-EXAMINE
CROSS-GRAINED
CROSSPATCHES
CROSS-SECTION
CROWNED HEADS
CROWN PRINCES
CRUSH BARRIER
CRYOPLANKTON
CRYPTANALYST
CRYPTOGRAPHY
CRYPTOLOGIST
CRYSTAL BALLS
CRYSTAL CLEAR
CRYSTAL GAZER
CRYSTALLITIC
CRYSTALLIZED
CUCKOO CLOCKS
CUMULATIVELY
CUMULONIMBUS
CUPBOARD LOVE
CURARIZATION
CURATORSHIPS
CURMUDGEONLY
CURTAILMENTS
CURTAIN CALLS
CURVACEOUSLY
CUT AND THRUST
CUTTLEFISHES
CYCLOPENTANE
CYCLOSTOMATE
CYCLOSTYLING
CYSTICERCOID
CYTOCHEMICAL
CYTOGENETICS
CYTOSKELETON
CYTOTAXONOMY
CZECHOSLOVAK

D

DACTYLICALLY
DAEMONICALLY
DAIRY FARMERS
DANGER SIGNAL
DANISH PASTRY
DARBY AND JOAN
DAY NURSERIES
DEACTIVATION
DEAF-MUTENESS

DEATH FUTURES
DEATH RATTLES
DEATH WARRANT
DEBARKATIONS
DEBAUCHERIES
DEBILITATING
DEBILITATION
DEBILITATIVE
DEBT OF HONOUR
DECALCOMANIA
DECALESCENCE
DECAPITATING
DECAPITATION
DECARBONIZER
DECASYLLABIC
DECASYLLABLE
DECELERATING
DECELERATION
DECENTRALIST
DECENTRALIZE
DECIMALIZING
DECIPHERABLE
DECIPHERMENT
DECISION TREE
DECISIVENESS
DECLAMATIONS
DECLARATIONS
DECLASSIFIED
DECLENSIONAL
DECLINATIONS
DECLINOMETER
DECOLLETAGES
DECOLONIZING
DECOLORATION
DECOMMISSION
DECOMPOSABLE
DECOMPRESSED
DECONGESTANT
DECONTROLLED
DECORATIVELY
DECORTICATOR
DEDUCIBILITY
DEERSTALKERS
DE-ESCALATING
DE-ESCALATION
DEFAMATORILY
DEFICIENCIES
DEFINITENESS
DEFINITIONAL
DEFINITIVELY
DEFLAGRATION

DEFLATIONARY	DENICOTINIZE	DESPOLIATION	DICTIONARIES
DEFLATIONIST	DENOMINATING	DESPONDENTLY	DIDACTICALLY
DEFLOCCULATE	DENOMINATION	DESPOTICALLY	DIENCEPHALIC
DEFORMATIONS	DENOMINATIVE	DESQUAMATION	DIENCEPHALON
DEFORMEDNESS	DENOMINATORS	DESSERTSPOON	DIESEL ENGINE
DEFRAUDATION	DENOUNCEMENT	DESSERT WINES	DIETETICALLY
DEGENERATING	DENSITOMETER	DESTABILIZED	DIFFERENTIAL
DEGENERATION	DENSITOMETRY	DESTINATIONS	DIFFICULTIES
DEGENERATIVE	DENTAL PLATES	DESTRUCTIBLE	DIGITAL VIDEO
DEGRADATIONS	DENTILINGUAL	DESULPHURIZE	DIGITIZATION
DEHUMANIZING	DENUNCIATION	DETERIORATED	DIGRESSIONAL
DEHUMIDIFIER	DENUNCIATORY	DETERMINABLE	DILAPIDATION
DEJECTEDNESS	DEONTOLOGIST	DETERMINANTS	DILATABILITY
DELAMINATION	DEPARTMENTAL	DETHRONEMENT	DILATATIONAL
DELIBERATELY	DEPENDENCIES	DETOXICATION	DILATOMETRIC
DELIBERATING	DEPILATORIES	DETRUNCATION	DILATORINESS
DELIBERATION	DEPOLITICIZE	DETUMESCENCE	DILETTANTISH
DELIBERATIVE	DEPOPULATING	DEUTERANOPIA	DILETTANTISM
DELICATESSEN	DEPOPULATION	DEUTERANOPIC	DILLYDALLIED
DELIGHTFULLY	DEPORTATIONS	DEUTOPLASMIC	DIMINISHABLE
DELIMITATION	DEPOSITORIES	DEUTSCHE MARK	DIMINISHMENT
DELIMITATIVE	DEPRAVEDNESS	DEUTSCHMARKS	DINING TABLES
DELIQUESCENT	DEPRECIATING	DEVALUATIONS	DINNER JACKET
DELITESCENCE	DEPRECIATION	DEVELOPMENTS	DIOPTRICALLY
DELTIOLOGIST	DEPRECIATORY	DEVIATIONISM	DIPHTHERITIC
DEMAGNETIZED	DEPREDATIONS	DEVIATIONIST	DIPHTHONGIZE
DEMAGNETIZER	DEPRESSINGLY	DEVILISHNESS	DIPLOBLASTIC
DEMENTEDNESS	DEPRIVATIONS	DEVIL-MAY-CARE	DIPLOCARDIAC
DEMILITARIZE	DERACINATION	DEVITALIZING	DIPLOMATISTS
DEMIMONDAINE	DERANGEMENTS	DEXTROGYRATE	DIPROPELLANT
DEMOCRATIZED	DEREGULATING	DIABOLICALLY	DIPSOMANIACS
DEMODULATION	DEREGULATION	DIAGEOTROPIC	DIRECT DEBITS
DEMOGRAPHERS	DERELICTIONS	DIAGRAMMATIC	DIRECT OBJECT
DEMOGRAPHICS	DERESTRICTED	DIALECTICIAN	DIRECTORATES
DEMOLISHMENT	DERISIVENESS	DIALECTOLOGY	DIRECTORSHIP
DEMONETIZING	DERIVATIONAL	DIALLING CODE	DIRECT SPEECH
DEMONIACALLY	DERIVATIVELY	DIALLING TONE	DIRIGIBILITY
DEMONOLOGIST	DERMATOPHYTE	DIALYTICALLY	DISABILITIES
DEMONOPOLIZE	DEROGATORILY	DIAMAGNETISM	DISABLEMENTS
DEMONSTRABLE	DESALINATING	DIAPOPHYSIAL	DISACCHARIDE
DEMONSTRABLY	DESALINATION	DIARTHRODIAL	DISADVANTAGE
DEMONSTRATED	DESCRIPTIONS	DIASTROPHISM	DISAFFECTION
DEMONSTRATOR	DESEGREGATED	DIATHERMANCY	DISAFFILIATE
DEMOTIVATING	DESENSITIZED	DIATOMACEOUS	DISAGGREGATE
DEMOTIVATION	DESENSITIZER	DIATONICALLY	DISAGREEABLE
DEMYSTIFYING	DESERVEDNESS	DIAZOMETHANE	DISAGREEABLY
DENATURALIZE	DESIDERATION	DIBRANCHIATE	DISAGREEMENT
DENATURATION	DESIDERATIVE	DICARBOXYLIC	DISALLOWABLE
DENBIGHSHIRF	DESIGNATIONS	DICHROMATISM	DISALLOWANCE
DENDROLOGIST	DESIRABILITY	DICHROSCOPIC	DISAMBIGUATE
DENG XIAOPING	DESPAIRINGLY	DICTATORSHIP	DISANNULMENT

DISAPPEARING	DISESTABLISH	DISSEMINATED	DOMESTICABLE
DISAPPOINTED	DISFORESTING	DISSEMINATOR	DOMESTICALLY
DISAPPOINTER	DISFRANCHISE	DISSENTIENCE	DOMESTICATED
DISAPPROVING	DISGORGEMENT	DISSERTATION	DOMESTICATOR
DISARRANGING	DISGUSTINGLY	DISSEVERANCE	DOMINO EFFECT
DISASSEMBLER	DISHEVELMENT	DISSIMILARLY	DONKEY JACKET
DISASSOCIATE	DISHONOURING	DISSIMULATED	DONKEYS YEARS
DISASTROUSLY	DISINCENTIVE	DISSIMULATOR	DONKEY'S YEARS
DISBELIEVERS	DISINFECTANT	DISSOCIATING	DOORKNOCKERS
DISBELIEVING	DISINFECTING	DISSOCIATION	DOORSTEPPING
DISBURSEMENT	DISINFECTION	DISSOCIATIVE	DOORSTOPPERS
DISCIPLESHIP	DISINFLATION	DISSOLUTIONS	DORSIVENTRAL
DISCIPLINARY	DISINGENUOUS	DISSYMMETRIC	DORSOVENTRAL
DISCIPLINING	DISINHERITED	DISTEMPERING	DOUBLE-ACTING
DISCLAMATION	DISINTEGRATE	DISTILLATION	DOUBLE AGENTS
DISCOGRAPHER	DISINTERMENT	DISTILLATORY	DOUBLE BASSES
DISCOLOURING	DISINTERRING	DISTILLERIES	DOUBLE-BEDDED
DISCOMFITING	DISJOINTEDLY	DISTINCTIONS	DOUBLE BLUFFS
DISCOMFITURE	DISLOCATIONS	DISTINCTNESS	DOUBLE DAGGER
DISCOMMODING	DISLODGEMENT	DISTORTIONAL	DOUBLE-DATING
DISCOMMODITY	DISLOYALTIES	DISTRACTEDLY	DOUBLE DEALER
DISCOMPOSING	DISMEMBERING	DISTRACTIBLE	DOUBLE-DEALER
DISCOMPOSURE	DISMOUNTABLE	DISTRACTIONS	DOUBLE-DECKER
DISCONCERTED	DISOBEDIENCE	DISTRAINABLE	DOUBLE-DOTTED
DISCONNECTED	DISOPERATION	DISTRAINMENT	DOUBLE FAULTS
DISCONNECTER	DISORGANIZED	DISTRIBUTARY	DOUBLE-GLAZED
DISCONSOLATE	DISORGANIZER	DISTRIBUTING	DOUBLE-HEADER
DISCONTENTED	DISORIENTATE	DISTRIBUTION	DOUBLE-PARKED
DISCONTINUED	DISPENSARIES	DISTRIBUTIVE	DOUBLE-TALKED
DISCORDANTLY	DISPENSATION	DISTRIBUTORS	DOUBLE-TONGUE
DISCOTHEQUES	DISPENSATORY	DISTURBANCES	DOUGHNUTTING
DISCOUNTABLE	DISPIRITEDLY	DITTOGRAPHIC	DOWN PAYMENTS
DISCOURAGING	DISPLACEABLE	DIURETICALLY	DOWNSHIFTING
DISCOURTEOUS	DISPLACEMENT	DIVARICATION	DOWN SHIFTING
DISCOVERABLE	DISPOSITIONS	DIVERSIFYING	DRACONIANISM
DISCOVERTURE	DISPOSSESSED	DIVERSIONARY	DRACONICALLY
DISCREDITING	DISPOSSESSOR	DIVERTICULAR	DRAG ONES FEET
DISCREETNESS	DISPUTATIONS	DIVERTICULUM	DRAMATICALLY
DISCRETENESS	DISPUTATIOUS	DIVERTIMENTO	DRAMATIZABLE
DISCRIMINANT	DISQUALIFIED	DIVINGBOARDS	DRAUGHTBOARD
DISCRIMINATE	DISQUALIFIER	DIVINIZATION	DRAWING BOARD
DISCURSIVELY	DISQUIETEDLY	DIVISIBILITY	DRAWING ROOMS
DISCUSSIONAL	DISQUISITION	DIVISIVENESS	DREADFULNESS
DISDAINFULLY	DISREGARDFUL	DOCTRINALITY	DREADNOUGHTS
DISEMBARKING	DISREGARDING	DOCTRINARIAN	DRESS CIRCLES
DISEMBARRASS	DISRELISHING	DODECAHEDRAL	DRESSING DOWN
DISEMBOWELED	DISREPUTABLE	DODECAHEDRON	DRESSING-DOWN
DISENCHANTED	DISREPUTABLY	DODECAPHONIC	DRESSING GOWN
DISENCHANTER	DISRUPTIVELY	DOGMATICALLY	DRESSING ROOM
DISENDOWMENT	DISSATISFIED	DO-IT-YOURSELF	DRY BATTERIES
DISENTANGLED	DISSEMBLANCE	DOMESDAY BOOK	DUCKING STOOL

DUMBFOUNDING
DUMORTIERITE
DUTCH AUCTION
DUTCH COURAGE
DUTY-FREE SHOP
DWARFISHNESS
DYNAMOMETRIC
DYSTELEOLOGY

E

EAGER BEAVERS
EARSPLITTING
EARTHSHAKING
EAST AYRSHIRE
EAST BERLINER
EASTER CACTUS
EASTER ISLAND
EASTER-LEDGES
EAST FLANDERS
EAST GERMANIC
EAST KILBRIDE
EASY ON THE
  EYE
EAT HUMBLE PIE
EATING APPLES
EAT ONES WORDS
EAU DE COLOGNE
EAVESDROPPED
EAVESDROPPER
EBULLIOSCOPY
ECCENTRICITY
ECCLESIASTIC
ECCLESIOLOGY
ECHINOCOCCUS
ECHINODERMAL
ECHOLOCATION
ECLECTICALLY
ECLIPTICALLY
ECOLOGICALLY
ECONOMETRICS
ECONOMICALLY
ECOTERRORIST
ECOTYPICALLY
ECSTATICALLY
ECTOPARASITE
ECUMENICALLY
EDACIOUSNESS
EDITORIALIST
EDITORIALIZE
EDULCORATION
EFFECTUALITY

EFFECTUATING
EFFECTUATION
EFFEMINATELY
EFFERVESCENT
EFFERVESCING
EFFLORESCENT
EFFORTLESSLY
EFFUSIOMETER
EFFUSIVENESS
EGOISTICALLY
EGYPTOLOGIST
EISTEDDFODIC
EJACULATIONS
EJECTOR SEATS
ELABORATIONS
ELASMOBRANCH
ELASTICATION
ELASTIC BANDS
ELECTRICALLY
ELECTRIC EYES
ELECTRICIANS
ELECTRIFYING
ELECTROCUTED
ELECTROGRAPH
ELECTROLYSER
ELECTROLYSIS
ELECTROLYTES
ELECTROLYTIC
ELECTROMETER
ELECTROMETRY
ELECTRONVOLT
ELECTROPHONE
ELECTROPLATE
ELECTROSCOPE
ELECTROSHOCK
ELECTROTONIC
ELECTROTONUS
ELECTROTYPER
ELEEMOSYNARY
ELEPHANT'S-EAR
ELEVENTH HOUR
ELIZABETHANS
ELLIPTICALLY
ELOCUTIONARY
ELOCUTIONIST
ELOQUENTNESS
ELYSEE PALACE
EMANCIPATING
EMANCIPATION
EMANCIPATIVE
EMANCIPATORY

EMARGINATION
EMASCULATING
EMASCULATION
EMASCULATIVE
EMBARKATIONS
EMBARRASSING
EMBELLISHING
EMBEZZLEMENT
EMBITTERMENT
EMBLAZONMENT
EMBRANCHMENT
EMBROCATIONS
EMBROIDERIES
EMBROIDERING
EMBRYOLOGIST
EMIGRATIONAL
EMOTIONALISM
EMOTIONALIST
EMOTIONALITY
EMOTIONALIZE
EMPATHICALLY
EMPHATICALLY
EMPLACEMENTS
EMULSIFIABLE
ENANTIOMORPH
ENARTHRODIAL
ENCEPHALITIC
ENCEPHALITIS
ENCHANTMENTS
ENCIPHERMENT
ENCIRCLEMENT
ENCLITICALLY
ENCOMPASSING
ENCOUNTERING
ENCROACHMENT
ENCRUSTATION
ENCUMBRANCER
ENCUMBRANCES
ENCYCLOPEDIA
ENCYCLOPEDIC
ENDAMAGEMENT
ENDANGERMENT
ENDEAVOURING
ENDOCARDITIC
ENDOCARDITIS
ENDOMORPHISM
ENDOPARASITE
ENDORSEMENTS
ENDOSKELETAL
ENDOSKELETON
ENDOTHELIOID

ENDOTHELIOMA
ENDOTHERMISM
ENDURABILITY
ENERGETICIST
ENFEEBLEMENT
ENFRANCHISED
ENFRANCHISER
ENGAGINGNESS
ENGENDERMENT
ENGINE DRIVER
ENGLISH HORNS
ENGLISHWOMAN
ENGRAFTATION
ENGROSSINGLY
ENHANCEMENTS
ENLARGEMENTS
ENLIGHTENING
ENLIVENINGLY
ENORMOUSNESS
ENSHRINEMENT
ENSILABILITY
ENTANGLEMENT
ENTEROKINASE
ENTERPRISING
ENTERTAINERS
ENTERTAINING
ENTHRONEMENT
ENTHUSIASTIC
ENTHYMEMATIC
ENTICINGNESS
ENTOMOLOGIST
ENTOMOLOGIZE
ENTRANCEMENT
ENTRANCINGLY
ENTREATINGLY
ENTRENCHMENT
ENTREPRENEUR
ENUMERATIONS
ENVIABLENESS
ENVIRONMENTS
ENVISAGEMENT
ENZOOTICALLY
ENZYMOLOGIST
EOSINOPHILIC
EPENCEPHALIC
EPENCEPHALON
EPHEMERALITY
EPICUREANISM
EPICYCLOIDAL
EPIDEMIOLOGY
EPIGLOTTIDES

EPIGLOTTISES	EUPHORICALLY	EXOPHTHALMOS	EXTORTIONIST
EPIGRAMMATIC	EUSTATICALLY	EXORBITANTLY	EXTRADITABLE
EPIMORPHOSIS	EVANGELISTIC	EXOTERICALLY	EXTRADITIONS
EPISCOPALIAN	EVANGELIZING	EXPANSIONARY	EXTRAMARITAL
EPISCOPALISM	EVAPORIMETER	EXPANSIONISM	EXTRAMUNDANE
EPISODICALLY	EVENING DRESS	EXPANSIONIST	EXTRANEOUSLY
EPISTEMOLOGY	EVEN-TEMPERED	EXPATRIATING	EXTRANUCLEAR
EPITHALAMIUM	EVENTFULNESS	EXPATRIATION	EXTRAPOLATED
EQUALITARIAN	EVERY MAN JACK	EXPECTATIONS	EXTRAPOLATOR
EQUALIZATION	EVISCERATING	EXPECTORATED	EXTRASENSORY
EQUATABILITY	EVISCERATION	EXPECTORATOR	EXTRAUTERINE
EQUESTRIENNE	EVOLUTIONARY	EXPEDIENTIAL	EXTRAVAGANCE
EQUIDISTANCE	EVOLUTIONISM	EXPERIENCING	EXTRAVAGANZA
EQUILIBRATOR	EVOLUTIONIST	EXPERIENTIAL	EXTROVERSION
EQUIPOLLENCE	EXACERBATING	EXPERIMENTAL	EXTROVERSIVE
EQUIVALENTLY	EXACERBATION	EXPERIMENTED	EYEWITNESSES
EQUIVOCALITY	EXACTINGNESS	EXPERIMENTER	
EQUIVOCATING	EXAGGERATING	EXPERT SYSTEM	**F**
EQUIVOCATION	EXAGGERATION	EXPLANATIONS	FABRICATIONS
EQUIVOCATORY	EXAGGERATIVE	EXPLANTATION	FABULOUSNESS
ERGASTOPLASM	EXAMINATIONS	EXPLICITNESS	FACELESSNESS
ERYTHROBLAST	EXASPERATING	EXPLOITATION	FACILITATING
ERYTHROCYTIC	EXASPERATION	EXPLOITATIVE	FACILITATION
ERYTHROMYCIN	EXCELLENCIES	EXPLORATIONS	FACILITATIVE
ESCAPE CLAUSE	EXCHANGEABLE	EXPOSITIONAL	FACTIONALISM
ESCAPOLOGIST	EXCHANGE RATE	EXPOSITORILY	FACTIONALIST
ESCUTCHEONED	EXCITABILITY	EXPOSTULATED	FACTIOUSNESS
ESOTERICALLY	EXCLAMATIONS	EXPOSTULATOR	FACTORY FARMS
ESSENTIALISM	EXCLUSIONARY	EXPRESSIONAL	FACTUALISTIC
ESSENTIALIST	EXCOGITATION	EXPRESSIVELY	FAINT-HEARTED
ESSENTIALITY	EXCOGITATIVE	EXPRESSIVITY	FAIT ACCOMPLI
ESTABLISHING	EXCORIATIONS	EXPROPRIABLE	FAITHFULNESS
ESTATE AGENCY	EXCRESCENCES	EXPROPRIATED	FAITH HEALERS
ESTATE AGENTS	EXCRUCIATING	EXPROPRIATOR	FAITH HEALING
ESTHETICALLY	EXCRUCIATION	EXPURGATIONS	FALLACIOUSLY
ESTRANGEMENT	EXCURSIONIST	EXSANGUINITY	FALLING STARS
ETERNITY RING	EXECUTIONERS	EX-SERVICEMAN	FALSE BOTTOMS
ETERNIZATION	EXECUTORSHIP	EX-SERVICEMEN	FAMILIARIZED
ETHERIZATION	EXEGETICALLY	EXTEMPORIZED	FAMILIARIZER
ETHNOCENTRIC	EXEMPLIFYING	EXTEMPORIZER	FAMILIARNESS
ETHNOGRAPHER	EXENTERATION	EXTENDEDNESS	FAMILY CIRCLE
ETHNOGRAPHIC	EXHAUSTIVELY	EXTENSOMETER	FAMILY DOCTOR
ETHNOLOGICAL	EXHIBITIONER	EXTERMINABLE	FANCIFULNESS
ETHNOLOGISTS	EXHILARATING	EXTERMINATED	FARADIZATION
ETHOXYETHANE	EXHILARATION	EXTERMINATOR	FARSIGHTEDLY
ETHYL ALCOHOL	EXHILARATIVE	EXTERNALIZED	FASCINATEDLY
ETYMOLOGICAL	EXHORTATIONS	EXTEROCEPTOR	FASTIDIOUSLY
ETYMOLOGISTS	EXIGUOUSNESS	EXTINGUISHED	FATHER FIGURE
EUCALYPTUSES	EXOBIOLOGIST	EXTINGUISHER	FATHERLINESS
EUHEMERISTIC	EXOPEPTIDASE	EXTORTIONARY	FATHERS-IN-LAW
EUPHONICALLY	EXOPHTHALMIC	EXTORTIONATE	FATIGABILITY

FAULT-FINDING
FAUTE DE MIEUX
FEARLESSNESS
FEARSOMENESS
FEATHERBRAIN
FEATURE FILMS
FEBRIFACIENT
FECKLESSNESS
FEDERALISTIC
FEEBLEMINDED
FEEL THE PINCH
FELDSPATHOSE
FELICITATING
FELICITATION
FELICITOUSLY
FEMINIZATION
FENESTRATION
FENNELFLOWER
FERLINGHETTI
FERMENTATION
FERMENTATIVE
FERRICYANIDE
FERRIS WHEELS
FERROCYANIDE
FERROSILICON
FERTILIZABLE
FEVERISHNESS
FIBRILLATION
FIBRILLIFORM
FIBRINOGENIC
FIBRINOLYSIN
FIBRINOLYSIS
FIBRINOLYTIC
FIBROBLASTIC
FICTIONALIZE
FICTITIOUSLY
FIDDLE-FADDLE
FIDDLESTICKS
FIELD GLASSES
FIELD MARSHAL
FIELD-TESTING
FIELDWORKERS
FIENDISHNESS
FIFTH COLUMNS
FIGURATIVELY
FIGURE-GROUND
FIGURE SKATER
FILIBUSTERED
FILIBUSTERER
FILM PREMIERE
FILTER-TIPPED

FINALIZATION
FINGERBOARDS
FINGERPLATES
FINGERPRINTS
FINGERSTALLS
FIRE BRIGADES
FIRECRACKERS
FIRE FIGHTERS
FIRE FIGHTING
FIRE HYDRANTS
FIRELIGHTERS
FIREPROOFING
FIRE STATIONS
FIRING SQUADS
FIRST COUSINS
FIRST-FOOTING
FIRST-NIGHTER
FIRST OFFENCE
FIRST REFUSAL
FISH AND CHIPS
FISH HATCHERY
FISSIPALMATE
FISSIROSTRAL
FLAGELLATING
FLAGELLATION
FLAGELLIFORM
FLAMBOYANTLY
FLAME-THROWER
FLAMMABILITY
FLATTERINGLY
FLAVOPROTEIN
FLEET ADMIRAL
FLICKERINGLY
FLITTERMOUSE
FLOATABILITY
FLOCCULATION
FLOORWALKERS
FLORICULTURE
FLOWCHARTING
FLUCTUATIONS
FLUIDEXTRACT
FLUIDIZATION
FLUORESCENCE
FLUORIDATING
FLUORIDATION
FLUORINATION
FLUOROCARBON
FLUOROMETRIC
FLUOROSCOPIC
FLUTTERINGLY
FLUVIOMARINE

FLYING DOCTOR
FLYING PICKET
FLYING SAUCER
FLYING SQUADS
FOCALIZATION
FOLKLORISTIC
FOOL'S-PARSLEY
FOOT-AND-MOUTH
FOOT FAULTING
FOOTSLOGGING
FORBEARINGLY
FORBIDDINGLY
FORCE-FEEDING
FORCEFULNESS
FORCIBLENESS
FORE-AND-AFTER
FORECLOSABLE
FORECLOSURES
FOREGONENESS
FOREKNOWABLE
FORENSICALLY
FOREORDAINED
FORESHADOWED
FORESHADOWER
FORESTALLING
FORESTALMENT
FORESTAYSAIL
FORETRIANGLE
FORGATHERING
FORGET-ME-NOTS
FORMALDEHYDE
FORMLESSNESS
FORMULARIZER
FORMULATIONS
FORT-DE-FRANCE
FORTUITOUSLY
FOSSILIZABLE
FOUNDATIONAL
FOUNTAINHEAD
FOUNTAIN PENS
FOURIERISTIC
FOURTH-DEGREE
FOURTH ESTATE
FOURTH OF JULY
FRACTIONALLY
FRACTIONATOR
FRAMES OF MIND
FRANCHE-COMTE
FRANCO GERMAN
FRANGIBILITY
FRANKFURTERS

FRANKINCENSE
FRATERNALISM
FRATERNITIES
FRATERNIZING
FRAUDULENTLY
FREAKISHNESS
FREE CHURCHES
FREE-FLOATING
FREESTANDING
FREE-SWIMMING
FREETHINKERS
FREETHINKING
FREEWHEELING
FREEZE-DRYING
FREIGHTLINER
FRENCH KISSES
FRENCH LOAVES
FRENCH POLISH
FRENETICALLY
FREQUENTABLE
FREUDIAN SLIP
FRIENDLINESS
FRIGHTENABLE
FROGMARCHING
FRONDESCENCE
FRONTBENCHER
FRONTBENCHES
FRONTIERSMAN
FRONTIERSMEN
FRONTISPIECE
FRONT-RUNNERS
FRUCTIFEROUS
FRUITFULNESS
FRUIT MACHINE
FRUMPISHNESS
FRUSTRATIONS
FUDDY-DUDDIES
FULLER'S EARTH
FULLY-FLEDGED
FULMINATIONS
FUNCTIONALLY
FUNDAMENTALS
FURFURACEOUS
FURUNCULOSIS
FUTILITARIAN
FUTUROLOGIST

G

GALACTAGOGUE
GALACTOMETER
GALACTOMETRY

GALL BLADDERS
GALLINACEOUS
GALLIVANTING
GALVANICALLY
GALVANOMETER
GALVANOMETRY
GALVANOSCOPE
GALVANOSCOPY
GAMESMANSHIP
GAMETOPHORIC
GAMETOPHYTIC
GAMOPETALOUS
GAMOPHYLLOUS
GAMOSEPALOUS
GARBAGE TRUCK
GARDEN CITIES
GASIFICATION
GASTIGHTNESS
GASTRONOMIST
GASTROPODOUS
GASTROSCOPIC
GASTRULATION
GATECRASHERS
GATECRASHING
GAVANIZATION
GEANTICLINAL
GENDER-BENDER
GENEALOGICAL
GENEALOGISTS
GENERALITIES
GENERALIZING
GENERAL STAFF
GENEROSITIES
GENEROUSNESS
GENICULATION
GENOTYPICITY
GENUFLECTING
GENUFLECTION
GEOCHEMISTRY
GEOGRAPHICAL
GEOLOGICALLY
GEOMAGNETISM
GEOMECHANICS
GEOPHYSICIST
GEOPOLITICAL
GEOSYNCLINAL
GERANIACEOUS
GERIATRICIAN
GERMANOPHILE
GERMANOPHOBE
GERONTOCRACY

GESTICULATED
GESTICULATOR
GET ONES CARDS
GET-TOGETHERS
GHOULISHNESS
GIANT KILLERS
GIBRALTARIAN
GIFT-WRAPPING
GIGANTICALLY
GIGANTICNESS
GINGER GROUPS
GINGERLINESS
GLABROUSNESS
GLACIOLOGIST
GLADIATORIAL
GLASSBLOWERS
GLASS-BLOWING
GLASS CEILING
GLASSCUTTERS
GLAUCOMATOUS
GLIMMERINGLY
GLISTENINGLY
GLITTERINGLY
GLOBETROTTER
GLOCKENSPIEL
GLORIOUSNESS
GLOSSOGRAPHY
GLOTTAL STOPS
GLOVE PUPPETS
GLUCOGENESIS
GLUCOGENETIC
GLUE-SNIFFERS
GLUE-SNIFFING
GLUTTONOUSLY
GLYCOGENESIS
GLYCOGENETIC
GLYCOPROTEIN
GLYPHOGRAPHY
GLYPTOGRAPHY
GNOMONICALLY
GNOTOBIOTICS
GOBBLEDEGOOK
GOBBLEDYGOOK
GOLDEN EAGLES
GOLDEN FLEECE
GOLDFISH BOWL
GOLD STANDARD
GONADOTROPIN
GOOD-HUMOURED
GOODY-GOODIES
GOOSEBERRIES

GOOSE PIMPLES
GOOSESTEPPED
GO OVER THE
 TOP
GORGEOUSNESS
GORMANDIZING
GOSSIPMONGER
GOVERNMENTAL
GOVERNORSHIP
GRACEFULNESS
GRACIOUSNESS
GRADE SCHOOLS
GRADUALISTIC
GRALLATORIAL
GRAMMATOLOGY
GRAM-NEGATIVE
GRAM-POSITIVE
GRANDFATHERS
GRAND MASTERS
GRANDMOTHERS
GRANDPARENTS
GRANODIORITE
GRANULOCYTIC
GRAPHOLOGIST
GRASSHOPPERS
GRATEFULNESS
GRATIFYINGLY
GRATUITOUSLY
GREASY SPOONS
GREAT BRITAIN
GREAT CIRCLES
GREAT RED SPOT
GREEN FINGERS
GREENGROCERS
GREENGROCERY
GREEN PEPPERS
GREGARIOUSLY
GRIEVOUSNESS
GRIZZLY BEARS
GROSSULARITE
GROUND FLOORS
GROUNDLESSLY
GROUNDSHEETS
GROUND STAFFS
GROUND STROKE
GROUNDSWELLS
GROUP CAPTAIN
GROUP THERAPY
GROVELLINGLY
GROWING PAINS
GRUESOMENESS

GUADALQUIVIR
GUARANTEEING
GUARDIANSHIP
GUERRILLAISM
GUESSTIMATES
GUEST WORKERS
GUILLOTINING
GUINEA-BISSAU
GUN CARRIAGES
GUTTERSNIPES
GUTTURALNESS
GYNAECOCRACY
GYROMAGNETIC

H

HABEAS CORPUS
HABERDASHERS
HABERDASHERY
HABILITATION
HABITABILITY
HABITATIONAL
HABITUALNESS
HACKING COUGH
HAEMATEMESIS
HAEMATOBLAST
HAEMATOCRYAL
HAEMATOGENIC
HAEMATOLOGIC
HAEMATOLYSIS
HAEMATOXYLIC
HAEMATOXYLIN
HAEMATOXYLON
HAEMOPHILIAC
HAEMOPOIESIS
HAEMOPOIETIC
HAEMORRHAGIC
HAEMORRHOIDS
HAGIOGRAPHER
HAGIOGRAPHIC
HAGIOLATROUS
HAIRDRESSERS
HAIRDRESSING
HAIRPIN BENDS
HAIR-RESTORER
HAIR'S BREADTH
HAIRSPLITTER
HAIR TRIGGERS
HALF-BROTHERS
HALF-HOLIDAYS
HALF MEASURES
HALF-TIMBERED

HALFWAY HOUSE
HALF-WITTEDLY
HALLOWEDNESS
HALLSTATTIAN
HALLUCINATED
HALLUCINATOR
HALLUCINOGEN
HALLUCINOSIS
HALOGENATION
HAMBLETONIAN
HAMMARSKJOLD
HAMMERHEADED
HAMPEREDNESS
HAMSTRINGING
HANDICAPPING
HANDKERCHIEF
HAND OVER FIST
HANDSOMENESS
HAPPENSTANCE
HAPPY-GO-LUCKY
HAPPY MEDIUMS
HAPTOTROPISM
HARD CURRENCY
HARD FEELINGS
HARD SHOULDER
HARE COURSING
HARLEQUINADE
HARLEY STREET
HARMLESSNESS
HARMONICALLY
HARMONIOUSLY
HARMONIZABLE
HARPSICHORDS
HARQUEBUSIER
HARTHACANUTE
HARVEST HOMES
HARVEST MOONS
HATCHET-FACED
HAUTE COUTURE
HAUTE CUISINE
HAUTE-GARONNE
HAUTS-DE-SEINE
HAZARD LIGHTS
HEADQUARTERS
HEADSHRINKER
HEADSTRONGLY
HEART ATTACKS
HEARTBREAKER
HEART DISEASE
HEARTENINGLY
HEART FAILURE

HEARTRENDING
HEARTSTRINGS
HEART TO HEART
HEART-TO-HEART
HEARTWARMING
HEATHENISHLY
HEAVENLINESS
HEAVYHEARTED
HEAVY PETTING
HEAVYWEIGHTS
HEBDOMADALLY
HEBETUDINOUS
HEBRAIZATION
HECTOCOTYLUS
HECTOGRAPHIC
HEDGEHOPPING
HEDGE SPARROW
HEEDLESSNESS
HEILONGJIANG
HEILUNGKIANG
HEIR APPARENT
HELICOIDALLY
HELIOCENTRIC
HELIOCHROMIC
HELIOGABALUS
HELIOGRAPHER
HELIOGRAPHIC
HELIOGRAVURE
HELIOLATROUS
HELIOTHERAPY
HELIOTROPISM
HELLENICALLY
HELLGRAMMITE
HELPING HANDS
HELPLESSNESS
HEMICHORDATE
HEMIHYDRATED
HEMIMORPHISM
HEMIMORPHITE
HEMIPARASITE
HEMISPHEROID
HEMOPHILIACS
HENDECAGONAL
HENOTHEISTIC
HERALDICALLY
HERBACEOUSLY
HERD INSTINCT
HERE AND THERE
HEREDITAMENT
HEREDITARILY
HEREINBEFORE

HERITABILITY
HERMANNSTADT
HERMENEUTICS
HERMENEUTIST
HERMETICALLY
HERMITICALLY
HERMOTENSILE
HEROD ANTIPAS
HEROICALNESS
HERPES ZOSTER
HERPETOLOGIC
HERRINGBONES
HERSTMONCEUX
HESITATINGLY
HETEROCERCAL
HETEROCYCLIC
HETERODACTYL
HETEROECIOUS
HETEROGAMETE
HETEROGAMOUS
HETEROGENOUS
HETEROGONOUS
HETEROGRAPHY
HETEROGYNOUS
HETEROLOGOUS
HETEROMEROUS
HETERONOMOUS
HETERONYMOUS
HETEROOUSIAN
HETEROPHYLLY
HETEROPLASTY
HETEROSEXISM
HETEROSEXUAL
HETEROTACTIC
HETEROZYGOTE
HETEROZYGOUS
HEXACOSANOIC
HEXAGRAMMOID
HEXAHYDRATED
HIBERNACULUM
HIBERNIANISM
HIDDEN AGENDA
HIERARCHICAL
HIERATICALLY
HIEROGLYPHIC
HIEROPHANTIC
HIGH FIDELITY
HIGH-HANDEDLY
HIGHLIGHTING
HIGHLY-STRUNG
HIGH-MINDEDLY

HIGH-PRESSURE
HIGH PROFILES
HIGH SHERIFFS
HIGH-SOUNDING
HIGH-SPIRITED
HINAYANISTIC
HINDQUARTERS
HIPPOCRENIAN
HIPPOPOTAMUS
HIRE PURCHASE
HISTOGENESIS
HISTOGENETIC
HISTOLOGICAL
HISTORICALLY
HIT A BAD
  PATCH
HOBBLEDEHOYS
HOBSON-JOBSON
HOHENZOLLERN
HOLIDAYMAKER
HOLISTICALLY
HOLOPHRASTIC
HOLOPLANKTON
HOLY OF HOLIES
HOME COUNTIES
HOME FROM HOME
HOMELESSNESS
HOMEOMORPHIC
HOMEOPATHIST
HOMESICKNESS
HOMING PIGEON
HOMOCHROMOUS
HOMOGENIZING
HOMOGONOUSLY
HOMOLOGATION
HOMOMORPHISM
HOMOPOLARITY
HOMOTAXIALLY
HOMOTHALLISM
HOMOZYGOUSLY
HONEYMOONERS
HONEYMOONING
HONEYSUCKLED
HONEYSUCKLES
HOPELESSNESS
HORIZONTALLY
HORNET'S NESTS
HORN OF PLENTY
HORRENDOUSLY
HORRIBLENESS
HORRIFICALLY

HORRIFYINGLY
HORS DE COMBAT
HORS D'OEUVRES
HORSEMANSHIP
HORSE TRADING
HORSE-TRADING
HORSEWHIPPED
HORSEWHIPPER
HORTICULTURE
HORTUS SICCUS
HOSPITALIZED
HOT-CROSS BUNS
HOT-GOSPELLER
HOUSE ARRESTS
HOUSEBREAKER
HOUSEFATHERS
HOUSEHOLDERS
HOUSE HUSBAND
HOUSEKEEPERS
HOUSEKEEPING
HOUSEMASTERS
HOUSEMOTHERS
HOUSE OF CARDS
HOUSE OF LORDS
HOUSEPARENTS
HOUSE PARTIES
HOUSE SPARROW
HOUSE-TO-HOUSE
HOUSE-TRAINED
HOUSEWARMING
HOUSEY HOUSEY
HOUSEY-HOUSEY
HUBBLE-BUBBLE
HUDDERSFIELD
HUGGER-MUGGER
HUMANITARIAN
HUMANIZATION
HUMILIATIONS
HUMMINGBIRDS
HUMOROUSNESS
HUMPTY DUMPTY
HUNGER STRIKE
HURDY-GURDIES
HURSTMONCEUX
HUSEIN IBN-ALI
HYALOPLASMIC
HYBRIDIZABLE
HYDNOCARPATE
HYDRASTININE
HYDROCARBONS
HYDROCEPHALY

HYDROCHLORIC
HYDRODYNAMIC
HYDROFLUORIC
HYDROGENATOR
HYDROGEN BOMB
HYDROGEOLOGY
HYDROGRAPHER
HYDROGRAPHIC
HYDROKINETIC
HYDROLYSABLE
HYDROMEDUSAN
HYDROTHERAPY
HYGIENICALLY
HYPERCORRECT
HYPERMARKETS
HYPNOTHERAPY
HYPNOTICALLY
HYPOCHONDRIA
HYPOCRITICAL
HYPOTHETICAL
HYSTERECTOMY
HYSTERICALLY

I

ICE-CREAM SODA
ICHNEUMON FLY
ICHNOGRAPHIC
ICHNOLOGICAL
ICHTHYOLOGIC
ICHTHYOPHAGY
ICONOCLASTIC
ICONOGRAPHER
ICONOGRAPHIC
ICONOLATROUS
ICONOLOGICAL
IDEALIZATION
IDENTIFIABLE
IDENTITY CARD
IDEOLOOGICAL
IDIOMORPHISM
IDIOSYNCRASY
IDOLATROUSLY
IGNITABILITY
ILLEGAL ENTRY
ILLEGALITIES
ILLEGIBILITY
ILLEGITIMACY
ILLEGITIMATE
ILLIBERALITY
ILLITERATELY
ILLOGICALITY

ILL-TREATMENT
ILLUMINATING
ILLUMINATION
ILLUMINATIVE
ILLUSIONISTS
ILLUSORINESS
ILLUSTRATING
ILLUSTRATION
ILLUSTRATIVE
ILLUSTRATORS
IMAGINATIONS
IMBECILITIES
IMMACULATELY
IMMEASURABLE
IMMEASURABLY
IMMEMORIABLE
IMMERSIONISM
IMMERSIONIST
IMMETHODICAL
IMMOBILIZING
IMMODERATELY
IMMODERATION
IMMORALITIES
IMMORTALIZED
IMMORTALIZER
IMMOVABILITY
IMMUNE SYSTEM
IMMUNIZATION
IMMUNOLOGIST
IMMUTABILITY
IMPARTIALITY
IMPEDIMENTAL
IMPENETRABLE
IMPENITENTLY
IMPERATIVELY
IMPERCEPTION
IMPERCEPTIVE
IMPERFECTION
IMPERFECTIVE
IMPERIALISTS
IMPERISHABLE
IMPERMANENCE
IMPERSONALLY
IMPERSONATED
IMPERSONATOR
IMPERTINENCE
IMPETIGINOUS
IMPLANTATION
IMPLEMENTING
IMPLICATIONS
IMPLICITNESS

IMPOLITENESS
IMPONDERABLE
IMPORTATIONS
IMPOVERISHED
IMPOVERISHER
IMPRECATIONS
IMPREGNATING
IMPREGNATION
IMPRESSIONAL
IMPRESSIVELY
IMPRISONMENT
IMPROPRIATOR
IMPROVEMENTS
IMPROVIDENCE
IMPUTABILITY
INACCESSIBLE
INACCESSIBLY
INACCURACIES
INACCURATELY
INACTIVATION
INADEQUACIES
INADEQUATELY
INADMISSIBLE
INADMISSIBLY
INADVERTENCE
INAPPLICABLE
INAPPLICABLY
INARTICULATE
IN ATTENDANCE
INAUDIBILITY
INAUGURATING
INAUGURATION
INAUSPICIOUS
INCALCULABLE
INCALCULABLY
INCALESCENCE
INCANDESCENT
INCANTATIONS
INCAPABILITY
INCAPACITATE
INCARCERATED
INCARCERATOR
INCARNATIONS
INCAUTIOUSLY
INCENDIARISM
INCESTUOUSLY
INCIDENTALLY
INCINERATING
INCINERATION
INCINERATORS
INCISIVENESS

INCIVILITIES	INDELIBILITY	INEXTIRPABLE	INSECTICIDAL
INCLINATIONS	INDELICATELY	INEXTRICABLE	INSECTICIDES
INCLINOMETER	INDEMNIFYING	INEXTRICABLY	INSECTIVORES
INCOGNIZANCE	INDENTATIONS	INFANTICIDAL	INSEMINATING
INCOHERENTLY	INDEPENDENCE	INFANTICIDES	INSEMINATION
INCOMMODIOUS	INDEPENDENCY	INFANT SCHOOL	IN SHORT ORDER
INCOMMUTABLE	INDEPENDENTS	INFATUATEDLY	INSINUATIONS
INCOMPARABLE	INDEX FINGERS	INFATUATIONS	INSOLUBILITY
INCOMPARABLY	INDEX FUTURES	INFECTIOUSLY	INSPECTINGLY
INCOMPATIBLE	INDIANAPOLIS	INFELICITOUS	INSPECTIONAL
INCOMPATIBLY	INDIAN SUMMER	INFESTATIONS	INSPECTORATE
INCOMPETENCE	INDICATIVELY	INFIBULATION	INSPIRATIONS
INCOMPETENTS	INDIFFERENCE	INFIDELITIES	INSPIRITMENT
INCOMPLETELY	INDIGENOUSLY	INFILTRATING	INSTALLATION
INCOMPLIANCE	INDIGESTIBLE	INFILTRATION	INSTILLATION
INCOMPUTABLE	INDIGESTIBLY	INFILTRATIVE	INSTITUTIONS
INCONCLUSIVE	INDIRECTNESS	INFILTRATORS	INSTRUCTIBLE
INCONFORMITY	INDISCIPLINE	INFLAMMATION	INSTRUCTIONS
INCONSEQUENT	INDISCREETLY	INFLAMMATORY	INSTRUMENTAL
INCONSISTENT	INDISCRETION	INFLATIONARY	INSUFFERABLE
INCONSOLABLE	INDISPUTABLE	INFLATIONISM	INSUFFERABLY
INCONSOLABLY	INDISPUTABLY	INFLATIONIST	INSUFFICIENT
INCONSONANCE	INDISSOLUBLE	INFLECTIONAL	INSUFFLATION
INCONSUMABLE	INDISSOLUBLY	INFLORESCENT	INSURABILITY
INCONTINENCE	INDISTINCTLY	INFOTAINMENT	INSURGENCIES
INCONVENIENT	INDIVIDUALLY	INFREQUENTLY	INSURRECTION
INCOORDINATE	INDIVIDUATOR	INFRINGEMENT	INTELLECTION
INCORPORABLE	INDOCTRINATE	INFUNDIBULAR	INTELLECTIVE
INCORPORATED	INDO-EUROPEAN	INFUNDIBULUM	INTELLECTUAL
INCORPORATOR	INDOLEACETIC	INFUSIBILITY	INTELLIGENCE
INCORPOREITY	INDOMETHACIN	INGLORIOUSLY	INTELLIGIBLE
INCORRIGIBLE	INDRE-ET-LOIRE	INGRATIATING	INTELLIGIBLY
INCORRIGIBLY	INDUSTRIALLY	INGRATIATION	INTEMPERANCE
INCRASSATION	INEFFABILITY	INHABITATION	INTENSIFIERS
INCREASINGLY	INEFFACEABLE	INHARMONIOUS	INTENSIFYING
INCRETIONARY	INEFFICIENCY	INHERITANCES	INTERACTIONS
INCRIMINATED	INELASTICITY	INHOSPITABLE	INTERCEPTING
INCRIMINATOR	INEQUALITIES	INHOSPITABLY	INTERCEPTION
INCRUSTATION	INERADICABLE	INHUMANITIES	INTERCEPTIVE
INCUBATIONAL	INERADICABLY	INIMICALNESS	INTERCEPTORS
INCUMBENCIES	INERTIA REELS	INIQUITOUSLY	INTERCESSION
INCURABILITY	INESCUTCHEON	INNOVATIONAL	INTERCESSORY
INDEBTEDNESS	INESSENTIALS	INNUTRITIOUS	INTERCHANGED
INDECISIVELY	INEXACTITUDE	INOBSERVANCE	INTERCHANGES
INDECLINABLE	INEXPEDIENCE	INOCULATIONS	INTERCONNECT
INDECOROUSLY	INEXPERIENCE	INORDINATELY	INTERCURRENT
INDEFEASIBLE	INEXPERTNESS	INOSCULATION	INTERDICTION
INDEFENSIBLE	INEXPLICABLE	INQUISITIONS	INTERDICTIVE
INDEFENSIBLY	INEXPLICABLY	INSALIVATION	INTERESTEDLY
INDEFINITELY	INEXPRESSIVE	INSALUBRIOUS	INTERFERENCE
INDEHISCENCE	INEXTENSIBLE	INSCRIPTIONS	INTERFERTILE

INTERFLUVIAL
INTERGLACIAL
INTERJECTING
INTERJECTION
INTERJECTORY
INTERLACEDLY
INTERLAMINAR
INTERLARDING
INTERLINKING
INTERLOCKING
INTERLOCUTOR
INTERMARRIED
INTERMEDIACY
INTERMEDIARY
INTERMEDIATE
INTERMINABLE
INTERMINABLY
INTERMINGLED
INTERMISSION
INTERMISSIVE
INTERMITTENT
INTERMIXABLE
INTERMIXTURE
INTERNALIZED
INTERNUNCIAL
INTEROCEPTOR
INTERPELLANT
INTERPELLATE
INTERPLEADER
INTERPOLATED
INTERPOLATER
INTERPOSABLE
INTERPRETERS
INTERPRETING
INTERPRETIVE
INTERREGNUMS
INTERROGATED
INTERROGATOR
INTERRUPTING
INTERRUPTION
INTERRUPTIVE
INTERSECTING
INTERSECTION
INTERSPATIAL
INTERSPERSED
INTERSTADIAL
INTERSTELLAR
INTERSTITIAL
INTERTEXTURE
INTERTWINING
INTERVENTION

INTERVIEWEES
INTERVIEWERS
INTERVIEWING
INTERVOCALIC
INTERWEAVING
IN THE LONG
 RUN
INTIMIDATING
INTIMIDATION
INTOLERANTLY
INTONATIONAL
INTOXICATING
INTOXICATION
INTOXICATIVE
INTRACARDIAC
INTRACRANIAL
INTRANSIGENT
INTRANSITIVE
INTRANUCLEAR
INTRAPRENEUR
INTRAUTERINE
INTRIGUINGLY
INTRODUCIBLE
INTRODUCTION
INTRODUCTORY
INTROJECTION
INTROJECTIVE
INTROVERSION
INTROVERSIVE
INTUITIONISM
INTUITIONIST
INTUMESCENCE
INTUSSUSCEPT
INVAGINATION
INVALIDATING
INVALIDATION
INVERCARGILL
INVERTEBRACY
INVERTEBRATE
INVERTED SNOB
INVESTIGABLE
INVESTIGATED
INVESTIGATOR
INVESTITURES
INVIGILATING
INVIGILATION
INVIGILATORS
INVIGORATING
INVIGORATION
INVIGORATIVE
INVISIBILITY

INVITATIONAL
INVOCATIONAL
INVOLUCELATE
INVOLUTIONAL
INVULNERABLE
INVULNERABLY
INVULTUATION
IRASCIBILITY
IRISH COFFEES
IRONING BOARD
IRRADIATIONS
IRRATIONALLY
IRREDEEMABLE
IRREDEEMABLY
IRREFRAGABLE
IRREGULARITY
IRRELEVANCES
IRRELEVANTLY
IRRELIEVABLE
IRREMEDIABLE
IRREMEDIABLY
IRREMISSIBLE
IRRESISTIBLE
IRRESISTIBLY
IRRESOLUTELY
IRRESOLUTION
IRRESOLVABLE
IRRESPECTIVE
IRRESPIRABLE
IRRESPONSIVE
IRREVERENTLY
IRREVERSIBLE
IRREVERSIBLY
IRRIGATIONAL
IRRITABILITY
ISOCHROMATIC
ISODIAMETRIC
ISOLATIONISM
ISOLATIONIST
ISOTOPICALLY
ITALIANESQUE

J
JACK-IN-THE-
 BOX
JACK O LANTERN
JACK-O'-
 LANTERN
JACK ROBINSON
JACKSONVILLE
JACOBS LADDER

JE NE SAIS
 QUOI
JEOPARDIZING
JET-PROPELLED
JIGSAW PUZZLE
JOHANNESBURG
JOURNALISTIC
JUDICATORIAL
JUGULAR VEINS
JUNIOR SCHOOL
JURISCONSULT
JURISDICTION
JURISDICTIVE
JURISPRUDENT
JUSTIFYINGLY
JUVENESCENCE

K
KALEIDOSCOPE
KARYOKINESIS
KARYOKINETIC
KARYOPLASMIC
KEEP ONES HEAD
KEEP THE PEACE
KERATOGENOUS
KERATOPLASTY
KERB CRAWLERS
KERB CRAWLING
KEYNESIANISM
KEY SIGNATURE
KILLER WHALES
KILOWATT-HOUR
KINAESTHESIA
KINAESTHETIC
KINDERGARTEN
KING'S COUNSEL
KING'S ENGLISH
KINROSS-SHIRE
KITCHENETTES
KLEPTOMANIAC
KLIPSPRINGER
KNACKER'S YARD
KNEE BREECHES
KNIGHT ERRANT
KNIGHT-ERRANT
KNOX-JOHNSTON
KOMI REPUBLIC
KOTA KINABALU
KREMLINOLOGY
KRISTIANSTAD
KYRGYZ STEPPE

L

LABORATORIES
LABOUR MARKET
LABOUR OF LOVE
LABOURSAVING
LABYRINTHINE
LACERABILITY
LACHRYMOSITY
LACTOPROTEIN
LADY'S FINGERS
LADY'S-SLIPPER
LAISSEZ-FAIRE
LAKE DISTRICT
LAMENTATIONS
LANDED GENTRY
LANDING CRAFT
LANDING FIELD
LANDING STAGE
LANDING STRIP
LANDLUBBERLY
LANGUISHMENT
LANGUOROUSLY
LANTERN-JAWED
LANTERNSLIDE
LAPIS LAZULIS
LARYNGOSCOPE
LARYNGOSCOPY
LASCIVIOUSLY
LASER PRINTER
LAST JUDGMENT
LATEENRIGGED
LATICIFEROUS
LATINIZATION
LAUNDERETTES
LAUNDRYWOMAN
LAUREATESHIP
LEADING LIGHT
LEAPFROGGING
LEASEHOLDERS
LEATHERINESS
LEAVE TAKINGS
LECTURESHIPS
LEGALIZATION
LEGIONNAIRES
LEGISLATRESS
LEGISLATURES
LEGITIMATELY
LEGITIMATION
LEGITIMATIZE
LEGITIMISTIC
LEGITIMIZING

LENTICELLATE
LEOPARD'S-BANE
LEPIDOPTERAN
LEPIDOPTERON
LETTER OPENER
LEUCOCYTOSIS
LEUCOCYTOTIC
LEUCOPOIESIS
LEUCOPOIETIC
LEUCORRHOEAL
LEVALLOISIAN
LEXICOGRAPHY
LEXICOLOGIST
LIBERALISTIC
LIBERALITIES
LIBERALIZING
LIBERAL PARTY
LIBERTARIANS
LIBERTICIDAL
LIBIDINOUSLY
LICENSE PLATE
LICENTIATION
LICENTIOUSLY
LICHTENSTEIN
LIE DETECTORS
LIFELESSNESS
LIGHT BRIGADE
LIGHT-HEARTED
LIGHTWEIGHTS
LIMNOLOGICAL
LINCOLNSHIRE
LINE DRAWINGS
LINE-ENGRAVER
LINEN BASKETS
LINE PRINTERS
LINE PRINTING
LINES OF SIGHT
LINGUA FRANCA
LIQUEFACIENT
LIQUEFACTION
LIQUEFACTIVE
LIRIODENDRON
LISTLESSNESS
LITERALISTIC
LITERARINESS
LITERATENESS
LITHOGRAPHED
LITHOGRAPHER
LITHOGRAPHIC
LITTERATEURS
LITTLE FINGER

LITTLE PEOPLE
LITURGICALLY
LIVERPUDLIAN
LIVER SAUSAGE
LIVERY STABLE
LIVING FOSSIL
LOCAL DERBIES
LOCALIZATION
LOCAL OPTIONS
LOCI CLASSICI
LOCKSMITHERY
LOCKSTITCHES
LODGING HOUSE
LOGANBERRIES
LOGANIACEOUS
LOGISTICALLY
LOLLAPALOOZA
LOMENTACEOUS
LONELY HEARTS
LONESOMENESS
LONG-DISTANCE
LONG DIVISION
LONG DRAWN OUT
LONG-DRAWN-OUT
LONGITUDINAL
LONGSHOREMAN
LONGSHOREMEN
LONG-STANDING
LONG VACATION
LONGWINDEDLY
LOOKING GLASS
LOOSE-JOINTED
LOOSE-TONGUED
LOPHOPHORATE
LOQUACIOUSLY
LOSS ADJUSTER
LOST PROPERTY
LOT-ET-GARONNE
LOUDSPEAKERS
LOUGHBOROUGH
LOVECHILDREN
LOWER AUSTRIA
LOWER CLASSES
LOW-WATER MARK
LUDWIGSHAFEN
LUGGAGE RACKS
LUGUBRIOUSLY
LUMBERJACKET
LUMINESCENCE
LUNCHEONETTE
LUSCIOUSNESS

LYMPHANGITIC
LYMPHANGITIS
LYMPHOMATOID
LYSERGIC ACID

M

MACCLESFIELD
MACHINATIONS
MACHINE CODES
MACHINE TOOLS
MACKINTOSHES
MACROCLIMATE
MACROCYTOSIS
MACROGRAPHIC
MACRONUCLEUS
MACROPHYSICS
MACROPTEROUS
MADEMOISELLE
MAGIC LANTERN
MAGISTRACIES
MAGISTRATURE
MAGNETICALLY
MAGNETIC HEAD
MAGNETIC POLE
MAGNETIC TAPE
MAGNETIZABLE
MAGNETOGRAPH
MAGNETOMETER
MAGNETOMETRY
MAGNIFICENCE
MAGNILOQUENT
MAGNITOGORSK
MAGNUM OPUSES
MAIDENLINESS
MAIDEN SPEECH
MAIDEN VOYAGE
MAID OF HONOUR
MAIDSERVANTS
MAILING LISTS
MAINE-ET-LOIRE
MAINTAINABLE
MAITRE D'HOTEL
MAJESTICALLY
MAJOR GENERAL
MAKE ENDS MEET
MALACOLOGIST
MALAPROPISMS
MALEDICTIONS
MALEFACTRESS
MALEVOLENILY
MALFEASANCES

MALFORMATION	MASS-PRODUCED	MENAGE A TROIS	METHODICALLY
MALFUNCTIONS	MASS-PRODUCER	MENDACIOUSLY	METHOTREXATE
MALIGNANCIES	MASTECTOMIES	MEN OF LETTERS	METICULOUSLY
MALIMPRINTED	MASTER-AT-ARMS	MENSTRUATING	METONIC CYCLE
MALLEABILITY	MASTERLINESS	MENSTRUATION	METROLOGICAL
MALNOURISHED	MASTERMINDED	MEPHITICALLY	METROPOLISES
MALNUTRITION	MASTER OF ARTS	MERCANTILISM	METROPOLITAN
MALOCCLUSION	MASTERPIECES	MERCANTILIST	METRORRHAGIA
MALPRACTICES	MASTERSTROKE	MERCHANDISED	MEZZO-RELIEVO
MALTESE CROSS	MASTIGOPHORE	MERCHANDISER	MEZZO-SOPRANO
MALTREATMENT	MASTURBATING	MERCHANTABLE	MICROANALYST
MAMMALOGICAL	MASTURBATION	MERCHANT BANK	MICROBALANCE
MAN ABOUT TOWN	MATABELELAND	MERCHANT NAVY	MICROBIOLOGY
MAN-ABOUT-TOWN	MATERIALISTS	MERCIFULNESS	MICROCEPHALY
MANAGERESSES	MATERIALIZED	MERCURIALIZE	MICROCIRCUIT
MANAGERIALLY	MATERIALIZER	MERCY KILLING	MICROCLIMATE
MANDARIN DUCK	MATHEMATICAL	MERETRICIOUS	MICROFILMING
MANEUVERABLE	MATINEE IDOLS	MERISTEMATIC	MICROGRAPHER
MANGEL-WURZEL	MATRIARCHIES	MEROPLANKTON	MICROGRAPHIC
MANIFESTABLE	MATRICLINOUS	MERRY-GO-ROUND	MICROGRAVITY
MANIPULATING	MATRICULATED	MESENTERITIS	MICROHABITAT
MANIPULATION	MATRICULATOR	MESENTERONIC	MICRONUCLEUS
MANIPULATIVE	MATRONLINESS	MESMERICALLY	MICROPHYSICS
MANIPULATORY	MATTER-OF-FACT	MESOCEPHALIC	MICROSCOPIST
MANNERLINESS	MATURATIONAL	MESOGASTRIUM	MICROSECONDS
MANOEUVRABLE	MAXIMIZATION	MESOGNATHISM	MICROSEISMIC
MAN OF LETTERS	MEALY-MOUTHED	MESOGNATHOUS	MICROSTOMOUS
MANSION HOUSE	MEAN BUSINESS	MESOMORPHISM	MIDDLE COURSE
MANSLAUGHTER	MEANDERINGLY	MESOMORPHOUS	MIDDLE FINGER
MANTELPIECES	MEANINGFULLY	MESOPOTAMIAN	MIDDLE SCHOOL
MANUFACTURAL	MEASUREMENTS	MESOTHORACIC	MIDDLEWEIGHT
MANUFACTURED	MECAMYLAMINE	MESSAGE STICK	MID GLAMORGAN
MANUFACTURER	MECHANICALLY	METAGALACTIC	MIDSUMMER DAY
MARCASITICAL	MEDALLIONIST	METAGNATHISM	MIDWESTERNER
MARIE GALANTE	MEDICAMENTAL	METAGNATHOUS	MIFEPRISTONE
MARITIME ALPS	MEDICINE BALL	METALANGUAGE	MIGHT AND MAIN
MARKET FORCES	MEDIOCRITIES	METALLICALLY	MILFORD HAVEN
MARKET GARDEN	MEDITATINGLY	METALLURGIST	MILITARISTIC
MARKETPLACES	MEDITATIVELY	METALWORKERS	MILITARIZING
MARKET PRICES	MEETINGHOUSE	METALWORKING	MILLEFEUILLE
MARKSMANSHIP	MEGACEPHALIC	METAMORPHISM	MILLENARIANS
MARLINESPIKE	MEGALOCARDIA	METAMORPHOSE	MILLIONAIRES
MARRIAGEABLE	MEGALOMANIAC	METAPHORICAL	MILTON KEYNES
MARSEILLAISE	MELANCHOLIAC	METAPHRASTIC	MIMEOGRAPHED
MARSHALL PLAN	MELANCHOLILY	METAPHYSICAL	MIND-BOGGLING
MARSHMALLOWS	MELODRAMATIC	METASOMATISM	MINDLESSNESS
MARSUPIALIAN	MELTING POINT	METATHORACIC	MINE DETECTOR
MARVELLOUSLY	MEMORABILITY	METEMPIRICAL	MINERALOGIST
MASQUERADERS	MEMORIALIZER	METEORICALLY	MINERAL WATER
MASQUERADING	MEMORIZATION	METEOROGRAPH	MINESWEEPERS
MASSOTHERAPY	MEN-ABOUT-TOWN	METHACRYLATE	MINESWEEPING

MINIATURISTS	MIXED DOUBLES	MONOTRICHOUS	MULTIGRAVIDA
MINICOMPUTER	MIXED ECONOMY	MONTPARNASSE	MULTILAMINAR
MINIFICATION	MIXED FARMING	MONUMENTALLY	MULTILATERAL
MINIMIZATION	MNEMONICALLY	MOONLIGHTERS	MULTILINGUAL
MINIMUM WAGES	MOBILIZATION	MOONLIGHTING	MULTINUCLEAR
MINISTRATION	MOCKINGBIRDS	MORALITY PLAY	MULTIPARTITE
MINISTRATIVE	MODERATENESS	MORALIZATION	MULTIPLIABLE
MINOR PLANETS	MODIFICATION	MORALIZINGLY	MULTIPLICAND
MINUTE STEAKS	MODIFICATORY	MORBIFICALLY	MULTIPLICATE
MIRACLE PLAYS	MODULABILITY	MORNING COATS	MULTIPLICITY
MIRROR IMAGES	MODUS VIVENDI	MORNING DRESS	MULTIPURPOSE
MIRTHFULNESS	MOHAVE DESERT	MORNING GLORY	MULTITASKING
MISADVENTURE	MOISTURIZING	MORPHALLAXIS	MULTIVALENCY
MISALIGNMENT	MOLLIFYINGLY	MORPHOLOGIES	MULTIVARIATE
MISALLIANCES	MOLLYCODDLED	MORPHOLOGIST	MUNICIPALITY
MISANTHROPES	MONADELPHOUS	MORRIS DANCER	MUNICIPALIZE
MISANTHROPIC	MONARCHISTIC	MORRIS DANCES	MUNIFICENTLY
MISAPPREHEND	MONASTICALLY	MORTARBOARDS	MUSEUM PIECES
MISBEHAVIOUR	MONETIZATION	MORTGAGEABLE	MUSICAL BOXES
MISCALCULATE	MONEYCHANGER	MORTIFYINGLY	MUSIC CENTRES
MISCARRIAGES	MONEY-GRUBBER	MORTISE LOCKS	MUSICIANSHIP
MISCEGENETIC	MONEYLENDERS	MOSQUITO NETS	MUSICOLOGIST
MISCELLANIES	MONEYLENDING	MOTHERFUCKER	MYRMECOPHILE
MISCELLANIST	MONEY SPINNER	MOTHERLINESS	MYSTERIOUSLY
MISCONCEIVED	MONEY-SPINNER	MOTHER NATURE	MYSTERY PLAYS
MISCONCEIVER	MONISTICALLY	MOTHERS-IN-LAW	MYSTERY TOURS
MISCONDUCTED	MONKEY-PUZZLE	MOTHER TONGUE	MYSTIFYINGLY
MISCONSTRUED	MONKEY WRENCH	MOTHPROOFING	MYTHOLOGICAL
MISDEMEANANT	MONOCHLORIDE	MOTIONLESSLY	MYTHOLOGISTS
MISDEMEANOUR	MONOCHROMIST	MOTIVATIONAL	MYTHOLOGIZER
MISDIRECTING	MONODRAMATIC	MOTORCYCLIST	MYXOMYCETOUS
MISDIRECTION	MONOFILAMENT	MOTORIZATION	
MISE-EN-SCENES	MONOGAMISTIC	MOTOR SCOOTER	**N**
MISINFORMANT	MONOGAMOUSLY	MOULDABILITY	NAIL SCISSORS
MISINFORMING	MONOMANIACAL	MOUNTAINEERS	NAMBY-PAMBIES
MISINTERPRET	MONOMETALLIC	MOUNTAIN LION	NAMEDROPPERS
MISJUDGEMENT	MONOMETRICAL	MOUNTAINSIDE	NAMEDROPPING
MISJUDGMENTS	MONOMORPHISM	MOUNTAINTOPS	NANOPLANKTON
MISLEADINGLY	MONOPETALOUS	MOURNFULNESS	NANSEN BOTTLE
MISPLACEMENT	MONOPHTHONGS	MOUTHBROODER	NARCISSISTIC
MISPRONOUNCE	MONOPHYLETIC	MOUTH-TO-MOUTH	NARCOTICALLY
MISQUOTATION	MONOPHYLLOUS	MOVABLE FEAST	NARRAGANSETT
MISREPORTING	MONOPOLISTIC	MUCILAGINOUS	NARROW GAUGES
MISREPRESENT	MONOPOLIZING	MUCOPURULENT	NARROW-MINDED
MISSING LINKS	MONOSEPALOUS	MUDDLE-HEADED	NARROW SQUEAK
MISSIONARIES	MONOSPERMOUS	MULLIGATAWNY	NASALIZATION
MISSPELLINGS	MONOSTROPHIC	MULTICHANNEL	NATIONAL DEBT
MISSTATEMENT	MONOSYLLABIC	MULTIFACETED	NATIONAL HUNT
MISTREATMENT	MONOSYLLABLE	MULTIFARIOUS	NATIONALISTS
MITHRIDATISM	MONOTHEISTIC	MULTIFOLIATE	NATIONALIZED
MIXED-ABILITY	MONOTONOUSLY	MULTIFORMITY	NATIONAL PARK

NATION STATES
NATIVITY PLAY
NATURALISTIC
NATURALIZING
NATUROPATHIC
NAUSEATINGLY
NAUSEOUSNESS
NAUTICAL MILE
NAVIGABILITY
NAVIGATIONAL
NEANDERTHALS
NEBULIZATION
NEBULOUSNESS
NECESSITATED
NECKERCHIEFS
NECROLOGICAL
NECROMANCERS
NECROPHILIAC
NECROPHILISM
NECROPOLISES
NEEDLESSNESS
NEGATIVENESS
NEGATIVE POLE
NEGATIVE SIGN
NEGATIVISTIC
NEGLECTFULLY
NEGOTIATIONS
NEIGHBOURING
NEMATOCYSTIC
NEOANTHROPIC
NEOCLASSICAL
NEOLOGICALLY
NEOTERICALLY
NEPHELOMETER
NEPHOLOGICAL
NERVE CENTRES
NERVE-RACKING
NETHERLANDER
NETTLE RASHES
NEURASTHENIA
NEURASTHENIC
NEUROANATOMY
NEUROBIOLOGY
NEUROLOGICAL
NEUROLOGISTS
NEUROPTEROUS
NEUROSCIENCE
NEUROSURGEON
NEUROSURGERY
NEUROTICALLY
NEUROTOMICAL

NEUTRALIZING
NEUTRON BOMBS
NEVERTHELESS
NEW BRUNSWICK
NEW CALEDONIA
NEWFOUNDLAND
NEW HAMPSHIRE
NEWS AGENCIES
NEWSPAPERMAN
NEW TESTAMENT
NEWTOWNABBEY
NEW ZEALANDER
NIAGARA FALLS
NICOTINAMIDE
NIDIFICATION
NIETZSCHEISM
NIGHTDRESSES
NIGHTINGALES
NIMBOSTRATUS
NITROBENZENE
NITROMETHANE
NO-CLAIM BONUS
NOCTAMBULISM
NOCTAMBULIST
NOCTILUCENCE
NOCTURNALITY
NOLENS VOLENS
NOMENCLATURE
NOMINALISTIC
NONADDICTIVE
NONAGENARIAN
NONALCOHOLIC
NONALIGNMENT
NONCHALANTLY
NONCOMBATANT
NONCOMMITTAL
NONCONDUCTOR
NONCORRODING
NONE SO PRETTY
NONESSENTIAL
NONEXISTENCE
NONEXPLOSIVE
NONFICTIONAL
NONFLAMMABLE
NONIDENTICAL
NONIDIOMATIC
NONMALIGNANT
NONOPERATIVE
NONPOISONOUS
NONPOLITICAL
NONRESIDENCE

NON RESIDENCE
NONRESIDENTS
NONRESISTANT
NONSCHEDULED
NONSECTARIAN
NON SEQUITURS
NONSTRATEGIC
NONTECHNICAL
NONVIOLENTLY
NORTH AMERICA
NORTH BRABANT
NORTHEASTERN
NORTHEASTERS
NORTHERNMOST
NORTH HOLLAND
NORTHUMBRIAN
NORTHWESTERN
NOTEWORTHILY
NOTICE BOARDS
NOTIFICATION
NOURISHINGLY
NOUVEAU RICHE
NOVOKUZNETSK
NUBIAN DESERT
NUCLEOPHILIC
NUMBERPLATES
NUMEROUSNESS
NUMINOUSNESS
NUMISMATISTS
NURSERY RHYME
NURSING HOMES
NUSA TENGGARA
NUTRITIONIST
NUTRITIOUSLY
NUTS AND BOLTS
NYCTITROPISM
NYMPHOLEPTIC
NYMPHOMANIAC

O

OBERAMMERGAU
OBITER DICTUM
OBJECT LESSON
OBLANCEOLATE
OBLATE SPHERE
OBLIGATIONAL
OBLIGATORILY
OBLITERATING
OBLITERATION
OBLITERATIVE
OBSCURANTISM

OBSCURANTIST
OBSEQUIOUSLY
OBSERVATIONS
OBSOLESCENCE
OBSOLETENESS
OBSTETRICIAN
OBSTREPEROUS
OBSTRUCTIONS
OCCASIONALLY
OCCUPATIONAL
OCEANOGRAPHY
OCTOGENARIAN
OCTOSYLLABIC
OCTOSYLLABLE
ODONTOGRAPHY
ODONTOLOGIST
ODONTOPHORAL
OESOPHAGUSES
OFFICE BLOCKS
OFFICEHOLDER
OFF ONES HANDS
OFF-THE-RECORD
OIL PAINTINGS
OKLAHOMA CITY
OLD-FASHIONED
OLD MANS BEARD
OLD PRETENDER
OLD SCHOOL TIE
OLD TESTAMENT
OLD WIVES'
   TALE
OLEORESINOUS
OLIGOTROPHIC
OLYMPIC GAMES
OMNIPRESENCE
ONEIROCRITIC
ONE-SIDEDNESS
ONE-TRACK MIND
ONE-UPMANSHIP
ONOMASIOLOGY
ONOMATOPOEIA
ONOMATOPOEIC
ON THE RAMPAGE
ONYCHOPHORAN
OOPHORECTOMY
OPEN-HANDEDLY
OPENING TIMES
OPEN-MINDEDLY
OPEN QUESTION
OPEN SANDWICH
OPEN VERDICTS

OPERA GLASSES
OPERATICALLY
OPHIOLOGICAL
OPHTHALMITIS
OPINION POLLS
OPPORTUNISTS
OPPOSABILITY
OPPOSITENESS
OPPOSITIONAL
OPPRESSINGLY
OPPRESSIVELY
OPSONIZATION
OPTIMIZATION
ORANGE ROUGHY
ORATORICALLY
ORBICULARITY
ORCHESTRA PIT
ORCHESTRATED
ORCHIDACEOUS
ORDINARINESS
ORGAN GRINDER
ORGANICISTIC
ORGANIZATION
ORGANOGRAPHY
ORGANOLEPTIC
ORGANOLOGIST
ORIEL WINDOWS
ORIENTALISTS
ORIENTATIONS
ORIENTEERING
ORNAMENTALLY
OROGENICALLY
OROLOGICALLY
ORTHOCEPHALY
ORTHODONTICS
ORTHOGENESIS
ORTHOGENETIC
ORTHOGRAPHER
ORTHOGRAPHIC
ORTHOMORPHIC
ORTHOPAEDICS
ORTHOPAEDIST
ORTHOPTEROUS
ORTHORHOMBIC
ORTHOTROPISM
ORTHOTROPOUS
OSCILLATIONS
OSCILLOGRAPH
OSCILLOSCOPE
OSSIFICATION
OSTENTATIOUS

OSTEOBLASTIC
OSTEOCLASTIC
OSTEOLOGICAL
OSTEOMALACIA
OSTEOPLASTIC
OSTRACIZABLE
OTHERWORLDLY
OUTBALANCING
OUTBUILDINGS
OUTDISTANCED
OUTGENERALED
OUTLANDISHLY
OUTMANOEUVRE
OUTNUMBERING
OUTRAGEOUSLY
OUTRIVALLING
OUTSTRETCHED
OUTSTRIPPING
OVERBALANCED
OVERBURDENED
OVERCAPACITY
OVERCAUTIOUS
OVERCHARGING
OVERCLOUDING
OVERCRITICAL
OVERCROPPING
OVERCROWDING
OVERDRESSING
OVEREMPHATIC
OVERESTIMATE
OVEREXPOSING
OVERGENEROUS
OVERINDULGED
OVERMASTERED
OVERPOPULATE
OVERPOWERING
OVERREACHING
OVERREACTING
OVERREACTION
OVERSHADOWED
OVERSHOOTING
OVERSIMPLIFY
OVERSLEEPING
OVERSTEPPING
OVERSTOCKING
OVERTHROWING
OVERWHELMING
OWNER-DRIVERS
OXYACETYLENE
OXYGENIZABLE

P
PACIFICATION
PACKAGE DEALS
PACKAGE TOURS
PACKING CASES
PADDLING POOL
PAEDOGENESIS
PAEDOGENETIC
PAEDOLOGICAL
PAGANIZATION
PAINTBRUSHES
PALAEOBOTANY
PALAEOGRAPHY
PALAEOLITHIC
PALATABILITY
PALATIALNESS
PALAZZO PANTS
PALEOGRAPHER
PALEONTOLOGY
PALETTE KNIFE
PALINGENESIS
PALINGENETIC
PALPITATIONS
PALYNOLOGIST
PAMPHLETEERS
PANCAKE ROLLS
PANCHROMATIC
PANDANACEOUS
PANDEMONIUMS
PANHELLENISM
PANHELLENIST
PANOPTICALLY
PANTECHNICON
PANTISOCRACY
PANTOGRAPHER
PANTOGRAPHIC
PAPERHANGERS
PAPERHANGING
PAPERWEIGHTS
PAPULIFEROUS
PARABOLOIDAL
PARACHRONISM
PARACHUTISTS
PARADE GROUND
PARADIGMATIC
PARADISE LOST
PARADISIACAL
PARAESTHESIA
PARAESTHETIC
PARAHYDROGEN
PARALANGUAGE

PARALLEL BARS
PARALLELISMS
PARALLELLING
PARALOGISTIC
PARALYSATION
PARAMAGNETIC
PARAMILITARY
PARAMORPHISM
PARAPHRASING
PARAPHRASTIC
PARASITICIDE
PARASITOLOGY
PARATHYROIDS
PARATROOPERS
PARENTHESIZE
PARISH CLERKS
PARISHIONERS
PARISYLLABIC
PARKING LIGHT
PARKING METER
PARLOUR GAMES
PAROCHIALISM
PARSIMONIOUS
PARSON'S NOSES
PART EXCHANGE
PARTHIAN SHOT
PARTIALITIES
PARTICIPANTS
PARTICIPATED
PARTICIPATOR
PARTICULARLY
PARTING SHOTS
PARTISANSHIP
PARTITIONING
PARTNERSHIPS
PART OF SPEECH
PARTY POOPERS
PASQUEFLOWER
PASSE PARTOUT
PASSE-PARTOUT
PASSIONATELY
PASSION PLAYS
PASTEURIZING
PAST PERFECTS
PATCH POCKETS
PATERNALISTS
PATERNOSTERS
PATHETICALLY
PATHOGENESIS
PATHOGENETIC
PATHOLOGICAL

PATHOLOGISTS
PATRIARCHATE
PATRIARCHIES
PATRICLINOUS
PATROL WAGONS
PATRON SAINTS
PAVING STONES
PAY ENVELOPES
PEACEFULNESS
PEAK DISTRICT
PEANUT BUTTER
PEARL HARBOUR
PEASE PUDDING
PECCADILLOES
PECKING ORDER
PEDANTICALLY
PEDIATRICIAN
PEEBLESSHIRE
PEJORATIVELY
PENALIZATION
PENALTY AREAS
PENDENTE LITE
PENITENTIARY
PENNSYLVANIA
PENNULTIMATE
PENNY PINCHER
PENNY WHISTLE
PENTARCHICAL
PEPTIC ULCERS
PERADVENTURE
PERAMBULATED
PERAMBULATOR
PERCEPTIONAL
PERCEPTIVELY
PERCEPTIVITY
PERCOLATIONS
PERCUTANEOUS
PEREGRINATOR
PEREMPTORILY
PERFECT PITCH
PERFIDIOUSLY
PERFOLIATION
PERFORATIONS
PERFORMANCES
PERFORMATIVE
PERICARDITIC
PERICARDITIS
PERICYNTHION
PERILOUSNESS
PERIMORPHISM
PERINEPHRIUM

PERINEURITIC
PERINEURITIS
PERIODICALLY
PERIODONTICS
PERIOD PIECES
PERIONYCHIUM
PERIPHERALLY
PERIPHRASTIC
PERITRICHOUS
PERMACULTURE
PERMANENT WAY
PERMANGANATE
PERMEABILITY
PERMISSIVELY
PERMITTIVITY
PERMUTATIONS
PERNICIOUSLY
PERPETRATING
PERPETRATION
PERPETRATORS
PERPETUATING
PERPETUATION
PERPETUITIES
PERPLEXITIES
PERSECUTIONS
PERSEVERANCE
PERSISTENTLY
PERSONA GRATA
PERSONALIZED
PERSONIFYING
PERSPECTIVES
PERSPICACITY
PERSPIRATION
PERSPIRATORY
PERSPIRINGLY
PERSUASIVELY
PERTINACIOUS
PERTURBATION
PERTURBINGLY
PERVERSENESS
PERVERSITIES
PERVIOUSNESS
PESTILENTIAL
PETALIFEROUS
PETERBOROUGH
PETIT LARCENY
PETRIFACTION
PETRODOLLARS
PETROGRAPHER
PETROGRAPHIC
PETROLOGICAL

PETROLOGISTS
PETROZAVODSK
PETTIFOGGING
PETTY LARCENY
PETTY OFFICER
PHAGOCYTOSIS
PHANEROGAMIC
PHANEROPHYTE
PHARMACOLOGY
PHARYNGOLOGY
PHARYNGOTOMY
PHELLODERMAL
PHENANTHRENE
PHENOLOGICAL
PHENOMENALLY
PHI BETA KAPPA
PHILADELPHIA
PHILADELPHUS
PHILANDERERS
PHILANDERING
PHILANTHROPY
PHILATELISTS
PHILHARMONIC
PHILISTINISM
PHILODENDRON
PHILOLOGICAL
PHILOLOGISTS
PHILOSOPHERS
PHILOSOPHIES
PHILOSOPHIZE
PHLEBOTOMIST
PHONEMICALLY
PHONE-TAPPING
PHONETICALLY
PHONETICIANS
PHONOGRAPHER
PHONOLOGICAL
PHONOLOGISTS
PHONOTACTICS
PHOSPHATURIA
PHOSPHATURIC
PHOSPHOLIPID
PHOSPHORESCE
PHOSPHORITIC
PHOTOACTINIC
PHOTOCATHODE
PHOTOCHEMIST
PHOTOCHROMIC
PHOTOCOMPOSE
PHOTOCOPIERS
PHOTOCOPYING

PHOTOCURRENT
PHOTODYNAMIC
PHOTOENGRAVE
PHOTOGEOLOGY
PHOTOGRAPHED
PHOTOGRAPHER
PHOTOGRAPHIC
PHOTOGRAVURE
PHOTOKINESIS
PHOTOKINETIC
PHOTOMETRIST
PHOTOMONTAGE
PHOTONEUTRON
PHOTONUCLEAR
PHOTOPHILOUS
PHOTOPOLYMER
PHOTOREALISM
PHOTOSPHERIC
PHOTOSTATTED
PHOTOTHERAPY
PHOTOTHERMIC
PHOTOTROPISM
PHRASAL VERBS
PHRASEOGRAPH
PHRENOLOGIST
PHYCOLOGICAL
PHYLETICALLY
PHYSICALNESS
PHYSIOCRATIC
PHYSIOGNOMIC
PHYSIOGRAPHY
PHYSIOLOGIES
PHYSIOLOGIST
PHYSOSTOMOUS
PHYTOGENESIS
PHYTOGENETIC
PHYTOHORMONE
PHYTOPHAGOUS
PICCANINNIES
PICKERELWEED
PICTURE BOOKS
PICTURE CARDS
PIECE OF EIGHT
PIECES OF WORK
PIGEONHOLING
PIGMENTATION
PILOT OFFICER
PINEAL GLANDS
PINK ELEPHANT
PIPE CLEANERS
PIPES OF PEACE

PISCICULTURE	POLICE STATES	PORTMANTEAUS	PRECIPITATES
PITCHFORKING	POLICYHOLDER	PORTMANTEAUX	PRECIPITATOR
PITIABLENESS	POLITICIZING	PORTS OF ENTRY	PRECISIANISM
PITILESSNESS	POLLEN COUNTS	POSITIVENESS	PRECISIONISM
PITTER-PATTER	POLLING BOOTH	POSITIVE POLE	PRECISIONIST
PLACENTATION	POLTERGEISTS	POSITIVISTIC	PRECLASSICAL
PLACE SETTING	POLYANTHUSES	POSSESSIVELY	PRECOCIOUSLY
PLAGIARISTIC	POLYCENTRISM	POSTAGE STAMP	PRECOGNITION
PLAGIARIZING	POLYCHAETOUS	POSTAL ORDERS	PRECOGNITIVE
PLAGIOCLIMAX	POLYCYTHEMIA	POSTDILUVIAL	PRECONCEIVED
PLAIN-CLOTHES	POLYEMBRYONY	POSTDILUVIAN	PRECONDITION
PLAIN SAILING	POLYETHYLENE	POSTDOCTORAL	PRECONSCIOUS
PLANETARIUMS	POLYISOPRENE	POSTER COLOUR	PREDECEASING
PLANETESIMAL	POLYMORPHISM	POSTER PAINTS	PREDECESSORS
PLANISPHERIC	POLYMORPHOUS	POSTGRADUATE	PREDESTINATE
PLANO-CONCAVE	POLYPETALOUS	POSTHUMOUSLY	PREDESTINING
PLANOGRAPHIC	POLYPHYLETIC	POSTMERIDIAN	PREDETERMINE
PLASTERBOARD	POLYPHYODONT	POST MERIDIEM	PREDICAMENTS
PLASTER CASTS	POLYRHYTHMIC	POSTPONEMENT	PREDICTIVELY
PLASTOMETRIC	POLYSEPALOUS	POSTPOSITION	PREDIGESTING
PLATONICALLY	POLYSULPHIDE	POSTPOSITIVE	PREDIGESTION
PLAUSIBILITY	POLYSYLLABIC	POSTPRANDIAL	PREDILECTION
PLAYER PIANOS	POLYSYLLABLE	POTATO BEETLE	PREDISPOSING
PLAYING CARDS	POLYSYNDETON	POTATO CRISPS	PREDOMINANCE
PLAYING FIELD	POLYTECHNICS	POTENTIALITY	PREDOMINATED
PLAYS ON WORDS	POLYTHEISTIC	POTTER'S WHEEL	PREDOMINATOR
PLEASANTNESS	POLYTONALIST	POTTING SHEDS	PRE-ECLAMPSIA
PLEASANTRIES	POLYTONALITY	POTTY-TRAINED	PRE-EMINENTLY
PLEASINGNESS	POLYURETHANE	POVERTY TRAPS	PRE-EMPTIVELY
PLEIOTROPISM	POMEGRANATES	POWER BROKERS	PRE-EXISTENCE
PLEOMORPHISM	PONS ASINORUM	POWERFULNESS	PREFABRICATE
PLIMSOLL LINE	PONTA DELGADA	POWER-SHARING	PREFECTORIAL
PLODDINGNESS	PONTIFICATED	POWER STATION	PREFERENTIAL
PLOUGHSHARES	PONTIFICATES	PRACTICALITY	PREFORMATION
PLUMBIFEROUS	PONY-TREKKING	PRACTITIONER	PREGNABILITY
PLUM PUDDINGS	POOR RELATION	PRAGMATISTIC	PREJUDGEMENT
PLUTOCRACIES	POOR-SPIRITED	PRAISEWORTHY	PREJUDGMENTS
PLUVIOMETRIC	POPOCATEPETL	PRASEODYMIUM	PREMARITALLY
PNEUMOCOCCUS	POPULAR FRONT	PRAYER WHEELS	PREMAXILLARY
PNEUMOTHORAX	POPULARIZING	PREAMPLIFIER	PREMEDITATED
POET LAUREATE	POPULOUSNESS	PREARRANGING	PREMEDITATOR
POINTILLISTS	PORNOGRAPHER	PREBENDARIES	PREMENSTRUAL
POINT OF ORDER	PORNOGRAPHIC	PRECARIOUSLY	PREMIERSHIPS
POINTS OF VIEW	PORPHYROPSIN	PRECEDENTIAL	PREMIUM BONDS
POINT-TO-POINT	PORT ADELAIDE	PRECENTORIAL	PREMONITIONS
POLARIMETRIC	PORT-AU-PRINCE	PRECEPTORATE	PREOCCUPYING
POLARIZATION	PORTCULLISES	PRECEPTORIAL	PREORDAINING
POLAROGRAPHY	PORTE-COCHERE	PRECESSIONAL	PREPARATIONS
POLE POSITION	PORTENTOUSLY	PRECIOUSNESS	PREPAREDNESS
POLE VAULTERS	PORTERHOUSES	PRECIPITANCE	PREPONDERANT
POLE VAULTING	PORT HARCOURT	PRECIPITATED	PREPONDERATE

PREPOSITIONS
PREPOSSESSED
PREPOSTEROUS
PRERECORDING
PREREQUISITE
PREROGATIVES
PRESBYTERATE
PRESBYTERIAL
PRESBYTERIAN
PRESBYTERIES
PRESCRIPTION
PRESCRIPTIVE
PRESENTATION
PRESENTATIVE
PRESENTIMENT
PRESERVATION
PRESERVATIVE
PRESIDENCIES
PRESIDENTIAL
PRESS CUTTING
PRESS GALLERY
PRESSGANGING
PRESSINGNESS
PRESS RELEASE
PRESSURIZING
PRESUMPTIONS
PRESUMPTUOUS
PRESUPPOSING
PRETTY-PRETTY
PREVAILINGLY
PREVARICATED
PREVARICATOR
PREVENTIVELY
PREVIOUSNESS
PRICKLY PEARS
PRIDE OF PLACE
PRIESTLINESS
PRIEST-RIDDEN
PRIGGISHNESS
PRIME NUMBERS
PRIMOGENITOR
PRIMORDIALLY
PRIMULACEOUS
PRIMUM MOBILE
PRINCELINESS
PRINCE REGENT
PRINCE RUPERT
PRINCIPAL BOY
PRINCIPALITY
PRINTABILITY
PRIORITIZING

PRISMATOIDAL
PRIVATE PARTS
PRIVY COUNCIL
PRIZEFIGHTER
PROBATIONARY
PROBATIONERS
PROBLEMATIZE
PROBOSCIDEAN
PROCATHEDRAL
PROCESSIONAL
PROCLAMATION
PROCLIVITIES
PROCONSULATE
PROCTOLOGIST
PRODIGIOUSLY
PRODUCTIONAL
PRODUCTIVELY
PRODUCTIVITY
PROFANATIONS
PROFESSIONAL
PROFESSORIAL
PROFICIENTLY
PROFITEERING
PROFITLESSLY
PROFIT MARGIN
PROFOUNDNESS
PROFUNDITIES
PROGESTERONE
PROGRAMMABLE
PROGRAMMATIC
PROGRESSIONS
PROGRESSIVES
PROHIBITIONS
PROJECTIONAL
PROLEGOMENAL
PROLEGOMENON
PROLETARIANS
PROLIFERATED
PROLIFICALLY
PROLIFICNESS
PROLONGATION
PROMISED LAND
PROMONTORIES
PROMULGATING
PROMULGATION
PROMULGATORS
PRONOMINALLY
PRONOUNCEDLY
PROOFREADERS
PROOFREADING
PROPAEDEUTIC

PROPAGANDISM
PROPAGANDIST
PROPAGANDIZE
PROPENSITIES
PROPHESIABLE
PROPHYLACTIC
PROPITIATING
PROPITIATION
PROPITIATIVE
PROPITIATORY
PROPITIOUSLY
PROPORTIONAL
PROPORTIONED
PROPOSITIONS
PROROGATIONS
PROSCRIPTION
PROSCRIPTIVE
PROSECUTABLE
PROSECUTIONS
PROSELYTIZED
PROSELYTIZER
PROSOPOPOEIA
PROSPECTUSES
PROSPEROUSLY
PROSTITUTING
PROSTITUTION
PROSTRATIONS
PROTACTINIUM
PROTAGONISTS
PROTECTIVELY
PROTECTORATE
PROTESTATION
PROTESTINGLY
PROTHALAMION
PROTHONOTARY
PROTOHISTORY
PROTOMORPHIC
PROTOPLASMIC
PROTOPLASTIC
PROTOSEMITIC
PROTOTHERIAN
PROTOTROPHIC
PROTOZOOLOGY
PROTRACTEDLY
PROTUBERANCE
PROVERBIALLY
PROVIDENTIAL
PROVINCETOWN
PROVINCIALLY
PROVISIONING
PROVOCATIONS

PRUDENTIALLY
PRUSSIAN BLUE
PSEPHOLOGIST
PSEUDONYMITY
PSEUDONYMOUS
PSEUDOPODIUM
PSYCHIATRIST
PSYCHOACTIVE
PSYCHOBABBLE
PSYCHOGNOSIS
PSYCHOGRAPHY
PSYCHOLOGIES
PSYCHOLOGISM
PSYCHOLOGIST
PSYCHOLOGIZE
PSYCHOMETRIC
PSYCHOPATHIC
PSYCHOSEXUAL
PSYCHOSOCIAL
PSYCHROMETER
PTERIDOPHYTE
PTERIDOSPERM
PTERODACTYLS
PUBLICATIONS
PUBLIC HOUSES
PUBLIC SCHOOL
PUBLIC SECTOR
PUBLIC SPIRIT
PUGNACIOUSLY
PULL A FAST
  ONE
PULVERULENCE
PUMPERNICKEL
PUNCHED CARDS
PUNITIVENESS
PURIFICATION
PURIFICATORY
PURISTICALLY
PURPLE HEARTS
PURPOSE-BUILT
PURPOSEFULLY
PURSE STRINGS
PUSSYFOOTING
PUSSY WILLOWS
PUT INTO WORDS
PUT ONES OAR
  IN
PUTREFACTION
PUTREFACTIVE
PYELOGRAPHIC
PYRIDOXAMINE

PYROCATECHOL
PYROCHEMICAL
PYROELECTRIC
PYROGNOSTICS
PYROLIGNEOUS
PYROMANIACAL
PYROMORPHITE
PYROPHYLLITE
PYROSULPHATE
PYROTECHNICS

Q
QUADRAGESIMA
QUADRANGULAR
QUADRAPHONIC
QUADRILLIONS
QUADRINOMIAL
QUADRIPLEGIA
QUADRIPLEGIC
QUADRIVALENT
QUADRUMANOUS
QUALIFYINGLY
QUANTIFIABLE
QUANTITATIVE
QUANTIZATION
QUANTUM LEAPS
QUAQUAVERSAL
QUARANTINING
QUARTER-BOUND
QUARTERFINAL
QUARTERLIGHT
QUARTER NOTES
QUARTER PLATE
QUARTERSTAFF
QUEEN CONSORT
QUEEN MOTHERS
QUELQUE CHOSE
QUESTIONABLE
QUESTIONABLY
QUESTION MARK
QUESTION TAGS
QUESTION TIME
QUEUE-JUMPERS
QUEUE-JUMPING
QUINDECAPLET
QUINQUENNIAL
QUINQUENNIUM
QUINTESSENCE
QUIXOTICALLY
QUIZZICALITY

R
RABBIT WARREN
RABBLE-ROUSER
RACE MEETINGS
RACEMIZATION
RADICALISTIC
RADIO BEACONS
RADIOBIOLOGY
RADIOCHEMIST
RADIOELEMENT
RADIOGRAPHER
RADIOGRAPHIC
RADIOISOTOPE
RADIOLOGICAL
RADIOLOGISTS
RADIONUCLIDE
RADIOTHERAPY
RAISE THE ROOF
RAISON D'ETRES
RALLENTANDOS
RAMBUNCTIOUS
RAMENTACEOUS
RAMIFICATION
RANGE FINDERS
RANKINE SCALE
RAPHAELESQUE
RAPSCALLIONS
RASTAFARIANS
RATIFICATION
RATIOCINATOR
RATIONALISTS
RATIONALIZED
RATIONALIZER
RATTLESNAKES
RAVENOUSNESS
RAYLEIGH DISC
RAZZLE-DAZZLE
REACH-ME-DOWNS
REACTIVATING
REACTIVATION
REACTIVENESS
READDRESSING
READJUSTABLE
READJUSTMENT
REAFFIRMANCE
REAFFORESTED
REALIGNMENTS
REALIZATIONS
REALLOCATION
REAL PROPERTY
REAPPEARANCE

REAPPRAISALS
REAPPRAISING
REAR ADMIRALS
REASSURANCES
REASSURINGLY
REAUMUR SCALE
REBELLIOUSLY
RECALCITRANT
RECALESCENCE
RECANTATIONS
RECAPITALIZE
RECAPITULATE
RECEIVERSHIP
RECEPTIONIST
RECESSIONALS
RECIDIVISTIC
RECIPROCALLY
RECIPROCATED
RECIPROCATOR
RECKLESSNESS
RECOGNITIONS
RECOGNIZABLE
RECOGNIZABLY
RECOGNIZANCE
RECOLLECTING
RECOLLECTION
RECOLLECTIVE
RECOMMENDING
RECOMMISSION
RECOMMITMENT
RECOMPENSING
RECONCILABLE
RECONCILABLY
RECONNOITRED
RECONNOITRER
RECONSECRATE
RECONSIDERED
RECONSTITUTE
RECONVERSION
RECORD PLAYER
RECREATIONAL
RECRIMINATED
RECRIMINATOR
RECUPERATING
RECUPERATION
RECUPERATIVE
RED BLOOD CELL
REDECORATING
REDEMANDABLE
REDEMPTIONAL
REDEPLOYMENT

REDEVELOPING
REDINTEGRATE
REDISTRIBUTE
RED-LETTER DAY
REDUCIBILITY
REDUNDANCIES
REDUPLICATED
REEFER JACKET
RE-EMPLOYMENT
RE-EXAMINABLE
REFLATIONARY
REFLECTINGLY
REFLECTIONAL
REFLECTIVITY
REFORMATIONS
REFRACTIONAL
REFRACTORILY
REFRESHINGLY
REFRESHMENTS
REFRIGERANTS
REFRIGERATED
REFRIGERATOR
REFURBISHING
REFUTABILITY
REGENERATING
REGENERATION
REGENERATIVE
REGISTRATION
REGULARIZING
REGURGITATED
REHABILITATE
REIMBURSABLE
REIMPOSITION
REIMPRESSION
REINCARNATED
REINVESTMENT
REITERATIONS
REJECTIONIST
REJUVENATING
REJUVENATION
RELATIONSHIP
RELATIVISTIC
RELENTLESSLY
RELINQUISHED
RELINQUISHER
REMAINDERING
REMAINDERMAN
REMEMBRANCER
REMEMBRANCES
REMINISCENCE
REMONSTRANCE

REMONSTRATED
REMONSTRATOR
REMORSEFULLY
REMOVABILITY
REMUNERATING
REMUNERATION
REMUNERATIVE
RENAISSANCES
RENEGOTIABLE
RENEWABILITY
RENFREWSHIRE
RENOUNCEMENT
RENUNCIATION
RENUNCIATIVE
REORGANIZING
REPARABILITY
REPATRIATING
REPATRIATION
REPERCUSSION
REPERCUSSIVE
REPLACEMENTS
REPLENISHING
REPLICATIONS
REPOSITORIES
REPOSSESSING
REPOSSESSION
REPREHENDING
REPREHENSION
REPREHENSIVE
REPREHENSORY
REPRESENTING
REPRESSIVELY
REPRIMANDING
REPROACHABLE
REPROACHABLY
REPROCESSING
REPRODUCIBLE
REPRODUCTION
REPRODUCTIVE
REPROGRAPHIC
REPUTABILITY
REQUEST STOPS
REQUIREMENTS
REQUISITIONS
RESCHEDULING
RESEARCHABLE
RESEMBLANCES
RESERVATIONS
RESERVEDNESS
RESETTLEMENT
RESIDENTIARY

RESIDENTSHIP
RESIGNATIONS
RESIGNEDNESS
RESINIFEROUS
RESINOUSNESS
RESOLUBILITY
RESOLUTENESS
RESOLUTIONER
RESOLVEDNESS
RESOUNDINGLY
RESOURCELESS
RESPECTFULLY
RESPECTIVELY
RESPLENDENCE
RESPONSIVELY
RESPONSORIAL
RESTATEMENTS
RESTAURATEUR
RESTLESSNESS
RESTORATIONS
RESTORATIVES
RESTRAINABLE
RESTRAINEDLY
RESTRICTEDLY
RESTRICTIONS
RESTRUCTURED
RESUPINATION
RESURRECTING
RESURRECTION
RESUSCITABLE
RESUSCITATED
RESUSCITATOR
RETICULATION
RETINOSCOPIC
RETRACTILITY
RETRENCHABLE
RETRENCHMENT
RETROCESSION
RETROCESSIVE
RETROFLEXION
RETROGRESSED
RETRO-ROCKETS
RETROVERSION
REUNIONISTIC
REVALUATIONS
REVEGETATION
REVELATIONAL
REVERBERATED
REVERBERATOR
REVERENDSHIP
REVERENTNESS

REVERSIONARY
REVISABILITY
REVISIONISTS
REVITALIZING
REVIVABILITY
REVIVALISTIC
REVOCABILITY
REVOKABILITY
REVULSIONARY
RHAPSODISTIC
RHAPSODIZING
RHESUS FACTOR
RHETORICALLY
RHETORICIANS
RHINOCEROSES
RHINOCEROTIC
RHINOLOGICAL
RHINOPLASTIC
RHIZOCARPOUS
RHODODENDRON
RHOMBOHEDRAL
RHOMBOHEDRON
RHYMING SLANG
RHYTHMICALLY
RHYTHM METHOD
RIBONUCLEASE
RICHTER SCALE
RICOCHETTING
RIDICULOUSLY
RIGHTFULNESS
RIGHT-HANDERS
RIGHT-HAND MAN
RIGHT-HAND MEN
RIGHTS ISSUES
RIGHT-WINGERS
RIGOROUSNESS
RING-STREAKED
RIO DE JANEIRO
ROAD MANAGERS
ROBBEN ISLAND
ROCKING CHAIR
ROCKING HORSE
ROCKUMENTARY
ROLLER BLINDS
ROLLER SKATED
ROLLER SKATER
ROLLER-SKATER
ROLLER SKATES
ROLLER TOWELS
ROLLICKINGLY
ROLLING MILLS

ROLLING STOCK
ROLLING STONE
ROLL OF HONOUR
ROLLTOP DESKS
ROMAN CANDLES
ROMAN NUMERAL
ROMANTICALLY
ROMANTICISTS
ROMANTICIZED
ROOMING HOUSE
ROOTLESSNESS
ROSE-COLOURED
ROSTROPOVICH
ROTARY TILLER
ROUGH DIAMOND
ROUND BRACKET
ROUND THE BEND
ROUTE MARCHES
ROYAL FLUSHES
ROYAL SOCIETY
RUBBER BRIDGE
RUBBER DINGHY
RUBBERNECKED
RUBBER PLANTS
RUBBER STAMPS
RULES OF THUMB
RUMINATINGLY
RUMINATIVELY
RUMMAGE SALES
RUMOURMONGER
RUNNING JUMPS
RUNNING MATES
RUN OF THE
   MILL
RUN-OF-THE-
   MILL
RURALIZATION
RUSTPROOFING
RUTHLESSNESS

S
SABBATARIANS
SACCHARINITY
SACRILEGIOUS
SADISTICALLY
SAFE AS HOUSES
SAFEBREAKERS
SAFEGUARDING
SAFETY ISLAND
SAFETY RAZORS
SAFETY VALVES

SAILING BOATS	SAUDI ARABIAN	SCRUTINIZING	SELF-RELIANCE
SAINT ANDREWS	SAUSAGE ROLLS	SCURRILOUSLY	SELF-REPROACH
SAINT AUSTELL	SAVING GRACES	SCUTELLATION	SELF-STARTERS
SAINT-ETIENNE	SAVINGS BANKS	SEAMSTRESSES	SELKIRKSHIRE
SAINT LAURENT	SAXONY-ANHALT	SEARCH ENGINE	SELLING PLATE
SAINT LEONARD	SAXOPHONISTS	SEARCHLIGHTS	SELLING POINT
SAINT-NAZAIRE	SCALABLENESS	SEASONALNESS	SEMANTICALLY
SAINT-QUENTIN	SCANDALIZING	SEASON TICKET	SEMICIRCULAR
SAINT VINCENT	SCANDALOUSLY	SEATON VALLEY	SEMIDETACHED
SALAMANDRINE	SCANDINAVIAN	SECESSIONISM	SEMIDIAMETER
SALESMANSHIP	SCAREMONGERS	SECESSIONIST	SEMIFINALIST
SALES PITCHES	SCARIFICATOR	SECLUDEDNESS	SEMIFLUIDITY
SALIFICATION	SCARLET FEVER	SECOND COMING	SEMINIFEROUS
SALINOMETRIC	SCARLET WOMAN	SECOND COUSIN	SEMIOTICIANS
SALMON LADDER	SCARLET WOMEN	SECOND-DEGREE	SEMIPALMATED
SALMON TROUTS	SCATOLOGICAL	SECOND NATURE	SEMIPRECIOUS
SALPIGLOSSIS	SCATTERBRAIN	SECOND PERSON	SEMITROPICAL
SALT LAKE CITY	SCENESHIFTER	SECOND-STRING	SEMIVITREOUS
SALUTARINESS	SCENOGRAPHER	SECRET AGENTS	SEMPITERNITY
SALUTATORILY	SCENOGRAPHIC	SECRETARIATS	SENARMONTITE
SALVATIONISM	SCHAFFHAUSEN	SECRETIONARY	SENSIBLENESS
SALVATIONIST	SCHEMATIZING	SECRET POLICE	SENSITOMETER
SAMARITANISM	SCHIZOMYCETE	SECTARIANISM	SENSITOMETRY
SAMOA ISLANDS	SCHIZOPHYTIC	SECTIONALISM	SENSORIMOTOR
SANCTIFIABLE	SCHIZOTHYMIA	SECTIONALIST	SENSUOUSNESS
SANCTIONABLE	SCHIZOTHYMIC	SECTIONALIZE	SEPARABILITY
SANDBLASTING	SCHOLARSHIPS	SECULARISTIC	SEPARATENESS
SAND BLASTING	SCHOLASTICAL	SECULARIZING	SEPARATISTIC
SANDPAPERING	SCHOOLFELLOW	SECURITY RISK	SEPTILATERAL
SAN FRANCISCO	SCHOOLHOUSES	SEDULOUSNESS	SEPTILLIONTH
SANGUINARILY	SCHOOL-LEAVER	SEGMENTATION	SEPTUAGESIMA
SANGUINENESS	SCHOOLMASTER	SEINE-ET-MARNE	SEPTUPLICATE
SANGUINOLENT	SCHORLACEOUS	SEISMOGRAPHS	SEQUENTIALLY
SANITARINESS	SCIENCE PARKS	SEISMOGRAPHY	SEQUESTRABLE
SAN PEDRO SULA	SCINTILLATED	SEISMOLOGIST	SEQUESTRATED
SAN SEBASTIAN	SCINTILLATOR	SEISMOSCOPIC	SEQUESTRATOR
SANTALACEOUS	SCLERENCHYMA	SELENOGRAPHY	SERIAL NUMBER
SANTO DOMINGO	SCLEROMETRIC	SELENOLOGIST	SERICULTURAL
SAONE-ET-LOIRE	SCOLOPENDRID	SELF-ABSORBED	SERINGAPATAM
SAPINDACEOUS	SCORNFULNESS	SELF-ANALYSIS	SERONEGATIVE
SAPONIFIABLE	SCOTCH TAPING	SELF-ASSEMBLY	SEROPOSITIVE
SAPROPHAGOUS	SCOTCH WHISKY	SELF-CATERING	SERVICEBERRY
SARCOMATOSIS	SCOTLAND YARD	SELF-COLOURED	SERVICE FLATS
SARDONICALLY	SCOUTMASTERS	SELF-DESTRUCT	SERVICE ROADS
SARSAPARILLA	SCRATCHINESS	SELF-EDUCATED	SESQUIALTERA
SASKATCHEWAN	SCRATCH PAPER	SELF-EFFACING	SET BY THE
SATIRIZATION	SCREWDRIVERS	SELF-EMPLOYED	EARS
SATISFACTION	SCRIMSHANDER	SELF-INTEREST	SEVENTEENTHS
SATISFACTORY	SCRIPTWRITER	SELFLESSNESS	SEVENTY-EIGHT
SATISFYINGLY	SCROBICULATE	SELF PORTRAIT	SEVERANCE PAY
SATURABILITY	SCRUPULOUSLY	SELF-PORTRAIT	SEXAGENARIAN

SEXCENTENARY
SEXTILLIONTH
SEXTUPLICATE
SHADOW-BOXING
SHAHJAHANPUR
SHAMATEURISM
SHAMEFACEDLY
SHAMEFULNESS
SHARECROPPER
SHAREHOLDERS
SHARPSHOOTER
SHARP-SIGHTED
SHARP-TONGUED
SHATTERINGLY
SHATTERPROOF
SHAVING CREAM
SHEATH KNIVES
SHEEPISHNESS
SHEEPSHEARER
SHEET ANCHORS
SHELLACKINGS
SHELLSHOCKED
SHEPHERD'S PIE
SHETLAND PONY
SHIFTINGNESS
SHIJIAZHUANG
SHILLY-SHALLY
SHIMMERINGLY
SHIPBUILDERS
SHIPBUILDING
SHIPWRECKING
SHIRTSLEEVES
SHIRTWAISTER
SHOCKABILITY
SHOCKINGNESS
SHOCKING PINK
SHOOTING STAR
SHOP STEWARDS
SHORT-CHANGED
SHORT-CHANGER
SHORT CIRCUIT
SHORTCOMINGS
SHORT-LISTING
SHORTSIGHTED
SHORT STORIES
SHORT-WAISTED
SHOT IN THE
  ARM
SHOW BUSINESS
SHOWSTOPPERS
SHOWSTOPPING

SHREWISHNESS
SHUDDERINGLY
SHUFFLEBOARD
SHUTTLECOCKS
SIAMESE TWINS
SICK HEADACHE
SIDEROSTATIC
SIDESLIPPING
SIDESTEPPING
SIDETRACKING
SIDE-WHEELERS
SIDE WHISKERS
SIDI-BEL-ABBES
SIERRA NEVADA
SIGHT-READERS
SIGHT-READING
SIGNIFICANCE
SIGN LANGUAGE
SILHOUETTING
SILICIFEROUS
SILICON CHIPS
SILIQUACEOUS
SILVERFISHES
SILVER LINING
SILVER MEDALS
SILVERSMITHS
SILVICULTURE
SIMILARITIES
SIMPLE-MINDED
SIMULTANEITY
SIMULTANEOUS
SINANTHROPUS
SINGLE-ACTING
SINGLE-ACTION
SINGLE-DECKER
SINGLE-HANDED
SINGLE-MINDED
SINGULARNESS
SINISTERNESS
SINISTRORSAL
SINKING FUNDS
SIPHONOPHORE
SIPHONOSTELE
SISTERLINESS
SISTERS-IN-LAW
SITTING DUCKS
SITTING ROOMS
SITUATIONISM
SKELETON KEYS
SKELMERSDALE
SKIPPING-ROPE

SKITTISHNESS
SKYROCKETING
SLANDEROUSLY
SLAUGHTERING
SLAUGHTEROUS
SLAVE DRIVERS
SLAVONICALLY
SLEDGEHAMMER
SLEEPING BAGS
SLEEPING CARS
SLEEPING PILL
SLEEPWALKERS
SLEEPWALKING
SLENDERIZING
SLIDING DOORS
SLIDING SCALE
SLIPPERINESS
SLIPPINGNESS
SLIPSTREAMED
SLOANE RANGER
SLOTHFULNESS
SLOT MACHINES
SLOVENLINESS
SLUGGARDNESS
SLUGGISHNESS
SLUMBERINGLY
SLUTTISHNESS
SMALL FORTUNE
SMALLHOLDERS
SMALLHOLDING
SMASH-AND-GRAB
SMILACACEOUS
SMOKESCREENS
SMOOTH-SPOKEN
SMORGASBORDS
SNAGGLETOOTH
SNAKE CHARMER
SNAP FASTENER
SNAPPISHNESS
SNEAKINGNESS
SNEAK PREVIEW
SNEAK THIEVES
SNICKERINGLY
SNIGGERINGLY
SNOBBISHNESS
SNOOPERSCOPE
SOCIALIZABLE
SOCIAL WORKER
SOCIOLOGICAL
SOCIOLOGISTS
SOCIOMETRIST

SODA FOUNTAIN
SOFT LANDINGS
SOFT-PEDALING
SOFT-PEDALLED
SOLARIZATION
SOLAR SYSTEMS
SOLICITATION
SOLICITOUSLY
SOLIDIFIABLE
SOLIFLUCTION
SOLILOQUIZED
SOLITARINESS
SOLITUDINOUS
SOLVENT ABUSE
SOMATOLOGIST
SOMATOPLEURE
SOMERSAULTED
SOMNAMBULANT
SOMNAMBULATE
SOMNAMBULISM
SOMNAMBULIST
SON ET LUMIERE
SONG AND DANCE
SONOROUSNESS
SOOTHINGNESS
SOPHISTICATE
SOPORIFEROUS
SOUL BROTHERS
SOULLESSNESS
SOUND BARRIER
SOUND EFFECTS
SOUNDPROOFED
SOUP KITCHENS
SOUSAPHONIST
SOUTH AMERICA
SOUTHEASTERN
SOUTHERNMOST
SOUTHERNWOOD
SOUTH HOLLAND
SOUTH OSSETIA
SOUTH SHIELDS
SOUTHWESTERN
SPACE CAPSULE
SPACE HEATERS
SPACE SHUTTLE
SPACE STATION
SPACIOUSNESS
SPEAKING TUBE
SPEARHEADING
SPECIALISTIC
SPECIALITIES

SPECIALIZING	SPORTFULNESS	STATION HOUSE	STOCKBREEDER
SPECIFICALLY	SPORTIVENESS	STATION WAGON	STOCKBROKERS
SPECIOUSNESS	SPORTSPERSON	STATISTICIAN	STOCKHOLDERS
SPECTACULARS	SPOT-CHECKING	STAYING POWER	STOCK-IN-TRADE
SPECTROGRAPH	SPOTLESSNESS	STEAK TARTARE	STOCKJOBBERS
SPECTROMETER	SPOTLIGHTING	STEAL THE SHOW	STOCKJOBBERY
SPECTROMETRY	SPOTTED DICKS	STEALTHINESS	STOCK MARKETS
SPECTROSCOPE	SPREAD-EAGLED	STEAMROLLERS	STOICHIOLOGY
SPECTROSCOPY	SPREADSHEETS	STEAM SHOVELS	STOKE-ON-TRENT
SPECULATIONS	SPRINGBOARDS	STEATOPYGOUS	STOMACHACHES
SPEECHIFYING	SPRING ONIONS	STEATORRHOEA	STOMACH PUMPS
SPEECHLESSLY	SPURIOUSNESS	STEEPLECHASE	STONECUTTING
SPEEDOMETERS	SQUAMOUSNESS	STEEPLEJACKS	STONEMASONRY
SPEEDWRITING	SQUARE DANCES	STELLIFEROUS	STONEWALLERS
SPELEOLOGIST	SQUARE-RIGGED	STENOGRAPHER	STONEWALLING
SPELLBINDERS	SQUARE-RIGGER	STENOGRAPHIC	STONY-HEARTED
SPELLBINDING	SQUEAKY-CLEAN	STENOTHERMAL	STOOLPIGEONS
SPELLCHECKER	SQUEEZEBOXES	STEPBROTHERS	STOREKEEPERS
SPENDTHRIFTS	SQUELCHINGLY	STEPCHILDREN	STOREKEEPING
SPERMATHECAL	SQUIRRELFISH	STEPDAUGHTER	STORM TROOPER
SPERMATOCYTE	STADDLESTONE	STEREOCHROME	STORMY PETREL
SPERMATOZOAL	STAFF OFFICER	STEREOCHROMY	STORYTELLERS
SPERMATOZOID	STAGECOACHES	STEREOGRAPHY	STORYTELLING
SPERMATOZOON	STAGE-MANAGED	STEREOISOMER	STOUTHEARTED
SPERMOGONIUM	STAGE MANAGER	STEREOMETRIC	STOVEPIPE HAT
SPHRAGISTICS	STAGE WHISPER	STEREOPHONIC	STRADIVARIUS
SPHYGMOGRAPH	STAGGERINGLY	STEREOPTICON	STRAGGLINGLY
SPICK AND SPAN	STAGING POSTS	STEREOSCOPIC	STRAIGHTAWAY
SPICK-AND-SPAN	STAINABILITY	STEREOTACTIC	STRAIGHTEDGE
SPIEGELEISEN	STAINED GLASS	STEREOTROPIC	STRAIGHTENED
SPINSTERHOOD	STAKEHOLDERS	STEREOTYPING	STRAIGHTENER
SPIRITEDNESS	STALACTIFORM	STEREOVISION	STRAIGHTNESS
SPIRIT LEVELS	STALLHOLDERS	STERILIZABLE	STRAINEDNESS
SPIRITUALISM	STALWARTNESS	STERNUTATION	STRAITJACKET
SPIRITUALIST	STAMMERINGLY	STERNUTATIVE	STRANGLEHOLD
SPIRITUALITY	STANDARDIZED	STERNUTATORY	STRANGULATED
SPIRITUALIZE	STANDARDIZER	STERNWHEELER	STRAPHANGERS
SPIRITUOSITY	STANDARD LAMP	STERTOROUSLY	STRAPHANGING
SPIROGRAPHIC	STANDARD TIME	STETHOSCOPES	STRATICULATE
SPITEFULNESS	STANDING ROOM	STETHOSCOPIC	STRATIGRAPHY
SPLASH GUARDS	STANDOFF HALF	STICHOMETRIC	STRATOCRATIC
SPLATTERPUNK	STAND-OFF HALF	STICK INSECTS	STRATOSPHERE
SPLENDIDNESS	STANLEY KNIFE	STICKLEBACKS	STRAWBERRIES
SPLENOMEGALY	STANNIFEROUS	STICKY WICKET	STREAMLINING
SPLIT SECONDS	STAR CHAMBERS	STIGMASTEROL	STREETS AHEAD
SPOKESPEOPLE	STAR-SPANGLED	STIGMATIZING	STREET VALUES
SPOKESPERSON	STARTING GATE	STILBOESTROL	STREETWALKER
SPONGIOBLAST	STATELY HOMES	STILETTO HEEL	STRENGTHENED
SPOON-FEEDING	STATEN ISLAND	STINKINGNESS	STRENGTHENER
SPORADICALLY	STATIONARILY	STIPULATIONS	STREPTOCOCCI
SPOROGENESIS	STATION BREAK	STIRRUP PUMPS	STREPTOMYCIN

STRETCHINESS
STRETCHMARKS
STRIDULATING
STRIDULATION
STRIDULATORY
STRIKINGNESS
STRIP CARTOON
STRIP MININGS
STROBE LIGHTS
STROBILATION
STROBOSCOPES
STROBOSCOPIC
STROMATOLITE
STRONG-MINDED
STRONG POINTS
STRONG-WILLED
STRONTIANITE
STROPHANTHIN
STROPHANTHUS
STRUCTURALLY
STRUGGLINGLY
STRYCHNINISM
STUBBORNNESS
STUDDINGSAIL
STUDIOUSNESS
STUFFED SHIRT
STUPEFACIENT
STUPEFACTION
STUPEFYINGLY
STUPENDOUSLY
STUTTERINGLY
STYLOGRAPHIC
STYRACACEOUS
SUBALTERNATE
SUBANTARCTIC
SUBAURICULAR
SUBCELESTIAL
SUBCLIMACTIC
SUBCOMMITTEE
SUBCONSCIOUS
SUBCONTINENT
SUBCUTANEOUS
SUBDEACONATE
SUBDIACONATE
SUBDIVISIONS
SUBERIZATION
SUBINFEUDATE
SUBJECTIVELY
SUBJECTIVISM
SUBJECTIVIST
SUBJECTIVITY

SUBJUNCTIVES
SUBMAXILLARY
SUBMERSIBLES
SUBMISSIVELY
SUBMITTINGLY
SUBNORMALITY
SUBORDINATED
SUBORDINATES
SUBPRINCIPAL
SUBSCRIPTION
SUBSCRIPTIVE
SUBSEQUENTLY
SUBSERVIENCE
SUBSIDIARIES
SUBSIDIARILY
SUBSIDIARITY
SUBSIDIZABLE
SUBSISTINGLY
SUBSTANTIATE
SUBSTANTIVAL
SUBSTANTIVES
SUBSTITUTING
SUBSTITUTION
SUBSTITUTIVE
SUBSTRUCTURE
SUBTEMPERATE
SUBTERRANEAN
SUBTRACTIONS
SUBURBANITES
SUBVERSIVELY
SUCCEDANEOUS
SUCCEEDINGLY
SUCCESSFULLY
SUCCESSIONAL
SUCCESSIVELY
SUCCINCTNESS
SUCTION PUMPS
SUDORIFEROUS
SUFFRAGETTES
SUFFRUTICOSE
SUGAR DADDIES
SUGGESTINGLY
SUGGESTIVELY
SUITABLENESS
SULPHONAMIDE
SULPHURATION
SUMMARIZABLE
SUMMERHOUSES
SUMMER SCHOOL
SUNDAY SCHOOL
SUPERABILITY

SUPERANNUATE
SUPERCHARGED
SUPERCHARGER
SUPERCILIARY
SUPERCILIOUS
SUPEREMINENT
SUPERFICIARY
SUPERGLACIAL
SUPERGRASSES
SUPERIMPOSED
SUPERLATIVES
SUPERMARKETS
SUPERNATURAL
SUPERPOSABLE
SUPERSEDABLE
SUPERSESSION
SUPERSTITION
SUPERSTRATUM
SUPERTANKERS
SUPERVENIENT
SUPPLEMENTAL
SUPPLEMENTED
SUPPLEMENTER
SUPPLETORILY
SUPPLICATING
SUPPLICATION
SUPPLICATORY
SUPPOSITIONS
SUPPOSITIOUS
SUPPRESSIBLE
SUPRAGLOTTAL
SUPRALIMINAL
SUPRAORBITAL
SUPRAPROTEST
SUPREMACISTS
SUPREME BEING
SUPREME COURT
SUREFOOTEDLY
SURFACE-TO-AIR
SURMOUNTABLE
SURPASSINGLY
SURPRISINGLY
SURREALISTIC
SURREJOINDER
SURRENDERING
SURROUNDEDLY
SURROUNDINGS
SURVEILLANCE
SURVEYORSHIP
SURVIVAL KITS
SUSCEPTIVITY

SUSPICIOUSLY
SUSTAININGLY
SWAGGERINGLY
SWALLOW DIVES
SWASHBUCKLER
SWEEPINGNESS
SWEET-AND-SOUR
SWEET PEPPERS
SWEET POTATOS
SWEET-TALKING
SWELTERINGLY
SWIMMING BATH
SWIMMING POOL
SWING THE LEAD
SWITCHBLADES
SWITCHBOARDS
SWIZZLE STICK
SWORD DANCERS
SYLLABICALLY
SYMBOLICALLY
SYMBOLOGICAL
SYMMETALLISM
SYMPATHIZERS
SYMPATHIZING
SYNAESTHESIA
SYNAESTHETIC
SYNAPTICALLY
SYNARTHROSIS
SYNCHROFLASH
SYNCHRONIZED
SYNCHRONIZER
SYNCHROSCOPE
SYNCLINORIUM
SYNDACTYLISM
SYNDETICALLY
SYNDICALISTS
SYNDIOTACTIC
SYNODIC MONTH
SYNONYMOUSLY
SYNOPTICALLY
SYNTHESIZERS
SYNTHESIZING
SYNTONICALLY
SYSTEMATIZED
SYSTEMATIZER
SYSTEMICALLY

T

TABERNACULAR
TABLE MANNERS
TABLE-TURNING

TACHEOMETRIC	TERATOLOGIST	THERMOSTABLE	TONSILLOTOMY
TACHYCARDIAC	TERCENTENARY	THERMOSTATIC	TOOTHBRUSHES
TACTLESSNESS	TEREBINTHINE	THERMOTROPIC	TOPDRESSINGS
TADZHIKISTAN	TERGIVERSATE	THEURGICALLY	TOP-HEAVINESS
TALCUM POWDER	TERMINATIONS	THICK-SKINNED	TOPOGRAPHERS
TALENT SCOUTS	TERRIBLENESS	THIEVISHNESS	TORMENTINGLY
TALKING POINT	TERRIFICALLY	THIGMOTACTIC	TORREFACTION
TAMBOURINIST	TERRIFYINGLY	THIGMOTROPIC	TORTUOUSNESS
TANGENTIALLY	TERRITORIALS	THINGAMAJIGS	TOTALITARIAN
TAPE MEASURES	TESSELLATION	THIOSINAMINE	TOTALIZATORS
TAPE RECORDER	TESTAMENTARY	THIOSULPHATE	TOURIST CLASS
TAPE STREAMER	TESTIMONIALS	THIRD PARTIES	TOUT ENSEMBLE
TARAMASALATA	TESTOSTERONE	THOROUGHBRED	TOWER HAMLETS
TARDENOISIAN	TEST-TUBE BABY	THOROUGHFARE	TOWER OF BABEL
TARTARIC ACID	TETANIZATION	THOROUGHNESS	TOWN PLANNERS
TASTEFULNESS	TETRACHORDAL	THOUGHTFULLY	TOWN PLANNING
TAUROMACHIAN	TETRACYCLINE	THREE QUARTER	TOXICOLOGIST
TAUTOLOGICAL	TETRAHEDRITE	THREE-QUARTER	TOXOPHILITIC
TAX COLLECTOR	TETRAPTEROUS	THREE-WHEELER	TRACEABILITY
TAXIDERMISTS	TETRASTICHIC	THROMBOCYTIC	TRACE ELEMENT
TECHNICALITY	TETRAVALENCY	THUNDERBOLTS	TRACHEOPHYTE
TECHNOBABBLE	TEUTONICALLY	THUNDERCLAPS	TRACHEOSTOMY
TECHNOGRAPHY	THALAMICALLY	THUNDERCLOUD	TRACHOMATOUS
TECHNOLOGIES	THALASSAEMIA	THUNDERFLASH	TRACING PAPER
TECHNOLOGIST	THALLOPHYTIC	THUNDERINGLY	TRACK RECORDS
TECTONICALLY	THANKFULNESS	THUNDEROUSLY	TRACTABILITY
TEENYBOPPERS	THANKSGIVING	THUNDERSTONE	TRACUCIANIST
TEETER-TOTTER	THAUMATOLOGY	THUNDERSTORM	TRADESCANTIA
TEETOTALLERS	THEANTHROPIC	THUNDER STORM	TRADESPEOPLE
TELAESTHESIA	THEATREGOERS	TICKLISHNESS	TRADING POSTS
TELAESTHETIC	THEATRICALLY	TIED COTTAGES	TRADING STAMP
TELAUTOGRAPH	THE HERMITAGE	TIME CAPSULES	TRADITIONIST
TELEGRAPHERS	THEISTICALLY	TIME EXPOSURE	TRADUCIANISM
TELEGRAPHESE	THEMATICALLY	TIME HONOURED	TRAFFICATORS
TELEGRAPHING	THEOCENTRISM	TIME-HONOURED	TRAFFIC LIGHT
TELEMEDICINE	THEOPHYLLINE	TIMELESSNESS	TRAGEDIENNES
TELEOLOGICAL	THEORETICIAN	TIME SWITCHES	TRAILBLAZING
TELEOLOGISTS	THEORIZATION	TIMOROUSNESS	TRAILER HOUSE
TELEPHONE BOX	THERAPEUTICS	TIRELESSNESS	TRAINBEARERS
TELEPHONISTS	THE REAL THING	TIRESOMENESS	TRAIN SPOTTER
TELEPRINTERS	THEREINAFTER	TITANIFEROUS	TRAINSPOTTER
TELEPROMPTER	THERMOCOUPLE	TITLEHOLDERS	TRAITOROUSLY
TELESHOPPING	THERMOGENOUS	TITTLE-TATTLE	TRAJECTORIES
TELEUTOSPORE	THERMOGRAPHY	TOASTING FORK	TRAMPISHNESS
TELEVISIONAL	THERMOLABILE	TOASTMASTERS	TRANQUILLITY
TELGENICALLY	THERMOMETERS	TOBACCONISTS	TRANQUILLIZE
TELLUROMETER	THERMOMETRIC	TOFFEE APPLES	TRANSACTIONS
TEMPERAMENTS	THERMOSCOPIC	TOGETHERNESS	TRANSCENDENT
TEMPERATURES	THERMOS FLASK	TOMFOOLERIES	TRANSCENDING
TENANT FARMER	THERMOSIPHON	TONE LANGUAGE	TRANSCRIBING
TEN-GALLON HAT	THERMOSPHERE	TONELESSNESS	TRANSCURRENT

TRANSDUCTION	TREMENDOUSLY	TUNNEL VISION	UNCINARIASIS
TRANSFERABLE	TRENDSETTERS	TURBELLARIAN	UNCLASSIFIED
TRANSFERENCE	TRENDSETTING	TURBIDIMETER	UNCOMMERCIAL
TRANSFERRING	TREPHINATION	TURBOCHARGED	UNCOMMONNESS
TRANSFIGURED	TRIBESPEOPLE	TURBOCHARGER	UNCONFORMITY
TRANSFORMERS	TRIBULATIONS	TURKISH BATHS	UNCONSENTING
TRANSFORMING	TRICHINIASIS	TURKMENISTAN	UNCONSIDERED
TRANSFORMISM	TRICHOCYSTIC	TURNING POINT	UNCONVINCING
TRANSFORMIST	TRICHOGYNIAL	TUVA REPUBLIC	UNCOVENANTED
TRANSFUSIBLE	TRICHOLOGIST	TU-WHIT TU-	UNCRITICALLY
TRANSFUSIONS	TRICHOPTERAN	WHOO	UNCTUOUSNESS
TRANSGRESSED	TRICHROMATIC	TWILIGHT ZONE	UNDECEIVABLE
TRANSGRESSOR	TRICK OR TREAT	TWISTABILITY	UNDEMOCRATIC
TRANSHUMANCE	TRIFURCATION	TWO-FACEDNESS	UNDERACHIEVE
TRANSITIONAL	TRIGGER HAPPY	TWO-WAY MIRROR	UNDERBELLIES
TRANSITORILY	TRIGGER-HAPPY	TYPIFICATION	UNDERCHARGED
TRANSLATABLE	TRIGLYCERIDE	TYPOGRAPHERS	UNDERCLOTHES
TRANSLATIONS	TRIGONOMETRY	TYRANNICALLY	UNDERCURRENT
TRANSLUCENCE	TRILINGUALLY	TYRANNICIDAL	UNDERCUTTING
TRANSLUCENCY	TRIMOLECULAR		UNDERDEVELOP
TRANSMIGRANT	TRIPARTITION	**U**	UNDERDRAWING
TRANSMIGRATE	TRIPHTHONGAL	UBIQUITOUSLY	UNDERDRESSED
TRANSMISSION	TRIPLE-TONGUE	UGLIFICATION	UNDEREXPOSED
TRANSMISSIVE	TRIPLICATION	UGLY CUSTOMER	UNDERGARMENT
TRANSMITTERS	TRIPOLITANIA	UGLY DUCKLING	UNDERGROUNDS
TRANSMITTING	TRIUMPHANTLY	ULTRAMONTANE	UNDERNOURISH
TRANSMOGRIFY	TRIUMVIRATES	ULTRAMUNDANE	UNDERPAYMENT
TRANSMUNDANE	TRIVIALITIES	UMBILICATION	UNDERPINNING
TRANSMUTABLE	TRIVIALIZING	UNACCEPTABLE	UNDERPLAYING
TRANSOCEANIC	TROCHAICALLY	UNACCUSTOMED	UNDERSCORING
TRANSPARENCY	TROCHOIDALLY	UNACQUAINTED	UNDERSELLING
TRANSPIRABLE	TROJAN HORSES	UNAFFECTEDLY	UNDERSHERIFF
TRANSPLANTED	TROLLEYBUSES	UNAFFORDABLE	UNDERSTAFFED
TRANSPLANTER	TROMBIDIASIS	UNAGGRESSIVE	UNDERSTATING
TRANSPONDERS	TROOP CARRIER	UNANSWERABLE	UNDERSTUDIED
TRANSPORTERS	TROPHALLAXIS	UNAPOLOGETIC	UNDERSTUDIES
TRANSPORTING	TROPOPHILOUS	UNAPPEALABLE	UNDERSURFACE
TRANSPORTIVE	TROUBLEMAKER	UNASSAILABLE	UNDERTAKINGS
TRANSPOSABLE	TROUBLE SPOTS	UNASSOCIATED	UNDERTRAINED
TRANSUDATORY	TROUSER PRESS	UNASSUMINGLY	UNDERUTILIZE
TRANSVAALIAN	TRUSTABILITY	UNATTAINABLE	UNDERVALUING
TRANSVERSELY	TRUSTEESHIPS	UNATTRACTIVE	UNDERWRITERS
TRANSVESTISM	TRUSTFULNESS	UNATTRIBUTED	UNDERWRITING
TRANSVESTITE	TRUTHFULNESS	UNBELIEVABLE	UNDERWRITTEN
TRANSYLVANIA	TRYPANOSOMAL	UNBELIEVABLY	UNDESIRABLES
TRAPSHOOTING	TRYPARSAMIDE	UNBIASEDNESS	UNDETERMINED
TRAUMATIZING	TUBERCULOSIS	UNCELEBRATED	UNDISCHARGED
TRAVEL AGENCY	TUMBLE-DRYERS	UNCHALLENGED	UNECONOMICAL
TRAVEL AGENTS	TUMBLE-DRYING	UNCHARITABLE	UNEMPLOYABLE
TREBLE CHANCE	TUMULTUOUSLY	UNCHARITABLY	UNEMPLOYMENT
TREELESSNESS	TUNELESSNESS	UNCHASTENESS	UNEVENTFULLY

UNEXPRESSIVE
UNEXPURGATED
UNFAITHFULLY
UNFATHOMABLE
UNFATHOMABLY
UNFAVOURABLE
UNFAVOURABLY
UNFLAGGINGLY
UNFLATTERING
UNFORGIVABLE
UNFORTUNATES
UNFREQUENTED
UNGAINLINESS
UNGOVERNABLE
UNGRATEFULLY
UNHESITATING
UNHYPHENATED
UNIDENTIFIED
UNIFOLIOLATE
UNILATERALLY
UNIMAGINABLE
UNIMPRESSIVE
UNINFLUENCED
UNINTERESTED
UNIONIZATION
UNISEXUALITY
UNITARIANISM
UNIVERSALISM
UNIVERSALIST
UNIVERSALITY
UNIVERSALIZE
UNIVERSITIES
UNKINDLINESS
UNLAWFULNESS
UNLIKELIHOOD
UNLIKELINESS
UNMANAGEABLE
UNMEASURABLE
UNMISTAKABLE
UNMISTAKABLY
UNMODERNIZED
UNOFFICIALLY
UNPARALLELED
UNPERFORATED
UNPLEASANTLY
UNPOPULARITY
UNPREJUDICED
UNPRINCIPLED
UNPRODUCTIVE
UNPROFITABLE
UNPUBLICIZED

UNQUESTIONED
UNREASONABLE
UNREASONABLY
UNRECKONABLE
UNRECOGNIZED
UNREFLECTIVE
UNREGENERACY
UNREGENERATE
UNRESERVEDLY
UNRESPONSIVE
UNRESTRAINED
UNRESTRICTED
UNSANCTIONED
UNSATURATION
UNSCIENTIFIC
UNSCRAMBLING
UNSCRUPULOUS
UNSEARCHABLE
UNSEASONABLE
UNSEASONABLY
UNSEEMLINESS
UNSEGREGATED
UNSETTLEMENT
UNSTEADINESS
UNSTRATIFIED
UNSTRUCTURED
UNSUCCESSFUL
UNSUPPORTIVE
UNSUSPECTING
UNTENABILITY
UNTHINKINGLY
UNTIMELINESS
UNTOUCHABLES
UNTOWARDNESS
UNTRAMMELLED
UNWIELDINESS
UNWORTHINESS
UNWRITTEN LAW
UPHOLSTERERS
UPHOLSTERING
UPPER AUSTRIA
UPRIGHT PIANO
UPROARIOUSLY
UP-TO-DATENESS
URANOGRAPHER
URANOGRAPHIC
URBANIZATION
URETHROSCOPE
URETHROSCOPY
URINOGENITAL
USER FRIENDLY

USER-FRIENDLY
USUFRUCTUARY
USURIOUSNESS
UTILITY ROOMS
UTTAR PRADESH
UXORIOUSNESS

V

VACCINATIONS
VACILLATIONS
VACUUM FLASKS
VACUUM-PACKED
VAINGLORIOUS
VALEDICTIONS
VALENCIENNES
VALORIZATION
VALUABLENESS
VANQUISHABLE
VANQUISHMENT
VANTAGEPOINT
VANTAGE POINT
VAPORESCENCE
VAPORIZATION
VAPOROUSNESS
VAPOUR TRAILS
VARICOLOURED
VASODILATION
VAUDEVILLIAN
VAUDEVILLIST
VEGETATIONAL
VELARIZATION
VELOCIRAPTOR
VENERABILITY
VENERATIONAL
VENGEFULNESS
VENIPUNCTURE
VENTRICOSITY
VERBENACEOUS
VERIDICALITY
VERIFICATION
VERIFICATIVE
VERTEBRATION
VERTICILLATE
VESICULATION
VESTAL VIRGIN
VIBRAPHONIST
VICE-CHAIRMAN
VICISSITUDES
VICTORIANISM
VICTORIA PLUM
VICTORIOUSLY

VIDEO NASTIES
VIGOROUSNESS
VILIFICATION
VILLAGE GREEN
VILLAHERMOSA
VILLEURBANNE
VINDICTIVELY
VINICULTURAL
VIN ORDINAIRE
VIOLONCELLOS
VIRGIN'S-BOWER
VIRIDESCENCE
VIRTUOUSNESS
VISCEROMOTOR
VISCOUNTCIES
VISITATIONAL
VISITATORIAL
VISITING CARD
VISITORS' BOOK
VITALIZATION
VITICULTURAL
VITICULTURER
VITREOUSNESS
VITUPERATION
VITUPERATIVE
VIVIFICATION
VIVISECTIONS
VIXENISHNESS
VOCABULARIES
VOCALIZATION
VOCIFERATING
VOCIFERATION
VOCIFEROUSLY
VOIDABLENESS
VOLCANICALLY
VOLTA REDONDA
VOLUMINOSITY
VOLUMINOUSLY
VOLUNTARYISM
VOLUNTARYIST
VOLUNTEERING
VOLUNTEERISM
VOLUPTUARIES
VOLUPTUOUSLY
VOMITURITION
VOTE OF THANKS
VOWELIZATION
VULCANIZABLE

W

WAGES COUNCIL

WAITING LISTS
WAITING ROOMS
WALKIE-TALKIE
WALKING STICK
WALLCOVERING
WALL PAINTING
WALLPAPERING
WANKEL ENGINE
WAREHOUSEMAN
WARMONGERING
WARS OF NERVES
WARWICKSHIRE
WASH DRAWINGS
WASTEFULNESS
WASTE PRODUCT
WATCHFULNESS
WATER BISCUIT
WATER BUFFALO
WATER CANNONS
WATER CLOSETS
WATERCOLOURS
WATERCOURSES
WATERING CANS
WATERING HOLE
WATERMANSHIP
WATER MEADOWS
WATERPROOFED
WATTENSCHEID
WAYS AND MEANS
WEATHERBOARD
WEATHER-BOUND
WEATHERCOCKS
WEATHERGLASS
WEATHERPROOF
WEATHER SHIPS
WEATHER VANES
WEDDING RINGS
WEIGHBRIDGES
WEIGHTLESSLY
WEIGHT LIFTER
WELFARE STATE
WELL-ADJUSTED

WELL-ASSORTED
WELL-ATTENDED
WELL BALANCED
WELL-BALANCED
WELL-DESERVED
WELL DISPOSED
WELL-DISPOSED
WELL-EDUCATED
WELL-EQUIPPED
WELL-FAVOURED
WELL-GROUNDED
WELL-INFORMED
WELL-MANNERED
WELL-PROVIDED
WELL-RECEIVED
WELL-SITUATED
WELL-TEMPERED
WELSH RAREBIT
WELTERWEIGHT
WENSLEYDALES
WEST BROMWICH
WESTERLINESS
WESTERN ISLES
WESTERNIZING
WESTERN SAMOA
WEST FLANDERS
WEST MIDLANDS
WEST VIRGINIA
WETTING AGENT
WHEELBARROWS
WHEELWRIGHTS
WHENCESOEVER
WHEREWITHALS
WHIGGISHNESS
WHIMPERINGLY
WHIMSICALITY
WHIPPING BOYS
WHIPPOORWILL
WHITE KNIGHTS
WHITE-LIVERED
WHITE SLAVERY
WHITEWASHING

WHITE WEDDING
WHOLE-HEARTED
WHOLE NUMBERS
WHORTLEBERRY
WICKET KEEPER
WIDE RECEIVER
WIFE SWAPPING
WIGTOWNSHIRE
WILDERNESSES
WILLIAMSBURG
WILL-O'-THE-
  WISP
WINDCHEATERS
WINDING SHEET
WINDOW SHADES
WIND TURBINES
WINEGLASSFUL
WINGLESSNESS
WINSTON-SALEM
WINTERBOURNE
WINTER SPORTS
WISCONSINITE
WISECRACKING
WITCHDOCTORS
WITCH-HUNTING
WITCHING HOUR
WITHDRAWABLE
WITHEREDNESS
WITH OPEN ARMS
WITH PLEASURE
WITHSTANDING
WITNESS BOXES
WOLF WHISTLES
WOLLASTONITE
WOMANISHNESS
WONDER-WORKER
WONDROUSNESS
WOODENHEADED
WOOLGATHERER
WOOLLY-HEADED
WORDLESSNESS
WORD OF HONOUR
WORKER-PRIEST

WORKING CLASS
WORKING ORDER
WORKING PARTY
WORKING WEEKS
WORKINGWOMAN
WORKSTATIONS
WORLD-BEATERS
WORLD-BEATING
WORLDSHAKING
WORLD WIDE WEB
WORMS EYE VIEW
WRATHFULNESS
WRETCHEDNESS
WRISTWATCHES
WRITER'S CRAMP
WRITING DESKS
WRITING PAPER
WRONGFULNESS

X

X CHROMOSOMES
XERODERMATIC
XIPHISTERNUM

Y

Y CHROMOSOMES
YELLOWHAMMER
YIELDINGNESS
YINDJIBARNDI
YOUTHFULNESS
YOUTH HOSTELS

Z

ZINCOGRAPHER
ZINCOGRAPHIC
ZOOCHEMISTRY
ZOOGEOGRAPHY
ZOOSPERMATIC
ZOOTOMICALLY
ZWITTERIONIC
ZYGAPOPHYSIS
ZYGOMORPHISM

A
ABBREVIATIONS
ABERDEENSHIRE
ABNORMALITIES
ABOLITIONISTS
ABORTIFACIENT
ABSORBABILITY
ACCELEROMETER
ACCENTUATIONS
ACCEPTABILITY
ACCESSIBILITY
ACCESSORINESS
ACCIDENT-PRONE
ACCLIMATIZING
ACCOMMODATING
ACCOMMODATION
ACCOMMODATIVE
ACCOMPANIMENT
ACCOMPLISHING
ACCOUTREMENTS
ACCREDITATION
ACCULTURATION
ACCUMULATIONS
ACETIFICATION
ACETYLCHOLINE
ACHILLES'
  HEELS
ACIDIFICATION
ACKNOWLEDGING
ACOTYLEDONOUS
ACQUAINTANCES
ACQUIESCENTLY
ACQUIRED TASTE
ACQUISITIVELY
ACRIMONIOUSLY
ACROBATICALLY
ACRYLONITRILE
ACTINOMORPHIC
ACTINOMYCOSIS
ACTINOMYCOTIC
ACTINOTHERAPY
ACTINOURANIUM
ACTUALIZATION
ADDITIONALITY
ADDRESSOGRAPH
ADENOIDECTOMY
ADIAPHORISTIC
ADMEASUREMENT
ADMINISTERING
ADMINISTRATOR
ADMISSIBILITY

ADMONISHINGLY
ADNYAMATHANHA
ADSORBABILITY
ADVANCED LEVEL
ADVENTURESSES
ADVENTUROUSLY
ADVERTISEMENT
AEROMECHANICS
AESTHETICALLY
AFFENPINSCHER
AFFIRMATIVELY
AFFORESTATION
AFTERTHOUGHTS
AGGIORNAMENTO
AGGLOMERATING
AGGLOMERATION
AGGLOMERATIVE
AGGLUTINATION
AGGLUTINATIVE
AGGRAVATINGLY
AGREEABLENESS
AGRICULTURIST
AGROBIOLOGIST
AIR COMMODORES
AIRCRAFTWOMAN
AIRWORTHINESS
AIX-EN-
  PROVENCE
ALBURY-WODONGA
ALCOHOLICALLY
ALCOHOLOMETER
ALDUS MANUTIUS
ALGEBRAICALLY
ALLEGORICALLY
ALLOCHTHONOUS
ALPHA AND
  OMEGA
ALTAI REPUBLIC
ALTERNATIVELY
ALUMINIFEROUS
ALUMINOTHERMY
AMALGAMATIONS
AMBASSADORIAL
AMBIDEXTERITY
AMBIGUGUITIES
AMBIGUOUSNESS
AMBITIOUSNESS
AMERICANIZING
AMERICAN SAMOA
AMNIOCENTESIS
AMORPHOUSNESS

AMPHIBLASTULA
AMPHIPROSTYLE
AMPHITHEATRES
AMPHITRICHOUS
AMPLIFICATION
AMUSEMENT PARK
ANACHRONISTIC
ANAEROBICALLY
ANAESTHETISTS
ANAESTHETIZED
ANAGRAMMATISM
ANAGRAMMATIST
ANAGRAMMATIZE
ANAL RETENTIVE
ANAPHORICALLY
ANAPHRODISIAC
ANATHEMATIZED
ANATOMIZATION
ANCHORPERSONS
ANDHRA PRADESH
ANEMOMETRICAL
ANESTHETIZING
ANFRACTUOSITY
ANGIOSPERMOUS
ANGLICIZATION
ANGLO-AMERICAN
ANGLO-CATHOLIC
ANIMADVERSION
ANIMADVERTING
ANIMALIZATION
ANISOMETROPIA
ANNEXATIONISM
ANNEXATIONIST
ANNIVERSARIES
ANNOUNCEMENTS
ANSWERABILITY
ANTAGONIZABLE
ANTHRAQUINONE
ANTHROPOMETRY
ANTHROPOPATHY
ANTHROPOPHAGI
ANTHROPOSOPHY
ANTI-APARTHEID
ANTIBACTERIAL
ANTICLIMACTIC
ANTICLINORIUM
ANTICLOCKWISE
ANTI-COMMUNIST
ANTIGENICALLY
ANTIHISTAMINE
ANTILOGARITHM

ANTIMACASSARS
ANTIMONARCHIC
ANTINOMICALLY
ANTIPERSONNEL
ANTIPRAGMATIC
ANTIPSYCHOTIC
ANTISPASMODIC
ANTISUBMARINE
APATHETICALLY
APERIODICALLY
APHELIOTROPIC
APLANATICALLY
APOCHROMATISM
APODICTICALLY
APOGEOTROPISM
APOSTROPHIZED
APPLE PIE
  ORDER
APPLICABILITY
APPORTIONABLE
APPORTIONMENT
APPRECIATIONS
APPREHENSIBLE
APPREHENSIONS
APPROPRIATELY
APPROPRIATING
APPROPRIATION
APPROXIMATELY
APPROXIMATING
APPROXIMATION
APPURTENANCES
AQUICULTURIST
ARABIAN DESERT
ARABIC NUMERAL
ARACHNOPHOBIA
ARBITRARINESS
ARBORICULTURE
ARCHAEOLOGIST
ARCHBISHOPRIC
ARCHIDIACONAL
ARCHIMANDRITE
ARCHIPELAGOES
ARCHITECTONIC
ARCHITECTURAL
ARGENTIFEROUS
ARGILLIFEROUS
ARGUMENTATION
ARGUMENTATIVE
ARGYLL AND
  BUTE
ARISTOCRACIES

ARITHMETICIAN
AROMATIZATION
ARRIERE-PENSEE
ARTERIOVENOUS
ARTESIAN WELLS
ARTICULATIONS
ARTIFICIALITY
ARTS AND
 CRAFTS
ARUNDINACEOUS
ASCERTAINABLE
ASCERTAINMENT
ASCHAFFENBURG
ASPERGILLOSIS
ASSASSINATING
ASSASSINATION
ASSAULT COURSE
ASSEMBLY LINES
ASSERTIVENESS
ASSET-STRIPPER
ASSEVERATIONS
ASSIDUOUSNESS
ASSIGNABILITY
ASSYRIOLOGIST
ASTHENOSPHERE
ASTHMATICALLY
ASTIGMATISTIC
ASTONISHINGLY
ASTRODYNAMICS
ASTROPHYSICAL
ASYNDETICALLY
ATACAMA DESERT
ATAVISTICALLY
ATHEISTICALLY
ATOMISTICALLY
ATROCIOUSNESS
ATTAINABILITY
ATTENTIVENESS
AT THE SAME
 TIME
ATTITUDINIZER
ATTRIBUTIVELY
AUBERVILLIERS
AUDACIOUSNESS
AUGMENTATIONS
AUNG SAN SUU
 KYI
AUSTRALASIANS
AUSTRO-ASIATIC
AUTECOLOGICAL
AUTHENTICALLY

AUTHENTICATED
AUTHENTICATOR
AUTHORITARIAN
AUTHORITATIVE
AUTHORIZATION
AUTOBIOGRAPHY
AUTOCATALYSIS
AUTOCHTHONISM
AUTOCHTHONOUS
AUTOMATICALLY
AUTOMATIC DOOR
AUTONOMICALLY
AUTOSTABILITY
AUXILIARY VERB
AXIOMATICALLY

B

BABY CARRIAGES
BACCALAUREATE
BACK FORMATION
BACKPEDALLING
BACKWARDATION
BACTERIOLYSIS
BACTERIOLYTIC
BACTERIOPHAGE
BALANCED DIETS
BALANCE SHEETS
BALKANIZATION
BALLISTICALLY
BALL LIGHTNING
BALNEOLOGICAL
BALSAMIFEROUS
BAMBOOZLEMENT
BANDSPREADING
BANKER'S
 ORDERS
BANTAMWEIGHTS
BARBAROUSNESS
BARBOUR JACKET
BAREFACEDNESS
BASIDIOMYCETE
BASOTHO-QWAQWA
BATTERING RAMS
BATTLE CRUISER
BATTLE-SCARRED
BEAST OF
 BURDEN
BEATIFICATION
BEAUFORT SCALE
BEAUTY PARLOUR
BEHAVIOURALLY

BEHAVIOURISTS
BELISHA BEACON
BELLES-LETTRES
BELLY-LANDINGS
BELO HORIZONTE
BENEFICIARIES
BENEFIT IN
 KIND
BERCHTESGADEN
BEWILDERINGLY
BIBLIOGRAPHER
BIBLIOGRAPHIC
BICENTENARIES
BIDIRECTIONAL
BIG BANG
 THEORY
BIGHEADEDNESS
BIGNONIACEOUS
BILLS OF
 HEALTH
BILLS OF
 LADING
BILLS OF
 RIGHTS
BIODEGRADABLE
BIOECOLOGICAL
BIOENERGETICS
BIOMETRICALLY
BIOSTATICALLY
BIOTECHNOLOGY
BIRD OF
 PASSAGE
BIRD'S-EYE
 VIEWS
BIREFRINGENCE
BLABBERMOUTHS
BLACK AND
 WHITE
BLACKBERRYING
BLACK COMEDIES
BLACKCURRANTS
BLACKGUARDISM
BLACK MOUNTAIN
BLACK PUDDINGS
BLAMELESSNESS
BLANDISHMENTS
BLANTYRE-LIMBE
BLASPHEMOUSLY
BLAST FURNACES
BLASTOGENESIS
BLIND MAN'S
 BUFF

BLOOD BROTHERS
BLOODCURDLING
BLOODLESSNESS
BLOOD PRESSURE
BLOOD RELATION
BLOTTING PAPER
BLUE MOUNTAINS
BLUE-PENCILLED
BLUESTOCKINGS
BLUNDERBUSSES
BOARDING CARDS
BOARDINGHOUSE
BOBO-DIOULASSO
BODY SNATCHERS
BODY STOCKINGS
BOILING POINTS
BOMBASTICALLY
BOOBY TRAPPING
BOON COMPANION
BORAGINACEOUS
BORDERS REGION
BOTTLE-FEEDING
BOTTOM DRAWERS
BOUGAINVILLEA
BOUILLABAISSE
BOUNDLESSNESS
BOUNTEOUSNESS
BOUNTIFULNESS
BOUSTROPHEDON
BOWLING ALLEYS
BOWLING GREENS
BRACHYCEPHALY
BRACHYPTEROUS
BRAINLESSNESS
BRAINSTORMING
BRASSICACEOUS
BRASS KNUCKLES
BROADMINDEDLY
BROKEN-HEARTED
BROMELIACEOUS
BRONCHIAL TUBE
BRONCHOSCOPIC
BROTHERLINESS
BROTHERS-IN-
 LAW
BROWNIE GUIDES
BROWNIE POINTS
BRUTALIZATION
BUBONIC PLAGUE
BUDGET DEFICIT
BUILDING BLOCK

BULLETIN BOARD
BUMPTIOUSNESS
BUNGEE JUMPING
BUNSEN BURNERS
BURDEN OF
    PROOF
BUREAUCRACIES
BUREAUCRATISM
BURGLAR ALARMS
BURNT OFFERING
BURY ST
    EDMUNDS
BUSH CARPENTER
BUSH TELEGRAPH
BUSINESS CLASS
BUSINESS SUITS
BUSINESSWOMAN
BUTCHER'S-
    BROOM
BUTTERFINGERS
BUTTER-FINGERS
BUTYRALDEHYDE

C
CABIN CRUISERS
CABINET-MAKERS
CABLE RAILWAYS
CAICOS ISLANDS
CALCARIFEROUS
CALCIFICATION
CALCULABILITY
CALENDAR MONTH
CALENDAR YEARS
CALLIGRAPHIST
CALLISTHENICS
CALORIFICALLY
CAMBRIDGE BLUE
CAMPANOLOGIST
CAMP FOLLOWERS
CAMPYLOBACTER
CANARY ISLANDS
CANCELLATIONS
CANNIBALISTIC
CANNIBALIZING
CANONIZATIONS
CAPACIOUSNESS
CAPARISONNING
CAPE COLOUREDS
CAPITAL LEVIES
CAPITULATIONS
CAPRIFICATION

CARAVANSERAIS
CARBOHYDRATES
CARBON DIOXIDE
CARBONIFEROUS
CARBONIZATION
CARBURIZATION
CARCINOMATOID
CARDIGANSHIRE
CARDINAL POINT
CARDIOGRAPHER
CARDIOGRAPHIC
CARDIOLOGICAL
CARICATURISTS
CARNIFICATION
CARPETBAGGERS
CARPET SWEEPER
CARRICKFERGUS
CARRIER PIGEON
CARTILAGINOUS
CARTOGRAPHERS
CARVING KNIVES
CASE HISTORIES
CASH DISPENSER
CASH REGISTERS
CASSEGRAINIAN
CASUISTICALLY
CATASTROPHISM
CATASTROPHIST
CATCHMENT AREA
CATECHIZATION
CATECHOLAMINE
CATEGORICALLY
CATER-CORNERED
CATHARTICALLY
CAT-O'-NINE-
    TAILS
CAUTERIZATION
CAYENNE PEPPER
CAYMAN ISLANDS
CELLULAR RADIO
CENTRAL REGION
CENTRE FORWARD
CEPHALIZATION
CEPHALOMETRIC
CEPHALOTHORAX
CEREBRAL PALSY
CEREBROSPINAL
CEREMONIALISM
CEREMONIALIST
CEREMONIOUSLY
CERTIFICATION

CERTIFICATORY
CERTIFIED MAIL
CERTIFIED MILK
CHAFING DISHES
CHAIN REACTION
CHAIN STITCHES
CHAIRMANSHIPS
CHAISE LONGUES
CHALCOGRAPHER
CHALCOGRAPHIC
CHALLENGEABLE
CHAMPIONSHIPS
CHANCELLERIES
CHANDERNAGORE
CHANDRASEKHAR
CHANGEABILITY
CHANGE OF
    HEART
CHANGE RINGING
CHANGING ROOMS
CHANNEL TUNNEL
CHANTRY CHAPEL
CHARACTERIZED
CHARACTERLESS
CHARGEABILITY
CHARGE ACCOUNT
CHARLOTTETOWN
CHARNEL HOUSES
CHARTER MEMBER
CHASTISEMENTS
CHASTITY BELTS
CHATEAUBRIAND
CHEERLESSNESS
CHEMISORPTION
CHEMORECEPTOR
CHESTERFIELDS
CHEVAL GLASSES
CHIAROSCURISM
CHIAROSCURIST
CHIEF JUSTICES
CHIEFS OF
    STAFF
CHIEFTAINSHIP
CHILDLESSNESS
CHIMNEYBREAST
CHIMNEY CORNER
CHIMNEYPIECES
CHIMNEYSTACKS
CHIMNEYSWEEPS
CHIROPRACTORS
CHLAMYDOSPORE

CHLOROBENZENE
CHLOROFORMING
CHLOROMYCETIN
CHLOROPLASTIC
CHONDRIOSOMAL
CHONDROMATOUS
CHOREOGRAPHED
CHOREOGRAPHER
CHOREOGRAPHIC
CHRISTIANIZER
CHRISTIAN NAME
CHRISTMAS CAKE
CHRISTMAS CARD
CHRISTMASTIDE
CHRISTMASTIME
CHRISTMAS TREE
CHRISTOLOGIST
CHROMATICALLY
CHROMATICNESS
CHROMATOLYSIS
CHROMATOPHORE
CHROMOPLASMIC
CHROMOPROTEIN
CHROMOSPHERIC
CHRONOBIOLOGY
CHRONOGRAPHER
CHRONOGRAPHIC
CHRONOLOGICAL
CHRYSANTHEMUM
CHURCHWARDENS
CICATRIZATION
CINEMATICALLY
CINEMATOGRAPH
CIRCULARIZING
CIRCUMAMBIENT
CIRCUMCISIONS
CIRCUMFERENCE
CIRCUMFLEXION
CIRCUMSCRIBED
CIRCUMSPECTLY
CIRCUMSTANCES
CIRCUMVALLATE
CIRCUMVENTING
CIRCUMVENTION
CIUDAD GUAYANA
CIVIL ENGINEER
CIVILIZATIONS
CIVIL SERVANTS
CLAIRAUDIENCE
CLANDESTINELY
CLAPPERBOARDS

CLARIFICATION
CLARINETTISTS
CLASSIFIED ADS
CLASSLESSNESS
CLASS STRUGGLE
CLAUSTROPHOBE
CLAVICHORDIST
CLEARANCE SALE
CLEAR-HEADEDLY
CLEARINGHOUSE
CLEISTOGAMOUS
CLERKS OF
    WORKS
CLIMACTERICAL
CLIMATOLOGIST
CLIMBING FRAME
CLIMBING IRONS
CLOSED-CIRCUIT
CLOSED SEASONS
CLOSING PRICES
CLOTHES HANGER
CLOTHESHORSES
CLUSTER-BOMBED
COACHBUILDERS
COACH STATIONS
COBELLIGERENT
COCAINIZATION
COCKER SPANIEL
COCKTAIL STICK
CODECLINATION
CODIFICATIONS
COEDUCATIONAL
COLD-BLOODEDLY
COLD-HEARTEDLY
COLLABORATING
COLLABORATION
COLLABORATIVE
COLLABORATORS
COLLATERALIZE
COLLETIVISTIC
COLLOQUIALISM
COLOUR SCHEMES
COMBAT FATIGUE
COMBINING FORM
COMMANDEERING
COMMANDERSHIP
COMMAND MODULE
COMMEMORATING
COMMEMORATION
COMMEMORATIVE
COMMENCEMENTS

COMMENDATIONS
COMMENSURABLE
COMMERCIALISM
COMMERCIALIST
COMMERCIALITY
COMMERCIALIZE
COMMISERATING
COMMISERATION
COMMISERATIVE
COMMISSARIATS
COMMISSIONERS
COMMISSIONING
COMMUNALISTIC
COMMUNAUTAIRE
COMMUNICATING
COMMUNICATION
COMMUNICATIVE
COMMUNICATORY
COMMUNITARIAN
COMMUNITY HOME
COMMUNIZATION
COMPANIONABLE
COMPANIONABLY
COMPANIONSHIP
COMPANIONWAYS
COMPARABILITY
COMPARATIVELY
COMPARTMENTAL
COMPASSIONATE
COMPASS POINTS
COMPATIBILITY
COMPATRIOTISM
COMPENDIOUSLY
COMPETITIVELY
COMPLAININGLY
COMPLAISANTLY
COMPLEMENTARY
COMPLEMENTING
COMPLICATEDLY
COMPLICATIONS
COMPLIMENTARY
COMPLIMENTING
COMPOSITIONAL
COMPREHENDING
COMPREHENSION
COMPREHENSIVE
COMPRESSIONAL
COMPUTABILITY
COMPUTATIONAL
COMPUTERIZING
CONCATENATING

CONCATENATION
CONCAVO-CONVEX
CONCENTRATING
CONCENTRATION
CONCENTRATIVE
CONCENTRICITY
CONCEPTUALISM
CONCEPTUALIST
CONCEPTUALIZE
CONCERT GRANDS
CONCERTINAING
CONCESSIONARY
CONCHOLOGICAL
CONCHOLOGISTS
CONCOMITANTLY
CONCRETE MIXER
CONCRETIONARY
CONCUPISCENCE
CONDEMNATIONS
CONDEMNED CELL
CONDENSED MILK
CONDESCENDING
CONDESCENSION
CONDITIONALLY
CONDUCIVENESS
CONDUCTOR RAIL
CONDYLOMATOUS
CONFABULATING
CONFABULATION
CONFABULATORY
CONFECTIONARY
CONFECTIONERS
CONFECTIONERY
CONFEDERACIES
CONFEDERATING
CONFEDERATION
CONFESSIONALS
CONFESSIONARY
CONFIGURATION
CONFIRMATIONS
CONFISCATIONS
CONFLAGRATION
CONFLAGRATIVE
CONFORMATIONS
CONFRATERNITY
CONFRONTATION
CONGLOMERATES
CONGLOMERATIC
CONGRATULATED
CONGRATULATOR
CONGREGATIONS

CONGRESSIONAL
CONGRESSWOMAN
CONJUGATIONAL
CONJUNCTIONAL
CONNECTING ROD
CONNING TOWERS
CONNOTATATIVE
CONQUISTADORS
CONSANGUINITY
CONSCIENTIOUS
CONSCIOUSNESS
CONSECUTIVELY
CONSEQUENTIAL
CONSERVANCIES
CONSERVATIVES
CONSERVATOIRE
CONSIDERATELY
CONSIDERATION
CONSISTENCIES
CONSOLIDATING
CONSOLIDATION
CONSPICUOUSLY
CONSPIRATRESS
CONSTELLATION
CONSTELLATORY
CONSTERNATION
CONSTITUTIONS
CONSTRAINEDLY
CONSTRICTIONS
CONSTRUCTIBLE
CONSTRUCTIONS
CONSULTANCIES
CONSULTATIONS
CONSUMMATIONS
CONTACT LENSES
CONTAINERIZED
CONTAMINATING
CONTAMINATION
CONTAMINATORS
CONTEMPLATING
CONTEMPLATION
CONTEMPLATIVE
CONTENTIOUSLY
CONTEXTUALISM
CONTEXTUALIZE
CONTINGENCIES
CONTINUATIONS
CONTORTIONIST
CONTRABANDIST
CONTRABASSIST
CONTRABASSOON

CONTRACEPTION
CONTRACEPTIVE
CONTRACTILITY
CONTRACTIONAL
CONTRACTUALLY
CONTRADICTING
CONTRADICTION
CONTRADICTIVE
CONTRADICTORY
CONTRAPUNTIST
CONTRAVENTION
CONTRIBUTIONS
CONTROVERSIAL
CONTROVERSIES
CONVALESCENCE
CONVALESCENTS
CONVERSATIONS
CONVERSAZIONE
CONVERTIPLANE
CONVEXO-CONVEX
CONVEYER BELTS
CONVOCATIONAL
CONVOLVULUSES
COOKING APPLES
COOPERATIVELY
CORDUROY ROADS
CORELIGIONIST
CO-RESPONDENCY
CO-RESPONDENTS
CORN EXCHANGES
CORPS DE
  BALLET
CORPUS CHRISTI
CORRESPONDENT
CORRESPONDING
CORRIGIBILITY
CORROBORATING
CORROBORATION
CORROBORATIVE
CORROBORATORS
CORRODIBILITY
CORROSIVENESS
CORRUPTIONIST
COSIGNATORIES
COSMOPOLITANS
COSMOPOLITISM
COST-EFFECTIVE
COSTERMONGERS
COTERMINOUSLY
COTTAGE CHEESE
COTTAGE LOAVES

COTTON-PICKING
COUNTENANCING
COUNTERACTING
COUNTERACTION
COUNTERACTIVE
COUNTERATTACK
COUNTERBLASTS
COUNTERCHARGE
COUNTERCLAIMS
COUNTERFEITED
COUNTERFEITER
COUNTERMANDED
COUNTERPOINTS
COUNTERPOISED
COUNTERPOISES
COUNTERSIGNED
COUNTERTENORS
COUNTERWEIGHT
COUNTINGHOUSE
COUNTRY COUSIN
COUNTRY DANCES
COUNTY BOROUGH
COUNTY COUNCIL
COURT CIRCULAR
COURTEOUSNESS
COURT MARTIALS
COURTS-MARTIAL
COVERED WAGONS
CRAFTSMANSHIP
CRANIOLOGICAL
CRASH BARRIERS
CRASH LANDINGS
CRASSULACEOUS
CREAM OF
  TARTAR
CREDIT ACCOUNT
CREDIT SQUEEZE
CREME DE
  MENTHE
CRIMINOLOGIST
CRISSCROSSING
CROSSBENCHERS
CROSSBREEDING
CROSSCHECKING
CROSSCURRENTS
CROSS-DRESSERS
CROSS-DRESSING
CROSS-EXAMINED
CROSS-EXAMINER
CROSS-HATCHING
CROSS-PURPOSES

CROSS-QUESTION
CROSS-REFERRED
CROSS-SECTIONS
CROSS-STITCHES
CROWN COLONIES
CROWN IMPERIAL
CROWN PRINCESS
CRUISE MISSILE
CRUISERWEIGHT
CRUSH BARRIERS
CRYOBIOLOGIST
CRYPTANALYSIS
CRYPTANALYTIC
CRYPTOCLASTIC
CRYPTOGRAPHER
CRYPTOGRAPHIC
CRYPTOZOOLOGY
CRYSTAL GAZERS
CRYSTAL GAZING
CRYSTALLINITY
CRYSTALLIZING
CUMULOSTRATUS
CURTAIN RAISER
CUSTODIANSHIP
CUT ONES
  LOSSES
CYANOBACTERIA
CYBERNETICIST
CYLINDRICALLY
CYTOCHEMISTRY
CYTOTAXONOMIC
CZECH REPUBLIC

D

DADAISTICALLY
DADDY LONGLEGS
DAGUERREOTYPE
DAGUERREOTYPY
DAMAGEABILITY
DAMNIFICATION
DANDIFICATION
DARK CONTINENT
DASTARDLINESS
DAUGHTER-IN-
  LAW
DEAD-CAT
  BOUNCE
DEAD RECKONING
DEATH WARRANTS
DEBTS OF
  HONOUR

DECAPITATIONS
DECEITFULNESS
DECENTRALIZED
DECEPTIVENESS
DECEREBRATION
DECK PASSENGER
DECLAMATORILY
DECLARATORILY
DECLASSIFYING
DECOMPOSITION
DECOMPRESSING
DECOMPRESSION
DECOMPRESSIVE
DECONGESTANTS
DECONTAMINANT
DECONTAMINATE
DECONTROLLING
DECORTICATION
DECREPITATION
DEDUCTIBILITY
DEFECTIVENESS
DEFENSIBILITY
DEFENSIVENESS
DEFERENTIALLY
DEFIBRILLATOR
DEFORESTATION
DEGLUTINATION
DEHYDROGENASE
DEHYDROGENATE
DEHYDROGENIZE
DELETERIOUSLY
DELIBERATIONS
DELICATESSENS
DELICIOUSNESS
DELINQUENCIES
DELIQUESCENCE
DELIRIOUSNESS
DEMAGNETIZING
DEMAGOGICALLY
DEMERARA SUGAR
DEMERITORIOUS
DEMILITARIZED
DEMOCRATIZING
DEMOLITIONIST
DEMONOLOGICAL
DEMONSTRATING
DEMONSTRATION
DEMONSTRATIVE
DEMONSTRATORS
DENATIONALIZE
DENDRITICALLY

DENDROLOGICAL	DIAMETRICALLY	DISCONTINUING	DISPUTABILITY
DENOMINATIONS	DIAPHRAGMATIC	DISCONTINUITY	DISQUALIFYING
DENSITOMETRIC	DIATHERMANOUS	DISCONTINUOUS	DISQUISITIONS
DENTAL SURGEON	DIATONIC SCALE	DISCOUNT STORE	DISRESPECTFUL
DENTICULATION	DIAZOTIZATION	DISCOURTESIES	DISSATISFYING
DENUNCIATIONS	DICHLAMIDEOUS	DISCREDITABLE	DISSEMINATING
DEODORIZATION	DICTATORIALLY	DISCREDITABLY	DISSEMINATION
DEONTOLOGICAL	DICTATORSHIPS	DISCREPANCIES	DISSEMINATIVE
DEOXIDIZATION	DIEFFENBACHIA	DISCRETIONARY	DISSEPIMENTAL
DEOXYGENATION	DIESEL ENGINES	DISCRIMINATED	DISSERTATIONS
DEPENDABILITY	DIFFERENTIALS	DISCRIMINATOR	DISSIMILARITY
DEPERSONALIZE	DIFFERENTIATE	DISEMBODIMENT	DISSIMILATION
DEPRECATINGLY	DIFFUSIBILITY	DISEMBOWELING	DISSIMILATIVE
DEPRECATORILY	DIGESTIBILITY	DISEMBOWELLED	DISSIMILATORY
DEPRESSOMOTOR	DIGITAL CAMERA	DISENABLEMENT	DISSIMILITUDE
DERMATOLOGIST	DILAPIDATIONS	DISENGAGEMENT	DISSIMULATING
DERMATOPHYTIC	DILLYDALLYING	DISENTAILMENT	DISSIMULATION
DERMATOPLASTY	DIMENSIONLESS	DISENTANGLING	DISSIMULATIVE
DESCRIPTIVELY	DIM-WITTEDNESS	DISFIGUREMENT	DISSOLUBILITY
DESCRIPTIVISM	DINNER JACKETS	DISFRANCHISED	DISSOLUTENESS
DESEGREGATING	DINNER SERVICE	DISGRACEFULLY	DISTASTEFULLY
DESEGREGATION	DIPHENYLAMINE	DISHARMONIOUS	DISTILLATIONS
DESENSITIZING	DIPSOMANIACAL	DISHONOURABLE	DISTINCTIVELY
DESPICABILITY	DIRECT CURRENT	DISHONOURABLY	DISTINGUISHED
DESSERTSPOONS	DIRECT OBJECTS	DISILLUSIONED	DISTINGUISHER
DESTABILIZING	DIRECTORSHIPS	DISINCENTIVES	DISTRESSINGLY
DESTRUCTIVELY	DISADVANTAGED	DISINFECTANTS	DISTRIBUTABLE
DESULTORINESS	DISADVANTAGES	DISINHERITING	DISTRIBUTIONS
DETACHABILITY	DISAFFECTEDLY	DISINTEGRABLE	DISTRUSTFULLY
DETERIORATING	DISAFFILIATED	DISINTEGRATED	DITRANSITIVES
DETERIORATION	DISAFFIRMANCE	DISINTEGRATOR	DIVERSIFIABLE
DETERIORATIVE	DISAFFORESTED	DISINTERESTED	DIVISIONALIZE
DETERMINATION	DISAGREEMENTS	DISINTERMENTS	DIVISION LOBBY
DETERMINATIVE	DISAPPEARANCE	DISINVESTMENT	DOCTRINAIRISM
DETERMINISTIC	DISAPPOINTING	DISMANTLEMENT	DOCUMENTARIES
DETESTABILITY	DISARTICULATE	DISMEMBERMENT	DOCUMENTARILY
DETRIMENTALLY	DISASSOCIATED	DISOBEDIENTLY	DOCUMENTARIST
DEUTEROGAMIST	DISBURDENMENT	DISOBLIGINGLY	DOCUMENTATION
DEVASTATINGLY	DISBURSEMENTS	DISORIENTATED	DODECAPHONISM
DEVELOPMENTAL	DISCHARGEABLE	DISPARAGEMENT	DODECAPHONIST
DEVIATIONISTS	DISCIPLINABLE	DISPARAGINGLY	DOGMATIZATION
DEVOLUTIONARY	DISCOLORATION	DISPASSIONATE	DOG'S
DEVOTIONALITY	DISCOMMODIOUS	DISPATCH BOXES	BREAKFAST
DEXTEROUSNESS	DISCOMPOSEDLY	DISPENSATIONS	DOLLARIZATION
DEXTROGLUCOSE	DISCONCERTING	DISPLACEMENTS	DOME OF THE
DIAGEOTROPISM	DISCONCERTION	DISPOSABILITY	ROCK
DIAGNOSTICIAN	DISCONFORMITY	DISPOSITIONAL	DOMESTICATING
DIALECTICIANS	DISCONNECTING	DISPOSSESSING	DOMESTICATION
DIALLING CODES	DISCONNECTION	DISPOSSESSION	DOMESTICATIVE
DIALLING TONES	DISCONNECTIVE	DISPOSSESSORY	DOMESTICITIES
DIALYSABILITY	DISCONTENTING	DISPROPORTION	DONKEY JACKETS

DOSIMETRICIAN
DOTHEBOYS HALL
DOUBLE-CHECKED
DOUBLE-CROSSED
DOUBLE-CROSSER
DOUBLE-CROSSES
DOUBLE-DEALERS
DOUBLE-DEALING
DOUBLE-DECKERS
DOUBLE FEATURE
DOUBLE FIGURES
DOUBLE-GLAZING
DOUBLE-JOINTED
DOUBLE OR
  QUITS
DOUBLE-PARKING
DOUBLE-TALKING
DOWNHEARTEDLY
DOWNING STREET
DOWN'S
  SYNDROME
DRAINING BOARD
DRAMATIC IRONY
DRAMATIZATION
DRAWING BOARDS
DRESSING GOWNS
DRESSING ROOMS
DRESSING TABLE
DRINKING WATER
DRUM MAJORETTE
DRYOPITHECINE
DUALISTICALLY
DUCKING STOOLS
DUCTLESS GLAND
DUMFRIESSHIRE
DUPLICABILITY
DUQUE DE
  CAXIAS
DUTCH AUCTIONS
DWELLING HOUSE
DYED-IN-THE-
  WOOL
DYSFUNCTIONAL
DYSMENORRHOEA

E

EAST-NORTHEAST
EAST-SOUTHEAST
EAVESDROPPERS
EAVESDROPPING
ECCENTRICALLY

ECCLESIASTICS
ECCLESIOLATER
ECCLESIOLATRY
ECONOMIZATION
ECTOPARASITIC
ECUMENICALISM
EDITORIALIZER
EDUCATED GUESS
EFFECTIVENESS
EFFERVESCENCE
EFFERVESCIBLE
EFFICACIOUSLY
EFFLORESCENCE
EGOCENTRICITY
EGOTISTICALLY
EGREGIOUSNESS
EGYPTOLOGICAL
EIGHTEEN HOLES
ELABORATENESS
ELECTIONEERER
ELECTRIC CHAIR
ELECTRIC FENCE
ELECTRIC SHOCK
ELECTRIFIABLE
ELECTROCUTING
ELECTROCUTION
ELECTROGRAPHY
ELECTROMAGNET
ELECTROMERISM
ELECTROMETRIC
ELECTROMOTIVE
ELECTROPHILIC
ELECTROPHONIC
ELECTROPHORUS
ELECTROPLATER
ELECTROSCOPIC
ELECTROSTATIC
ELECTROVALENT
ELEPHANTIASIC
ELEPHANTIASIS
ELEPHANT'S-
  FOOT
ELLESMERE PORT
EMBARRASSMENT
EMBELLISHMENT
EMBRYOLOGICAL
EMBRYONICALLY
EMILIA-ROMAGNA
EMINENCE GRISE
EMOTIONLESSLY
EMPHYSEMATOUS

EMPIRE-BUILDER
EMPIRICALNESS
EMPLOYABILITY
EMULSION PAINT
ENCAPSULATION
ENCAUSTICALLY
ENCEPHALOGRAM
ENCHANTRESSES
ENCOMPASSMENT
ENCOURAGEMENT
ENCOURAGINGLY
ENCROACHINGLY
ENCROACHMENTS
ENCULTURATION
ENCULTURATIVE
ENCUMBERINGLY
ENCYCLOPEDIAS
ENCYCLOPEDISM
ENCYCLOPEDIST
ENDOCRINOLOGY
ENDODONTOLOGY
ENDOLYMPHATIC
ENDOMETRIOSIS
ENDOPARASITIC
ENDOPEPTIDASE
ENERGETICALLY
ENFRANCHISING
ENGINE DRIVERS
ENIGMATICALLY
ENLIGHTENMENT
ENROLLED NURSE
ENTANGLEMENTS
ENTERTAINMENT
ENTHRALLINGLY
ENTHRONEMENTS
ENTOMOLOGICAL
ENTOMOLOGISTS
ENTOMOPHAGOUS
ENTOMOPHILOUS
ENTOMOSTRACAN
ENTREPRENEURS
ENUNCIABILITY
ENVIRONMENTAL
ENZYMOLOGICAL
EPIGRAMMATISM
EPIGRAMMATIST
EPIGRAMMATIZE
EPILEPTICALLY
EPIPHENOMENAL
EPIPHENOMENON
EPIPHYTICALLY

EPISCOPALIANS
EPITOMIZATION
EPIZOOTICALLY
EQUESTRIANISM
EQUILIBRATION
EQUILIBRISTIC
EQUIMOLECULAR
EQUIPONDERANT
EQUIPONDERATE
EQUIPOTENTIAL
EQUITABLENESS
EQUIVOCATIONS
ERGONOMICALLY
ERRONEOUSNESS
ERYSIPELATOUS
ESCAPOLOGISTS
ESCHATOLOGIST
ESPIRITO SANTO
ESPRIT DE
  CORPS
ESTABLISHMENT
ESTIMABLENESS
ESTRANGEMENTS
ETHNOCENTRISM
ETHNOGRAPHERS
ETHOLOGICALLY
ETIOLOGICALLY
EUROCOMMUNISM
EUSPORANGIATE
EVAPORABILITY
EVENTUALITIES
EVERLASTINGLY
EVERY WHICH
  WAY
EVOCATIVENESS
EXAGGERATEDLY
EXAGGERATIONS
EXAMINATIONAL
EXANTHEMATOUS
EXASPERATEDLY
EXCEPTIONABLE
EXCEPTIONALLY
EXCESSIVENESS
EXCHANGE RATES
EXCLAMATIONAL
EXCLAMATORILY
EXCLUDABILITY
EXCLUSIVENESS
EXCOMMUNICATE
EXCURSIVENESS
EXCUSABLENESS

EXECRABLENESS
EXEMPLARINESS
EXEMPLIFIABLE
EXEMPLI GRATIA
EXHIBITIONISM
EXHIBITIONIST
EXPANSIBILITY
EXPANSIONISTS
EXPANSIVENESS
EXPECTORATING
EXPECTORATION
EXPEDITIONARY
EXPEDITIOUSLY
EXPENDABILITY
EXPENSIVENESS
EXPERIMENTING
EXPERT SYSTEMS
EXPLANATORIES
EXPLANATORILY
EXPLOSIVENESS
EXPONENTIALLY
EXPORTABILITY
EXPOSTULATING
EXPOSTULATION
EXPOSTULATORY
EXPRESSIONISM
EXPRESSIONIST
EXPROPRIATING
EXPROPRIATION
EXPROPRIATORS
EXQUISITENESS
EXTEMPORARILY
EXTEMPORIZING
EXTENDIBILITY
EXTENSIBILITY
EXTENSIVENESS
EXTENUATINGLY
EXTERMINATING
EXTERMINATION
EXTERMINATIVE
EXTERMINATORS
EXTERNALIZING
EXTEROCEPTIVE
EXTERRITORIAL
EXTINGUISHANT
EXTINGUISHERS
EXTINGUISHING
EXTORTIONABLE
EXTORTIONISTS
EXTRACELLULAR
EXTRAGALACTIC

EXTRAJUDICIAL
EXTRAORDINARY
EXTRAPOLATING
EXTRAPOLATION
EXTRAPOLATIVE
EXTRAPOSITION
EXTRAVAGANCES
EXTRAVAGANTLY
EXTRAVAGANZAS
EXTRAVAGATION
EXTRAVASATION
EXTRAVASCULAR
EXTRINSICALLY
EYEBROW PENCIL
EYE-CATCHINGLY

F

FACETIOUSNESS
FACTORABILITY
FACTORIZATION
FAITHLESSNESS
FALLOPIAN TUBE
FALSIFICATION
FAMILIARITIES
FAMILIARIZING
FAMILY DOCTORS
FAMILY SUPPORT
FANTASTICALLY
FASCICULATION
FASCINATINGLY
FASCISTICALLY
FATHEADEDNESS
FATHER FIGURES
FAULTLESSNESS
FEATHERBEDDED
FEATHERSTITCH
FEATHER-VEINED
FEATHERWEIGHT
FEATURE-LENGTH
FEEDING BOTTLE
FELICITATIONS
FELLOW FEELING
FELONIOUSNESS
FEMMES FATALES
FEROCIOUSNESS
FERRIMAGNETIC
FERROCHROMIUM
FERROCONCRETE
FERROELECTRIC
FERROMAGNETIC
FERTILIZATION

FEUDALIZATION
FEUILLETONISM
FEUILLETONIST
FIBROVASCULAR
FICTIONALIZED
FIELD MARSHALS
FIELD OF
 VISION
FIGHTER-BOMBER
FIGURED BASSES
FIGURE OF
 EIGHT
FIGURE SKATERS
FIGURE-SKATING
FILIBUSTERING
FILING CABINET
FILM PREMIERES
FILTERABILITY
FINANCIAL YEAR
FINE-TOOTH
 COMB
FINGERPRINTED
FIRST MINISTER
FIRST OFFENDER
FISH-EYE
 LENSES
FISSION-FUSION
FLABBERGASTED
FLAGELLANTISM
FLAME-THROWERS
FLAVOPURPURIN
FLEET ADMIRALS
FLESH AND
 BLOOD
FLIGHT CAPITAL
FLIRTATIOUSLY
FLOATING-POINT
FLOATING VOTER
FLOODLIGHTING
FLORIANOPOLIS
FLORICULTURAL
FLORISTICALLY
FLOURISHINGLY
FLYING COLOURS
FLYING DOCTORS
FLYING OFFICER
FLYING PICKETS
FLYING SAUCERS
FOLLOW-THROUGH
FONTAINEBLEAU
FOOD POISONING
FOOD PROCESSOR

FOOLHARDINESS
FOOL'S
 PARADISE
FOOTBALL POOLS
FORAMINIFERAL
FORBIDDEN CITY
FOREIGN OFFICE
FOREJUDGEMENT
FOREKNOWINGLY
FOREKNOWLEDGE
FORENSICALITY
FOREORDAINING
FORESHADOWING
FORESHORTENED
FOREWARNINGLY
FORGETFULNESS
FORGIVINGNESS
FORKLIFT TRUCK
FORMALIZATION
FORMATIVENESS
FORMIDABILITY
FORTIFICATION
FORTITUDINOUS
FORTUNE HUNTER
FORTUNE-TELLER
FOSSILIFEROUS
FOSSILIZATION
FOUNDATIONARY
FRACTIONATION
FRACTIOUSNESS
FRACTOCUMULUS
FRACTOSTRATUS
FRAGMENTATION
FRANCHISEMENT
FREDERIKSBERG
FREEZING POINT
FREIGHTLINERS
FRENCH WINDOWS
FREQUENTATION
FREQUENTATIVE
FREUDIAN SLIPS
FRIDGE-FREEZER
FRIGHTENINGLY
FRIGHTFULNESS
FRINGE BENEFIT
FRIVOLOUSNESS
FRONTBENCHERS
FRONTISPIECES
FRONTOGENESIS
FRUITLESSNESS
FRUIT MACHINES

FRUMENTACEOUS
FULL-FASHIONED
FUNCTIONALISM
FUNCTIONALIST
FUNCTIONARIES
FUNDAMENTALLY
FUNNY BUSINESS
FUTURE PERFECT

G

GALLICIZATION
GALLOWS HUMOUR
GALVANOMETRIC
GALVANOSCOPIC
GALVANOTROPIC
GAMBREL-ROOFED
GAMETOGENESIS
GAMMA GLOBULIN
GARBAGE TRUCKS
GARDEN PARTIES
GARRULOUSNESS
GASTROSCOPIST
GEIGER COUNTER
GELANDESPRUNG
GELSENKIRCHEN
GENDER-BENDERS
GENERALISSIMO
GENERAL STRIKE
GENERATION GAP
GENTIANACEOUS
GENUFLECTIONS
GEOCHRONOLOGY
GEODYNAMICIST
GEOMETRICALLY
GEOMORPHOLOGY
GEOPOLITICIAN
GEOSTATIONARY
GEOTACTICALLY
GEOTROPICALLY
GERIATRICIANS
GERMANIZATION
GERMAN MEASLES
GERMANOPHILIA
GERMANOPHOBIA
GERONTOCRATIC
GERONTOLOGIST
GERRYMANDERED
GESTICULATING
GESTICULATION
GESTICULATIVE
GHETTO BLASTER

GLACIOLOGICAL
GLAMORIZATION
GLAMOROUSNESS
GLOBETROTTERS
GLOBETROTTING
GLOBULIFEROUS
GLOCKENSPIELS
GLORIFICATION
GLOSSOGRAPHER
GLUTINOUSNESS
GLYPHOGRAPHER
GLYPHOGRAPHIC
GLYPTOGRAPHER
GLYPTOGRAPHIC
GO-AS-YOU-
    PLEASE
GOING STRAIGHT
GOLDEN HAMSTER
GOLDEN JUBILEE
GOLDEN WEDDING
GOLDFISH BOWLS
GOOD AFTERNOON
GOOD-NATUREDLY
GOOD SAMARITAN
GOOSESTEPPING
GOVERNABILITY
GRACELESSNESS
GRADE CROSSING
GRAMINIVOROUS
GRAMMAR SCHOOL
GRAMMATICALLY
GRAM-MOLECULAR
GRANDCHILDREN
GRANDDAUGHTER
GRANDILOQUENT
GRANULOMATOUS
GRAPHEMICALLY
GRAPHICALNESS
GRAPHIC DESIGN
GRAPHOLOGISTS
GRAPPLING IRON
GRATIFICATION
GRAVEYARD SLOT
GRAVITATIONAL
GREAT YARMOUTH
GREEN-FINGERED
GROTESQUENESS
GROUND STROKES
GROUP CAPTAINS
GROUP PRACTICE
GUARDIAN ANGEL

GUATEMALA CITY
GUBERNATORIAL
GUIDED MISSILE
GUILELESSNESS
GUILTLESSNESS
GUNPOWDER PLOT
GYMNOSPERMISM
GYMNOSPERMOUS
GYNAECOCRATIC
GYNAECOLOGIST
GYNANDROMORPH

H

HACKING COUGHS
HAEMATOGENOUS
HAEMATOLOGIST
HAEMODIALYSIS
HAEMOPHILIOID
HAEMORRHOIDAL
HAGIOGRAPHIES
HAILE SELASSIE
HAIR-RESTORERS
HAIR-SPLITTING
HALE AND
    HEARTY
HALF-HEARTEDLY
HALFWAY HOUSES
HALICARNASSUS
HALLUCINATING
HALLUCINATION
HALLUCINATORY
HAMILCAR BARCA
HANDBRAKE TURN
HANDKERCHIEFS
HANG SENG
    INDEX
HAPHAZARDNESS
HARD-HEARTEDLY
HARD-LUCK
    STORY
HARD OF
    HEARING
HARD SHOULDERS
HARMONIZATION
HARUN AL-
    RASHID
HAVE NO TIME
    FOR
HAZARDOUSNESS
HEADSHRINKERS
HEALTHFULNESS
HEALTH VISITOR

HEARTBREAKING
HEARTBROKENLY
HEART DISEASES
HEARTLESSNESS
HEARTSICKNESS
HEARTSOMENESS
HEART-TO-
    HEARTS
HEATH ROBINSON
HEAVY HYDROGEN
HEAVY INDUSTRY
HEDGE SPARROWS
HEEBIE-JEEBIES
HEIRS APPARENT
HELLENIZATION
HELMINTHIASIS
HELMINTHOLOGY
HELTER SKELTER
HELTER-SKELTER
HEMICELLULOSE
HENDECAHEDRON
HEPTADECANOIC
HEPTAMETRICAL
HERBIVOROUSLY
HEREDITAMENTS
HEREFORDSHIRE
HERMAPHRODITE
HERNIORRHAPHY
HEROIC COUPLET
HERPES SIMPLEX
HERPETOLOGIST
HERTFORDSHIRE
HETEROGENEITY
HETEROGENEOUS
HETEROGENESIS
HETEROGENETIC
HETEROGRAPHIC
HETEROMORPHIC
HETEROPLASTIC
HETEROPTEROUS
HETEROSEXUALS
HETEROSPOROUS
HETEROSTYLOUS
HETEROTHALLIC
HETEROTROPHIC
HETEROZYGOSIS
HEURISTICALLY
HIERACOSPHINX
HIEROGLYPHICS
HIEROGLYPHIST

HIGH-AND-
   MIGHTY
HIGH CHURCHMAN
HIGHER-RATE
   TAX
HIGH EXPLOSIVE
HIGHLAND FLING
HIGH-PRESSURED
HIGH-WATER
   MARK
HILARIOUSNESS
HILDEBRANDIAN
HILDEBRANDINE
HISTOCHEMICAL
HOBSON'S
   CHOICE
HO CHI MINH
   CITY
HOIDENISHNESS
HOLE-AND-
   CORNER
HOLIDAYMAKERS
HOLIDAYMAKING
HOLY COMMUNION
HOME ECONOMICS
HOMEOMORPHISM
HOMILETICALLY
HOMOCHROMATIC
HOMOEROTICISM
HOMOGENEOUSLY
HOMOIOTHERMIC
HOMOLOGICALLY
HOMOLOGRAPHIC
HOMOOUSIANISM
HOMOSEXUALITY
HONEYDEW MELON
HONORIFICALLY
HORNS OF
   PLENTY
HORRIFICATION
HORRIPILATION
HORSE CHESTNUT
HORSEWHIPPING
HORTICULTURAL
HOSPITALIZING
HOT-GOSPELLERS
HOT-GOSPELLING
HOT-HEADEDNESS
HOUSEBREAKERS
HOUSEBREAKING
HOUSEHOLD NAME
HOUSE HUSBANDS

HOUSEMISTRESS
HOUSES OF
   CARDS
HOUSE SPARROWS
HOUSEWARMINGS
HOYDENISHNESS
HUCKLEBERRIES
HUMANITARIANS
HUMILIATINGLY
HUNDREDWEIGHT
HUNGER MARCHER
HUNGER MARCHES
HUNGER STRIKER
HUNGER STRIKES
HUNTING GROUND
HURRICANE LAMP
HYALURONIDASE
HYBRIDIZATION
HYDRAULICALLY
HYDROCEPHALIC
HYDROCEPHALUS
HYDROCHLORIDE
HYDRODYNAMICS
HYDROELECTRIC
HYDROGENATION
HYDROGEN BOMBS
HYDROKINETICS
HYDROLYSATION
HYPERCRITICAL
HYPOCHONDRIAC

I

IATROGENICITY
ICE-CREAM
   SODAS
ICHTHYOLOGIST
ICONOMATICISM
IDEALIZATIONS
IDENTICAL TWIN
IDENTITY CARDS
IDEOLOGICALLY
IDIOMATICALLY
IDIOSYNCRATIC
IGNOMINIOUSLY
ILL-CONSIDERED
ILLE-ET-
   VILAINE
ILLOCUTIONARY
ILLUMINATIONS
ILLUSIONISTIC
ILLUSTRATIONS

ILLUSTRIOUSLY
IMAGINATIVELY
IMAGISTICALLY
IMITATIVENESS
IMMATERIALISM
IMMATERIALIST
IMMATERIALITY
IMMATERIALIZE
IMMIGRATIONAL
IMMISCIBILITY
IMMORTALIZING
IMMUNIZATIONS
IMMUNOGENETIC
IMMUNOTHERAPY
IMPALPABILITY
IMPARIPINNATE
IMPARTIBILITY
IMPASSABILITY
IMPASSIONEDLY
IMPASSIVENESS
IMPECCABILITY
IMPECUNIOUSLY
IMPERCEPTIBLE
IMPERCEPTIBLY
IMPERFECTIONS
IMPERFORATION
IMPERIALISTIC
IMPERIOUSNESS
IMPERMISSIBLE
IMPERSONALITY
IMPERSONALIZE
IMPERSONATING
IMPERSONATION
IMPERSONATORS
IMPERTINENTLY
IMPERTURBABLE
IMPERTURBABLY
IMPETUOUSNESS
IMPLACABILITY
IMPONDERABLES
IMPORTUNATELY
IMPOSSIBILITY
IMPOVERISHING
IMPRACTICABLE
IMPRACTICABLY
IMPRACTICALLY
IMPRESSIONISM
IMPRESSIONIST
IMPROBABILITY
IMPROPRIATION
IMPROPRIETIES

IMPROVABILITY
IMPROVIDENTLY
IMPROVISATION
IMPULSIVENESS
INADVERTENTLY
INAPPROPRIATE
INATTENTIVELY
INAUGURATIONS
INCANDESCENCE
INCANTATIONAL
INCAPACITATED
INCAPSULATION
INCARCERATING
INCARCERATION
INCARDINATION
INCLINATIONAL
INCOMBUSTIBLE
INCOME SUPPORT
INCOMMUNICADO
INCOMPETENTLY
INCONCEIVABLE
INCONCEIVABLY
INCONDENSABLE
INCONGRUITIES
INCONGRUOUSLY
INCONSEQUENCE
INCONSIDERATE
INCONSISTENCY
INCONSPICUOUS
INCONSTANCIES
INCONTESTABLE
INCONTESTABLY
INCONVENIENCE
INCONVERTIBLE
INCONVINCIBLE
INCORPORATING
INCORPORATION
INCORPORATIVE
INCORPOREALLY
INCORRECTNESS
INCORRUPTIBLE
INCORRUPTIBLY
INCREDIBILITY
INCREDULOUSLY
INCREMENTALLY
INCRIMINATING
INCRIMINATION
INCRIMINATORY
INCRUSTATIONS
INCULPABILITY
INDEFATIGABLE

INDEFATIGABLY	INFLECTEDNESS	INSUPPORTABLE	INTERPOLATION
INDENTURESHIP	INFLEXIBILITY	INSURRECTIONS	INTERPOLATIVE
INDEPENDENTLY	INFLORESCENCE	INSUSCEPTIBLE	INTERPOSINGLY
INDESCRIBABLE	INFLUENCEABLE	INTANGIBILITY	INTERPOSITION
INDESCRIBABLY	INFLUENTIALLY	INTEGRABILITY	INTERPRETABLE
INDETERMINACY	INFORMATIONAL	INTEGUMENTARY	INTERRACIALLY
INDETERMINATE	INFORMATIVELY	INTELLECTUALS	INTERRELATION
INDETERMINISM	INFRINGEMENTS	INTELLIGENTLY	INTERROGATING
INDETERMINIST	INFURIATINGLY	INTEMPERATELY	INTERROGATION
INDIAN SUMMERS	INGENUOUSNESS	INTENTIONALLY	INTERROGATIVE
INDIFFERENTLY	INGRAINEDNESS	INTERACTIONAL	INTERROGATORS
INDISCERNIBLE	INGURGITATION	INTERACTIVELY	INTERROGATORY
INDISCRETIONS	INHOSPITALITY	INTERACTIVITY	INTERRUPTIBLE
INDISPENSABLE	INIMITABILITY	INTERBREEDING	INTERRUPTIONS
INDISPENSABLY	INJUDICIOUSLY	INTERCALARILY	INTERSECTIONS
INDISPOSITION	INLAND REVENUE	INTERCALATION	INTERSPERSING
INDISTINCTIVE	INNER MONGOLIA	INTERCALATIVE	INTERSPERSION
INDIVIDUALISM	INNOCUOUSNESS	INTERCELLULAR	INTERSTRATIFY
INDIVIDUALIST	INNOVATIONIST	INTERCEPTIONS	INTERTROPICAL
INDIVIDUALITY	INOCULABILITY	INTERCESSIONS	INTERVENTIONS
INDIVIDUALIZE	INOFFENSIVELY	INTERCHANGING	INTRACELLULAR
INDIVIDUATION	INOPERABILITY	INTERCLAVICLE	INTRAMUSCULAR
INDOCTRINATED	INOPPORTUNELY	INTERCOLUMNAR	INTRANSIGENCE
INDOCTRINATOR	INORGANICALLY	INTERCURRENCE	INTRAPERSONAL
INDOLEBUTYRIC	INQUISITIONAL	INTEREST GROUP	INTRATELLURIC
INDUPLICATION	INQUISITIVELY	INTERESTINGLY	INTRAVASATION
INDUSTRIALISM	INQUISITORIAL	INTERFACIALLY	INTRAVENOUSLY
INDUSTRIALIST	INSATIABILITY	INTERFERINGLY	INTRINSICALLY
INDUSTRIALIZE	INSCRIPTIONAL	INTERGALACTIC	INTRODUCTIONS
INDUSTRIOUSLY	INSECTIVOROUS	INTERGRADIENT	INTROGRESSION
INEDUCABILITY	INSENSIBILITY	INTERJECTIONS	INTROSPECTION
INEFFECTIVELY	INSENSITIVELY	INTERLACEMENT	INTROSPECTIVE
INEFFECTUALLY	INSENSITIVITY	INTERLAMINATE	INTUITIVENESS
INEFFICACIOUS	INSIDIOUSNESS	INTERLOCUTION	INVARIABILITY
INEFFICIENTLY	INSIGNIFICANT	INTERLOCUTORS	INVENTIVENESS
INELIGIBILITY	INSOLVABILITY	INTERLOCUTORY	INVENTORIABLE
INEVITABILITY	INSPECTORATES	INTERLUNATION	INVERTEBRATES
INEXHAUSTIBLE	INSPECTORSHIP	INTERMARRIAGE	INVERTED COMMA
INEXHAUSTIBLY	INSPIRATIONAL	INTERMARRYING	INVERTED SNOBS
INEXORABILITY	INSPIRITINGLY	INTERMEDIATOR	INVERTIBILITY
INEXPENSIVELY	INSTABILITIES	INTERMINGLING	INVESTIGATING
INEXPERIENCED	INSTALLATIONS	INTERMISSIONS	INVESTIGATION
INEXPRESSIBLE	INSTANTANEOUS	INTERMITTENCE	INVESTIGATIVE
INEXPRESSIBLY	INSTIGATINGLY	INTERNALIZING	INVESTIGATORS
INFALLIBILITY	INSTINCTIVELY	INTERNATIONAL	INVIDIOUSNESS
INFANT PRODIGY	INSTITUTIONAL	INTEROCEPTIVE	INVINCIBILITY
INFECTIVENESS	INSTRUCTIONAL	INTEROPERABLE	INVIOLABILITY
INFERENTIALLY	INSTRUCTIVELY	INTEROSCULATE	INVOLUNTARILY
INFILTRATIONS	INSUBORDINATE	INTERPELLATOR	IONIAN ISLANDS
INFINITESIMAL	INSUBSTANTIAL	INTERPERSONAL	IRONING BOARDS
INFLAMMATIONS	INSUFFICIENCY	INTERPOLATING	IRRATIONALITY

IRRECLAIMABLE
IRRECOVERABLE
IRRECOVERABLY
IRREFRANGIBLE
IRRELIGIONIST
IRREPLACEABLE
IRREPLEVIABLE
IRREPRESSIBLE
IRREPRESSIBLY
IRRESPONSIBLE
IRRESPONSIBLY
IRRETRIEVABLE
IRRETRIEVABLY
ISOAGGLUTININ
ISODIMORPHISM
ISODIMORPHOUS
ISOELECTRONIC
ISOGEOTHERMAL
ISOLATIONISTS
ISOMERIZATION
ISOSPONDYLOUS
ITALICIZATION

J

JACK-O'-
  LANTERNS
JARGONIZATION
JEFFERSON CITY
JELLIFICATION
JET PROPULSION
JIGGERY-POKERY
JIGSAW PUZZLES
JOBS COMFORTER
JOB'S
  COMFORTER
JOLLIFICATION
JUDICIOUSNESS
JUGLANDACEOUS
JUNIOR SCHOOLS
JURISPRUDENCE
JUSTICIARSHIP
JUSTIFICATION
JUSTIFICATORY
JUXTAPOSITION

K

KALEIDOSCOPES
KALEIDOSCOPIC
KANGAROO COURT
KANGCHENJUNGA

KARL-MARX-
  STADT
KERATOPLASTIC
KETTLEDRUMMER
KEY SIGNATURES
KIDDERMINSTER
KIDNEY MACHINE
KINDERGARTENS
KIND-HEARTEDLY
KINEMATICALLY
KINETIC ENERGY
KINETONUCLEUS
KING'S
  COUNSELS
KING'S
  EVIDENCE
KIRKCUDBRIGHT
KITCHEN GARDEN
KITTY-CORNERED
KLEPTOMANIACS
KNAVE OF
  HEARTS
KNIGHTS-ERRANT
KNOWLEDGEABLE
KNOWLEDGEABLY
KNUCKLE-DUSTER
KWANGSI-CHUANG

L

LABIALIZATION
LABORIOUSNESS
LABOURS OF
  LOVE
LACKADAISICAL
LACTOBACILLUS
LADY BOUNTIFUL
LADY-IN-
  WAITING
LAEVOROTATION
LAEVOROTATORY
LAMELLIBRANCH
LANCE CORPORAL
LANDING FIELDS
LANDING STAGES
LANDING STRIPS
LANDOWNERSHIP
LANTERNSLIDES
LAPAROSCOPIES
LARYNGOLOGIST
LARYNGOSCOPIC
LASER PRINTERS
LATCHKEY CHILD

LATEROVERSION
LATIN AMERICAN
LAUGHINGSTOCK
LAUNDRY BASKET
LEADING LADIES
LEADING LIGHTS
LEAMINGTON SPA
LEATHERJACKET
LECHEROUSNESS
LEGISLATORIAL
LEISHMANIASIS
LEISURELINESS
LEPIDOPTERIST
LEPIDOPTEROUS
LEPTOCEPHALUS
LEPTOPHYLLOUS
LETHARGICALLY
LETTER OPENERS
LETTER PERFECT
LETTER-PERFECT
LETTERPRESSES
LEVEL CROSSING
LEXICOGRAPHER
LEXICOGRAPHIC
LEXICOLOGICAL
LIBRARIANSHIP
LICENSE PLATES
LICENSING LAWS
LIEBFRAUMILCH
LIECHTENSTEIN
LIFE PRESERVER
LIGHT AIRCRAFT
LIGHT-FINGERED
LIGHT-HEADEDLY
LIGNIFICATION
LIMITLESSNESS
LINE-ENGRAVING
LINGUA FRANCAS
LIPARI ISLANDS
LITHOGRAPHING
LITIGIOUSNESS
LITTLE FINGERS
LIVERY COMPANY
LIVERY STABLES
LIVING FOSSILS
LOATHSOMENESS
LODGING HOUSES
LOGOGRAMMATIC
LONDON BRIGADE
LONG HOT
  SUMMER

LONGSUFFERING
LONG VACATIONS
LONS-LE-
  SAUNIER
LOSS ADJUSTERS
LOTHIAN REGION
LOWER EAST
  SIDE
LOW-PASS
  FILTER
LOW-WATER
  MARKS
LUBRICATIONAL
LUDICROUSNESS
LUNATIC FRINGE
LUNCHEONETTES
LYMPHADENITIS
LYMPHATICALLY
LYMPHOBLASTIC
LYMPHOCYTOSIS
LYMPHOCYTOTIC
LYMPHOPOIESIS
LYMPHOPOIETIC

M

MACARONICALLY
MACHIAVELLIAN
MACHICOLATION
MACHINABILITY
MACHINEGUNNED
MACRENCEPHALY
MACROCLIMATIC
MACROECONOMIC
MACROMOLECULE
MACRONUTRIENT
MADE-TO-
  MEASURE
MADHYA PRADESH
MADRIGALESQUE
MAGIC LANTERNS
MAGISTERIALLY
MAGNANIMOUSLY
MAGNETIC FIELD
MAGNETIC HEADS
MAGNETIC NORTH
MAGNETIC POLES
MAGNETIC TAPES
MAGNETIZATION
MAGNETOMETRIC
MAGNETOMOTIVE
MAGNETOSPHERE
MAGNIFICATION

MAGNIFICENTLY
MAGNILOQUENCE
MAGNITUDINOUS
MAGNOLIACEOUS
MAIDS OF
  HONOUR
MAJOR GENERALS
MALACOLOGICAL
MALACOSTRACAN
MALADJUSTMENT
MALADMINISTER
MALADROITNESS
MALFORMATIONS
MALFUNCTIONED
MALICIOUSNESS
MALIMPRINTING
MALTHUSIANISM
MANAGEABILITY
MANDARIN DUCKS
MANGEL-WURZELS
MANIFESTATION
MANIPULATABLE
MANIPULATIONS
MANTELSHELVES
MANUFACTURERS
MANUFACTURING
MANY-SIDEDNESS
MARAGING STEEL
MARCHIONESSES
MARKETABILITY
MARKET GARDENS
MARRIAGE LINES
MARRONS GLACES
MARTYRIZATION
MARTYROLOGIST
MASSACHUSETTS
MASSIF CENTRAL
MASS-PRODUCING
MASTERFULNESS
MASTERMINDING
MASTERS-AT-
  ARMS
MASTERS OF
  ARTS
MASTERSTROKES
MASTIGOPHORAN
MASTOIDECTOMY
MATCHLESSNESS
MATERFAMILIAS
MATERIALISTIC
MATERIALIZING

MATERNALISTIC
MATHEMATICIAN
MATRICULATING
MATRICULATION
MATRILOCALITY
MATURE STUDENT
MAXILLIPEDARY
MEALS ON
  WHEELS
MEANINGLESSLY
MEASURABILITY
MECHANIZATION
MEDIATIZATION
MEDIATORIALLY
MEDIEVALISTIC
MEDITERRANEAN
MEETINGHOUSES
MEGACEPHALOUS
MEGALOBLASTIC
MEGALOMANIACS
MEGALOPOLITAN
MELODIOUSNESS
MELODRAMATIST
MELTING POINTS
MELTON MOWBRAY
MENINGOCOCCUS
MENSTRUATIONS
MENSURATIONAL
MENTAL ILLNESS
MERCENARINESS
MERCERIZATION
MERCHANDISING
MERCHANT BANKS
MERCILESSNESS
MERCURIALNESS
MERCUROCHROME
MERCY KILLINGS
MERITOCRACIES
MERITORIOUSLY
MERRY-GO-
  ROUNDS
MERTHYR TYDFIL
MESENCEPHALIC
MESENCEPHALON
MESMERIZATION
MESSIANICALLY
METABOLICALLY
METABOLIZABLE
METACHROMATIC
METALANGUAGES
METALLIFEROUS

METALLIZATION
METALLOGRAPHY
METALLURGICAL
METALLURGISTS
METAMERICALLY
METAMORPHOSED
METAMORPHOSES
METAMORPHOSIS
METAPHOSPHATE
METAPHYSICIAN
METASTABILITY
METEMPIRICIST
METENCEPHALIC
METENCEPHALON
METEOROLOGIST
METHODIZATION
METHODOLOGIES
METHODOLOGIST
METHYL ALCOHOL
METRONIDAZOLE
METROPOLITANS
MEZZO-SOPRANOS
MICROANALYSIS
MICROANALYTIC
MICROCEPHALIC
MICROCHEMICAL
MICROCLIMATIC
MICROCOMPUTER
MICRODETECTOR
MICRONUTRIENT
MICROORGANISM
MICROPARASITE
MICROPHYSICAL
MICROTONALITY
MIDDLEBROWISM
MIDDLE EASTERN
MIDDLE ENGLAND
MIDDLE FINGERS
MIDDLE PASSAGE
MIDDLESBROUGH
MIDDLE SCHOOLS
MIDDLEWEIGHTS
MIDDLE WESTERN
MID-LIFE
  CRISES
MID-LIFE
  CRISIS
MIDWAY ISLANDS
MILK CHOCOLATE
MILLENNIALIST
MILLENNIUM BUG

MILLIONAIRESS
MIMEOGRAPHING
MINE DETECTORS
MINERALOGICAL
MINERALOGISTS
MINERAL WATERS
MINICOMPUTERS
MINISTERIALLY
MIRABILE DICTU
MIRROR WRITING
MIRTHLESSNESS
MISADVENTURES
MISCALCULATED
MISCEGENATION
MISCELLANEOUS
MISCHIEVOUSLY
MISCONCEIVING
MISCONCEPTION
MISCONDUCTING
MISCONSTRUING
MISDEMEANOURS
MISERABLENESS
MISGOVERNMENT
MISJUDGEMENTS
MISMANAGEMENT
MISPROPORTION
MISQUOTATIONS
MISSISSIPPIAN
MISSTATEMENTS
MISTRUSTFULLY
MISTRUSTINGLY
MISUNDERSTAND
MISUNDERSTOOD
MITOCHONDRIAL
MITOCHONDRION
MIXED BLESSING
MIXED METAPHOR
MOBILE LIBRARY
MOBILIZATIONS
MODERNIZATION
MODIFIABILITY
MODIFICATIONS
MODUS OPERANDI
MOHAMMEDANISM
MOLLIFICATION
MOLLYCODDLING
MOMENT OF
  TRUTH
MONEYCHANGERS
MONEY-GRUBBERS
MONEY-GRUBBING

379

MONEY-SPINNERS
MONKEY-PUZZLES
MONMOUTHSHIRE
MONOCHROMATIC
MONOCOTYLEDON
MONOGRAMMATIC
MONOMETALLISM
MONOMETALLIST
MONOMOLECULAR
MONONUCLEOSIS
MONOPHTHONGAL
MONOPSONISTIC
MONOSYLLABISM
MONOSYLLABLES
MONOTREMATOUS
MONSTROSITIES
MONS VENERISES
MONUMENTALITY
MOONLIGHT FLIT
MORALITY PLAYS
MORAL MAJORITY
MORNING PRAYER
MORPHEMICALLY
MORPHOGENESIS
MORPHOGENETIC
MORPHOLOGICAL
MORPHOPHONEME
MORRISDANCERS
MORTIFICATION
MOTHER COUNTRY
MOTHER-OF-
  PEARL
MOTHER TONGUES
MOTION PICTURE
MOTORCYCLISTS
MOTOR SCOOTERS
MOUNTAIN LIONS
MOUNTAINSIDES
MOUNTEBANKERY
MOUTH WATERING
MOUTH-WATERING
MOVABLE FEASTS
MOVING PICTURE
MUHAMMADANISM
MULTICELLULAR
MULTICOLOURED
MULTINATIONAL
MULTIPLE STORE
MULTITUDINOUS
MULTIVIBRATOR
MUMMIFICATION

MURDEROUSNESS
MUSICAL CHAIRS
MUSICOLOGICAL
MYCOBACTERIUM
MYRMECOLOGIST
MYSTIFICATION
MYTHICIZATION

N

NARCOANALYSIS
NARCOTIZATION
NARROW SQUEAKS
NATIONAL DEBTS
NATIONALISTIC
NATIONALITIES
NATIONALIZING
NATIONAL PARKS
NATIONAL TRUST
NATIVITY PLAYS
NATURAL NUMBER
NAUTICAL MILES
NEARSIGHTEDLY
NECESSARY EVIL
NECESSITARIAN
NECESSITATING
NECESSITATION
NECESSITATIVE
NECESSITOUSLY
NECKERCHIEVES
NECROPHILIACS
NEFARIOUSNESS
NEGATIVE POLES
NEGLIGIBILITY
NEGOTIABILITY
NEGRI SEMBILAN
NEIGHBOURHOOD
NEMATHELMINTH
NEOCLASSICISM
NEOCLASSICIST
NEOPLASTICISM
NERVELESSNESS
NERVOUS SYSTEM
NEUROFIBRILAR
NEUROMUSCULAR
NEUROSURGICAL
NEUROVASCULAR
NEW PROVIDENCE
NEW SOUTH
  WALES
NEW TECHNOLOGY
NICKELIFEROUS

NIGGARDLINESS
NIGHTCLUBBING
NIGHTMARISHLY
NIGHT WATCHMAN
NITRIFICATION
NITROBACTERIA
NITROGLYCERIN
NITROPARAFFIN
NO-CLAIMS
  BONUS
NO HOLDS
  BARRED
NOISELESSNESS
NOLI-ME-
  TANGERE
NOLLE PROSEQUI
NOMENCLATURES
NOMOGRAPHICAL
NOMOLOGICALLY
NONAGENARIANS
NONAGGRESSION
NONAPPEARANCE
NONATTENDANCE
NONCOMBATANTS
NONCOMPLIANCE
NONCONCURRENT
NONCONDUCTORS
NONCONFORMISM
NONCONFORMIST
NONCONFORMITY
NONCONTAGIOUS
NONCOOPERATOR
NONFUNCTIONAL
NONINDUSTRIAL
NONINFECTIOUS
NONPRODUCTIVE
NONRETURNABLE
NONSENSICALLY
NO OIL
  PAINTING
NORADRENALINE
NORFOLK ISLAND
NORFOLK JACKET
NORMALIZATION
NORTHALLERTON
NORTH AYRSHIRE
NORTH CAROLINA
NORTHEASTERLY
NORTHEASTWARD
NORTH OSSETIAN
NORTH SOMERSET
NORTH TYNESIDE

NORTHWESTERLY
NORTHWESTWARD
NOSOLOGICALLY
NOSTALGICALLY
NOTICEABILITY
NOTIFICATIONS
NOTORIOUSNESS
NUCLEAR ENERGY
NUCLEAR FAMILY
NUCLEAR WINTER
NUCLEONICALLY
NUCLEOPLASMIC
NUCLEOPROTEIN
NUISANCE VALUE
NULLIFICATION
NUMEROLOGICAL
NUMISMATOLOGY
NURSERY RHYMES
NURSERY SCHOOL
NYMPHAEACEOUS
NYMPHOMANIACS

O

OBJECTIONABLE
OBJECTIONABLY
OBJECTIVENESS
OBJECTIVISTIC
OBJECT LESSONS
OBLATE SPHERES
OBLIVIOUSNESS
OBNOXIOUSNESS
OBSERVATIONAL
OBSERVATORIES
OBSESSIVENESS
OBSTETRICALLY
OBSTETRICIANS
OBSTRUCTIONAL
OBSTRUCTIVELY
OBTAINABILITY
OBTRUSIVENESS
OCCASIONALISM
OCCIDENTALISM
OCCIDENTALIST
OCCIDENTALIZE
OCCLUSIVENESS
OCEANOGRAPHER
OCEANOGRAPHIC
OCTOGENARIANS
ODONTOBLASTIC
ODONTOGLOSSUM
ODONTOGRAPHIC

ODONTOLOGICAL
OFFENSIVENESS
OFFHANDEDNESS
OFFICEHOLDERS
OFFICIOUSNESS
OLD AGE
  PENSION
OLD-BOY
  NETWORK
OLD SCHOOL
  TIES
OLD WIVES'
  TALES
OLIGOPOLISTIC
OLIVE BRANCHES
OMMATOPHOROUS
ONE-NIGHT
  STAND
ONE-TRACK
  MINDS
ON THE
  PREMISES
ONTOGENICALLY
ONTOLOGICALLY
OPENHEARTEDLY
OPEN THE DOOR
  TO
OPERATIONALLY
OPERATIVENESS
OPHTHALMOLOGY
OPISTHOBRANCH
OPPORTUNENESS
OPPORTUNISTIC
OPPORTUNITIES
OPPOSITIONIST
OPPROBRIOUSLY
ORANGE BLOSSOM
ORCHESTRA PITS
ORCHESTRATING
ORCHESTRATION
ORDINARY LEVEL
ORDZHONIKIDZE
ORGAN GRINDERS
ORGANIZATIONS
ORGANOGENESIS
ORGANOGENETIC
ORGANOGRAPHIC
ORGANOLOGICAL
ORGANOTHERAPY
ORIENTALISTIC
ORIENTATIONAL
ORNAMENTATION

ORNITHISCHIAN
ORNITHOLOGIST
ORTHOCEPHALIC
ORTHOEPICALLY
ORTHOGNATHISM
ORTHOGNATHOUS
ORTHOHYDROGEN
ORTHOSTICHOUS
OSCILLOGRAPHY
OSTENSIBILITY
OSTEOMALACIAL
OSTEOMYELITIS
OTHER-DIRECTED
OUTBOARD MOTOR
OUTDISTANCING
OUTGENERALING
OUTGENERALLED
OUTMANOEUVRED
OUTSPOKENNESS
OUTSTANDINGLY
OVERABUNDANCE
OVERAMBITIOUS
OVERBALANCING
OVERBEARINGLY
OVERBURDENING
OVERCONFIDENT
OVERCRITICIZE
OVERCULTIVATE
OVERDEVELOPED
OVERELABORATE
OVEREMPHASIZE
OVERESTIMATED
OVERESTIMATES
OVERINDULGING
OVERMASTERING
OVERPOPULATED
OVERREACTIONS
OVERSHADOWING
OVERSTATEMENT
OVERSUBSCRIBE
OVERWEENINGLY
OVOVIVIPAROUS
OWNER-OCCUPIED
OWNER-OCCUPIER
OYSTERCATCHER

P

PADDLE STEAMER
PADDLING POOLS
PAEDIATRICIAN
PAINSTAKINGLY

PAINTBALL GAME
PALAEOECOLOGY
PALAEOGRAPHIC
PALAEONTOLOGY
PALAEOZOOLOGY
PALEOGRAPHERS
PALETTE KNIVES
PALYNOLOGICAL
PANCHROMATISM
PANDORA'S
  BOXES
PANIC DISORDER
PANIC STATIONS
PANIC-STRICKEN
PANORAMICALLY
PANSOPHICALLY
PANTECHNICONS
PAPAVERACEOUS
PAPILLOMATOUS
PARABOLICALLY
PARADE GROUNDS
PARADOXICALLY
PARAGOGICALLY
PARALLELOGRAM
PARALYTICALLY
PARAMAGNETISM
PARANOIACALLY
PARAPHERNALIA
PARASITICALLY
PARASITICIDAL
PARASYNTHESIS
PARASYNTHETON
PARENT COMPANY
PARENTHETICAL
PAR EXCELLENCE
PARKING GARAGE
PARKING LIGHTS
PARKING METERS
PARKINSON'S
  LAW
PARLIAMENTARY
PARROT-FASHION
PART EXCHANGES
PARTHENOCARPY
PARTICIPATING
PARTICIPATION
PARTICIPIALLY
PARTI-COLOURED
PARTICULARISM
PARTICULARIST
PARTICULARITY

PARTICULARIZE
PARTS OF
  SPEECH
PASSEMENTERIE
PASSIONFLOWER
PASSIONLESSLY
PASSIVIZATION
PATENT LEATHER
PATERFAMILIAS
PATERNALISTIC
PATHOGNOMONIC
PATRIOTICALLY
PATRISTICALLY
PATRONIZINGLY
PAY-AND-
  DISPLAY
PEACEABLENESS
PEACE DIVIDEND
PEACE OFFERING
PECKING ORDERS
PECTORAL CROSS
PECULIARITIES
PEDAGOGICALLY
PEDESTRIANIZE
PEDIATRICIANS
PEDUNCULATION
PELOPONNESIAN
PELTIER EFFECT
PEMBROKESHIRE
PENALTY CORNER
PENEPLANATION
PENETRABILITY
PENETRATINGLY
PENETRATIVELY
PENICILLATION
PENITENTIALLY
PENNILESSNESS
PENNSYLVANIAN
PENNY-DREADFUL
PENNY FARTHING
PENNY-FARTHING
PENNY-PINCHERS
PENNY-PINCHING
PENNY WHISTLES
PENTANOIC ACID
PEOPLE CARRIER
PEPPER-AND-
  SALT
PEPTONIZATION
PERAMBULATING
PERAMBULATION

PERAMBULATORS
PERAMBULATORY
PERCUSSION CAP
PERCUSSIONIST
PEREGRINATION
PERFECTIONISM
PERFECTIONIST
PERFUNCTORILY
PERICARPOIDAL
PERICHONDRIUM
PERIODIC TABLE
PERIOPERATIVE
PERISHABILITY
PERISSODACTYL
PERMANENT WAVE
PERMANENT WAYS
PERMUTATIONAL
PERPENDICULAR
PERSEVERATION
PERSONALISTIC
PERSONALITIES
PERSONALIZING
PERSONIFIABLE
PERSPECTIVISM
PERSPICACIOUS
PERVASIVENESS
PERVERTEDNESS
PETROCHEMICAL
PETROL STATION
PETROPAVLOVSK
PETTY OFFICERS
PHALLOCENTRIC
PHARMACEUTICS
PHARMACOGNOSY
PHARMACOPOEIA
PHARYNGOSCOPE
PHARYNGOSCOPY
PHELLOGENETIC
PHENCYCLIDINE
PHENOMENALISM
PHENOMENALIST
PHENOMENOLOGY
PHENOTHIAZINE
PHENYLALANINE
PHI BETA
  KAPPAS
PHILANTHROPIC
PHILHELLENISM
PHILOSOPHICAL
PHILOSOPHIZED
PHILOSOPHIZER

PHI-PHENOMENON
PHOSPHORYLASE
PHOTOCHEMICAL
PHOTOCOMPOSER
PHOTODYNAMICS
PHOTOELECTRIC
PHOTOELECTRON
PHOTOEMISSION
PHOTOEMISSIVE
PHOTOENGRAVER
PHOTO FINISHES
PHOTOGRAPHERS
PHOTOGRAPHING
PHOTOPERIODIC
PHOTORECEPTOR
PHOTOSTATTING
PHRASEOGRAPHY
PHRASEOLOGIST
PHRENOLOGICAL
PHYCOMYCETOUS
PHYLLOQUINONE
PHYSICALISTIC
PHYSICAL JERKS
PHYSIOGNOMIES
PHYSIOGNOMIST
PHYSIOGRAPHER
PHYSIOGRAPHIC
PHYSIOLOGICAL
PHYSIOLOGISTS
PHYSIOTHERAPY
PHYSOCLISTOUS
PHYSOSTIGMINE
PHYTOPLANKTON
PICTURESQUELY
PICTURE WINDOW
PIECES OF
  EIGHT
PIEZOELECTRIC
PIGEON-CHESTED
PIGHEADEDNESS
PILOT OFFICERS
PINK ELEPHANTS
PINKING SHEARS
PISCICULTURAL
PITCHED BATTLE
PLACE SETTINGS
PLAGIOTROPISM
PLAINTIVENESS
PLASTIC BULLET
PLATINIFEROUS
PLATINIRIDIUM

PLATINIZATION
PLATINUM-BLOND
PLATITUDINIZE
PLATITUDINOUS
PLATYHELMINTH
PLAYING FIELDS
PLENTEOUSNESS
PLENTIFULNESS
PLIMSOLL LINES
PLOUGHMANSHIP
PLURALIZATION
PNEUMATICALLY
PNEUMATOLYSIS
PNEUMATOMETER
PNEUMATOMETRY
PNEUMATOPHORE
PNEUMOGASTRIC
PNEUMONECTOMY
POETIC JUSTICE
POETIC LICENCE
POETS LAUREATE
POINTLESSNESS
POINTS OF
  ORDER
POINT-TO-
  POINTS
POISONOUSNESS
POLE POSITIONS
POLICE OFFICER
POLICE STATION
POLIOMYELITIS
POLLING BOOTHS
POLLINIFEROUS
POLYADELPHOUS
POLYCHROMATIC
POLYCOTYLEDON
POLYDACTYLOUS
POLYEMBRYONIC
POLYGALACEOUS
POLYGONACEOUS
POLYPHOSPHATE
POLYPROPYLENE
POLYPROTODONT
POLYSYLLABLES
POLYSYLLOGISM
POLYSYNTHESIS
PONDERABILITY
PONDEROUSNESS
PONTIFICATING
POOR RELATIONS
PORCELLANEOUS

PORNOGRAPHERS
PORT ELIZABETH
POSITIVE POLES
POSSIBILITIES
POSTAGE STAMPS
POSTCLASSICAL
POSTER COLOURS
POSTE RESTANTE
POSTGRADUATES
POSTMAN'S
  KNOCK
POST OFFICE
  BOX
POSTOPERATIVE
POSTPONEMENTS
POTATO BEETLES
POTENTIOMETER
POTTER'S
  WHEELS
POTTY-TRAINING
POWERLESSNESS
POWER POLITICS
POWER STATIONS
POWER STEERING
PRACTICAL JOKE
PRACTITIONERS
PRAGMATICALLY
PRAYER MEETING
PRAYING MANTIS
PREADAPTATION
PREADOLESCENT
PRECAUTIONARY
PRECEPTORSHIP
PRECIOUS METAL
PRECIOUS STONE
PRECIPITATELY
PRECIPITATING
PRECIPITATION
PRECIPITATIVE
PRECIPITOUSLY
PRECONCEPTION
PRECONDITIONS
PRECONIZATION
PREDATORINESS
PREDETERMINED
PREDETERMINER
PREDICABILITY
PREDICATIVELY
PREDILECTIONS
PREDOMINANTLY
PREDOMINATING

PREDOMINATION
PREFABRICATED
PREFABRICATOR
PREFERABILITY
PREFIGURATION
PREFIGURATIVE
PREFIGUREMENT
PREJUDGEMENTS
PRELIMINARIES
PRELIMINARILY
PREMATURENESS
PREMEDICATION
PREMEDITATION
PREMEDITATIVE
PREOCCUPATION
PREORDINATION
PREPARATORILY
PREPONDERANCE
PREPONDERATED
PREPOSITIONAL
PREPOSSESSING
PREPOSSESSION
PRE-RAPHAELITE
PREREQUISITES
PRESBYTERIANS
PRESCRIPTIBLE
PRESCRIPTIONS
PRESENTATIONS
PRESENTIMENTS
PRESERVATIVES
PRESS AGENCIES
PRESS CUTTINGS
PRESS RELEASES
PRESSURE GROUP
PRESSURE POINT
PRESUMPTIVELY
PRETENTIOUSLY
PRETERNATURAL
PREVARICATING
PREVARICATION
PREVARICATORS
PRICELESSNESS
PRIMARY COLOUR
PRIMARY SCHOOL
PRIMARY STRESS
PRIME MERIDIAN
PRIME MINISTER
PRIMITIVENESS
PRIMITIVISTIC
PRIMOGENITURE
PRINCE CONSORT

PRINCIPAL BOYS
PRINTED MATTER
PRINTING PRESS
PRISONER OF
  WAR
PRISON VISITOR
PRIVATE MEMBER
PRIVATE SCHOOL
PRIVATE SECTOR
PRIVATIZATION
PRIZEFIGHTERS
PRIZEFIGHTING
PROBABILISTIC
PROBABILITIES
PROCESS-SERVER
PROCLAMATIONS
PROCONSULATES
PROCRASTINATE
PROCTOLOGICAL
PRODUCIBILITY
PROFESSIONALS
PROFESSORIATE
PROFESSORSHIP
PROFITABILITY
PROFIT MARGINS
PROFIT SHARING
PROGNOSTICATE
PROGRESSIONAL
PROGRESSIVELY
PROGRESSIVISM
PROGRESSIVIST
PROHIBITIVELY
PROJECTIONIST
PROLEPTICALLY
PROLIFERATING
PROLIFERATION
PROLIFERATIVE
PROLONGATIONS
PROMENADE DECK
PROMINENTNESS
PROMISCUOUSLY
PROMISED LANDS
PROMISINGNESS
PROMOTIVENESS
PRONOMINALIZE
PRONOUNCEABLE
PRONOUNCEMENT
PRONUNCIATION
PROPAGABILITY
PROPAGANDISTS
PROPAGANDIZED

PROPAGATIONAL
PROPAROXYTONE
PROPHETICALLY
PROPHYLACTICS
PROPITIATIOUS
PROPORTIONATE
PROPORTIONING
PROPOSITIONAL
PROPOSITIONED
PROPRIETARILY
PROPRIETORIAL
PROPRIOCEPTOR
PROSCRIPTIONS
PROSELYTIZERS
PROSELYTIZING
PROSOPOPOEIAL
PROSTAGLANDIN
PROSTATECTOMY
PROTECTIONISM
PROTECTIONIST
PROTECTORATES
PROTEINACEOUS
PROTESTANTISM
PROTESTATIONS
PROTHETICALLY
PROTOCHORDATE
PROTOHISTORIC
PROTOLANGUAGE
PROTUBERANCES
PROTUBERANTLY
PROVINCIALISM
PROVINCIALITY
PROVING GROUND
PROVISIONALLY
PROVOCATIVELY
PROXIMATENESS
PSEPHOLOGICAL
PSEPHOLOGISTS
PSEUDOMORPHIC
PSYCHIATRISTS
PSYCHOANALYSE
PSYCHOANALYST
PSYCHOANALYZE
PSYCHOBIOLOGY
PSYCHODYNAMIC
PSYCHOGENESIS
PSYCHOGENETIC
PSYCHOGNOSTIC
PSYCHOGRAPHIC
PSYCHOHISTORY
PSYCHOKINESIS

PSYCHOKINETIC
PSYCHOLOGICAL
PSYCHOLOGISTS
PSYCHOMETRICS
PSYCHOPHYSICS
PSYCHOSOMATIC
PSYCHOSURGERY
PSYCHOTHERAPY
PSYCHOTICALLY
PSYCHROPHILIC
PTERIDOLOGIST
PTERIDOPHYTIC
PUBLIC COMPANY
PUBLIC SCHOOLS
PULVERIZATION
PUNCTILIOUSLY
PUNISHABILITY
PURITANICALLY
PURPLE PASSAGE
PURPOSELESSLY
PURPOSIVENESS
PUSILLANIMITY
PUSILLANIMOUS
PUT OUT OF
  SIGHT
PYRHELIOMETER
PYROPHOSPHATE

Q

QUADRICIPITAL
QUADRILATERAL
QUADRILLIONTH
QUADRIPARTITE
QUADRISECTION
QUADRIVALENCY
QUADRUPLICATE
QUADRUPLICITY
QUALIFICATION
QUALIFICATORY
QUALITATIVELY
QUANTUM THEORY
QUARTERFINALS
QUARTERMASTER
QUARTERSTAFFS
QUARTERSTAVES
QUARTZIFEROUS
QUEENS CONSORT
QUEEN'S
  COUNSEL
QUEEN'S
  ENGLISH

QUERULOUSNESS
QUESTIONINGLY
QUESTION MARKS
QUESTIONNAIRE
QUICK-TEMPERED
QUINDECENNIAL
QUINQUAGESIMA
QUINQUEVALENT
QUINTILLIONTH
QUINTUPLICATE
QUODLIBETICAL
QUOTATION MARK

R
RABBIT HUTCHES
RABBIT PUNCHES
RABBIT WARRENS
RABBLE-ROUSING
RACK-AND-
   PINION
RADIOACTIVATE
RADIOACTIVITY
RADIOCHEMICAL
RADIOGRAPHERS
RADIOISOTOPIC
RADIOTELEGRAM
RADIOTELETYPE
RAG-AND-BONE
   MAN
RAINBOW NATION
RAMIFICATIONS
RANCOROUSNESS
RANDOMIZATION
RAPPROCHEMENT
RAPTUROUSNESS
RAREFACTIONAL
RATEABLE VALUE
RATIOCINATION
RATIONALISTIC
RATIONALIZING
RATUSHINSKAYA
REACTIONARIES
READJUSTMENTS
READ-WRITE
   HEAD
REAFFIRMATION
REAFFORESTING
REALISTICALLY
REAPPOINTMENT
REARRANGEMENT
RECALCITRANCE

RECAPITULATED
RECEPTIONISTS
RECEPTION ROOM
RECESSIVENESS
RECIPROCALITY
RECIPROCATING
RECIPROCATION
RECIPROCATIVE
RECOGNITIONAL
RECOLLECTIONS
RECOMBINATION
RECOMMENDABLE
RECOMPENSABLE
RECOMPOSITION
RECONCILEMENT
RECONCILINGLY
RECONDITENESS
RECONDITIONED
RECONDITIONER
RECONNOITRING
RECONSIDERING
RECONSTITUENT
RECONSTITUTED
RECONSTRUCTED
RECONSTRUCTOR
RECORD-CHANGER
RECORD LIBRARY
RECORD PLAYERS
RECRIMINATING
RECRIMINATION
RECRIMINATIVE
RECRIMINATORY
RECRUDESCENCE
RECRYSTALLIZE
RECTIFICATION
RED BLOOD
   CELLS
REDEEMABILITY
REDEVELOPMENT
REDISTRIBUTED
RED-LETTER
   DAYS
REDUPLICATING
REDUPLICATION
REDUPLICATIVE
REEFER JACKETS
RE-ENFORCEMENT
RE-EXAMINATION
RE-EXPORTATION
REFERENCE BOOK
REFLEXIVENESS

REFORESTATION
REFORMATIONAL
REFORMATORIES
REFRACTOMETER
REFRACTOMETRY
REFRIGERATING
REFRIGERATION
REFRIGERATIVE
REFRIGERATORS
REFURBISHMENT
REGARDFULNESS
REGIMENTATION
REGISTRARSHIP
REGISTRATIONS
REGRETFULNESS
REGURGITATING
REGURGITATION
REHABILITATED
REIGN OF
   TERROR
REIMBURSEMENT
REIMPORTATION
REINCARNATING
REINCARNATION
REINFORCEMENT
REINSTATEMENT
REJUVENESCENT
RELATIONSHIPS
RELIGIOUSNESS
RELINQUISHING
REMINISCENCES
REMISSIBILITY
REMONSTRANCES
REMONSTRATING
REMONSTRATION
REMONSTRATIVE
REMORSELESSLY
REMOTE CONTROL
RENATIONALIZE
RENEGOTIATION
RENSSELAERITE
RENUNCIATIONS
REPEATABILITY
REPELLINGNESS
REPERCUSSIONS
REPLENISHMENT
REPOSEFULNESS
REPREHENDABLE
REPREHENSIBLE
REPREHENSIBLY
REPRESENTABLE

REPROACHFULLY
REPROACHINGLY
REPRODUCTIONS
REPROGRAPHICS
REPUBLICANISM
REPUBLICANIZE
REPUBLICATION
REPUBLISHABLE
REPULSIVENESS
REQUISITIONED
REQUISITIONER
RESENTFULNESS
RESISTIBILITY
RESISTIVENESS
RESOLVABILITY
RESOURCEFULLY
RESPIRABILITY
RESPIRATIONAL
RESPLENDENTLY
RESTAURANT CAR
RESTAURATEURS
RESTRAININGLY
RESTRICTIVELY
RESTRUCTURING
RESURRECTIONS
RESUSCITATING
RESUSCITATION
RESUSCITATIVE
RETAINABILITY
RETENTIVENESS
RETICULATIONS
RETINOSCOPIST
RETROACTIVELY
RETROACTIVITY
RETROGRESSING
RETROGRESSION
RETROGRESSIVE
RETROSPECTION
RETROSPECTIVE
RETURNABILITY
REUNIFICATION
REUTILIZATION
REVEALABILITY
REVELATIONIST
REVERBERATING
REVERBERATION
REVERBERATIVE
REVERBERATORY
REVERENTIALLY
REVERSIBILITY
REVOLUTIONARY

REVOLUTIONIST
REVOLUTIONIZE
RHABDOMANTIST
RHAPSODICALLY
RHIZOCEPHALAN
RHIZOMORPHOUS
RHODOCHROSITE
RHODODENDRONS
RIBEIRAO PRETO
RIGHTEOUSNESS
RIGHT TRIANGLE
ROAD ALLOWANCE
ROCK-AND-
  ROLLER
ROCKING CHAIRS
ROCKING HORSES
ROGUES'
  GALLERY
ROLLER COASTER
ROLLER-SKATERS
ROLLER SKATING
ROLLING STONES
ROLL OF
  HONOURS
ROLL-ON ROLL-
  OFF
ROMAN CATHOLIC
ROMAN NUMERALS
ROMANTICIZING
ROOMING HOUSES
RORSCHACH TEST
ROTARY TILLERS
ROTTEN BOROUGH
ROUGH AND
  READY
ROUGH-AND-
  READY
ROUGH DIAMONDS
ROUND BRACKETS
ROUND-THE-
  CLOCK
ROXBURGHSHIRE
ROYAL HIGHNESS
RUBBERNECKING
RUBBER-STAMPED
RUMOURMONGERS
RUTHERFORDIUM
RYUKYU ISLANDS

S
SABRE-RATTLING
SACCHARIMETER

SACCHAROMETER
SACRIFICEABLE
SACRIFICIALLY
SACRIFICINGLY
SACROSANCTITY
SADOMASOCHISM
SADOMASOCHIST
SAFETY CATCHES
SAFETY CURTAIN
SAFETY ISLANDS
SAFETY MATCHES
SAGACIOUSNESS
SAINT LAWRENCE
SAKHA REPUBLIC
SALACIOUSNESS
SALAD DRESSING
SALPINGECTOMY
SALVATION ARMY
SALVATIONISTS
SAM BROWNE
  BELT
SAN BERNARDINO
SANCTIMONIOUS
SAND-BLINDNESS
SANDWICH BOARD
SAN FRANCISCAN
SANGUINOLENCY
SANITARY TOWEL
SAN LUIS
  POTOSI
SANTA CATARINA
SAPROGENICITY
SARCASTICALLY
SARCOPHAGUSES
SATANICALNESS
SATIRICALNESS
SATISFACTIONS
SATURNINENESS
SCANDALMONGER
SCARIFICATION
SCATTERBRAINS
SCENESHIFTERS
SCEPTICALNESS
SCHEMATICALLY
SCHIZOCARPOUS
SCHIZOGENESIS
SCHIZOGENETIC
SCHIZOMYCETIC
SCHIZOPHRENIA
SCHIZOPHRENIC
SCHOLARLINESS

SCHOLASTICATE
SCHOLASTICISM
SCHOOLFELLOWS
SCHOOL-LEAVERS
SCHOOLMARMISH
SCHOOLMASTERS
SCHOOLTEACHER
SCIENTOLOGIST
SCILLY ISLANDS
SCINTILLATING
SCINTILLATION
SCLEROPROTEIN
SCOLOPENDRINE
SCORCHED EARTH
SCORIFICATION
SCRIPTWRITERS
SCRIPTWRITING
SCULPTURESQUE
SEANAD EIREANN
SEA OF
  TROUBLES
SEARCH PARTIES
SEARCH WARRANT
SEASON TICKETS
SEAWORTHINESS
SECESSIONISTS
SECLUSIVENESS
SECONDARINESS
SECOND COUSINS
SECOND-GUESSED
SECOND THOUGHT
SECRETARYSHIP
SECRETIVENESS
SECRET SERVICE
SECURITY RISKS
SEDENTARINESS
SEDIMENTARILY
SEDIMENTATION
SEDIMENTOLOGY
SEDITIOUSNESS
SEDUCTIVENESS
SEGREGATIONAL
SEINE-MARITIME
SEISMOGRAPHER
SEISMOGRAPHIC
SEISMOLOGISTS
SELECTIVENESS
SELENOGRAPHER
SELENOGRAPHIC
SELF-ABASEMENT
SELF-ADDRESSED

SELF-ANNEALING
SELF-APPOINTED
SELF-ASSERTION
SELF-ASSERTIVE
SELF-ASSURANCE
SELF-CONFESSED
SELF-CONFIDENT
SELF-CONSCIOUS
SELF-CONTAINED
SELF-DECEPTION
SELF-DECEPTIVE
SELF-DEFEATING
SELF-EVIDENTLY
SELF-IMPORTANT
SELF-INDUCTION
SELF-INDUCTIVE
SELF-INDULGENT
SELF-INFLICTED
SELF-KNOWLEDGE
SELF-PITYINGLY
SELF-POSSESSED
SELF-PROPELLED
SELF-RESTRAINT
SELF-RIGHTEOUS
SELF-SACRIFICE
SELF-SATISFIED
SELLER'S
  MARKET
SELLING-PLATER
SELLING POINTS
SEMASIOLOGIST
SEMIAUTOMATIC
SEMICONDUCTOR
SEMICONSCIOUS
SEMIDETACHEDS
SEMIFINALISTS
SEMIPALATINSK
SEMIPARASITIC
SEMIPERMEABLE
SEMIPORCELAIN
SEMPER FIDELIS
SEMPER PARATUS
SENIOR CITIZEN
SENSATIONALLY
SENSELESSNESS
SENSITIVENESS
SENSITIZATION
SENTENTIOUSLY
SENTIMENTALLY
SEQUENTIALITY
SEQUESTRATING

SEQUESTRATION
SERBO-CROATIAN
SERGEANT MAJOR
SERIALIZATION
SERIAL NUMBERS
SERICULTURIST
SERJEANT AT
  LAW
SERVICE CHARGE
SEVENTH HEAVEN
SEVEN-YEAR
  ITCH
SEWING MACHINE
SEXAGENARIANS
SEXPLOITATION
SHAKESPEAREAN
SHAMELESSNESS
SHAPELESSNESS
SHARP PRACTICE
SHARPSHOOTERS
SHEEPSHEARING
SHEPHERDESSES
SHIFTLESSNESS
SHIP'S
  CHANDLER
SHIRTWAISTERS
SHOCK ABSORBER
SHOOTING MATCH
SHOOTING STARS
SHOOTING STICK
SHOP ASSISTANT
SHORT-CHANGING
SHORT CIRCUITS
SHORT-TEMPERED
SHOULDER BLADE
SHOULDER STRAP
SHROVE TUESDAY
SICK HEADACHES
SIDESPLITTING
SIERRA LEONEAN
SIGHTLESSNESS
SIGMOIDOSCOPE
SIGMOIDOSCOPY
SIGNATURE TUNE
SIGNIFICANTLY
SIGNIFICATION
SIGNIFICATIVE
SILENT PARTNER
SILVER BIRCHES
SILVER JUBILEE
SILVER-TONGUED

SILVER WEDDING
SILVICULTURAL
SIMPLE MACHINE
SINGLE-DECKERS
SINGULARITIES
SIPHONOSTELIC
SIT ON THE
  FENCE
SITTING PRETTY
SITTING TARGET
SIXTEENTH NOTE
SKEET SHOOTING
SKIRTING BOARD
SLAP AND
  TICKLE
SLEDGEHAMMERS
SLEEPING PILLS
SLEEP LEARNING
SLEEPLESSNESS
SLEIGHT OF
  HAND
SLIDING SCALES
SLIPSTREAMING
SMALL FORTUNES
SMALLHOLDINGS
SMELLING SALTS
SMOOTH-TONGUED
SNAKE CHARMERS
SNAP FASTENERS
SNEAK PREVIEWS
SNOW BLINDNESS
SOCIAL CHAPTER
SOCIAL CLIMBER
SOCIALIZATION
SOCIAL SCIENCE
SOCIAL SERVICE
SOCIAL WORKERS
SOCIOECONOMIC
SOCIOLINGUIST
SODA FOUNTAINS
SOFT-PEDALLING
SOLAR CONSTANT
SOLDERING IRON
SOLDIERLINESS
SOLEMNIZATION
SOLICITATIONS
SOLICITORSHIP
SOLILOQUIZING
SOLVAY PROCESS
SOMATOPLASTIC
SOMATOPLEURAL

SOMERSAULTING
SOMNAMBULANCE
SOMNAMBULATOR
SOMNAMBULISTS
SONS-OF-
  BITCHES
SOPHISTICALLY
SOPHISTICATED
SOPHISTICATES
SOPHISTICATOR
SOPORIFICALLY
SORROWFULNESS
SOUL-SEARCHING
SOUNDING BOARD
SOUNDLESSNESS
SOUNDPROOFING
SOUTH CAROLINA
SOUTHEAST ASIA
SOUTHEASTERLY
SOUTHEASTWARD
SOUTHEND-ON-
  SEA
SOUTHERLINESS
SOUTHERN OCEAN
SOUTH TYNESIDE
SOUTHWESTERLY
SOUTHWESTWARD
SOVIETIZATION
SPACE INVADERS
SPACE SHUTTLES
SPACE STATIONS
SPASMODICALLY
SPEAKING TUBES
SPECIAL BRANCH
SPECIAL SCHOOL
SPECIFICATION
SPECIFICATIVE
SPECTACULARLY
SPECTROGRAPHY
SPECTROMETRIC
SPECTROSCOPES
SPECTROSCOPIC
SPECULATIVELY
SPEECH THERAPY
SPELEOLOGICAL
SPELEOLOGISTS
SPENDING MONEY
SPERMATICALLY
SPERMATOPHORE
SPERMATOPHYTE
SPHERICALNESS

SPHEROIDICITY
SPHINGOMYELIN
SPHYGMOGRAPHY
SPINE-CHILLING
SPINELESSNESS
SPINNING JENNY
SPINNING WHEEL
SPIRITUALISTS
SPIRITUALIZER
SPIT AND
  POLISH
SPITTING IMAGE
SPLAYFOOTEDLY
SPLENDIFEROUS
SPLINTER GROUP
SPONTANEOUSLY
SPORTSMANLIKE
SPORTSMANSHIP
SPREAD BETTING
SPREAD-EAGLING
SPRIGHTLINESS
SPRING CHICKEN
SPRING-CLEANED
SQUANDERINGLY
SQUARE-BASHING
SQUARE BRACKET
SQUEAMISHNESS
SQUIREARCHIES
STABILIZATION
STAFF OFFICERS
STAFFORDSHIRE
STAFF SERGEANT
STAGE MANAGERS
STAGE-MANAGING
STAGE WHISPERS
STALKING-HORSE
STAMINIFEROUS
STANDARDIZING
STANDARD LAMPS
STANDING ORDER
STANDOFFISHLY
STAPHYLOCOCCI
STARCH-REDUCED
STARTING BLOCK
STARTING GATES
STARTING PRICE
STATELESSNESS
STATE-OF-THE-
  ART
STATESMANLIKE
STATESMANSHIP

STATION BREAKS
STATION HOUSES
STATIONMASTER
STATION WAGONS
STATISTICALLY
STATISTICIANS
STEADFASTNESS
STEAMROLLERED
STEEPLECHASER
STEEPLECHASES
STEERING WHEEL
STENOGRAPHERS
STENOPETALOUS
STENOPHYLLOUS
STEPPING-STONE
STERCORACEOUS
STEREOGRAPHIC
STEREOSCOPIST
STEREOTROPISM
STEREOTYPICAL
STERILIZATION
STICKING POINT
STICK IN THE
  MUD
STICK-IN-THE-
  MUD
STIFF UPPER
  LIP
STILETTO HEELS
STIMULATINGLY
STIPENDIARIES
STIRLINGSHIRE
STOCKBREEDERS
STOCKBREEDING
STOCK EXCHANGE
STOICHIOMETRY
STOLONIFEROUS
STOMATOPLASTY
STOP AT
  NOTHING
STORM TROOPERS
STORMY PETRELS
STOVEPIPE HATS
STRAIGHTEDGES
STRAIGHTENING
STRAIGHT-FACED
STRAIGHT FIGHT
STRAIGHT RAZOR
STRAITJACKETS
STRANGLEHOLDS
STRANGULATING
STRANGULATION

STRATEGICALLY
STRATIGRAPHER
STRATIGRAPHIC
STRATOCUMULUS
STRATOSPHERIC
STRAW-COLOURED
STREETWALKERS
STRENGTHENING
STRENUOUSNESS
STREPTOCARPUS
STREPTOCOCCAL
STREPTOCOCCUS
STREPTOKINASE
STRIKEBREAKER
STRIP CARTOONS
STRIP LIGHTING
STROBILACEOUS
STROMATOLITIC
STRUCTURALISM
STRUCTURALIST
STUDENTS'
  UNION
STUDIO COUCHES
STUFFED SHIRTS
STYLISTICALLY
SUBCOMMITTEES
SUBCONTINENTS
SUBCONTRACTED
SUBCONTRACTOR
SUBDIVISIONAL
SUBEQUATORIAL
SUBIRRIGATION
SUBJECT MATTER
SUBLIEUTENANT
SUBMACHINE GUN
SUBORDINATING
SUBORDINATION
SUBORDINATIVE
SUBPOPULATION
SUBREPTITIOUS
SUBSCRIPTIONS
SUBSERVIENTLY
SUBSIDIZATION
SUBSTANTIALLY
SUBSTANTIATED
SUBSTANTIATOR
SUBSTANTIVELY
SUBSTANTIVIZE
SUBSTITUTABLE
SUBSTITUTIONS
SUBSTRUCTURAL

SUBSTRUCTURES
SUBTILIZATION
SUBVENTIONARY
SUFFICIENCIES
SUFFOCATINGLY
SUFFRAGANSHIP
SUFFRAGETTISM
SUFFUMIGATION
SULPHADIAZINE
SULPHURIC ACID
SUMMARIZATION
SUMMER SCHOOLS
SUMPTUOUSNESS
SUNDAY SCHOOLS
SUPERABUNDANT
SUPERADDITION
SUPERANNUATED
SUPERCALENDER
SUPERCHARGERS
SUPERCHARGING
SUPERCOLUMNAR
SUPERCRITICAL
SUPEREMINENCE
SUPERFETATION
SUPERFICIALLY
SUPERFLUIDITY
SUPERFLUOUSLY
SUPERHUMANITY
SUPERIMPOSING
SUPERINTENDED
SUPERLATIVELY
SUPERNATATION
SUPERNUMERARY
SUPERORDINATE
SUPERPHYSICAL
SUPERPOSITION
SUPERSENSIBLE
SUPERSTITIONS
SUPERSTITIOUS
SUPERVENIENCE
SUPPLANTATION
SUPPLEMENTARY
SUPPLEMENTING
SUPPLICATIONS
SUPPLY TEACHER
SUPPOSITIONAL
SUPPOSITORIES
SUPRANATIONAL
SURFACE-ACTIVE
SURREPTITIOUS
SURROGATESHIP

SURVIVABILITY
SUSTENTACULAR
SWASHBUCKLING
SWEET NOTHINGS
SWIMMING BATHS
SWIMMING POOLS
SWIZZLE STICKS
SWOLLEN HEADED
SWORDSMANSHIP
SYBARITICALLY
SYLLABOGRAPHY
SYLLEPTICALLY
SYLLOGISTICAL
SYLLOGIZATION
SYMBOLIZATION
SYMMETRICALLY
SYMPATHECTOMY
SYMPATHOLYTIC
SYMPATRICALLY
SYMPHONICALLY
SYMPHYSICALLY
SYNARTHRODIAL
SYNCHRONISTIC
SYNCHRONIZING
SYNDICALISTIC
SYNTACTICALLY
SYNTHETICALLY
SYPHILOLOGIST
SYRINGOMYELIA
SYRINGOMYELIC
SYSTEMATIZING
SYSTEMATOLOGY
SYSTEMIZATION
SYZYGETICALLY

T

TACHISTOSCOPE
TACHYPHYLAXIS
TAKE A BACK
  SEAT
TAKE THE
  PLEDGE
TALKATIVENESS
TALKING POINTS
TANGENTIALITY
TANTALIZATION
TANTALIZINGLY
TAPE RECORDERS
TAR AND
  FEATHER

TARN-ET-
  GARONNE
TARTARIZATION
TASTELESSNESS
TATAR REPUBLIC
TAX-DEDUCTIBLE
TAXONOMICALLY
TAYSIDE REGION
TEAR A STRIP
  OFF
TECHNOLOGICAL
TECHNOLOGISTS
TEETER-TOTTERS
TELAUTOGRAPHY
TELECOMMUTING
TELEGRAPH POLE
TELEMARKETING
TELENCEPHALIC
TELENCEPHALON
TELEPHOTO LENS
TELEPROMPTERS
TELEUTOSPORIC
TELEVISIONARY
TEMPERABILITY
TEMPERAMENTAL
TEMPERATENESS
TEMPESTUOUSLY
TEMPORARINESS
TEMPORIZATION
TEMPORIZINGLY
TENACIOUSNESS
TENANT FARMERS
TENDENTIOUSLY
TENDERHEARTED
TENDERIZATION
TEN-GALLON
  HATS
TENPIN BOWLING
TENTATIVENESS
TERGIVERSATOR
TERMINABILITY
TERMINATIONAL
TERMINOLOGIES
TERMINOLOGIST
TERPSICHOREAN
TERRACED HOUSE
TERRESTRIALLY
TERRORIZATION
TESTIFICATION
TETARTOHEDRAL
TETRABASICITY

TETRACHLORIDE
TETRADYNAMOUS
TETRASTICHOUS
TETRASYLLABIC
TETRASYLLABLE
THALASSOCRACY
THANKLESSNESS
THANKSGIVINGS
THEANTHROPISM
THEANTHROPIST
THEATRICALITY
THE CUT OF A
  CARD
THE GONDOLIERS
THE LIONS
  SHARE
THE MAGIC
  FLUTE
THENCEFORWARD
THEOLOGICALLY
THEORETICALLY
THERIOMORPHIC
THERMOCHEMIST
THERMODYNAMIC
THERMOGENESIS
THERMOGRAPHER
THERMOGRAPHIC
THERMONUCLEAR
THERMOPLASTIC
THERMOSETTING
THERMOS FLASKS
THERMOSTATICS
THERMOTHERAPY
THERMOTROPISM
THETFORD MINES
THIGMOTROPISM
THORACOPLASTY
THOROUGHBREDS
THOROUGHFARES
THOROUGHGOING
THOROUGHPACED
THOUGHTLESSLY
THOUGHT POLICE
THREATENINGLY
THREE-CORNERED
THREE-DAY
  EVENT
THREE LINE
  WHIP
THREE-LINE
  WHIP
THREMMATOLOGY

THUNDERCLOUDS
THUNDERSHOWER
THUNDERSTORMS
THUNDERSTRUCK
THYROIDECTOMY
TIME AFTER
  TIME
TIME-AND-
  MOTION
TIME-CONSUMING
TIME EXPOSURES
TIME SIGNATURE
TINTINNABULAR
TINTINNABULUM
TITILLATINGLY
TITTLE-TATTLED
TITTLE-TATTLER
TOAD-IN-THE-
  HOLE
TOASTING FORKS
TOILET-TRAINED
TOLERABLENESS
TOLERATIONISM
TOLERATIONIST
TONE LANGUAGES
TONGUE TWISTER
TONSILLECTOMY
TOOTHSOMENESS
TOPOGRAPHICAL
TOPOLOGICALLY
TORRE DEL
  GRECO
TORTOISESHELL
TOTIPALMATION
TOXICOLOGICAL
TOXICOLOGISTS
TOXOPLASMOSIS
TRACE ELEMENTS
TRACHEOTOMIST
TRADE UNIONISM
TRADE UNIONIST
TRADING ESTATE
TRADING STAMPS
TRADITIONALLY
TRAFFIC CIRCLE
TRAFFIC ISLAND
TRAFFIC LIGHTS
TRAFFIC WARDEN
TRAGICOMEDIES
TRAILER HOUSES
TRANQUILLIZED
TRANQUILLIZER

TRANSACTINIDE
TRANSACTIONAL
TRANSATLANTIC
TRANSCAUCASIA
TRANSCENDENCE
TRANSCENDENCY
TRANSCRIBABLE
TRANSCRIPTION
TRANSFIGURING
TRANSFORMABLE
TRANSGRESSING
TRANSGRESSION
TRANSGRESSIVE
TRANSGRESSORS
TRANSISTORIZE
TRANSLATIONAL
TRANSLATORIAL
TRANSLITERATE
TRANSLOCATION
TRANSMIGRATOR
TRANSMISSIBLE
TRANSMISSIONS
TRANSMITTANCE
TRANSMITTANCY
TRANSMUTATION
TRANSPARENTLY
TRANSPIRATION
TRANSPIRATORY
TRANSPLANTING
TRANSPORTABLE
TRANSPORT CAFE
TRANSPORTEDLY
TRANSPOSITION
TRANSSHIPMENT
TRANSVESTITES
TRANSYLVANIAN
TRAPEZOHEDRAL
TRAPEZOHEDRON
TRAUMATICALLY
TREACHEROUSLY
TREASURERSHIP
TREASURE TROVE
TREASURE-TROVE
TREASURY NOTES
TREMULOUSNESS
TREPONEMATOUS
TRIANGULARITY
TRIANGULATION
TRIATOMICALLY
TRIBOELECTRIC
TRICENTENNIAL

TRICHOLOGISTS
TRICHOMONADAL
TRICHROMATISM
TRIGONOMETRIC
TRILATERATION
TRILINGUALISM
TRIMETHADIONE
TRIPLOBLASTIC
TRIPOLITANIAN
TRISACCHARIDE
TROOP CARRIERS
TROPHALLACTIC
TROPHOBLASTIC
TROUBLEMAKERS
TRUCIAL STATES
TRUSTWORTHILY
TRUTH-FUNCTION
TUBERCULATION
TUBUAI ISLANDS
TUBULIFLOROUS
TURBOCHARGERS
TURBOCHARGING
TURBO-ELECTRIC
TURING MACHINE
TURNING CIRCLE
TURNING POINTS
TWO-WAY
  MIRRORS
TYPOGRAPHICAL
TYRANNIZINGLY
TYRANNOSAURUS
TYRANNOUSNESS

U

UGLY DUCKLINGS
ULTRANATIONAL
UMBELLIFEROUS
UMBILICAL CORD
UNACCOMPANIED
UNACCOUNTABLE
UNACCOUNTABLY
UNADULTERATED
UNADVENTUROUS
UNADVISEDNESS
UNASHAMEDNESS
UNBELIEVINGLY
UNBENDINGNESS
UNBLESSEDNESS
UNCEASINGNESS
UNCEREMONIOUS
UNCERTAINNESS

UNCHALLENGING
UNCHARISMATIC
UNCIRCUMCISED
UNCLEANLINESS
UNCOMFORTABLE
UNCOMFORTABLY
UNCOMPENSATED
UNCOMPETITIVE
UNCOMPLAINING
UNCOMPLICATED
UNCONCERNEDLY
UNCONDITIONAL
UNCONDITIONED
UNCONFORMABLE
UNCONSCIOUSLY
UNCONSTRAINED
UNCONSUMMATED
UNCONTENTIOUS
UNCOORDINATED
UNCROWNED KING
UNDECIDEDNESS
UNDERACHIEVED
UNDERACHIEVER
UNDERBREEDING
UNDERCARRIAGE
UNDERCHARGING
UNDERCURRENTS
UNDERDRAINAGE
UNDEREDUCATED
UNDEREMPLOYED
UNDERESTIMATE
UNDEREXPOSING
UNDEREXPOSURE
UNDERGARMENTS
UNDERGRADUATE
UNDERHANDEDLY
UNDER MILK
  WOOD
UNDERMININGLY
UNDERPAINTING
UNDERPINNINGS
UNDERSTANDING
UNDERSTRENGTH
UNDERSTUDYING
UNDISCIPLINED
UNDISTRIBUTED
UNEARTHLINESS
UNEMBARRASSED
UNENFORCEABLE
UNENLIGHTENED
UNEQUIVOCALLY

UNEXCEPTIONAL
UNEXPERIENCED
UNFALTERINGLY
UNFAMILIARITY
UNFASHIONABLE
UNFEELINGNESS
UNFLINCHINGLY
UNFORESEEABLE
UNFORGETTABLE
UNFORGETTABLY
UNFORTUNATELY
UNFOUNDEDNESS
UNGUARDEDNESS
UNHEALTHINESS
UNICAMERALISM
UNICAMERALIST
UNILATERALISM
UNILLUSTRATED
UNIMPEACHABLE
UNIMPEACHABLY
UNINHABITABLE
UNINHIBITEDLY
UNINTELLIGENT
UNINTENTIONAL
UNINTERRUPTED
UNITED KINGDOM
UNITED NATIONS
UNIVERSALNESS
UNIVERSAL TIME
UNMENTIONABLE
UNMUSICALNESS
UNNATURALNESS
UNNECESSARILY
UNOBTRUSIVELY
UNPATRONIZING
UNPRECEDENTED
UNPREDICTABLE
UNPRESSURIZED
UNPRETENTIOUS
UNQUALIFIABLE
UNQUESTIONING
UNREADABILITY
UNRELENTINGLY
UNRELIABILITY
UNREMITTINGLY
UNREPRESENTED
UNRUFFLEDNESS
UNSAVOURINESS
UNSELFISHNESS
UNSERVICEABLE
UNSIGHTLINESS

UNSOCIABILITY
UNSUBSTANTIAL
UNSUITABILITY
UNSUSTAINABLE
UNTHREATENING
UNTRADITIONAL
UNTRANSFORMED
UNWARRANTABLE
UNWILLINGNESS
UNWRITTEN LAWS
UPRIGHT PIANOS
UP TO THE
  MINUTE
UP-TO-THE-
  MINUTE
URETHROSCOPIC
UTI POSSIDETIS
UTTERABLENESS

V

VACILLATINGLY
VACUUM CLEANER
VALUE-ADDED
  TAX
VALUE JUDGMENT
VALUELESSNESS
VANTAGE POINTS
VAPOURABILITY
VAPOURISHNESS
VARICOSE VEINS
VARIOLIZATION
VASOINHIBITOR
VAULTING HORSE
VEGETARIANISM
VENEREOLOGIST
VENETIAN BLIND
VENTRILOQUIAL
VENTRILOQUISM
VENTRILOQUIST
VENTRILOQUIZE
VERACIOUSNESS
VERBALIZATION
VERBIFICATION
VERITABLENESS
VERMICULATION
VERMINOUSNESS
VERNACULARISM
VERNALIZATION
VERSIFICATION
VESTAL VIRGINS
VESTMANAEYJAR

VEXATIOUSNESS
VEXED QUESTION
VEXILLOLOGIST
VICARIOUSNESS
VICE PRESIDENT
VICIOUS CIRCLE
VICTIMIZATION
VICTORIA CROSS
VICTORIA PLUMS
VILIFICATIONS
VINDICABILITY
VINICULTURIST
VIOLONCELLIST
VIRGINIA BEACH
VIRGIN ISLANDS
VISCOUNTESSES
VISIONARINESS
VISITING CARDS
VISITORS'
  BOOKS
VISUALIZATION
VITRIFICATION
VITRIOLICALLY
VIVACIOUSNESS
VIVISECTIONAL
VOCIFERATIONS
VOICELESSNESS
VOLATILIZABLE
VOLCANIZATION
VOLCANOLOGIST
VOLUNTARINESS
VOLUNTARISTIC
VOTE OF
  CENSURE
VOTES OF
  THANKS
VOUCHSAFEMENT

VRAISEMBLANCE
VULCANIZATION
VULGARIZATION
VULNERABILITY

W

WALKIE-TALKIES
WALKING PAPERS
WALKING STICKS
WALL PAINTINGS
WALTHAM FOREST
WARM-HEARTEDLY
WASHINGTONIAN
WASTE PRODUCTS
WATCH THE
  CLOCK
WATER BISCUITS
WATER BUFFALOS
WATERING HOLES
WATERING PLACE
WATERPROOFING
WATER SOFTENER
WATER SUPPLIES
WATTLE AND
  DAUB
WEARISOMENESS
WEATHER-BEATEN
WEATHERBOARDS
WEIGHT LIFTERS
WEIGHT LIFTING
WELFARE STATES
WELL-APPOINTED
WELL-CONNECTED
WELL-DEVELOPED
WELL-PRESERVED
WELL-QUALIFIED
WELL-SUPPORTED

WELL-THOUGHT-
  OF
WELSH RAREBITS
WELTERWEIGHTS
WEST BERKSHIRE
WESTERN SAHARA
WEST GLAMORGAN
WEST-NORTHWEST
WEST-SOUTHWEST
WEST YORKSHIRE
WETTING AGENTS
WHEELER DEALER
WHEELER-DEALER
WHIMSICALNESS
WHIPPOORWILLS
WHITE ELEPHANT
WHITE WEDDINGS
WHOLESOMENESS
WHOOPING COUGH
WICKET KEEPERS
WIDE-AWAKENESS
WILDCAT STRIKE
WILHELMSHAVEN
WILL-O'-THE-
  WISPS
WILLOW PATTERN
WINDING SHEETS
WINDOW-DRESSER
WINDOW-SHOPPED
WINDOW-SHOPPER
WING COMMANDER
WITHDRAWNNESS
WITHERINGNESS
WITWATERSRAND
WOLVERHAMPTON
WOMEN'S
  STUDIES

WONDERFULNESS
WONDER-WORKING
WOODCRAFTSMAN
WOOLGATHERING
WORD BLINDNESS
WORD PROCESSOR
WORK-HARDENING
WORSHIPPINGLY
WORTHLESSNESS
WRONGHEADEDLY

X

XANTHOCHROISM
XEROPHTHALMIA
XEROPHTHALMIC
XINJIANG UYGUR

Y

YACHTSMANSHIP
YEOMAN SERVICE
YOUNG MARRIEDS

Z

ZEBRA CROSSING
ZEUGMATICALLY
ZIGZAGGEDNESS
ZINJANTHROPUS
ZOOGEOGRAPHER
ZOOGEOGRAPHIC
ZOOSPORANGIAL
ZOOSPORANGIUM
ZYGAPOPHYSEAL
ZYGODACTYLISM
ZYGODACTYLOUS

A

ABOVE-
  MENTIONED
ABSENT-
  MINDEDLY
ABSORBEFACIENT
ABSTEMIOUSNESS
ABSTRACTEDNESS
ABSTRACTIONISM
ACCLIMATIZABLE
ACCOMMODATIONS
ACCOMPANIMENTS
ACCOMPLISHABLE
ACCOMPLISHMENT
ACCOUNTABILITY
ACCUMULATIVELY
ACHONDROPLASIA
ACHROMATICALLY
ACKNOWLEDGMENT
ACQUIRED
  TASTES
ACROSS THE
  BOARD
ACROSS-THE-
  BOARD
ACTION
  STATIONS
ADENOCARCINOMA
ADMINISTRATION
ADMINISTRATIVE
ADMINISTRATORS
ADMINISTRATRIX
ADULT
  EDUCATION
ADVANCED
  LEVELS
ADVANTAGEOUSLY
AEROBALLISTICS
AEROMECHANICAL
AFFECTIONATELY
AFOREMENTIONED
AGGLOMERATIONS
AGGRANDIZEMENT
AGGRESSIVENESS
AGRICULTURISTS
AGROBIOLOGICAL
AGUASCALIENTES
AIR-
  CONDITIONED
AIR VICE-
  MARSHAL
ALCOHOLIZATION

ALLEGORIZATION
ALL-IN
  WRESTLING
ALLITERATIVELY
ALLOPATHICALLY
ALLOPATRICALLY
ALLOTROPICALLY
ALL OVER THE
  SHOP
ALPES
  MARITIMES
ALPHABETICALLY
ALSACE-
  LORRAINE
ALTRUISTICALLY
AMARANTHACEOUS
AMATEURISHNESS
AMBASSADORSHIP
AMBASSADRESSES
AMBIDEXTROUSLY
AMERICAN
  INDIAN
AMMONIFICATION
AMPHIARTHROSIS
AMPHIBOLOGICAL
AMPHIPROSTYLAR
AMUSEMENT
  PARKS
ANACARDIACEOUS
ANAESTHETIZING
ANAMNESTICALLY
ANAMORPHOSCOPE
ANATHEMATIZING
ANCIENT
  MARINER
ANDORRA LA
  VELLA
ANGINA
  PECTORIS
ANGLO-
  AMERICANS
ANGLO-
  CATHOLICS
ANIMADVERSIONS
ANISODACTYLOUS
ANTAGONIZATION
ANTHROPOLOGIST
ANTHROPOMETRIC
ANTHROPOPATHIC
ANTHROPOSOPHIC
ANTICHLORISTIC
ANTICIPATORILY

ANTIDEPRESSANT
ANTIHISTAMINES
ANTILOGARITHMS
ANTIMONARCHIST
ANTIPERSPIRANT
ANTIPHLOGISTIC
ANTIPRAGMATISM
ANTIQUATEDNESS
ANTIREPUBLICAN
ANTISEPTICALLY
ANTITHETICALLY
APARTMENT
  HOUSE
APOLOGETICALLY
APOPLECTICALLY
APOSTROPHIZING
APPENDECTOMIES
APPENDICECTOMY
APPLES AND
  PEARS
APPORTIONMENTS
APPRECIATIVELY
APPREHENSIVELY
APPRENTICESHIP
APPROPRIATIONS
APPROVED
  SCHOOL
APPROXIMATIONS
ARABIC
  NUMERALS
ARCHAEOLOGICAL
ARCHAEOLOGISTS
ARCHBISHOPRICS
ARCHETYPICALLY
ARCHIDIACONATE
ARCHIEPISCOPAL
ARCHIMANDRITES
ARCHITECTONICS
ARITHMETICALLY
ARITHMETICIANS
ARRONDISSEMENT
ARTICULATENESS
ARTIODACTYLOUS
AS CLEAR AS A
  BELL
AS DRUNK AS A
  LORD
AS SAFE AS
  HOUSES
ASSASSINATIONS
ASSAULT
  COURSES

ASSET-
  STRIPPING
ASSOCIATIONISM
AS THE CASE
  MAY BE
ASTIGMATICALLY
ASTROLOGICALLY
ASTRONAVIGATOR
ASTRONOMICALLY
ASTROPHYSICIST
ASYMMETRICALLY
ASYMPTOTICALLY
AT DAGGERS
  DRAWN
ATTRACTIVENESS
AUF
  WIEDERSEHEN
AUSPICIOUSNESS
AUTHENTICATING
AUTHENTICATION
AUTHENTICITIES
AUTHORITARIANS
AUTHORIZATIONS
AUTOBIOGRAPHER
AUTOBIOGRAPHIC
AUTOCRATICALLY
AUTOIONIZATION
AUTOMATIC
  PILOT
AUTOPHYTICALLY
AUTORADIOGRAPH
AUTOSUGGESTION
AUTOSUGGESTIVE
AUXILIARY
  VERBS
AWE-
  INSPIRINGLY

B

BACCALAUREATES
BACHELOR OF
  ARTS
BACK
  FORMATIONS
BACKHANDEDNESS
BACK-SEAT
  DRIVER
BACTERIOLOGIST
BACTERIOPHAGIC
BACTERIOSTASIS
BACTERIOSTATIC

BALANCE OF
  POWER
BALANCE OF
  TRADE
BALSAMINACEOUS
BANANA
  REPUBLIC
BANNER
  HEADLINE
BAROMETRICALLY
BASIDIOSPOROUS
BASTARDIZATION
BATCH
  PROCESSED
BATHING
  MACHINE
BATTLE
  CRUISERS
BE-ALL AND
  END-ALL
BEASTS OF
  BURDEN
BEATIFICATIONS
BEAUTIFICATION
BEAUTY
  PARLOURS
BEHIND THE
  TIMES
BELISHA
  BEACONS
BERBERIDACEOUS
BERKSHIRE
  DOWNS
BESIDE THE
  POINT
BEST BEFORE
  DATE
BIBLIOGRAPHERS
BIBLIOGRAPHIES
BIG GAME
  HUNTING
BIOCLIMATOLOGY
BIODEGRADABLES
BIOENGINEERING
BIOGENETICALLY
BIOGRAPHICALLY
BIOLUMINESCENT
BIPARTISANSHIP
BIRD OF
  PARADISE
BIRDS OF
  PASSAGE
BITUMINIZATION

BLACK
  MARKETEER
BLANK
  CARTRIDGE
BLOCK AND
  TACKLE
BLOOD
  POISONING
BLOOD
  PRESSURES
BLOOD
  RELATIONS
BLOOD
  SACRIFICE
BLOODTHIRSTILY
BLUE-
  PENCILLING
BOARDINGHOUSES
BOARDING
  SCHOOL
BOIS DE
  BOULOGNE
BOISTEROUSNESS
BOLOMETRICALLY
BOON
  COMPANIONS
BOUCHES-DU-
  RHONE
BOUGAINVILLEAS
BOUILLABAISSES
BOULEVERSEMENT
BOWDLERIZATION
BRACHYCEPHALIC
BRACHYDACTYLIA
BRACHYDACTYLIC
BREAD-AND-
  BUTTER
BREAKFAST
  TABLE
BREATHLESSNESS
BREMSSTRAHLUNG
BRIGHT AND
  EARLY
BRONCHIAL
  TUBES
BRONCHIECTASIS
BRONCHOSCOPIST
BRUSSELS
  SPROUT
BUILDING
  BLOCKS
BULLETIN
  BOARDS

BULLHEADEDNESS
BUREAU DE
  CHANGE
BURNT
  OFFERINGS
BUSMAN'S
  HOLIDAY

C
CADAVEROUSNESS
CALAMINE
  LOTION
CALENDAR
  MONTHS
CALLIGRAPHISTS
CAMPANOLOGISTS
CAMPANULACEOUS
CANTANKEROUSLY
CAPITALIZATION
CAPITAL
  LETTERS
CAPPARIDACEOUS
CAPRICIOUSNESS
CARBON
  MONOXIDE
CARCINOMATOSIS
CARDINAL
  POINTS
CARDIOVASCULAR
CARPET
  SWEEPERS
CARRIER
  PIGEONS
CARRYING
  CHARGE
CARTOGRAPHICAL
CARTRIDGE
  PAPER
CASEMENT
  WINDOW
CASH AND
  CARRIES
CASH
  DISPENSERS
CATCHMENT
  AREAS
CATECHETICALLY
CATEGORIZATION
CATHEDRAL
  CLOSE
CATHERINE
  WHEEL

CATHODE RAY
  TUBE
CAUGHT
  UNAWARES
CAUSES
  CELEBRES
CENSORIOUSNESS
CENTRAL
  HEATING
CENTRALIZATION
CENTRE
  FORWARDS
CENTRIFUGATION
CERCOPITHECOID
CHAIN
  REACTIONS
CHAISES
  LONGUES
CHANGEABLENESS
CHANTRY
  CHAPELS
CHARACTER
  ACTOR
CHARACTERISTIC
CHARACTERIZING
CHARGE
  ACCOUNTS
CHARITABLENESS
CHARLATANISTIC
CHARTER
  MEMBERS
CHECHENO-
  INGUSH
CHEMOSYNTHESIS
CHEMOSYNTHETIC
CHEMOTHERAPIST
CHEST OF
  DRAWERS
CHICKENHEARTED
CHIEF
  CONSTABLE
CHIEF
  EXECUTIVE
CHIEF
  INSPECTOR
CHIEFTAINSHIPS
CHILD
  PRODIGIES
CHIMNEYBREASTS
CHIMNEY
  CORNERS
CHINCHERINCHEE

CHINESE
LANTERN
CHINLESS
WONDER
CHLOROPHYLLOID
CHLOROPHYLLOUS
CHLOROTHIAZIDE
CHLORPROMAZINE
CHLORPROPAMIDE
CHOLINESTERASE
CHOREOGRAPHERS
CHOREOGRAPHING
CHRISTIAN
NAMES
CHRISTMAS
BOXES
CHRISTMAS
CAKES
CHRISTMAS
CARDS
CHRISTMAS
TREES
CHRISTOLOGICAL
CHROMATOGRAPHY
CHROMATOPHORIC
CHRYSANTHEMUMS
CIGARETTE
PAPER
CINCHONIZATION
CINEMATOGRAPHY
CIRCUIT
BREAKER
CIRCULAR
LETTER
CIRCUMAMBIENCE
CIRCUMAMBULATE
CIRCUMFERENCES
CIRCUMLOCUTION
CIRCUMLOCUTORY
CIRCUMNAVIGATE
CIRCUMNUTATION
CIRCUMSCISSILE
CIRCUMSCRIBING
CIRCUMSPECTION
CIRCUMSTANTIAL
CIRCUMVOLUTION
CIRCUMVOLUTORY
CIVIL
ENGINEERS
CLARIFICATIONS
CLASS-
CONSCIOUS

CLASSIFICATION
CLASSIFICATORY
CLAUSTROPHOBIA
CLAUSTROPHOBIC
CLEARANCE
SALES
CLEARINGHOUSES
CLEAR-
SIGHTEDLY
CLIMBING
FRAMES
CLOAK-AND-
DAGGER
CLOTHES
HANGERS
CLUB
SANDWICHES
CLUSTER
BOMBING
COCK-A-DOODLE-
DOO
COCKER
SPANIELS
COCKTAIL
LOUNGE
COCKTAIL
STICKS
COESSENTIALITY
COFFEE
KLATCHES
COINCIDENTALLY
COLD
SHOULDERED
COLLAPSIBILITY
COLLECTIVE
FARM
COLLECTIVE
NOUN
COLLECTOR'S
ITEM
COLLOQUIALISMS
COLORADO
BEETLE
COLOURFASTNESS
COLOURLESSNESS
COMBINING
FORMS
COMBUSTIBILITY
COMFORTABLY
OFF
COMFORT
STATION

COMMAND
MODULES
COMMENSURATION
COMMERCIALIZED
COMMISERATIONS
COMMISSIONAIRE
COMMITTEE
STAGE
COMMON
FRACTION
COMMON-OR-
GARDEN
COMMUNICATIONS
COMMUNITY
CHEST
COMMUNITY
HOMES
COMPLEMENTIZER
COMPREHENSIBLE
COMPREHENSIBLY
COMPREHENSIONS
COMPREHENSIVES
COMPULSIVENESS
CONCATENATIONS
CONCAVO-
CONCAVE
CONCELEBRATION
CONCENTRATIONS
CONCEPTUALIZED
CONCESSIONAIRE
CONCRETE
JUNGLE
CONCRETE
MIXERS
CONCRETE
POETRY
CONCRETIZATION
CONDEMNED
CELLS
CONDENSABILITY
CONDITIONALITY
CONDUCTOR
RAILS
CONDUPLICATION
CONFABULATIONS
CONFEDERATIONS
CONFIDENTIALLY
CONFIGURATIONS
CONFLAGRATIONS
CONFORMABILITY
CONFRONTATIONS
CONGLOMERATION

CONGLUTINATIVE
CONGRATULATING
CONGRATULATION
CONGRATULATORY
CONGREGATIONAL
CONJUNCTIVITIS
CONNECTING
RODS
CONQUISTADORES
CONRAIL,
CONRAIL
CONSANGUINEOUS
CONSCRIPTIONAL
CONSERVATIONAL
CONSERVATIVELY
CONSERVATOIRES
CONSERVATORIES
CONSIDERATIONS
CONSOLIDATIONS
CONSPIRATORIAL
CONSTABULARIES
CONSTANTINOPLE
CONSTELLATIONS
CONSTITUENCIES
CONSTITUTIONAL
CONSTRUCTIONAL
CONSTRUCTIVELY
CONSTRUCTIVISM
CONSTRUCTIVIST
CONSUETUDINARY
CONTAGIOUSNESS
CONTAINERIZING
CONTEMPORARIES
CONTEMPORARILY
CONTEMPTUOUSLY
CONTINENTALISM
CONTINENTALIST
CONTINENTALITY
CONTORTIONISTS
CONTRACEPTIVES
CONTRACT
BRIDGE
CONTRADICTIONS
CONTRAINDICANT
CONTRAINDICATE
CONTRAPOSITION
CONTRAPUNTALLY
CONTRAVENTIONS
CONTRIBUTORIAL
CONTROVERTIBLE
CONTUMACIOUSLY

CONTUMELIOUSLY
CONVENTIONALLY
CONVERSATIONAL
CONVERSAZIOOONI
CONVERTIBILITY
CONVEXO-
CONCAVE
COPPER-
BOTTOMED
CORELIGIONISTS
CORNISH
PASTIES
CORPORATION
TAX
CORRESPONDENCE
CORRESPONDENTS
CORRUPTIBILITY
CORTICOSTEROID
CORTICOSTERONE
CORTICOTROPHIN
COUNTERACTIONS
COUNTERATTACKS
COUNTERBALANCE
COUNTERFEITERS
COUNTERFEITING
COUNTERMANDING
COUNTERMEASURE
COUNTERMENSURE
COUNTERPOISING
COUNTERSHADING
COUNTERSIGNING
COUNTERSINKING
COUNTERVAILING
COUNTINGHOUSES
COUNTRY
COUSINS
COUNTY
COUNCILS
COURAGEOUSNESS
COURT-
MARTIALED
COURT OF
INQUIRY
COVERING
LETTER
CRADLE
SNATCHER
CRAMP ONES
STYLE
CREDIBILITY
GAP
CREDITABLENESS

CREDIT
ACCOUNTS
CREDIT
SQUEEZES
CREEPY-
CRAWLIES
CRIMINAL
RECORD
CRIMINOLOGICAL
CRIMINOLOGISTS
CROCODILE
TEARS
CROSS-
COUNTRIES
CROSS-
EXAMINERS
CROSS-
EXAMINING
CROSS-
FERTILIZE
CROSS-
POLLINATE
CROSS
REFERENCE
CROSS-
REFERENCE
CROSS-
REFERRING
CROSS-
SECTIONAL
CROWN AND
ANCHOR
CRUISE
MISSILES
CRYPTAESTHESIA
CRYPTOGRAPHERS
CSECHOSLOVAKIA
CUCURBITACEOUS
CURRENT
ACCOUNT
CURRICULA
VITAE
CURRUGATED
IRON
CURTAIN
RAISERS
CURVILINEARITY
CYANOCOBALAMIN
CYBERNETICALLY
CYTOTAXONOMIST

D

DAGUERREOTYPER

DAGUERREOTYPES
DANISH
PASTRIES
DATA
PROCESSING
DAUGHTERLINESS
DAUGHTERS-IN-
LAW
DAY OF
RECKONING
DEAD MANS
HANDLE
DEAD TO THE
WORLD
DECEIVABLENESS
DECENTRALIZING
DECIMALIZATION
DECLASSIFIABLE
DECLENSIONALLY
DECLINE AND
FALL
DECOLONIZATION
DECOLORIZATION
DECONTAMINATED
DECONTAMINATOR
DEFENESTRATION
DEFLOCCULATION
DEGENERATENESS
DEHUMANIZATION
DELECTABLENESS
DELIBERATENESS
DELIGHTFULNESS
DELOCALIZATION
DEMILITARIZING
DEMISEMIQUAVER
DEMOBILIZATION
DEMOCRATICALLY
DEMONETIZATION
DEMONSTRATIONS
DEMORALIZATION
DENATIONALIZED
DENOMINATIONAL
DENTAL
SURGEONS
DEPLORABLENESS
DEPOLARIZATION
DEPOSIT
ACCOUNT
DERMATOLOGICAL
DERMATOLOGISTS
DERMATOPLASTIC
DEROGATORINESS

DESTRUCTIONIST
DETERMINEDNESS
DEVIL'S
ADVOCATE
DEVITALIZATION
DEXTROROTATION
DEXTROROTATORY
DIABOLICALNESS
DIAGNOSTICALLY
DIALECTOLOGIST
DIAMOND
JUBILEE
DIAMOND
WEDDING
DIAPHANOUSNESS
DIAPHOTOTROPIC
DICHROMATICISM
DICOTYLEDONOUS
DIELECTRICALLY
DIESEL-
ELECTRIC
DIEU ET MON
DROIT
DIFFERENTIABLE
DIFFERENTIATED
DIFFERENTIATOR
DIFFRACTOMETER
DIGITALIZATION
DIG ONES HEELS
IN
DIMENHYDRINATE
DIMENSIONALITY
DINITROBENZENE
DINNER
SERVICES
DINOFLAGELLATE
DIPLOMATICALLY
DIPLOSTEMONOUS
DIRECTIONALITY
DIRECT
TAXATION
DISAFFILIATING
DISAFFILIATION
DISAFFORESTING
DISAPPEARANCES
DISAPPOINTEDLY
DISAPPOINTMENT
DISAPPROBATION
DISAPPROVINGLY
DISARRANGEMENT
DISARTICULATOR
DISASSOCIATING

DISASSOCIATION
DISBELIEVINGLY
DISCIPLINARIAN
DISCOLORATIONS
DISCOMPOSINGLY
DISCONNECTEDLY
DISCONNECTIONS
DISCONSOLATELY
DISCONSOLATION
DISCONTENTEDLY
DISCONTENTMENT
DISCONTINUANCE
DISCOUNTENANCE
DISCOUNT
  STORES
DISCOURAGEMENT
DISCOURAGINGLY
DISCOURTEOUSLY
DISCRIMINATING
DISCRIMINATION
DISCRIMINATORY
DISCURSIVENESS
DISEMBARKATION
DISEMBOGUEMENT
DISEMBOWELLING
DISEMBOWELMENT
DISENCHANTMENT
DISENFRANCHISE
DISENTHRALMENT
DISEQUILIBRIUM
DISESTABLISHED
DISFEATUREMENT
DISFIGUREMENTS
DISFORESTATION
DISFRANCHISING
DISGRUNTLEMENT
DISHEARTENMENT
DISILLUSIONING
DISINCLINATION
DISINFESTATION
DISINGENUOUSLY
DISINHERITANCE
DISINTEGRATING
DISINTEGRATION
DISINTEGRATIVE
DISJOINTEDNESS
DISORDERLINESS
DISORIENTATING
DISORIENTATION
DISPARAGEMENTS
DISPENSABILITY

DISPENSATIONAL
DISPUTATIOUSLY
DISQUALIFIABLE
DISQUIETEDNESS
DISRESPECTABLE
DISSERTATIONAL
DISSERVICEABLE
DISSIMULATIONS
DISSOCIABILITY
DISSOLVABILITY
DISSUASIVENESS
DISTENSIBILITY
DISTINGUISHING
DISTRIBUTIONAL
DISTRIBUTIVELY
DIURETICALNESS
DIVERTICULITIS
DIVERTICULOSIS
DIVERTISSEMENT
DNEPROPETROVSK
DOG IN THE
  MANGER
DO-IT-
  YOURSELFER
DOMESTIC
  ANIMAL
DOUBLE
  BREASTED
DOUBLE-
  BREASTED
DOUBLE-
  CHECKING
DOUBLE-
  CROSSERS
DOUBLE-
  CROSSING
DOUBLE
  ENTENDRE
DOUBLE
  FEATURES
DOUBTING
  THOMAS
DOWN IN THE
  DUMPS
DRAINING
  BOARDS
DRAMATIZATIONS
DRESSING
  TABLES
DRESS
  REHEARSAL
DRIVING
  LICENCE

DROP IN THE
  OCEAN
DRUM
  MAJORETTES
DUCKS AND
  DRAKES
DUCTLESS
  GLANDS
DWELLING
  HOUSES
DYER'S-
  GREENWEED
DYNAMOELECTRIC
DYSMENORRHOEAL

E

ECCENTRICITIES
ECCLESIASTICAL
ECCLESIOLOGIST
ECONOMETRICIAN
EDITIO
  PRINCEPS
EDUCATIONALIST
EFFERVESCENTLY
EFFERVESCINGLY
EFFORTLESSNESS
EGALITARIANISM
EGOCENTRICALLY
ELDER
  STATESMAN
ELDER
  STATESMEN
ELECTIONEERING
ELECTRA
  COMPLEX
ELECTROCHEMIST
ELECTROCUTIONS
ELECTRODEPOSIT
ELECTRODYNAMIC
ELECTROGRAPHIC
ELECTROKINETIC
ELECTRONICALLY
ELECTRONIC
  MAIL
ELECTROSTATICS
ELECTROSURGERY
ELECTROTHERMAL
ELECTROVALENCY
ELEMENTARINESS
ELLIPTICALNESS
EMBARRASSINGLY
EMBARRASSMENTS

EMBELLISHMENTS
EMBLEMATICALLY
EMOTIONALISTIC
EMPHATICALNESS
EMULSIFICATION
EMULSION
  PAINTS
ENANTIOMORPHIC
ENCAPSULATIONS
ENCEPHALOGRAPH
ENCOURAGEMENTS
ENDOCRINE
  GLAND
ENDOCRINOLOGIC
ENDOPHYTICALLY
ENDOSMOTICALLY
ENFANT
  TERRIBLE
ENFORCEABILITY
ENGAGEMENT
  RING
ENHARMONICALLY
ENLIGHTENINGLY
ENROLLED
  NURSES
ENTEROGASTRONE
ENTERPRISINGLY
ENTERTAININGLY
ENTERTAINMENTS
ENTOMOSTRACOUS
EPEXEGETICALLY
EPICONTINENTAL
EPIDEMIOLOGIST
EPIGENETICALLY
EPIGRAPHICALLY
EPISTEMOLOGIST
EQUIPONDERANCE
EQUIVOCATINGLY
ERYTHROBLASTIC
ERYTHROPOIESIS
ERYTHROPOIETIC
ESCAPE
  VELOCITY
ESCHATOLOGICAL
ESTABLISHMENTS
ESTATE
  AGENCIES
ESTERIFICATION
ETERNALIZATION
ETHERIFICATION
ETHNOCENTRISMS
ETHNOLOGICALLY

ETYMOLOGICALLY
EULOGISTICALLY
EUPHONICALNESS
EUPHORBIACEOUS
EUPHUISTICALLY
EUSTACHIAN
  TUBE
EUTROPHICATION
EVANGELICALISM
EVANGELIZATION
EVAPORATED
  MILK
EVEN-
  HANDEDNESS
EVENING
  DRESSES
EVIL-
  MINDEDNESS
EVOLUTIONISTIC
EXACERBATINGLY
EXAGGERATINGLY
EXASPERATINGLY
EXCEPTIONALITY
EXCLAUSTRATION
EXCOMMUNICABLE
EXCOMMUNICATED
EXCOMMUNICATOR
EXCRUCIATINGLY
EXHAUSTIBILITY
EXHAUSTIVENESS
EXHIBITIONISTS
EXHILARATINGLY
EXISTENTIALISM
EXISTENTIALIST
EXOTHERMICALLY
EXPANSIONISTIC
EXPENSE
  ACCOUNT
EXPERIMENTALLY
EXPOSTULATIONS
EXPRESSIONISTS
EXPRESSIONLESS
EXPRESSIVENESS
EXPROPRIATIONS
EXTEMPORANEOUS
EXTENDED
  FAMILY
EXTENSIONALITY
EXTINGUISHABLE
EXTINGUISHMENT
EXTORTIONATELY
EXTRACANONICAL

EXTRACTABILITY
EXTRANEOUSNESS
EXTRAVEHICULAR
EYEBROW
  PENCILS

F

FACTITIOUSNESS
FACTORY
  FARMING
FAINT-
  HEARTEDLY
FAIR-
  MINDEDNESS
FAIRY
  GODMOTHER
FAITS
  ACCOMPLIS
FALLACIOUSNESS
FALLOPIAN
  TUBES
FALSE
  PRETENCES
FALSIFICATIONS
FAMILY
  PLANNING
FARSIGHTEDNESS
FASTIDIOUSNESS
FATALISTICALLY
FATHERS AND
  SONS
FAVOURABLENESS
FEATHERBEDDING
FEATHERBRAINED
FEATHERWEIGHTS
FEDERALIZATION
FEEDING
  BOTTLES
FEEL THE
  DRAUGHT
FELICITOUSNESS
FEMININE
  ENDING
FEMME DE
  CHAMBRE
FERMENTABILITY
FERRIMAGNETISM
FERROMAGNESIAN
FERROMAGNETISM
FERROMANGANESE
FICTIONALIZING
FICTITIOUSNESS
FIDEICOMMISSUM

FIELDS OF
  VISION
FIELD
  TELEGRAPH
FIFTH
  COLUMNIST
FIGHTING
  CHANCE
FIGURATIVENESS
FIGURE OF
  SPEECH
FIGURES OF
  EIGHT
FILING
  CABINETS
FILLING
  STATION
FINANCIAL
  YEARS
FINE-TOOTH
  COMBS
FINGER
  PAINTING
FINGERPRINTING
FINSTERAARHORN
FIRST
  OFFENDERS
FISSIONABILITY
FLABBERGASTING
FLIGHT-
  RECORDER
FLIGHT
  SERGEANT
FLOATING
  VOTERS
FLOG A DEAD
  HORSE
FLORICULTURIST
FLOWER-OF-AN-
  HOUR
FLYING
  BUTTRESS
FLYING
  DUTCHMAN
FLYING
  OFFICERS
FOLLOW MY
  LEADER
FOLLOW-MY-
  LEADER
FOLLOW-
  THROUGHS
FOOD
  PROCESSORS

FORBIDDEN
  FRUIT
FORBIDDINGNESS
FOREIGN
  AFFAIRS
FOREORDAINMENT
FORESHORTENING
FORETHOUGHTFUL
FORE-
  TOPGALLANT
FORKLIFT
  TRUCKS
FORTHRIGHTNESS
FORTIFICATIONS
FORTUITOUSNESS
FORTUNE
  HUNTERS
FORTUNE-
  TELLERS
FORWARD-
  LOOKING
FOUNDING
  FATHER
FOUR-LETTER
  WORD
FRATERNIZATION
FREE
  ENTERPRISE
FREEZING
  POINTS
FRENCH
  DRESSING
FRENCH
  POLISHED
FRIDGE-
  FREEZERS
FRIENDLESSNESS
FRINGE
  BENEFITS
FROZEN
  SHOULDER
FRUCTIFICATION
FULLY-
  FASHIONED
FUNCTIONALISTS
FUNDAMENTALISM
FUNDAMENTALIST
FUNDAMENTALITY
FUNERAL
  PARLOUR
FURFURALDEHYDE
FUTURISTICALLY

G

GALACTOPOIESIS
GALACTOPOIETIC
GALVANOTROPISM
GASTROVASCULAR
GAVE UP THE
  GHOST
GEIGER
  COUNTERS
GELATINIZATION
GENEALOGICALLY
GENERALISSIMOS
GENERALIZATION
GENERAL
  STRIKES
GENTRIFICATION
GEOCENTRICALLY
GEOGRAPHICALLY
GERMAN
  SHEPHERD
GERONTOLOGICAL
GERRYMANDERING
GESTICULATIONS
GET ONES OWN
  BACK
GHETTO
  BLASTERS
GLANDULAR
  FEVER
GLOBE
  ARTICHOKE
GLOBETROTTINGS
GLORIFICATIONS
GLORY-OF-THE-
  SNOW
GLOSSY
  MAGAZINE
GLUCOCORTICORD
GOLDEN
  JUBILEES
GOLDEN
  WEDDINGS
GOLD-OF-
  PLEASURE
GOOD-FOR-
  NOTHING
GOOD-
  HUMOUREDLY
GOOD
  SAMARITANS
GRACE-AND-
  FAVOUR

GRADE
  CROSSINGS
GRAMMAR
  SCHOOLS
GRAMMATICALITY
GRAMMATOLOGIST
GRANDDAUGHTERS
GRANDILOQUENCE
GRANGERIZATION
GRAPHITIZATION
GRAPPLING
  IRONS
GRASP THE
  NETTLE
GRATIFICATIONS
GRATUITOUSNESS
GREGARIOUSNESS
GREGORIAN
  CHANT
GROUNDLESSNESS
GROUP
  PRACTICES
GUARDIAN
  ANGELS
GUIDED
  MISSILES
GUY FAWKES
  NIGHT
GYNAECOLOGICAL
GYNAECOLOGISTS
GYROSTABILIZER

H

HABERDASHERIES
HAEMACYTOMETER
HAEMAGGLUTININ
HAEMATOBLASTIC
HAEMATOGENESIS
HAEMATOPOIESIS
HAEMATOPOIETIC
HAEMATOTHERMAL
HAEMOCYTOMETER
HALFPENNYWORTH
HALFWITTEDNESS
HALICARNASSIAN
HALLUCINATIONS
HALLUCINOGENIC
HANDICRAFTSMAN
HANDSOME
  SALARY
HANGING
  GARDENS

HAPAX
  LEGOMENON
HARD
  CURRENCIES
HARD-
  HEADEDNESS
HARMONIOUSNESS
HARPSICHORDIST
HEAD LIKE A
  SIEVE
HEADMASTERSHIP
HEADSTRONGNESS
HEARTRENDINGLY
HEARTWARMINGLY
HEATHENISHNESS
HEBRAISTICALLY
HEGIRA
  CALENDAR
HELL FOR
  LEATHER
HELTER-
  SKELTERS
HEMEL
  HEMPSTEAD
HEMISPHEROIDAL
HENRIETTA
  MARIA
HEREDITABILITY
HEREDITARINESS
HERMAPHRODITES
HERMAPHRODITIC
HERMAPHRODITUS
HEROIC
  COUPLETS
HERO
  WORSHIPPED
HERPES
  LABIALIS
HETEROCHROMOUS
HETEROGONOUSLY
HETEROLECITHAL
HETEROMORPHISM
HETERONOMOUSLY
HETERONYMOUSLY
HETEROPHYLLOUS
HETEROPOLARITY
HETEROSEXUALLY
HIERARCHICALLY
HIGH
  COMMISSION
HIGH COURT
  JUDGE

HIGH
  EXPLOSIVES
HIGH-
  HANDEDNESS
HIGHLAND
  FLINGS
HIGH-
  MINDEDNESS
HIGH-
  PRESSURING
HIGH-
  PRINCIPLED
HIGH SPEED
  TRAIN
HIGH
  TECHNOLOGY
HIGH WATER
  MARKS
HIPPOPOTAMUSES
HISTOCHEMISTRY
HISTOLOGICALLY
HISTOLYTICALLY
HISTOPATHOLOGY
HISTOPLASMOSIS
HISTORICALNESS
HISTORIOGRAPHY
HISTRIONICALLY
HOEK VAN
  HOLLAND
HOLDING
  COMPANY
HOLD NO BRIEF
  FOR
HOLIER-THAN-
  THOU
HOMOCHROMATISM
HOMOGENIZATION
HOMOIOUSIANISM
HOMOPHONICALLY
HONEYDEW
  MELONS
HONOURABLENESS
HORATIUS
  COCLES
HORIZONTALNESS
HORRENDOUSNESS
HORROR-
  STRICKEN
HORSE
  CHESTNUTS
HORSE
  LATITUDES
HORTICULTURIST

HOSPITABLENESS
HOT WATER
  BOTTLE
HOT-WATER
  BOTTLE
HOUSEHOLD
  NAMES
HOUSEMAID'S
  KNEE
HOUSE OF
  COMMONS
HOUSING
  PROJECT
HUMIDIFICATION
HUMOURLESSNESS
HUNGER
  MARCHERS
HUNGER
  STRIKERS
HUNTING
  GROUNDS
HURRICANE
  LAMPS
HYDROCELLULOSE
HYDROCORTISONE
HYDROGENOLYSIS
HYDROLOGICALLY
HYDROMAGNETICS
HYDROMECHANICS
HYPERBOLICALLY
HYPERSENSITIVE
HYPOCHONDRIACS
HYPOCRITICALLY
HYPODERMICALLY
HYPOTHETICALLY
HYSTERECTOMIES

I

ICEBERG
  LETTUCE
ICHNEUMON
  FLIES
ICHTHYOPHAGOUS
IDEALISTICALLY
IDENTICAL
  TWINS
IDENTIFICATION
IDEOLOOGICALLY
IDIOSYNCRASIES
ILLEGALIZATION
ILLEGITIMATELY
ILLIMITABILITY

ILLUSTRATIONAL
ILLUSTRATIVELY
IMMETHODICALLY
IMMOBILIZATION
IMMUNOGENETICS
IMMUNOGLOBULIN
IMMUNOREACTION
IMPARISYLLABIC
IMPEACHABILITY
IMPERCEPTIVITY
IMPERMEABILITY
IMPERSONATIONS
IMPERTURBATION
IMPLAUSIBILITY
IMPLEMENTATION
IMPOLITENESSES
IMPRACTICALITY
IMPREGNABILITY
IMPRESSIONABLE
IMPRESSIONABLY
IMPRESSIONALLY
IMPRESSIONISTS
IMPRESSIVENESS
IMPROVISATIONS
INADVISABILITY
INALIENABILITY
INALTERABILITY
INAPPRECIATIVE
INAPPREHENSIVE
INAPPROACHABLE
INARTICULATELY
INARTISTICALLY
INAUSPICIOUSLY
INCANDESCENTLY
INCAPACITATING
INCAPACITATION
INCAUTIOUSNESS
INCESTUOUSNESS
INCOMMENSURATE
INCOMMODIOUSLY
INCOMMUNICABLE
INCOMPLETENESS
INCOMPRESSIBLE
INCONCLUSIVELY
INCONSIDERABLE
INCONSISTENTLY
INCONVENIENCED
INCONVENIENCES
INCONVENIENTLY
INCOORDINATION
INDECIPHERABLE

INDECIPHERABLY
INDECOROUSNESS
INDEFINITENESS
INDESTRUCTIBLE
INDESTRUCTIBLY
INDETERMINABLE
INDETERMINABLY
INDIAN
  ELEPHANT
INDIFFERENTISM
INDIFFERENTIST
INDIGENOUSNESS
INDIRECT
  OBJECT
INDIRECT
  SPEECH
INDISCRIMINATE
INDISPOSITIONS
INDISTINCTNESS
INDIVIDUALISTS
INDIVIDUALIZED
INDIVIDUALIZER
INDIVISIBILITY
INDOCTRINATING
INDOCTRINATION
INDOMITABILITY
INDUBITABILITY
INDUSTRIALISTS
INDUSTRIALIZED
INEFFECTUALITY
INELUCTABILITY
INERTIA
  SELLING
INESSENTIALITY
INESTIMABILITY
INEXCUSABILITY
INFECTIOUSNESS
INFLAMMABILITY
INFLAMMATORILY
INFRALAPSARIAN
INFRANGIBILITY
INFRASTRUCTURE
INGRATIATINGLY
INHABITABILITY
INHARMONIOUSLY
INHERITABILITY
INITIALIZATION
IN LOCO
  PARENTIS
INNUMERABILITY
INQUISITIONIST
INSANITARINESS

INSCRUTABILITY
INSEPARABILITY
INSIDER
  DEALING
INSIGNIFICANCE
INSTITUTIONARY
INSTRUCTORSHIP
INSUFFICIENTLY
INSUPERABILITY
INSUPPRESSIBLE
INSURMOUNTABLE
INSURRECTIONAL
INTEGRATIONIST
INTELLECTUALLY
INTELLIGENTSIA
INTENTIONALITY
INTERCESSIONAL
INTERCOMMUNION
INTERDEPENDENT
INTEREST
  GROUPS
INTERFERENTIAL
INTERFEROMETER
INTERFEROMETRY
INTERFERTILITY
INTERGRADATION
INTERJECTIONAL
INTERLOCUTRESS
INTERMEDIARIES
INTERMIGRATION
INTERMITTENTLY
INTERMITTINGLY
INTERMOLECULAR
INTERNAL
  MARKET
INTERNATIONALE
INTERNATIONALS
INTERPELLATION
INTERPENETRANT
INTERPENETRATE
INTERPLANETARY
INTERPOLATIONS
INTERPOSITIONS
INTERPRETATION
INTERPRETATIVE
INTERRELATIONS
INTERROGATIONS
INTERROGATIVES
INTERSECTIONAL
INTERSEXUALITY
INTERSPERSEDLY

INTERTWININGLY
INTERVENTIONAL
INTOLERABILITY
INTO THE
  BARGAIN
INTOXICATINGLY
INTRACTABILITY
INTRACUTANEOUS
INTRAMOLECULAR
INTRANSIGENTLY
INTRANSITIVELY
INTRODUCTORILY
INVERTED
  COMMAS
INVESTIGATIONS
INVIGORATINGLY
IODOMETRICALLY
IRRECONCILABLE
IRRECONCILABLY
IRREDUCIBILITY
IRREFUTABILITY
IRREGULARITIES
IRREMOVABILITY
IRREPARABILITY
IRREPROACHABLE
IRREPROACHABLY
IRRESOLUBILITY
IRREVOCABILITY
ISOPIESTICALLY

J

JACK-IN-THE-
  BOXES
JOB'S
  COMFORTERS
JOLLIFICATIONS
JOURNALIZATION
JURISDICTIONAL
JUSTICIABILITY
JUSTIFIABILITY

K

KAISERSLAUTERN
KAMENSK-
  URALSKI
KANGAROO
  COURTS
KEEP ONES CHIN
  UP
KEEP ONES HAND
  IN
KERATINIZATION

KEYHOLE
  SURGURY
KIDNEY
  MACHINES
KINDERGARTENER
KITCHEN
  GARDENS
KNICKERBOCKERS
KNIGHT-
  ERRANTRY
KNOCK ON THE
  HEAD
KNUCKLE-
  DUSTERS
KOSOVO-
  METOHIJA

L

LABOUR
  EXCHANGE
LAMELLIROSTRAL
LANCE
  CORPORALS
LAND ON ONES
  FEET
LARGE
  INTESTINE
LARGER THAN
  LIFE
LARYNGOLOGICAL
LARYNGOSCOPIST
LASCIVIOUSNESS
LATITUDINARIAN
LAUGHINGSTOCKS
LAUNDRY
  BASKETS
LAW OF THE
  JUNGLE
LEADING
  ARTICLE
LEADING
  STRINGS
LEAVE OF
  ABSENCE
LEFT-
  HANDEDNESS
LEFT IN THE
  LURCH
LEGALISTICALLY
LEGERDEMAINIST
LEGION OF
  HONOUR
LEGITIMIZATION

LENDING
  LIBRARY
LETS CALL IT A
  DAY
LETTER OF
  CREDIT
LEVEL
  CROSSINGS
LEXICOGRAPHERS
LIBERALIZATION
LIBERAL
  STUDIES
LIBERTARIANISM
LIBIDINOUSNESS
LICENTIATESHIP
LICENTIOUSNESS
LIFE
  EXPECTANCY
LIFE
  PRESERVERS
LIGHT
  AIRCRAFTS
LIGNOCELLULOSE
LIKE-
  MINDEDNESS
LINE ONES
  POCKET
LINGUISTICALLY
LISTEN TO
  REASON
LITHOLOGICALLY
LITTLE BY
  LITTLE
LITTLE GREEN
  MEN
LOCAL
  AUTHORITY
LOCUS
  CLASSICUS
LONGITUDINALLY
LONG-
  SUFFERANCE
LONGWINDEDNESS
LOOKING
  GLASSES
LOVING
  KINDNESS
LOXODROMICALLY
LUGUBRIOUSNESS

M

MACADAMIZATION
MACHINEGUNNING

MACROECONOMICS
MACROEVOLUTION
MACROMOLECULAR
MAGNETIC
  FIELDS
MAGNIFICATIONS
MAHALLA EL
  KUBRA
MAKE
  ALLOWANCES
MAKE THE
  RUNNING
MAKE UP ONES
  MIND
MALACOPHYLLOUS
MALACOSTRACOUS
MALE
  CHAUVINIST
MALFUNCTIONING
MALPIGHIACEOUS
MALTESE
  CROSSES
MANIFESTATIONS
MAN IN THE
  STREET
MANIPULABILITY
MANNERLESSNESS
MANOMETRICALLY
MANUFACTURABLE
MARCHING
  ORDERS
MARKET
  GARDENER
MARKET
  RESEARCH
MARTYROLOGICAL
MASON-DIXON
  LINE
MASSAGE
  PARLOUR
MASSOTHERAPIST
MASS
  PRODUCTION
MATERNITY
  LEAVE
MATHEMATICALLY
MATHEMATICIANS
MATTER OF
  COURSE
MATTER-OF-
  FACTLY
MATURE
  STUDENTS

MAUNDY
THURSDAY
MEANINGFULNESS
MECHANOTHERAPY
MEDDLESOMENESS
MEDITATIVENESS
MEGALOCEPHALIC
MEGALOMANIACAL
MEGAPHONICALLY
MEGASPOROPHYLL
MELANCHOLINESS
MENDACIOUSNESS
MENTAL
HOSPITAL
MEPHISTOPHELES
MERCAPTOPURINE
MERCHANT
NAVIES
MERETRICIOUSLY
MESDEMOISELLES
METACHROMATISM
METALLOGRAPHER
METALLOGRAPHIC
METAMORPHOSING
METAPHORICALLY
METAPHYSICALLY
METAPSYCHOLOGY
METASTATICALLY
METEMPSYCHOSIS
METEOROGRAPHIC
METEOROLOGICAL
METEOROLOGISTS
METHAEMOGLOBIN
METHODICALNESS
METHODOLOGICAL
METICULOUSNESS
MICROBAROGRAPH
MICROBIOLOGIST
MICROCEPHALOUS
MICROCHEMISTRY
MICROCIRCUITRY
MICROCOMPUTERS
MICROECONOMICS
MICROMETEORITE
MICROORGANISMS
MICROPARASITIC
MICROPROCESSOR
MICROPYROMETER
MICROSTOMATOUS
MICROSTRUCTURE
MIDDLE-
DISTANCE

MIGHT-HAVE-
BEENS
MILITARIZATION
MILITARY
POLICE
MILLENARIANISM
MINERALIZATION
MISAPPLICATION
MISAPPREHENDED
MISAPPROPRIATE
MISCALCULATING
MISCALCULATION
MISCONCEPTIONS
MISINFORMATION
MISINTERPRETED
MISINTERPRETER
MISREPRESENTED
MISREPRESENTER
MIXED
ECONOMIES
MIXED
METAPHORS
MOCK-
HEROICALLY
MOCK TURTLE
SOUP
MODERNIZATIONS
MOMENTS OF
TRUTH
MONGRELIZATION
MONKEY
BUSINESS
MONKEY
WRENCHES
MONOCARPELLARY
MONOCHROMATISM
MONOLITHICALLY
MONOPOLIZATION
MONOPROPELLANT
MONOSACCHARIDE
MOONLIGHT
FLITS
MORALISTICALLY
MORGANATICALLY
MORNING
GLORIES
MORPHOPHONEMIC
MOTHER
SUPERIOR
MOTIONLESSNESS
MOTION
PICTURES

MOTIVELESSNESS
MOUNTAINEERING
MOVING
PAVEMENT
MOVING
PICTURES
MUCOMEMBRANOUS
MUCOUS
MEMBRANE
MULTIFACTORIAL
MULTIFARIOUSLY
MULTILATERALLY
MULTINATIONALS
MULTIPLE
STORES
MULTIPLICATION
MULTIPLICATIVE
MUNICIPALITIES
MUSTARD
PLASTER
MYELENCEPHALIC
MYELENCEPHALON
MYOCARDIOGRAPH
MYOGRAPHICALLY
MYRMECOLOGICAL
MYRMECOPHAGOUS
MYRMECOPHILOUS
MYSTAGOGICALLY
MYSTERIOUSNESS

N

NANSEN
PASSPORT
NARCOSYNTHESIS
NARRATIVE
VERSE
NASOPHARYNGEAL
NASTY BIT OF
WORK
NATIONAL
ANTHEM
NATIVE
AMERICAN
NATURAL
HISTORY
NATURALIZATION
NATURAL
SCIENCE
NEANDERTHAL
MAN
NEBUCHADNEZZAR
NEGLECTFULNESS

NEIGHBOURHOODS
NEOCOLONIALISM
NEOCOLONIALIST
NERVOUS
SYSTEMS
NEUROPATHOLOGY
NEUTRALIZATION
NEWFOUNDLANDER
NEWS
CONFERENCE
NEWSWORTHINESS
NIGHT
BLINDNESS
NIGHT
WATCHMANS
NIL
DESPERANDUM
NINE DAYS'
WONDER
NITROCELLULOSE
NITROGLYCERINE
NOBLESSE
OBLIGE
NO-CLAIM
BONUSES
NOLO
CONTENDERE
NONATTRIBUTIVE
NONCOMMITTALLY
NONCONFORMISTS
NONCOOPERATION
NONCOOPERATIVE
NONDISJUNCTION
NONEQUIVALENCE
NONINFLAMMABLE
NONPROGRESSIVE
NON
PROSEQUITUR
NONRESIDENTIAL
NONRESTRICTIVE
NONSTIMULATING
NORFOLK
JACKETS
NORTHERN
LIGHTS
NORTH-
NORTHEAST
NORTH-
NORTHWEST
NORTHUMBERLAND
NOTEWORTHINESS
NOUVEAUX
RICHES

NO-WIN
 SITUATION
NUCLEAR
 REACTOR
NUCLEAR
 WINTERS
NURSERY
 SCHOOLS
NUTRITIOUSNESS
NYCTAGINACEOUS
NYMPHOMANIACAL

O

OBSEQUIOUSNESS
OBSERVABLENESS
OBSTREPEROUSLY
OBSTRUCTIONISM
OBSTRUCTIONIST
OCCUPATIONALLY
OCEAN
 GRAYHOUND
OCEANOGRAPHERS
OEDIPUS
 COMPLEX
OLD MAN OF THE
 SEA
OLD PEOPLE'S
 HOME
OLD TIME
 DANCING
OLIGARCHICALLY
OLIGOPSONISTIC
ONE-ARMED
 BANDIT
ONEIROCRITICAL
ONE-NIGHT
 STANDS
ON ONES BEAM
 ENDS
ON THE OTHER
 HAND
ON THE
 THRESHOLD
OPEN-
 HANDEDNESS
OPEN-
 MINDEDNESS
OPEN
 SANDWICHES
OPEN
 UNIVERSITY
OPERATING
 TABLE

OPERATIONALISM
OPHTHALMOSCOPE
OPHTHALMOSCOPY
OPPOSITE
 NUMBER
OPPRESSIVENESS
OPTIMISTICALLY
ORCHESTRATIONS
ORDINARY
 LEVELS
ORDINARY
 SEAMAN
ORDNANCE
 SURVEY
ORGANIZATIONAL
ORGANIZED
 CRIME
ORGANOGRAPHIST
ORGANOMETALLIC
ORNITHOLOGICAL
ORNITHOLOGISTS
OROBANCHACEOUS
OROGRAPHICALLY
ORTHOCHROMATIC
ORTHODOX
 CHURCH
ORTHOGENICALLY
ORTHOGRAPHICAL
ORTHOPHOSPHATE
OSCILLOGRAPHIC
OSMOMETRICALLY
OSTENTATIOUSLY
OSTEOARTHRITIC
OSTEOARTHRITIS
OSTEOLOGICALLY
OTOLARYNGOLOGY
OUTBOARD
 MOTORS
OUTGENERALLING
OUTLANDISHNESS
OUTMANOEUVRING
OUTRAGEOUSNESS
OVERCAPITALIZE
OVERCOMPENSATE
OVERDEVELOPING
OVERENTHUSIASM
OVERESTIMATING
OVERESTIMATION
OVERINDULGENCE
OVERPOPULATION
OVERPOWERINGLY
OVERPRODUCTION

OVERPROTECTION
OVERSIMPLIFIED
OVERSTATEMENTS
OVERSUBSCRIBED
OVER-THE-
 COUNTER
OVERWHELMINGLY
OWNER-
 OCCUPIERS
OXYHAEMOGLOBIN
OYSTERCATCHERS

P

PACHYDERMATOUS
PACKAGE
 HOLIDAY
PADDLE
 STEAMERS
PAEDIATRICIANS
PAEDOMORPHOSIS
PAGANISTICALLY
PALAEANTHROPIC
PALAEETHNOLOGY
PALAEOBOTANIST
PALATALIZATION
PALEONTOLOGIST
PAN-
 AMERICANISM
PANCAKE
 LANDING
PANGENETICALLY
PANHELLENISTIC
PAPILLOMATOSIS
PARABOLIZATION
PARALLELEPIPED
PARALLELOGRAMS
PARAPHERNALIAS
PARAPSYCHOLOGY
PARASITOLOGIST
PARATACTICALLY
PARENCHYMATOUS
PARKING
 GARAGES
PARSIMONIOUSLY
PARTHENOCARPIC
PARTICULARIZED
PARTICULARIZER
PARTURIFACIENT
PASSENGER
 TRAIN
PASSING THE
 BUCK

PASSIONATENESS
PASSIONFLOWERS
PASSIVE
 SMOKING
PASTEURIZATION
PAST
 PARTICIPLE
PATE DE FOIE
 GRAS
PATENT
 MEDICINE
PATHOLOGICALLY
PAVEMENT
 ARTIST
PEACE
 OFFERINGS
PENITENTIARIES
PENNY
 DREADFULS
PENNY-
 FARTHINGS
PENNY-
 HALFPENNY
PEPPERCORN
 RENT
PERAMBULATIONS
PERCEIVABILITY
PERCEPTIBILITY
PERCUSSION
 CAPS
PERCUSSIONISTS
PEREGRINATIONS
PEREMPTORINESS
PERFECT
 BINDING
PERFECTIBILITY
PERFECTIONISTS
PERFIDIOUSNESS
PERIMETRICALLY
PERISCOPICALLY
PERLOCUTIONARY
PERMANENT
 WAVES
PERMISSIBILITY
PERMISSIVENESS
PERNICIOUSNESS
PERNICKETINESS
PEROXIDE
 BLONDE
PERPENDICULARS
PERSONABLENESS
PERSONAL
 COLUMN

PERSONAL
ESTATE
PERSONAL
STEREO
PERSON-TO-
PERSON
PERSUADABILITY
PERSUASIVENESS
PERTINACIOUSLY
PETIT
BOURGEOIS
PETIT
LARCENIST
PETROCHEMICALS
PETROCHEMISTRY
PETROLEUM
JELLY
PETROL
STATIONS
PETTY
BOURGEOIS
PETTY
LARCENIES
PHANTASMAGORIA
PHANTASMAGORIC
PHARMACEUTICAL
PHARMACOLOGIST
PHARMACOPOEIAL
PHARMACOPOEIAS
PHARMACOPOEIST
PHARYNGOLOGIST
PHARYNGOSCOPIC
PHENOBARBITONE
PHENOTYPICALLY
PHILANTHROPIST
PHILATELICALLY
PHILOLOGICALLY
PHILOSOPHIZING
PHLEGMATICALLY
PHONOLOGICALLY
PHOSPHOPROTEIN
PHOSPHORESCENT
PHOSPHOROSCOPE
PHOTOCHEMISTRY
PHOTOCONDUCTOR
PHOTOENGRAVING
PHOTOGENICALLY
PHOTOGRAMMETRY
PHOTOPERIODISM
PHOTOSENSITIVE
PHOTOSENSITIZE
PHOTOSYNTHESIS

PHOTOSYNTHETIC
PHOTOTYPICALLY
PHRASEOGRAPHIC
PHRASEOLOGICAL
PHTHALOCYANINE
PHYTOGEOGRAPHY
PHYTOPATHOLOGY
PHYTOSOCIOLOGY
PICTURE
WINDOWS
PIEZOCHEMISTRY
PILGRIM
FATHERS
PINCER
MOVEMENT
PINNATIPARTITE
PINS AND
NEEDLES
PISCICULTURIST
PITCH-
BLACKNESS
PITCHED
BATTLES
PLAIN
CHOCOLATE
PLANCK
CONSTANT
PLASTER OF
PARIS
PLASTIC
BULLETS
PLASTICIZATION
PLASTIC
SURGEON
PLASTIC
SURGERY
PLATINOCYANIDE
PLATINUM
BLONDE
PLATITUDINIZER
PLEA
BARGAINING
PLEONASTICALLY
PLETHYSMOGRAPH
PLUMBER'S
FRIEND
PNEUMATIC
DRILL
PNEUMOBACILLUS
PNEUMOCONIOSIS
PNEUMODYNAMICS
POIKILOTHERMAL
POLEMONIACEOUS

POLICE
OFFICERS
POLICE
STATIONS
POLITICIZATION
POLLING
STATION
POLYCARPELLARY
POLYCHROMATISM
POLYMERIZATION
POLYNUCLEOTIDE
POLYPHONICALLY
POLYSACCHARIDE
POLYSYNTHESISM
PONTOON
BRIDGES
POOR-
SPIRITEDLY
POPULARIZATION
PORPHYROGENITE
PORTENTOUSNESS
PORTULACACEOUS
POSSESSIVENESS
POSTMILLENNIAL
POSTPOSITIONAL
POTENTIALITIES
PRACTICABILITY
PRACTICALITIES
PRACTICAL
JOKER
PRACTICAL
JOKES
PRAISEWORTHILY
PRAYER
MEETINGS
PREADOLESCENCE
PREARRANGEMENT
PRECARIOUSNESS
PRECIOUS
METALS
PRECIOUS
STONES
PRECIPITATIONS
PRECOCIOUSNESS
PRECONCEPTIONS
PREDACIOUSNESS
PREDESTINARIAN
PREDESTINATION
PREDETERMINATE
PREDETERMINERS
PREDETERMINING
PREDICTABILITY

PREDISPOSITION
PREFABRICATING
PREFABRICATION
PREFERENTIALLY
PREFIGURATIONS
PREMEDITATEDLY
PREOCCUPATIONS
PREORDINATIONS
PREPONDERANTLY
PREPONDERATING
PREPONDERATION
PREPOSSESSIONS
PREPOSTEROUSLY
PRE-
RAPHAELITES
PRESCRIPTIVELY
PRESCRIPTIVISM
PRESCRIPTIVIST
PRESENCE OF
MIND
PRESENTATIONAL
PRESENT
PERFECT
PRESERVABILITY
PRESIDENT
ELECT
PRESIDENT-
ELECT
PRESS
GALLERIES
PRESSURE
COOKER
PRESSURE
GROUPS
PRESSURE
POINTS
PRESSURIZATION
PRESUMPTUOUSLY
PRESUPPOSITION
PREVARICATIONS
PREVENTIVENESS
PRIMA
BALLERINA
PRIMARY
COLOURS
PRIMARY
SCHOOLS
PRIME
MINISTERS
PRINCE
CHARMING
PRINCES
CONSORT

PRINCIPALITIES
PRINCIPAL
  PARTS
PRINTED
  CIRCUIT
PRISONERS OF
  WAR
PRISON
  VISITORS
PRIVATE
  MEMBERS
PRIVATE
  SCHOOLS
PRIVATE
  SOLDIER
PRO BONO
  PUBLICO
PROCRASTINATED
PROCRASTINATOR
PROCRYPTICALLY
PRODIGIOUSNESS
PRODUCTION
  LINE
PRODUCTIVENESS
PROFESSIONALLY
PROFESSORIALLY
PROFESSORSHIPS
PROGESTATIONAL
PROGNOSTICATED
PROGNOSTICATOR
PROGRAMME
  MUSIC
PROHIBITIONARY
PROHIBITIONISM
PROHIBITIONIST
PROJECTIONISTS
PROLETARIANISM
PROLIFERATIONS
PROMENADE
  DECKS
PRONOUNCEMENTS
PRONUNCIATIONS
PROPAEDEUTICAL
PROPAGANDIZING
PROPER
  FRACTION
PROPITIOUSNESS
PROPORTIONALLY
PROPORTIONMENT
PROPOSITIONING
PROPRIETORALLY
PROPRIOCEPTIVE

PROSENCEPHALON
PROSPEROUSNESS
PROSTHETICALLY
PROSTHODONTICS
PROSTHODONTIST
PROTECTIONISTS
PROTECTIVENESS
PROTHONOTARIAL
PROTOZOOLOGIST
PROTRACTEDNESS
PROTRUSIVENESS
PROVENTRICULAR
PROVENTRICULUS
PROVIDENTIALLY
PROVINCIALISMS
PROVING
  GROUNDS
PSEUDOMORPHISM
PSYCHOANALYSED
PSYCHOANALYSIS
PSYCHOANALYSTS
PSYCHOANALYTIC
PSYCHOANALYZER
PSYCHOCHEMICAL
PSYCHODRAMATIC
PSYCHODYNAMICS
PSYCHOLINGUIST
PSYCHOLOGISTIC
PSYCHONEUROSIS
PSYCHONEUROTIC
PSYCHOPHYSICAL
PSYCHOSOMATICS
PSYCHOSURGICAL
PSYCHOTECHNICS
PTERIDOLOGICAL
PUBLIC
  NUISANCE
PUBLIC
  SPIRITED
PUBLIC-
  SPIRITED
PUGILISTICALLY
PUGNACIOUSNESS
PURCHASABILITY
PURPLE
  PASSAGES
PURPOSEFULNESS
PURSE
  STRINGSES
PUT THE SCREWS
  ON
PYELONEPHRITIS

PYRAMID
  SELLING
PYRHELIOMETRIC
PYROMETALLURGY
PYROMETRICALLY
PYROPHOTOMETER
PYROPHOTOMETRY
PYROTECHNICSES
PYRRHIC
  VICTORY

Q

QUADRAGENARIAN
QUADRILATERALS
QUALIFICATIONS
QUANTIFICATION
QUANTITATIVELY
QUARTERMASTERS
QUEEN'S
  COUNSELS
QUEEN'S
  EVIDENCE
QUESTION
  MASTER
QUESTIONNAIRES
QUICK ON THE
  DRAW
QUINQUEFOLIATE
QUINQUEPARTITE
QUINQUEVALENCY
QUINTESSENTIAL
QUOTATION
  MARKS

R

RADIOBIOLOGIST
RADIOCHEMISTRY
RADIO
  FREQUENCY
RADIOSENSITIVE
RADIOTELEGRAPH
RADIOTELEMETRY
RADIOTELEPHONE
RADIOTELEPHONY
RADIO
  TELESCOPE
RADIOTHERAPIST
RAILWAY
  STATION
RAMBUNCTIOUSLY
RAMPAGEOUSNESS
RANUNCULACEOUS

RAPPROCHEMENTS
RASTAFARIANISM
RATEABLE
  VALUES
RATE OF
  EXCHANGE
READY FOR
  ACTION
REAFFIRMATIONS
REAL-TIME
  SYSTEM
REARRANGEMENTS
REAR VIEW
  MIRROR
REASONABLENESS
REBELLIOUSNESS
RECAPITULATING
RECAPITULATION
RECAPITULATIVE
RECEPTION
  ROOMS
RECKLINGHAUSEN
RECOMMENCEMENT
RECOMMENDATION
RECOMMENDATORY
RECONCILIATION
RECONCILIATORY
RECONDITIONING
RECONNAISSANCE
RECONSTITUTING
RECONSTITUTION
RECONSTRUCTING
RECONSTRUCTION
RECONSTRUCTIVE
RECORD-
  BREAKING
RECOVERABILITY
RECREATION
  ROOM
RECRIMINATIONS
RECRUDESCENCES
RECTANGULARITY
RECTIFICATIONS
REDEVELOPMENTS
REDINTEGRATION
REDINTEGRATIVE
REDISTRIBUTING
REDISTRIBUTION
REFERENCE
  BOOKS
REFLECTIVENESS
REFRACTIVENESS

REFRACTOMETRIC
REFRACTORINESS
REFRANGIBILITY
REGARDLESSNESS
REGISTERED
POST
REGISTER
OFFICE
REGISTRATIONAL
REGISTRY
OFFICE
REGRESSIVENESS
REGULARIZATION
REHABILITATING
REHABILITATION
REHABILITATIVE
REIGNS OF
TERROR
REIMBURSEMENTS
REINCARNATIONS
REINFORCEMENTS
REINSTALLATION
REINSTATEMENTS
REINTRODUCTION
REJUVENESCENCE
RELATIVE
CLAUSE
RELENTLESSNESS
RELINQUISHMENT
REMARKABLENESS
REMEMBRANCE
DAY
REMONETIZATION
REMORSEFULNESS
REMUNERABILITY
REMUNERATIVELY
REORGANIZATION
REPETITIVENESS
REPLACEABILITY
REPORTED
SPEECH
REPRESENTATION
REPRESENTATIVE
REPRESSIVENESS
REPRIMANDINGLY
REQUISITIONARY
REQUISITIONING
RESPECTABILITY
RESPECTFULNESS
RESPONSIBILITY
RESPONSIVENESS

RESTAURANT
CARS
RESTRICTEDNESS
RESTRICTIONIST
RESURRECTIONAL
RETRACTABILITY
RETRIEVABILITY
RETROGRADATION
RETROGRADATORY
RETRO-
OPERATIVE
RETROSPECTIVES
REVERBERATIONS
REVEREND
MOTHER
REVISED
VERSION
REVITALIZATION
REVIVIFICATION
REVOLUTIONIZED
REVOLUTIONIZER
RHEUMATIC
FEVER
RHINENCEPHALIC
RHINENCEPHALON
RHIZOCEPHALOUS
RHYTHM AND
BLUES
RICINOLEIC
ACID
RIDICULOUSNESS
RIGHT
TRIANGLES
RIO GRANDE DO
SUL
ROADWORTHINESS
ROARING
FORTIES
ROCKET-
LAUNCHER
ROCKY
MOUNTAINS
ROENTGENOPAQUE
ROLLER
COASTERS
ROMAINE
LETTUCE
ROMAN
CATHOLICS
RORSCHACH
TESTS
ROTTEN
BOROUGHS

ROUGH-AND-
TUMBLE
RUBBER
DINGHIES
RUBBER-
STAMPING
RUBBING
ALCOHOL
RUDIMENTARILLY
RUNNING
REPAIRS
RUN THE
GAUNTLET
RUSH ONES
FENCES

S

SACRAMENTALISM
SACRAMENTALIST
SACRAMENTALITY
SACRAMENTARIAN
SACRILEGIOUSLY
SADOMASOCHISTS
SAFE-DEPOSIT
BOX
SAFETY
CURTAINS
SALAD
DRESSINGS
SALUBRIOUSNESS
SANCTIFICATION
SANDWICH
BOARDS
SANDWICH
COURSE
SANGUINARINESS
SANITARY
TOWELS
SANTIAGO DE
CUBA
SAPONIFICATION
SATELLITE
STATE
SATISFACTIONAL
SATISFACTORILY
SAVE ONES
BREATH
SAVINGS
ACCOUNT
SAWN-OFF
SHOTGUN
SAXIFRAGACEOUS
SCANDALIZATION

SCANDALMONGERS
SCANDALOUSNESS
SCATTERBRAINED
SCHEMATIZATION
SCHISMATICALLY
SCHIZOMYCETOUS
SCHIZOPHRENICS
SCHIZOPHYCEOUS
SCHOOLCHILDREN
SCHOOLMISTRESS
SCHOOLTEACHERS
SCIENCE
FICTION
SCIENTIFICALLY
SCINTILLOMETER
SCOTCH
WHISKIES
SCREEN
PRINTING
SCRUBBING
BRUSH
SCRUPULOUSNESS
SCRUTINIZINGLY
SCURRILOUSNESS
SEARCH
WARRANTS
SEASONABLENESS
SECOND-
GUESSING
SECOND
THOUGHTS
SECULARIZATION
SEGREGATIONIST
SELF-
ABNEGATION
SELF-
ABSORPTION
SELF-
ANALYTICAL
SELF-
CONFIDENCE
SELF-
CONTROLLED
SELF-
DESTRUCTED
SELF-
DISCIPLINE
SELF-
EFFACEMENT
SELF-
EMPLOYMENT
SELF-
GOVERNMENT

SELF-IMPORTANCE
SELF-INDUCTANCE
SELF-INDULGENCE
SELF-INFLICTION
SELF-INTERESTED
SELF-JUSTIFYING
SELF-POSSESSION
SELF-PROTECTION
SELF-RESPECTFUL
SELF-RESPECTING
SELF-SUFFICIENT
SELF-SUPPORTING
SEMAPHORICALLY
SEMASIOLOGICAL
SEMICENTENNIAL
SEMICONDUCTION
SEMICONDUCTORS
SEMIELLIPTICAL
SEMIPARASITISM
SENIOR CITIZENS
SENSATIONALISM
SENSATIONALIST
SENTIMENTALISM
SENTIMENTALIST
SENTIMENTALITY
SENTIMENTALIZE
SEPARATE TABLES
SEPARATIVENESS
SEPTUAGENARIAN
SEQUESTRATIONS
SERGEANT-AT-ARMS
SERGEANT MAJORS
SERIALIZATIONS
SERIOCOMICALLY
SERJEANT-AT-ARMS
SERVICEABILITY

SERVICE CHARGES
SERVICE STATION
SERVOMECHANISM
SESQUIPEDALIAN
SEWING MACHINES
SHAGGY-DOG STORY
SHAMEFACEDNESS
SHEET LIGHTNING
SHEPHERD'S-PURSE
SHERARDIZATION
SHETLAND PONIES
SHIHCHIACHUANG
SHILLY-SHALLIED
SHILLYSHALLIER
SHIP'S CHANDLERS
SHOCK ABSORBERS
SHOCK TREATMENT
SHOOTING STICKS
SHOP ASSISTANTS
SHOPPING CENTRE
SHORT-CIRCUITED
SHORTSIGHTEDLY
SHOTGUN WEDDING
SHOULDER BLADES
SHOULDER STRAPS
SIDEWALK ARTIST
SIGMOIDOSCOPIC
SIGNATURE TUNES
SIGNIFICATIONS
SILENT PARTNERS
SILICIFICATION

SILVER JUBILEES
SILVER WEDDINGS
SILVICULTURIST
SIMAROUBACEOUS
SIMPLE FRACTURE
SIMPLE INTEREST
SIMPLE MACHINES
SIMPLIFICATION
SIMPLIFICATIVE
SIMPLISTICALLY
SIMULTANEOUSLY
SINGLE-BREASTED
SINGLE-MINDEDLY
SINKIANG-UIGHUR
SINKING FEELING
SIPHONOPHOROUS
SITTING TARGETS
SIXTEENTH NOTES
SKATE ON THIN ICE
SKIRTING BOARDS
SLANDEROUSNESS
SLAP ON THE WRIST
SLATTERNLINESS
SLAUGHTERHOUSE
SLIPSHODDINESS
SLOTTED SPATULA
SLUGGARDLINESS
SLUMBEROUSNESS
SMALL INTESTINE
SOCIAL CLIMBERS
SOCIAL SCIENCES
SOCIAL SECURITY
SOCIAL SERVICES

SOCIOLOGICALLY
SOCIOPOLITICAL
SODIUM CHLORIDE
SOLDERING IRONS
SOLICITOUSNESS
SOLIDIFICATION
SOMNAMBULATION
SOMNAMBULISTIC
SOPHISTICATION
SOUL-DESTROYING
SOUNDING BOARDS
SOUTHEASTWARDS
SOUTHERN LIGHTS
SOUTH-SOUTHEAST
SOUTH-SOUTHWEST
SOUTHWESTWARDS
SPATIOTEMPORAL
SPEAKERS CORNER
SPECIALIZATION
SPECIAL LICENCE
SPECIAL SCHOOLS
SPECIFICATIONS
SPECTROGRAPHIC
SPECTROSCOPIST
SPEECHLESSNESS
SPERMATOGONIAL
SPERMATOGONIUM
SPERMATOPHORAL
SPERMATOPHYTIC
SPERMATORRHOEA
SPERMIOGENESIS
SPERMIOGENETIC
SPHEROIDICALLY
SPHYGMOGRAPHIC
SPINNING WHEELS
SPINTHARISCOPE
SPIRITLESSNESS
SPIRITUALISTIC
SPIROCHAETOSIS
SPIRONOLACTONE

SPITTING
  IMAGES
SPLINTER
  GROUPS
SPONGIOBLASTIC
SPORADICALNESS
SPRECHSTIMMUNG
SPRING
  CHICKENS
SPRING-
  CLEANING
SQUADRON
  LEADER
SQUARE
  BRACKETS
STAFF
  SERGEANTS
STAGE
  DIRECTION
STAMPING
  GROUND
STANDARD-
  BEARER
STANDING
  ORDERS
STANDOFF
  HALVES
ST ANDREWS
  CROSS
STAPHYLOCOCCAL
STAPHYLOCOCCUS
STAPHYLOPLASTY
STARTING
  BLOCKS
STARTING
  PISTOL
STARTING
  PRICES
START
  SOMETHING
STATE'S
  EVIDENCE
STATIONARINESS
STATIONMASTERS
STATUESQUENESS
STEAMROLLERING
STEAMTIGHTNESS
STEERING
  WHEELS
STEPPING-
  STONES
STERCORICOLOUS
STERCULIACEOUS

STEREOMETRICAL
STEREOSPECIFIC
STERTOROUSNESS
STICKING
  POINTS
STIGMATIZATION
STINGING
  NETTLE
STIPPLING
  BRUSH
STIR ONES
  STUMPS
STOCHASTICALLY
STOCKBROKERAGE
STOCK
  EXCHANGES
STOCKING-
  FILLER
STOICHIOMETRIC
STOLEN
  PROPERTY
STOPS AT
  NOTHING
STORE
  DETECTIVE
STORM IN A
  TEACUP
STRAIGHT
  FIGHTS
STRAIGHTJACKET
STRAIGHT
  JACKET
STRATICULATION
STRATIFICATION
STRAWBERRY
  MARK
STREET-
  CREDIBLE
STREPTOTHRICIN
STRETCHABILITY
STRETCHER
  PARTY
STRIDULOUSNESS
STRIKEBREAKERS
STRIKEBREAKING
STRONG
  LANGUAGE
STRONG-
  MINDEDLY
STUDENTS'
  UNIONS
STULTIFICATION

STUMBLING
  BLOCK
STUPENDOUSNESS
SUBALTERNATION
SUBCONSCIOUSLY
SUBCONTINENTAL
SUBCONTRACTING
SUBCONTRACTORS
SUBCUTANEOUSLY
SUBINFEUDATION
SUBINFEUDATORY
SUBJECTABILITY
SUBJECTIVISTIC
SUBJECT-
  RAISING
SUBLIEUTENANCY
SUBLIEUTENANTS
SUBMACHINE
  GUNS
SUBMERSIBILITY
SUBMICROSCOPIC
SUBMISSIVENESS
SUBSIDIARINESS
SUBSTANTIALISM
SUBSTANTIALIST
SUBSTANTIALITY
SUBSTANTIATING
SUBSTANTIATION
SUBSTANTIATIVE
SUBTERRESTRIAL
SUBVERSIVENESS
SUCCESSFULNESS
SUCCESSIVENESS
SUGGESTIBILITY
SUGGESTIVENESS
SULPHANILAMIDE
SULPHATHIAZOLE
SULPHISOXAZOLE
SULPHONMETHANE
SULPHURIZATION
SULPHUROUSNESS
SUPERABUNDANCE
SUPERANNUATION
SUPERCILIOUSLY
SUPERCONDUCTOR
SUPERELEVATION
SUPERFICIALITY
SUPERINCUMBENT
SUPERINDUCTION
SUPERINTENDENT
SUPERINTENDING

SUPERNATURALLY
SUPERNORMALITY
SUPERPHOSPHATE
SUPERSATURATED
SUPERSCRIPTION
SUPERSONICALLY
SUPERSTRUCTURE
SUPPLY
  TEACHERS
SUPPORTABILITY
SUPPORTING
  PART
SUPRAMOLECULAR
SUPRASEGMENTAL
SUREFOOTEDNESS
SURGICAL
  SPIRIT
SURPASSINGNESS
SURPRISINGNESS
SUSCEPTIBILITY
SUSPENDIBILITY
SUSPENSIVENESS
SUSPICIOUSNESS
SWIMMING
  TRUNKS
SWORD-
  SWALLOWER
SYMBIONTICALLY
SYMBOLICALNESS
SYMMETRIZATION
SYMPATHIZINGLY
SYMPTOMATOLOGY
SYNCHRONICALLY
SYNCRETIZATION
SYNERGETICALLY
SYNONYMOUSNESS
SYNTHESIZATION
SYNTHETIZATION
SYPHILITICALLY
SYSTEMATICALLY
SYSTEMS
  ANALYST

T

TACHISTOSCOPIC
TAKE IN GOOD
  PART
TALK OF THE
  DEVIL
TARTAN
  TROUSERS
TAUTOLOGICALLY

TECHNICALITIES
TELANGIECTASIS
TELANGIECTATIC
TELAUTOGRAPHIC
TELEGRAPH
  POLES
TELEMETRICALLY
TELEOLOGICALLY
TELEPATHICALLY
TELEPHONE
  BOXES
TELESCOPICALLY
TELETYPESETTER
TERCENTENARIES
TERGIVERSATION
TERGIVERSATORY
TERMINOLOGICAL
TERRACED
  HOUSES
TERRITORIALISM
TERRITORIALIST
TERRITORIALITY
TERRITORIALIZE
TERROR-
  STRICKEN
TEST-TUBE
  BABIES
TETRAETHYL
  LEAD
THAUMATROPICAL
THE
  AMBASSADORS
THE FOUR
  SEASONS
THE LIFE OF
  RILEY
THEOCENTRICITY
THEOCRATICALLY
THEOLOGIZATION
THEOSOPHICALLY
THERIANTHROPIC
THERMAESTHESIA
THERMOCHEMICAL
THERMODYNAMICS
THERMOELECTRIC
THERMOELECTRON
THERMOJUNCTION
THERMOMAGNETIC
THERMOPLASTICS
THIOCYANIC
  ACID
THOUGHTFULNESS

THREE-DAY
  EVENTS
THREE-
  HALFPENCE
THREE-LINE
  WHIPS
THREE-POINT
  TURN
THRIFTLESSNESS
THROMBOPLASTIC
THROMBOPLASTIN
THYMELAEACEOUS
THYROTOXICOSIS
TICKLED TO
  DEATH
TIERRA DEL
  FUEGO
TIME
  IMMEMORIAL
TIME
  SIGNATURES
TITTLE-
  TATTLING
TOAD OF TOAD
  HALL
TOILET
  TRAINING
TO-ING AND
  FRO-ING
TONGUE
  TWISTERS
TORTOISESHELLS
TRACTION
  ENGINE
TRADE
  UNIONISTS
TRADING
  ESTATES
TRADITIONALISM
TRADITIONALIST
TRADUCIANISTIC
TRAFFIC
  CALMING
TRAFFIC
  CIRCLES
TRAFFIC
  ISLANDS
TRAFFIC
  WARDENS
TRAGICOMICALLY
TRAITOROUSNESS
TRANQUILLIZERS
TRANQUILLIZING

TRANSCAUCASIAN
TRANSCENDENTAL
TRANSCENDENTLY
TRANSCENDINGLY
TRANSCRIPTIONS
TRANSFERENTIAL
TRANSFORMATION
TRANSFORMATIVE
TRANSGRESSIBLE
TRANSGRESSIONS
TRANSISTORIZED
TRANSITIONALLY
TRANSITIVENESS
TRANSITORINESS
TRANS-
  JORDANIAN
TRANSLITERATED
TRANSLITERATOR
TRANSMIGRATION
TRANSMIGRATIVE
TRANSMIGRATORY
TRANSMISSIVITY
TRANSMOGRIFIED
TRANSMUTATIONS
TRANSPARENCIES
TRANSPLANTABLE
TRANSPORTATION
TRANSPORT
  CAFES
TRANSPOSITIONS
TRANSVALUATION
TRANSVERSENESS
TRAUMATIZATION
TRAVEL
  AGENCIES
TRAVELLERS
  TALE
TRAVELSICKNESS
TREAD THE
  BOARDS
TREASURE
  ISLAND
TREASURE
  TROVES
TREMENDOUSNESS
TRICHINIZATION
TRICHOMONIASIS
TRICHOTOMOUSLY
TRICK OR
  TREATED
TRIDIMENSIONAL
TRINITROCRESOL

TRINITROPHENOL
TRISOCTAHEDRAL
TRISOCTAHEDRON
TRISTAN DA
  CUNHA
TRIVIALIZATION
TROPIC OF
  CANCER
TROUBLESHOOTER
TROUSER
  PRESSES
TUMULTUOUSNESS
TUNBRIDGE
  WELLS
TURBOGENERATOR
TURF
  ACCOUNTANT
TURKISH
  DELIGHT
TURN A DEAF
  EAR TO
TURNING
  CIRCLES
TWO-
  DIMENSIONAL
TYRANNICALNESS

U

UBIQUITOUSNESS
ULTIMOGENITURE
ULTRAMODERNISM
ULTRAMODERNIST
ULTRAMONTANISM
ULTRAMONTANIST
ULTRASONICALLY
ULTRASTRUCTURE
UMBILICAL
  CORDS
UNACCOMMODATED
UNACCOMPLISHED
UNACCOUNTED
  FOR
UNACCOUNTED-
  FOR
UNAPPRECIATIVE
UNAPPROACHABLE
UNAPPROPRIATED
UNAVOIDABILITY
UNBEARABLENESS
UNBECOMINGNESS
UNCOMPROMISING
UNCONSCIONABLE

UNCONSCIONABLY
UNCONTAMINATED
UNCONTROLLABLE
UNCONVENTIONAL
UNCONVINCINGLY
UNCORROBORATED
UNDERACHIEVERS
UNDERACHIEVING
UNDERCARRIAGES
UNDERESTIMATED
UNDERESTIMATES
UNDERGRADUATES
UNDERMENTIONED
UNDERNOURISHED
UNDERSECRETARY
UNDERSTANDABLE
UNDERSTANDABLY
UNDERSTANDINGS
UNDERSTATEMENT
UNDERVALUATION
UNDESIRABILITY
UNECONOMICALLY
UNENTHUSIASTIC
UNEVENTFULNESS
UNEXPECTEDNESS
UNFAITHFULNESS
UNFLAPPABILITY
UNFRIENDLINESS
UNFRUITFULNESS
UNGRATEFULNESS
UNHANDSOMENESS
UNHOLY
  ALLIANCE
UNICELLULARITY
UNIDENTIFIABLE
UNIDIRECTIONAL
UNIFORMITARIAN
UNINCORPORATED
UNINTELLIGENCE
UNINTELLIGIBLE
UNIPERSONALITY
UNIVERSALISTIC
UNIVERSAL
  JOINT
UNKNOWABLENESS
UNMENTIONABLES
UNPLEASANTNESS
UNPRACTICALITY
UNPREMEDITATED
UNPREPAREDNESS
UNPROFESSIONAL

UNQUESTIONABLE
UNQUESTIONABLY
UNRECOGNIZABLE
UNRESERVEDNESS
UNRESTRAINEDLY
UNSATISFACTORY
UNSCRUPULOUSLY
UNTHANKFULNESS
UNTHINKABILITY
UNTOUCHABILITY
UPSIDE-
  DOWNNESS
UPSTANDINGNESS
UPWARDLY-
  MOBILE
UST-
  KAMENOGORSK
UTILITARIANISM

V

VACUUM
  CLEANERS
VALERIANACEOUS
VALETUDINARIAN
VALUE
  JUDGMENTS
VASOINHIBITORY
VAULTING
  HORSES
VEGETABLE
  KNIFE
VEGETATIVENESS
VENDING
  MACHINE
VENETIAN
  BLINDS
VENTRILOQUISTS
VENTURE
  CAPITAL
VERISIMILITUDE
VERTICILLASTER
VERTICILLATION
VESPERTILIONID
VESTED
  INTEREST
VEXED
  QUESTIONS
VICE-
  CHANCELLOR
VICE-
  PRESIDENCY
VICIOUS
  CIRCLES

VICTORIOUSNESS
VIEW ON THE
  STOUR
VILLAINOUSNESS
VINDICTIVENESS
VISHAKHAPATNAM
VITRIFIABILITY
VITRIOLIZATION
VITUPERATIVELY
VIVISECTIONIST
VOCIFEROUSNESS
VOLATILIZATION
VOLCANOLOGICAL
VOLUMETRICALLY
VOLUMINOUSNESS
VOLUPTUOUSNESS
VOROSHILOVGRAD
VOTES OF
  CENSURE
VULGAR
  FRACTION
VULGARIZATIONS
VULVOVAGINITIS

W

WARRANTABILITY
WARRANT
  OFFICER
WASHING
  MACHINE
WATERCOLOURIST
WATERING
  PLACES
WATERPROOFNESS
WATER-
  REPELLENT
WATER-
  RESISTANT
WATER
  SOFTENERS
WATERTIGHTNESS
WEAK-
  MINDEDNESS
WEATHERABILITY
WEATHERPROOFED
WEATHER
  STATION
WEIGHTLESSNESS
WE LIVE AND
  LEARN
WELL-
  ACCUSTOMED

WELL-
  ACQUAINTED
WELL-
  DOCUMENTED
WESTERNIZATION
WET ONES
  WHISTLE
WHEELER-
  DEALERS
WHEELER-
  DEALING
WHIMSICALITIES
WHIPPERSNAPPER
WHITE BLOOD
  CELL
WHITE
  ELEPHANTS
WHOLE-
  HEARTEDLY
WHORTLEBERRIES
WILDCAT
  STRIKES
WILD GOOSE
  CHASE
WILD-GOOSE
  CHASE
WILLIAM AND
  MARY
WIND
  INSTRUMENT
WINDOW
  DRESSING
WINDOW-
  SHOPPERS
WINDOW
  SHOPPING
WINDOW-
  SHOPPING
WIND-
  POLLINATED
WING
  COMMANDERS
WOMEN'S
  MOVEMENT
WORCESTER
  SAUCE
WORD
  PROCESSING
WORD
  PROCESSORS
WORKING
  PARTIES
WORLD-
  WEARINESS

WORMWOOD
  SCRUBS
WORSHIPFULNESS
WORTHWHILENESS

X
XANTHOPHYLLOUS
XEROPHYTICALLY

Y
YOUTH
  HOSTELLER

Z
ZEBRA
  CROSSINGS
ZINGIBERACEOUS

A

A BUNDLE OF NERVES
ACANTHOCEPHALAN
ACCLIMATIZATION
ACCOMMODATINGLY
ACCOMPLISHMENTS
ACHONDROPLASTIC
ACHROMATIZATION
ACIDIMETRICALLY
ACKNOWLEDGEABLE
ACKNOWLEDGMENTS
ACOUSTIC COUPLER
ACQUISITIVENESS
ADMINISTRATIONS
A DROP IN THE OCEAN
AERODYNAMICALLY
AFFRANCHISEMENT
AGAINST THE GRAIN
AGGLUTINABILITY
AGRANULOCYTOSIS
AIR CHIEF MARSHAL
AIR-CONDITIONING
AIRCRAFT CARRIER
AIR VICE-MARSHALS
ALGORITHMICALLY
ALIMENTARY CANAL
ALIVE AND KICKING
ALPHABETIZATION
ALUMINOSILICATE
AMARYLLIDACEOUS
AMBASSADORSHIPS
AMERICAN INDIANS
AMERICANIZATION
A MONTH OF SUNDAYS
AMUSEMENT ARCADE
ANABOLIC STEROID
ANARCHISTICALLY
ANCYLOSTOMIASIS
ANIMAL HUSBANDRY
ANIMATED CARTOON
ANOMALISTICALLY
ANTARCTIC CIRCLE
ANTEPENULTIMATE
ANTHROPOCENTRIC
ANTHROPOGENESIS
ANTHROPOGENETIC
ANTHROPOLOGICAL
ANTHROPOLOGISTS
ANTHROPOMETRIST
ANTHROPOMORPHIC
ANTICHOLINERGIC

ANTICLERICALISM
ANTI-IMPERIALISM
ANTI-IMPERIALIST
ANTILOGARITHMIC
ANTINATIONALIST
ANTIPERISTALSIS
ANTIPERSPIRANTS
APARTMENT HOUSES
APOCALYPTICALLY
APPRENTICESHIPS
APPROACHABILITY
APPROPRIATENESS
APPROVED SCHOOLS
ARCHIEPISCOPATE
ARCHITECTURALLY
ARGUMENTATIVELY
ARTERIALIZATION
ASCLEPIADACEOUS
ASSIMILATIONIST
ASSOCIATE DEGREE
ASTRONAUTICALLY
ASTRONAVIGATION
ASTROPHYSICISTS
ATHEROSCLEROSIS
ATHEROSCLEROTIC
ATMOSPHERICALLY
AT THE DROP OF A
  HAT
ATTORNEY GENERAL
AUDIOMETRICALLY
AUTHORITATIVELY
AUTOBIOGRAPHIES
AUTOCORRELATION
AUTOGRAPHICALLY
AUTOMATIC PILOTS
AUTORADIOGRAPHY
AUTOTRANSFORMER
AVERSION THERAPY

B

BACHELOR'S DEGREE
BACK-SEAT DRIVERS
BACTERIOLOGICAL
BACTERIOLOGISTS
BACTERIOPHAGOUS
BALLROOM DANCING
BANANA REPUBLICS
BANNER HEADLINES
BANQUETING HOUSE
BASIDIOMYCETOUS
BATCH PROCESSING

BATHING MACHINES
BATHOMETRICALLY
BATHYMETRICALLY
BEATEN AT THE POST
BED AND BREAKFAST
BENEFIT OF CLERGY
BIBLIOGRAPHICAL
BIBLIOPHILISTIC
BINOCULAR VISION
BIOASTRONAUTICS
BIOGEOGRAPHICAL
BIOLUMINESCENCE
BIOTECHNOLOGIST
BIRDS OF A FEATHER
BIRDS OF PARADISE
BISYMMETRICALLY
BLACK MARKETEERS
BLACKWATER FEVER
BLAMEWORTHINESS
BLANK CARTRIDGES
BLOCK AND TACKLES
BLOOD-AND-THUNDER
BOARDING SCHOOLS
BONDED WAREHOUSE
BOW STREET RUNNER
BRAKE HORSE POWER
BREAKING THE NEWS
BRING AND BUY SALE
BROADMINDEDNESS
BROKEN-HEARTEDLY
BRUSSELS SPROUTS
BUBBLE AND SQUEAK
BUILDING SOCIETY
BUREAU DE CHANGES
BUSMAN'S HOLIDAYS
BUTTERFLY STROKE

C

CABLE TELEVISION
CANNIBALIZATION
CAPRIFOLIACEOUS
CARDIOPULMONARY
CARPOMETACARPUS
CARRYING CHARGES
CASEMENT WINDOWS
CATEGORIZATIONS
CATHERINE WHEELS
CATHETERIZATION
CATHODE RAY TUBES
CATHOLICIZATION
CENTRE OF GRAVITY

CEPHALOCHORDATE
CEPHALOTHORACIC
CEREBROVASCULAR
CEREMONIOUSNESS
CHAPTER AND VERSE
CHARACTERISTICS
CHARENT-MARITIME
CHARGE D'AFFAIRES
CHECKING ACCOUNT
CHEMICAL WARFARE
CHEMOTACTICALLY
CHEMOTROPICALLY
CHENOPODIACEOUS
CHESTS OF DRAWERS
CHIEF CONSTABLES
CHIEF INSPECTORS
CHINESE CHEQUERS
CHINESE LANTERNS
CHINLESS WONDERS
CHLORAMPHENICOL
CHOLECALCIFEROL
CHOLECYSTECTOMY
CHONDRIFICATION
CHROMATOGRAPHER
CHROMATOGRAPHIC
CHROMATOPHOROUS
CHRONOGRAMMATIC
CHRONOLOGICALLY
CHUCK-WILL'S-WIDOW
CHURCH OF ENGLAND
CIGARETTE HOLDER
CIGARETTE PAPERS
CINEMATOGRAPHER
CINEMATOGRAPHIC
CIRCUIT BREAKERS
CIRCULARIZATION
CIRCUMAMBULATOR
CIRCUMFERENTIAL
CIRCUMLOCUTIONS
CIRCUMNAVIGABLE
CIRCUMNAVIGATED
CIRCUMNAVIGATOR
CIRCUMSCRIPTION
CIRCUMSTANTIATE
CIRCUMVALLATION
CLANDESTINENESS
CLASSIFICATIONS
CLAUSTROPHOBICS
CLEAR-HEADEDNESS
CLERMONT-FERRAND
CLOUD CUCKOO LAND

CLOUD-CUCKOO-LAND
COCK-A-DOODLE-DOOS
COCKNEYFICATION
COCKTAIL LOUNGES
COFFEE-TABLE BOOK
COLD-BLOODEDNESS
COLD-HEARTEDNESS
COLD-SHOULDERING
COLLECTIVE FARMS
COLLECTIVE NOUNS
COLLECTOR'S ITEMS
COLLISION COURSE
COLORADO BEETLES
COLOUR BLINDNESS
COMBINATION LOCK
COMEDY OF MANNERS
COME INTO ONES OWN
COMFORT STATIONS
COMITY OF NATIONS
COMMERCIALISTIC
COMMERCIALIZING
COMMISSIONAIRES
COMMITTEE STAGES
COMMODIFICATION
COMMON FRACTIONS
COMMUNALIZATION
COMMUNICABILITY
COMMUNITY CENTRE
COMMUNITY CHESTS
COMPASSIONATELY
COMPETITIVENESS
COMPLICATEDNESS
COMPREHENSIVELY
COMPRESSIBILITY
COMPUTERIZATION
CONCEPTUALISTIC
CONCEPTUALIZING
CONCESSIONAIRES
CONCRETE JUNGLES
CONFECTIONERIES
CONFIDENCE TRICK
CONFIDENTIALITY
CONFIGURATIONAL
CONFRATERNITIES
CONGLOMERATIONS
CONGRATULATIONS
CONSCIENCE MONEY
CONSCIENTIOUSLY
CONSCRIPTIONIST
CONSENTING ADULT
CONSERVATIONISM

CONSERVATIONIST
CONSIDERATENESS
CONSPICUOUSNESS
CONSTITUTIONALS
CONSUMER DURABLE
CONTEMPORANEITY
CONTEMPORANEOUS
CONTEMPTIBILITY
CONTENTIOUSNESS
CONTORTIONISTIC
CONTRACTIBILITY
CONTRAINDICATED
CONTROVERSIALLY
CONVENIENCE FOOD
CONVENTIONALISM
CONVENTIONALIST
CONVENTIONALITY
CONVENTIONALIZE
CONVOLVULACEOUS
CORRELATIVENESS
CORRESPONDINGLY
COSMOPOLITANISM
COST-EFFECTIVELY
COTTAGE HOSPITAL
COTTAGE INDUSTRY
COUNTERATTACKED
COUNTERATTACKER
COUNTERBALANCED
COUNTERBALANCES
COUNTERCLAIMANT
COUNTERIRRITANT
COUNTER IRRITANT
COUNTERMEASURES
COUNTERPROPOSAL
COURT-MARTIALING
COURT-MARTIALLED
COURTS OF INQUIRY
COVERING LETTERS
CREASE RESISTANT
CREATIVE WRITING
CREDIBILITY GAPS
CRICKET PAVILION
CRIMINAL CLASSES
CROSS-FERTILIZED
CROSSOPTERYGION
CROSS-QUESTIONED
CROSS-QUESTIONER
CROSS-REFERENCES
CROSSWORD EDITORS
CROWN PRINCESSES
CRYSTALLIZATION

CRYSTALLOGRAPHY
CUCKOO IN THE NEST
CURRENT ACCOUNTS
CURRICULUM VITAE
CUT AND COME AGAIN
CYTOMEGALOVIRUS

D
DAYLIGHT ROBBERY
DAYS OF RECKONING
DECALCIFICATION
DECARBONIZATION
DECARBOXYLATION
DECIPHERABILITY
DECOMPOSABILITY
DECONTAMINATING
DECONTAMINATION
DECONTAMINATIVE
DECONTEXTUALIZE
DEFINITE ARTICLE
DEHYDROGENATION
DELIRIUM TREMENS
DELIVER THE GOODS
DEMAGNETIZATION
DEMOCRATIZATION
DEMONSTRABILITY
DEMONSTRATIONAL
DEMONSTRATIVELY
DEMULSIFICATION
DEMYSTIFICATION
DENATIONALIZING
DENITRIFICATION
DEPARTMENTALISM
DEPARTMENTALIZE
DEPARTMENT STORE
DEPARTURE LOUNGE
DEPENDENT CLAUSE
DEPOSIT ACCOUNTS
DERMATOGLYPHICS
DERMATOPHYTOSIS
DESCRIPTIVENESS
DESENSITIZATION
DESEXUALIZATION
DESTABILIZATION
DESTRUCTIBILITY
DESTRUCTIVENESS
DETRIBALIZATION
DEVELOPMENT AREA
DEVIL'S ADVOCATES
DEVITRIFICATION
DIALECTOLOGICAL

DIAMAGNETICALLY
DIAMOND JUBILEES
DIAMOND WEDDINGS
DIAPHOTOTROPISM
DICHOTOMIZATION
DIESEL-HYDRAULIC
DIFFERENTIATING
DIFFERENTIATION
DIGITAL COMPUTER
DIRECTION FINDER
DISADVANTAGEOUS
DISAPPOINTINGLY
DISAPPOINTMENTS
DISARTICULATION
DISCIPLINARIANS
DISCONCERTINGLY
DISCONTINUATION
DISCONTINUITIES
DISCONTINUOUSLY
DISCOUNTENANCED
DISCOURAGEMENTS
DISCRETIONARILY
DISENCUMBERMENT
DISENTANGLEMENT
DISESTABLISHING
DISHEARTENINGLY
DISHEARTENMENTS
DISILLUSIONMENT
DISINCLINATIONS
DISINFLATIONARY
DISINTERESTEDLY
DISORDERLY HOUSE
DISORGANIZATION
DISPASSIONATELY
DISREPUTABILITY
DISRESPECTFULLY
DISSATISFACTION
DISSATISFACTORY
DISSERTATIONIST
DISSIMILARITIES
DISTASTEFULNESS
DISTINCTIVENESS
DISTINGUISHABLE
DISTRACTIBILITY
DISTRUSTFULNESS
DITHYRAMBICALLY
DIVERSIFICATION
DIVISION LOBBIES
DO-IT-YOURSELFERS
DOLICHOCEPHALIC
DOMESTIC ANIMALS

DOMESTIC SCIENCE
DOMESTIC SERVICE
DORSIVENTRALITY
DOUBLE-BARRELLED
DOUBLE ENTENDRES
DOUBLE STANDARDS
DOUBLE WHITE LINE
DRAUGHTSMANSHIP
DRESSING STATION
DRESS REHEARSALS
DRIVE-BY SHOOTING
DRIVING LICENCES
DRUIDICAL CIRCLE
DUAL CARRIAGEWAY
DUAL CITIZENSHIP
DUTCH ELM DISEASE

E
EARTHSHATTERING
EAT ONES HEART OUT
ECCLESIASTICISM
ECCLESIOLOGICAL
EDUCATED GUESSES
EDUCATIONALISTS
ELECTRIC BLANKET
ELECTRIFICATION
ELECTROACOUSTIC
ELECTROANALYSIS
ELECTROANALYTIC
ELECTROCHEMICAL
ELECTRODIALYSIS
ELECTRODYNAMICS
ELECTROKINETICS
ELECTROLYSATION
ELECTROMAGNETIC
ELECTRONEGATIVE
ELECTROPHORESIS
ELECTROPHORETIC
ELECTROPOSITIVE
ELECTROSURGICAL
ELEVATED RAILWAY
EMANCIPATIONIST
EMINENCES GRISES
ENANTIOMORPHISM
ENCEPHALOGRAPHY
ENCHONDROMATOUS
ENCOMIASTICALLY
ENDOCRINE GLANDS
ENDOCRINOLOGIST
ENDOTHERMICALLY
ENDOWMENT POLICY

ENFRANCHISEMENT
ENGAGEMENT RINGS
ENTENTE CORDIALE
ENTREPRENEURIAL
ENVIRONMENTALLY
EPIDEMIOLOGICAL
EPISCOPALIANISM
EPISTEMOLOGICAL
EPITHELIOMATOUS
EQUALITARIANISM
ETERNAL TRIANGLE
ETHEREALIZATION
ETHNIC CLEANSING
ETHNOCENTRICITY
EUCHARISTICALLY
EUDIOMETRICALLY
EUPHEMISTICALLY
EUROPEANIZATION
EUSTACHIAN TUBES
EVERLASTINGNESS
EXCEPTIONALNESS
EXCHANGEABILITY
EXCLAMATION MARK
EXCOMMUNICATING
EXCOMMUNICATION
EXCOMMUNICATIVE
EXEMPLIFICATION
EXEMPLIFICATIVE
EXHIBITIONISTIC
EXPEDITIOUSNESS
EXPENSE ACCOUNTS
EXPERIMENTALISM
EXPERIMENTALIST
EXPERIMENTATION
EXPOSTULATINGLY
EXPRESSIONISTIC
EXTEMPORARINESS
EXTEMPORIZATION
EXTERIORIZATION
EXTERNALIZATION
EXTRACURRICULAR
EXTRALINGUISTIC
EXTRAORDINARILY

F

FAIRY GODMOTHERS
FAMILIARIZATION
FAMILY ALLOWANCE
FASHIONABLENESS
FATHER CHRISTMAS
FEATURELESSNESS

FELLOW TRAVELLER
FEUILLETONISTIC
FIDEICOMMISSARY
FIFTH COLUMNISTS
FIGURES OF SPEECH
FILLING STATIONS
FINISHING SCHOOL
FIRST LIEUTENANT
FLIBBERTIGIBBET
FLIGHT SERGEANTS
FLIRTATIOUSNESS
FOLDING ONES ARMS
FOOT-POUND-SECOND
FOREIGN EXCHANGE
FORESIGHTEDNESS
FORKED LIGHTNING
FORMULARIZATION
FOUNDATION STONE
FOUNDING FATHERS
FOUR-DIMENSIONAL
FOUR-LETTER WORDS
FOURTH DIMENSION
FRACTIONIZATION
FRAGMENTARINESS
FRANKFURT AM MAIN
FREE ASSOCIATION
FRENCH POLISHING
FRIENDLY SOCIETY
FROM STEM TO STERN
FULL-BLOODEDNESS
FUNDAMENTALISTS
FUNERAL DIRECTOR
FUNERAL PARLOURS
FUTILITARIANISM

G

GAME SET AND MATCH
GASTROENTERITIC
GASTROENTERITIS
GASTRONOMICALLY
GENERAL DELIVERY
GENERAL ELECTION
GENERALIZATIONS
GENERAL PRACTICE
GENTLEMAN-AT-ARMS
GENTLEMAN FARMER
GENTLEMANLINESS
GENTLEMEN-AT-ARMS
GERMAN SHEPHERDS
GET ONES SKATES ON
GIVE ONESELF AWAY

GIVE THE GAME AWAY
GLOBE ARTICHOKES
GLOSSY MAGAZINES
GLOUCESTERSHIRE
GLUCONEOGENESIS
GNOTOBIOTICALLY
GOLDEN HANDSHAKE
GOLDEN RETRIEVER
GOOD-FOR-NOTHINGS
GOOD-NATUREDNESS
GO OFF THE DEEP END
GORNO-BADAKHSHAN
GOVERNOR-GENERAL
GRAPHIC DESIGNER
GREGORIAN CHANTS
GUTTURALIZATION
GYNANDROMORPHIC

H

HACKNEY CARRIAGE
HAEMAGGLUTINATE
HAEMOFLAGELLATE
HAEMOGLOBINURIA
HALF-HEARTEDNESS
HALL OF RESIDENCE
HALLUCINATIONAL
HAMAMELIDACEOUS
HAMMER AND SICKLE
HARD-HEARTEDNESS
HARD LUCK STORIES
HARMONISTICALLY
HARVEST FESTIVAL
HAVE A BONE TO PICK
HEARTBREAK HOUSE
HEARTBREAKINGLY
HEARTBROKENNESS
HEAVY-HANDEDNESS
HEIR PRESUMPTIVE
HELIOCENTRICITY
HELIOMETRICALLY
HELIOTROPICALLY
HELLENISTICALLY
HELMINTHOLOGIST
HENDECASYLLABIC
HENDECASYLLABLE
HERBIVOROUSNESS
HEREDITARIANISM
HERMAPHRODITISM
HERMENEUTICALLY
HERO-WORSHIPPING
HETEROCHROMATIC

HETEROCHROMATIN
HETEROGENEOUSLY
HETEROSEXUALITY
HEXACHLOROPHENE
HEXYLRESORCINOL
HIGH COMMISSIONS
HIGHER EDUCATION
HIMACHAL PRADESH
HIPPOCRATIC OATH
HISPANICIZATION
HISTORIC PRESENT
HISTORIOGRAPHER
HISTORIOGRAPHIC
HOLOBLASTICALLY
HOLOGRAPHICALLY
HOLY ROMAN EMPIRE
HOMEOPATHICALLY
HOMOCENTRICALLY
HOMOGENEOUSNESS
HOMOPLASTICALLY
HOPE AGAINST HOPE
HORTICULTURALLY
HOSPITALIZATION
HOT-WATER BOTTLES
HOUSEHOLDERSHIP
HOUSEHOLD TROOPS
HOUSEWIFELINESS
HOUSING PROJECTS
HUMANITARIANISM
HUMANITARIANIST
HUNTINGDONSHIRE
HYDROBROMIC ACID
HYDROGENIZATION
HYDROMECHANICAL
HYDROMETALLURGY
HYPERCRITICALLY

I

ICEBERG LETTUCES
IDIOMORPHICALLY
IMMEASURABILITY
IMMERSION HEATER
IMMORTALIZATION
IMMUNOCHEMISTRY
IMMUNOGENICALLY
IMMUNOLOGICALLY
IMPECUNIOUSNESS
IMPENETRABILITY
IMPERISHABILITY
IMPONDERABILITY
IMPRESCRIPTIBLE

IMPRESSIONISTIC
IMPROBABILITIES
IMPROVISATIONAL
INACCESSIBILITY
INADMISSIBILITY
INAPPLICABILITY
INAPPROPRIATELY
INATTENTIVENESS
IN BLACK AND WHITE
INCALCULABILITY
INCIDENTAL MUSIC
INCOMMENSURABLE
INCOMMUNICATIVE
INCOMMUTABILITY
INCOMPARABILITY
INCOMPATIBILITY
INCOMPREHENSION
INCOMPREHENSIVE
INCOMPUTABILITY
INCONGRUOUSNESS
INCONSEQUENTIAL
INCONSIDERATELY
INCONSIDERATION
INCONSISTENCIES
INCONSOLABILITY
INCONSPICUOUSLY
INCONVENIENCING
INCORRIGIBILITY
INCREDULOUSNESS
INDECENT ASSAULT
INDEFEASIBILITY
INDEFENSIBILITY
INDEMNIFICATION
INDETERMINISTIC
INDIAN ROPE-TRICK
INDIGESTIBILITY
INDIRECT OBJECTS
INDISCRETIONARY
INDISPUTABILITY
INDISSOLUBILITY
INDIVIDUALISTIC
INDIVIDUALIZING
INDUSTRIALIZING
INDUSTRIOUSNESS
INEFFACEABILITY
INEFFECTIVENESS
INEXPENSIVENESS
INEXPLICABILITY
INEXTENSIBILITY
INEXTRICABILITY
INFANT PRODIGIES

INFINITESIMALLY
INFRASTRUCTURES
INFUNDIBULIFORM
INJUDICIOUSNESS
INOFFENSIVENESS
INOPPORTUNENESS
INQUISITIVENESS
INQUISITORIALLY
INSENSIBILITIES
INSIGNIFICANTLY
INSTALLMENT PLAN
INSTANTANEOUSLY
INSTRUMENTALISM
INSTRUMENTALIST
INSTRUMENTALITY
INSTRUMENTATION
INSUBORDINATELY
INSUBORDINATION
INSURANCE POLICY
INSURRECTIONARY
INSURRECTIONISM
INSURRECTIONIST
INTELLECTUALISE
INTELLECTUALISM
INTELLECTUALIST
INTELLECTUALITY
INTELLECTUALIZE
INTELLIGIBILITY
INTENSIFICATION
INTERCHANGEABLE
INTERCHANGEABLY
INTERCLAVICULAR
INTERCOLLEGIATE
INTERCONNECTION
INTERDEPENDENCE
INTERFEROMETRIC
INTERLAMINATION
INTERLOCUTORILY
INTERNALIZATION
INTERNAL REVENUE
INTERNATIONALES
INTERNATIONALLY
INTEROSCULATION
INTERPENETRABLE
INTERPRETATIONS
INTERROGATINGLY
INTERROGATIONAL
INTERROGATIVELY
INTERROGATORIES
INTERROGATORILY
INTERSCHOLASTIC

INTERVENTIONISM
INTERVENTIONIST
IN THE LAST RESORT
INTRANSIGENTIST
INTROSPECTIONAL
INTROSPECTIVELY
INTUSSUSCEPTION
INTUSSUSCEPTIVE
INVESTIGATIONAL
INVOLUNTARINESS
INVOLUNTATARILY
INVULNERABILITY
IRREDEEMABILITY
IRREFRAGABILITY
IRREMISSIBILITY
IRRESISTIBILITY
IRRESOLVABILITY
IRREVERSIBILITY

J
JACK-OF-ALL-TRADES
JAPANESE LANTERN
JEHOVAH'S WITNESS
JUMPING-OFF PLACE
JURISPRUDENTIAL
JUXTAPOSITIONAL

K
KABARDINO-BALKAR
KEEPS ONES HAND IN
KIND-HEARTEDNESS

L
LABOUR EXCHANGES
LABOUR INTENSIVE
LABOUR-INTENSIVE
LABYRINTHICALLY
LACKADAISICALLY
LADIES-IN-WAITING
LAISSEZ-FAIREISM
LARGE INTESTINES
LATERAL THINKING
LAUGHING JACKASS
LEADING ARTICLES
LEADING QUESTION
LET ONES HAIR DOWN
LETTERS OF CREDIT
LEVEL-HEADEDNESS
LIGHT-HEADEDNESS
LIGHT MACHINE GUN
LIGHTNING STRIKE

LIKE THE CLAPPERS
LILY OF THE VALLEY
LIVERY COMPANIES
LOCAL GOVERNMENT
LOGARITHMICALLY
LOIRE-ATLANTIQUE
LOPHOBRANCHIATE
LOURENCO MARQUES

M
MACHINE-READABLE
MACROCOSMICALLY
MACROSCOPICALLY
MACROSPORANGIUM
MAD AS A MARCH HARE
MAGNANIMOUSNESS
MAGNETOCHEMICAL
MAGNETOELECTRIC
MAGNETO ELECTRIC
MAGNIFYING GLASS
MALACOPTERYGIAN
MALASSIMILATION
MALE CHAUVINISTS
MALPRACTITIONER
MANIC-DEPRESSIVE
MANIFESTATIONAL
MANNERISTICALLY
MANOEUVRABILITY
MARKET GARDENERS
MARKET GARDENING
MARRIAGEABILITY
MARSHALLING YARD
MARXISM-LENINISM
MARXIST-LENINIST
MASSAGE PARLOURS
MASTER CRAFTSMAN
MASTER OF SCIENCE
MATERIALIZATION
MEANINGLESSNESS
MECHANISTICALLY
MEGALOCEPHALOUS
MELANCHOLICALLY
MELLIFLUOUSNESS
MEMORIALIZATION
MENDING ONES WAYS
MENISPERMACEOUS
MENSTRUAL PERIOD
MENTAL DEFECTIVE
MENTAL HOSPITALS
MENTALISTICALLY
MEPHISTOPHELEAN

MEROBLASTICALLY
METACINNABARITE
METAGENETICALLY
METALINGUISTICS
METALLURGICALLY
METAMATHEMATICS
METHODISTICALLY
METROPOLITANISM
MICROBIOLOGICAL
MICROBIOLOGISTS
MICROELECTRONIC
MICROPHOTOGRAPH
MICROPROCESSORS
MICROSCOPICALLY
MICROSPORANGIUM
MICROSPOROPHYLL
MIDDLE OF NOWHERE
MIDDLE-OF-THE-ROAD
MINIATURIZATION
MISAPPLICATIONS
MISAPPREHENDING
MISAPPREHENSION
MISAPPREHENSIVE
MISAPPROPRIATED
MISCALCULATIONS
MISCELLANEOUSLY
MISCHIEVOUSNESS
MISCONSTRUCTION
MISINTERPRETING
MISREPRESENTING
MISTRUSTFULNESS
MOBILE LIBRARIES
MODERNISTICALLY
MOLOTOV COCKTAIL
MONCHEN-GLADBACH
MONEY FOR OLD ROPE
MONOGRAPHICALLY
MONOUNSATURATED
MONTE CARLO RALLY
MONTMORILLONITE
MOOG SYNTHESIZER
MOONLIGHT SONATA
MORNING SICKNESS
MORPHOLOGICALLY
MORPHOPHONEMICS
MOTHER COUNTRIES
MOTHER SUPERIORS
MOVING STAIRCASE
MULTITUDINOUSLY
MUSCULOSKELETAL
MUSTARD AND CRESS

MUSTARD PLASTERS
MUTATIS MUTANDIS
MYTHOLOGIZATION

N
NAGORNO-KARABAKH
NATIONAL ANTHEMS
NATIONAL GALLERY
NATIONALIZATION
NATIONAL SERVICE
NATURAL SCIENCES
NEARSIGHTEDNESS
NEEDLE AND THREAD
NEGATIVE-RAISING
NEIGHBOURLINESS
NEOARSPHENAMINE
NEOLOGISTICALLY
NEUROHYPOPHYSIS
NEUROPATHICALLY
NEUROPHYSIOLOGY
NEUROPSYCHIATRY
NEUROPSYCHOLOGY
NEUROSURGICALLY
NEWS CONFERENCES
NIGHTMARISHNESS
NINE DAYS' WONDERS
NITROCHLOROFORM
NITROGENIZATION
NOMOGRAPHICALLY
NON COMPOS MENTIS
NONCONTRIBUTING
NONCONTRIBUTORY
NONINTERVENTION
NON INTERVENTION
NONINTOXICATING
NONPRODUCTIVITY
NON-PROFIT-MAKING
NONSENSICALNESS
NONSTANDARDIZED
NORTH COUNTRYMAN
NOTWITHSTANDING
NOUVELLE CUISINE
NO-WIN SITUATIONS
NUCLEAR FAMILIES
NUCLEAR REACTORS
NUCLEOSYNTHESIS
NUMBER-CRUNCHING

O
OBJECTIFICATION
OBSERVATION POST

OBSTRUCTIONISTS
OBSTRUCTIVENESS
OESTROGENICALLY
OLD AGE PENSIONER
OLD PEOPLE'S HOMES
OLIGOSACCHARIDE
OMNIDIRECTIONAL
ONCE IN A BLUE MOON
ONE-ARMED BANDITS
ONES HEART BLEEDS
ON THE BACK BURNER
OPEN-AND-SHUT CASE
OPENHEARTEDNESS
OPERATING SYSTEM
OPHTHALMOLOGIST
OPHTHALMOSCOPIC
OPINIONATEDNESS
OPISTHOGNATHISM
OPISTHOGNATHOUS
OPPOSITE NUMBERS
OPTICAL ILLUSION
OPTOELECTRONICS
ORIENTALIZATION
ORNITHORHYNCHUS
ORTHOCHROMATISM
ORTHOPSYCHIATRY
OSTEOPATHICALLY
OUT OF THE PICTURE
OVERCAPITALIZED
OVERCOMPENSATED
OVERDEVELOPMENT
OVERSIMPLIFYING
OXYTETRACYCLINE

P
PAINSTAKINGNESS
PALAEOBOTANICAL
PALAEOGRAPHICAL
PALAEONTOGRAPHY
PALAEONTOLOGIST
PALAEOZOOLOGIST
PALEONTOLOGISTS
PANCAKE LANDINGS
PANTHEISTICALLY
PARAGENETICALLY
PARAGRAPHICALLY
PARALLACTICALLY
PARASITOLOGICAL
PARASYMPATHETIC
PARENT COMPANIES
PARENTHETICALLY

PARLIAMENTARIAN
PARTHENOGENESIS
PARTHENOGENETIC
PARTICULARISTIC
PARTICULARITIES
PARTICULARIZING
PASSIFLORACEOUS
PASSIONLESSNESS
PAST PARTICIPLES
PATENT MEDICINES
PATHETIC FALLACY
PAVEMENT ARTISTS
PAYING IN ADVANCE
PELICAN CROSSING
PENTATONIC SCALE
PENTOTHAL SODIUM
PEPPERCORN RENTS
PEREGRINE FALCON
PERFUNCTORINESS
PERIODONTICALLY
PERIPATETICALLY
PERISTALTICALLY
PEROXIDE BLONDES
PERPENDICULARLY
PERPETUAL MOTION
PERSONAL COLUMNS
PERSONALITY CULT
PERSONALIZATION
PERSONAL PRONOUN
PERSONAL STEREOS
PERSONA NON GRATA
PERSONIFICATION
PERSPICACIOUSLY
PERSPICUOUSNESS
PESSIMISTICALLY
PHANTASMAGORIAS
PHARMACODYNAMIC
PHARMACOGNOSIST
PHARMACOGNOSTIC
PHARMACOLOGICAL
PHARMACOLOGISTS
PHARYNGOLOGICAL
PHENOLPHTHALEIN
PHENYLKETONURIA
PHILANTHROPISTS
PHILOSOPHICALLY
PHLEBOSCLEROSIS
PHOSPHATIZATION
PHOSPHOCREATINE
PHOSPHORESCENCE
PHOTOCONDUCTION

PHOTODEGRADABLE
PHOTOELASTICITY
PHOTOGRAMMETRIC
PHOTOJOURNALISM
PHOTOJOURNALIST
PHOTOLITHOGRAPH
PHOTOMECHANICAL
PHOTOMETRICALLY
PHOTOMICROGRAPH
PHOTOMULTIPLIER
PHOTOSENSITIZED
PHOTOTELEGRAPHY
PHOTOTOPOGRAPHY
PHOTOTRANSISTOR
PHOTOTYPESETTER
PHOTOTYPOGRAPHY
PHOTOZINCOGRAPH
PHYSICOCHEMICAL
PHYSIOTHERAPIST
PHYTOGEOGRAPHER
PHYTOPLANKTONIC
PICTURE-POSTCARD
PICTURESQUENESS
PIEZOMETRICALLY
PINCER MOVEMENTS
PITHECANTHROPUS
PLASMOLYTICALLY
PLASTIC SURGEONS
PLATINUM BLONDES
PLATYHELMINTHIC
PLEASURABLENESS
PLENIPOTENTIARY
PLEUROPNEUMONIA
PLIGHT ONES TROTH
PLOUGHMAN'S LUNCH
PLUMBAGINACEOUS
PLUMBER'S FRIENDS
PLUTOCRATICALLY
PNEUMATIC DRILLS
POIKILOTHERMISM
POISON-PEN LETTER
POLICE CONSTABLE
POLITICAL ASYLUM
POLLING STATIONS
POLYGENETICALLY
POLYGRAPHICALLY
POLYUNSATURATED
PORTMANTEAU WORD
POST OFFICE BOXES
POVERTY-STRICKEN
POWER OF ATTORNEY

PRAYING MANTISES
PREACHIFICATION
PRECANCELLATION
PRECIPITOUSNESS
PREDISPOSITIONS
PREFERENTIALITY
PREHISTORICALLY
PREPOSITIONALLY
PRESBYTERIANISM
PRESCRIPTIVISTS
PRESENCE CHAMBER
PRESENTABLENESS
PRESENTATIONISM
PRESENTATIONIST
PRESS CONFERENCE
PRESSURE COOKERS
PRESTIDIGITATOR
PRESTIGIOUSNESS
PRESUMPTIVENESS
PRESUPPOSITIONS
PRETENTIOUSNESS
PRETERNATURALLY
PRIMA BALLERINAS
PRIMARY STRESSES
PRINCE CHARMINGS
PRINTED CIRCUITS
PRINTING PRESSES
PRIVATE PROPERTY
PRIVATE SOLDIERS
PRIVY COUNCILLOR
PROBLEMATICALLY
PROCRASTINATING
PROCRASTINATION
PRODUCTION LINES
PROFESSIONALISM
PROFESSIONALIST
PROGENITIVENESS
PROGNOSTICATING
PROGNOSTICATION
PROGNOSTICATIVE
PROGNOSTICATORS
PROGRESSIVENESS
PROHIBITIONISTS
PROHIBITIVENESS
PROLETARIANNESS
PROMISCUOUSNESS
PROPER FRACTIONS
PROPORTIONALITY
PROPORTIONATELY
PROPYLENE GLYCOL
PROSELYTIZATION

PROSENCHYMATOUS
PROTOZOOLOGICAL
PROVOCATIVENESS
PSEPHOLOGICALLY
PSEUDOMUTUALITY
PSYCHEDELICALLY
PSYCHIATRICALLY
PSYCHOACOUSTICS
PSYCHOANALYSING
PSYCHOBIOLOGIST
PSYCHOGENICALLY
PSYCHOLOGICALLY
PSYCHOMETRICIAN
PSYCHOPATHOLOGY
PSYCHOSEXUALITY
PSYCHOTECHNICAL
PSYCHOTHERAPIST
PSYCHOTOMIMETIC
PTOLEMAIC SYSTEM
PUBLIC COMPANIES
PUBLIC NUISANCES
PUBLIC OWNERSHIP
PUBLIC RELATIONS
PULCHRITUDINOUS
PUNCTILIOUSNESS
PUNCTUATION MARK
PURITANICALNESS
PURPOSELESSNESS
PUSILLANIMOUSLY
PUT ONES FOOT DOWN
PUT OUT MORE FLAGS
PYROELECTRICITY

Q

QUADRUPLICATION
QUARRELSOMENESS
QUARTER SESSIONS
QUATERCENTENARY
QUEEN'S EVIDENCES
QUESTION MASTERS
QUICK-WITTEDNESS
QUINQUAGENARIAN
QUINTUPLICATION
QUODLIBETICALLY

R

RADIOACTIVATION
RADIOBIOLOGICAL
RADIOLOCATIONAL
RADIOMICROMETER
RADIOPHONICALLY

RADIOSCOPICALLY
RADIOTELEGRAPHY
RADIOTELEPHONIC
RADIO TELESCOPES
RADIOTHERAPISTS
RAILWAY STATIONS
RASTAFARIANISMS
RATE OF EXCHANGES
RATIONALIZATION
REAFFORESTATION
REAL-ESTATE AGENT
REARGUARD ACTION
RECAPITULATIONS
RECOGNIZABILITY
RECOMMENDATIONS
RECONCILABILITY
RECONNAISSANCES
RECONSIDERATION
RECONSTRUCTIBLE
RECONSTRUCTIONS
RECORD LIBRARIES
RECREATION ROOMS
REDOUBTABLENESS
REFRESHER COURSE
REGISTERED NURSE
REGISTER OFFICES
REGISTRY OFFICES
REGIUS PROFESSOR
REINDUSTRIALIZE
RELATIVE CLAUSES
RELATIVE PRONOUN
REMORSELESSNESS
REPETITIOUSNESS
REPRESENTATIONS
REPRESENTATIVES
REPROACHFULNESS
REPRODUCIBILITY
RESOURCEFULNESS
RESPECTABLENESS
RESPONSIBLENESS
RESTRICTIVENESS
RESURRECTIONARY
RESURRECTIONISM
RESURRECTIONIST
RESURRECTION MEN
RETROGRESSIVELY
RETROSPECTIVELY
REVEREND MOTHERS
REVOLUTIONARIES
REVOLUTIONARILY
REVOLUTIONIZING

RHOMBENCEPHALON
RIBONUCLEIC ACID
RIGHT-HANDEDNESS
RIGHT-MINDEDNESS
RITUALISTICALLY
ROBIN GOODFELLOW
ROGUES' GALLERIES
ROMANTICIZATION
ROUGH-AND-TUMBLES
ROUND-SHOULDERED
ROYAL HIGHNESSES
RUMBUSTIOUSNESS
RUSSIAN ROULETTE

S
SADOMASOCHISTIC
SALES RESISTANCE
SANCTIMONIOUSLY
SANDWICH COURSES
SAPROPHYTICALLY
SARRACENIACEOUS
SATURATION POINT
SAVINGS ACCOUNTS
SAWN-OFF SHOTGUNS
SCARBOROUGH FAIR
SCHISTOSOMIASIS
SCHOOL OF THOUGHT
SCINTILLATINGLY
SCLERODERMATOUS
SCRUMPTIOUSNESS
SEA ISLAND COTTON
SECONDARY MODERN
SECONDARY STRESS
SECOND CHILDHOOD
SECOND IN COMMAND
SECOND-IN-COMMAND
SECURITY COUNCIL
SEINE-SAINT-DENIS
SELECT COMMITTEE
SELF-CENTREDNESS
SELF-CONFIDENTLY
SELF-CONSCIOUSLY
SELF-DESTRUCTING
SELF-DESTRUCTION
SELF-DISCIPLINED
SELF-EXAMINATION
SELF-EXPLANATORY
SELF-IMPORTANTLY
SELF-IMPROVEMENT
SELF-INDULGENTLY
SELF-LIQUIDATING

SELF-POLLINATION
SELF-POSSESSEDLY
SELF-REPROACHFUL
SELF-RIGHTEOUSLY
SELF-SACRIFICING
SELF-SUFFICIENCY
SENSATIONALISTS
SENSE OF OCCASION
SENTENTIOUSNESS
SENTIMENTALISTS
SENTIMENTALIZED
SEPTUAGENARIANS
SERGEANTS-AT-ARMS
SERVICE STATIONS
SERVOMECHANICAL
SERVOMECHANISMS
SESQUICARBONATE
SHARP-WITTEDNESS
SHILLY SHALLYING
SHILLY-SHALLYING
SHOOTING GALLERY
SHOOTING MATCHES
SHOPPING CENTRES
SHORT-CIRCUITING
SHORT-HANDEDNESS
SHORTHAND TYPIST
SHOTGUN WEDDINGS
SHOWING ONES HAND
SHRINKING VIOLET
SHRINK RESISTANT
SICKNESS BENEFIT
SIDEWALK ARTISTS
SIESMOLOGICALLY
SIMPLE FRACTURES
SIMPLICIDENTATE
SIMPLIFICATIONS
SINGULARIZATION
SINISTRODEXTRAL
SITUATION COMEDY
SITUATION ETHICS
SLAUGHTERHOUSES
SLEEPING PARTNER
SLOTTED SPATULAS
SLOUGH OF DESPOND
SLOW ON THE UPTAKE
SMALL INTESTINES
SMALL-MINDEDNESS
SMELLS OF THE LAMP
SOCIAL DEMOCRATS
SOCIALISTICALLY
SOCIOLINGUISTIC

SOFT FURNISHINGS
SOFTHEARTEDNESS
SOLEMNIFICATION
SOUNDED THE ALARM
SOW DRAGONS TEETH
SPANISH-AMERICAN
SPANISH OMELETTE
SPECIALIZATIONS
SPECIAL LICENCES
SPECIAL PLEADING
SPECIFIC GRAVITY
SPECULATIVENESS
SPEECHIFICATION
SPEECH THERAPIST
SPERMATOGENESIS
SPERMATOGENETIC
SPINNING JENNIES
SPLIT INFINITIVE
SPONTANEOUSNESS
SPUR-OF-THE-MOMENT
SQUADRON LEADERS
SQUARE THE CIRCLE
STAGE DIRECTIONS
STAMPING GROUNDS
STANDARD-BEARERS
STANDARDIZATION
STANDOFFISHNESS
STAND ONES GROUND
STAPHYLOPLASTIC
STAPHYLORRHAPHY
STAR-OF-BETHLEHEM
STARS AND STRIPES
STARVATION WAGES
STATE DEPARTMENT
STEREOCHEMISTRY
STEREOISOMERISM
STEREOISOMETRIC
STICKING PLASTER
STINGING NETTLES
STOCKBROKER BELT
STOCKING-FILLERS
STOICHIOLOGICAL
STORE DETECTIVES
STRAIGHTFORWARD
STRAIGHTJACKETS
STRATIFICATIONS
STRAWBERRY MARKS
STRETCHER-BEARER
STUMBLING BLOCKS
SUBORDINATENESS
SUBSISTENCE CROP

SUBSPECIFICALLY
SUBSTANTIVENESS
SUGGESTIBLENESS
SULPHUREOUSNESS
SUNRISE INDUSTRY
SUPERADDITIONAL
SUPERCONDUCTION
SUPERCONDUCTIVE
SUPERCONDUCTORS
SUPERFLUOUSNESS
SUPERIMPOSITION
SUPERINCUMBENCE
SUPERINDUCEMENT
SUPERINTENDENCE
SUPERINTENDENCY
SUPERINTENDENTS
SUPERLATIVENESS
SUPERNATURALISM
SUPERNATURALIST
SUPERNUMERARIES
SUPERSTITIOUSLY
SUPERSTRUCTURAL
SUPERSTRUCTURES
SUPPLEMENTARILY
SUPPLEMENTATION
SUPPLY AND DEMAND
SUPPORTING PARTS
SURREPTITIOUSLY
SUSCEPTIBLENESS
SWIMMING COSTUME
SWIM WITH THE TIDE
SWORD OF DAMOCLES
SYCOPHANTICALLY
SYLLABIFICATION
SYMBOL-FORMATION
SYMBOLISTICALLY
SYMMETRICALNESS
SYMPATHETICALLY
SYMPATHOMIMETIC
SYMPTOMATICALLY
SYNCHRONIZATION
SYNCHRONOUSNESS
SYNECDOCHICALLY
SYNECOLOGICALLY
SYNOPTIC GOSPELS
SYSTEMATIZATION
SYSTEMS ANALYSTS

T

TACHOMETRICALLY
TACHYMETRICALLY

TAKEN FOR GRANTED
TAKE TO ONES HEELS
TARSOMETATARSAL
TARSOMETATARSUS
TECHNOLOGICALLY
TECHNOSTRUCTURE
TELEGRAPHICALLY
TELEPHONE NUMBER
TELEPHOTOGRAPHY
TELEPHOTO LENSES
TELESTEREOSCOPE
TELETYPESETTING
TEMPERAMENTALLY
TEMPESTUOUSNESS
TEN COMMANDMENTS
TENDENTIOUSNESS
TENDERHEARTEDLY
TERMINOLOOGICAL
TERRITORIAL ARMY
TETRABRANCHIATE
THALASSOTHERAPY
THATS MORE LIKE IT
THE BACK OF BEYOND
THE COAST IS CLEAR
THEOREMATICALLY
THE POWERS THAT BE
THERAPEUTICALLY
THERIANTHROPISM
THERMIONIC VALVE
THERMOBAROGRAPH
THERMOCHEMISTRY
THERMOSTABILITY
THICKHEADEDNESS
THICK-WITTEDNESS
THOUGHTLESSNESS
THREE-LEGGED RACE
THREE-POINT TURNS
THROMBOEMBOLISM
THYROCALCITONIN
TIGHTFISTEDNESS
TIGHTROPE WALKER
TIMES IMMEMORIAL
TOOK SOME BEATING
TOPOGRAPHICALLY
TOTALITARIANISM
TO THE MANNER BORN
TOWER OF STRENGTH
TRACTION ENGINES
TRADITIONALISTS
TRAINING COLLEGE
TRANSCRIPTIONAL

TRANSFERABILITY
TRANSFIGURATION
TRANSFIGUREMENT
TRANSFORMATIONS
TRANSGRESSINGLY
TRANSILLUMINATE
TRANSISTORIZING
TRANSLATABILITY
TRANSLITERATING
TRANSLITERATION
TRANSMOGRIFYING
TRANSMUTATIONAL
TRANSPARENTNESS
TRANSPLANTATION
TRANSPOSABILITY
TRANSPOSITIONAL
TRANSUBSTANTIAL
TREACHEROUSNESS
TREASONABLENESS
TRIBROMOETHANOL
TRICHLOROETHANE
TRICK OR TREATING
TRINITROBENZENE
TRINITROTOLUENE
TROPICALIZATION
TROUBLESHOOTERS
TROUBLESOMENESS
TRUSTWORTHINESS
TRYPANOSOMIASIS
TURF ACCOUNTANTS
TYPOGRAPHICALLY
TYRANNOSAURUSES

U

ULTRACENTRIFUGE
ULTRAFILTRATION
ULTRAMICROMETER
ULTRAMICROSCOPE
ULTRAMICROSCOPY
ULTRASTRUCTURAL
UNBELIEVABILITY
UNCEREMONIOUSLY
UNCHALLENGEABLE
UNCOMMUNICATIVE
UNCOMPLIMENTARY
UNCONCERNEDNESS
UNCONDITIONALLY
UNCONNECTEDNESS

UNCONSCIOUSNESS
UNDEMONSTRATIVE
UNDERCAPITALIZE
UNDEREMPLOYMENT
UNDERESTIMATING
UNDERESTIMATION
UNDERHANDEDNESS
UNDERPRIVILEGED
UNDERPRODUCTION
UNDERSTATEMENTS
UNDER-THE-COUNTER
UNDISTINGUISHED
UNEMPLOYABILITY
UNEQUIVOCALNESS
UNEXCEPTIONABLE
UNEXCEPTIONABLY
UNFLINCHINGNESS
UNFORTUNATENESS
UNHOLY ALLIANCES
UNINTERRUPTEDLY
UNIVERSAL JOINTS
UNKNOWN QUANTITY
UNOBTRUSIVENESS
UNPARLIAMENTARY
UNPRECEDENTEDLY
UNPREMEDITATION
UNPRETENTIOUSLY
UNPROFITABILITY
UNPRONOUNCEABLE
UNSOPHISTICATED
UNWHOLESOMENESS

V

VALETUDINARIANS
VALUE-ADDED TAXES
VASCULARIZATION
VASOCONSTRICTOR
VEGETABLE KNIVES
VEGETABLE MARROW
VENDING MACHINES
VENEREAL DISEASE
VENTRILOQUISTIC
VENTURESOMENESS
VERTIGINOUSNESS
VESPERTILIONINE
VESTED INTERESTS
VICE-CHANCELLORS
VICISSITUDINARY

VICTORIA CROSSES
VIDEOCONFERENCE
VIRGINIA CREEPER
VITAL STATISTICS
VIVISECTIONISTS
VOYEURISTICALLY
VULGAR FRACTIONS

W

WALRUS MOUSTACHE
WARM-BLOODEDNESS
WARM-HEARTEDNESS
WAR OF JENKINS EAR
WARRANT OFFICERS
WASHING MACHINES
WEATHERBOARDING
WEATHER BOARDING
WEATHER FORECAST
WEATHERPROOFING
WEATHER STATIONS
WELL-CONSTRUCTED
WELL-ESTABLISHED
WELL-INTENTIONED
WHIPPERSNAPPERS
WHISTLE-STOP TOUR
WHITE BLOOD CELLS
WHITED SEPULCHRE
WHITE MANS BURDEN
WILD-GOOSE CHASES
WIND INSTRUMENTS
WIND-POLLINATION
WINDSCREEN WIPER
WISHFUL THINKING
WRONGHEADEDNESS

X

XENOMORPHICALLY
XEROGRAPHICALLY

Y

YOURS FAITHFULLY
YOUTH HOSTELLERS
YOUTH HOSTELLING

Z

ZYGOPHYLLACEOUS

Words that contain letter Q not followed by U

Anqing City in China

Aqaba Port in Jordan, on the Gulf of Aqaba

Aqmola Former name of Astana, capital of Kazakhstan

Basotho-Qwaqwa Former Bantu Homeland in South Africa

Chongqing City in China

Dimashq Arabic name for Damascus, capital of Syria

faqir Muslim or Hindu holy man

inqilab Urdu word for revolution

Iqbal Sir Mohammed Iqbal, Indian Muslim poet, philosopher and political leader

Iraq Country in the Middle East

Iraqi **1** Inhabitant of Iraq **2** Relating to Iraq

Jiang Qing Chinese communist politician, widow of Mao Tse-Tung

Lailat-ul-Qadr Annual night of prayer and study for Muslims

Masqat Arabic name for Musca, capital of Oman

mbaqnaga A style of Black popular music in South Africa

Qabis Arabic name for Gabés, port in Tunisia

Qabis bin Said Sultan of Oman

Qaddafi Moamar al-Qaddafi, leader of Libya

Qaddish Jewish prayer, especially for the dead

qadi Muslim judge

Qairwan Holy city in Tunisia

QANTAS Australian national airline (Queensland and Northern Territory Aerial Services)

qat Type of bush found in Ethiopia

Qatar Country in Arabia

Qattara Depression Depression in the Sahara

qawwali Muslim religious song

Qeshm Iranian island

Qian Long Chinese emperor

qibla The direction of Mecca

Qingdao Port in China

Qinghai Province of China

qintar Albanian coin

Qiqihar City in China

Qishm Iranian island

Qom Holy city in Israel

qoph Hebrew letter Q

qorma Indian dish of meat and vegetables

Qu Qiu Bai Chinese communist leader and writer

Qwaqwa Former Bantu homeland in South Africa

qwerty Standard layout of English computer keyboard

Sercq French name for Sark in the Channel Islands

Si-ma Qian Ancient Chinese historian

Zaqaziq City in Eqypt

Zarqa City in Jordan

Words that start with letter X

xanthate Salt or ester of xanthic acid

xanthein Yellow pigment found in in flowers

xanthene Crystalline compound used dyes

xanthic Relating to xanthic acid

xanthin Orange-yellow pigment found in plants

xanthine Crystalline compound found in urine

Xanthippe The wife of Socrates: any nagging or quarrelsome woman

xanthism Abnormal yellowness of skin, fur, etc.

xanthocroi Relating to races having light hair and pale skin

xanthocroism Excessive yellowness in goldfish, etc.

xanthoma Yellow-brown patch or nodule on the skin

xanthophyll Yellow pigment found in plants

xanthous Relating to races having light hair and pale skin

Xanthus The chief city of ancient Lycia in Asia Minor

Xavier St Francis Xavier, Spanish Jesuit missionary

xebec Small, three-masted ship

xenia **1** Gift or offering **2** Influence of pollen upon the developing fruit

Xenocrates Greek philosopher

xenocryst Crystal of different origin found in igneous rock

xenogamy Cross-fertilization

xenogeneic Derived from an individual of a different species

xenogenesis Production of offspring unlike either parent

xenoglossia Ability to speak a language one has never learned

xenograft Graft of skin from an individual of a different species

xenolith Rock fragment of different origin found in igneous rock

xenomorphic (of a mineral) Having a different form from the surrounding rock

xenon Gasous chemical element

Xenophanes Greek philosopher and poet

xenophile Person who likes foreign people or things

xenophobe Person who dislikes foreign people or things

xenophobia Fear or hatred of foreign people and things

xenophon Greek general and historian

xeranthemum Several Mediterranean plants, especially the immortelle

xerarch (of plant successions) Originating in a dry habitat

Xeres Former name of Jerez in Spain

xeric (of plants) Growing in dry conditions

xeroderma Abnormal dryness of the skin

xerography Photo-copying process

xeromorphic (of plants) Having protection against excessive water loss

xerophilous Adapted to a dry habitat

APPENDIX

xerophthalmia Dryness in the eye

xerophyte Plant that is adapted to dry conditions

xerosere Plant succession originating in a dry habitat

xerosis Abnormal dryness of the skin or other tissues

Xerostomia Abnormal dryness of the mouth

Xerox Tradename for a photocopying process

xi Greek letter X

Xhosa Bantu people and language of South Africa

Xia Gui Chinese landscape painter

Xi An City in China

Xiang River in China

Ximenes Ximenes de Cinseros, Spanish cardinal and statesman

Xingu River in Brazil

Xining City in China

Xinjiang Uygur Administrative division of China

xiphisternum The lowest part of the breast bone

xiphoid (of bodily parts) Swordshaped

xiphosuran Horseshoe crab

Xizang Chinese name for Tibet

Xmas Christmas

xoanon Carved image of a god

Xochimilco Town and lake in Mexico

X-ray Electromagnetic radiation of very short wavelength, used in medical diagnosis etc.

Xuthus Son of Hellen in Greek mythology

Xuzhou City in China

xylan Yellow carbohydrate found in wood and straw

xylem Plant tissue that conducts water and nutrients

xylene Liquid hydrocarbon used as a solvent

xylidine Xylene derivative used in dyes

xylocarp Fruit with a hard woody shell

xylogenous (of insects etc,) Living in or on wood

xylograph Engraved wooden block or print made from one

xylography Art of printing from wooden blocks

xyloid Relating to or like wood

xylophagous (of insects etc.) Feeding on wood

xylophone Tuned wooden percussion instrument

xylorimba Large xylophone

xylose Sugar found in wood and straw, used in food for diabetics

xylotomous (of insects etc.) Boring into wood

xylotomy Preparation of wood sections for microscope examination

xylyl Derived from xylene

xyst 1 (in ancient Greece) Covered portico used for athletics 2 (in ancient Rome) Treelined garden walk

xyster Surgical file for scraping bone

Other titles published by A&C Black

Anagram Solver
John Daintith, 2006, £10.99
ISBN 0-7136-7510-1
Anagram Solver is the essential guide to cracking all types of quiz and crossword featuring anagrams. Containing over 200,000 words and phrases, this book includes plural noun forms, palindromes, idioms, first names and all parts of speech. Anagrams are grouped by the number of letters they contain with the letters set out in alphabetical order so that once the letters of an anagram are arranged alphabetically, finding the solution is as easy as locating the word in a dictionary.

Pocket Crossword Dictionary
B. J. Holmes, 2005, £5.99
ISBN 0-7136-7503-9
In a convenient pocket format, with its clear layout and easy-to-use cross-referencing, this handy crossword dictionary is an ideal companion for any crossword enthusiast. The Pocket Crossword Dictionary lists thousands of possible solutions, arranged under 13,000 headings. Entries also include synonyms, associated words, puns, plays on words and anagrams.

Solving Cryptic Crosswords
B. J. Holmes, 2005, £5.99
ISBN 0-7136-7738-4
This book offers hundreds of examples to illustrate how crossword clues work and helps readers understand how crosswords are created and how to interpret the clues. It includes real crossword grids with detailed explanations so readers can test themselves, and will be useful for beginners and improvers alike.

Specialist dictionaries

Dictionary of Accounting	0 7475 6991 6
Dictionary of Banking and Finance	0 7136 7739 2
Dictionary of Business	0 7136 7918 2
Dictionary of Computing	0 7475 6622 4
Dictionary of Economics	0 7136 8203 5
Dictionary of Environment and Ecology	0 7475 7201 1
Dictionary of Food Science and Nutrition	0 7136 7784 8
Dictionary of Human Resources and Personnel Management	0 7136 8142 X
Dictionary of ICT	0 7475 6990 8
Dictionary of Information and Library Management	0 7136 7591 8
Dictionary of Law	0 7475 6636 4
Dictionary of Leisure, Travel and Tourism	0 7475 7222 4
Dictionary of Marketing	0 7475 6621 6
Dictionary of Media Studies	0 7136 7593 4
Dictionary of Medical Terms	0 7136 7603 5
Dictionary of Nursing	0 7475 6634 8
Dictionary of Politics and Government	0 7475 7220 8
Dictionary of Publishing and Printing	0 7136 7589 6
Dictionary of Science and Technology	0 7475 6620 8
Dictionary of Sport and Exercise Science	0 7136 7785 6

Easier English™ titles

Easier English Basic Dictionary	0 7475 6644 5
Easier English Basic Synonyms	0 7475 6979 7
Easier English Dictionary: Handy Pocket Edition	0 7475 6625 9
Easier English Intermediate Dictionary	0 7475 6989 4
Easier English Student Dictionary	0 7475 6624 0
English Thesaurus for Students	1 9016 5931 3

Check Your English Vocabulary workbooks

Academic English	0 7475 6691 7
Business and Administration	0 7136 7916 6
Human Resources	0 7475 6997 5
Law	0 7136 7592 6
Living in the UK	0 7136 7914 X
Medicine	0 7136 7590 X
FCE +	0 7475 6981 9
IELTS	0 7136 7604 3
PET	0 7475 6627 5
TOEFL®	0 7475 6984 3
TOEIC	0 7136 7508 X

Visit our website for full details of all our books: **www.acblack.com**